The Undocumented PC

Second Edition

A Programmer's Guide to I/O, CPUs, and Fixed Memory Areas

Frank van Gilluwe

ADDISON-WESLEY DEVELOPERS PRESS
An imprint of Addison Wesley Longman, Inc.

Reading, Massachusetts • Harlow, England • Menlo Park, California
Berkeley, California • Don Mills, Ontario • Sydney
Bonn • Amsterdam • Tokyo • Mexico City

Library of Congress Cataloging-in-Publication Data

Van Gilluwe, Frank.
The undocumented PC : a programmer's guide to I/O, CPUs, and fixed memory areas / Frank van Gilluwe. -- 2nd ed.
p. cm.
includes index.
ISBN 0-201-47950-8
1. Microcomputers. 2. Electronic data processing documentation.
I. Title.
QA76.5.V27 1997
004.165--dc20 96-33409
CIP

A-W Developers Press is a division of Addison Wesley Longman, Inc.

Sponsoring Editor: Kathleen Tibbetts
Project Manager: Sarah Weaver
Production Coordinator: Erin Sweeney
Cover design: Robert Dietz
Set in 10-point Galliard by Octal Publishing, Inc.

1 2 3 4 5 6 7 8 9 - CRS - 0099989796
First printing, December 1996

Contents

Acknowledgments

Thanks go to Michael Schmit for reviewing this new edition and providing excellent feedback, corrections, and technical review. Thanks are also due to the many readers who took time to contact me and offer suggestions and ideas for this edition. This includes Bob Meister, who provided a detailed review of the first edition.

Thanks also go to Andrew Schulman and Mark Nelson, who were invaluable in providing their detailed technical review and suggestions for the first edition.

Special thanks are due Kathleen Tibbetts and the staff at Addison-Wesley for their work, excellent suggestions, and again accepting a book much larger than my original estimates.

Thanks to V Communications for equipment use, and the use of their internal menu software, used in making the UNPC program. Lastly, I need to thank all my family and friends for their continued support.

Preface

This second edition of *The Undocumented PC* provides extensive new material and updates major sections from the first edition. I'm still amazed at how much has changed in just two years. The MCA system was put to a merciful death, more new processor variants were released than in the first 10 years of the PC, and a number of new major operating systems took hold.

What's New?

This second edition changes every chapter in the book. Some chapters had simple updates such as adding the latest Windows 95 keyboard keys. In others, like the hard disk system chapter, it seemed like every page changed! Extensive material also was added to deal with the new CPUs that did not exist in the first edition. This includes Intel's Pentium Pro and MMX variants, AMD's 5_K86, Cyrix 5x86 and 6x86, and the obsolete NexGen CPUs.

Many programs in the first edition were enhanced and brought up to date. Like the first edition, complete documented source code is provided with the attached diskette. New features include the detection of PCI and related information, BIOS vendor and date, and a utility to show and describe BIOS data in detail. The keyboard view program was changed to work in more environments and show the untranslated scan code and translated scan code for any key.

For CPU detection, routines detect the presence of MMX, and identify the true instruction set (which is often different than you might expect). Many more CPU vendors are detected along with the CPU speed and internal CPU information. The Model Specific Register program now describes many undocumented registers by name and provides quick access to hidden registers.

Why the Undocumented PC?

If you're reading this for the first time, I must have caught your interest with the title *The Undocumented PC*. I hope you're as skeptical as I am, because many technical books in the past have promised a lot and delivered nothing more than a rehash of the same old tables of interrupts, OS commands, ASCII charts, and so forth. You will not be disappointed with this book.

You will find very little overlap with any other publication to date. Rather than just in-depth explanation, I've added information on related problems and concerns, and real code examples.

OK, what's the catch? I'm not all-knowing, and there are far more undocumented areas of the PC than can even be covered in this book. My approach has been to focus on the most useful areas that have been left undocumented or poorly documented, but are truly necessary in many development projects today.

With every new system design, it seems to be the manufacturer's objective to make it the most unreliable platform possible in the complex software area. How can I make such an incredible statement? It's just that the level of documentation provided by these manufacturers and consortiums is beyond belief. At least with early PCs you could obtain complete schematic diagrams and BIOS listings that could be used when the balance of the documentation lacked critical information. But even then, if you had difficulty reading a schematic or understanding cryptic assembly code, it could be very difficult to make good use of the information.

Today, what passes for documentation is rather pitiful. It's obvious these documents are prepared with little thought for the software and firmware developer. It has also become cost prohibitive to purchase what poor documentation exists. For example, if you were ever interested in supporting EISA- and MCA-based machines, you would need to spend hundreds of dollars to get the EISA and MCA specification documents. It's just one of the reasons these platforms never became very successful. Even when you have access to the entire technical works available, you will find a number of technical inaccuracies, missing information, and the extensive use of RESERVED used to hide information.

I have gone to great lengths to maintain an extremely high level of accuracy. This was accomplished in part by the development of working programs to confirm much of the information included in this book. In addition, extensive time was spent confirming information with the lowest level source of information. This includes examinaton of schematics, disassembled BIOS listings, and original IC data sheets.

In addition to the problems of just getting understandable and useful information for a task at hand, I have compiled informaton for both obsolete and current system standards. This includes the PC, XT, AT, ISA, MCA, EISA, and PCI systems. Many of the obsolete systems, such as MCA machines, are still in use, and can be supported with little effort.

Software tasks can usually be handled effectively from the operating system or through standard, well-documented functions. It's always wise to use these interfaces when appropriate. When these interfaces fail to provide the features or performance necessary for a task, it is necessary to go below the surface and use the underlying power of a system that manufacturers seem so determined to hide.

Now I'll give the manufacturers a little break. They have created a great machine with a wide range of capabilities. They have an understandable interest in hiding information from competitors. It also takes considerable effort to explain operations from a useful software perspective. Functional design changes are much easier when they are left undocumented because then, in theory, no one can use them! Today's marketplace also demands open interfaces. Most vendors claim their system is open to all. Just don't expect to be able to get much useful, cost-effective information from them.

I feel confident you will be pleased with my results. Every day, I'm sure there are newly documented designs being foisted onto the marketplace, but I believe this book covers a level of detail for the programmer that has truly been ignored far too long.

Frank van Gilluwe (74000.635@compuserve.com)

CHAPTER 1

Introduction

Undocumented information may be entertaining and interesting, but my focus is on those areas of the PC that are of genuine use to both software and hardware developers. You may wonder what could possibly remain undocumented when hundreds of technical books have been written about the PC! Well, over the last ten years, there seems to be an endless stream of important areas of the PC that are still undocumented or poorly documented. Many critical areas, such as the system BIOS and input/output ports, have been presented with so little detail that it is often impossible to actually understand and utilize these key areas of the system.

In particular, input and output ports are the most poorly documented areas of the system environment. Unlike the single line descriptions provided in the few manuals that even mention I/O, I've gone to great lengths to explain specific I/O ports and bits used to define each port, and in many cases have provided real examples of their use and possible problems that may occur.

Developers will find this reference invaluable in selecting port assignments for new hardware applications. One entire chapter covers specific issues relating to adapter card development, from a software perspective.

You may be asking yourself, how complete is *The Undocumented PC?* I've been gathering this information over the last ten years for use in the popular disassembler, Sourcer, which I wrote. As a disassembler, Sourcer takes executable files and BIOS ROMs, and converts them into readable assembly code with comments on interrupts, I/O ports, and much more. To keep Sourcer up to date, I've had to examine many documents and listings, and look below the surface to understand both how and why specific BIOS functions and I/O ports are used.

To organize this information, the book includes a chapter on each major system functional block. Each chapter explores a subject to the lowest levels, explains any BIOS functions available, and wraps up with detailed descriptions of related I/O ports. Most chapters also include interesting programs to demonstrate how to access the functions described. These program examples include complete source code, so modification or inclusion into your own programs is easy.

Some of the most interesting highlights include how to explore for undocumented information, described in Chapter 2; the numerous undocumented processor instructions described in Chapter 3; and complete source code in Chapter 4 for detecting system and processor types, processor vendor, processor speed, and programs for finding future undocumented instructions. Chapters 5, 6, and 7 explain adapter card development, BIOS data areas, and the interrupt vector table. The remaining chapters go into detail on each subsystem.

Sources of Information

When I began this book, I knew that a considerable amount of information was poorly documented, missing, or undocumented. I took an unusual bottom-up approach in developing the information contained in this book. In most cases, I first reviewed the original manufacturer's IC data sheets used for a particular subsystem. I then examined how the chip was actually connected on standard motherboards. This involved both using system schematics, and in a few cases, actually tracing system circuitry. I also examined disassembled BIOS code from a number of different manufacturers to see how they interacted with the subsystems at these lower levels. I also created test programs to verify the operation of some subsystems. Lastly, I looked at the *official* documentation. This included IBM technical references, which have been the primary source for many other technical books.

I was not surprised to find the IBM technical reference a poor source for reliable low-level information. It's obvious that much of the IBM documentation comes directly from programmer's notes in various IC data sheets. What surprised me was the number of times this information is either wrong or misleading due to actual implementation. For example, a feature inside a chip may be impossible to use because of the hardware implementation. These are *fully* documented as if someone could actually use them. In too many cases, the explanations of functions are so terse, they're useless to the programmer.

Please don't take this to mean I think the IBM technical references are worthless, as they have pieces of truly useful information. Of course this brings up the second problem I'm sure you've encountered. The documentation that is necessary to develop software to work with all the variant systems such as the PC, XT, AT, ISA, MCA, EISA, and PCI systems is scattered over many documents. To avoid these complications, I've highlighted any differences a programmer needs to know with each BIOS function and port description.

Too many technical references like to use the word *reserved* when avoiding the real details of what is going on, but the real meaning of *reserved* is never clear. What the vendor means to say, I think, is one of the following:

- Currently unused, but it might be used in the future.
- Unused and unlikely to ever be used.
- Used for some function that is not available in the PC architecture.
- Used for some hidden function.
- Used for some function that can cause unpredictable actions.
- Was used in older PCs, but is now obsolete.
- Vendor has no clue what it is used for.

I have endeavored to avoid the use of *reserved* throughout this book. In fact, I'll be honest and admit I cannot fathom what a reserved function is used for. In most cases, my analysis has shown *reserved* means unused.

System Types

In many places throughout this book I reference specific machine types with abbreviations such as AT, EISA, and others. These indicate a specific family of systems that have a common hardware design and similar BIOS functionality. A plus sign (+) is added to indicate that the specified function or I/O port is supported on that family and all others that came later. For example, AT+ indicates the function is supported on all AT machines, as well as EISA, PCI, and obsolete MCA machines.

Type	Description
PC	early 8088-based computers
XT	early 8088-based computers with hard disk capabilities, but still no built-in CMOS clock or CMOS configuration memory
AT	80286, 386, 486, and a few Pentium+ CPU-based systems with an Industry Standard Architecture (ISA) bus
MCA	80286, 386, 486, and Pentium CPU-based systems with a Micro-Channel Architecture (MCA) bus. All IBM PS/2 models 50 and above use the MCA bus.
EISA	386, 486, and Pentium CPU-based systems with an Extended Industry Standard Architecture (EISA) bus
PCI	486, Pentium, and Pentium Pro CPU-based systems with the Peripheral Component Interconnect (PCI) bus

Figure 1-1. Programmer's System Diagram

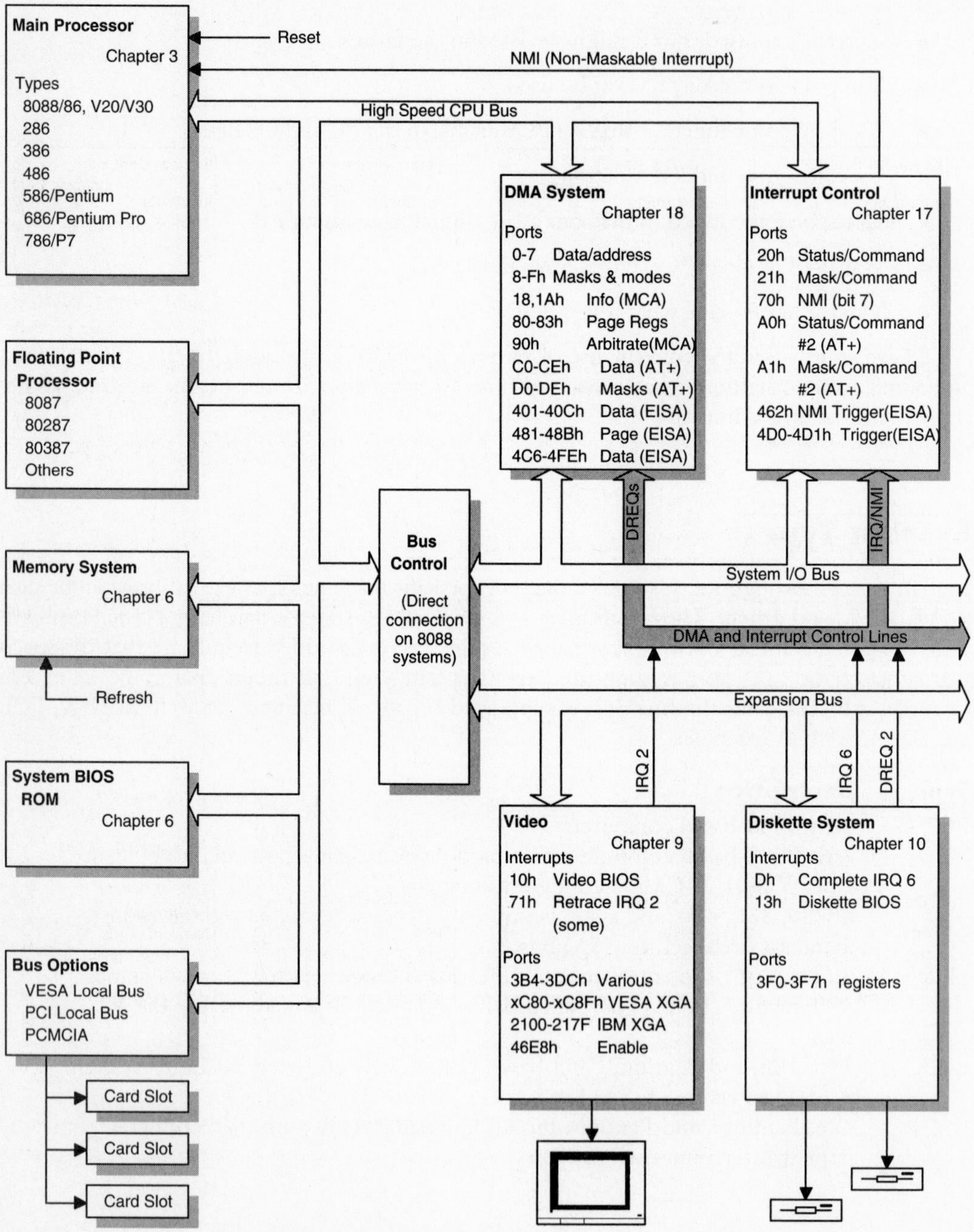

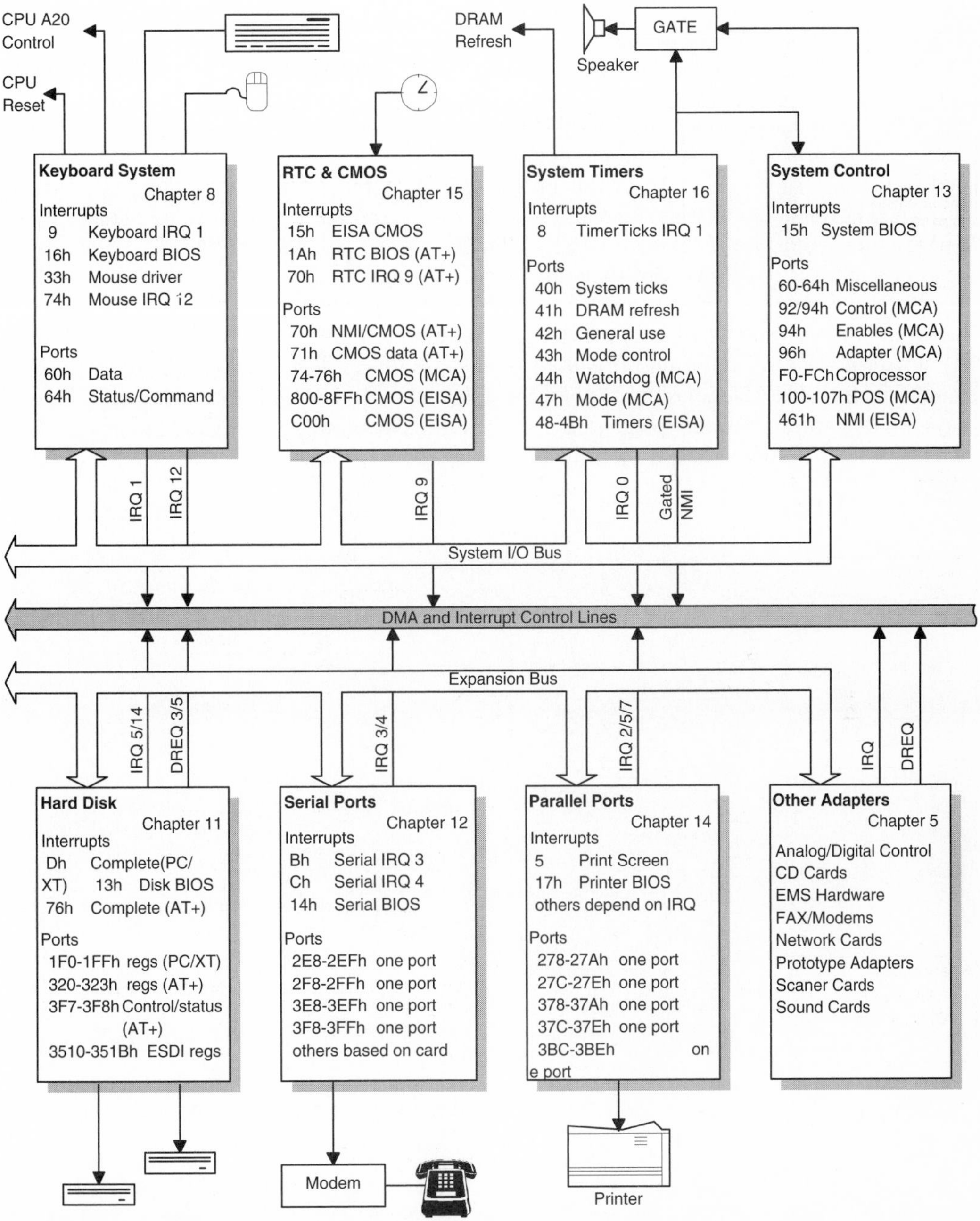
CPU A20 Control
CPU Reset
DRAM Refresh
GATE
Speaker
Keyboard System
Chapter 8
Interrupts
9 Keyboard IRQ 1
16h Keyboard BIOS
33h Mouse driver
74h Mouse IRQ 12
Ports
60h Data
64h Status/Command
RTC & CMOS
Chapter 15
Interrupts
15h EISA CMOS
1Ah RTC BIOS (AT+)
70h RTC IRQ 9 (AT+)
Ports
70h NMI/CMOS (AT+)
71h CMOS data (AT+)
74-76h CMOS (MCA)
800-8FFh CMOS (EISA)
C00h CMOS (EISA)
System Timers
Chapter 16
Interrupts
8 TimerTicks IRQ 1
Ports
40h System ticks
41h DRAM refresh
42h General use
43h Mode control
44h Watchdog (MCA)
47h Mode (MCA)
48-4Bh Timers (EISA)
System Control
Chapter 13
Interrupts
15h System BIOS
Ports
60-64h Miscellaneous
92/94h Control (MCA)
94h Enables (MCA)
96h Adapter (MCA)
F0-FCh Coprocessor
100-107h POS (MCA)
461h NMI (EISA)
IRQ 1
IRQ 12
IRQ 9
IRQ 0
Gated NMI
System I/O Bus
DMA and Interrupt Control Lines
Expansion Bus
IRQ 5/14
DREQ 3/5
IRQ 3/4
IRQ 2/5/7
IRQ
DREQ
Hard Disk
Chapter 11
Interrupts
Dh Complete(PC/XT)
13h Disk BIOS
76h Complete (AT+)
Ports
1F0-1FFh regs (PC/XT)
320-323h regs (AT+)
3F7-3F8h Control/status (AT+)
3510-351Bh ESDI regs
Serial Ports
Chapter 12
Interrupts
Bh Serial IRQ 3
Ch Serial IRQ 4
14h Serial BIOS
Ports
2E8-2EFh one port
2F8-2FFh one port
3E8-3EFh one port
3F8-3FFh one port
others based on card
Parallel Ports
Chapter 14
Interrupts
5 Print Screen
17h Printer BIOS
others depend on IRQ
Ports
278-27Ah one port
27C-27Eh one port
378-37Ah one port
37C-37Eh one port
3BC-3BEh one port
Other Adapters
Chapter 5
Analog/Digital Control
CD Cards
EMS Hardware
FAX/Modems
Network Cards
Prototype Adapters
Scaner Cards
Sound Cards
Modem
Printer

Programmer's System Diagram

Although you may have a good understanding of the basic system, I thought it would be worthwhile to present the system from the perspective of a single programming target, regardless of the actual processor and bus design used. Some programming aspects are dependent on the CPU or bus design, but much of the system is independent from these unique system aspects. Many hardware features such as bus width, cache memory, and local bus, have little to do with programming and have no programming interface.

Figure 1-1 shows what I call the Programmer's System Diagram. It outlines all of the major hardware blocks in the system and how they interconnect. Each hardware block is shown with any interrupts and I/O ports used within the subsystem. Each block also references the chapter that explains more about the individual subsystem.

Keep in mind that different vendors and platforms may connect the blocks up differently in hardware, but the functional software design is always the same. Any programming differences are noted in the interrupts and ports used by the subsystem. If a vendor drifts from the basic standard, a considerable amount of software will no longer work on that machine. The early days of compatible PCs were plagued by vendors drifting from the standard. The few that got their act together and made a truly compatible machine are still with us today, while the rest are history.

CHAPTER 2

Exploring the Undocumented PC

Introduction

There will always be new areas in the realm of the PC that manufacturers leave undocumented. This is not always by intent, but often in the rush to release a new system, adapter, or software, the related documentation is a low priority. This is especially true if the documentation is not required to make the equipment function at some base level. If and when documentation does become available, it seems to be presented in a form least usable by the software professional!

With some of the techniques I'll explain here, you should be able to see through the manufacturer's documentation smoke screen and improve your understanding of critical interfaces, operations, and data areas. I'll also show how to avoid the pitfalls of misleading and downright inaccurate documentation.

Key #1: Find the original source documents.

Look for the original source documents on the subsystem of interest. This includes schematic diagrams, IC specification sheets, IC application notes, and IC programmer references. With these documents in hand, and an understanding of both hardware and software, the exact nature of most subsystems can be thoroughly understood. Be aware that many complex ICs are used in every PC. These parts, in many cases, have some features and capabilities that are not possible in a PC design. For example, the 8254 programmable timer IC has a number of modes that can be programmed for each counter. Due to the way the timer IC is connected in the hardware of the PC, many modes are not possible or make no sense. A thorough understanding of the IC in combination with an examination of the actual schematic diagram will bring these limitations to light. Of course I've already done this work for subsystems in the PC, but you may have an interest in examining some new design or adapter card.

It is common for technical references to simply lift the information from an IC manual without considering the actual implementation of the part. Often modes and functions that are documented in some technical references are available in the IC, but are not available in any PC family design.

Unfortunately, there are still a number of problems in applying these techniques to make sense of the system. Very few manufacturers make internal schematic diagrams available. IBM's last published schematics were included in the *Technical Reference—Personal Computer AT*, published in 1985. Even in this reference, IBM removed a significant amount of information and used cryptic nomenclature to make the schematics more difficult to understand. Many programmers find a normal schematic diagram difficult to read, let alone one that has important information missing!

With newer PCI, MCA, and EISA systems, the task of understanding the subsystems at the lowest levels becomes almost impossible. Schematics are not available, and most newer systems use custom LSI ICs for which little or no data is available. At this point, other approaches must be used to understand the capabilities of the subsystem of interest.

Key #2: Has someone already done the work for you?

I hope you'll find all the answers you seek in this book. But, as I stated earlier, there are always new adapters, subsystems, and even new system designs being created. Some subsystems have been thoroughly examined and have been extremely well documented. The VGA display system falls into this category. There are many excellent technical references now available to cover many angles on writing software for the VGA adapter.

It's somewhat of a crap shoot, but see whether the manufacturer of the adapter or subsystem has a programmer's technical reference for their hardware. Smaller companies tend to be more receptive to releasing information that helps make their product a standard. Larger companies usually have information available, but it is usually difficult to find the right document and there is usually a costly fee for the document.

Since you are looking at documents that are extracted from the hardware design, keep in mind that additional features and capabilities are often available. These extra features may be left out because of a sinister vendor wishing to keep a competitive edge, or more likely because the feature has limited use or the technical writer failed to fully comprehend the hardware from a software perspective.

Key #3: Look at how someone else did it.

Even if you were lucky enough to find the source documents provided by the vendor, they rarely show how software is written to use the subsystem of interest. Examining how the BIOS interacts with the hardware subsystem will greatly increase your understanding of the subsystem. The BIOS (Basic Input/Output System) controls how programs often access hardware in the system.

One source is the original BIOS listings for the IBM AT. The last official BIOS listing was published in IBM's *Technical Reference—Personal Computer AT* manual. While it is an excellent source on the inner workings of original AT BIOS routines, it's out of date. These listings were produced from a large number of small programs, making it difficult to follow jumps and calls through the listings. There is no cross-reference, and since the listing is not on a disk, searching for data or subroutines is a pain.

Other sources include the Windows and NT Device Driver Kits (DDK) from Microsoft. These packages include considerable assembly source code showing how Windows and NT connect into the PC hardware. In some cases, these routines bypass the BIOS routines for performance. The DDK includes routines to replace portions of the BIOS for the keyboard, diskette, and some hard disk BIOSes. The DDK also contains code for interfacing with the serial ports, the mouse, and many video standards.

The last approach requires disassembling the BIOS or driver to see how someone else interacts with the hardware. I wrote a commercial product, Sourcer with the BIOS Pre-Processor, to do just that. It's also one of the major reasons I've discovered many undocumented hardware and software aspects of the PC system.

Through the process of disassembly, it is possible to see exactly how other manufacturers wrote software. Disassembly also brings to light the use of undocumented interrupts, I/O ports, instructions, and other tricks that many major vendors routinely use in their software. We'll examine the entire process of disassembly in significant detail in the next section.

Disassembly

The Need for Disassembly

One of the most frustrating aspects of software development occurs when source code or code documentation is needed but is unavailable. Disassembly of executable code may offer the only realistic solution. The lack of source code occurs far more frequently than most people realize and for a wide variety of reasons.

Most developers find that having source code listings contributes to the understanding of another product. If it is necessary to develop a new program that will complement or add to an existing product, fully understanding the interfaces can be critical to success. Once the interfaces are understood, your application development can proceed.

Disassembly Options

Every DOS computer sold includes a basic debugging tool called DEBUG, which can be helpful in solving problems. Unfortunately, DEBUG only provides a limited ability to disassemble executable programs and show the resultant assembly code.

More advanced products like Borland's Turbo Debugger can also disassemble, but the main focus is on debugging programs under development, where the source code already exists. The results produced by these debuggers and other interactive disassemblers are limited because they only show one screen of code at a time. The output cannot be easily written to a file or printed, the code has no assembler directives, and it can be very difficult to understand.

These products do nothing to separate code from data and easily become misaligned, requiring constant work to get them back on track.

Why Is Disassembly So Difficult ?

The 8088 family of microprocessors is one of the most difficult instruction sets to properly disassemble. These CPUs have a very large and complex instruction set, with many small variations. One of the biggest difficulties occurs with memory references. Figure 2-1 shows one line from a listing.

Figure 2-1. Memory reference from source code listing

```
0492  A1  20C2          mov      ax,Memory_spot
```

The simple move instruction is easy to write and assemble, as the assembler knows what segment and offset Memory_spot resides in. When the processor executes this instruction the processor calculates the location of Memory_spot from the value 20C2h in the binary instruction and the current value in the DS segment register. Disassembly from just the binary instruction is inadequate because the segment register value is not known. Given only the binary instructions "A1 20C2" a disassembler has 65,536 possibilities in memory where the data could reside! Figure 2-2 shows how debuggers display the same instruction, when no source code is provided. There is no clue to the current segment value unless the program is actually run to this location. Of course that may not be possible in real-time software or when looking inside BIOS ROMs.

Figure 2-2. Debugger Disassembly

```
22B1:  0492  A1 20C2          MOV     AX,[20C2]
```

Resolving offsets pose an even trickier problem. In the first line of the listing in Figure 2-3, the SI register is loaded with the offset to String_data. The assembler knows where String_data resides, and builds a binary instruction with this value. When executing this line of code, the processor inserts the binary offset location of String_data into SI. The segment of String_data is unimportant until SI is used later. In this example, the third instruction changes the ES segment value, and the fourth instruction uses the ES segment register with the SI register to reference memory.

Figure 2-3. Offset Operation from Source Listing

```
011C  BE 4E02          mov     si,offset String_data
011F  B8 6000          mov     ax,data_seg
0122  8E C0            mov     es,ax
0124  26:8B 14         mov     dx,es:[si]
```

Debuggers generally avoid doing any analysis and in this case will just display the value coded in the instruction. Figure 2-4 shows what DEBUG does with this same code.

Figure 2-4. Code from DEBUG

DEBUG Output				Comments
5C22:011C	BE024E	MOV	SI,4E02	no offset
5C22:011F	B8C260	MOV	AX,60C2	no segment
5C22:0122	8EC0	MOV	ES,AX	
5C22:0124	26	ES:		segment override is not
5C22:0125	8B14	MOV	DX,[SI]	on the proper line

While technically correct, the disassembly from DEBUG makes the understanding of the program difficult at best. DEBUG also prevents the program from being easily modified, since all offsets and segments are hard-coded hex values.

Commented Disassembly

About ten years ago I developed a special disassembler to solve many of the problems encountered with DEBUG and other disassemblers. I wanted to see disassembled output with comments about what is going on. I also wanted the output to appear similar to what any good assembler programmer would write, and avoid the "machine" look of DEBUG. Over the years my disassembler, Sourcer, was marketed and enhanced by V Communications to accomplish these goals. From executable files, Sourcer produces assembly source code, with comments on complicated instructions, I/O port usage, and interrupt sub-functions. Sourcer performs a complete analysis of the program using multiple passes to generate complete assembly source code.

By looking at the entire program at one time and performing an internal simulation of the code, the quality of the output is greatly enhanced. This makes the code much easier to understand. Sourcer also inserts the necessary assembler directives to help allow resultant source code to be reassembled with the least effort.

Let's look at a tiny 932-byte file called KEYID.EXE. This program prompts the user to select from one of three options and display the ASCII key, scan code, or Num-Lock state. Although the program is not overly useful, KEYID does provide a good starting point in examining the complexities of disassembly.

First, I used DEBUG to disassemble the code. The result is shown in Figure 2-5. It isn't clear what the program does or how it does it. This is typical of interactive debuggers and disassemblers. If the program was even ten times larger, the disassembly task would become quite unmanageable. I've noted in the comments column some of the more significant problems.

Figure 2-5. Using DEBUG to disassemble KEYID.EXE

DEBUG				**Comments about Debug**
C:> DEBUG KEYID.EXE				run DEBUG
-U 0 L1A8				unassemble at 0, 1A8h bytes
22E8:0000	4B	DEC	BX	this area is really data
22E8:0001	45	INC	BP	but DEBUG cannot separate
22E8:0002	59	POP	CX	what is code and what is
22E8:0003	49	DEC	CX	data or determine what
22E8:0004	44	INC	SP	type of data it is
22E8:0005	207631	AND	[BP+31],DH	
22E8:0008	2E	CS:		
22E8:0009	3030	XOR	[BX+SI],DH	
22E8:000B	2028	AND	[BX+SI],CH	
22E8:000D	63	DB	63	further DEBUG errors
22E8:000E	2920	SUB	[BX+SI],SP	
22E8:0010	3139	XOR	[BX+DI],DI	
22E8:0012	3933	CMP	[BP+DI],SI	
22E8:0014	204656	AND	[BP+56],AL	
22E8:0017	47	INC	DI	
22E8:0018	B8F422	MOV	AX,22F4	this is the code start, but
22E8:001B	8ED8	MOV	DS,AX	it's not obvious
22E8:001D	B409	MOV	AH,09	
22E8:001F	BA0E00	MOV	DX,000E	
22E8:0022	CD21	INT	21	what does this do ?
22E8:0024	26	ES:		confusing override placement
22E8:0025	803E800002	CMP	BYTE PTR [0080],02	
22E8:002A	7509	JNZ	0035	no label

Figure 2-5. Continued

```
22E8:002C 26            ES:
22E8:002D A18100        MOV    AX,[0081]      what segment is data in ?
22E8:0030 86C4          XCHG   AL,AH
22E8:0032 EB0C          JMP    0040           no label
22E8:0034 90            NOP                   is this executable ?
22E8:0035 B409          MOV    AH,09
22E8:0037 BA2000        MOV    DX,0020        value or offset ?
22E8:003A CD21          INT    21             what does this do ?
22E8:003C FECC          DEC    AH
22E8:003E CD21          INT    21             no clue what this does
22E8:0040 2C31          SUB    AL,31
22E8:0042 3C02          CMP    AL,02
22E8:0044 77EF          JA     0035
22E8:0046 32E4          XOR    AH,AH
22E8:0048 D0E0          SHL    AL,1
22E8:004A 8BD8          MOV    BX,AX
22E8:004C FFA7CE00      JMP    [BX+00CE]      where does this go ?
22E8:0050 B409          MOV    AH,09          how does this get executed ?
   ...  skipping over confusing code
22E8:00A6 B44C          MOV    AH,4C
22E8:00A8 CD21          INT    21
22E8:00AA 0000          ADD    [BX+SI],AL     seems very unlikely
22E8:00AC 0000          ADD    [BX+SI],AL      (actually this is
22E8:00AE 0000          ADD    [BX+SI],AL      the stack, and is
22E8:00B0 0000          ADD    [BX+SI],AL      shown as a single line
22E8:00B2 0000          ADD    [BX+SI],AL      "  db  30 dup (0) "
22E8:00B4 0000          ADD    [BX+SI],AL      in Sourcer's output)
22E8:00B6 0000          ADD    [BX+SI],AL
   ...  skipping over confusing code
22E8:00CA 0000          ADD    [BX+SI],AL
22E8:00CC 0000          ADD    [BX+SI],AL
```

Figure 2-5. Continued

```
22E8:00CE 4B            DEC    BX               no indication that this
22E8:00CF 45            INC    BP                is a new segment, and
22E8:00D0 59            POP    CX                again mistakes data for
22E8:00D1 20494E        AND    [BX+DI+4E],CL     code
22E8:00D4 44            INC    SP
22E8:00D5 45            INC    BP
   ...  skipping over confusing code
22E8:019A 36            SS:                     really data strings, and
22E8:019B 37            AAA                      is not code
22E8:019C 3839          CMP    [BX+DI],BH
22E8:019E 41            INC    CX
22E8:019F 42            INC    DX
22E8:01A0 43            INC    BX
22E8:01A1 44            INC    SP
22E8:01A2 45            INC    BP
22E8:01A3 46            INC    SI
22E8:01A4 86C4          XCHG   AL,AH            this is beyond the
22E8:01A6 90            NOP                      the end of the file!
22E8:01A7 B44F          MOV    AH,4F
-Q                                              enough already, let's exit
```

With the same KEYID program, Figure 2-6 shows the source code generated automatically by Sourcer. Notice that the output looks more like source code written by a programmer, rather than machine generated. Sourcer inserts directives for the assembler, and identifies each segment and procedure in the program. In addition, the comments shown in the listing are automatically created by Sourcer.

Sourcer also separates code from data and sets the data types based on contextual usage. Code and data separation is one of the most complex tasks for a disassembler, since the binary file has no direct information about what is code or data. This is one of the major reasons why debuggers without source code do such a poor job of disassembly.

Figure 2-6. Disassembly of KEYID.EXE by Sourcer

```
PAGE  59, 132

;
;██████████████████████████████████████████████████████████████████
;██                                                              ██
;██                          KEYID                               ██
;██                                                              ██
;██       Created:   28-Apr-96                                   ██
;██       Version:   1.00                                        ██
;██       Passes:    5          Analysis Options on: none        ██
;██       (c) 1996 FVG                                           ██
;██                                                              ██
;██████████████████████████████████████████████████████████████████

keybd_flags_1   equ     17h
psp_cmd_size    equ     80h
psp_cmd_tail    equ     81h

;------------------------------------------------------ seg_a  ----

seg_a           segment byte public
                assume cs:seg_a , ds:seg_a , ss:stack_seg_b

                db      'KEYID v1.00 '
copyright       db      '(c) 1996 FVG'

;██████████████████████████████████████████████████████████████████
;
;                        Program Entry Point
;
;██████████████████████████████████████████████████████████████████
```

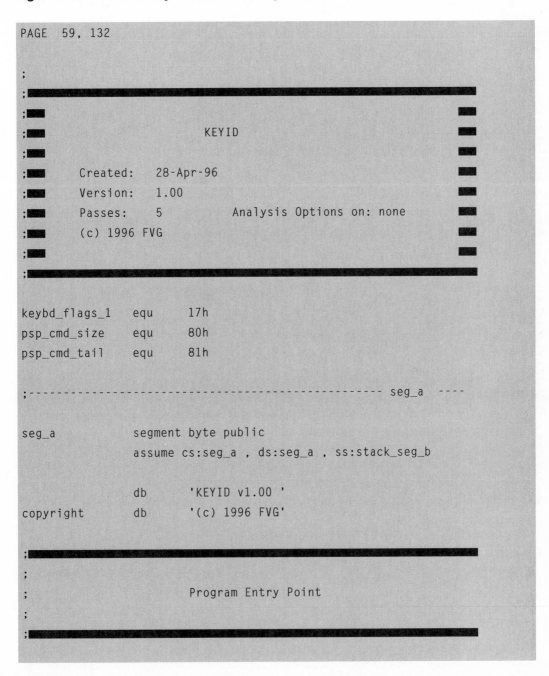

Figure 2-6. Continued

```
keyid   proc    far

start:
        mov     ax,seg_c
        mov     ds,ax
        mov     ah,9
        mov     dx,offset data_9   ; ('KEY IDENTIFIER    ')
        int     21h                ; DOS Services  ah=function 09h
                                   ;  display char string at ds:dx
        cmp     byte ptr es:psp_cmd_size,2
        jne     loc_1              ; Jump if not equal
        mov     ax,es:psp_cmd_tail
        xchg    al,ah
        jmp     short loc_2
        db      90h
loc_1:
        mov     ah,9
        mov     dx,offset data_10  ; ('  Press 1 for ascii char ')
        int     21h                ; DOS Services  ah=function 09h
                                   ;  display char string at ds:dx
        dec     ah
        int     21h                ; DOS Services  ah=function 08h
                                   ;  get keybd char al, no echo
loc_2:
        sub     al,31h             ; '1'
        cmp     al,2
        ja      loc_1              ; Jump if above
        xor     ah,ah              ; Zero register
        shl     al,1               ; Shift w/zeros fill
        mov     bx,ax
        assume  ds:seg_c
        jmp     word ptr data_15[bx] ;*3 entries
```

Figure 2-6. Continued

```
; -----Indexed Entry Point-----------------------------------------

loc_3:
        mov     ah,9
        mov     dx,offset data_11  ; ('  Press key for ascii cha')
        int     21h                ; DOS Services  ah=function 09h
                                   ;  display char string at ds:dx
        mov     ah,1
        int     21h                ; DOS Services  ah=function 01h
                                   ;  get keybd char al, with echo
        jmp     short loc_7
        db      90h

; -----Indexed Entry Point-----------------------------------------

loc_4:
        mov     ah,9
        mov     dx,offset data_12  ; ('  Press key for display o')
        int     21h                ; DOS Services  ah=function 09h
                                   ;  display char string at ds:dx
        xor     ah,ah              ; Zero register
        int     16h                ; Keyboard i/o  ah=function 00h
                                   ;  get keybd char in al, ah=scan
        mov     bx,offset data_18
        mov     al,ah
        and     ax,0F00Fh
        xlat                       ; al=[al+[bx]] table
        mov     dl,al
        mov     al,ah
        mov     cl,4
        ror     al,cl              ; Rotate
        xlat                       ; al=[al+[bx]] table
        mov     ah,0Eh
        xor     bh,bh              ; Zero register
```

Figure 2-6. Continued

```
        int     10h                 ; Video display   ah=functn 0Eh
                                    ;  write char al, teletype mode
        mov     al,dl
        int     10h                 ; Video display   ah=functn 0Eh
                                    ;  write char al, teletype mode
        mov     al,68h
        int     10h                 ; Video display   ah=functn 0Eh
                                    ;  write char al, teletype mode
        jmp     short loc_7
        db      90h

; -----Indexed Entry Point-----------------------------------------

loc_5:
        mov     ax,40h
        mov     es,ax
        test    byte ptr es:keybd_flags_1,20h  ; ' '
        jz      loc_6               ; Jump if zero
        mov     byte ptr data_13+14h,31h  ; ('0') '1'
        nop
loc_6:
        mov     ah,9
        mov     dx,offset data_13   ; ('  Numlock BIOS flag=0 ')
        int     21h                 ; DOS Services  ah=function 09h
                                    ;  display char string at ds:dx
loc_7:
        mov     ah,4Ch
        int     21h                 ; DOS Services  ah=function 4Ch
                                    ;  terminate with al=return code
        db      0, 0, 0, 0, 0, 0

keyid   endp
```

Figure 2-6. Continued

```
seg_a   ends

;----------------------------------------- stack_seg_b  ---

stack_seg_b     segment word stack 'STACK'

      db      30 dup (0)

stack_seg_b     ends

;--------------------------------------------- seg_c  ----

seg_c   segment byte public
        assume cs:seg_c , ds:seg_c , ss:stack_seg_b

        db      14 dup (0)
data_9  db      'KEY IDENTIFIER , 0Dh, 0Ah, '$'
data_10 db      '  Press 1 for ascii char', 0Dh, 0Ah
        db      '  Press 2 for scan code', 0Dh, 0Ah
        db      '  Press 3 for numlock flag', 0Dh
        db      0Ah, 0Dh, 0Ah, '$'
data_11 db      '  Press key for ascii char - $'
data_12 db      '  Press key for display of scan '
        db      'code - $'
data_13 db      '  Numlock BIOS flag=0$'
data_15 dw      offset loc_3           ; Data table (indexed access)
data_16 dw      offset loc_4
data_17 dw      offset loc_5
data_18 db      '0123456789ABCDEF'

seg_c   ends
        end     start
```

Instead of an ASM type output, suitable for reassembly, Sourcer can also create a listing similar to what MASM or TASM creates. This is very useful in understanding how a program works. Sourcer adds cross-reference information wherever a label or data item is defined.

In addition, an interrupt and I/O port usage summary is generated. Figure 2-7 shows a Sourcer output listing of the BEEPA program. The BEEPA program uses the timer to generate a two-second beep.

Figure 2-7. Disassembly Listing of BEEPA.COM by Sourcer

```
                        PAGE  59,132

                        ;██████████████████████████████████████████████████████████
                        ;██                                                      ██
                        ;██                         BEEPA                        ██
                        ;██                                                      ██
                        ;██      Created:    29-Apr-96                           ██
                        ;██      Passes:     5        Analysis Options on: QRS   ██
                        ;██                                                      ██
                        ;██████████████████████████████████████████████████████████

                        seg_a   segment byte public
                                assume  cs:seg_a, ds:seg_a

                                org     100h

                        beepa   proc    far

9382:0100               start:
9382:0100  B0 B6                mov     al,0B6h
9382:0102  E6 43                out     43h,al         ; port 43h, 8253 timer control
9382:0104  B8 00EE              mov     ax,0EEh
9382:0107  EB 00                jmp     short $+2      ; delay for I/O
9382:0109  EB 00                jmp     short $+2      ; delay for I/O
9382:010B  E6 42                out     42h,al         ; port 42h, 8253 timer 2 spkr
9382:010D  8A C4                mov     al,ah
9382:010F  EB 00                jmp     short $+2      ; delay for I/O
9382:0111  EB 00                jmp     short $+2      ; delay for I/O
```

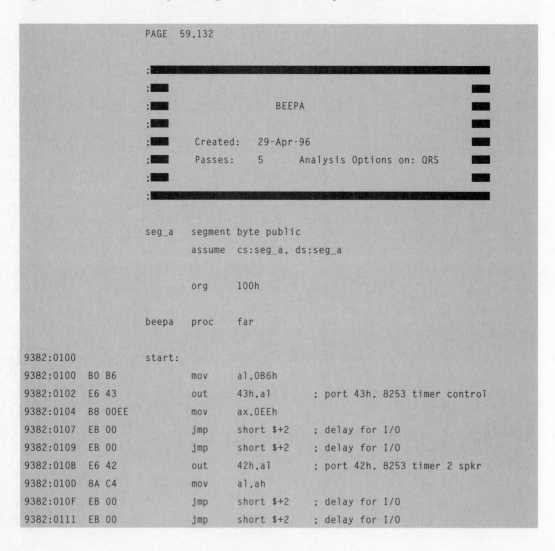

Figure 2-7. Continued

```
9382:0113  E6 42          out    42h,al        ; port 42h, 8253 timer 2 spkr
9382:0115  E4 61          in     al,61h        ; port 61h, 8255 port B, read
9382:0117  0C 03          or     al,3
9382:0119  EB 00          jmp    short $+2     ; delay for I/O
9382:011B  EB 00          jmp    short $+2     ; delay for I/O
9382:011D  E6 61          out    61h,al        ; port 61h, 8255 B - spkr, etc
9382:011F  B4 86          mov    ah,86h
9382:0121  B9 0008        mov    cx,8
9382:0124  BA 0000        mov    dx,0
9382:0127  CD 15          int    15h           ; General services, ah=func 86h
                                               ;  wait cx:dx microseconds
9382:0129  E4 61          in     al,61h        ; port 61h, 8255 port B, read
9382:012B  24 FC          and    al,0FCh
9382:012D  EB 00          jmp    short $+2     ; delay for I/O
9382:012F  EB 00          jmp    short $+2     ; delay for I/O
9382:0131  E6 61          out    61h,al        ; port 61h, 8255 B - spkr, etc
                                               ;  al = 0, speaker off
9382:0133  B4 4C          mov    ah,4Ch
9382:0135  CD 21          int    21h           ; DOS Services  ah=function 4Ch
                                               ;  terminate with al=return code

                 beepa    endp

                 seg_a    ends

                          end    start

                 ███████ CROSS REFERENCE - KEY ENTRY POINTS ███████

                   seg:off    type       label
                  ---- ----   ----    ------------------------------
                  9382:0100   far     start
```

Figure 2-7. Continued

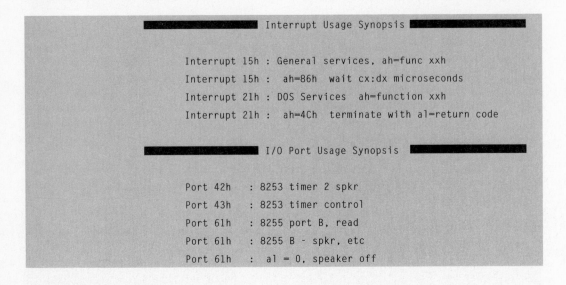

```
                    Interrupt Usage Synopsis

        Interrupt 15h : General services, ah=func xxh
        Interrupt 15h :  ah=86h  wait cx:dx microseconds
        Interrupt 21h : DOS Services  ah=function xxh
        Interrupt 21h :  ah=4Ch  terminate with al=return code

                    I/O Port Usage Synopsis

        Port 42h    : 8253 timer 2 spkr
        Port 43h    : 8253 timer control
        Port 61h    : 8255 port B, read
        Port 61h    : 8255 B - spkr, etc
        Port 61h    :  al = 0, speaker off
```

One quick way to get a general idea of the function of a program is to look at the end of the Sourcer listing. There you will find a summary of interrupts and I/O ports used. From the summary at the end of the BEEPA listing, note that interrupt 15h is used for a wait function, and I/O ports are used for the timer and speaker gate. This program would need considerable modification to work on a non-IBM compatible system like the NEC 9800 series computer, popular in Japan.

Other portions of a listing can often provide a quick view into a disassembled program. Looking back on the earlier KEYID program disassembly, the beginning of the program has a few equates created by Sourcer. These equates are shown in Figure 2-8 from the Sourcer listing of KEYID.

Figure 2-8. Equates from KEYID Disassembly

```
keybd_flags_1    equ     17h             ; (0040:0017=0)
psp_cmd_size     equ     80h             ; (81EF:0080=0)
psp_cmd_tail     equ     81h             ; (81EF:0081=0)
```

These equates are created by Sourcer to identify data references outside the bounds of the program. Sourcer has an internal database of common references into the BIOS, PSP, and other areas.

In the first equate, the program uses the keyboard flags in the BIOS data area at 40:17h. This BIOS reference could be a problem for running the program on a non-IBM compatible system.

The KEYID program also accesses data in PSP at offset 80 and 81h. It is clear the program reads information from the command line that was stored by DOS at PSP offset 81h. Searching the program for the keyword *psp_cmd_size* will identify the area of code that handles command line input.

Another key area of interest is the cross reference at the end of the listing. The cross-reference summary shows key entry points and shows interrupt entry points into the program. Figure 2-9 shows a portion of the cross-reference section for a disassembly of the system BIOS. From this information, you can quickly locate key routines in the program.

Figure 2-9. Partial Cross Reference from Sourcer's BIOS Analysis

```
           CROSS REFERENCE - KEY ENTRY POINTS

  seg:off     type          label
---- ----     ----     -------------------------------

0000:7C00     far      run_boot_sector
F000:00F0     near     ROM_exception
F000:0100     near     system_reset
F000:0F1F     near     int_19h_bootup
F000:15F7     near     int_2_NMI
F000:3CCC     near     int_13h_floppy
F000:4A41     near     int_13h_hrd_dsk
F000:529B     near     int_10h_video
  .
  .
```

With TSR programs, Sourcer identifies interrupt entry points by examining any interrupt 21h, function 25h calls. This is the DOS function used to hook an interrupt. Through Sourcer's simulation, it is usually able to identify the entry point of the hooked service routine and assign a descriptive label like *int_33h_entry*.

It is wise to review the code. Sourcer helps by placing a warning star comment ";*" on lines that indicate potential trouble spots. For example, in the Sourcer KEYID listing, the indexed jump instruction has such a warning star. This one line is repeated in Figure 2-10.

Figure 2-10. Example of Warning Star

```
81FF:004C    jmp    word ptr data_15[bx]  ;*(820B:00CE=50h) 3 entries
```

Sourcer needed to make a number of assumptions in processing this complex instruction. Sourcer located and identified three entries in a table of offsets starting at data_15. Then each offset in the table was linked to a specific location within the program. In this case, Sourcer performed the task perfectly. Index jumps often occur in the BIOS, and Sourcer's ability to automatically build the table of offsets makes understanding a BIOS routine much easier.

Should a change be necessary, Sourcer has a definition facility that provides complete control over the results. With this facility you can control segment types for 16- or 32-bit code, add your own descriptive labels and comments, and define special data types. The definition facility also allows setting of all of Sourcer's format control options such as uppercase versus lowercase, label styles, and other user preferences.

When generating assembly code, Sourcer also allows the selection of a target assembler. Every assembler produces slightly different binary code given the identical source code. This is due in part to the Intel instruction set, which offers a number of ways to encode the same instruction. Sourcer can "tune" its output for a specific assembler version to aid in reassembling the code. In most cases, the resultant assembly code can be reassembled to be byte identical to the original binary file.

Sourcer handles a wide variety of inputs formats. These include multisegment EXE files, COM files, device drivers (both .SYS and .EXE types), chained device drivers, disassembly from ROM or RAM, and Windows 32-bit VxDs. Sourcer also has an optional pre-processor, Windows Source, to handle Windows EXEs, DLLs, VxDs, device drivers, resources, WIN32S, OS/2 32-bit programs, and several other formats.

Disassembly can be performed by anyone, but some knowledge of assembly language is necessary to understand the results. Sourcer greatly simplifies this task. With advanced tools such as Sourcer, solving problems and understanding undocumented interfaces is feasible.

Disassembling the BIOS

The task of disassembling the BIOS is far more complex than that of an ordinary EXE or device driver. The BIOS is comprised of a number of independent routines and data tables. Each BIOS is implemented in different ways so that routines and data end up in completely different locations. The locations also tend to change between different versions from the same manufacturer.

Different BIOSes provide a wide range of functions. For the system BIOS there are currently five major types: the PC, XT, AT (ISA & PCI), EISA, and MCA. The system BIOS controls the power on tests, basic disk control, simple video control, printers, serial ports, and other key functions. For adapter cards, there are countless BIOSes. A few of the more popular adapter BIOSes include the hard disk, video, and network cards.

A few years ago I developed a companion to Sourcer, the BIOS Pre-Processor, to automate the disassembly of a BIOS. The BIOS Pre-Processor works with Sourcer to generate a complete listing of the BIOS with detailed comments. The Pre-Processor analyzes the BIOS ROM and the system to determine interrupt entry points, where data areas reside, the size of the data areas, and other key information about the BIOS under analysis. The Pre-Processor then labels this information descriptively. Instead of a generic label (or no labels if using a debugger), key references are in English. For example, the video service routine entry label appears as *int_10h_video*. Many data references also appear descriptively throughout the code, with labels like *baud_rate_tbl* and *hdsk_cylinders*.

The end result is a very readable listing of the BIOS. I've had customers who have seen a manufacturer's original BIOS source code and tell me the Sourcer-generated listings are clearer than their own original source code! Figure 2-11 shows a partial output of Printer BIOS service routine generated by Sourcer after the BIOS Pre-Processor has run. This printer BIOS routine handles three functions. Each function is handled through the use of an indexed call instruction. In this case, Sourcer builds the table of three subroutine offsets, and identifies the three subroutines starting with *sub_75*.

Figure 2-11. Partial Disassembly Listing of BIOS by Sourcer

```
mbios.lst        SYSTEM BIOS                Sourcer Listing                 Page 35

F000:08E5  0910       data_75 dw     offset sub_75        ; Data table (indexed)
                                                          ;  xref F000:0903

F000:08E7  091D       data_76 dw     offset sub_76        ;  xref F000:0903
F000:08E9  092F       data_77 dw     offset sub_77        ;  xref F000:0903

                      ;
                      ; ████████████████████████████████████ int 17h ██████
                      ;
                      ;   PRINTER SERVICES
                      ;
                      ;   Call with:  ah = function code
                      ;               dx = printer number 0-2 (may allow 0-3)
                      ;
                      ;   Returns:    ah = status bits
                      ;                 7     6      5    4      3   2  1   0
                      ;                not  acknow-  no  select  I/O  unused  no
                      ;                busy  ledge  paper        error        response
                      ;                -------- from printer --------
```

Figure 2-11. Continued

```
                    ;
                    ;   Functions:
                    ;       ah = 0   Send character to printer, al = character
                    ;       ah = 1   Printer port initialization
                    ;       ah = 2   Get printer status in ah

F000:08EB                int_17h_printer proc    far           ;  xref F000:0504
F000:08EB  53                    push    bx
F000:08EC  51                    push    cx
F000:08ED  1E                    push    ds
F000:08EE  06                    push    es
F000:08EF  80 FC 03              cmp     ah,3
F000:08F2  73 15                 jae     loc_135               ; Jump if above or =
F000:08F4  E8 FFE4               call    sub_74
F000:08F7  8B FA                 mov     di,dx
F000:08F9  D1 E7                 shl     di,1                  ; Shift w/zeros fill
F000:08FB  26:8B 55 08           mov     dx,es:@prn_port_1[di] ; (0040:0008=378h)
F000:08FF  8A DC                 mov     bl,ah
F000:0901  32 FF                 xor     bh,bh                 ; Zero register
F000:0903  FF 97 08E5            call    word ptr data_75[bx] ;*(F000:08E5=910h)
                                                               ;   3 entries
F000:0907  EB 02                 jmp     short loc_136
F000:0909                loc_135:                              ;  xref F000:08F2
F000:0909  B4 09                 mov     ah,9
F000:090B                loc_136:                              ;  xref F000:0907
F000:090B  07                    pop     es
F000:090C  1F                    pop     ds
F000:090D  59                    pop     cx
F000:090E  5B                    pop     bx
F000:090F  CF                    iret                          ; Interrupt return
                         int_17h_printer endp
```

Figure 2-11. Continued

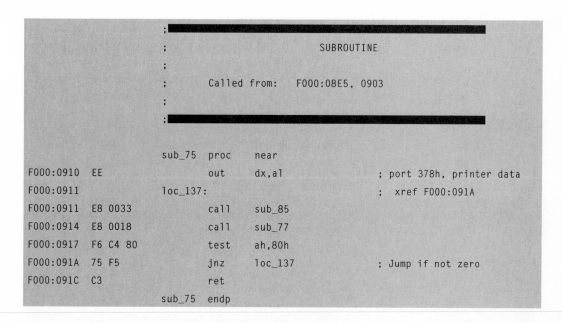

```
                        ;
                        ;                              SUBROUTINE
                        ;
                        ;       Called from:   F000:08E5, 0903
                        ;
                        ;

                        sub_75  proc    near
F000:0910  EE                   out     dx,al                   ; port 378h, printer data
F000:0911               loc_137:                                ;  xref F000:091A
F000:0911  E8 0033              call    sub_85
F000:0914  E8 0018              call    sub_77
F000:0917  F6 C4 80             test    ah,80h
F000:091A  75 F5                jnz     loc_137                 ; Jump if not zero
F000:091C  C3                   ret
                        sub_75  endp
```

IOSPY—The I/O Port Monitor TSR

In many cases, it's handy to see the status of an I/O port while running or debugging other programs. IOSPY is a terminate and stay resident utility (TSR) included on the disk that continuously monitors specified ports and displays the current state on screen. IOSPY has a number of options to handle almost any I/O port.

To use IOSPY, just run IOSPY with the port number desired. Up to eight ports can be monitored at one time. A number of global and local options control how IOSPY operates. When activated (by turning on scroll-lock), a Spyport is shown for each port specified. The Spyport includes the port number, the current value read from the port, the last different value read from the port, and a short text identifier. The first time IOSPY is run, the last value will be blank until the port has a change in value. A Spyport appears on screen as:

```
port  27Ah=FFh  last=0Eh  Printer
```

Global options are not related to any specific I/O port. They include:

- -a Always-on mode is active. By default, IOSPY is active only when scroll-lock is on.
- -c Clear all ports, but remain resident (occurs when no port number appears before the -c option).

-d This option shows the Spyport information outside of the normal 25-row screen on a color VGA system. The VGA controller is set up to use 31 lines of text. The port status information is shown below the normal 25-line screen, without obstructing DOS or a running program. DOS is told the screen is still 80 columns by 25 lines, and most well-behaved programs will only display information in the 25-line window. This special mode is not usable for graphics programs or programs that perform custom video control. This feature is unlikely to work on laptop screens as well, since IOSPY sets the VGA controller to 500 scan line mode.

-m On a dual monitor system, this option forces the port status information to appear on the monochrome adapter. No checks are made to see if the monochrome adapter is truly present.

-n No background color change. Without this option, the background color is briefly changed whenever the port value changes.

-u Uninstall. IOSPY can be removed when no other TSR has been installed after IOSPY that hooks interrupt 1Ch. Uninstall will work even if IOSPY has been loaded into high memory. If the -d option was used, IOSPY also restores the VGA screen to normal 80x25 operation.

Local options are specific to an I/O port. Each I/O port monitored can have different local options. By default, no local options are active. A port number is specified, and the options that appear after the port number are associated with that port.

-b Beep when the specified I/O port changes value. IOSPY will use the hardware timer 2. If another program uses timer 2, the beep function may overwrite the timer 2 mode and timing function.

-c Clear the specified port from IOSPY's list of ports to monitor.

-f Filter the incoming data. This option is useful if the data is changing too quickly to see. The quickly changing data are still shown, but instead of showing the last changed value, a filtered value is shown, updated once every 400 ms.

-hXX Hex value pre-write mode is enabled. For I/O ports that use two ports to access information, this option will write the hex value XX to the specified port, and then read status from the port number plus one (or plus two if a 16-bit port). This is useful for looking at CMOS registers and many VGA registers.

-s Sixteen-bit I/O operation is used for the selected port instead of the default of 8-bit operation (most I/O ports are 8-bit).

-w Write back to the port the previously read value. Used when reading the port causes bits to change in the same register. For example some of the serial port status registers clear bits when the register is read. Interrupts are disabled between the read and the write.

'text' Override the default text string provided by IOSPY. The text string can be up to 10 characters long, though only the first 8 characters are shown in 16-bit mode.

Multiple ports can be specified at one time, or additional ports can be added after IOSPY is installed. After a port has been loaded, IOSPY can be rerun with the same port number with new options to update the resident copy of IOSPY.

For example, to monitor the printer status at port 279h and printer control at port 27Ah, the following command line is entered. Turn on Scroll-lock to see the status information.

```
iospy 279 27A
```

The result of this example will appear as two lines in the upper right corner of the screen. The Spyport appears on screen as:

```
port  279h=FFh            Printer
port  27Ah=FFh            Printer
```

A more complex example uses the global always-on option (-a), and displays the port information below the 80x25 screen (-d). This example monitors the CMOS equipment byte number 14h, (ports 70 and 71h). If the CMOS equipment byte changes in value, beep (-b). The text 'CMOS equip' will be associated with port pair 70/71h. The example also monitors the serial port line status register 3FBh. Since the line status register clears bits when read, the port value must be written back after a read, so a program depending on these error flags has the proper information.

```
iospy -a -d  70 -h14 -b 'CMOS equip' 3FB -w
```

With this example, beneath the first 25 lines of the screen, the Spyport information appears.

```
---------------------------------------- iospy------------
port  71h=0Fh          CMOS equip    port 3FBh=02h          RS232 line
```

Keep in mind that some ports are write only, and reading the port will not produce valid information. Since IOSPY monitors ports every timer tick (once every 54 ms), the displayed information is always valid, but it is possible the port may have been changed to other values between IOSPY snapshots.

The IOSPY TSR is designed to operate reliably from either high or low memory. When loading high, IOSPY will require about 6K bytes to load, before reducing to a resident size of under 1.3K bytes. The small resident size is primarily due to its implementation in assembly language.

One last note about using IOSPY on serial ports. Remember that if you read incoming data from a serial port, the data will appear on screen, but will be lost to the software using the serial port. The Writeback option will not work since a write to the serial port tells the UART to transmit the byte. For monitoring status on the serial port, some registers will require writing the data back after a read. Use the program SSPY to monitor serial port status. It is a subset of the IOSPY program, specifically designed to monitor serial port status activity. Refer to Chapter 12, Serial Ports, for more information and details on SSPY.

Although IOSPY source code is not included on the disk, it is similar in nature to the SSPY program which does include source code on the disk. IOSPY works by hooking the interrupt 8 timer interrupt. The resident portion gets called every 54 ms, and reads the current status of the specified ports and updates the screen information using direct screen writes.

UNPC—I/O Port Viewer

Sometimes it is desirable to see if a specific port or range of ports is being used and what values the ports hold. I've created an I/O viewer that continuously displays the contents of any group of 256 ports. To run the I/O viewer, run UNPC, select *I/O Port Viewer*, and then *View I/O Ports.*

UNPC will continuously read and display the first 256 I/O ports. Use the PgUp and PgDn keys to move through other groups of ports. F1 provides additional details. Figure 2-12 shows how the I/O port viewer appears on screen.

Figure 2-12. UNPC I/O Viewer

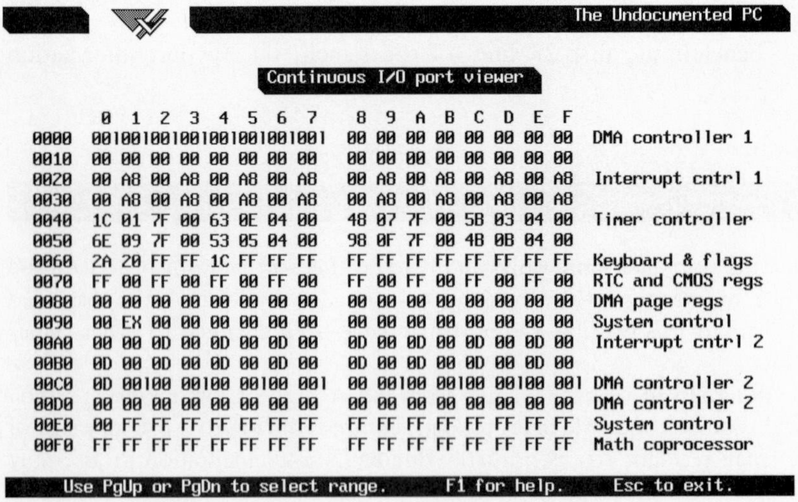

The Undocumented PC
Continuous I/O port viewer
0 1 2 3 4 5 6 7 8 9 A B C D E F
0000 00100100100100100100100100 00 00 00 00 00 00 00 00 DMA controller 1
0010 00 00 00 00 00 00 00 00 00 00 00 00 00 00 00 00
0020 00 A8 00 A8 00 A8 00 A8 00 A8 00 A8 00 A8 00 A8 Interrupt cntrl 1
0030 00 A8 00 A8 00 A8 00 A8 00 A8 00 A8 00 A8 00 A8
0040 1C 01 7F 00 63 0E 04 00 48 07 7F 00 5B 03 04 00 Timer controller
0050 6E 09 7F 00 53 05 04 00 98 0F 7F 00 4B 0B 04 00
0060 2A 20 FF FF 1C FF FF FF FF FF FF FF FF FF FF FF Keyboard & flags
0070 FF 00 FF 00 FF 00 FF 00 FF 00 FF 00 FF 00 FF 00 RTC and CMOS regs
0080 00 00 00 00 00 00 00 00 00 00 00 00 00 00 00 00 DMA page regs
0090 00 EX 00 00 00 00 00 00 00 00 00 00 00 00 00 00 System control
00A0 00 00 0D 00 0D 00 0D 00 0D 00 0D 00 0D 00 0D 00 Interrupt cntrl 2
00B0 0D 00 0D 00 0D 00 0D 00 0D 00 0D 00 0D 00 0D 00
00C0 0D 00100 00100 00100 001 00 00100 00100 00100 001 DMA controller 2
00D0 00 00 00 00 00 00 00 00 00 00 00 00 00 00 00 00 DMA controller 2
00E0 00 FF FF FF FF FF FF FF FF FF FF FF FF FF FF FF System control
00F0 FF FF FF FF FF FF FF FF FF FF FF FF FF FF FF FF Math coprocessor
Use PgUp or PgDn to select range. F1 for help. Esc to exit.

Be aware that system ports and many adapter cards do not fully decode I/O ports, making them appear at multiple places. For example, a printer port at 279h may appear every 400h in the I/O port address range. This means reading port 279h is the same as ports 679h, A79h, E79h, 1279h, etc. Some system ports, like the interrupt controller ports 20h and 21h, may appear repeated every two ports starting at 22h and 23h through 3Eh and 3Fh. This *port duplication* is caused by the motherboard or adapter vendor saving a few cents in logic and poorly decoding I/O addresses. Newer systems are less prone to do this. EISA systems are specifically designed to avoid these problems.

As I noted in the discussion of IOSPY, some I/O ports require special handling. First, a few 8-bit ports must be read twice to get a resultant 16-bit value. Use the spacebar to toggle if the low or high portion is shown from a read-twice port. Some ports cause system problems if read. These ports are excluded and appear on screen as a red EX. Lastly, some ports lose their contents if read, and must be written back after being read. Writeback ports are shown in blue.

All of these special cases can be changed on a port-by-port basis. From the prior menu (press Esc if you are in the I/O port viewer), you can select Exclusions, Writebacks, or Read-Twice. Each of these allow setting the respective option for I/O ports. Use the spacebar to toggle the state of the port that the cursor appears on. In addition, the Insert and Delete keys allow activation or clearing a group of ports, or resetting the flags to the original defaults. Any option changes will be automatically saved upon exit of UNPC. If you wish to exit without saving the changes, just press Ctrl-C.

The I/O port viewer works by simply reading each I/O port and displaying the value on the screen as fast as possible. Once all of the current group of 256 ports have been read, the process repeats. The speed of updates depends on the CPU speed, expansion bus speed, and the video adapter performance. Even though the screen appears in graphics mode, it is really in text mode, using custom fonts borrowed (with permission) from V Communications. This maintains the best possible screen update performance.

CHAPTER 3

The CPU and Undocumented Instructions

Most 80x86 CPUs are well documented in related CPU manuals and other books. Since the balance of this book covers undocumented ports and usage, the first part of this chapter reviews input and output on the 80x86 family of CPUs. There is very little new or undocumented in this part, but the information will be useful if you are unclear or unfamiliar with using ports to control and access information on the PC.

A somewhat more interesting section follows, covering timing issues related to I/O ports. The timing section explains when delays are needed between I/O port accesses. A sample program is provided as one means to ensure port timing overlaps do not occur.

For those individuals who hate assembly code, you'll find a section on how to access CPU hardware through high-level languages such as C and C++. This includes access to registers, interrupts, and I/O ports. An example program is provided in both C and assembly to contrast the differences.

Later, I explain various versions of the CPU and the differences among vendors' CPUs. This includes many offerings from AMD/NexGen, Cyrix, IBM, Intel, NEC, and Texas Instruments.

The middle section of this chapter is one of the most interesting parts of the book. It covers undocumented instructions on various CPUs. This includes extensive details on LOADALL, and other less known "undocumented" instructions.

The chapter wraps up with specific topics relating to the CPU. This includes explanations of hidden memory, suspend/resume, in-circuit-emulation, and reset. Routines are provided to produce a reliable system reset, and to get control before CTRL-ALT-DEL resets the system.

Input/Output Basics

Input and Output refer to the ability of the processor to communicate with devices external to the processor. For example, when the processor wishes to send a character to the printer, the CPU outputs a character. The reverse action occurs when the processor receives information. When a key is pressed on the keyboard, the character is input to the processor as shown in Figure 3-1.

Figure 3-1. Processor Input and Output

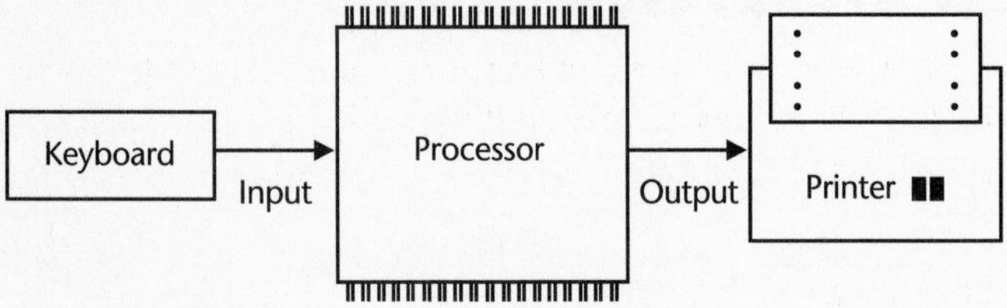

Other examples of input devices on a PC include mice, digitizing tablets, trackballs, modems, networks, disk drives, and tape drives. Output device types include displays, plotters, modems, networks, disk drives, and tape drives. Many devices are used for both for input and output. A storage device, such as a disk drive, needs to save output from the processor. To read data from the disk drive the data is input to the processor.

Input and output are generally sent as bytes or words and, on the latest processors, can be send as double words. This means that the processor can transfer 8, 16, or 32 bits of information at one time.

The Intel 80x86 family of processors offers two ways to access input and output devices. The processors provide specific instructions to access a dedicated I/O address space. The I/O address space is the most common way PCs perform input and output. As an alternative, hardware designers can define I/O as positions in the memory address space, commonly called memory-mapped I/O. This is rarely employed to avoid memory conflicts in PCs.

I/O Addressing

The 80x86 family can access 65,536 individual 8-bit ports. Two 8-bit ports can be combined to create a 16-bit port. On 386 processors and above, four 8-bit ports can be used to create a 32-bit port. Instructions are provided to access the first 256 ports using an immediate byte to define the port number. Alternatively, the DX register is used to specify any of the possible 65,536 ports. Table 3-1 summarizes this information for the different address types.

Table 3-1. I/O Address Types

Port Number Defined by	Number of Ports	Recommended Alignment	Data Size	Port Numbering
immediate byte	256	byte	8-bit	0,1,2,3,..... 255
immediate byte	128	word	16-bit	0,2,4,6,..... 254
immediate byte	64	double word	32-bit	0,4,8,16,.... 252
DX register	256	byte	8-bit	0,1,2,3,... 65535
DX register	128	word	16-bit	0,2,4,6,... 65534
DX register	64	double word	32-bit	0,4,8,16,.. 65532

Aligning the port size to the related boundary assures that all the bits are transferred in a single cycle. This means a 16-bit port should use even port addresses, such as 0, 2, and 4. A 32-bit port should use port addresses divisible by four, such as 0, 4, and 8. The CPU design allows nonaligned ports, but the access will require more bus cycles which slows access through a non-aligned port.

I/O Instructions

There are four basic I/O instructions available on all 8088 and later processors. Two additional instructions were added with the 80188 processor to handle multiple accesses in one instruction. A summary of the basic instructions is shown in Table 3-2.

Table 3-2. I/O Port Instruction Summary

Instruction	Operands	Description
IN	reg, imm	Input, where register=AL/AX/EAX
IN	reg, DX	Input, where register=AL/AX/EAX
INS		Input saved at memory at ES:[DI]
OUT	imm, reg	Output, where register=AL/AX/EAX
OUT	DX, reg	Output, where register=AL/AX/EAX
OUTS		Output from memory at ES:[DI]

Input from Port

The IN instruction transfers a data byte, word, or double word from the specified port into the specified register, AL, AX, or EAX. The short immediate form can be used to read from any of the first 256 ports, 0 to 0FFh. The DX forms are used to access any input port 0 to 0FFFFh.

IN	AL, PORT#	Input byte from immediate port number into AL (for port numbers 0 to 0FFh only)
IN	AX, PORT#	Input word from immediate port number into AX (for port numbers 0 to 0FFh only)

IN	EAX, PORT#	Input double word from immediate port number into EAX (for port numbers 0 to 0FFh, 386 and later only)
IN	AL, DX	Input byte from port DX into AL
IN	AX, DX	Input word from port DX into AX
IN	EAX, DX	Input double word from port DX into EAX (386 and later only)

Code Examples:

```
        in      al, 60h
        in      ax, 20h
        in      eax, 42h
        mov     dx, 60h
        in      al, dx
        mov     dx, 3E27h
        in      ax, dx
        mov     dx, 177Ch
        in      eax, dx
```

Input String

The INS (input string) instruction transfers a byte, word, or double word from the port specified by the DX register. When operating in 16-bit address-size mode, the destination is ES:[DI]. When operating in 32-bit address-size mode, the destination is ES:[EDI]. The ES segment register is always used, as no segment overrides are allowed.

After the transfer is made, the DI/EDI register is updated by the size of the transfer. A cleared direction flag (from a previous CLD instruction) will cause the DI/EDI register to increment. A set direction flag (from a previous STD instruction) will cause the DI/EDI register to decrement. For a byte transfer, the DI/EDI register changes by one, word transfers change DI/EDI by two, and double word transfers change DI/EDI by four.

The REP (repeat) prefix is commonly used with INS to input a string of length CX. INS is not valid on 8088/8086 processors. INSD (double word) and all 32-bit address-size forms are valid only on 80386 and later processors.

16-Bit Address-size mode

INSB	Input byte from port DX into ES:[DI], then increment/decrement DI by one.
INSW	Input word from port DX into ES:[DI], then increment/decrement DI by two.
INSD	Input double word from port DX into ES:[DI], then increment/decrement DI by four. (386 and later only)

32-Bit Address-size mode (386 and later only)

INSB	Input byte from port DX into ES:[EDI], then increment/decrement EDI by one.
INSW	Input word from port DX into ES:[EDI], then increment/decrement EDI by two.
INSD	Input double word from port DX into ES:[EDI], then increment/decrement EDI by four.

Code Examples:

```
        mov     es, seg in_buffer   ; es:di = ptr to buffer
        mov     di, offset in_buffer
        mov     dx, 123h            ; dx = port number 123h
        cld                         ; clear direction flag
        insb                        ; input 1 byte to in_buffer
                                    ;  DI points to in_buffer+1
```

```
        mov     es, seg in_buffer   ; es:di = ptr to buffer
        mov     di, offset in_buffer
        mov     dx, 60h             ; dx = port number 60h
        mov     cx, 30              ; cx = number of times to input
        cld                         ; clear direction flag
        rep     insw                ; input 30 words to in_buffer,
                                    ;  at completion, register DI
                                    ;  points to in_buffer+60
```

Warnings

When the CPU is running in virtual 8086 mode with a 386 or later processor, trapping of the INS instruction can cause problems. The protected mode manager gets control when the trapped INS instruction is issued. Unfortunately, the trapping process cannot restart the first input byte/word from INS. Although trapping individual ports is avoided because of performance effects, the protected mode manager may have to trap some ports for system reliability. Trapping of the DMA ports is a prime example of this.

Protected mode environments include all memory managers like EMM386, Windows Enhanced mode, and newer operating systems like OS/2, Windows 95 and NT. When the software will be used in these environments, I highly recommended that you avoid INS in your code.

Output to Port

OUT	PORT#, AL	Output byte in AL to immediate port number (for port numbers 0 to 0FFh only)
OUT	PORT#, AX	Output word in AX to immediate port number (for port numbers 0 to 0FFh only)
OUT	PORT#, EAX	Output double word in EAX to immediate port number (for port numbers 0 to 0FFh, 386 and later only)
OUT	DX, AL	Output byte in AL to port DX
OUT	DX, AX	Output word in AX to port DX
OUT	DX, EAX	Output double word in EAX to port DX (386 and later only)

Code Examples:

```
        out     60h, al
        out     20h, ax
        out     42h, eax
        mov     dx, 60h
        out     dx, al
        mov     dx, 3E27h
        out     dx, ax
        mov     dx, 177Ch
        out     dx, eax
```

Output String

The OUTS (output string) instruction transfers a byte, word, or double word from the source register to the port specified by the DX register. When operating in 16-bit address-size mode, the source is DS:[SI]. When operating in 32-bit address-size mode, the source is DS:[ESI]. DS is the default segment register, and OUTS allows other segment overrides.

After the transfer is made, the SI/ESI register is updated by the size of the transfer. A cleared direction flag (from a previous CLD instruction) will cause the SI/ESI register to increment. A set direction flag (from a previous STD instruction) will cause the SI/ESI register to decrement. For a byte transfer, the SI/ESI register changes by one, word transfers change SI/ESI by two, and double word transfer change SI/ESI by four.

The REP (repeat) prefix is commonly used with OUTS to output a string of length CX. OUTS is not valid on 8088/8086 processors. OUTSD (double word) and all 32-bit address-size forms are valid only on 80386 and higher processors.

16-Bit Address-size mode

OUTS	DX, BYTE PTR DS:[SI]	Output byte to port DX from DS:[SI], then increment/decrement SI by one. Any segment register can be used in place of DS.
OUTS	DX, WORD PTR DS:[SI]	Output word to port DX from DS:[SI], then increment/decrement SI by two. Any segment register can be used in place of DS.
OUTS	DX, DWORD PTR DS:[SI]	Output double word to port DX from DS:[SI], then increment/decrement SI by four. Any segment register can be used in place of DS. This form is only valid on 386 and later processors.
OUTSB		Output byte to port DX from DS:[SI], then increment/decrement SI by one.

OUTSW		Output word to port DX from DS:[SI], then increment/decrement SI by two.
OUTSD		Output double word to port DX from DS:[SI], then increment/decrement SI by four. This form is only valid on 386 and later processors.

32-Bit Address-size mode (386 and later only)

OUTS	DX, BYTE PTR DS:[ESI]	Output byte to port DX from DS:[ESI], then increment/decrement ESI by one. Any segment register can be used in place of DS.
OUTS	DX, WORD PTR DS:[ESI]	Output word to port DX from DS:[ESI], then increment/decrement ESI by two. Any segment register can be used in place of DS.
OUTS	DX, DWORD PTR DS:[ESI]	Output double word to port DX from DS:[ESI], then increment/decrement ESI by four. Any segment register can be used in place of DS. This form is only valid on 386 and later processors.
OUTSB		Output byte to port DX from DS:[ESI], then increment/decrement ESI by one.
OUTSW		Output word to port DX from DS:[ESI], then increment/decrement ESI by two.
OUTSD		Output double word to port DX from DS:[ESI], then increment/decrement ESI by four. This form is only valid on 386 and later processors.

Code Examples:

```
mov     gs, seg out_buffer ; gs:si = ptr to buffer
mov     si, offset out_buffer
mov     dx, 234h           ; dx = port number
cld                        ; clear direction flag
outsb    dx, gs:[si]       ; output 1 byte from out_buffer
                           ;   SI points to out_buffer+1
```

```
mov     ds, seg out_buffer ; ds:si = ptr to buffer
mov     si, offset out_buffer
mov     dx, 234h           ; dx = port number
mov     cx, 20             ; cx = number of times to output
```

```
        cld                             ; clear direction flag
        rep     outsw                   ; output 20 words from out_buffer,
                                        ; at completion, register SI
                                        ; will point to out_buffer+40
```

Instruction Timing

Table 3-3 below shows the number of clock cycles each instruction requires for each processor. The times assume the instruction has been prefetched and is ready for execution, that it has no wait states, that there are no exceptions while processing the instruction, and that it starts on a double word boundary. This means you are unlikely to get these best-case numbers.

In protected mode (PM) on the 386 through Pentium, two timings are shown. The first time is when the current privilege level is less or equal to the I/O privilege level. The second time occurs when the current privilege level is greater than the I/O privilege level. The I/O privilege level (IOPL) is in the EFLAGS register and defines the right to use I/O related instructions. Intel does not document instruction timings for the Pentium Pro.

Table 3-3. I/O Instruction Timings

				--80386--		-------80486-------			------Pentium------		
Instruction	**Opcode**	**8088**	**80286**	**Real**	**PM**	**Real**	**VM**	**PM**	**Real**	**VM**	**PM**
IN AL, imm8	E4 ib	10	5	12	6/26	14	27	8/28	7	19	4/21
IN AX, imm8	E5 ib	10	5	12	6/26	14	27	8/28	7	19	4/21
IN EAX, imm8	E5 ib			12	6/26	14	27	8/28	7	19	4/21
IN AL, DX	EC	8	5	13	7/27	14	27	8/28	7	19	4/21
IN AX, DX	ED	8	5	13	7/27	14	27	8/28	7	19	4/21
IN EAX, DX	ED			13	7/27	14	27	8/28	7	19	4/21
INSB	6C		5	15	9/29	17	30	10/32	9	22	6/24
INSW	6D		5	15	9/29	17	30	10/32	9	22	6/24
INSD	6D			15	9/29	17	30	10/32	9	22	6/24
OUT imm8, AL	E6 ib	10	3	10	4/24	16	29	11/31	12	24	9/26
OUT imm8, AX	E7 ib	10	3	10	4/24	16	29	11/31	12	24	9/26
OUT imm8, EAX	E7 ib			10	4/24	16	29	11/31	12	24	9/26
OUT DX, AL	EE	8	3	10	5/25	16	29	11/31	12	24	9/26
OUT DX, AX	EF	8	3	10	5/25	16	29	11/31	12	24	9/26
OUT DX, EAX	EF			10	5/25	16	29	11/31	12	24	9/26
OUTSB	6E		5	14	8/28	17	30	10/32	13	25	10/27
OUTSW	6F		5	14	8/28	17	30	10/32	13	25	10/27
OUTSD	6F			14	8/28	17	30	10/32	13	25	10/27

Note: imm8 is the port number as an immediate byte.

Timing Problems

If the same I/O device is accessed twice in succession, it is possible for the second access to get erroneous data. This occurs with systems that can execute an adapter bus cycle faster than the I/O device accepts. Some newer systems are designed so I/O operations cannot overrun an attached I/O device. All current systems fit into this category (EISA, PCI, VLB), and require no extra delays when accessing the same I/O device.

To slow down the code on older systems, programs typically include a short jump between I/O operations to the same device. For example, the following approach creates a one microsecond delay between I/O operations to the same device, assuming the system is a 386 at 20 MHz.

```
out     dx, al              ; output
jmp     short $+2           ; delay
jmp     short $+2           ; delay
in      al, dx              ; input
```

As CPUs get faster and faster, how much delay is appropriate? On an 8 MHz backplane bus, the system can access an I/O device twice in about 750 nS. This is typically too fast. It is recommended that a delay of about 1 uS be maintained before another I/O access is made to the same I/O device of unknown performance specifications. This will ensure I/O operations do not overrun each other. Of course, if firmware is being written for a specific hardware device, these delays may be unnecessary when the hardware handles I/O at full speed.

Stringing a number of jump instructions together is the easiest way to create this short delay for faster systems. Table 3-4 shows the number of jump delay instructions that should be used for different systems. Note the number of cycles to execute a short jump instruction does vary with CPU. The software should provide this delay based on the maximum expected system speed.

Table 3-4. I/O Delays with Jump Instructions

CPU	CPU Speed	CPU Cycle	Cycles per Jump	Number of Jumps
8088	5 MHz	200 nS	15	0
80286	8 MHz	125 nS	9	1
80286	16 MHz	63 nS	9	2
80386	20 MHz	50 nS	9	2
80386	40 MHz	25 nS	9	4
80486	25 MHz	40 nS	5	5
80486	66 MHz	15 nS	5	14
Pentium	66 MHz	15 nS	1	67
Pentium	100 MHz	10 nS	1	100

To make old software work reliably on fast systems, the motherboard designer usually resorts to adding extra wait-states for each I/O access. These wait-states prevent the CPU from accessing an I/O device too quickly. In these cases, a few short jumps even on fast machines, is usually adequate. The next code example, Code Sample 3-1, shows an alternative way to ensure the necessary delay is always maintained.

Code Sample 3-1. I/O Delay

The following routine is designed to ensure a sufficient I/O delay period regardless of the CPU or bus speed. The first time IO_DELAY is called, the routine measures the CPU performance and saves an adjustment factor. IO_DELAY uses the Real-Time Clock (RTC), if present, to measure the speed of instruction executions over a 5 ms period. If the RTC is not present, IO_DELAY assumes the system is a PC or XT, and forces a minimal delay.

The result is a delay routine that always takes at least 1 uS. The delay is controlled by the variable IO_COUNT, which is calculated the first time the routine is called. The first time the routine is called, it will take 5 ms to calibrate the time. If desired, IO_DELAY can be called once during initialization for calibration before use.

On a very slow system, like an 8088 at 5 MHz, the shortest delay with IO_COUNT set to 1 will actually cause a delay of about 16 uS including a near call to the subroutine. With faster CPUs and clock speeds, the overhead becomes minimal.

In all the other routines supplied with this book, we've used a MACRO called IODELAY, which inserts a short delay using two short jump instructions. The macro can be changed to call IO_DELAY instead.

```
;---------------------------------------------------------------
;    I/O DELAY
;       Delay to ensure successive I/O operations to the same
;       device are not too fast on a fast CPU. First time
;       iodelay is called, a 5 ms delay occurs to calibrate
;       the delay loop.
;
;       Called with:    nothing
;
;       Returns:        delay of 1 to 16 uS
;
;       Regs used:      none (no flags altered)

io_delay proc    near
        push    cx
        mov     cx, cs:[io_count]
        jcxz    io_init             ; only if cx = 0 (first time)
io_delay_loop:
        loop    io_delay_loop       ; 13 cycles per loop on a 386
```

```
        pop     cx
        ret

; first time run, so determine initialization value and save

io_init:
        pushf
        push    ax
        push    bx
        push    dx
        push    es

        mov     ax, cs
        mov     es, ax
        mov     ax, 8300h           ; set wait interval
        mov     cx, 0
        mov     dx, 5000            ; delay 5 ms, until wait flag
        mov     bx, offset io_flag  ;  is set
        int     15h                 ; start 5 ms delay
        jc      io_failed_15        ; not implemented or
                                    ;  in progress

; the RTC timer has begun, and will set bit 7 of the wait flag
; when 5 ms elapses. Meanwhile, the software loop counts down
; slowly for slow systems, and fast for fast systems. The loop
; is 30 cycles on a 386 CPU. Other CPUs will vary slightly from
; this.

        dec     cx                  ; cx = FFFFh

io_delay_loop2:
        test    cs:[io_flag], 80h   ; flag set after 5 ms
        jnz     io_5ms_done         ; jump if 5 ms complete
        jmp     short $+2
        loop    io_delay_loop2
```

```
        mov     ax, 100              ; gets here if  >> 400 MHz CPU,
        jmp     io_set               ;  so use really large number

; cx = countdown from FFFF

io_5ms_done:
        mov     ax, 0FFFFh
        sub     ax, cx               ; get number of times looped
        mov     bx, 1500             ; adjustment factor
        xor     dx, dx               ; dx zeroed for divide
        div     bx                   ; ax= dx:ax/cx
        cmp     ax, 0
        je      io_1_delay           ; set at least 1 delay
        jmp     io_set               ; ax = delay value

io_failed_15:
        or      ah, ah               ; int 15 supported or busy?
        jz      io_exit              ; jump if busy, try later
                                     ; old systems fail int 15h
io_1_delay:
        mov     ax, 1                ; minimum delay period
io_set:
        mov     cs:[io_count], ax    ; load delay value
io_exit:
        pop     es
        pop     dx
        pop     bx
        pop     ax
        popf
        pop     cx
        ret
io_delay endp

io_count dw     0                    ; 0 = non-initialized count
io_flag  db     0                    ; bit 7=1 at end of 5ms wait
```

CPU Modes Relating to I/O

The 386 through Pentium Pro processors provide three modes of operation. These are referred to as Real mode, Protected mode, and Virtual 86 mode.

Real mode is similar in concept to an 8088 processor. All resources, such as I/O ports, are always accessible to all software users. No provisions are available to limit access to I/O addresses.

Two other processor modes, Protected and Virtual 86, can limit access to I/O. This means that an advanced operating system such as Windows or OS/2 can control who is allowed to read or write I/O ports. In the DOS environment, memory managers run in protected mode to provide a wide array of memory services on top of DOS running in virtual 8086 mode. In some cases, memory managers need to control access, or "trap" selected I/O addresses.

One example is the need to control access to the DMA (Direct Memory Access) controller hardware that resides in every PC. DMA is used to make transfers between one part of memory and the I/O bus, without the help of the processor. In real mode, this operates fine. Software will communicate to the DMA controller through I/O ports, and indicate where the data will come from, where the data will go, and how many bytes to transfer.

Under DOS, one of a memory manager's tasks is to move extended memory around for EMS services and high loading of TSRs. The processor translates addresses, so software will see the expanded memory mapped-in by the memory manager. Now let's get back to the DMA controller. The DMA hardware operates on the physical memory, but the software that controls DMA only understands the virtual memory. If a request is made by software to send some bytes into a virtual area of memory, the DMA will comply by sending the information to a nonexistent "hole" in memory!

To deal with this problem, the memory manager "traps" the I/O to the DMA controller. If anyone attempts to access the DMA I/O ports, the memory manager gets control before the I/O operation occurs. The manager can then look to see what addresses are being programmed into the DMA controller. If these addresses would go into a virtual area, the memory manager alters the values sent to the DMA controller so the memory addresses point to where the real memory exists in the physical map.

There are many uses for the trapping of I/O operations by an operating system or other low-level resource management programs. Trapping allows multitasking software to help protect one program from another. Trapping can also provide a means to emulate different hardware that may not even exist.

Hardware Access Through C and C++

Up to now, we've shown the actual binary instructions and examples of assembly instructions to access I/O and interrupts on the PC. Many high-level languages also provide direct access to hardware I/O and interrupts. Some of this is through in-line assembly, but actual high-level instructions are often provided.

Registers

Most interrupts require that values be set into registers before execution, and may return values in a register. To access the CPU registers from C code, the REGS structure in DOS.H provides a set of register definitions. For example, to load value 70h into DX prior to issuing an interrupt via the int86x function:

```
        regs.x.dx = 0x70;                  // in assembly:    mov  dx, 70h
```

Most compilers allow all the standard 8- and 16-bit registers, but only the newest versions support 32-bit registers and the new FS and GS registers on 80386 and later processors. Generally, the IP (instruction pointer) register is not supported. The standard pseudovariables supported are shown in Table 3-5.

Table 3-5. CPU Pseudovariables in C

Assembly	Variable *	Type	REGS
ah	_AH	unsigned char	regs.h.ah
al	_AL	unsigned char	regs.h.al
ax	_AX	unsigned int	regs.x.ax
bh	_BH	unsigned char	regs.h.bh
bl	_BL	unsigned char	regs.h.bl
bx	_BX	unsigned int	regs.x.bx
ch	_CH	unsigned char	regs.h.ch
cl	_CL	unsigned char	regs.h.cl
cx	_CX	unsigned int	regs.x.cx
dh	_DH	unsigned char	regs.h.dh
dl	_DL	unsigned char	regs.h.dl
dx	_DX	unsigned int	regs.x.dx
bp	_BP	unsigned int	regs.x.bp
di	_DI	unsigned int	regs.x.di
si	_SI	unsigned int	regs.x.si
sp	_SP	unsigned int	regs.x.sp
cs	_CS	unsigned int	regs.x.cs
ds	_DS	unsigned int	regs.x.ds
es	_ES	unsigned int	regs.x.es
ss	_SS	unsigned int	regs.x.ss
(flags)	_FLAGS	unsigned int	regs.x.flags

* *Not in all compilers (Borland does include these)*

Interrupts

Most libraries included with the compiler provide routines to easily call interrupts on the PC system. The application issues the interrupt function with a set of CPU registers that are passed to the interrupt and a set of registers are returned from the interrupt.

Be aware that these C functions have several limits in the PC environment. There is no support for 32-bit registers, nor is there support for the SS, FS, or GS segment registers. Should the interrupt require any of these registers, you must revert to assembly language. I am unaware of any standard function that requires any of these registers.

Table 3-6 shows common functions used by both Borland and Microsoft. Other language vendors have similar functions available. Other functions are also available from both Borland and Microsoft to access the DOS interrupt 21h and a few other special case forms unique to each vendor's implementation.

Table 3-6. Common Interrupt Functions

Function	Description
int86	Issue an interrupt. User specifies a set of input and output registers. Returns the AX value through the function after the interrupt completes. Syntax: `int int86(int interrupt_#, &inregs, &outregs);`
int86x	Issue an interrupt. User specifies a set of input and output registers, and DS and ES segment registers. Returns the AX value through the function after the interrupt completes. Syntax: `int int86x(int interrupt_#, &inregs, &outregs, &segregs);`

These general purpose routines are easy to use, but are not always as efficient or as fast as coding in assembly. Most functions update all the registers going into the interrupt, even if some or most of the registers are ignored by the interrupt. Similarly, they often save all the registers into variables, even if only a few are changed by the interrupt.

For interrupt functions requiring a far pointer or returning a far pointer, it is necessary to convert between the C far pointer and the segment:offset pair required by the CPU. Three macros are provided to accomplish this, as shown in Table 3-7.

Table 3-7. Pointer Conversions

Function	Description
FP_OFF	Get the offset portion of a C far pointer. Syntax: `unsigned FP_OFF(void far *p);`
FP_SEG	Get the segment portion of a C far pointer. Syntax: `unsigned FP_SEG(void far *p);`
MK_FP	Convert a segment and offset into a C far pointer. Only Borland offers this function, as no equivalent appears in Microsoft's C 7.0. Syntax: `void far *MK_FP(unsigned segment, unsigned offset);`

Interrupt Control

In some instances it is necessary to disable or enable interrupts. Two functions are normally provided for this. In both Borland and Microsoft compilers, these are the _disable and _enable functions. _disable is the same function as the assembly instruction CLI, and clears the processor's interrupt flag. _enable is the same as the assembly instruction STI, which sets the processor's interrupt flag.

I/O Ports

Four basic library functions provide direct access to I/O devices. Functions are provided for both byte and word forms, but keep in mind most ports are accessed as bytes. Tables 3-8 and 3-9 show the four allowable combinations for both Borland and Microsoft:

Table 3-8. Borland I/O Port Functions

Function	Description
inportb	Input byte from specified port. Syntax: `unsigned char inportb(int portid);`
inport	Input word from specified port. Syntax: `int inport(int portid);`
outportb	Output byte to specified port. Syntax: `void outportb(int portid, unsigned char value);`
outport	Output word to specified port. Syntax: `void outport(int portid, int value);`

Table 3-9. Microsoft I/O Port Functions

Function	Description
inp	Input byte from specified port. Syntax: `int _inp(unsigned portid);`
inpw	Input word from specified port. Syntax: `unsigned char _inpw(int portid);`
outp	Output byte to specified port. Syntax: `int _outp(unsigned portid, int value);`
outpw	Output word to specified port. Syntax: `unsigned _outpw(unsigned portid, unsigned char value);`

C and Assembly Code Examples

To compare assembly language, Borland C, and Microsoft C, I've created a subroutine to beep the speaker for two seconds. The routine demonstrates outputs, inputs, and interrupts. The first example in Code Sample 3-2 shows how the code appears in assembly language. The source code resides in the file BEEPA.ASM. For Borland C and Turbo C, see Code Sample 3-3. The source code resides in the file BEEPB.C. For Microsoft C, see Code Sample 3-4. The Microsoft source code is in the file BEEPM.C.

Code Sample 3-2. Assembly Code for BEEPA

```
;----------------------------------------------------------------------
;                          Two Second Beep
;----------------------------------------------------------------------
include undocpc.inc
cseg    segment para public
        assume  cs:cseg, ds:cseg
        org     100h            ; build as COM program
; first set up Timer 2 for 5 KHz signal
beepa   proc    near
        mov     al, 0B6h          ; timer 2 mode set
        out     43h, al           ; set mode
        mov     ax, 0EEh          ; for 5 KHz: 1190/5 = 0EEh
        IODELAY
        out     42h, al           ; set LSB of counter
        mov     al, ah
        IODELAY
        out     42h, al           ; set MSB of counter
; Activate Speaker
        in      al, 61h
        or      al, 3             ; connect speaker to timer 2
        IODELAY
        out     61h, al
; Wait for 2 seconds
        mov     ah, 86h           ; system wait function
        mov     cx, 1Eh           ; cx:dx = 1E8480h for 2 seconds
        mov     dx, 8480h         ;   (1E8480h = 2,000,000 uS)
        int     15h               ; wait for 2 seconds
; Turn off speaker
        in      al, 61h
        and     al, 0FCh          ; turn off speaker
        IODELAY
        out     61h, al
```

```
; Exit to DOS
        mov     ah, 4Ch
        int     21h
beepa   endp
cseg    ends
        end
```

Code Sample 3-3. Borland C Code for BEEPB

```
/*---------------------------------------------------------------------
                    Two Second Beep - Borland C
---------------------------------------------------------------------*/
#include "dos.h"
int main(void)
{
        static union REGS ourregs;
        // first set up Timer 2 for 5 KHz signal
        outportb(0x43, 0xB6);   // timer 2 mode set
                                // for 5kHz: 1190/5 = 0xEE
        outportb(0x42, 0xEE);   // set LSB of counter
        outportb(0x42, 0);      // set MSB of counter
        // Activate Speaker and connect timer to speaker by
        //   only setting bits 0 and 1 of port 0x61. Other
        //   bits are left unchanged by reading bits first.
        outportb(0x61, (inportb(0x61) | 0x03));
        // Wait for 2 seconds, using interrupt 15, function 86
        ourregs.h.ah = 0x86;
        ourregs.x.cx = 0x1E;     // 0x1E8480 = 2,000,000 uS
        ourregs.x.dx = 0x8480;
        int86(0x15, &ourregs, &ourregs);  // issue interrupt 15
        // turn off speaker
        outportb(0x61, (inportb(0x61) & 0xFC));
        return 0;
}
```

Code Sample 3-4. Microsoft C Code for BEEPM

```
/*---------------------------------------------------------------------
                    Two Second Beep - Microsoft C
---------------------------------------------------------------------*/
#include "dos.h"
int main(void)
{         static union _REGS ourregs;
        // first set up Timer 2 for 5 KHz signal
        _outp(0x43, 0xB6);        // timer 2 mode set
                                  // for 5 KHz: 1190/5 = 0xEE
        _outp(0x42, 0xEE);        // set LSB of counter
        _outp(0x42, 0);           // set MSB of counter
        // Activate Speaker and connect timer to speaker by
        //   only setting bits 0 and 1 of port 0x61. Other
        //   bits are left unchanged by reading bits first.
        _outp(0x61, (_inp(0x61) | 0x03));
        // Wait for 2 seconds, using interrupt 15, function 86
        ourregs.h.ah = 0x86;
        ourregs.x.cx = 0x1E;       // 0x1E8480 = 2,000,000 uS
        ourregs.x.dx = 0x8480;
        _int86(0x15, &ourregs, &ourregs); // issue interrupt 15
        // turn off speaker
        _outp(0x61, (_inp(0x61) & 0xFC));
}
```

Summary of CPUs

Table 3-10 shows the major processor family used on the PC today. The 80188/80186 is not included because its design is incompatible for use on the PC. The 80188/80186 CPUs have enjoyed some success in the embedded controller market, where on-chip integration of some peripherals provide a cost and size advantage over the 8088. New 386 and 486 variants have also been produced for the embedded controller market, and are not covered here.

Table 3-10. Intel Processor Families and Characteristics

CPU	Intel Released	Internal Bus Size	External Bus Size	Introductory Speed	Maximum Address
8088	June 1978	16	8	5 MHz	1 MB
80286	February 1982	16	16	6 MHz	16 MB
80386	October 1985	32	32	16 MHz	4 GB
80486	August 1989	32	32	20 MHz	4 GB
Pentium	March 1993	64	64	66 MHz	4 GB
Pentium Pro	April 1995	64	64	150 MHz	4 GB
P55C (MMX)	Spring 1997*	64	64	200 MHz	4 GB

* *Pentium with MMX; Beta testing begun in Spring 1996; release due in Spring 1997*

The following section identifies some of the most common processors parts, vendors, and differences among each of the parts within a family. It's important to note that starting with the 386 a wide number of variations were produced. To identify these variations, vendors are using a bewildering array of confusing suffixes such as DX, DX2, DX4, SX, SL, SLC, SLC2, DLC, and others. Three common Intel parts are the 386SX, 486SX, and 486SL. These are similar sounding suffixes, yet the 386SX only has a 16-bit external data bus, while the 486SX and 486SL use a 32-bit bus. The 386SX and 486SX do not have floating-point math built in, but the 486SL does. The only two letters with any significance are D and L. The "D" indicates a full 32-bit external bus part. Part numbers without a "D" suffix may or may not have a 32-bit external bus. "L" in the suffix indicates the CPU offers some type of low power mode. CPU part numbers that end in the number "2" or "4" indicate the CPU uses clock doubler or tripler technology for faster internal processing. All other suffixes are often meaningless, other than to identify a variation of the part. The processors listed are in order of approximate release. All parts from a single vendor are listed together for each family.

Part	Vendors	Family
8088	Intel and others	8086

The 8088 was selected by IBM for the PC and is obsolete today. The 8088 provides a 16-bit internal CPU with an 8-bit external data bus, and optional connections for a floating-point processor, the 8087.

Part	Vendors	Family
8086	Intel and others	8086

This is software identical to the 8088, but provides a 16-bit external bus, and larger prefetch queue. This results in about 15 to 20 percent performance improvement over the 8088. The 8086 was only used by a few PC vendors, such as AT&T. It had more success in the imbedded system market.

Part	Vendors	Family
V20	NEC	8086

The V20 was a pin-for-pin replacement of the 8088 that provided 10–15% improved performance. The V20 also came with a few additional instructions and the ability to process older 8080 code. Many speed-hungry 8088 users rushed out and replaced their 8088 with the V20. Other than the useless POP CS instruction, abandoned on all later CPU families, the V20 executes every instruction of the 8088. A few undocumented instructions on the 8088 do not work on the V20.

Part	Vendors	Family
80286	Intel and others	286

The 80286 was the first 8088-compatible CPU with major enhancements in performance, features, and memory addressability. The speed was boosted from 5 MHz on the 8088 to 8 MHz. In addition, the address range was extended from 1 MB on the 8088 to 16 MB.

Since the 286 design was completed around the time the IBM PC was introduced, most of the 286's new protected-mode features were unusable by real-mode DOS software. IBM and Intel were going in different directions at the time. Later, when the first versions of OS/2 and Windows appeared in the marketplace, the 286 was too underpowered for most users to accept these environments, driving the need for even faster CPUs.

When additional math performance was required, the optional 80287 floating-point coprocessor was used. Intel produced a high performance math coprocessor, the 80287XLT.

Part	Vendors	Family
80386DX	Intel and AMD	386

With the 80386, Intel delivered a dramatic boost in power, usable features, and address space. The first versions of this 32-bit processor quadrupled the performance over the 80286. Of course, when this part was introduced, almost every software product was still written for the 8088, which slightly reduced maximum possible benefits.

The biggest breakthrough has been the newly created Virtual 86 mode. This has allowed software vendors to deliver all sorts of new capabilities in software. Just a few of these features include Expanded Memory Management in software, high-loading of TSRs and device drivers, multitasking operating systems like Windows and OS/2, multiple DOS boxes, and many more. The 80386 became the minimum daily requirement for most users in the early 1990s.

Other major advancements include boosted performance by reducing the number of clocks for most instructions, a range of built-in debugging features, and access to up to 4 GB of memory.

A number of companies have attempted to clone the 80386, but most have fallen away under Intel's legal barrage. The only clone still in the running is AMD's Am386. Most of AMD's parts built in 1993 use Intel masks and microcode. Surprisingly, AMD offers the fastest part, at 40 MHz. IBM also produced a pseudo-386 part for a while, but more about that later.

Many instructions were added to the base 286 instruction set along with a number of new 32-bit addressing modes. Most of these are well documented. The undocumented 286 LOADALL instruction was dropped, and a new 386 LOADALL with a different opcode was added. Refer to the section, Undocumented Instructions, for more about LOADALL.

The 80386DX was intended to have an optional math coprocessor, the 80387DX. This part was delayed initially, and some vendors attached a lower cost 16-bit 80287 math coprocessor to provide the only possible solution at the time.

Part	Vendors	Family
80386SX	Intel	386

This is functionally identical to a 80386DX part internally, but uses a 16-bit external data bus and 24-bit address bus. This means the CPU takes twice as long to transfer data and code externally. In addition, the 386SX can only address a maximum of 16 MB.

The 386SX has been used in a large number of computers because of its lower relative cost compared with the 386DX. The 16-bit external bus also simplifies the motherboard design to further reduce costs.

The floating-point processor for the 80386SX is the 80387SX. The 387SX uses a 16-bit external data bus and software identical to the 80387DX.

Part	Vendors	Family
386SL	Intel	386

This was Intel's low-power 386 for laptops. The 386SL offers complete 80386 compatibility, low-power modes, suspend and resume capabilities, and integrates a memory and cache controller.

This is functionally identical to a 80386DX part internally, but it only provides a 16-bit external data bus and a 24-bit address bus. This means external data and code transfers take twice as long as with a 386DX part of the same speed. In addition, the 386SL can only address a maximum of 16 MB. The part is implemented in static logic, unlike most other CPUs in Intel's family. This is useful to save power, by stopping the CPU clock during long periods of inactivity, or for user-controlled suspend and resume.

A companion floating-point processor, the 80387SL, provides as many of the low-power features as the 387SL. However, the 387SL uses a 16-bit external data bus.

Part	Vendors	Family
386SXL/DXL	AMD	386

These parts are similar to the standard 386DX and 386SX parts, but offer static operation for low-power modes. Unlike Intel's 386SL, the 386SXL/DXL does not provide a suspend and resume feature.

Part	Vendors	Family
386SXLV	AMD	386

This part is similar to Intel's 80386SL, offering both low-power modes and suspend and resume capability. The suspend and resume operates differently from the Intel part, and requires unique code.

Part	Vendors	Family
386DXLV	AMD	386

This is the only 386 part that offers a 32-bit external address bus, low-power modes, and suspend and resume capabilities. The AMD 386DXLV provides a faster 386 solution for laptops.

Part	Vendors	Family
386SLC	IBM	386

I refer to the 386SLC as a fake 386. A closer look shows this part to be a 486 "wolf in sheep-skin." It turns out this part has everything a 486SX part has except one PC incompatible feature no one uses! The 386SLC has a full 8 KB of internal cache, supports every 80486SX instruction, and the chip has been reworked for improved instruction performance with the same clock speed of the 80486! The 386SLC even has some additional instructions for power-saving capabilities similar to Intel's 80486SL.

This seems too good to be true! For the most part it is true, but IBM's part does have one limit. The part uses an external 16-bit data bus and 24-bit address bus, like Intel's 386SX. This should not be confused with the 80486SX, which offers a full 32-bit external data and addresses busses.

Why doesn't IBM call this part a 486? There appear to be two reasons, but this is pure conjecture on my part. First, they have even a better part they call a 486SLC2, which has an internal 16 KB cache. The 386SLC label helps differentiate these parts. The second, and I think more likely reason, has to do with saving money. I suspect IBM's royalty agreement with Intel required a much lower royalty on a 386 part than a 486 part!

Although somewhat unlikely, the 386SLC may be a 486SLC with one-half the 16 KB cache defective. Perhaps the manufacturing process can bond out the chip as a 486 or 386 depending on how the die passes manufacturing tests. This would improve the overall yields, and save money at the same time. I've been unable to convince a few friends to pop the lids off the chips to see if IBM is using the same die. Of course, this would destroy the chips, so I can understand their reluctance!

What's really missing on IBM's 80386SLC? All 486 CPUs provide an alignment check feature to generate an interrupt when data are not properly aligned. I've never seen anyone use this feature, most likely because alignment check issues interrupt 11h, in direct conflict with the system BIOS's equipment configuration function. Alignment check is controlled by bit 18 in EFLAGS. This bit can be toggled on the 486 part, and cannot be toggled on the 386 part. For years, many developers have used this trick as the de facto standard for identifying a 486 part.

Additional interesting instructions supported on the 386SLC include LOADALL, RDMSR, and WRMSR. Each of these are explained in the next section on undocumented instructions. To be fair to IBM, they do document these instructions, but few programmers are likely to have this information.

Part	Vendors	Family
80486DX	Intel	486

The 80486 was the next major advancement in the Intel family of processors. Looking back, the 80486 seems a lot less earth-shattering than the first release of the 80386. The 80486 can be looked on as a 80386 with a few significant add-ons. The 486DX includes an integrated 8 KB cache and a complete floating-point processor inside the CPU. Of course both of these features were available externally on most 386 systems. In addition the 80486 hardware and microcode were further improved over prior designs to boost performance. It was a major achievement to put all this on a single chip. The best part was the total compatibility with all prior processors.

The 80486 has many variants. It's offered in a wide range of speeds and low-power versions and was the initial target of a number of Intel competitors.

The latest variations provide a clock-doubler or tripler techniques in which the internal CPU clock is faster than the external bus clock. Intel assigns a DX2, DX4 suffix to the part number. (DX4 means clock tripling not quadrupling!) This further enhances performance without complex high-speed motherboard designs. In many cases, these clock-enhanced CPUs can be installed in older 486 systems to provide an instant boost in performance.

New instructions added include BSWAP, CMPXCHG (which changed opcodes between the A and B steps), INVD, INVLPG, WBINVD, and XADD. All of these are reasonably well documented. The undocumented 386 LOADALL instruction was removed.

Part	Vendors	Family
80486SX	Intel	486

The 80486SX is identical to the 80486DX except for the lack of a built-in floating-point processor (FPU). In fact, the early SX parts were rumored to be DX parts with defective FPUs or disconnected FPUs. This would have improved the overall yield and provided a lower cost part. The 486SX, unlike the 386SX, retains a full 32-bit internal and external bus support.

To detect if a 80486 is a DX or SX part, the control register CR0, bit 4 cannot be toggled on a DX part, indicating the FPU is built in. On a SX part, this bit can be toggled, even if an external FPU is attached.

The companion math coprocessor is the 80487SX FPU. From a software view, it is identical to the FPU in a 80486DX.

Part	Vendors	Family
80486SL	Intel	486

Unlike the 486SX, the 80486SL offers full 486DX functionality with the floating-point processor. In addition, the 486SL provides power management capabilities for low-power designs, clock control, bus and memory controllers built in. It is intended for use with the 82360 companion peripheral components chip. These two parts together form the basis for a complete AT system.

Part	Vendors	Family
486SLC2	IBM	486

This is a hybrid between the 486SX and a 386SX. From a programming point of view, this part has all of the instructions of an 80486SX, plus a few extras. This means all 80486 instructions are supported, except there is no floating-point math coprocessor built in. IBM's 486 also provides power management features for laptop designs. Like the 386SX, the 486SLC2 has a 16-bit external data bus, and a 24-bit address bus. Unlike any other 386/486 CPU, IBM's 486SLC has a large 16 KB internal cache. This chip also provides clock-doubling, so the internal CPU runs at twice the speed of the external bus. With all of these feature enhancements, IBM claims a three times improvement in performance over a 386SX part of the same external bus speed.

A newer part, the 486SLC3, became available at the end of 1993. This variant uses a clock tripler technology to run the internal CPU at three times the external bus rate. The 486SLC3 provides an internal speed of 75Mhz to 99 MHz, depending on the part.

Additional interesting instructions supported on the 486SLC include LOADALL, RDMSR, and WRMSR. Each of these are explained in the next section on undocumented instructions. As I noted with the IBM 386SLC part, IBM does document these instructions.

Part	Vendors	Family
486SLC	Cyrix	486

This is the first 486 clone chip developed without Intel's seal of approval. After years of legal wrangling with Intel, it appears Cyrix has succeeded.

From my tests, Cyrix has done a very good job at duplicating the 486 CPU. The 486SLC offers significant performance improvements on most instructions, given the same clock speed, but only offers a 1 KB built-in cache. The Cyrix part also provides low-power options for laptops. Like Intel's 486SX this part does not have the floating-point processor built in. Unlike the 486SX, the 486SLC only has an external 16-bit data bus, and a 24-bit address bus, more in line with a 386SX. Because this Cyrix part has so many hardware differences from Intel's parts, it becomes difficult to say whether it is better or worse than Intel's 486.

The only instruction difference we've noted on Cyrix parts is the lack of the undocumented UMOV instruction, used primarily with emulators. This is not significant, especially because Intel has dropped UMOV from the Pentium.

Cyrix stopped production on 486 parts at the end of 1995 to focus on higher performance parts.

Part	Vendors	Family
486DLC	Cyrix	486

The Cyrix 486DLC is pin-for-pin equivalent to Intel's 486SX. In provides full 32-bit data and address busses. In addition, many instructions have been improved to take fewer cycles, boosting performance. The 486DLC only has a 2 KB internal cache, as compared with Intel's full 8 KB cache. Like its smaller brother the 486SLC, the 486DLC has various low-power modes useful in laptop designs.

The only instruction difference we've noted on Cyrix parts is the lack of the undocumented UMOV instruction, used primarily with emulators. This is not significant, especially because Intel has dropped UMOV from the Pentium.

Cyrix stopped production on 486 parts at the end of 1995.

Part	Vendors	Family
486SLC	Texas Instruments	486

This part is identical to the Cyrix part. Cyrix developed the part, and TI was one of the manufactureres used by Cyrix. This was done to attempt to avoid legal problems with Intel, since TI has an extensive cross-licensing agreement with Intel. TI no longer produces these parts.

Part	Vendors	Family
486DLC	Texas Instruments	486

This part is identical to the Cyrix part. See above for the details.

Part	Vendors	Family
486SXLV	AMD	486

This part is similar to an Intel 486SX, but uses much less power. The Am486SXLV includes additional low-power modes and has suspend and resume capability. Like the 486SX, the 486SXLV provides a full external 32-bit address bus and internal 8K cache. No internal math coprocessor is provided.

Part	Vendors	Family
486DXLV	AMD	486

This part is similar to an Intel 486DX, but uses much less power. The Am386DXLV includes additional low-power modes and has suspend and resume capability. The 486DXLV provides a full external 32-bit address bus, internal 8K cache, and a built-in math coprocessor. Newer DX2 and DX4 variations use internal clock doubling and tripling to boost performance. As of this writing, AMD produces the fastest 486 variant at 120 MHz. The DX2 and DX4 parts include support for CPUID. Newest versions also provide an improved write-back cache design.

Part	Vendors	Family
Am5x86	AMD	486

The 5x86 is really a fast 486 chip (133 MHz, DX4). It was badged by AMD as a "586" class part since it performs similar to a 75 MHz Pentium. There are no Pentium unique instructions nor any of the additional logic for boosting performance. Because it really is a 486, the CPU identification program in the next chapter will identify this as a fast 486 part.

Part	Vendors	Family
Pentium	**Intel**	**586**

The Pentium, from a software perspective, is very similar to the 80486, with only a few additional instructions. From a hardware view, a truly mind-boggling array of new approaches provide a big performance boost. The Pentium also implements System Management Mode, typically used in designs requiring power savings and save and resume features.

From the hardware side, the Pentium provides a long list of enhancements. These include an 8 KB data cache and a separate 8 KB instruction cache, a 64-bit internal *and* external data bus, a 256-bit internal code bus, dual 64-byte prefetch queues with writebacks, dual instruction pipeline to process two instructions at the same time, and a branch prediction table for the last 256 branches. In addition, an improved floating-point coprocessor is built in that boosts floating performance by as much as ten times.

New, well-documented instructions for the Pentium include CMPXCHG8B, CPUID, MOV to and from CR4. Other undocumented or poorly documented instructions include RDMSR, RDTSC, RSM, and WRMSR, which are described in detail in the next section on undocumented instructions. The Pentium has removed all MOV to and from test register instructions, and the undocumented UMOV instruction that is provided on all Intel 386 and 486 parts.

The Pentium also has a number of new enhancements that Intel originally decided to hide from programmers. A secret document, Appendix H, is referenced extensively in the Pentium manual for many "reserved" functions and fields. Intel publicly indicated, in 1995, that all this information would be released, and the latest Pentium manuals do document some information that was previously hidden. Unfortunately, the newest Pentium manuals (purchased from Intel 6/96) still keep information hidden. It still has an unavailable Appendix H for advanced feature information. I have yet to talk to anyone outside of Intel who has ever seen the elusive Appendix H. What is very weird is that most of this "hidden information" appears to have been included in the standard Pentium Pro manuals. Go figure!

These new "undocumented" features are controlled through two bits in Control Register 4 (CR4). The Protected-Mode Virtual Interrupt (PVI) bit helps reduce the interrupt overhead. The Virtual-8086 Mode Extensions (VME) bit can eliminate trapping the often-used CLI and STI interrupt disable and enable instructions.

Two new status flag bits are defined to handle these new features. In the EFLAGS register, the Virtual Interrupt Pending (VIP) flag is used with the Virtual Interrupt Flag (VIF) to virtualize the interrupt flag.

Part	Vendors	Family
5x86	**Cyrix**	**586**

The 5x86 competes with Intel's Pentium, but requires a slightly higher clock rate perform similar to a Pentium. Like the Pentium, it provides a 64-bit internal data path. The 5x86 does not handle 64-bit wide data externally, but only 32-bits external to the part. It includes a 16 KB of internal cache and an 80-bit floating-point unit. Other advanced features include the ability to process more than one instruction at a time, branch prediction logic, and power management features. Unlike the Pentium, the 5x86's pin-out and bus design is 486-compatible and most Pentium unique instructions are not supported. This makes it a low-cost solution for 486 system upgrades and it competes favorably with lower-end Pentium processors.

This part has also been sold under IBM and SGS labels.

Part	Vendors	Family
Nx586	NexGen	586

The Nx586 used to be the closest performance competitor with Intel's Pentium. Benchmarks generally show the Nx586 is faster for the same processor speed. It provides full internal and external 64-bit buses, branch prediction, and the ability to process multiple instructions at the same time. It goes beyond the Pentium with a 32 KB on-board L1 cache (like the Pentium Pro). It does not include a built-in floating-point processor, but NexGen also has a FPU part available. The Nx586 is not pin or motherboard compatible with any Intel parts.

From a software perspective, the Nx586 is a speedy 486 part. No Pentium instructions are available, and the 486 alignment check feature is not supported (rarely if ever used). Most CPU identification tests use the alignment test to determine whether a CPU is a 486 or a 386, and the test will indicate that NexGen is a 386. The CPU identification test I've included in the next chapter will identify the Nx586 as a 586 class part with a 486 instruction set. NexGen was planning to implement the CPUID instruction in a mask revision. To my knowledge, the CPUID support was never released.

NexGen was purchased by AMD at the end of 1995 and subsequently discontinued the Nx586. AMD's really wanted NexGen's technology and NexGen's 686 CPU, which was in development. The Nx586 is not the same as the Cyrix 5x86, or AMD's 5x86 and 5_K86 parts.

Part	Vendors	Family
5_K86	AMD	586

The 5_K86 competes with Intel's Pentium. It provides the full Pentium instruction set and functionality. Unlike the Pentium, it uses a 32-bit internal and external data paths. This keeps it pin compatible with the 486. It includes a 16 KB of internal cache and an 80-bit floating-point unit. It does not have other Pentium advancements, such as branch prediction logic or the ability to process multiple instructions at the same time.

Part	Vendors	Family
Pentium Pro	Intel	686

The Pentium Pro provides the highest 86 family performance to date. From a software perspective, it is almost identical to the Pentium, with only a few additional instructions. From a hardware view, further enhancements have been made to boost performance. The Pentium Pro includes an internal 16 KB L1 cache, and internal 256 KB or 512 KB L2 cache. It also has hardware for multiprocessor support and includes an out-of-order execution engine with a very long pipeline. It provides the biggest boost to 32-bit software.

Older 16-bit software may not realize significant improvements when compared with the same clock speed Pentiums. The problem occurs when software (primarily 16-bit) makes many changes to the code segment registers. Each code segment change requires a flush of the large instruction pipeline, which defeats the benefit of the out-order-execution feature.

New, well-documented instructions for the Pentium Pro include CMOV, FCMOV, FCOMI, and RDPMC. The Read/Write Model specific Registers have been documented and expanded over the Pentium. New memory management features are also included.

Part	Vendors	Family
6x86	Cyrix	686

The 6x86 competes with Intel's Pentium and Pentium Pro processors. Unlike the Cyrix 5x86, this part has a full 64-bit external interface. Other features are similar to the 5x86 such as a 16 KB of internal cache and an 80-bit floating-point unit. Other advanced features include the ability to process more than one instruction at a time, branch prediction logic, and power management features. Unique features that are transparent to software to boost performance include register renaming, out-of-order execution, and data forwarding. This part supports a few of the unique Pentium instructions, but not all.

This part has also been sold under IBM and SGS labels.

Part	Vendors	Family
P55C (Pentium MMX)	Intel	586

The MMX are new instructions for improved math performance typically used in multimedia environments. Depending on who you talk to, MMX stands for Multi-Media eXtensions or Matrix Math eXtensions. Intel's current position is that MMX does not stand for anything, and prefers the name MMX Technology. These instructions and operation are detailed on Intel's web site (www.intel.com). The MMX instructions are designed to boost performance by processing 64-bits of data as a group of bytes, words, or dwords in a single operation. The MMX instructions are supported on the CPU when the CPUID feature bit 23 is 1. Processors with MMX instructions are expected to be released at the beginning of 1997. Intel plans to release a version of the Pentium Pro with MMX instructions later in 1997.

The P55C is similar to the standard Pentium, but has a number of enhancements in addition to the MMX instructions. These enhancements include a larger 32 KB L1 cache (16 KB for data and 16 KB for code) and new branch prediction logic. This Pentium also implements the Read Performance Monitoring Counters (RDPMC) instruction that is documented in the Pentium Pro manual.

Undocumented Instructions

You may be wondering how I define an undocumented instruction, because we are dealing with some murky waters here. To me an undocumented instruction is any instruction not currently documented in Intel's published processor documentation. Most of these undocumented instructions are not terribly useful. Some undocumented instructions have alternative documented instructions to perform the same function. What is interesting is the fact there are undocumented instructions on every 80x88 family CPU. In a few cases, undocumented instructions provide secret access to unusual features of the processor.

Although these instructions are sometimes tempting to use, in most cases they should be avoided or used only when absolutely necessary. It is also wise to protect against instruction failure, in the event the instruction is not supported on a future chip version. At a minimum, it is smart to have a user-setable option in order to skip the use of any undocumented instruction.

To see if your specific CPU has properly implemented undocumented instructions I've identified, run CPUTYPE. To test for additional hidden undocumented CPU instructions, run CPUUNDOC. The CPUUNDOC program tries all possible instruction combinations that have not been assigned. It skips any instruction we've already identified as undocumented. In my tests with many CPUs, I haven't seen any other instructions appear. The test should be run in real mode (i.e., with no memory manager running, nor from a DOS box of Windows 95, NT, or OS/2). CPUUNDOC will not find any instruction that requires operation in protected mode, or that needs special register values or special mm-reg-r/m fields.

Few if any assemblers support undocumented instructions. We've described many of the undocumented instructions in macros that can be used with all the current assemblers. The diskette file UNDOCPC.INC has these macros. Simply include the UNDOCPC.INC at the beginning of your assembly program:

```
        include  undocpc.inc
```

Summary of Undocumented Instructions

Instruction	Description	Platform
AAD	Adjust AX Before BCD Divide	All, except V20
AAM	Adjust AX After BCD Multiply	All, except V20
CPUID	CPU Identification	Some 486+
IBTS	Insert Bit String	Intel 80386 A step
ICEBP	In-Circuit-Emulator Break-Point	Most 386+
IN/OUT	Ports 22h/23h access to CPU Functions	Most Cyrix CPUs
LOADALL	Load All Processor Registers	Some 286-486
POP CS	Load CS from Stack	8088/8086
RDMSR	Read Model Specific Register	Some 386+
RDTSC	Read Time Stamp Counter	Pentium+
RSM	Resume From System Management Mode	Some 386+
SETALC	Set AL to Carry	All, except V20
SHL	Shift Left by Count	80188+
SHL	Shift Left by 1	All
SMI	System Management Interrupt Entry	AMD 386DXLV/SXDLV

Summary of Undocumented Instructions (Continued)

Instruction	Description	Platform
TEST	Test Register with Immediate	All
UMOV	User Move Register Instructions	Some 386/486
WRMSR	Write Model Specific Register	Some 386+
XBTS	Extract Bit String	Intel 80386 A step

Undocumented Instruction Detail

Inst	Description	Processors
AAD	Adjust AX Before BCD Divide	All, except V20

```
D5h, imm        aad                 ; convert base to binary
D5h, imm        aad                 ; convert base to binary
```

The standard form of the AAD instruction is well documented and supported on all processors. In its default form, it takes the value in AH times 10, and adds it to AL. The result is placed in AX. This is used to convert two BCD characters into binary. For example, if AX has the value 0907h (BCD 97), then AAD converts this to (9 * 10) + 7 = 0061h. This is necessary for division of BCD numbers, and other functions.

In the documented form, the assembler always makes the immediate opcode byte 0Ah. What is undocumented is the ability to convert other bases like hex or octal into binary. Instead of letting the assembler force the second opcode byte to be 0Ah (for base 10), hand coding the instruction allows any base value. With the opcodes bytes D5h, followed by an immediate value N, the CPU takes the following action:

```
AL = (AH * N) + AL
AH = 0
```

The two most common uses are to convert hex, base 16 and octal, base 8 into binary, using just a single instruction! To convert two hex digits into binary, the opcodes D5h, 10h are used. This takes the undocumented action:

```
AL = (AH * 10h) + AL
AH = 0
```

To convert two octal digits into binary, the opcodes D5h, 08h are used. This takes the undocumented action:

```
AL = (AH * 8) + AL
AH = 0
```

This undocumented ability of AAD has been used in a few commercial applications, and works on all 80x86 CPUs except for the V20. Assuming the N value is already in a register, an 8-bit multiply instruction is slightly faster on the 8088, but slightly slower on all later CPUs.

Inst	Description	Processors
AAM	**Adjust AX After BCD Multiply**	**All, except V20**

```
D4h, imm          aam                    ; convert base to binary
```

The standard f orm of the AAM instruction is well documented and supported on all processors. In its default form, AAM divides the value in AL by 10, and inserts the result in AH, with the remainder in AL. After multiplying two BCD digits together, the standard AAM converts the result in AX back into two BCD digits.

In the documented form, the assembler always makes the immediate opcode byte 0Ah. Using other values for the immediate opcode value can divide other numbers. Instead of letting the assembler force the second opcode byte to be 0Ah (for base 10), hand coding the instruction allows alternate divide values. With the opcodes bytes D4h, followed by an immediate value N, the CPU takes the following action:

```
AH = AL / N
AL = AL MOD N
```

To separate a hex byte so the upper nibble is in AH, and the lower nibble in AL, the opcodes D4h, 10h are used. This takes the undocumented action:

```
AH = AL / 10h
AL = AL MOD 10h
```

With a value of 7Fh in AL, the end result is AX=070Fh. The undocumented ability of AAM works on all 80x86 CPUs except for the NEC V20.

Inst	Description	Processors
CPUID	**Adjust AX After Processor Identification**	**Some 486+, Pentium+**

```
0Fh, A2h          cpuid
```

CPUID is used to identify the CPU type, vendor, and specific features available on the CPU. While this instruction is well documented, it returns different information depending on the vendor and is not supported on older parts. Intel introduced the instruction on the Pentium processor, and has added it to new 486 masks produced after the Pentium was released. Older AMD, Cyrix and NexGen parts do not have CPUID. The new AMD 5K86 supports it.

To determine if the CPU supports the CPUID instruction, bit 21 of EFLAGS can be toggled. For example, once you have identified the CPU is at least a 386, then the following code is used to detect CPUID support:

```
cli                        ; disable interrupts
pushdf                     ; push flags to look at
pop     eax                ; move eflags to eax
mov     ebx, eax           ; save for later
xor     eax, 200000h       ; toggle bit 21
push    eax
popdf                      ; load modified eflags to CPU
pushfd                     ; push eflags to look at
pop     eax                ; get new eflags value
push    ebx                ; push original flags
sti                        ; enable interrupts
xor     eax, ebx           ; check if bit changed
jnz     CPUID_ok           ; jump if CPUID supported
jmp     no_CPUID           ; no CPUID instruction
```

To use the CPUID instruction, EAX is first loaded with a function number. The CPUID instruction is issued, and the results appear in various registers, depending on the function.

Get Vendor String, EAX = 0

Returns: EAX = Maximum function value supported by CPUID instruction. Value is 1 for most CPUs. The Pentium Pro returns 2.

EBX, ECX, EDX = Vendor string in ASCII. The first ASCII byte starts in the low byte of EBX (bits 7-0). The last byte of the string resides in the high byte of EDX (bits 31-24). Current known vendor strings include:

"AuthenticAMD"	(currently in use)
"CyrixInstead"	(currently in use)
"GenuineIntel"	(currently in use)
"NexGenDriven"	(unknown if ever used)
"UMC UMC UMC "	(discontinued?)

Get Version and Feature Information, EAX = 1

Returns: EAX = Version Information:

Bits	31-14	Reserved for future use (zeros)
	13-12	Processor type
		0 0 = Original OEM Processor
		0 1 = Backward pin compatible variation (Intel OverDrive)
		1 0 = Dual Pentium class processor configuration
		1 1 = Reserved for future
	11-8	Family
		3 = 386
		4 = 486
		5 = 586 and Pentium
		6 = 686 and Pentium Pro
		7 = P7 class
	7-4	Model
	3-0	Stepping number

EBX and ECX = Zero (reserved for future)

EDX = Feature Information (documented in Intel's Pentium Pro manual)

Bits	31-24	Reserved for future and/or undocumented
	23	CPU includes MMX support
	22-16	Reserved for future and/or undocumented
	15	CMOV instruction supported
	14	Machine Check Global Capability supported
	13	Page Global enable flag supported
	12	Memory Type Range Registers supported
	11-10	Reserved for future and/or undocumented
	9	Advanced Programable Interrupt controller (APIC) resides on chip and is enabled
	8	CMPXCH8B instruction supported
	7	Machine Check Exception supported
	6	Physical address extension to 36-bits supported
	5	Model Specific Registers supported
	4	Time Stamp Counter supported
	3	4 MB Page size extensions supported
	2	Debugging extensions supported
	1	Virtual 8086 Mode enhancements supported
	0	Floating-point Unit resides on the CPU chip

Cache and TLB Information, EAX = 2 (Currently Pentium Pro+ only)

This function indicates the types of caches implemented within the CPU.

Returns: EAX = Cache Information

Bit	31	0—if information in register valid
	30-24	Cache type
	23-16	Cache type
	15-8	Cache type
	7-0	Number of times to issue CPUID with function 2 to get all of the cache information. The first Pentium Pro release returns a value of 1.

EBX, ECX, EDX = Cache Information

Bit	31	0—if information in register valid
	30-24	Cache type
	23-16	Cache type
	15-8	Cache type
	7-0	Cache type

Cache Types:

0 = Null descriptor

1 = Instruction Translation Lookaside Buffer (TLB): 4 KB Pages, 4-way set associative cache, 64 entries

2 = Instruction Translation Lookaside Buffer (TLB): 4 MB Pages, 4-way set associative cache, 4 entries

3 = Data Translation Lookaside Buffer (TLB): 4 KB Pages, 4-way set associative cache, 64 entries

4 = Data Translation Lookaside Buffer (TLB): 4 MB Pages, 4-way set associative cache, 8 entries

6 = Instruction cache: 8 KB, 4-way set associative, 32 byte line size

0Ah = Data cache: 8 KB, 2-way set associative, 32 byte line size

41h = Unified cache: 128 KB, 4-way set associative, 32 byte line size

42h = Unified cache: 256 KB, 4-way set associative, 32 byte line size

43h = Unified cache: 512 KB, 4-way set associative, 32 byte line size

Inst	Description	Processors
IBTS	Insert Bit String	Intel 80386 A step

```
0Fh, A7h, r/m   ibts    regW/memW, ax, cl, reg
```

The insert bit string instruction take a string of bits from the second operand and places them in the first operand.

Only the very first 80386, referred to as the "A step," included the IBTS instruction. It was eliminated in the next step to make room for additional microcode. It has not been duplicated by any competitor because its presence signifies a very old 80386 chip that has a few quirks.

The same opcode was reused in the first 80486 for the CMPXCHG instruction. It was discovered that some applications written prior to the 80486 were checking for the presence of the IBTS instruction, and were falsely thinking the new 80486 was an old 80386 A step part. So Intel moved the CMPXCHG instruction to a new opcode on the 80486 B step of the part! The end result is that most developers find it's way too much trouble to figure all this out, and they avoid using the IBTS or CMPXCHG instructions. Also see the XBTS instruction later in this chapter.

The word forms of this instruction will appear as dword forms depending on the current mode (16- or 32-bit), and if a size override prefix is used.

Inst	Description	Processors
ICEBP	In-Circuit-Emulator Break-Point	Most 386+

```
F1h             icebp                 ; breakpoint or interrupt 1
```

This instruction has several operational modes. It can be used as a single byte interrupt, similar to INT 3, except that interrupt 1 is called instead. In other modes, it is used by an In-Circuit-Emulator (ICE) or software to interrupt the current process and gain control of the system.

The operation of ICEBP will vary depending on the chip vendor for 386 and later CPUs. The information is VERY UNDOCUMENTED, meaning some information may not be applicable to all vendors, and/or some stepping of parts may behave differently. See the SMI instruction using the same F1h opcode for AMD's 386 part.

Interrupt Mode

The ICEBP instruction behaves as a single byte access to interrupt 1 in the default mode on 80386 and later CPUs after a hardware reset. This mode is maintained as long as Debug Register 7 bit 12 remains zero (an undocumented bit). On IBM's 386 and 486 CPUs the Model specific Register 1000h, bit 5, must also remain at zero (see the WRMSR instruction on how to change this bit).

Interrupt 1 is normally reserved for the single step interrupt, but when it is issued from the ICEBP instruction in this mode (the trap flag, bit 8 in the FLAGS register) is not set. When the interrupt 1 handler completes, instruction execution continues, unlike single step mode.

In-Circuit-Emulator Mode

Some special versions of the Intel 80386 and 80486, and all IBM 386SLC and 486SLC CPUs, are usable with emulators. Intel provides their ICE bondout versions with additional wires for connection to the emulator hardware. IBM's parts include the necessary connections. All parts must have additional hardware to take advantage of this feature.

Setting debug register 7, bit 12 to 1 changes the ICEBP instruction mode to In-Circuit-Emulator mode. When the ICEBP instruction is encountered, the CPU switches from normal user memory to hidden memory. The emulator hardware breakpoint handler now gains control. Hidden memory is described in detail later in this chapter under In-Circuit-Emulation.

When using a CPU without the necessary connections for hidden memory, if ICEBP is encountered in In-Circuit-Emulator mode, the system will hang: the CPU will attempt to switch to hidden memory, which does not exist on non-bondout chips and is unlikely to exist on motherboards with IBM's CPU. The system must have hidden memory, as provided in an ICE system, or ICEBP will attempt to execute undefined data. Two other cases can cause problems if In-Circuit-Emulator mode is active and no hidden memory is available. If software issues interrupt 1 using the standard INT 1 instruction, or if a single-step is attempted (which also invokes interrupt 1), the system will crash. In these cases, the CPU attempts to switch to hidden memory when interrupt 1 is issued, no matter who issues the interrupt.

In Emulator Mode, ICEBP is used to stop the emulator at a specific point in your program. In many cases you may not know (or care) where the program is loaded. By inserting a ICEBP in your source code at a point of interest, the emulator can be set to stop at that point.

With Intel's emulator, the ICE is first halted. The ICE command "GO TIL 0" is issued. This sets the debug register bit 14 to 1. Whenever the ICEBP instruction is encountered, the emulator will stop. On Intel's emulator, a warning is displayed on screen: "Unknown breakpoint at address xxxx:xxxx:xxxxxxxx."

ICEBP works in all modes, including real, V86, and protected mode, and will also work correctly even if paging is enabled.

Register Save Mode

IBM and possibly other vendors offer an additional ICEBP mode to both switch to hidden memory and to save every register in the CPU. Like the In-Circuit-Emulator mode, the debug register 7 bit 12 must be set to 1. In addition, the Register Save Mode is enabled by setting the Model Specific Register 1000h, bit 5 to 1. See the WRMSR instruction on how to set this bit. When enabled, if ICEBP is encountered, the system switches to hidden memory, stores the entire register set, switches to real mode, resets all registers in the CPU, and jumps to the ICE or Suspend code. In addition all code and data fetches bypass the internal CPU cache, so cache contents are not altered.

For a laptop's Suspend/Resume feature, ICEBP performs the same action as asserting the Power Interrupt (PWI) pin. See the section on Suspend and Resume Modes later in this chapter for more about this feature.

An In-Circuit-Emulator can display or alter the ICEBP saved registers in hidden memory. To resume, the LOADALL instruction is issued; it reloads all the CPU's registers, exits hidden memory, and begins execution at the loaded CS:IP value. See the LOADALL instruction for the definition of all these registers, which are in the same order as registers saved by ICEBP.

Inst	Description	Processors
IN/OUT	Ports 22h/23h access to CPU	Most Cyrix CPUs

```
E4h, 2xh        in    al, 2xh           ; input port
E6h, 2xh        out   2xh, al           ; output port
```

Cyrix CPUs access internal machine registers through ports 22h and 23h. To access these registers, it is necessary to output a register value in AL to port 22h. If this value is within a valid range, after a short 6 clock delay (or more), the specified register can be read or written through port 23h. You must write the register value to port 22h before each read or write. Invalid accesses (sequence errors or out of range register values) will send the I/O request to the external bus.

The following registers are available:

Register	Description	Cyrix Processor
20h	Performance Control Register	5x86
C0h	Configuration Control Register 0	486SLC/DLC, 6x86
C1h	Configuration Control Register 1	486SLC/DLC, 5x86, 6x86
C2h	Configuration Control Register 2	486S/S2/D/D2/DX/DX2/DX4, 5x86, 6x86
C3h	Configuration Control Register 3	486S2/D2/DX/DX2/DX4, 5x86, 6x86
C4h	Address region 0, bits 31-24	486DLC, 6x86
C5h	Address region 0, bits 23-16	486SLC/DLC, 6x86
C6h	Address region 0, bits 15-12	486SLC/DLC, 6x86
C7h	Address region 1, bits 31-24	486DLC, 6x86
C8h	Address region 1, bits 23-16	486SLC/DLC, 6x86
C9h	Address region 1, bits 15-12	486SLC/DLC, 6x86
CAh	Address region 2, bits 31-24	486DLC, 6x86
CBh	Address region 2, bits 23-16	486SLC/DLC, 6x86
CCh	Address region 2, bits 15-12	486SLC/DLC, 6x86
CDh	Address region 3, bits 31-24	486DLC, 6x86
CDh	SMM region start, bits 31-24	486S/S2/D/D2/DX/DX2/DX4, 5x86
CEh	Address region 3, bits 23-16	486SLC/DLC, 6x86
CEh	SMM region start, bits 23-16	486S/S2/D/D2/DX/DX2/DX4, 5x86
CFh	Address region 3, bits 15-12	486SLC/DLC, 6x86
CFh	SMM region start, bits 15-12	486S/S2/D/D2/DX/DX2/DX4, 5x86
D0h	Address region 4, bits 31-24	6x86
D1h	Address region 4, bits 23-16	6x86
D2h	Address region 4, bits 15-12	6x86
D3h	Address region 5, bits 31-24	6x86
D4h	Address region 5, bits 23-16	6x86
D5h	Address region 5, bits 15-12	6x86
D6h	Address region 6, bits 31-24	6x86

Register	Description	Cyrix Processor
D7h	Address region 6, bits 23-16	6x86
D8h	Address region 6, bits 15-12	6x86
D9h	Address region 7, bits 31-24	6x86
DAh	Address region 7, bits 23-16	6x86
DBh	Address region 7, bits 15-12	6x86
DCh	Region control 0	6x86
DDh	Region control 1	6x86
DEh	Region control 2	6x86
DFh	Region control 3	6x86
E0h	Region control 4	6x86
E1h	Region control 5	6x86
E2h	Region control 6	6x86
E3h	Region control 7	6x86
E8h	Configuration Control Register 4	5x86, 6x86
E9h	Configuration Control Register 5	6x86
F0h	Power Management	5x86
FEh	Device Identification register 0	486S2/D2/DX/DX2/DX4, 5x86,6x86
FFh	Device Identification register 1	486S2/D2/DX/DX2/DX4, 5x86,6x86

Cyrix CPU I/O Port Register Detail

Note: Bits not specified for a CPU type are considered reserved for that CPU type.

Register	Description	Cyrix Processor
20h	Performance Control Register	5x86

PCR0	bit	7 = 0	Memory reads and writes can be reorganized for optimum performance
		6 = x	Reserved
		5 = x	Reserved
		4 = x	Reserved
		3 = x	Reserved
		2 = 1	Improve performance by avoiding a prefetch queue flush if jump destination is already in the queue
		1 = 1	Branch prediction is enabled
		0 = 1	Improve performance by enabling the return stack. RET instructions will speculatively execute the code following the related CALL instruction.

Register	Description	Cyrix Processor
C0h	Configuration Control Register 0	486SLC/DLC, 6x86

CCR0	bit	7 = 1	Enable the suspend feature (SUSP input and SUSPA output pins) *
		6 = 0	Cache set to 2 way set associative *
		1	Cache is directly mapped *
		5 = 1	Flush internal cache when beginning HOLD state *
		4 = 1	Enable the FLUSH input pin *
		3 = 1	Enable the KEN input pin *
		2 = 1	Enable the A20M input pin *
		1 = 0	Address region 640 KB to 1 MB is cacheable
		0 = 1	The first 64 KB of each 1 MB of address is set to noncacheable *

** Reserved values on 6x86 and may have another function or be unused*

Register	Description	Cyrix Processor
C1h	Configuration Control Register 1	486SLC/DLC, 5x86, 6x86

CCR1	bit	7 = 1	Address region 3 is designated as SMM address space (6x86 only) *
		6 = x	Reserved
		5 = x	Reserved
		4 = 0	Do not negate the LOCK pin during bus cycles to improve performance (6x86 only)
		3 = 1	All data accesses get system memory instead of SMI memory when in an SMI service routine (5x86 only)
		2 = 1	Test SMI memory—Access SMI memory instead of system memory within the SMI address range (5x86 & 6x86 only) *
		1 = 1	Enable SMI# I/O pin and SMIACT# output pin for SMM feature (5x86 & 6x86 only) *
		0 = 1	Enable output pins RPLSET and RPLVAL# (486 only)

** Write access to these bits are only allowed when bit 0 of CCR3 is enabled (Register C3h)*

Register	Description	Cyrix Processor
C2h	Configuration Control Register 2	486S/S2/D/D2/DX/DX2/ DX4, 5x86, 6x86

CCR2	bit	7 = 1	Enable SUSP# input and SUSPA# output pins for Suspend feature
		6 = 1	Enable use of 16-byte burst write-back cycles

5 = 1	Enable cache coherency on bus arbitration by writing back all dirty cache data when HOLD is requested and prior to asserting HLDA (486 only)
4 = 1	Write protect region 1, memory addresses 640 KB to 1 MB (6x86) All writes in the memory address range 640 KB to 1 MB that hit the internal cache, are also issued on the external bus (486 & 5x86 only)
3 = 1	CPU entries suspend mode when HLT instruction executes.
2 = 0	CR0 bit 29 (internal cache write-back mode) can be modified
1 = 1	Enable write-back cache interface. Enable INVAL and WM_RST input pins (486 and 5x86 only), the CACHE# and HITM# output pins (5x86 only), and the HITM# pin (486 only).
0 = 1	Reserved

Register	Description	Cyrix Processor
C3h	Configuration Control Register 3	486S2/D2/DX/DX2/DX4, 5x86, 6x86

CCR3 bit

7 = x 6 = x 5 = x 4 = x	Access to port 22h/23h control (5x86 and 6x86 only) 0 = Only configuration registers C0-CFh, FEh and FFh are accessible 1 = All configuration registers are available
3 = 0	SMM pins function as defined in Intel's 486SL CPU (5x86 only)
1	SMM pins function as defined in standard Cyrix SMM mode (5x86 only)
2 = 0	Linear address burst cycles use "1+4" Pentium compatible sequencing (5x86 and 6x86 only)
1	Linear address burst cycles use linear sequencing (5x86 and 6x86 only)
1 = 0	Non-Maskable Interrupt is not recognized during SMM mode
0 = 1	Write protect SMM configuration register bits CCR0, bits 1, 2, 3; CCR3 bits 1, 3; and all SMM address region registers. These bits and registers are always writable while in SMM mode. Once this bit is set, only a CPU reset can clear the bit. These bits and registers are writable during SMM mode regardless of the state of this bit. SMM functions are intended to be set up once by the BIOS and never modified after that point.

Register	Description	Cyrix Processor
C4h	Address region 0, bits 31-24	486DLC, 6x86

Specify location of a region of memory. Bits 31-12 of the memory address appear in three consecutive 8-bit registers. The region size is specified in the third register of the group. Memory regions are noncacheable memory on the 486DLC. On the 6x86, the corresponding region control register defines the type of region.

Register	Description	Cyrix Processor
C5h	Address region 0, bits 23-16	486SLC/DLC, 6x86

Bits 23 through 16 of the region memory address. See register C4h for more details.

Register	Description	Cyrix Processor
C6h	Address region 0, bits 15-12	486SLC/DLC, 6x86

Bits 15 through 12 of the region memory address appear as the upper four bits of this register. The lower four bits indicate the size. See register C4h for more details.

bit	7 = x	Bit 15 of region starting address		
	6 = x	Bit 14 of region starting address		
	5 = x	Bit 13 of region starting address		
	4 = x	Bit 12 of region starting address		
	3 = x	Size of region*	Regions 0 to 6	Region 7
	2 = x	0 =	Disabled	Disabled
	1 = x	1 =	4 KB	256 KB
	0 = x	2 =	8 KB	512 KB
		3 =	16 KB	1 MB
		4 =	32 KB	2 MB
		5 =	64 KB	4 MB
		6 =	128 KB	8 MB
		7 =	256 KB	16 MB
		8 =	512 KB	32 MB
		9 =	1 MB	64 MB
		A =	2 MB	128 MB
		B =	4 MB	256 MB
		C =	8 MB	512 MB
		D =	16 MB	1 GB
		E =	32 MB	2 GB
		F =	4 GB	4 GB

* *Only regions 0 to 3 are available on the 486*

Register	Description	Cyrix Processor
C7h	Address region 1, bits 31-24	486DLC, 6x86

See region 0, register C4h for details.

Register	Description	Cyrix Processor
C8h	Address region 1, bits 23-16	486SLC/DLC, 6x86

See region 0, register C5h for details.

Register	Description	Cyrix Processor
C9h	Address region 1, bits 15-12	486SLC/DLC, 6x86

See region 0, register C6h for details.

Register	Description	Cyrix Processor
CAh	Address region 2, bits 31-24	486DLC, 6x86

See region 0, register C4h for details.

Register	Description	Cyrix Processor
CBh	Address region 2, bits 23-16	486SLC/DLC, 6x86

See region 0, register C5h for details.

Register	Description	Cyrix Processor
CCh	Address region 2, bits 15-12	486SLC/DLC, 6x86

See region 0, register C6h for details.

Register	Description	Cyrix Processor
CDh	Address region 3, bits 31-24	486DLC, 6x86

See region 0, register C4h for details.

Register	Description	Cyrix Processor
CDh	SMM region start, bits 31-24	486S/S2/D/D2/DX/DX2/ DX4, 5x86

Specify location of the SMM region of memory. Bits 31-12 of the memory address appear in three consecutive 8-bit registers. The region size is specified in the third register of the group.

Register	Description	Cyrix Processor
CEh	Address region 3, bits 23-16	486SLC/DLC, 6x86

See region 0, register C5h for details.

Register	Description	Cyrix Processor
CEh	SMM region start, bits 23-16	486S/S2/D/D2/DX/DX2/ DX4, 5x86

Bits 23 through 16 of the SMM memory address. See register CDh for more details.

Register	Description	Cyrix Processor
CFh	Address region 3, bits 15-12	486SLC/DLC, 6x86

See region 0, register C6h for details.

Register	Description	Cyrix Processor
CFh	SMM region start, bits 15-12	486S/S2/D/D2/DX/DX2/ DX4, 5x86

Bits 15 through 12 of the SMM memory address and the size of the SMM memory region. See register C6h for more details.

Register	Description	Cyrix Processor
D0h	Address region 4, bits 31-24	6x86

See region 0, register C4h for details.

Register	Description	Cyrix Processor
D1h	Address region 4, bits 23-16	6x86

See region 0, register C5h for details.

Register	Description	Cyrix Processor
D2h	Address region 4, bits 15-12	6x86

See region 0, register C6h for details.

Register	Description	Cyrix Processor
D3h	Address region 5, bits 31-24	6x86

See region 0, register C4h for details.

Register	Description	Cyrix Processor
D4h	Address region 5, bits 23-16	6x86

See region 0, register C5h for details.

Register	Description	Cyrix Processor
D5h	Address region 5, bits 15-12	6x86

See region 0, register C6h for details.

Register	Description	Cyrix Processor
D6h	Address region 6, bits 31-24	6x86

See region 0, register C4h for details.

Register	Description	Cyrix Processor
D7h	Address region 6, bits 23-16	6x86

See region 0, register C5h for details.

Register	Description	Cyrix Processor
D8h	Address region 6, bits 15-12	6x86

See region 0, register C6h for details.

Register	Description	Cyrix Processor
D9h	Address region 7, bits 31-24	6x86

See region 0, register C4h for details.

Register	Description	Cyrix Processor
DAh	Address region 7, bits 23-16	6x86

See region 0, register C5h for details.

Register	Description	Cyrix Processor
DBh	Address region 7, bits 15-12	6x86

See region 0, register C6h for details.

Register	Description	Cyrix Processor
DCh	Region control 0	6x86

Define the type and control of the related address region.

bit	7 = x	Reserved
	6 = x	Reserved
	5 = 1	The LBA# output pin is not asserted for access to the related region
	4 = 1	The address region is write-through
	3 = 1	Write gathering for address region enabled (improves performance)
	2 = 1	Weak locking enabled for region
	1 = 1	Weak write ordering enabled for region
	0 = 1	Disables caching for region (regions 0 through 6 only)
	1	Enable caching for region (region 7 only)

Register	Description	Cyrix Processor
DDh	Region control 1	6x86

See region control 0, register DCh for details.

Register	Description	Cyrix Processor
DEh	Region control 2	6x86

See region control 0, register DCh for details.

Register	Description	Cyrix Processor
DFh	Region control 3	6x86

See region control 0, register DCh for details.

Register	Description	Cyrix Processor
E0h	Region control 4	6x86

See region control 0, register DCh for details.

Register	Description	Cyrix Processor
E1h	Region control 5	6x86

See region control 0, register DCh for details.

Register	Description	Cyrix Processor
E2h	Region control 6	6x86

See region control 0, register DCh for details.

Register	Description	Cyrix Processor
E3h	Region control 7	6x86

See region control 0, register DCh for details.

Register	Description	Cyrix Processor
E8h	Configuration Control Register 4	5x86, 6x86

CCR4	bit	7 = 1	Enable the CPUID instruction. Also allow bit 21 of EFLAGS (the CPUID supported if writable flag) to be writable (6x86 only).
		6 = x	Reserved
		5 = x	Reserved
		4 = 1	Enable the Directory Table Entry cache
		3 = 1	Enable memory read bypassing (5x86 only)
		2 = x	Minimum number of bus clock cycles between I/O accesses
		1 = x	0 = no clock delay
		0 = x	1 = 2 clock delay
			2 = 4 clock delay
			3 = 8 clock delay
			4 = 16 clock delay
			5 = 32 clock delay
			6 = 64 clock delay
			7 = 128 clock delay

Register	Description	Cyrix Processor
E9h	Configuration Control Register 5	6x86

CCR5	bit	7 = x	Reserved
		6 = x	Reserved
		5 = 1	Enable all Address Region registers (C4h to DBh)
		4 = 1	Assert the LBA# output pin for all memory accesses to region 640 KB to 1 MB
		3 = x	Reserved
		2 = x	Reserved
		1 = x	Reserved
		0 = 0	New cache lines are allocated for both read and write misses
		1	New cache lines are only allocated for read misses

Register	Description	Cyrix Processor
F0h	Power Management	5x86

PMR bit

7 = x	Reserved
6 = x	Reserved
5 = x	Reserved
4 = x	Reserved
3 = x	Reserved
2 = 1	Half speed clock—The CPU runs at half the speed of the external bus, and bits 0 and 1 are ignored. When an external bus transfer takes place, the internal clock increases in frequency for the duration of the transfer, and returns to half speed upon completion.
1 = x 0 = x	Internal Clock/Bus Clock ratio (also see bit 2) 0 = 1:1 1 = 2:1 (default if CLKMUL pin = 0 at powerup) 2 = reserved 3 = 3:1 (default if CLKMUL pin = 1 at powerup)

Register	Description	Cyrix Processor
FEh	Device Identification register 0	486S2/D2/DX/DX2/DX4, 5x86,6x86

Read only register of the CPU type. See register FFh for a list of known and ids.

Register	Description	Cyrix Processor
FFh	Device Identification register 1	486S2/D2/DX/DX2/DX4,6x86

Read only register of the CPU step (bits 7 to 4), and revision (bits 3 to 0). A partial list of ids include:

FEh Register	FFh Register	Part Name
0	n/a	Cx486SLC
1	n/a	Cx486DLC
2	n/a	Cx486SLC2
3	n/a	Cx486DLC2
4	n/a	Cx486SRx (retail upgrade of Cx486SLC)
5	n/a	Cx486DRx (retail upgrade of Cx486SLC)
6	n/a	Cx486SRx2 (retail upgrade of Cx486SLC2)
7	n/a	Cx486DRx2 (retail upgrade of Cx486DLC2)

10h	n/a	Cx486S (B step)
11h	n/a	Cx486S2 (B step)
12h	n/a	Cx486Se (B step)
13h	n/a	Cx486S2e (B step)
1Ah	5	Cx486DX-40
1Bh	8	Cx486DX2-50
1Bh	Bh	Cx486DX2-66
1Bh	31h	Cx486DX2-v80
1Fh	36h	Cx486DX4-v100
28h	n/a	5x86 1xs
29h	n/a	5x86 2xs
2Ah	n/a	5x86 1xp
2Bh	n/a	5x86 2xp
2Ch	n/a	5x86 4xs
2Dh	n/a	5x86 3xs
2Eh	n/a	5x86 4xp
2Fh	n/a	5x86 3xp
30h	?	6x86 1xs
31h	?	6x86 2xs
32h	?	6x86 1xp
33h	?	6x86 2xp
34h	?	6x86 4xs
35h	?	6x86 3xs
36h	?	6x86 4xp
37h	?	6x86 3xp

n/a Register is not available on this part
? Unknown register value(s)

Inst	Description	Processors
LOADALL	**Load All Processor Registers**	**Some 286-486**

ABC

```
0Fh, 05h      loadall      ; load registers from 0:800h (286 only)
0Fh, 07h      loadall      ; load registers from es:edi (386-486)
```

The LOADALL instruction was first implemented on the 80286 to load every register in the CPU in one operation. This includes a number of hidden, inaccessible registers. The opcode was changed in the 80386, and dropped entirely in Intel's 80486. Surprisingly, some other CPU manufacturer, such as IBM and AMD, have included it in their 486s.

Intel used the LOADALL instruction for testing the CPU after fabrication, and as a means for the In-Circuit-Emulator (ICE) to load the entire state of the CPU in one operation. Intel had never expected LOADALL to be used by any program and hid its existence. Some clever programmers found out and noticed it was a slick way to quickly access extended memory (above 1 MB) without going into protected mode.

When accessing extended memory on a system, the only alternative to LOADALL is to switch to protected mode. This process on a 286 is very slow. The program (perhaps by using XMS functions) must switch to protected mode, transfer the extended memory to the desired main memory area, and then reset the CPU to return the real mode. Using a special mode of the BIOS, the BIOS can resume after a reset in user code rather than rerunning the power-on-self-test routines. Several BIOS routines are also available to access extended memory, but they perform the same slow technique.

Using LOADALL in real mode, the program can load hidden descriptor cache registers and keep the system in real mode. The hidden descriptor cache registers are used by the CPU to limit access to memory. Descriptor cache registers were intended to be used to limit a program's access and protect the operating system and other programs in a multitasking operating system environment. By default after BIOS initialization, these registers are set to only allow access to the first 1 MB of memory to simulate an 8088 environment.

LOADALL is the only really viable solution to accessing extended memory on an 80286. To make a usable memory manager on an 80286 requires the use of the LOADALL instruction. You will find that even Microsoft uses it to provide XMS services in HIMEM.SYS, which is shipped with both DOS and Windows.

It is also interesting to note that most 80386 BIOSes hook the bad opcode interrupt 6. If the instruction causing the bad opcode was an 80286 LOADALL, it reformats the data and executes an 80386 LOADALL.

Emulators and laptop "sleep" modes can also use the LOADALL to restart the CPU to a known state after an emulator breakpoint or suspend operation. In this situation, all of the registers have been previously saved. To get all the internal registers, some newer chips provide special enhancements usually related to power-down sleep modes.

When using the LOADALL instruction, no checks are made on any of the data loaded. Invalid values may cause unpredictable CPU operation. You should be very familiar with protected mode programming and related registers and descriptor tables before using this instruction. The processor may hang if a CPU fault occurs during the execution of LOADALL. A page fault is one type of fault that will cause the CPU to hang. LOADALL can only be executed when the privilege level is 0. This means it's OK in real mode. The AMD 486DXLV part restricts LOADALL operation from system management mode only, and generates an illegal opcode interrupt when attempted in any other processor state.

LOADALL on the 80286

When executed, the CPU reads 51 words from physical memory at address 0:800h. These 51 words are loaded into registers and various descriptors. Table 3-11 shows the LOADALL table for an 80286. Table 3-12 shows the layout of the six byte descriptors.

Table 3-11. LOADALL Table of Words, 80286

Memory Address	Words	Register Loaded
800h	3	none
806h	1	MSW—Machine Status Word
808h	7	none
816h	1	TR—Task Register
818h	1	Flags
81Ah	1	IP
81Ch	1	LDTR—Local Descriptor Table Register
81Eh	1	DS
820h	1	SS
822h	1	CS
824h	1	ES
826h	1	DI
828h	1	SI
82Ah	1	BP
82Ch	1	SP
82Eh	1	BX
830h	1	DX
832h	1	CX
834h	1	AX
836h	3	ES Descriptor
83Ch	3	CS Descriptor
842h	3	SS Descriptor
848h	3	DS Descriptor
84Eh	3	GDT Descriptor (Global Descriptor Table)
854h	3	LDT Descriptor (Local Descriptor Table)
85Ah	3	IDT Descriptor (Interrupt Descriptor Table)
860h	3	TSS Descriptor (Task State Segment)

Table 3-12. LOADALL Descriptor Bytes, 80286

Offset	Bytes	Description
0	3	24-bit physical base address
3	1	For IDT and GDT, set to 0 Segment Access rights byte—See an Intel CPU manual for detailed description of alternative values. For CS: 9Bh = executable only 93h = executable, read, and writeable For DS/ES/SS: 93h = read and writeable For LDT: 82h = specifies it is an LDT For TSS: 89h = task state OK for switch
4	2	16-bit segment limit in bytes Use FFFFh to access all 64K bytes in a segment

LOADALL on the 386/486

When LOADALL is executed, the CPU reads 10 double words from the memory address pointed to by ES:EDI+100h, and then reads 51 additional double words from memory at ES:EDI. Even if the system is in protected mode, ES must contain a real mode segment value and not a selector.

Similar to the 80286 LOADALL functionally, the 61 double words are loaded into registers and various descriptors. Table 3-13 shows the basic LOADALL table for 80386. Table 3-16 shows the basic layout of the descriptors. Be aware that some AMD parts (386 and 486) use a somewhat different table than Intel or IBM.

It is my understanding that Intel does not provide LOADALL on 80486 and later CPUs. My own testing confirms this, but Intel may have hidden it with special register setups or other convoluted schemes.

Table 3-13. LOADALL Table of Dwords for 386/486

ES:EDI Offset	Dwords	Register Loaded
00h	1	CR0
04h	1	EFLAGS
08h	1	EIP
0Ch	1	EDI
10h	1	ESI
14h	1	EBP
18h	1	ESP
1Ch	1	EBX
20h	1	EDX
24h	1	ECX
28h	1	EAX

Table 3-13. Continued

ES:EDI Offset	Dwords	Register Loaded
2Ch	1	DR6
30h	1	DR7
34h	1	TR (Task State Selector Register)
38h	1	LDTR (Local Descriptor Table Register)
3Ch*	1	GS
40h*	1	FS
44h*	1	DS
48h*	1	SS
4Ch*	1	CS
50h*	1	ES
54h	3	TSS Descriptor (Task State Selector)
60h	3	IDT Descriptor (Interrupt Descriptor Table)
6Ch	3	GDT Descriptor (Global Descriptor Table)
78h	3	LDT Descriptor (Local Descriptor Table)
84h	3	GS Descriptor
90h	3	FS Descriptor
9Ch	3	DS Descriptor
A8h	3	SS Descriptor
B4h	3	CS Descriptor
C0h	3	ES Descriptor
CCh**	1	Length of table
D0h**	12	These dwords are unused and not loaded by LOADALL
100h	1	Temporary register TST
104h	1	Temporary register IDX
108h	1	Temporary register H
10Ch	1	Temporary register G
110h	1	Temporary register F
114h	1	Temporary register E
118h	1	Temporary register D
11Ch	1	Temporary register C
120h**	1	Temporary register B
124h**	1	Temporary register A

* *Upper word of Dword always zero*
** *Value ignored during AMD 486 LOADALL*

IBM's 386 and 486 chips both support LOADALL. These parts provide an option to load the normal 61 words, or the full set of registers in the IBM CPU, 73 double words. To enable the 73-word mode, bit 5 of the Model Specific Register 1000h must be set on. The additional information saved after the first 61 double words is shown in Table 3-14.

Table 3-14. Optional LOADALL Dwords on IBM's 386/486

These registers loaded only if the Model specific Register 1000h has its Enable ICE, bit 14 set. (See WRMSR instruction.)

ES:EDI Offset	Dwords	Register Loaded
128h	1	CR2
12Ch	1	CR3
130h	1	MSR—Model specific Register 1001h, bits 0-31
134h	1	MSR—Model specific Register 1001h, bits 32-63
138h	1	MSR—Model specific Register 1000h, bits 0-14
13Ch	1	DR0
140h	1	DR1
144h	1	DR2
148h	1	DR3
14Ch*	1	PEIP—Previous Hidden Memory space instruction pointer

** The Previous Hidden Memory space instruction pointer is never loaded into the CPU by LOADALL, but is shown where it occurs if the registers are dumped from the CPU. See the section in this chapter on Suspend and Resume Modes for more about hidden memory space.*

Table 3-15. Additional LOADALL Dwords on AMD's 486DXLV

ES:EDI Offset	Dwords	Register Loaded
128h*	1	PEIP—Previous Hidden Memory space instruction pointer
12Ch**	7	unused
148h	2	unused, and not loaded by SMI
150h	22	Floating-Point Internal Registers

** The Previous Hidden Memory space instruction pointer is never loaded into the CPU by LOAD-ALL, but is shown where it occurs if the registers are dumped from the CPU. See the section in this chapter on Suspend and Resume Modes for more about hidden memory space.*
*** Values ignored during AMD 486 LOADALL (RES4)*

Table 3-16. LOADALL Descriptor Bytes, 386/486

Offset	Bytes	Description	
0	0	unused, set to 0	
1	1	For IDT and GDT, set to 0 For all others—Access rights byte Bit 7, the present bit is redefined as a valid bit. A bit value of 0 indicates the descriptor is invalid, and if the descriptor is used, will cause a General Protection Fault (interrupt Dh). Segment Access rights byte—See an Intel CPU manual for detailed description of alternative values.	
		For CS:	9Bh = executable only 93h = executable, read and writeable
		For DS/ES/FS/GS/SS:	93h = read and writeable
		For LDT:	82h = specifies it is an LDT
		For TSS:	89h = task state OK for switch
2	2	unused, set to 0	
4	4	32-bit physical base address	
8	4	32-bit limit	

Using LOADALL

As I stated earlier, the most prevalent use of LOADALL is to access all memory from real mode. While LOADALL appears to be a trap door into the CPU, it does require the CPU to be at privilege level 0. Any operating system with some level of security never lets applications run at privilege level 0. This includes OS/2, NT, and many others. Of course DOS does not have any security whatsoever, and when running without a memory manager, it is running in real mode, allowing LOADALL to function.

First, I need to digress to explain a little more about descriptors. To access a memory address at B8006h (which happens to be the video buffer area), a segment register is loaded with B800h, and an instruction is used to access byte 6 in the DS segment. What is hidden from application programs is the descriptor for the DS segment. To determine the actual memory address, the CPU takes a "base" value from the hidden descriptor register and adds it to the DS segment and adds in the offset. Figure 3-2 shows how this works.

Figure 3-2. Memory Address Calculation, First MB

	Value	Multiplier	Result	Range of Control
Memory offset	= 0006h	1	6h	64 KB
DS segment value	= B800h	10h	B8000h	1 MB
Descriptor Base address	= 000000h	1	0	16 MB*

Generated memory address:			B0006h	

** 4 GB with 32-bit base (386+), 16 MB if 24-bit base (286)*

After a CPU reset, the descriptors base address is automatically set to 0. In this manner the application can access any byte in the first 1 MB. (I'm going to ignore the HMA case of accessing an extra 64K-16 bytes by using segment FFFF). Now when we wish to access memory in the third megabyte starting at physical address 200000h, we have to change the descriptor base address, as shown in Figure 3-3 below.

Figure 3-3. Memory Address Calculation, Third MB

	Value	Multiplier	Result	Range of Control
Memory offset	= 0000h	1	0h	64 KB
DS segment value	= 0000h	10h	00000h	1 MB
Descriptor Base address	= 200000h	1	200000h	16 MB*

Generated memory address:			200000h	

** 4 GB with 32-bit base (386+), 16 MB if 24-bit base (286)*

The program can load DS with values from 0 to FFFF, and access any memory in the third megabyte. With the base address at 200000h, the user cannot access memory outside this 1 MB range with DS segment values. So far it seems straightforward, except in real mode there is no way (other than LOADALL) to change the value of the descriptor! Now I've made a fair number of simplifications to make this easier to understand. If you are unfamiliar with all this, the *Intel Pentium Processor User's Manual* is a good place to brush up on descriptors and related topics.

So the big trick to accessing memory beyond 1 MB in real mode is to use LOADALL to change the descriptor base address of a segment. If we need to transfer memory from the first megabyte to the third megabyte, the DS descriptor base address could be left at zero, and the ES descriptor base address set to 200000h. Of course, all the other registers also must be set properly. After LOADALL executes, the DS segment register will allow access to any location in the first megabyte, and ES will allow access to any location in the third megabyte. Memory can easily be transferred using any of a number of different instructions. For example, MOVSB can be used to transfer bytes from DS:[SI] to ES:[DI].

Using LOADALL for Real Mode Paging

The 80386 and 80486 can remap any 4K byte physical block to a different logical address. This is referred to as *paging*. When paging is activated, software only sees the logical addresses. This is handy to remap slow BIOS ROMs into fast 32-bit RAM, provide EMS emulation, make memory appear in the PC's Upper Memory Blocks (UMBs), and other tricks. Intel designed paging for use by a protected mode program, such as an operating system or memory manager. Unfortunately, making a protected mode system that runs DOS programs is very difficult. Protected mode also slows the system by 5 to 10 percent in most cases, and can slow down the system considerably more in situations where very high interrupt rates are occurring.

LOADALL can be used to eliminate the performance limitations of protected mode on 80386 and later CPUs that support LOADALL. The LOADALL instruction is used to create a special (and somewhat incompatible) undocumented mode called Real Mode Paging or "Big Real Mode." Obviously, protected mode offers a range of additional features over real mode, but if paging is the only protected mode feature needed, LOADALL is the only way to accomplish it.

CR0 controls when the system is in protected mode and when paging is active. Only one move instruction can load CR0, and the CPU will not allow the paging bit to be set if the system is not in protected mode. Here's where the LOADALL comes in. As we stated before, no checks are made to the values loaded by LOADALL. If CR0 is loaded with the paging bit set, but the protected mode is not set, the CPU goes into undocumented Real Mode Paging mode.

When setting up CR0 for the LOADALL, all of the reserved bits of CR0 must be set to zero. This may seem strange, since if CR0 is read, the reserved bits are all set to 1.

Resume from System Management Mode "LOADALL"

AMD, Cyrix and Intel offer a new instruction, Resume from System Management mode (RSM) on some CPUs in place of LOADALL. This instruction is basically the same as LOADALL, with a different opcode. The major difference is the CPU logic only allows the RSM instruction in a very special System Management Mode. This is described in more detail under the RSM and Suspend and Resume sections later in this chapter.

It's interesting to note that Pentium's RSM instruction now performs some checking on the values loaded into the CPU. In particular, it will not allow the paging bit of CR0 to be set without the protected mode bit. This means it's impossible to set up the Real Mode Paging described earlier.

Inst	Description	Processors
POP CS	Load CS from Stack	8088/8086

ABC

```
0Fh          pop cs          ; load CS from stack
```

All 8088 and 8086 CPUs implement the POP CS instruction. When executed, the top of the current stack is loaded into the Current instruction segment, CS register. This is not a very useful instruction. Unlike a Return Far instruction, which updates both the CS and IP registers from the stack at the same time, I have not been able to figure out any useful purpose for POP CS.

I suspect it may have been a microcode mistake or it may have been left in just to save a slight bit of chip logic. If you look at an opcode map, it so happens that the four POP segment register instructions all use the same base bit pattern, 000nn111. The nn value defines the segment register:

Instruction	nn	opcode
POP ES	00	07h
POP CS	01	0Fh
POP SS	10	17h
POP DS	11	1Fh

All later processors, including the NEC V20/V30 CPUs, reuse the POP CS opcode for the first byte of a new group of instructions.

Inst	Description	Processors
RDMSR	Read Model Specific Register	Some 386+

```
0Fh, 32h        rdmsr                ; read model specific register
                                     ;   ecx into edx:eax
```

This instruction reads specific Model Specific Registers. The register to read is supplied in ECX. Upon return, the 64-bit register value is loaded into EDX:EAX. See the instruction Write Model Specific Register (WRMSR) for complete details and register contents.

RDMSR is only allowed in real mode and protected mode at privilege level 0. Otherwise, a General Protection Fault occurs.

See the sample program at the end of this chapter (CPURDMSR) to hunt for possible undocumented registers. We've run it on a standard Intel 80486, and not found any Model Specific Registers. On the Pentium there are a number of undocumented registers, which are defined for cache information, the Translation Lookaside Buffer (TLB), and other information. Other CPUs may have hidden registers, but keep in mind that hidden registers may exist that CPURDMSR does not identify. This might be the case if undocumented bits need to be set to access other undocumented registers, or if registers other than ECX need special values to unlock the access.

Inst	Description	Processors
RDTSC	Read Time Stamp Counter	Pentium+

```
0Fh, 31h        rdtsc                ; get the time stamp counter
                                     ;  into edx:eax
```

This is a new instruction on the Pentium CPU that gets the current contents of the internal Time Stamp Counter. The 64-bit time stamp counter is set to zero by a reset, and begins counting at the CPU rate. For a 200 MHz clock, this means 200,000,000 counts occur per second. This instruction was not documented by Intel for the first three years of the Pentium release. It has now been documented in the latest Pentium manuals.

If the current privilege level is 0, RDTSC instruction can be used any time. When the privilege level of the program is not zero, RDTSC can only be read if the TSD bit 2 is cleared in CR4.

The Time Stamp Counter can also be accessed by the Model Specific Register commands, using register 10h. With the WRMSR instruction, the Time Stamp Counter can be changed to a new value.

This is a great way to easily time events precisely, without any concern about other users. The time stamp counter value is read and saved at the start of an event, and again at event completion. The difference in values is the event duration. Because of the 64-bit size of the timer, it will only roll over after about 8,000 years of continuous operation, an unlikely event in my lifetime.

To see how simple it is to measure extremely short and long events, it takes only six instructions to get the event duration! Unfortunately, this only works on a 586+ CPU, and you need to know the clock frequency to determine the elapsed time period. See the sample routine CPUSPEED in the program CPUTYPE for getting the CPU speed.

```
          rdtsc                              ; get time stamp
          mov     [count_hi], edx            ; save value
          mov     [count_lo], eax
     <<<< Event or code to time goes here >>>>
          rdtsc                              ; get second time stamp
          sub     eax, [count_lo]            ; calculate difference
          sbb     edx, [count_hi]
                                             ; edx:eax = event duration
```

You may desire as much accuracy as possible. Depending on what the timing is for, you may need to consider disabling interrupts and NMI. This avoids possible interruptions that could affect the measurements. To slightly improve the accuracy, one directive and two instructions are added in front of the prior example:

```
          ALIGN 4
          mov     [temp_lo], eax             ; save the event duration
          mov     [temp_hi], edx             ;    from the prior steps
```

This ensures all data variables are in the L1 cache. Otherwise, the first use of COUNT_HI and COUNT_LO may or may not have a cache hit, causing a few cycles of uncertainty.

If a few cycles make a difference, the following code fragment removes the slight amount of time for the execution of the RDTSC and register saves in the prior example. It is executed immediately after the code that calculates the difference.

Keep in mind that code and data alignment may also cost a few cycles, so an ALIGN 4 statement should be used before the code to keep everything on an even footing. Another ALIGN 4 should appear before the data definition (not shown).

```
mov     [temp_lo], eax      ; save the event duration
mov     [temp_hi], edx      ;   from the prior steps
rdtsc                       ; get time stamp
mov     [count_hi], edx     ; save value
mov     [count_lo], eax
rdtsc                       ; get second time stamp
sub     eax, [count_lo]     ; calculate difference
sbb     edx, [count_hi]     ; edx:eax is the overhead time
sub     [temp_lo], eax
sbb     [temp_hi], edx
mov     eax, [temp_lo]
mov     edx, [temp_hi]      ; edx:eax has the adjusted
                            ;  event duration
```

Except for the Pentium Pro, the processor does not ensure all previous instructions have been executed prior to RDTSC. It is also possible that instructions following RDTSC could be executed before the read operation is performed. This does not affect our prior example, because the two prior instructions must be executed prior to RDTSC, and the two instructions following RDTSC cannot be executed prior to RDTSC.

The RDTSC instruction is now documented in the Pentium Pro manual, but not in Pentium manual editions dated 1995 or earlier.

Inst	Description	Processors
RSM	**Resume From System Management Mode**	**Some 386+**

```
0Fh, AAh        rsm                     ; resume from SMI
```

RSM loads all the CPU's registers previously saved by the System Management Interrupt. It does not reload any floating-point registers if present, and does not alter the Model Specific Registers on the Pentium and Pentium compatibles. Execution then begins at the point where the last System Management interrupt occurred.

Its function is similar to LOADALL, except it can only be executed while in System Management Mode. Attempting to execute RSM from any other mode, real, protected or V86, will cause a bad opcode fault, interrupt 6.

Refer to the section in this chapter on Suspend and Resume Modes for additional details. Table 3-14 in the Suspend and Resume section shows the Intel CPU Registers saved in Hidden Memory that are loaded back into the CPU by the RSM instruction.

RSM is supported in Intel's 80386SL, 80486SL, and Pentium processors. The Cyrix/TI 486SLC/e also uses this instruction, although far fewer registers are restored on the Cyrix part. This instruction is described in some, but not all, Intel CPU manuals, and is described in the Cyrix SMM programmer's guide.

Inst	Description	Processors
SETALC	**Set AL to Carry**	**All, except V20**

```
D6h         setalc                    ; mov carry into al
```

This instruction sets all bits in AL to the value of the carry bit. If carry is not set, AL becomes zero. If carry is set, AL is set to FFh. No flags are affected by this instruction.

My tests show this alternate instruction form is supported in every chip from all vendors except for NEC's V20. I have seen a few older commercial applications use this instruction in their code. You can expect all future CPUs will have to support SETALC if they want to maintain compatibility with old code.

The following code sequence duplicates the functionality of this undocumented instruction:

```
            pushf                     ; save flags
            mov      al, 0            ; clear al
            jnc      not_set          ; jump if no carry
            dec      al               ; set to FFh
       not_set:
            popf                      ; restore flags
```

Inst	Description	Processors
SHL	**Shift Left by Count**	**80188+**

```
C0h, r/m    shl      regB/memB, imm   ; shift byte left by immediate
C1h, r/m    shl      regW/memW, imm   ; shift word left by immediate
C1h, r/m    shl      regD/memD, imm   ; shift dword left by immediate
```

Shift left by an immediate count has been a standard instruction since the 80188. What is not documented is that a second opcode form performs the identical action.

The difference between the standard form and the undocumented form is the REG field of the MM-REG-R/M byte. The documented form has the 3-bit REG field fixed at 100. The undocumented form uses a 3-bit REG field of 110.

This alternate form is not very useful. I've seen one brave person use this undocumented form in the code generated by a shareware assembler. I expect the idea was to be able to tell whether anyone used the assembler to create code without purchasing a license for the assembler.

My tests show this alternate instruction form is supported in every chip from all vendors. Since there is code out there that uses this form, it's going to be supported for a long time.

Inst	Description	Processors
SHL	**Shift Left by 1**	**All**

```
D0h, r/m      shl    regB/memB, 1    ; shift byte left by 1
D1h, r/m      shl    regW/memW, 1    ; shift word left by 1
D1h, r/m      shl    regD/memD, 1    ; shift dword left by 1
```

Shift left by one has been in every processor since the 8088. What is not documented is that a second opcode form performs the identical action.

The difference between the standard form and the undocumented form is the REG field of the MM-REG-R/M byte. The documented form has the 3-bit REG field set to 100. The undocumented form uses a 3-bit REG field of 110.

This alternate form is not very useful. Similar to the undocumented form of Shift left by Count, I've only seen the undocumented form in code generated from a shareware assembler.

My tests show this alternate instruction form is supported in every chip from all vendors. Since there is code out there that uses this form, it's going to be supported for a long time.

Inst	Description	Processors
SMI	**System Management Mode Entry**	**AMD 386SXLV, DXLV 486DXLV**

```
F1h           smi                    ; call SMI interrupt handler
```

This instruction is unique to AMD's low-power parts. It provides a software means to enter System Management Mode, where hidden memory becomes available. On most other processors F1h is used for the ICE breakpoint. See the ICEBP for these alternate uses. Similar to the IBM part, the LOADALL is used to resume normal operation after System Management Mode. The UMOV instructions are used to access user memory while system management mode is active. System management mode is covered in more detail later in the section on Suspend and Resume.

AMD's newer DX2 and DX4 486 variants and the $Am5_K86$ do not support SMI but revert to a hardware only activation.

Inst	Description	Processors
TEST	**Test Register with Immediate**	**All**

```
F6h, r/m      test    regB/memB, imm   ; AND byte with immediate
F7h, r/m      test    regW/memW, imm   ; AND word with immediate
F7h, r/m      test    regD/memD, imm   ; AND dword with immediate
```

The test with immediate instruction has been in every processor since the 8088. What is not documented is a second opcode form that performs the identical action.

The difference between the standard form and the undocumented form is the REG field of the MM-REG-R/M byte. The documented form has the 3-bit REG field set to 000. The undocumented form uses a 3-bit REG field of 001.

This alternate form is not very useful. Similar to the undocumented form of Shift left, I've only seen the undocumented form in code generated from a shareware assembler.

My tests show this alternate instruction form is supported in every chip from all vendors. Since there is code out there that uses this form, it's going to be supported for a long time.

Inst	Description	Processors
UMOV	**User Move Register Instructions**	**Some 386/486**

```
0Fh, 10h, r/m   mov   regB1/memB, regB2   ; move byte from register 2
                                          ;   to register 1 or memory
0Fh, 11h, r/m   mov   regW1/memW, regW2   ; move word from register 2
                                          ;   to register 1 or memory
0Fh, 12h, r/m   mov   regB1, regB2/memB   ; move byte from register 2
                                          ;   or memory to register 1
0Fh, 13h, r/m   mov   regW1, regW2/memW   ; move word from register 2
                                          ;   or memory to register 1
```

To understand the User Move instructions, you need to understand hidden memory described in the sections Suspend and Resume Modes and In-Circuit-Emulation. When the CPU is in a state that has hidden memory active, the user memory area is normally inaccessible. The UMOV allows the transference of data to and from the user memory area while hidden memory is active. When hidden memory is not active, UMOV acts identical to normal MOV instructions, opcodes 88h through 8 Bh.

The instruction is supported on all 386 and 486 processors, except for Cyrix CPUs, which have no need for hidden memory. What is odd is the UMOV instruction acts like a two-byte NOP on the Cyrix. No fault is generated. The UMOV instructions were inexplicably left out of the Pentium and later Intel processor instruction sets.

UMOV is typically used by an emulator to access data and instruction information in the user space while hidden memory is active. For example, after an ICE breakpoint has occurred the hidden memory space is active. To display a disassembly at the instruction that caused the breakpoint, code bytes must be read from user memory at the point of the breakpoint. UMOV is the only way to accomplish this, because when hidden memory is active, normal MOV instructions (and almost all other instructions) operate on hidden memory.

UMOV is also useful in identifying a Cyrix 486 CPU from other vendors 486 CPUs. Once it is determined that the CPU is not a Pentium processor, a check is made to see whether UMOV is an allowable instruction. The Bad Opcode interrupt 6 should be hooked first as a safety net, in case a future CPU drops this instruction. Once the CPU is identified as a 386 or 486, the UMOV instruction is executed. A check is made to see if the UMOV transferred the specified data, or if a bad opcode interrupt occurred. If neither of these events occurred, the CPU must be a Cyrix. Of course this might change in the future with additional vendors entering the CPU fray. See the CPUVENDOR subroutine in the CPUTYPE program for an example of using UMOV to help determine the CPU vendor.

The word forms of this instruction will appear as dword forms depending on the current mode, 16-bit or 32-bit, and whether a size override prefix is used. No flags are altered by this instruction.

Inst	Description	Processors
WRMSR	**Write Model Specific Register**	**Some 386+**

```
0Fh, 30h        wrmsr                     ; write edx:eax into model
                                          ;  specific register ecx
```

A number of CPU chip versions include new registers to support functions specific to that CPU. These registers are defined for a specific processor and are unlikely to be supported in the same way on different models or vendors. Currently only Intel's Pentium CPUs, AMD's $Am5_K86$, and IBM's 386 and 486 CPUs, have Model Specific Registers.

In general, Model Specific Registers were intended for the system BIOS and not for general application use. Changing model specific registers from an application may cause undesirable results, depending on the hardware system implementation and how the BIOS expects these flags to be set.

To write to a specific register, ECX is loaded with the register number, and a 64-bit value is loaded into EDX:EAX. The WRMSR instruction is then issued. It is allowed only in real mode and protected mode at privilege level 0. Otherwise, a General Protection Fault occurs.

To read the contents of a register, see the Read Model Specific Register instruction RDMSR. Before any bit changes are made to a Model Specific Register, the current value should be read. Any desired bits are changed, leaving all other bits unchanged. The new dword register value is then written back to the Model Specific Register. For example:

```
                mov     ecx, 1000h
                rdmsr                     ; get register 1000h
                or      eax, 20h          ; set bit 5 on in edx:eax
                wrmsr                     ; write register 1000h
```

Register Summary

Register	Description	Processor
0	Machine Check Address	Pentium, Pentium Pro, $Am5_K86$
1	Machine Check Type	Pentium, Pentium Pro, $Am5_K86$
2	Parity Reversal Register (TR1)	Pentium
4	End Bit Test Register (TR2)	Pentium
5	Cache Data Test Register (TR3)	Pentium
6	Cache Status Test Register (TR4)	Pentium
7	Cache Control Test Register (TR5)	Pentium
8	TLB Command Test Register (TR6)	Pentium
9	TLB Data Test Register (TR7)	Pentium
Bh	BTB Tag Test Register (TR9)	Pentium
Ch	BTB Target Test Register (TR10)	Pentium
Dh	BTB Command Test Register (TR11)	Pentium
Eh	New Feature Control (TR12)	Pentium
10h	Time Stamp Counter	Pentium, Pentium Pro, $Am5_K86$
11h	Control/Event Select Register	Pentium
12h	Counter 0	Pentium
13h	Counter 1	Pentium
1Bh	APICBASE	Pentium Pro
2Ah	Power-On Functions	Pentium Pro
79h	BIOS Update Trigger Register	Pentium Pro
82h	Array Access Register	$Am5_K86$
83h	Hardware Configuration Register	$Am5_K86$
8Bh	BIOS Update Signature Register	Pentium Pro
C1h	Performance Counter 0 Control	Pentium Pro
C2h	Performance Counter 1 Control	Pentium Pro
FEh	Memory Type Range Register	Pentium Pro
179h	Machine Check Global Capabilities	Pentium Pro
17Ah	Machine Check Global Status	Pentium Pro
17Bh	Machine Check Global Control	Pentium Pro
186h	Event Select 0 Register	Pentium Pro
187h	Event Select 1 Register	Pentium Pro
1D9h	Debug Control MSR Register	Pentium Pro
1DBh	Last Branch from IP	Pentium Pro
1DCh	Last Branch to IP	Pentium Pro
1DDh	Last Interrupt from IP	Pentium Pro
1DEh	Last Interrupt to IP	Pentium Pro
1E0h	ROB_CR_BKUPTMPDR6	Pentium Pro
200h-20Fh	Memory Type Range Register Physical Base & Mask (8 registers each)	Pentium Pro
250h	Memory Type Range Register fix 64K_0	Pentium Pro
258h-259h	Memory Type Range Register fix 16K (2 registers)	Pentium Pro

Register Summary (Continued)

Register	Description	Processor
268h-26Fh	Memory Type Range Register fix 4K (8 registers)	Pentium Pro
2FFh	Memory Type Range Register type	Pentium Pro
400h	Machine Check 0 Control	Pentium Pro
401h	Machine Check 0 Status	Pentium Pro
402h	Machine Check 0 Address	Pentium Pro
403h	Machine Check 0 Miscellaneous	Reserved for future Pentium
404h	Machine Check 1 Control	Pentium Pro
405h	Machine Check 1 Status	Pentium Pro
406h	Machine Check 1 Address	Pentium Pro
407h	Machine Check 1 Miscellaneous	Reserved for future Pentium
408h	Machine Check 2 Control	Pentium Pro
409h	Machine Check 2 Status	Pentium Pro
40Ah	Machine Check 2 Address	Pentium Pro
40Bh	Machine Check 2 Miscellaneous	Reserved for future Pentium
40Ch	Machine Check 4 Control	Pentium Pro
40Dh	Machine Check 4 Status	Pentium Pro
40Eh	Machine Check 4 Address	Pentium Pro
40Fh	Machine Check 4 Miscellaneous	Reserved for future Pentium
410h	Machine Check 3 Control	Pentium Pro
411h	Machine Check 3 Status	Pentium Pro
412h	Machine Check 3 Address	Pentium Pro
413h	Machine Check 3 Miscellaneous	Reserved for future Pentium
1000h	Processor Operation Register	IBM 386/486SLC
1001h	Cache Region Control Registers	IBM 386/486SLC
1002h	Processor Operation Register 2	IBM 486SLC2
1004h	Processor Control Register	IBM 486SBL3

* *All Pentium Pro MSRs are documented to some degree in the Pentium Pro manual. No further knowledge about the contents of these registers is known. Use the CPURDMSR program to view the current contents of any desired registers.*

In my tests, registers that are not supported cause a double fault CPU interrupt 8 to be issued.

Register Detail

Register 0	Machine Check Address	Pentium, Pentium Pro, Am5$_K$86

The Machine Check feature is used to record a data read parity error or a bus error. When either of these errors occur, the 64-bit address of the faulting location is saved in this register. The type of fault is stored with other related information in Model Specific Register 1. When the error occurs, if the Machine Check interrupt is enabled, interrupt 12h is issued. I have not seen any use for writing a value into register 0, but there appears to be no restriction on doing so.

The Pentium Pro provides this register as a Pentium compatible register. The preferred method is to detect a Pentium Pro and use the detailed information provided in the machine check MSR's starting at 400h. These are described in detail in the Pentium Pro manual.

Register 1 — Machine Check Type — Pentium, Pentium Pro, $Am5_K86$

When a fault address is stored in the Machine Check Address, this register holds the type of fault. Bit 0 of this register is set to 1 to indicate this register and register 0 are both valid. When bit 0 is 0, the other bits in this register are undefined, and register 0 is also undefined.

The act of reading this register clears bit 0, making register 0 undefined. So just to make your life a little more difficult, the CPU requires the Machine Check Address register 0 to be read first and saved. Then Machine Check Type register 1 is read to see whether the address previously read is valid. Seems just a bit strange to me, but I'm sure a few gates were saved.

I have not seen any use for writing a value into register 1, but there appears to be no restriction on doing so.

The Pentium Pro provides this register as a Pentium compatible register. The preferred method is to detect a Pentium Pro and use the detailed information provided in the machine check MSR's starting at 400h. These are described in detail in the Pentium Pro manual.

bits	63-5 = 0	Reserved, and presumed unused
	4 = 1	The LOCK hardware line was asserted (1) when the error occurred.
	3 = 0	Error occurred in an I/O cycle
	1	Error occurred in a memory cycle
	2 = 0	Error occurred in a data cycle
	1	Error occurred in a code fetch cycle
	1 = 0	Error occurred in a write cycle
	1	Error occurred in a read cycle
	0 = 0	No error latched, all other bits undefined (see text)
	1	Error information latched

Register 2 — Parity Reversal Register (TR1) — Pentium

This register is used to test the parity logic in various internal areas of the Pentium. When activated for a specific type of internal memory, the logic reverses the sense of parity generation for a write (or read if testing the microcode). With parity reversal activated, a write and read is made to the related item. A parity error should be generated to indicate the logic is working properly.

The parity error will set the IERR# pin active and the processor may shutdown. To avoid a shutdown, bit 1 is set to 1. Bit 0 of this register is read to confirm the parity error occurred (should be 1 if parity error). All bits are writable, but only bit 0 is readable.

bits	63-14 = x	Reserved (unused or hidden bits)
	13 = 1	Reverse parity on microcode read
	12 = 1	Reverse parity on data TLB (Translation Look-aside Buffer) data
	11 = 1	Reverse parity on data TLB (Translation Look-aside Buffer) tag
	10 = 1	Reverse parity on data cache data
	9 = 1	Reverse parity on data cache tag
	8 = 1	Reverse parity on code TLB (Translation Look-aside Buffer) data
	7 = 1	Reverse parity on code TLB (Translation Look-aside Buffer) tag
	6 = 1	Reverse parity on code cache data (odd bits 255, 253, ... 131, 129)
	5 = 1	Reverse parity on code cache data (even bits 254, 252, ... 130, 128)
	4 = 1	Reverse parity on code cache data (odd bits 127, 125, ... 3, 1)
	3 = 1	Reverse parity on code cache data (even bits 126, 124, ... 2, 0)
	2 = 1	Reverse parity on code cache tag
	1 = 0	Parity error sets bit 0 = 1, asserts IERR# line, and shuts down the CPU
	1	Parity error only sets bit 0 = 1 and asserts IERR# line
	0 = 1	Parity error occurred

Register 4 — End Bit Test Register (TR2) — Pentium

Registers 4 through 7 (TR 2 to TR 5) are used for testing the on-chip caches. Similar functions were provided on the 80486 through the MOV TRx instructions, which no longer exist on the Pentium. Writing to any cache test register during normal operation can cause unpredictable behavior. You should thoroughly understand the cache operation and related terminology before attempting a test of the cache.

To assure proper test results, external inquire cycles must be inhibited. This is accomplished by setting register CR0 Cache Disable (bit 30), and CR0 Not Writethrough (bit 29) to 1. You must avoid the use of INVD, WBINVD, and INVLPG instructions during a specific test (before or after a test is acceptable).

Sequence for writing into a cache through the test registers:

1) Inhibit external inquiry cycles (CR0 bits 30 and 29 are set to 1).
2) For each 4-byte access (remember that a cache line requires eight 4-byte accesses):
   a) Write the desired address into TR5 (WRMSR register 7), TR5 control bits 0 & 1 are set to "0".
   b) Write the data into TR3 (WRMSR register 5).
   c) If writing into the instruction cache, set the end bits in TR2 (WRMSR register 4).
3) Write the desired tag, LRU and valid bits into TR4 (WRMSR register 6).
4) Perform a testability write by loading TR5 (WRMSR register 7), but with TR5 control bit 1 set to "0", and bit 0 set to "1".

Sequence for reading an entry from the cache through the test registers:

1) Inhibit external inquiry cycles (CR0 bits 30 and 29 are set to 1).
2) For each 4-byte access (remember that a cache line requires eight 4-byte accesses):
   a) Write the desired address into TR5 (WRMSR register 7), with TR5 control bit 1 set to "1" and bit 0 set to "0".
   b) Read the data from TR3 (RDMSR register 5).
   c) If reading from the instruction cache, read the end bits in TR2 (RDMSR register 4).
   d) Read the tag, LRU, and valid bits from TR4 (RDMSR register 6).

Sequence to invalidate the entire code cache:

Write to TR5 (WRMSR register 7), with TR5 CD bit 13 set to "0", and TR5 control bits 1 and 0 set to "1".

Sequence to invalidate the entire data cache (modified lines are not written back):

Write to TR5 (WRMSR register 7), with TR5 CD bit 13 set to "1", and TR5 WB bit set to "0", and TR5 control bits 1 and 0 set to "1".

Sequence to invalidate one cache line (and writeback if modified):

Write to TR5 (WRMSR register 7), with TR5 CD bit 13 set to "1", and TR5 WB bit set to "1", and TR5 control bits 1 and 0 set to "1". The cache line address is also specified in TR5.

The End Bit Test Register (TR2) is only used when dealing with the instruction cache. Each of the four bits relate to each of the four bytes in TR3. A bit is set to "1" when the related byte in TR3 is the last byte of an instruction. This information is used to decode two instructions in one clock cycle. Incorrect end bit values are automatically corrected, but the bad end bits will prevent the processing of two instructions in one clock.

bits	63-4 = x	Unused
	3 = 1	Byte 3 (bits 31-24) of TR3 holds the last byte of an instruction

2 = 1	Byte 2 (bits 23-16) of TR3 holds the last byte of an instruction
1 = 1	Byte 1 (bits 15-8) of TR3 holds the last byte of an instruction
0 = 1	Byte 0 (bits 7-0) of TR3 holds the last byte of an instruction

Register 5 — Cache Data Test Register (TR3) — Pentium

This register holds four bytes to be read or written to a portion of a cache line. See model specific register 4 (End Bit Test Register) on how to use this register.

bits	63-32 = x	Unused
	31-24 = x	Byte 3 data
	23-16 = x	Byte 2 data
	15-8 = x	Byte 1 data
	7-0 = x	Byte 0 data

Register 6 — Cache Status Test Register (TR4) — Pentium

This register holds status information for cache operations. See model specific register 4 (End Bit Test Register) on how to use this register.

bits	63-32 = x	Unused
	31-8 = x	Tag
	7-3 = x	Unused
	2 = 0	Points to WAY 0
	1	Points to WAY 1
	1 = x	Cache line state
	0 = x	

If Data Cache (TR5, bit 13=1) bit 1	bit 0	If Code Cache (TR5, bit 13=0) bit 1	bit 0
0	0 = Invalid state	0	0 = Invalid state
0	1 = Share state	0	1 = Valid state
1	0 = in E state	1	0 = Invalid state
1	1 = in M state	1	1 = Valid state

Register 7 — Cache Control Test Register (TR5) — Pentium

This register sets the cache address, type of cache, and read/write control. See model specific register 4 (End Bit Test Register) on how to use this register.

bits	63-15 = x	Unused
	14 = 0	Cache is writethrough (data cache only)
	1	Cache is writeback (data cache only)
	13 = 0	Code cache
	1	Data cache
	12 = 0	Entry is Way 0
	1	Entry is Way 1
	11-5 = x	Cache address (selects cache line, one out of the 128 32-byte sets)
	4-2 = x	Cache address (selects one of eight 4-byte areas in a cache line to be accessed through TR2)
	1 = x	Test control
	0 = x	

bit 1	bit 0
0	0 = normal operation
0	1 = testability write
1	0 = testability read
1	1 = flush cache

Register 8 — TLB Command Test Register (TR6) — Pentium

Registers 8 and 9 (TR6 and TR7) are used for testing the translation lookaside buffers (TLBs). Writing to any TLB test register during normal operation can cause unpredictable behavior. You should thoroughly understand the TLB operation and related terminology before attempting a test of a TLB. There are three TLBs in the Pentium as shown in Table 3-17.

Table 3-17. Translation Lookaside Buffers

TLB Type	Entries	Page Size
Data	64	4 KB
Data	8	4 MB
Code	32	4 KB or 4 MB (handles both sizes in code TLB)

Sequence for writing an entry into a TLB through the test registers:

1) Write the physical address, related bits, and bit 4 = 1 (Hit bit) into TR7.
2) Write the linear address, related bits, page size, and bit 0 = 0 (writeTLB) into TR6.

Sequence for reading an entry from TLB through the test registers:

1) Write the linear address, related bits, page size, and bit 0 = 1 (read TLB) into TR6.
2) Read TR7. And check the state of bit 4, the Hit bit.
   a) If the Hit bit is zero, the read was a miss, and the physical address is undefined.

b) If the Hit bit is one, the read had a hit. The translated physical address and related bits are valid from reading TR7. Read TR6 to get the four bits 10-8 (Valid, Dirty, User and Writable bits).

Note: The linear address bits 31-12 in TR6 are automatically cleared after the read cycle as part of a valid code TLB test. Data TLB tests do not clear these bits.

The TLB Command Test Register (TR6) defines the linear address and related control and status bits.

bits	63-32 = x	Unused	
	31-12 = x	Linear address	
	11 = 0	TLB entry is invalid	
	1	TLB entry is valid	
	10 = 0	No write was made to the related page of memory	
	1	Write(s) were made to the related page of memory	
	9 = 0	User can access the page of memory when in any privilege level (0-3)	
	1	User can only access the page of memory when in privilege level 0	
	8 = 0	Writeable mode is off, page is read-only	
	1	Page is writeable	
	7-3 = x	Reserved	
	2 = x	TLB selection	
	1 = x	bit 2	bit 1
		x	0 = code TLB (size bit is ignored)
		0	1 = data TLB 4 KB page size
		1	1 = data TLB 4 MB page size
	0 = 0	TLB write	
	1	TLB read	

Register 9 TLB Data Test Register (TR7) Pentium

This register is used for testing the translation lookaside buffers (TLBs). See model specific register 8 (TR6) for details.

bits	63-32 = x	Unused
	31-12 = x	Physical address
	11 = x	Page level cache disable
	10 = x	Page level write through
	9 = x	LRU bit 2

8 = x	LRU bit 1
7 = x	LRU bit 0
6 = x	Reserved
5 = x	Reserved
4 = 0	Prior read was a miss
1	Prior read was a hit (when writing this register, this bit is set to 1)
3 = x	Entry pointer (one of four ways)
2 = x	
1 = x	Reserved
0 = x	Reserved

Register Bh   BTB Tag Test Register (TR9)   Pentium

Registers B through D (TR9 to TR11) are used for testing the Branch Target Buffer (BTB). To assure proper test results, the branch prediction logic is disabled. This is accomplished by first setting model specific register F (TR12) bit 0 to 1. Writing to any BTB test register during normal operation can cause unpredictable behavior.

Sequence for writing an entry into the BTB through the test registers:

1) Disable branch prediction (TR12 bit 0 set to 1) if not already disabled.
2) Write TR9 (WRMSR register 0Bh) with the tag address and history
3) Write TR10 (WRMSR register 0Ch) with the target address
4) Write TR11 (WRMSR register 0Dh) with the set select value, entry and testability write (bit 1 = 0, and bit 0 = 1)

Sequence for reading an entry from the BTB through the test registers:

1) Write TR11 (WRMSR register 0Dh) with the set select value, entry and testability read (bit 1 = 1, and bit 0 = 0)
2) Read TR9 (RDMSR register 0Bh) to get the tag address and history
3) Read TR10 (RDMSR register 0Ch) to get the target address

The BTB Tag Test Register (TR9) defines the tag address and history bits.

bits	63-32 = x	Unused
	31-6 = x	Tag address
	5-2 = x	Reserved
	1-0 = x	History

Register Ch   BTB Target Test Register (TR10)   Pentium

This register is used for testing the branch target buffer (BTB). See model specific register B (TR9) for details.

bits	63-32 = x	Unused
	31-0 = x	Target address

Register Dh — BTB Command Test Register (TR11) — Pentium

This register is used for testing the branch target buffer (BTB). See model specific register B (TR9) for details.

bits	63-12 = x	Unused	
	11-6 = x	Set select (one of 64 sets)	
	5 = x	Reserved	
	4 = x	Reserved	
	3-2 = x	Entry (one of four ways)	
	1 = x	Control bits	
	0 = x	bit 1	bit 0
		0	0 = normal operation
		0	1 = testability write
		1	0 = testability read
		1	1 = flush

Register Eh — New Feature Control Register (TR12) — Pentium

This register controls new features introduced in the Pentium CPU.

bits	63-10 = x	Reserved (maybe unused or additional hidden bits)
	9 = x	IO Trap reset—Used as part of the SMM (System Management Mode) to restart IO accesses trapped by SMM.
	8 = 0	When branch tracing enabled (see bit 1 below), normal branch trace message bus cycles are generated
	1	When branch tracing enabled (see bit 1 below), issue fast branch trace message bus cycle (this feature available only on newer Pentium parts)
	7 = x	Reserved (undocumented function)
	6 = 1	Auto halt disabled (not available on all Pentium varients)
	5 = x	Reserved (undocumented function)
	4 = 1	Disable internal APIC (for Pentiums with integrated APIC)
	3 = 0	Normal cache operation
	1	The L1 (internal data & code) cache is disabled, but not cleared. This does not affect any L2 external cache, if present.

2 = 0	Normal multiple instruction pipe operation (both U and V pipes available)
1	Inhibit the V instruction pipe
1 = 1	Tracing Enabled. This bit allows an emulator to trace all types of branching conditions. When enabled, and the CPU branches, the address of the target is output to the bus in a special cycle. The emulator can then record the address into its trace buffer. In this case, branches include jumps, calls, returns, interrupts, and a few other special cases, such as segment descriptor loads. This feature is intended for testing and emulator use only, and has no effect on program operation.
0 = 0	Normal branch prediction enabled
1	Disable addition of new entries into the branch prediction buffer. Existing entries will still be processed.

Register 10h Time Stamp Counter — Pentium, Pentium Pro, Am5$_K$86

The Time Stamp Counter is described in detail under the undocumented RDTSC instruction. This register provides an alternate way to read the Time Stamp Counter and a means to change the value of the register.

Register 11h Performance Monitor Control and Event Select — Pentium

The Pentium processor provides two 40-bit counters used to count the occurrences of various internal events or number of clocks during an event. This register is used to control each counter and specify which event to monitor. The counters are stored in registers 12h and 13h. These counters must be set to a known value (typically zero) before use. In addition, the counter must be disabled, and a preset value loaded before switching to a new event.

To use the event counters for performance monitoring, the Time Stamp Counter can be used. In this case, the RDMSR instructions is used with register 10h or the RDTSC instruction is used. The time stamp value is saved before the event starts, and again after the event to be monitored completes. The difference yields a very precise clock cycle measurement.

bits	63-32 = 0	Unused
	31-26 = x	Reserved (unused or hidden bits)
	25 = x	PM1 processor pin control for Counter 1 (in register 13h) 0 = when counter increments, signal on external PM1 pin 1 = when counter overflows, signal on external PM1 pin

24 = x	Counter 1 control—events count clocks or number of events (see specific events for how this bit should be set) 0 = Count the number of events 1 = Count the number of clocks during the event	
23 = x	Counter 1 privilege level	
23 = x	bit 23 22 0 0 = Disable counter 0 1 = Count while the privilege level is 0, 1 or 2 1 0 = Count while the privilege level is 3 1 1 = Count in any privilege level	
21 = x	Event to monitor for counter 1 (items are all occurrence based, except for those marked with an asterisk "*" count the clocks which occur during the event)	
20 = x		
19 = x	0	= Data read
18 = x	1	= Data write
17 = x	2	= Data cache TLB (Translation Lookaside Buffer) miss
16 = x	3	= Data read miss
	4	= Data write miss
	5	= Write hit to M or E state lines in data cache
	6	= Data cache lines written back
	7	= External snoops
	8	= Data cache snoop hits
	9	= Memory accesses in both pipes
	Ah	= Bank conflicts
	Bh	= Misaligned data memory or I/O references
	Ch	= Code read
	Dh	= Code TLB (Translation Lookaside Buffer) miss
	Eh	= Code cache miss
	Fh	= Any segment register loaded
	12h	= Actual branches (including jmps, calls, rets, ints, etc.)
	13h	= BTB (Branch Target Buffer) hits
	14h	= Taken branch or BTB (Branch Target Buffer) hit
	15h	= Pipeline flushes
	16h	= Instruction executed
	17h	= Instructions executed in the V-pipe

18h = Clocks while a bus cycle is in progress (bus utilization)*
19h = Number of clocks stalled due to full write buffers*
1Ah = Instruction pipeline stalled while waiting for data memory read*
1Bh = Stall on write to an E or M state line in data cache*
1Ch = Locked bus cycle
1Dh = I/O read or write cycle
1Eh = Noncacheable memory reads
1Fh = Instruction pipeline stalled because of an address generation interlock*
22h = FLOPs (Floating point Operations)
23h = Breakpoint match on DR0 register
24h = Breakpoint match on DR1 register
25h = Breakpoint match on DR2 register
26h = Breakpoint match on DR3 register
27h = Hardware interrupts
28h = Data read or write
29h = Data read miss or write miss

15-10 = x Reserved (unused or hidden bits)

9 = x PM0 processor pin control for Counter 0 (in register 12h)
0 = when counter increments, signal on external PM0 pin
1 = when counter overflows, signal on external PM0 pin

8 = x Counter 0 control—events count clocks or number of events (see specific events for how this bit should be set)
0 = Count the number of events
1 = Count the number of clocks during the event

7 = x | Counter 0 privilege level
6 = x | bit 7 6

bit 7	bit 6	
0	0	= Disable counter
0	1	= Count while the privilege level is 0, 1 or 2
1	0	= Count while the privilege level is 3
1	1	= Count in any privilege level

5-0 = x Event to monitor for counter 0 (see bits 21-16 for event types)

Register 12h Event Counter 0 Pentium

This 40-bit counter is used to count the occurrences of various internal events or number of clocks during an event. See register 11h for event types and other details.

Register 13h Event Counter 1 Pentium

This 40-bit counter is used to count the occurrences of various internal events or number of clocks during an event. See register 11h for event types and other details.

Register 82h Array Access Register Am5$_K$86

This function allows for the testing of the various cache memory that resides on the Am5$_K$86 chip. This includes the 8 KB data cache, 8 KB code cache, and both the 4 KB and 4 MB TLB caches. The test type in EDX is not altered by the WRMSR after execution. A RDMSR on register 82h will not alter EDX. This makes it easier to write and read various data values without reloading EDX. Use the WRMSR first to write the test data, and then RDMSR to check whether the data written was correct.

Table 3-18 shows the register contents for each type of test. The "Way" indicates the column to test, and the "Set" indicates the row to test. In some cases, an additional 3 bits define which dword to use (out of 8). The Array ID is always in the lower byte (bits 7-0) of EDX. All unspecified bits should be set to zero.

Table 3-18. Array Register Contents

	In EDX				In EAX
Accessed Array	**Way Bits**	**Set Bits**	**Dword Bits**	**Array ID**	**Valid Bits**
Data Cache: Data	29-28	18-13	12-10	E0h	31-0
Data Cache: Linear Tag	29-28	18-13	none	E1h	27-0
Data Cache: Physical Tag	29-28	18-13	none	ECh	22-0
Instruction Cache: Instructions	29-28	19-12	11-9*	E4h	25-0
Instruction Cache: Linear Tag	29-28	19-12	none	E5h	19-0
Instruction Cache: Physical Tag	29-28	19-12	none	EDh	20-0
Instruction Cache: Valid Bits	29-28	19-12	none	E6h	18-0
Instruction Cache: Branch Bits	29-28	19-12	none	E7h	18-0
4 KB TLB: Page	29-28	12-8	none	E8h	21-0
4 KB TLB: Linear Tag	29-28	12-8	none	E9h	19-0
4 MB TLB: Page	29-28**	none	none	EAh	11-0
4 MB TLB: Linear Tag	29-28**	none	none	EBh	14-0

* *Referred to as opcode bytes (1 of 8), not dword*

** *Referred to as Entry (1 of 4), not way*

bits	63-32	Array Pointer (edx)
	31-0	Array Data (eax)

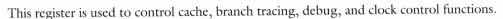

Register 83h Hardware Configuration Register Am5$_K$86

This register is used to control cache, branch tracing, debug, and clock control functions.

bits	63-8	Reserved (set to 0 for WRMSR)
	7 = 0	Enable Data Cache
	1	Disable Data Cache
	6 = 0	Enable Instruction Cache
	1	Disable Instruction Cache
	5 = 0	Enable Branch Prediction
	1	Disable Branch Prediction
	3-1 = x	Debug Control (nonspecified bit combinations reserved)

bit 3	bit 2	bit 1
0	0	0 = Disable debug control
0	0	1 = Enable branch-tracing messages
1	0	0 = Activate probe mode on debug trap

	0 = 0	Enables stopping of CPU clocks in HALT and Stop Grant states
	1	Disables stopping of CPU clocks in HALT and Stop Grant states

Register 1000h Processor Operation Register IBM 386/486SLC

This register controls a variety of custom features only available on these IBM chips. Bits 15 to 17 are available on the 486SLC but are reserved on the 386SLC. The functions for all the bits specified in EDX:EAX are:

bits	63-19	Reserved, and presumed unused
	18 = 1	Low power PLA mode—Additional dynamic parts of the CPU are powered down during the low-power halt state. (Unavailable or undocumented in 386SLC)
	17 = 1	Force all reads from external memory, even if cache is enabled. It is used for factory CPU testing. (Unavailable or undocumented in 386SLC)
	16 = 1	Switch the internal cache from odd to even parity. This forces the generation of an internal cache parity error. It is intended for factory CPU testing. (Unavailable or undocumented in 386SLC)

15 = 1 Enable Cacheability of floating point operand reads. If an external Intel FPU is used, this bit must be zero. If a Cyrix FPU is used, setting this bit on boosts opcode transfer performance.

14 = 0 Enable the ERROR input pin to Intel Compatible ERROR. The ERROR line is unused on all PC compatible designs, and was intended by Intel to signal errors from a math FPU.

1 Switch ERROR pin to a Hidden Memory Address Strobe output line. This is used to access hidden memory during Suspend or Emulation operations if supported in the motherboard. See the section on Suspend and Resume for more about hidden memory. This bit can only be set the first time WRMSR 1000h is issued after a hardware reset. Further attempts at changing the value are ignored to avoid an ERROR input clashing with the Strobe output option.

13 = 1 Enable Low Power Halt mode. A HALT instruction will cause the CPU to stop its internal clock to save power.

12 = 1 Wait for Ready after Output. After an output instruction is issued, the processor will wait until the CPU READY line is active before executing the next instruction. This allows working with devices that may be powered off and require extra time to come back online.

11 = 1 Cache Reload Status Bit—When an internal cache reload occurs, this bit is set by the CPU.

10 = 0 Internal Cache enable is determined by external hardware line input.

1 Internal Cache enable is determined within the CPU using the limits set from the Model specific Register 1001h. The pin that would be used as an input (when this flag is 0) becomes an output indicating whether a memory cycle is a cacheable cycle. This bit can only be set the first time WRMSR 1000h is issued after a hardware reset. Further attempts at changing the value are ignored.

9 = 1 Disable Cache Lock Mode—Allows the CPU to recognize a locked Read-Modify-Write cycle, but does not cache the cycle.

8 = x Reserved for unknown function or unused

7 = 1 Internal Cache Enabled—This is a similar function to the Cache Enable bit in the EFLAGS register of Intel's CPUs.

6 = 1 Disable caching for the region of memory E0000 to E0FFFh. This 4K area is used for Double Byte Character Support (DBCS) on a Japanese system, and should not be cached when DBCS is used.

5 = 1 Enable Power Interrupt PWI—Allows the PWI pin to control Suspend mode. See section on Suspend and Resume Modes. It also controls the number of bytes saved and restored. Also see LOADALL for additional information.

4 = 1	Enable Flush Snooping. This is used for specific motherboard designs. It flushes the internal CPU cache when the processor is in HOLD and a CPU signal line is activated. It can be used when bit 3 is zero.
3 = 1	Enable Snoop Input—When the CPU is in HOLD by hardware the CPU still monitors data on the bus. If a write occurs by another CPU or device to a memory location that is also in the cache, the cache item is invalidated.
2 = 1	Enable A20 Mask—The AT+ system must include some logic, normally external to the CPU, to mask the CPU address line A20. This is done to simulate an 8088 address space. This IBM CPU contains logic inside the CPU to optionally perform the same function. When this bit is on, address line 20 is disabled unless paging is active (paging is set in CR0 bit 31). When A20 mask bit is off, control is either external or the entire address range is accessible.
1 = 1	Cache Parity Enable—The internal CPU cache parity checking is enabled. If a parity error occurs, the cache is flushed, disabled (bit 7 is set to 0), parity error flag set (bit 0 is set to 1), and parity disabled (bit 1 is set to 0). The NMI handler is called to deal with the parity error.
0 = 1	Parity Error occurred in internal cache memory—Write a zero to clear this flag. See bit 1 for more details. This flag can be set by a parity error even if parity is disabled, but no actions are taken when parity is disabled.

Register 1001h Cache Region Control Registers — IBM 386/486SLC

When caching is enabled, the specific regions of physical memory that are allowed to be cached are set with this register. Caching also specifies any ROM memory areas, so the cache can ignore attempted writes into ROM space. Normally these registers are set by the BIOS POST operation based on the total amount and types of memory in the system. The 64 bits from EDX:EAX have the following contents:

bits	63-40	Reserved and presumed unused
	39-32	Extended Memory Cache limit—Specifies the number of contiguous 64K blocks starting at the 1 MB boundary that can be cached. For example, a value of 0Fh indicates 15 megabytes are cacheable.
	31-16	Read Only Cache blocks—Each bit represents a 64K region of memory in the first Megabyte of memory space that has ROM memory. Bit 31 is set to indicate the last 64K at segment F000h is ROM. Bit 30 is set to indicate the 64K block at E000h is ROM, and so forth. A write to an area set as ROM will not be updated in cache memory.
	15-0	First Megabyte Cacheable—Each bit represents a 64K region of memory in the first megabyte of memory space that can be cached. Bit 15 is set to indicate the last 64K at segment F000h can be cached. Bit 0 is set to indicate the first 64K block at 0 that can be cached.

Register 1002h Processor Operation Register 2 — IBM 486SLC2

This register controls different clock modes to allow the internal CPU clock to run twice as fast as the external clock. It also controls the process of changing the external clock frequency.

Because the internal clock can run at twice the frequency as the outside clock, it cannot be changed on-the-fly for a turbo mode feature. The CPU must be advised that a clock frequency change is requested. This request can be made either by setting a software bit or from an external pin on the chip. The CPU will respond on a hardware line when it is acceptable to change the incoming clock speed. Once the input clock frequency change has been made, the software request or hardware request should be removed, so the CPU can resume the normal clock state.

bits	63-30	Reserved and presumed unused
	29 = 1	Enable External Dynamic Frequency Shift—This option allows the motherboard to control the CPU clock frequency shift. The system BIOS should be the only one to control this function because it is dependent on the motherboard design.
	28 = 1	Dynamic Frequency Shift Ready—When a request is made for a frequency shift by hardware or setting bit 27 or when the CPU is ready for the shift, this flag is set.
	27 = 1	Dynamic Frequency Request—Setting this bit to 1 requests the CPU to prepare for a clock input frequency change. When bit 28 is set, the input clock can be changed.
	26 = x	Clock mode
	25 = x	
	24 = x	
	23-0	Reserved and presumed unused

Clock mode (bits 26–24):

bit 26	bit 25	bit 24
0	0	0 = divide incoming clock by 2 (same as a 386SX)
0	1	1 = use incoming clock, no divide, for doubling internal CPU speed
1	0	0 = 3:1 clock mode (unconfirmed)

Register 1004h Processor Control Register — IBM 486SBL3

This register controls options on the IBM 486BL3, Blue Lightning CPU (unconfirmed).

bits	63-24	Reserved and presumed unused
	23 = 0	DD1 hardware
	1	DD0 hardware (for OS/2 boot)
	22 = 0	MOV CR0 decode for DD0, DD1A, DD1B and DD1D hardware
	1	MOV CR0 decode for DD1C hardware
	21 = x	Unknown
	20 = 0	Cache remains on
	1	Cache disabled when not in use (low-power mode)

19 = x	Unknown
18 = 0	NOP instruction cycles (DD0 uses 2 cycles, DD1 uses 3 cycles)
1	NOP instruction cycles (DD0 uses 3 cycles, DD1 uses 2 cycles)
17-0 = x	Unknown

Inst	Description	Processors
XBTS	**Extract Bit String**	**Intel 80386 A step**

```
0Fh, A6h, r/m   xbts    regW, regW/memW, ax, cl
```

The extract bit string instruction takes a string of bits from the first operand and places them in the second operand.

This instruction only exists in the very first 80386, referred to as the A step. It was eliminated in the next step to make room for additional microcode. It has not been duplicated by any competitor, since its presence signifies a very old 80386 chip that has a few quirks.

The same opcode was re-used in the first 80486 for the CMPXCHG instruction. It was discovered that some applications written prior to the 80486 were checking for the presence of the XBTS instruction, and were falsely thinking the new 80486 was an old 80386 A step part. So Intel moved the CMPXCHG instruction to a new opcode on the 80486 B step of the part! The end result is that most developers find it's way too much trouble to figure all this out, and just avoid using the CMPXCHG instruction. Also see the IBTS instruction earlier in this chapter.

The word forms of this instruction will appear as dword forms depending on the current mode (16- or 32-bit), and if a size override prefix is used.

Hidden Address Space

Some versions of the 386 and later CPUs provide features for a Suspend mode and assist with In-Circuit-Emulation. These features are accomplished in part by using hidden or "alternate" memory, not normally accessible from any program. This can only be used when both the CPU supports hidden memory and the hardware on the motherboard is designed to support hidden memory. Currently IBM-manufactured CPUs have this feature (386SLC and 486SLC), as does the Intel 80386SL, 80486SL and Pentium parts, and some AMD, Cyrix and TI parts. Keep in mind that many IBM computers use non-IBM CPUs that do not support these features, and IBM has sold motherboards to other vendors, which include IBM-made CPUs.

In most cases, three undocumented instructions are used for the suspend and emulation features. These include the In-Circuit-Emulator breakpoint (ICEBP), User Move Register (UMOV), and Load All Registers (LOADALL). In addition, the features may be controlled by the Read and Write Model Specific Register (RDMSR and WRMSR) instructions. Also note the RSM instruction. All of these instructions are described in detail in the previous section on undocumented instructions.

Suspend and Resume Modes

Many laptops offer the ability to suspend operations by pressing a button or by closing the lid. Typical designs save the entire processor state and power down the CPU. At a later time, the CPU is powered up, and the registers are restored. The operating system and application resume where they left off, completely unaware of the interruption.

Older processors such as the 80286 and 80386DX/SX have created serious problems in making a reliable suspend and resume feature. Some registers are inaccessible, making a full capture of the CPU state very questionable. It is not uncommon to hear of suspend acting more like the undesirable feature "Hang system now!"

The four major 80x86 CPU manufacturers, AMD, Cyrix, IBM, and Intel have each provided unique and separate solutions to these problems. Table 3-19 summarizes the differences in operation among vendors for suspend and resume. It shows which means are available to activate system management mode (SMM) used for suspend and resume, and the number of bytes saved by the activation of SMM. The more bytes that are saved by SMM will reduce the software effort to save the CPU state, but at the cost of greater delay in getting in and out of SMM.

Table 3-19. System Management Designs

Vendor's Part		**Activation by: Hardware**	**Activation by: Software**	**Number of Bytes Saved**	**Hidden RAM Save Area**	**Hidden SMM Code Area**
AMD	386SXLC	Yes	SMI	228	6000:0h	FFFFFFF0h (reset)
	386DXLC	Yes	SMI	228	6000:0h	FFFFFF0h (reset)
	486DXLC	Yes	SMI	364	6000:0h	FFFFFFF0h (reset)
	486DX2	Yes	No	512 ***	3000:FE00h	3000:8000h
	486DX4	Yes	No	512 ***	3000:FE00h	3000:8000h
	Am5$_K$86	Yes	No	512 ***	3000:FE00h	3000:8000h
Cyrix	486SLC	Yes	HALT	none	none	none
	486DLC	Yes	HALT	none	none	none
	486SLC/e*	Yes	No	35	user defined	user defined
	6x86	Yes	SMINT	48	user defined	user defined
IBM	386SLC	Yes	ICEBP	284	6000:0h	FFFFFFF0h (reset)
	486SLC	Yes	ICEBP	284	6000:0h	FFFFFFF0h (reset)
Intel	386SL	Yes	Timer **	512 ***	3000:FE00h	3000:8000h
	486SL	Yes	Timer **	512 ***	3000:FE00h	3000:8000h

Table 3-19. Continued

Vendor's Part	Activation by: Hardware	Activation by: Software	Number of Bytes Saved	Hidden RAM Save Area	Hidden SMM Code Area
Pentium	Yes	No	512 ***	3000:FE00h	3000:8000h
Pentium Pro	Yes	No	512 ***	3000:FE00h	3000:8000h

* *SMM was not available on A step of this part.*

** *The companion 82360SL chip provides a timer that can initiate System Management Mode upon a software settable timeout period.*

*** *Vendor only defines a maximum possible number of bytes saved.*

One difficult problem can occur with the suspend and resume feature. The feature can be activated during the execution of a repeat string instruction. The worst case is during a REP INS, when an input transaction is in progress. Execution must begin where it left off, which might be partway through the instruction. Each manufacturer has solutions to address this, although it may require considerable software to make it work reliably.

The following section summarizes the various vendors' approach to suspend and resume. Many vendors refer to this capability by other names, such as System Management Mode, or Power Management Interrupt. For complete details on using these special modes, you will need the vendor's complete documentation. In many cases, suspend and resume features are undocumented in the vendor's IC data book, but separate documents specifically detail the operation. Many of these sources are listed in the bibliography.

AMD 386SXLC, 386DXLC, 486DXLC

A special System Management Interrupt (SMI) line into the CPU signals the CPU to enter code for the suspend feature. The SMI is a special nonmaskable interrupt with a higher priority than all other interrupts, including NMI. In addition, a special SMI instruction can initiate the same action.

The CPU takes a number of actions different from any other interrupt when SMI is activated. First, it saves the entire set of CPU registers to hidden memory starting at address 6000:0h. Hidden memory can only be accessed by this special state, and coexists with normal user memory at the same address. The motherboard must be specially designed to support hidden memory. See Figure 3-4 for the layout of hidden memory. Some portion of hidden memory will be RAM, while the power down suspend code will typically be in ROM. Depending on the implementation, only a small part of the hidden address space has actual memory.

Figure 3-4. Hidden Memory on an AMD 486DXLC

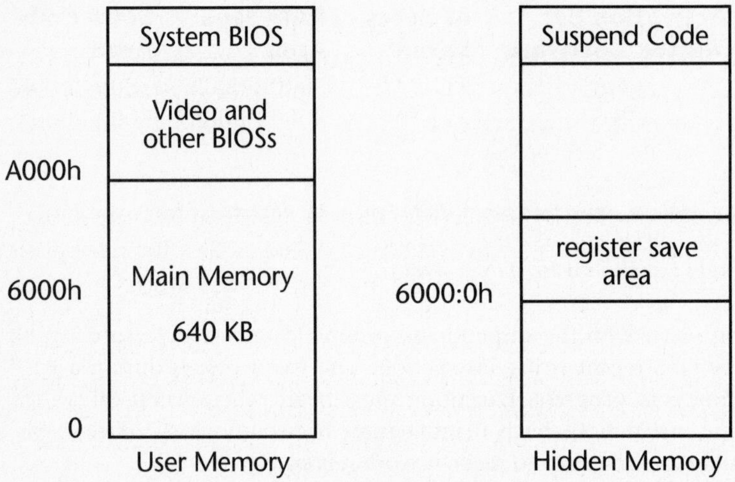

Once all the registers have been saved, the CPU resets almost all registers to the same state as a first-time power up. The SMI activation does not change the contents of the CPU's cache memory, when the CPU has internal cache memory. The CPU will be forced into real mode, even if it was in protected or V86 mode before. All interrupts are disabled including NMI.

The CPU then begins execution at FFFFF0h in hidden memory in 16-bit real mode. Overrides can still be used to execute 32-bit code. The internal cache is not used while executing code from hidden memory, to prevent changes to cache contents. The power down suspend code can then take additional actions if necessary, such writing to an I/O port to shut off power to various peripherals. If it is necessary to write or read data to the user memory area while hidden memory is active, the UMOV instruction is used.

To resume, the code must execute the LOADALL instruction. AMD calls it a RES4 instruction, but it does the same thing as 386 LOADALL, and uses the same opcode. LOADALL is executed with ES:EDI set to 6000:0h. This takes all the registers from hidden memory and loads them into the CPU. At the completion of LOADALL, execution resumes exactly where the SMI first occurred.

Cyrix and TI 486SLC, 486DLC

These Cyrix/TI parts have the simplest design from a software point of view. They require no special software at all! The Cyrix/TI parts have a special low-power mode controlled from hardware. When activated, the CPU completes the current instruction. If a math coprocessor is present, the CPU waits for the coprocessor to complete its last operation. The CPU then goes into a very low-power mode, keeping all the contents of the registers valid. At this point the hardware can stop the CPU clock. While in standby mode, the CPU will typically use a negligible 100 microamps: low enough for most battery systems to power the CPU for a long time.

To resume from a hardware-activated suspend operation, the clock is started and the suspend line into the CPU is released. The CPU then continues from the location that suspend was first activated.

A suspend mode can also be entered from software by issuing a HLT (halt) instruction. This is useful when software detects little or no activity is occurring, and power savings is needed. The HLT instruction causes the CPU to go into a standby mode. The CPU clock remains on. In this case, the CPU takes more power, about 5 milliamps.

When the CPU is in standby after a HALT instruction is issued, an NMI or any unmasked hardware interrupt will resume operations. The CPU will begin processing by entering the interrupt service handler associated with the last interrupt.

Cyrix and TI 486SLC/e

This is a newer variant of the 486 that offers a more conventional Suspend and Resume feature, but with a number of interesting twists. Like the other vendors, a dedicated SMI interrupt pin is triggered to initiate System Management Mode. There is no software means to trigger SMM on this part. Once triggered a very small subset of the CPU registers are saved. This means the duration from SMM entry to exit can be about one-fifth of any other CPU. This might be useful in some special purposes, but it is not important for the standard Suspend and Resume feature.

Unlike all other vendors, the location where the CPU registers are saved and the code space for SMM is defined in software. This can add some flexibility no one else offers. The space allocated to SMM can also be defined from 4 KB to 32 MB.

Once in System Management Mode, it may be necessary to save additional registers. Cyrix defines a number of unique instructions to save other registers as necessary. These additional instructions are usable when the CPU is in privilege level 0, and the CPU's SMI pin is active low. When SMI is not active, and the CPU is in privilege level 0, the instruction will also function if the SMAC bit is set in Configuration Register 1. These configuration registers only appear on Cyrix/TI parts, and are accessed through port 22h and 23h. When failing to meet either of the above conditions, these new instructions will trigger the bad opcode interrupt. These new instructions are summarized in Table 3-20. Cyrix documents these instructions in detail in the SMM programmer's guide.

Table 3-20. Special Cyrix/TI Instructions

Base Instruction	Opcode	Description
RSDC	0F 79	Restore segment register and its descriptor
RSLDT	0F 7B	Restore local descriptor table register and its descriptor
RSM	0F AA	Resume from system management mode (same as Intel)
RSTS	0F 7D	Restore task state register and its descriptor
SVDC	0F 78	Save segment and its descriptor
SVLDT	0F 7A	Save local descriptor table register and its descriptor
SVTS	0F 7C	Save task state registers and its descriptor

To resume normal operation from SMM, the program must first restore any altered registers using standard instructions and the special instructions in Table 3-20. Then the RSM instruction is executed to restore the registers previously saved by entering System Management Mode. At the completion of RSM, execution resumes exactly where the SMI first occurred.

Cyrix 6x86

The 6x86 is very similar to the 486SLC/e previously described. The major difference is the addition of the SMINT instruction to initiate SMM in software. Additional registers are also stored when SMM is activated.

IBM 386SLC and 486SLC

A special Power Interrupt (PWI) line into the CPU signals the CPU to enter code for the suspend feature. The PWI is a special nonmaskable interrupt with a higher priority than all other interrupts including NMI. This feature is enabled by setting the Enable PWI bit 5 of Model Specific Register 1000h (see the WRMSR instruction).

The CPU takes a number of actions different from any other interrupt when PWI is activated. First, it saves the entire set of CPU registers to hidden memory starting at address 6000:0h. This operation is very similar to the older 486 AMD parts. To reiterate, hidden memory can only be accessed by this special state, and coexists with normal user memory at the same address. The motherboard must be specially designed to support hidden memory. See Figure 3-5 for a layout of hidden memory. Some portion of hidden memory will be RAM, while the power down suspend code will be in ROM. Depending on the implementation, only a small part of the hidden address space has actual memory.

Figure 3-5. Hidden Memory on an IBM CPU

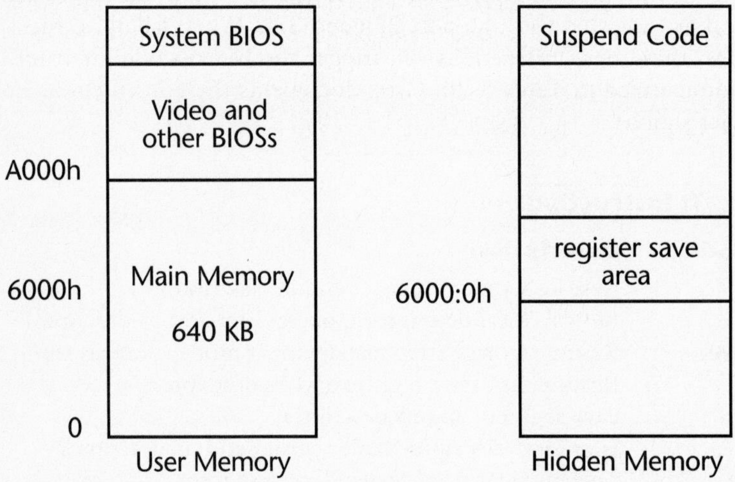

Once all the registers have been saved, the CPU resets almost all registers to the same state as a first-time power up. The PWI mode does not change the contents of the CPU's cache memory or the model specific registers. This means the CPU will be in real mode, even if it was in protected or V86 mode before. All interrupts are disabled including NMI.

The CPU then begins execution at FFFFF0h in hidden memory in 16-bit real mode. Overrides can still be used to execute 32-bit code. The internal cache is not used while executing code from hidden memory, to prevent changes to cache contents. The power down suspend code can then take additional actions when necessary, such as writing to an I/O port to shut off power peripherals or even the CPU itself. If it is necessary to write or read data to the user memory area while hidden memory is active, the UMOV instruction is used.

To resume when powered off, the CPU is reset so the system BIOS takes control in user memory. The system BIOS must check to see if the reset is from a prior suspend operation. If so, the processor enables PWI (bit 5 in Model specific Register 1000h) and issues a LOADALL instruction, with ES:EDI set to 6000:0h. This takes all the registers from hidden memory and loads them into the CPU. At completion of LOADALL, execution resumes exactly where the PWI interrupt first occurred.

Intel 80386SL, 80486SL, Pentium, Pentium Pro, AMD 5_K86

IBM and Intel/AMD share a similar design, but have a number of significant differences. A special Systems Management Interrupt (SMI) line into the CPU signals the CPU to enter code for the suspend feature. The SMI is a special nonmaskable interrupt with a higher priority than all other interrupts including NMI.

The CPU takes a number of actions different from any other interrupt when SMI is activated. First, it saves the entire set of CPU registers to hidden memory starting at address 3000:FE00h. Hidden memory can only be accessed by this special state, and coexists with normal user memory at the same address. The motherboard must be specially designed to support hidden memory. See Figure 3-6 for a layout of hidden memory. Typically only 32K of memory will be RAM starting at 3000:8000h when hidden mode is active.

Figure 3-6. Hidden Memory on an Intel CPU

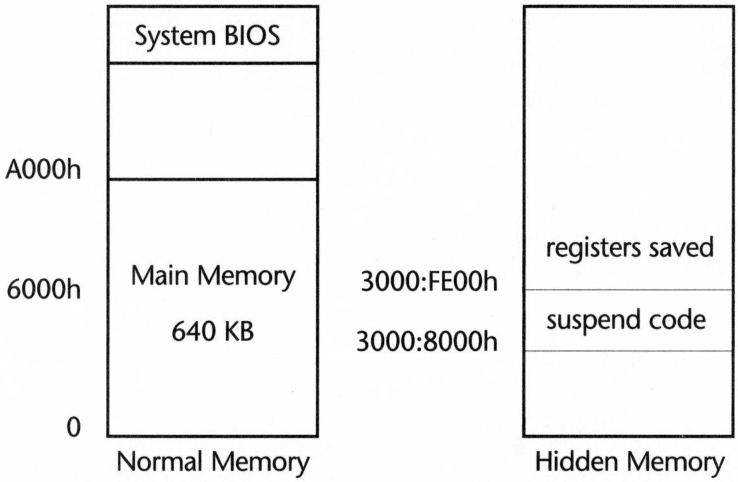

The registers loaded into hidden memory are shown in Table 3-21. Most registers can be changed if needed, but reserved locations must not be altered or the processor may malfunction. Reserved memory includes space for future processors and registers the vendor does not want to divulge. Specific registers saved in reserved areas include CR1, CR2, CR4 and all descriptors. Registers not saved include DR0-DR7 and all floating-point registers STn, FCS, FSW, tag word, FIP, and floating-point opcode and operand pointers.

Table 3-21. CPU Registers Saved in Hidden Memory

Memory Offset	Words	Register Loaded
FE00	124	Reserved
FEF8	2	State Dump Base—This holds the internal register value of the segment for the Suspend code and storage of this table. It defaults to 3000h. If changed, it must align on a 32K (800h) boundary. The first time RSM is executed this value is loaded back into the CPU's internal dump base register. The new base segment is used for future SMI interrupt Register Saves and Suspend Code execution.
FEFC	1	System Management Mode Bits bit 0 = 1 CPU supports I/O Trap restart bit 1 = 1 CPU supports state dump base changes
FFFE	1	System Management Mode Revision Number
FF00	1	I/O Trap restart—Always set to zero when saved. See RSM instruction for actions taken if this word is set to FFFFh by the suspend code.
FF02	1	Halt auto restart—This value is set to 1 if SMI occurred while the CPU was in a HALT instruction. Otherwise it is set to 0. See RSM instruction for action taken depending on the state of this dword.
FF04	66	Reserved
FF88	2	GDT Base
FF8C	4	Reserved
FF94	2	IDT Base
FF98	8	Reserved
FFA8	1	ES
FFAA	1	Reserved
FFAC	1	CS
FFAE	1	Reserved
FFB0	1	SS
FFB2	1	Reserved
FFB4	1	DS
FFB6	1	Reserved
FFB8	1	FS
FFBA	1	Reserved

Table 3-21. Continued

Memory Offset	Words	Register Loaded
FFBC	1	GS
FFBE	1	Reserved
FFC0	1	LDTR—Local Descriptor Table Register
FFC2	1	Reserved
FFC4	1	TR—Task Register
FFC6	1	Reserved
FFC8	2	DR7
FFCC	2	DR6
FFD0	2	EAX
FFD4	2	ECX
FFD8	2	EDX
FFDC	2	EBX
FFE0	2	ESP
FFE4	2	EBP
FFE8	2	ESI
FFEC	2	EDI
FFF0	2	EIP
FFF4	2	EFLAGS
FFF8	2	CR3
FFFC	2	CR0

Note: The offsets shown match the Intel Pentium manual and not the Pentium Pro manual. The Intel Pentium Pro manual has contradictory offset information that in one place matches the Pentium, and on the same page shows different offsets!

Once all the registers have been saved, the CPU resets almost all registers to the same state as a first-time power up. The SMI mode does not change the contents of the CPU's cache memory. The Pentium's model specific registers are also untouched by SMI mode. If the cache is enabled in SMM mode, the cache contents could be altered. The CPU will be in real mode, even if it was in protected or V86 mode before.

The CPU then begins execution at 3000:8000h in hidden memory. The suspend code can then take additional actions if necessary, such as reducing or stopping the CPU clock to save power.

The state of the floating-point unit is unaffected by System Management Mode. Because it is not saved automatically, use of floating-point instructions should be avoided in suspend code.

To resume from System Management Mode, a RSM instruction is issued. This instruction loads all registers previously saved at 3000:FF00h back into the CPU. RSM can only be issued while in System Management Mode. At the completion of RSM, normal execution resumes from user memory. See the RSM instruction for additional details.

In-Circuit-Emulation

For emulation operations, a special breakpoint occurs, causing the entire state of the CPU to be saved in memory. The emulator can then display the state of the CPU at the breakpoint. To restart the instruction at the breakpoint, the emulator restores the original instruction, and reloads the saved CPU state.

Emulation operation is similar to the suspend and resume mode previously described for Intel and IBM. In this case, hidden memory holds the code for the ICE rather than the suspend code. Refer to instructions UMOV, LOADALL, and ICEBP for more details.

CPU Reset

The CPU is set to its first-time power-on state by activation of the hardware reset line. The hardware reset line is triggered at power on and on some systems from a reset button. With AT systems and later, the keyboard controller can also generate a hardware reset (see Chapter 8, The Keyboard System).

Upon reset, the CPU sets itself to a known state, real mode, with interrupts disabled and key registers set to a known state. The system memory contents are unaffected by a hardware reset, if system power was not lost during the reset. With the 386 and later processors, a self test is run, and AX returns 0 if the self test passed. DH is set to the family type, 3 for 386, 4 for 486, 5 for Pentium, and 6 for the Pentium Pro. Some vendors also return a number in the upper nibble of DH, to indicate subfamilies, like the 386SL. The DL register will contain the revision number, often referred to as the chip stepping number.

The reset will cause the processor to jump to the system BIOS and begin code execution. On the 8088 this was at address F000:FFF0. For the 80286 and later it is the top of addressable memory, less 16 bytes. For example, on a 486 with a 32-bit address bus, the physical address will be FFFFFFF0h. The motherboard design usually double maps the system BIOS at the very top of the address range, as well as at the top of the 1 MB area. An access to F000:FFF0 gets the same contents as physical address FFFFFFF0h.

Now the 286+ CPU takes an unusual step. When the very first far jump or far call occurs, the CPU limits execution access to memory within the first 1 MB. Most system BIOS manufacturers have a far jump at FFFFFFF0h that goes to the beginning of initialization code in the F000 segment. This signals the CPU to set the upper address lines to zero. At this point the system appears very much like the old 8088, limited to 1 MB of total address space. The system BIOS is responsible to complete setting up registers, descriptors, and other requirements for operation to match the system on which it is running.

After the system BIOS gains control, an AT+ system reads the shutdown register byte Fh from CMOS. This byte tells the system BIOS how to proceed. It may just perform a normal BIOS initialization, or it can directly jump to the bootstrap loader, or to a prespecified routine. This control was provided so the 80286 could be switched from protected mode back to real mode. The CMOS shutdown register Fh is described in Chapter 15 (CMOS Memory and Real-Time Clock).

Resetting the CPU

There seem to be many approaches to resetting the CPU from software, but only a few will work reliably. Some approaches will appear to work on one machine while they fail to work reliably on another.

Misconception #1: Jump to the Bootstrap Vector The BIOS has an interrupt that loads the bootstrap loader program from the hard disk or diskette drive and begins execution of the loader. This occurs when the bootstrap interrupt vector 19h is issued. It should *never* be called from an application. Since this bypasses much of the BIOS, it might seem to be a quick way to reboot the system. What usually goes wrong is that the TSRs and device drivers hook various interrupts. The system BIOS loads the bootstrap program from the drive into the fixed address 0:7C00h without concern about whether a TSR or a driver might still be running at the same address. The bootstrap program, once begun, will load more into memory, possibly destroying other TSRs and drivers. Keep in mind that many interrupt vectors will be pointing into TSRs and drivers that are no longer in memory! When an interrupt is issued that points to the nonexistent TSR or driver, the system will crash.

Misconception #2: Jump to the Reset Start Address F000:FFFF When the processor has a hardware reset, the CPU begins execution at F000:FFF0. It seems natural to just jump to F000:FFFF to begin the system BIOS initialization code. In most cases, this will work fine on a 8088. With any later CPU this may appear to work in some circumstances, but it is very likely to fail and hang the system. The system BIOS has been written to expect that the CPU is in a full reset condition, in real mode, and key registers are in a known state. Jumping into the system BIOS does not assure any of these conditions. The system could be in V86 mode, debug breakpoints might still be active, interrupts could be still enabled, and a host of other potential problems could cause the system BIOS to hang.

Three Ways to Reset The only way to initiate a hardware reset on an 8088-based PC is to jump to address F000:FFF0. As we noted before, this technique should never be used on a system with a 286 or later CPU.

With AT systems and later, the processor can be reset under software control. This is accomplished by sending a command to pulse the reset line to the keyboard controller microcontroller. Code showing how to accomplish this is provided in Chapter 8, The Keyboard System, under Code Sample 8-4.

On MCA and on some EISA systems, a much easier and faster approach is available. The system control port defines a bit for fast reset without going through the keyboard controller. This is a much faster reset, and should be used when switching from protected mode to real mode. The code for doing this appears as:

```
in      al, 92h         ; get system control port
IODELAY
or      al, 1           ; set bit 0 for fast reset
out     92h, al         ; do it!
hlt                     ; Halt - should not get here
```

You may wish to review the system control port (92h), for other bits that can be set for other actions, such as disabling the A20 address line.

Warm Boot and Cold Boot When first powering up a system, the BIOS checks a value in RAM to see whether the system is in a warm boot (i.e., already powered up) or a cold boot. Most BIOSes will test all memory and take other necessary actions during a cold boot. A warm boot indicates no memory test is needed, and the system can start up much faster.

When you press Ctrl-Alt-Del, the keyboard BIOS sets the warm boot RAM value to 1234h to signal this is a warm boot. Some systems use other values, as shown in Table 3-22, to signal information to the BIOS. The warm boot flag resides in the BIOS data area as a word at 40:72h. If initiating a reset through software, the warm boot flag should be set for the desired type of boot up. To ensure a cold boot, set the warm boot flag to 0.

Table 3-22. Boot Flag Values

Value	Function
0000h	Cold boot—check memory, all memory altered
1234h	Warm boot—skip memory checks, memory may be altered
4321h	Warm boot—skip memory checks and leave RAM unchanged
0064h	Cycle BIOS tests for manufacturing burn-in (some vendors)

Getting Control Before Reset

In some situations, it is highly desirable to get control before the reset process begins. For example, a disk cache may have information in RAM that it has not written back to the disk yet. The disk cache program needs to flush these buffers before a reset. If they are not updated, disk files, and even the disk structure itself could be left in an incomplete state.

On an 8088-based system, the only way to intercept a reset is to provide a complete replacement for the keyboard BIOS interrupt 9h. Due to system differences among vendors, this can be very difficult. When interrupt 9 is replaced, the key combination of Ctrl-Alt-Del (the reset combination) can be intercepted.

AT and later systems all provide a trap point for the Ctrl-Alt-Del command. In this case, interrupt 15h is hooked to a special handler. The handler looks for AH set to 4Fh indicating a key has been pressed, but not yet processed by the interrupt 9 keyboard BIOS. If 4Fh is detected, the carry flag is checked to ensure it is set. If the carry flag is not set, the key should be ignored, and no further checks are necessary. Assuming the carry flag is set, the AL register is checked to see whether it's the DEL key scan code 71h. If so, then the BIOS keyboard flags byte at 40:17h is checked to see if Ctrl and Alt keys are currently pressed. If Ctrl and Alt are down, bits 2 and 3 will both be set to 1. At this point you known the user must have pressed Ctrl-Alt-Del, and any desired actions can occur before the reset.

When returning from the interrupt 15h hook, be sure not to alter AX and to keep the carry flag set. This will allow other handlers that may have hooked interrupt 15h to take necessary actions. When the keyboard handler regains control from interrupt 15h, it will then reset the system.

This mechanism does not protect against a reset by writing directly to the keyboard controller or the system control port. If the program is running in protected mode, like Windows or a memory manager, and a 386 or later CPU is used, it is possible to trap I/O port 60h, 64h, and 92h. These ports are watched to see if anyone attempts to reset the system this way. Again, if a reset is about to occur, any necessary actions can be taken.

Code Sample 3-5 shows a code fragment illustrating the hooked interrupt 15h handler to detect Ctrl-Alt-Del. It assumes interrupt 15h has been pointed to int_15h_hook and the previous interrupt 15h pointer has been saved at old_int_15h.

Code Sample 3-5. Resident Reset Handler

```
; ---------------------------------------------------------------------
;  Resident handler to detect if CTRL-ALT-DEL pressed

int_15h_hook    proc    far
        pushf
        push    ax
        push    ds
        cmp     ah, 4Fh                 ; interrupt 9 key function ?
        jne     skip_finished           ; jump if not

        cmp     al, 71h                 ; delete key down ?
        jne     skip_finished
        mov     ax, 40h
        mov     ds, ax                  ; point to BIOS data area
        test    byte ptr ds:[17h], 4    ; is ALT down ?
        jz      skip_finished           ; jump if not
        test    byte ptr ds:[17h], 2    ; is Ctrl down ?
        jz      skip_finished           ; jump if not

; The user has pressed CTRL-ALT-DEL
```

```
    <<<<User unique code goes here (e.g., write out disk cache)>>>>

; Done, now let any other TSRs and Drivers that hook interrupt 15h a
;   chance to detect CTRL-ALT-DEL.

skip_finished:
        pop     ds
        pop     ax
        popf
        jmp     dword ptr cs:old_int_15h  ; process old int_15h

int_15h_hook    endp

old_int_15h     dd      0          ; old pointer saved here
```

CHAPTER 4

System and Equipment Detection

In this chapter, I show how to detect various system types and extensive details about the CPU. To my knowledge, most of this information has never been published before *The Undocumented PC.* These detection functions are easily inserted into other programs as a subroutine. Many example programs are provided to demonstrate the operation of each function.

One routine detects the system bus type, PC, ISA, EISA, MCA, and PCI. A number of other routines are used to detect the CPU class from the 8088 through the Pentium Pro, the true instruction set of the processor (which may not match the class!), the floating-point processor type, CPU vendor identification, internal CPU speed analysis, and determination of the internal CPU cache size. In addition, a group of programs check the functionality of undocumented instructions I've identified and look for additional undocumented instructions.

Other chapters describing specific hardware have routines to detect the video adapter type, diskette drive types, hard drive types and capacities, serial port types, and parallel port types. Refer to the specific chapter for further information. All of these routines are summarized in Appendix A, Programs on Disk. The complete source code for every routine is included on the supplied diskette.

It is necessary to have reliable methods for checking what system resources are available. This becomes complicated due to the wide range of processors, adapters, and systems with which most software must be compatible. Some of this information is easily available, but may be misleading. The remainder requires some tricky work to pry configuration secrets from the system.

In an ideal world, hardware developers would provide an easy means of telling what the hardware is, and specify the version and revision of the hardware. The twisted hoops we must jump through to get this information are unbelievable. In some cases, equipment detection routines must rely on undocumented techniques to flush out the needed information. Whenever possible this has been avoided.

The Easy Stuff

IBM did try and make our lives easier with two BIOS functions to tell us about the system: interrupt 11h (equipment determination) and interrupt 12h (memory size determination). These worked great on the original PC. Although they provide useful information, even on today's computers, they fail to show the whole picture. Remember, back then we had the choice of only one processor, the 8088, we were limited to 360K 5.25-inch diskette drives, and we had a choice of only two video adapters, CGA or Monochrome.

INT

Int	Description	Platform
11h	Equipment Determination	All

This interrupt returns a word in AX containing flags describing the system. This interrupt simply reads the BIOS equipment word at 40:10h. The equipment word is initialized by the system BIOS during the Power-On-Self-Test (POST).

Because it is not updated after POST is run, other device drivers or programs can add to the equipment list without updating this word. Equipment determination should only be used for knowledge of what is minimally in the system.

Returns in AX:

bit	15 = x 14 = x	Number of parallel printer ports detected by POST (0 to 3)
	13 = 0	Unused (most systems), or modem not installed
	= 1	Internal modem installed (some systems)
	12 = 0	Unused (all AT+ systems), or no game port installed
	1	Game port installed (PC & XT)
	11 = x 10 = x 9 = x	Number of serial ports attached (0 to 4)

8 = 0	Unused		
7 = x	Number diskette drives (if bit 0 is 1)		
6 = x		bit 7	bit 6
		0	0 = 1 drive
		0	1 = 2 drives
		1	0 = 3 drives (PC & XT only)
		1	1 = 4 drives (PC & XT only)
5 = x	Initial video mode type		
4 = x		bit 5	bit 4
		0	0 = EGA/VGA or later adapter
		0	1 = CGA color 40 columns by 25 rows
		1	0 = CGA color 80 columns by 25 rows
		1	1 = Monochrome 80 columns by 25 rows
3 = 0	Unused (see text below)		
2 = 1	Mouse port installed on system board (see text below)		
1 = 1	Math coprocessor installed		
0 = 1	Boot diskette drive installed		

There are a number of limitations with the equipment word. First, some systems allow a fourth parallel port. This equipment word cannot indicate the presence of a fourth parallel port. The internal modem flag is valid when set to 1, but many systems will have a modem without this flag being set. In the rare situation of an AT+ system with more than two drives, only the first two drives (a: and b:) are counted for the number of diskette drives.

Bits 3 and 2 were used by the original PC to show how much system memory was on the motherboard (16K, 32K, 48K, or 64K). If you assume your software will never run on the original PC (a very good bet), you can ignore the conflict with bit 2. For AT+ systems that have a mouse port installed in the system board, bit 2 is set. If a mouse is attached to a serial port or bus mouse card, bit 2 will not be set. The mouse bit does not indicate whether mouse support is available, because the driver must be installed for the mouse to work with applications.

The math coprocessor flag will probably be set when a math coprocessor is installed. The math flag is also set when the system has a 486DX, Pentium, or later CPU with a built-in math coprocessor. Note that Code sample 4-4 does *not* use interrupt 11h to determine if a coprocessor is present, but actually checks for valid math coprocessor responses.

Int	Description	Platform
12h	Memory Size Determination	All

INT

The total amount of main memory in the system is returned in AX using this interrupt. This is the total contiguous memory starting at 0, up to the end of main memory. This interrupt simply returns the word stored in the BIOS data area at 40:13h. For a system limited to 640K, the value returned in AX will be 640 (280h), the number of 1,024-byte blocks.

Some systems have the capability of offering additional main memory. A few memory managers can rearrange memory when a system is based on the 386 or later CPU. Ignoring my plug for Memory Commander from V Communications, Memory Commander can transparently move the VGA BIOS and display buffer and expand main memory up to a best-case scenario of 924K. In this situation, the memory size value will be 924.

Remember the memory size word is the total amount of main memory, not the amount available. The CPU and BIOS use a portion of this memory at the bottom, and the operating system will use additional memory at the bottom, just above the BIOS data. Also be aware that some BIOSes and a few adapter cards steal some of the main memory from the top for their own use. In these cases, the total main memory is reduced by 1 to 4K. This area is commonly referred to as the extended BIOS data area.

A number of viruses, such as Michelangelo, also steal memory from the top of the system. The virus loads itself at the top of main memory, and then reduces the value at 40:13h, to indicate to the system that there is now less memory. In actuality the memory is still present, and contains the virus code.

System Detection

It is critical to detect the system type before using any feature unique to a platform. This includes the original PC, XT, AT, EISA, MCA, and PCI type systems. With most AT systems and later, IBM provided a specific service to get a pointer into ROM with details about the system. This interrupt 15h service cannot be used on older systems, and does not help identify EISA or PCI systems. Refer to Chapter 13, System Functions, Interrupt 15h, Function C0h for more about this function.

Code sample 4-1 shows a reliable way to establish on which system the software is running. This routine can be used with other detection routines to get a complete picture of the system.

Code Sample 4-1. System Detection

To detect the system type for most systems today, interrupt 15h, function C0h returns a pointer into the system BIOS of key system data. This includes the model and submodel type, duplicated at the end of the BIOS, and a bit indicating whether the system uses a Micro Channel (MCA) bus.

The model byte appears at the next to the last byte of the BIOS at F000:FFFE. The submodel byte follows. A few memory managers alter the contents of these bytes, so it is important to avoid reading these bytes directly from memory. Most manufacturers today follow the IBM model conventions, but many older 286 and earlier clone systems may have anything in the model and submodel bytes, so do not rely completely on these bytes. This detection routine cross-checks model information with the processor type.

To detect an EISA system, the text string "EISA" appears at F000:FFD9. Because EISA systems are always 32-bit systems, an EISA system must have a 386 or later processor.

To see the results of the SYSVALUE subroutine on your system, run the SYSTYPE program. The results of SYSTYPE from one system are shown in Figure 4-1. The SYSVALUE subroutine returns the system type, as shown on the "System type" line. In addition, PCI detection is shown on the following line. PCI information comes from the subroutine PCI_DETECT. The BIOSINFO routine shows details about the BIOS ROM used in the system.

Figure 4-1. Result of SYSTYPE on One Pentium System

```
SYSTEM ANALYSIS                          v2.00 (c) 1994, 1996 FVG
System type:      AT / ISA (Industry Standard Architecture)
                  PCI v 2.00 (Peripheral Component Interconnect)
System BIOS:      American Megatrends Inc
                  Date: 25-Jul-94
                  BIOS supports LBA disks (> 504 MB)
                  Motherboard is made in USA
Diskette a:       2.88MB 3.5" (80 tracks, 36 sectors per track)
Diskette b:       1.2MB 5.25" (80 tracks, 15 sectors per track)
Hard Drive 0:     IDE controller, LBA active
                  Total size = 1545 MB (with diagnostic cylinder)
                  785 Cylinders, 64 Heads, 63 Sectors per track
Hard Drive 1:     AT or IDE type controller
                  Total size = 503 MB (with diagnostic cylinder)
                  1022 Cylinders, 16 Heads, 63 Sectors per track
Video Adapter:    SVGA, programs should use color attributes.
Video Vendor:     ATI MACH64
```

The SYSVALUE subroutine inside SYSTYPE to determine the system type is shown below.

```
;-------------------------------------------------------------
;    SYSTEM TYPE DETECTION SUBROUTINE
;       Determine the type of system the software is running
;       on.
;
;       Called with:    nothing
;
;       Returns:        al = System type
```

```
;                               0 if PC (8088 based)
;                               1 if XT (8088 based)
;                               2 if PC convertible (8088 based)
;                               3 if PC jr (8088 based)
;                               4 other pre-80286 based machine
;                               8 if XT (80286 based)
;                              10h if AT or ISA
;                              20h if EISA
;                              40h if MCA
;
;       Regs used:      ax, bx
;                       eax, ebx (386 or later)
;
;       Subs called:    cpu386

sysvalue proc    near
        push    cx
        push    dx
        push    es

        call    far ptr cpu386      ; get the cpu type in al
        mov     cl, al              ; save cpu class

; Avoid directly reading BIOS ROM, because a few memory managers
; like 386MAX alter bytes at the end of the BIOS.

        push    cx                  ; save cpu number on stack
        mov     ah, 0C0h
        int     15h                 ; get BIOS config data es:bx
        pop     cx
        jc      sys_skp1            ; jump if no config support
                                    ;   (old BIOS)
        mov     dl, es:[bx+2]       ; get model byte
        mov     dh, es:[bx+3]       ; get submodel byte
```

```
        mov     al, 40h              ; assume MCA
        test    byte ptr es:[bx+5], 2
        jnz     sys_Exit             ; exit if MCA
        jmp     sys_skp2

; we only get here on older PCs in which a memory manager
;  can not be run

sys_skp1:                            ; ok, get BIOS model directly
        mov     ax, 0F000h
        mov     es, ax               ; point into system BIOS
        mov     dx, es:[0FFFEh]      ; get model & submodel byte

; now use the model and submodel bytes im DX to determine machine

sys_skp2:
        xor     al, al               ; assume PC (al=0)
        cmp     dl, 0FFh
        je      sys_Exit             ; jump if PC
        inc     al                   ; assume XT (al=1)
        cmp     dl, 0FEh
        je      sys_Exit             ; jump if XT
        cmp     dl, 0FBh
        je      sys_Exit             ; jump if XT
        inc     al                   ; assume PC convertible (al=2)
        cmp     dl, 0F9h
        je      sys_Exit             ; jump if convertible
        inc     al                   ; assume PCjr (al=3)
        cmp     dl, 0FDh
        je      sys_Exit             ; jump if PCjr
        inc     al                   ; assume other pre-286 (al=4)
        cmp     cl, 2                ; cl=CPU type - pre-286 ?
        jb      sys_Exit             ; jump so
        ja      sys_skp3             ; jump if 386 or above
```

```
; possible a 286 XT - use the model and submodel bytes to
;  determine

        mov     al, 8                   ; assumption for 286XT
        cmp     dx, 02FCh               ; model code for 286XT ?
        je      sys_exit                ; jump if so

; check if EISA system by looking for the "EISA" string at
;  address F000:FFD9

sys_skp3:
        mov     ax, 0F000h
        mov     es, ax
        mov     al, 10h                 ; assume a standard AT/ISA
        cmp     word ptr es:[0FFD9h], 'IE'
        jne     sys_exit                ; jump if not EISA
        cmp     word ptr es:[0FFDBh], 'AS'
        jne     sys_exit                ; jump if not EISA
        mov     al, 20h                 ; EISA machine
sys_Exit:
        pop     es
        pop     dx
        pop     cx
        ret
sysvalue endp
```

The PCI_DETECT subroutine inside SYSTYPE is used to determine PCI presence. The routine uses an interrupt 1Ah function to detect PCI and the PCI version.

```
;-------------------------------------------------------------
;    PCI DETECTION SUBROUTINE
;       Determine if the BIOS supports PCI, and if so, get the
;       PCI BIOS version.
;
;       Called with:    nothing
```

```
;
;       Returns:        carry = 0 if PCI BIOS present and:
;                         bx = version in BCD
;                       carry = 1 if no PCI BIOS support
;
;       Regs used:      ax, bx
;                       edx (386 or later)
;
;       Subs called:    cpu386

.386

pci_detect proc    near
        push    cx

        call    far ptr cpu386      ; get the cpu type in al
        cmp     al, 3               ; 386 or better ?
        jae     pci_check           ; jump if so
        stc                         ; set carry flag (no PCI)
        jmp     pci_exit

pci_check:
        mov     ax, 0B101h          ; function for PCI detect
        mov     edx, " PCI"         ; signifier
        int     1Ah                 ; check if present

pci_exit:
        pop     cx
        ret
pci_detect endp

.8086
```

The BIOSVEN subroutine returns key information about the System BIOS. Information includes the vendor identification and BIOS date (in a uniform format). Depending on the vendor, additional information may include LBA support, chipset used, where the motherboard was manufactured, and the vendor ASCII string. The BIOSVEN routine calls several special subroutines which are not reprinted here. Full source is included on the diskette.

```
;-------------------------------------------------------------
;    BIOS INFO SUBROUTINE
;        Determine the BIOS vendor and other key information
;
;        Called with:    al = system type (from sysvalue)
;
;        Returns:        al = BIOS
;                              0 unknown LBA support status
;                              1 no LBA support
;                              2 LBA support
;                        ah = Motherboard manufacturing location
;                              0 = unknown
;                              1 = outside USA (from AMI code)
;                              2 = by American Megatrends
;                              3 = in USA (from AMI code)
;                        dl = vendor value
;                              0 = unknown
;                              1 = American Megatrends
;                              2 = Award Software International
;                              3 = Phoenix Technologies
;                              4 = Chips & Technologies
;                              5 = Compaq
;                              6 = DTK
;                              7 = Eurosoft
;                              8 = Faraday (Western Digital)
;                              9 = Hewlett Packard
;                              10 = Landmark Research International
;                              11 = Microid Research
;                              12 = Olivetti
;                              13 = Quadtel
```

```
;                               14 = Toshiba
;                               15 = Western Digital
;                               16 = IBM
;                               17 = IBM (old)
;                         es:bx = Chipset string (ASCIIZ, 10 char max)
;                         es:si = Vendor string (ASCIIZ, 40 char max)
;                         es:di = BIOS Date (ASCIIZ, form yy-mm-dd)
;
;       Regs used:        ax, bx
;
;       Subs called:      find_string, compare_date


;   table of strings, length of string appears first (31 chars max)
;   biosven strings must be in caps, and only symbols below 30h
;   allowed are spaces or an ampersand
;   Recommend AMI, Award, and Phoenix be placed first, since other
;   vendors have sometimes used one of these first three.
;   IBM should appear last, since many BIOSes include an IBM
;   string in the BIOS like "IBM Compatible".

biosven         db      19, 'AMERICAN MEGATRENDS'  ; near top
                db      5,  'AWARD'                ; near top
                db      7,  'PHOENIX'              ; near top
                db      20, 'CHIPS & TECHNOLOGIES'
                db      6,  'COMPAQ'
                db      3,  'DTK'
                db      4,  'ERSO'
                db      8,  'EUROSOFT'
                db      7,  'FARADAY'
                db      7,  'HEWLETT'
                db      8,  'LANDMARK'
                db      7,  'MICROID'
                db      5,  'MYLEX'
                db      8,  'OLIVETTI'
```

```
                db      7,  'QUADTEL'
                db      7,  'TOSHIBA'
                db      15, 'WESTERN DIGITAL'
                db      8,  'IBM CORP'              ; near end
                db      7,  'IBM 198'               ; near end
                db      0

biosc_string    db      10 dup (0)
biosv_string    db      40 dup (0)
biosd_string    db      '00/00/00', 0   ; date in yy/mm/dd form
motherboard     db      0               ; temp for motherboard
LBA_support     db      0               ; temp for LBA

ami_LBA_date    db      '94/07/25'      ; LBA ok on AMI BIOS date+

; the following strings are used to look for vendor specific
; information:   * = any char, # = digit 0-9

ami1_string     db      31, '##-####-******-########-######-' ; new
ami2_string     db      15, '-####-######-K#'                 ; old

award_string    db      22, '##/##/##-***-####-####'

find_date1      db      8, '##/##*##'
find_date2      db      8, '##-##-##'

bios_size       dw      0               ; bytes to look at in BIOS

biosinfo proc    near
        push    ds
        push    cs
        pop     ds
```

```
        mov     bx, 0F000h          ; assume bios starts at F000
        mov     cx, 0FFE0h          ; number of bytes to check
        cmp     al, 8               ; old PC/XT ?
        ja      biosi_skp1          ; jump if not
        mov     bx, 0FE00h          ; use smaller BIOS limit
        mov     cx, 01FE0h          ; number of bytes to check
biosi_skp1:
        mov     [bios_size], cx
        mov     es, bx
        mov     si, offset biosven
        mov     dx, 1               ; dl is BIOS vendor number

biosi_loop1:
        cmp     byte ptr [si], 0    ; no more strings to check?
        je      biosi_skp5

        call    find_string         ; see if string [si] appears
                                    ;   in the BIOS at es:0
        jc      biosi_skp3          ; jump if found
        inc     dx
        mov     al, [si]
        xor     ah, ah
        add     si, ax              ; move to next string
        inc     si
        jmp     biosi_loop1         ; try next vendor string

        ; vendor string found, start of string at es:bx

biosi_skp3:
        mov     si, offset biosv_string
        mov     cx, 39              ; string limit
biosi_loop2:
        mov     al, es:[bx]
        cmp     al, 20h             ; allows spaces
```

```
        jb      biosi_skp5
        je      biosi_skp4
        cmp     al, '&'             ; allow ampersand
        je      biosi_skp4
        cmp     al, 30h             ; skip some symbols
        jb      biosi_skp5
        cmp     al, 7Eh             ; skip chars > 7Eh
        ja      biosi_skp5
biosi_skp4:
        mov     [si], al            ; save character
        inc     si
        inc     bx
        loop    biosi_loop2

biosi_skp5:
        cmp     [biosv_string], 0  ; no string found?
        jne     biosi_skp6
        mov     dl, 0               ; set unknown flag

        ; now look for vendor specific information

biosi_skp6:
        cmp     dl, 1               ; AMI?
        jne     biosi_skp7          ; jump if not

        mov     cx, [bios_size]
        mov     si, offset ami1_string
        call    find_string         ; see if string [si] appears
                                    ;   in the BIOS, start at es:0
        jnc     biosi_ami1          ; jump if not found
        mov     al, es:[bx]         ; get motherboard byte
        add     bx, 24              ; point to date string
        jmp     biosi_ami2
```

```
biosi_ami1:
        mov     si, offset ami2_string
        call    find_string         ; see if string [si] appears
                                    ;   in the BIOS at es:0
        jnc     biosi_skp7          ; jump if not found
        mov     ax, [bx-4]          ; get 4 chipset chars
        mov     word ptr [biosc_string], ax
        mov     ax, [bx-2]
        mov     word ptr [biosc_string+2], ax
        mov     al, es:[bx+1]       ; get motherboard byte
        add     bx, 6               ; point to date string
biosi_ami2:
        sub     al, 2Fh             ; convert AMI code to our
        and     al, 0FEh            ;  motherboard ids
        shr     al, 1
        cmp     al, 3
        ja      biosi_ami3          ; skip save if invalid value
        mov     [motherboard], al   ; save

        ; covert AMI date at es:bx to yy-mm-dd form
biosi_ami3:
        mov     di, offset biosd_string
        mov     ax, es:[bx]
        mov     [di+3], ax          ; insert month
        mov     ax, es:[bx+2]
        mov     [di+6], ax          ; insert day
        mov     ax, es:[bx+4]
        mov     [di], ax            ; insert year

        ; AMI began LBA support in BIOSes 25-07-94 and later

        mov     [LBA_support], 1    ; no LBA assumed
        mov     di, offset ami_LBA_date
        mov     si, offset biosd_string
        call    compare_date        ; compare
```

```
        jnc     biosi_done2         ; jump if date earlier
        mov     [LBA_support], 2    ; LBA should be supported
biosi_done2:
        jmp     biosi_done

biosi_skp7:
        cmp     dl, 2               ; Award
        jne     biosi_skp8          ; jump if not

        mov     cx, [bios_size]
        mov     si, offset award_string
        call    find_string         ; see if string [si] appears
        jnc     biosi_skp8          ; jump if not found

        mov     ax, es:[bx+9]       ; get chipset chars
        mov     word ptr [biosc_string], ax
        mov     al, es:[bx+11]
        mov     [biosc_string+2], al

        mov     di, offset biosd_string
        mov     ax, es:[bx]
        mov     [di+3], ax          ; insert month
        mov     ax, es:[bx+3]
        mov     [di+6], ax          ; insert day
        mov     ax, es:[bx+6]
        mov     [di], ax            ; insert year
        jmp     biosi_done

        ; generic search for BIOS date

biosi_skp8:
        push    es
        mov     ax, 0FFFFh
        mov     es, ax
        mov     cx, 15              ; see if string in last 15 chars
```

```
        mov     si, offset find_date2
        call    find_string
        jc      biosi_date_found   ; jump if date found
        mov     si, offset find_date1 ; try alternate format
        call    find_string
        jc      biosi_date_found
        pop     es
        push    es
        mov     cx, [bios_size]    ; look over all of the BIOS
        call    find_string
        jc      biosi_date_found   ; jump if date found
        mov     si, offset find_date2
        call    find_string
        jnc     biosi_skp10        ; jump if date not found

biosi_date_found:
        mov     di, offset biosd_string
        mov     ax, es:[bx+6]
        mov     [di], ax           ; insert year

        ; check if date in US or international order

        mov     ax, es:[bx]        ; if US this is the month
        mov     cx, es:[bx+3]      ; if US this is the day
        xchg    al, ah
        cmp     ax, '12'           ; greater than 12, not US
        xchg    al, ah
        jbe     biosi_skp9         ; jump if seems to be US order
        xchg    ax, cx             ; change to US order
biosi_skp9:
        mov     [di+3], ax         ; insert month
        mov     [di+6], cx         ; insert day
biosi_skp10:
        pop     es
```

```
biosi_done:
        cmp     byte ptr [biosd_string], '8'     ; 1980s ?
        je      biosi_skp11                      ; if no, NO LBA
        cmp     byte ptr [biosd_string], '9'     ; 1990s ?
        jne     biosi_skp12                      ; if not, unknown
        cmp     byte ptr [biosd_string+1], '4'   ; 1994 or after ?
        jae     biosi_skp12                      ; if so, unknown
biosi_skp11:
        mov     [LBA_support], 1    ; no LBA in 1980-1993 BIOSs
biosi_skp12:
        mov     ah, [motherboard]
        mov     al, [LBA_support]
        mov     bx, offset biosc_string ; BIOS chipset id
        mov     si, offset biosv_string ; BIOS vendor
        mov     di, offset biosd_string ; BIOS date string
        push    ds
        pop     es
        pop     ds
        ret
biosinfo endp
```

CPU Information

Currently there are six families of processors (CPUs) commonly used in the PC architecture, and three standard external floating-point processors (FPUs). Many CPUs have variants, depending on the manufacturer. A few of the current variants for the 486 include versions with and without floating point, different on-chip cache sizes, and different external bus widths. For example, Cyrix and TI offer two 486 models with 1K or 2K internal cache memory, while Intel's 80486 is 8K, and IBM's 80486 cache is 16K. I've created a number of routines to help identify exactly what CPU the system contains. Run the CPUTYPE program to display a complete CPU analysis. CPUTYPE has command line options as follows:

```
CPUTYPE         normal operation
CPUTYPE -       disable internal/external FPU detect
CPUTYPE +       include raw timings from cache timings tests
```

The minus option disables those tests deemed slightly risky. For example, to determine whether an FPU is internal to the chip, like an 80486DX, or is external to the chip like an 80486SX, the test must perform a protected mode instruction. Some older generation memory managers will cause a protection fault and stop the program. Most memory managers created in 1993 or later will emulate the actions transparently.

The plus option will add the actual cache timing test results, for those processors with an internal active cache. The cache size test determines how long the CPU takes to perform multiple reads from a block of memory. Data blocks are tested in sizes ranging from .5K to 64K. The timing results are normalized to show the relative difference between cache size tests of .5K, 1K, 2K, 4K, 8K, 16K, 32K, and 64K. A significant difference between two timings indicate the end of the cache. On the Pentium and Pentium Pro, only the data cache size is measured.

The CPUTYPE program is used to demonstrate each of the various subroutines used to identify specific information about the CPU. Complete source code for CPUTYPE is included on the diskette, but is not shown here. Figure 4-2 shows the result of running CPUTYPE.

Figure 4-2. Result of CPUTYPE on a Pentium with MMX

```
CPU ANALYSIS AND INFORMATION v2.00 (c) 1994, 1996 FVG
CPU class:               Pentium/586 (FPU inside CPU)
CPU instruction set:     Pentium   Includes MMX (Matrix-Math extensions)
CPU vendor:              Intel
Internal CPU speed:      167 Mhz
Prefetch queue size:     64
CPUID - Vendor string:   GenuineIntel
Other info:              Stepping: 1   Model: 4   Family: 5   Max reg: 1
Features (008001BF):     Yes  Floating-point processor in CPU chip
                         Yes  Support for enhanced virtual 80x86 mode
                         Yes  I/O breakpoints supported
                         Yes  Page size extensions supported
                         Yes  Time stamp counter support
                         Yes  Model specific registers supported
                         No   2 MB paging/36-bit addressing supported
                         Yes  Support for machine check exception
                         Yes  Support for CMPXCHG8B instruction
                         No   Internal APIC in CPU
Current CPU mode:        Real
Internal CPU cache:      Enabled, with write-back
  Data L1 cache size:    16 KB
  Code L1 cache size:    16 KB (assumed, not measured)
```

The specific CPU detection subroutines I've written are summarized here. These routines include:

CPUVALUE	Used to detect the CPU, from the 8088 to P8.
FPUTYPE	Used to detect whether a floating-point processor (FPU) is present and to identify which type.
FPULOC	Determines whether the FPU is located internal or external to the CPU.
CPUQ	Find the size of the prefetch queue in bytes.
CPUSTEP	Determine the CPU chip version.
CPUMODE	See if the processor is in real or protected mode.
CPUVENDOR	Determine the CPU Vendor (AMD, Cyrix, IBM, Intel, NEC, NexGen, or TI).
CPUSPEED	Measure the internal speed of the CPU in megahertz.
CPU_CACHE	Show if the CPU's internal cache is enabled.
CPU_D_SIZE	Determine the internal data cache size.

Code Sample 4-2. Processor Identification

The following subroutine determines the actively running CPU type. It uses a few undocumented tricks to accomplish proper detection. This approach has worked reliably in a large number of commercial products. How the program works is described in detail with the code. CPUTYPE detects the following CPU classes: 8088/8086, V20/V30, 80188/80186, 80286, 80386, 80486, Pentium/586, Pentium Pro/686. The future P7 and P8 processors are also handled.

While the CPU class is interesting, the CPU instruction set is often critical. With non-Intel parts, the class may not match the set of instructions supported. For example, an older IBM 386 part actually supports the full 486 instruction set. As another example, the Cyrix 6x86 only supports the 486 instruction set (with a few, but not all Pentium instructions). The CPUTYPE program returns both the class and the actual working instruction set, based on Intel's lead.

If you intend to write all of your code for a single processor, CPU identification may be unnecessary. For the most part, 8088 code will run on any processor, and does not need special detection. For any other processor, it is necessary to be sure instructions and CPU architecture differences are handled, depending on the CPU in the system.

One note of caution is in order. To detect the differences between the 80386, 80486, and Pentium processors, it is necessary to try and change some flags. This is the only means recommended by Intel, and will work reliably in most instances. The act of changing the flags may cause a protection fault depending on the CPU mode. Because most systems today run in protected (V86) mode, the memory manager or operating system is responsible for handling the protection fault and will emulate the action of the flag changes transparently to the CPUTYPE program. This means the instruction POPFD acts as if nothing was amiss. This is all fine except when the protected code has bugs that incorrectly handle the emulation. Windows 3.1 in enhanced mode, under some conditions, will incorrectly emulate POPFD. The CPUTYPE subroutine I've designed will make additional tests to properly get around this rare problem.

In some cases, only the detection of 32-bit or non-32-bit processor is necessary. See Code Sample 4-3 for a simpler version of the CPUVALUE program that detects 8080 through the 386.

```
;-------------------------------------------------------------
;    CPU IDENTIFICATION SUBROUTINE
;       Identify the CPU, from 8088 to the P8.  Routine works
;       even if the 386 or later CPU is in V86 mode.  Note that
;       interrupts are enabled at exit, even if they were
;       disabled on entry.  If it is necessary to run this
;       routine with interrupts disabled, just remove all CLI
;       and STI instructions, so long as interrupts are
;       always disabled before running.
;
;       The "CPU class" is the class of CPU as specified by
;       the vendor.  It is a rough indicator of performance.
;
;       The "CPU standard instruction set" identifies the
;       highest level of Intel compatible instruction set
;       that can be used for the CPU.  For example, the
;       NexGen 5x86 has 586 level performance, but only
;       supports instructions defined for the Intel 80386.
;
;       Called with:    nothing
;
;       Returns:        al = CPU family
;                              0 if 8088/8086 or V20/V30
;                              1 if 80186/80188
;                              2 if 80286
;                              3 if 80386
;                              4 if 80486
;                              5 if Pentium/586
;                              6 if Pentium Pro/686
```

```
;                          7 if 786 (future)
;                          8 if 886 (future)
;                    ah =  bit 0 = 0 if CPUID unavailable
;                                  1 if CPUID ok
;                          bit 1 = 0 if not V20/V30
;                                  1 if NEC V20/V30
;                          bit 2 = 0 if no 486+ Alignment Check
;                                  1 supports Alignment Check
;                    bl = CPU standard instruction set
;                          0 if 8088/8086
;                          1 if 80186/80188
;                          2 if 80286
;                          3 if 80386
;                          4 if 80486
;                          5 if Pentium
;                          6 if Pentium Pro or better
;
;       Regs used:       ax, bx
;                        eax, ebx (386 or later)
;
;       Subs called:     hook_int6, restore_int6, bad_op_handler

.8086   ; all instructions 8088/8086 unless overridden later

cpuvalue proc    far
        push    cx
        push    dx
        push    ds
        push    es

; 8088/8086 test - Use rotate quirk - All later CPUs mask the CL
;   register with 0Fh, when shifting a byte by cl bits.  This
;   test loads CL with a large value (20h) and shifts the AX
;   register right.  With the 8088, any bits in AX are shifted
```

```
;   out, and becomes 0.  On all higher level processors, the
;   CL value of 20h is anded with 0Fh, before the shift.  This
;   means the effective number of shifts is 0, so AX is
;   unaffected.

        mov     cl, 20h                 ; load high CL value
        mov     ax, 1                   ; load a non-zero value in AX
        shr     ax, cl                  ; do the shift
        cmp     ax, 0                   ; if zero, then 8088/86
        jne     up186                   ; jump if not 8088/86

; V20/V30 test - It is now either a V20/V30 or a 8088.  I'll use
;   another undocumented trick to find out which.  On the 8088,
;   0Fh performs a POP CS.  On the V20/V30, it is the start of
;   a number of multibyte instructions.  With the byte string
;   0Fh, 14h, C3h the CPU will perform the following:
;               8088/8086                  V20/V30
;             pop     cs                 set1   bl, cl
;             adc     al, 0C3h

        xor     al, al                  ; clear al and carry flag
        push    cs
        db      0Fh, 14h, 0C3h          ; instructions (see above)
        cmp     al, 0C3h                ; if al is C3h then 8088/8086
        jne     upV20
        mov     ax, 0                   ; set 8088/8086 flag
        jmp     uP_Exit

upV20:
        pop     ax                      ; correct for lack of pop cs
        mov     ax, 200h                ; set V20/V30 flag
        jmp     uP_Exit

; 80186/80188 test - Check what is pushed onto the stack with a
;   PUSH SP instruction.  The 80186 updates the stack pointer
```

```
;   before the value of SP is pushed onto the stack.  With all
;   higher level processors, the current value of SP is pushed
;   onto the stack, and then the stack pointer is updated.

up186:
        mov     bx, sp              ; save the current stack ptr
        push    sp                  ; do test
        pop     ax                  ; get the pushed value
        cmp     ax, bx              ; did SP change ?
        je      up286               ; if not, it's a 286+
        mov     ax, 1               ; set 80186 flag
        jmp     uP_Exit

; 80286 test A - We'll look at the top four bits of the EFLAGS
;   register.  On a 286, these bits are always zero.  Later
;   CPUs allow these bits to be changed.  During this test,
;   We'll disable interrupts to ensure interrupts do not change
;   the flags.

up286:
        cli                         ; disable interrupts
        pushf                       ; save the current flags

        pushf                       ; push flags onto stack
        pop     ax                  ; now pop flags from stack
        or      ax, 0F000h          ; try and set bits 12-15 hi
        push    ax
        popf                        ; set new flags
        pushf
        pop     ax                  ; see if upper bits are 0

        popf                        ; restore flags to original
        sti                         ; enable interrupts
        test    ax, 0F000h          ; were any upper bits 1 ?
```

```
        jnz     up386plus           ; if so, not a 286

; 80286 test B - If the system was in V86 mode, (386 or higher)
;   the POPF instruction causes a protection fault, and the
;   protected mode software must emulate the action of POPF. If
;   the protected mode software screws up, as occurs with a
;   rarely encountered bug in Windows 3.1 enhanced mode, the
;   prior test may look like a 286, but it's really a higher
;   level processor. We'll check if the protected mode bit is
;   on.  If not, it's guaranteed to be a 286.

.286P                               ; allow a 286 instruction
        smsw    ax                  ; get machine status word
        test    ax, 1               ; in protected mode ?
        jz      is286               ; jump if not (must be 286)

; 80286 test C - It's very likely a 386 or greater, but it is
;   not guaranteed yet.  There is a small possibility the system
;   could be in 286 protected mode so we'll do one last test. We
;   will try out a 386 unique instruction, after vectoring the
;   bad-opcode interrupt vector (int 6) to ourselves.

        call    hook_int6           ; do it!
        mov     [badoff], offset upbad_op3  ; where to go if bad
.386
        xchg    eax, eax            ; 32 bit nop (bad on 286)

        call    restore_int6        ; restore vector
        jmp     up386plus           ; only gets here if 386
                                    ;  or greater!

; Interrupt vector 6 (bad opcode) comes here if system is a
;   80286 (assuming the 286 protected mode interrupt 6 handler
;   will execute the bad-opcode interrupt).
```

```
upbad_op3:
        call    restore_int6
is286:
        mov     ax, 2                   ; set 80286 flag
        jmp     uP_Exit

; CPUID test - If bit 21 is changeable, it indicates the CPU
;   supports the CPUID instruction.  During this test, we'll
;   disable interrupts to ensure no interrupt will change any
;   flags.

.586                                    ; allow 486 instructions

up386plus:
        cli                             ; disable interrupts
        mov     cx, sp                  ; save the current stack ptr
        and     sp, NOT 3               ; align stack, avoids AC fault
        pushfd                          ; push flags to look at
        pop     eax                     ; get eflags
        mov     ebx, eax                ; save for later
        xor     eax, 200000h            ; toggle bit 21
        push    eax
        popfd                           ; load modified eflags to CPU
        pushfd                          ; push eflags to look at
        pop     eax                     ; get current eflags
        push    ebx                     ; push original onto stack
        popfd                           ; restore original flags
        mov     sp, cx                  ; restore stack ptr
        sti                             ; enable interrupts
        xor     dl, dl                  ; DL = temp flag, 0=no CPUID
        xor     eax, ebx                ; check if bit changed
        jz      up386                   ; jump if no change, no CPUID
        inc     dl                      ; set flag that CPUID is ok
```

```
; 80386 test - Bit 18 in EFLAGS is not settable on a 386, but is
;   changeable on the 486 and later CPUs.  Bit 18 is used to
;   flag alignment faults. During this test, we'll disable
;   interrupts to ensure no interrupt will change any flags.


up386:
        cli                             ; disable interrupts
        mov     cx, sp                  ; save the current stack ptr
        and     sp, NOT 3               ; align stack, avoids AC fault
        pushfd                          ; push flags to look at
        pop     eax                     ; get eflags
        mov     ebx, eax                ; save for later
        xor     eax, 40000h             ; toggle bit 18, AC flag
        push    eax
        popfd                           ; load modified eflags to CPU
        pushfd                          ; push eflags to look at
        pop     eax                     ; get current eflags
        push    ebx                     ; push original onto stack
        popfd                           ; restore original flags
        mov     sp, cx                  ; restore stack ptr
        sti                             ; enable interrupts
        xor     eax, ebx                ; check if bit changed
        jz      upNoAC                  ; no Alignment Check
        or      dl, 4                   ; DL = temp flag, bit 2=1 AC ok
        jmp     up486                   ; changed, so 486 or later

        ; looks like a 386 - check for NexGen Nx586

upNoAC:
        push    dx                      ; save temp flags (CPUID & AC)
        mov     ax, 5555h               ; init AX with non-zero
        xor     dx, dx                  ; set zero flag to 1
        mov     cx, 2
```

```
        div     cx                  ; Nx586 processor does not
        pop     dx                  ;   modify zero flag on DIV
        mov     ax, 3               ; assume 386 family
        jnz     upCPUID             ; not Nx586 if zero flag 0
        mov     ax, 5               ; set 586 family
        jmp     upCPUID

up486:
        mov     ax, 4               ; set 486 family
        test    dl, 1
        jnz     upCPUID             ; If CPUID valid, use it

        ; Check for Cyrix, which may look like a 486 so far.
        ; For some dumb reason they provide a option to turn
        ; off the CPUID instruction in many versions, and
        ; the BIOS initializes the CPUID to off!  This
        ; makes the Cyrix 5x86 & 6x86 look like a 486 on
        ; less robust CPU identification programs.

        ; To check for Cyrix, a divide instruction on
        ; non-Cyrix CPUs will change the state of some
        ; flags (undefined).  Cyrix will leave the flags
        ; cleared (except bit 1 is always 1 on all 286+ CPUs).

        xor     ah, ah
        sahf                        ; clear flags
        mov     ax, 10              ; actual values for the
        mov     cl, 4               ;  divide not important
        div     cl                  ; perform a divide
        lahf                        ; get the flags
        and     ah, 0FDh            ; ignore bit 1
        cmp     ah, 0               ; are flags zero?
        je      is_Cyrix            ; if so, it is Cyrix
```

```
        mov     ax, 4
        jmp     upInSet             ; must be 486 non-Cyrix

        ; We now know that it is a Cyrix 486 or better part,
        ; without CPUID operating. Now we find out which
        ; type of part by using the Cyrix unique system
        ; registers port 22h and port 23h.

is_Cyrix:
        mov     al, 0FEh
        call    read_cyrix_reg      ; get device ID reg 0 (FEh)
        mov     bl, al              ; save Cyrix CPU type value
        mov     ax, 4               ; assume 486 type
        and     bl, 0F0h            ; ignore lower nibble
        cmp     bl, 060h            ; undefined ?
        jae     upInSet             ; must be old Cyrix 486
        cmp     bl, 10h             ; defined as 486 part ?
        jbe     upInSet             ; jump if so
        mov     al, bl              ; convert to 5 or 6
        shr     al, 4
        add     al, 3
        jmp     upInSet             ; AX=5 5x86, AX=6 6x86

; If allowed, use the CPUID instruction to get the CPU class.
;   The CPUID returns a family number 0 or higher for the
;   processor type.  As of 1996, recent Intel 486s, and many
;   later processors (Pentium, Pentium Pro) support the CPUID
;   instruction.  Other vendors may also include support in
;   new CPU releases.

upCPUID:
        test    dl, 1               ; CPUID instruction missing?
        jz      upInSet             ; jump if no CPUID
```

```
        push    ecx                 ; CPUID changes eax to edx
        push    edx                 ;
        mov     eax, 1              ; get family info function
        CPUID                       ; macro for CPUID instruction
        and     eax, 0F00h          ; find family info
        shr     eax, 8              ; move to al
        mov     ah, 1               ; set flag that CPUID ok
        pop     edx
        pop     ecx


; AL has the CPU family (386 or higher) so we now need to test
; for the validity of the instruction set.  We will try a
; 486, Pentium, and Pentium Pro unique instructions, after
; vectoring the bad-opcode interrupt vector (int 6) to
; ourselves.

upInSet:
        mov     ah, dl              ; CPUID & AC flags for exit
        cmp     al, 3               ; if below 386, we are done!
        jb      up_Exit

        push    ax
        call    hook_int6           ; do it!
        mov     [badoff], offset upbad_op4  ; where to go if bad
.486
        xadd    al, ah              ; exchange & add (486+)
        bswap   eax                 ; byte swap (486+)

        call    restore_int6        ; restore vector
        pop     ax                  ; 486 instruction is ok

        ; now try Pentium instruction
```

```
        cmp     al, 4                   ; if a 486, we are done!
        jbe     up_Exit

        push    ax
        call    hook_int6               ; do it!
        mov     [badoff], offset upbad_op5  ; where to go if bad
.586
        mov     eax, cs:[0]             ; use any address
        not     eax                     ; ensure compare fails
                                        ;   to avoid changing cs:[0]
        cmpxchg8b qword ptr cs:[0] ; compare & exchange (Pentium+)

        call    restore_int6            ; restore vector
        pop     ax                      ; Pentium instruction is ok

        ; now try Pentium Pro instruction

        cmp     al, 5                   ; if a Pentium, we are done!
        jbe     up_Exit

        push    ax
        call    hook_int6               ; do it!
        mov     [badoff], offset upbad_op6  ; where to go if bad

;        cmovne   ax, bx                ; conditional move, not-equal
                                        ;   (Pentium Pro)
        db      0Fh, 45h, 0C3h          ; byte encoding of CMOVNE since
                                        ;  most assemblers can't encode it
        call    restore_int6            ; restore vector
        pop     ax                      ; Pentium Pro instruction is ok
        jmp     up_Exit

; Interrupt vector 6 (bad opcode) comes here if CPU does not
;   support 486 instruction set
```

```
upbad_op4:
        call    restore_int6
        pop     ax
        mov     bl, 3                ; instruction set 386
        jmp     uP_Exit2

; Interrupt vector 6 (bad opcode) comes here if CPU does not
;   support Pentium instruction set

upbad_op5:
        call    restore_int6
        pop     ax
        mov     bl, 4                ; instruction set 486
        jmp     uP_Exit2

; Interrupt vector 6 (bad opcode) comes here if CPU does not
;   support Pentium Pro instruction set

upbad_op6:
        call    restore_int6
        pop     ax
        mov     bl, 5                ; instruction set Pentium
        jmp     uP_Exit2

up_Exit:
        mov     bl, al               ; set the instruction set
up_Exit2:
        pop     es
        pop     ds
        pop     dx
        pop     cx
        ret
cpuvalue endp
.8086                                ; return to 8086 instructions
```

Code Sample 4-3. Simple Processor Identification

Unlike Code Sample 4-2, this routine is a much smaller and simpler routine. It detects only whether the CPU is a 8088, 80186, 286 or a 386 or better.

```
;-------------------------------------------------------------
;    CPU 386 IDENTIFICATION SUBROUTINE
;       Identify the CPU type, from 8088 to 386+.  This is
;       subset of the more extensive CPUVALUE program.  It is
;       used when identification of CPUs above the 386 is
;       not necessary (i.e. 32-bit support or not)
;
;       Called with:    nothing
;
;       Returns:        al = CPU type
;                             0 if 8088/8086 or V20/V30
;                             1 if 80186/80188
;                             2 if 80286
;                             3 if 80386 or better
;
;       Regs used:      ax, bx
;                       eax (32-bit CPU only)
;
;       Subs called:    hook_int6, restore_int6, bad_op_handler

.8086   ; all instructions 8088/8086 unless overridden later

cpu386  proc    far
        push    cx
        push    dx
        push    ds
        push    es

; 8088/8086 test - Use rotate quirk - All later CPUs mask the CL
;   register with 0Fh, when shifting a byte by cl bits.  This
```

```
;   test loads CL with a large value (20h) and shifts the AX
;   register right.  With the 8088, any bits in AX are shifted
;   out, and becomes 0.  On all higher level processors, the
;   CL value of 20h is anded with 0Fh, before the shift.  This
;   means the effective number of shifts is 0, so AX is
;   unaffected.

        mov     cl, 20h             ; load high CL value
        mov     ax, 1               ; load a non-zero value in AX
        shr     ax, cl              ; do the shift
        cmp     ax, 0               ; if zero, then 8088/86
        jne     up186               ; jump if not 8088/86
        jmp     uP_Exit

; 80186/80188 test - Check what is pushed onto the stack with a
;   PUSH SP instruction.  The 80186 updates the stack pointer
;   before the value of SP is pushed onto the stack.  With all
;   higher level processors, the current value of SP is pushed
;   onto the stack, and then the stack pointer is updated.

up186:
        mov     bx, sp              ; save the current stack ptr
        push    sp                  ; do test
        pop     ax                  ; get the pushed value
        cmp     ax, bx              ; did SP change ?
        je      up286               ; if not, it's a 286+
        mov     ax, 1               ; set 80186 flag
        jmp     uP_Exit

; 80286 test A - We'll look at the top four bits of the EFLAGS
;   register.  On a 286, these bits are always zero.  Later
;   CPUs allow these bits to be changed.  During this test,
;   We'll disable interrupts to ensure interrupts do not change
;   the flags.
```

```
up286:
        cli                             ; disable interrupts
        pushf                           ; save the current flags

        pushf                           ; push flags onto stack
        pop     ax                      ; now pop flags from stack
        or      ax, 0F000h              ; try and set bits 12-15 hi
        push    ax
        popf                            ; set new flags
        pushf
        pop     ax                      ; see if upper bits are 0

        popf                            ; restore flags to original
        sti                             ; enable interrupts
        test    ax, 0F000h              ; were any upper bits 1 ?
        jnz     up386plus               ; if so, not a 286

; 80286 test B - If the system was in V86 mode, (386 or higher)
;   the POPF instruction causes a protection fault, and the
;   protected mode software must emulate the action of POPF. If
;   the protected mode software screws up, as occurs with a
;   rarely encountered bug in Windows 3.1 enhanced mode, the
;   prior test may look like a 286, but it's really a higher
;   level processor. We'll check if the protected mode bit is
;   on.  If not, it's guaranteed to be a 286.

.286P                                   ; allow a 286 instruction
        smsw    ax                      ; get machine status word
        test    ax, 1                   ; in protected mode ?
        jz      is286                   ; jump if not (must be 286)

; 80286 test C - It's very likely a 386 or greater, but it is
;   not guaranteed yet.  There is a small possibility the system
;   could be in 286 protected mode so we'll do one last test. We
```

```
;   will try out a 386 unique instruction, after vectoring the
;   bad-opcode interrupt vector (int 6) to ourselves.

        call    hook_int6           ; do it!
        mov     [badoff], offset upbad_op3  ; where to go if bad
.386
        xchg    eax, eax            ; 32 bit nop (bad on 286)

        call    restore_int6        ; restore vector
        jmp     up386plus           ; only gets here if 386
                                    ;  or greater!

; Interrupt vector 6 (bad opcode) comes here if system is a
;   80286 (assuming the 286 protected mode interrupt 6 handler
;   will execute the bad-opcode interrupt).

upbad_op3:
        call    restore_int6
is286:
        mov     ax, 2               ; set 80286 flag
        jmp     uP_Exit

up386plus:
        mov     ax, 3               ; 32-bit CPU (386 or later)

up_Exit:
        pop     es
        pop     ds
        pop     dx
        pop     cx
        ret
cpu386  endp
.8086                               ; return to 8086 instructions
```

Code Sample 4-4. Floating-point Processor Detector

This routine determines whether a floating-point processor is available and which type: 8087, 80287, or 80387. The routine also determines whether an 80287 FPU is attached to an 80386 CPU. Note that the routine returns a value of 4 or higher for those CPU classes that have an integrated FPU. The routine verifies whether an FPU is available, but does not indicate whether the 80486 CPU is a DX version (with FPU internal) or an 80486SX version that has an external 80387 FPU. Use the routine FPULOC shown in Code sample 4-5 to detect where the FPU is located.

The FPUTYPE routine requires the CPUVALUE routine to have been previously run, and the CPU type saved in the variable CPU_VAL.

```
;------------------------------------------------------------
;    FLOATING-POINT DETECTION SUBROUTINE
;       Determines if the math coprocessor is present by
;       checking the FPU's status and control words.  Also
;       detects if a 80386 system has a 80287 or 80387 FPU.
;
;       Called with:    ds = cs (to handle local variable fpu_temp)
;                       ds:[cpu_val] set with CPU class
;                       ds:[cpu_inst] set with CPU instruction set
;
;       Returns:        al = FPU type
;                             0 if no FPU
;                             1 if 8087
;                             2 if 80287
;                             3 if 80387 or equivalent
;                             4 if 80486 with FPU
;                             5 if Pentium (586) with FPU
;                             6 if Pentium Pro (686) with FPU
;                             7 if P7 (786) with FPU
;
;       Regs used:      ax

fpu_temp dw     0                       ; temp word for detector
```

```
.386
.387                                    ; allow math instructions

fputype proc    near
        fninit                          ; initialize FPU (reset)
        mov     [fpu_temp], 1234h       ; set any non zero value
        fnstsw  [fpu_temp]              ; get status word from FPU
        and     [fpu_temp], 0FFh        ; only look at bottom 8 bits
        jnz     fput_not_found          ; if non-zero, no FPU
        fnstcw  [fpu_temp]              ; get control word from FPU
        and     [fpu_temp], 103Fh       ; strip unneeded bits
        cmp     [fpu_temp], 3Fh         ; are the proper bits set ?
        je      fput_present            ; jump if so, FPU present

fput_not_found:
        mov     ax, 0                   ; FPU not present
        jmp     fput_Exit

; FPU was found, so see which type, 8087, 80287, or 80387

fput_present:
        mov     ax, 1                   ; assume 8087
        cmp     [cpu_val], 2            ; CPU below 286 ?
        jb      fput_Exit               ; if so, must be 8087
        mov     ax, 2                   ; assume 80287
        je      fput_Exit               ; if 80286, then FPU is 80287
        xor     ah, ah
        mov     al, [cpu_inst]          ; get cpu, 80386 or higher ?
        cmp     al, 3                   ; 386 ?
        je      fput_386
        mov     al, [cpu_val]
        jmp     fput_Exit               ; jump if 486 or higher
```

```
; 80386 could have a 80287 or 80387 FPU.  To find out, check if
;   -infinity is equal to +infinity.  If not, it's an 80387.

fput_386:
        fld1                        ; push +1 onto stack
        fldz                        ; push +0 onto the stack
        fdiv                        ; 1/0 = infinity
        fld     st                  ; load +infinity onto stack
        fchs                        ; now -infinity on stack
        fcompp                      ; compare + and - infinity
        fstsw   [fpu_temp]          ; status of compare in temp
        test    [fpu_temp], 4000h   ; equal ? (test zero bit)
        jnz     fput_Exit           ; jump if not (387, al= 3)
        mov     al, 2               ; +/- infinity equal, 80287

fput_Exit:
        ret
fputype endp
.8086
```

Code Sample 4-5. Floating-point Processor Location

This routine finds the location of the FPU on the 80486 and Pentium CPUs. The 80486SX has no FPU on the CPU, but can have an 80387 on the motherboard to provide FPU operations. This routine indicates where the FPU resides.

To detect the FPU location, it is necessary to see if bit 4 in CR0 can be changed. This requires execution of the MOV CR0, EAX protected mode instruction. Some protected mode products like some older memory managers may not allow this instruction. The memory manager will generate a General Protection Fault, aborting the routine. Current memory managers emulate the MOV CR0 instruction so this test can be made safely. Because of this problem, I would not recommend including this routine in any commercial package. When using this routine, it is wise to include some type of option to allow a user to bypass the routine. For example, the CPUTYPE program that demonstrates this routine has a command line option to skip this test.

The FPULOC routine requires the FPUTYPE routine to have been previously run, and the FPUTYPE saved in the variable FPU_VAL.

```
;------------------------------------------------------------
;
;   FLOATING POINT ON CHIP SUBROUTINE
;       For the 80486/Pentium, a check is made to see if the FPU
;       is on the CPU chip or is separate. The Extension Type
;       bit 4 in CR0 is checked to see if it can be changed.
;       If it can't be changed, the CPU has the FPU inside the
;       chip. If the bit can be changed, it's outside the CPU.
;
;                  ********** IMPORTANT **********
;         Changing the CR0 register while in V86 mode causes
;         a CPU fault that should be handled transparently by
;         the protected mode software such as memory manager.
;
;       Called with:    ds:[fpu_val] set with FPU type
;
;       Returns:        al = 0 if FPU not on CPU or no FPU
;                            1 if FPU inside CPU
;
;       Regs used:      ax

.386P

fpuloc proc     near
        xor     al, al                  ; assume FPU not in CPU
        cmp     [fpu_val], 4            ; 486 or higher CPU with FPU?
        jb      fpul_exit               ; exit if not
        push    bx
        push    eax
        mov     eax, cr0
        mov     bx, ax                  ; save lower portion
        and     eax, 0FFFFFFEFh         ; attempt to set 16-bit mode
        mov     cr0, eax
```

```
        mov     eax, cr0
        xchg    ax, bx
        mov     cr0, eax                ; restore cr0 to original
        pop     eax
        mov     al, bl
        shr     al, 4                   ; return ET bit in bit 0
        pop     bx
fpul_exit:
        ret
fpuloc  endp
.8086
```

Code Sample 4-6. Prefetch Queue Size Detector

This routine determines the size of the instruction prefetch queue of the CPU. The prefetch queue is a first-in-first-out buffer holding instructions to be executed. Its size varies with different families of processors and different vendors.

Its implementation is a bit strange. To find the length of the queue, I use the fact that the queue cannot be written to. Self-modifying code is used to modify the next instructions to execute. A single repeat store-string-byte (REP STOSB) instruction will overwrite a number of no-operation (NOP) instructions. The NOPs are overwritten with the byte value for an increment BX (INC BX) instruction. The instructions in memory are *always* overwritten, but those in the prefetch queue are not.

I've created a small example to help clarify the self-modifying code operation. The example is shown in Figure 4-3. I've assumed a 4-byte prefetch queue. The REP STOSB will always write the correct information into memory, but the CPU fails to update the bytes loaded into the prefetch queue. As soon as the REP STOSB instruction completes, the CPU executes the NOPs in the prefetch queue. The BX register will not be incremented by the length of the prefetch queue. In this example, we have processed 6 instructions but BX is 2, so the length of the queue is 4.

Figure 4-3. Four Byte Prefetch Queue Operation

	Before REP STOSB Executes		After REP STOSB Executes	
Offset	**PreFetch Queue**	**Memory**	**PreFetch Queue**	**Memory**
x	REP	REP	REP	REP
x+1	STOSB	STOSB	STOSB	STOSB
x+2	NOP	NOP	NOP	INC BX
x+3	NOP	NOP	NOP	INC BX
x+4*	NOP	NOP	INC BX	INC BX
x+5*	NOP	NOP	INC BX	INC BX

* *Bytes that have not been prefetched yet*

After spending many hours with different designs, I found the following routine is the most stable (method 1) for pre-Pentium designs. All interrupts are disabled during the test, the prefetch queue is flushed, aligned on a paragraph boundary, and 16 slow divide instructions are executed to help give the processor time to load up the prefetch queue.

Unfortunately, I've noticed some systems indicate shorter prefetch queues than expected. Intel has not released specific information on how the prefetch queue gets loaded or even the length of the prefetch queue on some processors. Because of the variances seen with some CPUs, it is not always possible to rely on the results of the prefetch queue routine.

On the Pentium, this test will appear to show no prefetch queue. The Pentium is the first CPU in the family to check if a write will affect the prefetch queue. If so, the Pentium updates the prefetch queue. To solve this, an alternate method was devised (method 2). The Pentium has one quirk that we can exploit to get an accurate prefetch queue measurement. It's a slight variant of the previous design where we self modify our own code.

The basic AT design, still in use today, has an option to turn off the A20 address line externally from the CPU. This is the default way the system powers up, and it normally remains this way while real mode is active. This emulates the original 8088 design so that addresses above 1 MB will wrap back to low memory.

We move our method 2 prefetch queue code into low memory below 64 KB. We then set the data reference to segment FFFFh. By adding 16 to the offset, we address the identical area in low memory! The A20 line from the CPU goes high, but is ignored by the external A20 logic, causing an address wrap. Now any writes to memory are not updated in the prefetch queue, and we can measure its size.

The problem with method 2 is the A20 line must be off. The routine verifies A20 is off before running, but does not attempt to turn off A20 when it is active. It will return a error value when A20 is enabled.

My next surprise was that both methods failed to provide an accurate value on the Pentium Pro. On close examination of the Pentium Pro hardware manual, A20 disable logic is provided inside the CPU. Although it is very clever of the Pentium Pro to update the prefetch queue on what should be considered incorrect addresses, it could be considered a bug (I suspect Intel will disagree!). I can find no reason why it should matter either way, except to properly detect the prefetch queue size.

```
;--------------------------------------------------------------
;    CPU PREFETECH QUEUE DEPTH SUBROUTINE
;       This routine returns the depth of the prefetch
;       queue.  Each processor uses a different size queue,
;       in which self-modifying code does not work.  This
;       routine cleverly uses self-modifying code to determine
;       the queue size.
;
;       For Pentium+ processor, A20 must be disabled
;       (i.e. no memory manager) to get the prefetech q size.
;       This uses an alternate method 2.  The Pentium Pro changed
;       the prefetch logic again, so both methods produce
;       incorrect results on the Pentium Pro.
;
;       Called with:    [cpu_val]
;                        al = Method to use
;                             0 = automatic
;                             1 = force method 1
;                             2 = force method 2
;
;       Returns:        ax = CPU prefetch size
;                             0 if can't be measured if A20 enabled
;                                on Pentium type processors
;                             2 unable to measure (CPU updates the
;                                prefetch queue writes
;                             4 if 8088/8086
;                             8 if 80286
;                             16 if 80386
;                             32 if 80486
;                             64 if Pentium
;
```

```
;       Regs used:      ax

QSIZE   equ     80h                     ; maximum queue size
int_backup      db      256 dup(0) ; temp storage for int table

cpuQ    proc    far
        push    bx
        push    cx
        push    dx
        push    di
        push    es

; The first method works fine for any CPU that does not update
; the prefetch q dynamically.  Pentium class CPUs cannot use this
; technique, and resort to an alternate.

        cmp     al, 0                   ; check method to use first
        je      cpuq_auto
        cmp     al, 1
        je      cpuq_method1
        jmp     cpuq_method2

cpuq_auto:
        cmp     [cpu_val], 5            ; Pentium class?
        jb      cpuq_method1            ; jump if not
        jmp     cpuq_method2

; The Queue size test works by issuing a large number of
;   very slow DIV instructions to allow the CPU to load
;   up the prefetch queue while the slow instructions
;   are being executed.  Next the REP STOB instruction
;   will overwrite some number of NOP instructions
;   with "INC BX".  If there was no prefetch queue, all
;   of the NOP instructions would be converted to INC BX.
;   If there was a 16 byte prefetch queue, the change is
```

```
;   made to memory, but not the NOPs in the prefetch
;   queue.

cpuq_method1:
        mov     ax, cs              ; Initialize queue in
        mov     es, ax              ;   code segment
        mov     cx, QSIZE           ; queue size
        mov     di, offset qdata    ; queue location
        mov     al, 90h             ; set to all NOPs to start
        cld
        rep     stosb               ; all Queue bytes NOPs

        xor     bx, bx              ; start value for count
        mov     cx, QSIZE           ; number of bytes to modify
        mov     di, offset qdata+QSIZE-1 ; ptr where to modify
        std                         ; write backwards from end
        mov     al, 80h
        out     70h, al             ; disable NMI
        cli                         ; disable interrupts
        mov     ax, 43h             ; 43h = "inc bx"
        mov     dl, 1               ; divisor 1 (no effect to AL)
        jmp     short upqflush      ; flush prefetch queue
ALIGN 16                            ; align code on para boundary
upqflush:
        div     dl                  ; load up prefetch q with
        div     dl                  ;   lots of slow instructions
        div     dl
        div     dl
        div     dl
        div     dl
        div     dl
        div     dl
        rep     stosb               ; al to es:[di+39h] thru [di]
qdata   db      QSIZE dup (90h)     ; NOP instructions
```

```
        xor     al, al
        out     70h, al             ; enable NMI
        sti
        cld
        mov     ax, QSIZE+2         ; size (less 2 for REP STOSB)
        sub     ax, bx              ; ax = queue size
cpuq_exit2:
        jmp     cpuq_exit

;   This alternate method checks if A20 disabled.  If so, a trick
;   is done to fool the Pentium class CPU to not update the
;   prefetch q so we can get an accurate measurement.  This is
;   accomplished by executing the code in the first 64KB of memory,
;   and having the code alterations performed with a segment value
;   of FFFF.  With proper design, the writes wrap to low memory
;   (i.e. that's what A20 disabled does), but the processor is not
;   smart enough to see that we are writing to an area that is in
;   the prefetch queue!  This routine fails to work on the Pentium
;   Pro, since it does update the prefetch queue.

cpuq_method2:
        call    check_A20           ; is A20 enabled ?
        xor     ax, ax              ; assume it is
        cmp     cx, 1
        je      cpuq_exit2          ; exit with AX=0 if enabled

        ; save the contents of low memory we are going to use
        ; (which starts at the interrupt vector C0h through FFh)

        push    ds
        xor     ax, ax
        mov     ds, ax
        push    cs
        pop     es
```

```
        mov     si, 300h            ; interrupt C0 vector location
        mov     di, offset int_backup
        mov     cx, 128
        cld
        rep     movsw               ; save interrupts C0 to FF
                                    ;  which are unlikely to be in use

        ; now move the queue test code into low memory

        cli                         ; disable interrupts
        push    cs
        pop     ds
        xor     ax, ax
        mov     es, ax
        mov     si, offset cpuq_code
        mov     di, 300h
        mov     cx, 128
        rep     movsw               ; load code into low memory
        db      0EAh                ; far jump to cpu_code in low mem
        dw      300h, 0             ;  at 0:300

        ; the following code is moved to low memory before execution

ALIGN 16                            ; align code on para boundary
cpuq_code:
        mov     ax, cs              ; Initialize queue in
        mov     es, ax              ;   code segment
        mov     cx, QSIZE           ; queue size
        mov     di, offset qdata2 - offset cpuq_code + 300h
                                    ; queue location
        mov     al, 90h             ; set to all NOPs to start
        cld
        rep     stosb               ; all Queue bytes NOPs
```

```
        xor     bx, bx                  ; start value for count
        mov     cx, QSIZE               ; number of bytes to modify
        mov     di, offset qdata2+QSIZE-1 - offset cpuq_code + 300h + 10h
                                        ; di points to end of queue
        mov     ax, 0FFFFh
        mov     es, ax                  ; change segment to FFFFh
        std                             ; write backwards from end
        mov     al, 80h
        out     70h, al                 ; disable NMI
        mov     ax, 43h                 ; 43h = "inc bx"
        mov     dl, 1                   ; divisor 1 (no effect to AL)
        db      0EAh                    ; hard coded jump to upqflush
        dw      offset upqflush2 - offset cpuq_code + 300h, 0
                                        ; flush prefetch queue
ALIGN 16                                ; align code on para boundary
upqflush2:
        div     dl                      ; load up prefetch q with
        div     dl                      ;   lots of slow instructions
        div     dl
        div     dl
        div     dl
        div     dl
        div     dl
        div     dl
        rep     stosb                   ; al to es:[di+39h] thru [di]
qdata2  db      QSIZE dup (90h)         ; NOP instructions
        xor     al, al
        out     70h, al                 ; enable NMI
        cld
        mov     ax, QSIZE+2             ; size (less 2 for REP STOSB)
        sub     ax, bx                  ; ax = queue size
        db      0EAh                    ; hard coded far jump back to
        dw      offset cpuq_ret         ;  cpuq routine
        dw      seg cpuq_ret
```

```
        ; AX = queue size;  restore interrupt vector memory

cpuq_ret:
        xor     si, si
        mov     es, si
        push    cs
        pop     ds
        mov     di, 300h             ; interrupt C0 vector location
        mov     si, offset int_backup
        mov     cx, 128
        cld
        rep     movsw                ; restore interrupts C0 to FF
        sti                          ; enable interrupts
        pop     ds

cpuq_exit:
        pop     es
        pop     di
        pop     dx
        pop     cx
        pop     bx
        ret
cpuQ    endp
```

Code Sample 4-7. Processor Version Detector

The CPU version indicates a revision level of a specific chip. Just like most software programs, each CPU type has multiple revisions (called steppings) to fix minor bugs or hardware abnormalities. In some cases the revision is made to shrink the size of the CPU chip for faster performance and reduced production costs.

It is rarely necessary to know which CPU version is being used on a program, although there are always a few exceptions! For example, some instructions were only supported on the A step of the 80386, but were dropped in all later versions. While correcting some abnormalities of this first released 386 version, Intel ran out of microcode space in the CPU. To make additional room, they chopped out a few instructions. Of course, if you wanted to use these instructions, you had better test that the 386 CPU is an A step.

This routine uses a number of techniques to help identify the CPU version. Although I've found no problems using this routine on a number of systems, I would not recommend using the routine in a commercial application. The routine uses too many undocumented tricks that could potentially fail on some future CPU or system.

Before running this routine, the CPU_VAL and CPU_INFO bytes must be set from the results of CPUVALUE. The routine outputs its results using the DOS output string function.

```
;-------------------------------------------------------------
;    CPU STEP
;       If the CPUID instruction is supported, get info from
;       it, otherwise, check if BIOS supports function that
;       has the CPU step information.  Message displayed
;       depending on results.
;
;       Call with:      ds:[cpu_val] set with CPU
;                       ds:[cpu_info] set with CPUID flag
;                       ds:[cpu_mfg] = 7 or 8 if Cyrix
;
;       Returns:        display step information
;
;       Regs used:      eax, ebx, ecx, edx, di
;
;       Subs called:    hex2ascii, xferbytes, hook_int6,
;                       restore_int6, bad_op_handler

bver    db      '  CPU version from BIOS: '
bvernum db                               '    h  '
bvercom db      '                  '
        db      CR, LF, '$'

novermg db      '  CPU version detection: '
        db      'Not supported in this BIOS or CPU'
        db      CR, LF, '$'

idtxtmg db      '  CPUID - Vendor string: '
idtext  db      '             ', CR, LF, '$'
```

```
stepmsg db      '    Other info:          Stepping: '
stepval db      '    Model: '
modval  db      '    Family: '
famval  db      '    Max reg: '
caseval db      '  ', CR, LF, '$'
featmsg db      '    Features ('
featval db      'xxxxxxxx): '
featb0  db      'No   Floating-point processor in CPU chip   '
        db      CR, LF
        db      '                                        '
featb1  db      'No   Support for enhanced virtual 80x86 mode'
        db      CR, LF
        db      '                                        '
        db      'No   I/O breakpoints supported              '
        db      CR, LF
        db      '                                        '
        db      'No   Page size extensions supported         '
        db      CR, LF
        db      '                                        '
        db      'No   Time stamp counter support             '
        db      CR, LF
        db      '                                        '
        db      'No   Model specific registers supported     '
        db      CR, LF
        db      '                                        '
        db      'No   2 MB paging/36-bit addressing supported'
        db      CR, LF
        db      '                                        '
        db      'No   Support for machine check exception    '
        db      CR, LF
        db      '                                        '
        db      'No   Support for CMPXCHG8B instruction      '
        db      CR, LF
        db      '                                        '
```

```
        db      'No   Internal APIC in CPU                    '
        db      CR, LF
        db      '$'

stepa   db      '  CPU version detection: '
        db      'Step A (earliest released version)'
        db      CR, LF, '$'

cid0msg db      '  Cyrix ID register 0:   Part ID:  '
cidval  db      '    ', CR, LF, '$'
cid1msg db      '       ID register 1:   Stepping: '
cstpval db      '      Revision: '
crevval db      '  ', CR, LF, '$'

; table of step values and what they mean

bvt     dw      303h
        db      '(80386 step B1)'
bvte    dw      305h
        db      '(80386 step D0)'
        dw      308h
        db      '(80386 step D1)'
        dw      400h
        db      '(80486 step A0)'
        dw      401h
        db      '(80486 step B2)'
        dw      403h
        db      '(80486 step B3)'
        dw      404h
        db      '(80486 step B4)'
        dw      405h
        db      '(80486 step B5)'
        dw      406h
        db      '(80486 step B6)'
```

```
        dw      407h
        db      '(80486 step C1)'
        dw      2300h
        db      '(80386SX)      '
        dw      0A301h
        db      '(386SLC step 1)'       ; IBM
        dw      0A412h
        db      '(486SLC)       '       ; IBM
        dw      0A422h
        db      '(486SLC2)      '       ; IBM
        dw      0FFFFh
.586
cpustep proc    near
        cmp     [cpu_val], 3        ; 386 or later ?
        jae     cpust_skp1
        jmp     cpust_no_BIOS_rev

cpust_skp1:
        test    [cpu_info], 1       ; CPUID supported ?
        jnz     cpust_idok          ; jump if so

; The Cyrix 6x86 can disable CPUID, so let's try and enable it

        cmp     [cpu_mfg], 7        ; Cyrix ?
        je      cpust_isCyrix       ; jump if so
        cmp     [cpu_mfg], 8        ; Cyrix ?
        jne     cpust_noid          ; jump if not
cpust_isCyrix:
        mov     ah, 0E8h
        call    read_cyrix_reg      ; get Config reg 4 (E8h)
        or      al, 80h             ; attempt to enable CPUID
        call    write_cyrix_reg
        call    read_cyrix_reg      ; see if bit 7 is on
        test    al, 80h
```

```
        jz      cpust_noid          ; jump if no CPUID enable

cpust_idok:
        mov     eax, 0              ; get vendor string function
        CPUID                       ;   for CPUID
        mov     di, offset idtext
        mov     eax, ebx
        call    xfer_bytes          ; xfer 4 text bytes from eax
        mov     eax, edx
        call    xfer_bytes          ; xfer 4 text bytes from eax
        mov     eax, ecx
        call    xfer_bytes          ; xfer 4 text bytes from eax
        OUTMSG  idtxtmg             ; display vendor string

        mov     eax, 1              ; get stepping information
        CPUID                       ;   for CPUID in al

        ; save feature flags and insert stepping id

        push    edx
        push    eax
        and     al, 0Fh             ; only lower 4 bits
        call    hex2ascii           ; convert al to ascii in bx
        mov     stepval, bh         ; xfer ascii byte
        pop     eax

        ; insert model from CPUID instruction

        push    eax
        shr     al, 4               ; get model number
        and     al, 0Fh             ; only lower 4 bits
        call    hex2ascii           ; convert al to ascii in bx
        mov     modval, bh          ; xfer ascii byte
        pop     eax
```

```
        ; insert family from CPUID instruction

        shr     ax, 8                   ; get family number
        and     al, 0Fh                 ; only lower 4 bits
        call    hex2ascii               ; convert al to ascii in bx
        mov     famval, bh              ; xfer ascii byte

        ; get the number of CPUID cases

        mov     eax, 0                  ; get number of cases
        CPUID                           ;   for CPUID in al
        call    hex2ascii
        mov     di, offset caseval
        cmp     bl, '0'                 ; if upper nibble zero, skip
        je      cpust_skp1a
        mov     [di], bl                ; insert upper nibble
        inc     di
cpust_skp1a:
        mov     [di], bh                ; insert lower nibble
        OUTMSG  stepmsg


        ; now output feature bits from CPUID instruction (edx)

        pop     edx
        push    edx
        mov     cx, 4                   ; handle 4 bytes of edx
        mov     di, offset featval

cpust_loop1:
        rol     edx, 8
        mov     al, dl
        call    hex2ascii               ; convert al to ascii in bx
```

```
        mov     [di], bx            ; insert ASCII byte into string
        add     di, 2
        loop    cpust_loop1

        pop     edx
        mov     cx, 9               ; 9 feature bits displayed
        mov     di, offset featb0

cpust_loop2:                        ; set feature to YES or NO
        test    dl, 1
        jz      cpust_skp2
        mov     word ptr [di], 'eY' ; insert 'Yes'
        mov     byte ptr [di+2], 's'
cpust_skp2:
        add     di, offset featb1 - offset featb0
        ror     edx, 1
        loop    cpust_loop2

        OUTMSG  featmsg

; Check if Cyrix and use I/O port method (unique to Cyrix)

cpust_noid:
        cmp     [cpu_mfg], 7        ; Cyrix ?
        je      cpust_isCyrix2
        cmp     [cpu_mfg], 8        ; Cyrix ?
        jne     cpust_anyid         ; if not, try BIOS method
cpust_isCyrix2:
        mov     al, 0FEh
        call    read_cyrix_reg      ; get device ID reg 0 (FEh)

        push    ax
        call    hex2ascii
        mov     di, offset cidval
```

```
        cmp     bl, '0'             ; if upper nibble zero, skip
        je      cpust_skp2a
        mov     [di], bl            ; insert upper nibble
        inc     di
cpust_skp2a:
        mov     [di], bh            ; insert lower nibble
        OUTMSG  cid0msg             ; display id value
        pop     ax

        ; now try and get the stepping and revision numbers

        and     al, 0F0h
        cmp     al, 0F0h
        je      cpust_anyid         ; no ID register
        mov     al, 0FFh
        call    read_cyrix_reg      ; get device ID reg 1 (FFh)
        cmp     al, 0
        je      cpust_anyid         ; if zero, assume invalid
        cmp     al, 0FFh
        je      cpust_anyid         ; if 0FFh, assume invalid
        push    ax
        and     al, 0F0h            ; only upper 4 bits
        call    hex2ascii           ; convert al to ascii in bx
        mov     cstpval, bh         ; xfer ascii byte
        pop     ax
        and     al, 0Fh             ; only lower 4 bits
        call    hex2ascii           ; convert al to ascii in bx
        mov     crevval, bh         ; xfer ascii byte
        OUTMSG  cid1msg             ; display stepping & revision
        jmp     cpust_exit

; if CPUID was previously used, then we are done!
```

```
cpust_anyid:
        test    [cpu_info], 1       ; CPUID supported ?
        jz      cpust_bios          ; jump if not
        jmp     cpust_exit          ; done

; Try the BIOS function for the ID.
;   Unfortunately the BIOS function is not supported by most
;   manufacturers' BIOSes.

cpust_bios:
        mov     ax, 0C910h          ; BIOS get chip revision
        int     15h                 ;   returned in cx
        jc      cpust_chk_A_step    ; carry if unsuccessful
        jcxz    cpust_chk_A_step    ; 0=not supported
        mov     al, ch
        mov     di, offset bvernum
        call    hex2ascii
        mov     [di], bx
        add     di, 2
        mov     al, cl
        call    hex2ascii
        mov     [di], bx
        add     di, 4
        mov     si, offset bvt      ; get text for step
        mov     dx, offset bver     ; output message

cpust_loop:
        cmp     word ptr [si], 0FFFFh ; at end ?
        je      cpust_out_msg       ; jump if so
        cmp     [si], ax            ; version match ?
        je      cpust_bios_match    ; jump if so
        add     si, offset bvte - offset bvt
        jmp     cpust_loop
```

```
cpust_bios_match:
        mov     cx, offset bvte - offset bvt -1
        cld
        rep     movsb                   ; xfer CPU & step text
        jmp     cpust_out_msg

; Ok - neither the CPUID or the BIOS supports getting the CPU
;   step, so a few checks may determine if a 386 or 486 is
;   revision A or if it is a later revision.

cpust_chk_A_step:
        call    hook_int6               ; hook the bad-opcode int
        cmp     [cpu_val], 3            ; 386 only ?
        jne     cpust_rev_486           ; jump if above
        mov     [badoff], offset cpust_no_rev ; for bad opcode
        mov     ax, 1
        mov     bx, 1
        mov     cl, 1
        mov     dx, 1
        db      0Fh, 0A6h, 0DAh         ; xbts  bx, dx, ax, al
        nop                             ;  (only valid on 386 A step)
        nop
        OUTMSG  stepa                   ; use Step A message
        jmp     cpust_restore

cpust_rev_486:
        cmp     [cpu_val], 4            ; 486 only ?
        jne     cpust_no_rev            ; jump if not
        mov     [badoff], offset cpust_no_rev ; for bad opcode
        db      0Fh, 0A6h, 0DAh         ; cmpxchg   bx, dx
        nop                             ;  (only valid on 486 A step)
        nop
        OUTMSG  stepa                   ; use Step A message
        jmp     cpust_restore
```

```
cpust_no_rev:
        OUTMSG  novermg             ; no support in BIOS message
cpust_restore:                      ; restore interrupt vector 6
        call    restore_int6        ; restore the int 6 handler
        jmp     cpust_exit

cpust_no_BIOS_rev:
        mov     dx, offset novermg ; no support in BIOS message
cpust_out_msg:
        mov     ah, 9
        int     21h
cpust_exit:
        ret
cpustep endp
```

Code Sample 4-8. Processor Mode Detector

This routine identifies if the CPU is in protected mode. If the CPU supports protected mode, checks are made to determine the mode (real or protected) and the current privilege level. If the CPU is an 80386 or later in protected mode, it is assumed the CPU is in V86 mode (the routine would need to be modified for incorporation in a protected-mode program). The CPU does have a Virtual 86 mode bit, but it is not readable by a program that is running in V86 mode!

The CPUMODE routine requires the CPUVALUE routine to have been previously run, and the CPU type saved in the variable CPU_VAL.

```
;-------------------------------------------------------------
;     CPU MODE
;        Check if the 286 or later CPU is in real, protected or
;        V86 mode.  It is assumed that if the 80386 or later
;        processor is in protected mode, we must be in V86 mode.
;
;        Call with:      ds:[cpu_val] set
;
;        Returns:        al = 0 protected mode not supported
```

```
;                               1 if real mode
;                               2 if protected mode
;                               3 if V86 mode
;                           ah = privilege level 0 to 3
;
;       Regs used:      ax

.386P                                   ; allow 286/386 instructions

cpumode proc    near
        push    cx
        xor     cx, cx                  ; assume no protected mode
        cmp     [cpu_val], 2            ; 286 CPU or later ?
        jb      cpum_Exit               ; jump if not
        mov     cx, 1                   ; assume real mode flag
        smsw    ax                      ; get machine status word
        test    ax, 1                   ; in protected mode ?
        jz      cpum_Exit               ; jump if not (real mode)

cpu_not_real:
        mov     cl, 2                   ; protected mode
        pushf
        pop     ax                      ; get flags
        and     ax, 3000h               ; get I/O privilege level
        shr     ax, 12
        mov     ch, al                  ; save privilege
        cmp     [cpu_val], 2            ; if 286, then protected
        je      cpum_Exit               ; jump if so

; On 386 or later, we have to assume V86 mode.  Note that the
;  next four lines of code (commented out) might seem the
;  correct way to detect V86 mode.  It will not work, since the
;  PUSHFD instruction clears the VM bit before placing it on the
;  stack.  This is undocumented on the 386 and 486, but
```

```
;  documented on the Pentium/Pentium Pro.

;        pushfd                      ; save flags on stack
;        pop     eax                 ; get extended flags
;        test    eax, 20000h         ; V86 mode ?
;        jz      cpum_out_mode       ; jump if not

        mov     cl, 3               ; return V86 mode

cpum_Exit:
        mov     ax, cx              ; return status
        pop     cx
        ret
cpumode endp
.8086
```

Code Sample 4-9. Vendor Identification

This routine identifies the CPU vendor, when the chip is not identical to Intel's part. It is capable of detecting AMD, Cyrix, IBM, Intel, NEC, and NexGen parts.

At this time, AMD produces a 386 CPU identical to Intel, making it a bit more difficult to tell them apart. Well, actually it's impossible to tell apart the 33 Mhz and 25 Mhz speed versions, but only AMD makes a 40 Mhz 386 part, and only Intel has made parts slower than 25 Mhz. This routine does not make this fine determination, but by using the CPUSPEED program after running CPUVENDOR, a few further tests can refine these details, if necessary. I did not incorporate this test inside the CPUVENDOR program, because the CPUSPEED program needs the result from this routine! The CPUTYPE program, which displays the results from these routines, does include code to detect the difference between Intel's and AMD's CPUs using the results from CPUSPEED.

```
;-------------------------------------------------------------
;    CPU VENDOR IDENTIFICATION SUBROUTINE
;       Determines the CPU manufacturer by checking a number
;       of unique aspects of each vendors chips.
;
```

```
;       Called with:    ds:[cpu_val] set with CPU type
;                       ds:[cpu_info] set with additional CPU info
;                       ds:[cpu_inst] set with instruction set
;
;       Returns:        al = Vendor number
;                               0 = Unknown, 8088 to 80286
;                               1 = Unknown vendor in CPUID string
;                               2 = NEC V20/V30
;                               3 = Intel or AMD, not IBM not Cyrix
;                               4 = Intel
;                               5 = AMD, only one to make 40Mhz 386
;                                       or from CPUID
;                               6 = IBM, only 386/486 with RDMSR
;                               7 = Cyrix or TI, no UMOV support
;                               8 = Cyrix (from CPUID or 586+)
;                               9 = NexGen (from CPUID or tests)
;                               10 = UMC
;                       transfers CPUID string to ds:[idstring]
;
;       Regs used:      ax, bx, ecx, dx
;
;       Subs called:    hook_int6, restore_int6, bad_op_handler
;                       hook_intD, restore_intD

.586P                                   ; allow CPUID instruction



vendnam db      4,  5, 'INTEL'  ; used to find vendors in CPUID
        db      8,  5, 'CYRIX'  ;  first byte is vendor number
        db      9,  6, 'NEXGEN' ;  2nd byte is the string length
        db      10, 3, 'UMC'    ;  remaining bytes are string in
        db      5,  3, 'AMD'    ;  capital letters
        db      0
```

```
cpuvendor  proc   near
        push    ds
        push    es

        mov     al, 2               ; assume NEC
        test    [cpu_info], 2       ; V20/V30 ? (only NEC makes this)
        jnz     cpuv_exit           ; jump if so
        mov     al, 0               ; assume unknown vendor
        cmp     [cpu_val], 2        ; get cpu number
        jbe     cpuv_exit           ; jump if 286 or less
        test    [cpu_info], 1       ; CPUID valid ?
        jz      cpuv_NexGen         ; jump if not

        mov     eax, 0              ; get vendor string function
        CPUID                       ;   for CPUID into ebx, ecx, edx
        mov     di, offset idstring
        mov     eax, ebx
        call    xfer_bytes          ; xfer 4 text bytes from eax
        mov     eax, edx
        call    xfer_bytes          ; xfer 4 text bytes from eax
        mov     eax, ecx
        call    xfer_bytes          ; xfer 4 text bytes from eax

; Search CPUID string for known manufacturers

        mov     ax, ds
        mov     es, ax
        push    cs
        pop     ds
        mov     si, offset vendnam
        mov     di, offset idstring
        mov     cx, 12              ; 12 bytes to look at
```

```
cpuv_loop1:
        cmp     byte ptr [si], 0    ; no more strings to check?
        je      cpuv_skp3           ; jump if not found

        mov     dl, [si]            ; save vendor number
        inc     si                  ; point to length byte
        call    find_string2        ; see if string [si] appears
                                    ;   in the cpustring at es:[di]
        jc      cpuv_skp2           ; jump if found
        mov     al, [si]
        xor     ah, ah
        add     si, ax              ; move to next string
        inc     si
        jmp     cpuv_loop1          ; try next vendor string

cpuv_skp2:
        mov     al, dl              ; set vendor number
        jmp     cpuv_exit

cpuv_skp3:
        mov     al, 1               ; unknown vendor
        jmp     cpuv_exit

; Check if it might be a NexGen - The instruction class will be
;   a 586, with an instruction set of 486, but alignment check
;   will not be supported.

cpuv_NexGen:
        cmp     [cpu_val], 5        ; 586 class?
        jne     cpuv_Cyrix          ; jump if not
        cmp     [cpu_inst], 4       ; 486 instructions supported?
        jne     cpuv_Cyrix          ; jump if not
        test    [cpu_info], 4       ; is AC supported?
        jnz     cpuv_Cyrix          ; if so, not NexGen
```

```
        mov     al, 9               ; set NexGen
        jmp     cpuv_Exit

; Check if it might be a Cyrix CPU - The DIV instruction does
;   not modify the flags.  This test is only made if CPUID
;   is not supported.

cpuv_Cyrix:
        xor     ah, ah
        sahf                        ; clear flags
        mov     ax, 10              ; actual values for the
        mov     cl, 4               ;  divide not important
        div     cl                  ; perform a divide
        lahf                        ; get the flags
        and     ah, 0FDh            ; ignore bit 1
        cmp     ah, 0               ; are flags zero?
        jne     cpuv_skp4           ; if not, not clear what it is

        mov     al, 7               ; set Cyrix or TI
        cmp     [cpu_val], 4        ; if above 486, must be Cyrix
        jbe     cpuv_Cyrix2
        mov     al, 8               ; clearly Cyrix
cpuv_Cyrix2:
        jmp     cpuv_Exit

; We'll check if it's an older Cyrix/TI CPU.  Cyrix does not need
;  the UMOV instruction, and is not supported.  (The Pentium+
;  does not support UMOV either, but the Pentium vendor has
;  already been detected, since it supports CPUID).

cpuv_skp4:
        call    hook_int6           ; hook the bad-opcode int
        call    hook_intD           ; hook general protection fault
        mov     [badoff], offset cpuv_badop  ; where to go if bad
        mov     al, 05Ah
```

```
        mov     bh, 0A5h
        clc                             ; clear carry
        db      0Fh, 10h, 0F8h          ; umov al, bh
        db      90h, 90h
        jc      cpuv_badop              ; carry should not be set
        cmp     al, bh
        jne     cpuv_badop              ; al should = bh
        jmp     cpuv_try_IBM            ; UMOV ok, likely Intel/AMD/IBM

; UMOV not supported on 386+ CPU, so must be Cyrix

cpuv_badop:
        mov     al, 7
        cmp     [cpu_val], 4            ; if above 486, must be Cyrix
        jbe     cpuv_Cyrix3
        mov     al, 8                   ; clearly Cyrix
cpuv_Cyrix3:
        jmp     cpuv_restore

; See if it's an IBM CPU.  Only IBM's chips support the Read
;   Model Specific Register (RDMSR) with ecx=1000h
;   WARNING: A bug in Windows enhanced mode will make Windows
;   shutdown if this is attempted. The CPUTYPE program will
;   not call this routine if Windows is running.

cpuv_try_IBM:
        mov     [badoff], offset cpuv_badop2 ; where to go if bad
        mov     ecx, 1000h
        RDMSR                           ; read model specific reg
        db      90h, 90h                ; safety NOPs
        mov     al, 6                   ; RDMSR works, must be IBM!
        jmp     cpuv_restore

cpuv_badop2:
```

```
        mov     al, 3                   ; not IBM, likely Intel or AMD

cpuv_restore:
        call    restore_intD            ; restore the int D handler
        call    restore_int6            ; restore int 6 vector
cpuv_exit:
        pop     es
        pop     ds
        ret
cpuvendor endp
.8086                                   ; return to 8086 instructions
```

Code Sample 4-10. Measuring CPU Speed

This routine measures the internal speed of the CPU in megahertz. Because the microcode differs between most vendors parts the instruction timing also differs between these parts. To correct for this, the CPUVENDOR program must first identify the vendor. The routine can then select a vendor-specific scaling factor to compensate for these differences.

The routine does an excellent job of measuring the internal CPU speed, independent of external cache designs. For CPUs with faster internal operation than the external bus speed, this routine returns the internal CPU speed. For example, a 100 Mhz 486DX2 chip runs at 100 Mhz inside, but 33 Mhz externally. The CPUSPEED routine will report the CPU as a 100 Mhz part.

Future chip vendors and future chip versions are likely to return a value faster than the real CPU speed, unless the vendor is identified and a suitable compensation value is assigned.

The routine uses the CLI instruction to keep interrupts from affecting the timing. Note, however, that V86 environments such as Windows enhanced mode emulate the CLI and STI instructions, maintaining a virtual interrupt flag. In such environments, interrupts are generally still enabled, even after a CLI.

```
;-------------------------------------------------------------
;    CPU SPEED DETERMINATION SUBROUTINE
;       Determines the CPU speed by accurately measuring
;       a short loop.
;
;       Called with:    ds:[cpu_val] set with CPU type
```

```
;                       ds:[cpu_mfg] set with CPU vendor
;
;       Returns:        ax = Speed in Mhz
;                       bx = raw timing value
;
;       Regs used:      ax, bx, cx

; Data Speed table - The first word is the number of times
;   to repeat the loop.  Larger numbers take longer, and are
;   used to compensate for faster CPUs.  The second word is a
;   factor adjustment to end up with the speed in Mhz.  For
;   example, on a 80486 at 33 Mhz, the 2nd word is 16550 = (33
;   * 2006 ticks)/4.  A table is included for each vendor.
;   If first word is zero, the timing is unknown (or in most
;   cases, the vendor/processor never existed).  Entries
;   with an "*" are assumed to match the Intel standard.

TIMING_TYPES    equ     8          ; number of CPUs per vendor
; Timing for type Unknown (0)
type0   dw       1, 10848          ; *8088  - loop duration, adjust
        dw       1, 10848          ; *80186  (5Mhz =  ~8345 ticks)
        dw       2, 3234           ; *80286  (12Mhz = ~1035 ticks)
        dw      10, 16200          ; *80386  (33Mhz = ~1917 ticks)
        dw      10, 16550          ; *80486  (33Mhz = ~2006 ticks)
        dw      20, 34318          ; *Pentium (60Mhz = ~2269 ticks)
        dw      20, 30935          ; *Pentium Pro
        dw       0, 0              ; *P7
; Timing for type Unknown (1)
type1   dw       1, 10848          ; *8088  - loop duration, adjust
        dw       1, 10848          ; *80186  (5Mhz =  ~8345 ticks)
        dw       2, 3234           ; *80286  (12Mhz = ~1035 ticks)
        dw      10, 16200          ; *80386  (33Mhz = ~1917 ticks)
        dw      10, 16550          ; *80486  (33Mhz = ~2006 ticks)
        dw      20, 34318          ; *Pentium (60Mhz = ~2269 ticks)
```

```
        dw     20, 30935        ; *Pentium Pro
        dw      0, 0            ; *P7
; Timing for type NEC V20/V30 (2)
type2   dw      1, 10848        ; 8088  - loop duration, adjust
        dw      1, 10848        ; *80186  (5Mhz =  ~8345 ticks)
        dw      2, 3234         ; *80286  (12Mhz = ~1035 ticks)
        dw     10, 16200        ; *80386  (33Mhz = ~1917 ticks)
        dw     10, 16550        ; *80486  (33Mhz = ~2006 ticks)
        dw     20, 34318        ; *Pentium (60Mhz = ~2269 ticks)
        dw     20, 30935        ; *Pentium Pro
        dw      0, 0            ; *P7
; Timing for type Intel (3)
type3   dw      1, 10848        ; 8088  - loop duration, adjust
        dw      1, 10848        ; 80186  (5Mhz =  ~8345 ticks)
        dw      2, 3234         ; 80286  (12Mhz = ~1035 ticks)
        dw     10, 16200        ; 80386  (33Mhz = ~1917 ticks)
        dw     10, 16550        ; 80486  (33Mhz = ~2006 ticks)
        dw     20, 34318        ; Pentium (60Mhz = ~2269 ticks)
        dw     20, 30935        ; *Pentium Pro
        dw      0, 0            ; P7
; other vendor timings inserted here (see CPUTYPE source code)

cpuspeed proc   near
        push    dx
        push    si
        mov     ah, TIMING_TYPES
        shl     ah, 1
        shl     ah, 1                 ; times 4 bytes per entry
        mov     al, [cpu_mfg]         ; get cpu manufacturer
        mul     ah                    ; ax = table index
        mov     si, ax
        add     si, offset type0      ; table of values

        mov     al, [cpu_val]         ; get cpu number
```

```
        xor     ah, ah
        shl     ax, 1
        shl     ax, 1                   ; times 4 bytes per entry
        add     si, ax                  ; point SI to value for CPU

; now setup timer 2 to time instruction execution

        mov     al, 0B0h                ; Timer 2 command, mode 0
        out     43h, al                 ; send command
        IODELAY
        mov     al, 0FFh                ; counter value FFFF
        out     42h, al                 ; send lsb to counter
        IODELAY
        out     42h, al                 ; send msb to counter
        IODELAY

; all interrupts, including NMI, are shut off to prevent any
; interrupts from affecting the timing

        cli                             ; disable interrupts
        mov     al, 80h
        out     70h, al                 ; disable NMI
        IODELAY
        in      al, 61h                 ; read the current contents
        IODELAY
        or      al, 1                   ; set gate bit on
        out     61h, al                 ; turn on timer (begins timing)
        xor     dx, dx
        mov     bx, 1
        mov     ax, [si]

; this loop executes a bunch of slow divide instructions

cpus_loop1:
        mov     cx, 10h                 ; loop value
```

```
cpus_loop2:
        div     bx                      ; ax = dx:ax/1  dx=rem
        div     bx                      ; (lots of cycles per inst)
        div     bx
        div     bx
        div     bx
        div     bx
        div     bx
        div     bx
        div     bx
        div     bx
        div     bx
        div     bx
        div     bx
        div     bx
        loop    cpus_loop2
        dec     ax
        jnz     cpus_loop1              ; loop x times for the CPU

; when the loop completes, the timer is stopped, and interrupts
; are re-enabled.

        in      al, 61h                 ; read the current contents
        IODELAY
        and     al, 0FEh                ; set gate bit off
        out     61h, al                 ; disable the counter
        xor     al, al
        out     70h, al                 ; enable NMI
        sti                             ; enable interrupts

; now the timer contents are read, and the duration of
; instruction execution is determined

        mov     al, 80h                 ; latch output command
```

```
        out     43h, al              ; send command
        IODELAY
        in      al, 42h              ; get lsb of counter
        IODELAY
        mov     dl, al
        in      al, 42h              ; get msb of counter
        mov     dh, al               ; dx = counter value
        mov     ax, 0FFFFh           ; starting value
        sub     ax, dx               ; ax = duration count
        mov     cx, ax
        mov     bx, ax               ; save for exit
        mov     ax, cx
        cmp     word ptr [si+2], 0 ; no factor adjust ?
        je      cpus_skp2            ; exit with value

; now compensate for each CPU type and vendor, since every
; type executes instructions with different timings
; (i.e. a divide on a 8088 takes from 144 to 162 clocks
; depending on the values, while a Pentium takes 25 clocks)

        mov     ax, [si+2]           ; get factor
        xor     dx, dx
        shl     ax, 1
        rcl     dx, 1
        shl     ax, 1
        rcl     dx, 1                ; factor * 4
        div     cx                   ; factor adjust (ax=dx:ax/cx)

; return the CPU speed in Mhz in AX

cpus_skp2:
        pop     si
        pop     dx
        ret
cpuspeed endp
```

Code Sample 4-11. Processor Cache Detector

This routine returns the status of the internal CPU cache on a 386 or later CPU. Surprisingly, some 386 parts, such as IBM's, have a cache! Here's a case where my first attempt proved to be a mess. Different vendors are now using different means to control the cache. Why they are not following Intel's lead is unclear. The cache is usually controlled by the system BIOS. These differences are not important to most programmers, unless you are writing a BIOS.

The CPUMODE routine requires the CPUVALUE routine to have been previously run, and the CPU type saved in the variable CPU_VAL. In addition CPUVENDOR must have been run, and the vendor type saved in CPU_MFG.

```
;---------------------------------------------------------
;    CPU CACHE
;       Check if the later CPU cache is enabled and cache
;       flags.  Cyrix, IBM, and Intel all handle the cache
;       information a little differently.
;
;       Call with:      ds:[cpu_val] set to CPU
;                       ds:[cpu_info] for CPUID flag
;                       ds:[cpu_mfg] set to manufacturer
;
;       Returns:        al = 0 if no cache
;                            1 if cache disabled
;                            2 if enabled, no write-through
;                            3 if enabled, write-through
;                            4 if enabled, write-back
;
;       Regs used:      eax, bx

.586P                                ; allow 486 instructions
cpu_cache proc  near
        xor     bl, bl               ; assume no cache
        cmp     [cpu_val], 3         ; cache only in 486+, and some 386
        jb      cpuc_type            ; jump if none
        mov     bh, [cpu_mfg]
        cmp     bh, 6                ; IBM ?
```

```
        je      cpuc_ibm            ; jump if so
        cmp     bh, 7               ; Cyrix ?
        je      cpuc_cyrix          ; jump if so
        cmp     bh, 8               ; Cyrix ?
        je      cpuc_cyrix          ; jump if so

; Use Intel method of detection (486 and later only)

        cmp     [cpu_val], 4        ; cache only in 486+
        jb      cpuc_type           ; jump if none
        mov     eax, cr0            ; get control register
        inc     bl                  ; has an internal cache
        test    eax, 40000000h      ; cache disabled ?
        jnz     cpuc_type           ; jump if so
        inc     bl                  ; return cache is enabled
        test    eax, 20000000h      ; write-through ?
        jnz     cpuc_type           ; jump if not
        inc     bl                  ; write-through enabled
        jmp     cpuc_type

; IBM method of cache enable detection

cpuc_ibm:
        mov     ecx, 1000h          ; get register 1000h
        RDMSR                       ; read model specific reg
        mov     bl, 1               ; has a cache, assume disabled
        test    eax, 80h            ; cache enabled ?
        jz      cpuc_type           ; jump if not
        mov     bl, 3               ; cache with write-through
        jmp     cpuc_type

; Cyrix is similar to Intel, but if enabled, always has write-through
```

```
cpuc_cyrix:
        mov     eax, cr0            ; get control register
        mov     bl, 1               ; has an internal cache
        test    eax, 40000000h      ; cache disabled ?
        jnz     cpuc_type           ; jump if so
        mov     bl, 3               ; write-through enabled

; if cache is enabled, older designs use write-through whereas
; newer designs (like most 586 class) support write-back cache.

cpuc_type:
        cmp     bl, 3               ; write-through enabled?
        jne     cpuc_Exit           ; jump if not
        cmp     [cpu_val], 4        ; check cpu type
        jb      cpuc_exit           ; jump if 386 (no write-back)
        ja      cpuc_586            ; jump if 586+
        cmp     [cpu_mfg], 5        ; 486 enhanced from AMD ?
        jne     cpuc_Exit           ; jump if not
        test    [cpu_info], 1       ; only AMD 486 with CPUID
        jz      cpuc_Exit           ; jump if not
        jmp     cpuc_writeback      ; it is write-back cache
cpuc_586:
        cmp     [cpu_mfg], 9        ; NexGen?
        je      cpuc_Exit           ; if so, not write-back
cpuc_writeback:
        inc     bl                  ; set to write-back enabled
cpuc_Exit:
        mov     al, bl              ; return status in al
        ret
cpu_cache endp
.8086
```

Code Sample 4-12. Processor Data Cache Size Analysis

Once it is determined the CPU has an internal cache, and it is enabled, this routine determines the size of that cache. For 386 and 486 CPUs that have a cache, a single cache exists for both data and code. However, a separate code and data cache exist on the Pentium and Pentium Pro.

This routine tests the cache based on timing successively larger reads of data. The routine begins by reading a block of 512 bytes, 128 times. In successive tests, the block size is doubled while the repeat rate is halved. Upon completion, after reading a 64K block, the times required for each block are compared to see where the largest difference occurs. When the CPU must start using external data instead of the internal cache, reading the block of data will take at least 5 percent more time. With a slow system or no external cache, the first block to use external memory is more than twice as slow as the blocks that use the internal CPU cache.

If the CPU does not have a cache or if the external cache is as fast as the internal CPU cache, the cache size returned is zero. The routine checks to be sure the differences in timing are greater than 5 percent. The routine returns a size of zero if the differences between timings are less than 5 percent. This would occur, for example, if run on an 80386 that has no internal cache, or when the 80486 cache was disabled.

```
;------------------------------------------------------------
;    FIND DATA CACHE SIZE
;       Determine the internal CPU data cache size.  Results
;       will not be valid on a CPU without an internal cache.
;
;       Call with:      nothing
;
;       Returns:        ax = cache size * 1KB
;
;       Regs used:      ax, bx, cx, si, di
;
;       Subs called:    read_n_time

timings     dw  0               ; .5 K timing
            dw  0               ; 1 K
            dw  0               ; 2 K
            dw  0               ; 4 K
            dw  0               ; 8 K
            dw  0               ; 16 K
```

```
          dw  0                    ; 32 K
          dw  0                    ; 64 K

cache_d_size proc  near
        mov     di, offset timings ; array of timings
        mov     bh, 8              ; get 8 sets of values
        mov     bl, 0              ; number of times to reread
                                   ;  (bl=0 means 256 times)
        mov     cx, 256            ; start at .5K (256 words)

chd_loop:
        call    read_n_time        ; read cx words @ ds:0,
                                   ;   returns duration in ax

        mov     [di], ax           ; save value
        add     di, 2
        shr     bl, 1              ; number of group reads/2
        cmp     bl, 0              ; if first time, bl=0 (256)
        jne     chd_skp1
        mov     bl, 128            ; second time uses 128
chd_skp1:
        shl     cx, 1              ; number of bytes * 2
        dec     bh
        jnz     chd_loop

        mov     bp, 1              ; cache size 1=1KB
        mov     dx, bp
        mov     di, offset timings
        mov     cx, 7              ; 8 timings
        xor     bx, bx             ; first time - minimal value

chd_loop3:
        mov     ax, [di]
        sub     ax, [di+2]         ; difference between times
```

```
        jns     chd_not_neg
        not     ax                      ; get positive difference
chd_not_neg:
        cmp     ax, bx                  ; which is larger ?
        jb      chd_skp2
        mov     bx, ax                  ; save new large value
        mov     dx, bp                  ; save cache size
chd_skp2:
        shl     bp, 1
        add     di, 2
        loop    chd_loop3
        shr     dx, 1                   ; adjust back

; now check that there was sufficient difference to matter
;   (i.e. maximum difference should be greater that 5% of first
;   timing value)

        mov     cx, dx                  ; save size
        mov     ax, bx                  ; bx
        mov     bx, [timings]           ; get 1st timing value
        xor     dx, dx
        div     bx                      ; ax = ax/bx, dx=remainder
        or      ax, ax
        jnz     chd_ok                  ; if ax > 0, then valid
        cmp     dx, 5                   ; if > 5% ok
        ja      chd_ok                  ; jump if so
        xor     cx, cx                  ; return zero
chd_ok:
        mov     ax, cx
        ret
cache_d_size endp


;-------------------------------------------------------------
;    READ AND TIME
;       Read CX words from memory, starting at ds:0.   Reread
```

```
;       the data BL times. Time the duration required for
;       block of reads using hardware timer 2.  Interrupts are
;       disabled during the test to improve results.
;
;       Call with:      cx = number of words to read (0FFFh max)
;                       bl = number of times to repeat read
;                       bl = 0 for 256 times
;
;       Returns:        ax = duration of reads (ax*838nS = time)
;
;       Regs used:      ax

read_n_time  proc    near
        push    dx
        push    si
        mov     al, 0B0h            ; Timer 2 command, mode 0
        out     43h, al             ; send command
        IODELAY
        mov     al, 0FFh            ; counter value FFFF
        out     42h, al             ; send lsb to counter
        IODELAY
        out     42h, al             ; send msb to counter
        IODELAY
        cli                         ; disable interrupts
        in      al, 61h             ; read the current contents
        IODELAY
        or      al, 1               ; set gate bit on
        out     61h, al             ; activate counter
        cld
        push    bx

read_again:
        push    cx
        xor     si, si              ; start from 0
```

```
        rep     lodsw                   ; read block
        pop     cx
        dec     bl                      ; number of times to cycle
        jnz     read_again

        pop     bx
        in      al, 61h                 ; read the current contents
        IODELAY
        and     al, 0FEh                ; set gate bit off
        out     61h, al                 ; disable the counter
        sti                             ; enable interrupts

        mov     al, 80h                 ; latch output command
        out     43h, al                 ; send command
        IODELAY
        in      al, 42h                 ; get lsb of counter
        IODELAY
        mov     dl, al
        in      al, 42h                 ; get msb of counter
        mov     dh, al                  ; dx = counter value
        mov     ax, 0FFFFh              ; starting value
        sub     ax, dx                  ; ax = duration count
        pop     si
        pop     dx
        ret
read_n_time endp
```

Code Sample 4-13. Undocumented Instruction Tests

This next routine tests the known undocumented instructions for the specific CPU. I know that sounds like a contradiction in terms, but I'm referring to the undocumented instructions that I described in Chapter 3, The CPU and Undocumented Instructions. Each of these undocumented instructions is tested to verify the instruction operates as specified in Chapter 3.

In case the CPU hangs while running this test, the routine first displays which instruction is about to be tested. When the test completes, it displays the result of the test. To avoid hanging the system, the routine hooks both the bad opcode interrupt and the double-fault interrupt.

Although it might be possible for an unknown instruction to hang the system, I've never had this routine crash while testing on a number of systems.

To see the results on your CPU, run the program CPUUNDOC. The screen will appear something like Figure 4-4.

Figure 4-4. Test Run of CPUUNDOC on an Intel Pentium System

```
UNDOCUMENTED INSTRUCTION TESTS v2.00 (c) 1994, 1996 FVG
Undocumented Instruction Summary for this CPU
Might support:   UMOV              (0Fh, 10h-13h)  Failed test.
Should support:  RDTSC             (0Fh, 31h)      Tested OK.
Should support:  SHL     AL,imm    (C0h, reg=110)  Tested OK.
Should support:  SHL     AX,imm    (C1h, reg=110)  Tested OK.
Should support:  SHL     AL,1      (D0h, reg=110)  Tested OK.
Should support:  SHL     AX,1      (D1h, reg=110)  Tested OK.
Should support:  AAM     imm       (D4h, 8)        Tested OK.
Should support:  AAD     imm       (D5h, 10h)      Tested OK.
Should support:  SETALC            (D6h)           Tested OK.
Should support:  ICEBP             (F1h)           Tested OK.
Should support:  TEST    AL,1      (F6h, reg=001)  Tested OK.
Should support:  TEST    AX,1      (F7h, reg=001)  Tested OK.
```

The specific instructions tested depend on the CPU. Some instructions like ICEBP, are not tested when the system is not in real mode, as the action may cause problems on some CPUs. See CPUUNDOC for the complete listings. All of the interesting parts are shown in the CHKUNDOC subroutine shown below.

```
;---------------------------------------------------------------
;    CHECK UNDOCUMENTED
;        Check and display undocumented instructions. Most
;        undocumented instructions are tested to ensure the
;        instruction works as described. The result of the
;        test is displayed.
;
;        Specific undocumented instructions are only tested
;        when it is known to work for some or all CPUs in
;        a family. For example, POP CS is only tested on
;        8088/8086 CPUs, as it conflicts with documented
;        instructions on all other CPUs.
```

```
;
;       Call with:      ds:[cpu_val] set with CPU
;                       ds:[cpu_info] set with CPU info
;                       ds:[cpu_prot] set with CPU protection
;                           status
;
;       Returns:        display undocumented information
;
;       Regs used:      ax, bx, cx, dx


cpu_val  db     0                   ; CPU value from CPUVALUE
cpu_info db     0                   ; flags from CPUVALUE
cpu_prot db     0                   ; protected state

ud_flags     db 0                   ; bit 1 = 1 if INT 1 occurred

old_int6_seg dw 0                   ; temp storage for old int 6
old_int6_off dw 0                   ;  vector (bad opcode)

badoff       dw 0                   ; temp return offset if bad
                                    ;  offset interrupt 6 called

;  text for undocumented instructions

ud_header db CR, LF
          db '  Undocumented Instruction Summary for this CPU'
          db CR, LF, '$'
ud_popcs  db 'Should support:    POP     CS      (0Fh)          $'
ud_ldall2 db 'Should support:    LOADALL         (0Fh, 05h)     $'
ud_ldall3 db 'Should support:    LOADALL         (0Fh, 07h)     $'
ud_umov   db 'Might support :    UMOV            (0Fh, 10h-13h) $'
ud_rdtsc  db 'Should support:    RDTSC           (0Fh, 31h)     $'
ud_xbts   db 'Only 386 rev A:    XBTS            (0Fh, A6h)     $'
ud_ibts   db 'Only 386 rev A:    IBTS            (0Fh, A7h)     $'
```

```
ud_shlal3 db 'Should support:    SHL     AL,imm  (C0h, reg=110) $'
ud_shlax3 db 'Should support:    SHL     AX,imm  (C1h, reg=110) $'
ud_shlal  db 'Should support:    SHL     AL,1    (D0h, reg=110) $'
ud_shlax  db 'Should support:    SHL     AX,1    (D1h, reg=110) $'
ud_aam    db 'Should support:    AAM     imm     (D4h, 8)       $'
ud_aad    db 'Should support:    AAD     imm     (D5h, 10h)     $'
ud_setalc db 'Should support:    SETALC          (D6h)          $'
ud_icebp  db 'Should support:    ICEBP           (F1h)          $'
ud_testal db 'Should support:    TEST    AL,1    (F6h, reg=001) $'
ud_testax db 'Should support:    TEST    AX,1    (F7h, reg=001) $'

ud_tested db ' Tested OK.', CR, LF, '$'
ud_untest db ' Not tested.', CR, LF, '$'
ud_untstv db ' Untested (V86 mode).', CR, LF, '$'
ud_failed db ' Failed test.', CR, LF, '$'
ud_notA   db ' Failed, not rev A.', CR, LF, '$'

chk_undoc proc  near
        OUTMSG  ud_header           ; undocumented summary header

; first, if a 286 or later, trap the bad opcode interrupt 6

        cmp     [cpu_val], 2        ; 286 or later ?
        jb      ud_skp1
        call    hook_int6           ; hook the bad opcode interrupt

; begin tests for undocumented instructions

ud_skp1:
        cmp     [cpu_val], 0        ; 8088 or V20 ?
        jne     ud_skp2             ; jump if not
        test    [cpu_info], 2       ; V20/V30 ?
        jnz     ud_skp2             ; jump if so (no POP CS)
        OUTMSG  ud_popcs            ; undocumented POP CS
        push    cs
```

```
        POPCS
        nop
        OUTMSG  ud_tested           ; tested ok

ud_skp2:
        cmp     [cpu_val], 2        ; 286 ?
        jne     ud_skp3             ; jump if not
        OUTMSG  ud_ldall2           ; LOADALL
        OUTMSG  ud_untest           ; not tested

ud_skp3:
        cmp     [cpu_val], 3        ; 386 ?
        jne     ud_skp4             ; jump if not
        OUTMSG  ud_ldall3           ; LOADALL
        OUTMSG  ud_untest           ; not tested
ud_skp4:
        cmp     [cpu_val], 3        ; 386 or later
        jb      ud_skp6
        OUTMSG  ud_umov             ; UMOV might be supported
        mov     [badoff], offset ud_skp5  ; for bad opcodes
        mov     bx, 5A5Ah
        xor     ax, ax
        db      0Fh, 10h, 0D8h      ; mov al, bl
        db      4 dup (90h)         ; nops
        cmp     al, 5Ah
        jne     ud_skp5             ; test failed
        xor     ax, ax
        db      0Fh, 11h, 0D8h      ; mov ax, bx
        db      4 dup (90h)         ; nops
        cmp     ax, 5A5Ah
        jne     ud_skp5             ; test failed
        xor     ax, ax
        db      0Fh, 12h, 0C3h      ; mov al, bl
        db      4 dup (90h)         ; nops
        cmp     al, 5Ah
```

```
        jne     ud_skp5             ; test failed
        xor     ax, ax
        db      0Fh, 13h, 0C3h      ; mov ax, bx
        db      4 dup (90h)         ; nops
        cmp     ax, 5A5Ah
        jne     ud_skp5             ; test failed
        OUTMSG  ud_tested           ; tested ok
        jmp     ud_skp6
ud_skp5:
        OUTMSG  ud_failed           ; failed UMOV test

ud_skp6:
        cmp     [cpu_val], 5        ; Pentium ?
        jb      ud_skp9             ; jump if not
        OUTMSG  ud_rdtsc            ; RDTSC
        mov     [badoff], offset ud_skp8   ; for bad opcodes
.586
        mov     eax, 0
        mov     edx, 0
        RDTSC                       ; read time stamp register
        nop
        nop
        cmp     eax, 0              ; returned value in edx:eax
        jne     ud_skp7             ;  will be ticks after reset
        cmp     edx, 0              ;  so a value of zero means
        je      ud_skp8             ;  RDTSC is not working!
.8086
ud_skp7:
        OUTMSG  ud_tested           ; ok !
        jmp     ud_skp9

ud_skp8:
        OUTMSG  ud_failed           ; failed

ud_skp9:
```

```
        cmp     [cpu_val], 3        ; 386 only ?
        jne     ud_skp13
        OUTMSG  ud_xbts             ; undocumented xbts
        mov     [badoff], offset ud_skp10  ; for bad opcodes
        mov     ax, 1
        mov     bx, 1
        mov     cl, 1
        mov     dx, 1
        db      0Fh, 0A6h, 0DAh     ; xbts  bx, dx, ax, al
        nop
        nop
        OUTMSG  ud_tested
        jmp     ud_skp11
ud_skp10:
        OUTMSG  ud_notA             ; failed, not A step of 386

ud_skp11:
        OUTMSG  ud_ibts             ; undocumented ibts
        mov     [badoff], offset ud_skp12  ; for bad opcodes
        mov     ax, 1
        mov     bx, 1
        mov     cl, 1
        mov     dx, 1
        db      0Fh, 0A7h, 0DAh     ; ibts  bx, dx, ax, al
        nop
        nop
        OUTMSG  ud_tested
        jmp     ud_skp13
ud_skp12:
        OUTMSG  ud_notA             ; failed, not A step of 386

ud_skp13:
        cmp     [cpu_val], 2        ; 80286 or later
        jae     ud_skp14            ; jump if so
        jmp     ud_skp22            ; jump if not
```

```
ud_skp14:
        OUTMSG  ud_shlal3           ; undocumented shl/sal
        mov     [badoff], offset ud_skp15 ; for bad opcodes
        mov     al, 1
        db      0C0h, 0F0h, 5       ; shl  al, 1
        db      4 dup (90h)         ; nops
        cmp     al, 20h             ; did shift occur ?
        jne     ud_skp15            ; jump if not
        OUTMSG  ud_tested
        jmp     ud_skp16

ud_skp15:
        OUTMSG  ud_failed

ud_skp16:
        OUTMSG  ud_shlax3           ; undocumented shl/sal
        mov     [badoff], offset ud_skp17 ; for bad opcodes
        mov     ax, 10h
        db      0C1h, 0F0h, 5       ; shl  ax, 5
        db      4 dup (90h)         ; nops
        cmp     ax, 200h            ; did shift occur ?
        jne     ud_skp17            ; jump if not
        OUTMSG  ud_tested
        jmp     ud_skp18
ud_skp17:
        OUTMSG  ud_failed
ud_skp18:
        OUTMSG  ud_shlal            ; undocumented shl/sal
        mov     [badoff], offset ud_skp19 ; for bad opcodes
        mov     al, 2
        db      0D0h, 0F0h          ; shl  al, 1
        db      4 dup (90h)         ; nops
        cmp     al, 4               ; did shift occur ?
        jne     ud_skp19            ; jump if not
```

```
        OUTMSG  ud_tested
        jmp     ud_skp20
ud_skp19:
        OUTMSG  ud_failed

ud_skp20:
        OUTMSG  ud_shlax            ; undocumented shl/sal
        mov     [badoff], offset ud_skp21 ; for bad opcodes
        mov     ax, 200h
        db      0D1h, 0F0h          ; shl  ax, 1
        db      4 dup (90h)         ; nops
        cmp     ax, 400h            ; did shift occur ?
        jne     ud_skp21            ; jump if not
        OUTMSG  ud_tested
        jmp     ud_skp22
ud_skp21:
        OUTMSG  ud_failed

ud_skp22:
        OUTMSG  ud_aam           ; undocumented AAM, with non 0Ah immediate
        mov     [badoff], offset ud_skp22a ; for bad opcodes
        mov     ah, 0FFh            ; garbage value (should be ignored)
        mov     al, 12h
        db      0D4h, 8             ; AAM, immediate=8
        db      4 dup (90h)         ; nops
        cmp     al, 2
        jne     ud_skp22a           ; jump if not working
        cmp     ah, 2
        jne     ud_skp22a           ; jump if not working
        OUTMSG  ud_tested           ; tested ok
        jmp     ud_skp22b
ud_skp22a:
        OUTMSG  ud_failed
```

```
ud_skp22b:
        OUTMSG  ud_aad           ; undocumented AAD, with non 0Ah immediate
        mov     [badoff], offset ud_skp22c ; for bad opcodes
        mov     ax, 0705h
        db      0D5h, 10h          ; AAD, immediate=10h
        db      4 dup (90h)        ; nops
        cmp     al, 75h
        jne     ud_skp22c          ; jump if not working
        cmp     ah, 0
        jne     ud_skp22c          ; jump if not working
        OUTMSG  ud_tested          ; tested ok
        jmp     ud_skp22d
ud_skp22c:
        OUTMSG  ud_failed

ud_skp22d:
        OUTMSG  ud_setalc          ; undocumented SETALC
        mov     [badoff], offset ud_skp23 ; for bad opcodes
        stc                        ; set carry
        SETALC                     ; set al from carry
        db      4 dup (90h)        ; nops
        cmp     al, 0FFh
        jne     ud_skp23           ; jump if not working
        clc
        SETALC                     ; set al from carry
        db      4 dup (90h)        ; nops
        cmp     al, 0
        jne     ud_skp23           ; jump if not working
        OUTMSG  ud_tested          ; tested ok
        jmp     ud_skp24
ud_skp23:
        OUTMSG  ud_failed

ud_skp24:
        cmp     [cpu_val], 3       ; 386 or later
```

```
        jb      ud_skp27
        OUTMSG  ud_icebp            ; ICEBP might be supported
        cmp     [cpu_prot], 2       ; in protected/v86 mode ?
        jb      ud_skp25            ; jump if not (ok to test)
        OUTMSG  ud_untstv           ; untested message (v86)
        jmp     ud_skp27

ud_skp25:
        mov     [badoff], offset ud_skp26 ; for bad opcodes
        push    es
        xor     ax, ax
        mov     es, ax
        cli                         ; disable interrupts
        mov     dx, es:[4]          ; get offset of int 1
        mov     cx, es:[4+2]        ; get segment
        mov     ax, offset int1test
        mov     es:[4], ax          ; set new vector
        mov     ax, cs
        mov     es:[4+2], ax
        sti                         ; enable interrupts
.386P
        mov     eax, dr7            ; get debug register
        and     eax, 0FFFFEFFFh     ; clear bit 12 to allow ICEBP
        mov     dr7, eax            ; set it
        ICEBP                       ; issue int 1
        db      4 dup (90h)         ; nops
.8086
        cli                         ; disable interrupts
        mov     es:[4], dx          ; restore original int 1
        mov     es:[4+2], cx
        sti                         ; enable interrupts
        pop     es
        test    [ud_flags], 2       ; did int 1 occur ?
        jz      ud_skp26
```

```
        OUTMSG  ud_tested           ; tested ok
        jmp     ud_skp27

ud_skp26:
        mov     [ud_flags], 0       ; clear bad opcode flag
        OUTMSG  ud_failed           ; failed ICEBP test

ud_skp27:
        OUTMSG  ud_testal           ; undocumented test al
        mov     [badoff], offset ud_skp28 ; for bad opcodes
        mov     al, 1
        db      0F6h, 0C8h, 01h     ; test al, 1
        db      4 dup (90h)         ; nops
        jz      ud_skp28            ; jump if failed
        mov     al, 0
        db      0F6h, 0C8h, 01h     ; test al, 1
        db      4 dup (90h)         ; nops
        jnz     ud_skp28            ; jump if failed
        OUTMSG  ud_tested
        jmp     ud_skp29
ud_skp28:
        OUTMSG  ud_failed

ud_skp29:
        OUTMSG  ud_testax           ; undocumented test ax
        mov     [badoff], offset ud_skp30 ; for bad opcodes
        mov     ax, 100h
        db      0F7h, 0C8h, 0, 1    ; test ax, 100h
        db      4 dup (90h)         ; nops
        jz      ud_skp30            ; jump if failed
        mov     ax, 0
        db      0F7h, 0C8h, 0, 1    ; test ax, 100h
        db      4 dup (90h)         ; nops
        jnz     ud_skp30            ; jump if failed
```

```
        OUTMSG  ud_tested
        jmp     ud_skp31
ud_skp30:
        OUTMSG  ud_failed

ud_skp31:
        cmp     [cpu_val], 2        ; 286 or later ?
        jb      ud_skp32            ; jump if not

        call    restore_int6
ud_skp32:
        ret

;----------------------------------------------------------------
; Interrupt vector 1 comes here if the ICEBP instruction is
;   supported.

int1test:
        mov     cs:[ud_flags], 2    ; set flag that we got here
        iret
```

Code Sample 4-14. Find New Undocumented Instructions

The prior routine tests all known undocumented instructions, but what about new secret instructions on future CPUs? This next routine hunts through every possible CPU instruction to locate hidden instructions.

CPUTEST works by executing an instruction not currently defined for the CPU, and seeing whether the bad opcode or double fault interrupt is issued. If neither of these interrupts occurs, the routine flags the instruction as doing something, although the routine does not know what. Although not totally bullet-proof, CPUTEST has verified no hidden instructions appear in the current batch of CPUs that I have not already documented.

If a new vendor comes out with a compatible chip, this routine should help determine whether new hidden instructions exist. Since the program has no idea what the instruction might do, interrupts are disabled, and the stack is switched over to an alternate stack until the instruction completes. Although one test is made for each instruction, it is possible that some special values must be set in a register for the instruction to operate. The RDMSR instruction is a good example of this situation, where ECX has a very limited set of values in which the RDMSR works.

The program also detects whether MMX instructions are supported by the CPU. If MMX is supported, the MMX instructions are excluded from CPUTEST.

The routine displays the opcode it is going to test before it is tested. Should the instruction do something unusual like hang the system, the display will be left showing the opcode combination that caused the fault. To see the results of this program on your system, run CPUTEST. A sample run is shown in Figure 4-5.

Figure 4-5. Partial Output of CPUTEST on an Intel 486DX System

```
ANALYSIS LOOKS FOR UNDOCUMENTED CPU INSTRUCTIONS
Testing instruction: 0Fh, 04h            Instruction invalid.
Testing instruction: 0Fh, 0Ah            Instruction invalid.
Testing instruction: 0Fh, 0Bh            Instruction invalid.
Testing instruction: 0Fh, 0Ch            Instruction invalid.
Testing instruction: 0Fh, 0Dh            Instruction invalid.
Testing instruction: 0Fh, 0Eh            Instruction invalid.
Testing instruction: 0Fh, 0Fh            Instruction invalid.
Testing instruction: 0Fh, 14h            Instruction invalid.
Testing instruction: 0Fh, 15h            Instruction invalid.
.
.
Testing instruction: 0Fh, C7h, 32h       Instruction invalid.
Testing instruction: 0Fh, C7h, 3Ah       Instruction invalid.
No hidden undocumented instructions found on this CPU.
```

Because the code for CPUTEST is not all that interesting or revealing, I've omitted it from the book. Complete source code for this routine is on the supplied diskette.

Code Sample 4-15. Find and Display Model Specific Registers

The new instructions, Read and Write Model Specific Registers (RDMSR and WRMSR), first appeared on IBM's 386 and 486 parts. Intel has also included model specific registers with the Pentium and Pentium Pro, and now AMD includes registers on the 5_K86. This instruction allows access to internal 64-bit CPU registers for special functions and features. The instruction uses ECX to specify which Model Specific Register to access. This means there are over 4 billion possible register locations!

This routine tests every possible Model Specific Register to display both known and hidden registers. On an Intel 486 33 Mhz, the routine takes about six hours to test all 4 billion combinations, and shows that standard Intel 486 parts do not use any Model Specific Registers yet. On 586+ type parts, this test runs much faster. All of the valid registers I've found on different CPUs below 80000000h have ECX values from zero to 1004h. These are all shown within a few seconds, so it is not necessary to run the complete test. As an option, you can use the "2" command line option to stop after testing the first 2000h possible register locations. In all cases, you can use Control-Break to exit the test before completion.

On the Pentium there appears a duplicate set of 32 registers starting at ECX values 80000000h. These are similar or identical to those that start at 0. To quickly view these registers, run the CPURDMSR program with the command line option "-".

The Model Specific Register instructions cause a bad opcode fault or a double fault if the register is not valid for the CPU. The CPURDMSR program hooks both of these interrupts to determine which registers are valid. Figure 4-6 shows the result of running CPURDMSR on a Pentium. This test only runs in real mode, and will exit if any other CPU mode is active.

Figure 4-6. Output of CPURDMSR on the Intel Pentium

```
DETECT AND DISPLAY MODEL SPECIFIC REGISTERS v2.00 (c) 1994, 1996 FVG
Command line options:+ to display every register tested
                     - to display 32 undocumented regs at 8000000h
Ctrl-Break to exit tests.

Register    Returned 64-bit value        Description
00000000h   edx:eax=00000000:00017AC0h   machine check address
00000001h   edx:eax=00000000:00000008h   machine check exception type
00000002h   edx:eax=00000000:00000004h   parity reversal test
00000004h   edx:eax=00000000:00000000h   instruction cache end bit test
00000005h   edx:eax=00000000:00000000h   cache data test
00000006h   edx:eax=00000000:00000000h   cache tag test
00000007h   edx:eax=00000000:0000000Eh   cache control test
00000008h   edx:eax=00000000:00000000h   TLB command test
00000009h   edx:eax=00000000:00000000h   TLB data test
0000000Bh   edx:eax=00000000:00000000h   branch target buffer tag test
0000000Ch   edx:eax=00000000:00000000h   branch target buffer target test
0000000Dh   edx:eax=00000000:0000001Ah   branch target buffer control test
0000000Eh   edx:eax=00000000:0000001Ch   new feature control
00000010h   edx:eax=00000100:E9BF4ABFh   time stamp counter
00000011h   edx:eax=00000000:00000000h   counter event selection and control
00000012h   edx:eax=00000000:00000000h   counter 0
00000013h   edx:eax=00000000:00000000h   counter 1
00000014h   edx:eax=00000000:00000000h   undocumented
FFFFFFFFh
```

This routine does not check if the Write Model Specific Register is allowable, because it is unclear what the processor might do if the register is changed. Many of these registers are used for test purposes and can cause unpredictable results if a write is attempted.

Again, since the code for CPURDMSR is not all that interesting or revealing, I've omitted it from the book. Complete source code for this routine is on the supplied diskette.

Code Sample 4-16. Display Time Stamp Counter

With the Pentium, one new undocumented instruction was added, RDTSC. This reads the hidden Time Stamp Counter, a new feature in the Pentium. The Time Stamp Counter is described in detail in Chapter 3 in the section, Undocumented Instructions.

This routine simply reads the Time Stamp Counter, using this new undocumented instruction, and displays the 64-bit return value on screen. The program runs continuously until Ctrl-Break is pressed.

Figure 4-7 shows the result of running CPURDTSC. The CPURDTSC is a rather simple program and is included with source code on the diskette. I've omitted the code from the book.

Figure 4-7. Display Time Stamp Counter

```
READ TIME STAMP COUNTER                          v1.00
This routine shows the current contents of the Time Stamp Counter
(opcode 0Fh, 31h). Use Ctrl-Break to stop test.

EDX:EAX value returned:
0000002D:36E39086h

Test aborted due to Ctrl-Break.
```

CHAPTER 5

Adapter Card Development

Creating a hardware card that has a BIOS ROM and uses I/O ports is relatively easy, but critical design decisions can make user's installation and operation either painless or pure torture! Of course this will either make your customer support group very happy, or ensure that they have to deal with endless problems. Many of the problems addressed in this section are oriented toward AT bus machines, though many points are also applicable to MCA and EISA architectures. MCA and EISA help eliminate some of the problems with flexible software-definable ROM and RAM. EISA systems also offer flexible port address selection in hardware. Of course, the AT architecture dominates the market. Intel's Plug and Play approach makes it even easier for users who have Plug and Play systems.

The ROM Header and Initialization

During the system BIOS Power-On-Self-Test (POST) operation, POST scans memory segments starting at C000 through the start of the system BIOS (typically EF80). POST looks for the presence of a ROM at each 2K boundary. The scan for ROMs is performed in several parts. Early in the POST, segments C000 through C780 are scanned for a video ROM, so the video BIOS can be initialized. This allows the POST to use the display for showing error conditions if they occur. Later, POST begins scanning at segment C800 to segment DF80 for other potential adapter ROMs.

Systems that use a 128K system BIOS, such as IBM's PS/2 line, stop scanning at DF80. Other systems that use a 64 KB system BIOS or smaller may continue to scan to segment EF80.

The original IBM AT standard had segment E000 reserved for an optional system BIOS that, to my knowledge, was never used. POST would only look at segment E000 for a header word of AA55h. If found, after a checksum validation, the system BIOS would jump to the initialization code at offset 3. The header size byte at offset 2 is not defined and is never checked. No additional scanning is performed after segment E000.

Valid ROMs are recognized by the detection of the header word AA55h. The full ROM header appears as:

```
byte 0  55h
byte 1  AAh
byte 2  Size of the ROM in 512-byte pages. (7Fh maximum)
byte 3  First byte of code for initialization
```

For example, the first bytes of one VGA BIOS appear as:

```
C000:0000  55 AA 40 EB 04 37 34 30-30 E9 A2 14 00 00 49 42  U*@k.7400i"...IB
C000:0010  4D 20 56 47 41 20 43 6F-6D 70 61 74 69 62 6C 65  M VGA Compatible
```

In this example, the 32 KB BIOS ROM size is specified with the byte 40h at offset 2. The initialization code (which jumps around the description string) begins at offset 3.

When POST detects a ROM with the header indicated, it first adds up all the bytes in the ROM as specified by the size byte. The lower byte of this sum should always return a zero. If not, the ROM initialization is skipped. If the checksum does add up to zero, the POST will then make a far call to the ROM's initialization routine at offset 3.

The ROM can now take any necessary initialization actions such as setting up the adapter card's hardware, hooking interrupt vectors, and other tasks. At the completion, the ROM must return control to the POST routine by issuing a RETF instruction.

A few old clone machines have bugs in the POST code which cause the POST to call the adapter's initialization routine *twice* during POST. This problem should be considered when writing the initialization routine.

MCA ROM Scan

On MCA-type machines, early on, the POST starts scanning at segment C000. The scan continues through segment DF80 looking for a video adapter ROM. In addition to the standard ROM header previously described, it looks for an identification string to determine if the card is a video adapter. An MCA video adapter ROM has the following additional information:

```
byte 0Ch        Video identification string (77h, 0CCh, 'VIDEO ')
byte 30h        Programmable Option Select (POS) for port 102
byte 31h        Programmable Option Select (POS) for port 103
byte 32h        Programmable Option Select (POS) for port 104
byte 33h        Programmable Option Select (POS) for port 105
```

Later in the POST, the same area from segment C000 to DF80 is rescanned for any non-video ROMs to initialize.

Setting the ROM Size and Starting Address

Offset 2 of the header contains the size of the ROM in 512-byte pages. Some common values for the ROM size are:

```
10h = 8K
20h = 16K
30h = 24K
40h = 32K
80h = 64K
```

The amount of memory used is very important in today's crammed computers. Gone are the days when no one cared about the adapter's memory requirements. As an adapter card uses more memory space, less is available for other adapters. Adapter ROMs also reduce the user's ability to load TSRs and drivers high. For ROM requirements over 32K, alternatives should be carefully considered. Some of these alternatives include a separate device driver that uses EMS or XMS memory, or paging a larger ROM into a smaller memory address space under I/O control.

ROMs only come in specific sizes (e.g., a 24K ROM is not practical). The smart designer will only use the necessary memory address space. Should the firmware require only 24K, the adapter hardware will likely use a 32K ROM. It's usually a simple matter to specify in the ROM header that the ROM appears to the system as 24K. In addition, a good design does not connect to the bus when addressing the unused portion of the ROM. In this example the last 8K of the 32K ROM will not conflict if another adapter attempts to use that address area.

Some of the early clone VGA adapter cards specified use of 24K in the ROM header, but neglected to turn off the addressing of the last 8K of the 32K ROM. This has caused all kinds of conflicts with other adapter cards and with other software that rely on accurate header information.

Most 386 and later CPU-based computers use memory management software such as DOS's EMM386, Memory Commander, QEMM, or 386MAX. All of these can reclaim unused high memory areas. Due to limitations of the processor, paging of high memory only occurs on 4K boundaries, and has a minimum size of 4K. For this reason, it's best to pick the starting address for an adapter ROM on a 4K boundary. A 4K+2K boundary will make 2K of upper memory unavailable for high loading.

Of course the most flexible design is a software-setable ROM starting address. This reduces conflicts with other adapters, and can allow the user to control the exact placement of the adapter. The display adapter ROM is normally placed at C000 when not built into the system BIOS. Non-video adapters should avoid the 32K area at C000 to prevent overlaps and out-of-sequence initialization.

ROM Code

The adapter's BIOS ROM is responsible for the card's initialization and operation. Many cards also transfer control or share control with a companion device driver. The device driver serves as the interface with the operating system. In some cases the device driver can replace a defective or outdated BIOS ROM routine.

A few rules should be followed to maximize system compatibility and compatibility with other software.

RULE 1: Avoid writes to the ROM.

Writing to ROM usually indicates a bug in the program, since the ROM cannot be written to. It's unlikely that this is intentional, but I've seen a few commercial adapter BIOSs make this error. Should the adapter ROM be shadowed using a memory manager, writing to ROM will cause a General Protection Fault. Shadowing is the trick of copying the slow 8-bit ROM BIOS contents into fast 32 or 64-bit wide RAM, and mapping the RAM at the old ROM address. This can dramatically speed up BIOS services. Current memory managers handle the general protection fault transparently, ignoring the invalid write. The reason this is important is the significant performance degradation if many writes occur. The General Protection Fault is one of the slowest processes of the CPU and memory management software, even if it just returns without performing any action.

RULE 2: Avoid fixed segments in the ROM.

Having fixed segments means a specific ROM address is hard-coded and the ROM can only exist at one address. As an example, a BIOS ROM located at D000 makes a far jump or call with D000 hard-coded as the segment. We have never seen a need to hard code a segment in ROM code that requires less than 64K of memory space. Jumps and calls instructions should always be made relative to the instruction pointer. Relative addresses also make for faster and more compact code. When installing interrupt vectors for the ROM, using the CS segment value rather than hard-coding a segment avoids these problems.

Even if the card provides no hardware ability to use an alternate ROM address, advanced memory managers like Memory Commander and 386MAX can improve system flexibility by moving ROMs to different addresses. Of course this only works when the code segment is not embedded into the code.

Tricks to Getting Necessary RAM

Some types of adapter cards already have a well-defined means of including RAM memory. For example, a VGA card reserves 128K at A000h. The adapter can use this area in a number of ways including switching pages of memory from a much larger amount of total adapter memory.

Most other adapters have no pre-specified method if they require RAM. This RAM can be supplied in a number of ways, each with advantages and drawbacks.

METHOD #1: Supply the RAM on the card.

This can be the most reliable means to have RAM, but adds cost and complexity to the adapter card. It's also hard to avoid conflicts with memory management software.

Major problems occur when a memory manager is unaware of the adapter's RAM, and perceives the RAM address as unused space. The memory manager changes the CPU's page map to fit RAM into all unused gaps in high memory. The memory manager will then load TSRs and device drivers into these areas. If the adapter's RAM area is not excluded from the memory manager, the adapter's RAM will be inaccessible. When the adapter's ROM or device driver reads or writes to the area of the adapter RAM, the adapter will read the wrong data or write on top of a TSR or device driver! Usually a system crash will result.

The current generation of memory managers will attempt to locate RAM areas to exclude. This requires the memory manager to read and write data to the adapter card's RAM memory. This has its own set of risks, but the memory manager will restore the memory to its original state. The manager assumes the act of reading and writing to the RAM will not trigger some other event.

Two approaches can greatly reduce these conflicts. First, the adapter's RAM address can be included as part of the adapter's ROM. For example, the adapter's ROM may indicate the adapter is reserving 32K for its use (see previous section). In actuality the adapter may have a 24K space for ROM, followed by an 8K RAM area. In this case, any software that scans for ROMs will not touch the 8K RAM area. This approach does require the RAM contents to be a known value at initialization so the POST's checksum is valid.

A second approach uses a false header that makes the RAM appear as a ROM. For example, the first word in the RAM is always AA55h, followed by the size of the RAM in 512-byte pages. The fourth byte is an RETF instruction (CBh). Should the BIOS or other software attempt to initialize the ROM, the RETF returns control to the caller without any action. Any software that scans for ROMs will skip the RAM area if the adapter has this header written in the first 4 bytes. If the RAM address follows the associated ROM, the ROM BIOS can initialize the RAM to the required values.

Both of these solutions will eliminate many problems, unless a system shadows the adapter ROM area. As noted earlier, this means the ROM is copied to RAM and the RAM is relocated to the same address as the original ROM. This shadowed RAM is always write protected so using either of the two methods outlined above will fail. Normally automatic shadowing of adapter ROMs is avoided, since speed-related problems often crop up. The video BIOS and system BIOS are almost always shadowed on new systems.

METHOD #2: Steal RAM from the top of the DOS main memory area.

This is handy if only a small amount of memory is needed, typically under 10 KB. Using DOS memory can save cost on the adapter card, but can create its own problems. Users are grasping for every byte of main memory possible. Reducing the user's main memory is never well received. A large number of viruses also take away memory from the top of the main memory space. It may be difficult to detect if the system is infected with a virus or if the adapter card is taking the memory, further confusing both the user and technical support staffs.

To steal memory from the main memory area during the adapter ROM initialization, the word at address 40:13h is decremented by 1 for each 1,024 bytes needed. This word holds the total amount of main memory in 1K increments. To determine the starting segment of the area to use, multiply the new value at 40:13h by 40h. You must save this segment value, since other adapter cards and programs may also take additional memory from the top, changing the value at 40:13h.

METHOD #3: Use a few bytes in the BIOS or Interrupt data areas.

There are a number of bytes that are generally not used at the end of the low BIOS data area, segment 40h (in the range of offsets CFh to FFh). Use of this memory is *not* recommended. A BIOS manufacturer may use some of these bytes in the future, and there is no easy way to ensure no conflicts are occurring.

It is also possible to store a limited amount of data in unused interrupt locations. This is a better approach than using the BIOS data area, but it is also subject to conflicts. Some system BIOSes already do this. For example, some AMI BIOSes that do not shadow the main BIOS ROM, save user-defined hard-disk type information starting at 0:300h (interrupts C0h through C7h).

If you must use one of these approaches, be sure to have some means to check the validity of the stored information, such as a checksum, just in case someone else overwrites it! Also, if someone hooks the interrupt vector where data is stored, the system will likely crash. The interrupt handler will attempt to pass control down the interrupt chain. At some point control may be passed to the vector address that holds data bytes. The system will then jump to a garbage address, usually causing a system hang.

METHOD #4: Use I/O accessed memory.

When a limited amount of memory is needed and the speed of access is not critical, several I/O port addresses can be used to access memory on the adapter. Typically one port is used to set an address, and a second port is used to transfer data. This method avoids many of the conflicts we've shown so far, but does require a slightly more complex hardware interface.

The system's CMOS memory at ports 70h and 71h uses this method. Now that I have brought up the fact there is CMOS memory, I strongly suggest avoiding the temptation to use it. CMOS is very limited, and unused bytes are hard to identify. Different BIOS manufacturers use these bytes for different purposes. See the chapter on CMOS RAM, Chapter 15, for more details if you are tempted to use it.

METHOD #5: Use a device driver to reserve the necessary RAM.

Using a device driver is an effective way to get the exact amount of memory and no more. Again, as with method #2, limited system memory is reduced, potentially preventing larger applications from operating. To some degree this objection can be overcome. First, if the device driver is designed to load high by a memory manager, this reduces the problem on many systems. Secondly, if EMS and/or XMS memory is detected, allocate as much of the needed memory from EMS or XMS.

Use of a device driver has two major considerations. First, if the adapter requires a device driver, the services the adapter provides will not be available until the CONFIG.SYS file is processed. This may become fairly complex for a disk controller, but is of little concern for most network adapters.

Carefully consider when the device driver is actually needed. With the large number of drivers and the special services they provide, it's difficult to require the driver to be "first" in CONFIG.SYS. Obviously, only one device driver can be "first." The best design eliminates this type of requirement to avoid problems for both users and technical support staff. Use of a device driver also has the risk of not being loaded. The user may set up the system improperly or may accidentally delete the device driver. If options are passed to the driver on the DEVICE= line, the user may make errors or incorrectly change options. These potential problems should be considered with any design.

Another consideration is how the adapter will function with other operating systems. A simple self-contained disk controller such as an IDE type will work with all the major operating systems (DOS, OS/2, NT, UNIX, etc.). If the adapter is to be used with other operating systems, a separate device driver will likely be required for each system.

METHOD #6: Use DMA.

Many situations can be handled without any addressable adapter memory. For these adapters, information is transferred through Direct Memory Access (DMA). The adapter can transfer large amounts of memory to the system or applications without having addressable memory on the adapter. Almost all systems transfer diskette data through DMA. Many network and scanner cards also use DMA to transfer data. Refer to the chapter on DMA for more about this process.

Unfortunately, using DMA is not without its own problems. There are a limited number of DMA channels that are available on the system. It's a big problem to locate which DMA channel to use during installation. There is no mechanism in place to accurately determine which DMA channels are already reserved for other adapters. It's almost unbelievable, but users are typically told to try different DMA channel selections until the adapter works! Considering most users have no idea what this is all about, use of DMA can create another technical support nightmare.

Plug and Play systems and EISA systems reduce the problem of DMA channel assignment. These systems provide a configuration program that usually resolves DMA channel usage and conflicts.

METHOD #7: Use very high RAM addresses.

With the 386DX and later CPUs, the 32-bit address range allows for a huge address space of 4 gigabytes. Even a 286 can access 16 megabytes of memory. An adapter can steal some of the unused address space for their use. This assumes the adapter's RAM will not conflict with actual system RAM. The RAM can be accessed through the BIOS service interrupt 15h, function 87h. If the adapter's code runs in protected mode, the memory is directly accessible.

Two major problems can occur with high RAM addresses. First, the adapter RAM can overlap with system memory. System memory conflicts have to be dealt with by informing the user of system memory limitations. Be aware that on 386 and later CPUs, many memory managers do not allow access to memory space not under its control. The manager is likely to prevent access to any address range outside system memory.

The second problem occurs if the system provides the needed address signals to the adapter card. A standard 16-bit ISA card slot can only access the first 16 megabytes of memory. An 8-bit card slot is not usable, because 8-bit slots only allow access to the first 1 megabyte of memory. A VESA local bus, PCI, MCA, or EISA specific card can access the entire 4 gigabyte address range.

METHOD #8: Is any RAM really necessary?

In some cases, the adapter may only need a small amount of temporary memory. Consider using the stack memory. This may afford a small amount of memory that, if used in a temporary fashion, may be sufficient. For reliable system operation, the amount of stack memory should be limited to less than 10 words. If too much is used, the stack may overflow when other adapters, TSRs, and adapters are used. The stack should never be considered long-term memory. Stack memory is useful while an adapter routine is handling an interrupt, but not much else.

Selecting I/O Port Numbers

There is no perfect way to ensure selected I/O port numbers will not conflict with other adapters—I'm sure you expected to hear that! You can however intelligently pick I/O port addresses that will likely minimize problems and conflicts.

The best I/O port choice is that of similar adapter cards, which cannot be used at the same time. For example, the VGA has a number of well-defined I/O ports. Using the same port assignments for a new video adapter, which replaces the system's VGA adapter, would be a smart choice. If the new adapter works *with* the old VGA adapter, then a different set of I/O ports must be selected. This approach works well for other adapter types such as sound cards, scanners, etc. Find the addresses used by other similar type adapters, and use the same port addresses.

The next best approach is to pick any number not already used. The index at the end of this book shows many common port assignments.

The best insurance is to use as few I/O ports as possible, and to allow more than one set of port addresses. This does complicate the hardware and installation instructions, but will often make the difference between failed and successful installation. If the product has some type of installation program, the program should be able to confirm the adapter is installed and using the desired I/O ports. Again this can help solve a lot of problems and reduce the headaches for both the user and your customer support group.

Lots of Ports?

The CPU designates a total of 65,536 I/O ports for a system. In reality, on the PC family of systems, there are far fewer ports. On non-MCA type systems, the motherboard and many adapter cards do not decode I/O address lines A10 and above. Address lines A10 to A15 become "don't cares," which are ignored by the system and adapter cards. This cuts the number to only 1024 useful ports. This may still seem like a lot, but there are far more manufacturers producing products that require ports than there are unique ports.

Ports 0 to FFh are reserved for the system motherboard. If an adapter card attempts to use an unused port in the range 0 to FFh, a major conflict exists. Most motherboards do not fully decode all port numbers. For example, the interrupt controller uses ports 20h and 21h, and no ports are defined for 22h to 3Fh on most systems. It would seem like there are 30 additional undefined ports from 22h to 3Fh. Not so!

Most systems ignore address lines A1 through A4 for I/O addresses 20h to 3Fh. This means that the interrupt controller is addressed not only at ports 20h and 21h, but at every port number through 3Fh! Reading port 3Eh is identical to reading port 20h. Because of this sloppy decoding, which varies from manufacturer to manufacturer, an adapter card developer would be foolish to attempt to use any port number 0 to FFh for a general purpose adapter card.

Motherboard designers can assign additional ports within the 0 to FFh range by proper I/O address decoding. Many systems that contain advanced chip sets use ports 22h and 23h to access advanced features of that chip set. This, of course, means they must decode at least I/O address lines 0 and 1 to avoid an overlap with the interrupt controller at port 20h.

Be aware that many newer motherboards include adapter cards built onto the motherboard. The most common ones are serial and parallel ports. Many PCI and MCA systems also include a VGA adapter, disk and diskette controllers. All these built-in adapters use ports in the range 100h to 3FFh. In addition, MCA systems reserve ports 100h to 107h for their Programmable Option Select (POS) functions.

Table 5-1 summarizes the port assignment ranges for non-EISA systems. The table shows how the port addresses are duplicated after port number 400h.

Table 5-1. System Port Assignment Ranges—PC/XT/AT/MCA

I/O Port Range	Used By
0000-00FF	System motherboard (i.e., DMA, Timers, keyboard controller, etc.)
0100-03FF	Optional adapter cards (i.e., VGA, Disk, Network, etc.)
0400-04FF	duplicate of 0-FF
0500-07FF	duplicate of 100-3FF
.	.
.	.
.	.
FC00-FCFF	duplicate of 0-FF
FD00-FFFF	duplicate of 100-3FF

EISA systems improve on AT-type systems by providing a clever approach to maintaining compatibility with older systems while expanding the number of assignable ports. EISA systems fully decode the I/O address lines. This allows a new area 400h to 4FFh to be used for additional system board functions. In addition, each EISA adapter slot is provided with 1024 unique ports for that slot. By defining ports based on the physical slot, EISA systems avoid any conflicts.

To make this work, an EISA adapter card must be able to change its port numbers to reflect the proper slot. The EISA configuration program is responsible for accomplishing this. Table 5-2 summarizes the EISA port assignment ranges.

Table 5-2. System Port Assignment Ranges—EISA

I/O Port Range	Used By
0000-00FF	ISA compatible system motherboard (e.g., DMA, Timers, keyboard controller, etc.)
0100-03FF	ISA optional adapter cards (e.g., VGA, Disk, Network, etc.)
0400-04FF	EISA system motherboard (DMA extensions, Unique EISA registers, etc.)
0500-07FF	duplicate of 100-3FF
0800-08FF	Additional EISA system motherboard reserved
0900-0BFF	duplicate of 100-3FF
0C00-0CFF	Additional EISA system motherboard reserved
0D00-0FFF	duplicate of 100-3FF
x000-x0FF	Available for EISA Slot x
x100-x3FF	duplicate of 100-3FF
x400-x4FF	Available for EISA Slot x
x500-x7FF	duplicate of 100-3FF
x800-x8FF	Available for EISA Slot x
x900-xBFF	duplicate of 100-3FF
xC00-xCFF	Available for EISA Slot x
xD00-xFFF	duplicate of 100-3FF

Where x = 1 to F, representing EISA adapter slot numbers 1 to 15.

Disappearing ROM and RAM

A few adapter manufacturers thought it would be clever if the adapter ROM and RAM appear only when the adapter's device driver is run. What a mistake! IBM's token ring adapter card is one of the best known cases. Ask any network administrator who has had to contend with this beast, and you'll find someone who would rather use *anything* but this card!

There are two major reasons to avoid "disappearing" ROM and RAM. First, it's very easy to install another adapter card at the same address as the "disappearing" card. Most advanced installation software will scan the ROMs in memory to help identify where a new adapter card can be installed. If the "disappearing" adapter is not active, the user may set the second adapter at the same address. This will certainly cause a big headache for all concerned.

The second problem comes with the current generation of memory managers. The most popular ones, Memory Commander, QEMM, and 386MAX, all scan for adapter cards to locate safe areas to use in loading TSRs and drivers high. Any ROM and RAM areas found are automatically excluded from use. If the adapter is not active, the area that would normally be reserved for the card will instead be switched to high-loading memory. Again this causes big headaches and lots of customer support for all involved.

Switches and Jumpers

Generally, most engineers attempt to design adapter cards with a minimum of switches and jumpers. They both add cost and are easily set incorrectly. EISA systems have the capability of avoiding all switches and jumpers because of a clever design that provides slot unique I/O ports and non-volatile slot specific configuration information. MCA adapter cards also attempt to eliminate switches and jumpers with reasonable success using the system's non-volatile configuration information. Intel's Plug and Play approach offers an excellent way to mediate and automate card configurations. For all other systems, which represent most of the market, it's almost a requirement to have at least one set of alternate I/O ports. Other functions may also necessitate jumpers and switches. For example, most EGA and VGA adapters have switches that specify the adapter configuration and avoid conflicts with other video adapter cards.

When developing a card that contains switches and/or jumpers, if at all possible, the settings should be labeled on the card in a non-cryptic manner. This may seem like common sense, but it's rarely done in practice. Sooner or later someone will need to understand what has been set. It's quite surprising how infrequently companies label this information, despite that fact that there is no added cost when the information is included as part of the printed component mask of the circuit board. Oh well, enough said about companies that love throwing money away on unnecessary technical support and fostering customer confusion.

Plug and Play

In 1994, Intel introduced a new concept for the automatic configuration of adapter cards. Many BIOSes started supporting Plug and Play in 1995, and now almost all new systems include Plug and Play support. Of course most existing systems are not yet Plug and Play. This means you will likely need a solution for older legacy systems when you provide Plug and Play support for new systems. See Appendix C for details on obtaining the complete Plug and Play specification, and other related materials and books.

CHAPTER 6

BIOS Data and Other Fixed Data Areas

The CPU, BIOS, and common adapter cards have all established a number of fixed data areas used to perform various functions in the first megabyte of address space. These addresses are generally common among all 80x86 IBM compatible computers, regardless of the operating system or hardware design. Any differences are noted with the specific address description.

Fixed data areas include the CPU's interrupt vector table, data stored inside the interrupt vector table, and BIOS and adapter card data. I've also included a great deal of information on the undocumented extended BIOS data area. Chapter 7 (Interrupt Vector Table) details interrupt vectors and data stored in the interrupt vector table.

BIOS Data Area

This area contains critical data information used by the system BIOS ROM. The BIOS data can be easily accessed by programs for special situations. On all systems this area starts at segment 40h in memory. This memory is typically addressed in two ways. The first is using segment 40h and an offset starting at 0. The second uses segment 0, with the data beginning at offset 400h. Both forms are commonly used to access the same information.

The BIOS data area also holds information for some common adapter cards such as the serial and parallel ports, and video adapters. When this optional equipment is not installed, the data values remain set to zero, and are unused.

BIOS data items relate to a service or function of the BIOS. These relationships are explained in detail under the chapter for the specific service.

Summary of BIOS Data Area

Address	Function	Size	Platform
40:00h	Serial I/O address, port 1	word	All
40:02h	Serial I/O address, port 2	word	All
40:04h	Serial I/O address, port 3	word	All
40:06h	Serial I/O address, port 4	word	All
40:08h	Parallel I/O address, port 1	word	All
40:0Ah	Parallel I/O address, port 2	word	All
40:0Ch	Parallel I/O address, port 3	word	All
40:0Eh	Extended BIOS Data Area Segment	word	AT+
	Parallel I/O address, port 4	word	PC, XT
40:10h	Equipment word	word	All
40:12h	Manufacturing test	byte	All
40:13h	Main memory size in kilobytes	word	All
40:15h	Error codes	word	AT+
	Adapter memory size	word	PC, XT
40:17h	Keyboard, shift flags, set 1	byte	All
40:18h	Keyboard, shift flags, set 2	byte	All
40:19h	Keyboard, Alt-Numpad Work Area	byte	All
40:1Ah	Keyboard, Head of buffer pointer	word	All
40:1Ch	Keyboard, End of buffer pointer	word	All
40:1Eh	Keyboard buffer	16 words	All
40:3Eh	Diskette, recalibrate status	byte	All
40:3Fh	Diskette, motor status	byte	All
40:40h	Diskette, motor timeout counter	byte	All
40:41h	Diskette, controller status return code	byte	All
40:42h	Diskette & Disk controller status bytes	7 bytes	All
40:49h	Video mode	byte	All
40:4Ah	Video, number of columns	word	All
40:4Ch	Video, total number of bytes per page	word	All
40:4Eh	Video, current page offset	word	All
40:50h	Video, cursor position, pages 0 to 7	8 words	All
40:60h	Video, cursor shape	word	All
40:62h	Video, active display page	byte	All
40:63h	Video, I/O port number base	word	All
40:65h	Video, internal mode register	byte	All

Summary of BIOS Data Area (Continued)

40:66h	Video, color palette	byte	All
40:67h	General Use offset	word	XT+
	Cassette, Time count at data edge	word	PC
40:69h	General Use segment	word	XT+
	Cassette, CRC register	word	PC
40:6Bh	Last interrupt that occurred	byte	XT+
	Cassette, Last value read	byte	PC
40:6Ch	Timer ticks count	dword	All
40:70h	Timer ticks 24 hour rollover flag	byte	All
40:71h	Keyboard, Ctrl-Break flag	byte	All
40:72h	Warm boot flag	word	All
40:74h	Hard disk, status of last operation	byte	XT+
40:75h	Hard disk, number attached	byte	XT+
40:76h	Hard disk, control byte	byte	XT+
40:77h	Hard disk, port offset	byte	XT
40:78h	Parallel printer 1, timeout	byte	XT+
40:79h	Parallel printer 2, timeout	byte	XT+
40:7Ah	Parallel printer 3, timeout	byte	XT+
40:7Bh	Parallel printer 4, timeout	byte	XT+
40:7Ch	Serial 1, timeout	byte	XT+
40:7Dh	Serial 2, timeout	byte	XT+
40:7Eh	Serial 3, timeout	byte	XT+
40:7Fh	Serial 4, timeout	byte	XT+
40:80h	Keyboard, Pointer to start of buffer	word	XT+
40:82h	Keyboard, Pointer to end of buffer	word	XT+
40:84h	Video, number of rows	byte	EGA+
40:85h	Video, pixels per character	word	EGA+
40:87h	Video, options	byte	EGA+
40:88h	Video, switches	byte	EGA+
40:89h	Video, save area 1	byte	VGA+
40:8Ah	Video, save area 2	byte	VGA+
40:8Bh	Diskette, configuration data	byte	AT+
40:8Ch	Hard disk, status register	byte	AT+
40:8Dh	Hard disk, error register	byte	AT+
40:8Eh	Hard disk, task complete flag	byte	AT+
40:8Fh	Diskette, controller information	byte	AT+
40:90h	Diskette 0, media state	byte	AT+
40:91h	Diskette 1, media state	byte	AT+
40:92h	Diskette 0, operational starting state	byte	AT+
40:93h	Diskette 1, operational starting state	byte	AT+
40:94h	Diskette 0, current cylinder	byte	AT+
40:95h	Diskette 1, current cylinder	byte	AT+

Summary of BIOS Data Area (Continued)

40:96h	Keyboard, status flags 3	byte	AT+
40:97h	Keyboard, status flags 4	byte	AT+
40:98h	User's wait flag pointer	dword	AT+
40:9Ch	User's wait count	dword	AT+
40:A0h	Wait flag	byte	AT+
40:A1h	Local Area Network	7 bytes	AT+
40:A8h	Video, parameter control block pointer	dword	EGA+
40:CEh	Clock, days since 1980 (some BIOSs)	dword	AT+
50:00h	Print screen status	byte	All

Detailed BIOS Data Area

Location	Description	Size	Platform
40:00h	Serial I/O Address, Port 1	word	All

This word value is used to store the first I/O port number for serial port 1. Normally serial port 1 is at I/O address 3F8h, but any serial I/O port can be stored in this word.

Location	Description	Size	Platform
40:02h	Serial I/O Address, Port 2	word	All

This word value is used to store the first I/O port number for serial port 2. Normally serial port 2 is at I/O address 2F8h, but any serial I/O port can be stored in this word.

Location	Description	Size	Platform
40:04h	Serial I/O Address, Port 3	word	All

This word value is used to store the first I/O port number for serial port 3. Any serial I/O port can be stored in this word.

Location	Description	Size	Platform
40:06h	Serial I/O Address, Port 4	word	All

This word value is used to store the first I/O port number for serial port 4. Any serial I/O port can be stored in this word.

Location	Description	Size	Platform
40:08h	Parallel I/O Address, Port 1	word	All

The parallel I/O port number is stored in this word. Typical I/O address values are 3BCh, 378h, or 278h, but any parallel I/O port can be stored in this word. It is accessed as PRN or LPT1 from most OSes.

Location	Description	Size	Platform
40:0Ah	Parallel I/O Address, Port 2	word	All

The parallel I/O port number is stored in this word. Typical I/O address values are 378h or 278h, but any parallel I/O port can be stored in this word. It is accessed as LPT2 from most OSes.

Location	Description	Size	Platform
40:0Ch	Parallel I/O Address, Port 3	word	All

The parallel I/O port number is stored in this word. Normally parallel port 3 is set to I/O address 278h, but any parallel I/O port can be stored in this word. It is accessed as LPT3 from most OSes.

Location	Description	Size	Platform
40:0Eh	EBDA Segment	word	AT+

40:0Eh	EBDA Segment	word	AT+
	Parallel I/O Address, Port 4	word	PC, XT

On AT+ systems, when an extended BIOS data area is used, this word holds the segment of the extended BIOS data area. The extended BIOS data area typically uses 1K of RAM at the top of main memory at 639K. See the section, Extended BIOS Data Area, later in this chapter for more information.

On the PC and XT, and in some cases when no extended BIOS data are used, this word can be used to store a fourth parallel port I/O address. The I/O port address must be loaded by an application or driver. Unlike parallel ports 1, 2, and 3, POST does not set this word. It is accessed as LPT4 from most OSes.

Location	Description	Size
40:10h	Equipment Word	word

This holds configuration information determined by POST. Its value can be accessed directly in RAM or obtained by interrupt 11h, Equipment Determination.

AT+ Systems

bit	15 = x	Number of parallel printer ports detected by POST (0 to 3)
	14 = x	
	13 = 1	Internal modem installed (some systems)
	12 = 0	Unused
	11 = x	Number of serial ports attached (0 to 4)
	10 = x	
	9 = x	

	8 = 0	Unused	
	7 = x	Number diskette drives (if bit 0 is 1)	
	6 = x	bit 7	bit 6
		0	0 = 1 drive
		0	1 = 2 drives
	5 = x	Initial video mode type	
	4 = x	bit 5	bit 4
		0	0 = EGA or later adapter determines type
		0	1 = Color 40 columns by 25 rows
		1	0 = Color 80 columns by 25 rows
		1	1 = Monochrome 80 columns by 25 rows
	3 = 0	Unused	
	2 = 1	Mouse port installed on system board	
	1 = 1	Math coprocessor installed	
	0 = 1	Boot diskette drive installed	

PC/XT Systems

bit	15 = x	Number of parallel printer ports detected by POST (0 to 3)	
	14 = x		
	13 = 0	Unused	
	12 = 1	Game port attached	
	11 = x	Number of serial ports attached (0 to 4)	
	10 = x		
	9 = x		
	8 = 0	Unused	
	7 = x	Number diskette drives (if bit 0 is 1)	
	6 = x	bit 7	bit 6
		0	0 = 1 drive
		0	1 = 2 drives
		1	0 = 3 drives
		1	1 = 4 drives
	5 = x	Initial video mode type	
	4 = x	bit 5	bit 4
		0	0 = Unused
		0	1 = Color 40 columns by 25 rows
		1	0 = Color 80 columns by 25 rows
		1	1 = Monochrome 80 columns by 25 rows

3 = x	System memory board size		
2 = x		bit 3	bit 2
		0	0 = 16K
		0	1 = 32K
		1	0 = 48K
		1	1 = 64K (Wow!)
1 = 1	Math coprocessor installed (XT only)		
0 = 1	Boot diskette drive installed		

Location	Description	Size	Platform
40:12h	Manufacturing Test	byte	All

This byte is used to indicate a manufacturing test mode. Manufacturing test mode is usually initiated by connecting a test jumper on the motherboard. This is read during POST and the jumper status loaded into this byte. Manufacturing test mode is typically used to initiate a continuous test cycle for system burn-in and to assist with some types of repairs. The operations of the manufacturing test vary with each BIOS vendor.

Non-MCA Systems

bits	7-1 = x	Unused, and may be in any state
	0 = 0	Normal operation
	1	Manufacturing test mode

MCA Systems

bit	7 = x	POST flag, unknown function
	6 = x	Unused
	5 = x	Unused
	4 = 1	POST flag, slot 4 has adapter ID=EDAFh
	3 = 1	POST flag, video type 80x25 color
	2 = x	POST flag, unknown function
	1 = x	Unused
	0 = 0	Normal operation
	1	Manufacturing test mode

Location	Description	Size	Platform
40:13h	Main Memory Size	word	All

This word contains the size of the main memory in 1024-byte blocks. If an extended BIOS data area is used, the main memory size is reduced by the size of that area. For a typical 640K system, this word will contain the value 280h.

Many viruses will also steal some memory at the top of the main memory area. This results in keeping the virus active, such as hooking key interrupts to this "hidden" area. When the virus becomes active during the boot process, it stores itself in the top of main memory and reduces the main memory value by the amount it needs to stay resident.

Location	Description	Size	Platform
40:15h	Error Codes	word	AT+
	Adapter Memory Size	word	PC, XT

On current systems, these two bytes are assignable by the BIOS vendor for any purpose. On the IBM AT it is used to store manufacturing test error codes.

On the PC/XT this word indicates the size of main memory that is not on the system board. The value is the RAM size in kilobytes. It is referred to in some technical references by the confusing term *I/O Channel Size*. The obsolete term *I/O Channel* is simply the adapter card bus.

Location	Description	Size	Platform
40:17h	Keyboard Shift Flags 1	byte	All

This byte holds the current status of the keyboard shift and toggle states. It is maintained by the low-level keyboard handler, interrupt 9.

Caps Lock, Num Lock, and Scroll Lock, all provide LED status on the AT keyboard. The interrupt 9 handler is responsible for updating the keyboard LED state from these flags. There is no visual indicator provided for the state of the Insert toggle bit.

bit	7 = 1	Insert on
	6 = 1	Caps Lock on
	5 = 1	Num Lock on
	4 = 1	Scroll Lock on
	3 = 1	Alt key down (left or right)
	2 = 1	Control key down (left or right)
	1 = 1	Left Shift key down
	0 = 1	Right Shift key down

Location	Description	Size	Platform
40:18h	Keyboard Shift Flags 2	byte	All

This byte holds the current status of the keyboard shifts and toggle states. It is maintained by the low-level keyboard handler, interrupt 9.

bit	7 = 1	Insert key down
	6 = 1	Caps Lock key down
	5 = 1	Num Lock key down
	4 = 1	Scroll Lock key down
	3 = 1	Pause activated
	2 = 1	Sys Req key down (except 83 key keyboards)
	1 = 1	Left Alt key down (101/102 key keyboards only)
	0 = 1	Left Ctrl key down (101/102 key keyboards only)

Location	Description	Size	Platform
40:19h	Keyboard Alt-Numpad Work Area	byte	All

The keyboard handler, interrupt 9, will create a value from 0 to FFh when the decimal value is entered on the num-pad while the ALT key is held down. This byte is used as a temporary work area by the keyboard handler to create the final value as each num-pad key is entered.

Location	Description	Size	Platform
40:1Ah	Keyboard, Head of Buffer Pointer	word	All

This word contains the offset in segment 40 from where to retrieve the next key in the keyboard buffer. If this value points to the same address as in location 40:1Ch, the end of buffer pointer, there are no keys currently in the buffer.

As a key is removed from the buffer, this pointer is incremented by 2, until the last word of the buffer is reached. At that point it is reset to the start of the keyboard buffer area. In so doing, a FIFO type buffer is created to ensure the first key stored in the buffer is always the first out. Interrupt 16h (the intermediate keyboard handler) is responsible for removing keys from the buffer upon request and updating this pointer.

Location	Description	Size	Platform
40:1Ch	Keyboard, End of Buffer Pointer	word	All

This word contains the offset in segment 40 used to store the tail of the keyboard buffer. If this value points to the same location as in location 40:1Ah, the head of buffer pointer, there are no keys currently in the buffer.

As a key is added to the buffer, this pointer is incremented by 2 until the last word of the buffer is reached. At that point it is reset to the start of the keyboard buffer area. In doing so, an FIFO type buffer is created to ensure that the last key stored in the buffer is always the last one out. Interrupt 9h (the low-level keyboard handler) is responsible for adding keys to the buffer. In addition, interrupt 16h offers a function to force keys into the buffer.

When the action of adding a new key to the queue would cause the end pointer to equal the head of the buffer pointer, the buffer is considered full. This means that the 16-word buffer at RAM address 40:1Eh can hold 15 keys. When the buffer is full, additional keys are discarded by the keyboard handler interrupt 9. An error beep is generated for each discard.

Location	Description	Size	Platform
40:1Eh	Keyboard Buffer	16 words	All

This 16-word FIFO buffer holds up to 15 keys. A saved key has its scan code in the upper byte of the word. The lower byte holds the ASCII conversion of the scan code. Two pointers at RAM address 40:1Ah and 40:1Ch control the first and last entries of the buffer.

Location	Description	Size	Platform
40:3Eh	Diskette, Recalibrate Status	byte	All

If any bit 0 to 3 is set to zero, the specified drive is uncalibrated and must be recalibrated before the next seek. A recalibration is performed by the controller by retracting the read/write head to track 0. The controller then attempts to obtain a sufficient signal to confirm track 0 is valid. The drive becomes uncalibrated after a system reset and whenever a new diskette is inserted into the drive.

The diskette BIOS, interrupt 13h, issues a command to the diskette controller and must remain in a tight loop waiting for bit 7 to become active. When the diskette controller completes an operation, it issues IRQ 6, which invokes interrupt Eh. The diskette BIOS interrupt Eh handler sets bit 7 in this byte as a flag for diskette operation complete. When bit 7 is set, the diskette BIOS knows the operation is complete. The diskette BIOS then clears the bit and proceeds to its next task or exits if all tasks are complete.

bit	7 = 1	Diskette hardware interrupt has occurred (int 0Eh from the diskette controller hardware)
	6 = x	Unused
	5 = x	Unused
	4 = x	Unused
	3 = 0	Drive 3 uncalibrated (PC/XT only)
	2 = 0	Drive 2 uncalibrated (PC/XT only)
	1 = 0	Drive 1 uncalibrated
	0 = 0	Drive 0 uncalibrated

Location	Description	Size	Platform
40:3Fh	Diskette; Motor Status	byte	All

This byte holds status information about the current state of each diskette drive. If the motor timeout counter at address 40:40h expires, all four motor-on bits are cleared.

bit	7 = 0	Current operation - Read or Verify
	1	Current operation - Write or Format that requires delay
	6 = x	Unused
	5 = x	Drive select
	4 = x	bit 5 bit 4

	0	0 = drive 0
	0	1 = drive 1
	1	0 = drive 2 (PC/XT only)
	1	1 = drive 3 (PC/XT only)
3 = 1	Drive 3 motor on (PC/XT only)	
2 = 1	Drive 2 motor on (PC/XT only)	
1 = 1	Drive 1 motor on	
0 = 1	Drive 0 motor on	

Location	Description	Size	Platform
40:40h	Diskette, Motor Timeout	byte	All

BIOS

This byte is used to keep the diskette motor running for a set time after the last diskette access. When any diskette activity occurs, this byte is loaded with a countdown value. Interrupt 8, the timer tick, decrements this counter each tick. Should the count decrement to zero, the interrupt 8 handler turns off any active diskette drive motors.

The length of the delay until the motor is turned off is set by the third byte of the diskette parameter table (see Chapter 10, Table 10-2). Most systems have this set at 25h to let the motor run for 2 seconds before it is turned off. If another diskette action occurs before the counter expires, the timer is reset to begin the countdown again.

Location	Description	Size	Platform
40:41h	Diskette Controller Return Code	byte	All

BIOS

If the BIOS interrupt 13h diskette handler detects an invalid value for an AH subfunction, then the error condition is stored in this byte. For diskette controller functions, this return code is based on the two returned status bytes from the controller. See Chapter 10 (Diskette System) for expanded return status code descriptions.

Value	**Status**
0	Operation successful
1	Invalid value passed or unsupported function
2	Missing address mark
3	Diskette is write protected
4	Requested sector not found
6	Diskette change line active
8	DMA overrun
9	Data boundary error
0Ch	Media type not found
10h	CRC error during read
20h	Diskette controller or drive problem
40h	Seek operation failed
80h	Timeout—The diskette drive failed to respond

Location	Description	Size	Platform
40:42h	Disk & Diskette Controller Status Register 0	byte	All

This byte along with the next six bytes are used for the diskette controller on all systems. For systems with a PC/XT-type hard disk controller, the first four bytes are also used to hold the controller's sense data when an error is detected. See Chapter 11 (Hard Disk System) for details about these four bytes for the hard disk.

At the completion of a diskette operation, the BIOS interrupt 13h handler reads status register 0 from the controller. This byte is defined as shown.

bit	7 = x	Interrupt code
	6 = x	bit 7 bit 6
		0 0 = Normal completion of command occurred
		0 1 = Abnormal termination of command while executing
		1 0 = Invalid command attempted
		1 1 = Abnormal termination, ready line on, or diskette changed
	5 = 1	Commanded seek completed
	4 = 1	Drive fault—Either a fault signal was received from the drive or unable to complete recalibrate due to track 0 signal failure
	3 = 1	Drive not ready—occurs when read/write attempted while the drive is not ready or an attempt is made to read/write side 1 of a single-sided diskette (160K, which is very obsolete)
	2 = x	Head state when interrupt occurred
	1 = x	Drive unit selected when interrupt occurred
	0 = x	bit 1 bit 0
		0 0 = drive 0
		0 1 = drive 1
		1 0 = drive 2 (PC/XT only)
		1 1 = drive 3 (PC/XT only)

Location	Description	Size	Platform
40:43h	Diskette Controller Status Register 1	byte	All

At the completion of a diskette operation the BIOS interrupt 13h handler reads status register 1 from the controller, and stores it here.

bit	7 = 1	Controller attempted to access a sector beyond the last cylinder on the diskette
	6 = 0	Unused
	5 = 1	CRC error detected on read

	4 = 1	DMA overrun—the DMA did not transfer data to or from the controller fast enough, such that a timeout occurred in the controller
	3 = 0	Unused
	2 = 1	Data problem—Cannot find sector, or cannot read the diskette ID field
	1 = 1	Attempted write or format inhibited due to write protection
	0 = 1	Missing address mark—attempts to read the diskette's ID address mark failed after two passes of the index hole

Location	Description	Size	Platform
40:44h	Diskette Controller Status Register 2	byte	All

At the completion of a diskette operation the BIOS interrupt 13h handler reads status register 2 from the controller, and stores it here.

bit	7 = 0	Unused
	6 = 1	A deleted data address mark was encountered while reading diskette dataor verifing data
	5 = 1	CRC error detected in data field
	4 = 1	Wrong cylinder—The cylinder read differs from the one specified by the controller
	3 = 1	The condition of equal is satisfied during verification
	2 = 1	During verify, the controller cannot find a sector on the cylinder that matches the verify condition
	1 = 1	Bad cylinder—The cylinder read differs from the one specified by the controller and has the value FFh
	0 = 1	The address mark (or deleted address mark) cannot be found while reading diskette.

Location	Description	Size	Platform
40:45h	Diskette Controller Cylinder Number	byte	All

At the completion of a diskette operation the BIOS interrupt 13h handler reads the cylinder number. This is the cylinder track number after the executed command completes. Some BIOSes do not save this byte.

Location	Description	Size	Platform
40:46h	Diskette Controller Head Number	byte	All

At the completion of a diskette operation the BIOS interrupt 13h handler reads the head number. A value 0 indicates head 0 used for side 0 of the diskette. The value 1 indicates head 1 for side 1 of the diskette. This is the head number at command completion. Some BIOSes do not save this byte.

Location	Description	Size	Platform
40:47h	Diskette Controller Sector Number	byte	All

At the completion of a diskette operation the BIOS interrupt 13h handler reads the sector number. This is the sector number at command completion. Some BIOSes do not save this byte.

Location	Description	Size	Platform
40:48h	Diskette Controller Bytes Written	byte	All

At the completion of a diskette operation the BIOS interrupt 13h handler reads the number of bytes written in a sector. Some BIOSes do not save this byte.

Location	Description	Size	Platform
40:49h	Video Mode	byte	All

The active video mode number is stored here. In Chapter 9, Video System, the possible modes for different adapters are shown.

Location	Description	Size	Platform
40:4Ah	Video Columns	word	All

After a video mode is set, the video BIOS stores the number of columns in this word. In graphics modes the value represents the number of columns of text possible using the video BIOS functions to write text. For 80-column modes, the value stored is 50h.

Location	Description	Size	Platform
40:4Ch	Video—Bytes per Page	word	All

The video BIOS stores the number of bytes per page for the last video mode set.

Be aware that different system and video BIOS manufacturers may store slightly different values in this word. For example, in mode 3 the display can show 2000 characters on screen (4000 total bytes including attributes). Between each page are 96 unused bytes. Some systems will then indicate there are 4000 bytes per page, while others will indicate 4096.

Location	Description	Size	Platform
40:4Eh	Video—Current Page Offset	word	All

The video BIOS stores the offset of the current page in this word. For page zero in all modes, the stored offset is 0. In the case of video mode 3, the offset for page 1 would be 1000h (4096).

Location	Description	Size	Platform
40:50h	Video—Cursor Position Page 0	word	All

This word holds the cursor position for page 0. The low byte holds the row where the cursor appears and the high byte holds the column. These entries are zero-based. The top left corner has a word value of 0000. For a video mode with 80 columns and 25 rows, the bottom right corner cursor position would have a value of 4F18h.

Location	Description	Size	Platform
40:52h	Video—Cursor Position Page 1	word	All

This word holds the cursor position for page 1. See location 40:50h for details.

Location	Description	Size	Platform
40:54h	Video—Cursor Position Page 2	word	All

This word holds the cursor position for page 2. See location 40:50h for details.

Location	Description	Size	Platform
40:56h	Video—Cursor Position Page 3	word	All

This word holds the cursor position for page 3. See location 40:50h for details.

Location	Description	Size	Platform
40:58h	Video—Cursor Position Page 4	word	All

This word holds the cursor position for page 4. See location 40:50h for details.

Location	Description	Size	Platform
40:5Ah	Video—Cursor Position Page 5	word	All

This word holds the cursor position for page 5. See location 40:50h for details.

Location	Description	Size	Platform
40:5Ch	Video—Cursor Position Page 6	word	All

This word holds the cursor position for page 6. See location 40:50h for details.

Location	Description	Size	Platform
40:5Eh	Video—Cursor Position Page 7	word	All

This word holds the cursor position for page 7. See location 40:50h for details.

Location	Description	Size	Platform
40:60h	Video—Cursor Shape	word	All

This word holds the cursor shape. The low byte holds the ending scan line number, while the upper byte at address 40:61h holds the starting scan line. With video mode 3 the character cell is normally 16 scan lines high on a VGA. To turn off the cursor, set the ending scan line number above the starting scan line number. Table 6-1 shows some typical cursor shapes in this mode.

Table 6-1. Sample Cursor Shapes

Shape	Value
two line cursor at bottom	0607h
lower half cursor	0307h
upper half or quarter cursor	0003h
full box cursor	0007h
blank cursor	0100h

Location	Description	Size	Platform
40:62h	Video—Active Display Page	byte	All

The video BIOS stores the current page number in this byte. The default after any video mode is set is always page 0. Keep in mind the allowable number of pages differs in some modes depending on the video hardware.

Location	Description	Size	Platform
40:63h	Video—I/O Port Number Base	word	All

This word holds the base port number of the active video adapter. Table 6-2 details the standard port number used, depending on the adapter and monitor used.

Table 6-2. Base Video Port Address

Adapter	Port used with Monochrome Monitor	Port used with Color Monitor
MGA/HGA	3B4h	n/a
CGA	3D4h (composite mono)	3D4h
EGA	3B4h	3D4h
VGA/SVGA	3B4h	3D4h
XGA	3B4h	3D4h

Location	Description	Size	Platform
40:65h	Video—Internal Mode Register	byte	All

This byte contains the last value sent to the video adapter's internal mode register at port 3D8h on CGA-type adapters, and 3B8h on MDA adapters. The EGA/VGA adapter has no equivalent port, but the EGA/VGA video BIOS maintains this value for downward compatibility for video modes 0 to 7. Table 6-3 shows the standard values for different video modes.

bit	7 = 0	Unused
	6 = 0	Unused
	5 = 0	Screen attribute bit 7 controls background intensity
	1	Screen attribute bit 7 controls blinking
	4 = 1	Mode 6, 640x200 graphics operation, 2 colors (monochrome)
	3 = 1	Enable video signal
	2 = 0	Color operation
	1	Monochrome operation
	1 = 1	Modes 4 and 5, 320x200 graphics operation
	0 = 1	Text modes 2 and 3, 80 columns x 25 rows

Table 6-3. Internal Mode Bits for Each Video Mode

		Bits							
Video Mode	**Description**	**7**	**6**	**5**	**4**	**3**	**2**	**1**	**0**
0	40x25 text, mono	0	0	?	0	?	1	0	0
1	40x25 text, color	0	0	?	0	?	0	0	0
2	80x25 text, mono	0	0	?	0	?	1	0	1
3	80x25 text, color	0	0	?	0	?	0	0	1
4	320x200 graphics, mono	0	0	x	0	?	1	1	0
5	320x200 graphics, color	0	0	x	0	?	1	1	0
6	640x200 graphics, mono	0	0	x	1	?	1	1	0
7	80x25 text, mono	0	0	?	x	?	x	x	1

x = don't care
? = depends on user options, default 1

Location	Description	Size	Platform
40:66h	Video—Color Palette	byte	All

This byte contains the last value sent to the video adapter's internal color register at port 3D9h on CGA type adapters. EGA/VGA adapter has no equivalent port, but the EGA/VGA video BIOS maintains this value for downward compatibility for video modes 0 to 6.

bit	7 = 0	Unused
	6 = 0	Unused
	5 = 0	Mode 5 foreground colors—green/red/yellow
	1	Mode 5 foreground colors—cyan/magenta/white
	4 = 0	Normal background colors
	1	Intensified background colors—text modes only
	3 = x	Intensified Border color in text 40x25 mode and background color on graphics mode 5.
	2 = x	Red
	1 = x	Green
	0 = x	Blue

Location	Description	Size	Platform
40:67h	General Use Offset	word	XT+
	Cassette, Time Count	word	PC

On XT+ systems, this word is used as a temporary value for a variety of purposes including stack pointer for protected mode on 286+ systems, the offset portion of a pointer for ROM initialization, and other temporary functions.

On AT+ systems it is also used as a return pointer with address 69h during some reset operations. After a reset, the CMOS shutdown byte 0Fh instructs the POST how to proceed. A number of options are provided to jump to the far address stored in these two words. This allows the system to switch from protected mode back to real mode, which can only be done with a processor reset.

On PC systems this word contains a count used for timing data bits with the obsolete cassette drive.

Location	Description	Size	Platform
40:69h	General Use Segment	word	XT+
	Cassette, CRC Register	word	PC

On XT+ systems, this word is used as a temporary value for a variety of purposes including stack pointer for protected mode on 286+ systems, the segment portion of a pointer for ROM initialization, and other temporary functions.

On AT+ systems it is also used as a return pointer along with offset 40:67h during some reset operations. See location 40:67h for additional details.

On PC systems this word is used for cassette CRC operations.

Location	Description	Size	Platform
40:6Bh	Last Interrupt	byte	XT+
	Cassette, Last Value Read	byte	PC

On XT+ systems, this byte stores the hardware IRQ bit when an invalid interrupt occurs. Part of the BIOS initialization process will point all unused interrupt vectors to a single BIOS interrupt handler. This handler checks if the interrupt was caused by a hardware event. If not, this value is loaded with FFh. If a hardware interrupt did occur, the offending hardware interrupt that occurred is stored here.

bit	7 = 1	IRQ 7 hardware interrupt occurred
	6 = 1	IRQ 6 hardware interrupt occurred
	5 = 1	IRQ 5 hardware interrupt occurred
	4 = 1	IRQ 4 hardware interrupt occurred
	3 = 1	IRQ 3 hardware interrupt occurred
	2 = 1	IRQ 2 hardware interrupt occurred (IRQ 8 to 15 on AT)
	1 = 1	IRQ 1 hardware interrupt occurred
	0 = 1	IRQ 0 hardware interrupt occurred

As an example, a hardware interrupt occurs on IRQ 3 (interrupt 0Bh) and the vector points to the unused BIOS interrupt handler. The unused interrupt handler detects that IRQ 3 was the one to make the request, and loads the binary value 00001000 into this byte. Bit 2 will be set when any interrupt occurs on IRQ 8 through 15 (AT+ only).

On the PC platform this byte holds the last data byte read from the cassette.

Location	Description	Size	Platform
40:6Ch	Timer Ticks Count	dword	All

This double word holds the current count of timer ticks. It is incremented by every call to the interrupt 8 BIOS timer ticks service routine. Interrupt 8 is issued when timer 0 rolls over, once every 54.9 ms.

If the count reaches 1800B2h, equivalent to 24 hours worth of ticks, the count is reset. In addition, the timer ticks rollover flag is set at RAM address 40:70h. The BIOS clears this counter during the POST power on sequence. For AT+ systems, the operating system will normally read the CMOS clock value and set the timer ticks count so that rollover will occur at midnight.

Location	Description	Size	Platform
40:70h	Timer Ticks Rollover Flag	byte	All

This flag is set to 1 each time the timer ticks count at 40:6Ch is reset. This normally occurs once every 24 hours. The flag is reset when the BIOS time of day service routine function 0 is issued.

A lot of confusion exists about this flag. The rollover flag has two states, 0 and 1. The flag never increments beyond 1. In normal operation the operating system periodically issues a BIOS time of day interrupt 1Ah with function 0. This gets the current ticks count and this flag. After the flag is read, the BIOS service handler clears the flag. A problem occurs should an application program issue an interrupt 1Ah, function 0, before the operating system does. In this case, the flag information is lost to the operating system, and the operating system's date does not change at midnight. Programmers should avoid the use of Interrupt 1Ah, function 0. Simply read the values directly from memory, at 40:6Ch and 40:70h.

Location	Description	Size	Platform
40:71h	Keyboard Control-Break Flag	byte	All

When the key combination Ctrl-Break has been pressed, bit 7 is set. In addition, when Ctrl-Break occurs, the keyboard BIOS issues interrupt 1Bh for handling the Ctrl-Break action.

bit	7 = 1	Control-Break key has been pressed
	6-0 = x	Unused, but may be in any state

Location	Description	Size	Platform
40:72h	Warm Boot Flag	word	All

This word is used to signal a warm boot. When the three keys Alt, Ctrl, and Delete are pressed together, the keyboard BIOS sets the Warm Boot Flag to 1234h. On the PC and XT the keyboard BIOS then jumps to the beginning of the Power-On-Self-Test (POST) routines. On the AT+ the keyboard BIOS issues a hardware CPU reset, which also runs the POST routine. POST checks the warm boot flag. If the value is 1234h, the memory tests are skipped, and if an optional EGA+ video adapter is installed, its memory check is also skipped.

Two other values are used on the PS/2 and some AT+ system BIOSes. Value 4321h indicates the POST must skip memory tests and leave memory unchanged. Value 64h is used for manufacturing test. When POST sees a warm boot flag value of 64h, the POST tests are cycled continuously. This can be useful to detect problems during burn-in or to help identify intermittent problems.

Location	Description	Size	Platform
40:74h	Hard Disk—Status of Last Operation	byte	XT+

When a hard disk operation completes, the status from that operation is stored in this byte. Return codes are shown in Table 6-4. Not all hard disk service routines generate every code shown. Refer to Chapter 11 (Hard Disk System) for detailed information on each return code.

Table 6-4. Hard Disk Return Status Codes

Hex Code	Description
0	Successful operation
1	Bad command or parameter
2	Missing address mark
3	Removable media write protected
4	Requested sector not found
5	Reset failed
6	Removable media disk changed
7	Drive parameter activity failed
8	DMA overrun
9	Data boundary error
Ah	Bad sector flag detected
Bh	Bad track detected
Dh	Invalid number of sectors on format
Eh	Control data address mark detected
Fh	DMA arbitration level out of range
10h	ECC error during read
11h	ECC corrected data error
20h	Hard disk controller or drive problem
31h	No media in removable media drive
40h	Seek operation failed
80h	Timeout
AAh	Drive is not ready or is not selected
B0h	Volume not locked in drive
B1h	Volume locked in drive
B2h	Volume not removable
B3h	Volume in use
B4h	Lock count exceeded
B5h	Valid eject request failed
BBh	Undefined error occurred
CCh	Write fault on selected drive
E0h	Status error flagged with controller error code zero (no error!)
FFh	Sense operation failed

Location	Description	Size	Platform
40:75h	Hard Disk—Number Attached	byte	XT+

This byte indicates the number of hard disks detected by POST. A maximum of two hard drives is supported by the PC and XT BIOS, and most other BIOSes dated before 1996. Most newer BIOSes (1996 and later) support four hard drives. Disk controllers that provide their own BIOS are only limited by the controller's capability. I've seen a few systems that incorrectly include IDE CD-ROM drives in this count of hard drives.

Location	Description	Size	Platform
40:76h	Hard Disk—Control Byte	byte	XT+

This byte holds temporary control flags for the hard disk BIOS. During many hard disk operations, the BIOS loads this byte from the disk parameter table control byte at offset 8. If either bit 6 or 7 is on, no retries are attempted if an error occurs. On some systems, bit 3 is used to indicate the drive has more than eight heads. This byte is not used on PS/2 BIOSes that directly support ESDI drives.

bit	7 = 1	Disable retries on disk error
	6 = 1	Disable retries on disk error
	5 = 0	Unused
	4 = 0	Unused
	3 = 1	Drive has more than eight heads
	2 = 0	Unused
	1 = 0	Unused
	0 = 0	Unused

Location	Description	Size	Platform
40:77h	Hard Disk—Port Offset	byte	XT

This byte holds a temporary offset to the hard disk port number. It is only used in XT hard disk BIOSes and a few early hard disk adapter BIOSes.

Location	Description	Size	Platform
40:78h	Parallel Printer 1 Timeout	byte	XT+

This byte holds a fixed value used by the printer interrupt 17h handler. When the printer BIOS is outputting a character to the printer, the BIOS uses this value as the maximum delay while the printer is busy. If the printer is still busy after this delay, the BIOS returns with a failed error code.

The POST sets the initial value to 14h on most systems. In most BIOSes the timeout period is based on instruction delays. The duration will vary depending on the system clock speed and typically ranges from 2 to 8 uS per count. For a timeout value of 14h, this means a waiting period of 40 to 160 uS. All AT+ systems and a few XT BIOSes use this word.

Location	Description	Size	Platform
40:79h	Parallel Printer 2 Timeout	byte	XT+

This holds the timeout value for parallel printer 2. Refer to 40:78h for a detailed description.

Location	Description	Size	Platform
40:7Ah	Parallel Printer 3 Timeout	byte	XT+

This holds the timeout value for parallel printer 3. Refer to 40:78h for a detailed description.

Location	Description	Size	Platform
40:7Bh	Parallel Printer 4 Timeout	byte	XT
	VDS Support	byte	AT+

This holds the timeout value for parallel printer 4. Refer to 40:78h for a detailed description. Some systems do not allow a fourth printer. In this case, the byte is unused or may be used for another unrelated purpose.

On AT+ systems, Virtual DMA Services (VDS) uses bit 5 to indicate if VDS is active. To help the VDS supplier properly chain interrupt 4Bh, MCA systems use bit 3 as a flag.

For MCA systems only, if bit 3 is one, interrupt 4Bh must be chained by the VDS provider. This means the VDS provider passes unused VDS function numbers to the old interrupt 4Bh handler. If bit 3 is zero, then the interrupt 4Bh segment vector must be checked at 0:12Ch. If the segment value at 0:12Ch is not 0, E000, or F000, then the VDS provider must chain interrupt 4Bh. If the segment value is 0, E000 or F000, then VDS must not chain interrupt 4Bh. In this case, invalid VDS functions are simply returned. The prior interrupt 4Bh vector is ignored.

When not used as Printer Timeout:

bit	7 = 0	Unused
	6 = 0	Unused
	5 = 1	VDS services supported
	4 = 0	Unused
	3 = 1	Chaining required on interrupt 4Bh (see text)
	2 = 0	Unused
	1 = 0	Unused
	0 = 0	Unused

Location	Description	Size	Platform
40:7Ch	Serial 1 Timeout	byte	XT+

This byte holds a fixed timeout value used by the serial port interrupt 14h handler. When the serial port BIOS sends a character, the BIOS uses this value as the maximum delay while waiting for the Data Terminal Ready (DTR) and Request To Send (RTS) lines to become active. The BIOS then uses the timeout value again to wait until status indicates the controller is ready to transmit. If either timeouts occur, the interrupt handler returns an error condition.

Similar actions occur while receiving a character. First, the timeout value is used while waiting for Data Set Ready (DSR) line to become active. Then the BIOS uses the timeout value again to wait until the serial controller status indicates the receive buffer has a character.

If either condition fails to occur within the timeout duration, the interrupt handler returns an error condition.

The POST sets the initial value to 1 on most systems. Each count is equivalent to about 2 ms of delay. Since the timeout is based on instruction delays, the duration will vary depending on the system clock speed and BIOS implementation.

Location	Description	Size	Platform
40:7Dh	Serial 2 Timeout	byte	XT+

This byte holds the timeout value for serial port 2. Refer to address 40:7Ch for a detailed description.

Location	Description	Size	Platform
40:7Eh	Serial 3 Timeout	byte	XT+

This byte holds the timeout value for serial port 3. Refer to address 40:7Ch for a detailed description.

Location	Description	Size	Platform
40:7Fh	Serial 4 Timeout	byte	XT+

This byte holds the timeout value for serial port 4. Refer to address 40:7Ch for a detailed description.

Location	Description	Size	Platform
40:80h	Keyboard—Start of Buffer	word	XT+

This word holds a pointer to the start of the keyboard buffer in segment 40h. The system default buffer start is at address 1Eh. As keys are added and removed from the buffer, this value does not change, unlike the keyboard head and tail pointers.

Location	Description	Size	Platform
40:82h	Keyboard—End of Buffer	word	XT+

This word holds a pointer to the byte past end of the keyboard buffer in segment 40h. The system default buffer end is at address 3Eh. As keys are added and removed from the buffer, this value does not change, unlike the keyboard head and tail pointers.

Location	Description	Size	Platform
40:84h	Video—Number of Rows	byte	EGA+

This byte holds the number of rows on screen, less one. For a 25-line display the stored value is 18h. It is only applicable to video adapters with their own BIOS ROM, such as the EGA/VGA and others.

Location	Description	Size	Platform
40:85h	Video—Pixels per Character	word	EGA+

This word holds the number of scan lines per character. For a typical VGA text character in a 16-pixel-high by 9-pixel-wide cell, the stored value is 10h. It is only applicable to video adapters with their own BIOS ROM, such as the EGA/VGA and others.

Location	Description	Size	Platform
40:87h	Video—Options	byte	EGA+

The options of the video adapter are stored in this byte. It is only applicable to video adapters with their own BIOS ROM, such as the EGA/VGA.

bit	7 = x	Copied from bit 7 of the last video mode set
	0	clear display buffer RAM when video mode set
	1	do not clear display buffer RAM when video mode set
	6 = x	Memory on video card
	5 = x	bit 6 bit 5 0 0 = 64K 0 1 = 128K 1 0 = 192K 1 1 = 256K or more
	4 = x	Unused
	3 = 1	Video adapter active
	2 = 1	Wait for display enable
	1 = 0	Color monitor attached (use ports 3Dxh)
	1	Monochrome monitor attached (use ports 3Bxh)
	0 = 0	CGA emulation of cursor (see int 10h, function 12h, cursor size control)

Location	Description	Size	Platform
40:88h	Video—Switches	byte	EGA+

The switch and feature connector settings from the advanced video adapter are stored in this byte. It is only applicable to video adapters with their own BIOS ROM, such as the EGA/VGA.

The adapter switch setting bits 0 to 3 directly relates to the EGA/VGA switches SW1 to SW4. When a switch is in the closed-on position, the value saved for the switch is zero. Bits 0 to 3 control which adapter is the active display during the boot process and is referred to as the primary display. In addition, the switch selections allow for an optional CGA or MDA type secondary display.

A number of newer adapters eliminate the switches by using non-volatile memory on the adapter. In this case, the adapter's setup software controls these bits.

Be aware that the switches are only read once during the video start-up operations. After that point, some video options may change the state of the lower four bits. For example, Interrupt 10h, function 12h, subfunction 30h changes the number of scan lines, and loads new values into the lower nibble of this byte.

The rarely used feature connector has two lines which are read when the video BIOS POST runs. The feature connector also has an output state line. The two feature lines 0 and 1 are first read while the output state line is set to 0. Next the state line is set to 1, and the two feature lines are read again. The feature line values are saved in bits 4 through 7.

bit	7 = x	Value of the Feature 0 line on the feature connector, in state 0
	6 = x	Value of the Feature 1 line on the feature connector, in state 0
	5 = x	Value of the Feature 0 line on the feature connector, in state 1
	4 = x	Value of the Feature 1 line on the feature connector, in state 1
	3 = x	Adapter type switch settings
	2 = x	
	1 = x	
	0 = x	

bit 3	2	1	0	Primary	Secondary
0	0	0	0	= MDA	color 40x25
0	0	0	1	= MDA	color 80x25
0	0	1	0	= MDA	hi-res 80x25
0	0	1	1	= MDA	hi-res enhanced
0	1	0	0	= CGA 40x25	monochrome
0	1	0	1	= CGA 80x25	monochrome
0	1	1	0	= color 40x25	MDA
0	1	1	1	= color 80x25	MDA
1	0	0	0	= hi-res 80x25	MDA
1	0	0	1	= hi-res enhanced	MDA
1	0	1	0	= monochrome	CGA 40x25
1	0	1	1	= monochrome	CGA 80x25
1	1	0	0	= Unused	
1	1	0	1	= Unused	
1	1	1	0	= Unused	
1	1	1	1	= Unused	

Location	Description	Size	Platform
40:89h	Video—Save area 1	byte	VGA+

This byte holds information for advanced video BIOSes, VGA or later. Some video BIOS vendors may use this byte for other uses. The two scan line bits 7 and 4 take effect only after a mode set. Bit 7 is cleared after the new scan line setting takes place.

bit	7 = 0	Scan lines 350 or 400 (see bit 4)
	1	Scan lines 200 (bit 4=0)
	6 = x	Unused on IBM and most other systems, although some vendors use this bit for their own purposes
	5 = 0	Unused
	4 = 0	Scan lines 200 or 350 (see bit 7)
	1	Scan lines 400 (bit 7=0)
	3 = 0	Set color registers to defaults on any mode set
	1	Do not change color registers on any mode set
	2 = 0	Color monitor attached
	1	Monochrome monitor attached
	1 = 0	Normal colors
	1	Convert color register values to gray scales
	0 = 1	All available modes are allowable on attached monitor

Location	Description	Size	Platform
40:8Ah	Video—Save area 2	byte	VGA+

This bytes holds information for some advanced video BIOSes, VGA or later.

Location	Description	Size	Platform
40:8Bh	Diskette—Configuration Data	byte	AT+

This byte holds the data transfer rate information for the diskette drive. It is used to save time when the controller has already established the proper data rate for a diskette.

The data rate at the start of an operation is used when the media type has not been established. Different rates are used in part to determine the correct diskette type. For a system with a 1.44 MB drive and a 720 KB diskette, the BIOS first tries a 500 K bits per second rate. When that fails, the BIOS tries the 250 K bits per second rate. For a 720 KB diskette, 250 K bits per second is the correct rate.

Not all BIOSes save the last drive stepping rate. In this case, bits 4 and 5 may be unused on these systems.

bit 7 = x, 6 = x — Last data rate sent to the diskette controller

bit 7	bit 6
0	0 = 500 K bits/s
0	1 = 300 K bits/s
1	0 = 250 K bits/s
1	1 = Rate not set yet, or 1 M bits/s on some systems

5 = x, 4 = x — Last drive stepping rate sent to the diskette controller

bit 5	bit 4

	0	0 = 8 ms
	0	1 = 7 ms (typical)
	1	0 = 6 ms (typical)
	1	1 = 5 ms
3 = x	Data rate set at the start of operation	
2 = x	bit 3	bit 2
	0	0 = 500 K bits/s
	0	1 = 300 K bits/s
	1	0 = 250 K bits/s
	1	1 = 1 M bits/s (when supported)
1 = x	Unused on most systems, unknown function on some clones	
0 = x	Unused on most systems, unknown function on some clones	

Location	Description	Size	Platform
40:8Ch	Hard Disk—Status	byte	AT+

The actual status from the hard disk controller port 1F7h is stored in this byte. Some BIOSes do not support this function. See port 1F7h described in Chapter 11 (Hard Disk System).

Location	Description	Size	Platform
40:8Dh	Hard Disk—Error	byte	AT+

The error register from the disk controller port 1F1h is stored in this byte. Some BIOSes do not support this function. See port 1F1h described in Chapter 11.

Location	Description	Size	Platform
40:8Eh	Hard Disk—Task Complete Flag	byte	AT+

The hard disk BIOS sets this value to 0 at the start of a disk controller task. The disk controller hardware signals when the task is complete with IRQ 14, interrupt 76h. The interrupt 76h handler then sets this byte to 0FFh. Early BIOSes do not support this function.

Location	Description	Size	Platform
40:8Fh	Diskette—Controller Information	byte	AT+

This byte is used for diskette controller information. It is supported on most AT+ BIOSes.

bit	7 = 0	Unused
	6 = 1	Drive 1 type has been determined
	5 = 1	Drive 1 is multi-rate
	4 = 1	Drive 1 has a diskette changed detection line

3 = 0	Unused
2 = 1	Drive 0 type has been determined
1 = 1	Drive 0 is multi-rate
0 = 1	Drive 0 has a diskette changed detection line

Some early AT BIOS documentation incorrectly states the function of this byte is to indicate when the system has a disk/diskette adapter card. These early AT systems left this byte unused.

Location	Description	Size	Platform
40:90h	Diskette 0—Media State	byte	AT+

This byte contains diskette media state information for AT+ systems, drive 0. A value of 0 indicates no drive.

bit 7 = x, 6 = x — Data transfer rate

bit 7	bit 6
0	0 = 500 K bits/s
0	1 = 300 K bits/s
1	0 = 250 K bits/s
1	1 = 1 M bits/s

5 = 1	Double stepping required (1.2 MB drive with 360 K diskette)
4 = 1	Known media in diskette drive
3 = 0	Unused

2 = x, 1 = x, 0 = x — Determination of last access

bit 2	1	0
0	0	0 = Trying 360 K media in 360 K drive
0	0	1 = Trying 360 K media in 1.2 M drive
0	1	0 = Trying 1.2 M media in 1.2 M drive
0	1	1 = Known 360 K media in 360 K drive
1	0	0 = Known 360 K media in 1.2 M drive
1	0	1 = Known 1.2 M media in 1.2 M drive
1	1	0 = Unused State
1	1	1 = 720 K media in 720 K drive or 1.44 M media in 1.44 M drive

Location	Description	Size	Platform
40:91h	Diskette 1—Media State	byte	AT+

This byte contains diskette media state information for AT+ systems, drive 1. A value of 0 indicates no drive.

bit 7 = x	Data transfer rate				
6 = x	bit 7	bit 6			
	0	0 = 500 K bits/s			
	0	1 = 300 K bits/s			
	1	0 = 250 K bits/s			
	1	1 = 1 M bits/s			
5 = 1	Double stepping required (1.2 MB drive with 360 K diskette)				
4 = 1	Known media in diskette drive				
3 = 0	Unused				
2 = x	Determination of last access				
1 = x	bit	2	1	0	
0 = x		0	0	0 =	Trying 360 K media in 360 K drive
		0	0	1 =	Trying 360 K media in 1.2 M drive
		0	1	0 =	Trying 1.2 M media in 1.2 M drive
		0	1	1 =	Known 360 K media in 360 K drive
		1	0	0 =	Known 360 K media in 1.2 M drive
		1	0	1 =	Known 1.2 M media in 1.2 M drive
		1	1	0 =	Unused state
		1	1	1 =	720 K media in 720 K drive or 1.44 M media in 1.44 M drive

Location	Description	Size	Platform
40:92h	Diskette 0—Operational Starting State	byte	AT+

This byte holds starting state information for diskette drive 0. Some BIOSes do not use this byte.

bit 7 = x	Data transfer rate	
6 = x	bit 7	bit 6
	0	0 = 500 K bits/s
	0	1 = 300 K bits/s
	1	0 = 250 K bits/s
	1	1 = 1 M bits/s
5 = x	Unknown function	
4 = x	Unknown function	
3 = 0	Unused	
2 = 1	Drive type has been determined	
1 = 1	Drive is multirate	
0 = 1	Drive has diskette changed detection line	

Location	Description	Size	Platform
40:93h	Diskette 1—Operational Starting State	byte	AT+

This byte holds starting state information for diskette drive 1. Some BIOSes do not use this byte.

bit	7 = x	Data transfer rate
	6 = x	bit 7 bit 6
		0 0 = 500 K bits/s
		0 1 = 300 K bits/s
		1 0 = 250 K bits/s
		1 1 = 1 M bits/s
	5 = x	Unknown function
	4 = x	Unknown function
	3 = 0	Unused
	2 = 1	Drive type has been determined
	1 = 1	Drive is multirate
	0 = 1	Drive has diskette changed detection line

Location	Description	Size	Platform
40:94h	Diskette 0—Current Cylinder	byte	AT+

This byte holds the current cylinder that drive 0 is positioned on.

Location	Description	Size	Platform
40:95h	Diskette 1—Current Cylinder	byte	AT+

This byte holds the current cylinder that drive 1 is positioned on.

Location	Description	Size	Platform
40:96h	Keyboard—Status Flags 3	byte	AT+

This is a status byte for advanced keyboards. Bits 6 and 7 are used to read the keyboard ID. This ID is typically the value ABh followed by 41h. This is done after reset to check if the keyboard is attached and responding.

bit	7 = 1	In process of reading two byte ID of keyboard
	6 = 1	Last keyboard byte input is first ID char, now get second
	5 = 1	Force Num Lock on after getting keyboard ID (reset)
	4 = 1	101 to 104 key keyboard
	3 = 1	Right alt key depressed

2 = 1	Right control key depressed
1 = 1	When scan code received is E0h, this flag is set and the next byte fromthe keyboard is read
0 = 1	When scan code received is E1h, this flag is set and the next byte fromthe keyboard is read
= 1	Keyboard installed (early ATs)

Location	Description	Size	Platform
40:97h	Keyboard—Status Flags 4	byte	AT+

This byte holds additional keyboard status information and LED state information.

bit	7 = 1	Keyboard transmit error
	6 = 1	LED update in progress
	5 = 1	Keyboard sent a Resend byte, FEh
	4 = 1	Keyboard sent an Acknowledge byte, FAh
	3 = 0	Unused
	2 = 1	Caps Lock LED on
	1 = 1	Num Lock LED on
	0 = 1	Scroll Lock LED on

Location	Description	Size	Platform
40:98h	User's Wait Flag Pointer	dword	AT+

The General BIOS Services, interrupt 15h, function 83h, provides a user timer service. The user calls the function with the number of microseconds to wait and a pointer to user's flag byte. The user's pointer is stored in this double word in segment:offset form.

The flag byte's bit 7 is initialized by the user to 0. When the user-specified time period expires, the user's flag byte, bit 7 is set to 1. See 40:9Ch for more about the related counter.

Location	Description	Size	Platform
40:9Ch	User's Wait Count	dword	AT+

This double word is used as a countdown timer for the user timer service, interrupt 15h, function 83h. This function loads the user's wait time in microseconds into this double word. When activated, every 976 uS this counter is decremented by 976. When the count goes below zero, the user's wait flag byte, bit 7, is set to 1. See RAM address 40:98h for the user's wait flag pointer.

The CMOS Real-Time Clock's periodic interrupt output is connected to IRQ 8. With the proper setup, the Real-Time Clock generates a periodic signal at a 1,024 Hz rate. This means an interrupt occurs every 976 microseconds. IRQ 8 is fed to interrupt 70h, which decrements this double word counter by 976.

The maximum time delay is a value of FFFFFFFFh. This converts to a time delay of 71 minutes. There are two accuracy errors in this counting mechanism. The count is changed by

976 every 976.562 microseconds. This means the countdown is 0.06 percent fast. A more critical effect occurs when small values are used. As an extreme example, to time one millisecond, the counter is loaded with 1,000. The timer then trips after two interrupts, 1.95 milliseconds later. This results in a 95 percent inaccuracy!

Location	Description	Size	Platform
40:A0h	Wait Flag	byte	AT+

This byte is used for the delay service of interrupt 15h, function 86h. The function is called with a double word value of delay in microseconds. This flag is related to the wait counter and wait flag pointer, at locations 40:9Ch and 40:98h.

Bit 0 is used to control the status of wait. Interrupt 15h, function 86h, sets the user wait flag pointer to this byte. This means that bit 7 is set when the time period elapses.

bit	7 = 1	Wait time elapsed (if this address is stored in the User's Wait Flag Pointer at 40:98h)
	6 = x	Unused
	5 = x	Unused
	4 = x	Unused
	3 = x	Unused
	2 = x	Unused
	1 = x	Unused
	0 = 0	No wait is in progress
	1	Wait in progress

Location	Description	Size	Platform
40:A1h	Local Area Network Bytes	7 bytes	AT+

These seven bytes are documented by IBM as reserved for the local area network. They are not used within the system BIOS. There is no specification on how these bytes are to be used by a specific network.

Location	Description	Size	Platform
40:A8h	Video—Parameter Control Block Pointer	dword	EGA+

This double word points to a table of additional pointers for the advanced video system, such as the VGA adapter. This table of pointers is shown in Table 6-5. The pointer is stored in segment:offset form.

Table 6-5. Video Save Table

Offset	Type	Pointer To
0	dword	Video parameters
4	dword	Parameter save area
8	dword	Alphanumeric character set
Ch	dword	Graphics character set
10h	dword	Second save table pointer (see Table 6-6)
14h	dword	Unused (0:0)
18h	dword	Unused (0:0)

The value at offset 10h in Table 6-5 points to a second table of information:

Table 6-6. Second Video Save Table

Offset	Type	Pointer To
0	word	Total bytes in this table
2	dword	Combination code table
6	dword	Second alphanumeric character set
Ah	dword	User palette table
Eh	dword	Unused (0:0)
12h	dword	Unused (0:0)
16h	dword	Unused (0:0)

Refer to Chapter 9, Video System, for detailed information.

Location	Description	Size	Platform
40:CEh	Clock—Days since 1980	word	AT+

In some BIOSes, this word holds the current number of days since 1980.

Location	Description	Size	Platform
50:00h	Print Screen Status	byte	All

The print screen function is initiated by the low-level keyboard BIOS when the Print-Screen key is pressed. The keyboard BIOS issues interrupt 5, the print screen handler. This handler controls the status of the print screen operation through this status byte. This byte is accessed at address 40:100h as well as at 50:0.

The byte holds the following values and functions:

00h =	Print screen ready
01h =	Print screen in progress
FFh =	Error occurred while printing—Out of paper, Error signaled from printer, or timeout while waiting to become non-busy

Extended BIOS Data Area

Some system BIOSes store additional data just below the top of DOS. The most common use of this Extended BIOS Data Area (EBDA) is to hold data for a motherboard mouse port, hard disk parameters, and disk track buffers.

The extended BIOS data area segment is normally stored in the word at 40:0Eh. Since this word was originally used to hold the printer port 4 port number, not all BIOSes follow this semi-undocumented standard. This pointer is typically set to 9FC0h on a 640K system, representing a 1K extended BIOS data area. Though rare, a few systems reserve 2K or even 4K for the extended BIOS data area.

A quick way to see if an extended BIOS data area is active on a system is to run the DOS MEM command. For a 640K system without memory management, a system with no extended BIOS data will normally return 640K or 655360 bytes total conventional memory. When the extended BIOS data area is used, this number will be smaller.

The main memory size word at 40:13h is reduced by the extended BIOS data area size. This word is normally set to 280h, indicating 640K of main memory. If the value is somewhat less, like 27Fh, then 1K just below the display area is likely being used for the extended BIOS data area. Some systems, like a few SCSI based older Hewlett-Packard systems, use 4K for hard disk information.

The only legitimate use for the area below the display adapter is for an extended BIOS data area. Be aware that a number of viruses also use this technique to hide the virus code in the same area. Most viruses will use between 2K and 4K.

Since this information is mostly undocumented, it is unclear if most vendors follow IBM. Phoenix appears to follow IBM for systems that included BIOS mouse support and a watchdog timer. Some functions described are not supported in different models. This information may change in future BIOS versions, but some items such as the mouse have remained consistent for the last six years or so.

Extended BIOS Data Usage Summary

The following list shows the common usage of the Extended BIOS Data Area. This includes data relating to the mouse, watchdog timer, keyboard, diskette, and hard disk. The segment location is flexible, but is typically at 9FC0h on a system with 640K of main memory. The segment from 40:0Eh is shown as "EBDA."

Address	Function	Size
EBDA:0	Size of Extended BIOS Data Area	byte
EBDA:17h	Number of POST Error Entries	byte
EBDA:18h	Error Log	5 words
EBDA:22h	Mouse device driver far call	dword
EBDA:26h	Mouse flags 1	byte
EBDA:27h	Mouse flags 2	byte
EBDA:28-2Fh	Mouse data	8 bytes
EBDA:39h	Watchdog timer	word

Address	Function	Size
EBDA:3D-4Ch	Hard disk 0 parameter table	16 bytes
EBDA:4D-5Ch	Hard disk 1 parameter table	16 bytes
EBDA:68h	Cache control	byte
EBDA:6Eh	Repeat rate of keyboard	byte
EBDA:6Fh	Delay until keyboard repeats	byte
EBDA:70h	Number of hard drives attached	byte
EBDA:71h	DMA channel for hard drive	byte
EBDA:72h	Hard disk interrupt status	byte
EBDA:73h	Hard disk operation flags	byte
EBDA:74h	Old interrupt 76h vector pointer	dword
EBDA:78h	Hard disk DMA type	byte
EBDA:79h	Hard disk, status of last operation	byte
EBDA:7Ah	Hard disk, timeout value	byte
EBDA:7E-8Dh	Hard disk controller return status words	8 words
EBDA:E7h	Diskette Drive Type	byte
EBDA:ECh	Hard Disk Parameters Loaded	byte
EBDA:EEh	CPU family ID	byte
EBDA:EFh	CPU stepping	byte
EBDA:117h	Keyboard ID	word
EBDA:11Ah	Non-BIOS interrupt 18h flag	byte
EBDA:11Dh	User Interrupt 18h far pointer	dword

Detailed Extended BIOS Data Area

Location	Description	Size
EBDA:0	Size of Extended BIOS Data Area	byte

This byte specifies the number of 1,024-byte blocks in the extended BIOS data area. With a typical EBDA size of 1024 bytes, this value is 1.

Location	Description	Size
EBDA:17h	Number of POST Error Entries	byte

On most PS/2 systems, when a POST error occurs, the POST code is saved to the error log. This value indicates how many errors have been saved in the error log. After the 5th error, no additional errors are saved.

Location	Description	Size
EBDA:18h	Error Log	5 words

When POST detects errors, the POST codes are stored in this error log, one word per error. EBDA:17h is used as an index into the log. When a new error is detected, it is placed in the next unused log word. Up to a maximum of five errors can be saved in this log.

Location	Description	Size
EBDA:22h	Mouse Device Driver Far Call	dword

This double word is a pointer to the mouse device driver code. When a mouse event occurs, data is passed on the stack to the device driver. See Chapter 13, interrupt 15h, function C2h, subfunction 7 for more details.

Location	Description	Size
EBDA:26h	Mouse Flags 1	byte

This byte holds a number of flags relating to the motherboard mouse port controller.

bit	7 = 1	Command in progress
	6 = 1	Mouse sent a Resend byte, FAh
	5 = 1	Mouse sent an Acknowledge byte, FEh
	4 = 1	Mouse transmit error byte, FCh
	3 = 1	Unexpected value received
	2 = x	Index count 0 to 7—used to retrieve 1 to 8 bytes from the controller,
	1 = x	decremented each time interrupt 74h issued (mouse interrupt).
	0 = x	Each successive byte is stored in EBDA starting at 28h.

Location	Description	Size
EBDA:27h	Mouse Flags 2	byte

This byte holds a number of flags relating to the motherboard mouse port operation.

bit	7 = x	Device driver far call flag
	6 = x	Unused or unknown function
	5 = x	Unused or unknown function
	4 = x	Unused or unknown function
	3 = x	Unused or unknown function
	2 = x	Package count (1-8 bytes). This is the number of bytes received from
	1 = x	the mouse.
	0 = x	

Location	Description	Size
EBDA:28-2Fh	Mouse Data	8 bytes

These eight bytes are used to save incoming data from the keyboard/mouse controller. The number of bytes specified by the package count, EBDA:27h, are collected. When all of these bytes have been loaded into this area, the data from this area pushed onto the stack and a far call is made to the mouse device driver.

Location	Description	Size
EBDA:39h	Watchdog Timer	word

This word holds the Watchdog timer initial count value. A value of 0 indicates the Watchdog timer is not active.

Location	Description	Size
EBDA:3D-4Ch	Hard Disk 0 Parameter Table	16 bytes

When an IDE drive is used, the parameter table for hard disk 0 is stored in these 16 bytes. See Chapter 11, Hard Disk System, for the structure of the hard disk parameter table.

Location	Description	Size
EBDA:4D-5Ch	Hard Disk 1 Parameter Table	16 bytes

When an IDE drive is used, the parameter table for hard disk 1 is stored in these 16 bytes. See Chapter 11, Hard Disk System, for the structure of the hard disk parameter table.

Location	Description	Size
EBDA:68h	Cache Control	byte

This byte is used to control the CPU cache, for those CPUs that have an on-chip cache. This includes all 486 CPUs and IBM's 386SLC CPU.

bit	7 = 0	Unused
	6 = 0	Unused
	5 = 0	Unused
	4 = 0	Unused
	3 = 0	Unused
	2 = 0	Unused
	1 = 0	Cache tested ok (this bit may serve a different function)
	1	Cache failed, do not use
	0 = 0	CPU cache enabled
	1	CPU cache disabled

Location	Description	Size
EBDA:6Eh	Repeat Rate of Keyboard	byte

The last repeat rate sent to the keyboard is stored here. The value saved is identical to the value used by interrupt 16h, function 3. See Chapter 8, The Keyboard System, for additional details.

Location	Description	Size
EBDA:6Fh	Delay Until Keyboard Repeats	byte

The last delay value sent to the keyboard is stored here. This is the time to wait after a key is pressed down until auto-repeat begins. The value saved is identical to the value used by interrupt 16h, function 3. See Chapter 8, The Keyboard System, for additional details.

Location	Description	Size
EBDA:70h	Number of Hard Drives Attached	byte

Number of hard drives attached, 0 to 2, as detected by POST.

Location	Description	Size
EBDA:71h	DMA channel for hard drive	byte

Defines the 16-bit DMA channel to use for hard disk system. POST defaults to using DMA channel 5.

Location	Description	Size
EBDA:72h	Hard disk interrupt status	byte

The interrupt status from the hard disk controller is stored in this byte when a disk operation is complete. It is also set to 1Fh if any timeout occurs waiting for controller response or waiting too long for an interrupt complete.

Location	Description	Size
EBDA:73h	Hard disk operation flags	byte

Bit 7 is set to 1 if the hard disk controller issues an interrupt. This bit is set by the interrupt 76h operation complete routine. Bit 6 is set when the controller has been reset, and cleared once a DMA operation for the controller has begun. Other bits appear unused.

bit	7 = 1	Disk controller issued an operation complete interrupt
	6 = 1	Controller has been reset
	5 = 0	Unused
	4 = 0	Unused
	3 = 0	Unused
	2 = 0	Unused
	1 = 0	Unused
	0 = 0	Unused

Location	Description	Size
EBDA:74	Old interrupt 76h vector pointer	dword

The hard disk first-time initialization code stores the old interrupt 76h vector in this location before replacing the vector with a pointer to the Operation Complete routine. If the Operation Complete routine, interrupt 76h, is issued by someone other than the hard disk controller, the BIOS passes control to the original interrupt 76h routine using this dword pointer.

Location	Description	Size
EBDA:78	Hard disk DMA type	byte

This is a temporary storage byte for the DMA extended mode register. The DMA extended mode register is defined in Chapter 18, under DMA Services, port 18h, command 7xh.

The interrupt 13h BIOS handler loads a value to indicate that a 16-bit DMA transfer will be performed, the read/write selection, and other information. Once the hard disk controller indicates it is ready for DMA setup, this value is loaded into the DMA extended mode register. A value of 44h is typically used for reads, and 4Ch for writes.

Location	Description	Size
EBDA:79	Hard disk, status of last operation	byte

The status of the last disk operation is saved in this byte. It is returned by interrupt 13h function 1 (Get status of last disk operation).

Location	Description	Size
EBDA:7A	Hard disk, timeout value	byte

This value is set by POST to indicate how long the disk services BIOS should wait for the controller to indicate its operation is complete. If the controller does not interrupt the system within the timeout period, the BIOS service aborts the current operation and returns a timeout error.

Location	Description	Size
EBDA:7E-8D	Hard disk controller return status words	8 words

A group of words read from the hard disk controller, such as status blocks and other data, are stored into these locations. The number of words read from the controller and stored here depends upon the controller operation, but will always be eight words or less. See the PS/2's ESDI port 3510h in Chapter 11, Hard Disk System, for details of the returned status words.

Location	Description	Size
EBDA:E7h	Diskette Drive Type	byte

This indicates if a drive is present and what type, 3.5" or 5.25". It is used by the diskette BIOS to determine the proper parameters for the drive.

bit	7 = 1	Diskette drive is present
	6 = 0	Unused
	5 = 0	Unused
	4 = 0	Unused
	3 = 0	Unused
	2 = 0	Unused
	1 = 0	Diskette drive 1 is 3.5"
	1	Diskette drive 1 is 5.25"
	0 = 0	Diskette drive 0 is 3.5"
	1	Diskette drive 0 is 5.25"

Location	Description	Size
EBDA:ECh	Hard Disk Parameters Loaded	byte

This indicates if the hard disk BIOS has loaded the IDE drive parameters in to the Extended BIOS data area (starting at EBDA:3D).

bit	7 = 1	Hard disk parameters loaded
	6-0 = 0	Unused

Location	Description	Size
EBDA:EEh	CPU family ID	byte

When the CPU is reset, the family ID is placed into the DH register. For example a 486 has a family ID of 4. The BIOS saves this value in this location. It is returned by interrupt 15h, AX=C9h.

Location	Description	Size
EBDA:EFh	CPU stepping	byte

When the CPU is reset, the stepping revision number is placed into DL register. The BIOS saves this value in this location. It is returned by interrupt 15h, AX=C9h.

Location	Description	Size
EBDA:117	Keyboard ID	word

This word holds the keyboard ID. The most common IBM keyboard used today in the USA has an ID of 41ABh.

Location	Description	Size
EBDA:11A	Non-BIOS Interrupt 18h Flag	word

If a program or TSR uses interrupt 18h (the BASIC interrupt), the BIOS may rehook this interrupt, saving the user's pointer at EBDA:11Dh. Before calling the user's vector, bit 0 of this byte is set to 1. The purpose of this pointer is not certain, but it may be related to the on-screen system setup offered in some systems.

bit	7-1 = 0	Unused
	0 = 1	Before calling user's interrupt 18h

Location	Description	Size
EBDA:11D	User Interrupt 18h Far Pointer	dword

If a program or TSR uses interrupt 18h (the BASIC interrupt), the BIOS may rehook this interrupt, saving the pointer in this double word. The purpose of this pointer is not certain, but it may be related to the on-screen system setup offered in some systems.

Display Memory

The system reserves 128K for the display buffer area. In many cases some of this buffer space is unused, depending on the adapter used. Many advanced memory managers can reuse these vacant spots in the display area as Upper Memory Blocks (UMBs)—see Table 6-7. UMBs can hold TSRs and drivers to increase the available low DOS space for applications.

Table 6-7. Video Display Buffer

Address	Size	Function
A000:00h	64K	EGA/VGA/XGA/SVGA Graphics display area and text font storage area. Some video modes and video chip operations will use up to 128K of address space for resolutions above 800x600.
B000:00h	4K	MDA display area, text only. EGA+ emulations allow up to eight text pages for a total of 32K of address space. This area is commonly used as an extra upper memory block area when no mode 7 video is used, and no very high resolution graphics, such as 1024x768 are used.
B000:00h	64K	Hercules Graphics mode, two pages
B800:00h	32K	CGA/EGA+ color text modes, eight pages

Adapter ROMs and UMB Memory

The area above the display buffer was originally defined for adapter ROM firmware. It is now fought tooth and nail by hardware and software vendors as the last unclaimed region of easily accessible memory. Though a number of standards help make everything coexist peacefully, many vendors have bent these standards to make high memory far more messy than it ought to be! See Chapter 5, Adapter Card Development, for more on this subject.

CHAPTER 7

Interrupt Vector Table

Most of this chapter describes interrupts directly related to hardware, which are generally undocumented or poorly documented. BIOS interrupt functions are described in greater detail in chapters relating to the specific BIOS subsystem. Other interrupts that are well documented are only briefly summarized. Refer to the bibliography for some excellent sources of interrupt vector descriptions not expanded upon here.

Interrupt vectors are normally stored in the first 1,024 bytes of memory, and hold 256 double-word interrupt pointers. These are divided into interrupts dedicated for the CPU, BIOS interrupts, common adapter card interrupts, operating system interrupts, and user/application interrupts. Beginning with the 286 CPU, the interrupt vector table could be switched to any location in memory when in protected mode. This is very useful to advanced operating systems and protected mode software.

There are conflicts between the BIOS supported functions and a number of CPU exceptions. Intel specified that interrupts 0 to 1Fh were all reserved for internal CPU use. On the 8088 only the first four interrupts were actually used, so IBM decided to use others for BIOS functions. This was a purely arbitrary decision, because IBM could have chosen any of the remaining 224 interrupts. This is one of the few places where IBM really blundered in the system design.

Once the PC became a major standard, it was too late to change the BIOS interrupt assignments. Fortunately, the interrupt functions Intel has added to later CPUs do not conflict with the BIOS/DOS-based real-mode PC environment. One of many possible examples of overlapped BIOS and CPU interrupts occurs at interrupt 0Ch. Intel defined the CPU stack fault exception as interrupt 0Ch on 386 and later CPUs. This same interrupt is often used for the serial port. If the system is in V86 or protected mode, the protected mode handler is designed to determine if the interrupt was caused by a stack fault or by the serial UART. The handler will vector to the stack fault handler code in protected mode or switch to the serial port code.

In real mode, the conflicts between the BIOS and CPU are ignored. In my prior example, the assumption is made that stack faults never occur. Of course we all know that software is always perfect and never has bugs that could cause a fault! If the impossible happens, and a stack fault does occur, the system is likely to crash. Since there is not much you can do about it, the BIOS simply ignores it, and lets the system come tumbling down.

Interrupts 20h to 3Fh are supposed to be reserved for DOS. Most interrupts 20h to 2Fh are used by DOS, but it does not use any of the interrupts from 30h to 3Fh. Instead, a number of standards have evolved that make use of the interrupts from 30h to 3Fh. Table 7-1 summarizes how interrupts are used by the vast majority of systems and software.

Some interrupt vectors are used for data storage. When this occurs, that particular interrupt vector isn't available for other uses. These data storage entries are shown with a type "data."

Table 7-1. Interrupt Vector Table Summary

Int	Address	Type	Function
0	0:00h	CPU	Divide error
1	0:04h	CPU	Single Step
2	0:08h	CPU	Non-Maskable Interrupt
3	0:0Ch	CPU	Breakpoint Instruction
4	0:10h	CPU	Overflow Instruction
5	0:14h	BIOS	Print Screen
		CPU, 286+	Bound Range Exceeded
6	0:18h	CPU, 286+	Invalid Opcode
7	0:1Ch	CPU, 286+	Coprocessor Not Available
8	0:20h	Hardware	IRQ 0—System Timer
		CPU, 286	Exception due to interrupt out of range
		CPU, 386+	Double exception
9	0:24h	Hardware	IRQ 1—Keyboard
		CPU, 286+	Coprocessor Segment Overrun
A	0:28h	Hardware	IRQ 2—General Adapter Use/Cascade
		CPU, 386+	Invalid TSS

Table 7-1. Continued

Int	Address	Type	Function
B	0:2Ch	Hardware	IRQ 3—Serial Port
		CPU, 386+	Segment Not Present
C	0:30h	Hardware	IRQ 4—Serial Port
		CPU, 386+	Stack Exception
D	0:34h	Hardware	IRQ 5—General Adapter Use
		CPU, 286	Segment overrun exception
		CPU, 386+	General Protection Fault
E	0:38h	Hardware	IRQ 6—Diskette Controller
		CPU, 386+	Page Fault
F	0:3Ch	Hardware	IRQ 7—Printer 1
10	0:40h	BIOS	Video
		CPU, 286+	Coprocessor error (not used)
11	0:44h	BIOS	Equipment Configuration
		CPU, 486+	Alignment Check
12	0:48h	BIOS	Memory Size
		CPU, Pentium+	Machine Check
13	0:4Ch	BIOS	Disk/Diskette Services
14	0:50h	BIOS	Serial Communications
15	0:54h	BIOS	System Services
16	0:58h	BIOS	Keyboard Services
17	0:5Ch	BIOS	Printer Services
18	0:60h	BIOS	ROM BASIC/Boot Failure
19	0:64h	BIOS	Bootstrap Loader
1A	0:68h	BIOS	Time-Of-Day
1B	0:6Ch	BIOS	Keyboard Control-Break
1C	0:70h	BIOS	User Timer Tick
1D	0:74h	BIOS Data	Video Initialization Data Pointer
1E	0:78h	BIOS Data	Diskette Configuration Pointer
1F	0:7Ch	BIOS Data	Graphics Character Set Pointer
20	0:80h	DOS	Terminate Program
21	0:84h	DOS	General Services
22	0:88h	DOS Data	Termination Address
23	0:8Ch	DOS Data	Control-C Handler Address
24	0:90h	DOS Data	Critical Error Handler Address
25	0:94h	DOS	Absolute Disk Read
26	0:98h	DOS	Absolute Disk Write
27	0:9Ch	DOS	Terminate and Stay Resident (Obsolete)
28	0:A0h	DOS	DOS Idle
29	0:A4h	DOS	Display Character
2A	0:A8h	DOS	NETBIOS
2B	0:ACh	DOS	Unused

Table 7-1. Continued

Int	Address	Type	Function
2C	0:B0h	DOS	Unused
2D	0:B4h	DOS	Unused
2E	0:B8h	DOS	DOS Command Execute
2F	0:BCh	DOS	Multiplex
30	0:C0h	DOS Data	Jump into DOS for CP/M services (5 bytes)
31	0:C4h	User	DPMI (in protected mode)
32	0:C8h	User	Unused
33	0:CCh	User	Mouse
34	0:D0h	User	Floating Point, emulate instruction D8h
35	0:D4h	User	Floating Point, emulate instruction D9h
36	0:D8h	User	Floating Point, emulate instruction DAh
37	0:DCh	User	Floating Point, emulate instruction DBh
38	0:E0h	User	Floating Point, emulate instruction DCh
39	0:E4h	User	Floating Point, emulate instruction DDh
3A	0:E8h	User	Floating Point, emulate instruction DEh
3B	0:ECh	User	Floating Point, emulate instruction DFh
3C	0:F0h	User	Floating Point Emulation
3D	0:F4h	User	Floating Point Emulation
3F	0:FCh	User	Overlay Manager/Other
40	0:100h	BIOS, AT+	Revectored Diskette Services
41	0:104h	BIOS Data	Hard Disk 0 Configuration Pointer
42	0:108h	EGA+	Old Video Interrupt Vector
43	0:10Ch	EGA+ Data	Full Graphics Character Set Pointer
46	0:118h	BIOS Data	Hard Disk 1 Configuration Pointer
4A	0:128h	BIOS, AT+	Alarm occurred
4B	0:12Ch	User	Virtual DMA Services
67	0:19Ch	User	EMS Memory
70	0:1C0h	Hardware, AT+	IRQ 8—CMOS Real-Time Clock
71	0:1C4h	Hardware, AT+	IRQ 9—General Adapter Use
72	0:1C8h	Hardware, AT+	IRQ 10—General Adapter Use
73	0:1CCh	Hardware, AT+	IRQ 11—General Adapter Use
74	0:1D0h	Hardware, AT+	IRQ 12—Mouse Port
75	0:1D4h	Hardware, AT+	IRQ 13—Math Coprocessor Error
76	0:1D8h	Hardware, AT+	IRQ 14—Primary Hard Disk Controller
77	0:1DCh	Hardware, AT+	IRQ 15—General Adapter Use
C0-C3	0:300h	BIOS Data	User defined hard disk 0 data (16 bytes)
C4-C7	0:310h	BIOS Data	User defined hard disk 1 data (16 bytes)

Interrupt Vectors and Data Descriptions

Int	Description	Type
0	Divide Error	8088+

While attempting to execute a divide instruction, an improper operation occurred. An interrupt 0 is issued if the instruction's divisor is 0. Since a divide by zero creates an infinite value, it is never allowed. A zero divisor usually indicates a bug in a program. Interrupt 0 is also issued if the result overflows the quotient. For example, if AX = FFFFh, BL=1, the instruction DIV BL (which means AL = AX/BL) will have a quotient of FFFFh, which cannot fit into the resultant register AL.

If an application program does not provide a divide error handler, most operating systems will attempt to kill the application and exit back to the OS. Depending on the nature of the program causing the divide overflow, this does not always work and the system may hang.

The return address indicates the location of the problem, but differs slightly between CPU types. On the 8088, 8086, 80188, and 80186 CPUs, the far return address points to the instruction *after* the divide instruction that caused the divide error. On the 80286 and later CPUs, the return address points to the instruction that caused the divide error. If the instruction has prefixes like ES, the pointer refers to the first prefix of the instruction that caused the divide error.

Int	Description	Type
1	Single Step	All CPUs

When the CPU is in single-step mode for debugging, this interrupt is called after each instruction execution. However, the general interrupt instruction is a special case. When the INT instruction is encountered (like INT 13h), all of the code for the specified interrupt is processed. When the interrupt returns, the CPU issues interrupt 1, as if a single instruction was executed.

The 80386 CPU and later also use this interrupt for additional debugging functions. These special debugging functions include interrupting when an instruction or address breakpoint occurred, a task switch breakpoint occurred, or an In-Circuit-Emulator (ICE) conflict fault occurred. The bits in the debug registers DR6 and DR7 are used to determine which condition occurred as shown in Table 7-2. Table 7-3 helps explain the various related flags.

Table 7-2. Debug Interrupt Determination

Test Conditions	Why Interrupt Occurred
BS=1	Single Step
B0=1 and (GE0=1 or LE0=1)	Breakpoint from DR0 occurred
B1=1 and (GE1=1 or LE1=1)	Breakpoint from DR1 occurred
B2=1 and (GE2=1 or LE2=1)	Breakpoint from DR2 occurred
B3=1 and (GE3=1 or LE3=1)	Breakpoint from DR3 occurred
BD=1	Debug registers unavailable since ICE in use
BT=1	Task switch breakpoint

Table 7-3. Debug Flags

Flag	Description	Register	Bit
B0	Breakpoint for debug register 0	DR6	0
B1	Breakpoint for debug register 1	DR6	1
B2	Breakpoint for debug register 2	DR6	2
B3	Breakpoint for debug register 3	DR6	3
BD	Conflict with ICE (In-Circuit-Emulator)	DR6	13
BS	Break-Single Step	DR6	14
BT	Breakpoint for Task	DR6	15
GE0	Global enable for debug register 0	DR7	1
GE1	Global enable for debug register 1	DR7	3
GE2	Global enable for debug register 2	DR7	5
GE3	Global enable for debug register 3	DR7	7
LE0	Local enable for debug register 0	DR7	0
LE1	Local enable for debug register 1	DR7	2
LE2	Local enable for debug register 2	DR7	4
LE3	Local enable for debug register 3	DR7	6

INT

Int	Description	Type
2	Non-Maskable Interrupt	All CPUs

The CPU has a separate hardware input line that cannot be turned off by the CPU. It is used for critical failures like DRAM parity errors and coprocessor errors, if a coprocessor is attached. All PC systems offer the ability to "mask off" the NMI function in hardware, external from the CPU. This is controlled through port 70h. Refer to Chapter 17, Interrupt Control and NMI, for additional details.

A few of the common uses in the PC environment include: RAM parity error detection, math coprocessor errors, watch-dog time-outs, power loss (from UPS hardware), and break-out operations on some hardware debuggers.

INT

Int	Description	Type
3	Breakpoint Instruction	All CPUs

The CPU provides a special single-byte instruction to issue interrupt 3. It is used by older debuggers like DEBUG to insert a breakpoint into code. At the breakpoint location, the debugger saves the current instruction byte and replaces it with the interrupt 3 instruction, CCh. When the CCh instruction is executed, interrupt 3 occurs and vectors back into the debugger.

In a few cases interrupt 3 is used by an application program for a critical interrupt function. The purpose is to make it difficult to analyze what the program does. Copy protection schemes are the prime users of this technique. By using this interrupt, the program will fail to function correctly when breakpoints are used by a debugger that requires interrupt 3. To make the debugger's breakpoints fail, the program points the interrupt 3 vector to its own code. Unlike a normal interrupt hook, the program's interrupt 3 handler does not pass control to the original interrupt 3 handler, the debugger. If a breakpoint is inserted into the code by the debugger and the breakpoint is encountered, the interrupt does not return to the debugger, but instead goes into the application program's handler. The application can then terminate or perform other nasty actions. Of course any 386+ debugger avoids these problems by using the debug registers for hardware breakpoints.

Int	Description	Type
4	Overflow Instruction	All CPUs

INT

A special single-byte interrupt overflow instruction causes interrupt 4 if the overflow flag is set. I suspect the original idea was to handle math error conditions through an interrupt handler. I've never seen this instruction actually used in any commercial program.

Int	Description	Type
5	Print Screen- Bound Range Exceeded	BIOS 80188+

INT

This is the first of a number of interrupts in which IBM-defined BIOS functions conflict with Intel defined exceptions on 80186 or later CPUs. Interrupt 5 is called from the low-level keyboard handler, interrupt 9, when the Print-Screen key is pressed. The system BIOS handler for interrupt 5 scans the current text screen and outputs the data to the printer. Most advanced video BIOSes, like the VGA, provide a software-controlled option to replace old system BIOS routine with their own. This allows the Print-Screen function to print out text from screens that are wider than 80 columns or larger than 25 rows. See Chapter 14, Parallel Ports and Print Screen, for more details.

The CPU will also issue an interrupt 5 upon execution of the BOUND instruction if the array index it checks is outside the bounds of the array. The BOUND instruction was not available on the 8088/8086 processor, but is supported on all later CPUs. The BOUND instruction is rarely used, probably because of the conflict with the BIOS Print-Screen function. If it is used for BOUND exception handling, a far return re-executes the failed BOUND instruction.

Int	Description	Type
6	Invalid Opcode	80188+

INT

When an invalid opcode is issued this interrupt occurs. For example, the instruction bytes 0Fh, 17h have never been assigned on 80186 and later CPUs. If execution of 0Fh, 17h were attempted, the CPU would issue interrupt 6. Some instructions only allow a register or memory reference for an operand, but not both. If the wrong type is used, it will create an invalid opcode exception. Instructions that can cause this include BOUND, LDS, LES, LFS, LGS, LSS, LGDT, and LIDT instructions.

Invalid opcode exception is not supported on the 8088/8086 processor, but is supported on the 80186/80188, and all later CPUs. It is used by some advanced debuggers to help identify program bugs, but would not occur in normal operation. The program CPUUNDOC on the supplied disk uses the Invalid Opcode interrupt to look for possible undocumented instructions.

Int	Description	Type
7	Coprocessor Not Available	80286+

For 80286 or later CPUs, if ESCAPE instruction opcodes D8h to DFh or the WAIT instruction are executed and no math coprocessor is connected, the CPU issues interrupt 7. It is used by some compilers to emulate math coprocessor instructions, should the system have no math coprocessor. Most compilers today provide faster math coprocessor emulation without using interrupt 7. See the group of interrupts starting at 34h for one alternative technique for math coprocessor emulation.

80286 status bits in the machine status word determine whether or not math instructions are to be emulated in software using this interrupt. On the 80386 and later processors an ESCAPE instruction will trigger interrupt 7 if the Emulate Bit in CR0 is set. Both ESCAPE and WAIT instructions will trigger interrupt 7 if either the Task Switched bit or Monitor Processor Extension bits of CR0 are set.

Int	Description	Type
8	IRQ 0—System Timer	Hardware
	Double Fault	80286+

Interrupt 8 is used for system timing. It is connected in hardware to IRQ 0, from system timer 0. Timer 0 trips interrupt 8 every 54.9 ms. See Chapter 16, System Timers, for more details.

On 80286 CPUs and later, interrupt 8 is issued when a double fault occurs. A double fault occurs when, while processing one CPU fault, the handler causes a second fault to occur. For example, an invalid instruction is attempted to be executed. This causes the Bad Opcode interrupt 6 to be issued. If, at the same time, the stack pointer is set to FFFFh, the CPU attempts to push the bad opcode address onto the stack, and a stack fault is issued. This causes a double fault interrupt 8 to be called. In real mode, the stack is still a problem, so getting to interrupt 8 causes another stack fault (the third fault). The CPU halts, since it cannot deal with an error of this magnitude.

Since a double fault is both rare and difficult to recover from, both the BIOS and DOS ignore double faults.

Not all faults will cause a double fault to occur. If any of the faults in Table 7-4 are in progress, and another fault from this table occurs, a double fault is issued. There is one exception to this rule. If processing any fault from this list (except a page fault) and a page fault occurs, a double fault is not generated.

Table 7-4. Double Fault Types

Interrupt	Fault Description
0	Divide Error
A	Invalid Task State Segment (TSS)
B	Segment not present
C	Stack fault
D	General Protection Fault (GPF)
E	Page Fault

Int	Description	Type
9	Keyboard Coprocessor—Segment Overrun	Hardware 286/386

INT

Interrupt 9 is used for the low-level keyboard handler. It is connected in hardware to IRQ 1, from the keyboard controller. Refer to Chapter 8, The Keyboard System, for more details.

If the 80286 or 80386 CPU is in protected mode, and while transferring the coprocessor instruction to the coprocessor a page or segment violation occurs, interrupt 9 is issued. Since the keyboard handler never operates in protected mode, no conflicts occur. On the 80486 and later CPUs, the Coprocessor Segment Overrun interrupt was moved to interrupt 0Dh.

Int	Description	Type
A	IRQ 2—Invalid TSS	Hardware 80286+

INT

Hardware IRQ 2 causes interrupt A to occur. This is a non-dedicated interrupt used by some adapter cards. On AT+ systems with two interrupt controllers, IRQ 2 is used for the cascade function of the controller. IRQ 9 is connected to the same hardware line as the old IRQ 2 line. The BIOS then plays a few tricks to end up here should IRQ 9 occur. This maintains compatibility with older cards. Refer to interrupt 71h and Chapter 17, Interrupt Control and NMI, for more details. IRQ 2 is typically used for some network adapter cards, some MIDI interfaces, and optionally on some EGA/VGA cards every time vertical retrace occurs.

For 80286 or later CPUs, interrupt A occurs if, during a task switch, the new Task State Selector (TSS) is invalid. This can only occur with protected-mode software, and indicates a serious bug in the software.

Int	Description	Type
B	Serial Port Segment Not Present	Hardware 80286+

INT

Hardware IRQ 3 causes interrupt B to occur. This is a non-dedicated interrupt used by adapter cards, and is typically used by serial ports 2 and 4, and some network adapter cards. For more about how the serial port uses this interrupt, see Chapter 12, Serial Ports.

For 80286 and later CPUs, interrupt B occurs in protected mode when the processor detects a loaded segment is not present in the system. It can be used by a protected mode operating system to implement a segment based virtual memory system. For example, OS/2 version 1.x used this method for virtual memory. Its usage does not conflict with IRQ 3, since the protected mode handler can detect if the interrupt occurred from hardware or the CPU. See Chapter 17, under Warnings, on how to determine if an interrupt was caused by hardware or the CPU. Refer to an Intel programmer's reference manual on the 80286 or later CPU for more about the Segment Not Present exception.

INT

Int	Description	Type
C	IRQ 4	Hardware
	Stack Exception	80286+

Hardware IRQ 4 causes interrupt C to occur. This non-dedicated interrupt is used by adapter cards, and is typically used by serial ports 1 and 3. For more about how the serial port uses this interrupt, see Chapter 12, Serial Ports.

For 80286 and later CPUs, interrupt C appears when a limit violation occurs while changing the SS register or a stack underflow or overflow. Its usage does not conflict with IRQ 4, since the protected-mode handler can detect if the interrupt occurred from hardware or the CPU. See Chapter 17, Interrupt Control and NMI, under Warnings, on how to determine if an interrupt was caused by hardware or the CPU. Refer to an Intel programmer's reference manual on the 80286 or later CPU for more about the stack exception.

INT

Int	Description	Type
D	IRQ 5	Hardware
	General Protection Fault	80286+

Hardware IRQ 5 causes interrupt D to occur. This is a non-dedicated interrupt used by adapter cards. On the PC and XT, interrupt D was used by the hard disk adapter. For more about hard disk usage, see Chapter 11, Hard Disk System. On AT+ systems interrupt D is typically used for parallel port 2 or a network card.

For 80286 and later CPUs, interrupt D occurs whenever serious errors (that fail to fit into any other class) are detected by the CPU. It is the responsibility of the protected-mode handler to determine if a fault occurred or if IRQ 5 needs servicing. See Chapter 17, Interrupt Control and NMI, under Warnings, on how to determine if an interrupt was caused by hardware or the CPU. Although a general protection fault usually indicates a serious bug or problem, there are two general protection faults more common than others. These are faults due to a privileged instruction and a fault caused by execution or data access across a segment boundary.

This fault is generated if a privileged instruction is not allowed for the current privilege level. Unfortunately, Intel was a little too protective of some needed instructions. For example, reading CR0 is considered privileged and will cause a fault in V86 mode (MOV EAX, CR0). If a memory manager is used, the CPU passes control through this interrupt if a program attempts to read CR0. The better managers will simulate this useful instruction and place the contents of CR0 into EAX.

Segment boundary faults fall into two categories, code and data. A code fault occurs if the instruction pointer wraps. For example, in 16-bit mode, a non-branching instruction is executed at offset FFFFh. A data fault will occur if the program attempts to read or write across the segment boundary. For example, in 16-bit mode, a dword is read from offset FFFDh.

Though the CPU exception does not conflict with the IRQ 5 usage, it can slow the response to handling IRQ 5 while in V86 mode. Refer to Chapter 17, Interrupt Control and NMI, for more details on the performance problem with general protection faults and IRQ 5. See Chapter 17, under Warnings, on how to determine if an interrupt was caused by hardware or the CPU.

Int	Description	Type
E	IRQ 6—Diskette Controller Page Fault	Hardware 80386+

INT

The diskette controller issues an interrupt E at the conclusion of the current operation. The interrupt E handler sets bit 7 in the diskette recalibrate status byte at 40:3Eh. On AT+ systems interrupt 15h is also issued with function ax=9101h to indicate the diskette controller operation is complete. See Chapter 10, Diskette System, for additional details.

On 80386 CPUs and later, interrupt E will occur when paging is enabled and the system is unable to access the specified page. Paging is the ability of the 386 and later processors to map physical memory to different logical addresses. This remapping technique is used by all memory managers to, among other features, create high memory in the gaps above the display adapter. Interrupt E may indicate an error in the protected-mode code, or in a number of cases it may be intentionally used for protection, dynamic mapping, virtual memory, and other functions.

The CPU issued interrupt will never occur in real mode. In V86 mode, the protected-mode handler must determine if the interrupt was caused by a page fault or a hardware interrupt and take the appropriate action. See Chapter 17, Interrupt Control and NMI, under Warnings, on how to determine if an interrupt was caused by hardware or the CPU.

Int	Description	Type
F	IRQ 7—Printer 1	Hardware

INT

Each printer port can issue an interrupt when the Acknowledge line from the printer is asserted (ACK=0). This ability can be disabled from within the printer controller. When enabled on the printer 1 adapter, printer acknowledge causes interrupt F to be called. The BIOS interrupt 17h handler does not use this interrupt, and the default is to disable the printer interrupt. Refer to Chapter 14, Parallel Ports and Print Screen, for additional details.

The interrupt controller also uses this interrupt in the unlikely case of an unknown hardware interrupt occurring. This might happen if a hardware interrupt request occurs too briefly, or if noise appears on an interrupt request line. There is no support provided in the system BIOS for this situation, and it is generally ignored.

INT

Int	Description	Type
10h	Video Coprocessor Error (unused)	BIOS 80386+

This interrupt is issued by software to access video functions. Refer to Chapter 9, Video System, for additional details.

If you look at any of the current 80386 or later Intel CPU manuals, they seem to indicate interrupt 10h is a reserved CPU function for coprocessor errors. This would be true if the math coprocessor was connected as Intel suggests. In AT+ systems, the coprocessor error output is connected to IRQ 13, interrupt 75h. Refer to interrupt 75h for additional details.

The 80386 and later CPUs have a separate ERROR input line that Intel had intended for connecting the ERROR output line and the math coprocessor. Even the 486DX, the Pentium, and the Pentium Pro, which have a built-in math coprocessor, have an ERROR input line. If the CPU's ERROR line could be activated, it would cause interrupt 10h to occur. On all properly designed AT+ systems, the CPU ERROR input is unused, and will never cause interrupt 10h. Of course a few clone boards have botched this, and followed Intel's suggested approach instead of the real-world approach. As long as no math coprocessor is installed, even these systems will work fine.

INT

Int	Description	Type
11h	Equipment Configuration Alignment Check	BIOS 80486+

This interrupt returns the equipment configuration determined by POST. It simply returns the contents of the equipment word at address 40:10h in AX. Refer to the equipment word described for address 40:10h for the bit contents (Chapter 6, BIOS Data and Other Fixed Data Areas).

On 80486 and later CPUs, an option is provided to trap references to misaligned memory addresses. The option is enabled by setting the Alignment Check bit in EFLAGS. If enabled, and the CPU is in privilege mode 3, and a memory reference is made to a misaligned address, interrupt 11h is issued. For AT+ systems, the Alignment Check feature is disabled to avoid conflicts with the Equipment Configuration use of interrupt 11h.

A misaligned address is any data reference that is not evenly divisible by its size. For example, a 4-byte DWORD data item can be accessed at offset 0, but offsets 1, 2, and 3 initiate the Alignment Check interrupt. Developers sometimes use this function to help identify misaligned data references that can slow down critical portions of code.

Another use of the Alignment Check feature is to add extra information to pointers. For example, the lower two bits of a dword pointer could signify four different pointer types. For example, before the pointer is used, the lower bits might signify the data type:

bit 1	bit 0	Data type
0	0	= byte
0	1	= word
1	0	= dword
1	1	= qword

Before the pointer is used, the lower two bits are always cleared. The Alignment Check would be used to flag a pointer error, should these additional bits not be properly cleared. It would be better coding practice to avoid such a convoluted design, and avoid reliance on Alignment Check completely.

Int	Description	Type
12h	Memory Size	BIOS
	Machine Check	Pentium

This interrupt returns the total main memory in kilobytes. It simply returns the contents of the main memory word at address 40:13h in AX. For 640K of main memory, this value is 280h.

On the Pentium and Pentium Pro CPUs, a new Machine Check exception will issue interrupt 12h. Machine Check is an optional function of the Pentium class processors that flag parity errors on data reads and unsuccessful completions of a bus cycle. If a Machine Check occurs, the program in operation cannot be restarted. Of course it's not clear whether any code will operate properly if parity errors are occurring, but it may be possible to display some indication of the problem before shut down.

To enable the Machine Check feature, the Machine Check Enable bit 6 in CR4 is enabled. If the feature is used, it can be shared with the standard BIOS function. To work together, the interrupt 12h handler must look at the Machine Check Type register, bit 0:

```
mov     ecx, 1                  ; machine check type
rdmsr                           ; read model specific register
test    eax, 1                  ; edx:eax = Type register
jz      get_memory_size         ; jump if not Machine Check
<<<<<< machine check code here (not restartable) >>>>>>
hlt
```

The address used when the parity error or the bus cycle problem occurs is automatically saved in the 64-bit Machine Check address. The value is undefined if a Machine Check has not occurred. This can be read as follows:

```
mov     ecx, 0                  ; machine check address
rdmsr                           ; read model specific register
                                ; edx:eax = address
```

For parity errors, the Parity Enable pin on the Pentium chip must be set high AND the data read must be detected to have odd parity AND the Machine Check feature must be enabled. For bus cycle errors, the Bus Check pin on the Pentium chip must be set high AND the Machine Check feature must be enabled. See Chapter 3, The CPU and Undocumented Instructions, for more about the Read Model Specific Register instructions and related registers.

INT

Int	Description	Type
13h	Disk/Diskette Services	BIOS

This interrupt is issued by software to access both the hard disk and the diskette drives. Refer to Chapter 10, Diskette System, and Chapter 11, Hard Disk System, for full details. Also refer to interrupt 40h, used to hold the diskette BIOS service interrupt vector.

INT

Int	Description	Type
14h	Serial Communications	BIOS

This interrupt is issued by software to initialize and send or receive data to a serial port. Chapter 12, Serial Ports, describes the Serial BIOS interrupt.

INT

Int	Description	Type
15h	System Services	BIOS

On the original PC, interrupt 15h was used to control the cassette drive. I'm sure glad I never had to use one! With later systems it evolved to a catch-all of different functions that failed to fit into other categories. Refer to Chapter 13, System Functions, for additional details.

INT

Int	Description	Type
16h	Keyboard Services	BIOS

This interrupt is issued by software to provide the primary interface between the keyboard buffer and the operating system and applications. Chapter 8, The Keyboard System, covers interrupt 16h operations.

INT

Int	Description	Type
17h	Printer Services	BIOS

This interrupt is issued by software to initialize and send or receive data to or from a printer port. Chapter 14 covers interrupt 17h in detail.

INT

Int	Description	Type
18h	ROM BASIC/Boot Failure	BIOS

When no boot device is found, this interrupt is called. Non-IBM systems usually just return a message that a boot floppy is required. On IBM machines this vectors into ROM BASIC. Almost no other manufacturer puts BASIC in the BIOS like IBM. I understand that the original agreement between Microsoft and IBM offered IBM a reduction in royalties if every machine included Microsoft's BASIC in ROM. Because of this, every IBM system still has the obsolete ROM BASIC as part of the system BIOS.

A new BIOS boot specification document (4Q 1995) reuses this interrupt to potentially allow booting from other devices, such as a CD-ROM. Should a boot device (like the hard disk) fail to boot, it issues interrupt 18h so an attempt can be made to boot from another device. See Appendix C, Bibliography, for information on the BIOS Boot Specification document.

Int	Description	Type
19h	Bootstrap Loader	BIOS

INT III I

Once the BIOS completes POST operations, it issues interrupt 19h to load the boot sector from track 0, sector 1 of the boot device. This data are transferred into memory starting at the fixed location 0:7C00h. After 512 bytes have been loaded, control is passed to the start of the loaded code at 0:7C00h. DL holds the drive number where the sector was read. If there is any problem, interrupt 18h is issued.

Many people have the misconception that the system can be reset by simply issuing an interrupt 19h. Interrupt 19h should only be called by the BIOS, after hardware has been properly reset, and BIOS data and interrupt vectors are set correctly for this boot-up phase. Should an application attempt interrupt 19h, the system will likely hang, depending on the state of the BIOS data area and interrupt vector table. See the end of Chapter 3, The CPU and Undocumented Instructions, for the proper way to reset the system.

Int	Description	Type
1Ah	Time-Of-Day	BIOS

INT III I

This interrupt is issued by software to access the time-of-day functions. It is not supported on the original PC. The time-of-day functions are detailed in Chapter 15, CMOS Memory and Real-Time Clock.

Int	Description	Type
1Bh	Keyboard Control-Break	BIOS

INT III I

The low-level keyboard handler, interrupt 9, detects a Control-Break key combination. When this occurs, the keyboard buffer is cleared, the BIOS Control-Break flag is set at address 40:71h, and the keyboard handler issues interrupt 1Bh. It is normally used by the operating system to trap when Control-Break occurs. When the operating system is DOS, this interrupt is vectored into a small routine inside DOS. This routine records that a Control-Break occurred. At a later time, when any DOS interrupt 21h function is allowed, DOS calls the user's Control-Break handler. The user's Control-Break handler address is stored at 0:8Ch (the interrupt 23h vector). See interrupt 23h for additional details.

Int	Description	Type
1Ch	User Timer Tick	BIOS

Before the BIOS system timer routine completes, it issues interrupt 1Ch. The BIOS service handler for 1Ch is the smallest service handler possible: the BIOS simply returns without any action by issuing IRET.

The only purpose of this interrupt is to signal an application program once every 54.9 ms. To accomplish this, the application program hooks interrupt 1Ch. See Interrupt 8 and Chapter 16, System Timers, for more information.

Int	Description	Type
1Dh	Video Initialization Data Pointer	Data

This is a far pointer to the initialization values for the CGA and monochrome video adapters. It usually points into ROM, but can be pointed into a user table. When a mode is changed, the appropriate group of 16 bytes of data is loaded into the 6845 CRT controller. Port 3D4h is used on the CGA for specifying which internal register to use, and port 3D5h is used to send the data to the controller. The 16 bytes are loaded into registers 0 to 15 on the controller. For MDA, the same action occurs, except ports 3B4h and 3B5h are used. Table 7-5 describes the contents of this table.

Table 7-5. Video Initialization Parameter Table

Offset	Bytes	Description
0	16	Setup data for CRT controller, 40 columns by 25 lines (mode 0, 1)
10h	16	Setup data for CRT controller, 80 columns by 25 lines (mode 2, 3)
20h	16	Setup data for CRT controller, setup data, graphics (mode 4, 5, or 6)
30h	16	Setup data for CRT controller, 80 columns by 25 lines (mode 7)
40h	2	Video buffer size, CGA 40x25 mode (800h)
42h	2	Video buffer size, CGA 80x25 mode (1000h)
44h	2	Video buffer size, CGA graphics mode (4000h)
46h	2	Unused
48h	8	Number of columns for modes 0 to 7
4Ah	8	Internal CRT controller mode sent to port 3B8h/3D8h for video modes 0 to 7

Int	Description	Type
1Eh	Diskette Configuration Pointer	Data

A table of diskette configuration information is pointed to by this far pointer. It usually points into ROM, but can be pointed instead at a user table. A summary of the Diskette Parameter Table is shown in Table 7-6. Additional details are provided in Chapter 10, Diskette System.

Table 7-6. Diskette Parameter Table Summary

Offset	Bytes	Description
0	1	Step rate and head unload time
1	1	Head load time and DMA mode flag
2	1	Delay for motor turn off after last access
3	1	Bytes per sector
4	1	Number of sectors per track
5	1	Gap length between sectors
6	1	Data length if bytes per sector = 0
7	1	Gap length between sectors during format
8	1	Format byte value
9	1	Head settling time
A	1	Delay until motor startup reaches normal speed

Int	Description	Type
1Fh	Graphics Character Set Pointer	Data

INT
III I

With the CGA adapter, graphics modes 4, 5, and 6 support the ability to use the video interrupt handler to write characters to the screen. It supports ASCII characters 0 to 127 in the system BIOS. The BIOS does not contain the fonts for characters 128 to 255 and sets this pointer to 0:0.

This pointer can be loaded with a user-supplied font table for characters 128 to 255. The table of font patterns consists of 8 bytes of data per character. For example, the 8 bytes for the letter "I" are shown below.

```
Letter_I        db      01111000b       ; top of "I"
                db      00110000b       ; center portion
                db      00110000b       ;   is two bits wide
                db      00110000b
                db      00110000b
                db      00110000b
                db      01111000b       ; bottom of "I"
                db      00000000b       ; blank line
```

NOTE: The remaining interrupt vectors not included below are used for the operating system, adapters, or general use. A number of technical references included in the bibliography detail those interrupts not included here.

Int	Description	Type
21h	General Services	DOS

This interrupt is used for a wide range of operating system services. See any DOS technical book for complete details. See the book *Undocumented DOS* for many hidden functions and inner details of DOS.

Int	Description	Type
22h	Termination Address	Data

When a DOS application completes, the system must terminate the current process. This vector location holds a pointer to executable code. Upon termination, control is passed to this code. If a critical error occurs and the completion code is 2 (terminate), this address is used to terminate the current application prematurely. It is not a callable interrupt vector and should never be issued as an interrupt.

Int	Description	Type
23h	Control-C Address	Data

This location contains the address for DOS to jump to if a Control-C or Control-Break occurs during all DOS I/O operations and most DOS functions. The state of the DOS break flag does not affect this operation. Even with BREAK OFF, DOS will still go to the address stored at this vector when Control-C or Control-Break is issued. It is not a callable interrupt vector and should never be issued as an interrupt.

The Control-C handler is always called at a point when it is safe to use all available DOS services. If an application changes this address to point into user code, one of three actions can be taken by the user's Control-C handler:

1. Take any action deemed necessary, such as saving a flag that Control-C occurred. The Control-C handler issues an IRET at completion. Of course all registers must be preserved by the handler.
2. Take any action deemed necessary, and issue an RETF at completion with a carry flag indicator. DOS proceeds normally if the carry is clear. If the carry flag is set, DOS terminates the current application.
3. Take any action deemed necessary and jump directly back into the application without returning to DOS. The Control-C function is designed to allow this case without issuing an IRET or RETF.

Int	Description	Type
24h	Critical Error Handler Address	Data

If an error is detected by DOS during an operation, DOS uses the address stored at this location to pass control to an error handler. The primary responsibility of the critical error handler is to inform the operating system how to proceed after an error occurs. It is not a callable interrupt vector and should never be issued as an interrupt.

DOS supplies an error handler by default. The DOS error handler displays the message "Abort, Retry, Ignore, or Fail?", and handles the error condition based on the user response.

An application may take over the error handling for improved handling or to avoid the DOS "Abort, Retry ..." message from appearing in the middle of a screen. If an application puts its own error handler address in this vector address, it will be called when an error occurs. The address does not need to be restored on program exit, as DOS will automatically reset the address when the program terminates. The application program that gets control will receive the following information from DOS:

```
ah = flags about error condition and allowed options
            bit 7 = 0  disk error (usually after some number of retries)
                    1  error type depends on device attributes, found at
                         bp:[si+4]. If bit 15 = 0, then the error occurred
                         in the memory image of the file allocation table.
                         If bit 15 = 1, then the error is in a character
                         device.
                6 = 0  Unused
                5 = 0  "Ignore" error option not allowed
                    1  "Ignore" error option allowed (only DOS 3.0 and later)
                4 = 0  "Retry" option not allowed
                    1  "Retry" option allowed (only DOS 3.0 and later)
                3 = 0  "Fail" option not allowed
                    1  "Fail" option allowed (only DOS 3.0 and later)
                2 = x | Location of error, if disk error
                1 = x |         bit 2  bit 1
                                0      0   = DOS area
                                0      1   = File allocation table
                                1      0   = Root directory
                                1      1   = other areas
                0 = 0  error occurred during read operation
                    1  error occurred during write operation
al = drive number when ah, bit 7 = 0  (0=a:, 1=b:, 2=c:, etc.)
bp:si = pointer to a device-header control block
```

```
di = error code
        bits 15-8 = x  undefined
        bits 7-0 = error code:
                  0     Write protect error occurred
                  1     Unknown unit
                  2     Drive not ready
                  3     Unknown command issued
                  4     Data error or bad CRC
                  5     Incorrect drive-request structure length
                  6     Seek error
                  7     Unknown media type
                  8     Sector not found
                  9     Printer out of paper
                  Ah    Write fault
                  Bh    Read fault
                  Ch    General failure
                  Dh    Sharing violation*
                  Eh    Lock violation*
                  Fh    Invalid disk change*
                  10h   File Control Block (FCB) unavailable*
                  11h   Sharing buffer overflow*
                  12h   Code page mismatch*
                  13h   Out of input*
                  14h   Insufficient disk space*
                * DOS version 3.0 or later
```

The error handler should preserve all registers, including the stack pointer. While the error handler is operating, it can only access limited DOS interrupt 21h functions, including 1 through Ch, 50h, 51h, 59h, 62h, and some subfunctions of function 33h. Upon error handler completion, it issues an IRET and returns an action code in the AL register as follows:

```
0       Ignore error
1       Retry
2       Terminate program using address stored at 0:88h (int 23h vector)
3       Fail system call in progress (Only in DOS 3.0 or later)
```

Int	Description	Type
30h	Jump into DOS for CP/M Services	Data

INT III I

DOS inserts a 5-byte far jump instruction starting at location 0:C0h. This instruction jumps into an area of DOS to handle old CP/M functions. This function is obsolete and undocumented, and the new DPMI service handler in protected mode uses interrupt 31h, which destroys the last byte of this 5-byte far jump.

Int	Description	Type
34h	Floating Point Emulation	User

INT III I

Many compilers, including those from Microsoft and Borland, use interrupts 34h to 3Dh for floating point emulation. The compiler codes interrupts 34h through 3Bh to emulate the math coprocessor instructions by using an interrupt followed by the original instruction bytes of the floating point instruction. For example, a normal math coprocessor instruction is:

```
D8 C1           FADD    ST, ST(1)
```

All D8 math instructions are built by the compiler to use interrupt 34h. The emulated instruction will appear as:

```
CD 34           INT     34h
C1              db      0C1h
```

The first time this specific interrupt 34h is executed in the program, the interrupt 34h handler (which is part of the program) checks if the system has a math coprocessor. If the system does have a math coprocessor, it modifies the code to the correct coprocessor instruction. In this example, the three bytes CD, 34, and C1 become 9B (wait), D8, and C1. The interrupt routine changes the return address to the start of the instruction and reruns the real instruction. In this manner, there is only a performance penalty the very first time the instruction is executed. Although we were all taught to avoid self-modifying code like the plague, this clever approach saves code space while maximizing performance on all types of systems.

Now if the interrupt 34h handler found there was no math coprocessor, the routine must then emulate the instruction. Since interrupt 34h was called, the handler knows it is an instruction in the D8 family. The handler then looks at the bytes following the interrupt instruction to fully define which instruction was being requested. The handler can then emulate the specific instruction. After the emulation is complete, the handler must return after the C1 byte of our example. Keep in mind that different instructions can use more than one byte after the interrupt.

INT

Int	Description	Type
35h	Floating Point Emulation	User

Emulate math coprocessor instructions that start with opcode D1h. See interrupt 34h for details.

INT

Int	Description	Type
36h	Floating Point Emulation	User

Emulate math coprocessor instructions that start with opcode D2h. See interrupt 34h for details.

INT

Int	Description	Type
37h	Floating Point Emulation	User

Emulate math coprocessor instructions that start with opcode D3h. See interrupt 34h for details.

INT

Int	Description	Type
38h	Floating Point Emulation	User

Emulate math coprocessor instructions that start with opcode D4h. See interrupt 34h for details.

INT

Int	Description	Type
39h	Floating Point Emulation	User

Emulate math coprocessor instructions that start with opcode D5h. See interrupt 34h for details.

INT

Int	Description	Type
3Ah	Floating Point Emulation	User

Emulate math coprocessor instructions that start with opcode D6h. See interrupt 34h for details.

INT

Int	Description	Type
3Bh	Floating Point Emulation	User

Emulate math coprocessor instructions that start with opcode D7h. See interrupt 34h for details.

Int	Description	Type
3Ch	Floating Point Emulation	User

INT

This indicates an ES override is required on the next emulated math instruction. If a math coprocessor is active, the handler will overwrite the interrupt 3Ch instruction bytes CD and 3C with 9B (wait) and 26 (ES prefix override). See interrupt 34h for more about emulated floating point interrupts.

Int	Description	Type
3Dh	Floating Point Emulation	User

INT

This indicates a WAIT instruction should be emulated. The WAIT instruction is used in some cases after a floating point instruction. The instruction causes the CPU to wait until any possible errors, caused by the prior instruction, are handled. If a math coprocessor is active, the handler will overwrite the interrupt 3Dh instruction bytes CD and 3D with 90 (nop) and 9B (wait). See interrupt 34h for more about emulated floating point interrupts.

Int	Description	Type
40h	Revectored Diskette Services	BIOS

INT

When a hard disk is detected, the BIOS shifts the Diskette BIOS services from interrupt 13h to interrupt 40h. It then points the interrupt 13h vector to the hard disk BIOS services handler. When the hard disk handler is called, it checks if DL, bit 7 is zero. If so, it issues an interrupt 40h to handle the diskette operation. When DL, bit 7 is 1, the specified hard disk action is performed.

Int	Description	Type
41h	Hard Disk 0 Configuration Pointer	Data

INT

This entry is a far pointer to configuration information of hard disk 0. The BIOS ROM contains a number of preset drive types. This pointer often points to one entry within the BIOS table of drive types. Table 7-7 outlines the contents of the Disk Parameter Table. Most newer BIOSes offer a user-defined drive type that sets this pointer to type information stored in RAM. For example, older AMI BIOSes have an option to store the user hard disk configuration in the interrupt table at address 0:C00h. Most systems today place the user-defined data into an area of the shadowed main BIOS ROM. Shadowing moves the BIOS ROM contents into RAM. After the user values are written into the BIOS RAM area, the area is write protected. Complete details are provided in Chapter 11, Hard Disk System.

Table 7-7. Hard Disk Parameter Table Summary

Offset	Size	Description	System
0	word	Maximum number of cylinders	XT/AT+
2	byte	Maximum number of heads	XT/AT+

Table 7-7. Continued

Offset	Size	Description	System
3	word	Cylinder for start of reduced write current	XT only
5	word	Cylinder for start of write pre-compensation	XT/AT+
7	byte	Maximum ECC burst length	XT only
8	byte	Control byte	XT/AT+
9	byte	Standard timeout value	XT only
A	byte	Format drive command timeout value	XT only
B	byte	Check drive command timeout	XT only
C	word	Landing zone	AT+
E	byte	Number of sectors per track	AT+
F	byte	Unused	All

Warnings

Be aware that a number of technical references incorrectly indicate the pointer stored in interrupt 41h is for hard disk 1. It is always a pointer for hard disk 0.

INT

Int	Description	Type
42h	Old Video Interrupt Vector	EGA+

When a video BIOS ROM is initialized by the system BIOS, the video BIOS saves the old video interrupt 10h vector in the interrupt 42h location. The video BIOS then places its own vector in interrupt 10h. In most cases interrupt 42h will point into the system BIOS video handler, which is no longer used.

INT

Int	Description	Type
43h	Full Graphics Character Set Pointer	Data

The EGA/VGA and later video adapters use this far pointer to get the font patterns to use for text characters while in graphics modes. For video modes 4, 5 and 6 the font pattern is for the first 128 characters (see interrupt 1Fh for the pointer to the upper 128 characters font). For all other graphics modes, this points to a table of font patterns for all 256 characters.

Normally this pointer is set by the video service routines, interrupt 10h, function 11h. It allows the pointer to be set to the various font patterns stored in the video BIOS ROM. These services also allow the setting of a user font.

Warnings

A number of technical references show this pointer incorrectly stored in vector 44h at address 0:110h, due to an error in the original IBM EGA documentation.

Int	Description	Type
46h	Hard Disk 1 Configuration Pointer	Data

This entry is a far pointer to configuration information of hard disk 1. The BIOS ROM contains a number of preset drive types. This pointer often points to one entry within the BIOS table of drive types.

Most newer BIOSes offer a user defined drive type that sets this pointer to type information stored in RAM. For example, some BIOSes have an option to store the user hard disk configuration in the interrupt table at address 0:C10h. See Chapter 11, Hard Disk System, for additional details. The hard disk table is the same form as shown in Table 7-7.

Warnings

Be aware that a number of technical references incorrectly indicate this pointer is for hard disk 0.

Int	Description	Type
4Ah	Alarm Occurred	BIOS

Interrupt 4Ah is a user-supplied interrupt handler that is called when the CMOS alarm is triggered. The user uses BIOS services 1Ah to set the alarm time. When the alarm time matches the current time, interrupt 70h is issued. The interrupt 70h handler, in turn, issues interrupt 4Ah. This is described in more detail in Chapter 15, under interrupt 1Ah.

Int	Description	Type
70h	IRQ 8—CMOS Real Time Clock	Hardware

For AT+ systems the CMOS Real Time Clock interrupt line is connected to IRQ 8. This line is activated under the periodic and alarm modes of the RTC chip. Both of these modes can operate at the same time without conflict.

In the RTC's periodic mode, the interrupt line is toggled at a periodic frequency. This mode is used by the BIOS to time a duration set by interrupt 15h, functions 83h and 86h. The RTC is programmed to interrupt at a frequency of 1024 Hz. The interrupt 70h handler decrements the double word counter at 40:9Ch. When it expires, the periodic interrupt mode is turned off, and the user's flag byte is set to 80h. The user's flag double word pointer is stored at address 40:98h.

For the alarm mode, the interrupt occurs when the preset alarm time matches the current CMOS time. The alarm time is set using BIOS interrupt 1Ah, function 6h. To be notified of the alarm the user must hook interrupt 4Ah. When the alarm occurs, the interrupt 70h handler issues an interrupt 4Ah to execute the user's alarm handler.

See Chapter 15 for additional information.

Int	Description	Type
71h	IRQ 9—General Adapter Use	Hardware

For AT+ systems, this interrupt is unassigned and is available for an adapter connected to IRQ 9. Considerable confusion surrounds IRQ 9 and its unusual relationship with IRQ 2.

First, a little background is necessary. With the design of the AT, IBM added a second interrupt controller to provide seven additional hardware interrupts. The design of the interrupt controller allows two controllers to work together in a special "chained" mode. This requires one of the first eight interrupts requests to be dedicated to the chaining process. IBM selected IRQ 2 for this function, which means IRQ 2 is no longer available to the system.

To maintain complete compatibility with the PC/XT's single interrupt controller, IRQ 9 is handled in a special way. AT+ systems attach the IRQ 9 line to the same adapter bus connector line as was used on the XT/PC for IRQ 2. Often systems and vendors refer to IRQ 2, which is really IRQ 9. When IRQ 9 is activated, the interrupt controller issues interrupt 71h.

Now with some clever BIOS footwork, the AT system is made to be 100% compatible with hardware and software that expects IRQ 2. To do this, the BIOS interrupt 71h handler issues an End-Of-Interrupt (EOI) to the second controller only. The BIOS then issues an interrupt 0Ah. This simulates the services of the original PC/XT, which vectors IRQ 2 to interrupt 0Ah. In this fashion, the AT+ system makes the system appear both software and hardware identical to older PC/XT standard.

Because of the unusual handling of IRQ 9, there are often errors in various technical references. Some refer to the physical IRQ 9 line incorrectly as IRQ 2, even though it merely has the apparent function of IRQ 2. From a software standpoint, this is not very important. As a programmer you can consider all systems (PC, XT, AT+) as having either a real IRQ 2 or a virtual IRQ 2, for which the programming is identical.

The first two entries of Table 7-8 show how the same adapter card will operate on the PC/XT and AT+ systems. As an alternative, the third entry shows a card designed only for the AT+. The third entry bypasses the BIOS interrupt 71h handler and directly handles interrupt 71h. Generally this is not recommended, as other adapters fail if they use the virtual IRQ 2.

Table 7-8. IRQ 2 and IRQ 9 Operations

System	Real IRQ	Virtual IRQ	Interrupt Handler
PC or XT	2	none	0Ah
AT+	9	2	0Ah
AT+	9	none	71h

Int	Description	Type
72h	IRQ 10—General Adapter Use	Hardware

This interrupt is unassigned and is available for a 16-bit adapter connected to IRQ 10.

Int	Description	Type
73h	IRQ 11—General Adapter Use	Hardware

INT

This interrupt is unassigned and is available for a 16-bit adapter connected to IRQ 11.

Int	Description	Type
74h	IRQ 12—Mouse Port	Hardware

INT

On systems with a built-in mouse port, IRQ 12 is used to inform the BIOS that data is available from the mouse. Refer to Chapter 8, The Keyboard System, for more details about the mouse port. For systems without a built-in mouse port, the interrupt is unassigned and is available for a 16-bit adapter connected to IRQ 12.

Int	Description	Type
75h	IRQ 13—Math Coprocessor Error	Hardware

INT

On IBM and 100% compatible clone AT+ systems the interrupt/error line from the math coprocessor is attached to IRQ 13h. When activated, interrupt 75h occurs.

On a PC/XT the math coprocessor interrupt line is connected to NMI, interrupt 2. AT+ systems maintain compatibility with the PC/XT design through the interrupt 75h BIOS handler. This handler sends the required End-Of-Interrupt signals to both interrupt controllers and then issues an interrupt 2, the non-maskable interrupt.

A few clone AT+ systems have the coprocessor interrupt/error line miswired on the motherboard. See interrupt 10h for additional explanation of this problem.

On EISA systems, this interrupt is also used for the DMA adapter. When a DMA is in chaining mode, it signals the system when the DMA needs the next set of memory addresses for a chained DMA operation in progress. See Chapter 18, DMA Services and DRAM Refresh, about the EISA DMA use of interrupt 75h.

Int	Description	Type
76h	IRQ 14—Hard Disk Controller	Hardware

INT

For AT+ systems, when the primary hard disk controller completes an action, it signals IRQ 14. The primary controller can handle up to two devices. AT and EISA system's interrupt 76h handler sets the byte at 40:8Eh to FFh to flag operation completion. The interrupt 76h handler also issues an interrupt 15h with function ax=9100h to indicate the hard disk controller operation is complete. Refer to Chapter 11, Hard Disk System, for more details.

Int	Description	Type
77h	IRQ 15—General Adapter Use	Hardware

INT

This interrupt is unassigned and is available for a 16-bit adapter connected to IRQ 15. For systems with two IDE controllers (for up to 4 IDE devices), this interrupt is typically used for the secondary controller. The secondary controller is used for the third and fourth hard disks or related IDE devices.

Int	Description	Type
C0-C3h	Hard Disk 0 User Defined Data	Data

On some AT+ systems, the BIOS can provide a user-defined set of hard disk parameters. The pointer to this group of 16 bytes is shown under interrupt 41h, described previously. When a user-defined entry is created, it is saved in the CMOS memory. The system's POST transfers 16 bytes from CMOS into RAM starting at location 300h. The pointer stored at RAM location 0:104h (interrupt 41h) points to this data. Not all BIOSes support user-defined hard disk types, and of those that do, many do not store the information here.

Int	Description	Type
C4-C7h	Hard Disk 1 User Defined Data	Data

On some AT+ systems, the BIOS can provide a user-defined set of hard disk parameters. The pointer to this group of 16 bytes is shown under interrupt 46h, described previously. When a user-defined entry is created, it is saved in the CMOS memory. The system's POST transfers 16 bytes from CMOS into RAM starting at location 310h. The pointer stored at RAM location 0:118h (interrupt 46h) points to this data. Not all BIOSes support user-defined hard disk types, and of those that do, many do not store the information here.

CHAPTER 8

The Keyboard System

On the surface, the keyboard system seems relatively simple. The keyboard system gets far more confusing as you look into the lowest levels. Keyboard control has changed dramatically between the first PC, the AT, and MCA systems. In fact there are now two microprocessors to run the keyboard system, separate from the main CPU!

The chapter explains all of the detailed steps that occur—from when a key is pressed to when an application gets the key. This includes following the process through the two microcontrollers, several interrupt services, and much more.

As you may already know, there are several layers of keyboard code translation. I'll show how this works with a complete table of the keyboard-to-controller codes, controller-to-system codes, and resultant ASCII codes. Unlike any tables I've seen before, these are organized in alphabetical order for easy reference.

Later in the chapter, we describe how you access the keyboard controllers, with complete source code to send and receive information, and change the keyboard LED states. An example program ties all of these routines together to show the rarely seen keyboard-to-controller codes and scan codes.

Lastly, I've compiled the most extensive list of I/O port functions and commands needed to access the keyboard controllers and hardware mouse port. This list covers many undocumented functions and features of the keyboard controller. For example, the keyboard controller also handles the A20 address line, used to access memory above one megabyte.

Introduction

The keyboard system converts keystrokes into usable code for application programs. The system also performs a number of services for applications, the operating system, and direct actions depending on the key combinations pressed. The keyboard system is comprised of the keyboard itself, a keyboard interface on the motherboard, a low-level BIOS interrupt service handler (interrupt 9), an intermediate BIOS interrupt service handler (interrupt 16h), and the operating system interface.

Each of these parts combine to provide key input to an application that is running on top of the operating system. Unfortunately, in an attempt to make it easier for applications to access keyboard information, a variety of problems were created. Many applications must access the keyboard below the operating system interface to provide required functions. Some of these functions include:

- Access to unavailable key combinations
- Interception of keys
- Key substitution
- Keyboard "stuffing"
- Shift key state detection
- Performance enhancements
- Repeat rate and delay control
- Terminate and Stay Resident (TSR) hot keys

The operating system and intermediate BIOS services should be used whenever possible because of identical operation on all platforms. In addition, these interfaces are generally well documented. We'll only spend a limited amount of space covering these services. Refer to any good book on services for the operating system you use. Several references are listed in the bibliography. To accomplish more advanced tasks, you'll need to understand and be able to access the lower-level functional parts of the keyboard system.

Basic Operation

The keyboard has an 8031 or 8048 single chip microcontroller to handle all keyboard actions. This controller scans the keys for depressions and releases, and on the AT keyboard, controls the three LEDs. It encodes the key pressed and released information into Kscan codes. This information is then sent over a dedicated bidirectional serial link to the motherboard. In addition, the controller inside 101+ key keyboards simulates some key combinations for compatibility with older designs.

The original PC/XT motherboard contains hardware to convert the serial keyboard data into a byte of data. This byte is read from one port of the 8255 programmable interface chip. The system's keyboard BIOS software communicates with the 8255 port to get keyboard information, such as scan codes.

In the AT, the old PC/XT design was replaced by a far more sophisticated organization. An 8042 single-chip microcontroller is used to link the system with the keyboard. This controller is responsible for all keyboard serial link communications, data validity checking, buffering data between the BIOS and the keyboard, and translation of Kscan codes into scan codes.

Unlike the original PC and XT, the AT's keyboard serial link was made bidirectional so the motherboard controller can send commands to the keyboard. The motherboard controller also handles several system functions, completely unrelated to the keyboard, such as enabling the A20 address line and issuing a hardware system reset. This system arrangement is shown in Figure 8-1.

Figure 8-1. The Keyboard Controller

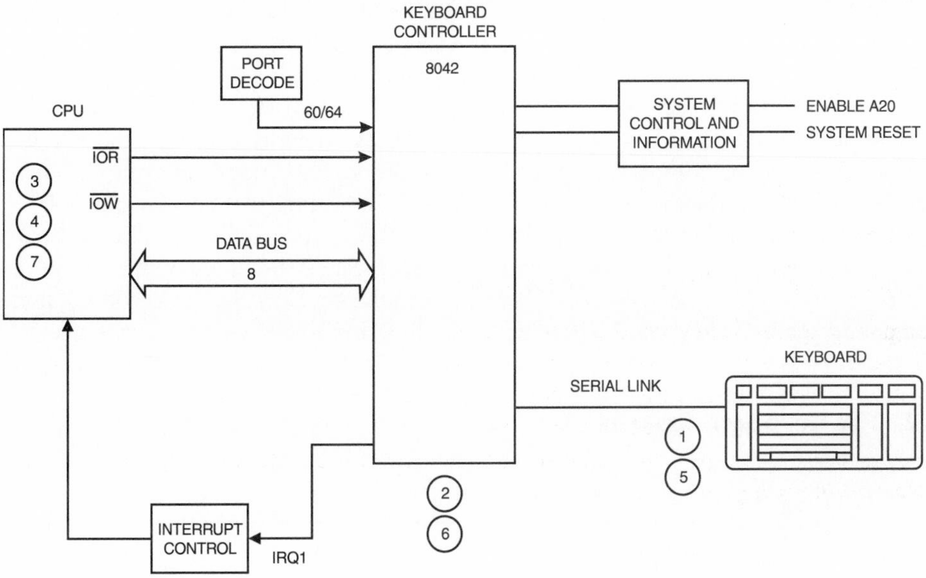

A Typical Key Press Operation on the AT

When the "P" key is pressed, a series of actions are set into motion. First, the 8031 controller inside the keyboard detects that the "P" key is depressed and sends a Kscan code value of 4Dh over the keyboard serial link. The 8042 keyboard controller on the motherboard receives the Kscan byte. The 8042 translates the Kscan code 4Dh into the system scan code value 19h, and places the value in its output buffer. This resultant scan code matches the scan codes produced by the PC/XT keyboard for software compatibility. The motherboard controller then issues an interrupt request indicating that data are available. The interrupt request calls the interrupt 9 handler, the keyboard BIOS. The keyboard BIOS reads the scan code from the motherboard controller and translates the scan code into an ASCII byte 70h. For this example, we've assumed no shift keys are active at the same time. In other words, the "P" key generates a lower-case "p." The keyboard handler puts both the scan code and the ASCII byte into the next available spot in the 16-word FIFO keyboard buffer. Lastly, the keyboard interrupt is cleared, and the keyboard BIOS exits, returning control to the task running at the time of the keyboard interrupt.

The operating system or application program uses interrupt 16h, the intermediate keyboard BIOS service, to access the keyboard buffer. Interrupt 16h functions are used to find if a key is available and to determine the value of a key. The Get Key function of interrupt 16h returns the oldest key in the buffer with both the scan code and ASCII value. For the "P" key pressed, the function returns the value 1970h. The intermediate keyboard BIOS then removes the key from the keyboard buffer.

When the "P" key is released another series of actions is set into motion. The microcontroller in the keyboard detects that the "P" key has been released and sends the release code value of F0h followed by the Kscan code value of 4Dh on the keyboard serial link. The 8042 keyboard controller on the motherboard receives the two bytes. The 8042 translates the Kscan code 4Dh into the system scan code value 19h, and sets bit 7 high as an indication that the key was released. The combined value, 99h, is then placed in the motherboard controller's output buffer. The motherboard controller then issues an interrupt request indicating that data are available.

The interrupt request calls the interrupt 9 handler, the keyboard BIOS. The keyboard BIOS reads the scan code from the motherboard controller. Since the "P" key released information that serves no function, the keyboard BIOS ignores the key. Finally, the keyboard interrupt is cleared, and again the keyboard BIOS exits. Figure 8-2 shows the keyboard system.

Figure 8-2. The Keyboard System

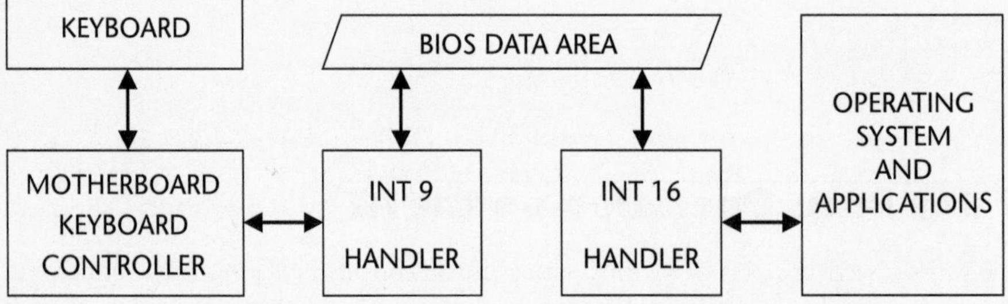

A Typical Key-Pressed Operation on the PC/XT

When the "X" key is pressed, a different series of actions is set into motion from those that occur with current AT designs. First, the 8048 microcontroller inside the keyboard detects that the "X" key is depressed and sends the scan code value of 2Dh over the keyboard serial link. The motherboard logic converts the serial data back into a byte and saves the byte in a latch. The output of this latch is connected to port C of the 8255 programmable interface chip. No translation of the scan code is performed as is required in an AT+ system. The motherboard hardware logic also issues an interrupt request indicating the motherboard has data available from the keyboard. The interrupt request calls the interrupt 9 handler, the keyboard BIOS. The keyboard BIOS reads the scan code from port C of the 8255 and translates the scan code into an ASCII byte 78h. For this example, we've assumed that no shift keys were depressed at the same time. The keyboard BIOS puts both the scan code and the ASCII byte into the next available spot in the 16-word FIFO keyboard buffer. Lastly, the keyboard interrupt is cleared and the keyboard BIOS exits.

Just like AT+ systems previously described, the operating system or application program uses interrupt 16h, the intermediate keyboard BIOS, to access the keyboard buffer. Interrupt 16h functions are used to find out if a key is available and the value of the key. The Get Key function of interrupt 16h returns the oldest key in the buffer with the scan code and ASCII code. For the "X" key pressed, the function returns the value 2D78h. The intermediate keyboard BIOS then removes the key from the keyboard buffer.

When the "X" key is released the next set of actions occur. The microcontroller in the keyboard detects the "X" key has been released and sends the release code value of ADh. This is just the "X" scan code of 2Dh with bit 7 set on to indicate the key was just released. Just as when the key was pressed, the value is sent over the serial link, and presented to the 8255 port. An interrupt is generated to signal that new data are available.

The interrupt request calls the interrupt 9 handler, the keyboard BIOS. The keyboard BIOS then reads the scan code from the 8255 port. Since the "X" key released information serves no function, the handler ignores the key. The keyboard interrupt is cleared, and again the handler exits.

Controller Communications

On the AT+, ports 60h and 64h communicate with the motherboard keyboard controller. Port 60h is used to write and read information that is passed to or from the keyboard. Port 64h is used to read status from the motherboard keyboard controller and to send commands to the motherboard keyboard controller. These are explained in much greater detail later in this chapter.

On the PC and XT, port 60h is used to read data directly from the keyboard. Several bits in port 61h enable and disable the keyboard. Port 61h is described in Chapter 13, System Functions.

Keyboard to Motherboard Data

The motherboard controller communicates with the keyboard over a single serial line. A synchronized clock line is provided from the motherboard to the keyboard when data are sent from the keyboard. Each 11-bit serial frame consists of a start bit, 8 data bits, an odd parity bit, and a stop bit.

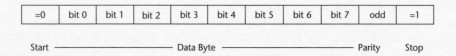

=0	bit 0	bit 1	bit 2	bit 3	bit 4	bit 5	bit 6	bit 7	odd	=1

Start ———— Data Byte ———— Parity Stop

In the idle state, both the data and clock lines are high. To begin sending the data to the motherboard, the keyboard sends the start bit on the data line (0). The motherboard responds by starting the clock line, with the first clock pulse going low. The clock is continued, with the keyboard sending each bit in turn. At the 11th clock, the keyboard sends the stop bit (1), and the clock line resumes its idle high state.

The data byte sent normally has key-pressed information. In addition, Table 8-1 shows commands that are sent from the keyboard to the motherboard. Only the communication value FFh is supported on PC and XT keyboards.

Table 8-1. Communication Values, Keyboard to Motherboard

Value	Description
0	Overrun—The internal 16-character first-in-first-out buffer has filled, and key action(s) may have been lost. This buffer is unrelated to the 16-word keyboard-buffer in the BIOS data area. (On keyboards that have multiple scan code sets, value 0 occurs only with sets 2 or 3. Overruns using set 1 cause a value FFh to be generated.)
AAh	Self-Test OK—The self-test diagnostic passed.
EEh	Echo—The return value after an Echo command.
F0h	Break Prefix—After a key is released, the keyboard sends a F0h followed by the Kscan code number of the key released. (AT+ only)
FAh	Acknowledgment—After a command is received by the keyboard, the keyboard returns this acknowledgment byte. The Echo and Resend commands do not initiate an acknowledgment byte.
FCh	Self-Test Failed—The self-test diagnostic failed.
FDh	Internal Failure—A periodic test of the keyboard's internal sense amplifier failed.
FEh	Resend—A resend command is sent whenever an invalid command or parity error was received by the keyboard.
FFh	Overrun—The internal 16-character first-in-first-out buffer has filled, and key action(s) may have been lost. (On keyboards that have multiple scan code sets, such as the PS/2, FFh occurs only with set 1. Overrun occurring with sets 2 and 3 generate a 0 value).

If the data from the AT+ type keyboard have a parity error, the motherboard controller automatically sends a retry message to the keyboard. If the parity error is not cleared after a number of attempts, the motherboard controller gives up and declares the attempted data unreadable. The parity error status bit is set and the motherboard controller's output buffer, port 60h, is set to the parity error code. The error code value depends on the internal controller command byte as sent to port 64h, using sub-command 60h. If the command byte bits 5, 6, and 7 are all 0, the error value is 00h; otherwise the error value is FFh.

A key depression sends a scan or Kscan code to the keyboard controller. If the key is held down, then the code repeats at the typematic rate. When the key is released, except for the Pause key, the "release" byte F0h is sent followed by a second byte with the key's code. The Pause key does not generate a release code.

Internal to the keyboard is a first-in-first-out buffer. On the PC/XT this buffer holds 20 bytes, and on the AT+ keyboards it is 16 bytes. Should too many keyboard actions occur, and the buffer fills to capacity, the next action will cause an overrun code of 0 to be inserted where key information was lost. This buffer should not be confused with the 16 key buffer that the keyboard BIOS routine handles. Should a keystroke require multiple bytes, the entire sequence must fit within the available buffer. If it does not fit, an overrun occurs, and the key is lost.

On AT+ systems, when a proper key-pressed Kscan code is received by the motherboard controller the code is normally translated into a system scan code. This scan code can then be read from port 60h. For example, when the Escape key is pressed, the keyboard sends the Kscan code 76h to the keyboard controller. In normal operation this is translated to the system scan code of 01h. The normal scan conversion can be turned off by clearing bit 6 of the command byte 20h at port 64h.

The AT+ keyboard responds to all transmissions, except the commands Echo and Respond. The keyboard sends the byte value FAh indicating successful receipt of the last transmission. If the motherboard controller fails to get a proper response within 25 milliseconds, the motherboard controller sets both the receive and transmit timeout bits and loads the error value FEh into the motherboard controller's output buffer (read port 60h).

Non-scan code values that the AT+ keyboard sends are shown in Table 8-2. All other values indicate a key-pressed scan code number. These values are read from port 60h.

Table 8-2. Software Readable Communication Values from the Keyboard

Value	Description
0	Keyboard parity error (when command byte bits 5, 6, & 7 = 000)
F1h	Password not installed (after command A4h). Not used in all systems
FAh	Keyboard acknowledge of previous data sent to keyboard
FCh	Mouse transmit error. Not used in all systems
FEh	Keyboard fails to provide proper acknowledgment
FFh	Keyboard parity error (when command byte bits 5, 6, & 7 are not 000)

Motherboard to Keyboard Data on the AT

The serial format previously described is also used to send data from the motherboard controller to the keyboard. In the idle state, both the data and clock lines are high. To begin sending the data to the keyboard, the motherboard sends the start bit on the data line (0). The keyboard responds by starting the clock line, with the first clock pulse going low. A problem is flagged if this clock does not start within 15 milliseconds, or if the first clock cycle is more than 2 milliseconds long. The problem is indicated by the transmit timeout bit 5 being set in the motherboard controller status byte. In addition, an error value of FEh is loaded into the controller's output buffer that can be read from port 60h.

With normal operation, the clock is continued. The motherboard controller sends each data bit in turn. At the 11th clock, the motherboard sends the stop bit (1), and the clock line resumes its idle high state.

Keyboard BIOS—Low Level

When the motherboard receives a byte from the keyboard, the motherboard flags the system by issuing a hardware interrupt IRQ 1. This initiates an interrupt 9 service, handled by the keyboard system BIOS.

The interrupt 9 service routine on AT+ systems takes the following actions:

1. Temporarily disables the keyboard and interrupts since the routine is not reentrant.
2. Reads the byte from the keyboard controller
3. Issues a Key Intercept Interrupt 15h, ah=4Fh, al=key. If upon return the carry flag is cleared, ignore the key and exit (see below for more details)
4. Checks for keyboard commands Resend, Acknowledge, or Overrun, and handles the command as needed
5. Updates LEDs if a change has occurred with the Caps, Num, or Scroll Locks
6. Processes the key (see below)
7. Enables interrupts, issues EOI to interrupt controller, and re-enables the keyboard

When the keyboard controller sends an extended scan code, the first byte read is zero on a PC/XT, and E0h on AT+ keyboards. This indicates a second byte must be read to get the extended scan code byte.

The act of processing the key depends on the key combination. A number of special actions are taken by the keyboard BIOS when specific key combinations are detected. In these cases the key is not inserted into the keyboard buffer. These special key combinations are shown in Table 8-3.

Table 8-3. Special Key Combinations

Key Combination	Keyboard BIOS Action
Ctrl-Alt-Del	Issue a system reset, but skip a retest of the memory (warm boot)
Ctrl-Break	Clear the keyboard buffer and issue an interrupt 1Bh
Ctrl-Print Screen	Toggle keyboard echo to printer
Ctrl-Num Lock	Pause until another key is pressed and absorb that key
Pause	Pause until another key is pressed and absorb that key
Print Screen	Issue an interrupt 5
System Request	Issue an interrupt 15h, ax=8500h when pressed, and interrupt 15h, ax=8501h when released
Alt-Keypad	Convert up to three digits from the keypad (0 to 255) into a hex value and insert the number into the BIOS key buffer as if a key was pressed.
Shift keys	Save the new shift state (Ctrl, Alt, Shift, Insert, Caps Lock, Num Lock, Scroll Lock)
Other	Convert scan code with shifts states into ASCII. If the BIOS key buffer is full, beep; otherwise store a word into the key buffer with the upper byte containing the scan code and the lower byte containing the ASCII character.

Some BIOS manufacturers also provide special key combinations for other purposes. These tend to vary among different manufacturers, and even vary among different versions from the same manufacturer.

Table 8-4. Nonstandard Key Combinations

Key Combination	Keyboard BIOS Action
Ctrl-Alt-Gray Minus	Set the processor clock to low-speed mode. This was useful on fast systems to run old programs that were speed-sensitive. Though rarely used today, it is sometimes handy to see problems that occur too quickly. (Gray Minus is on the Num Pad)
Ctrl-Alt-Gray Plus	Set the processor clock to high-speed mode. (Gray Plus is on the Num Pad)
Ctrl-Alt-Left Shift-Gray Minus	Turn off the system cache. This was provided to support older cache systems that could cause problems with programs that perform self-modifying code and other non-recommended coding practices. (Newer caches offer a write-back method that avoids this problem.) To reactivate the cache, use Ctrl-Alt_Gray Plus.
Ctrl-Alt-Esc	Invoke the BIOS setup program.
Ctrl-Alt-S	Invoke the BIOS setup program.
Ctrl-Alt-Ins	Invoke the BIOS setup program.

Many laptops also have special key functions for monitoring remaining battery power, setting color shading on a monochrome display, and other functions. These have no standardization, and seem to be different for every laptop model made! (OK, a few manufacturers are somewhat consistent within their own product line, but it seems quite rare.)

Keyboard BIOS—Intermediate Level

To access the keyboard buffer and status, applications and operating systems use the keyboard BIOS services from interrupt 16h. These services get data from the keyboard buffer, obtain the status of the keyboard, and read shift key states. If possible, access to the keyboard should be made at this level or through the operating system.

Interrupt 16h is comprised of up to ten services depending on the BIOS implementation:

Function	Description	Platform
ah=0	Read keyboard input	All
ah=1	Check keyboard status	All
ah=2	Get shift flag status	All
ah=3	Set typematic rate and delay	AT+ (some)
ah=4	Keyboard click adjustment	PCjr, Convertible
ah=5	Store key data into buffer	AT+ (most)
ah=9	Typematic capabilities	AT+ (some)
ah=Ah	Get keyboard ID	Some
ah=10h	Read extended keyboard input	AT+ (most)
ah=11h	Check extended keyboard status	AT+ (most)
ah=12h	Get extended shift flag status	AT+ (most)
ah=13h	DBCS Shift Control	DOS/V
ah=14h	Shift status display control	DOS/V

INT

Int	Func	Description	Platform
16h	0	Read Keyboard Input	All

This function reads the next available key. If a key is in the keyboard buffer, the two-byte value is removed from the buffer and returned in AX. If no key is available, the function waits until a key is available before returning.

On AT systems, if no key is available, an Interrupt 15h, function AX=9002h is issued. This alerts the operating system that this function is waiting for a key, and another task might be performed until a key is received. When a key is received after this wait, the keyboard BIOS issues an Interrupt 15h, function AX=9102h to indicate the interrupt is complete. The key is then removed from the buffer and returned to the original caller.

Called with:	ah = 0
Returns:	ah = scan code
	al = ASCII character
	A value of 0 indicates a non-ASCII function key, like F1, was pressed. AH is then used to determine which function key was pressed.
Notes:	When using extended keyboards, unique key combinations are converted to key functions available on 84 key keyboards. Use function AH=10h to get unique extended key information. Key functions from extended keyboards that have no equivalent on 84 key keyboards are thrown away.

Int	Func	Description	Platform
16h	1	Check Keyboard Status	All

INT
III I

This function checks if a key is waiting in the key buffer. If a key is available the scan code and ASCII equivalent value are returned in AX, but are not removed from the buffer.

Called with:	ah = 1
Returns:	zero flag = 1, no key is available
	zero flag = 0, a key is in the buffer and:
	ah = scan code
	al = ASCII character
	A value of 0 indicates a non-ASCII function key, like F1, was pressed. AH is then used to determine which function key was pressed.
Notes:	When using extended keyboards, unique key combinations are converted to key functions available on 84-key keyboards. Use function AH=11h to get unique extended key information. Key functions from extended keyboards that have no equivalent on 84-key keyboards are ignored.

Int	Func	Description	Platform
16h	2	Get Shift Flag Status	All

INT
III I

This function returns the state of the shift flags stored in the BIOS data area at 40:17h.

Called with:	ah = 2		
Returns:	al = Shift and Toggle status		
	bit	7 = 1	Insert on
		6 = 1	Caps Lock on
		5 = 1	Num Lock on
		4 = 1	Scroll Lock on
		3 = 1	Alt key down

2 = 1	Control key down
1 = 1	Left Shift key down
0 = 1	Right Shift key down

ah = value may not be preserved

Notes: When using extended keyboards, additional flag status is available by using function AH=12h.

INT Int	Func	Description	Platform
16h	3	Typematic Rate and Delay	AT+ (some)

Almost all AT systems or later, and a few XT systems, offer the ability to set the typematic rate. The typematic rate is the number of times per second a depressed key repeats. In addition, this function sets the typematic delay. This delay is the time from when a key is first pressed to when the start of the first repeated key is generated.

This function has six subfunctions that are only available on some BIOSes. Interrupt 16h, function AH=9 determines which subfunctions are supported. Refer to function AH=9 for additional details. All AT+ systems support subfunction 5, which sets the typematic rate and delay.

Subfunction AL=0 (if function AH=9 allows it)

Called with: ax = 300h

Returns: Return the keyboard to its defaults: typematic on, and default typematic rate and delay

Subfunction AL=1 (PCjr only)

Called with: ax = 301h

Returns: Typematic delay increased

Subfunction AL=2 (PCjr only)

Called with: ax = 302h

Returns: Slows the typematic rate

Subfunction AL=3 (PCjr only)

Called with: ax = 303h

Returns: Typematic delay increased and slows the typematic rate

Subfunction AL=4 (if function AH=9 allows it)

Called with: ax = 304h

Returns: Turn off typematic feature

Subfunction AL=5 (AT+ and some XT systems)

Called with: ax = 305h

bl = typematic rate to set

Hex	Characters Per Second	Hex	Characters Per Second
0	30.0	10	7.5
1	26.7	11	6.7
2	24.0	12	6.0
3	21.8	13	5.5
4	20.0	14	5.0
5	18.5	15	4.6
6	17.1	16	4.3
7	16.0	17	4.0
8	15.0	18	3.7
9	13.3	19	3.3
A	12.0	1A	3.0
B	10.9 *	1B	2.7
C	10.0	1C	2.5
D	9.2	1D	2.3
E	8.6	1E	2.1
F	8.0	1F	2.0

*typical default value

bh = delay until typematic begins

0 = 250 ms
1 = 500 ms
2 = 750 ms
3 = 1,000 ms

Returns: Typematic rate and delay set to values specified

Subfunction AL=6 (if function AH=9 allows it)

Called with: ax = 306h

Returns: bl = the typematic rate (see the prior subfunction for values)

bh = the delay value until typematic begins

0 = 250 ms
1 = 500 ms
2 = 750 ms
3 = 1,000 ms

Int	Func	Description	Platform
16h	4	Keyboard Click	Convertible, PCjr

This function controls the electronic keyboard click sound on the PC Convertible and PCjr. A few older laptops also provided this function.

Called with: ah = 4
al = 0 to set the keyboard click off
1 to set the keyboard click on

Int	Func	Description	Platform
16h	5	Store Key data into Buffer	AT+ (most)

Almost all AT systems or later, and a few XT systems, offer the ability to load key data into the keyboard buffer as if a key was pressed. This "stuffed" key is placed at the end of the keyboard FIFO buffer, and does not affect keys already in the buffer. This is useful to provide a simple macro capability or to control other applications. See Code Sample 8-7 later in this chapter to detect whether this function is supported.

Called with: ah = 5
cl = ASCII character
ch = Keyboard scan code

Returns: al = 0 when operation is successful
1 if the keyboard buffer is full

Int	Func	Description	Platform
16h	9	Typematic Capabilities	AT+ (some)

This determines which interrupt 16h function 3 subfunctions are supported. It returns bits indicating which specific subfunctions are available. Function 3, subfunction 5 is available on all AT+ class machines, so it is unnecessary to check if it is supported.

Now the operation gets a little more confusing! Before function 9 is issued, an interrupt 15h, function AH=C0h must be issued to confirm that interrupt 16h function 9 is supported. The following code shows how this is done. This function is explained in more detail under interrupt 15h in Chapter 13, System Functions.

```
        mov     ah, 0C0h                   ; get ptr es:bx to
        int     15h                        ;   ROM configuration
        jc      not_supported              ; exit if unavailable
        test    byte ptr es:[bx+6], 40h    ; int 16h, ah=9 support?
        jz      not_supported              ; exit if not supported
        mov     ah, 9                      ; do it
        int     16h
```

Once it is determined that interrupt 16h, function 9 is supported, function 9 is issued:

Called with: ah = 9

Returns: al = typematic capabilities

bit	7 = x	Unused
	6 = x	Unused
	5 = x	Unused
	4 = x	Unused
	3 = 1	Int 16h, function ax=306h supported
	2 = 1	Int 16h, function ax=305h supported
	1 = 1	Int 16h, function ax=304h supported
	0 = 1	Int 16h, function ax=300h supported

Int	Func	Description	Platform
16h	Ah	Get Keyboard ID	Some

INT III I

Gets the keyboard ID word from the keyboard. This function uses port 60h command F2h to get the ID word from the keyboard. This function is not supported on most AT and PS/2 systems, but is supported on the IBM PS/2 model 55, for the Japanese market. The keyboard ID codes are valid for IBM keyboards in Japan only, and may be different for other vendors.

The Japanese "G" and "P" style keyboards are similar to those used in the U.S., but provide several additional function keys for the input of Japanese characters. The "A" style keyboard is an older design offering an additional 24 special purpose keys. When using interrupt 16h, functions 0, 1, 10h, and 11h, all these keyboards act identically.

Called with: ah = Ah

Returns: bx = Keyboard ID

0000 = no keyboard attached
41AB = New "G" keyboard in translate mode
54AB = New "P" keyboard in translate mode
83AB = New "G" keyboard in pass-through mode

84AB = New "P" keyboard in pass-through mode
90AB = Old "G" keyboard
91AB = Old "P" keyboard
92AB = Old "A" keyboard

Int	Func	Description	Platform
16h	10h	Read Extended Keyboard Input	AT+ (most)

This function reads the next available key. If a key is in the keyboard buffer the two-byte value is removed from the buffer and returned in AX. If no key is available, the function waits until a key is available before returning. This function is supported on almost all AT+ systems and some XT systems. See Code Sample 8-7 to detect if this function is supported.

On AT systems, if no key is available, an Interrupt 15h, function AX=9002h is issued. This alerts the operating system that this function is waiting for a key, and another task might be performed until a key is received. When a key is received after this wait, the keyboard BIOS issues an Interrupt 15h, function AX=9102h to indicate the interrupt is complete. The key is then removed from the buffer and returned to the original caller.

Called with: ah = 10h

Returns: ah = scan code or special character ID
al = ASCII character
A value of 0 or E0 indicates a non-ASCII function key, like F1, was pressed. AH is then used to determine which key function was pressed.

Notes: This function differs from function 0. Extended keyboard key data bytes are returned unaltered. This allows differentiation of keys such as the Gray Plus key, and the shifted Plus key. With function 0, pressing either key will return ax=0D2Bh. With function 10h, the shifted Plus returns ax=0D2Bh, and the Gray Plus returns ax=4E2Bh. Refer to Table 8-5 on Keyboard Codes.

Some extended key combinations will only return a value using functions 10h and 11h and are ignored for functions 0 and 1. For example, Alt-Esc is ignored when using functions 0 and 1. These are shown in Table 8-5 shaded in gray.

Int	Func	Description	Platform
16h	11h	Check Extended Keyboard Status	AT+

This function checks if a key is waiting in the key buffer. If a key is available the value is returned in AX, but is not removed from the buffer. This function is supported on all AT+ systems and some XT systems. See Code Sample 8-7 to detect if this function is supported.

Called with: ah = 11h

Returns: zero flag = 1, no key is available

zero flag = 0, a key is in the buffer

ah = scan code or special character ID

al = ASCII character

A value of 0 or E0 indicates a non-ASCII function key, like F1, was pressed. AH is then used to determine which key function was pressed.

Notes: This function differs from function 1. Extended keyboard key data bytes are returned unaltered. This allows differentiation of keys such as the Gray Plus key, and the shifted Plus key. With function 0, pressing either key will return ax=0D2Bh. With function 10h, the shifted Plus returns ax=0D2Bh, and the Gray Plus returns ax=4E2Bh. Refer to Table 8-5 on Keyboard Codes.

Int	Func	Description	Platform
16h	12h	Get Extended Shift Flag Status	AT+

This function returns the state of the shift flags stored in the BIOS data area at 40:17h into AL. In addition, extended shift flags from BIOS data areas 40:18h and 40:96h are combined and inserted into AH. This function is supported on all AT+ systems and some XT systems.

Called with: ah = 12h

Returns: al = Shift and Toggle status

bit	7 = 1	Insert on
	6 = 1	Caps Lock on
	5 = 1	Num Lock on
	4 = 1	Scroll Lock on
	3 = 1	Alt key down
	2 = 1	Control key down
	1 = 1	Left Shift key down
	0 = 1	Right Shift key down

ah = Extended Shift status

bit	7 = 1	Sys Req key down
	6 = 1	Caps Lock key down
	5 = 1	Num Lock key down
	4 = 1	Scroll Lock key down
	3 = 1	Right Alt key down
	2 = 1	Right Ctrl key down
	1 = 1	Left Alt key down
	0 = 1	Left Ctrl key down

Int	Func	Description	Platform
16h	13h	DBCS Shift Control	DOS/V

This function gets and sets the Double Byte Character Set (DBCS) shift status information when the Japanese Front-End-Processor (FEP) is installed. The FEP is responsible for the input of Japanese characters and conversion into double byte characters.

Subfunction	Description	Int	Function
AL=0	Set DBCS Shift Status	16h	AH=13h

This subfunction loads the DBCS shift status.

Before changing the shift status, the current status should be obtained using function 1301h. The bits described can be changed, but the internal status bits should not be altered. This means bits 3, 4, 5, and 8 to 15 should be written with the same value read from function 1301h.

Katakana, Hiragana, and Romaji are different forms of the Japanese language, Kanji.

```
Called with:    ax = 1300h
                dx = Shift status
                     bits 15-8 = x  Internal status (see text)
                             7 = 0  No Katakana to Kanji conversion
                                 1  Katakana to Kanji conversion mode
                             6 = 0  Romaji off
                                 1  Romaji on
                             5 = x  Internal status (see text)
                             4 = x  Internal status (see text)
                             3 = x  Internal status (see text)
                             2 = x | Character Input Mode
                             1 = x |   bit 2    bit 1
                                       0        0 = alphanumeric
                                       0        1 = Katakana
                                       1        0 = Hiragana
                                       1        1 = unused
                             0 = 0  Half size
                                 1  Full size
Returns:        nothing
```

Subfunction	Description	Int	Function
AL=1	Get DBCS Shift Status	16h	AH=13h

INT

This subfunction gets the current DBCS shift status. If the FEP is not installed, the DX register is returned with zero.

Called with: ax = 1301h

Returns: dx = Shift status

bits 15-8 = x	Internal status	
7 = 0	No Katakana to Kanji conversion	
1	Katakana to Kanji conversion mode	
6 = 0	Romaji off	
1	Romaji on	
5 = x	Internal status	
4 = x	Internal status	
3 = x	Internal status	
2 = x	Character Input Mode	
1 = x	bit 2	bit 1
	0	0 = alphanumeric
	0	1 = Katakana
	1	0 = Hiragana
	1	1 = unused
0 = 0	Half size	
0 = 1	Full size	

Int	Func	Description	Platform
16h	14h	Shift Status Display Control	DOS/V

INT

This function controls the shift status row(s), which appears at the bottom line on the display. The shift status row(s) show the current character input mode and other related information. The Front-End-Processor (FEP) is responsible for handling this function, and will use interrupt 10h, function 19h to control the display of Japanese DBCS shift information.

The shift status display provides three subfunctions:

AL=	Description
0	Enable Shift Status Display
1	Disable Shift Status Display
2	Get State of Shift Status Display

Subfunction	Description	Int	Function
AL=0	Enable Shift Status Display	16h	AH=14h

Instruct the FEP, if installed, to display shift status on the bottom row of the display.

Called with: ax = 1400h
Returns: nothing

Subfunction	Description	Int	Function
AL=1	Disable Shift Status Display	16h	AH=14h

Instruct the FEP, if installed, to turn off the display shift status on the bottom row of the display.

Called with: ax = 1401h
Returns: nothing

Subfunction	Description	Int	Function
AL=2	Get State of Shift Status Display	16h	AH=14h

Gets the current state of the shift status display from the FEP.

Called with: ax = 1402h
Returns: al = 0 Shift status display enabled
1 Shift status display disabled or FEP not installed

Keyboard BIOS Data Areas

The low-level keyboard BIOS (interrupt 9) and the intermediate keyboard BIOS (interrupt 16h) use a number of areas in the BIOS to store flags and key pressed information. All of the BIOS data area is covered in Chapter 6, BIOS Data and Other Fixed Data Areas, but data specific to the keyboard system are also described here.

Location	Description	Size
40:17h	Keyboard flags, Shift and Toggle status	Byte

Interrupt 9 maintains these flags of Shift keys and Toggle keys.

bit	7 = 1	Insert on
	6 = 1	Caps Lock on
	5 = 1	Num Lock on
	4 = 1	Scroll Lock on
	3 = 1	Alt key down
	2 = 1	Control key down
	1 = 1	Left Shift key down
	0 = 1	Right Shift key down

Location	Description	Size
40:18h	Keyboard flags, Current Shifts state	Byte

Interrupt 9 stores the current state of key positions for toggle and shift keys in this byte.

bit	7 = 1	Insert key down
	6 = 1	Caps Lock key down
	5 = 1	Num Lock key down
	4 = 1	Scroll Lock key down
	3 = 1	Pause activated
	2 = 1	Sys Req key down
	1 = 1	Left Alt key down
	0 = 1	Left Ctrl key down

Location	Description	Size
40:19h	Alt Number Entry Scratch Pad	Byte

This is a work area used by the BIOS. When entering a decimal number with the Alt key and num-pad keys, this byte stores digits entered.

Location	Description	Size
40:1Ah	Keyboard Head Pointer	Word

The Keyboard Head Pointer is the offset in segment 40h of the first key in the keyboard buffer. If the keyboard head pointer is equal to the keyboard tail pointer no keys are in the buffer.

Location	Description	Size
40:1Ch	Keyboard Tail Pointer	Word

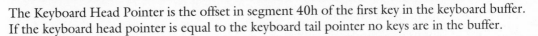

The Keyboard Tail Pointer is the offset in segment 40h where the next incoming key value will be placed in the keyboard buffer. If the keyboard head pointer is equal to the keyboard tail pointer no keys are in the buffer.

Location	Description	Size
40:1Eh	Keyboard Buffer	16 Words

The keyboard buffer is a 16-word FIFO that holds up to 15 key scan code/ASCII values from interrupt 9. The intermediate keyboard BIOS, interrupt 16h reads keys from this buffer. The head and tail pointers point to the first and last entries.

Location	Description	Size
40:71h	Control-Break Flag	Byte

Bit 7 = 1 if the Ctrl-Break key has been pressed. This bit is set by the low level interrupt 9 keyboard routine.

Location	Description	Size
40:80h	Keyboard Buffer Start	Word

The keyboard buffer start holds the offset to the beginning of the keyboard buffer in segment 40h (AT+ only).

Location	Description	Size
40:82h	Keyboard Buffer End	Word

The keyboard buffer end holds the offset to the end of the keyboard buffer in segment 40h (AT+ only).

Location	Description	Size
40:96h	Keyboard Status	Byte

This byte holds keyboard status information used by interrupt 9h (AT+ only).

bit	7 = 1	Reading ID of keyboard
	6 = 1	Last code is first ID character
	5 = 1	Forced num lock
	4 = 1	101+ key keyboard
	3 = 1	Right Alt key down
	2 = 1	Right Ctrl key down
	1 = 1	Last scan coded was E0h
	0 = 1	Last scan coded was E1h

Location	Description	Size
40:97h	Keyboard Internal Flags	Byte

This byte holds keyboard flags for interrupt 9 operations with the keyboard controller and the current keyboard LED states (AT+ only).

bit	7 = 1	Keyboard transmit error
	6 = 1	LED update in progress
	5 = 1	Keyboard sent a Resend
	4 = 1	Keyboard sent an Acknowledge
	3 = 0	Unused
	2 = 1	Caps Lock LED on
	1 = 1	Num Lock LED on
	0 = 1	Scroll Lock LED on

Hot Keys and Access to Undefined Keys

It is necessary for TSRs to get access to keys, such as hot-key combinations prior to the normal BIOS keyboard service routine. Applications may also need to detect key combinations that are not supported by the BIOS keyboard service routine. For example, a program might need to intercept the Print-Screen key and perform additional actions, such as sending printer setup information in advance of the screen data.

To accomplish this on pre-AT class machines, it is necessary to replace the standard keyboard BIOS interrupt 9 handler. Unfortunately, only one program can replace the keyboard BIOS handler. There is no way to pass this information onto another keyboard handler once the key is input. This causes a number of conflicts when two or more programs attempt to get direct access to the key input stream.

With the AT, IBM's engineers added the ability to hook the keyboard stream. After the BIOS routine reads a key scan code, the BIOS immediately makes a call to interrupt 15h, with AH=4Fh. The AL register has the scan code of the key that was read. The carry flag is set to indicate the key is valid. Now multiple applications can hook interrupt 15h, and look for function 4Fh. Should an important key combination occur, the application can take one of three actions:

1. Ignore the key, and pass the key onto other hooked applications and back to the BIOS keyboard handler to process. The carry flag is left set in this case.
2. Remove the key as if the key never occurred. This is useful for TSR hot-keys. The TSR records that the hot key occurred so it can take action at a later time. The TSR clears the carry flag to indicate to any other application that hooked interrupt 15h, and to the BIOS keyboard handler, that there is no longer a key to process. The BIOS will still be responsible for clearing the interrupt request.

3. Substitute a different key scan code for the one that occurred. In this scenario, the value in AL is changed, but the carry flag is left on. Any other applications hooking interrupt 15h after this application and the BIOS keyboard handler will see only the new key. Remember that the changed key must be a scan code value and is not ASCII.

Scan Codes

Many technical references seem to have the obligatory scan code tables, but I've found them hard to use, and lacking in detail. The tables below will have some of the same information everyone else has, but I've added the complete lists of the keyboard to motherboard controller Kscan codes supplied from the AT+ keyboard. These Kscan codes are different from the system scan codes delivered by the motherboard controller to the low level BIOS keyboard handler, interrupt 9. I also think you'll find this list is better organized for quick reference.

The translation performed by the motherboard controller can be turned off. The motherboard controller's command byte, bit 6, controls if the Kscan codes are to be translated into system scan codes (see port 64h). This is useful if you need to detect unusual key combinations, like Shift-F1-Q that would normally be filtered out by the motherboard controller. MCA systems have several optional keyboard scan code sets. See port 60h, command F0h for more details. Scan code set 2, the default on MCA systems, is identical to the Kscan codes shown in Table 8-5.

Only the keyboard "make" codes are shown, which appear when a key is depressed. When a key is released, the Kscan code is normally preceded by an F0h byte. For example, when the letter "B" is pressed, the Kscan code 32h is sent. When the "B" key is released, the Kscan codes F0h and 32h are sent. If the key was already preceded by an E0h extended function byte, the release code has the E0h extended function byte, followed by F0h, followed by the Kscan code. For example, when the right-Ctrl is pressed, the two-byte make code is E0,14. Upon key release the Kscan bytes are E0,F0,14.

The motherboard controller translates the release code into the system scan code with bit 7 set to 1. Release scan codes are filtered by the low level BIOS routine, interrupt 9, and are not placed into the BIOS keyboard buffer.

Table 8-5. Keyboard Codes

U.S. Key Legend	Keybd Size	Kscan Code	Scan Code	——ah/al from int 16h (scan/ASCII)—— No-Shift		Shifted		Control	Alt
A		1C	1E	1E/61	a	1E/41	A	1E/01	1E/00
B		32	30	30/62	b	30/42	B	30/02	30/00
C		21	2E	2E/63	c	2E/43	C	2E/03	3E/00
D		23	20	20/64	d	20/44	D	20/04	20/00
E		24	12	12/65	e	12/45	E	12/05	12/00
F		2B	21	21/66	f	21/46	F	21/06	21/00
G		34	22	22/67	g	22/47	G	22/07	22/00
H		33	23	23/68	h	23/48	H	23/08	23/00
I		43	17	17/69	i	17/49	I	17/09	17/00
J		3B	24	24/6A	j	24/4A	J	24/0A	24/00
K		42	25	25/6B	k	25/4B	K	25/0B	25/00
L		4B	26	26/6C	l	26/4C	L	26/0C	26/00
M		3A	32	32/6D	m	32/4D	M	32/0D	32/00
N		31	31	31/6E	n	31/4E	N	31/0E	31/00
O		44	18	18/6F	o	18/4F	O	18/0F	18/00
P		4D	19	19/70	p	19/50	P	19/10	19/00
Q		15	10	10/71	q	10/51	Q	10/11	10/00
R		2D	13	13/72	r	13/52	R	13/12	13/00
S		1B	1F	1F/73	s	1F/53	S	1F/13	1F/00
T		2C	14	14/74	t	14/54	T	14/14	14/00
U		3C	16	16/75	u	16/55	U	16/15	16/00
V		2A	2F	2F/76	v	2F/56	V	2F/16	2F/00
W		1D	11	11/77	w	11/57	W	11/17	11/00
X		22	2D	2D/78	x	2D/58	X	2D/18	2D/00
Y		35	15	15/79	y	15/59	Y	15/19	15/00
Z		1A	2C	2C/7A	z	2C/5A	Z	2C/1A	2C/00
0)		45	0B	0B/30	0	0B/29	)		81/00
1!		16	02	02/31	1	02/21	!		78/00
2@		1E	03	03/32	2	03/40	@	03/00	79/00
3#		26	04	04/33	3	04/23	#		7A/00
4$		25	05	05/34	4	05/24	$		7B/00
5%		2E	06	06/35	5	06/25	%		7C/00
6^		36	07	07/36	6	07/5E	^	07/1E	7D/00
7&		3D	08	08/37	7	08/26	&		7E/00
8*		3E	09	09/38	8	09/2A	*		7F/00
9(		46	0A	0A/39	9	0A/28	(		80/00

Table 8-5. Continued

U.S. Key Legend	Keybd Size	Kscan Code	Scan Code	——ah/al from int 16h (scan/ASCII)——					
				No-Shift		Shifted		Control	Alt
1 End		69	4F	4F/00		4F/31	1	75/00	###
2 Down		72	50	50/00		50/32	2	91/00	###
3 PgDn		7A	51	51/00		51/33	3	76/00	###
4 Left		6B	4B	4B/00		4B/34	4	73/00	###
5 (center)		73	4C	4C/00		4C/35	5	8F/00	###
6 Right		74	4D	4D/00		4D/36	6	74/00	###
7 Home		6C	47	47/00		47/37	7	77/00	###
8 Up		75	48	48/00		48/38	8	8D/00	###
9 PgUp		7D	49	49/00		49/39	9	84/00	###
0 Insert		70	52	52/00		52/30	0	92/00	###
'"		52	28	28/27	’	28/22	"		28/00
,<		41	33	33/2C	,	33/3C	<		33/00
-_		4E	0C	0C/2D	-	0C/5F	_	0C/1F	82/00
.>		49	34	34/2E	.	34/2E	>		34/00
/?		4A	35	35/2F	/	35/3F	?		35/00
;:		4C	27	27/3B	;	27/3A	:		27/00
=+		55	0D	0D/3D	=	0D/2B	+		83/00
[{		54	1A	1A/5B	[	1A/7B	{	1A/1B	1A/00
|	102-	5D	2B	2B/5C	\	2B/7C	|	2B/1C	2B/00
]}		5B	1B	1B/5D	]	1B/7D	}	1B/1D	1B/00
`~		0E	29	29/60	`	29/7E	~		29/00
BackSpace		66	0E	0E/08		0E/08		0E/7F	0E/00
Tab		0D	0F	0F/09		0F/00		94/00	A5/00
Enter-main		5A	1C	1C/0D		1C/0D		1C/0A	1C/00
Space		29	39	39/20		39/20		39/20	39/20
Del.		71	53	53/00		53/2E	.	93/00	
Gray-		7B	4A	4A/2D	-	4A/2D	-	8E/00	4A/00
Gray+		79	4E	4E/2B	+	4E/2B	+	90/00	4E/00
Enter		5A	1C	1C/0D		1C/0D		1C/0A	1C/00
Escape		76	01	01/1B		01/1B		01/1B	01/00
* PrintSrcn	83/84	7C	37	37/2A	*			96/00	37/00
F1		05	3B	3B/00		54/00		5E/00	68/00
F2		06	3C	3C/00		55/00		5F/00	69/00
F3		04	3D	3D/00		56/00		60/00	6A/00
F4		0C	3E	3E/00		57/00		61/00	6B/00
F5		03	3F	3F/00		58/00		62/00	6C/00
F6		0B	40	40/00		59/00		63/00	6D/00
F7		83	41	41/00		5A/00		64/00	6E/00
F8		0A	42	42/00		5B/00		65/00	6F/00

Table 8-5. Continued

U.S. Key Legend	Keybd Size	Kscan Code	Scan Code	——ah/al from int 16h (scan/ASCII)—— No-Shift	Shifted	Control	Alt
F9		01	43	43/00	5C/00	66/00	70/00
F10		09	44	44/00	5D/00	67/00	71/00
F11	101	78	57	85/00	87/00	89/00	8B/00
F12	101	07	58	86/00	88/00	8A/00	8C/00
Enter-num	101	E0,5A	E0/1C	E0/0D 1C/0D	E0/0D 1C/0D	E0/0A 1C/0A	A6/00
Gray /	101	E0,4A[2]	E0,35	E0/2F / 35/2F /	E0/2F / 36/2F /	95/00	A4/00
Gray *	101	7C	37	37/2A *	37/2A *	96/00	37/00
Gray End	101	E0,69[1]	E0,4F	4F/E0	4F/E0	75/E0	9F/00
Gray Down	101	E0,72[1]	E0,50	50/E0	50/E0	91/E0	A0/00
Gray PgDn	101	E0,7A[1]	E0,51	51/E0	51/E0	76/E0	A1/00
Gray Left	101	E0,6B[1]	E0,4B	4B/E0	4B/E0	73/E0	9B/00
Gray Right	101	E0,74[1]	E0,4D	4D/E0	4D/E0	74/E0	9D/00
Gray Home	101	E0,6C[1]	E0,47	47/E0	47/E0	77/E0	97/00
Gray Up	101	E0,75[1]	E0,48	48/E0	48/E0	8D/E0	98/00
Gray PgUp	101	E0,7D[1]	E0,49	49/E0	49/E0	84/E0	99/00
Gray Ins	101	E0,70[1]	E0,52	52/E0	52/E0	92/E0	A2/00
Gray Del	101	E0,71[1]	E0,53	53/E0	53/E0	93/E0	A3/00
L-Ctrl		14	1D				
L-Shift		12	2A				
R-Shift		59	36				
CapsLock		58	3A				
NumLock		77	45				
ScrollLock		7E	46				
L-Alt		11	38				
R-Alt	101	E0,11	E0,38				
R-Ctrl	101	E0,14	E0,1D				
PrintScrn[3]	101	E0,12, E0,7C	E0,2A, E0,37			72/00	
Pause	101	E0,14, 77,E1[4]	E1,1D, E1,45				
SysReq	84+	84	54				
keya	102	5D					
keyb	102	61					
left window	104	E0,1F	E0,5B				
right window	104	E0,27	E0,5C				
list bit	104	E0,2F	E0,5D				

Table 8-5. Continued

Scan code table notes:

All values in hex.

"xx,xx" indicates multiple bytes make up the scan code for that key. The first byte E0h indicates a second byte must be read to determine the key.

"xx/xx" indicates the ah/al pair values that are stored in the BIOS key buffer. Interrupt 16h, functions 0, 1, 10h and 11h, return the scan code in ah, and ASCII (if key has ASCII equivalent) in al. With functions 0 and 1 only, if the al table value is E0, the actual return value is 00.

***Gray shaded** scan codes indicates nothing returned in int 16h, functions 0 and 1. Only functions 10h and 11h return value in gray box.*

When Alt key and 1 to 3 digits are entered on the numeric pad, the decimal number, 0 to 255, is converted to an ASCII character.

Keyboard Size:

blank = applicable to all keyboards
83/84 = Only on 83/84 key keyboards
84+ = Available on 84, 101, 102, and 104 key keyboards (not on 83 key keyboard)
101 = Available on 101, 102, and 104 key keyboards only
102- = Not available on 102 key keyboard
102 = Only available on 102 key keyboard (non-U.S. keyboards)
104 = Windows 95 type keyboards with 3 extra keys beyond 101 key style

[1] *On the 101+ keyboard, these keys should take the indicated action regardless of the state of the Shift key and NumLock key. To ensure this and maintain Kscan code compatibility with 84 key keyboards, additional Kscan codes are sent depending on the state of the Shift and NumLock. If the shift is down or NumLock is on (but not both) then extra codes are sent to make it appear as if the shift/NumLock is not on during the key activation. This is done to fool the motherboard controller into always producing the specified function. (Remember that the old 84-key keyboard has these functions on the num-pad and they are activated depending on the num-lock and shifts). The following example shows the Kscan codes for the Gray HOME key, E0,6C. The end result is the motherboard controller issues a HOME scan code function regardless of the Shift and NumLock states. Note that the Kscan code for the Shift key is 12.*

Shift	***Num-Lock***	***Make Kscan Codes***	***Release Kscan Codes***
Off	*Off*	*E0,6C*	*E0,F0,6C*
Off	*On*	*E0,12,E0,6C*	*E0,F0,6C,E0,F0,12*
Down	*Off*	*E0,F0,12,E0,6C*	*E0,F0,6C,E0,12*
Down	*On*	*E0,6C*	*E0,F0,6C*

Table 8-5. Continued

[2]On 101+ key keyboards, the Kscan code is modified depending on the state of the keyboard Shift. If the Shift is down, then extra codes are sent to make it appear as if the shift key is up during the key activation. This is done to fool the motherboard controller into always creating a "/" key function, otherwise it would create a "|" function as specified on the 84-key keyboard. Note that the Kscan code for the Shift key is 12.

Shift	*Make Kscan Codes*	*Release Kscan Codes*
Off	*E0,4A*	*E0,F0,4A*
Down	*E0,F0,12,E0,4A*	*E0,F0,4A,E0,12*

[3]On 101+ key keyboards, the PrintScrn key must activate print screen regardless of the Shift state. If Alt is also pressed then the Sys-Req function is issued. Since the Print Screen key must maintain compatibility with 84 key keyboards, the keyboard must fool the motherboard controller by sending additional Kscan codes to make it appear the Print Screen key or Sys-Req was pressed. Kscan code 12 is for the Shift, Kscan 7C is the PrintScrn key, and 84 is the Sys-Req key.

Shift	*Ctrl*	*Alt*	*Make Kscan Codes*	*Release Kscan Codes*	*Function*
Off	*Off*	*Off*	*E0,12,E0,7C*	*E0,F0,7C,E0,F0,12*	*Prt Scrn*
Off	*Off*	*Down*	*84*	*F0,84*	*Sys Req*
Off	*Down*	*Off*	*E0,7C*	*E0,F0,7C*	*Prt Scrn*
Down	*Off*	*Off*	*E0,7C*	*E0,F0,7C*	*Prt Scrn*

[4]On 101+ key keyboards, the Ctrl-Pause key must simulate the Ctrl-Break function of the 84 key keyboard. When Ctrl is active while Pause is depressed, the keyboard generates a "Ctrl-Break" code. Note that this key has no release code, so one is included as part of the make code.

Ctrl	*Make Kscan Codes*	*Function*
Off	*E1,14,77,E1,F0,14,F0,77*	*Pause*
Down	*E0,7E,E0,F0,7E*	*Ctrl-Break*

Foreign Keyboards

Only a few keys differ between foreign keyboards and the U.S. keyboard shown in Table 8-5. Only those key legends that differ are noted in Tables 8-6 and 8-7. The Kscan codes will correspond to that of the U.S. keyboard, but the system scan codes will differ depending on the key function and the BIOS handler used.

Table 8-6. 84-Key Foreign Keyboards

<table>
<tr><th>U.S. key legend</th><th>French legend</th><th>German legend</th><th>Italian legend</th><th>Spanish legend</th><th>U.K. legend</th></tr>
<tr><td>A</td><td>Q</td><td></td><td></td><td></td><td></td></tr>
<tr><td>M</td><td>,?</td><td></td><td></td><td></td><td></td></tr>
<tr><td>Q</td><td>A</td><td></td><td></td><td></td><td></td></tr>
<tr><td>W</td><td>Z</td><td></td><td></td><td></td><td></td></tr>
<tr><td>Y</td><td></td><td>Z</td><td></td><td></td><td></td></tr>
<tr><td>Z</td><td>W</td><td>Y</td><td></td><td></td><td></td></tr>
<tr><td>0)</td><td>à0</td><td>0=</td><td>0=</td><td></td><td></td></tr>
<tr><td>1!</td><td>&1</td><td></td><td></td><td>1¡</td><td></td></tr>
<tr><td>2@</td><td>é2</td><td>2"</td><td>2"</td><td>2¿</td><td>2"</td></tr>
<tr><td>3#</td><td>"3</td><td>3§</td><td>3£</td><td></td><td>3£</td></tr>
<tr><td>4$</td><td>'4</td><td></td><td></td><td></td><td></td></tr>
<tr><td>5%</td><td>(5</td><td></td><td></td><td></td><td></td></tr>
<tr><td>6^</td><td>§6</td><td>6&</td><td>6&</td><td>6/</td><td></td></tr>
<tr><td>7&</td><td>è7</td><td>7/</td><td>7/</td><td></td><td></td></tr>
<tr><td>8*</td><td>!8</td><td>8(</td><td>8(</td><td></td><td></td></tr>
<tr><td>9(</td><td>Ç9</td><td>9)</td><td>9)</td><td></td><td></td></tr>
<tr><td>'"</td><td>`%</td><td>Ä</td><td>`a#</td><td>;:</td><td>'@</td></tr>
<tr><td>,<</td><td>;.</td><td>,;</td><td>,;</td><td>,?</td><td></td></tr>
<tr><td>-_</td><td>)°</td><td>ß?</td><td>'?</td><td></td><td></td></tr>
<tr><td>.></td><td>:/</td><td>.:</td><td>.:</td><td>.!</td><td></td></tr>
<tr><td>/?</td><td>=+</td><td>-_</td><td>-_</td><td>'"</td><td></td></tr>
<tr><td>;:</td><td>M</td><td>ö</td><td>ò@</td><td>Ñ</td><td></td></tr>
<tr><td>=+</td><td>-_</td><td>'`</td><td>ì^</td><td></td><td></td></tr>
<tr><td>[{</td><td>^¨</td><td>ü</td><td>èé</td><td>'"</td><td></td></tr>
<tr><td>\|</td><td>µ£</td><td>#^</td><td>ù§</td><td>Ç</td><td></td></tr>
<tr><td>]}</td><td>$*</td><td>+*</td><td>+*</td><td>`^</td><td>#~</td></tr>
<tr><td>`~</td><td><></td><td><></td><td><></td><td><></td><td>\|</td></tr>
</table>

Table 8-7. 102-Key Foreign Keyboards

U.S. Legend	Belgian	Canadian (French)	Danish	Dutch	French	German	Italian	Latin America	Norwegian	Portugese	Spanish	Swedish	Swiss	U.K.
A	Q				Q									
C				C¢										
M	,?	Mµ		Mµ	,?	Mµ								
0		0§												
P		P¶												
Q	A				A	Q@		Q@						
S				Sß										
W	Z				Z									
X				X»										
Y						Z							Z	
Z	W			Z«	W	Y							Y	
0)	à}0	0¼)	0}=	0'	à@0	0}=	0=	0=	0}=	0}=	0=	0}=	0=	
1!	&|1	1±!		11!	&1						1|!		1!+	
2@	é@2	2@"	2@"	2²"	é~2	2²"	2"	2"	2@"	2@"	2@"	2@"	2@"	2"
3#	"#3	3£/	3£#	3³#	"#3	3³§	3£		3£#	3£#	3#·	3£#	3#*	3£
4$	'4	4¢$	4$¤	4¼$	'{4				4$¤	4§$		§4$¤	4Ç	
5%	(5	5¤%		5½%	([5									
6^	§^6	6¬?	6&	6¾&	-|6	6&	6&	6&	6&	6&	6¬&	6&	6&	
7&	è7	7|&	7{/	7£_	è`7	7{/	7/	7/	7{/	7{/	7/	7{/	7/	
8*	!8	8²*	8[(	8{(	_\8	8[(	8(	8(	8[(	8[(	8(	8[(	8(	
9(	Ç{9	9³)	9])	9})	Ç^9	9])	9)	9)	9])	9])	9)	9])	9)	
'"	ù'%	`{`	0	'`	ù%	Ä	à#°	{^[	Æ	º ª	'{"	Ä	äàää	'@
,<	;.	'_'	,;	,;	;.	,;	,;	,;	,;	,;	,;	,;	,;	
-_	)°	-½_	+?	/\?	)]°	ß\?	'?	'\?	+?	'?	'?	+\?	'`?	
.>	:/	._.	.:	.•:	:/	.:	.:	.:	.:	.:	.:	.:	.:	
/?	=~+	'É	-_	-=	!§	-_	-_	-_	-_	-_	-_	-_	-_	
;:	M	;~:	Æ	+±	M	Ö	ò@Ç	Ñ	0	Ç	Ñ	Ö	öééö	
=+	-_	=¾+	'|`	°ç~	=}+	'`	ì^	¿¡	\'`	«»	¡¿	'`	^~`	
[{	^["	^[^	Å	¨^	^¨	Ü	è[é	'¨	Å	+¨*	`[^	Å	üééü	
]}	$]*	]¨	¨~^	*|	$¤£	+~*	+]*	~*	¨~^	'`	+]*	¨~^	¨!	
`~	23	#\\|	½§	@¬§	2	^°	\\|	|¬°	|§	\\|	<>	§½	§°	
key a	µ`£	<}>	'*	<>	*µ	#'	ù§	}`]	,*	~^	}Ç	,*	$£	#~
key b	<\>	«°»	<\>	]|[	<>	<|>	<>	<>	<>	<>	<>	<|>	<\>	\\|

Keys with 3 legends indicates the 2nd legend occurs when the AltCar key is pressed (under BIOS control). Keys with 4 legends (Swiss only) indicates that the 2nd legend occurs when the AltCar key is pressed, and the 4th legend occurs when Shift-AltCar is pressed. AltCar is the same as Alt-R on U.S. keyboards. Key a and key b do not exist on U.S. keyboards. The U.S. keyboard key “ \|” does not exist on foreign keyboards.

A20 Access to Extended Memory

A lock on the A20 address line has been provided on the keyboard controller for backwards compatibility with the 8088 on all AT systems and later. A little background is necessary to help understand the A20 lockout.

1MB Segment Wrap

The 286 and all later CPUs provide 16 MB or more of memory address range as compared with the 8088's 1 MB maximum memory address range. A quirk with the 8088 addressing scheme allowed a program to access the lowest 64 KB area using any segment:offset pair that exceeded the 1 MB limit. For example, the segment offset FFFF:50 will access the same byte as 0:40. Although there is no reason for software to ever use this quirk, bugs in a few very old programs used segment:offset pairs that wrap the 1 MB boundary. Since these programs seemed to work correctly, no actions were taken to correct the defects.

The 286 provides 16 MB of addressability, and provides its own quirk when accessing memory with a segment:offset pair that would cause a wrap on the 8088. Instead, the 286 CPU accesses 64 KB just above the 1 MB boundary. Table 8-8 helps to illustrate the differences in addressing memory between the 8088 and the 80286.

Table 8-8. CPU Memory Access at the 1 MB Boundary

Segment:Offset Address	8088 Physical Address	80286 Physical Address	Notes
FFFF:0	0FFFF0h	0FFFF0h	Same physical address
FFFF:10	0	100000h	1 M difference
FFFF:FFFF	0FFEFh	10FFEFh	1 M difference, limit is 16 bytes from end of 64 KB block

A20 Gate

To make the 80286 system appear identical to the 8088 addressing, IBM added external hardware to the 80286 to force the A20 address line to zero. This hardware is referred to as the A20 gate. When the A20 gate is in its default state, access to memory at 1MB will actually access memory in the first 64K, just like the 8088. Table 8-9 shows the result if the examples in Table 8-8 are used when the A20 address line is forced to zero.

Table 8-9. System Memory Access at the 1 MB Boundary (A20 Zero)

Segment:Offset Address	8088 Physical Address	80286 Physical Address	Notes
FFFF:0	0FFFF0h	0FFFF0h	Same physical address
FFFF:10	0	0	Same physical address
FFFF:FFFF	0FFEFh	0FFEFh	Same physical address

To allow memory access above the 1 M boundary, the A20 gate is enabled. The state of the CPU's address line 20 is then passed unaltered. This allows access to 64 K (less 16 bytes) just above the 1 MB boundary in all CPU modes, real and protected. To access the remainder of extended memory, it is necessary to go into protected mode, or use tricks I've described with the undocumented LOADALL instruction.

The 64K area just above the 1MB area is referred to as the High Memory Area (HMA). Recent versions of DOS can load portions of itself into the HMA to save space in the lower 640K. To make the HMA work, the A20 line must be enabled.

A20 Gate Status

Although the state of the A20 gate can be checked using the keyboard controller command D0h, a few systems fail to follow the IBM standard. In addition, reading the status from the keyboard controller takes a fair amount of code to follow the proper protocols. This chapter has additional details on using keyboard controller commands, and command D0h.

I've created a code fragment, shown in Code Sample 8-1, as an alternative means of getting the current A20 status. It is designed to work on any system. To determine the A20 state, the routine first compares the word at address 0:0 with data at address FFFF:10h. If the values are different, A20 is enabled. If the values are the same, the routine temporarily inverts the word at 0:0. The routine then compares the word at address 0:0 with data at address FFFF:10h. If the two words are the same, then A20 is presumed disabled and this routine returns an AX value of zero. If A20 is enabled, these two words will have different values and the routine returns 1 in AX.

Code Sample 8-1. Get the Current A20 Status

```
;    Get A20 Status
;
;       Called with:    nothing
;
;       Returns:        ax = 0  A20 disabled
;                            1  A20 enabled
;                       interrupts enabled
;
;       Regs Used:      ax

getA20  proc    near
        push    cx
        push    di
```

```
        push    si
        push    ds
        push    es

        mov     di, 10h
        mov     ax, 0FFFFh
        mov     es, ax                  ; es:di = FFFF:10h
        xor     ax, ax                  ; default ax=0
        mov     si, ax
        mov     ds, ax                  ; ds:si = 0:0
        mov     cx, ax

        cli                             ; disable interrupts
        mov     ax, es:[di]             ; get value at FFFF:10h
        cmp     ax, [si]                ; same as 0:0 ?
        je      getA20_skip1            ; jump if unknown state
        inc     cx                      ; A20 enabled (compare fails)
        jmp     getA20_exit

getA20_skip1:
        not     word ptr ds:[si]        ; invert word
        mov     ax, es:[di]             ; get value at FFFF:10h
        cmp     ax, [si]                ; same as 0:0 ?
        je      getA20_skip2            ; jump if disabled
        inc     cx                      ; A20 enabled (compare fails)
getA20_skip2:
        not     word ptr ds:[si]        ; restore word back to original

getA20_exit:
        sti                             ; enable interrupts
        mov     ax, cx                  ; return state in ax
        pop     es
        pop     ds
        pop     si
```

```
        pop     di
        pop     cx
        ret
getA20  endp
```

A20 Gate Control

In general, few programs are concerned with A20 gate control. The four groups of programs that handle the A20 gate include the BIOS, some advanced operating systems like NT and OS/2, memory managers, and DOS extenders.

If you need to go into protected mode, I would strongly recommend using the BIOS service interrupt 15h, function 89h, described in Chapter 13, System Functions. As part of this service, the A20 gate is handled to allow full access to extended memory.

In 99.9% of PC systems, the keyboard controller is used to handle the A20 gate. This may seem a bit odd, but the keyboard controller has some additional output lines which were not needed for keyboard operations. The remaining small percentage of systems that do not use the keyboard controller for A20 control are not fully IBM compatible, and are considered obsolete today. I've ignored these systems in the rest of this section.

One command is commonly used to set the A20 state, keyboard controller command D1h. Command D1h controls A20, reset, keyboard data, and other vendor dependent items. To avoid affecting other system functions, you must read the current status using command D0h first. With the current status in hand, the A20 bit can be changed before writing the new data back. Code Sample 8-2 shows how this is done. It uses keyboard controller subroutines described later in this chapter.

Code Sample 8-2. A20 Control

```
;    Set A20 Status
;
;       Called with:    ah = 0 to disable A20
;                            1 to enable A20
;
;       Returns:        A20 state changed
;
;       Regs Used:      cx

setA20  proc    near
```

```
        push    ax
        cli                             ; disable interrupts

; get the keyboard controller output status

        mov     bl, 0D0h                ; read port command
        call    keyboard_cmd            ; activate
        call    error_cmd               ; handle possible error
        call    keyboard_read           ; read value into AL
        mov     bl, al
        pop     ax                      ; get back settings
        mov     al, bl                  ; ah=keyboard controller value
        push    ax

; now write the old output status with the new A20 state

        mov     bl, 0D1h                ; command to change controller port
        call    keyboard_cmd            ; activate
        call    error_cmd               ; handle possible error
        pop     ax                      ; ah=new state (0 or 1)
                                        ; al=value from controller
        cmp     ah, 0                   ; disable A20 ?
        je      setA20_disable          ; jump if so
        or      al, 2                   ; set bit 1 to enable A20
        jmp     setA20_skip

setA20_disable:
        and     al, 0FDh                ; clear bit 1 to disable A20
setA20_skip:
        call    keyboard_write          ; send command to keyboard
        call    error_write             ; handle possible error
        sti
        ret
setA20  endp
```

On a few systems, two alternate keyboard controller commands are available. Command DDh disables A20, and command DFh enables A20. Using these commands is simpler and faster, but most vendors do not support these options.

Because A20 control is not the same on all systems, after changing the state, it is wise to verify the true A20 state has been selected (see Code Sample 8-1).

Warnings

Before reading any information from port 60h, the controller output buffer status should be checked to ensure a byte is available. Read port 64h to get the status and check that bit 0 is 1. If bit 0 is 0, then no valid information is available. MCA systems with a Type 1 controller (described below) must wait at least 7 microseconds after bit 0 transitions from 0 to 1, before reading the data from port 60h. Code to do this is shown in the Keyboard_read subroutine.

Before writing any information to port 60h, the controller input buffer must be empty. Read port 64h to get the status and check that bit 1 is 0. If bit 1 is 1, then the controller's input buffer is still full and cannot be written to.

When sending commands to the keyboard that are followed by data bytes to the keyboard, the controller should be disabled prior to the command. The following code excerpt shows how the typematic rate is set. Remember, you can't single step through this code, because the keyboard is disabled.

```
mov     bl, 0ADh
call    keyboard_cmd         ; disable keyboard (AD)
mov     al, 0F3h
call    keyboard_write       ; typematic rate command (F3)
mov     al, 0
call    keyboard_write       ; set fastest typematic rate (0)
mov     bl, 0AEh
call    keyboard_cmd         ; enable keyboard (AE)
```

MCA systems have two different types of motherboard controllers, Type 1 and Type 2. There are a few minor differences in operation and functions. The following code fragment detects the controller type by checking if the command byte's translate bit can be set to 1. Only type 1 controllers will allow this.

```
        mov     bl, 20              ; get command byte function
        call    keyboard_cmd
        call    keyboard_read
        mov     ah, al              ; save the command byte
        mov     bl, 60              ; set command byte function
        call    keyboard_cmd
        mov     al, ah              ; restore command byte
        or      al, 40h             ; set the keyboard translate bit
        call    keyboard_write      ; write new command
                                    ; Now re-read the command
        mov     bl, 20              ; get command byte function
        call    keyboard_cmd
        call    keyboard_read
        mov     bh, al              ; save result
        mov     bl, 60              ; set command byte function
        call    keyboard_cmd
        mov     al, ah              ; restore command byte
        call    keyboard_write      ; write original command byte
        and     bh, 0BFh            ; bh=0 if Type 2, bh=40h if Type 1
```

Keyboard Connection and Signals

The keyboard is connected through a 5-pin DIN connector on most ISA/EISA systems, though some use the newer connector design found on the PS/2.

Pin Number	Line
1	Keyboard Clock
2	Keyboard Serial Data
3	Unused
4	Ground
5	Power (+5.0 VDC)

Male End (from keyboard)

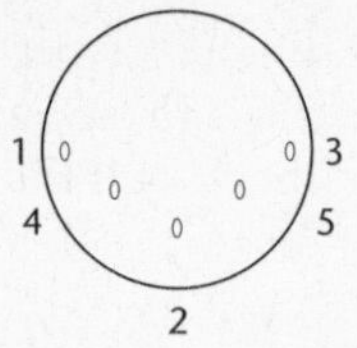

An alternate keyboard connector, a 6-pin miniature DIN connector, is typically used on most laptops and newer PCI systems, and all PS/1 and PS/2 machines. This same connector pinout is also used for the mouse on many systems.

Pin Number	Line
1	Serial Data
2	Unused
3	Ground
4	Power (+5.0 VDC)
5	Clock
6	Unused

Male End (from keyboard)

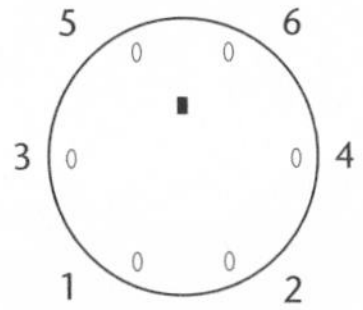

The signal and clock lines are driven from a open collector driver, with a 10K ohm pull-up resistor. This allows both the keyboard and the motherboard to each drive the clock and data lines when needed. These connector pinouts are useful to monitor the serial link with a logic analyzer or serial communications analyzer.

Code Sample 8-3. Controller Access

The next four routines handle basic keyboard functions to read and write bytes, and send commands to the controller. In addition the setLEDs routine loads the state of the three LEDs on the keyboard. They are all intended for AT+ systems.

```
;-------------------------------------------------------------------
;    KEYBOARD_READ
;       read a byte from the keyboard into al (port 60h).
;
;       Called with:    nothing
;
;       Returns:        if ah=0, al=byte read from keyboard
;                       if ah=1, no byte ready after timeout
;
;       Regs Used:      al

keyboard_read   proc    near
        push    cx
        push    dx

        xor     cx, cx              ; counter for timeout (64K)
```

```
key_read_loop:
        in      al, 64h             ; keyboard controller status
        IODELAY
        test    al, 1               ; is a data byte ready ?
        jnz     key_read_ready      ; jump if now ready to read
        loop    key_read_loop

        mov     ah, 1               ; return status - bad
        jmp     key_read_exit

key_read_ready:
        push    cx                  ; delay routine needed for
        mov     cx, 16              ;   MCA Type 1 controller.
key_read_delay:                     ;   Insures a 7 uS or longer
        IODELAY
        loop    key_read_delay      ;   Assumes CPU is 80486,
        pop     cx                  ;   66Mhz or slower

        in      al, 60h             ; now read the byte
        IODELAY
        xor     ah, ah              ; return status - ok
key_read_exit:
        pop     dx
        pop     cx
        ret
keyboard_read   endp

;----------------------------------------------------------------------
;    KEYBOARD_WRITE
;       Send byte AL to the keyboard controller (port 60h).
;       Assumes no BIOS interrupt 9 handler active.
;
;       If the routine times out due to the buffer remaining
;       full, ah is non-zero.
```

```
;
;       Called with:    al = byte to send
;                       ds = cs
;
;       Returns:        if ah = 0, successful
;                       if ah = 1, failed
;
;       Regs Used:      ax

keyboard_write  proc    near
        push    cx
        push    dx
        mov     dl, al                  ; save data for keyboard

        ; wait until keyboard receive timeout is clear (usually is)

        xor     cx, cx                  ; counter for timeout (64K)
kbd_wrt_loop1:
        in      al, 64h                 ; get keyboard status
        IODELAY
        test    al, 20h                 ; receive timeout occurred?
        jz      kbd_wrt_ok1             ; jump if not
        loop    kbd_wrt_loop1           ; try again
                                        ; fall through
        mov     ah, 1                   ; return status - failed
        jmp     kbd_wrt_exit

kbd_wrt_ok1:
        in      al, 60h                 ; dispose of anything in buffer

        ; wait for input buffer to clear (usually is)

        xor     cx, cx                  ; counter for timeout (64K)
kbd_wrt_loop:
```

```
        in      al, 64h             ; get keyboard status
        IODELAY
        test    al, 2               ; check if buffer in use
        jz      kbd_wrt_ok          ; jump if not in use
        loop    kbd_wrt_loop        ; try again
                                    ; fall through, still busy
        mov     ah, 1               ; return status - failed
        jmp     kbd_wrt_exit

        ; write data (temporally stored in DL)

kbd_wrt_ok:
        mov     al, dl
        out     60h, al             ; data to controller/keyboard
        IODELAY

        ; wait until input buffer clear (usually is)

        xor     cx, cx              ; counter for timeout (64K)

kbd_wrt_loop3:
        in      al, 64h             ; get keyboard status
        IODELAY
        test    al, 2               ; check if buffer in use
        jz      kbd_wrt_ok3         ; jump if not in use
        loop    kbd_wrt_loop3       ; try again
                                    ; fall through, still busy
        mov     ah, 1               ; return status - failed
        jmp     kbd_wrt_exit

        ; wait until output buffer clear

kbd_wrt_ok3:
        mov     ah, 8               ; larger delay loop (8 * 64K)
kbd_wrt_loop4:
```

```
        xor     cx, cx                  ; counter for timeout (64K)
kbd_wrt_loop5:
        in      al, 64h                 ; get keyboard status
        IODELAY
        test    al, 1                   ; check if buffer in use
        jnz     kbd_wrt_ok4             ; jump if not in use
        loop    kbd_wrt_loop5           ; try again
                                        ; fall through, still busy
        dec     ah
        jnz     kbd_wrt_loop4
kbd_wrt_ok4:
        xor     ah, ah                  ; return status ok
kbd_wrt_exit:
        pop     dx
        pop     cx
        ret
keyboard_write  endp

;-----------------------------------------------------------------
;    KEYBOARD_CMD
;       Send a command in register BL to the keyboard controller
;       (port 64h).
;
;       If the routine times out due to the buffer remaining
;       full, ah is non-zero.
;
;       Called with:    bl = command byte
;                       ds = cs
;
;       Returns:        if ah = 0, successful
;                       if ah = 1, failed
;
;       Regs Used:      ax, cx
```

```
keyboard_cmd    proc    near
        xor     cx, cx              ; counter for timeout (64K)
cmd_wait:
        in      al, 64h             ; get controller status
        IODELAY
        test    al, 2               ; is input buffer full?
        jz      cmd_send            ; ready to accept command ?
        loop    cmd_wait            ; jump if not
                                    ; fall through, still busy
        jmp     cmd_error

cmd_send:                           ; send command byte
        mov     al, bl
        out     64h, al             ; send command
        IODELAY

        xor     cx, cx              ; counter for timeout (64K)
cmd_accept:
        in      al, 64h             ; get controller status
        IODELAY
        test    al, 2               ; is input buffer full?
        jz      cmd_ok              ; jump if command accepted
        loop    cmd_accept          ; try again
                                    ; fall through, still busy
cmd_error:
        mov     ah, 1               ; return status - failed
        jmp     cmd_exit
cmd_ok:
        xor     ah, ah              ; return status ok
cmd_exit:
        ret
keyboard_cmd    endp
```

```
;----------------------------------------------------------------
;    SET LEDs
;       Send 3 bits from BL to the keyboard LEDs (handy for
;       debugging TSRs). Does NOT update the keyboard flags. The
;       next LED update will restore the 3 keyboard LEDs. In the
;       unlikely event that an LED update is in progress, the
;       update is skipped.
;
;           40:97h = keyboard_flags2
;                  bit 7 = 1 if keyboard transmit error occurred
;                  bit 6 = 1 if LED update is in progress
;                  bit 5 = 1 if resend received
;                  bit 4 = 1 if acknowledgment received
;
;       This routine also assumes the standard int 9 BIOS
;       keyboard handler maintains keyboard status in
;       keyboard_flags2 at 40:97h.
;
;       Called with:    bl, bit 0=1 to turn on Scroll Lock LED
;                               1=1 to turn on Num Lock LED
;                               2=1 to turn on Caps Lock LED
;                       other bits 3-7 ignored
;
;       Regs Used:      ax

setLEDs proc    near
        push    es
        mov     ax, 40h
        mov     es, ax                  ; es points to BIOS data
        cli                             ; ints off while update
        test    byte ptr es:[97h], 40h  ; already updating ?
        jnz     setLED_return3          ; return if so

        or      byte ptr es:[97h], 40h  ; set update in-progress
```

```
        mov     al, 0EDh                    ; Update LED command
        call    keyboard_write              ; send keyboard command
        test    byte ptr es:[97h], 80h      ; xmit error ?
        jnz     setLED_return1              ; exit if xmit error
        mov     al, bl
        and     al, 7                       ; only send 3 LED bits
        call    keyboard_write              ; LED data to keyboard
        test    byte ptr es:[97h], 80h      ; xmit error ?
        jz      setLED_return2              ; jump if not
setLED_return1:
        mov     al, 0F4h                    ; enable keyboard
        call    keyboard_write              ;  since error occurred
setLED_return2:
        and     byte ptr es:[97h], 3Fh      ; error off & update
setLED_return3:
        sti                                 ; enable interrupts
        pop     es
        ret
setLEDs endp
```

Code Sample 8-4. System Reset

This fragment is used to force a system reset on all AT+ systems by sending a command to the keyboard controller. Chapter 3, The CPU and Undocumented Instructions, goes into more depth about resetting the processor.

```
        mov     bl, 0FEh          ; reset system command
        call    keyboard_cmd      ; should not return!
        hlt
```

Code Sample 8-5. View Scan and Kscan Codes

KEYSCAN shows how the various elements of this chapter can be connected together to make a working program. In KEYSCAN the motherboard controller is set to optionally skip translation of Kscan codes from the AT keyboard. As a key is pressed, the unaltered Kscan code appears. These codes are normally translated by the 8042 motherboard controller into XT compatible system scan codes, with extensions for new keys. To see the Kscan codes, the command line option "K" is used. Otherwise, only the normal scan codes are shown.

The code sample takes over complete keyboard processing, and does not use BIOS services for its operation. The KEYSCAN program also shows the key release codes from the keyboard. In Kscan mode, the keyboard sends a F0h byte followed by the Kscan code for a released key. Some controllers in the non-translate mode alter this two-byte release code into a single Kscan byte with bit 7 set on. To exit the program, press Escape.

The entire program is not shown; only the main portions. Refer to the supplied diskette for complete source code.

```
;-----------------------------------------------------------------
;                            KEYSCAN
;-----------------------------------------------------------------
;
;    This program demonstrates the lowest level interactions
;    with the keyboard and keyboard controller.  It also
;    shows the Kscan codes between the keyboard and controller
;    and the scan codes translated by the controller and fed
;    normally to the BIOS interrupt 9 handler.
;
;    KEYSCAN performs the following actions:
;       Slows the keyboard repeat rate to the slowest allowed
;       Turns on all the keyboard LEDs (just to show how
;         it's done)
;       Displays the command byte we write for translation mode
;       Shows one of two types of scan codes when any key is
;         pressed.  The default (no command line option) shows
;         the typical scan code when a key is pressed (this
;         is what is sent to INT 9 normally). Uses the command
;         line option -k to show the Kscan codes which come
;         from the keyboard, before translated by the keyboard
```

```
;         controller.
;       Escape by pressing the Esc key or 50 key presses
;       Normal keyboard operation is restored
;       The LED state is restored
;       Keyboard repeat rate is set to 24 cps, with a 500 ms
;         delay before repeat starts
;
;    For all computers equipped with a 8042 style keyboard
;    controller (not for PC/XT).
;
;    (c) Copyright 1994, 1996  Frank van Gilluwe
;    All rights reserved.
;
;    V2.00 - Adds the option for Kscan codes or Scan codes.
;            Keyboard repeat rate slowed during operation.
;            Restores keyboard LED state on exit
;            Shows the Escape key scan code when pressed
;            Exit if 50 keys pressed and released or Escape
;            Improved KEYBOARD_WRITE to work with latest PCs

include undocpc.inc

cseg    segment para public
        assume  cs:cseg, ds:cseg, ss:stacka

keyscan         proc near

message1 db     CR, LF
         db     'KEYBOARD INFORMATION AND SCAN CODES'
         db     '            v2.00 (c) 1994, 1996 FVG'
         db     CR, LF
         db     '------------------------------'
         db     '---------------------------------------------'
         db     CR, LF
```

```
        db     '  To exit, press Escape', CR, LF, CR, LF, '$'

message2 db    '  Displays the normal scan code for each'
         db    ' key pressed.', CR, LF
         db    '  Use command line option -k to see the'
         db    ' untranslated scan codes.'
         db    CR, LF, CR, LF, '$'

message3 db    '  Displays the untranslated Kscan code for'
         db    ' each key pressed.', CR, LF, CR, LF, '$'

message4 db    'New keyboard command byte = '
commandb db    '  ', CR, LF, CR, LF, '$'

message5 db    'Returned scan code = '
scanbytN db    '  ', CR, LF, '$'

message6 db    'Returned Kscan code = '
scanbytK db    '  ', CR, LF, '$'

message7 db    'Keyboard read timeout error', CR, LF, '$'

message8 db    CR, LF
         db    'Complete - 50 keys pressed and released'
         db    CR, LF, '$'

message9 db    CR, LF
         db    'Complete - Escape key pressed', CR, LF, '$'

cmd_line db    0                    ; 'K' if no translation

start:
        xor    bl, bl
        cmp    byte ptr ds:[80h], 1 ; any characters on line ?
```

```
        jbe     no_options              ; jump if not
        mov     bl, ds:[83h]            ; get option on cmd line
no_options:
        mov     ax, cs
        mov     ds, ax
        mov     es, ax
        and     bl, 0dfh                ; convert to upper case
        mov     [cmd_line], bl          ; save option
        OUTMSG  message1                ; display initial message
        cmp     [cmd_line], 'K'         ; Translation or not?
        je      no_translate
        OUTMSG  message2                ; normal translation
        jmp     slow_rate

no_translate:

        OUTMSG  message3                ; show Kscan codes

; although not necessary, we'll change the repeat rate to the
; slowest rate so it is easy to see the key pressed and
; release codes

slow_rate:
        mov     ax, 305h                ; set typematic rate
        mov     bx, 031Fh               ; use 1 sec delay, 2 cps
        int     16h                     ; do it!

set_LEDs_on:
        mov     bl, 7                   ; turn all LEDs on
        call    setLEDs
```

```
; Send command to turn off keyboard interrupt IRQ1 (bit 0=0) so
;   the BIOS will not handle anything from the keyboard.
;   If Kscan mode, set keyboard translation off (bit 6=0)

        cli                           ; disable interrupts
        mov     bl, 60h               ; set command byte function
        call    keyboard_cmd          ; activate
        call    error_cmd             ; display if error (ah=1)
        mov     al, 24h               ; turn off use of IRQ 1
                                      ;  (int 9), no translation
        cmp     [cmd_line], 'K'       ; Kscan mode ?
        je      load_cmd              ; jump if so
        mov     al, 64h               ; translation ok
load_cmd:
        call    keyboard_write        ; send command to keyboard
        call    error_write           ; if error, display

; flush any remaining keys out of the buffer

flush_all:
        in      al, 64h               ; get status
        test    al, 1                 ; any keys to read ?
        jz      read_command
        call    keyboard_read         ; read until buffer empty
        jmp     flush_all


; Now read the just programmed command byte and display it

read_command:
        mov     bl, 20h               ; get command byte function
        call    keyboard_cmd          ; activate
        call    error_cmd             ; display if error (ah=1)
        call    keyboard_read         ; read command byte into al
```

```
        or      ah, ah              ; valid ?
        jnz     error               ; jump if not
        mov     bx, offset commandb
        call    hex                 ; convert to ascii
        OUTMSG  message4            ; display new command byte

        mov     dx, 100             ; maximum key press and
                                    ;   releases before exit

; Display each key pressed scan code screen or the release of
;   the escape key exits program

next_key:
        call    keyboard_read       ; read command byte into al
        or      ah, ah              ; valid ?
        jnz     next_key            ; loop if no key

display_key:
        push    ax                  ; save key for later
        push    dx
        cmp     [cmd_line], 'K'     ; Kscan type?
        je      display_kscan

        mov     bx, offset scanbytN
        call    hex                 ; convert to ascii
        OUTMSG  message5            ; display scan information
        jmp     display_next

display_kscan:
        mov     bx, offset scanbytK
        call    hex                 ; convert to ascii
        OUTMSG  message6            ; display Kscan information

display_next:
```

```
        pop     dx
        pop     ax

        mov     bl, 76h              ; Escape key Kscan code
        cmp     [cmd_line], 'K'
        je      check_if_esc
        mov     bl, 1                ; Escape key scan code
check_if_esc:
        cmp     al, bl               ; Escape key ?
        je      escape               ; exit if so
        dec     dx
        jnz     next_key             ; if under 100, get next
        OUTMSG  message8             ; display done
        jmp     done

; Escape pressed - so restore controller to normal operation

escape:
        OUTMSG  message9             ; display done
done:
        mov     bl, 60h              ; set command byte function
        call    keyboard_cmd         ; activate
        call    error_cmd            ; display if error (ah=1)
        mov     al, 45h              ; reset to normal
        call    keyboard_write       ; send command to keyboard
        call    error_write          ; if error, display
        jmp     exit


; Display keyboard read timeout error message

error:
        OUTMSG  message7             ; display error message
```

```
exit:
        sti
        mov     bl, 0AEh            ; enable keyboard
        call    keyboard_cmd        ; do-it
        call    error_cmd           ; display if error (ah=1)

; return the keyboard LEDs to the proper state

        mov     ax, 40h
        mov     es, ax
        mov     bl, es:[97h]        ; get the real LED flags
        call    setLEDs

; reset the repeat rate to something closer to normal

        mov     ax, 305h            ; set typematic rate
        mov     bx, 102h            ; use 500 msec delay, 24 cps
        int     16h                 ; do it!

        mov     ah, 4Ch
        int     21h                 ; exit
keyscan endp
```

Code Sample 8-6. Swap Keys TSR

This is a small TSR that swaps the functions of the CapsLock key and the Ctrl key. The TSR demonstrates how easy it is to change keys around to suit a user preference. When run, the TSR hooks interrupt 15h, function 4Fh to look at the incoming system scan codes. When CapsLock or Ctrl occurs, the scan code is changed. Running the TSR a second time performs a double swap, effectively returning key operation to normal.

```
;-----------------------------------------------------------------
;                          CTRL2CAP
;-----------------------------------------------------------------
;
;   TSR to swap the functions of the Ctrl and CapsLock keys.
;   System scan code for Ctrl = 1Dh, and for CapsLock = 3Ah
;
;   For all AT and later computers (not for PC/XT).
;
;   (c) Copyright 1993, 1996  Frank van Gilluwe
;    All Rights Reserved.

include undocpc.inc


cseg    segment para public
        assume  cs:cseg, ds:cseg, ss:tsrstk

;
; This is the resident handler to detect if CAPS or CTRL pressed
;   and swaps the system scan codes if so.

int_15h_hook    proc    far
        pushf
        cmp     ah, 4Fh                 ; interrupt 9 key function ?
        jne     skip_change             ; jump if not

        cmp     al, 3Ah                 ; caps make ?
        je      caps_make               ; jump if so
        cmp     al, 0BAh                ; caps release ?
        je      caps_release            ; jump if so

        cmp     al, 1Dh                 ; ctrl make ?
        je      ctrl_make               ; jump so
```

```
        cmp     al, 9Dh             ; ctrl release ?
        je      ctrl_release        ; jump if so
        jmp     skip_change

caps_make:
        mov     al, 1Dh             ; switch to ctrl make
        jmp     finish_int15
caps_release:
        mov     al, 9Dh             ; switch to ctrl release
        jmp     finish_int15
ctrl_make:
        mov     al, 3Ah             ; switch to caps make
        jmp     finish_int15
ctrl_release:
        mov     al, 0BAh            ; switch to caps release

finish_int15:
skip_change:
        popf
        jmp     cs:old_int_15h      ; process old int_15h

int_15h_hook    endp

old_int_15h     dd      0           ; old pointer saved here


;================================================================
; Start of nonresident installation portion

ctrl2cap        proc    far



start:
        push    cs
```

```
        pop     ds

; get the current interrupt 15h vector and save

        mov     al, 15h
        mov     ah, 35h
        int     21h             ; get current int 15h pointer
        mov     word ptr old_int_15h, bx
        mov     word ptr old_int_15h+2, es

; install our new interrupt 15h routine

        mov     dx, offset int_15h_hook
        mov     al, 15h
        mov     ah, 25h
        int     21h             ; install our interrupt

        OUTMSG  installmsg         ; display installed message

; now determine the size to remain resident (paragraphs)
;   and become a TSR

        mov     dx, (offset start - offset int_15h_hook) SHR 4
        add     dx, 11h            ; add PSP size + 1 paragraph
        mov     ax, 3100h          ; exit to DOS as tsr
        int     21h
ctrl2cap        endp


installmsg db   CR, LF
        db      'CTRL2CAP TSR Installed'
        db      ' - Ctrl key swapped with Caps-Lock'
        db      CR, LF, '$'
```

```
cseg    ends

;=========================================================== stack ====

tsrstk  segment para stack

        db      150 dup (0)

tsrstk  ends

        end     start
```

Code Sample 8-7. Functionality Detect

A number of interrupt 16h functions are not supported in all system BIOSes. The next two subroutines detect if functions 5, 9, 10h, 11h, 12h are available. The program KEYBIOS on the supplied diskette displays the results of these two subroutines.

```
;----------------------------------------------------------------------
;    KEYTYPE
;       Find out whether keyboard BIOS supports extended functions
;       interrupt 16h, functions 5, 10h, 11h, and 12h. To do
;       this, the keyboard buffer is flushed, and any prior
;       keys are discarded. The routine then tries to stuff
;       the key value FFFF into the buffer and read it using
;       the keyboard BIOS extended key functions.
;
;       Returns:        if ah=0, extended functions supported
;                       if ah=1, extended function not supported
;
;       Regs Used:      ax

keytype proc    near
```

```
        push    cx
key_loop1:
        mov     ah, 1               ; function 1, get status
        int     16h
        jz      key_try5            ; jump if no keys in buffer
        mov     ah, 0               ; function 0, get key
        int     16h                 ; discard key
        jmp     key_loop1           ; loop until buffer empty

key_try5:
        mov     ah, 5               ; try function 5
        mov     cx, 0FFFFh          ; put in bogus key value
        int     16h
        cmp     al, 0               ; al = 0 ok, 1 failed
        ja      key_no_ext

        mov     cx, 16              ; try up to 16 times
key_loop2:
        mov     ah, 11h             ; function 11h, get status
        int     16h
        jz      key_no_ext          ; jump if no key in buffer
        mov     ah, 10h             ; function 10h, get key
        int     16h
        cmp     ax, 0FFFFh          ; did key appear ?
        je      key_ok              ; jump if so, success!
        loop    key_loop2           ; try next key

; extended BIOS functions not supported

key_no_ext:
        mov     ah, 1
        jmp     key_ret

; the keyboard BIOS does support extended functions
```

```
key_ok:
        xor     ah, ah
key_ret:
        pop     cx
        ret
keytype endp



;---------------------------------------------------------------
;    KEY9
;       Find out if keyboard BIOS supports extended functions
;       interrupt 16h, function 9. This determination is
;       made after it is determined that other extended
;       functions are supported. In addition, it uses int 15h
;       function C0h to make this determination.
;
;       Returns:        if ah=0, extended function 9 supported
;                       if ah=1, extended function 9 not
;                                supported
;
;       Regs Used:      ax

key9    proc    near
        push    bx
        push    es
        mov     ah, 0C0h        ; get ptr es:bx to the
        int     15h             ;  ROM configuration
        jc      key9_not        ; jump if not supported
        test    byte ptr es:[bx+6], 40h  ; check for support
        jz      key9_not        ; jump if not supported

; interrupt 16h, function 9 is supported
```

```
        mov     ah, 0
        jmp     key9_exit

key9_not:
        mov     ah, 1
key9_exit:
        pop     es
        pop     bx
        ret
key9 endp
```

Port Summary

This is a list of ports used to communicate with the keyboard and the motherboard controller.

Port	Type	Function	Platform
60h	I/O	Keyboard Data	AT+
60h	Input	Keyboard Data	PC/XT
64h	I/O	Keyboard Controller Status & Commands	AT+

Command Confusion

Different commands are sent to the keyboard and the motherboard keyboard controller. In addition the controller has a "command byte." Each of these provide significantly different functions, but can be confused because of the similar terminology. The following key should help clarify each command type.

- Keyboard Command—Commands to the keyboard controller are always written to port 60h.
- Motherboard Controller Command—Commands to the motherboard keyboard controller are always written to port 64h.
- Command Byte—The keyboard controller command byte is accessed through a command to the keyboard controller.

Some commands will transfer data either to the motherboard keyboard controller or to the keyboard itself. Data is always transferred through port 60h. I hope as you read specific port functions, this will become clearer.

Port Detail

Port	Type	Description	Platform
60h	I/O	Keyboard Data	AT+

This port connects to the motherboard keyboard controller, typically an 8042 microcontroller. The port is used for both input and output. Information, such as a key pressed scan code, is read from this port. Sending a byte to port 60h will write data to the motherboard controller. In most cases the data are passed on to the keyboard as a command or data. Sending a byte to port 64h is treated as a command to the motherboard controller, and in some cases is followed by data to port 60h.

Note that status bits 0 and 1 of port 64h indicate the controller's buffer state. If port 64h bit 1 is 0, then a write is acceptable to port 60h. If port 64h bit 0 is 1, then a read is acceptable from port 60h.

Input (bits 0-7)—Read a byte from the motherboard keyboard controller.

Output (bits 0-7)—Write a byte to the motherboard keyboard controller.

The following list summarizes valid command functions.

Command Summary

Number	Port 60h Commands
E6h	Set Mouse Scaling to 1:1
E7h	Set Mouse Scaling to 2:1
E8h	Set Mouse Resolution
E9h	Get Mouse Information
EDh	LED Write
EEh	Diagnostic Echo
F0h	Set/Get Alternate Scan Codes
F2h	Read Keyboard ID
F2h*	Read Mouse ID
F3h	Set Typematic Information
F3h*	Set Mouse Sample Rate
F4h	Keyboard Enable
F4h*	Mouse Enable
F5h	Set Defaults and Disable Keyboard
F6h	Set Defaults and Disable Mouse
F7h	Set all keys to Typematic
F8h	Set all keys to Make/Release
F9h	Set all keys to Make
FAh	Set all keys to Typematic/Make/Release
FBh	Set a key to Typematic
FCh	Set a key to Make/Release

Number	Port 60h Commands
FDh	Set a key to Make Only
FEh	Resend
FFh	Keyboard Reset
FFh*	Mouse Reset

**These commands are prefixed with a D4h command to port 64h.*

Command Detail

Command	Description	Port
E6h	Set Mouse Scaling to 1:1	60h

Sets the mouse scaling factor to 1:1 for systems equipped with a built-in mouse port. Command D4h to port 64h must be issued before this command.

Command	Description	Port
E7h	Set Mouse Scaling to 2:1	60h

Sets the mouse scaling factor to 2:1 for systems equipped with a built-in mouse port. Command D4h to port 64h must be issued before this command.

Command	Description	Port
E8h	Set Mouse Resolution	60h

Sets the mouse resolution for systems equipped with a built-in mouse port. Command D4h to port 64h must be issued before this command. After E8h is sent to port 60h, it is followed with the resolution value byte, also to port 60h. The resolution byte holds a code for the four possible resolutions as follows:

0 = 25 dpi, 1 count per millimeter
1 = 50 dpi, 2 counts per millimeter
2 = 100 dpi, 4 counts per millimeter
3 = 200 dpi, 8 counts per millimeter

Command	Description	Port
E9h	Get Mouse Information	60h

Get information and settings from the mouse. Command D4h to port 64h must be issued before this command. After E9h is sent to port 60h, three bytes are read from port 60h. These three bytes contain the following information:

First byte—Status

bit	7 = 0	unused
	6 = 0	stream mode
	1	remote mode
	5 = 0	disabled
	1	enabled
	4 = 0	scaling set to 1:1
	1	scaling set to 2:1
	3 = 0	unused
	2 = 1	left button pressed
	1 = 1	unused
	0 = 1	right button pressed

Second byte—resolution

0 = 25 dpi, 1 count per millimeter
1 = 50 dpi, 2 counts per millimeter
2 = 100 dpi, 4 counts per millimeter
3 = 200 dpi, 8 counts per millimeter

Third byte—sample rate value, in reports per second (i.e. 64h = 100 reports per second)

Command	Description	Port
EDh	LED Write	60h

After sending a EDh LED write command byte to port 60h, a second byte is written to port 60h to set the LED state on the keyboard.

bit	7 = 0	Unused
	6 = 0	Unused
	5 = 0	Unused
	4 = 0	Unused
	3 = 0	Unused
	2 = 1	Caps Lock LED on
	1 = 1	Num Lock LED on
	0 = 1	Scroll Lock LED on

Command	Description	Port
EEh	Diagnostic Echo	60h

Commands the keyboard to echo back a byte. The returned byte will also be value EEh. Useful as a basic diagnostic function.

Command	Description	Port
F0h	Set/Get Alternate Scan Codes	60h

On MCA systems and a few others, the keyboard can be instructed to select from three sets of Kscan codes. A value is sent to port 60h as follows:

0 read the current scan code set
1 activate scan code set 1 (unavailable on Type 2 controller)
2 activate scan code set 2 (default)
3 activate scan code set 3

To read the current scan code set on Type 1 controllers the motherboard controller must not translate incoming Kscan codes. To turn off keyboard translation, the controller command bit 6 is set to 0. Then this F0h command is sent to port 60h, followed by subfunction byte value 0. Then port 60h is read to get the current scan code value. The controller command should then be reissued to resume normal translation (bit 6 set to 1).

Scan code set 1 makes the keyboard appear similar to a PC/XT keyboard, where the keyboard generates system scan codes. No translation is necessary by the motherboard controller. Scan code set 2 causes the keyboard to generate Kscan codes that require translation by the motherboard controller. On 101+ key keyboards some keys generate different output depending on the state of the Shift and Num Lock keys. In these cases, a single key pressed may cause the keyboard to send up to 5 bytes to the controller. Scan set 2 is the normal for all AT+ systems.

The PS/2 offers yet a third alternative. Scan code set 3 generates a single byte code for any key pressed. No key is affected by any shift state. Since scan code set 3 is not supported on other AT+ systems, the only useful purpose I can fathom is testing the keyboard during manufacturing.

Command	Description	Port
F2h	Read Keyboard ID	60h

Gets the two keyboard ID bytes by reading port 60h twice after this command. Be sure to wait at least 10 ms for the keyboard to respond. Not supported on all keyboards.

Command	Description	Port
F2h	Read Mouse ID	60h

Gets the two mouse ID bytes by reading port 60h twice after this command. Command D4h to port 64h must be issued before this command. Be sure to wait at least 10 ms for the keyboard to respond. Only supported on some systems.

Command	Description	Port
F3h	Set Typematic Information	60h

This command sets the keyboard repeat rate and the time delay until a key held down begins repeating. A second byte is sent after the F3h command to load the new rate and delay values. See warning section in this chapter for an example of setting the typematic rate information.

bit	7 = 0	Unused
	6 = x	Set the delay before keyboard repeat occurs
	5 = x	bit 6 bit 5
		0 0 = 250 mS delay
		0 1 = 500 mS delay (default after reset)
		1 0 = 750 mS delay
		1 1 = 1000 mS delay
	4 = x	Repeat rate (see Table 8-10)
	3 = x	
	2 = x	
	1 = x	
	0 = x	

Table 8-10. Repeat Rate Table

Bits 4 3 2 1 0	Hex	Characters Per Second	Bits 4 3 2 1 0	Hex	Characters Per Second
0 0 0 0 0	0	30.0	1 0 0 0 0	10	7.5
0 0 0 0 1	1	26.7	1 0 0 0 1	11	6.7
0 0 0 1 0	2	24.0	1 0 0 1 0	12	6.0
0 0 0 1 1	3	21.8	1 0 0 1 1	13	5.5
0 0 1 0 0	4	20.0	1 0 1 0 0	14	5.0
0 0 1 0 1	5	18.5	1 0 1 0 1	15	4.6
0 0 1 1 0	6	17.1	1 0 1 1 0	16	4.3
0 0 1 1 1	7	16.0	1 0 1 1 1	17	4.0
0 1 0 0 0	8	15.0	1 1 0 0 0	18	3.7
0 1 0 0 1	9	13.3	1 1 0 0 1	19	3.3
0 1 0 1 0	A	12.0	1 1 0 1 0	1A	3.0
0 1 0 1 1	B	10.9 *	1 1 0 1 1	1B	2.7
0 1 1 0 0	C	10.0	1 1 1 0 0	1C	2.5
0 1 1 0 1	D	9.2	1 1 1 0 1	1D	2.3
0 1 1 1 0	E	8.6	1 1 1 1 0	1E	2.1
0 1 1 1 1	F	8.0	1 1 1 1 1	1F	2.0

**Default after reset*

Command	Description	Port
F3h	**Set Mouse Sample Rate**	**60h**

Loads the mouse sample rate. Command D4h to port 64h must be issued before this command. Then the command F3h is issued to port 60h, followed by the sample rate to port 60h. The sample rate value is in reports per second. For example, a value 50 indicates the mouse will report back 50 times per second. This is only supported on some systems.

Command	Description	Port
F4h	**Keyboard Enable**	**60h**

If a transmit error occurs, the keyboard is automatically disabled. This command re-enables the keyboard, and clears the keyboard's internal 16 character buffer.

Command	Description	Port
F4h	**Mouse Enable**	**60h**

Enables the mouse. Command D4h to port 64h must be issued before this command. Then the command F4h is issued to port 60h. Only supported on some systems.

Command	Description	Port
F5h	**Set Defaults and Disable Keyboard**	**60h**

Resets the keyboard to its default state. Its output buffer is cleared, the three LEDs are set off, and the typematic rate and delay are set to their defaults. The keyboard scan is disabled.

Command	Description	Port
F5h	**Set Defaults and Disable Mouse**	**60h**

Sets the defaults and disables the mouse. Command D4h to port 64h must be issued before this command. Then the command F5h is issued to port 60h. Only supported on some systems.

Command	Description	Port
F6h	**Set Defaults**	**60h**

Resets the keyboard to its default state. The internal keyboard output buffer is cleared, the three LEDs are set off, and the typematic rate and delay are set to their defaults. If the keyboard was enabled, it continues to scan for key state changes.

Command	Description	Port
F7h	Set all keys to Typematic	60h

On MCA systems, and a few others, this command clears the internal keyboard buffer and sets all keys to automatically repeat when held down beyond the typematic delay period. See subcommand F3h for more about the typematic options. This only affects operation when scan code set 3 is set. See keyboard command F0h for more about scan code set 3.

Command	Description	Port
F8h	Set all keys to Make/Release	60h

On MCA systems, and a few others, this command clears the internal keyboard buffer and sets all keys to issue a code when the key is first depressed, and another code when a key is released. This only affects operation when scan code set 3 is set. See subcommand F0h for more about scan code set 3.

Command	Description	Port
F9h	Set all keys to Make	60h

On MCA systems, and a few others, this command clears the internal keyboard buffer and sets all keys to issue a code when the key is first depressed. No code is generated when a key is released. This only affects operation when scan code set 3 is set. See subcommand F0h for more about scan code set 3.

Command	Description	Port
FAh	Set all keys to Typematic/Make/Release	60h

On MCA systems, and a few others, this command clears the internal keyboard buffer and sets all keys to issue a code when the key is first depressed, and another code when a key is released. All keys automatically repeat when held down beyond the typematic delay period. See subcommand F3h for more about the typematic options. This only affects operation when scan code set 3 is set. See subcommand F0h for more about scan code set 3.

Command	Description	Port
FBh	Set a key to Typematic	60h

On MCA systems, and a few others, this command clears the internal keyboard buffer and sets a specified key to automatically repeat when held down beyond the typematic delay period. See subcommand F3h for more about the typematic options. After this subcommand is issued, another write is made to port 60h with the Kscan code of the key.

Command	Description	Port
FCh	Set a key to Make/Release	60h

On MCA systems, and a few others, this command clears the internal keyboard buffer and sets a specified key to issue a code when the key is first depressed, and another code when a key is released. After this subcommand is issued, another write is made to port 60h with the Kscan code of the key.

Command	Description	Port
FDh	Set a key to Make Only	60h

On MCA systems, and a few others, this command clears the internal keyboard buffer and sets a specified key to issue a code when the key is first depressed. No code is generated when a key is released. After this sub-command is issued, another write is made to port 60h with the Kscan code of the key.

Command	Description	Port
FEh	Resend	60h

After a transmission error from the keyboard, the resend command instructs the keyboard to resend its last byte. This is normally used by the controller, and is not sent by the keyboard BIOS.

Command	Description	Port
FFh	Keyboard Reset	60h

Forces a total reset of the keyboard. The keyboard will perform a self-test. Its output buffer is cleared, the three LEDs are set off, and the typematic rate and delay are set to their defaults.

Command	Description	Port
FFh	Mouse Reset	60h

Resets the mouse and sets the mouse to the disabled state. Command D4h to port 64h must be issued before this command. Then the command FFh is issued to port 60h. Only supported on some systems.

Port	Type	Description	Platform
60h	Input	Keyboard Data	PC/XT

On the PC and XT, the communication with the keyboard is limited to reading information from the keyboard. No facility is available to send commands to the keyboard.

The motherboard hardware converts the serial keyboard data into a 8-bit scan code number. It is read from port C of the 8255 chip, from port 60h. Remember the scan codes are the direct keyboard scan codes, and are not re-translated as normally occurs on the AT+ type machines.

When the keyboard sends an extended scan code, the first byte read is zero. This indicates a second byte must be read to get the extended scan code byte.

Input (bits 0-7)—Key-pressed information

Port	Type	Description	Platform
64h	I/O	Keyboard Controller Status & Commands	AT+

This port connects directly to the motherboard keyboard controller, typically an Intel 8042 microprocessor. Motherboard controller status is read from this port at any time. Control data for the 8042 processor are written to the processor from both ports 60h and 64h. When sending data to the motherboard controller from port 60h, it is a data write. Outputting to port 64h indicates a command write. Refer to port 60h for related information.

The PS/2 changes a few definitions, as specifically shown. The major change is the addition of a second serial device port, typically used for a mouse.

Input (bits 0-7)—Controller status (AT/EISA)

bit 7 r = 1	Parity error on serial link from keyboard (last byte was even parity and only odd parity is allowed).
6 r = 1	Receive timeout occurred, indicating the keyboard began sending information, but did not complete the transmission with the proper timeout delay.
5 r = 1	Transmit timeout occurred, indicating the keyboard transmission exceeded the preset time limit. This will occur if the time to transmit one byte is too long, or if the byte was sent, but the response exceeded the timeout delay. This error also occurs if the response to a timeout has a parity error (then both parity and transmit timeout bits are set).
4 r = 0	Inhibit keyboard (from keyboard lock switch). This flag is updated whenever sending data to the keyboard controller. On password controlled systems, 0 indicates keyboard is inhibited until the password is verified.
3 r = 0	Data was sent to the controller last (using port 60h)
1	Command was sent to the controller last (using port 64h)
2 r = 0	Power-on caused reset.
1	Successful completion of the motherboard controller self-test. The bit status can also be set from the system flag bit in command 60h (see Output, commands).
1 r = 0	The motherboard controller's input buffer is empty. A write can be made to port 60h or 64h.

1	The motherboard controller's input buffer is full. Until the motherboard controller has emptied the buffer, no writes should occur to ports 60h or 64h or the data/command will be lost.
0 r = 0	The motherboard controller's output buffer is empty. A read from port 60h will not be valid.
1	The motherboard controller's output buffer has a byte available to read. Use port 60h to read the byte.

Input (bits 0-7)—Controller status (MCA PS/2)

bit 7 r = 1 — Parity error on serial link from keyboard (last byte was even parity and only odd parity is allowed).When a parity error occurs, FFh is loaded into the output buffer (read from port 60h).

6 r = 1 — General timeout occurred indicates one several possible error conditions have occurred. When this occurs, FFh is loaded into the output buffer (read from port 60h). The possible error conditions are:

a) The keyboard began sending information, but did not complete the transmission with the proper timeout delay.

b) The keyboard transmission exceeded the preset time limit. This will occur if the time to transmit one byte is too long, or if the byte was sent, but the response exceeded the timeout delay. The error will also occur if the response to a timeout has a parity error (then both parity and transmit timeout bits are set).

5 r = 1 — Mouse Output buffer full, depends on bit 0 as well:

bit 5	bit 0
0	0 = both buffers empty
0	1 = motherboard controller output buffer full
1	0 = not used
1	1 = mouse output buffer full

4 r = 0	Inhibit keyboard (from keyboard lock switch). This flag is updated whenever sending data to the motherboard controller. On password-controlled systems, 0 indicates keyboard is inhibited until the password is verified.
3 r = 0	Data was sent to the controller last (using port 60h)
1	Command was sent to the controller last (using port 64h)
2 r = 0	Power-on caused reset.
1	Successful completion of the motherboard controller self-test. The bit status can also be set from the system flag bit in command 60h (see Output, commands).
1 r = 0	The motherboard controller's input buffer is empty. A write can be made to port 60h or 64h.

1	The motherboard controller's input buffer is full. Until the motherboard controller has emptied the buffer, no writes should occur to ports 60h or 64h or the data/command will be lost.
0 r = 0	The motherboard controller's output buffer is empty. A read from port 60h will not be valid.
1	The motherboard controller's output buffer has a byte available to read. Use port 60h to read the byte. See bit 5 for which buffer (keyboard or mouse) is full.

Output (bits 0-7)—Send command byte to Controller

The following lists command functions. The byte indicated is sent to port 64h.

Command Summary

Number	Port 64h Commands
20h	Get Command Byte
21h-3Fh	Read Controller RAM
60h	Write Command Byte
61h-7Fh	Write Controller RAM
A4h	Check If Password Installed
A5h	Load Password
A6h	Check Password
A7h	Disable Mouse Port
A8h	Enable Mouse Port
A9h	Test Mouse Port
AAh	Self Test
ABh	Interface Test
ACh	Diagnostic Dump
ADh	Disable Keyboard
AEh	Enable Keyboard
C0h	Read Input Port
C1h	Continuous Input Port Poll, Low
C2h	Continuous Input Port Poll, High
D0h	Read Output Port
D1h	Write Output Port
D2h	Write Keyboard Output Buffer
D3h	Write Mouse Output Buffer
D4h	Write To Mouse
DDh	Disable A20 Address Line
DFh	Enable A20 Address Line
E0h	Read Test Inputs
F0h-FDh	Pulse Output Bit
FEh	System Reset

Command Detail

Command	Description	Port
20h	Get Command Byte	64h

Reads the current keyboard command byte. First a command byte 20h is sent to port 64h. Then port 60h is used to read this value. The keyboard command byte is set by command 60h below. The bit values for the command byte are listed under command 60h as well.

Command	Description	Port
20h-3Fh	Read Controller RAM	64h

Reads the internal motherboard controller's RAM. The address is the command value less 20h. To read byte 9, use command 29h. These functions may not be available on all controllers. To get the specified byte, the command is followed by a read from port 60h.

On MCA systems Type 1 controllers can access all 31 locations. Type 2 controllers can only access RAM bytes 0, 13h to 17h, 1Dh, and 1Fh.

Offset	**Function**
0	Command byte—see command 60h for details
13h	Security on—non-zero when password enabled (MCA)
14h	Security off—non-zero when password matched (MCA)
16h	Password discard 1—If the make code equals this byte during password entry, it is discarded. (MCA)
17h	Password discard 2—If the make code equals this byte during password entry, it is discarded. (MCA)

Command	Description	Port
60h	Write Command Byte	64h

Writes a command byte to the controller. The next byte written to port 60h is then retained as the new motherboard controller's command byte. During most normal operations the command byte value will be 45h. The bits in the command byte are defined as:

Command byte—For ISA/EISA

bit 7 = 0	Unused, set to 0
6 = 0	No conversion of keyboard scan codes.
1	Standard Scan conversion - the scan code from the keyboard is converted into the normal scan codes used in PCs (1 is normal operation).
5 = 0	Check parity from keyboard, with scan conversion (0 is normal operation).
1	Ignore parity from keyboard, no scan code conversion.

4 = 0	Enable keyboard.
1	Disable keyboard by forcing the keyboard clock low. Data cannot be sent to or received from the keyboard.
3 = 1	Override keyboard inhibit function. Port 64h bit 4 is set to 1, ignoring the keyboard lockout switch (this is used for a keyboard test during power-up).
2 = 0	System flag status bit indicates reset by power on.
1	System flag after successful controller self-test.
1 = 0	Unused, set to 0.
0 = 0	Do not send interrupt when keyboard output buffer full
1	Output buffer full causes interrupt (IRQ 1).

Command byte—For MCA & PS/2

bit 7 = 0	Unused, set to 0
6 = 0	No conversion of keyboard scan codes.
1	Standard Scan conversion - the scan code from the keyboard is converted into the normal scan codes used in PCs (1 is normal operation). MCA Type 2 controllers cannot set this bit to 1. In this case scan code conversion is set using keyboard command F0h to port 60h.
5 = 0	Enable mouse.
1	Disable mouse by forcing the mouse serial clock line low. Data cannot be sent to or received from the mouse.
4 = 0	Enable keyboard.
1	Disable keyboard by forcing the keyboard clock low. Data cannot be sent to or received from the keyboard.
3 = 0	Unused, set to 0.
2 = 0	System flag status bit indicates reset by power on.
1	System flag after successful controller self-test.
1 = 0	Do not send interrupt when mouse output buffer full
1	Mouse output buffer full causes interrupt (IRQ 12)
0 = 0	Do not send interrupt when keyboard output buffer full
1	Output buffer full causes interrupt (IRQ 1).

Command	Description	Port
60h-7Fh	Write Controller RAM	64h

Writes the internal motherboard controller's RAM. The address is the command value less 60h. To write to byte 5, use command 65h. These functions may not be available on all controllers. To write the specified byte, the command is followed by a write to port 60h.

On MCA systems type 1 controllers can access all 31 locations. Type 2 controllers can only access RAM bytes 0, 13h to 17h, 1Dh, and 1Fh.

Offset	Function
0	Command byte—see command 60h for details
13h	Security on—non-zero when password enabled (MCA)
14h	Security off—non-zero when password matched (MCA)
16h	Password discard 1—If the make code equals this byte during password entry, it is discarded (MCA).
17h	Password discard 2—If the make code equals this byte during password entry, it is discarded (MCA).

Command	Description	Port
A4h	Check If Password Installed	64h

This command checks if a password has been previously stored in the motherboard controller. The command returns one of two status values, which is read from port 60h. F1 is returned when no password is installed, and FA is returned when a password is installed. Many systems do not support this password method (but all MCA systems do).

Command	Description	Port
A5h	Load Password	64h

To load a new password, once the load password command is issued, successive password bytes are written to the motherboard controller at port 60h. The password is complete when a 0 is sent. The password must be stored in scan code format (not ASCII). Many systems do not support this password method (but all MCA systems do).

Command	Description	Port
A6h	Check Password	64h

When the motherboard controller has a valid password, this command instructs the controller to match incoming keystrokes with the password. Upon successful password match, the keyboard is enabled. Many systems do not support this password method (but all MCA systems do).

Command	Description	Port
A7h	Disable Mouse Port	64h

Disables the mouse by setting bit 5 of the command byte high. The clock line to the mouse is then set low, preventing any data from being received or sent to the mouse (MCA only).

Command	Description	Port
A8h	Enable Mouse Port	64h

Enables the mouse by setting bit 5 of the command byte low. The clock line to the mouse becomes active, if previously set low (MCA only).

Command	Description	Port
A9h	Test Mouse Port	64h

Initiates a test of the serial link between the controller and the mouse. It tests both the mouse data and clock lines. The test results are read from port 60h. The following values indicate the result:

00h—No errors detected.
01h—The mouse clock line is stuck low.
02h—The mouse clock line is stuck high.
03h—The mouse data line is stuck low.
04h—The mouse data line is stuck high.

Command	Description	Port
AAh	Self Test	64h

Initiates an internal self-test of the motherboard controller. If no errors are detected, the value 55h will be read from port 60h.

Command	Description	Port
ABh	Interface Test	64h

Initiates a test of the serial link between the controller and the keyboard. It tests both the keyboard data and clock lines. The test results are read from port 60h. The following values indicate the result:

00h—No errors detected.
01h—The keyboard clock line is stuck low.
02h—The keyboard clock line is stuck high.
03h—The keyboard data line is stuck low.
04h—The keyboard data line is stuck high.

Command	Description	Port
ACh	Diagnostic Dump	64h

Gets 16 bytes of the controller's RAM, the current controller input and output port states and the controller's program status word. This information is read from port 60h.

Command	Description	Port
ADh	Disable Keyboard	64h

Disables the keyboard by setting bit 4 of the command byte high. The clock line to the keyboard is then set low, preventing any data from being received or sent to the keyboard.

Command	Description	Port
AEh	Enable Keyboard	64h

Enables the keyboard by setting bit 4 of the command byte low. The clock line to the keyboard becomes active, if previously set low.

Command	Description	Port
C0h	Read Input Port	64h

Reads the 8042 controller's input port, P1. The byte can then be read by reading port 60h. This command should only be issued if the controller's output port is empty. Bit assignments typically vary from system to system.

When reading port 60h after command C0h is issued, the following data are returned on the original IBM AT.

bit	7 = 1	Keyboard Inhibit switch on
	6 = 0	Color Text/Graphics is default video adapter on power up
	1	Monochrome adapter is default video adapter on power up
	5 = 0	Manufacturing jumper is installed
	1	Normal
	4 = 0	RAM size select switch = 512K
	1	RAM size select switch = 256K
	3 = x	Unused
	2 = x	Unused
	1 = x	Unused
	0 = x	Unused

When reading port 60h after command C0h is issued, the following byte is returned on PS/2 MCA systems.

bit	7 = 0	Unused
	6 = 0	Unused
	5 = 0	Unused
	4 = 0	Unused
	3 = 0	Unused
	2 = 0	Keyboard power normal
	1	No keyboard power
	1 = x	Mouse serial data in
	0 = x	Keyboard serial data in

Command	Description	Port
C1h	Continuous Input Port Poll, Low	64h

The low 4 bits of the 8042 motherboard controller port P1, are continuously polled and placed into the status register bits 4 to 7. The status register contents are read from port 64h. This continues until another controller command is received. This function is not implemented on all systems, but is available on all MCA systems that have a Type 1 controller. Type 2 controllers do not support this function.

Command	Description	Port
C2h	Continuous Input Port Poll, High	64h

The high 4 bits of the 8042 motherboard controller port P1, are continuously polled and placed into the status register bits 4 to 7. The status register contents are read from port 64h. This continues until another controller command is received. This function is not implemented on all systems, but is available on all MCA systems that have a Type 1 controller. Type 2 controllers do not support this function.

Command	Description	Port
D0h	Read Output Port	64h

Read the 8042 controller's output port P2. The byte can then be read by reading port 60h. This command should only be issued if the controller's output port is empty.

The following bit assignments are for the original IBM AT.

bit	7 = x	Data to keyboard line
	6 = x	Keyboard data clock
	5 = 0	Input buffer empty
	4 = 1	Keyboard output buffer is full (connected to IRQ 1). When the output buffer has been read from port 60h, this bit is cleared.
	3 = x	Unused

	2 = x	Unused
	1 = x	A20 status. The current state of the A20 line, where 0 indicates A20, is disabled. Some systems always leave this bit set, regardless of the actual A20 state.
	0 = 0	Main processor reset (This value cannot be read, since by nature, the system is in a reset mode).
	1	Normal

The following bit assignments are for MCA systems.

bit	7 = x	Data to keyboard
	6 = x	Keyboard data clock
	5 = 1	Controller output buffer is full, with a mouse byte (connected to IRQ 12). When the output buffer has been read from port 60h, this bit is cleared.
	4 = 1	Controller output buffer is full, with a keyboard byte (connected to IRQ 1). When the output buffer has been read from port 60h, this bit is cleared.
	3 = x	Data to mouse
	2 = x	Mouse data clock
	1 = 0	Disable A20 address line, causing writes to addresses above 1MB to wrap to low memory. This simulates operation of a 8088 machine, and is the power-on default.
	1	Enable A20 address line and allow access to memory above 1MB.
	0 = 0	Main processor reset (This value cannot be read, since by nature, the system is in a reset mode).
	1	Normal

Command	Description	Port
D1h	Write Output Port	64h

★★★

The next byte written to port 60h is transferred to the controller's output port P2.

The following bit assignments are for the original IBM AT.

bit	7 = x	Data to keyboard
	6 = x	Keyboard data clock
	5 = 0	Input buffer empty
	4 = 1	Activate IRQ 1 (interrupt 9). When the output buffer has been read from port 60h, this bit is cleared.
	3 = x	Unused
	2 = x	Unused
	1 = 0	Disable A20 address line, causing writes to addresses above 1MB to wrap to low memory. This simulates operation of a 8088 machine, and is the power-on default.

	1	Enable A20 address line and allow access to memory above 1MB.
	0 = 0	Reset the main processor (hardware reset)
	1	Normal

MCA systems with a Type 1 controller allow all bits in the output port to be changed. Type 2 controllers ignore all bits except for bit 1 to control the A20 line. The following bit assignments are for MCA systems only.

bit	7 = x	Data to keyboard
	6 = x	Keyboard data clock
	5 = 1	Activate IRQ 12 (interrupt 74h). When the output buffer has been read from port 60h, this bit is cleared.
	4 = 1	Activate IRQ 1 (interrupt 9h). When the output buffer has been read from port 60h, this bit is cleared.
	3 = x	Data to mouse
	2 = x	Mouse data clock
	1 = 0	Disable A20 address line, causing writes to addresses above 1 MB to wrap to low memory. This simulates operation of a 8088 machine, and is the power-on default.
	1	Enable A20 address line and allow access to memory above 1MB.
	0 = 0	Reset the main processor (hardware reset)
	1	Normal

Command	Description	Port
D2h	Write Keyboard Output Buffer	64h

The controller's output buffer is loaded with the byte next written to port 60h. Once the byte is written to port 60h and the controller's command byte allows IRQ 1 (bit 0 = 1), then IRQ 1 is activated as if initiated by the keyboard. This function is not available on all AT+ systems, but is available on all MCA systems.

Command	Description	Port
D3h	Write Mouse Output Buffer	64h

The controller's output buffer is loaded with the byte next written to port 60h. Once the byte is written to port 60h and the controller's command byte allows IRQ 12 (bit 1 = 1), then IRQ 12 is activated as if initiated by the mouse. This function is not available on all AT+ systems, but is available on all MCA systems.

Command	Description	Port
D4h	Write To Mouse	64h

The next byte written to port 60h is transferred to the mouse. This function is not available on all AT+ systems, but is available on all MCA systems.

Command	Description	Port
DDh	Disable A20 Address Line	64h

Disables the A20 address line. This limits memory to the first 1MB, similar to the original 8088 address range. This command is not supported on most systems.

Command	Description	Port
DFh	Enable A20 Address Line	64h

Enables the A20 address line. This allows accessing memory above 1MB. This command is not supported on most systems.

Command	Description	Port
E0h	Read Test Inputs	64h

Get the state of the 8042 test input lines, T0 and T1. The byte is obtained by reading port 60h. This command should only be issued if the controller's output port is empty.

bit	7 = x	Unused
	6 = x	Unused
	5 = x	Unused
	4 = x	Unused
	3 = x	Unused
	2 = x	Unused
	1 = x	Keyboard data
	0 = x	Keyboard clock

Command	Description	Port
F0h-FDh	Pulse Output Bit	64h

These commands allow pulsing selective controller output bits. The lower 4 bits of the command F0h to FFh directly control the four output bits of port P2 on the controller. Commands F0h to FDh, and FFh serve no useful purpose. See command FEh below for system reset. On MCA systems with a type 2 controller, none of these commands are supported.

Command	Description	Port
FEh	System Reset	64h

Issues a hardware reset by setting the system reset line low for approximately 6 microseconds. See Chapter 3, The CPU and Undocumented Instructions, for more about CPU reset.

CHAPTER 9

Video System

If you bought this book to fully understand the video system, you've got the wrong book! Well, unlike every other subsystem in the PC, the video system has been covered in reasonable detail in some IBM technical references, and has been expanded upon in numerous books. There is so much material alone just about video adapters, how they work, and related information, that it would easily take another book this size just for video!

There is not much left undocumented when it comes to the video system, but quite a bit of information is scattered around. Many of the BIOS functions have been so poorly documented that they are difficult to use. This chapter consolidates the key information and explains BIOS interrupt calls in greater detail. I've uncovered several interesting undocumented BIOS functions for the VGA Pel Mask. I/O ports for the various adapters are summarized, but only previously undocumented ports are expanded upon.

I've included complete details on the Relocated Screen Interface Specification (RSIS). This simple interface can make many programs operate under a wider range of environments, such as DOS/V, a special Japanese version of DOS. A program that uses RSIS with an advanced memory manager like Memory Commander will gain 100 to 300K of additional DOS main memory without any performance penalties. Many programmers find converting an existing program to RSIS takes less than 30 minutes.

The video adapters covered in this chapter include the MGA, HGA, CGA, MCGA, EGA, VGA, SVGA, XGA, and the VESA XGA. In addition, BIOS functions for RSIS and DOS/V are also included. There is only a limited amount of coverage for the obsolete PGA, PCjr, and the PC Convertible video systems.

Near the end of this chapter are included a number of code samples for RSIS and a complete routine for detecting which video adapter a machine has, the correct attributes to use, and other useful information.

Introduction

The video adapter has become one of the most complex parts of the system. Many standards have evolved over the years. Since the video area is usually the biggest bottleneck to performance, most programs bypass the very slow BIOS screen routines and directly write into the screen buffer. To add further complications, all adapter designs since 1988 support multiple monitor types.

Many of the video adapter hardware designs were exciting technological developments when released, but were a bear to program. The difficulty in creating a program for a specific video adapter was hampered by documentation that briefly described the many registers in an adapter, but offered no examples or even basic information about dependencies between registers. In addition, early hardware designs seemed to take perverse pleasure in providing write-only registers. This made it impossible to detect what state the video system was in. TSR programs that need to save and restore the state of the video system were extremely difficult to write. To make matters worse, many functions were scattered across registers, in seemingly random fashion. Some of these problems have been corrected over the years. One of the biggest difficulties for the professional programmer is just dealing with the large number of different standards.

One issue all programmers must face is the relentless progression of new standards. As of this writing, the latest IBM adapter is the XGA. Over the last several years, the orientation has been to limit any significant documentation to programmers. I suspect a few people at IBM will disagree with this, but starting with the VGA, more and more important parts shifted into the undocumented realm. With the advent of many highly integrated custom ICs, it became very tough to figure out how to make the best use of these advanced video adapters, and to scope out how they work. This lack of support for the programmer is one of the prime reasons new adapters take many years for anyone to support them, and why some standards never make it. One way out of this problem is to develop software as if the last adapter in existence was the VGA.

I'm not going to go into much detail about how the different video adapters work or how they should be best programmed. Many books have covered these topics in great depth. See Appendix C, Bibliography, for a number of good references.

Video Adapter Standards

Most video adapter standards today have been created by IBM from various adapters it has manufactured. Only two non-IBM created standards have found common acceptance, the Hercules monochrome Graphics Adapter (HGA) and the Super VGA (SVGA).

CGA—Color Graphics Adapter

The CGA provided basic text mode, using an eye-straining 8x8 character cell font. It did offer 16 colors, and provided the only graphics capability when the PC was launched. It supported a CGA color monitor, composite (TV-like) color and composite monochrome monitors. Many CGA adapters suffer from "snow" when screen writes are made, and they require special programming to avoid it during video buffer access. The CGA is obsolete today, and most programmers ignore support for it in current designs.

MDA—Monochrome Display Adapter

The MDA supports a 9x14 text cell, the highest resolution for many years. No graphics are available on this adapter. Only a monochrome monitor is supported.

HGA—Hercules Graphics Adapter

The HGA was the first successful video adapter design outside of IBM. It was identical to the MDA, except it provided two pages of monochrome graphics at almost twice the resolution of the CGA.

PGA—Professional Graphics Adapter

The PGA provided high-resolution color graphics. Because of the very high cost, and some software compatibility issues, the PGA never caught on. I've never talked to anyone who actually programmed PGA-specific software, and it's considered completely obsolete today.

EGA—Enhanced Graphics Adapter

The EGA took a long time to become successful, but established a high-resolution color graphics standard, and provided full-color high-resolution 8x14 cell characters. Sixteen-color graphics were provided for resolutions up to 640x350. The EGA is more complicated than its MDA and CGA predecessors, but offers a rich assortment of features and advantages over prior adapters. These include custom font loading, selection of 16 colors from a palette of 64, a number of new graphics modes, and much more. It requires an EGA monitor for advanced features.

Although a few systems still use the EGA adapter, no new systems have been built in the last few years using this standard. EGA adapter cards are no longer available, having been completely replaced with the newer VGA standard. Most programmers today treat the EGA as an obsolete adapter.

MCGA

This standard was used on the old PS/2 AT bus machines, prior to the 80386. These systems had the MCGA video hardware built on the motherboard. To my knowledge it was never available as a separate adapter card. The MCGA is a subset of features of the VGA, and only offers a maximum resolution of 640x480. The text cell is 8x16.

VGA—Video Graphics Array

The VGA was a new standard created by IBM for the PS/2 MicroChannel line of computers. A separate AT bus adapter version was also made available. The VGA adapter also allows replacement of the built-in MCGA video adapter supplied with the first PS/2 AT bus systems. The

VGA provides increased resolution over the EGA in both text and graphics modes. The standard text cell was increased to 9x16, and graphics resolution increased to 640x480. The VGA is functionally downward compatible with the EGA, and it also eliminated all the nasty write-only registers we all learned to hate on the EGA.

The VGA is becoming obsolete, but the VGA is still present in many systems in use today. Because its programming operation is somewhat simpler that newer standards, many programmers still use the VGA as the core video design target.

SVGA—Super VGA

The SVGA adapter was created outside of IBM, partly due to IBM's slow response to the need for a higher-resolution adapter. The market was becoming very chaotic with many vendors introducing new custom capabilities incompatible with each other. They finally got together and formed the Video Electronic Standards Association (VESA). VESA created the SVGA standard to access these higher modes of operation. All SVGA adapters support 800x600 graphics resolution, and most also provide 1024x768 resolution. Depending on the amount of memory, 16, 256, or even more colors are available in these high-resolution graphics modes.

One of the best features of the SVGA standard is its capability to allow vendors to add new higher resolutions that a program can detect and use. This gives the SVGA standard extensive future capabilities, not limited by an inflexible standard.

Almost all systems purchased today include a SVGA adapter in some form.

XGA—Extended Graphics Adapter

The latest offering from IBM is the XGA. This further expands the capabilities beyond the VGA. Custom text characters can be built up to an incredible 255x255 cell size. Resolution is more than doubled over the stock VGA, to provide up to 1024x768 for graphics. Many other features are provided to help boost video performance and support faster operations under graphical user interfaces such as OS/2 and Windows. The Video Electronics Standards Association has further expanded the XGA standard for additional flexibility. Those XGA adapters that provide the VESA extensions are referred to as the VESA XGA.

Even after a number of years in the market, the XGA and compatibles have not sold well. The XGA holds only a small part of the video adapter market. Very little software code is available that requires an XGA.

JEGA, AX-VGA—Japanese Adapters

These two adapters are functionally similar to the standard EGA and VGA counterparts, but include hardware support for Japanese Double Byte Characters. These adapters have several new modes and alter the way a number of standard modes work for the Japanese environment. Consult the AX Technical Reference Guide if you are interested in these details. It is listed in Appendix C, Bibliography, under BIOS and Systems.

Adapter Names

Throughout the balance of this chapter we use the common abbreviations for all adapter names. In addition, many references have a plus prefix. This indicates the reference relates to the specified adapter and all adapters that are supersets of the adapter. Table 9-1 shows what adapters are included for each abbreviation.

Table 9-1. Adapter Name Groupings

Adapter	Includes
EGA+	EGA, VGA, SVGA, XGA, VESA XGA
VGA+	VGA, SVGA, XGA, VESA XGA
XGA+	XGA, VESA XGA

In some cases, we've indicated whether DOS/V supports a specific function. DOS/V is a version of MS-DOS that works on VGA+ type adapters to provide the Double Byte Character Set (DBCS), typically required for Asian character sets. Although DOS/V is not an adapter, it may restrict or change the operation of some video BIOS functions. DOS lets any standard VGA adapter display the large set of DBCS Japanese characters.

BIOS Services

Interrupt 10h provides the following services:

Function	Description	Adapters
ah=0	Set Video Mode	All
ah=1	Set Cursor Type	All
ah=2	Set Cursor Position	All
ah=3	Read Cursor Position and Type	All
ah=4	Read Light Pen Position	All
ah=5	Select Active Display Page	All
ah=6	Scroll Active Page Up	All
ah=7	Scroll Active Page Down	All
ah=8	Read Character and attribute	All
ah=9	Write Character and attribute	All
ah=A	Write Character Only	All
ah=B	Set Color Palette	All
ah=C	Write Dot	All
ah=D	Read Dot	All
ah=E	Write in Teletype Mode	All
ah=F	Read Current Video State	All
ah=10	Set Palette Register Functions	MCGA/EGA/VGA+
ah=11	Character Generation Functions	All
ah=12	Miscellaneous Functions	All
ah=13	Write String	All
ah=14	LCD Control	PC Convertible
ah=15	Get Display Type	PC Convertible
ah=18	Request for Font Pattern	DOS/V

Function	Description	Adapters
ah=1A	Read/Write Display Combination Code	VGA+
ah=1B	Return Video System State Information	VGA+
ah=1C	Save/Restore Video State	VGA+
ah=1D	Shift Status Line Functions	DOS/V
ah=1F	Display Mode Information	XGA+
ah=4E	VESA XGA Subfunctions	VESA XGA
ah=4F	Super VGA Subfunctions	SVGA
ah=FE	Get Relocated Screen address	All
ah=FF	Update Relocated Screen	All

INT

Int	Func	Description	Platform
10h	0	Set Video Mode	All

Sets the current video mode. The mode selected specifies the type of video, text or graphics, the screen density, and the physical screen buffer location. A list of the most common modes is shown in Table 9-2. Before selecting a mode, the type of adapter and current display must be established. Functions do not return a failure code if an improper mode is selected, but an invalid mode number will be ignored and the adapter will likely remain in the last valid mode set.

With the MCGA, EGA, and all later adapters, bit 7 of the mode signifies if the display buffer should be cleared during the mode change. If bit 7 is set to zero, the buffer is cleared. On CGA, MDA, and HGA bit 7 must be zero, and the display is always cleared. When clearing the screen, text modes are filled with ASCII spaces, and the attribute of 7. Graphics modes clear the screen buffer to all zeros.

Called with: ah = 0
al, bit 7 = 0 Clear display buffer
1 Leave contents of display buffer as-is
bits 6-0 = video mode (0 to 7Fh)

Returns: mode set if valid for adapter
BIOS value 40:49h set to the video mode

Upon system power-up, a system with a color monitor will default to mode 3. A system with a monochrome monitor will default to mode 7. These defaults are controlled by switches on PC/XT motherboards, or are recorded in CMOS memory by the BIOS setup program on AT+ systems.

The display segment in Table 9-2 is the actual physical segment of the display buffer. See interrupt 10h, function FEh to determine the actual logical display segment.

Table 9-2. Video Modes by Adapter Family

Mode	MDA	CGA	MCGA	EGA	VGA	SVGA	XGA	DOS/V	AX & VGA	Pixels horiz	Pixels vert	Char size	Max pgs	Display seg	Description
0		x	x	x	x	x	x			320	200	8x8	8	B800	Text, 40 columns, 25 rows monochrome (color burst off for composite output)
			x	x	x	x	x			320	350	8x14	8	B800	
			x							320	400	8x16	8	B800	
					x	x	x			360	400	9x16	8	B800	
1		x	x	x	x	x	x			320	200	8x8	8	B800	Text, 40 columns, 25 rows, 16 colors
			x	x	x	x	x			320	350	8x14	8	B800	
			x							320	400	8x16	8	B800	
					x	x	x			360	400	9x16	8	B800	
2		x								640	200	8x8	4	B800	Text, 80 columns, 25 rows, mono (color burst off for composite output)
			x	x	x	x	x			640	200	8x8	8	B800	
			x	x	x	x	x			640	350	8x14	8	B800	
			x							640	400	8x16	8	B800	
					x	x	x			720	400	9x16	8	B800	
								x		640	475	8x19	1	none	
3		x								640	200	8x8	4	B800	Text, 80 columns, 25 rows, 16 colors
			x	x	x	x	x			640	200	8x8	8	B800	
			x	x	x	x	x			640	350	8x14	8	B800	
			x							640	400	8x16	8	B800	
					x	x	x			720	400	9x16	8	B800	
								x		640	475	8x19	1	none	
4		x	x	x	x	x	x			320	200	8x8	1	B800	Graphics, 4 colors
5		x	x	x	x	x	x			320	200	8x8	1	B800	Graphics, mono (color burst off)
6		x	x	x	x	x	x			640	200	8x8	1	B800	Graphics, 2 colors
7	x									720	350	9x14	1	B000	Text, 80 columns, 25 rows, mono
				x	x	x	x			720	350	9x14	8	B000	
					x	x	x			720	400	9x16	8	B000	
8-C															PCjr & Invalid modes
D				x	x	x	x			320	200	8x8	8	A000	Graphics, 16 colors
E				x	x	x	x			640	200	8x8	4	A000	Graphics, 16 colors
F				x	x	x	x			640	350	8x14	2	A000	Graphics, 2 colors
10h				x	x	x	x			640	350	8x14	2	A000	Graphics, 16 colors
11h			x		x	x	x	x		640	480	8x16	1	A000	Graphics, 2 colors
12h					x	x	x	x		640	480	8x16	1	A000	Graphics, 16 colors
13h			x		x	x	x			320	200	8x8	1	A000	Graphics, 256 colors
14h							x			640	400	8x16	4	B800	Text, 132 columns, 25 rows, 16 colors
52h									x	640	480	8x19	1	A000	Graphics, 16 colors KANJI display and superimpose ability
53h									x	640	480	8x19	1	A000	Graphics, 16 colors KANJI display, no superimpose ability
6Ah						x				800	600		1	A000	Graphics, 16 colors
72h								x		640	480	8x19	1	A000	Graphics, 16 colors
73h								x		640	475	8x19	1	none	Text, 80 columns, 25 rows (emulated in a graphics mode)
100h*						x				640	400		1	A000	Graphics, 256 colors

Table 9-2. Continued

Mode	MDA	CGA	MCGA	EGA	VGA	SVGA	XGA	DOS/V	AX & VGA	Pixels horiz	Pixels vert	Char size	Max pgs	Display seg	Description
101h*						x				640	480		1	A000	Graphics, 256 colors
102h*						x				800	600		1	A000	Graphics, 16 colors
103h*						x				800	600		1	A000	Graphics, 256 colors
104h*						x				1024	768		1	A000	Graphics, 16 colors
105h*						x				1024	768		1	A000	Graphics, 256 colors
106h*						x				1024	1024		1	A000	Graphics, 16 colors
107h*						x				1024	1024		1	A000	Graphics, 256 colors

** Requires special mode set for SVGA card, using function 4Fh, subfunction 2.*
"None" in the segment buffer column indicates the DOS/V DBCS (Double Byte Character Set) driver requires the use of interrupt 10h, function FEh to get the segment and offset of a virtual buffer.

Modes 0 and 2 are functionally identical to modes 1 and 3 on the EGA and all later adapters, and allow full color. What is not well documented is how mode 2 is used by most software vendors. For text-based applications, almost everyone uses mode 3. An application checks the current mode using interrupt 10h, function 0Fh. If mode 2 is set, the application should switch to using black, white, and bright white attributes. In this manner, a user can simply set mode 2 to make applications operate in monochrome mode. To set the text mode on a DOS system, the MODE program is run at the DOS prompt:

To set mode 0, black and white 40 columns:	MODE BW40
To set mode 1, color 40 columns:	MODE CO40
To set mode 2, black and white 80 columns:	MODE BW80
To set mode 3, color 80 columns:	MODE CO80

INT

Int	Func	Description	Platform
10h	1	Set Cursor Type	All

For text modes, this function defines the position of the cursor within the cell and the number of lines to blink for the cursor. Only one cursor type is provided in the video system, regardless of the active page number. The cursor type is stored in a word in the BIOS data area at 40:60h.

See Function 12h, subfunction BL=34h on how a VGA system can change the cursor size set by the Set Cursor Type function, relative to the character cell size.

Called with:	ah = 1
	ch = top line in cell to use for cursor (0 to 31)
	cl = bottom line in cell to use for cursor (0 to 31)
Returns:	cursor updated
	ax = unaltered on most, but value changed on some BIOSes

Unless cursor type emulation has been turned off, the character cell size is assumed to be 8 scan lines for all adapters. This includes the EGA/VGA and later adapters that really display 14 or 16 scan lines per character. Common values for cursor types include:

cx = 0607h Two line cursor near or at the bottom of cell
cx = 0307h Half box cursor at bottom of cell
cx = 0003h Half or quarter box cursor at top of cell
cx = 0007h Full box cursor
cx = 0100h No cursor

Int	Func	Description	Platform
10h	2	Set Cursor Position	All

INT

Sets the cursor position for the specified video page. The BIOS maintains a separate cursor location for each page. These cursor position values are stored in 8 words in the BIOS data area starting at 40:50h.

Called with:	ah = 2
	bh = video page (0 is the default after mode set)
	dh = row (0 is the topmost row)
	dl = column (0 is the leftmost column)
Returns:	cursor position updated

Int	Func	Description	Platform
10h	3	Read Cursor Position and Type	All

INT

Gets the cursor position for the specified video page and the cursor type. The BIOS maintains a separate cursor location for each page. These cursor position values are stored in 8 words in the BIOS data area starting at 40:50h. See function 1 for more about the cursor type.

Called with:	ah = 3
	bh = video page (0 is the default after mode set)
Returns:	ch = type, top line in cell for cursor
	cl = type, bottom line in cell for cursor
	dh = row (0 is the topmost row)
	dl = column (0 is the leftmost column)

INT	Int	Func	Description	Platform
	10h	4	Read Light Pen Position	CGA, EGA

Gets the current light pen position. Support for the light pen was dropped with the VGA.

Called with: ah = 4

Returns: if no light pen, not activated, or not supported:

- ah = 0
- bx, cx, dx = undefined

if valid, activated, light pen:

- ah = 1
- bx = pel column (0 to 319, modes 4, 5, and D) (0 to 639, modes 6, E-10h)
- ch = raster line (0 to 199, modes 4-6)
- cx = raster line (0 to 199, modes D-E, EGA only) (0 to 349, modes F-10, EGA only)
- dh = row of character that pen is positioned on
- dl = column of character that pen is positioned on

INT	Int	Func	Description	Platform
	10h	5	Select Active Display Page	All

Many modes offer multiple pages. This function selects which page is active. This provides the fastest means to switch between two full video pages. Inactive pages may be written at any time, without affecting the currently active, displayed page. The active page number is stored in the BIOS data area at 40:62h.

Many BIOSes do not check for valid page values, and may take unpredictable actions if an out of range value is used. When DOS/V is used, only page 0 is supported.

Called with: ah = 5
al = active page number, zero based

Returns: specified page selected

INT	Int	Func	Description	Platform
	10h	6	Scroll Active Page Up	All

The described window on the active page is scrolled up by the number of rows specified in AL. The contents scrolled off the top are lost. The color attributes of the new blank bottom line(s) are specified by BH. This function is available for all modes, including graphics. In graphics modes, the default character size in scan lines per character indicates how many scan lines are scrolled up per row.

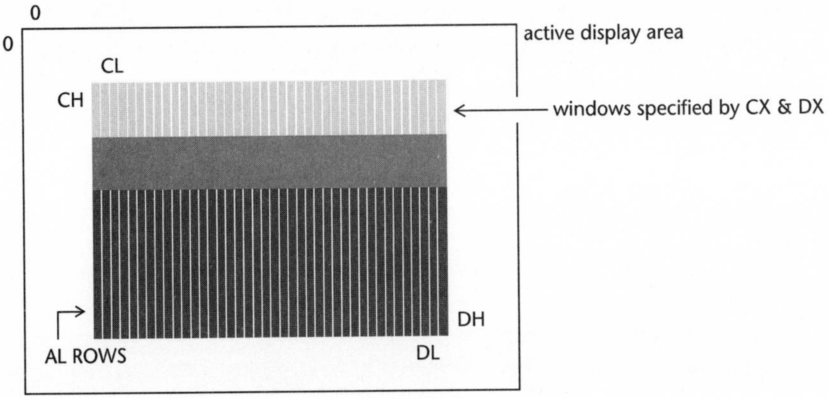

Called with: ah = 6
al = number of rows to scroll up (0 blanks area by scrolling all rows up)
bh = attribute to use on blank bottom line(s)
ch = top row of scroll (0 = topmost row)
cl = left column of scroll (0 = leftmost column)
dh = bottom row of scroll
dl = right column of scroll

Returns: specified area of screen scrolled up

Int	Func	Description	Platform
10h	7	Scroll Active Page Down	All

INT

The active page is scrolled down by the number of rows specified in AL. The contents scrolled off the bottom are lost. The color attributes of the new blank top line(s) are specified by BH. This function is available for all modes, including graphics. In graphics modes, the default character size in scan lines per character indicates how many scan lines are scrolled down per row.

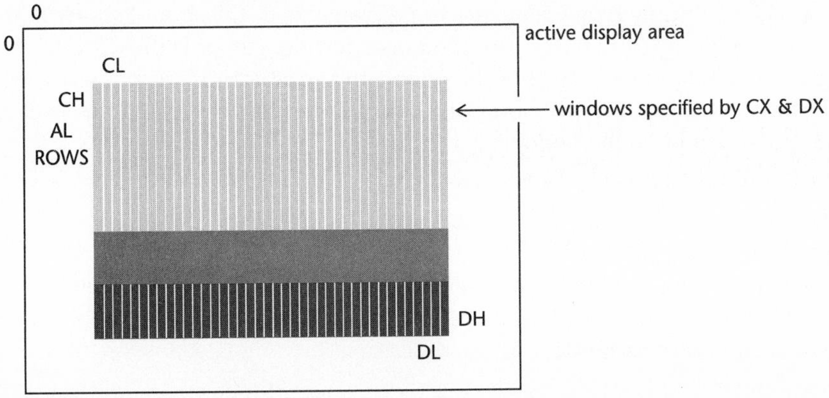

Called with: ah = 7
al = number of rows to scroll down (0 blanks area by scrolling all rows down)
bh = attribute to use on blank top line(s)
ch = top row of scroll (0 = topmost row)
cl = left column of scroll (0 = leftmost column)
dh = bottom row of scroll
dl = right column of scroll
Returns: specified area of screen scrolled down

INT

Int	Func	Description	Platform
10h	8	Read Character and Attribute	All

Gets the character and attribute at the current cursor position of the specified page. In graphics modes, this function can be quite slow. With graphics, if a match is not made with the default ROM character table, AL is set to zero.

Called with: ah = 8
bh = page number
Returns: al = character read
ah = attribute if text mode, undefined if graphics mode

INT

Int	Func	Description	Platform
10h	9	Write Character and Attribute	All

Writes the character and attribute to the current cursor position of the specified page. This function allows the same character and attribute to be repeated multiple times. For graphics modes, the repeat count should not allow characters to be written beyond the end of the current line.

When using any character number 80h or above in graphics modes 4, 5, or 6, the graphics font is specified from the dword pointer stored at 0:7Ch. This pointer must be set by the application. The graphics font pointer is not set by the adapter or system BIOS.

When DOS/V's DBCS (Double Byte Character Set) driver is used, CX should always be 1. The leading byte of the double byte character is written first, and the cursor is moved one column right by the caller. Then the trailing byte of the double byte character is written using this function again. For consistent color on both halves of a double byte character, both the leading and trailing attribute bytes should be the same.

Called with: ah = 9
al = character to write (0-255)
bh = page number (except mode 13h), background color (0-255, mode 13h only)
bl = attribute if text mode

foreground color if graphics (up to 15, except mode 13h) background is set to 0 (black).

bit 7 = 1 if color value to be XORed with the current color bits at these locations foreground color if graphics (0-255 mode 13h only)

cx = count of characters to repeat

Returns: screen updated

Int	Func	Description	Platform
10h	A	Write Character Only	All

INT III I

Writes the character to the current cursor position of the specified page. The current attribute is left unchanged. This function allows the same character to be repeated multiple times. For graphics modes, it is recommended to use function 9. Although undocumented, using function A in graphics mode will work identically to function 9, and the value in BL register is used to specify the color.

When DOS/V's DBCS (Double Byte Character Set) driver is used, CX should always be 1. The leading byte of the double byte character is written first, and the cursor is moved one column right by the caller. Then the trailing byte of the double byte character is written using this function again.

Called with: ah = Ah
al = character to write (0-255)
bh = page number
cx = count of characters to repeat

Returns: screen updated

Int	Func	Description	Platform
10h	B	Set Color Palette	All

INT III I

This function is used to set color options on modes 0 to 6 only. More advanced color options are provided on the EGA and later adapters using function 10h.

If the current video mode is a text mode 0 to 3, the option allows setting the border color. In addition, it allows changing the blink attribute bit 7 to a high-intensity background color option. When the blink attribute bit is set, the character will either blink, or will expand the normal 8 background colors to 16. When using graphics modes 4, 5, or 6, this function selects the colors to use.

The VGA adapter cannot display a border in the rarely used modes 0, 1, 4, or 5. This function may not be supported if using DOS/V.

Called with: ah = Bh
bh = 0 (text modes 0-3)
bl, bits 0-3 = border color (0-15)
bit 4 = 0 blinking option
1 intensified background option

0 (graphics mode 4 or 5)
    bl = background color (0-15)
0 (graphics mode 6)
    bl = foreground color (0-15)
1 (graphics mode 4 or 5)
    bl = 0 foreground colors green/red/brown
        1 foreground colors cyan/magenta/white

Returns: color selections activated

Int	Func	Description	Platform
10h	C	Write Dot	All

This function writes one pixel at the specified address. This is an extremely slow way to write graphics. You should strongly consider writing directly to the display memory. All graphics modes are supported. This function should not be used in text modes as characters or attribute information will be changed.

Called with: ah = Ch
al = color value (all graphics modes except 13h)
bl, bits 0-3 = color (0-15, depending on color range allowed by mode)
    bit 7 = 0 replace pixel
        1 XOR pixel with current pixel color value (0-255, mode 13h only)
bh = page number (ignored if only 1 page allowed)
cx = column number (0-639 or more, depending on mode)
dx = row number (0-479 or more, depending on mode)

Returns: pixel updated

Int	Func	Description	Platform
10h	D	Read Dot	All

This function reads one pixel at the specified address. This is an extremely slow way to read graphics. You should strongly consider reading directly from display memory. All graphics modes are supported. This function should not be used in text modes, as the value returned will have no meaning.

Called with: ah = Dh
bh = page number (ignored if only 1 page allowed)
cx = column number (0-639 or more, depending on mode)
dx = row number (0-479 or more, depending on mode)

Returns: al = pixel color at specified location

Int	Func	Description	Platform
10h	E	Write in Teletype Mode	All

This function sends a character to the display at the current cursor position on the active display page. As necessary, it automatically wraps lines, scrolls, and interprets some control characters for specific actions. It supports text and graphics modes.

The only bytes that are interpreted as a command are 7, 8, A, and D. These values take the following actions:

Value	Name	Description
7	bell	Generates a 1/2 second beep using timer 2.
8	backspace	The cursor is moved back one column, unless already at column 0, in which case the command is ignored.
A	linefeed	Moves the cursor down one row, unless already at the last row, in which case the screen is scrolled up one row.
D	return	The cursor moves to column 0.

When scrolling up in text mode, the new row uses the same attribute as appears at the prior cursor position. In graphics mode, black is used as the background color on a new row.

Called with: ah = Eh
al = character to write
bh = active page number (only required on the oldest PC BIOSs, ignored on all XT+ BIOSs)
bl = foreground color (graphics modes only)

Returns: character displayed or command executed

Int	Func	Description	Platform
10h	F	Read Current Video State	All

Gets the current video mode, number of columns, and the active page number. These values are obtained from the BIOS data area. The number of columns is stored at 40:4Ah, the video mode is stored at 40:49h, and the active page is stored at 40:62h. DOS/V supports only one page in any mode.

Called with: ah = Fh

Returns: ah = number of text columns on screen
al = video mode
bit 7 = 0 if the last mode set cleared the video buffer
1 if the last mode set left the video buffer as-is
bits 6-0 = video mode number (see Table 9-2)
bh = active page

Int	Func	Description	Platform
10h	10	Set Color Register Functions	MCGA/EGA/VGA+

This function provides a number of subfunctions to control the various color palette registers in advanced adapters. The MCGA standard has a number of restrictions as noted with each subfunction.

See function 12h, subfunction 31h, on the ability to lock color register values so a mode set will not change the color registers. Also see function 12h, subfunction 33h, on the ability to force color register settings to be automatically converted to gray scales on a VGA or better adapter.

Table 9-3 shows the standard colors for each attribute. On an EGA or later adapter, each attribute can be changed to one of the 64 colors in Table 9-4. With a VGA or better, each attribute color can also be described with 18-bits of color information. The colors I've described in Table 9-4 will be affected by the monitor and monitor settings. They should only be used as a guide, and assume a well-adjusted monitor.

Table 9-3. Standard Color Values

Color Register	Hex Value	Description
0	0	black
1	1	blue
2	2	green
3	3	cyan
4	4	red
5	5	magenta
6	14	brown
7	7	white
8	38	gray
9	39	bright blue
10	3A	bright green
11	3B	bright cyan
12	3C	bright red
13	3D	bright magenta
14	3E	bright yellow
15	3F	bright white

Table 9-4. Color Descriptions, 64 Colors

Value	Description	Value	Description
0	black	20	dark red
1	blue	21	deep blue-purple
2	green	22	green
3	cyan	23	cyan
4	red	24	bright red-orange
5	magenta	25	deep pink
6	dull yellow	26	orange
7	white	27	pink
8	dark blue	28	dark purple
9	medium blue	29	medium blue
A	army green	2A	green-gray
B	baby blue	2B	medium blue
C	ruby red	2C	cherry red
D	lavender	2D	deep magenta
E	light gold	2E	light orange
F	light lavender	2F	light lavender
10	dark green	30	dark army green
11	medium-dark blue	31	blue-purple
12	fluorescent green	32	bright green-yellow
13	green-cyan	33	light green-cyan
14	brown	34	orange-red
15	medium purple	35	hot pink
16	bright yellow-green	36	lemon yellow
17	faded green	37	warm white
18	dark cyan	38	gray
19	deep blue	39	bright blue
1A	bright green	3A	bright green
1B	bright cyan	3B	bright cyan
1C	faded red	3C	bright red
1D	purple	3D	bright magenta
1E	bright yellow-green	3E	bright yellow
1F	ice blue	3F	bright white

Although the following list of subfunctions skips some subfunction numbers, these are unused and will simply return without any action on an EGA/VGA adapter. Future adapters may utilize currently unused subfunctions.

AL=	Set Color Registers' Subfunctions	Adapters/Drivers
0	Sets single color register	VGA+, EGA, MCGA, DOSV
1	Sets border color	VGA+, EGA
2	Sets all color registers and border	VGA+, EGA, DOSV
3	Background blink or intensify	VGA+, EGA, MCGA
7	Reads single color register	VGA+, DOSV
8	Reads border color	VGA+
9	Reads all color registers and border	VGA+, DOSV
10h	Sets single 18-bit color register	VGA+, MCGA
12h	Sets multiple 18-bit color registers	VGA+, MCGA
13h	Selects color page	VGA+
15h	Reads single 18-bit color register	VGA+, MCGA
17h	Reads multiple 18-bit color registers	VGA+, MCGA
18h	Writes VGA Pel Mask register	VGA+
19h	Reads VGA Pel Mask register	VGA+
1Ah	Reads color page state	VGA+
1Bh	Converts colors to grayscales	VGA+, MCGA

Subfunction Detail for Function 10h

INT

Subfunction	Description	Int	Function
AL=0	Set Single Color Register	10h	AH=10h

On the EGA and VGA+ adapters, this subfunction is used to set one of the 16 color registers to 1 out of 64 colors. The most common default color values for the 16 registers are shown in Table 9-3. Other values are loaded for some graphics modes, and some video vendors adjust the brown color value to appear more pleasing on their hardware. The 64 color choices are shown in Table 9-4.

IBM recommends that only the BX value 712h be used on the MCGA adapter. This switches the system from 16 colors to 8 consistent colors. Other adapters can use this special value to lock the upper 8 colors to the same colors as the lower 8 colors. After 8 constant color mode is invoked, changes to the upper 8 color registers are ignored. Locking the upper 8 colors is typically done when using a 512 character font, so that colors stay consistent over the entire font. A video mode set returns the system to normal 16-color mode.

Called with:	ax = 1000h	
	bl = register number to set (0-15, 18)	
	bh = new value (0-63)	
Returns:	color register updated	

Subfunction	Description	Int	Function
AL=1	Set border color	10h	AH=10h

INT

Sets the border color to one out of 64 colors, as listed in Table 9-4. This subfunction is not supported on the MCGA. The VGA adapter cannot display a border in the rarely-used modes 0, 1, 4, 5, or D.

Called with: ax = 1001h
bh = new value (0-63)
Returns: border color updated

Subfunction	Description	Int	Function
AL=2	Set all color registers and border	10h	AH=10h

INT

Sets the colors for all 16-color registers and the border color. Each register selects from one of the 64 colors shown in Table 9-4. This subfunction is not supported on the MCGA. The VGA adapter cannot display a border in the rarely-used modes 0, 1, 4, 5, or D.

Called with: ax = 1002h
es:bx = pointer to 17-byte color table
bytes 0 to F specify color registers
byte 10h specifies border color
Returns: color registers and border updated

Subfunction	Description	Int	Function
AL=3	Background blink or intensify	10h	AH=10h

INT

For text modes, bit 7 of the attribute normally controls if the background should blink or not. It can also be used to expand the normal 8 background colors to a full 16 colors. This function selects how bit 7 of the attribute byte will affect the background.

Called with: ax = 1003h
bl = 0 use attribute bit 7 for intensified colors
1 use attribute bit 7 for blinking
Returns: attribute control saved

Subfunction	Description	Int	Function
AL=7	Read single color register	10h	AH=10h

INT

Reads one of the 16-color registers. Color values are shown in Table 9-4. This subfunction is supported only on VGA and better adapters.

Called with: ax = 1007h
bl = register number to get (0-15)
Returns: bh = register value (0-63)

Subfunction	Description	Int	Function
AL=8	Read border color	10h	AH=10h

Gets the current boarder color. Color values are shown in Table 9-4. This subfunction is supported only on VGA and better adapters.

Called with: ax = 1008h
Returns: bh = border color value (0-63)

Subfunction	Description	Int	Function
AL=9	Read all color registers and border	10h	AH=10h

Reads all 16-color registers and the border color register. Color values are shown in Table 9-4. This subfunction is supported only on VGA and better adapters.

Called with: ax = 1009h
es:bx = pointer save area for 17-byte color table
bytes 0 to F will hold the color registers
byte 10h will hold the border color
Returns: 17 color bytes loaded into table

Subfunction	Description	Int	Function
AL=10h	Set single 18-bit color register	10h	AH=10h

On the VGA+ and MCGA adapters, this function is used to set one of the 64 18-bit color registers. With the VGA+/MCGA, each of the 64 colors in Table 9-4 is controlled by three 6-bit registers, one each for green, red, and blue intensity. This allows changing any of the 64 EGA type colors into any custom color. This subfunction is not supported on the EGA.

Called with: ax = 1010h
bx = register number to set (0-63)
ch = green value (0-63)
cl = blue value (0-63)
dh = red value (0-63)
Returns: color register updated

Subfunction	Description	Int	Function
AL=12h	Set multiple 18-bit color registers	10h	AH=10h

INT

On the VGA+ and MCGA adapters, this function is used to set multiple 18-bit color registers. With the VGA+/MCGA, each of the 64 colors in Table 9-4 is controlled by three 6-bit registers, one each for green, red, and blue intensity. This allows changing a group of the 64 EGA type colors into new custom colors. This subfunction is not supported on the EGA.

Called with: ax = 1012h
bx = first color register to set (0-63)
cx = number of color registers to set (1-64)
es:bx = pointer to table of color triads-The table is made up of three color bytes for each register, in the order red, green, blue (each color byte value has a range of 0-63)

Returns: color registers updated

Subfunction	Description	Int	Function
AL=13h	Select color page	10h	AH=10h

INT

The VGA+ offers multiple pages of 18-bit color registers, which can be quickly switched. Switching the color page is much faster than reloading all the color registers. This is often used by games to generate special effects, and even limited animation if cleverly structured. There is only one color page for mode 13h, so this function is not valid while mode 13h is active.

Whenever a mode is set with Interrupt 10h, function 0, the system defaults to the paging mode with four color pages, with the first page active. Only the first page of 64 color registers is initialized.

Called with: ax = 1013h
bl = 0 Select paging mode
bh = 0 use 4 pages, where each page has 64 color registers (default after power-up)
bh = 1 use 16 pages, where each page has 16 color registers
bl = 1 Select color page number
bh = color page number
when in 4 color page mode, page range is 0-3
when in 16 color page mode, page range is 0-15

Returns: color page or mode selected

Subfunction	Description	Int	Function
AL=15h	Read single 18-bit color register	10h	AH=10h

INT

On the VGA+ and MCGA adapters, this function is used to read one of the 64 18-bit color registers. This subfunction is not supported on the EGA.

Called with: ax = 1015h
bx = register number to read (0-63)
Returns: ch = green value (0-63)
cl = blue value (0-63)
dh = red value (0-63)

INT	Subfunction	Description	Int	Function
	AL=17h	Read multiple 18-bit color registers	10h	AH=10h

On the VGA+ and MCGA adapters, this function is used to read multiple 18-bit color registers. This subfunction is not supported on the EGA.

Called with: ax = 1017h
bx = first color register to read (0-63)
cx = number of color registers to read (1-64)
es:bx = pointer to table where to store color triads. The table is made up of three color bytes for each register, in the order red, green, blue
Returns: es:bx table loaded with specified color register values

INT	Subfunction	Description	Int	Function
	AL=18h	Write VGA Pel Mask register	10h	AH=10h

This undocumented function simply loads the VGA Pel mask register, at port 3C6h. The Pel Mask register is loaded with the value FFh during a BIOS mode set. Subfunction 18h seems to be supported on most, if not all, vendor's BIOSes, but it is never called from the video BIOS. The Pel Mask register is also an undocumented I/O port on the VGA.

The Pel Mask register can be used for providing the fastest possible color changes. The VGA has an internal table of 256 colors, although most modes only use the first 16. When a color is to be displayed, the color's address is selected by hardware. The hardware ANDs the table address with the contents of the Pel Mask register. With the default Pel Mask of 0FFh, all 256 colors are displayed. The Pel Mask register can limit access to the color registers, without affecting the contents of video memory or the color register contents.

For example, when the default colors are loaded, table entry 0 and 1 are used to access the black and blue colors. Loading the pel mask with the value 1, means that only attributes 0 (black), 1 (blue), are allowed. Any other attribute will result in either black or blue appearing on screen. If the attribute was cyan, indicating table address 3, the address is ANDed with the pel mask of 1, resulting in blue on screen rather than cyan. If the pel mask value was 5, only black, blue, red or magenta colors will appear on screen.

Called with: ax = 1018h
bl register value
Returns: Pel Mask register loaded

Subfunction	Description	Int	Function
AL=19h	Read VGA Pel Mask register	10h	AH=10h

This undocumented function reads the undocumented VGA Pel mask register, at port 3C6h. Subfunction 19h seems to be supported on most, if not all, vendor's BIOSes, but it is never called from the video BIOS. See subfunction 18h for additional details.

Called with: ax = 1019h

Returns: bh = 0

bl = contents of Pel Mask register

Subfunction	Description	Int	Function
AL=1Ah	Read color page state	10h	AH=10h

INT

Gets the color page mode and active color page. See subfunction 13h for more details. This subfunction is supported only on VGA+ adapters.

Called with: ax = 101Ah

Returns: bh = active color page (0-15)

bl = color page mode (0-1)

Subfunction	Description	Int	Function
AL=1Bh	Convert colors to grayscales	10h	AH=10h

INT

This subfunction takes a value in the 18-bit color register and converts it into a grayscale value. This works by taking a percentage of each color and adding them together. The resultant value is then loaded into the red, green, and blue components of the 18-bit color value. The following example helps show how the VGA+ adapter performs this transformation on one register. The percentage weights are fixed by the adapter as shown.

Starting Color	Value	Percent Weight by Color	Result	Ending Color Values
blue	58	11 %	6	→ 33
green	26	59 %	15	→ 33
red	39	30 %	12	→ 33
			sum = 33	

Called with: ax = 101Bh

bx = first color register to sum (0-63)

cx = number of color registers to sum (1-64)

Returns: specified color registers converted to grayscales

INT

Int	Func	Description	Platform
10h	11	Character Generation Functions	MCGA/EGA/VGA+

This function provides a number of subfunctions to set and get character generation features on the MCGA, EGA, and VGA+ adapters. Different adapters have slight differences as noted in each subfunction.

Although the list of subfunctions skips over some subfunction numbers, these are unused and will simply return without any action on an EGA/VGA adapter. Future adapters may assign currently unused subfunctions to new uses.

AL=	Character Generator Subfunctions	Adapters/Drivers
0	Load User Font	VGA+, EGA, MCGA, DOSV
1	Load 8x14 Font	VGA+, EGA, MCGA
2	Load 8x8 Font	VGA+, EGA, MCGA
3	Select Font Mode	VGA+, EGA, MCGA
4	Load 8x16 Font	VGA+, MCGA
10h	Load User Font After Mode Set	VGA+, EGA, MCGA
11h	Load 8x14 Font After Mode Set	VGA+, EGA, MCGA
12h	Load 8x8 Font After Mode Set	VGA+, EGA, MCGA
14h	Load 8x16 Font After Mode Set	VGA+, MCGA
20h	Set Int 1Fh Graphics Font Pointer	VGA+, EGA, MCGA
21h	Set Int 43h Graphics Font Pointer	VGA+, EGA, MCGA
22h	Load 8x14 Font into Int 43h	VGA+, EGA, MCGA
23h	Load 8x8 Font into Int 43h	VGA+, EGA, MCGA
24h	Load 8x16 Font into Int 43h	VGA+, MCGA
30h	Get Font Information	VGA+, EGA, MCGA

Subfunction Detail for Function 11h

INT

Subfunction	Description	Int	Function
AL=0	Load User Font	10h	AH=11h

Loads a user-specified font character into the adapter's font memory. Internal to the adapter are a number of 32x256 font pages. Each 32-byte font block in a font page describes the bits to use for each text character. In most cases only a portion of the 32 bytes make up the complete character. For example, the EGA's standard 8x14 font is made up of 14 bytes. The character "T" appears as:

	bits
byte	76543210
0	00000000
1	01111110
2	01111110

3	01011010
4	00011000
5	00011000
6	00011000
7	00011000
8	00011000
9	00011000
10	00111100
11	00000000
12	00000000
13	00000000

When loading a user font, only supply the number of bytes per character that make up the character cell. For an 8x14 font, the user font table will have 14x256 bytes. Nine bit-wide fonts only use eight bits per row. The ninth column is created by the video adapter hardware. For characters 0-BFh and E0-F0h, the ninth column is always blank. For characters C0-DFh the eighth column is duplicated in the ninth column. This makes line graphic font characters continuous when placed adjacent on screen.

All font characters for text modes are stored in the red plane, plane number 2, in the high-resolution graphics memory area. A switch to graphics mode Dh or above clears the font information, and a switch to a text mode resets the default font. Performing a font load while in a graphics mode will create red dots on the top half of a blank graphics screen.

If we had previously supplied an 8x14 font table of 256 characters, and wished to only reload the one character "T", the registers are set: BH=14, BL=0, CX=1, DX='T', ES:BP=start of table. The size of the font table for this example will be 14x256 or 3584 bytes long, although only the 14 bytes that make up the "T" will actually be used.

This function does not set the number of scan lines on the screen. See subfunction 30h to do this. The number of rows on screen are determined by the number of scan lines divided by the number of rows in each character.

This is the only subfunction allowable for function 11h with DOS/V. DOS/V allows only font page 0.

Called with:	ax = 1100h
	bh = number of bytes per character (1-32)
	bl = font page
	cx = number of font characters to load (1-256)
	dx = character number in table (0-255)
	es:bp = beginning of user font table
Returns:	font updated

INT	Subfunction	Description	Int	Function
	AL=1	Load 8x14 Font	10h	AH=11h

Loads the adapter's internal 8x14 font into the specified font page. Resets the adapter to use the 8x14 font. The MCGA adapter cannot display an 8x14 font and will issue subfunction 4 and display an 8x16 font if subfunction 1 is attempted.

Called with:	ax	= 1101h
	bl	= font page
Returns:	8x14 font loaded	

INT	Subfunction	Description	Int	Function
	AL=2	Load 8x8 Font	10h	AH=11h

Loads the adapter's internal 8x8 font into the specified font page. Resets the adapter to use the 8x8 font.

Called with:	ax	= 1102h
	bl	= font page
Returns:	8x8 font loaded	

INT	Subfunction	Description	Int	Function
	AL=3	Select Font Page Mode	10h	AH=11h

This subfunction specifies which font pages are active. Up to two font pages can be active at one time making a maximum of 512 characters possible on the screen at the same time. The EGA and MCGA provide a total of four font pages, and the VGA and later adapters provide eight font pages.

To access 512 characters, the attribute byte, bit 3, normally just controls the color intensity of the foreground. In 512 character mode, it also controls which of two fonts are displayed. To get eight consistent colors, it is necessary to change the color registers so the first eight registers are the same as the second set of eight registers. See interrupt 10h, function AL=10h, subfunction 0 for a special mode to accomplish this.

Table 9-5 shows which page is selected based on the attribute bit 3 and the font page mode value (BL) on the EGA and MCGA. If the selected page is the same for both states of the attribute intensity bit, then only 256 characters are accessible. For example, if the font page mode was set to 8, then 512 characters are enabled, with font page 0 used when the attribute bit 3 was zero. Font page 2 would be used when the attribute bit 3 was one. Table 9-6 shows the page selected on VGA+ adapters for all possible font page modes.

Table 9-5. Font Page Selections, MCGA and EGA

Page Mode	Page Selected — Attribute — Bit 3=0	Bit 3=1	Page Mode	Page Selected — Attribute — Bit 3=0	Bit 3=1
0	0	0	8	0	2
1	1	0	9	1	2
2	2	0	A	2	2
3	3	0	B	3	2
4	0	1	C	0	3
5	1	1	D	1	3
6	2	1	E	2	3
7	3	1	F	3	3

Table 9-6. Font Page Selections, VGA+

Page Mode	Page Selected — Attribute — Bit 3=0	Bit 3=1	Page Mode	Page Selected — Attribute — Bit 3=0	Bit 3=1
0	0	0	20	0	4
1	1	0	21	1	4
2	2	0	22	2	4
3	3	0	23	3	4
4	0	1	24	0	5
5	1	1	25	1	5
6	2	1	26	2	5
7	3	1	27	3	5
8	0	2	28	0	6
9	1	2	29	1	6
A	2	2	2A	2	6
B	3	2	2B	3	6
C	0	3	2C	0	7
D	1	3	2D	1	7
E	2	3	2E	2	7
F	3	3	2F	3	7
10	4	0	30	4	4
11	5	0	31	5	4
12	6	0	32	6	4
13	7	0	33	7	4
14	4	1	34	4	5
15	5	1	35	5	5

Table 9-6. Continued

Page Mode	Page Selected Attribute Bit 3=0	Page Selected Attribute Bit 3=1	Page Mode	Page Selected Attribute Bit 3=0	Page Selected Attribute Bit 3=1
16	6	1	36	6	5
17	7	1	37	7	5
18	4	2	38	4	6
19	5	2	39	5	6
1A	6	2	3A	6	6
1B	7	2	3B	7	6
1C	4	3	3C	4	7
1D	5	3	3D	5	7
1E	6	3	3E	6	7
1F	7	3	3F	7	7

Called with: ax = 1103h
bl = font page mode (see text)
Returns: font page mode set

INT	Subfunction	Description	Int	Function
	AL=4	Load 8x16 Font	10h	AH=11h

Loads the adapter's internal 8x16 font into the specified font page. Resets the adapter to use the 8x16 font. This subfunction is available on the MCGA and VGA+ adapters only, and is not supported on the EGA.

Called with: ax = 1104h
bl = font page
Returns: 8x16 font loaded

INT	Subfunction	Description	Int	Function
	AL=10h	Load User Font After Mode Set	10h	AH=11h

This subfunction loads a user font, similar to subfunction 0. Unlike subfunction 0, this subfunction can only be issued immediately after a mode set and performs a number of actions. Page zero must be active (the mode set always sets page 0 active). The number of rows saved in the BIOS data area at address 40:84h is calculated from the integer value:

$$\text{Maximum Rows (zero based)} = \frac{\text{Scan Lines}}{\text{Character Height}} - 1$$

For example, if an 8x20 font was loaded, while the scan lines were set to 400, the result would be (400/20)–1 = 19. Since it is zero based, 19 really means there are 20 rows.

The number of bytes in the page is recalculated and saved in the BIOS data area at 40:4Ch. The Rows value is obtained from the BIOS data area at 40:84h, and the columns is obtained from 40:4Ah. The bytes per page calculation is:

Bytes per Page = (Rows + 1) * Columns * 2

Some of the CRT Controller Registers, accessed through port 3D5h, are updated with new values. These include:

Maximum Scan Line Register	(index 9)	= character height – 1
Cursor Start Register	(index A)	= character height – 2
Cursor End Register	(index B)	= character height – 1
Vertical Display End Register	(index 12h)	=
		for 200 Scan Line Mode:
		((Rows + 1) * Character Height * 2) – 1
		for 350 scan lines and above:
		((Rows + 1) * Character Height) – 1

If the system is currently in monochrome mode 7, then the CRT Controller underline register is also updated:

Underline Location Register (index 14h) = Character Height – 1

On the MCGA, this subfunction is not implemented, and will issue subfunction 0 if attempted.

Called with:	ax = 1110h
	bh = number of bytes per character (2-32)
	bl = font page
	cx = number of font characters to load (1-256)
	dx = character number in table (0-255)
	es:bp = beginning of user font table
Returns:	font updated

INT Subfunction	Description	Int	Function
AL=11h	Load 8x14 Font After Mode Set	10h	AH=11h

Loads the adapter's internal 8x14 font into the specified font page. This is similar to subfunction 1, except a mode set must be issued immediately before subfunction 11h is issued. See subfunction 10h for the actions taken.

This subfunction is used to set an 8x14 ROM font after a text video mode has been set. The MCGA adapter cannot display an 8x14 font and will issue subfunction 4 and display an 8x16 font if subfunction 11h is attempted.

Called with:	ax = 1111h
	bl = font page
Returns:	8x14 font loaded

INT Subfunction	Description	Int	Function
AL=12h	Load 8x8 Font After Mode Set	10h	AH=11h

Loads the adapter's internal 8x8 font into the specified font page. This is similar to subfunction 2, except a mode set must be issued immediately before subfunction 12h is issued. See subfunction 10h for actions taken.

This subfunction is used to set an 8x8 ROM font after a text video mode has been set. On the MCGA, this subfunction is not implemented, and will issue subfunction 2 if attempted.

Called with:	ax = 1112h
	bl = font page
Returns:	8x8 font loaded

INT Subfunction	Description	Int	Function
AL=14h	Load 8x16 Font After Mode Set	10h	AH=11h

Loads the adapter's internal 8x16 font into the specified font page. This is similar to subfunction 4, except a mode set must be issued immediately before subfunction 14h is issued. See subfunction 10h for actions taken.

This subfunction is used to set an 8x16 ROM font after a text video mode has been set. This subfunction is only available on VGA+ adapters, and is not supported on the EGA. On the MCGA, this subfunction is not implemented, and will issue subfunction 4 if attempted.

Called with:	ax = 1114h
	bl = font page
Returns:	8x16 font loaded

Subfunction	Description	Int	Function
AL=20h	Set Int 1Fh Graphics Font Pointer	10h	AH=11h

INT

Saves the pointer to a user-supplied table of graphics characters. This table is only used by graphics modes 4, 5, and 6 for characters 128 to 255. The table is configured as 128 8-byte characters, for an 8x8 cell character.

The pointer is stored in interrupt vector 1Fh address 0:7Ch. This function performs no actions other than loading the user pointer into the interrupt 1Fh vector address.

Called with: ax = 1120h
es:bp = pointer to user supplied font table of characters 128 to 255
Returns: pointer loaded

Subfunction	Description	Int	Function
AL=21h	Set Int 43h Graphics Font Pointer	10h	AH=11h

INT

Saves the supplied pointer to a table of graphics characters. While in modes 4, 5, or 6, this pointer identifies a font table of the first 128 characters. See subfunction 20h for handling the upper 128 characters. On all other graphics modes, this pointer identifies the complete 256 font table to use.

The pointer is stored in interrupt vector 43h address 0:10Ch. The number of scan lines per character is stored in the BIOS data area at 40:85h. The number of display rows is stored at 40:84h. This function performs no actions other than loading specified values into memory. This subfunction should only be used immediately after a graphics video mode set.

Called with: ax = 1121h
bl = number of character rows selection
0 = number of rows specified in DL
1 = 14 rows
2 = 25 rows
3 = 43 rows
cx = number of bytes per character (1-32)
dl = number of rows (if bl=0)
es:bp = pointer to ROM or user-supplied font table
Returns: pointer loaded and BIOS values updated

INT	Subfunction	Description	Int	Function
	AL=22h	Load 8x14 Font Into Int 43h	10h	AH=11h

This function simply loads a pointer to the 8x14 ROM font into the interrupt 43h vector location at 0:10Ch. It is identical to subfunction 21h, with CX set to 14, and with ES:BP pointing to the 8x14 ROM font. The BL register is set to the number of rows.

This function performs no other actions other than loading specified values into memory. This subfunction is designed to be used immediately after a graphics video mode set.

The MCGA adapter cannot display an 8x14 font and will issue subfunction 24h to load the 8x16 font pointer if subfunction 22h is attempted.

Called with: ax = 1122h
bl = number of character rows selection
0 = number of rows specified in DL
1 = 14 rows
2 = 25 rows
3 = 43 rows
dl = number of rows (if bl=0)

Returns: 8x14 pointer loaded and BIOS values updated

INT	Subfunction	Description	Int	Function
	AL=23h	Load 8x8 Font into Int 43h	10h	AH=11h

This function simply loads a pointer to the 8x8 ROM font into the interrupt 43h vector location at 0:10Ch. It is identical to subfunction 21h, with CX set to 8, and with ES:BP pointing to the 8x8 ROM font. The BL register is set to the number of rows.

This function performs no actions other than loading specified values into memory. This subfunction is designed to be used immediately after a graphics video mode set.

Called with: ax = 1123h
bl = number of character rows selection
0 = number of rows specified in DL
1 = 14 rows
2 = 25 rows
3 = 43 rows
dl = number of rows (if bl=0)

Returns: 8x8 pointer loaded and BIOS values updated

Subfunction	Description	Int	Function
AL=24h	Load 8x16 Font into Int 43	10h	AH=11h

INT

This function simply loads a pointer to the 8x16 ROM font into the interrupt 43h vector location at 0:10Ch. It is identical to subfunction 21h, with CX set to 16, and with ES:BP pointing to the 8x16 ROM font. The BL register is set to the number of rows.

This function performs no actions other than loading specified values into memory. This subfunction is designed to be used immediately after a graphics video mode set. This subfunction is available on the MCGA and VGA+ adapters only, and is not supported on the EGA.

Called with: ax = 1124h
bl = number of character rows selection
0 = number of rows specified in DL
1 = 14 rows
2 = 25 rows
3 = 43 rows
dl = number of rows (if bl=0)

Returns: 8x16 pointer loaded and BIOS values updated

Subfunction	Description	Int	Function
AL=30h	Get Font Information	10h	AH=11h

INT

Gets information about a specific font, and gets the current bytes per character and rows. The current bytes per character value is loaded from the BIOS data area at 40:85h. The current character rows value is read directly from 40:84h, and is the number of text rows on screen, less one. These two values are independent of the font table selected.

The font tables are in the form of one byte for every 8-bit row of the character cell. An 8x16 font will be 16x256, or 4096 bytes long.

The two special 9-bit replacement tables are used to specify a small number of characters to replace in an 8-bit-wide font. For example, the lower case "m" character is wider in the 9x14 font than in the 8x14 font. Rather than waste ROM space with a completely separate 9x14 font, only the few characters that are different are stored. About 20 characters are typically provided with replacements for the standard 8-bit-wide characters.

These replacement tables are organized as a byte indicating the character value, followed by the bytes that make up the character. For a 9x14 font, 15 bytes are used per character. The character value 0 is used to signify the end of the table. The BIOS provides no means to accept these special tables using a BIOS call. The characters must be loaded one at a time, using subfunction 0 or 10h.

BH values of 6 and 7 are not supported on the EGA. BH values 5 and 7 are not supported on the MCGA. MCGA, BL=2 will return a pointer to the 8x16 font.

Called with: ax = 1130h
bh = which font table pointer to return
0 = get the pointer stored in int 1Fh
1 = get the pointer stored in int 43h
2 = 8x14 ROM font (characters 0-255)
3 = 8x8 ROM font (characters 0-255)
4 = 8x8 ROM font (characters 128-255)
5 = special table of characters to replace 8x14 character with 9x14
6 = 8x16 ROM font (characters 0-255)
7 = special table of characters to replace 8x16 character with 9x16

Returns: cx = current bytes per character
dx = current character rows – 1
es:bp = pointer to font table

Int	Func	Description	Platform
10h	12	Miscellaneous Functions	MCGA/EGA/VGA+

This function supports a number of subfunctions that fail to fall into any well-defined group. This function is sometimes referred to as the Alternate Select, because one subfunction selects an alternate print-screen.

None of these subfunctions are available while DOS/V is installed.

AL=	Miscellaneous Subfunctions	Adapters
10	Get Information	VGA+, EGA, MCGA
20	Install Alternate Print Screen	VGA+, EGA, MCGA
30	Select Scan Lines for Text Modes	VGA+, MCGA
31	Color Register Loading Options	VGA+, MCGA
32	Video Enable/Disable	VGA+, MCGA
33	Sum Colors to Gray scales	VGA+, MCGA
34	Cursor Size Control	VGA+
35	Display Switch	VGA+, MCGA
36	Video Screen On/Off	VGA+
37	Mainframe Interactive Support	XGA+

Subfunction	Description	Int	Function
BL=10h	Get Information	10h	AH=12h

This subfunction gets information previously saved in the BIOS data area. The color type is obtained from 40:87, bit 1. The amount of memory comes from the bits 6 and 5 at 40:87. The switches and feature connector bits are stored at 40:88, where the upper four bits are the feature connector bits, which are shifted down by 4, before returning the value in CH. The switch settings, shown in Table 9-7, control how the adapter is configured at start up. Some adapters retain these switch settings using nonvolatile memory, and require a setup program to alter the values. With all EGA+ compatible adapters, the switch value returned by this function will correspond to the original EGA/VGA switch settings, even if no switches are provided or the actual switches are used for other purposes.

Table 9-7. Original EGA+ Adapter Switches

Bits				**Configuration**	
3	**2**	**1**	**0**	**Primary (Default)**	**Secondary**
0	0	0	0	MDA/HGA 80x25 monochrome	EGA/VGA+ 40x25 color
0	0	0	1	MDA/HGA 80x25 monochrome	EGA/VGA+ 80x25 color
0	0	1	0	MDA/HGA 80x25 monochrome	EGA/VGA+ 80x25 color
0	0	1	1	MDA/HGA 80x25 monochrome	EGA/VGA+ 80x25 color
0	1	0	0	CGA 40x25 color	EGA/VGA+ 80x25 monochrome
0	1	0	1	CGA 80x25 color	EGA/VGA+ 80x25 monochrome
0	1	1	0	EGA/VGA+ 40x25 color	MDA/HGA 80x25 monochrome*
0	1	1	1	EGA/VGA+ 80x25 color	MDA/HGA 80x25 monochrome*
1	0	0	0	EGA/VGA+ 80x25 color	MDA/HGA 80x25 monochrome*
1	0	0	1	EGA/VGA+ 80x25 color	MDA/HGA 80x25 monochrome*
1	0	1	0	EGA/VGA+ 80x25 monochrome	CGA 40x25 color*
1	0	1	1	EGA/VGA+ 80x25 monochrome	CGA 80x25 color*

**Indicates optional adapter, and is not required*

Called with: ah = 12h
bl = 10h

Returns: bh = color/monochrome type
0 = color mode, using 3Dxh ports
1 = monochrome mode, using 3Bxh ports
bl = amount of memory on adapter
0 = 64K
1 = 128K
2 = 192K
3 = 256K or more
ch = feature connector bits
bits 7-4 = 0
bit 3 = Feature connector line 0, in state 1
bit 2 = Feature connector line 1, in state 1
bit 1 = Feature connector line 0, in state 2
bit 0 = Feature connector line 1, in state 2

cl = switches to control adapter type
bits 7-4 = 0
bits 3-0 = switches (see Table 9-7)

INT Subfunction	Description	Int	Function
BL=20h	Install Alternate Print Screen	10h	AH=12h

This routine replaces the current interrupt 5 print screen handler with one from the video BIOS. This function is generally poorly understood. The original PC and XT print screen functions only look at 25 rows regardless of how many are actually displayed. With the capability of having more than 25 display rows with EGA and VGA adapters, the old print screen handler needs to be replaced. This subfunction replaces the old print screen handler with a new one that handles more than 25 rows on screen.

It is only necessary to install this alternate print screen if more than 25 rows of text are going to be displayed and the system is a PC or XT. With the AT and all later systems, the standard BIOS print screen was updated to handle more than 25 rows.

Since this just replaces the current interrupt 5 vector without hooking the old vector, it can cause system stability problems. If another device driver or TSR had hooked interrupt 5, they will no longer get control when interrupt 5 is issued. I highly recommend examining the interrupt 5 vector before issuing this subfunction. If the interrupt 5 vector is pointing to the system BIOS, at segment F000, then it is acceptable to replace the print screen handler using this function. Otherwise a warning or error message should be displayed, and the subfunction should not be issued.

If you are writing a TSR that needs to know the state of the print screen, do not hook interrupt 5. You can always see the state of the print screen by reading the byte at 50:0. See Chapter 6, BIOS Data and Other Fixed Data Areas, for more about the print screen status at location 50:0.

Called with: ah = 12h
bl = 20h
Returns: new print screen handler installed

INT Subfunction	Description	Int	Function
BL=30h	Select Scan Lines for Text Modes	10h	AH=12h

Sets the number of scan lines to appear on screen. The new scan lines setting does not take effect until the next mode set. Subsequent same mode sets do not change the number of scan lines. Unfortunately, this subfunction does not support scan line values for 480 or more scan line settings. This function is only supported on VGA+ adapters.

This function is ignored if the adapter is inactive, as bit 3 at 40:87 signifies. If the adapter is in monochrome mode, an attempt to set 200 scan lines is ignored. When accepted, this subfunction simply updates the Advanced Video switches byte at 40:88h to make it look like an alternate mode was set. In addition, the Advanced Video Save Area 1 byte at 40:89 has the 200/350 and 400 scan line bits updated.

Called with:	ah	= 12h
	al	= scan line value after mode set
		0 = 200 scan lines (CGA resolution)
		1 = 350 scan lines (EGA resolution)
		2 = 400 scan lines (VGA resolution)
	bl	= 30h
Returns:	al	= 12h (indicating subfunction supported)

Subfunction	Description	Int	Function
BL=31h	Color Register Loading Options	10h	AH=12h

INT

Controls whether the color registers are updated after a mode set. Normally, as part of a mode set, the 64 8-bit color registers, the border color register, and the 256 18-bit color registers are set to the default values. This function makes it possible to prevent any of these color registers from being updated during a mode set.

The status of this load option is stored at 40:89, bit 3. This subfunction is only available on MCGA and VGA+ adapters.

Called with:	ah	= 12h
	al	= Color load state
		0 = Enable normal color register loads
		1 = Disable color register loads
	bl	= 31h
Returns:	al	= 12h (indicating subfunction supported)

Subfunction	Description	Int	Function
BL=32h	Video Enable/Disable	10h	AH=12h

INT

This controls whether the VGA+ adapter will respond to I/O ports and use of the video memory area. When disabled, the VGA card is no longer accessible from the system, with the exception of this command. This means I/O ports are ignored, and the entire video memory address mapped by the VGA+ card from A000 to BFFF disappears!

This subfunction does not blank the screen or turn off the video output to the monitor. The actual video adapter is still active, and the display contents will remain frozen on screen until video is enabled and the screen updated. The video BIOS ROM remains active in memory while video is disabled.

The low-level action taken by this subfunction is to write the value 0 to port 46E8h to disable video, and write value E to this same port to enable video. Some adapters may use other

I/O ports to enable and disable video. This subfunction is only available on MCGA and VGA+ adapters.

Called with: ah = 12h
al = Video Adapter State
0 = Enable video
1 = Disable video
bl = 32h
Returns: al = 12h (indicating subfunction supported)

INT

Subfunction	Description	Int	Function
BL=33h	Sum Colors to Grayscales	10h	AH=12h

On a VGA grayscale monitor, it is desirable to always maintain colors at some grayscale level. Very few applications support grayscale monitors. With this option set, an application using colors will usually be easy to read on a grayscale monitor. This function sets a flag to force grayscales in the color registers during a video mode set or during the update to any color register with function 10h.

The status of summing is stored as an inverted bit at 40:89, bit 1. This subfunction is only available on MCGA and VGA+ adapters.

Called with: ah = 12h
al = Grayscale Summing Mode
0 = Enabled
1 = Disabled
bl = 33h
Returns: al = 12h (indicating subfunction supported)

INT

Subfunction	Description	Int	Function
BL=34h	Cursor Size Control	10h	AH=12h

The cursor size is set using function 1 by specifying a start and end address. When the Cursor Size Control allows scaling, the values passed in function 1 are altered to maintain a cursor size relative to the current character cell size. This is the default condition. With no scaling, the function 1 cursor size is not changed.

For example, if a half block cursor is desired, and a program assumes an 8x8 character cell. The program sets the cursor start at 3 and cursor end at 7. Now if the system is really in a mode with an 8x16 character cell, the cursor size would seem wrong. The scaling mode will readjust this request to get an approximate half block cursor, even though the wrong values were used. The size control reliably handles any font from 8 to 32 scan lines high, and supports no cursor, overbar cursor, underline cursor, half-cell, and full-cell cursors.

The status of cursor size control is stored at 40:87, bit 0. This subfunction is only available on VGA+ adapters.

Called with: ah = 12h
al = Cursor Size Control
0 = Scale size to character height (default)
1 = No scaling of cursor
bl = 34h
Returns: al = 12h (indicating subfunction supported)

Subfunction	Description	Int	Function
BL=35h	Display Switch	10h	AH=12h

INT

This function is used when a system is equipped with a VGA on the motherboard. Display Switch allows switching between the motherboard VGA and an alternate VGA adapter. Most PS/2 systems have the VGA system installed on the motherboard.

The two problems this subfunction solves are the shared usage of key BIOS data area bytes in segment 40h, and I/O addresses that may overlap each other.

The first time this function is used, it must be called with AL=0 to save the video system state in a user-supplied buffer, 128 bytes long. This also disables the add-in VGA adapter. The second step is to activate the motherboard VGA by using AL=1. After these initial steps are made, all future switching is performed by issuing AL=2 to disable the active VGA, and issuing AL=3 to enable the previously inactive VGA. Each time the AL=2, AL=3 pair of commands is issued, the display will toggle between the motherboard VGA and the adapter VGA.

This subfunction is only supported on MCGA and VGA+ systems and adapters.

Called with: ah = 12h
al = Steps for switching between VGAs
0 = First time save of video state and disables VGA+ adapter card
1 = First time enable motherboard VGA
2 = Switch off active VGA+
3 = Switch on previously inactive VGA+
bl = 35h
es:dx = pointer to 128-byte switch state save area (not required for AL=1)
Returns: al = 12h (indicating subfunction supported)

Subfunction	Description	Int	Function
BL=36h	Video Screen On/Off	10h	AH=12h

INT

This subfunction blanks the screen. Video memory and the video mode are unaffected by this command. When the screen is enabled, the prior screen contents are restored.

This subfunction is only supported on VGA+ systems.

Called with: ah = 12h
al = Video Screen
0 = Blank screen
1 = Enable screen
bl = 36h
Returns: al = 12h (indicating subfunction supported)

INT	Subfunction	Description	Int	Function
	BL=37h	Mainframe Interactive Support	10h	AH=12h

For XGA adapters only, this new function switches the normal text attribute definition to one compatible with mainframes. Table 9-8 shows both the normal and mainframe definitions for the attribute byte.

Table 9-8. Attribute Byte Description

Bit	Description (VGA Normal)	Bit	Description (Mainframe Type)
7 = 0	Normal background	7 = 0	Background color 0
1	blink normal rate, 50% duty cycle or intensified background (see AH=10h, AL=3)	1	blink double rate, 75% on duty cycle or use color 8 for background (see AH=10h, AL=3)
6 = x	Background color, bits 4, 5, & 6 select from 1 of 8 colors	6 = 0	Normal
		1	Reverse video
5 = x	Background color	5 = 0	Normal
		1	Underline on
4 = x	Background color	4 = 0	Normal
		1	The left and rightmost dots of the underline area is set to the foreground color if bit 5=0. These dots are set to the background color if bit 5=1
3 = x	Foreground Intensity and character font select	3 = x	Foreground Intensity and character font select
2 = x	Foreground color, bits 0, 1, & 2 select from 1 of 8 colors	2 = 1	Foreground color, bits 0, 1, & 2 select from 1 of 8 colors
1 = x	Foreground color	1 = 1	Foreground color
0 = x	Foreground color	0 = 1	Foreground color

This subfunction is only supported on the XGA adapter.

Called with:	ah	= 12h
	al	= Text attribute byte 0 = Normal VGA type attributes 1 = Mainframe type attributes
	bl	= 37h
Returns:	al	= 12h (indicating subfunction supported)

Int	Func	Description	Platform
10h	13h	Write String	All

INT III I

This function writes a string of characters on the display at a specified position. As necessary, the function will automatically wrap lines, scroll, and interpret some control characters for specific actions. Two subfunctions supports text and graphics modes, and two subfunctions allow attributes for text modes only.

When using Double Byte Character Set (DBCS) with DOS/V, each DBCS character counts as two "characters" in all of the following subfunctions.

The only characters that are interpreted as commands include 7, 8, A, and D. These values take the following actions:

Value	**Name**	**Description**
7	bell	Generates a 1/2 second beep using timer 2.
8	backspace	The cursor is moved back one column, unless already at column 0, in which case the command is ignored.
A	linefeed	Moves the cursor down one row, unless already at the last row, in which case the screen is scrolled up one row.
D	return	The cursor moves to column 0.

When scrolling up in text mode the new row uses the same attribute as appears at the prior cursor position. In graphics mode, black is used as the background color on a new row.

These subfunctions are provided for writing strings:

AL=	**Write String Subfunctions**	**Platforms**
0	Write Characters, Cursor unaffected	All
1	Write Characters, Move Cursor	All
2	Write Characters & Attributes, Cursor unaffected	All
3	Write Characters & Attributes, Move Cursor	All
10h	Read Chars & Attribute for DBCSs, Cursor unaffected	DOS/V
11h	Read Chars & Attributes for DBCSs, Cursor unaffected	DOS/V
20h	Write Chars & Attribute for DBCSs, Cursor unaffected	DOS/V
21h	Write Chars & Attributes for DBCSs, Cursor unaffected	DOS/V

Subfunction	Description	Int	Function
AL=0	Write Characters, Cursor Unaffected	10h	AH=13h

Writes the supplied string to the display. The cursor position is unaffected by this subfunction. This function is valid in both text and graphics modes.

Called with: ax = 1300h
bh = page number
bl = attribute byte
cx = number of characters in string
dh = row where to start (0 is the topmost row)
dl = column where to start (0 is the leftmost column)
es:bp = pointer to character string

Returns: characters displayed

Subfunction	Description	Int	Function
AL=1	Write Characters, Move Cursor	10h	AH=13h

Writes the supplied string to the display. The cursor position is moved along with the characters written to the screen. This function is valid in both text and graphics modes.

Called with: ax = 1301h
bh = page number
bl = attribute byte
cx = number of characters in string
dh = row where to start (0 is the topmost row)
dl = column where to start (0 is the leftmost column)
es:bp = pointer to character string

Returns: characters displayed

Subfunction	Description	Int	Function
AL=2	Write Characters & Attributes, Cursor Unaffected	10h	AH=13h

Writes the supplied string to the display. Each character in the string is followed by its related attribute byte. This means the string has the form: character, attribute, character, attribute, etc. The cursor position is unaffected by this subfunction. This function is valid only in text modes.

Called with: ax = 1302h
bh = page number

cx = number of characters in string
dh = row where to start (0 is the topmost row)
dl = column where to start (0 is the leftmost column)
es:bp = pointer to character/attribute string

Returns: characters and attributes displayed

Subfunction	Description	Int	Function
AL=3	Write Characters & Attributes, Move Cursor	10h	AH=13h

INT

Writes the supplied string to the display. Each character in the string is followed by its related attribute byte. This means the string has the form: character, attribute, character, attribute, etc. The cursor position is moved along with the characters written to the screen. This function is valid only in text modes.

Called with: ax = 1303h
bh = page number
cx = number of characters in string
dh = row where to start (0 is the topmost row)
dl = column where to start (0 is the leftmost column)
es:bp = pointer to character/attribute string

Returns: characters and attributes displayed

Subfunction	Description	Int	Function
AL=10h	Read Chars & Attribute for DBCSs Cursor Unaffected	10h	AH=13h

INT

Reads characters and matching attributes from the screen into the user-supplied buffer. Each character in the string is followed by its related attribute byte. This means the string has the form: character, attribute, character, attribute, etc. The cursor position is unaffected by this subfunction. This subfunction is valid only with DOS/V.

Called with: ax = 1310h
bh = 0
cx = number of characters in string
dh = row where to start (0 is the topmost row)
dl = column where to start (0 is the leftmost column)
es:bp = pointer to character/attribute buffer

Returns: es:bp = pointer to characters and attributes read from screen

INT	Subfunction	Description	Int	Function
	AL=11h	Read Chars & Attributes for DBCSs, Cursor Unaffected	10h	AH=13h

Reads characters and matching attributes from the screen into the user-supplied buffer. Each character in the string is followed by its related three attribute bytes. This means the string has the form: character, attribute0, attribute1, attribute2, character, attribute0, attribute1, attribute2, etc. There are three attributes per character, where attribute0 is the same as normal text modes and attribute2 is always zero. Attribute1 has the following definition:

Attribute1 bit	7 = 1	underline cell, using foreground color
	6 = 1	reverse foreground and background attributes used in attribute0 byte (may not function depending on implementation)
	5 = 0	unused
	4 = 0	unused
	3 = 1	vertical white grid line in cell
	2 = 1	horizontal white grid line in cell
	1 = 0	unused
	0 = 0	unused

The cursor position is unaffected by this subfunction. This subfunction is valid only when video mode 73h is used in DOS/V.

Called with:	ax = 1311h
	bh = 0
	cx = number of characters in string
	dh = row where to start (0 is the topmost row)
	dl = column where to start (0 is the leftmost column)
	es:bp = pointer to character/attribute buffer
Returns:	es:bp = pointer to characters and attributes read from screen

INT	Subfunction	Description	Int	Function
	AL=20h	Write Chars & Attribute for DBCSs, Cursor Unaffected	10h	AH=13h

Writes characters and matching attributes to the display from a user-supplied buffer. Each character in the string is followed by its related attribute byte. This means the string has the form: character, attribute, character, attribute, etc. The cursor position is unaffected by this subfunction. This subfunction is valid only with DOS/V.

Called with: ax = 1320h
bh = 0
cx = number of characters in string
dh = row where to start (0 is the topmost row)
dl = column where to start (0 is the leftmost column)
es:bp = pointer to string of characters and attributes
Returns: characters and attributes displayed

Subfunction	Description	Int	Function
AL=21h	Write Chars & Attributes for DBCSs, Cursor Unaffected	10h	AH=13h

INT

Writes characters and matching attributes to the display from a user-supplied buffer. Each character in the string is followed by its related three attribute bytes. This means the string has the form: character, attribute0, attribute1, attribute2, character, attribute0, attribute1, attribute2, etc. See subfunction 11h for the definition of these attributes.

The cursor position is unaffected by this subfunction. This subfunction is valid only when video mode 73h is used in DOS/V.

Called with: ax = 1321h
bh = 0
cx = number of characters in string
dh = row where to start (0 is the topmost row)
dl = column where to start (0 is the leftmost column)
es:bp = pointer to string of characters and attributes
Returns: characters and attributes displayed

Int	Func	Description	Platform
10h	14h	LCD Control	PC Convertible

INT

The obsolete PC Convertible laptop could control how high-intensity characters appear on screen. The LCD screen used on the PC Convertible could only show pixels as on or off without gray levels. Other laptops that do not provide VGA grayscale support may also implement this function.

Three subfunctions are used to control how the font appears.

AL=	**LCD Font Control Subfunctions**
0	Load User-Specified Font
1	Load ROM Font
2	High Intensity Attribute Affect

Subfunction	Description	Int	Function
AL=0	Load User Specific Font	10h	AH=14h

Called with: ax = 1400h
bh = number of bytes per character (1-32)
bl = font page (0 or 1)
cx = number of characters to load (1-256)
dx = starting character number (0-255) (used as an offset where to begin loading)
es:di = pointer to user supplied font bytes

Returns: font characters loaded

Subfunction	Description	Int	Function
AL=1	Load ROM Font	10h	AH=14h

Called with: ax = 1401h
bl = font page (0 or 1)

Returns: font characters loaded from ROM

Subfunction	Description	Int	Function
AL=2	High Intensity Attribute Affect	10h	AH=14h

Called with: ax = 1402h
bl = How to interpret high-intensity attribute
0 = Ignore
1 = show character in reverse image
2 = show character with underline
3 = show character from alternate font page

Returns: selection saved

Int	Func	Description	Platform
10h	15h	Get Display Type	PC Convertible

The PC Convertible display type and information can be read using this command. This function may be supported on other early laptops.

Called with: ah = 15h

Returns: ax = alternate display adapter type

0 = no alternate adapter
5140h = LCD
5153h = CGA display
5151h = Monochrome display
es:di = pointer to 7 word type table
word 1 = display model number
word 2 = # of vertical pixels per meter
word 3 = # of horizontal pixels per meter
word 4 = total number of vertical pixels
word 5 = total number of horizontal pixels
word 6 = horizontal distance between adjacent pixels, center to center, in micrometers
word 7 = vertical distance between adjacent pixels, center to center, in micrometers

Int	Func	Description	Platform
10h	18h	Request for Font Pattern	DOS/V

INT

This function transfers the font pattern between the user buffer and the system font buffer. It is only supported on systems with DOS/V.

Subfunction	Description	Int	Function
AL=0	Get Font Pattern	10h	AH=18h

INT

Called with: ax = 1800h
bx = 0
cx = single- or double-byte character (single byte in cl, ch=0)
dx = pixels character width and height
0810h = 8 x 16 single-byte font
0813h = 8 x 19 single-byte font
1010h = 16 x 16 double-byte font
1818h = 24 x 24 user-supplied double-byte font
es:di = pointer to buffer where to store font image

Returns: al = 0 if successful, any other value indicates error
es:di = pointer to user buffer where font bytes loaded

Subfunction	Description	Int	Function
AL=1	Set Font Pattern	10h	AH=18h

Called with: ax = 1801h
bx = 0
cx = single- or double-byte character (single byte in cl, ch=0)
dx = pixels character width and height
0810h = 8 x 16 single-byte font
0813h = 8 x 19 single-byte font
1010h = 16 x 16 double-byte font
1818h = 24 x 24 user-supplied double-byte font
es:di = pointer to font image

Returns: al = 0 if font image loaded into system font buffer, any other value indicates error

Int	Func	Description	Platform
10h	1Ah	Read/Write Display Combination Code	VGA+

This function returns information about the adapter emulation of older adapters, and the basic type of monitor attached. The VGA BIOS determines this information during initialization. The adapter codes are shown in Table 9-9. This function is only supported on VGA+ systems.

Table 9-9. Adapter Codes

Code	Adapter and Display
0	No display
1	Monochrome or HGA
2	CGA
4	EGA with color EGA monitor
5	EGA with monochrome monitor
6	PGA with color PGA monitor
7	VGA with analog monochrome VGA monitor
8	VGA with analog color VGA monitor
B	MCGA with analog monochrome VGA monitor
C	MCGA with analog color VGA monitor
FF	Unknown

Subfunction	Description	Int	Function
AL=0	Read Display Combination Code	10h	AH=1Ah

INT

Called with: ax = 1A00h

Returns: al = 1Ah (indicating subfunction supported)
bh = active display code (see Table 9-9)
bl = alternate display code (see Table 9-9)

Subfunction	Description	Int	Function
AL=1	Write Display Combination Code	10h	AH=1Ah

INT

Called with: ax = 1A01h
bh = active display code (see Table 9-9)
bl = alternate display code (see Table 9-9)

Returns: al = 1Ah (indicating subfunction supported)

Int	Func	Description	Platform
10h	1Bh	Return Video System State Information	VGA+

INT

Loads user-supplied memory with a 64-byte table of information about the current video state. This table comprises a number of BIOS data area bytes, register information, ROM data, and values only saved in the VGA adapter itself. Table 9-10 shows the contents of the table. Data originating from the BIOS data area are explained in more detail in Chapter 6, BIOS Data and Other Fixed Data Areas.

This function is only supported on VGA+ systems, and may not be supported when DOS/V is used.

Table 9-10. Video State Table

Hex Offset	Size	Description	Read from
0	dword	Far pointer to functionality state table in ROM (see Table 9-11)	ROM
4	byte	Video mode	40:49h
5	word	Number of character columns	40:4Ah
7	word	Total number of bytes per page	40:4Ch
9	word	Current page offset	40:4Eh
B	8 words	Cursor Position, pages 0 to 7 (high byte=row, low byte=column)	40:50h
1B	word	Cursor shape (starting and ending cell row)	40:60h
1D	byte	Active display page	40:62h
1E	word	Video I/O port number base	40:63h

Table 9-10. Continued

Hex Offset	Size	Description	Read from
20	byte	Current mode register value for CGA/MDA	40:65h
21	byte	Current CGA color palette register value	40:66h
22	byte	Character rows on screen (value 40:84h+1)	40:84h
23	word	Scan lines per character	40:85h
25	byte	Active display code (Table 9-9)	
26	byte	Alternate display code (Table 9-9)	
27	word	Number of different colors supported for this mode (2-FFFF)	ROM
29	byte	Number of display pages for this mode (1-8)	ROM
2A	byte	Scan lines currently on display	
		0 = 200 scan lines	
		1 = 350 scan lines	
		2 = 400 scan lines	
		3 = 480 scan lines	
2B	byte	Font page when attribute intensity bit = 0	
2C	byte	Font page when attribute intensity bit = 1	
2D	byte	Miscellaneous state bits	
		bit 7 = 0 Unused	
		6 = 0 Unused	
		5 = 0 Attribute bit 7 controls intensity	
		1 Attribute bit 7 controls blinking	
		4 = 0 No cursor size control (see AH=12h, bl=34h for Cursor Size Control)	40:87
		1 Normal size control	40:89
		3 = 0 Color registers are set to default on any mode set	40:89
		2 = 0 Color display attached	40:89
		1 Monochrome display attached	40:89
		1 = 1 Grayscale summing active	
		0 = 0 Only color modes supported	
		1 All available modes are allowable on attached monitor	
2E	3 bytes	Unused (may be used by some vendors)	

Table 9-10. Continued

Hex Offset	Size	Description	Read from
31	byte	Video memory value (from bits 6 & 5 of 40:87) 0 = 64K 1 = 128K 2 = 192K 3 = 256K or more	40:87
32	1 byte	Save pointer state information bit 7 = 0 Unused 6 = 0 Unused 5 = 1 Display combination code active 4 = 1 Palette override active 3 = 1 Graphics font override active 2 = 1 Alpha font override active 1 = 1 Dynamic save area active 0 = 1 512-character set active	
33	13 bytes	Unused (may be used by some vendors)	

Table 9-11. Functionality State Table (from Table 9-10)

Hex Offset	Size	Description	Read from
0	byte	Allowed video modes bit x = 1 Mode x allowed	ROM
1	byte	Allowed video modes bit x = 1 Mode x+8 allowed	ROM
2	byte	Allowed video modes bit 7 = 0 Unused 6 = 0 Unused 5 = 0 Unused 4 = 0 Unused 3 = 1 Mode 13h allowed 2 = 1 Mode 12h allowed 1 = 1 Mode 11h allowed 0 = 1 Mode 10h allowed	ROM
3	4 bytes	Unused (reserved for future)	ROM

Table 9-11. Continued

Hex Offset	Size	Description		Read from
7	byte	Number of scan lines available in text modes		ROM
		bit 7 = 0	Unused	
		6 = 0	Unused	
		5 = 0	Unused	
		4 = 0	Unused	
		3 = 0	Unused	
		2 = 1	400-scan line mode supported	
		1 = 1	350-scan line mode supported	
		0 = 1	200-scan line mode supported	
8	byte	Number of font pages usable at the same time		ROM
9	byte	Maximum number of font pages		ROM
A	byte	Miscellaneous functions 1		ROM
		bit 7 = 1	Supports multiple pages of 256-color registers	
		6 = 1	Supports 256 18-bit color regs	
		5 = 1	Supports 64 8-bit color regs	
		4 = 1	Supports cursor shape control (see function AH=12h, BL=34h)	
		3 = 1	Supports option to disable color registers updates on mode set (see AH=12h, BL=31h)	
		2 = 1	Supports character font loads (see AH=11h)	
		1 = 1	Supports grayscale summing (see AH=12h, BL=33h)	
		0 = 0	Only color modes allowed	
		1	All modes are acceptable with the attached monitor	
B	byte	Miscellaneous functions 2		ROM
		bit 7 = 0	Unused	
		6 = 0	Unused	
		5 = 0	Unused	
		4 = 0	Unused	
		3 = 1	Supports Display combination code (see function AH=1Ah)	
		2 = 0	Supports selection of background blink/intensity select (see function AX=1003h)	
		1 = 1	Supports save and restore state (see function AH=1Ch)	
		0 = 1	Supports light pen (see AH=4)	
B	2 bytes	Unused (reserved for future)		ROM

Table 9-11. Continued

Hex Offset	Size	Description	Read from
E	byte	Save pointer functions allowed	ROM
		bit 7 = 0 Unused	
		6 = 0 Unused	
		5 = 1 Display combination code	
		4 = 1 Color register override	
		3 = 1 Graphics font override	
		2 = 1 Text font override	
		1 = 1 Dynamic save area	
		0 = 1 512-character font	
F	byte	Unused (reserved for future)	ROM

Called with: ah = 1Bh
es:di = pointer to 64-byte table where to have state information stored

Returns: al = 1Bh (indicating subfunction supported)

Int	Func	Description	Platform
10h	1Ch	Save/Restore Video State	VGA+

This function is used to save and restore the entire state of the VGA adapter. This is one of the most welcome features on the VGA for anyone who has had to develop a TSR that works in all video modes.

Once the state is saved, the mode can be changed. For a TSR, first the video state is saved using this function. The display memory that will be overwritten must also be saved. If going from a graphics mode to a text mode this must include portions of red plane 2 where the text character font is stored. The mode is changed, using a mode value with bit 7 set high. This prevents the adapter from erasing the video buffer. The TSR can then "pop-up" on the display.

To exit, the TSR changes the mode back to the original mode, updates the display buffer, and then restores the state information. If you're lucky, it will all work!

A program may not need to save and restore all the information, depending on what actions are intended. Some TSRs that are space-limited may choose to save and restore the key information, such as the hardware and BIOS data area information, and ignore the color registers. Table 9-12 shows the options that are available.

Table 9-12. Save and Restore State Options

CX Bits	Value	Description
0	1	Save/Restore video hardware state
1	1	Save/Restore video BIOS data areas
2	1	Save/Restore Digital to Analog Converter (DAC) and color registers
3-15	0	Unused

The Save/Restore Video State function has three subfunctions. It is only supported on VGA+ adapters, but is not supported when DOS/V is running.

AL=	**Save/Restore State Subfunctions**
0	Get buffer size for save state
1	Save Adapter State
2	Restore Adapter State

INT

Subfunction	Description	Int	Function
AL=0	Get buffer size for save state	10h	AH=1Ch

Before saving the video state it's a good idea to find out how much memory is going to be required. This function returns the number of 64-byte blocks required, depending on the information requested to save. Different vendors will return different values, and unfortunately, there is no stated upper limit! In my own analysis, a typical number of 64-byte blocks required on a SVGA adapter for state options are:

Save/Restore video hardware state:	2 (128 bytes)
Save/Restore video BIOS data areas:	2 (128 bytes)
Save/Restore DAC and color registers:	D (832 bytes)
All three options together:	F (960 bytes)

Be prepared for possible larger space requirements.

Called with:	ax = 1C00h
	cx = requested states (see Table 9-12)
Returns:	al = 1Ch (indicating subfunction supported)
	bx = number of 64-byte blocks required

INT

Subfunction	Description	Int	Function
AL=1	Save Adapter State	10h	AH=1Ch

Called with:	ax = 1C01h
	cx = requested states (see Table 9-12)
	es:bx = pointer where to save state
Returns:	al = 1Ch (indicating subfunction supported)

INT

Subfunction	Description	Int	Function
AL=2	Restore Adapter State	10h	AH=1Ch

Called with:	ax = 1C02h
	cx = requested states (see Table 9-12)
	es:bx = pointer where to get state to restore
Returns:	al = 1Ch (indicating subfunction supported)

Int	Func	Description	Platform
10h	1Dh	Shift Status Line Functions	DOS/V

This function controls the bottom status lines. The bottom status lines are used to display shift status and to help enter double-byte characters when the Input Assist Subsystem driver is installed. The BIOS value, indicating the number of displayed rows, at address 40:84 is reduced by one when the status line is activated, and incremented by one when turned back off. This function is only intended for use by the FEP (Front End Processor) driver.

Subfunction	Description	Int	Function
AL=0	Activate Shift Status Line	10h	AH=1Dh

Called with: ax = 1D00h
bx = number of lines at bottom to reserve for shift status (typically 1)

Returns: nothing

Subfunction	Description	Int	Function
AL=1	Deactivate Shift Status Line	10h	AH=1Dh

Called with: ax = 1D01h
bx = number of lines at bottom reserved for shift status (typically 1)

Returns: nothing

Subfunction	Description	Int	Function
AL=2	Get Number of Shift Status Lines	10h	AH=1Dh

Called with: ax = 1D02h

Returns: bx = number of lines activated for shift status (typically 1)

Int	Func	Description	Platform
10h	1Fh	Display Mode Information	XGA+

This function loads a buffer with information about all the XGA adapters in the system. The XGA architecture allows for up to eight XGAs in a system, and each adapter uses specific memory and I/O addresses to avoid conflicts.

Subfunction	Description	Int	Function
AL=0	Get XGA Information Buffer Length	10h	AH=1Fh

This buffer returns the buffer size required for the next subfunction, AL=1. For the following subfunction, a typical system will require 32 bytes for each XGA adapter in the system. This means if a system has three adapters, the next subfunction will require a buffer of at least 96 bytes.

This subfunction is only supported on the XGA adapter. This subfunction is ideal for identifying the presence of an XGA adapter. A non-XGA will not alter any registers, returning an AX value of 1F00h.

Called with:	ax	= 1F00h
Returns:	al	= 1Fh (indicating subfunction supported)
	bx	= number of bytes required for buffer

INT	Subfunction	Description	Int	Function
	AL=1	Get XGA Information	10h	AH=1Fh

The XGA adapter information is loaded into the user-supplied buffer space. See subfunction 0 to get the size of the buffer required. Table 9-13 shows the information stored in the buffer for one adapter. When multiple adapters are used, the returned buffer will contain multiple blocks of data, one block for each XGA.

Table 9-13. XGA Information Buffer

Offset	Size	Description
0	word	Offset in bytes to next XGA adapter information
2	byte	Slot number the XGA card resides in
3	byte	XGA implementation function level 3 = Base XGA implementation 5 = XGA-N1 implementation (includes additional XGA capabilities)
4	byte	XGA implementation resolution level 0 = Base XGA implementation with 45 MHz max Pel rate 3 = XGA-N1 implementation with 90 MHz max Pel rate
5	word	Vendor ID
7	word	Vendor specified
9	word	Adapter I/O base address
B	word	Segment where memory mapped XGA coprocessor registers appear in system address space
D	word	Location in physical memory of the 1 MB aperture (a value of 3 indicates the aperture starts at 3 MB, a value of 0 indicates aperture is not allocated)
F	word	Location in physical memory of the 4 MB aperture (a value of 8 indicates the aperture starts at 8 MB, a value of 0 indicates aperture is not allocated)
11	word	Location in system memory of the video memory buffer (a value of 4 indicates the buffer starts at 4 MB)
13	word	Composite ID of the attached display determined by POST
15	byte	Total memory on adapter (in 256 K multiples, so that a value of 8 indicates the card has 2 MB of memory)

This subfunction is only supported on the XGA adapter.

Called with:	ax = 1F01h
	es:di = buffer where to place information
Returns:	al = 1Fh (indicating subfunction supported)
	es:di = buffer loaded with XGA information

Int	Func	Description	Platform
10h	4Eh	VESA XGA Subfunctions	VESA XGA

INT

This function is used for a number of services unique to VESA XGA adapters. These may not be supported on IBM's XGA adapters. All manufacturers of VESA XGA cards subscribe to this common interface, but may not choose to implement every function. Upon completion of any function, status must be checked to confirm the function is supported and completed successfully.

The VESA XGA function has a number of subfunctions only supported on VESA XGA adapters.

AL=	VESA XGA Subfunctions
0	Get VESA XGA Environment Information
1	Get VESA XGA Subsystem Information
2	Get VESA XGA Mode Information
3	Set VESA XGA Video Mode
4	Get Current VESA XGA Video Mode
5	Set VESA XGA Feature Connector State
6	Get VESA XGA Feature Connector State

Subfunction	Description	Int	Function
AL=0	Get VESA XGA Environment Information	10h	AH=4Eh

INT

Loads the user-supplied buffer with 256 bytes of information about the capabilities of the VESA XGA adapter. The contents of this buffer are described in Table 9-14.

Table 9-14. VESA XGA Environment Information Table

Offset	Size	Description
0	4 bytes	VESA XGA Signature—Should be "VESA" indicating the XGA adapter follows the Video Electronics Standards Association standards.
4	word	VESA version number (for example 0100h = version 1.00)
6	dword	Vendor String—This is a far pointer to vendor supplied string, zero terminated. The string usually contains manufacturer's name and card model, but it is left to the vendor to specify the text.

Table 9-14. Continued

Offset	Size	Description
A	dword	Environment Flag bits 31-3 Unused, normally set to 0 bit 2 = 0 Bus mastering not available in this system 1 Bus mastering is available in this system as determined by the VESA XGA POST 1 = x | System Bus Architecture 0 = x | bit 1 bit 0 0 0 = Micro Channel (MCA) 0 1 = AT/ISA 1 0 = undefined 1 1 = EISA
E	word	Number of XGAs—This holds the total number of XGAs currently installed on the system (up to 8).
14	240 bytes	Unused—The remainder of the buffer is reserved for future specifications. The VESA XGA BIOS returns all zeros in this area.

Called with: ax = 4E00h
es:di = buffer where to place information

Returns: if successful:
ax = 004Eh
es:di = buffer loaded with information
all other AX values indicate VESA XGA is not installed

INT	Subfunction	Description	Int	Function
	AL=1	Get VESA XGA Subsystem Information	10h	AH=4Eh

Loads the user-supplied buffer with 256 bytes of information and pointers about the VESA XGA adapter. The contents of this buffer are described in Table 9-15.

Table 9-15. VESA XGA Subsystem Information Table

Offset	Size	Description
0	dword	Vendor String—This is a far pointer to vendor-supplied string, zero terminated. The string usually contains manufacturer's name and card model, but it is left to the vendor to specify the text.
4	dword	Capabilities Flags bits 31-8 Unused, normally set to 0 bit 7 = 0 DMA Channel disabled or not an AT system 1 DMA Channel enabled on AT system 6 = x, 5 = x, 4 = x DMA Channel, 0 to 7, assigned for acquiring bus mastership on an AT system (set to zero on all other systems) 3 = 0 Unused 2 = 0 Unused 1 = x, 0 = x System Bus Architecture bit 1 bit 0 0 0 = Micro Channel (MCA) 0 1 = AT/ISA 1 0 = undefined 1 1 = EISA
8	dword	ROM Pointer—Pointer to XGA's BIOS ROM. If zero, no ROM is installed. Pointer is in segment:offset form.
C	dword	Memory Mapped Register Pointer—Pointer is in segment:offset form.
10	word	I/O base address for this XGA adapter
12	dword	Video Display Memory Pointer—Start of the Physical display memory. Pointer is in 32-bit form.
16	dword	A 32-bit pointer to the 4 MB aperture—Zero indicates the 4 MB aperture is not enabled.
1A	dword	A 32-bit pointer to the 1 MB aperture—Zero indicates the 1 MB aperture is not enabled.
1E	dword	A 32-bit pointer to the 64 KB aperture—Zero indicates the 64 KB aperture is not enabled.
22	dword	A 32-bit pointer to a vendor-defined aperture greater than 4 MB. Zero indicates the vendor aperture is not available.
26	word	Size of vendor-defined aperture in 64K blocks

Table 9-15. Continued

Offset	Size	Description
28	dword	Pointer to list of supported video modes—This is a segment:offset pointer to a list of XGA video modes supported by the adapter. Each entry in the list is a word. The end of the list is identified by FFFFh. This list can include VESA specified mode numbers as well as vendor unique modes. The list may include modes not allowed due to monitor or adapter memory limitations. See subfunction 2 on how to get additional information about which modes are currently allowed.
2C	word	Total memory—number of 64K blocks. A value of 20h indicates the XGA adapter has 2 MB of memory.
2E	dword	Vendor ID number
32	206 bytes	Unused—The remainder of the buffer is reserved for future specifications. The VESA XGA BIOS returns all zeros in this area.

Called with: ax = 4E01h
es:di = buffer where to place information

Returns: if successful:
ax = 004Eh
es:di = buffer loaded with information
all other AX values indicate VESA XGA is not installed

INT	Subfunction	Description	Int	Function
	AL=2	Get VESA XGA Mode Information	10h	AH=4Eh

Get detailed information about a specific video mode. The prior subfunction, number 1, returns a buffer that includes a pointer to a list of video modes supported by the adapter. This subfunction provides details about each of these modes. No support is provided for video modes not included in the list. The user-supplied buffer must be 256 bytes long. See Table 9-16 for the contents of this table.

Table 9-16. Video Mode Information Table

Offset	Size	Description
0	word	Mode Attributes bits 15-5 Unused, normally set to 0 bit 4 = 0 Text mode, VGA registers active and XGA registers inactive 1 Graphics mode, VGA registers inactive and XGA registers active 3 = 0 Unused, normally set to 0 2 = 0 BIOS output functions are not supported for this video mode (scroll, write char, write teletype mode, write pixel, etc.) 1 BIOS output functions supported 1 = 0 Unused, normally set to 0 0 = 0 Mode not supported due to limits imposed by the attached monitor or amount of memory on adapter card 1 Video mode supported
2	word	Bytes per Logical Scan Line—The total number of bytes that make up one logical scan line. A logical scan line may be longer than the physical "displayed" scan line.
4	word	Horizontal Resolution—In graphics, the number of pixels per horizontal line, and in text modes, the number of characters per row.
6	word	Vertical Resolution—In graphics, the number of pixels vertically, and in text modes, the number of character rows.
8	byte	Character Cell Width
9	byte	Character Cell Height
A	byte	Number of Memory Planes—This indicates the number of color bit planes required to make up the video memory. For a standard VGA 16-color mode, there are normally four planes.
B	byte	Bits per Pixel—The number of color/shade bits per screen dot. For 256-color mode, there must be eight bits per pixel.

Table 9-16. Continued

Offset	Size	Description
C	byte	Memory Organization 0 = text mode (character and attribute) 1 = CGA graphics 2 = Hercules graphics 3 = 4-plane 4 = packed pixel 5 = 256-color nonchain 4 6 = direct color 7 = YUV-24 8-FF = reserved for future VESA modes
D	byte	Number of Image Pages—Total number of pages that the adapter can handle at one time for this mode.
E	byte	Red Mask Size—The number of bits used to define the red intensity for a single pixel when using the Direct Color memory organization. In the YUV-24 memory organization, this byte holds the number of bits that make up the V component. This value is unused in all other memory organizations.
F	byte	Red Field Position—This value specifies the position of the least significant red or V component bit within the data field of a single pixel, when using the Direct Color or YUV-24 memory organizations. This value is unused in all other memory organizations.
10	byte	Green Mask Size—The number of bits used to define the green intensity for a single pixel when using the Direct Color memory organization. In the YUV-24 memory organization, this byte holds the number of bits that make up the Y component. This value is unused in all other memory organizations.
11	byte	Green Field Position—This value specifies the position of the least significant green or Y component bit within the data field of a single pixel, when using the Direct Color or YUV-24 memory organizations. This value is unused in all other memory organizations.
12	byte	Blue Mask Size—The number of bits used to define the blue intensity for a single pixel when using the Direct Color memory organization. In the YUV-24 memory organization, this byte holds the number of bits that make up the U component. This value is unused in all other memory organizations.
13	byte	Blue Field Position—This value specifies the position of the least significant blue or U component bit within the data field of a single pixel, when using the Direct Color or YUV-24 memory organizations. This value is unused in all other memory organizations.

Table 9-16. Continued

Offset	Size	Description
14	byte	Reserved Mask Size—The number of bits used to define the noncolor component, such as intensity for a single pixel when using the Direct Color or YUV-24 memory organization. This value is unused in all other memory organizations.
15	byte	Reserved Field Position—This value specifies the position of the least significant noncolor component bit, such as intensity, within the data field of a single pixel, when using the Direct Color or YUV-24 memory organizations. This value is unused in all other memory organizations.
16	234 bytes	Unused—The remainder of the buffer is reserved for future specifications. The VESA XGA BIOS returns all zeros in this area.

Called with: ax = 4E02h
cx = video mode number from subfunction 1 list
es:di = buffer where to place information

Returns: if successful:
ax = 004Eh
es:di = buffer loaded with information
if function supported, but invalid mode:
ax = 014Eh
if function not supported, al is not 4Eh

Subfunction	Description	Int	Function
AL=3	Set VESA XGA Video Mode	10h	AH=4Eh

INT

Changes the video mode. This function allows both VGA type 8-bit modes (by setting bits 14-8 to zero) and 15-bit VESA XGA modes. See subfunctions 1 and 2 about VESA XGA modes and support. See Table 9-2 for common video modes.

Called with: ax = 4E03h
bx, bit 15 = 0 clear video memory
1 leave video memory as-is
14-0 = video mode number
cx, bits 15-1 = 0 unused
bit 0 = 0 Set feature connector to default state
1 Do not change state of feature connector
dx = XGA handle (which XGA adapter)

Returns: If successful:
ax = 004Eh

if function supported, but invalid mode:

ax = 014Eh

if function not supported, al is not 4Eh

INT	Subfunction	Description	Int	Function
	AL=4	Get Current VESA XGA Video Mode	10h	AH=4Eh

The current video mode is returned. This includes both standard VGA modes 0 to 13h and the new 15-bit VESA XGA modes. This subfunction does not return the video clear bit. See interrupt 10h, function F to get the video clear bit.

Called with: ax = 4E04h

dx = XGA handle (which XGA adapter)

Returns: if successful:

ax = 004Eh

bx, bit 15 = 0 (fixed at zero)

14-0 = video mode number

if function supported, but failed:

ax = 014Eh

if function not supported, al is not 4Eh

INT	Subfunction	Description	Int	Function
	AL=5	Set VESA XGA Feature Connector State	10h	AH=4Eh

This subfunction controls the direction of data on the XGA's feature connector. This subfunction also provides the ability to enable or disable the data transferred through the feature connector.

Called with: ax = 4E05h

bx, bits 15-2 = 0 Unused

bit 1 = 0 Input mode on feature connector

1 Output mode on feature connector

bit 0 = 0 Disable feature connector data

1 Enable feature connector data

dx = XGA handle (which XGA adapter)

Returns: if successful:

ax = 004Eh

if function supported, but failed:

ax = 014Eh

if function not supported, al is not 4Eh

Subfunction	Description	Int	Function
AL=6	Get VESA XGA Feature Connector State	10h	AH=4Eh

INT

This subfunction gets the current state of the VESA XGA feature connector. See prior subfunction 4E05h on how to set these options.

Called with: ax = 4E06h
dx = XGA handle (which XGA adapter)

Returns: if successful:
ax = 004Eh
bx, bits 15-2 = 0 Unused
bit 1 = 0 Input mode on feature connector
1 Output mode on feature connector
bit 0 = 0 Feature connector is disabled
1 Feature connector is enabled
if function supported, but failed:
ax = 014Eh
if function not supported, al is not 4Eh

Int	Func	Description	Platform
10h	4Fh	Super VGA Subfunctions	SVGA

INT

This function is used for a number of services unique to Super VGA adapters. All manufacturers of SVGA cards subscribe to this common interface, but may not choose to implement every function. Upon completion of any function, status must be checked to confirm the function is supported and completed successfully.

The Super VGA function has a number of subfunctions. Function 4Fh is only supported on SVGA adapters.

AL=	SVGA Subfunctions
0	Get SVGA General Information
1	Get SVGA Mode Information
2	Set SVGA Video Mode
3	Get Current SVGA Video Mode
4	Get Save State Buffer Size (DL=0)
4	Save the SVGA State (DL=1)
4	Restore the SVGA State (DL=2)
5	Set SVGA Memory Window Position (BH=0)
5	Get SVGA Memory Window Position (BH=1)
6	Set Logical Scan Line Length (BL=0)
6	Get Logical Scan Line Length (BL=1)
7	Set Logical Display Start (BL=0)
7	Get Logical Display Start (BL=1)
4D	Video Cursor Interface Request

INT Subfunction	Description	Int	Function
AL=0	Get SVGA General Information	10h	AH=4Fh

Loads the user-supplied buffer with 256 bytes of information about the capabilities of the SVGA adapter. The contents of this buffer are described in Table 9-17.

Table 9-17. SVGA General Information Table

Offset	Size	Description
0	4 bytes	SVGA Signature—Should be "VESA" indicating the SVGA adapter follows the Video Electronics Standards Association standards.
4	word	VESA version number (for example 0102h = version 1.02)
6	dword	Vendor String—This is a far pointer to vendor-supplied string, zero terminated. This string usually contains the manufacturer's name and card model, but it is left to the vendor to specify the text.
A	dword	Capabilities—This dword is currently undefined and is reserved for possible use in future specifications
E	dword	Mode List—This is a far pointer to a list of SVGA video modes supported by the adapter. Each entry in the list is a word. The end of the list is identified by an FFFFh value. This list can include VESA specified mode numbers as well as vendor unique modes. The list may include modes not supported due to monitor or adapter memory limitations. See subfunction 1, following this subfunction, on how to get additional information about modes supported.
12	word	Total Memory—This word shows the total amount of video memory that the adapter has. Multiply this word by 64K to get the total memory size. For example, a value of 10h indicates the card has 1 MB of memory.
14	236 bytes	Unused—The remainder of the buffer is reserved for future specifications. Most vendors return all zeros in this area.

Called with: ax = 4F00h
es:di = buffer where to place information

Returns: if successful:
ax = 004Fh
es:di = buffer loaded with information
if function supported, but failed:
ax = 014Fh
if function not supported, al is not 4Fh

Subfunction	Description	Int	Function
AL=1	Get SVGA Mode Information	10h	AH=4Fh

Gets detailed information about a specific video mode. Subfunction 0 returns a pointer to a list of video modes supported by the adapter. This subfunction provides details about each mode. No support is provided for video modes not included in the list. The user-supplied buffer must provide for the return of up to 256 bytes of information. See Table 9-18 for the contents of this table. To ensure all unused bytes are zero, the buffer should be set to all zeros prior to issuing this subfunction.

The SVGA provides a windowing scheme in which part of the video screen is defined as one of two windows. Information about the SVGA windowing system for each mode is also described.

Table 9-18. Video Mode Information Table

Offset	Size	Description	
0	word	Mode Attributes	
		bits 15-5	Unused, normally set to 0
		bit 4 = 0	Text mode
		1	Graphics mode
		3 = 0	Monochrome mode, base I/O address is 3B4h
		1	(video modes 7 or 0Fh are monochrome modes)
		2 = 0	Color mode, base I/O address is 3D4h
		1	BIOS output functions are not supported for this video mode (scroll, write char, write teletype mode, write pixel, and so forth.)
		1	BIOS output functions supported
		1 = 0	No extended mode information
		1	Extended mode information starts at offset 12h
		0 = 0	Mode not supported due to limits imposed by the attached monitor or amount of memory on adapter card
		1	Video mode supported
2	byte	Window A Attributes	
		bits 7-3	Unused, normally set to 0
		bit 2 = 0	Window A not writeable
		1	Window A writeable
		1 = 0	Window A not readable
		1	Window A readable
		0 = 0	Window A not supported
		1	Window A supported

Table 9-18. Continued

Offset	Size	Description
3	byte	Window B Attributes bits 7-3 Unused, normally set to 0 bit 2 = 0 Window B not writeable 1 Window B writeable 1 = 0 Window B not readable 1 Window B readable 0 = 0 Window B not supported 1 Window B supported
4	word	Window Granularity—The smallest boundary, in kilobytes that the Window can be placed in video memory.
6	word	Window Size—The number of kilobytes of memory the Window requires.
8	word	Window A Segment—The segment in video memory where Window A begins.
A	word	Window B Segment—The segment in video memory where Window B begins.
C	dword	Window Scheme Function Pointer—This holds a far pointer to the Window Scheme function handler. This pointer may change for different modes. See function 4F05h for details. AX and DX are not preserved by a call to the Window Scheme Function handler, and no return status is provided from the Window Scheme Function handler.
10	word	Bytes per Logical Scan Line—A logical scan line can be larger than the displayed scanline.

The following extended mode information is only valid if the Mode Attributes, word 0, bit 1 is 1.

Offset	Size	Description
12	word	Horizontal Resolution—In graphics, the number of pixels per horizontal line, and in text modes, the number of characters per row.
14	word	Vertical Resolution—In graphics, the number of pixels vertically, and in text modes, the number of character rows.
16	byte	Character Cell Width
17	byte	Character Cell Height
18	byte	Number of Memory Planes—This indicates the number of color planes required to make up the video memory. For a standard VGA 16-color mode, there are four planes.
19	byte	Bits per Pixel—The number of color/shade bits per screen dot. For a 256-color mode, there must be eight bits per pixel.

Table 9-18. Continued

Offset	Size	Description
1A	byte	Number of Banks—For graphics modes, this byte holds the number of scan line banks per scan line grouping. Modes 4-6 have two banks, and Hercules mode has four banks. For modes that do not have scan line banks, the value returned is 1. Modes D-13h do not have scan line banks.
1B	byte	Memory Organization 0 = text mode (character and attribute) 1 = CGA graphics 2 = Hercules graphics 3 = 4-plane 4 = packed pixel 5 = 256-color nonchain 4 6-F = reserved for future VESA modes 10-FF = vendor defined
1C	byte	Bank Size in Kilobytes—For graphics modes that have groups of scan lines, the memory size for each bank in 1 KB increments. For modes that do not support banks, this value is set to zero.
1D	byte	Number of Image Pages—Total number of pages that the adapter can handle at one time for this mode.
1E	byte	Page Function (always set to 1)
1F	224 bytes	Unused—The remainder of the buffer is reserved for future specifications. Most SVGA BIOSes will return all zeros in this area.

Called with: ax = 4F01h
cx = video mode number from subfunction 0
es:di = buffer where to place information

Returns: if successful:
ax = 004Fh
es:di = buffer loaded with information
if function supported, but invalid mode:
ax = 014Fh
if function not supported, al is not 4Fh

Subfunction	Description	Int	Function
AL=2	Set SVGA Video Mode	10h	AH=4Fh

INT

Changes the video mode. This function allows both VGA type 8-bit modes (by setting bits 14-8 to zero) and 15-bit SVGA modes. See subfunctions 0 and 1 about SVGA modes and support. See Table 9-2 for common video modes.

Called with: ax = 4F02h
bx, bit 15 = 0 clear video memory
1 leave video memory as-is
14-0 = video mode number
Returns: if successful:
ax = 004Fh
if function supported, but invalid mode:
ax = 014Fh
if function not supported, al is not 4Fh

INT	Subfunction	Description	Int	Function
	AL=3	Get Current SVGA Video Mode	10h	AH=4Fh

The current video mode is returned. This includes both standard VGA modes 0 to 13h, and new 15-bit SVGA modes. This subfunction does not return the video clear bit. See interrupt 10h, function F to get the video clear bit.

Called with: ax = 4F03h
Returns: if successful:
ax = 004Fh
bx, bit 15 = 0 (fixed at zero)
14-0 = video mode number
if function supported, but failed:
ax = 014Fh
if function not supported, al is not 4Fh

INT	Subfunction	Description	Int	Function
	AL=4, DL=0	Get Save State Buffer Size	10h	AH=4Fh

Gets the size of the buffer that is required to save the required SVGA states. See the following two subfunctions for details about saving and restoring the SVGA state.

Called with: ax = 4F04h
cx = Save type
bits 15-4 = 0 unused
3 = 1 SVGA state save
2 = 1 video DAC (color registers)
1 = 1 video BIOS data state
0 = 1 video hardware state
dl = 0

Returns: if successful:
    ax = 004Fh
    bx = number of 64-byte blocks for buffer
  if function supported, but failed:
    ax = 014Fh
  if function not supported, al is not 4Fh

Subfunction	Description	Int	Function
AL=4, DL=1	Save the SVGA State	10h	AH=4Fh

INT

Saves the current state of the SVGA adapter in a user-supplied buffer. See the prior subfunction Get Save State Buffer Size to find the buffer size necessary. To save the entire state of the SVGA adapter, use a CX value of 000F. This subfunction does not save the contents of the video display memory.

Called with: ax = 4F04h
  cx = Save type
    bits 15-4 = 0 unused
      3 = 1 save SVGA state
      2 = 1 save video DAC (color registers)
      1 = 1 save video BIOS data state
      0 = 1 save video hardware state
  dl = 1
  es:bx = pointer to user-supplied buffer

Returns: if successful:
    ax = 004Fh
    es:bx = loaded with save state data
  if function supported, but failed:
    ax = 014Fh
  if function not supported, al is not 4Fh

Subfunction	Description	Int	Function
AL=4, DL=2	Restore the SVGA State	10h	AH=4Fh

INT

Restores the SVGA state previously saved. To restore the entire state of the SVGA adapter, use a CX value of 000F. This subfunction assumes that the state was previously saved in the user-supplied buffer and the same save type, CX, is used both for saving and restoring the state. This subfunction does not restore the contents of the video display memory.

Called with: ax = 4F04h
cx = Save type
bits 15-4 = 0 unused
3 = 1 save SVGA state
2 = 1 save video DAC (color registers)
1 = 1 save video BIOS data state
0 = 1 save video hardware state
dl = 2
es:bx = pointer to save state buffer

Returns: if successful:
ax = 004Fh
if function supported, but failed:
ax = 014Fh
if function not supported, al is not 4Fh

INT	Subfunction	Description	Int	Function
	AL=5, BH=0	Set SVGA Memory Window Position	10h	AH=4Fh

This subfunction sets the specified window, A or B, position in memory. Information about the capabilities of SVGA window for a mode is obtained from interrupt 10, function 4F01h. Function 4F01h shows the window granularity, size, and segment.

The same function can be issued using a far call to the Window Scheme Function Pointer, also returned from function 4F01h. See function 4F01h for additional information about directly calling this function.

Called with: ax = 4F05h
bh = 0
bl = 0 for window A1 for window B
dx = window position in memory (in window granularity units)

Returns: if successful:
ax = 004Fh
if function supported, but failed:
ax = 014Fh
if function not supported, al is not 4Fh

INT	Subfunction	Description	Int	Function
	AL=5, BH=1	Get SVGA Memory Window Position	10h	AH=4Fh

This subfunction gets the specified window, A or B, position in memory.

The same function can be issued using a far call to the Window Scheme Function Pointer, returned from function 4F01h. See function 4F01h for additional information about calling this function directly.

Called with: ax = 4F05h
bh = 1
bl = 0 for window A1 for window B

Returns: if successful:
ax = 004Fh
dx = window position in memory (in window granularity units)
if function supported, but failed:
ax = 014Fh
if function not supported, al is not 4Fh

Subfunction	Description	Int	Function
AL=6, BL=0	Set Logical Scan Line Length	10h	AH=4Fh

INT

The SVGA allows a logical display to be larger than the actual display. This subfunction sets the size of the logical display. It is valid for both text and graphics modes. In all modes, it is necessary to supply logical width in pixels. For a text mode, this means multiplying the number of columns desired by the Character Cell Width. The Character Cell Width is obtained from subfunction 4F01h.

If the requested width is beyond the capabilities of the video adapter or mode, the largest allowable width is selected. The information about what was really selected is returned. See subfunction 4F07h to specify the starting location of the displayed window.

Called with: ax = 4F06h
bl = 0
cx = desired width in pixels

Returns: if successful:
ax = 004Fh
bx = bytes per scan line (logical)
cx = actual pixels per scan line
dx = maximum number of scan lines
if function supported, but failed:
ax = 014Fh
if function not supported, al is not 4Fh

Subfunction	Description	Int	Function
AL=6, BL=1	Get Logical Scan Line Length	10h	AH=4Fh

Gets the logical and actual scan line width information. See the prior subfunction for additional details.

Called with: ax = 4F06h
bl = 1

Returns: if successful:
ax = 004Fh
bx = bytes per scan line (logical)
cx = actual pixels per scan line
dx = maximum number of scan lines
if function supported, but failed:
ax = 014Fh
if function not supported, al is not 4Fh

Subfunction	Description	Int	Function
AL=7, BL=0	Set Logical Display Start	10h	AH=4Fh

Sets the position of the larger logical display to appear within the visible on-screen display. The top left corner of a specified position in the logical page is displayed on the top left corner of the visible display. See subfunction 4F06h to define a logical display larger than the visible display.

Set Logical Display Start is valid for both text and graphics modes. In all modes, it is necessary to supply the position in pixels. For a text mode, this means multiplying the number of columns position by the Character Cell Width and the number of rows position by the Character Cell Height. The Character Cell Width and Height are obtained from subfunction 4F01h.

This function allows smooth hardware pan and scroll capabilities. It is also used to quickly display complete screens from a large logical screen for animation and special effects.

Called with: ax = 4F07h
bx = 0 (bh is reserved and must be zero)
cx = position in the logical display of the first displayed pixel of the scan line in dx
dx = position in the logical display of the first displayed scan line

Returns: if successful:
ax = 004Fh
if function supported, but failed:
ax = 014Fh
if function not supported, al is not 4Fh

Subfunction	Description	Int	Function
AL=7, BL=1	Get Logical Display Start	10h	AH=4Fh

INT

Gets the position of the larger logical display that currently appears on the visible portion of the display. See the prior subfunction 4F07h, BL=0, for additional details.

Called with: ax = 4F07h
bl = 1

Returns: if successful:
ax = 004Fh
bh = 0
cx = position in the logical display of the first displayed pixel of the scan line in dx
dx = position in the logical display of the first displayed scan line
if function supported, but failed:
ax = 014Fh
if function not supported, al is not 4Fh

Subfunction	Description	Int	Function
AL=4D	Video Cursor Interface Request	10h	AH=4Fh

INT

This function is part of a VESA standard to display a mouse cursor in all VGA and SVGA video modes. The VCI standard provides a common interface to SVGA hardware cursor support by the mouse driver. The purpose of the standard is to allow all current and future video modes to be supported by a single mouse driver. Operation is handled by the mouse driver and SVGA card, and does not have any functions usable by an application.

The complete Video Cursor Interface Standard is covered in detail in the VESA standard #VS911021. See Appendix C, Bibliography, for ordering this specification.

Called with: ax = 4F4Dh
bx = Number of bytes of RAM buffer available for VCI use
ds:0 = starting address of RAM buffer for VCI
es:di = address of the VCI driver call back function

Returns: if successful:
ax = 004Fh
cx = Number of bytes actually used by VCI
es:di = pointer where to call the VCI handler
if function supported, but failed:
ax = 014Fh
if function not supported, al is not 4Fh

Int	Func	Description	Platform
10h	FEh	Get Relocated Screen Address	All

This function gets the relocated screen address from a RSIS environment. The program must first determine the default display segment for the current mode, A000, B000 or B800. This segment value is passed in this function to see if an alternate relocated address should be used. It returns the address to use for all subsequent operations, even if no RSIS support is provided in the system.

With some systems, such as IBM's DOS/V for Japan, this function must be used, or nothing will appear on screen. DOS/V only returns a relocated address for video mode 3. Some environments, like DesqView and Memory Commander, can provide an RSIS compliant application with up to 300K of additional DOS memory, so its use can be very advantageous. There is an entire section later in this chapter about RSIS.

Even though the function asks for an offset, an offset value of zero should be passed in all cases. In all situations I've seen, the RSIS provider will then return a zero offset. Although it's possible some future design might return a non-zero offset, it appears unlikely.

Called with: ah = FEh
es:di = pointer to nonrelocated display base address
(A000:0, B000:0, or B800:0)

Returns: es:di = pointer to actual base segment:offset to use in direct screen writes

Int	Func	Description	Platform
10h	FFh	Update Relocated Screen	All

This function instructs the environment to update the screen. The function takes the character information written to the relocated screen buffer and writes the characters to the proper window on screen.

Currently I know of only two environments that require this function. IBM and Microsoft have released DOS/V, a special version of DOS for Japan, which lets any standard VGA adapter display the large set of DBCS Japanese characters. The display adapter remains in graphics mode at all times. A DOS text-based program can be converted in short order to work under DOS/V. All the program must do is issue Int 10h, function FEh to get the relocated screen, and then whenever the screen is changed, issue this call.

The simplest support can issue this function with CX=780h to update all 24 lines at one time. Performance is greatly improved by only updating those areas of the screen that change rather than the entire screen. This function, (when used for DOS/V), is only used in video mode 3, and ignored for all others.

The very obsolete TopView program from IBM also used this function to display multiple windows on screen, from different applications.

Called with:	ah = FFh
	cx = number of characters that have been modified (each DBCS character counts as two)
	es:di = pointer to the first character in the relocated video buffer that has changed
Returns:	display updated

Other Interrupts Related to the Video System

Int	Func	Description	Platform
42h	xx	Old Interrupt 10h	EGA+

INT III I

When a video adapter has its own BIOS code, the system BIOS will run the adapter's initialization code during system POST. The video BIOS transfers the old interrupt 10h video services pointer to interrupt 42h. The video BIOS then replaces the interrupt 10h vector with a pointer to its own interrupt 10h handler.

If the interrupt function called by a program is not supported by the adapter's BIOS, it is then passed to interrupt 42h, the system video BIOS. If the system BIOS does not support the function, it is ignored. When a system has two video adapters, and one is a CGA or MDA/Hercules adapter, the system BIOS is usually used for functions relating to these adapters.

In general, only interrupt 10h should be issued for all video operations, and use of interrupt 42h should be avoided.

Int	Func	Description	Platform
6Dh	xx	Alternate Interrupt 10h	VGA+

INT III I

This is an alternate way to call the VGA adapter directly. If the interrupt 10h was hooked by a number of TSRs, this interrupt will avoid passing control through those TSRs. I cannot see any reason to ever issue interrupt 6Dh. Because it's undocumented, it's easy to expect some clone VGAs may not support interrupt 6Dh.

In many VGA adapters, the video BIOS interrupt 10h simply issues an interrupt 6Dh.

Relocated Screen Interface Specification (RSIS)

There are a number of advantages in moving the screen buffer area for an application to a different portion of memory. A variety of environments can provide multiple simultaneous use of portions of the screen, or recover additional memory for the applications benefit. A moved screen buffer is considered to be relocated.

Programs that utilize the BIOS or system services for all screen reads and writes require no changes and are RSIS compliant by default. However, most commercial programs write directly to the screen area for maximum performance, based on rigid positioning established by the original IBM PC. IBM designated 128K of video memory starting at segment 0A000h.

This specification provides a well-defined means for any application to take advantage of a relocated screen. Depending on what services the environment is providing, there can be significant performance and feature enhancement to the application. Once implemented, the RSIS compliant application will retain its compatibility with other DOS environments. RSIS compliant programs are entirely transparent to the application user, and require no user input to take advantage of these features.

Making an application RSIS compliant is very easy, and usually involves a few small changes depending on how the program uses the video system. Examples in C and assembly are included later in this chapter.

Hardware and Software Considerations

No compatibility issues occur when making an application program RSIS compliant. After conversion, the application remains compatible with all industry standard compatible PCs. This includes the PC, XT, AT, EISA, and MCA. RSIS will also allow some programs to work properly with some non-IBM-compatible Japanese systems.

RSIS does not specify how a screen is relocated, nor is this important. Different environments can relocate the screen in a variety of ways following the RSIS specification.

Making a Program RSIS Compliant

There are up to five basic steps to making your code RSIS compliant. Detailed code examples are provided later for both C and assembly code. These can be adapted to any language.

- **Step 1**: When the program begins, the program's initialization code must determine where the current base screen address is using the RSIS function call.
- **Step 2:** All direct screen writes should use the base screen address determined in step 1 above.
- **Step 3:** If the video mode is changed, the new screen address needs to be acquired. If the video mode requires a change to graphics, a check is made to ensure this is allowable under the current environment options.
- **Step 4:** If multiple text pages are used, a check is necessary to verify the desired page is available.
- **Step 5:** For DOS/V compatibility only, when a change is made to the display, interrupt 10h, function FFh is issued to update the real display.

The RSIS Function Call

The key information is provided by interrupt 10h, function FEh as follows:

Called with: ah = FEh

es:di = pointer to non-relocated display base address (A000:0, B000:0, or B800:0)

Returns: es:di = pointer to actual base segment:offset to use in direct screen writes

The nonrelocated display location is simply the display address you already determined for direct video writes. The segment values are A000h for EGA/VGA graphics, B000h for monochrome text and Hercules graphics, and B800h for color text and CGA graphics. Table 9-2 shows the default display segment for different video modes. The offset will also be zero.

Interrupt 10h function FEh should be issued at the start of the program and after the video mode is changed, since the RSIS environment may need to alter the relocation address when switching between text and graphics.

If an environment is present which relocates the video screen, the environment will intercept this interrupt function and return the actual relocated screen address in ES:DI. The RSIS provider is responsible for managing the relocation process, not the application program.

This function is not provided by the BIOS. If no RSIS environment is present, the BIOS will not alter the registers, leaving ES:DI pointing to the correct screen address.

Special Considerations

Nonstandard Video Modes Since there are a number of conflicting modes used on nonstandard video adapters, no attempt has been made to address the use of these modes. If modes are used above IBM's defined mode 13h, and they use A000h as the video segment, the routines provided will function correctly and retain RSIS compatibility.

VESA Standards The Video Electronic Standards Association (VESA) has produced a standard for support of video modes and resolutions above the VGA's mode 13h for video hardware manufacturers. You should thoroughly understand VESA's Super VGA specification if you plan to use any of these modes. VESA modes are set differently from standard modes. The VESA Super VGA specification details how to detect if the card supports these modes, and how to set the mode. If you instruct the VESA compatible card to use A000h as the beginning of the video segment, the following program fragment can be used *after* the VESA mode has been set:

```
        mov     dx, 0A000h              ; Start of the screen buffer
        mov     es, dx                  ; set es:di to unaltered screen
        xor     di, di                  ;   segment address
        mov     ah, 0FEh                ; get alternate buffer address
        int     10h                     ; get es:di new seg or left as is
        mov     cs:screen_segment, es   ; save screen segment
        mov     cs:screen_offset, di    ; save screen offset
```

XGA and 8514/A All of the RSIS code shown will work correctly when using the VGA features of the XGA and 8514/A adapters. If you are writing code to use the special non-VGA features of the 8514/A or XGA, there is no method to redirect the screen buffers in these non-VGA modes.

Hercules Adapters Adapters such as the Hercules monochrome adapters and the Hercules InColor Card, use the display I/O status register to indicate if the card is present in the system. These cards provide two pages of graphics using the segment B000h. The video mode 7 remains in effect during the use of Hercules specific graphics. All of the routines will function correctly with these cards.

Code Sample 9-1. Getting the Relocated Screen Address, C Code

Most programs determine where the screen buffer resides during initialization. The usual method checks if mode 7 (monochrome) is in use, and if so, uses B000:0000h as the buffer start. If any other text mode is in use, B800:0000h is used at the screen buffer start. To make a program RSIS compliant, after the segment determination is made, a special call using interrupt 10h function 0FEh, is made to see if an alternate address should be used. The sample code below shows a routine that is run during initialization. The code sets the actual screen segment and offset to use during the remainder of the program.

```
regs.x.ax = 0x0F00;
int86x(0x10, &regs, &regs, &sregs); //  INT 10h, get video mode
regs.x.ax = regs.x.ax & 0x007F;     //  strip bits to leave mode
if (regs.x.ax == 0x0007)
    regs.x.es = 0xB000h             //  default monochrome segment
else regs.x.es = 0xB800h;           //  default color text segment
regs.x.ax = 0xFE00;
regs.x.di = 0;                      //  default buffer offset
int86x(0x10, &regs, &regs, &sregs); //  INT 10h, get alternate buffer
screen_segment = sregs.es;          //  screen buffer segment
screen_offset = regs.x.di;          //  screen buffer offset
```

Code Sample 9-2. Getting the Relocated Screen Address, Assembly Code

No Video Mode Changes (Text Based)

Most programs determine where the screen buffer resides during initialization. The usual method checks if mode 7 (monochrome) is in use, and if so, B000:0000h as the buffer start. If any other mode is in use, then B800:0000h is used as the screen buffer start. To make a program RSIS compliant, after the segment determination is made, a special call using interrupt 10h function 0FEh, is made to see if an alternate address should be used. Sample code below shows a subroutine that is called during initialization. The code sets the actual screen segment and offset to use during the remainder of the program.

```
;--------------------------------------------------------------------------
;   SCREEN INITIALIZATION
;       Get current screen buffer address for direct display
;       writes.
;
;       Called with:    nothing
;
;       Returns:        cs:screen_segment set
;                       cs:screen_offset set
;
;       Regs used:      none

screen_segment  dw      0                   ; screen buffer segment
screen_offset   dw      0                   ; screen buffer offset

init_screen proc    near
        push    ax                          ; save all registers used
        push    bx
        push    dx
        push    di
        push    es

        mov     ah, 0Fh                     ; get video mode function
        int     10h                         ; put current video mode into al,
```

```
                                        ;   this function also affects bh
        and     al, 7Fh                 ; strip bit 7 (not part of mode)
        mov     dx, 0B000h              ; assume monochrome buffer address
        cmp     al, 7                   ; monochrome mode ?
        je      video_skip              ; jump if so
        mov     dx, 0B800h              ; if not, use color buffer address
video_skip:
        mov     es, dx                  ; set es:di to unaltered screen
        xor     di, di                  ;   segment address
        mov     ah, 0FEh                ; get alternate buffer address
        int     10h                     ; get es:di new seg or left as-is

        mov     cs:screen_segment, es   ; save screen segment
        mov     cs:screen_offset, di    ; save screen offset

        pop     es                      ; restore all registers used
        pop     di
        pop     dx
        pop     bx
        pop     ax
        ret
init_screen     endp
```

Programs that Change Video Modes (Text and Graphics)

The following subroutine can be used in place of changing the video mode. A simple substitution can be made for all places where an Int 10h, function AH equal to 0 occurs.

Unlike the standard mode set, this subroutine sets the carry flag if a graphics mode was attempted, but not set. This may occur if an expected adapter card is not present, or the current screen memory allocation is not sufficient for the desired video mode. Some environments can reduce the available display memory, preventing use of a particular video mode. If the carry bit is set on return, the mode cannot be used, and a video mode with a smaller memory requirements should be used, or an error message should be displayed.

The subroutine first checks for unique EGA+ modes, 0Dh or above. If it is a mode below 0Dh, the mode is set, and the screen buffer address is set. If a unique EGA+ graphics modes 0Dh or above is attempted, the subroutine first checks if it is allowable. If it is allowable, the mode is changed, and the screen buffer address is set. If it is not allowed, the mode is *not* set, and the carry flag is set.

```
;----------------------------------------------------------------
;   SET VIDEO MODE
;       Replacement routine for standard BIOS interrupt 10h,
;       function 0, set mode. Updates the screen address for
;       all direct screen writes. Also checks for mode
;       allowance and identifies problems.
;
;       Called with:    al = video mode
;
;       Returns:        if requested mode not supported:
;                         carry = 1
;                       if requested mode supported:
;                         carry = 0
;                         cs:screen_segment set
;                         cs:screen_offset set
;
;       Regs used:      none

screen_segment  dw      0               ; screen buffer segment
screen_offset   dw      0               ; screen buffer offset


set_mode proc   near
        push    ax                      ; save all registers used
        push    bx
        push    cx
        push    di
        push    es

        mov     bl, al                  ; get new mode
        and     bl, 7Fh                 ; strip upper bit
        cmp     bl, 0Dh                 ; mode for EGA/VGA only ?
        jb      set_the_mode            ; jump if not

        mov     ah, 12h                 ; Alternate selection function
        mov     bl, 10h                 ; EGA/VGA get info subfunction
        mov     bh, 0FFh                ; check value
        int     10h                     ; check if EGA/VGA (also alters cx)
```

```
        cmp     bh, 1                   ; if value above 1, not EGA/VGA
        ja      no_mode_set             ; jump if no EGA/VGA graphics
set_the_mode:
        mov     ah, 0                   ; set new mode function
        int     10h                     ; mode to set is in al

        mov     bl, al                  ; save mode
        and     bl, 7Fh                 ; strip upper bit
        mov     ax, 0A000h              ; assume normal EGA/VGA graphics seg
        cmp     bl, 0Dh                 ; mode D or above ?
        jae     check_alternate         ; jump if so
        mov     ax, 0B800h              ; assume color text or CGA graphics
        cmp     bl, 7                   ; mono text ?
        jne     check_alternate         ; jump if not mono
        mov     ax, 0B000h              ; normal mono screen segment

check_alternate:
        mov     es, ax                  ; set es:di to unaltered screen
        xor     di, di                  ;   segment address
        mov     ah, 0FEh                ; get alternate buffer address
        int     10h                     ; get es:di new seg or left as is

        mov     cs:screen_segment, es   ; save screen segment
        mov     cs:screen_offset, di    ; save screen offset
        clc                             ; carry cleared, mode set success
        jmp     short set_done
no_mode_set:
        stc                             ; EGA/VGA mode not allowed now
set_done:
        pop     es                      ; restore all registers used
        pop     di
        pop     cx
        pop     bx
        pop     ax
        ret
set_mode endp
```

Code Sample 9-3. Writing to Display Memory

The following excerpt shows a text screen being written from a buffer. The example is presented as just one of many possible ways to handle direct screen writes. The code assumes the values for the screen segment and offset were previously obtained. This routine does not support the snow problem with obsolete CGA adapters. For faster performance on a 486 or better CPU, the `loop` instruction can be replaced with the two instructions `dec cx`, and `jnz next_char`.

```
        mov     es, cs:screen_segment        ; where screen buffer resides
        mov     di, cs:screen_offset
        mov     ds, segment program_screen   ; address of program's screen
        mov     si, offset program_screen    ;  80x25 text characters
        mov     cx, 80*25                    ; size of screen
        mov     al, 7                        ; screen attribute, white
        cld
next_char:
        movsb                                ; xfer char to screen
        stosb                                ; xfer attribute to screen
        loop    next_char
```

Screen Update Function for DOS/V

The new Japanese operating system, DOS/V, always runs in graphics mode, even though most programs operate as if text mode is active. DOS/V requires the use of the relocated screen address *and* when the screen needs to be updated, the screen update function must be called. The following code fragment will tell DOS/V to update the entire screen. If only partial screen changes are made, a significant boost in display performance is made by only updating the portion of the screen that was changed. See interrupt 10h, function FFh for more information.

```
        mov     ah, 0FFh
        mov     cx, 1920              ; update 24 * 80 characters
        mov     bx, screen_offset     ; start of buffer
        mov     es, screen_segment    ; (from int 10h, func FEh)
        int     10h                   ; update screen
```

When DOS/V is not present, the interrupt 10h, function FFh is ignored and performs no actions.

Multiple Pages

When writing to multiple pages, the program can change either the screen segment value or screen offset value to write to the correct page. For example, simply add the (page size) * (the page number) to the screen_offset. If it is necessary to write to a second page (page 1) in mode 3, where the page size is 1000h bytes, add 1000h to the screen_offset to obtain the offset of where to write the screen.

In some environments, the screen buffer is reduced to less than the standard size. For example, if the allocated screen buffer is only 8K while in text mode 3, only two pages of 80x25 are allowed. To see if the desired page is allowable, attempt to activate the page and check if the page becomes active. If the page is not changed, then the requested screen page is unavailable. The following example attempts to go from page 0, the default when the last mode was set, to page 1.

```
        mov     ah, 5                   ; select active display page
        mov     al, 1                   ; set to page 1
        int     10h                     ; do it!

        push    ax
        mov     ah, 0Fh                 ; read current display state
        int     10h                     ; get active page in bh
        pop     ax                      ; recover desired page in al
        cmp     al,bh                   ; is the current page correct ?
        je      page_set_ok             ; jump if so

page_not_set:
        .                               ; code for page unavailable
        .
page_set_ok:
        .                               ; code for new page is set
```

Once a page is found to be available, all lower numbered pages are available and the pages will be available for the duration of the program. It is not necessary to recheck page availability once it is known the page is valid, unless the video mode is changed.

How Environments Provide RSIS Support

This section is provided for environment developers who wish to provide relocated screen services. Application developers can ignore this section.

Responsibilities

Environments that supply a relocated screen address are responsible for providing the correct segment and offset where screen data can be written. This alternate address must have sufficient memory, to perform all of the functions specified by the program, and handle all possible modes appropriate to an application.

The environment must intercept interrupt 10h, function 0FEh to provide the correct screen address, without alteration to unused registers. The actions of this function are described in the description of interrupt 10h, function FEh.

RSIS Environments

There are three known types of environments that need to relocate the video buffer address: multi-application, memory management, and foreign language support.

The multi-application environment relocates the application's video buffer to a RAM address unique for each running application. This allows the environment to control what portion of the application's screen appears on the display. In this manner, the application program sees a complete video screen, but the multi-application environment controls how much of an application's screen information really appears on the screen.

When the multi-application environment first loads, the environment's code should also use interrupt 10h, function 0FEh to establish the relocated buffer address. Whenever a video mode changes, the multi-application environment should re-establish the correct relocated buffer address.

The memory management environment changes the physical address of video memory to a higher address. This is done to gain additional main system memory. The amount of usable video memory can also be controlled to reclaim unneeded video memory depending on specific application needs.

The memory management interception of interrupt 10h function 0FEh should only occur at the lowest level of the interrupt chain. In the case of a system with both a multi-application environment and memory management running, the memory manager will not normally see requests for an alternate screen address directly from an application program.

The third use for RSIS is an operating system which needs to display more than 512 characters on the screen at one time. DOS/V uses this scheme. DOS/V keeps the display in a graphics mode so the thousands of Japanese characters can be displayed. Two bytes are used to describe ASCII and Japanese characters. The character values are written to a relocated screen buffer by the application, and converted by the operating system to display on the graphics screen.

Environments That Use RSIS

The following partial list of environments support some or all RSIS features. An RSIS-compliant application program will gain improved functionality and/or performance when used under these environments.

Environment	Publisher	Description
DOS/V*	IBM Corporation	DOS allows Japanese characters on a VGA
TopView*	IBM Corporation	Multi-application*
DesqView	Quarterdeck Office Systems	Multi-application
Memory Commander	V Communications, Inc.	386/486/Pentium Memory Management and DOS expansion

* *TopView and DOS/V requires a secondary interrupt function to update the screen. See interrupt 10h, function FFh.*

Code Sample 9-4. Detecting the Video Adapter

The following subroutine finds the exact adapter type, from the MDA to the VESA XGA. This routine also determines the attributes that should be used by the program based on the monitor and settings the user has made to the system. For some adapters, this subroutine also returns a pointer to a vendor string with the vendor's name.

The three attribute types are Color, Monochrome, and Grayscale. Do not use this information as to where the video buffer appears. It is only intended to convey the types of attributes to use on screen. There are a few cases where monochrome or grayscale are used, yet the video buffer segment is at B800h, normally considered the color text video memory area!

Grayscale monitors were introduced with the VGA, but have never become very popular. Most monochrome laptops support grayscale modes. Many applications ignore grayscale support and will incorrectly assume the monitor is color, making the display difficult to read. If you do not want to specifically support grayscale operation, just use black, white, and bright white attributes if the grayscale attributes value is returned.

The VIDEO_TEXT source code is located in the SYSTYPE program. For example, the result of running SYSTYPE on one system appears in Figure 9-1.

Figure 9-1. Video Results of SYSTYPE

```
SYSTEM ANALYSIS                    V1.00 (c) 1994, 1996 FVG
Video Adapter:VGA, programs should use color attributes.
Video Vendor:  Orchid Technology Fahrenheit VA
```

```
;
;   VIDEO TYPE DETECT
;
;       Find the video type, type attributes and possible
;       vendor string. This routine assumes the display is
;       in a text mode to determine the attribute byte CL.
;
;       The attributes option indicates what attributes a
;       program should use, color, monochrome, or gray scales.
;
;       Called with:    nothing
;
;       Returns:        al = video type
;                               0 = MDA
;                               1 = HGA
;                               2 = CGA
;                               3 = MCGA
;                               4 = EGA
;                               5 = VGA
;                               6 = SVGA
;                               7 = XGA
;                               8 = VESA XGA
;                       ch = attribute type
;                               0 = color
;                               1 = monochrome
;                               2 = gray scale (some MCGA or VGA+)
;                       cl = vendor string present in es:bx
;                               0 = no vendor string
;                               1 = vendor string
;                       es:si = vendor string, zero terminated
;                                 (if cl = 1)
;
;       Regs used:      ax, cx, si, es
```

```
infobuf db      256 dup (0)          ; buffer for video info
hercstr db      'Hercules', 0        ; Vendor string if Hercules

video_type proc    near
        push    bx
        push    dx
        push    di
        push    bp
        mov     bp, 4                ; bp = temp video type, 4=EGA

; --- check if EGA or later using get video information function

        mov     ah, 12h              ; get video info function
        mov     bh, 5Ah              ; test value
        mov     bl, 10h              ; subfunction EGA+ info
        int     10h
        cmp     bh, 1                ; must be 0, color or 1, mono
        ja      below_EGA            ; jump if not EGA+

; --- it is an EGA or later, so now test for VGA

        push    bx                   ; save color info for later
        mov     ax, 1A00h            ; get display code
        int     10h
        cmp     al, 1Ah              ; is function supported ?
        je      vid_VGA              ; if so, at least a VGA
        jmp     type_found           ; jump if not (must be EGA)

; --- at least a VGA, now test for SVGA

vid_VGA:
        inc     bp                   ; assume VGA (5)
        push    cs
        pop     es
```

```
        mov     di, offset infobuf ; buffer for video info
        mov     ax, 4F00h           ; return SVGA info
        int     10h

        cmp     al, 4Fh
        jne     XGA_test            ; jump if not SVGA
        inc     bp                  ; assume SVGA (6)

; --- at least a VGA/SVGA, now test for XGA/VESA XGA

XGA_test:
        mov     ax, 1F00h           ; get XGA information size
        int     10h
        cmp     al, 1Fh             ; is function supported ?
        jne     type_found          ; jump if not, is VGA or SVGA
        mov     bp, 7               ; set to XGA

; --- at least a XGA, now test for VESA XGA

        mov     di, offset infobuf ; buffer for video info
        mov     ax, 4E00h           ; return VESA XGA info
        int     10h
        cmp     ax, 004Eh           ; is function supported ?
        jne     type_found          ; jump if not
        inc     bp                  ; VESA XGA (8)
        jmp     type_found

; --- arrives here if adapter is below an EGA

below_EGA:
        mov     bp, 3               ; assume MCGA (3)
        mov     ax, 1A00h           ; get display code
        int     10h
        cmp     al, 1Ah             ; is function supported ?
```

```
        jne     vid_not_MCGA        ; jump if not MCGA
        mov     ah, 0Fh
        int     10h                 ; get video mode
        mov     cx, 100h            ; assume mono, no vendor
        cmp     al, 7
        je      vid_chk_gray        ; if mono, check gray
        mov     ch, 0               ; looks like color!
        je      vid_chk_gray        ; check gray scales

; --- not MCGA, test for CGA or MDA/HGA

vid_not_MCGA:
        dec     bp                  ; assume CGA (2)
        mov     ah, 0Fh             ; get video mode
        int     10h
        cmp     al, 7               ; mode 7 monochrome ?
        je      vid_mono_type       ; jump if so
        xor     cx, cx              ; return color, no vendor
        jne     vid_mono_type
        jmp     vid_mono_chk        ; must be CGA

; --- Must be MDA or HGA, so find out which. The HGA
;     (Hercules Graphics Adapter) toggles an undefined bit on
;     the MDA. Check to see if this bit changes state 10 times
;     or more.

vid_mono_type:
        dec     bp                  ; assume HGA (1)
        xor     bl, bl              ; start count at 0
        mov     dx, 3BAh            ; status port on HGA/MDA
        xor     ah, ah              ; ah used for prior status
        mov     cx, 0FFFFh          ; test for a long time
vid_loop:
        in      al, dx              ; read status port
```

```
        IODELAY
        and     al, 80h              ; isolate HGA toggle bit
        cmp     al, ah               ; has it changed ?
        je      vid_no_toggle        ; jump if not
        inc     bl                   ; bit changed, increment
        cmp     bl, 10               ; more than 10 toggles ?
        jae     vid_herc             ; if so, it's a Hercules card
vid_no_toggle:
        loop    vid_loop             ; read again until cx 0

; --- falls through if MDA (bit does not toggle)

        dec     bp                   ; set to MDA (0)
        mov     cx, 100h             ; mono attribute, no vendor
        jmp     vid_exit

; --- adapter is Hercules type

vid_herc:
        mov     cx, 101h
        push    cs
        pop     es
        mov     si, offset hercstr ; set string to Hercules
        jmp     vid_exit

; --- For MCGA/EGA/VGA/XGA put the attribute type in CL

type_found:
        pop     bx                   ; get attribute type (0 or 1)
        mov     ch, bh
vid_chk_gray:
        mov     ax, 1A00h
        int     10h
        cmp     al, 1Ah              ; check if supported
```

```
        jne     vid_string          ; jump if can't be gray scale
        cmp     bl, 7               ; gray scale monitor?
        je      vid_is_gray         ; jump if so
        cmp     bl, 0Bh             ; gray scale monitor?
        je      vid_is_gray         ; jump if so
        cmp     bp, 5               ; VGA or later ?

        mov     ax, 40h             ; BIOS data area
        mov     es, ax
        test    byte ptr es:[89h], 2  ; gray scale summing on ?
        jz      vid_string          ; not gray scale
vid_is_gray:
        mov     ch, 2               ; set ch to gray scale

vid_string:
        xor     cl, cl              ; assume no vendor string
        cmp     bp, 6               ; SVGA ?
        je      vid_skp1            ; jump if so
        cmp     bp, 8               ; VESA XGA ?
        jne     vid_mono_chk        ; jump if not
vid_skp1:
        mov     di, offset infobuf ; get buffer of SVGA info
        mov     si, cs:[di+6]       ; get offset and segment to
        mov     ax, cs:[di+8]       ;   the vendor string
        mov     es, ax              ; es:bx points to string
        inc     cl                  ; vendor string valid

; The last check is made to see if video mode 2 is set,
; indicating monochrome attributes should be used (if we
; haven't already detected monochrome operation)

vid_mono_chk:
        cmp     ch, 0               ; set to color ?
        jne     vid_exit            ; jump if not
```

```
        mov     ah, 0Fh
        int     10h                     ; get video mode
        and     al, 7Dh
        cmp     al, 0                   ; video mode 0 or 2 ?
        jne     vid_exit                ; jump if not
        mov     ch, 1                   ; use monochrome attributes

vid_exit:
        mov     ax, bp                  ; return adapter type in al
        pop     bp
        pop     di
        pop     dx
        pop     bx
        ret
video_type endp
```

Port Summary

This is a list of ports used to control all the major video adapter types.

Port	Type	Function	Adapters
3B4h	Output*	Video Controller Register Select	MDA, HGA, EGA+
3B5h	I/O	Video Controller Data	MDA, HGA, EGA+
3B8h	Output	Video Adapter Control	MDA, HGA
3BAh	Input	Video Adapter Status	MDA, HGA
3BAh	Input	Video Status Register 1 (mono)	EGA+
3BAh	Output	Video Feature Control (mono)	EGA+
3BFh	Output	Hercules Control Register (mono)	HGA
3C0h	Output	Video Attribute Controller Registers	EGA+
3C1h	Input	Video Attribute Controller Registers	VGA+
3C2h	Output	Video Miscellaneous Output Register	EGA+
3C2h	Input	Video Status Register 0	EGA+
3C3h	I/O	Video Adapter Enable	VGA
3C4h	Output*	Video Sequencer Register Select	EGA+
3C5h	Output*	Video Sequencer Data	EGA+
3C6h	I/O	Video Pel Mask Register	VGA+
3C7h	I/O	Video Digital to Analog Converter	VGA+
3C8h	I/O	Video Digital to Analog Converter	VGA+

Port	Type	Function	Adapters
3C9h	I/O	Video Digital to Analog Converter	VGA+
3CAh	Input	Video Feature Control Register	VGA+
3CCh	Output*	Video Graphics 1 Position	EGA+
3CDh	Output	Video Graphics 2 Position	EGA+
3CEh	Output*	Video Graphics Controller Register Select	EGA+
3CFh	Output*	Video Graphics Controller Data	EGA+
3D4h	Output*	Video Controller Register Select	CGA, EGA+
3D5h	Output*	Video Controller Data	CGA, EGA+
3D8h	Output	Video Adapter Mode Control	CGA
3D9h	Output	Video Adapter Color Select	CGA
3DAh	Input	Video Adapter Status	CGA
3DAh	Input	Video Status Register 1 (color)	EGA+
3DAh	Output	Video Feature Control (color)	EGA+
3DBh	Output	Video Adapter Clear Light Pen Latch	CGA
3DCh	Output	Video Adapter Preset Light Pen Latch	CGA
xC80h	I/O	EISA Video ID	VESA XGA
xC81h	I/O	EISA Video ID	VESA XGA
xC82h	I/O	EISA Video ID	VESA XGA
xC83h	I/O	EISA Video ID	VESA XGA
xC84h	I/O	EISA Video Expansion Board Control	VESA XGA
xC85h	I/O	EISA Setup Control	VESA XGA
xC88h	I/O	EISA Video Programmable Option Select 0	VESA XGA
xC89h	I/O	EISA Video Programmable Option Select 1	VESA XGA
xC8Ah	I/O	EISA Video Programmable Option Select 2	VESA XGA
xC8Bh	I/O	EISA Video Programmable Option Select 3	VESA XGA
xC8Ch	I/O	EISA Video Programmable Option Select 4	VESA XGA
xC8Dh	I/O	EISA Video Programmable Option Select 5	VESA XGA
xC8Eh	I/O	EISA Video Programmable Option Select 6	VESA XGA
xC8Fh	I/O	EISA Video Programmable Option Select 7	VESA XGA
21z0h	I/O	Video Operating Mode Register	XGA+
21z1h	I/O	Video Aperture Control	XGA+
21z2h	I/O	Video Unused or Unknown Function	XGA+
21z3h	I/O	Video Unused or Unknown Function	XGA+
21z4h	I/O	Video Interrupt Enable	XGA+
21z5h	I/O	Video Interrupt Status	XGA+
21z6h	I/O	Video Virtual Memory Control	XGA+
21z7h	I/O	Video Virtual Memory Interrupt Status	XGA+
21z8h	I/O	Video Aperture Index	XGA+
21z9h	I/O	Video Memory Access Mode	XGA+
21zAh	I/O	Video Index for Data	XGA+
21zBh	I/O	Video Data, byte wide	XGA+
21zCh	I/O	Video Data, word & Double word wide	XGA+

Port	Type	Function	Adapters
21zDh	I/O	Video Data	XGA+
21zEh	I/O	Video Data	XGA+
21zFh	I/O	Video Data	XGA+
46E8h	I/O	Video Adapter Enable	VGA

**These ports are write only on the EGA, read/write on others*
x indicates the EISA slot number in which the XGA adapter is installed
z indicates which XGA when a system has multiple XGA adapters

Port Detail of Undocumented Video I/O Ports

Port	Type	Description	Adapters
3C3h	I/O	Video Adapter Enable	VGA, SVGA

This port controls whether a video card is accessible. When disabled, all I/O ports except this one are ignored and the video memory from A000 to BFFF is disconnected from the bus. The video card retains the current state and the display remains unchanged. The enable/disable bit is primarily used to switch between a motherboard VGA and an adapter card VGA. The MCA's POS registers are also controlled using another bit of this port.

This port is only implemented on motherboard versions of the VGA. Port 46E8h is used for the identical function on VGA adapter cards.

I/O (bits 0-7)

bit	7 r/w = x	Unused or vendor defined
	6 r/w = x	Unused or vendor defined
	5 r/w = x	Unused or vendor defined
	4 r/w = 1	Setup for POS registers (MCA systems only)
	3 r/w = 0	Disable video I/O ports & video buffer
	1	Enable video I/O ports & video buffer
	2 r/w = x	Unused or vendor defined
	1 r/w = x	Unused or vendor defined
	0 r/w = x	Unused or vendor defined

Port	Type	Description	Adapters
3C6h	I/O	Video DAC Pixel Mask	VGA+

This port limits the number of colors or shades possible on the screen at one time. It is used by the BIOS to make various modes function as specified. For example, graphics mode 5 is limited to four colors.

The video adapter uses a Digital-to-Analog Converter (DAC) to take the three 6-bit color values and convert them into three analog voltages for the red, green, and blue signals to the monitor. The DAC has 256 of these 6-bit color triads. Each one of these color triads will display the associated color value when addressed by the VGA hardware.

The pixel address mask "disconnects" specified address lines to the DAC, so that even if a higher color address is specified by hardware, the DAC brings up a lower address. Each bit in the mask controls 1 of the 8 address bits to the 256 color registers. For example, a value of 0Fh loaded into this register will limit color addresses to the first 16 color triads. A hardware color register access of triad 2 is the same as 12h, 22h, 32h, and so forth with this mask value.

It is not clear if all vendors support reading this register. The video BIOS never reads the register.

I/O (bits 0-7)

bit	7 w = 0	Ignore address line 7 (treated as zero)
	6 w = 0	Ignore address line 6 (treated as zero)
	5 w = 0	Ignore address line 5 (treated as zero)
	4 w = 0	Ignore address line 4 (treated as zero)
	3 w = 0	Ignore address line 3 (treated as zero)
	2 w = 0	Ignore address line 2 (treated as zero)
	1 w = 0	Ignore address line 1 (treated as zero)
	0 w = 0	Ignore address line 0 (treated as zero)

Port	Type	Description	Adapters
3C7h	I/O	Video DAC Color Register Address	VGA+

This port accesses an 18-bit color register inside the DAC. The address 0 to 255 is written into this register before reading or writing to port 3C9h to get the data. Reading this port returns the current address.

I/O (bits 0-7) Color Register Address

Port	Type	Description	Adapters
3C8h	I/O	Video DAC Color Register Initialize	VGA+

This port initializes an 18-bit color register inside the DAC. The address, 0 to 255, is written into this register to specify which color register to initialize. A read simply indicates what the current register is.

I/O (bits 0-7) Color Register Address to Initialize

Port	Type	Description	Adapters
3C9h	I/O	Video DAC Color Register Data	VGA+

This port reads or writes a color register. The address must have been set once using port 3C7h. Since each color register is made up of three 6-bit groups, three reads or writes are necessary to access all 18-bits. The first byte accessed is red, then green, and finally blue. Each byte holds the lower 6-bits of the color value. The upper two bits are ignored. Future VGA adapters with different hardware may use all 8 bits in each register to provide 24-bit color capability.

After the three bytes of one color register are accessed, the address value is automatically incremented. The next color register can be accessed without sending a new address to port 3C7h.

I/O (bits 0-7) Color Register Data (3-bytes, red/green/blue)

Port	Type	Description	Adapters
46E8h	I/O	Video Adapter Enable	VGA, SVGA

This port controls whether a video card is accessible. When disabled, all I/O ports except this one are ignored and the video memory from A000 to BFFF is disconnected from the bus. The video card retains the current state and the display remains unchanged. The enable/disable bit is primarily used to switch between a motherboard VGA and an adapter card VGA. The MCA's POS registers are also controlled using another bit of this port.

This port is only implemented on adapter card versions of the VGA. Port 3C3h is used for the identical function on a motherboard-mounted VGA.

I/O (bits 0-7)

bit	7 r/w = x		Unused or vendor defined
	6 r/w = x		Unused or vendor defined
	5 r/w = x		Unused or vendor defined
	4 r/w = 1		Setup for POS registers (MCA systems only)
	3 r/w = 0		Disable video I/O ports and video buffer
		1	Enable video I/O ports and video buffer
	2 r/w = x		Unused or vendor defined
	1 r/w = x		Unused or vendor defined
	0 r/w = x		Unused or vendor defined

CHAPTER 10

Diskette System

The documentation for the diskette BIOS in the past has been better than for most other subsystems. The basic controller interface has remained basically the same since the first PC. The AT added a few new BIOS services, and the newest systems add support for 2.88 MB diskette drives.

I've expanded on the diskette BIOS services and error codes to provide a great deal of additional information and help clarify what is necessary to reliably use the BIOS and hardware services. In addition, I've written a diskette drive detector that identifies everything from the very obsolete 320K drives to the latest 2.88 MB drives. Complete source code is included later in this chapter.

When accessing the diskette controller directly, I've covered all the common ports used and the deeper details within each port. These ports also show the specific values required for the configuration and operation of each type of diskette drive supported by systems today. The few hardware documents that exist for the diskette controller are poorly organized for programmers. I've presented all controller commands and values in a form that is easy to understand and use.

The section on warnings covers a number of poorly understood problems in using the diskette BIOS services and controller.

Introduction

Diskette drives are accessed by hardware on an adapter card and BIOS software built within the main system BIOS. This combination provides the ability to easily format, read, and write diskettes. Beginning with the AT, BIOS support was reduced from four diskette drives to a maximum of two drives. Additional drives beyond these limits will require special adapter hardware and drivers, like DRIVER.SYS in DOS. Most operating systems, including DOS, have no set limit on the number or types of diskette drives.

The diskette system is shown in Figure 10-1. The diskette controller is the heart of the system and connects to each diskette drive in the system. All communications flow between the system and the drive through the controller. The system accesses the controller through I/O commands and returned status. Some commands also interrupt the processor when the requested operation is complete. Transfer of read and write sector data between the adapter and the system is handled through DMA transfers. The system uses DMA channel 2 for these transfers. DMA operations are transparent to the user if the BIOS is used to read and write data to the diskette. Chapter 18, DMA Services and DRAM Refresh, covers the DMA processes in detail.

Figure 10-1. Diskette System

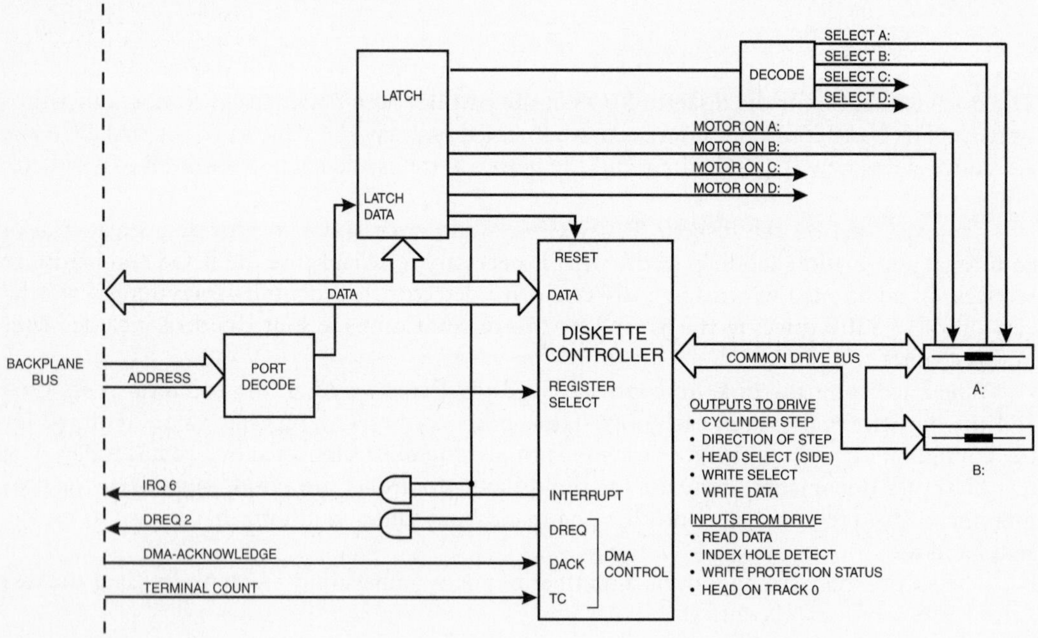

Throughout this chapter are references to common terminology relating to the structure of the diskette. Each diskette is divided into cylinders, tracks, and sectors, as shown in Figure 10-2. The smallest component is the sector, which normally holds 512 bytes of data. A number of sectors are grouped together to form a track. For example, a 1.44 MB diskette has 18 sectors per track. Other media types have from 9 to 36 sectors per track, depending on the density the number of bits per inch that can be reliably stored on the media. Two tracks, one on each side of the diskette, are grouped to define a cylinder. Finally the diskette has either 40 or 80 cylinders, depending on the media type.

Figure 10-2. Diskette Media Structure

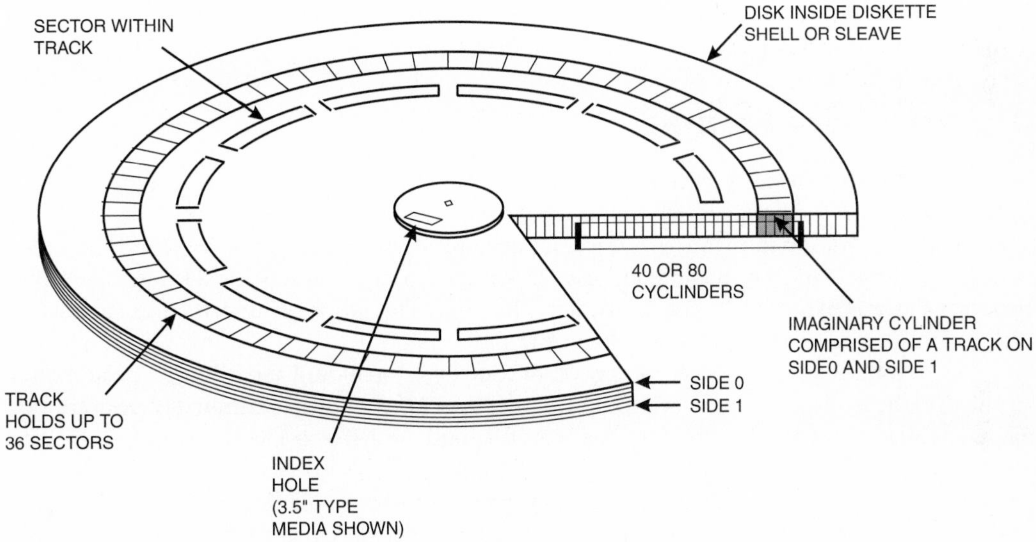

Diskette Drive Media Chart

Table 10-1 shows how the 512 byte sectors make up the total capacity of the diskette. The table also shows the transfer rate used, in bits per second. This is the speed at which data is transferred between the drive and the controller. The transfer rate varies depending on diskette capacity, the drive type, and the speed at which the diskette is spun, in RPM. The faster the diskette is spun and the more data packed per linear inch of the media, the higher the transfer rate. The transfer rate is always fixed for a given drive and media, and is not defined by software.

Table 10-1. Media Chart

Drive	Diskette	Tracks Per Side	Sectors Per Track	RPM	Transfer Rate
360 KB, 5.25"	360 KB	40	9	300	250 Kbps
1.2 MB, 5.25"	360 KB	40	9	360	300 Kbps
1.2 MB, 5.25"	1.2 MB	80	15	360	500 Kbps
720 KB, 3.5"	720 KB	80	9	360	250 Kbps
1.44 MB, 3.5"	720 KB	80	9	360	250 Kbps
1.44 MB, 3.5"	1.44 MB	80	18	360	500 Kbps
2.88 MB, 3.5"	720 KB	80	9	360	250 Kbps
2.88 MB, 3.5"	1.44 MB	80	18	360	500 Kbps
2.88 MB, 3.5"	2.88 MB	80	36	360	1 Mbps

Diskette Data Format

Each track on the diskette is comprised of gaps, sync pulses, and data such as address marks, sector ID, Cyclic Redundancy Checks (CRC), and the actual sector's data. It is helpful to understand the information on the track in making sense of various error conditions, like "missing address mark." A missing address mark error simply indicates the address byte values are not what was expected by the controller The controller strips off information such as the address mark before the data is sent to the system.

The sector ID information is comprised of four bytes including the cylinder, head, sector, and sector size code. These are controlled by the user of the format command, and are normally equal to the physical cylinder, head, sector, and actual sector code size. This is not a requirement, and old copy protection schemes would write weird values into the sector's ID bytes to help identify the original diskette. An operating system, like DOS, always formats the sector's ID with the cylinder, head, sector, and sector code size equal to the physical position.

Figure 10-3 shows the layout of data on all diskette types currently used on PCs.

Figure 10-3. Contents of One Diskette Track

Track bytes
- Index pulse Gap area, 80 bytes of 4Eh
- Track sync pulse, 12 bytes of 0h
- Track index address marks, 3 bytes of C2h, followed by 1 byte FCh
- Track gap area, 50 bytes of 4Eh
- Sector bytes (repeats for each sector)
  - Sector sync pulse, 12 bytes of 0
  - Index address mark, 3 bytes of A1h, followed by 1 byte FEh
  - Cylinder byte (normally 0 to 79, depending on media)
  - Head byte (normally 0 or 1)
  - Sector number byte (normally 1 to 36, depending on media)
  - Sector size code (normally 2 to indicate a 512 byte sector)
  - CRC byte covering the four prior bytes
  - Sector gap, 22 bytes of 4Eh on 360 KB through 1.44 MB media; 41 bytes of 4Eh on 2.88 MB media
  - Sector sync pulse, 12 bytes of 0
  - Data address mark, 3 bytes of A1h, followed by 1 byte FBh or F8h (values indicate normal or deleted data)
    - Data, number of bytes as specified by sector size code
    - CRC byte of sector's data
  - Sector gap, size as set by format command
  - Additional Sectors for track (up to 36 total, depending on media)
- End of track gap

Diskette Parameter Table

The diskette drive parameter table holds information about the disk drive. This table is used by the BIOS to program the diskette controller and specify various timings in control of the diskette drive. The pointer to the parameter table is stored in the location of interrupt 1Eh, at 0:78h. Be aware that some technical references do not understand how the parameter table works and have misleading or incorrect information!

The diskette parameter table is a great concept when only one drive type exists in the system, as in the original PC and XT systems. The parameter table also works fine in older PS/2s where there is only a choice of one or two of the same type drives, like 3.5" 1.44 MB. The diskette parameter table is used to fully define the parameters for the drive.

The big problem occurs when the BIOS supports two or more different types of drives, as occurs on many systems. A system might have two drives from the five possible diskette drives available today (360 KB, 1.2 MB, 720 KB, 1.44 MB, or 2.88 MB). There is no mechanism to make the diskette parameter table support multiple drives. As a result, most system BIOS manufactures write the BIOS diskette service handler to ignore most bytes in the diskette parameter table.

Multi-type diskette drive support in the BIOS is handled differently depending on the BIOS manufacturer. The diskette parameter table the BIOS POST points to after initialization will usually be valid for one drive only, and even then the table may be ignored!

When the BIOS diskette service routines do use values from the diskette parameter table, the BIOS usually just passes values directly to the diskette controller without any checks. The BIOS assumes the values in the table are valid. The contents of the diskette parameter table are shown in Table 10-2.

Table 10-2. Diskette Parameter Table Contents

Offset	Description		
0	Diskette controller (see port 3F5h, specify command, byte 2 for complete details)		
	bit	7 = x	Step rate (timing changes with data rate)
		6 = x	Typical values include:
		5 = x	Ah = 3 ms on a 2.88 MB drive
		4 = x	Ah = 6 ms on a 1.44 MB drive
			Ah = 12 ms on a 720 KB drive (some systems)
			Dh = 3 ms on a 1.2 MB drive
			Dh = 6 ms on a 720 KB drive (some systems)
			Dh = 6 ms on a 360 KB drive
		3 = x	Head unload time (timing changes with data rate)
		2 = x	Typical values include:
		1 = x	1 = 16 ms on a 1.44 MB drive (PS/1 and PS/2 only)
		0 = x	1 = 27 ms on a 720 KB drive (PS/1 and PS/2 only)
			Fh = 120 ms on a 2.88 MB drive
			Fh = 240 ms on 1.44 MB and 1.2 MB drives
			Fh = 480 ms on 720 KB and 360 KB drives
1	Diskette controller (see port 3F5h, specify command, byte 3 for complete details)		
	bit	7 = x	Head load time (timing changes with data rate)
		6 = x	The typical value is 0000001 for a load time of:
		5 = x	2 ms on a 2.88 MB drive
		4 = x	4 ms on 1.44 MB and 1.2 MB drives
		3 = x	8 ms on 720 KB and 360 KB drives
		2 = x	
		1 = x	
		0 = 0	DMA used for diskette operations (normal)
		1	no DMA used

Table 10-2. Continued

Offset	Description
2	Drive inactive motor turn-off delay Initial delay value to countdown while diskette inactive. It is decremented by the interrupt 8 timer service handler once every 54 ms. A typical value of 25h sets a delay of 2 seconds.
3	Bytes per sector code 0 = 128 bytes (or variable if using data length byte at offset 6) 1 = 256 bytes 2 = 512 bytes (standard used on all PC diskettes) 3 = 1,024 bytes 4 = 2,048 bytes (not possible on all media) 5 = 4,096 bytes (not possible on all media) 6 = 8,192 bytes (not possible on all media) 7 = 16,384 bytes (not possible on all media, not supported on all diskette controllers) 8 to FFh not valid
4	Sectors per track (common values are shown) 9 = 9 sectors for 360 KB and 720 KB diskettes 0Fh = 15 sectors for 1.2 MB diskettes 12h = 18 sectors for 1.44 MB diskettes 24h = 36 sectors for 2.88 MB diskettes
5	Gap length used between sectors (common values shown) 1Bh = for 1.2 MB, 1.44 MB, and 2.88 MB diskettes 2Ah = for 360 KB and 720 KB diskettes
6	Data Length This byte specifies the sector size if the bytes per sector code at offset 3 is 0. The sector length can be from 1 to 255 bytes. All PC drive media use 512 byte sectors, so this byte is not important, and is normally set to FFh.
7	Format gap length Size of the gap between sectors while formatting (common values shown) 50h = for 360 KB, 720 KB, and 2.88 MB diskettes 54h = for 1.2 MB diskettes 6Ch = for 1.44 MB diskettes
8	Fill byte for format Sector data is set to the fill byte during the format operation. The standard fill byte value is F6h.
9	Head settling time The BIOS software delay, in milliseconds, to wait after a seek for the head to settle on the correct track. All drives use a default delay of 15 milliseconds (0Fh).

Table 10-2. Continued

Offset	Description
A	Wait for motor startup time During a write operation, this value specifies the time delay in eighths of a second to wait, after first turning on the diskette motor. Most systems use a default value of 8 to set the duration to one second. Some PS/2 systems only wait half a second as a default, presuming a faster spin up on 3.5" drives. There is no preset delay period for reads, as the controller just begins reading until the data becomes stable.

BIOS Initialization

With the PC and XT, the system BIOS only understands 360 KB type drives. Switches on the motherboard tell the BIOS how many drives are configured. Once the switches are read, the controller is reset.

With AT+ systems the POST reads information from CMOS RAM byte 10h to understand which diskette drives are present and their drive types. POST then issues a software reset to the controller. With the CMOS information, POST programs the controller with the data rate appropriate for the boot drive. See Chapter 15 for more about the CMOS byte.

For all systems, after the controller has been reset and is ready, the motor is turned on. After a delay of about one second, POST issues a seek command to move the head to an inner cylinder of the diskette. If this is successful, the drive is ready to be used as the potential boot device. The motor is then turned off until POST is ready to attempt to boot from the diskette drive.

As part of the final initialization steps, a far pointer to the diskette parameter table in the system BIOS ROM is loaded into the interrupt vector table at 0:78h. The POST checks if a hard disk is present. If so, the BIOS copies the diskette interrupt 13h vector to interrupt 40h. The BIOS then replaces the old interrupt 13h with a new pointer to a service handler for the hard disk. Functions passed to the hard disk interrupt 13h for a diskette drive are revectored to the original diskette service handler, now at interrupt 40h.

Programs should always use interrupt 13h for diskette services. If interrupt 40h is used directly, any TSRs and device drivers that hook interrupt 13h will be bypassed, and a system crash is possible.

Diskette BIOS

Diskette services are accessed through interrupt 13h. Most functions require a number in DL to specify which drive to select. On the AT and all later systems, the BIOS supports only diskette drive 0 (A: in DOS), and drive 1 (B: in DOS). The original PC and XT both supported up to four diskette drives. Note that all diskette adapters use a disk controller that supports up to four diskette drives, but most newer adapters do not provide connections to the third and forth drive. The few adapter cards that allow four diskette drives must supply a special BIOS ROM to support the third and fourth drives.

Upon completion of a service, the diskette BIOS returns a status byte in the AH register. The status byte indicates if the operation was a success or contains an error code. This return status byte is also stored in the BIOS data area at address 40:41h. The status return values are described in detail in Table 10-3.

Table 10-3. Return Status Codes in AH

Hex Code	Description
0	Operation successful, no error occurred
1	Invalid value passed or unsupported function
2	Missing address mark—No sector address mark matched the request
3	Diskette is write protected
4	Requested sector not found or requested sector is past the last cylinder on the diskette
6	Diskette change line active—Except for the 360 KB drive, all other drives provides a hardware line to the controller to alert the controller whenever a diskette is removed, changed, or missing.
8	DMA overrun—the DMA did not transfer data to or from the controller fast enough, such that a timeout occurred in the controller.
9	Data boundary error—The DMA operation must be completely within a 64K page. This means the DMA operation attempted to cross a physical 64K boundary, like an address at FFFFh, 1FFFFh, 2FFFFh, etc.
C	Media type not found
10	CRC error during read—The CRC recorded on the diskette sector did not match a calculated CRC from the sector's data. The data is very likely to be wrong.
20	Diskette controller or drive problem—This is returned in two cases: 1) Abnormal termination of a command within the controller. 2) The returned drive status bytes have an invalid value, likely indicating a controller malfunction.
40	Seek operation failed—An attempt to move to a specific cylinder on the diskette failed.
80h	Timeout—The diskette drive failed to respond.

Diskette BIOS Services

Some technical references indicate a few interrupt 13h functions, like AH=6, 7, and 9, are "reserved." They are either used by the hard disk that shares this interrupt, or are currently unused, and to my knowledge, have never been used.

Interrupt 13h for diskettes provides the following eleven services. See Chapter 11, Hard Disk System, for interrupt 13h services relating to the hard disk.

Function	Description	Platform
ah=0	Diskette Controller reset	All
ah=1	Read Diskette Status	All
ah=2	Read Diskette Sectors	All
ah=3	Write Diskette Sectors	All
ah=4	Verify Diskette Sectors	All
ah=5	Format Diskette Track	All
ah=8	Read Diskette Drive Parameters	AT+
ah=15h	Read Diskette Drive Type	AT+
ah=16h	Get Diskette Change Line Status	AT+
ah=17h	Set Diskette Type For Format (old)	AT+
ah=18h	Set Diskette Type For Format (new)	AT+

INT

Int	Fun	Description	Platform
13h	0	Diskette-Controller-Reset	All

Commands the diskette controller to reset, and commands the controller to reset the specified drive.

Called with: ah = 0
dl = drive number, 0 to 3

Returns: ah = return status (see Table 10-3)
carry = 0 successful, = 1 if error occurred

INT

Int	Func	Description	Platform
13h	1	Read Diskette Status	All

Upon return from each diskette service, the return status value is saved in the BIOS data area at 40:41h. This function returns the value currently stored from 40:41h, which represents the status from the last operation. Unlike most other functions, no drive number is used.

Called with: ah = 1

Returns: ah = return status (see Table 10-3)
carry = 0 successful, = 1 if error occurred

INT

Int	Func	Description	Platform
13h	2	Read Diskette Sectors	All

Reads a number of 512 byte diskette sectors starting from the specified location. The data read is placed into RAM at the location specified by ES:BX. The buffer must be sufficiently large to hold the data AND must not cross a 64K linear address boundary. See the warnings section for more details.

Because the diskette motor may be off when the read request is made, some older BIOSes return an error on each attempt to read until the motor reaches proper speed. At least three attempts should be made before an error is confirmed. Most newer BIOSes wait until the motor is up to speed, and then perform the operation.

Called with: ah = 2
al = number of sectors to read, 1 to 36*
ch = track number, 0 to 79*
cl = sector number, 1 to 36*
* see media chart (Table 10-1) for limits
dh = head number, 0 or 1
dl = drive number, 0 to 3
es:bx = pointer where to place information read from diskette

Returns: ah = return status (see Table 10-3)
al = number of sectors actually read (see warnings section)
carry = 0 successful, = 1 if error occurred

Int	Func	Description	Platform
13h	3	Write Diskette Sectors	All

INT III I

Writes a number of diskette sectors starting from the specified location. The data is read from RAM at the location specified by ES:BX. The buffer must not cross a 64K linear address boundary. See the warnings section for more details.

Because the diskette motor may be off when the read request is made, some older BIOSes return an error on each attempt to read until the motor reaches proper speed. At least three retries should be made before an error is confirmed. Most newer BIOSes wait until the motor is up to speed, and then perform the operation.

Called with: ah = 3
al = number of sectors to write, 1 to 36*
ch = track number, 0 to 79*
cl = sector number, 1 to 36*
* see media chart (Table 10-1) for limits
dh = head number, 0 or 1
dl = drive number, 0 to 3
es:bx = pointer where to get information to write to the diskette

Returns: ah = return status (see Table 10-3)
al = number of sectors actually written (see warnings section)
carry = 0 successful, = 1 if error occurred

Int	Func	Description	Platform
13h	4	**Verify Diskette Sectors**	All

Verifies a number of diskette sectors starting from the specified location. This command does not actually check byte-for-byte that the data match a buffer's contents. Instead, the controller attempts to read the specified contents and then calculates a CRC. The controller then compares its calculated CRC with the CRC previously stored on the diskette. If the sectors are located, read and the CRC matches, the data is considered verified.

Most technical references indicate a buffer at ES:BX is required for the verify operation. It is not used on AT, MCA, or EISA based BIOSes. Some older BIOSes may use the buffer, but the actual contents are not checked! When a buffer is supplied, the buffer must not cross a 64K linear address boundary.

This function is commonly used to determine if a diskette resides in a drive. To do this, the drive should first be reset with function 0, and then followed with a verify. To speed the result, specify only one sector to verify at track 0, sector 1, head 0.

Since the diskette motor may be off when the verify request is made, some older BIOSes return an error on each attempt to verify until the motor reaches proper speed. At least three retries should be made before an error is confirmed. Most newer BIOSes wait until the motor is up to speed, and then perform the operation.

Called with: ah = 4
al = number of sectors to verify, 1 to 36*
ch = track number, 0 to 79*
cl = sector number, 1 to 36*
* see media chart (Table 10-1) for limits
dh = head number, 0 or 1
dl = drive number, 0 to 3
es:bx = unused buffer (see text above)

Returns: ah = return status (see Table 10-3)
al = number of sectors actually verified (see warnings section)
carry = 0 successful, = 1 if error occurred

Int	Func	Description	Platform
13h	5	**Format Diskette Track**	All

Formats a track on the diskette drive. Each sector of data includes additional information for the controller, which is written with the format command. Some of this information can be specified by the user, such as the track number, head number, sector number, and sector size. In addition the controller writes various gaps, synchronization pulses, CRC bytes, and fills the sector data area with a "fill" byte. All PC BIOSes use F6h as the fill byte, but this can be changed by modifying the diskette parameter table.

The user information is supplied in a table pointed to by ES:BX. This address table contains one entry for each sector to be formatted. To format an 18-sector track requires 18 entries, each four bytes long. The address table has the following contents:

Byte	Description
0	Track number 0 to FFh
1	Head number 0 to FFh
2	Sector number 1 to FFh
3	Sector size: 0 = 128 bytes 1 = 256 bytes 2 = 512 bytes (standard used on all PC diskettes) 3 = 1,024 bytes 4 = 2,048 bytes (not supported on all systems) 5 = 4,096 bytes (not supported on all systems) 6 = 8,192 bytes (not supported on all systems or media) 7 = 16,384 bytes (not supported on all systems or media) 8 to FFh not valid

A DOS-compatible format uses the address table track, head and sector number matching the actual track, head, and sector number, with a 512 byte sector size. Some copy protection schemes change the one for one mapping or use nonstandard sector sizes. For example, it is perfectly allowable to format a track with different sector sizes on the same track, missing sectors, or even changing the sector numbering order.

One protection scheme writes the sectors in reverse order on one track of the diskette. By timing the duration to read a normal track and the "reversed" track and comparing the result, a program can establish if it is the original protected diskette. A operating system's disk copy does not see the odd ordering and will not transfer the "reversed" sector numbering, so a copy is easily detected.

Many drives allow more than one format. The 3.5" 2.88 MB drive supports 2.88 MB, 1.44 MB and 720 KB diskettes. Before formatting a diskette, the media type should be established. Function 18h, set media type for format, is used for this purpose. Function 18h returns error information if a problem exists for the intended operation. For older systems that do not support 3.5" drives, and do not support function 18h, function 17h should be used to set the media type. For very old systems, like the original PC, and most XT models, the BIOS cannot support multiple media type drives, and no extra steps are required to format a diskette on the 360 KB 5.25" drive.

Called with: ah = 5

al = number of sectors to format, 1 to 36* (typically set to the total sectors per track for the media)

ch = track number, 0 to 79*

* see media chart Table 10-1 for limits

dh = head number, 0 or 1
dl = drive number, 0 to 3
es:bx = pointer to address table (see text above)

Returns: ah = return status (see Table 10-3)
carry = 0 successful, = 1 if error occurred

Int	Func	Description	Platform
13h	**8**	**Read Diskette Drive Parameters**	**AT+**

Gets the drive parameter table pointer and data about the specified drive. The drive type is read from CMOS location 10h, and is used to return other information. Remember this data is *not* the limits of the media in the drive, but the maximum capability of the specified drive. See Code Sample 11-2, the DISKTEST program in Chapter 11, Hard Disk System, for a method to detect the current media type in a drive.

Called with: ah = 8
dl = drive number, 0 or 1

Returns: ah = return status (see Table 10-3)
carry = 0 successful, = 1 if error occurred
if successful and the drive type is known
al = 0
bh = 0
bl = drive type value from CMOS memory
0 = CMOS not present, CMOS checksum invalid, or battery dead.
1 = 360 KB, 5.25"
2 = 1.2 MB, 5.25"
3 = 720 KB, 3.5"
4 = 1.44 MB, 3.5" (when supported)
5 = 2.88 MB, 3.5" (when supported)
6 to FFh = unspecified (for future drives)
ch = maximum track number (see below for values)
cl = maximum sector number (see below for values)
dh = maximum head number (always 1)
dl = number of diskette drives installed (0 to 2, does not include drives not supported by BIOS)
es:di = pointer to the 11 byte diskette drive parameter table (see Table 10-2)
if successful, but requested drive is not installed:
ax = bx = cx = dh = es = 0

if successful, but the drive number is above 1, or the drive type is unknown when the CMOS information is unavailable:

ax = bx = cx = dx = es = 0

dl = number of diskette drives installed (0 to 2, does not include drives not supported by BIOS)

The maximum track number (zero based) and sector number (one based) for standard drives are:

Drive Type	Maximum Track #	Maximum Sector #	CX Return Value
360 KB, 5.25"	39	9	2709h
1.2 MB, 5.25"	79	15	4F0Fh
720 KB, 3.5"	79	9	4F0Fh
1.44 MB, 3.5"	79	18	4F12h
2.88 MB, 3.5"	79	36	4F24h

Int	Func	Description	Platform
13h	15h	Read Diskette Drive Type	AT+

INT
III I

Checks if the drive is currently available, and if the change line is supported. See interrupt 13h, function 16h for more about the change line. The 40 track drives for 360 KB diskettes never have a change line. Drives that have 80 tracks, such as 1.2 MB, 1.44 MB, and 2.88 MB all have a change line.

Called with: ah = 15h

dl = drive number, 0 or 1

Returns: if successful

ah = 0 Drive not present

1 drive present, does not support change line

2 drive present, supports change line

carry = 0

if failed

ah = 1, function not supported (i.e., PC/XT)

carry = 1

Int	Func	Description	Platform
13h	16h	Get Diskette Change Line Status	AT+

INT
III I

The 1.2 MB, 1.44 MB, and 2.88 MB drives detect when a diskette is removed and replaced. The change line is active when no diskette is present or if a new disk has been inserted, but the media type has not been checked yet. Once the media type is established, the change line is no longer active.

If the diskette drive type is unknown, function 15h should be called first to establish if the change line is supported for the drive.

Called with:	ah = 16h		
	dl = drive number, 0 to 3		
Returns:	if successful		
		ah = 0	change line not active
		1	invalid drive number (only 0 or 1 allowed)
		6	the change line is active or the change line is not supported
		80h	drive is not present
		carry = 0	
	if failed		
		ah = 1, function not supported (i.e. PC/XT)	
		carry = 1	

Int	Func	Description	Platform
13h	17h	Set Diskette Type For Format (old)	AT+

This function specifies the media type on some types of diskette drives. The diskette type is set prior to issuing the format function 5, but is unnecessary if the correct media type has already been set or the default type is acceptable. It is only used for 360 KB, 1.2 MB, and 720 KB drives. It is not used for 1.44 MB or 2.88 MB drives.

This function was replaced by a more flexible function 18h, which supports newer drive types. When available, function 18h should be used in place of this function.

Called with:	ah = 17h		
	al = 1		360 KB diskette in a 360 KB drive
		2	360 KB diskette in a 1.2 MB drive
		3	1.2 MB diskette in a 1.2 MB drive
		4	720 KB diskette in a 720 KB drive
		all other values invalid	
	dl = drive number, 0 or 1		
Returns:	ah = return status (see Table 10-3)		
	carry = 0 successful, = 1 if error occurred		

Int	Func	Description	Platform
13h	18h	Set Diskette Type For Format (new)	AT+

This function specifies the media type on all types of diskette drives. The diskette type is set prior to issuing the format function 5, but is unnecessary if the correct media type has already been set or the default type is acceptable. This can help format lower density diskettes on high capacity drives. For example, to format a 720 KB diskette on a 2.88 MB drive, CX is set to 4F0Fh, the value for a 720 KB diskette.

This function was not implemented on the very first AT BIOS, which does not support 1.44 MB drives. These older BIOSes require the use of the less flexible function 17h.

Called with: ah = 18h
ch = maximum track number for format (see below for values)
cl = maximum sector number for format (see below for values)
dl = drive number, 0 or 1

Returns: ah = return status (see Table 10-3)
es:di = pointer to the 11 byte diskette drive parameter table (see Table 10-2).
carry = 0 successful, = 1 if error occurred

The CX value to use is listed below to format a specific media type. If the system does not support the specified media, an error is returned.

Diskette to Format	Maximum Track #	Maximum Sector #	CX Value
360 KB, 5.25"	39	9	2709h
1.2 MB, 5.25"	79	15	4F0Fh
720 KB, 3.5"	79	9	4F0Fh
1.44 MB, 3.5"	79	18	4F12h
2.88 MB, 3.5"	79	36	4F24h

Diskette BIOS Data

The diskette BIOS (interrupt 13h) uses a number of bytes in the BIOS data area for its operations. Table 10-4 shows those data locations and functions. Additional details are covered in Chapter 6, BIOS Data and Other Fixed Data Areas.

Table 10-4. BIOS Data

Address	Size	Description
40:3Eh	byte	Recalibrate Status—If any bit 0 to 3 is set to zero the specified drive is uncalibrated and must be recalibrated before the next seek. The drive becomes uncalibrated after a system reset and whenever a new diskette is inserted into the drive. bit 7 = 1 Diskette interrupt occurred (int 0Eh) 6 = x Unused 5 = x Unused 4 = x Unused 3 = 0 Drive 3 uncalibrated (PC/XT only) 2 = 0 Drive 2 uncalibrated (PC/XT only) 1 = 0 Drive 1 uncalibrated 0 = 0 Drive 0 uncalibrated
40:3Fh	byte	Motor Status—State of diskette drive motors and operations bit 7 = 0 Current operation—Read or Verify, so no delay is necessary if turning motor on 1 Current operation—Write or Format that requires a short wait if turning the motor on (see offset AH in diskette parameter table) 6 = x Unused 5 = x | Drive select 4 = x | bit 5 bit 4 0 0 = drive 0 0 1 = drive 1 1 0 = drive 2 1 1 = drive 3 3 = 1 Drive 3 motor on 2 = 1 Drive 2 motor on 1 = 1 Drive 1 motor on 0 = 1 Drive 0 motor on
40:40h	byte	Motor Timeout—Counter for diskette motor inactivity timeout. Initial value is from diskette parameter table, offset 2.
40:41h	byte	Diskette controller return code from last operation (see Table 10-3).
40:42h	7 bytes	Diskette Controller result registers

Table 10-4. Continued

Address	Size	Description
40:8Bh	byte	Configuration Data—This byte holds the data transfer rate information for the diskette drive. Not all BIOSes save the last drive stepping rate. In this case, bits 4 and 5 may be unused on these systems.
		bit 7 = x, 6 = x — Last data rate sent to the controller
		bit 7 bit 6
		0 0 = 500K bits/s
		0 1 = 300K bits/s
		1 0 = 250K bits/s
		1 1 = Rate not set yet, or 1M bits/s on some systems
		5 = x, 4 = x — Last drive stepping rate sent to the controller
		bit 5 bit 4
		0 0 = 8 ms
		0 1 = 7 ms (typical)
		1 0 = 6 ms (typical)
		1 1 = 5 ms
		3 = x, 2 = x — Data rate set at the start of operation
		bit 3 bit 2
		0 0 = 500K bits/s
		0 1 = 300K bits/s
		1 0 = 250K bits/s
		1 1 = 1M bits/s (when supported)
		1 = x, 0 = x — Unused on most, unknown function on some clones
40:8Fh	byte	Diskette Controller Information
		bit 7 = x Unused
		6 = 1 Drive 1 type has been determined
		5 = 1 Drive 1 is multirate
		4 = 1 Drive 1 has diskette changed detection line
		3 = x Unused
		2 = 1 Drive 0 type has been determined
		1 = 1 Drive 0 is multirate
		0 = 1 Drive 0 has diskette changed detection line
40:90h	byte	Diskette 0—Media State
		bit 7 = x, 6 = x — Data transfer rate
		bit 7 bit 6
		0 0 = 500K bits/s
		0 1 = 300K bits/s
		1 0 = 250K bits/s
		1 1 = 1M bits/s (if supported)

Table 10-4. Continued

Address	Size	Description				
		5 = 1	Double stepping required (1.2 MB drive with 360 KB diskette)			
		4 = 1	Known media in diskette drive			
		3 = 0	Unused			
		2 = x	Determination of last access			
		1 = x	bit 2	bit 1	bit 0	
		0 = x	0	0	0 =	Trying 360 KB media in 360 KB drive
			0	0	1 =	Trying 360 KB media in 1.2 MB drive
			0	1	0 =	Trying 1.2 MB media in 1.2 MB drive
			0	1	1 =	Known 360 KB media in 360 KB drive
			1	0	0 =	Known 360 KB media in 1.2 MB drive
			1	0	1 =	Known 1.2 MB media in 1.2 MB drive
			1	1	0 =	unused state
			1	1	1 =	720 KB media in 720 KB drive or 1.44 MB media in 1.44 MB drive
40:91h	byte	Diskette 1—Media State (see 40:90h)				
40:92h	byte	Diskette 0—Operational Starting State				
		bit 7 = x	Data transfer rate			
		6 = x	bit 7	bit 6		
			0	0 = 500K bits/s		
			0	1 = 300K bits/s		
			1	0 = 250K bits/s		
			1	1 = 1M bits/s		
		5 = x	Unknown function			
		4 = x	Unknown function			
		3 = 0	Unused			
		2 = 1	Drive type has been determined			
		1 = 1	Drive is multirate			
		0 = 1	Drive has diskette changed detection line			
40:93h	byte	Diskette 1—Operational Starting State (see 40:92h)				
40:94h	byte	Diskette 0—Current Cylinder—This byte holds the current cylinder that drive 0 is positioned on.				
40:95h	byte	Diskette 1—Current Cylinder—This byte holds the current cylinder that drive 1 is positioned on.				

Common Diskette Controller Parts

These are some of the common diskette controller parts used in systems over the last 10 years. All of these controllers are based on the 765 controller, used in the first IBM PC. From a software view, all the parts function the same as the original 765, but may offer additional enhancements or additional commands.

765 (NEC uPD765A) This IC (or a 100% compatible part) is used on many diskette adapter cards. Several manufacturers have produced functionally identical ICs. The 765 has 15 commands used to read, write, and format diskettes.

72065A (NEC uPD72065A) This is similar to the original 765 with a few hardware enhancements and three additional commands for power standby control and reset.

72065B (NEC uPD72065B) The B version adds one new command to determine which chip version is present. Otherwise functionally identical to the 72065A.

8272 (Intel 8272A) Functionally identical to 765.

82077 (Intel 82077AA) One of the newest ICs that combines all the logic necessary for a complete PC compatible diskette controller. The 82077 adds a number of enhancements over older controllers, including an FIFO mode for input and output data, and support for 2.88 MB drives. The 82077 has 8 new commands over the 765/8272 design.

82078 (Intel 82078) Provides all features of Intel's 82077. In addition the 82078 offers the option of 2 Mbps data rate for tape drives, new commands for faster operation, and hardware media and drive type identification.

Sending Commands to the Diskette Controller

The diskette controller has an extensive list of commands to perform various actions, such as formatting a track or reading a sector. These commands are typically followed with information bytes such as starting track and sector. Once the command is accepted, the controller performs the action. In most cases, after the command execution has completed, the controller returns a number of status bytes. Depending on the command the controller may also issue IRQ 6 (interrupt Eh) to signal the completion of the task. This entire process is coordinated by two bits in the Main Status register.

The process is begun by reading the data transfer mode from the Main Status register, at port 3F4h. When bits 7 and 6 become 1 and 0 respectively, a command is ready to be written to the controller. The command byte is sent to the data register, port 3F5h. The Main Status register is monitored to detect when the diskette controller is ready for each successive parameter byte as may be specified by the command. When all the parameters have been accepted, the controller proceeds to execute the command.

During command execution, if data is read or written, the Main Status register does not need to be checked. Data is read or written through the data register, port 3F5h. For DMA operations that are normally used in diskette data reads and writes, the data is transferred as previously set up through the DMA controller.

When the execution phase is complete, successful or not, most commands provide result information. Again the Main Status register is checked before reading each result byte. In this case, one result byte is ready to be read when both bits 7 and 6 become "1." The byte is read from the controller data port 3F5h. When the status bytes have all been read, and the command's operation complete, the Main Status register will indicate it is ready for the next command.

Refer to port 3F5h later in this chapter for commands, parameters, and result information.

Warnings

Operating the diskette controller is one of the most complex actions a program performs in directly accessing the hardware. If at all possible, interrupt 13h BIOS services should be used as the interface, as the BIOS deals with a number of subtle differences between the different PC platforms.

BIOS Sector Limits

In general the BIOS only supports a maximum data transfer of two tracks of data at one time. For the highest reliability I recommend never reading more than one track at a time.

In all cases, reading a track worth of data assumes the first sector is at the start of side 0. For reading two tracks in one operation the controller will read the sectors from side 0, and if necessary, switch the head to side 1 to read additional sectors. This means you *must* know exactly where the data is relative to the physical track and head. In addition the media of the diskette can be different than the drive type. When a 2.88 MB drive reads a track, it reads a total of 36 sectors. If that same 2.88 MB drive is used to read a tracks from a 720 KB diskette, only 9 sectors can be read at one time. This is important to know since there is no BIOS service to tell the current media type, but only the drive type.

The program DISKTEST, described in the Chapter 11, Hard Disk System, determines the diskette media type and tests the number of sectors that can reliably be read at one time. In my tests, most systems will correctly read up to two tracks of data at a time. A few systems failed to correctly transfer more than one track in one operation.

DISKTEST also shows the AL return value after the read operation. All systems show the number of sectors transferred, but some BIOSes will return a value limited to the maximum number of sectors per one track. This means if two tracks are read, the AL return value may incorrectly indicate only one track was read.

Transferring Data Across the 64 KB Boundary Problem

When transferring data to or from the diskette (functions 2 and 3), it is critical that the buffer area does not cross a 64 KB *physical* boundary. Using a low offset value in the BX register does not assure you will not cross a boundary. You must look at the ES value. For example, a buffer at ES:BX of 1FFF:0 will fail to work on most systems. In this example, after the first 16 bytes are handled, the data will appear on the next physical 64 KB section of memory. Most programs are designed to be relocatable, which requires that you add specific code to find a suitable place for your diskette buffer memory. This problem is one of the most common mistakes novice programmers make when using diskette services, since it will appear to work on many systems. If you are using a disk cache program, the disk cache (if written correctly) will shield you from seeing this problem.

Software Timing Problems

Older diskette subsystems are probably the most unstable portion of the PC. This is due in part to a number of timing loops implemented in software by the BIOS. The diskette BIOS code should be matched to the CPU and CPU speed, but many clones and system alterations cause BIOS software timing loops to become too short. For example, if the BIOS code is written for an 80486, 33 MHz, and the BIOS were run on a 100 MHz part, all of the software timing loops would run in about one third of normal time. This will often result in failures to read or write data and inappropriate timeouts. Another common problem is BIOS shadowing. This is the ability of the system or memory manager to copy the slow 8-bit wide system BIOS ROM into 32-bit-wide fast RAM. This could mean timing loops will execute much faster, depending on how they are coded. This is less of a problem for newer systems with larger prefetch queues, as provided in the 80486 and later CPUs, and systems with on-board memory caches.

Timing is controlled through three approaches. The most stable approach is using the system timer, interrupt 8 (see Chapter 16, System Timers). A countdown software loop is commonly used for shorter time periods. The loop cycles a preset number of times. In these cases the timing is entirely dependent on how fast each instruction in the loop takes for the given CPU and CPU speed. A much shorter delay is created by a simple short jump to the next instruction (jmp short $+2). Table 10-5 shows major functions within the diskette BIOS handler that rely on timing for various functions.

Table 10-5. Timed Functions Within Most Diskette BIOS Handlers

Function	Timing	Typical Delay
Time for motor to reach normal speed from off (write operation only)	software loop	500 milliseconds
Duration of motor on until off without additional diskette access	int 8	2 seconds
Time to wait for response from diskette controller	software loop	500 milliseconds
Head settling time after seek to track	software loop	25 milliseconds
Time to wait for diskette controller operation complete interrupt	software loop	2 seconds
Duration between successive I/O operations to controller	software jump	0.5 microseconds

Some newer systems use a clever approach to create reliable short timing loops. The refresh bit 4 in port 61h toggles on every other DRAM refresh cycle. This refresh bit can be counted to create short timing loops unaffected by CPU speed. Unfortunately, there is no standard for the duration of the refresh timing cycle, so it may only be useful to a BIOS designer for a specific motherboard.

Code Sample 10-1. Diskette Drive Detection

This routine checks if a specified diskette drive is attached, and determines its maximum capacity. The program works in systems having up to four diskette drives, using a single card diskette controller card. Of course the AT/EISA/MCA BIOS only supports two diskette drives, but a four-drive controller with its own BIOS will allow up to four drives on these systems.

The routine is included as a subroutine in SYSTYPE.ASM. Run SYSTYPE to see the results of DISKTYPE on the four possible diskette drives in a system.

```
;-------------------------------------------------------------------
;    DISKETTE DRIVE TYPE DETECTION SUBROUTINE
;        Determine the type of diskette drive
;
;        Called with:    dl = drive to check (0=a:, 1=b:, etc.)
;
;         Returns:        al = drive type
;                                0 = no drive
;                                1 = 360 KB
;                                2 = 1.2 MB
;                                3 = 720 KB
;                                4 = 1.44 MB
;                                5 = 2.88 MB
;                                6 = 320 KB  (obsolete)
;                                7 = unknown type
;
;        Regs used:      ax
```

```
dsktype proc    near
        push    bx
        push    cx
        push    dx
        push    es

        int     11h                 ; equipment check
        test    ax, 1               ; any drives ?
        jz      dskt_none           ; jump if not
        and     al, 0C0h            ; get # of drives bits
        mov     cl, 2
        rol     al, cl              ; convert to # of drives
        cmp     al, dl              ; is drive available ?
        jb      dskt_none           ; jump if not

; first we'll try getting the drive parameters from the BIOS

        mov     ah, 8
        int     13h                 ; get drive parameters
        jc      dskt_skp1           ; jump if failed
        mov     al, bl              ; get drive type
        cmp     al, 5               ; unknown type if >> 5
        jbe     dskt_done
        mov     al, 7               ; set to unknown type
        jmp     dskt_done

; Older systems can't supply drive info, so use diskette table.
;   First the drive is reset. This forces systems that change
;   the diskette parameter pointer for different drive types
;   to update the pointer to the correct drive type. Interrupt
;   vector 1Eh now points to the correct diskette parameter
;   table. Only 360 KB and 1.2 MB drives should get here.
```

```
dskt_skp1:
        xor     ah, ah
        int     13h                 ; reset drive
        xor     ax, ax
        mov     es, ax
        mov     bx, es:[1Eh*4]      ; get offset of table
        mov     ax, es:[1Eh*4+2]    ; get segment of table
        mov     es, ax              ; es:bx points to table
        mov     ah, es:[bx+4]       ; get sectors per track
        mov     al, 1               ; assume 360 KB
        cmp     ah, 9               ; 9 sectors per track ?
        je      dskt_done           ; jump if so
        inc     al
        cmp     ah, 15              ; 15 sectors per track
        je      dskt_done           ; jump if so
        mov     al, 6               ; unknown type
        cmp     ah, 8               ; 8 sectors per track
        je      dskt_done           ; jump if so
        inc     al                  ; al=7, unknown type
        jmp     dskt_done

dskt_none:
        xor     al, al
dskt_done:
        pop     es
        pop     dx
        pop     cx
        pop     bx
        ret
dsktype endp
```

Port Summary

This is a list of ports used to control the diskette controller. Note that registers supported will vary by platform as noted.

Port	Type	Function	Platform
3F0h	Input	Diskette Controller Status Register A	PS/2
3F1h	Input	Diskette Controller Diagnostic Register	Limited
3F1h	Input	Diskette Controller Status Register B	PS/2
3F2h	I/O	Diskette Controller Digital Output Register	All
3F3h	I/O	Diskette Controller Tape Drive Register	Limited
3F3h	Input	Diskette Controller Drive Status Register	PS/2
3F4h	Input	Diskette Controller Main Status Register	All
3F4h	Output	Diskette Controller Data Rate Select Register	None
3F5h	I/O	Diskette Controller Data	All
3F6h	I/O	Diskette Controller Reserved	All
3F7h	Input	Diskette Controller Digital Input Register	AT+
3F7h	Output	Diskette Controller Configuration Control Register	AT+

Port Detail

Port	Type	Description	Platform
3F0h	Input	Diskette Controller Status Register A	PS/2

This register returns the state of the interrupt pin from the controller and the current status on various drive cable lines. It is only supported on PS/2 products and its functions and states differ between MCA and AT type PS/2 machines. This register is not supported on AT or ISA compatible systems.

PS/2 MCA Bus Only

Inputs from the diskette drive cable will reflect the states from the attached diskette drive. The outputs to the diskette drive, Interrupt pending, Step, Head select, and Direction will all be zero after a hardware reset.

Input (bits 0-7)

bit	7 r	= 1	Interrupt Pending—Tracks the current state of the interrupt request line from the controller
	6 r	= 0	Second diskette drive attached (input from diskette cable)
	5 r	= 1	Step—Monitors the current state of the STEP line output to the diskette cable

4 r	= 0	The diskette drive indicates the head is currently on track 0 (input from diskette cable)
3 r	= 0	Head 0 is selected on the cable (diskette side 0)
	1	Head 1 is selected on the cable (diskette side 1)
2 r	= 0	The diskette drive indicates it is at the beginning of the track (input from diskette cable)
1 r	= 0	The diskette drive indicates the diskette is write protected (input from diskette cable)
0 r	= 0	Out direction—The head moves from the center of the diskette towards the outside edge
	1	In direction—The head moves from the outer edge towards the center.

PS/2 AT Bus Only (i.e., model 30 and others)

Inputs from the diskette drive cable will reflect the states from the attached diskette drive. The outputs to the diskette drive, Interrupt pending, DMA request, and Step Flip/Flop will all read zero after a hardware reset. Head select and direction bits will both read high after a hardware reset.

Input (bits 0-7)

bit	7 r	= 1	Interrupt Pending—Tracks the current state of the interrupt request line from the controller
	6 r	= 1	DMA request—Tracks the current state of the DMA request line from the controller
	5 r	= 1	Step Flip/Flop is set when the STEP output line goes active. It is reset when the Digital Input Register is read (Port 3F7h) or a hardware or software reset occurs.
	4 r	= 1	The diskette drive indicates the head is currently on track 0 (input from diskette cable)
	3 r	= 0	Head 1 is selected on the cable (diskette side 1)
		1	Head 0 is selected on the cable (diskette side 0)
	2 r	= 1	The diskette drive indicates it is at the beginning of the track (input from diskette cable)
	1 r	= 1	The diskette drive indicates the diskette is write protected (input from diskette cable)
	0 r	= 0	In direction—The head moves from the outer edge toward the center.
		1	Out direction—The head moves from the center of the diskette toward the outside edge

Port	Type	Description	Platform
3F1h	Input	Diskette Controller Diagnostic Register	Limited

This register is used on a few adapter cards to indicate if the controller accepts more than one drive type. This was the first mechanism to allow both a 360 KB and 1.2 MB drive to be used on the same system. This register is supported on early AT systems and some clones.

Input (bits 0-7)

bit	7 r = x	Adapter type
	6 r = x	01010 = supports multiple drive types (360 KB and 1.2 MB)
	5 r = x	
	4 r = x	
	3 r = x	
	2 r = x	Unknown or unused
	1 r = x	Unknown or unused
	0 r = x	Unknown or unused

Port	Type	Description	Platform
3F1h	Input	Diskette Controller Status Register B	PS/2

This register returns the current status of diskette controller outputs and inputs on various drive cable lines. It is only supported on PS/2 products and its functions and states differ between MCA and AT type PS/2 machines. This register is not supported by ISA or EISA compatible systems.

PS/2 MCA Bus Only

A software or hardware reset clears the Read and Write flip/flop bits. A hardware reset will also clear the drive select and motor select bits.

Input (bits 0-7)

bit	7 r = 1	Fixed at 1
	6 r = 1	Fixed at 1
	5 r = 1	Drive 0 selected—Monitors the controller's output Drive A select line
	4 r = x	Write data Flip/Flop—Toggles with each data write to the diskette drive
	3 r = x	Read data Flip/Flop—Toggles with each data write to the diskette drive
	2 r = 1	Write enable—State of the write enable output line

	1 r = 1	Drive 1 motor enabled—State of the drive 1 motor enable output line
	0 r = 1	Drive 0 motor enabled—State of the drive 0 motor enable output line

PS/2 AT Bus Only (i.e., model 30 and others)

A software or hardware reset clears the Read, Write and Write enable flip/flop bits. A read from the Digital Input Register (Port 3F7h) also resets these flip/flop bits.

Input (bits 0-7)

bit	7 r = 0	Second diskette drive attached (input from diskette cable)
	6 r = 0	Drive 1 selected—Monitors the controller's output Drive 1 select line (inverted)
	5 r = 0	Drive 0 selected—Monitors the controller's output Drive 0 select line (inverted)
	4 r = x	Write data Flip/Flop—Set on the active going edge of the data write line output to the diskette drive
	3 r = x	Read data Flip/Flop—Set on the active going edge of the data read line output to the diskette drive
	2 r = 1	Write enable Flip/Flop—Set on the active going edge of the write enable line
	1 r = 0	Drive 3 selected—Monitors the controller's output Drive 3 select line (inverted, may appear as different drive letter to system)
	0 r = 0	Drive 2 selected—Monitors the controller's output Drive 2 select line (inverted, may appear as different drive letter to system)

Port	Type	Description	Platform
3F2h	I/O	Diskette Controller Digital Output Register	All

This register controls the drive selection, drive motors, and DMA operation. Most adapter cards only support drives 0 and 1 (A: and B:). In this case, drive outputs 3 and 4 from the diskette controller chip are not connected and perform no function. Normally a drive is selected and its motor is turned on at the same time.

When a drive is selected, software must delay the head load time before a read or write is made. This is the time interval between the head first contacting the diskette and the first rear or write occurring. This delay avoids read and write problems when the head bounces after contacting the diskette. On the original PC with the obsolete 320 KB diskette drive, the head load time was 35 ms. With current drives, 8 ms or less is sufficient. The actual head load time is specified in the diskette parameter table, byte 1.

I/O (bits 0-7)

bit	7 r/w = 1	Motor on, drive 3 *
	6 r/w = 1	Motor on, drive 2 *
	5 r/w = 1	Motor on, drive 1
	4 r/w = 1	Motor on, drive 0
	3 r/w = 0	DMA & Interrupt capabilities disabled—inhibits the hardware DMA request line to the system, and ignores DMA acknowledge and Terminal Count inputs from the system. Also disables the interrupt request to the system. DMA and interrupt capabilities are always enabled on a PS/2 MCA system, and this bit may be ignored.
	1	DMA & Interrupt capabilities enabled (proper setting for all PS/2 MCA systems).
	2 r/w = 0	Software reset of the diskette controller and internal FIFO. The controller remains in reset mode until this bit is set to 1. This bit is cleared by a hardware reset and remains in reset mode until the bit is set by software to 1.
	1	Normal operation
	1 r/w = x	Drive select
	0 r/w = x	

bit 1	bit 0	
0	0	= Select drive 0
0	1	= Select drive 1
1	0	= Select drive 2 *
1	1	= Select drive 3 *

**May not be supported*

Port	Type	Description	Platform
3F3h	I/O	Diskette Controller Tape Drive Register	Limited

Some diskette controllers provide the ability to support one tape drive attached to the diskette drive cable. This register is used to select which drive (1 to 3), is associated with the tape drive. It is not supported on most diskette adapter controllers.

Drive 0 is always reserved for a diskette boot drive, and cannot be assigned to a tape drive.

I/O (bits 0-1)

bit	7 r = x	unused, tristated so any value can appear
	6 r = x	unused, tristated so any value can appear
	5 r = x	unused, tristated so any value can appear

4 r = x	unused, tristated so any value can appear	
3 r = x	unused, tristated so any value can appear	
2 r = x	unused, tristated so any value can appear	
1 r/w = x	Drive select	
0 r/w = x	bit 1	bit 0
	0	0 = No tape drive
	0	1 = Drive 1 is a tape drive
	1	0 = Drive 2 is a tape drive
	1	1 = Drive 3 is a tape drive

Port	Type	Description	Platform
3F3h	Input	Diskette Controller Drive Status Register	PS/2

Newer PS/2 systems support this status information register. The Drive Status Register indicates the diskette media type and drive capability. This extra status information makes PS/2s equipped with a 2.88 MB drive operate far more reliably and quickly than most other approaches I've seen. The key is having the drive indicate the type of media. On most other machines, the 2.88 MB vs. 1.44 MB line is disconnected or not available, requiring a slow software check to determine which kind of diskette is currently in the drive.

Input (bits 0-1)

bit 7 r = x	Media type from drive (valid only if a drive is selected)	
6 r = x	bit 7	bit 6
	0	0 = undefined (should not occur)
	0	1 = 2.88 MB diskette media
	1	0 = 1.44 MB diskette media
	1	1 = 720 KB diskette media
5 r = x	Drive type (valid only if a drive is selected)	
4 r = x	bit 5	bit 4
	0	0 = 1.44 MB, 3.5"
	0	1 = 2.88 MB, 3.5"
	1	0 = 1.2 MB, 5.25"
	1	1 = undefined (should not occur)
3 r = x	Drive to use for booting	
2 r = x	bit 3	bit 2
	0	0 = diskette drive 0
	0	1 = diskette drive 1

1	0	= diskette drive 2 (if supported)
1	1	= undefined (should not occur)

1 r = x unused or unknown function

0 r = x unused or unknown function

Port	Type	Description	Platform
3F4h	Input	Diskette Controller Main Status Register	All

This read-only register shows the current status of the controller and commands sent to the controller. The data transfer mode bit must be checked to load command bytes and get status bytes from the controller. When no access is permitted, the BIOS must go into a loop checking this register until the controller is ready to allow additional writes or reads through port 3F5h.

Input (bits 0-7)

bit		
7 r = x 6 r = x	Data transfer mode (using Port 3F5h) bit 7 bit 6 0 0 = No access is permitted 0 1 = No access is permitted 1 0 = data ready to be written 1 1 = data ready to be read	
5 r = 1	Execute phase of command in progress (non-DMA mode only)	
4 r = 1	A read or write command is in progress	
3 r = 1	Drive 3 busy * **	
2 r = 1	Drive 2 busy * **	
1 r = 1	Drive 1 busy *	
0 r = 1	Drive 0 busy *	

**Diskette drive is in the seek or recalibrate portion of command*
***May not be supported*

Port	Type	Description	Platform
3F4h	Output	Diskette Controller Data Rate Select Register	Limited

This write-only register is primarily used to set the data rate. It is not supported on most diskette controllers. The register also controls an alternate reset and power down mode and write precompensation. To set the data rate for 2.88 MB media, the value 3 is written to this register, assuming the controller supports the new 1 Mbps data rate.

With the PC family, the default write precompensation values are normally used. Write precompensation is the technique used to adjust for a phenomena with magnetic media that "shift" some bit patterns. When these data patterns are detected, the controller shifts the timing of a bit slightly faster or slower to compensate for the phenomena. Once the precompensated data is written, the data is read normally.

A software reset does not change the current data rate or write precompensation values. A hardware reset sets the data rate to 250 Kbps and the write precompensation to 125 ns.

This register is valid on PS/2 systems, although IBM does not define bits 5 through 7. On older PS/2s, a data rate select of 300 Kbps is not supported. The 300 Kbps data rate is required to read a 360 KB diskette in a 1.2 MB drive.

Output (bits 0-7)

bit 7	w = 0	Normal
	1	Software reset—Bit is automatically set to normal (0) after a reset cycle, unlike the Digital Output Register, which remains in reset mode.
6	w = 0	Normal
	1	Power down mode, drive outputs are tristated and the internal oscillator is shut down. A software or hardware reset returns the system to normal.
5	w = 0	Use internal Phase-Lock-Loop (normal)
	1	External Phase-Lock-Loop (requires external hardware and is never used in PC diskette controller designs)
4	w = x	Write Precompensation
3	w = x	
2	w = x	

bit 4	bit 3bit 2	
0	00	= Use default (see bits 0 & 1)
0	01	= 41.67 ns
0	10	= 83.34 ns
0	11	= 125.00 ns
1	00	= 166.67 ns
1	01	= 208.33 ns
1	10	= 250.00 ns
1	11	= 0 (no precompensation)

1	w = x	Data rate select
0	w = x	

bit 1	bit 0	Rate	Default Write Precompensation
0	0 =	500 Kbps	125 ns
0	1 =	300 Kbps	125 ns
1	0 =	250 Kbps	125 ns
1	1 =	1 Mbps*	41.67 ns

* *1 Mbps not supported on all controllers*

Port	Type	Description	Platform
3F5h	I/O	Diskette Controller Data	All

All disk data transfers and command parameters are sent through this port. Controllers with FIFO support and the FIFO mode active will send data through the diskette controller's 16 byte FIFO. The Main status register, Port 3F4h, bits 6 and 7, are monitored by software to regulate reads and writes.

Standard Command Parameters and Status

Most commands require the same parameters be loaded after the command, and return the same set of status bytes when the execution phase is complete. The standard parameters are shown in Table 10-6 and the standard status results are shown in Table 10-7.

Table 10-6. Standard Parameters (output to controller)

Byte 0: Command (see Command Summary)
Byte 1: Drive select and head select byte

bit 7 = 0	unused or Enable count off		
1	Enable count on (valid only on Verify command)		
6 = 0	unused		
5 = 0	unused		
4 = 0	unused		
3 = 0	unused		
2 = x	Head number (0=side 0, 1=side 1)		
1 = x	Drive select		
0 = x	bit 1	bit 0	
	0	0 =	Select drive 0
	0	1 =	Select drive 1
	1	0 =	Select drive 2 (may not be supported)
	1	1 =	Select drive 3 (may not be supported)

Byte 2: Cylinder number—Track numbers are the same as the cylinder number (0 to 79 depending on media).
Byte 3: Head number byte (0=side 0, 1=side 1)
Byte 4: Sector byte for action, or first sector byte if multisector operation (1 to 37 depending on media)
Byte 5: Sector size code byte (normally 2)

0 = 128 bytes
1 = 256 bytes
2 = 512 bytes (standard used on all PC family diskettes)
3 = 1,024 bytes
4 = 2,048 bytes (not possible on all media)
5 = 4,096 bytes (not possible on all media)

Table 10-6. Continued

6 = 8,192 bytes (not possible on all media)
7 = 16,384 bytes (not possible on all media, not supported on some controllers)
8 to FFh not valid

Byte 6: End of track byte—The last sector number possible on a track (see media chart, Table 10-1)

Byte 7: Gap length between sectors byte (from diskette parameter block) 5.25" 360 KB and 1.2 MB media uses a gap length value of 2Ah. The 3.5" 720 KB to 2.88 MB media all use a gap length value of 1Bh. Sector sizes other than the standard 512 byte size requires different gap length values.

Byte 8: Custom sector size byte—unused on all PC family systems, and should be set to FFh. If the sector size value was set to 0, this byte controls the number of bytes, 1 to 255.

Table 10-7. Standard Status Results (input from controller)

Byte 0: Status register 0

bit 7 = x | Interrupt code
6 = x |

bit 7	bit 6	
0	0 =	Normal termination, no errors
0	1 =	Abnormal termination, execution started but did not complete
1	0 =	Invalid command attempted
1	1 =	Abnormal termination due to the drive's ready line changing (since the drive ready line is permanently tied high, this error can't occur)

5 = 1 Seek End—A seek or recalibrate command completed, or a read or write with an implied seek completed.
4 = 1 Equipment check—The drive did not signal detection of track 0 during a recalibrate command, or a relative seek command attempted to move to a negative track number (i.e., attempted to step outward past track 0)
3 = 0 Ready status (permanently set to 0)
2 = x Current head number (0=side 0, 1=side 1)
1 = x | Current drive select
0 = x |

bit 1	bit 0	
0	0 =	Select drive 0
0	1 =	Select drive 1
1	0 =	Select drive 2 (may not be supported)
1	1 =	Select drive 3 (may not be supported)

Table 10-7. Continued

Byte 1: Status register 1

bit	7 = 1	Sector past end of track error—An attempt was made to access sector a sector past the final sector on the track.
	6 = 0	Unused
	5 = 1	Data error—A CRC error was detected in the ID field or data field of a sector.
	4 = 1	Overrun or Underrun error—The CPU or DMA transferred the data too fast or slow, such that at least one byte was lost.
	3 = 0	Unused
	2 = 1	No data error—While attempting to Read data or Read deleted data, the controller could not find the specified sector. The No data error also occurs if the Read ID command cannot read the ID without an error. A Read track command that cannot find the correct sector sequence will also generate this error.
	1 = 1	Write protect error—The write protect line is active while attempting to execute a Write data, Write deleted data, or a Format track command.
	0 = 1	Missing address mark error—Two index pulses occurred from the drive (i.e., at least one full diskette revolution) without finding the ID address mark at the specified track. This error also occurs if the controller cannot detect a data address or deleted data address mark on the specified track.

Byte 2: Status register 2

bit	7 = 0	Unused
	6 = 1	Control mark error—While expecting a specific data type (Read data or Read deleted data) the opposite type of data address mark was detected. If a normal Read data command was issued, a Deleted data address mark was encountered. If a Read Deleted data command was issued, a non-deleted data address mark was encountered.
	5 = 1	Data CRC error—The controller detected a CRC error in the data field of the sector.
	4 = 1	Wrong Cylinder—The track address maintained in the controller fails to match the track number in the sector ID field. This error condition also sets Status register 1, bit 2 to the value 1.
	3 = 0	Unused (except Scan commands—see scan command)
	2 = 0	Unused (except Scan commands—see scan command)
	1 = 1	Bad Cylinder—Same condition as wrong cylinder above, but the track number in the sector ID is FFh, indicating the cylinder has been previously marked as defective and has hard errors. This error condition also sets Status register 1, bit 2 on.
	0 = 1	Missing address mark—Immediately prior to the actual stored data of the sector, an address mark byte is stored. The address mark can only have one of two values 0F8h, or 0FEh, indicating either normal data follows, or delete data follows. This error occurs when neither of these values is detected.

Table 10-7. Continued

Byte 3: Cylinder number at completion—Track numbers are the same as the cylinder number (0 to 79 depending on media).
Byte 4: Head number at completion (0=side 0, 1=side 1)
Byte 5: Sector at completion (1 to 37 depending on media)
Byte 6: Sector size code at completion (see standard parameters byte 5 for sector size codes, 2 = 512 bytes)

Port 3F5h Command Summary

There are a number of possible commands for the diskette controller, but only those necessary to program the controller are shown. Some of the omitted commands are for very low-density, obsolete disk formats never used in any PC family system. Other omitted commands are duplicates of the commands listed, but provide reduced performance without any benefit. The description will note those commands that are never used by the BIOS diskette service routines, but that could still be useful.

Commands that are only available on enhanced controllers are indicated with Enhanced and are unavailable on standard diskette controllers. Use the version command 10h to detect an enhanced controller. Even though the version command itself is an Enhanced command, the status returned for a normal controller will be valid. The controller returns 80h in the result byte for all invalid commands.

Hex Value	Description	Controller
3	Specify	All
4	Sense Drive Status	All
7	Recalibrate	All
8	Sense Interrupt Status	All
E	Dump Registers	Enhanced
F	Seek	All
10	Version	All
12	Perpendicular 2.88 MB Mode	Enhanced
13	Configure	Enhanced
14	Unlock FIFO Functions	Enhanced
34	Exit Standby Mode	72065 only
35	Go to Standby Mode	72065 only
36	Hard Reset	72065 only
42	Read Track	All
4A	Read ID	All
4D	Format Track	All
8F	Relative Seek Outward	Enhanced
94	Lock FIFO Functions	Enhanced
C5	Write Data	All
C6	Read Normal and Deleted Data	All

Hex Value	Description	Controller
C9	Write Deleted Data	All
CC	Read Deleted Data	All
CF	Relative Seek Inward	Enhanced
D1	Scan Equal All	All
D6	Verify	Enhanced
E6	Read Normal Data	All
F1	Scan Equal	All
F6	Verify	Enhanced

Command Detail

Command	Description	Port
3h	Specify	3F5h

This command loads three internal timers of the controller and selects normal DMA mode or non-DMA mode. Every PC system I've ever seen uses DMA for the diskette system. The range of the timing values automatically gets shorter with faster data rates. This means one value will often work for more than one media type.

Step Rate Timer

The step rate timer controls the time interval between steps for the track stepping motor. The step rate nibble selects a time that depends on the data rate selection. The shortest interval occurs with the value Fh, and the longest interval with 0. Most systems use the value Ah for 1.44 MB and 2.88 MB drives, and value Dh for all others.

Selected data rate:	1 Mbps	500 Kbps	300 Kps	250 Kbps
media for rate:	2.88 MB	1.44 MB/1.2 MB	360 KB*	720 KB/360 KB
	step rate (ms)			
value 0	8.0	16	26.7	32 (longest delay)
value 1	7.5	15	25.0	30
:				
value A	3.0	6	10.0	12
value B	2.5	5	8.33	10
value C	2.0	4	6.67	8
value D	1.5	3	5.0	6
value E	1.0	2	3.33	4
value F	0.5	1	1.67	2 (shortest delay)

* *360 KB media in 1.2 MB drive*

Head Unload Timer

The head unload time is the time interval to wait after the completion of a read/write command and for the controller to remove the diskette heads from the media. This interval is set so the head can remain on the media during successive sector reads and writes, but unloads the head when no immediate activity is occurring to save both media and head wear. The shortest time is with value 1, increasing through value F, and value 0 being the longest delay.

Most systems use the value F, except for the PS/2, which uses the value 1. I see no reason why most BIOS manufacturers choose such long unload times, when the standard load times are so short. The performance effect appears minimal. I can only assume they stick with the values IBM set in the original PC/XT/AT.

Selected data rate:	1 Mbps	500 Kbps	300 Kps	250 Kbps
media for rate:	2.88 MB	1.44 MB/1.2 MB	360 KB*	720 KB/360 KB
	head unload time (ms)			
value 0	128	256	426	512 (longest delay)
value 1	8	16	26.7	32 (shortest delay)
:				
value E	112	224	373	448
value F	120	240	400	480

** 360 KB media in 1.2 MB drive*

The Head Load Timer

The head load time is the interval between the head being loaded (i.e., contacting the diskette) and the first read or write occurring. This delay is required, since the head bounces when first loaded for a short period. Reads or writes during this period will have erroneous data. The delay is normally set to a value of 1 or 2 in most systems.

Selected data rate:	1 Mbps	500 Kbps	300 Kps	250 Kbps
media for rate:	2.88 MB	1.44 MB/1.2 MB	360 KB*	720 KB/360 KB
	head load time (ms)			
value 0	128	256	426	512 (longest delay)
value 1	1	2	3.3	4 (shortest delay)
value 2	2	4	6.7	8
value 3	3	6	10.0	12
:				
value 7Fh	127	254	423	308

** 360 KB media in 1.2 MB drive*

Command byte 0 = 3

byte 1	bit	7 = x	Step rate time (0-Fh)
		6 = x	see above for timing values
		5 = x	
		4 = x	
		3 = x	Head unload time (0-Fh)
		2 = x	
		1 = x	
		0 = x	
byte 2	bit	7 = x	Head load time (0-7Fh)
		6 = x	
		5 = x	
		4 = x	
		3 = x	
		2 = x	
		1 = x	
		0 = 0	DMA mode (normal selection)
		1	non-DMA mode

Execution—The specified parameters are loaded

Result—No result bytes, no interrupt

Command	Description	Port
4h	Sense Drive Status	3F5h

Gets the current status for the specified drive. This includes the current state of several lines from the diskette drive, and the head and drive select lines to the drive.

Command byte 0 = 4

byte 1 = Drive select and head select byte (see standard parameters in Table 10-6)

Execution—Get status

Result—No interrupt

byte 0 = Status Register 3

bit	7 = 0	No drive fault (permanently tied to 0 on all systems)
	6 = 1	Write protected diskette (from drive)
	5 = 1	Drive ready (permanently tied to 1 on all systems)
	4 = 1	Head is on track 0 (from drive)
	3 = 1	Two-sided (permanently tied to 1 on all systems)
	2 = 0	Head select, side 0 (to drive)
	1	Head select, side 1 (to drive)

1 = x	Drive selected	
0 = x	bit 1	bit 0
	0	0 = drive 0 selected
	0	1 = drive 1 selected
	1	0 = drive 2 selected
	1	1 = drive 3 selected

Command	Description	Port
7h	Recalibrate	3F5h

Recalibrate commands the selected diskette drive to move its head to track 0. This is used so all subsequent operations are correctly indexed to the start of the diskette, track 0. This command is required whenever a new diskette is inserted and to initialize the controller and drive.

In the execution phase, recalibrate monitors the hardware line from the diskette drive that indicates when the drive is at track 0. The command steps the head outward until the drive's track 0 line becomes active. During execution, the controller is set to a non-busy state, which allows the recalibrate command to be issued to another diskette drive. This can be used to speed up the initialization of multiple drives.

If more than 79 steps are issued without the track 0 signal becoming active, the command terminates. The error condition is noted with Status register 0's equipment check bit set. The seek end bit is set to 1 in Status register 0 whether the command completes successfully or not.

Upon command completion, no status bytes are returned, but the controller issues an interrupt, Eh, to indicate the operation is complete. A Sense Interrupt Status command, described next, should be issued to verify the command completed successfully. The Sense interrupt command returns Status register 0 and the current cylinder number, which should be zero.

Command byte 0 = 7
byte 1 = 0 to select drive 0
1 to select drive 1
2 to select drive 2
3 to select drive 3

Execution—Retract head to track 0

Result—No result bytes, but issues an interrupt

Command	Description	Port
8h	Sense Interrupt Status	3F5h

This command clears an interrupt issued by the controller and returns the reason the interrupt occurred. The Sense Interrupt Status command should only be issued after an interrupt occurred, and will return an error value of 80h in status register 0 if an interrupt was not active.

The controller will issue an interrupt when various commands complete their execution phase. This includes all Read and Write commands, Read ID, Format track, Verify, all Seek commands, and Recalibrate. Sense Interrupt Status must be issued immediately after the completion of the Seek commands and the Recalibrate command to terminate their operation and to verify the head position is correct.

Command byte 0 = 8

Execution—Get status

Result—No interrupt

byte 0 = Status Register 0 (see detail in standard status results in Table 10-7)

byte 1 = Current cylinder number (0 to 79)

Command	Description	Port
Eh	Dump Registers (Enhanced)	3F5h

This command returns a number of internal registers from advanced controllers. It is intended only for debugging diskette controller software. This command is not used by PC family BIOS ROMs.

Command byte 0 = Eh

Execution—Internal registers read for result

Result—No interrupt

byte 0 = Current cylinder number for drive 0

byte 1 = Current cylinder number for drive 1

byte 2 = Current cylinder number for drive 2

byte 3 = Current cylinder number for drive 3

byte 4 = Step rate and head unload time (see byte 1 of specify command #3)

byte 5 = Head load time and DMA mode option (see byte 2 of specify command #3)

byte 6 = The final sector number of the current track

byte 7 = Perpendicular information (see byte 1 of the Perpendicular 2.88 MB Mode command #12, undefined on nonenhanced controllers)

byte 8 = Configure information (see byte 2 of the Configure command #13)

byte 9 = Write precompensation start (see byte 3 of the Configure command #13)

Command	Description	Port
Fh	Seek	3F5h

The controller moves the specified drive's head to the specified cylinder. This action is normally performed before a read or write operation.

Upon command completion, no status bytes are returned, but the controller issues an interrupt, Eh, to indicate the operation is complete. After command completion, a Sense Interrupt Status command 8 and a Read ID command 4Ah should be issued to verify the command completed successfully. The result status from the Read ID command should be verified that the head is now at the desired cylinder.

Command byte 0 = Fh

byte 1 = Drive select and head select byte (see standard parameters in Table 10-6)

byte 2 = cylinder number when to position head (0 to 79 depending on media)

Execution—Position head over specified cylinder

Result—No result bytes, but issues an interrupt

★★★

Command	Description	Port
10h	Version (Enhanced)	3F5h

The Version command checks if this is a standard diskette controller or if the controller is an enhanced version. The NEC 765 chip is the standard controller (and many clones have been made of this chip). The enhanced controller includes the Intel 82077 diskette controller, a superset of the standard controller. The enhanced controller includes FIFO operations, 2.88 MB diskette support, and other features. The NEC 72065B also supports the version function, and provides a few enhanced features (but not 2.88 MB support).

Even though this command is documented for an enhanced controller only, it is safe to use the Version command on all systems. A controller that does not support the Version command will always return 80h, the invalid command status. This command is not used by PC family BIOS ROMs.

Command byte 0 = 10h

Execution—Get status

Result—No interrupt

byte = 80h for standard controller

= 81h for Intel 82077

= 90h for NEC 72065B

★★★

Command	Description	Port
12h	Perpendicular 2.88 MB Mode (Enhanced)	3F5h

The 2.88 MB drive uses a perpendicular recording method on 2.88 MB media to double the number of bits per inch over 1.44 MB media. This command allows the controller to automatically change the sector gap size and write timing whenever a 2.88 MB drive is accessed. As part of the initialization, all 2.88 MB drives should be recorded with one issuance of this command, with bits 0 and 1 both set to 1. BIOS ROMs that support 2.88 MB diskettes will use this command. Note that bit 7 must be set to 1 to allow the drive type bits 2 through 5 to change.

The design of the 2.88 MB drive requires a separate erase head for its unique perpendicular recording method. All prior drive types could simply overwrite data with the write head. The new erase head in 2.88 MB drives physically preceeds the read/write head by about 200 micrometers. When a write begins, the erase head is turned on at the same time. With the high density of the 2.88 MB media, the 200 micrometer head separation means about 38 bytes are not erased as the write head begins writing data behind the erase head. This is not an issue for a format, where all the data is written for the entire track, but becomes an issue when writing data inside a sector on the track. The gap before the sector's data is only 22 bytes long on all prior media types. To compensate for this, the sector gap length is increased to 44 bytes on 2.88 MB media. Bits 0 and 1 control this function. The net effect is that the operation of 2.88 MB drive becomes transparent to the software once this command is issued.

Command	byte 0 = 12h	
	byte 1 - bit 7 = 0	Prevent change to bits 2-5
	bit 7 = 1	Allow change to bits 2-5
	6 = 0	Fixed at 0
	5 = 1	Drive 3 is 2.88 MB
	4 = 1	Drive 2 is 2.88 MB
	3 = 1	Drive 1 is 2.88 MB
	2 = 1	Drive 0 is 2.88 MB
	1 = 0	No sector gap alteration for 2.88 MB
	1	Gap expanded as necessary for 2.88 MB
	0 = 0	No write enable timing alteration
	1	Alter write enable timing to allow pre-erase loads on 2.88 MB drive

Execution—Updates internal register

Result—No result bytes and no interrupt

Command	Description	Port
13h	Configure (Enhanced)	3F5h

★★★

The configure command sets a number of controller options on an enhanced diskette controller. It is not supported on non-enhanced controllers, and is not used by PC family BIOS ROMs.

The implied seek feature is used to automatically perform a seek to the specified cylinder as part of the read/write command before the read or write operation occurs. This enhanced feature is not available on standard controllers.

To retain compatibility with the original diskette controller, the FIFO is disabled. Custom software could take advantage of FIFO mode.

The polling feature scans for changes in the drive change line for each drive and issues an interrupt if a change does occur. Polling is put on hold while the diskette head is loaded (i.e. in an operation).

Command byte 0 = 13h

byte 1 = 0

byte 2 - bit	7 = 0	unused
	6 = 0	no implied seek (default)
	1	implied seek on read or write
	5 = 0	Enable FIFO
	1	Disable FIFO (default)
	4 = 0	Polling enabled (default)
	1	Polling disabled
	3 = x	FIFO threshold value
	2 = x	0 = 1-byte threshold
	1 = x	1 = 2-byte threshold
	0 = x	F = 16-byte threshold

byte 3 = Write precompensation starting track—Indicates which track number write precompensation should begin (0 to 79 depending on media, defaults to 0)

Execution—Configuration information recorded internally

Result—No result bytes and no interrupt

Command	Description	Port
14h	Unlock FIFO Functions (Enhanced)	3F5h

This command is issued to allow a software reset to clear the current FIFO options set with the Configure command 13h. When lock is inactive, a software reset will disable the FIFO, set the FIFO threshold to 1 byte, and set the write precompensation to start on track 0. This command is not used by PC family BIOS ROMs.

Command byte 0 = 14h

Execution—Allows FIFO functions to be changed by reset

Result—No interrupt

byte 0 = 0 indicating unlock command accepted

Command	Description	Port
34h	Exit Standby Mode (72065 only)	3F5h

Returns the diskette controller from standby mode. See command 35h for more about standby mode.

Command byte 0 = 34h
Execution—Return to normal mode from standby
Result—No interrupt
byte 0 = 80h

Command	Description	Port
35h	Go to Standby Mode (72065 only)	3F5h

The diskette controller is placed in a low-power standby mode. The diskette controller's internal clock is stopped, and the controller awaits return to normal mode. Return to normal mode occurs if an Exit Standby Mode command 34h is received, or the controller is reset by software or hardware.

Command byte 0 = 35h
Execution—Diskette controller goes into standby mode
Result—No result bytes and no interrupt

Command	Description	Port
36h	Hard Reset (72065 only)	3F5h

Resets the diskette controller as if a hardware reset occurred.

Command byte 0 = 36h
Execution—Controller reset occurs
Result—No result bytes and no interrupt

Command	Description	Port
42h	Read Track	3F5h

Reads all the data on the specified track. The controller begins reading data from the first sector after the index hole, and continues through the last sector on the track. Unlike a normal read command E6h, Read Track does not check the actual sector number stored in the ID fields of each sector. This command will also read data from sectors with both normal or bad sectors marked with deleted IDs. The last sector to be read in the track is specified in the standard parameter's byte 6, End of track. This value has the number of sectors to read, normally the total number of sectors on the track. This command is not used by PC family BIOS ROMs.

Command byte 0 = 42h
bytes 1 to 8 = standard parameters (Table 10-6)
Execution—Read track
Result—Issues an interrupt
bytes 0 to 6 = standard status results (Table 10-7)

Command	Description	Port
4Ah	Read ID	3F5h

This command locates the current track the head is positioned on. The controller begins reading from the current track, without waiting for an index pulse. It then looks for a sector address mark and related sector ID information. When the first valid address mark is encountered, the data is saved, and the command completes by updating the status bytes with the information read.

If two index pulses occur (i.e., at least one full revolution), without detecting a valid sector address mark, an error is returned in status register 0, as an abnormal termination. In addition, Status register bit 0, the missing address mark error flag is set. This error would likely occur if the track was never formatted.

Command byte 0 = 4Ah

byte 1 = Drive select and head select byte (see standard parameters in Table 10-6)

Execution—The first correct ID information on the current cylinder is read and placed in the standard status

Result—Issues an interrupt

bytes 0 to 6 = standard status results (Table 10-7)

Command	Description	Port
4Dh	Format Track	3F5h

The format track command writes a full track of sectors onto the diskette. Once the command bytes are loaded, the controller waits for the drive's index pulse, indicating the start of the track. The controller then begins writing information onto the disk including gaps, sync pulses, ID and data fields, address marks, and CRC fields for each sector.

For each sector, the four sector ID bytes must be provided from the CPU, as they are not generated by the controller. I've shown these as bytes w, x, y, and z during the execution phase. This means the DMA process must have been set up prior to issuance of this command, and a data buffer created which has the sector ID information. For a 9-sector track on a 720 KB drive, the buffer must have 36 bytes.

Allowing the user to control the sector ID information for each sector allows odd ordering, or even impossible information, like sector 99. Of course, a sector number may not be accessible if it's too strange, or may only be useful for copy protection schemes. One valid reason for using a nonsequential sectors is to interleave sectors for a system incapable of handling the incredibly fast data rate of the diskette controller (I'm being sarcastic). A 2:1 interleave factor on a 9-sector diskette places sectors in the order 1, 6, 2, 7, 3, 8, 4, 9, 5. When the data is read, the controller skips every other sector. This is never done on a PC, since every 80x86 processor is capable of easily handling the maximum data rate. A 2.88 MB drive, at 1 Mbps can send data at the blindingly fast snail's pace of 125 K bytes per second! All other drives are two to four times slower.

Refer to Figure 10-3 earlier in this chapter for a detailed view of the contents of a track, which are set by the format command.

Command byte 0 = 4Dh
byte 1 = Drive select and head select *
byte 2 = Sector size code (2=512 bytes) *
byte 3 = Number of sectors to be formatted
byte 4 = Gap length between sectors *
byte 5 = Filler byte for initial data within the sector (value 0F6h for all PC family diskette formats)
*See standard parameters in Table 10-6 for full explanation

Execution—Format entire cylinder, with four bytes of sector ID information for each sector on the track (see text).
byte w = Cylinder number
byte x = Head number (0=side 0, 1=side 1)
byte y = Sector number (usually 1 to 36)
byte z = Sector size code (2=512 bytes)

Result—Issues an interrupt
byte 0 = Status Register 0 (see standard status results in Table 10-7)
byte 1 = Status Register 1 (see standard status results in Table 10-7)
byte 2 = Status Register 2 (see standard status results in Table 10-7)
byte 3 = undefined
byte 4 = undefined
byte 5 = undefined
byte 6 = undefined

Command	Description	Port
8Fh	Relative Seek Outward (Enhanced)	3F5h

This command is very similar to the ordinary seek command. It specifies a number of cylinders to move outward toward the outside edge, relative to the current position. See the Seek command, Fh, for further details. It is intended for future diskettes that might have more than 256 tracks. It is not used by any PC family BIOS ROMs. Also see the relative seek inward command CFh.

Command byte 0 = 8Fh
byte 1 = Drive select & head select byte (see standard parameters in Table 10-6)
byte 2 = number of cylinders to move from current cylinder outward to lower numbered cylinders

Execution—Moves specified cylinders outward

Result—No result bytes, but issues an interrupt

Command	Description	Port
94h	Lock FIFO Functions (Enhanced)	3F5h

This command prevents a software reset from changing the current FIFO options set with the Configure command 13h. When lock is active, a software reset will not change the current FIFO state (enabled or disabled), the FIFO threshold, or the write precompensation values. This command is not used by PC family BIOS ROMs.

Command byte 0 = 94h

Execution—Prevent FIFO functions from being changed by reset

Result—No interrupt

byte 0 = 10h, indicating lock command accepted

Command	Description	Port
C5h	Write Data	3F5h

The BIOS diskette interrupt servicer uses this command to write data to the disk. A write must first set up the DMA controller for the transfer using DMA channel 2. Next a seek command is issued to position the head over the correct track.

During the execution phase of this command, the head is loaded, and after the head load timeout period, data is read from the track. When the sector address from the diskette sector matches the sector specified in the loaded parameters, the DMA transfer begins. After a full sector of data has been written, if the DMA's terminal count line has not expired, the controller's sector number is incremented, and the next sector is transferred through the DMA process. Data is written to the specified sectors, with an address mark ID that indicates it is "normal data." The write process also determines the sector's CRC and writes this byte into the CRC field after the sector data.

This command uses the multitrack option. Multi-track with multiple sector transfers will automatically switch from head 0 to head 1, and continue writing sectors to side 1. This means the maximum number of sectors that can be written by a single issuance of this command is the number of sectors per track times two. For a 1.44 MB diskette with 18 sectors per track, a total of 36 sectors, or 18,432 bytes can be read at a time (36 sectors times 512 bytes per sector).

Command byte 0 = C5h

bytes 1 to 8 = standard parameters (Table 10-6)

Execution—Write data with "normal data" ID

Result—Issues an interrupt

bytes 0 to 6 = standard status results (Table 10-7)

Command	Description	Port
C6h	Read Normal and Deleted Data	3F5h

★★★

This command is identical to the Read Normal Data command E6h, except the controller reads all sectors. These include those sectors marked with the ID "deleted data" and "normal data." See the Read Normal Data command for additional details. This command is not used by PC family BIOS ROMs.

Command byte 0 = C6h
bytes 1 to 8 = standard parameters (Table 10-6)

Execution—Reads data from sectors

Result—Issues an interrupt
bytes 0 to 6 = standard status results (Table 10-7)

Command	Description	Port
C9h	Write Deleted Data	3F5h

★★★

This command is identical to the Write Data command C5h, except the controller marks each sector with the "deleted data" sector ID. See the Write Data command for additional details. This command is not used by PC family BIOS ROMs.

This command was intended to mark sectors that have errors, so they will be ignored by normal reads. It is sometimes used by copy protection schemes to hide data on a diskette, since the BIOS will only use controller commands that skip over a sector that is marked with the "deleted data" ID.

Command byte 0 = C9h
bytes 1 to 8 = standard parameters (Table 10-6)

Execution—Write data with "deleted data" ID

Result—Issues an interrupt
bytes 0 to 6 = standard status results (Table 10-7)

Command	Description	Port
CCh	Read Deleted Data	3F5h

★★★

This command is identical to the Read Normal Data command E6h, except the controller reads those sectors marked with the ID "deleted data." The command skips any sectors marked "normal data." See the Read Normal Data command for additional details. This command is not used by PC family BIOS ROMs.

Command byte 0 = CCh
bytes 1 to 8 = standard parameters (Table 10-6)

Execution—Reads data from sectors with the deleted data ID
Result—Issues an interrupt
bytes 0 to 6 = standard status results (Table 10-7)

★★★

Command	Description	Port
CFh	Relative Seek Inward (Enhanced)	3F5h

This command is very similar to the ordinary seek command. It is used to specify a number of cylinders to move inward towards the diskette center, relative to the current position. See the Seek command, Fh, for further details. It is intended for future diskettes that might have more than 256 tracks. It is not used by any PC family BIOS ROMs. Also see command 8Fh for relative seek outward.

Command byte 0 = CFh
byte 1 = Drive select and head select byte (see standard parameters in Table 10-6)
byte 2 = number of cylinders to move from current cylinder inward to higher numbered cylinders.
Execution—Moves specified cylinders inward
Result—No result bytes, but issues an interrupt

★★★

Command	Description	Port
D1h	Scan Equal All	3F5h

The controller performs a byte-for-byte check with data from the system and that which is recorded on the diskette. It is a true verification that the data on the diskette matches a buffer's contents. There are several other scan commands to stop when the first diskette byte is found that is lower or higher in value than the buffer's related byte. The functions are not very useful. Refer to the diskette controller's hardware reference if you are interested in these optional commands.

All sectors are read, regardless of the ID type ("deleted data" or "normal data"). Scan Equal and other scan commands are not used by PC family BIOS ROMs. See similar command F1h to skip sectors with "deleted data" IDs.

Command byte 0 = D1h
bytes 1 to 8 = standard parameters (Table 10-6)
Execution—Scan until failure to match or done
Result—No interrupt
bytes 0 to 6 = standard status results (Table 10-7)
Register 2 holds the status of the scan, in bits 3 and 2. A value of 01 for bits 3 and 2 respectively indicates that all the data are equal. A value of 10 indicates a mismatch.

Command	Description	Port
D6h	Verify (Enhanced)	3F5h

Checks the information on the specified sectors for possible errors. The data is read from each sector and a new CRC is determined. This is compared with the CRC read from the diskette for the sector. If they fail to match, the verify fails. This verify command includes any sectors with the "deleted data" ID. This command is not used by PC family BIOS ROMs.

Command byte 0 = D6h

bytes 1 to 8 = standard parameters in Table 10-6 except as follows:

If bit 7=1 in the drive select and head select byte, then the custom sector size byte becomes a count of sectors to verify

Execution—No system data transfer occurs

Result—Issues an interrupt

bytes 0 to 6 = standard status results (Table 10-7)

Command	Description	Port
E6h	Read Normal Data	3F5h

The BIOS diskette interrupt servicer uses this command to read data from the disk. A read must first set up the DMA controller for the read, using DMA channel 2. Next a seek command is issued to position the head over the correct track.

During the execution phase of the Read Normal command, the head is loaded, and after the head load timeout period, data is read from the track. When the sector address from the diskette sector matches the sector specified in the loaded parameters, the DMA transfer begins. After a sector's worth of data has been transferred, if the DMA's terminal count line has not expired, the controller's sector number is incremented, and the next sector is transferred through the DMA process. Any sector that has the "deleted data" ID is ignored.

This command uses the multi-track option. Multi-track with multiple sector transfers will automatically switch from head 0 to head 1, and continue reading sectors from side 1. This means the maximum number of sectors that can be read by a single issuance of this command is the number of sectors per track times two. For a 2.88 MB diskette with 36 sectors per track, a total of 72 sectors, or 36,864 bytes can be read at a time (72 sectors times 512 bytes per sector).

Command byte 0 = E6h

bytes 1 to 8 = standard parameters (Table 10-6)

Execution—Reads data from sectors

Result—Issues an interrupt

bytes 0 to 6 = standard status results (Table 10-7)

Command	Description	Port
F1h	Scan Equal	3F5h

The controller performs a byte-for-byte check with data from the system and that which is recorded on the diskette. It is a true verification that the data on the diskette matches a buffer's contents. There are several other scan commands to stop when the first diskette byte is found that is lower or higher in value than the buffer's related byte. These functions are not very useful. Refer to the diskette controller's hardware reference if you are interested in these optional commands.

Any sector that has the "deleted data" ID is ignored. Scan Equal is not used by PC family BIOS ROMs. See similar command D1h to include sectors with "deleted data" IDs.

Command byte 0 = F1h

bytes 1 to 8 = standard parameters (Table 10-6)

Execution—Scan until failure to match or done

Result—No interrupt

bytes 0 to 6 = standard status results (Table 10-7)

Register 2 holds the status of the scan, in bits 3 and 2. A bit value of 01 for bits 3 and 2 respectively indicates that all the data are equal. A bit value 10 indicates a mismatch.

Command	Description	Port
F6h	Verify (Enhanced)	3F5h

Checks the information on the specified sectors for possible errors. The data is read from each sector and a new CRC is determined. This is compared with the CRC on the diskette for the sector. If they fail to match, the verify fails. This verify commands ignores any sectors with the "deleted data" ID. This command is not used by PC family BIOS ROMs.

Command byte 0 = F6h

bytes 1 to 8 = standard parameters in Table 10-6 except as follows:

If bit 7=1 in the drive select and head select byte, then the custom sector size byte becomes a count of sectors to verify

Execution—No system data transfer occurs

Result—Issues an interrupt

bytes 0 to 6 = standard status results (Table 10-7)

Port	Type	Description	Platform
3F6h	I/O	Diskette Controller Reserved	All

This register address is unused and is reserved for possible future diskette controller features.

Port	Type	Description	Platform
3F7h	Input	Diskette Controller Digital Input Register	AT+

The Digital Input Register shows the state of the disk change line for the currently selected drive. All 3.5" diskette drives and the 1.2 MB 5.25" drive all support a disk change line. This line signals a new diskette has been placed in the drive, or there is no diskette in the drive.

This Port is shared with the hard disk controller, except on PS/2 systems. If the hard disk controller is present, the hard disk controller returns information in the lower 6 bits. Since only bit 7 is returned from the diskette controller, I've shown them as "unused, tristated." This means if no hard disk adapter is used, these "unused" bits can return any value.

AT+ systems (except PS/2 AT and MCA bus systems)
Input (bit 7)

bit	7 r = 0	Diskette is present and has not been changed
	1	Diskette missing or changed
	6 r = x	unused, tristated so any value can appear
	5 r = x	unused, tristated (see text)
	4 r = x	unused, tristated (see text)
	3 r = x	unused, tristated (see text)
	2 r = x	unused, tristated (see text)
	1 r = x	unused, tristated (see text)
	0 r = x	unused, tristated (see text)

PS/2 MCA Bus Only
Input (bits 0-7)

bit	7 r = 0	Diskette is present and has not been changed
	1	Diskette missing or changed
	6 r = 1	Fixed at 1
	5 r = 1	Fixed at 1
	4 r = 1	Fixed at 1
	3 r = 1	Fixed at 1
	2 r = x	Data rate selection
	1 r = x	

bit 2	bit 1	Rate
0	0 =	500 Kbps
0	1 =	300 Kbps (not supported on all models)
1	0 =	250 Kbps
1	1 =	1 Mbps (not supported on all models)

	0 r = 0	High-density data rate selected (500 Kbps or 1 Mbps)
	1	Low-density data rate selected (250 Kbps or 300 Kbps) (default after hardware reset)

PS/2 AT Bus Only (i.e., model 30 and others)

Input (bits 0-7)

bit	7 r = 0	Diskette is present and has not been changed
	1	Diskette missing or changed
	6 r = 0	Fixed at 0
	5 r = 0	Fixed at 0
	4 r = 0	Fixed at 0
	3 r = 0	DMA & Interrupt capabilities disabled (see Port 3F2h)
	1	DMA & Interrupt capabilities enabled
	2 r = x	no precompensation bit status from Configuration control register, Port 3F7h, bit 2 (currently not used for any purpose!)
	1 r = x	Data rate selection
	0 r = x	

bit 1	bit 0	Rate
0	0 =	500 Kbps
0	1 =	300 Kbps (not supported on all models)
1	0 =	250 Kbps
1	1 =	1 Mbps (not supported on all models)

Port	Type	Description	Platform
3F7h	Output	Diskette Controller Configuration Control Register	AT+

This register is used to set the current data rate. It is write-only on all but the PS/2, where, depending on the bus type, the register is readable. See the Digital Input Register for exact details on reading back the rate selection.

AT+ and PS/2 MCA bus systems (except PS/2 AT bus systems)

Output (bits 0-1)

bit	7 w = x	unused
	6 w = x	unused
	5 w = x	unused
	4 w = x	unused
	3 w = x	unused
	2 w = x	unused

1 w = x	Data rate selection			
0 w = x		bit 1	bit 0	Rate
		0	0 =	500 Kbps
		0	1 =	300 Kbps (not supported on all models)
		1	0 =	250 Kbps
		1	1 =	1 Mbps (not supported on all models)

PS/2 AT Bus Only (i.e., model 30 and others)
Output (bits 0-2)

bit	7 w = x	unused
	6 w = x	unused
	5 w = x	unused
	4 w = x	unused
	3 w = x	unused
	2 w = x	no precompensation bit—performs no current function other than bit can be read from the Digital Input Register at Port 3F7h. Cleared by hardware reset only.

1 w = x	Data rate selection			
0 w = x		bit 1	bit 0	Rate
		0	0 =	500 Kbps
		0	1 =	300 Kbps (not supported on all models)
		1	0 =	250 Kbps
		1	1 =	1 Mbps (not supported on all models)

CHAPTER 11

Hard Disk System

This is one of the longest chapters in the book, and it still does not cover all of the hard disk systems in use today. I've concentrated on the drives and controllers supported by the system BIOS and, to a lesser degree, on nonstandard controllers that replace the system BIOS services with their own custom disk BIOS.

In examining other technical documents, I was surprised at how poorly the documentation was assembled, the large number of errors, and ignorance of the subtle, but often very important differences between the various standards in use today.

I have spent a significant amount of effort looking into the actual BIOS code used from various vendors and examining hardware controllers to confirm the accuracy of the BIOS information presented later in this chapter. In addition, a software utility called DISKTEST can identify some of the more blatant BIOS errors I came across in testing different systems.

Although much of the chapter is crucial information if you wish to thoroughly understand the disk system, the section on BIOS interrupts is particularly important for those interested in developing advanced code. This section includes a very detailed list of error return codes, with real explanations as to what causes errors. This is followed by a description of the BIOS interrupt functions, including a number of undocumented details and functions.

For those brave souls who need to bypass the system BIOS, you'll find a comprehensive discussion of how the BIOS works with the controller. This includes an extensive list of I/O ports with detailed descriptions. Considerable caution should be used when bypassing the BIOS because many undocumented variations exist among different vendors.

Throughout this chapter I talk about PS/2s as using an ESDI controller and drive. This is not strictly true. During the final couple of years of the PS/2's production, various models used IDE and SCSI drives. Now that the PS/2 MCA based line of computers has been discontinued, software support for these machines is less of an issue. I've maintained details about the PS/2's ESDI interface for those users who need to support these legacy systems.

Introduction

Like diskette drives, a hard disk is simply a number of spinning platters that are capable of recording and playing back binary signals. The drive can be directed to a specific spot to begin writing or reading data. Most hard drives are based on magnetic media, although some drives provide optical media.

Most systems today contain at least one hard drive. Even diskless workstations use the network server to act like a hard drive to the user. The BIOSes on all AT-, EISA-, and MCA-type machines support up to two hard drives on the system. Most AT systems with a date of 1995 or later support up to four drives. The PC and XT used a BIOS on an adapter card independent of the system BIOS. With most systems, even if you seem to have more than two drives, the operating system is likely mapping multiple logical drives onto one or two hard disks, or a special disk adapter has replaced the system BIOS disk functions to allow more drives.

Similar to Chapter 10 on the diskette system, there are many references to common terminology relating to the structure of the hard disk. Each hard disk is divided into heads, cylinders, tracks, and sectors, as shown in Figure 11-1. The smallest component is the sector, which holds 512 bytes of data. A number of sectors are grouped together to form a track. A cylinder is a vertical group of tracks, usually two times the number of platters.

Figure 11-1. Hard Disk Media Structure

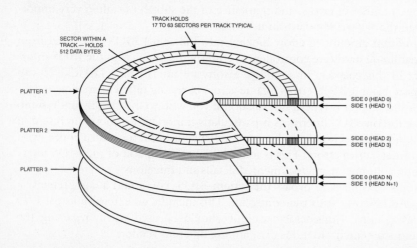

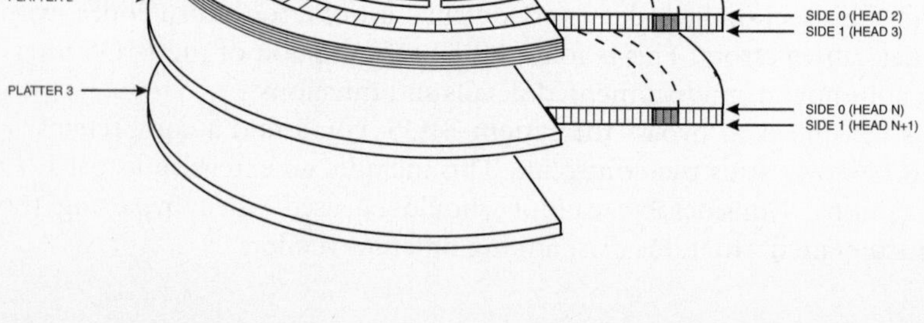

A hard disk is defined by a combination of sectors per track, tracks per cylinder and cylinders, and is normally set by the drive manufacturer. For example, one of the first 10 MB drives used on the XT had 17 sectors per track, 306 cylinders, and four heads:

(512 bytes per sector) * (17 sectors per track) * (306 cylinders) * (4 heads) =10,653,696 bytes

It's important to note that unlike old MFM drives, most drives today mask the actual layout of the real drive. From a software point of view, this is rarely important. Software always thinks of the drive as having a fixed number of sectors per track, heads, and cylinders. Most drives have a built-in translation from the structure presented from software to the internal drive mapping. Some of these conversions have become extremely complex, with the drive reserving sectors and cylinders to correct for media defects, which are invisible to software. Some of the highest capacity drives also use techniques to have more sectors per track on the outer cylinders, and fewer sectors per track on the inner cylinders. This boosts the drive capacity by always packing the maximum bit density on every track. All of this remapping is made invisible to software accessing the drive.

To access the hard disk drive, a program communicates with the operating system specifying a filename. The operating system determines the physical location on the disk for the file. Older OSes, like DOS, use BIOS services, interrupt 13h to perform the low-level work. The hard disk BIOS routinely communicates with the hard disk controller. Finally, the controller communicates with the drive to read or write the requested data. At the lowest level, there are a number of interface standards used by different drive vendors.

Figure 11-2 shows a basic hard disk subsystem. The diagram illustrates the original PC and AT standards, commonly referred to as ST-506. Although this standard is obsolete today, most system BIOSes still access the controller through the same mechanism. The interface between the controller and the physical drive has become blurred with many drives having the controller merged into the drive. With advances in servo control of the drive, position information is embedded into the drive itself, and the internal controller-to-drive functions may be quite different depending on the vendor. The good news is, we as programmers rarely have to care what happens beyond the controller once we have a conceptual model to work from.

Figure 11-2. Hard Disk Subsystem

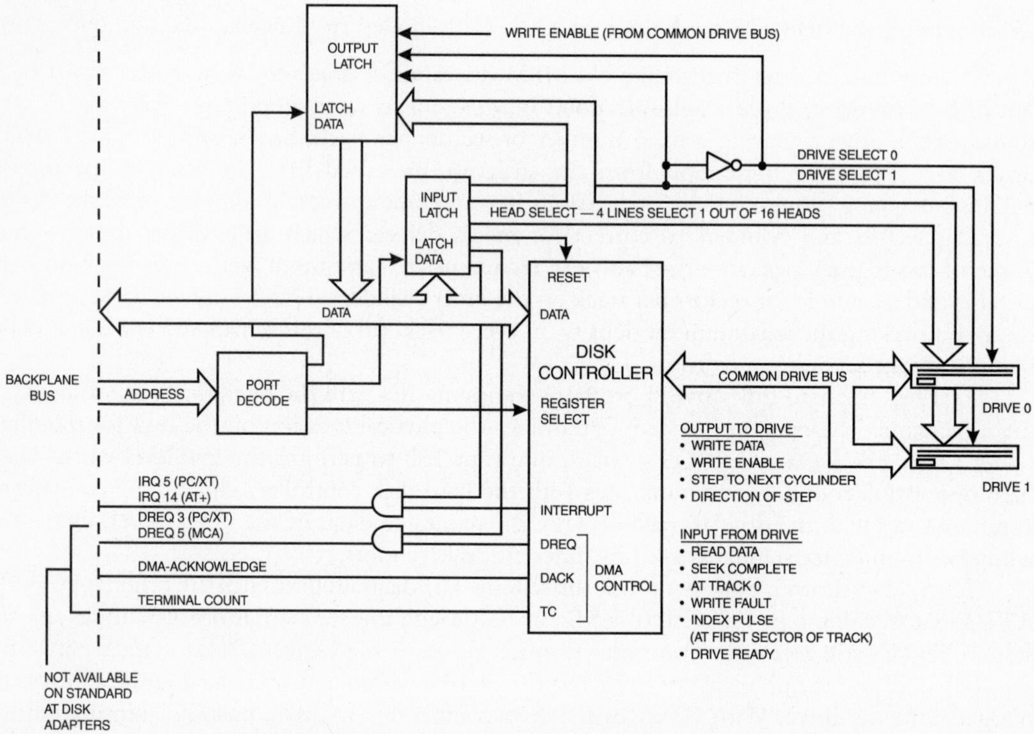

Will the Real Disk Size Please Stand Up?

Hard drive manufacturers used to mislead users into believing the hard drive has more data capacity than it actually has. The most common problem in the 1980s was that manufacturers would show only the unformatted capacity of the drive. Of course, you can't use a drive until it has been formatted by the operating system. Formatting is the process where each sector is defined, with identification information so a specific sector can be located on the disk. Additional bits on the disk are used for required gaps, sector identification information and Error Checking and Correction (ECC) codes. This means the formatted capacity is about 5 to 10 percent less than the unformatted capacity.

When is a 200 MB formatted drive not 200 megabytes? Most drive manufacturers now state the formatted size of a drive, but some vendors use several tricks to make the drive appear to have more capacity than you will ever get on a PC. The most common trick is to use a non-standard or large-sector size. For example, the capacity of a 200 MB formatted drive might be specified with 2,048-byte sectors. Every PC platform requires 512-byte sectors. Each sector can easily have 50 or more bytes of required overhead, but by using 2,048-byte sectors, the disk capacity might increase by 5–10%. Figure 11-3 helps illustrate how a larger sector size reduces the amount of disk space required.

Figure 11-3. Disk Capacity with Sector Size

Space required for 4 sectors, 512 bytes per sector

sector 1	sector 2	sector 3	sector 4
ooddddddddd	ooddddddddd	ooddddddddd	ooddddddddd

Space required for 1 sector, 2048 bytes per sector

sector 1
ooddddddddddddddddddddddddddddddddddddddddd

Key: o = overhead, such as ID, gaps, and ECC codes
d = data byte area

Another trick used to make a drive appear larger is the inclusion of spare sectors to which you have no access. SCSI drives and some other drive types include spare sectors and spare cylinders. These spares are used by the manufacturer to replace defective sectors on the disk. The number of sectors reserved for spares is rarely divulged.

Beware of drives with more than 512 MB. All PCs older than 1995, and some operating systems, cannot handle more than 1,024 cylinders, normally required for more than 512 MB capacity. Excess cylinders are inaccessible and can't be counted as part of the usable capacity on a PC system. This means a drive with 1,080 cylinders having a 540 MB capacity could only use 1,024 cylinders—a usable capacity of 512 MB. Also the BIOS often reserves one or two cylinders for diagnostics, which further reduces the usable capacity. In this case the drive manufacturer is being fair, but the system will limit the maximum capacity. New PCs and controllers get around this problem by replacing the BIOS and operating system interfaces with ones that handle these larger drives. The standard method for handling large IDE drives is referred to as Logical Block Addressing (LBA), but more on LBA later.

These outlined tricks are fairly common in the drive industry. This means it is almost impossible to get an accurate usable disk capacity number from the manufacturer unless it clearly states that the formatted size is for a standard DOS PC platform. Since most manufacturers resort to these tricks, when comparing one drive to another, you can expect 10% variance in usable capacity. To be fair to the drive industry, it is showing best-case numbers that are rarely possible on the PC platform, but might be possible on another platform, such as UNIX. Isn't competition fun!

Interface Standards and Controllers

The most common interface standards are listed in Table 11-1. These standards define the hardware connections and signals between the controller and the drive itself. Each standard requires a controller specific to the drive type. This means each hard disk controller card can only handle disks of the same type. For example, you cannot connect a SCSI drive and an IDE drive to the same hard disk controller, even though the controller may support two drives.

The ST-506/ST-512 interface is obsolete today, but still exists in many machines shipped in the past. The ESDI interface, an enhancement to the ST-506, is also obsolete today. With the PC platform, IDE and EIDE drives have completely taken over the single-user system market. The SCSI remains the prime choice for multi-drive servers and multitasking operating systems.

Table 11-1. Common Drive Interface Standards

ST-506/ST-412	Seagate Technology 506 Interface
ESDI	Enhanced Small Device Interface
IDE	Integrated Drive Electronics (using the AT Attachment standard)
EIDE	Enhanced Integrated Drive Electronics
SCSI I and II	Small Computer System Interface

With PC and XT systems, the controllers for the most part supported only the ST-506/ ST-412 interface standard. The hard disk BIOS support appears on the adapter card, because very few of these systems had a system BIOS with hard disk services. I refer to these controllers as PC/XT controllers. All PC/XT controllers use an 8-bit data path. PC/XT controllers established the basic interrupt 13h BIOS interface, of which a subset is still used by most controllers today. The lower level I/O to the controller is unique to the PC/XT system, and was changed significantly for the AT.

For the operating system to communicate with the drive, most AT and EISA systems use the built-in system BIOS hard disk services. These services provide a well-defined communication path to the controller. I will refer to these types of controllers as AT controllers, because this is the most prevalent standard currently in use. AT controllers come in many forms, and are available for the ESDI, IDE, EIDE, and SCSI standards in Table 11-1. AT-bus controllers are based on a 16-bit data path design. AT controllers that use the VLB or PCI bus normally support a 32-bit data path. Currently the EIDE is the most popular controller-to-drive interface standard. All AT controllers use the same I/O interface detailed later in this chapter.

Older PS/2 BIOSes are written to support only ESDI drives on an ESDI controller. These PS/2 BIOSes are not designed to support any other type of controller or drive. This is true of both Micro Channel and AT bus PS/2 systems. Throughout the balance of this chapter I'll refer to the PS/2 interface as the PS/2 ESDI controller. Be aware that ESDI drives on the AT system do not use the PS/2 ESDI design, even though the actual interface between the controller and drive are the same. Other standards can be supported in the PS/2 with additional hardware and a hard disk BIOS that replaces the system BIOS's disk handler.

The PS/1 is an AT-type system that uses an AT-type controller. Except for a few additional extensions unique to the PS/1, the PS/1's controller can be considered a superset of the standard AT controller.

The SCSI interface standard allows for seven devices to be attached to a single controller. Because the standard system BIOS only allows for the operation of two generic drives, most SCSI adapters include a driver or BIOS ROM, which replaces the system BIOS services when communicating with the SCSI drive. This allows access to all seven possible devices. This is true for the PC, XT, AT, EISA, and the PS/2. A few SCSI adapters use the AT's BIOS software, circumventing the need for its own BIOS ROM. These "ROMless" SCSI adapters can support a maximum of two drives.

Because of the range of interface standards commonly used today, I don't recommend writing directly to the controller, with few exceptions. For high performance requirements, when the drive interface is known, it may be desirable to talk directly with the controller. Windows 3.11 and Windows 95 are good examples. Windows provides a FastDisk option to bypass the BIOS hard disk handler with its own much faster 32-bit code. In this case, no native controller support is supplied for other interfaces without special drivers, such as SCSI or PS/2 ESDI. Of course it makes no sense to replace the hard disk BIOS on PC and XT systems because the CPU can't support 32-bit code.

The big advantage of the AT Controller interface is its simplicity. No special device drivers or BIOS ROMs, which waste memory space, are needed. Every current and future operating system that runs on the AT platform will work. With other interfaces, the controller manufacturer or the operating system vendor must provide special support for that drive interface. In many cases, support for alternate controllers may never become available or it may take many months or even years to get support for a non-AT controller-based system.

So now that it's apparent that everyone should use the AT standard drive interface, why doesn't everyone? Well, it comes down to our never-ending goal of better performance and features. For systems with a single drive, the AT controller standard will usually provide the best performance in the system. In addition, the IDE interface is simpler to install and provides a significant cost advantage over SCSI. On the other hand, a well-designed SCSI interface can provide a dramatic boost in performance when multiple drives are used on a server or multitasking operating system. This occurs because the SCSI adapter is capable of executing tasks on multiple drives at the same time. With a two-drive IDE system, only one drive is accessed at a time.

If many drives are required, some SCSI adapters can be used to provide up to 15 devices on a system. Currently most systems are limited to four IDE devices, although there are adapters available that support up to eight IDE devices on one system. With both SCSI and IDE, devices can be a mix of disk drives, tape backup systems, CD drives, and other hardware.

One final note about drive types: IDE, ESDI, and SCSI drives mask the internal disk layout from the user. Any combination of heads, cylinders, and sectors that stay within the capacity of the drive are valid. This makes setup very easy. The controller converts the virtual mapping into the actual internal drive mapping. All this is handled transparently by the system.

Drive Operations

The basic disk drive is a rather simple device. The drive spins a number of platters and moves a set of heads across the cylinders. Circuitry in the drive is used to select which head is active. Only one head can be active at a time. Of course, the real tricks are making the drive reliable, fast, and capable of holding more data—but that's someone else's job!

Data is stored on the drive in a serial stream on each track of the disk. When the controller reads from the disk, the controller must separate out various gaps, sector identification information, Error Checking and Correction (ECC) bytes, and the actual data. To write a sector, the controller moves the heads to the proper sector location and then the sector's bytes are converted to a serial stream and sent to the drive. The exact format of information on each track is completely defined by the controller.

ST-506 Type Drives

The drive informs the controller with very limited position information. Once every revolution the drive signals the controller that the heads are over the start of a track. This is the index pulse. In addition, when the heads are positioned on cylinder 0, another signal is sent to the controller.

To position the heads over a cylinder, the controller pulses the step line once to move the heads by one cylinder. A direction line indicates whether the heads should be moved inward or outward. The controller must keep track of how many steps have been made in each direction, so the controller knows on which cylinder the heads are positioned. When the position is uncertain, like after powering up, the controller performs a Recalibrate. Recalibrate simply sends step pulses, with the outward direction selected. When the drive signals that its heads have reached cylinder 0, the pulses are stopped, and the controller now knows where the heads are positioned.

To find a sector within a track for reads or writes, the controller reads the sector ID fields for each sector until the proper match is made to the desired sector. At this point the read continues or the write begins.

Drives Used with IDE, EIDE, ESDI, and SCSI Standards

Most newer drives are tightly coupled with the controller. The exact method used to position heads on the disk is vendor specific. The most common methods use a servo mechanism that keeps accurate position information. The drive can be thought of as one long sequential list of sectors. To select a new position, the controller simply converts the cylinder, head number, and sector number into a relative sector number. The drive is then positioned to the relative sector number to begin the read or write operation.

Large IDE Drives

The standard interrupt 13h disk services and the IDE drive interface each have a different set of cylinder, head, and sector limits shown in Table 11-2. This creates a resultant maximum, based on the lowest value between the BIOS and the IDE standards. Table 11-2 also shows the maximum possible drive size based on the BIOS limits, IDE limits, and the resultant limits. This is where the nasty 504 MB drive limit comes from.

Table 11-2. BIOS and IDE Drive Limits

	Maximum BIOS Value	Maximum IDE Value	Resultant Maximum
Cylinders	1,024	65,536	1,024
Heads	256	16	16
Sectors	63	255	63
Largest Drive	8 GB	130 GB	.5 GB (504 MB)

To get past the 504 MB limit, and still allow all software and operating systems to work unmodified, a new approach, now called Logical Block Addressing (LBA), was created. This uses the standard BIOS limits, and *translates* the Cylinder/Head/Sector address to fit the requirements of the IDE drive interface. For example, a 1 GB IDE drive has 2,048 cylinders, 16 heads, and 63 sectors. With LBA active, this same drive is made to look like a 1,024 cylinder, 32 head, 63 sector 1 GB drive to software. The translation technique allows standard interrupt 13h services to address to up to 8 GB of data. Software using interrupt 13h services do not need to know translations that are performed by the BIOS or when the LBA address is passed directly to an IDE drive. Most system BIOSes with a 1995 date or later provide LBA support.

To move past the 8 GB limit (without going to SCSI), a new Enhanced BIOS (EBIOS) standard has been created. This provides a new set of interrupt 13h services (starting at function 41h). EBIOS services allow access to IDE drives up to 130 GB in size. EBIOS services also support future drive standards that allow access to drives up to 2,048 GB in size! Software must be written to use these new standards, because only limited backward compatibility exists. As of this writing, only a few operating systems, like Windows 95, support systems equipped with EBIOS services, but many more will quickly follow.

Disk Parameter Table

Two hard disk parameter tables hold information about each hard drive in the system. The table is used by the BIOS to program the disk controller and specify various timings to control the drive. The pointer to the parameter table for drive 0 is stored in the location of interrupt 41h, at 0:104h. Drive 1's parameter table pointer is stored in the location of interrupt 46h, at 0:118h. By convention, all unused bytes in the disk parameter table are set to zero. Table 11-3 shows the contents of the disk parameter table.

Table 11-3. Disk Parameter Table Contents

Offset	Size	Description
0	word	Cylinders, maximum number on drive
2	byte	Heads, maximum number on drive, not exceeding limit Limit — Controller Type 8 — PC/XT controller 16 — AT controller and system BIOS (no LBA) 32 — PS/2 ESDI controller 255 — IDE and EIDE with LBA
3	word	Starting cylinder for reduced write current (XT only, unused on all others)
5	word	Starting write precompensation cylinder—This is used to induce a slight delay in the data stream sent to the drive. On drives that require write precompensation, it is activated for the specified cylinder through the innermost cylinder, usually half of the cylinders on the drive. All IDE- and EIDE-type drives do not need any precompensation and ignore the value. Any value greater than the maximum cylinders prevents write precompensation.
7	byte	Maximum ECC data burst length (XT only, unused on all others)
8	byte	Control byte (AT and all later systems) bit 7 = x, 6 = x — Retry operation if failed bit 7 / bit 6 0 / 0 = retry on error 0 / 1 = no retries 1 / 0 = no retries 1 / 1 = no retries 5 = 1 — The disk manufacturer's defect map resides on a cylinder at max cylinders + 1 (ignored on some controller/BIOSes) 4 = 0 — unused 3 = 1 — More than eight heads on the drive (ignored on some controllers/BIOSes) 2 = 0 — must be fixed at zero (no reset) 1 = 0 — must be fixed at zero (disable IRQ) 0 = 0 — unused

Table 11-3. Continued

Offset	Size	Description
		Control byte (XT only) bit 7 = 0 Retry up to four times if there is a problem with disk access 1 Disable retries if there is a problem with disk access. 6 = 1 Disable normal retry when an ECC (Error Check and Correction) occurs during a read. 5 = 0 unused 4 = 0 unused 3 = 0 unused 2 = x, 1 = x, 0 = x Drive step speed bit 2 / bit 1 / bit 0 / Step rate 0 0 0 = 3 ms 1 0 0 = 200 ms 1 0 1 = 70 ms (normal) 1 1 0 = 3 ms 1 1 1 = 3 ms
9	byte	Normal timeout value (XT only, unused on all others)
A	byte	Timeout value for format disk drive (XT only, unused on all others)
B	byte	Timeout value for check disk drive (XT only, unused on all others)
C	word	Cylinder for landing zone (AT and later systems only, unused on XT)
E	byte	Number of sectors per track (AT and later systems only, unused on XT)
F	byte	unused

An altered disk parameter table is provided as part of the Enhanced Disk Drive Specification. It breaks the 8 GB limit for EIDE drives. It is only used when a drive has more than 1,024 cylinders AND EBIOS services are provided by the system BIOS or a disk controller BIOS. Table 11-4 shows the contents of the EBIOS disk parameter table.

Table 11-4. EBIOS Disk Parameter Table Contents

Offset	Size	Description
0	word	Logical Cylinders, up to 1,024
2	byte	Logical Heads, up to 255
3	byte	Translated table signature byte—Always A0h
4	byte	Physical sectors per track
5	word	unused (obsolete precompensation word)
7	byte	unused

Table 11-4. Continued

Offset	Size	Description
8	byte	Drive control byte
		bit 7 = x, 6 = x: Retry operation if failed bit 7 / bit 6 0 / 0 = retry on error 0 / 1 = no retries 1 / 0 = no retries 1 / 1 = no retries
		5 = 1 The disk manufacturer's defect map resides on a cylinder at max cylinders + 1 (ignored on some controller/BIOSes)
		4 = 0 unused
		3 = 1 More than eight heads on the drive (ignored on some controllers/BIOSes)
		2 = 0 must be fixed at zero (no reset)
		1 = 0 must be fixed at zero (disable IRQ)
		0 = 0 unused
9	word	Physical Cylinders, up to 65,535
11	byte	Physical Heads, up to 16
12	word	unused (obsolete landing zone word)
14	byte	Logical Sectors per Track, up to 63
15	byte	checksum of bytes 0 to 14

Drive Type Table

The system BIOS ROM contains a table of popular drives, but it is usually limited to 20 or 30 drive types. Each entry in the drive type table is a 16-byte disk parameter table as shown in Table 11-3. Different platforms and manufacturers have assigned different drives to each type. Because of these inconsistencies, it can never be assumed a drive type number always represents a specific drive.

On very old systems and some adapter cards, the hard disk type was selected by switches or jumpers on the adapter card. This became impractical as the number and variety of drives expanded.

With current systems, the drive type is selected from system setup. It is performed from a setup program diskette or by using a special key combination during booting to trigger the system BIOS setup program. With the drive type selected for each hard drive, the type number is saved into CMOS memory. Refer to the CMOS chapter for additional details on registers used for storing the drive types. See Table 11-5 on the drive types assigned by IBM for most AT and PS/2 class systems. Other vendors rarely use the same entries shown in Table 11-5.

Notice that type 15 is never assigned. Because of the original expectation that there would never be more than 15 drive types in existence, only a single byte of CMOS memory was assigned for two drives. Of course, this limit was quickly exceeded, so another extended CMOS byte was assigned for each drive. The extended CMOS byte is used as the drive type when the original CMOS nibble type is 15. This is handled transparently by the setup program, however it explains why drive type 15 cannot be used.

A number of newer add-in disk controllers provide a feature allowing any drive parameters to be used in a system that may not have an appropriate table entry. These adapters typically have users set the CMOS memory to use a disk type 1. When the controller's BIOS gets control, it appears as if type 1 was set. If so, it auto detects the true drive capacity and uses the generated drive parameters.

Table 11-5. Drive Parameters for Each Drive Type

Type	Total Size	Maximum Cylinders	Heads	Sectors	Write Pre-Comp Cylinder	Landing Zone	Defect Map
0	no drive						
1	10 MB	306	4	17	128	305	No
2	20 MB	615	4	17	300	615	No
3	30 MB	615	6	17	300	615	No
4	62 MB	940	8	17	512	940	No
5	46 MB	940	6	17	512	940	No
6	20 MB	615	4	17	-1 (none)	615	No
7	30 MB	462	8	17	256	511	No
8	30 MB	733	5	17	-1 (none)	733	No
9	112 MB	900	15	17	-1 (none)	901	No
10	20 MB	820	3	17	-1 (none)	820	No
11	35 MB	855	5	17	-1 (none)	855	No
12	50 MB	855	7	17	-1 (none)	855	No
13	20 MB	306	8	17	128	319	No
14	43 MB	733	7	17	-1 (none)	733	No
15	reserved (see text)						
16	20 MB	612	4	17	0 (all)	663	No
17	40 MB	977	5	17	300	977	No
18	57 MB	977	7	17	-1 (none)	1023	No
19	60 MB	1024	7	17	512	732	No
20	30 MB	733	5	17	300	732	No
21	43 MB	733	7	17	300	732	No
22	30 MB	733	5	17	300	733	No
23	10 MB	306	4	17	0 (all)	336	No
24*	10 MB	612	4	17	305	663	No

Table 11-5. Continued

Type	Total Size	Maximum Cylinders	Heads	Sectors	Write Pre-Comp Cylinder	Landing Zone	Defect Map
25	10 MB	306	4	17	-1 (none)	340	No
26	20 MB	612	4	17	-1 (none)	670	No
27	41 MB	698	7	17	300	732	Yes
28	41 MB	976	5	17	488	977	Yes
29	10 MB	306	4	17	0 (all)	340	No
30	20 MB	611	4	17	306	663	Yes
31	43 MB	732	7	17	300	732	Yes
32	43 MB	1023	5	17	-1 (none)	1023	Yes
33	29 MB	614	4	25	-1 (none)	663	Yes

* *Some of the oldest AT BIOSes only have zeros for entries past type 23.*

Almost all BIOSes produced in the 1990s provide at least two user-settable drive types, commonly specified as type 47. With type 47, the system BIOS stores the parameter table values for each drive in CMOS. This allows complete flexibility for all available drives and future drives. Some older BIOS vendors allow one user-definable disk type, but most offer two. Most BIOSes produced in 1995 and later support four drives, and dispense with the drive table concept.

If the system BIOS does not offer user-settable drive parameters, the desired parameters need to be inserted into a blank entry in the BIOS's drive type table. This means identifying a suitable location, and using an EPROM programmer to change the contents of the BIOS EPROM. Most BIOS ROMs during POST checksum the ROM, so bytes in the ROM must add up to 0 if any changes are made. You can use a byte in another unused type entry to make the ROM checksum add up to zero. Be aware that a few manufacturers, like AMI, have a more convoluted checksum process that must be bypassed. To avoid these hassles, consider updating your BIOS ROM to one that supports user-changeable drive parameters.

Nonstandard drive types like SCSI and ESDI, do not use the drive parameter table. The drive parameters are stored on the drive. In these cases, the drive type is set to 0 in the BIOS, so the system BIOS will not attempt to access the nonstandard drive.

IDE drives can use any drive type in which the total capacity of the drive is not exceeded. For example, a 100 MB drive could use any entry in Table 11-5 except type 9. Unfortunately, the closest fit is type 4, which only allows access to 62 MB. If the BIOS has user-settable drive parameters, a much better set of values that use the full capacity of the drive can be entered. Most IDE drive manufacturers provide a set of suggested drive parameters to get the full drive capacity.

BIOS Initialization

The BIOS begins the initialization of the hard disk by moving the interrupt 13h vector for the diskette drive (previously installed by the BIOS) to interrupt 40h. Next, a new interrupt vector 13h is loaded to point into the hard disk handler. When software attempts to access the diskette drive using interrupt 13h, the hard disk handler determines whether a diskette function is intended, and, if so, calls interrupt 40h to handle the diskette function.

The hard disk BIOS initialization obtains the disk drive type. On a few old disk controller cards that have their own hard disk BIOS ROMs, the BIOS reads switches or jumpers to select the drive type. With the AT and later systems, hard disk support was built into the system BIOS. The AT system BIOS initialization routine gets the drive type from CMOS memory.

Once the drive type is obtained, it is used as an index to the drive type table in ROM. This table of disk parameters normally begins at address F000:E401. Since each parameter table is 16 bytes long, the BIOS multiplies the type number times 16 to locate the desired disk parameter table entry. The pointer to the entry for drive 0 is saved in the interrupt vector 41h, and the pointer for drive 1's parameters is saved in vector 46h. Newer BIOSes have no table of drive parameters in ROM, and allow the user to assign the values needed. These are stored in CMOS memory. Usually some type of automatic detection is also provided within the BIOS setup to set the drive parameter values.

Each hard drive is checked using the BIOS diagnostic, interrupt 13h, function 14h. Upon passing the diagnostic, the drive is recalibrated with function 11h, and the last sector is verified. The last sector is calculated from the drive's parameter table entry. Like the diskette controller, a verify simply reads the sector and ECC bytes, and only verifies that the ECC is valid for the bytes read. If the verify fails, an error message is normally displayed to indicate a drive failure occurred.

Should any drive or drive controller fail during initialization, the hard disk parameters and hard disk handler are left in place by the BIOS. This allows drives to continue to be accessed by diagnostic software, even though the hard disk system may have a problem.

Hard Disk BIOS

Hard disk services are accessed through interrupt 13h. All functions require a number in DL to specify the drive to use. Set bit 7 high in DL to indicate a hard disk is being accessed, otherwise the diskette drives are accessed. To access hard drive 0 (c: in DOS), set DL to 80h. Similarly, drive 1 is accessed when DL is set to 81h. Older system BIOSes only support two hard drives. To access additional drives, a controller card must supply replacement routines for the standard hard disk services in the system BIOS. Most system BIOSes with a date code of 1995 or later support up to four IDE-style hard disks.

Upon completion of a service, a status byte is returned in the AH register. The status byte indicates whether the operation was successful by returning zero; otherwise, it contains an error code. This status byte is also stored in the BIOS data area at address 40:74h. The status codes are described in Table 11-6. Some codes are unique to specific controllers.

Table 11-6. Return Status Codes in AH

Hex Code	Description
0	Operation successful, no error occurred.
1	Invalid value passed or the function attempted is not supported.
2	Missing address mark—This error occurs if no sector address mark matched the request, or if the disk address (cylinder, head, sector) was beyond the end of the disk. On a PS/2 ESDI system, this error may also be returned if no index or selector pulse is detected.
3	Removable media write protected.
4	Requested sector not found—The cylinder and head were valid, but the requested sector could not be located. On a PS/2 ESDI system, this error is also generated if the controller cannot read the first and last Relative Block Address flags.
5	Reset failed—After commanding the controller to reset, the controller remained busy or the status was incorrect after the reset.
6	Disk changed—The drive media has been changed (removable media only)
7	Drive parameter activity failed—A request was made for drive parameters on a drive that does not exist.
8	DMA overrun—The DMA did not transfer data to or from the controller fast enough, such that a timeout occurred in the controller.
9	Data boundary error—An attempt was made to read or write data that would cause a segment wrap. This occurs on some controllers if more than 80h sectors are read, or if 80h sectors are read and the buffer is not aligned on a paragraph boundary (80h sectors * 512 byte sectors = 64K). For some disk operations (functions Ah and Bh) ECC bytes are added to the sector to make a total of 516 bytes. This means slightly less than 64K bytes of data can be transferred, usually only 7Fh sectors worth, or this error may occur. (Some drives return 7 bytes of ECC information, which further limits the maximum number of sectors to 7Eh.)
A	Bad sector flag detected—Each sector has a flag which can be used to mark the sector as bad. This is set by a special format command to mark a sector as bad. A sector is usually marked as bad after a surface analysis detects the sector's data area is unreliable or defective.
B	Bad track detected—During the last operation a bad track flag was detected. No retries were made. Each track has a flag used to indicate the entire track is defective and should not be used. Attempting to read from a bad track will generate this error message.

Table 11-6. Continued

Hex Code	Description
D	Invalid number of sectors on format—This is returned on PS/2 systems only, and indicates a number of possible problems while using the Low Level Format ESDI Drive, function 1Ah. Problems include: 1. Timeout due to controller remaining busy too long, or remaining busy after a command request. 2. The format command issues interrupt 15h, AH=0Fh and function AX=9000h during the operation. If a program hooks these functions and sets the carry flag, the format operation is terminated. This error code is returned. 3. The sequence of the format was wrong, and indicates a BIOS coding error (should never occur). 4. The controller fails the format because the primary or secondary defect map is unusable or defective, or a checksum error occurred, or a diagnostic error occurred.
E	Control data address mark detected—This message is identified in the PS/2 BIOS Technical reference. It is not clear what this error indicates on a PS/2 system, and it may never be issued. It is clearly never issued on PC/XT/AT-type systems.
F	DMA arbitration level out of range—This message is identified in the PS/2 BIOS Technical reference. It is not clear what this error indicates on a PS/2 system, and it may never be issued. It is clearly never issued on PC/XT/AT type systems.
10h	ECC error during read—This is returned if: 1. The sector ID has an error. The controller can detect, but not correct, errors in the sector ID. This may require a reformat of the cylinder. 2. The data from the sector is so mangled that even the ECC can't fix it. 3. If a controller diagnostic was being run, the controller's internal ECC generator test failed.
11h	ECC corrected data error—The sector had a data error that was corrected by the ECC mechanism. Note that the number of consecutive bits in error is returned in AL. Also be aware that ECC correction has a small probability of error (about 1 out of 100,000 errors corrected will be incorrect).
20h	Hard disk controller or drive problem—This is returned if: 1. The drive's index signal was missing. The index signal should occur once every revolution, and is sent to the controller over an individual line (old drives only). 2. The drive signaled the controller with a write fault. 3. Recalibrate failure—After stepping the maximum number of cylinders outward, the drive failed to signal that it reached cylinder 0. 4. The drive fail to become ready after a timeout period.

Table 11-6. Continued

Hex Code	Description
	5. Upon execution of one of the controller diagnostics, the controller found a problem. 6. An interface fault included a parity error, attention or command complete error (PS/2 only).
31h	No media in removable media drive—An operation was attempted on a removable media drive that cannot be honored without media in the drive.
40h	Seek operation failed—This is returned if: 1. An attempt to move to a specific valid cylinder on the disk failed. After the drive was commanded to move to a specific cylinder, the drive failed to signal that the seek was completed over the dedicated "seek complete" line. 2. After a Check drive ready function, the drive is still seeking the desired cylinder (not an error). 3. After a seek operation (including read and writes), the cylinder and/or head address failed to match the specified seek address.
80h	Timeout—The disk drive failed to respond or is busy executing a command.
AAh	Drive is not ready or is not selected. This code is also returned if the PS/2 drive has been parked using interrupt 13h, function 19h.
B0h	Volume not locked in drive—This error is returned when an attempt is made to unlock a removable media drive that is already unlocked. See Interrupt 13h, function 45h.
B1h	Volume locked in drive—An attempt was made to eject the media from a locked removable media drive. See Interrupt 13h, function 46h.
B2h	Volume not removable—An attempt was made to eject the media from a drive that does not have removable media. See Interrupt 13h, function 46h.
B3h	Volume in use—This error might be issued by an operating system when an attempt is made to eject a removable media drive that is still being used. See Interrupt 15h, function 52h.
B4h	Lock count exceeded—More locks were attempted on a drive that are allowed. See Interrupt 13h, function 45h.
B5h	Valid eject request failed—The removable media drive refused to eject the drive. This may be due to a drive switch or option, or due to a hardware fault in the drive.
BBh	Undefined error occurred—The controller issued an error code that was unknown by the BIOS. In theory, this error should never occur.
CCh	Write fault on selected drive—Each drive has a hardware line that indicates a write problem on the selected drive.

Table 11-6. Continued

Hex Code	Description
E0h	Status error without error—On an AT controller the status port 1F7h, error bit 0 was set. This indicates an error should be recorded in the error register. When looking at the error register port 1F1h, no error was recorded. This error code will not be issued on PS/2 systems. In theory, this error condition should never occur. It's unclear when the controller could create this error, unless the controller is defective, or other commands are issued to the controller between getting the status and reading the error register.
FFh	Sense operation failed—An attempt to get error data from the controller failed either due to a timeout while failing to respond, while remaining busy, or due to an invalid controller status.

Special Notes About BIOS Functions

In general a PC/XT controller denotes an adapter card with its own BIOS code that is used on PC and XT systems. The PC/XT controller is similar to, but has a few differences from, those disk services built into the AT BIOS. The PS/2 system BIOS has disk services for ESDI drives that also differ slightly from the AT standard. Many ESDI controllers used on AT and EISA systems appear more like the AT standard than the methods used in the PS/2. These differences are explained in the various services and data tables.

Although the valid drive numbers are specified as 80h and 81h, other nonstandard approaches may allow higher numbers. Older disk BIOS services for the PC/XT, AT, and PS/2 type controllers are limited to two physical drives. Other hardware, such as SCSI controllers, may allow seven devices per controller. These nonstandard controllers must replace the interrupt 13h handler to provide similar functionality and access more than two drives.

Some technical references indicate BIOS functions, like AH=Ah, Bh, and Eh are reserved. Many of these are real functions, however. Some functions are exclusive to specific systems such as the XT. Some functions, as noted, may not be supported on nonstandard drives such as ESDI and SCSI.

The hard disk BIOS provides the following interrupts and services:

Int	Function	Description	Platform
0Dh		Operation Complete	PC/XT
13h	ah=0	Disk Controller Reset	All
13h	ah=1	Read Disk Status	All
13h	ah=2	Read Disk Sectors	All
13h	ah=3	Write Disk Sectors	All
13h	ah=4	Verify Disk Sectors	All
13h	ah=5	Format Disk Track	PC/XT/AT/EISA
13h	ah=6	Format Disk Track with Bad Sectors	PC/XT

Int	Function	Description	Platform
13h	ah=7	Format Multiple Cylinders	PC/XT
13h	ah=8	Read Disk Drive Parameters	All
13h	ah=9	Initialize Drive Parameters	All
13h	ah=Ah	Read Disk Sectors with ECC	PC/XT/AT/EISA
13h	ah=Bh	Write Disk Sectors with ECC	PC/XT/AT/EISA
13h	ah=Ch	Seek	All
13h	ah=Dh	Alternate Disk Reset	All
13h	ah=Eh	Read Sector Buffer	PC/XT/PS/1
13h	ah=Eh	ESDI Undocumented Diagnostic	PS/2
13h	ah=Fh	Write Sector Buffer	PC/XT/PS/1
13h	ah=Fh	ESDI Undocumented Diagnostic	PS/2
13h	ah=10h	Check Drive Ready	All
13h	ah=11h	Recalibrate	All
13h	ah=12h	Controller RAM Diagnostic	PC/XT
13h	ah=13h	Drive Diagnostic	PC/XT
13h	ah=14h	Controller Internal Diagnostic	All
13h	ah=15h	Read Disk Drive Size	AT +
13h	ah=19h	Park Heads	PS/2
13h	ah=1Ah	Format ESDI Drive	PS/2
13h	ah=1Bh	Get ESDI Manufacturing Header	PS/2
13h	ah=1Ch	ESDI Special Functions	PS/2
13h	ah=21h	Read Disk Sectors, Multiple Blocks	PS/1
13h	ah=22h	Write Disk Sectors, Multiple Blocks	PS/1
13h	ah=23h	Set Controller Features Register	PS/1
13h	ah=24h	Set Multiple Blocks	PS/1
13h	ah=25h	Get Drive Information	PS/1
13h	ah=41h	Check if Extensions Present	EBIOS
13h	ah=42h	Extended Read Sectors	EBIOS
13h	ah=43h	Extended Write Sectors	EBIOS
13h	ah=44h	Extended Verify Sectors	EBIOS
13h	ah=45h	Lock and Unlock Drive	EBIOS
13h	ah=46h	Eject Media Request	EBIOS
13h	ah=47h	Extended Seek	EBIOS
13h	ah=48h	Get Extended Drive Parameters	EBIOS
13h	ah=49h	Get Extended Disk Change Status	EBIOS
13h	ah=4Ah	Initiate Disk Emulation	Bootable CD-ROM
13h	ah=4Bh	Terminate Disk Emulation	Bootable CD-ROM
13h	ah=4Ch	Initiate Disk Emulation and Boot	Bootable CD-ROM
13h	ah=4Dh	Return Boot Catalog	Bootable CD-ROM
13h	ah=4Eh	Set Hardware Configuration	EBIOS
15h	ah=52h	Removable Media Eject Hook	EBIOS

Int	Function	Description	Platform
4Fh	ax=8100h	SCSI Command, Common Access Method	SCSI
4Fh	ax=8200h	SCSI Presence check, Common SCSI	Access Method
76h		Operation Complete	AT/EISA
76h		Operation Complete	PS/2

Int	Description	Platform
0Dh	Hard Disk Operation Complete	PC,XT

INT

When the PC/XT hard disk controller completes the current command and any requested data transfers, the controller signals a hardware interrupt request, IRQ 5. If no higher priority interrupts are active, and interrupts are enabled, this interrupt 0Dh service routine is called. This routine resets the hardware interrupt and disables the DMA channel.

The Hard Disk Operation Complete service routine in the BIOS performs three specific actions. First, the nonspecific End-Of-Interrupt command 20h is sent to the interrupt controller port 20h. This clears the interrupt that just called us. Next the DMA port channel 3 is masked off. Lastly, the routine disables IRQ 5 on the interrupt controller. The routine then exits.

When the next hard disk command is issued, the disk BIOS for the PC/XT will re-enable hardware interrupt 5 and DMA channel 3.

Int	Func	Description	Platform
13h	0	Disk Controller Reset	All

INT

Commands both the diskette and hard disk controllers to reset. The drive parameters are sent to the controller, and the Recalibrate command is issued to position the drive heads at cylinder 0. To only reset the hard disk controller and not the diskette controller, use the Alternate Reset, function 0Dh.

For two drive systems, the drive number 80h or 81h does not matter because both drives are reset. If the system only has one drive, and the value 81h is passed as the drive number, no action occurs with the hard disk controller.

This function is normally used after a failure to read, write, verify or format, before retrying the same operation.

Called with:	ah = 0
	dl = drive number, 80h or 81h (see text)
Returns:	ah = return status (see Table 11-5)
	carry = 0 successful, = 1 if error occurred

Int	Func	Description	Platform
13h	1	Read Disk Status	All

Upon return from each disk service, the return status value is saved in the BIOS data area at 40:74h. This function returns the value currently stored from 40:74h, which represents the status from the last operation. After getting the status, this function sets the old status at 40:74h to zero.

Be aware that some BIOSes have a bug that alters the value of AL, even though the official IBM specification indicates AL should not be altered.

Called with: ah = 1
dl = drive number, 80h or 81h

Returns: ah = return status (see Table 11-5)
al altered (on some systems)
40:74h set to zero
carry = 0 if ah is zero (no error)
= 1 if ah is non-zero (status has error code)

Int	Func	Description	Platform
13h	2	Read Disk Sectors	All

Seeks to the specified location and reads a number of 512-byte disk sectors. The read data is placed into RAM at the location specified by ES:BX.

The buffer must be sufficiently large to hold the data read and must not exceed a total of 64K. If the transfer size is within 16 bytes of 64K, make sure BX is paragraph aligned, or a data boundary error may occur.

Interestingly enough, the BIOS will normalize ES:BX so that it is acceptable (although confusing) to transfer a block of sectors that would appear to cause a segment wrap. For example, reading a block of 32K with ES:BX set to a 32K buffer at xxxx:FFF0h is acceptable. The BIOS converts this to xxxx+FFF:0000h for the purpose of the data transfer.

If an attempt is made to transfer more than one full track of sectors, various vendors' BIOSes react differently. The operation may seem to work, with a successful return code, but the BIOS may fail to read the data correctly! See Code Sample 11-2, DISKTEST, for a full explanation of this problem.

Should a hard uncorrectable error occur on a sector (any error other than 11h), the operation is immediately terminated, and sectors still to be read are ignored.

Upon return, if the error code is 11h, the data transferred to the buffer is likely to be valid. Error 11h indicates an error was detected and corrected by the controller's ECC mechanism. IBM indicates the ECC mechanism that they use has a miscorrection probability of 1 out of 100,000 error corrections. Most operating systems ignore error 11h, and assume the data is valid. When the ECC corrected status occurs, the AL register has the error burst length as the number of consecutive bits in error.

For most other error conditions except 1, 4, or 9, it is recommended the disk be reset with function 0 and the read operation be re-attempted.

Called with: ah = 2
al = number of sectors to read (see text)
ch = cylinder number (lowest 8 bits of the 10-bit cylinder number, 0 based)
cl, bits 6 & 7 = cylinder number bits 8 and 9
bits 0 - 5 = starting sector number (1-63)
dh = starting head number (0 to 255)
dl = drive number (80h + zero based hard drive number)
es:bx = pointer where to place information read from disk

Returns: ah = return status (see Table 11-5)
al = burst error length if ah=11h; undefined on most BIOSes for other ah return status values
carry = 0 successful, = 1 if error occurred

Int	Func	Description	Platform
13h	3	Write Disk Sectors	All

INT III I

Seeks to the specified location and writes a number of 512-byte disk sectors. The data is written to the disk from RAM at the location specified by ES:BX. The buffer must be sufficiently large for the data and must not exceed a total of 64K. If the transfer size is within 16 bytes of 64K, make sure BX is paragraph aligned, or a data boundary error could occur.

If an attempt is made to transfer more than one full track of sectors, various vendors' BIOSes react differently. The operation may seem to work, with a successful return code, but the BIOS may fail to write the data correctly! See Code Sample 11-2, DISKTEST, for a full explanation of this problem.

For most error conditions except for 1, 4, or 9, it is recommended the disk be reset with function 0 and the write operation be re-attempted.

Called with: ah = 3
al = number of sectors to write (see text)
ch = cylinder number (lowest 8 bits of the 10-bit cylinder number, 0 based)
cl, bits 6 & 7 = cylinder number bits 8 and 9
bits 0 - 5 = starting sector number (1-63)
dh = starting head number (0 to 255)
dl = drive number (80h + zero based hard drive number)
es:bx = pointer where to get information to write to the disk

Returns: ah = return status (see Table 11-5)
carry = 0 successful, = 1 if error occurred

Int	Func	Description	Platform
13h	4	Verify Disk Sectors	All

Verifies a number of disk sectors starting from the specified location. This command does not actually check that each byte matches a buffer's contents. Instead, the controller reads the specified contents from the disk and verifies that the calculated ECC matches the ECC previously stored on the disk. If the sectors are located, read, and the ECC is valid, the data is considered verified.

Some technical references indicate the ES:BX pointer should be specified for older PC/XT/AT BIOSes. I believe these are in error, as all IBM documentation and controller IC documentation I've examined indicate no buffer is used for verifies. This is consistent with the way the controller checks ECC information from sectors read off the disk, and never has a need for comparison buffer.

If an attempt is made to verify more than one full track of sectors, various vendors' BIOSes react differently. The operation may seem to work, with a successful return code, but the BIOS may fail to verify the data correctly! See Code Sample 11-2, DISKTEST, for a full explanation of this problem.

For most error conditions except 1, 4, or 9, it is recommended the disk be reset with function 0 and the verify operation be re-attempted.

Called with:
- ah = 4
- al = number of sectors to verify (see text)
- ch = cylinder number (lowest 8 bits of the 10-bit cylinder number, 0 based)
- cl, bits 6 & 7 = cylinder number bits 8 and 9
  - bits 0 - 5 = starting sector number (1-63)
- dh = starting head number (0 to 255)
- dl = drive number (80h + zero based hard drive number)
- es:bx = unused buffer (see text above)

Returns:
- ah = return status (see Table 11-5)
- carry = 0 successful, = 1 if error occurred

Int	Func	Description	Platform
13h	5	Format Disk Track	PC/XT/AT/EISA

Formats the specified track on the disk drive. Each sector within the track is written with the sector's assigned number, the sector type, initial sector data, and ECC bytes.

For AT and later systems, a table of sector information is provided from a buffer pointed to by ES:BX. This 512-byte table contains two bytes for each sector in the track to be formatted. The table contents are shown in Table 11-7.

Table 11-7. Format Sector Data Table

Byte	Description
0	Sector type
	0 = good
	20h = unassign from the alternate location for this sector
	40h = assign this sector to an alternate location
	80h = bad
1	Sector number 1 to 128

The first byte indicates if the sector is good or bad. A sector might be marked as bad if it is determined the sector has hard or soft errors. It's also used as a software copy protection scheme to mark an otherwise good sector as bad. Some controllers provide the ability to substitute an alternate sector in place of a bad sector. Sector types 20h and 40h control this mechanism. The second byte has the sector number to be written into the sector. For an interleave of one, the sector numbering is sequential.

The PC/XT allows setting the interleave for each track. Unlike the slow PC/XT, systems today are fast enough to process sectors sequentially from the drive. Without interleave on the PC/XT, by the time the first sector was read, the heads have already moved past the start of the next sector. This means the drive must wait one full revolution to get to the next sector! Interleave dramatically speeds up disk access, by ordering the sectors on the disk relative to the capacity of the system to process the sectors.

As an example, Figure 11-4 shows the buffer contents to format a track with an interleave of two on a 17-sector drive and physical sector 8 marked as bad. The physical sector numbers are above the bytes in the table. These are not part of the 512-byte data table.

Figure 11-4. 512-Byte Format Data Buffer

	sector 1	sector 2	sector 3	sector 4	sector 5	sector 6	sector 7	sector 8
es:bx ->	0, 1	0, 10	0, 2	0, 11	0, 3	0, 12	0, 4	80h, 13
	sector 9	sector 10	sector 11	sector 12	sector 13	sector 14	sector 15	sector 16
	0, 5	0, 14	0, 6	0, 15	0, 7	0, 16	0, 8	0, 17
	sector 17	unused	unused					
	0, 9	0, 0	0, 0	all remaining bytes are zero (fill to 512 byte limit)				

An interleave of 1 indicates the sectors are numbered consecutively. Higher interleave values are used to bring the data off the disk somewhat slower, but within the capacity of the system. Most PC/XTs use interleaves of 2 or higher for the best performance. If the interleave is set too low for the system, a dramatic reduction in performance occurs while the disk must spin one full revolution to get to each sector (the worst case scenario). For PC/XT systems, first use interrupt 13h, function 0Fh (Write Sector Buffer) to set the data contents for the format. PC systems normally use F6h as the byte for format data.

This function is not supported on a PS/2 with ESDI drives. Use function 1Ah, Low-Level Format ESDI Drive.

For most error conditions except 1, 4, or 0Dh, it is recommended the disk be reset with function 0 and the operation be reattempted.

Called with:	ah = 5
	al = interleave, 1 to 10h (this value is for PC/XT type controllers only, and is unused for all other controllers)
	ch = cylinder number (lowest 8 bits of the 10-bit cylinder number, 0 based)
	cl, bits 6 & 7 = cylinder number bits 8 and 9
	bits 0 - 5 = starting sector number (1-63)
	dh = starting head number (0 to 255)
	dl = drive number (80h + zero based hard drive number)
	es:bx = pointer to address table (AT controllers and later, unused on PC/XT)
Returns:	ah = return status (see Table 11-5)
	carry = 0 successful, = 1 if error occurred

Int	Func	Description	Platform
13h	6	Format Disk Track with Bad Sectors	PC/XT

Formats one track on the disk drive and marks each sector as bad. This function is the same as function 5, except every sector in the track is marked as bad. This is useful when soft or hard errors have been detected, and it is necessary to exclude the track from use. This function is available on the PC/XT only.

For most error conditions except 1, 4, or 0Dh, it is recommended the disk be reset with function 0 and the format operation be re-attempted.

Called with:	ah = 6 (PC/XT only)
	al = interleave, 1 to 10h
	ch = cylinder number (lowest 8 bits of the 10-bit cylinder number, 0 based)
	cl, bits 6 & 7 = cylinder number bits 8 and 9
	dh = starting head number (0 to 255)
	dl = drive number (80h + zero based hard drive number)
Returns:	ah = return status (see Table 11-5)
	carry = 0 successful, = 1 if error occurred

Int	Func	Description	Platform
13h	7	Format Multiple Cylinders	PC/XT

INT
III I

Formats all cylinders starting with the cylinder number passed in CX. This function is similar to function 5, except multiple cylinders are formatted. To format the entire drive, set CX to zero. This function is available on the PC/XT only.

For most error conditions except 1, 4, or 0Dh, it is recommended the disk be reset with function 0 and the format operation be re-attempted.

Called with:
- ah = 7 (PC/XT only)
- al = interleave, 1 to 10h
- ch = starting cylinder number (lowest 8 bits of the 10-bit cylinder number, 0 based)
- cl, bits 6 & 7 = cylinder number bits 8 and 9
- dl = drive number (80h + zero based hard drive number)

Returns:
- ah = return status (see Table 11-5)
- carry = 0 successful, = 1 if error occurred

Int	Func	Description	Platform
13h	8	Read Disk Drive Parameters	All

INT
III I

Gets the drive parameters for the specified drive. For AT-type disk controllers, the data is indirectly read using the pointer stored in either vector 41h or 46h, depending on whether drive 0 or 1 is specified.

On PC/XT type disk controllers, the data is indirectly read using the pointer stored in interrupt vector 41h if the switches for the specified drive are both ON. Otherwise, the switches on the PC/XT controller card are used to index into one of four parameter table entries, where the pointer at interrupt vector 41h is the base of the table. See Table 11-8 for these switch settings (in function 9).

On controllers, such as SCSI and PS/2 ESDI systems, parameter information stored on the disk is returned. Current IDE controllers provide a LBA (Logical Block Addressing) mode to access drives that are greater than 504 MB in size. If LBA is active, the returned parameters have been modified to provide access to the entire drive.

The maximum cylinder number must be increased by one to get the total number of cylinders, which does not include the diagnostic cylinder. The BIOS always reserves one cylinder for diagnostic purposes. This cylinder can be accessed, but data may be destroyed on the diagnostic cylinder during controller and drive tests. Add one more cylinder to the total if the real total number of cylinders is desired. It's been reported that some Zenith PC systems reserve an additional cylinder for unknown reasons. In this case the number of cylinders returned will be three less than the total number of cylinders specified in the disk parameter table.

The maximum head number must be increased by one to get the total number of heads on the drive (1 to 256). When defining your code, keep in mind a byte will not hold the maximum head count (256).

The function will fail if an attempt is made to get drive parameters from a drive number out of range, when a drive does not exist, or when no hard disk controller is active. This function does *not* return a pointer to the drive type table as is commonly indicated in many other technical references.

Called with: ah = 8
dl = drive number (80h + zero based hard drive number)

Returns: if successful
ah = 0
al = undefined
carry = 0
ch = maximum cylinder number (lowest 8 bits of the 10-bit cylinder number, 0 based)
cl, bits 6 & 7 = cylinder number bits 8 and 9
bits 0 - 5 = maximum sector number (1-63)
dh = maximum head number (0 to 255)
dl = number of drives

if failed (but at least one drive is active)
ah = 7
carry = 1
al = cx = dx = 0

if failed (because no hard disk exists)
ah = 1
carry = 1
al = bx = cx = dx = es = 0

INT

Int	Func	Description	Platform
13h	9	Initialize Drive Parameters	All

Initializes the specified drive controller with the drive type parameters.

For AT or later systems using standard drives (i.e., not ESDI), if drive 0 is selected, the parameters are used to initialize the drive from the pointer stored at interrupt vector 41h at address 0:104h. If drive 1 is selected, then interrupt vector 46h at address 0:118h points to the table of parameters to use for initialization. A PS/2 ESDI drive does not use the parameter table mechanism, as the parameters are stored on the drive. For a PS/2 ESDI drive, this command performs no action, and immediately returns success. For other non-AT controllers such as SCSI, this function also performs no action, and return success.

For the PC/XT, interrupt 41h points to the start of the drive type table, which is only four entries long. Switches for the specified drive are read from the disk controller card to determine which of the four drive types to use. The switch settings are shown in Table 11-8.

Table 11-8. Hard Disk Type Selection—PC/XT Controller

Uses Table Entry	Drive 0 Switch 1	Drive 0 Switch 2	Drive 1 Switch 3	Drive 1 Switch 4
0	on	on	on	on
1	on	off	on	off
2	off	on	off	on
3	off	off	off	off

On a PC/XT, if the drive number is between 80h and 87h, then both drives 0 and 1 are initialized (this is not a documentation error, but the way the PC/XT BIOS code actually works).

Called with: ah = 9
dl = drive number (80h + zero based hard drive number)

Returns: ah = return status (see Table 11-6)
carry = 0 successful, = 1 if error occurred

Int	Func	Description	Platform
13h	0Ah	Read Disk Sectors with ECC	PC/XT/AT/EISA

INT III I

Reads multiple sectors into a buffer starting at ES:BX. Each 512-byte sector transferred to the buffer includes an additional 4-byte ECC code. This means each sector requires 516 bytes of buffer space. Should a data error be detected on a sector, the operation immediately stops, and the failed sector is *not* corrected.

Some ESDI drives have an option to use a 7-byte ECC code, which means each sector will be 519 bytes long. The 7-byte ECC improves the error correction capabilities, but most controllers default to 4-byte mode to make them fully compatible with older software.

If an attempt is made to read more than one full track of sectors, various vendors' BIOSes react differently. The operation may seem to work, with a successful return code, but the BIOS may fail to read the data correctly! See Code Sample 11-2, DISKTEST, for a full explanation of this problem.

This function is supported on PC, XT, AT, and EISA systems, but not on PS/2 systems using ESDI drives. Normally interrupt 13h, function 2 is used by applications and the operating system to read multiple sectors.

For most error conditions except 1, 4, or 9, it is recommended the disk be reset with function 0 and the operation be re-attempted.

Called with: ah = 0Ah
al = Number of sectors to read (see text)
ch = cylinder number (lowest 8 bits of the 10-bit cylinder number, 0 based)
cl, bits 6 & 7 = cylinder number bits 8 and 9
bits 0 - 5 = starting sector number (1-63)
dh = starting head number (0 to 255)
dl = drive number (80h + zero based hard drive number)
es:bx = pointer where to store read sectors

Returns: ah = return status (see Table 11-5)
carry = 0 successful, = 1 if error occurred

Int	Func	Description	Platform
13h	0Bh	Write Disk Sectors with ECC	PC/XT/AT/EISA

Writes multiple sectors into a buffer starting at ES:BX. Each 512-byte sector must have its associated 4-byte ECC code. This means each sector requires 516 bytes of buffer space.

Some ESDI drives have an option to use a 7-byte ECC code, which means each sector will be 519 bytes long. The 7-byte ECC improves the error correction capabilities, but most controllers default to 4-byte mode to make them fully compatible with older software.

If an attempt is made to write more than one full track of sectors, various vendors' BIOSes react differently. The operation may seem to work, with a successful return code, but the BIOS may fail to write the data correctly! See Code Sample 11-2, DISKTEST, for a full explanation of this problem.

This function is supported on PC, XT, AT, and EISA systems, but not PS/2 systems using ESDI drives. Normally interrupt 13h, function 3 is used by applications and the operating system to write multiple sectors.

For most error conditions except 1, 4, or 9, it is recommended the disk be reset with function 0 and the operation be re-attempted.

Called with: ah = 0Bh
al = Number of sectors to write (see text)
ch = cylinder number (lowest 8 bits of the 10-bit cylinder number, 0 based)
cl, bits 6 & 7 = cylinder number bits 8 and 9
bits 0 - 5 = starting sector number (1-63)
dh = starting head number (0 to 255)
dl = drive number (80h + zero based hard drive number)
es:bx = pointer where to get sectors to write

Returns: ah = return status (see Table 11-5)
carry = 0 successful, = 1 if error occurred

Int	Func	Description	Platform
13h	**0Ch**	**Seek**	**All**

INT

Moves the head on the drive to the specified cylinder. For BIOS read, write, and verify sectors functions, the seek operation is automatic (functions 2, 3, 4, Ah, and Bh). No data is transferred with this function.

For most error conditions, except 1 or 4, it is recommended the disk be reset with function 0 and the operation be re-attempted.

Called with: ah = 0Ch
ch = cylinder number (lowest 8 bits of the 10-bit cylinder number, 0 based)
cl, bits 6 & 7 = cylinder number bits 8 and 9
dh = starting head number (0 to 255)
dl = drive number (80h + zero based hard drive number)

Returns: ah = return status (see Table 11-5)
carry = 0 successful, = 1 if error occurred

Int	Func	Description	Platform
13h	**0Dh**	**Alternate Disk Reset**	**All**

INT

Commands the hard disk controller to reset. The drive parameters are sent to the controller, and the recalibrate command is issued to position the drive heads at cylinder 0. This performs the same action as interrupt 13h function 0 (Disk Controller Reset), except the diskette controller is not reset.

For two-drive systems, the drive number (80h or 81h) does not matter, since both drives are reset. If the system only has one drive, and the value 81h is passed as the drive number, no action occurs with the hard disk controller.

Called with: ah = 0Dh
dl = drive number, 80h or 81h

Returns: ah = return status (see Table 11-5)
carry = 0 successful, = 1 if error occurred

Int	Func	Description	Platform
13h	**0Eh**	**Read Sector Buffer**	**PC/XT/PS/1**

INT

Reads the disk controller's internal sector buffer into ES:BX. This is used for diagnostic purposes only, and is available on PC/XT systems and the PS/1. Some other systems may support this function, but most do not. No data is read from the disk drive.

Called with: ah = 0Eh (PC/XT and PS/1 only)
dl = drive number, 80h or 81h
es:bx = pointer where store sector buffer
Returns: ah = return status (see Table 11-5)
carry = 0 successful, = 1 if error occurred

INT	Int	Func	Description	Platform
	13h	0Eh	ESDI Undocumented Diagnostic	PS/2

Issues a reserved command 11h to the ESDI controller after setting input parameters to point to cylinder 0, sector 1, head 0. The operation appears to use DMA. It is unknown what is tested with this function.

Called with: ah = 0Eh (ESDI PS/2 only)
dl = drive number, 80h or 81h
Returns: ah = return status (see Table 11-5)
carry = 0 successful, = 1 if error occurred

INT	Int	Func	Description	Platform
	13h	0Fh	Write Sector Buffer	PC/XT/PS/1

Writes data from ES:BX into the disk controller's internal sector buffer. This is used for diagnostic purposes and to set up the data contents for a format using function 5. No data is written onto the disk drive by this function alone. This function is available on PC/XT and PS/1 systems. Other systems may support this function, but most do not.

For a format, this function loads the data used by the format command to initialize each sector. The DOS standard requires a 512-byte buffer of all F6h bytes. Other operating systems may prefer different bytes.

Called with: ah = 0Fh (PC/XT and PS/1 only)
dl = drive number, 80h or 81h
es:bx = pointer to data to be written into disk controller (512 bytes)
Returns: ah = return status (see Table 11-5)
carry = 0 successful, = 1 if error occurred

INT	Int	Func	Description	Platform
	13h	0Fh	ESDI Undocumented Diagnostic	PS/2

Issues a reserved command 10h to the ESDI controller after setting input parameters to point to cylinder 0, sector 1, head 0. The operation appears to use DMA. It is unknown what is tested with this function.

Called with: ah = 0Eh (ESDI PS/2 only)
dl = drive number, 80h or 81h
Returns: ah = return status (see Table 11-5)
carry = 0 successful, = 1 if error occurred

Int	Func	Description	Platform
13h	10h	Check Drive Ready	All

INT

Checks if the specified hard disk is ready for a command. A return status of zero indicates the controller is not busy and the specified disk is ready.

Called with: ah = 10h
dl = drive number (80h + zero based hard drive number)
Returns: ah = return status (see Table 11-5)
carry = 0 successful, = 1 if error occurred

Int	Func	Description	Platform
13h	11h	Recalibrate	All

INT

Moves the specified drive's head 0 to cylinder 0.

For most error conditions, except for Invalid value passed error number 1, it is recommended the disk be reset with function 0 and the operation be re-attempted.

Called with: ah = 11h
dl = drive number (80h + zero based hard drive number)
Returns: ah = return status (see Table 11-5)
carry = 0 successful, = 1 if error occurred

Int	Func	Description	Platform
13h	12h	Controller RAM Diagnostic	PC/XT

INT

Initiates an internal test of the disk controller's sector buffer. This function is only available on PC/XT systems. If the test is successful, ah is set to zero.

Called with: ah = 12h (PC/XT only)
dl = drive number, 80h or 81h
Returns: ah = return status (see Table 11-5)
carry = 0 successful, = 1 if error occurred
al = 0

Int	Func	Description	Platform
13h	13h	Drive Diagnostic	PC/XT

Initiates an internal diagnostic test through the disk controller of the attached drive. This function is only available on PC/XT systems. If the test is successful, ah is set to zero.

Called with: ah = 13h (PC/XT only)
dl = drive number, 80h or 81h

Returns: ah = return status (see Table 11-5)
carry = 0 successful, = 1 if error occurred
al = 0

Int	Func	Description	Platform
13h	14h	Controller Internal Diagnostic	All

Initiates an internal disk controller self-test. This function is supported by the PC/XT and all later systems, but is undocumented for AT+ systems. If the test is successful, ah is set to zero.

Called with: ah = 14h
dl = drive number (80h + zero based hard drive number)

Returns: ah = return status (see Table 11-5)
carry = 0 successful, = 1 if error occurred
al = 0

Int	Func	Description	Platform
13h	15h	Read Disk Drive Size	AT+

Checks if the drive is valid and gets the number of 512-byte sectors on the hard drive. No access to the disk controller or drive is made with this command. The size is determined from the current drive parameter table for the specified drive, using the following calculation:

Total Sectors = (Number of heads) * (Number of sectors per track) * (Number of cylinders - 1)

Notice that this function removes one cylinder from the total size for diagnostics. Surprisingly, the BIOS code never uses this cylinder, but some disk controller designs may use the cylinder for diagnostics, so it's best to avoid use of this last cylinder. The diagnostic cylinder is fully accessible by any other disk service.

Called with:	ah = 15h
	dl = drive number (80h + zero based hard drive number)
Returns:	if successful
	ax = 3 Hard disk accessible
	carry = 0
	cx:dx = total number of sectors (32-bit)
	if failed
	ax = 0 Drive not present
	carry = 1
	cx = dx = 0

Int	Func	Description	Platform
13h	19h	Park Heads	PS/2

INT

Parks the heads of the specified drive in a safe area, defined by the drive manufacturer. A stop motor command is issued and the drive is locked out from further use until the system is powered down and back up again. After this command is issued, any other attempts to access the parked drive will return the Drive Not Ready error code AAh.

This function is only supported on PS/2 systems using ESDI type drives (both MCA and ISA bus types).

Called with:	ah = 19h
	dl = drive number, 80h or 81h
Returns:	ah = return status (see Table 11-6)
	carry = 0 successful, = 1 if error occurred

Int	Func	Description	Platform
13h	1Ah	Low-Level Format ESDI Drive	PS/2

INT

For PS/2 systems with ESDI drives, this command performs either a low-level format of the entire drive or can perform several related services, such as a surface analysis check for defects. All data on the selected drive is destroyed by the completion of this command (unformat utilities cannot recover the information). The partition information must be loaded and a high-level format must occur before the drive is usable. In DOS, this is accomplished with FDISK and FORMAT.

An optional defect table can be provided to inform the format process to skip specified defects. Each entry in the defects table is four bytes long, and is described in Table 11-9, the Defect Table entry structure.

Table 11-9. Defect Table Entry Structure

Offset	Size	Description		
0	byte	Relative Sector Address, LSB (bits 0-7)		
1	byte	Relative Sector Address, (bits 8-15)		
2	byte	Relative Sector Address, MSB (bits 16-24)		
3	byte	Flag and defect count byte		
		bit	7 = 1	Sector is the last logical sector on track
			6 = 1	Sector is the first logical sector on track
			5 = 1	Sector is in the last logical sector on the cylinder
			4 = 1	Logical sectors are pushed onto next track
			3 = x	Number of defects in a row (see below)
			2 = x	
			1 = x	
			0 = x	

The number of defects in a row value is the number of sectors pushed onto this cylinder from the previous cylinder. This occurs when a cylinder has more defects than can be contained in reserved defect areas on that cylinder. All sectors on one cylinder use the same "Number of defects in a row" number. This defect management approach assumes later cylinders will have less defects than normal, and the pushed sector(s) from one cylinder will fit on subsequent cylinders. The controller keeps track of pushed sectors to transparently manage access to these pushed sectors.

The Low-Level format is passed the CL register with control bits to indicate various subfunctions and operations. Bit 4 is used to issue an interrupt 15h, function AH=0Fh when each cylinder operation is complete. The interrupt 15h function is called with an operation code specified in AL. An AL value of 1 indicates a surface analysis, and 2 indicates a format. This feature allows a format program to hook the interrupt, and by counting each occurrence, display what cylinder is being formatted. By hooking interrupt 15h, AH=0Fh, a reliable means to stop the format in process is provided. The carry flag must be clear upon return from int 15h, AH=0Fh for the format to continue. Set the carry flag if the operation needs to be aborted.

To perform a surface analysis, the drive must be first formatted with control bit 3 set to zero. Once the format is complete, the surface analysis can be launched by setting control bit 3 on. To save the results of the surface analysis test, also set bit 2 on. This saves the defect information from the surface analysis in the secondary defect map. If the surface analysis results are to be ignored, clear bit 2.

Control bits 0 and 1 indicate if the defect maps should be used. In normal operation, both maps would be used. Leave both bits cleared to use both defect maps.

Called with:	ah	= 1Ah
	al	= 0 no defect table used
		> 0 number of entries in the defect table
	cl	= control bits

bits 7 to 5 = 0
4 = 1 Send interrupt after every cylinder completed (see text)
3 = 1 To perform surface analysis (see text)
2 = 1 Save the results from the surface analysis into the secondary defect map
1 = 1 Indicates the secondary defect map is ignored
0 = 1 Indicates the primary defect map is ignored (the map that was set by the drive manufacturer)

dl = drive number, 80h or 81h
es:bx = pointer to defect table

Returns: ah = return status (see Table 11-5)
carry = 0 successful, = 1 if error occurred

Int	Func	Description	Platform
13h	1Bh	Get ESDI Manufacturing Header	PS/2

For PS/2 systems with an ESDI drives, this command gets the manufacturing header and can be used to extract the primary defect map from the drive. Its operation is similar to a standard read sectors function. The first sector read with this command contains the manufacturing header with the number of defect entries, followed by the first entries of the defect map. Reading additional sectors will obtain the entire defect map. This function does not check for the end of the defect map, and will read the requested number of sectors, even if the defect map uses fewer sectors than requested. This function is undocumented.

Called with: ah = 1Bh
al = number of sectors to read
dl = drive number, 80h or 81h
es:bx = pointer where to place information read from disk

Returns: ah = return status (see Table 11-6)
carry = 0 successful, = 1 if error occurred

Int	Func	Description	Platform
13h	1Ch	ESDI Special Functions	PS/2

For PS/2 systems with an ESDI drives, this command selects from a number of subfunctions internal to the system BIOS. Other registers may be required for specific subfunctions, as this entire function is undocumented. In general, these subfunctions should only be used if replacing other interrupt 13h hard disk system services on a PS/2 system with replacement service routines.

Called with:	ah = 1Ch
	dl = drive number, 80h or 81h
	al = subfunction
Returns:	ah = return status (see Table 11-6)
	carry = 0 successful, = 1 if error occurred

AL=	ESDI Special Subfunction Commands
0	returns "not implemented" error (no action)
1	undocumented controller command 0612h, no DMA
2	undocumented controller command 0612h, no DMA
3	undocumented controller command 0612h, no DMA
4	undocumented controller command 0612h, no DMA
5	undocumented controller command 0612h, no DMA
6	undocumented controller command 0612h, no DMA
7	returns "not implemented error" (no action)
8	get command complete status
9	get device status
A	get configuration of drive
B	get configuration of controller
C	get Programmable Option Select (POS) information
D	undocumented controller command 0614h, no DMA
E	translate Relative Sector Address
F	undocumented controller command 0614h, no DMA
10h	unknown non-controller subfunction
11h	unknown non-controller subfunction
12h	undocumented controller command 0612h, no DMA

Subfunction Detail

INT

Subfunction	Description	Int	Function
AL=8	Get Command Complete Status	13h	AH=1Ch

Gets the Command Complete Status Block of the last completed command for the selected drive. When a command completes, the controller issues IRQ 14, interrupt 76h, indicating the status is ready to be read. When using this subfunction, ES:BX points to the buffer where to store the Command Complete Status Block. See port 3510h, output, Get command complete status (command 607h) and Table 11-22 for the details of the Command Complete Status Block.

Subfunction	Description	Int	Function
AL=9	Get Device Status	13h	AH=1Ch

INT

Gets the Device Status Block of the last completed command for the selected drive. When a command completes, the controller issues IRQ 14, interrupt 76h, indicating the status is ready to be read. When using this subfunction, ES:BX points to the buffer where to store the Device Status Block. See port 3510h, output, Get device status (command 608h) and Table 11-23 for the details of the Device Status Block.

Subfunction	Description	Int	Function
AL=Ah	Get Configuration of Drive	13h	AH=1Ch

INT

Commands the controller to return the Configuration Status Block for the drive. This has information similar to the drive parameter table, including the maximum number of cylinders, tracks, and other information. When using this subfunction, ES:BX points to the buffer where to store the Configuration Status Block. See port 3510h, output, Get configuration (command 609h) and Table 11-24 for the details of the Configuration Status Block.

Subfunction	Description	Int	Function
AL=Bh	Get Configuration of Controller	13h	AH=1Ch

INT

Commands the controller to return the Configuration Status Block for the controller. This gets the version of the microcode in the controller. When using this subfunction, ES:BX points to the buffer where to store the Configuration Status Block. See port 3510h, output, Get configuration (command 6E9h) and Table 11-26 for the details of the Configuration Status Block.

Subfunction	Description	Int	Function
AL=Ch	Get POS Information	13h	AH=1Ch

INT

Gets the contents of the Programmable Option Select (POS) registers. When using this subfunction, ES:BX points to the buffer where to store the Configuration Status Block. See port 3510h, output, Get Programmable Option Select Information (command 6EAh) and Table 11-27 for the details of the POS Information Status Block.

Subfunction	Description	Int	Function
AL=Eh	Translate Relative Sector Address	13h	AH=1Ch

INT

The ESDI drive maintains two types of addressing, Relative Sector Address (RSA) and Absolute Sector Address (ASA). The RSA is used to read, write, verify, and do other normal actions. The Relative Sector Address hides defects and makes the entire disk appear as one long linear array. If it is necessary to deallocate a defective sector, the Absolute Sector Address is required. This function converts an RSA into ASA.

See port 3510h, output, Translate Relative Sector Address (command 6EBh) for additional details.

Int	Func	Description	Platform
13h	21h	Read Disk Sectors, Multiple Blocks	PS/1

This function is similar to the Read Disk Sectors function 2, except interrupts are not generated at the end of every sector transfer, but only after a group of sectors are transferred. The Set Multiple Blocks function 24h must be issued prior to this function. See Set Multiple Blocks function 24h for additional information.

This function is undocumented and not supported on most AT controllers.

Called with:
- ah = 21h
- al = number of blocks of sectors to read
- ch = cylinder number (lowest 8 bits of the 10-bit cylinder number, 0 based)
- cl, bits 6 & 7 = cylinder number bits 8 and 9
  - bits 0 - 5 = starting sector number (1-63)
- dh = starting head number (0 to 255)
- dl = drive number (80h + zero based hard drive number)
- es:bx = pointer where to place information read from disk

Returns:
- ah = return status (see table 11-5)
- al = burst error length if ah=11h
- carry = 0 successful, = 1 if error occurred

Int	Func	Description	Platform
13h	22h	Write Disk Sectors, Multiple Blocks	PS/1

This function is similar to the Write Disk Sectors function 3, except interrupts are not generated at the end of every sector transfer, but only after a group of sectors are transferred. The Set Multiple Blocks function 24h must be issued prior to this function. See Set Multiple Blocks function 24h for additional information.

This function is undocumented and not supported on most AT controllers.

Called with:
- ah = 22h
- al = number of blocks of sectors to write
- ch = cylinder number (lowest 8 bits of the 10-bit cylinder number, 0 based)
- cl, bits 6 & 7 = cylinder number bits 8 and 9
  - bits 0 - 5= starting sector number (1-63)
- dh = starting head number (0 to 255)
- dl = drive number (80h + zero based hard drive number)
- es:bx = pointer where to get information to write to the disk

Returns:
- ah = return status (see Table 11-6)
- carry = 0 successful, = 1 if error occurred

Int	Func	Description	Platform
13h	23h	Set Controller Features Register	PS/1

This controls various internal features of the controller. Other registers may contain values necessary for a feature, depending on the vendor. It is not known if all the described features are supported by the PS/1 controller. Features that are enabled and disabled set internal flags in the controller. Once accepted, another Set Features function can be used without changing the prior feature setting. Table 11-10 shows the feature options.

Table 11-10. Controller Feature Options

Hex Value	Feature
1	Enable 8-bit data transfers instead of normal 16-bit transfers
2	Enable write cache
22	Write Same, user-specified area
33	Disable Retries
44	Specify length of ECC bytes returned on Read/Write with ECC
54	Set cache segments, value in the Sector Count register
55	Disable look-ahead feature
66	Disable reverting to power-on defaults
77	Disable ECC
81	Disable 8-bit data transfers, use 16 bits (normal)
82	Disable write cache
88	Enable ECC (normal)
99	Enable Retries (normal)
AA	Enable look-ahead feature
BB	Return 4 bytes on Read/Write with ECC commands
CC	Enable reverting to power-on defaults
DD	Write Same, entire disk

This function is undocumented and not supported on most AT controllers.

Called with: ah = 23h
al = function number
dl = drive number (80h + zero based hard drive number)
other registers may be necessary

Returns: ah = return status (see Table 11-5)
carry = 0 successful, = 1 if error occurred

Int	Func	Description	Platform
13h	24h	Set Multiple Blocks	PS/1

The controller provides a feature to transfer multiple groups of sectors at a time. The number of sectors per block is loaded by this function. Valid block sizes are 2, 4, 8, and 16. Larger blocks may be supported if the controller's internal buffer is greater than 8K.

Following this function would be Read or Write Disk Sectors, Multiple Blocks function 21h or 22h. The Read or Write Disk Sectors function begins the transfer of the specified block of sectors. The controller will only interrupt the system when each block of sectors completes.

If, for example, five sectors were transferred with a block size of 2, the first two sectors are transferred, followed by two more, and the last block would send the remainder, 1 sector. Only three interrupts would have been generated for this example, rather than the normal interrupt for each sector.

The Multiple Block feature is intended for higher performance operation. This function is undocumented and may have other unknown operational requirements.

Called with: ah = 24h
al = number of sectors per block, 2, 4, 8, or 16
dl = drive number (80h + zero based hard drive number)

Returns: ah = return status (see Table 11-5)
carry = 0 successful, = 1 if error occurred

Int	Func	Description	Platform
13h	25h	Get Drive Information	PS/1

This function gets 256 words of drive information that is stored on the drive. The command will only work with drives like IDE that hold this data on the disk. This command is not supported on most AT controllers. See Table 11-16 under port 1F7h, command ECh for the drive information table.

Int	Func	Description	Platform
13h	41h	Check If Extensions Present	EBIOS

This function is used to determine which, if any, EBIOS functions are supported for a specified hard drive. Both the returned carry bit and BX register must be checked before any other returned EBIOS values are valid.

Called with: ah = 41h
bx = 55AAh
dl = drive number (80h + zero based hard drive number)

Returns: if successful
carry = 0
ah = major version of EBIOS extensions

21h = version 1.1 specification (don't ask why)

al = altered

bx = AA55h

cx = Support bits

bits 15-3 = 0	unused (for future enhancements)
2 = 1	Enhanced Disk Drive (EDD) support, BIOS subfunctions 41h, 48h, and 4Eh are available
1 = 1	Drive locking and ejecting support, BIOS subfunctions 41h, 45h, 46h, 48h, and 49h are available, and interrupt 15h, function 52h
0 = 1	Enhanced drive access support, BIOS subfunctions 41h, 42h, 43h, 44h, 47h, and 48h are available

if failed

carry = 1 or BX is not AA55h

Int	Func	Description	Platform
13h	42h	Extended Read Sectors	EBIOS

INT

When supported by EBIOS services, read sectors from the disk into memory. This extended function requires a Disk Address Packet to specify the number of sectors to transfer, where on the disk to begin reading, and where to load the data into memory. See Table 11-11 for the exact form of the Disk Address Packet.

Table 11-11. Disk Address Packet for Extended Disk Services

Offset	Size	Description
0	byte	Size of this packet in bytes. Current packets are 16 bytes long so a value of 10h should be used. Larger values are acceptable, but smaller values will cause the function to be rejected.
1	byte	currently unused, must be set to 0
2	byte	Number of sectors to process, from 1 to 127. Larger values will be rejected. A value of zero is not rejected, but no data is transferred.
3	byte	currently unused, must be set to 0
4	word	memory offset for transfer (read/write only)
6	word	memory segment for transfer (read/write only)
8	qword	Starting logical sector for transfer, in 64-bits. For a drive that does not support logical sectors, the address is converted by the EBIOS to a Cylinder-Head-Sector address. The relationship between the Logical sector and the selected Cylinder-Head-Sector is defined by the following formula: Logical Sector = (((Cylinder * Max Heads) + Head) * Max Sector) + Sector – 1

Called with: ah = 42h
dl = drive number (80h + zero based hard drive number)
ds:si = pointer to Disk Address Packet (see Table 11-11)

Returns: if successful
ah = 0
carry = 0
if fails
carry = 1
ah = return status (see Table 11-6)
Disk Address Packet byte 2 indicates the number of sectors read successfully

Int	Func	Description	Platform
13h	43h	Extended Write Sectors	EBIOS

When supported by EBIOS services, write sectors to the disk from memory. This extended function requires a Disk Address Packet to specify the number of sectors to transfer, where on the disk to begin writing, and where to get the data from memory. See Table 11-11 for the exact form of the Disk Address Packet.

An option is provided to verify the write on some EBIOS implementations. Function 48h can be used to see if this feature is available. Write with verify off is similar to the standard BIOS function 3, Write Sectors.

Called with: ah = 43h
al = 0 or 1 to write with verify off
= 2 to write with verify (if supported)
dl = drive number (80h + zero based hard drive number)
ds:si = pointer to Disk Address Packet (see Table 11-10)

Returns: if successful
ah = 0
carry = 0
if fails
carry = 1
ah = return status (see Table 11-6)
Disk Address Packet byte 2 indicates the number of sectors written successfully

Int	Func	Description	Platform
13h	44h	Extended Verify Sectors	EBIOS

INT

When supported by EBIOS services, verify that sectors do not have errors. This extended function requires a Disk Address Packet to specify the number of sectors to verify and where on the disk to begin the verification. This function uses no memory. See Table 11-11 for the exact form of the Disk Address Packet.

Called with: ah = 44h
dl = drive number (80h + zero based hard drive number)
ds:si = pointer to Disk Address Packet (see Table 11-10)

Returns: if successful
ah = 0
carry = 0
if fails
carry = 1
ah = return status (see Table 11-6)
Disk Address Packet byte 2 indicates the number of sectors verified successfully

Int	Func	Description	Platform
13h	45h	Lock and Unlock Drive	EBIOS

INT

For hard drives that offer removable media, this function allows you to lock, unlock, or check the current lock status of a drive. A locked drive will not allow the software eject function to operate (function AH=46h). Each removable drive has a lock count associated with it, which allows up to 255 locks to be applied to the drive. The lock count is maintained by the BIOS. If three locks have been issued to a drive, then three unlock commands must be issued before the drive is actually unlocked. If an attempt is made to unlock a drive that is already in the unlock state, a *Drive not locked* error code is returned (AH=B0h). If you exceed the number of allowed locks on a drive, a *Lock count exceeded* error code is returned (AH=B4h).

Called with: ah = 45h
al = Operation (values 3 to FFh are invalid)
0 = Lock volume in drive (increment lock count)
1 = Unlock volume in drive (decrement lock count)
2 = Return lock/unlock status
dl = drive number (80h + zero based hard drive number)

Returns: if successful
carry = 0
ah = 0

al = 0 Drive is currently unlocked
1 Drive is currently locked

if fails

carry = 1

ah = return status (see Table 11-6)

Int	Func	Description	Platform
13h	46h	Eject Media Request	EBIOS

For a hard drive with removable media, this function will eject the media if the drive is currently unlocked. See function 45h for more about drive locking and unlocking.

If the selected removable media drive has unlocked media in the drive, the EBIOS code will issue an Interrupt 15h, function 52h. Typically an operating system hooks the interrupt 15h function so it can either flush any buffers to the drive before ejection, or prevent the ejection from occurring. If the Interrupt 15h hook does not fail the eject, the drive is commanded to eject the media.

The ejection request can fail under a number of error conditions. These errors include: an attempt to eject a nonremovable media drive (AH=B1h), no media in the removable drive (AH=31h), the removable media drive is locked (AH=B1h), a hardware failure (AH=B5h), or an error return code supplied from the Interrupt 15h, function 52h hook.

Called with: ah = 46h
al = 0
dl = drive number (80h + zero based hard drive number)

Returns: if successful
carry = 0
ah = 0
if failed
carry = 1
ah = return status (see Table 11-5)

Int	Func	Description	Platform
13h	47h	Extended Seek	EBIOS

Similar to the standard BIOS's function 7, move the heads of the disk to the location specified in the Disk Address Packet (see Table 11-10). The three fields, Number of sectors to transfer, memory offset and memory segment are not used by this function.

Called with: ah = 47h
dl = drive number (80h + zero based hard drive number)
ds:si = pointer to Disk Address Packet (see Table 11-10)

Returns: if successful
carry = 0
ah = 0
if fails
carry = 1
ah = return status (see Table 11-6)

Int	Func	Description	Platform
13h	48h	Get Extended Drive Parameters	EBIOS

INT III I

Get the extended drive parameter table information (see Table 11-12). A buffer must be provided in memory for the function to work. The first word of the table must be initialized to the maximum buffer size the user provides. A buffer size of less than 26 will fail. A buffer size of 26 to 29 will load 26 bytes of information into the table. Buffer sizes of 30 bytes or above will return 30 bytes of information if the EBIOS has Enhanced Disk Drive support (see Interrupt 13h, function 41h), or otherwise will return the first 26 bytes of information.

Table 11-12. Extended Drive Parameters

Offset	Size	Description		
0	word	Size of this buffer, at least 26 bytes long (see text).		
2	word	Information flags		
		bits 15-7	= 0	unused
		6	= 0	Media is present in drive
			1	No removable media present and the values for cylinders, heads, and sectors are all set to the maximum (removable media only)
		5	= 1	Drive is lockable (removable media only)
		4	= 1	Drive has change line support (removable media only)
		3	= 1	Drive supports write with verify
		2	= 1	Device is removable
		1	= 1	The heads and sector values at offset 8 and 12 are valid
		0	= 1	DMA boundary errors are automatically avoided by EBIOS
4	dword	Total number of addressable cylinders. This value is 1 greater than the zero based maximum cylinder number.		
8	dword	Total number of addressable heads. This value is 1 greater than the zero based maximum head number.		
12	dword	Number of sectors per track. This value is the same as the 1 based maximum sector number.		

Table 11-12. Continued

Offset	Size	Description
16	qword	Total number of addressable sectors. This is a 64-bit value.
24	word	Number of bytes per sector (typically 512).
26	dword	Optional segment:offset pointer to the Enhanced Disk Drive configuration parameters. This value is only returned if offset 0 of this table was set to 30 or higher, and Enhanced Disk Drive support is provided (as indicated from Interrupt 13h, function 41h). A return value of FFFF:FFFFh indicates the pointer is invalid.

Called with: ah = 48h

dl = drive number (80h + zero based hard drive number)

ds:si = pointer to Extended Drive Information Table (see Table 11-12)

Returns: if successful, the table is filled in and,

carry = 0

ds:si = pointer to Extended Drive Information Table (see Table 11-12)

if fails

carry = 1

ah = return status (see Table 11-5)

INT	Int	Func	Description	Platform
	13h	49h	Get Extended Disk Change Status	EBIOS

For removable media drives, see if the media was changed. A media change is tagged any time the media is removed, or if the drive is unlocked and relocked, even if the media was never removed.

Called with: ah = 49h

dl = drive number (80h + zero based hard drive number)

Returns: if successful, and the change-line was not active (no media change occurred)

carry = 0

ah = 0

if successful, and the change-line was active

carry = 1

ah = 6 (the normal error code indicating the removable media was changed)

if fails

carry = 1

ah = return status (see Table 11-5)

Int	Func	Description	Platform
13h	4Ah	Initiate Disk Emulation	Bootable CD-ROM

Pass a table of values to a BIOS that supports the Bootable CD-ROM extensions, version 1.0 or later. Table 11-13 is used to specify the drive letter to use. See the Bootable CD-ROM specification for more details on booting from a CD-ROM device (Appendix C, Bibliography).

Table 11-13. Bootable CD-ROM Specification Table

Offset	Size	Description
0	byte	Size of this packet in bytes. Current packets are 13 bytes
1	byte	Which boot media to emulate CD-ROM as bit 7 = 1 Image contains SCSI drivers 6 = 1 Image contains IDE driver 5 = 0 Unused 4 = 0 Unused 3 = x Emulation type 2 = x 0 = No emulation 1 = x 1 = 1.2 MB diskette 0 = x 2 = 1.44 MB diskette 3 = 2.88 MB diskette 4 = Hard disk (C:)
2	byte	Drive number of emulated drive 0 = diskette boot image 80h = hard disk boot image All other values indicate a non-bootable drive
3	byte	Controller number for CD-ROM drive (i.e. 0 = first controller)
4	dword	Sector on device where disk image begins (Logical sector, where first sector is address 0)
8	word	Device specification if IDE device (byte 1 of this table, bit 6 = 1) bits 15-1 = 0 unused bit 0 = 0 if CD-ROM is set to master 1 if CD-ROM is set to slave if SCSI device (byte 1 of this table, bit 7 = 1) bits 15-8 = x bus number bits 7-0 = x SCSI logical unit number of the CD device (LUN)
Ah	word	Optional cache buffer segment—If non-zero, a user supplied 3 KB buffer is used at the specified segment, offset 0, to buffer CD-ROM read operations.

Table 11-13. Continued

Offset	Size	Description
Ch	word	Boot load segment—This is the segment where boot image is to be loaded from device. This value is only used when issuing interrupt 13h, function 4Ch. A zero value will load the image to 7C0:0h.
Eh	word	Sector Count—The total number of sectors to load into memory at the load segment. This value is only used when issuing interrupt 13h, function 4Ch.
10h	byte	Low cylinder value—CH register value from interrupt 13h, function 8.
11h	byte	Sector and high cylinder value—CL register value from interrupt 13h, function 8.
12h	byte	Head count—DH register value from interrupt 13h, function 8.

Called with: ax = 4A00h
ds:si = Pointer to table of values for CD-ROM booting (see Table 11-13)

Returns: carry = 0 The specified drive is emulating
1 The system is not in emulation mode
ah = return status (see Table 11-6)

Int	Func	Description	Platform
13h	4Bh	Terminate Disk Emulation	Bootable CD-ROM

Ends the CD-ROM emulation of a boot device. The diskette or hard drive numbering returns to normal, as if no CD-ROM boot had occurred.

Called with: ah = 4Bh
al = subfunction (see below)
dl = drive number to terminate, use 7Fh to terminate all
ds:si = Pointer to an empty table of values (see Table 11-13)

Returns: carry = 0 The system is released
1 The system was not in emulation mode
ah = return status (see Table 11-6)
ds:si = Pointer to completed table of values (see Table 11-13)

AL=	Terminate Disk Emulation Subfunction Commands
0	Terminate emulation and return status
1	Return status only

Subfunction Detail

Subfunction	Description	Int	Function
AL=0	Terminate emulation and return status	13h	AH=4Bh

INT

End the CD-ROM boot emulation, and return drives to normal numbering. Also return the status and a completed table of values in DS:SI.

Subfunction	Description	Int	Function
AL=1	Return status only	13h	AH=4Bh

INT

Return the status and a completed table of values in DS:SI. The emulation state is not changed.

Int	Func	Description	Platform
13h	4Ch	Initiate Disk Emulation and Boot	Bootable CD-ROM

INT

Using the passed table of values, reboot the system from the CD-ROM device by emulating the CD-ROM as a diskette or hard disk drive. This function only returns if the table does not have a pointer to a valid boot image.

Called with:	ax = 4C00h	
	ds:si = Pointer to table of values for CD-ROM booting (see Table 11-13)	
If returns:	carry = 1	System failed to boot
	ah = return status (see Table 11-6)	

Int	Func	Description	Platform
13h	4Dh	Return Boot Catalog	Bootable CD-ROM

INT

Obtain the requested number of sectors from a CD-ROM's boot catalog. See Table 11-14 for the table of values that must be passed by this function. Depending on the user's buffer size, the catalog can be transferred in as little as 1 sector at a time.

Table 11-14. Boot Catalog Request Table

Offset	Size	Description
0	byte	Size of this packet in bytes. Current packets are 8 bytes
1	byte	Number of sectors to transfer
2	dword	User pointer (segment:offset) where to transfer the boot catalog
6	word	First sector to transfer (set to 0 for the first call)

Called with:	ax = 4D00h
	ds:si = Pointer to table of values for boot catalog transfer (see Table 11-14)

Returns:	carry = 0	Transfer was successful
	1	Failed, since device is not an emulated CD, or if the values in Table 11-14 were out of bounds.
	ah = return status (see Table 11-6)	

INT

Int	Func	Description	Platform
13h	4Eh	Set Extended Hardware Configuration	EBIOS

Set various hardware features for a device. When two drives (master and slave) are attached to the same IDE controller, some options set for either the master or slave drive will also affect the other drive on the same controller. All of the subfunctions will return a value AH=1 if the command has affected other drive(s) than the one specified.

There are currently seven subfunctions available:

AL=	Description
0	Enable Prefetch
1	Disable Prefetch
2	Set Maximum PIO Transfer Mode
3	Set PIO Mode 0
4	Set Default PIO Transfer Mode
5	Enable Int 13h DMA Maximum Mode
6	Disable Int 13h DMA

INT

Subfunction	Description	Int	Function
AL=0	Enable Prefetch	13h	AH=4Eh

This subfunction enables the IDE Prefetch feature. The Prefetch feature reads additional sectors from the disk when any read occurs. For example, if sector X is requested, the controller will read sector X, and may continue to read sectors following X into a buffer in the controller. It is likely that the next requested sector will be X+1, and the controller now has this sector in memory for instant response. Generally the controller's buffer is large enough to hold a complete track of sectors.

Another related prefetch trick is often used to boost performance. When the drive moves to the desired track, on the average, the controller must wait for one half a revolution of the disk before the desired sector is readable. Since reading a block of contiguous sectors is very common, the controller will begin reading as soon as the head is on the desired track. The sectors are read into a track buffer as the disk rotates to the requested sector. When the desired sector is transferred, and other sequential sectors are transferred, at some point the buffer holds all the remaining sectors for the track. At this point the controller no longer needs to wait for reading further sectors, and can quickly transfer the remaining desired sectors stored in its track buffer.

Called with: ax = 4E00h
dl = drive number (80h + zero based hard drive number)

Returns: if successful
carry = 0
ah = 0
al = 0 if command only affects the specified drive
1 if command affects other drives
if fails
carry = 1
ah = return status (see Table 11-6)

Subfunction	Description	Int	Function
AL=1	Disable Prefetch	13h	AH=4Eh

INT

This subfunction disables the IDE Prefetch feature. See Enable Prefetch for more about the Prefetch feature.

Called with: ax = 4E01h
dl = drive number (80h + zero based hard drive number)

Returns: if successful
carry = 0
ah = 0
al = 0 if command only affects the specified drive
1 if command affects other drives
if fails
carry = 1
ah = return status (see Table 11-5)

Subfunction	Description	Int	Function
AL=2	Set Maximum PIO Transfer Mode	13h	AH=4Eh

INT

Enable the highest performance Programmed I/O (PIO) mode which the controller offers. Data is transferred between the controller and the system through input and output instructions. This function will also disable the use of DMA for the drive.

Called with: ax = 4E02h
dl = drive number (80h + zero based hard drive number)

Returns: if successful
carry = 0
ah = 0

al = 0 if command only affects the specified drive
1 if command affects other drives

if fails

carry = 1
ah = return status (see Table 11-6)

INT	Subfunction	Description	Int	Function
	AL=3	Set PIO Mode 0	13h	AH=4Eh

Enable the lowest performance Programmed I/O (PIO) mode which the controller offers. Data is transferred between the controller and the system through input and output instructions. This function will also disable the use of DMA for the drive.

Called with: ax = 4E03h
dl = drive number (80h + zero based hard drive number)

Returns: if successful

carry = 0
ah = 0
al = 0 if command only affects the specified drive
1 if command affects other drives

if fails

carry = 1
ah = return status (see Table 11-5)

INT	Subfunction	Description	Int	Function
	AL=4	Set Default PIO Mode	13h	AH=4Eh

Enable the default Programmed I/O (PIO) mode in the controller. Data is transferred between the controller and the system through input and output instructions. This function will also disable the use of DMA for the drive.

Called with: ax = 4E04h
dl = drive number (80h + zero based hard drive number)

Returns: if successful

carry = 0
ah = 0
al = 0 if command only affects the specified drive
1 if command affects other drives

if fails

carry = 1
ah = return status (see Table 11-5)

Subfunction	Description	Int	Function
AL=5	Enable Int 13h DMA Maximum Mode	13h	AH=4Eh

INT

Enable the highest performance DMA mode in the controller. Data is transferred between the controller and the system through one channel of the DMA controller. For multitasking operating systems, this is best choice. Once the DMA operation is set up, the sectors are transferred to or from memory without CPU involvement. This function also disables any PIO mode set.

Called with: ax = 4E05h
dl = drive number (80h + zero based hard drive number)

Returns: if successful
carry = 0
ah = 0
al = 0 if command only affects the specified drive
1 if command affects other drives
if fails
carry = 1
ah = return status (see Table 11-6)

Subfunction	Description	Int	Function
AL=6	Disable Int 13h DMA	13h	AH=4Eh

INT

Turn off the disk DMA transfer mode for the drive. One of the three PIO options should be set before accessing the drive (subfunctions 2, 3, or 4).

Called with: ax = 4E06h
dl = drive number (80h + zero based hard drive number)

Returns: if successful
carry = 0
ah = 0
al = 0 if command only affects the specified drive
1 if command affects other drives
if fails
carry = 1
ah = return status (see Table 11-6)

INT

Int	Func	Description	Platform
15h	52h	Removable Media Eject	EBIOS

This function is issued by EBIOS when interrupt 13h, function 46h, eject removable media is issued. It should not be called by a program. A program or operating system can hook this interrupt so it can be alerted when an attempt is made to eject removable media. The program can perform some action, such as flushing a disk cache, and let the ejection occur. The program can also prevent the media ejection. This is useful if a critical disk read or write is in progress. To prevent ejection, one of two error return codes must be set, B1h to indicate an error condition "Volume Locked in Drive," or B3h to indicate "Volume in use."

Called with: ah = 52h
dl = drive number (80h + zero based hard drive number)

Returns: if successful, the ejection is allowed
carry = 0
ah = 0
if fails, no ejection is allowed at this time
carry = 1
ah = B1h Volume locked in drive
B3h Volume in use

INT

Int	Func	Description	Platform
4Fh	8100h	SCSI Command, Common Access Method	SCSI

Many newer SCSI cards use the Common Access Method (CAM) to provide vendor-independent access to the SCSI card. This function is used to send commands to the SCSI adapter. It is only supported from a SCSI hard disk adapter card BIOS or SCSI device driver.

The function points to a CAM control block of data, which defines the command and parameters for the command. For the current details on CAM control blocks, refer to the document SCSI-2 Common Access Method Transport and SCSI Interface Module shown in Appendix C.

Called with: ax = 8100h
es:bx = pointer to CAM control block

Returns: ah = 0 if successful, any other value for failure

Int	Func	Description	Platform
4Fh	8200h	SCSI Presence check, Common Access Method	SCSI

Many newer SCSI cards use the Common Access Method (CAM) to provide vendor-independent access to the SCSI card. Very few systems provide SCSI BIOS support as part of the system, but provide support through a BIOS on the SCSI adapter card. This function checks to see if the SCSI adapter card is present and supports CAM specifications. If CAM is supported, commands are passed through interrupt 4Fh, function 8100h.

Called with: ax = 8200h
cx = 9765h
dx = CBA9h

Returns: if installed:
ah = 0
cx = 9ABCh
dx = 5678h
es:di pointer to string SCSI_CAM

Int	Description	Platform
76h	Hard Disk Operation Complete	AT/EISA

For AT and EISA systems, the Hard Disk Complete interrupt occurs when the hard disk controller command and related data transfers are complete. The controller signals with IRQ 14. If no higher priority interrupts are active, and interrupts are enabled, the interrupt 76h service routine is called.

The routine first sets the disk operation complete flag, indicating the active hard disk operation is complete. To do this, the BIOS data item at 40:8Eh is set to FFh through I/O ports 20h and A0h, both interrupt controllers are issued the nonspecific End-Of-Interrupt command 20h to clear the current interrupt. Interrupts are then re-enabled. The routine also issues an operation complete message to the system by calling interrupt 15h, with AX=9100h. Other software can hook interrupt 15h to be alerted every time a disk operation completes.

Before this interrupt occurs, the disk BIOS is in a tight loop looking at the disk operation complete flag. Interrupt 76h is issued by the controller. The interrupt 76h handler sets the operation complete flag, and exits. The disk BIOS service sees the change in the operation complete flag and proceeds to wrap up the disk operation by getting controller status and returning to the interrupt 13h caller.

Multitasking operating systems cannot tolerate the disk BIOS waiting in a tight loop. Fortunately, the BIOS provides a mechanism to give control to the OS during the wait period. For details of this mechanism, see interrupt 15h, function 90h, device busy, in Chapter 13, System Functions.

INT

Int	Description	Platform
76h	Operation Complete	PS/2

The PS/2 Operation Complete is similar to that on AT systems. The disk controller signals IRQ 14. If no higher priority interrupts are active, and interrupts are enabled, this interrupt 76h service routine is called.

Unlike the AT, the routine is designed to be used for multiple purposes, of which the hard disk controller is the only current user. This is accomplished by first checking the hard disk controller to see if the controller caused the interrupt. The Basic Status register at port 3512h bit 0 is checked to see if the disk controller is issuing an interrupt. The bit will be set if the controller issued an interrupt. If the controller did not issue the interrupt, the system BIOS routine returns, allowing any other device that hooked interrupt 76h to take desired actions.

If the controller did issue the interrupt, the Controller Interrupt Status is obtained from port 3513h and saved in the Extended BIOS Data Area (EBDA) at offset 72h. The disk operation complete flag is set by setting bit 7 at offset 73h in the EBDA.

Both interrupt controllers are issued the nonspecific End-Of-Interrupt command 20h to clear the current interrupt. Interrupts are then re-enabled. The routine also issues an operation complete message to the system by calling interrupt 15h, with AX=9100h. Other software can hook interrupt 15h to be alerted every time a disk operation completes.

Before this interrupt occurs, the disk BIOS will be in a tight loop looking at the disk operation complete flag. Interrupt 76h is issued by the disk controller, which sets the operation complete flag, and exits. The disk BIOS service routine regains control, sees the flag set, and proceeds to the next step. This interrupt is used somewhat differently than in the AT design. See the section Typical Read Sector Operation, and the sub-section PS/2 EISA Type Controllers and BIOS, later in this chapter for additional details.

Disk BIOS Data

The disk BIOS (interrupt 13h) uses a number of bytes in the BIOS data area for its operations. Table 11-15 shows these data locations and functions. The PS/2 also uses many values in the Extended BIOS Data Area. Additional details are covered in Chapter 6.

Table 11-15. Hard Disk BIOS Data

Address	Size	Description
40:42h	4 bytes	Disk Controller Returned Status Bytes—For systems with the PC/XT-type hard disk controller, the four bytes following these four bytes are also used to hold the controller's sense data when an error is detected. See port 320h under Request Sense Status for details about these bytes. The diskette controller also stores temporary information in these bytes.
40:74h	byte	Status of Last Operation—When a hard disk operation completes, the status from that operation is stored in this byte. Status codes were previously described in Table 11-5. Most hard disk services cannot issue every possible error code. This byte is also used to store the temporary status, when an ECC error is detected, but corrected. The ECC error is saved here, but the operation continues to completion. At the end of the operation, if an ECC error had occurred on any sector, the return status from an interrupt 13h function is set to 11h, ECC Error Corrected.
40:75h	byte	Number of Hard Disks Attached—This byte indicates the number of hard disks detected by POST. Older BIOSes support a maximum of two drives, while newer system BIOSes often support up to four drives. Disk controllers that provide their own BIOS are only limited by the controller's capability. A few BIOS ROMs have a bug that will incorrectly count an attached CD-ROM drive as a hard disk.
40:76h	byte	Hard Disk Control Byte—This byte holds temporary control flags for the hard disk BIOSes. It is only used in some hard disk BIOSes. There appears to be no standard assignment of bits for those that use this byte.
40:77h	byte	Hard Disk Port Offset—This byte holds a temporary offset to the hard disk port number. It is only used in PC/XT hard disk BIOSes and a few other early hard disk adapters.
40:8Ch	byte	Hard Disk Status—The actual status from the hard disk controller is stored in this byte. Some BIOSes do not support this function.
40:8Dh	byte	Hard Disk Error—The error register from the disk controller is stored in this byte. Some BIOSes do not support this function.
40:8Eh	byte	Hard Disk Task Complete Flag—The hard disk BIOS sets this value to 0 at the start of a disk controller task. The disk controller hardware signals when the task is complete with IRQ 14, interrupt 76h. The interrupt 76h handler then sets this byte to 0FFh. PC/XT BIOSes do not use this method of completion, and do not use this byte.

Sending Commands to the Disk Controller

The disk controller has an extensive list of commands to perform various actions, such as format a track, or write a sector. Commands are typically sent as part of Command Data Block, used to describe parameters and address information necessary to carry out the command. Once the command is accepted, the controller performs the action. When the command execution is complete, the controller issues an interrupt. This disk complete message uses interrupt Dh on the PC and XT systems. On the AT and all later systems, interrupt 76h is used to indicate the command is complete. The hard disk BIOS handler then obtains a block of data from the controller to check if the command was successful or if any errors occurred.

A Typical Read Sector Operation

This is a long section, but it will help clear the way to a better understanding of disk operations. Many aspects of the disk system are tied together, including the BIOS and the lowest levels of the controller. This section covers the three most common systems, PC/XT, AT/EISA, and the PS/2 ESDI hard disk systems. Other than the initial operations that are common to all three types, the remaining operations are quite different among these three standards. All cases assume a single primary controller. Other controllers are accessed through an alternate set of ports, if supported by the BIOS.

Common Read Sector Operations

First, we'll begin by assuming the controller has been reset, the drive table parameters have been loaded for the drive in use, and the drive has been recalibrated. Recalibration simply moves the heads to cylinder 0, a position that the drive confirms to the controller.

The operating system or application must convert its file system position into a disk address, made up of a cylinder, a head, and a sector on a track. Once the position on the disk is determined, the hard disk service routine, interrupt 13h, function 2 can be called to read sectors.

Interrupt 13h, function 2 is passed the disk address where data will be read from the device. This address is defined by a cylinder, a head number, and a sector. The number of sectors to be read and a pointer where to store the sectors read from the disk are passed to function 2. Of course the drive number, 0 or greater is also specified, with bit 7 set to indicate the operation is for the hard disk, and not for the diskette drive.

The steps necessary to complete the Read operation are dependent on the controller used in the system. We'll examine three common controllers, the PC/XT, AT, and PS/2 EISA, one at a time.

PC/XT Type Controller and BIOS

After checking that the drive number is valid, the BIOS handler builds a Command Data Block for a read command. The Command Data Block has the following contents:

Byte 0—Command (a value 8 indicates read)
Byte 1—Drive and Head number
Byte 2—Cylinder (upper 2 bits) and Sector number
Byte 3—Cylinder number (lower 8 bits)
Byte 4—Number of sectors to read
Byte 5—Control byte (a value 5 indicates normal retries and normal step timing)

Next a check is made to ensure the number of sectors is not out of range for the DMA operation. A maximum of 64K can be transferred at one time. If within range, DMA channel 3 is set up to be able to transfer the requested number of bytes from the disk adapter card to memory at the specified address.

The controller is set to a busy state by sending any value to port 322h, the Hard Disk Controller Select Pulse. The DMA and Interrupt masks are then cleared by sending the value 3 to port 323h. This allows the controller to issue the DMA and interrupt requests at the appropriate times. The Controller Hardware Status is checked from port 321h to ensure the controller is ready. The busy latch should be set, and the controller should be expecting command input, and request ready. This means the lower 4 bits of the status byte should be 0Dh when it's ready.

When the disk controller is ready, the six bytes of the previously created Command Data Block are sent one byte at a time to the controller over port 320h. As a confirmation that the six bytes were received, the hardware status is checked one more time. Bit 0 should be cleared, indicating the controller is not accepting any more bytes. If it is not cleared, then there may be a problem with the controller.

The controller issues a DMA request for channel 3 by asserting the DREQ 3 line. The BIOS unmasks DMA channel 3, by sending to the DMA mask register, port Ah, the value 3. At the same time, the BIOS clears the mask bit in the interrupt controller so IRQ 5 will be allowed. The BIOS then goes into a wait loop for the data transfer to complete.

At this point various handshaking of signals in hardware results in the controller reading data from the disk, and DMA transferring the data over the data bus to memory. When the requested number of sectors have been transferred, the controller signals the system with the PC/XT interrupt request 5 (IRQ 5), the Hard Disk Operation Complete Interrupt 0Dh. All of this occurs in hardware without any software intervention.

The BIOS detects the completion of the transfer and performs its final cleanup. The controller's DMA and interrupt masks are set by writing zero to port 323h. The Controller Status is read from port 320h to see if any error occurred from the command. If no error occurred, the operation is complete and returns the success code, 0 in AL. If an error did occur, the error information is retrieved from the controller and the error status is passed back to the user in AL. Now wasn't that simple!

AT/IDE-Type Controllers and BIOS

The hard disk BIOS checks that the desired drive is a valid operating drive, and verifies that less than 64K of data is specified by the operation. In this example, if more than 128 sectors were requested, the DMA boundary error is issued, even though the AT controller does not use DMA! I'll explain more about how the BIOS skips DMA in a moment.

Many system BIOSes only allow a maximum of 64K to be transferred in one operation. All controllers can transfer up to 128K, and some BIOSes will support transfers up to 128K. For general programming use, 64K or less is the only safe amount that can be trusted, because there are many bugs in different system BIOSes using more than 64K. See the DISKTEST program later in this chapter for more about this problem.

A minor but important limit is the starting offset of the buffer where the data will be written. If the lowest nibble of the offset is non-zero, then only 127 sectors can be transferred. Requesting 128 sectors will cause the same DMA boundary error to occur. This makes sense, since the transfer of 64K occurs by incrementing the offset. Surprisingly, the upper three nibbles of the offset do not matter. A buffer offset of FFF0h is fully acceptable to transfer 64K. In this case, the data read from the disk will be written starting at the segment:FFF0h bytes, for 64K. The system BIOS normalizes the address to segment+FFF:0000h before the transfer is made. No segment wrap can occur.

The controller is checked to ensure it is not busy by reading Status port 1F7h and checking bit 7. It is cleared when the controller is ready. The Head and Drive select register port 1F6h can now be loaded with the drive value. Again the Status port 1F7h is checked, but this time bit 6 is checked to confirm the selected drive is ready. Bit 6 is 1 when the drive is ready. The Write Fault bit 5, must also be clear, because the controller cannot accept a command if the drive is indicating a write fault from some prior operation.

The system BIOS then obtains the drive parameters for the drive. The pointer for the table is stored in interrupt vector 41h for drive 0, and vector 46h for drive 1. The control byte from the disk parameter table, offset 8, is loaded into the Adapter Control register, port 3F7h. This informs the hard disk adapter if more than eight heads are used on the drive.

If the operation was a write command, it is necessary to load the Write Precompensation register port 1F1h. The value is obtained from the disk parameter table, offset 3. The write precompensation value is not used by the controller for a read command and is ignored if loaded. This value is also ignored by all IDE type drives.

The other controller registers are loaded with the number of sectors to read, and with the disk address comprised of the starting sector, the cylinder, the head, and the drive. These registers span ports 1F2h through 1F6h. The Head and Drive select register will normally set bit 7 on to perform Error Checking and Correction (ECC). The Head and drive select register bits 6 and 5 are set to 0 and 1, respectively, to specify 512-byte sectors. Although the controller is capable of other sector sizes, only 512-byte sectors are used on all PC-based systems. Most AT controllers only accept a maximum of 1,024 cylinders, 64 sectors, and 16 heads. Larger values should only be used if it is clearly known the controller will accept it. IDE drives can accept more than 1,024 cylinders. (See the prior section, *Large IDE Drives* about BIOS limitations).

To summarize the registers loaded:

Register	Name	Loaded with
1F1h	Write Precompensation	Write Precompensation cylinder
1F2h	Sector Count	Number of sectors to read
1F3h	Sector Number	Starting sector number
1F4h	Cylinder Low	Starting cylinder, lower 8 bits
1F5h	Cylinder High	Starting cylinder, upper 8 bits
1F6h	Drive and Head	Drive number 0 or 1, Head 0-15 and bits 7 to 5 = 101

One last step is required before commanding the controller to begin. The interrupt controller's mask must be cleared for IRQ 14. This will allow the system to acknowledge when the controller is ready for each sector's transfer. This will become clear shortly.

To launch the read operation, now that all of the controller's registers are properly set up, the Read command, 20h is written to the Command register at port 1F7h. Once the controller accepts the command, the data is read from the drive into the controller's sector buffer. While this is occurring, the system BIOS waits in a loop for the operation complete flag to be set.

When one complete sector has been read, the controller issues a Data Ready Interrupt, IRQ 14h. In this case, IRQ 14 is handled by interrupt 76h, which simply sets the operation complete flag. The system BIOS detects that this flag is set and will directly read the 256 words from the controller's sector buffer. The 16-bit port 1F0h is read to get this data. This is significantly different from the PC/XT and PS/2 BIOS operations. They use DMA to transfer the information in a strictly hardware method, whereas the AT just reads the data words in a software loop from port 1F0h. Most current systems support 32-bit data transfers, when the hardware is equipped to double the transfer speed.

After the data has been read, a check is made to see if any errors occurred. Status port 1F7h is read, and the various error conditions are checked. Any fatal errors require exiting the routine. If an ECC-corrected error was detected, it can be safely ignored. A flag could be set to return status to the user that an ECC error was detected, but corrected.

If no fatal errors occurred, the original sector count number is decremented. If the sector count is still non-zero, the next sector is read. The sector count in the controller is not changed by software in this case, but a copy of the original value passed from the interrupt 13h call is decremented.

When all of the desired sectors have been read from the disk, and written to memory, the system BIOS returns the status of the operation.

PS/2 EISA-Type Controllers and BIOS

Similar to the last two approaches, the drive number is validated and the BIOS handler builds a Command Data Block for a read command. The Command Data Block has the following contents:

Word 0—Command, Read data from drive 0 (4601h) or from drive 1 (4621h)
Word 1—Number of Sectors to transfer

Word 2—Relative Sector Address, least significant word
Word 3—Relative Sector Address, most significant word

Unlike the last two approaches, the PS/2 BIOS must convert the cylinder, head, and sector address into the Relative Sector Address, required by the PS/2 ESDI controller. PS/2 systems I've examined only support a maximum drive combination of 1,024 cylinders, 64 heads, and 32 sectors, or about 1,073 MB total. To get the Relative Sector Address, the following equation is used:

Relative Sector Address = (cylinder * 2048) + (head * 32) + (sector number)

In addition, the PS/2's hard disk busy light is set on. The BIOS activates the disk busy light by setting the uppermost bit in port 92h.

At this point a significant amount of handshaking goes on with the controller to load the command, process it, and clean up behind it. You can skip the next few paragraphs if you're not interested in the fine details!

With the Command Data Block defined, the controller's interrupt mask is cleared by sending the value 1 to port 3512h, the Basic Control register. Next the Basic Status register is read, port 3512h, and checked to see that the controller is not busy. The Not Busy bit 4 should be zero.

A command request is issued to the attention register, port 3510h. Issuing the value 2 signals the controller that the command will be for drive 0. Value 22h is used when the command is for drive 1.

If the controller is working correctly, it should become busy. Reading the Basic Status at port 3512h verifies that bit 4, the Busy Flag, is now set. From the same register, bit 2 being cleared signifies the controller is ready for the Command Data Block. In the case of our Read command, there are four words to be sent to the controller over port 3510h. After every word is sent, the BIOS must check that the Basic Status register's bit 2 is clear before the next word can be sent.

The BIOS flags the system that it is going to wait for the command to be accepted by issuing interrupt 15h, function AX=9000h. The BIOS then goes into a timing loop waiting for the Disk Complete interrupt.

Command acceptance is signaled by the controller issuing a hardware interrupt request, IRQ 14, which calls Interrupt 76h. The interrupt 76h BIOS routine flags the operation is complete by setting the Disk Complete Flag in RAM. In the case of the PS/2, bit 7 is set in byte 73h of the extended BIOS data area. Interrupt 76h also issues an interrupt 15h, function AX=9100h to alert any other interested applications or operating systems that the disk operation is now complete.

The disk BIOS, which has been in a loop waiting for the interrupt to complete, sees the Disk Complete Flag set, and then reads the Interrupt Status register, port 3513h. If the controller is ready for the transfer, the controller returns the "Data Transfer Ready" interrupt status. The lower five bits of the interrupt status will be 0Bh.

The disk BIOS now sets up the DMA controller for the upcoming data transfer. The address in RAM where to transfer the data from the disk is loaded into DMA channel 5. The actual operation is begun by sending the value 3 to the basic control register at port 3512h. This allows both DMA requests and interrupt requests to occur.

The BIOS flags the system again that it is going to wait for the data transfer to complete. The disk BIOS issues an interrupt 15h, function AX=9000h. The BIOS goes into a timing loop waiting for the Disk Complete interrupt. At the same time the data transfer begins between the controller and memory through DMA. No software is involved in the actual transfer of data.

The controller issues IRQ 14, interrupt 76h, when the transfer is complete, or if any problems occurred. The interrupt 76h handler sets the Disk Complete Flag and issues an operation complete, interrupt 15h, AX=9100h.

The disk BIOS, which has been in a loop waiting for the interrupt to complete, sees the Disk Complete Flag set, and then reads the Interrupt Status register, port 3513h. If the operation was a success, the lower five bits of the interrupt status will be the value 1. Any other value indicates there was some problem with the transfer.

For error conditions, the Basic Status register port 3512h is read, and bit 3 will be set if additional status is available. The status words can be read from port 3510h. After each word, the Basic Status register is checked to see if additional status words are available. These status words indicate the exact nature of the error, and the Relative Sector Address of the error.

To complete the operation, the End-Of-Interrupt code is sent to the attention register, port 3513h. A value 2 is used for drive 0, and 22h for drive 1. The entire operation is now complete, and the status is returned to the original caller.

Warnings

Operating the disk controller is one of the most complex actions a program can perform in directly accessing the hardware. If at all possible, the operating system should be used to access the disk. (DOS's generic IOCTL provides many useful low-level disk functions.) If this is not possible, then interrupt 13h should be used as the interface, since interrupt 13h transparently handles a number of significant differences among the different controllers and disk types.

Directly accessing the controller assumes that you know exactly which controller the system is using. Use extreme caution if the system uses disk compression, such as DoubleSpace, SuperStor, Stacker, or other such products. Although the contents of the disk are fully accessible, the actual data is encoded in one of many proprietary formats. Direct disk access will bypass these compression programs.

For reliable BIOS operation, never read more than a single track's worth of data at one time. There are many BIOSes that produce unreliable operation when attempting to read across a track boundary. See Code Sample 11-2 for a simple test that demonstrates this problem.

Code Sample 11-1. Disk Drive Detection

This routine checks if a given disk drive is attached, and determines its maximum capacity. The program should work with normal and nonstandard drives. The routine also detects some of the common types of controllers such as the old PC/XT controller, newer AT controllers, IDE, PS/2 ESDI, and common SCSI controllers. Note that some ESDI and SCSI controllers do not have their own hard disk BIOS, and rely on the standard system BIOS for all services. In these cases, the disk drive detection routine will indicate whether it is using an AT-type controller.

To use this routine to get the total disk size, multiply the total number of cylinders times the number of heads times the number of sectors per track.

The routine is included in SYSTYPE.ASM. Run SYSTYPE to see the results of the HDRVTYPE subroutine. On one system, the portion of SYSTYPE related to disk drive detection appears in Figure 11-5.

Figure 11-5. Partial Results from SYSTYPE

```
SYSTEM ANALYSIS                                            v2.00
Hard Drive 0:    IDE Controller, LBA active
                     Total Size = 1,545 MB (with diagnostic cylinder)
                     785 Cylinders, 64 Heads, 63 Sectors per track
Hard Drive 1:    AT or IDE type Controller
                     Total Size = 503 MB (with diagnostic cylinder)
                     1,022 Cylinders, 16 Heads, 63 Sectors per track
```

```
;---------------------------------------------------------------
;  HARD DISK DRIVE TYPE DETECTION SUBROUTINE
;    Determine if a hard drive is attached, its likely type,
;    and the capacity of that drive.
;
;    Called with:  ds = cs
;            dl = drive to check, 80h=drive 0, etc.
;
;    Returns:     al = drive type
;                 0 = no drive or no controller
;                 1 = XT type controller
;                 2 = AT or IDE type controller
;                 3 = SCSI type controller
;                 4 = PS/2 ESDI type controller
;                 5 = unknown controller type
;                 6 = IDE controller, LBA active
```

```
;           cx = total number of cylinders (includes
;              the diagnostic cylinder)
;           dx = total number of heads (1-256)
;           ah = number of 512 byte sectors (1-63)
;    Regs used:    ax

; local data for routine

hd_parm_seg   dw   0              ; pointer to disk
hd_parm_off   dw   0              ; parameter table
hd_cylinder   dw   0              ; temp # from table
ESDIbuf       db   1024 dup (0)   ; ESDI info buffer

hdsktype proc  near
    push  bx
    push  es
    xor   bp, bp                  ; used for temp drive type
    cmp   dl, 80h                 ; at least 80h ?
    jb    hdsk_skp1               ; exit if not

; first we will get the number of drives attached

    push  dx
    mov   dl, 80h                 ; ask for drive 0
    mov   ah, 8
    int   13h                     ; read disk drive parameters
    pop   ax
    add   dl, 7Fh
    cmp   al, dl                  ; drive for this number ?
    jbe   hdsk_skp2
hdsk_skp1:
    jmp   hdsk_none               ; jump if out of range
```

```
; now determine the controller/disk type

hdsk_skp2:
    inc   bp              ; bp=1 assume XT type drive
    mov   dl, al          ; dl = drive number
    push  dx
    mov   ah, 15h
    int   13h
    pop   dx
    cmp   ah, 1                     ; invalid request status ?
    je    hdsk_skp4                 ; if so, XT type & exit
    inc   bp                        ; set type to AT
    cmp   ah, 3                     ; confirm valid hard disk
    je    hdsk_skp3
    jmp   hdsk_none                 ; exit if not

; let's check if it's a drive which does not use the drive
;  parameter table like SCSI and some ESDI drives.

hdsk_skp3:
    inc   bp                        ; assume SCSI
    cmp   dl, 87h                   ; if aboce 87h, assume SCSI
    jbe   hdsk_skp5
hdsk_skp4:
    jmp   hdsk_info                 ; jump if so

hdsk_skp5:
    mov   bx, 4*41h                 ; assume ptr to vector 41h
    cmp   dl, 80h                   ; drive 0 ?
    je    hdsk_skp6                 ; jump if so
    mov   bx, 4*46h                 ; pointer to vector 46h
hdsk_skp6:
    xor   ax, ax
    mov   es, ax
```

```
    mov   si, es:[bx]     ; offset of parameter table
    mov   ax, es:[bx+2]    ; segment of parameter table
    mov   [hd_parm_seg], ax ; save pointer
    mov   [hd_parm_off], si
    mov   es, ax         ; es:si ptr to table

; we now have a pointer to the disk parameter table, but there
;  are two types! Check if string at offset 2 is not 'IBM ', then
;  use normal table (cylinder at offset 0). Otherwise use
;  old PS/2 style, where cylinder is at offset 19h.

    cmp   word ptr es:[si+2], 'BI' ; string 'IBM ' ?
    jne   hdsk_skp7                ; jump if not
    cmp   word ptr es:[si+4], ' M'
    jne   hdsk_skp7
    add   si, 19h                  ; adjust to PS/2 style
hdsk_skp7:
    mov   ax, es:[si]              ; get cylinders from table
    mov   [hd_cylinder], ax        ; save
    cmp   ax, 0                    ; invalid # of cylinders ?
    jne   hdsk_skp8                ; jump if ok (non-zero)
    jmp   hdsk_info                ; we will assume SCSI

hdsk_skp8:
    dec   bp                       ; assume AT type (2)
    push  dx
    mov   ah, 8
    int   13h                      ; get disk parameters
    call  hdconvert                ; convert into useful values
    cmp   ax, 1021                 ; near end of IDE limit?
    jb    hdsk_skp8a               ; jump if not
    cmp   [hd_cylinder], 1020
    jae   hdsk_skp8b               ; jump if ok
    jmp   hdsk_skp9                ; unlikly AT or IDE type
```

```
hdsk_skp8a:
    cmp   ax, [hd_cylinder] ; are they within 3 cylinders?
    ja   hdsk_skp9          ; jump if not
    add   ax, 3
    cmp   ax, [hd_cylinder] ; are they within 3 cylinders?
    jb   hdsk_skp9          ; jump if not

                            ; is AT type, check if LBA active (heads > 16)

hdsk_skp8b:
    cmp   dx, 16            ; more than 16 heads ?
    jbe   hdsk_info2        ; jump if not
    mov   bp, 6             ; set to AT type with LBA on (6)
hdsk_info2:
    pop   dx
    jmp   hdsk_info         ; if so, likely AT type

; Not likely AT type, since cylinders do not match up!
; First we'll try an older Future Domain SCSI test

; Future Domain SCSI test - Interrupt 13h, function 18h will
; return invalid command with DL >= 80h, if no Future Domain
; SCSI card is present

hdsk_skp9:
    pop   dx
    inc   bp                ; assume SCSI
    push  dx
    mov   ah, 18h
    int   13h               ; Future Domain SCSI ?
    pop   dx
    jc   hdsk_skp10         ; jump if not
    cmp   ax, 4321h         ; confirmation number
    jne   hdsk_skp10
```

```
    jmp   hdsk_info

; Now check if possible PS/2 ESDI drive

hdsk_skp10:
    push  cs
    pop   es
    push  dx
    mov   ax, 1B0Ah
    mov   bx, offset ESDIbuf
    int   13h                         ; Get ESDI config
    pop   dx
    jc   hdsk_skp11                   ; jump if not PS/2 ESDI
    cmp   bx, offset ESDIbuf
    jne   hdsk_skp11
    mov   ax, cs
    mov   bx, es
    cmp   ax, bx                      ; is CS = ES ?
    jne   hdsk_skp11                  ; jump if not
    inc   bp
    jmp   hdsk_info

; General SCSI test (not drive specific)

hdsk_skp11:
    xor   ax, ax
    mov   es, ax
    cmp   word ptr es:[4*4Fh+2], 0    ; vector valid ?
    je   hdsk_skp12                   ; jump if not
    push  dx
    mov   ax, 8200h
    mov   cx, 8765h
    mov   dx, 0CBA9h
    int   4Fh                         ; check for SCSI CAM
```

```
    cmp   dx, 5678h
    pop   dx
    jne   hdsk_skp12              ; jump if not
    cmp   ah, 0
    jne   hdsk_skp12              ; jump if not
    cmp   cx, 9ABCh
    jne   hdsk_skp12              ; jump if not
    jmp   hdsk_info

hdsk_skp12:
    mov   bp, 5                   ; Indicate unknown
                                  ; controller type

; now get the disk parameter for the specified drive

hdsk_info:
    mov   ah, 8
    int   13h                     ; read disk drive parameters
    call  hdconvert               ; convert to useful value
    xchg  cx, ax                  ; put in proper registers
    mov   bl, al                  ; sectors
    mov   ax, bp                  ; get drive type
    mov   ah, bl                  ; insert sectors
    jmp   hdsk_exit

hdsk_none:
    xor   al, al                  ; no drive with this number
    xor   cx, cx
    xor   dx, dx
hdsk_exit:
    pop   es
    pop   bx
    ret
hdsktype endp
```

```
;-----------------------------------------------------------------------
;  HARD DISK CONVERT
;     The cylinder number is in cx. This routine
;     properly combines them back into a 10 bit
;     cylinder number in AX. The number is increased by
;     one for the diagnostic cylinder, and by one more, since
;     the number is zero based. The upper two bits in CL are
;     cleared to get the sector number. One is added
;     to the head number, since it is zero based.
;
;     Called with:  ch = lower 8 bits of cylinder number
;             cl upper two bits are
;                bits 9 & 8 of cylinder
;              lower six bits is sector number
;             dh = head number
;
;     Returns:    ax = total combined cylinders
;             cl = sector number
;             dx = total heads (1-256)
;
;     Regs used:   cx, dh

hdconvert proc  near
    mov   ax, cx                    ; get fragmented cylinder #
    rol   al, 1
    rol   al, 1
    and   al, 3
    xchg  al, ah                    ; ax = # of cylinders
    and   cx, 3Fh                   ; mask for sector number
    mov   dl, dh
    xor   dh,dh
    inc   dx                        ; adjust for head count
    ret
hdconvert endp
```

Code Sample 11-2. Interrupt 13h Disk Read Test

The DISKTEST program is used to check how a specific BIOS handles block reads of up to 128K. It is not intended as a test of the disk system, but points out some serious BIOS bugs common on many systems. Both the executable and source code are provided on the diskette. Since the source code is not very important, I've refrained from printing it in the book.

The test first reads 128K of data from the disk, one sector at a time. This operation is always successful unless the drive has a real serious problem. Next, DISKTEST performs a series of tests having the BIOS read progressively more sectors in a single call. The data read is compared with the reference data to assure that the BIOS and controller are reading the data correctly. The results of each test are displayed.

To use DISKTEST, add a command line value for the disk drive to test: for floppy diskettes, 0 or 1; and for hard disks, 80 or 81. For example, to test the C: hard drive, use the command line:

```
DISKTEST 80
```

The test results of DISKTEST on one system are shown in Figure 11-6. In this case, at least 81h sectors can be read reliably. This BIOS properly returned an error when the read failed.

Figure 11-6. Results from DISKTEST

```
DISKTEST - Interrupt 13h Sector Read Test    v2.00 (c) 1994, 1996 FVG
Loading 128 KB, 1 sector at a time, for reference data in tests.
................................................................................


Number of sectors being read: 01h  Compare passed, returns AH=0, AL=00h.
Number of sectors being read: 33h  Compare passed, returns AH=0, AL=00h.
Number of sectors being read: 66h  Compare passed, returns AH=0, AL=00h.
Number of sectors being read: 7Fh  Compare passed, returns AH=0, AL=00h.
Number of sectors being read: 80h  Compare passed, returns AH=0, AL=00h.
Number of sectors being read: 81h  Compare passed, returns AH=0, AL=00h.
Number of sectors being read: C0h  Failed. Error number = 09h
```

I was surprised to find many BIOSes incorrectly handle standard data transfers. The results of DISKTEST, on a variety of systems, fell into one of five categories, as follows.

1. Works fine and allows up to FFh sectors to be transferred (rare).
2. Allows up to 80h sectors to be transferred, but hangs if 81h or more sectors are attempted.
3. Works fine and allows up to 80h sectors to be transferred, but the BIOS indicates success if more than 81h sectors are attempted, even though the data is incorrect.
4. The BIOS issues an error code that read was unsuccessful when attempting to read more than 80h sectors.
5. When reading more than one track's worth of data, the BIOS indicates success, but the data is incorrect.

The test will perform a number of retries if any error condition is returned. This is especially important for laptop hard drives and diskettes, where the motor may take a short time to spin up to speed.

What does it all mean? For hard disk drives, a maximum of one track's worth of sectors is always reliable. If it is necessary to read any more than one track at a time, be sure to test the system before allowing it. Reading a full track also requires first reading the first sector on the track. It is not reliable on some systems to read across a track boundary.

For example, if a drive has 17 sectors per track, and you need to read 8 sectors starting at sector 15, two operations are required. The first three sectors are read from the first track (head 0, sectors 15, 16, and 17). Next, five more sectors are read, using head 1, starting at sector 0. This obtains logical sectors 18 through 22.

Port Summary

This is a list of ports used to control the hard disk controller. The registers supported will vary by platform as noted. On the original AT only one controller was specified, which allowed for two drives. Most systems with BIOS dates 1995 or later, will support two controllers, for up to four drives. Some systems and special controllers provide support for up to eight drives across four controllers. These port assignments are typical, but some vendors may use other alternate ports.

Port	**Type**	**Function**	**Platform**
70h	I/O	Hard Disk Data (4th controller)	AT/EISA
71h	Input	Hard Disk Error Register (4th controller)	AT/EISA
71h	Output	Hard Disk Write Precompensation (4th controller)	AT/EISA
72h	I/O	Hard Disk Sector Count (4th controller)	AT/EISA
73h	I/O	Hard Disk Sector Number (4th controller)	AT/EISA

Port	Type	Function	Platform
74h	I/O	Hard Disk Cylinder Low (4th controller)	AT/EISA
75h	I/O	Hard Disk Cylinder High (4th controller)	AT/EISA
76h	I/O	Hard Disk Drive and Head (4th controller)	AT/EISA
77h	Input	Hard Disk Status (4th controller)	AT/EISA
77h	Output	Hard Disk Command (4th controller)	AT/EISA
F0h	I/O	Hard Disk Data (3rd controller)	AT/EISA
F1h	Input	Hard Disk Error Register (3rd controller)	AT/EISA
F1h	Output	Hard Disk Write Precompensation (3rd controller)	AT/EISA
F2h	I/O	Hard Disk Sector Count (3rd controller)	AT/EISA
F3h	I/O	Hard Disk Sector Number (3rd controller)	AT/EISA
F4h	I/O	Hard Disk Cylinder Low (3rd controller)	AT/EISA
F5h	I/O	Hard Disk Cylinder High (3rd controller)	AT/EISA
F6h	I/O	Hard Disk Drive and Head (3rd controller)	AT/EISA
F7h	Input	Hard Disk Status (3rd controller)	AT/EISA
F7h	Output	Hard Disk Command (3rd controller)	AT/EISA
170h	I/O	Hard Disk Data (2nd controller)	AT/EISA
171h	Input	Hard Disk Error Register (2nd controller)	AT/EISA
171h	Output	Hard Disk Write Precompensation (2nd controller)	AT/EISA
172h	I/O	Hard Disk Sector Count (2nd controller)	AT/EISA
173h	I/O	Hard Disk Sector Number (2nd controller)	AT/EISA
174h	I/O	Hard Disk Cylinder Low (2nd controller)	AT/EISA
175h	I/O	Hard Disk Cylinder High (2nd controller)	AT/EISA
176h	I/O	Hard Disk Drive and Head (2nd controller)	AT/EISA
177h	Input	Hard Disk Status (2nd controller)	AT/EISA
177h	Output	Hard Disk Command (2nd controller)	AT/EISA
1F0h	I/O	Hard Disk Data	AT/EISA
1F1h	Input	Hard Disk Error Register	AT/EISA
1F1h	Output	Hard Disk Write Precompensation	AT/EISA
1F2h	I/O	Hard Disk Sector Count	AT/EISA
1F3h	I/O	Hard Disk Sector Number	AT/EISA
1F4h	I/O	Hard Disk Cylinder Low	AT/EISA
1F5h	I/O	Hard Disk Cylinder High	AT/EISA
1F6h	I/O	Hard Disk Drive and Head	AT/EISA
1F7h	Input	Hard Disk Status	AT/EISA
1F7h	Output	Hard Disk Command	AT/EISA
276h	Input	Hard Disk Alternate Status (4th controller)	AT/EISA
276h	Output	Hard Disk Adapter Register (4th controller)	AT/EISA
277h	Input	Hard Disk Drive Address Register (4th controller)	AT/EISA
2F6h	Input	Hard Disk Alternate Status (3rd controller)	AT/EISA
2F6h	Output	Hard Disk Adapter Register (3rd controller)	AT/EISA
2F7h	Input	Hard Disk Drive Address Register (3rd controller)	AT/EISA
320h	Input	Hard Disk Controller Status	PC/XT

Port	Type	Function	Platform
320h	Output	Hard Disk Commands	PC/XT
321h	Input	Hard Disk Controller Status	PC/XT
321h	Output	Hard Disk Controller Reset	PC/XT
322h	Input	Hard Disk Get Type Switches	PC/XT
322h	Output	Hard Disk Controller Select Pulse	PC/XT
323h	Output	Hard Disk DMA and Interrupt Masks	PC/XT
376h	Input	Hard Disk Alternate Status (2nd controller)	AT/EISA
376h	Output	Hard Disk Adapter Register (2nd controller)	AT/EISA
377h	Input	Hard Disk Drive Address Register (2nd controller)	AT/EISA
3F6h	Input	Hard Disk Alternate Status	AT/EISA
3F6h	Output	Hard Disk Adapter Control Register	AT/EISA
3F7h	Input	Hard Disk Drive Address Register	AT/EISA
3510h	Input	ESDI Hard Disk Status (16-bit)	PS/2
3510h	Output	ESDI Hard Disk Commands (16-bit)	PS/2
3512h	Input	ESDI Hard Disk Basic Status	PS/2
3512h	Output	ESDI Hard Disk Basic Control	PS/2
3513h	Input	ESDI Hard Disk Interrupt Status	PS/2
3513h	Output	ESDI Hard Disk Attention	PS/2
3518h	Input	ESDI Hard Disk Status (16-bit), Secondary	PS/2
3518h	Output	ESDI Hard Disk Commands (16-bit), Secondary	PS/2
351Ah	Input	ESDI Hard Disk Basic Status, Secondary	PS/2
351Ah	Output	ESDI Hard Disk Basic Control, Secondary	PS/2
351Bh	Input	ESDI Hard Disk Interrupt Status, Secondary	PS/2
351Bh	Output	ESDI Hard Disk Attention, Secondary	PS/2

Port Detail

Port	Type	Description	Platform
70h	**I/O**	**Hard Disk Data (4th controller)**	**AT/EISA**

Alternate address for a fourth hard disk adapter. See port 1F0h, I/O.

Port	Type	Description	Platform
71h	**Input**	**Hard Disk Error Register (4th controller)**	**AT/EISA**

Alternate address for a fourth hard disk adapter. See port 1F1h, Input.

Port	Type	Description	Platform
71h	Output	Hard Disk Write Precompensation (4th controller)	AT/EISA

Alternate address for a fourth hard disk adapter. See port 1F1h, Output.

Port	Type	Description	Platform
72h	I/O	Hard Disk Sector Count (4th controller)	AT/EISA

Alternate address for a fourth hard disk adapter. See port 1F2h, I/O.

Port	Type	Description	Platform
73h	I/O	Hard Disk Sector Number (4th controller)	AT/EISA

Alternate address for a fourth hard disk adapter. See port 1F3h, I/O.

Port	Type	Description	Platform
74h	I/O	Hard Disk Cylinder Low (4th controller)	AT/EISA

Alternate address for a fourth hard disk adapter. See port 1F4h, I/O.

Port	Type	Description	Platform
75h	I/O	Hard Disk Cylinder High (4th controller)	AT/EISA

Alternate address for a fourth hard disk adapter. See port 1F5h, I/O.

Port	Type	Description	Platform
76h	I/O	Hard Disk Drive and Head (4th controller)	AT/EISA

Alternate address for a fourth hard disk adapter. See port 1F6h, I/O.

Port	Type	Description	Platform
77h	Input	Hard Disk Status (4th controller)	AT/EISA

Alternate address for a fourth hard disk adapter. See port 1F7h, Input.

Port	Type	Description	Platform
77h	Output	Hard Disk Command (4th controller)	AT/EISA

Alternate address for a fourth hard disk adapter. See port 1F7h, Output.

Port	Type	Description	Platform
F0h	I/O	Hard Disk Data (3rd controller)	AT/EISA

Alternate address for a third hard disk adapter. See port 1F0h, I/O.

Port	Type	Description	Platform
F1h	Input	Hard Disk Error Register (3rd controller)	AT/EISA

Alternate address for a third hard disk adapter. See port 1F1h, Input.

Port	Type	Description	Platform
F1h	Output	Hard Disk Write Precompensation (3rd controller)	AT/EISA

Alternate address for a third hard disk adapter. See port 1F1h, Output.

Port	Type	Description	Platform
F2h	I/O	Hard Disk Sector Count (3rd controller)	AT/EISA

Alternate address for a third hard disk adapter. See port 1F2h, I/O.

Port	Type	Description	Platform
F3h	I/O	Hard Disk Sector Number (3rd controller)	AT/EISA

Alternate address for a third hard disk adapter. See port 1F3h, I/O.

Port	Type	Description	Platform
F4h	I/O	Hard Disk Cylinder Low (3rd controller)	AT/EISA

Alternate address for a third hard disk adapter. See port 1F4h, I/O.

Port	Type	Description	Platform
F5h	I/O	Hard Disk Cylinder High (3rd controller)	AT/EISA

Alternate address for a third hard disk adapter. See port 1F5h, I/O.

Port	Type	Description	Platform
F6h	I/O	Hard Disk Drive and Head (3rd controller)	AT/EISA

Alternate address for a third hard disk adapter. See port 1F6h, I/O.

Port	Type	Description	Platform
F7h	Input	Hard Disk Status (3rd controller)	AT/EISA

Alternate address for a third hard disk adapter. See port 1F7h, Input.

Port	Type	Description	Platform
F7h	Output	Hard Disk Command (3rd controller)	AT/EISA

Alternate address for a third hard disk adapter. See port 1F7h, Output.

Port	Type	Description	Platform
170h	I/O	Hard Disk Data (2nd controller)	AT/EISA

Alternate address for a second hard disk adapter. See port 1F0h, I/O.

Port	Type	Description	Platform
171h	Input	Hard Disk Error Register (2nd controller)	AT/EISA

Alternate address for a second hard disk adapter. See port 1F1h, Input.

Port	Type	Description	Platform
171h	Output	Hard Disk Write Precompensation (2nd controller)	AT/EISA

Alternate address for a second hard disk adapter. See port 1F1h, Output.

Port	Type	Description	Platform
172h	I/O	Hard Disk Sector Count (2nd controller)	AT/EISA

Alternate address for a second hard disk adapter. See port 1F2h, I/O.

Port	Type	Description	Platform
173h	I/O	Hard Disk Sector Number (2nd controller)	AT/EISA

Alternate address for a second hard disk adapter. See port 1F3h, I/O.

Port	Type	Description	Platform
174h	I/O	Hard Disk Cylinder Low (2nd controller)	AT/EISA

Alternate address for a second hard disk adapter. See port 1F4h, I/O.

Port	Type	Description	Platform
175h	I/O	Hard Disk Cylinder High (2nd controller)	AT/EISA

Alternate address for a second hard disk adapter. See port 1F5h, I/O.

Port	Type	Description	Platform
176h	I/O	Hard Disk Drive and Head (2nd controller)	AT/EISA

Alternate address for a second hard disk adapter. See port 1F6h, I/O.

Port	Type	Description	Platform
177h	Input	Hard Disk Status (2nd controller)	AT/EISA

Alternate address for a second hard disk adapter. See port 1F7h, Input.

Port	Type	Description	Platform
177h	Output	Hard Disk Command (2nd controller)	AT/EISA

Alternate address for a second hard disk adapter. See port 1F7h, Output.

Port	Type	Description	Platform
1F0h	I/O	Hard Disk Data (16/32-bit)	AT/EISA

This I/O port transfers data to and from the hard disk controller. Generally 256 words, or a sector's worth of data, are transferred at a time. Unlike the PC/XT and PS/2 ESDI controllers, which use DMA to transfer data, the hard disk BIOS for the AT controller transfers the data directly through this port.

Before the first sector of data can be transferred, the BIOS must wait for the controller to signal that data is available. The Hard Disk Status at port 1F7h, Data Request bit 3 will go high when the controller is ready for data to be transferred.

The data is transferred as a block of 256 words or 128 double words, usually with an input or output string instruction INSW/INSD or OUTSW/OUTSD. Use of 32-bit transfers are only allowed when both the PC bus and the controller hardware support it. For example, most VLB- and PCI-based controllers support 32-bit data transfers through this port. Interrupts should be disabled during the transfer of each sector. Refer to the section on Common Read Sector Operations for an example of how this register is used.

Port	Type	Description	Platform
1F1h	Input	Hard Disk Error Register	AT/EISA

The error register holds the failure status of the command last executed, or diagnostic mode error status. In normal operating mode, if an error occurred during a command, the error bit is set on in the status register, port 1F7h, bit 0. Only if this bit is on is the error register valid for normal operation.

Input (0-7) Normal Operation, when error bit set

bit 7 r = 1 Bad Sector Detected—The bad block bit was set in the sector's ID field. The bad block bit is only set by the format command to signify a sector with hard data errors. The sector should not be used or the disk address specified was incorrect.

6 r = 1 Uncorrectable Data Error—The sector's data has errors beyond the ability of the controller's error correction mechanism to fix.

5 r = 1 Media Changed—The removable media has been removed, and another media has been inserted. The media type and capacity should be determined before use. This error condition is not supported on most controllers, and returns a zero from unsupported controllers. If supported, this bit can only be cleared with an Acknowledge Removable Media Change command, DBh. See port 1F7h for details.

4 r = 1 ID or Target Sector Not Found—The controller was unable to locate the specified cylinder, sector, or head address. This error may also indicate there was an error in the ID field, read from the sector. The controller will normally try eight or more times to locate and/or reread sectors in attempt to get to the requested address.

3 r = 1 Media Change Requested—The removable media drive's release media button or latch has been activated by a user. The software may be required to unlock the drive and/or eject the media, using a vendor-specific command. This error condition is not supported on most controllers, and returns a zero from unsupported controllers.

2 r = 1 Command Aborted—This flag is set if the specified command is undefined or if a command was issued while a drive was busy or had a write fault. Check the status bits at port 1F7h or 3F6h for the drive busy and write fault conditions.

1 r = 1 Track 0 Not Found—During a recalibrate command, the heads were moved the maximum number of cylinders supported by the controller outward, and the track 0 line from the drive never went active.

0 r = 1	Address Mark Not Found—During a read sector command, after the proper sector ID was found, no address mark was detected. The sector likely has a hard error, and should be removed from use.

While in any diagnostics mode, or after a reset, when the controller goes through a self-test, the error register contents indicate the result of the diagnostic test.

Input (0-7) Diagnostics Error Status (Drive 0 selected, default case)

Hex Value	Description
1	No error detected, drive 0 and 1
2	Device error
3	Sector buffer (inside controller) error
4	ECC circuitry failure
5	Control processor error
81	Drive 1 failed, no error on drive 0
82	Drive 1 failed, device error on drive 0
83	Drive 1 failed, sector buffer error on drive 0
84	Drive 1 failed, ECC circuitry failure on drive 0
85	Drive 1 failed, Control processor error or drive 0

To obtain the error status for drive 1 after the diagnostic test completes, this register is read. Bit 7 will be set indicating a problem with drive 1, if drive 1 is present. Write 10h to the Drive and Head Register port 1F6h to set the drive bit to drive 1. Reading this Error register again will return the status of drive 1. Not all controllers can get diagnostic failure information from drive 1.

Input (0-7) Diagnostics Error Status (Drive 1 selected after diagnostic)

Hex Value	Description
1	No error detected
2	Device error
3	Sector buffer (inside controller) error
4	ECC circuitry failure
5	Control processor error

Port	Type	Description	Platform
1F1h	Output	Hard Disk Write Precompensation	AT/EISA

Some older disk drives, during write operations, require write precompensation on inner cylinders of the drive. This register specifies on which cylinder (if any) write precompensation will begin. It loads a byte value of the cylinder divided by four from the location where write precompensation should begin. To begin write precompensation at cylinder 512, use a value 512/4 or 128. A value of FFh indicates no write precompensation will occur on the drive.

Since few drives today need write precompensation, new controllers (IDE) have eliminated this feature and reused this byte for custom features unique to the controller. To help maintain backward compatibility, the storage of a value is ignored unless a specific feature command is issued after the write (see port 1F7h, commands E9h and EFh).

Port	Type	Description	Platform
1F2h	I/O	Hard Disk Sector Count	AT/EISA

For read and write operations this register holds the number of sectors to transfer. A value of zero indicates 256 sectors are to be transferred. Although the controller is capable of transferring up to 128K in a single operation, many system BIOSes have serious bugs when handling more than 64K in a single transfer.

When the command completes, this register will hold the number of sectors remaining. A value of zero indicates all the sectors were transferred. A non-zero value indicates the number of sectors that need to be transferred in order to complete the original request.

Other commands, such as format and initialize drive, define this register for alternate purposes. See the specific commands for details.

Port	Type	Description	Platform
1F3h	I/O	Hard Disk Sector Number	AT/EISA

This register holds the starting sector number for any disk access command. When a commanded controller operation is complete the register holds the current sector number of the drive.

On IDE drives, when LBA mode is active (see port 1F6h), this port holds bits 0 to 7 of the 28-bit LBA.

Port	Type	Description	Platform
1F4h	I/O	Hard Disk Cylinder Low	AT/EISA

This register stores the lower 8-bytes of the starting cylinder number for any disk access, such as read, write, verify, or seek. When a commanded controller operation is complete the register holds the lower 8-bytes of the current cylinder number of the drive.

On IDE drives, when LBA mode is active (see port 1F6h), this port holds bits 8 to 15 of the 28-bit LBA.

Port	Type	Description	Platform
1F5h	I/O	Hard Disk Cylinder High	AT/EISA

This register stores the high byte of the starting cylinder number for any disk access, such as read, write, verify, or seek. When a commanded controller operation is complete the register holds the upper bits of the current cylinder number of the drive.

Older controllers only support a combined 10-bit cylinder number and ignore bits 2 through 7 in this register. If an attempt were made to write to cylinder 1,024, the older controller would write to cylinder 0!

Most current EIDE controllers support cylinder numbers beyond 10 bits using additional bits in this register.

On IDE drives, when LBA mode is active (see port 1F6h), this port holds bits 16 to 23 of the 28-bit LBA.

Port	Type	Description	Platform
1F6h	I/O	Hard Disk Drive and Head Register	AT/EISA

The drive and head is specified in this register. When a commanded controller operation is complete, the head number is updated to the current head number. IDE drives are fixed at a 512-byte sector size, and bit 6 is reused as a LBA (Logical Block Address) indicator. When LBA is active, the lower four bits are used along with the Sector Number and Cylinder ports to define a 28 bit LBA address.

I/O (bits 0-7) Non-IDE Drives

bit	Value	Description
bit	7 r/w = 1	Extend data field for ECC (used in all cases). This makes the on-disk sector size 512 bytes + 7 ECC bytes. All systems use this format.
	6 r/w = 0 5 r/w = 1	Sector size

bit 6	bit 5	bytes per sector
0	0	= 256
0	1	= 512 (used in all cases)
1	0	= 1024
1	1	= 128

bit	Value	Description
	4 r/w = 0	Drive 0 select (master)
	1	Drive 1 select (slave)
	3 r/w = x 2 r/w = x 1 r/w = x 0 r/w = x	Head number (0 to 15)

I/O (bits 0-7) IDE Drives—Normal Cylinder-Head-Sector mode

bit	Value	Description
bit	7 r/w = 1	Must be set to 1
	6 r/w = 0	Address drive using Cylinder-Head-Sector address
	5 r/w = 1	Must be set to 1

4 r/w = 0	Drive 0 select (master)
1	Drive 1 select (slave)
3 r/w = x	Head number (0 to 15)
2 r/w = x	
1 r/w = x	
0 r/w = x	

I/O (bits 0-7) IDE Drives—LBA (logical block address) mode

bit	7 r/w = 1	Must be set to 1
	6 r/w = 1	LBA mode flag
	5 r/w = 1	Must be set to 1
	4 r/w = 0	Drive 0 select (master)
	1	Drive 1 select (slave)
	3 r/w = x	Bit 27 of the LBA address
	2 r/w = x	Bit 26 of the LBA address
	1 r/w = x	Bit 25 of the LBA address
	0 r/w = x	Bit 24 of the LBA address

Port	Type	Description	Platform
1F7h	Input	Hard Disk Status	AT/EISA

This port returns the controller status. Reading this port causes any pending interrupt to be cleared, and provides an implied interrupt acknowledge. Use port 3F6h, Input, to get this status information without clearing a pending interrupt and to avoid sending an interrupt acknowledge.

If the controller busy bit 7 is on, all other bits are undefined. In addition, when busy, reading any controller port 1F0 to 1F7 will return undefined results. When the busy bit transitions from busy to not busy, the remaining bits in this register and values in ports 1F0 to 1F7 will become valid 400 ns after the transition.

When an interrupt is caused by an Aborted Command (usually due to a timeout error) bits 6, 5, and 4 are latched and are not updated until this register is read.

Input (bits 0-7)

bit	7 r = 0	Controller is not busy
	1	Controller busy, bits 0-6 undefined (see text)
	6 r = 0	Selected Drive not ready
	1	Selected Drive ready to respond to a command from the controller and if bit 4 is set, it is ready for a read, write or seek.
	5 r = 1	Write fault occurred from selected drive

4 r = 1	Seek is complete on the selected drive and the heads are now at the requested position
3 r = 1	Data Request is active—The controller indicates it is ready to send or receive words through its sector buffer. Refer to Data port 1F0h for details.
2 r = 1	Corrected data—The data read from the disk had a correctable data error that was corrected by the vendor's ECC algorithm. The condition does not stop a multisector data transfer.
1 r = 1	Index pulse—On older drives, this bit reflects the index pulse state and is set on once every revolution of the disk. Currently, vendors can use this for other purposes or leave the bit unused.
0 r = 0	No error
1	Error occurred in the previous command—The error register indicates the nature of the error. This bit is cleared when the next command is sent to the controller.

Port	Type	Description	Platform
1F7h	Output	Hard Disk Command	AT/EISA

Commands are issued to the controller through this port. Before issuing a command the controller should be ready (not busy). The busy status is read from the Status register, port 1F7h, bit 7. The interrupt request is automatically cleared when a new command is loaded. All registers required for the command must have been loaded before the command is issued.

Unless otherwise noted, each command must have the disk address, made up of the drive number, cylinder, head, and sector. The sector count must be loaded. Write and Format commands must also have the write precompensation cylinder value set when used with older non-IDE type drives.

See port 1F0h for the normal method of transferring data words to and from the controller. Some controllers with their own hard disk BIOS may use DMA, unlike the normal non-DMA I/O transfers made by the system BIOS.

Any command marked with "(limited)" indicates extensions that may or may not be supported by the controller, and are never issued by a system BIOS dated 1994 or older. These added commands are for specific vendor hardware, such as removable media drives and special power-down operations, and/or refer to the latest ATA specifications (ATA-1, ATA-2, and ATA-3 specifications).

Hex Value	Commands
00	No operation
1x	Recalibrate
20	Read Multiple Sectors, with retries
21	Read Multiple Sectors, no retries
22	Read Sector and ECC data, with retries
23	Read Sector and ECC data, no retries
30	Write Multiple Sectors, with retries
31	Write Multiple Sectors, no retries
32	Write Sector and ECC data, with retries
33	Write Sector and ECC data, no retries
3C	Write Multiple Sectors and Verify (limited)
40	Verify Multiple Sectors, with retries
41	Verify Multiple Sectors, no retries
50	Format Track
7x	Seek
90	Drive Diagnostic
91	Initialize Drive Parameters
92	Download Microcode
94	Standby Immediate (limited)
95	Idle Immediate (limited)
96	Standby (limited)
97	Idle (limited)
98	Check Power Mode (limited)
99	Set Sleep Mode (limited)
B0	SMART Operations (limited)
C4	Read Multiple Blocks (limited)
C5	Write Multiple Blocks (limited)
C6	Set Multiple Blocks Mode (limited)
C8	Read DMA, with retries (limited)
C9	Read DMA, no retries (limited)
CA	Write DMA, with retries (limited)
CB	Write DMA, no retries (limited)
DB	Acknowledge Removable Media Change (limited)
DC	Removable Media Post-Boot (limited)
DD	Removable Media Pre-Boot (limited)
DE	Removable Media Door Lock (limited)
DF	Removable Media Door Unlock (limited)
E0	Standby Immediate (limited)
E1	Idle Immediate (limited)
E2	Standby (limited)
E3	Idle (limited)

Hex Value	Commands
E4	Read Buffer (limited)
E5	Check Power Mode (limited)
E6	Set Sleep Mode (limited)
E8	Write Buffer (limited)
E9	Write Same (limited)
EC	Get Device Information (limited)
ED	Media Eject (limited)
EE	Get Device Information DMA (limited)
EF	Set Features (limited)
F1	Security Set Password (limited)
F2	Security Unlock (limited)
F3	Security Erase Prepare (limited)
F4	Security Erase Unit (limited)
F5	Security Freeze Lock (limited)
F6	Security Disabled Password (limited)

Command Detail

Command	Description	Port
0	No Operation	1F7

Perform no operation on the drive, and respond with the aborted command, bit 2 = 1, in the error register.

Command	Description	Port
1xh	Recalibrate	1F7h

Any command, 10h to 1Fh, will position the head on cylinder 0. Only the head value needs to be specified. This operation ignores all other registers.

Command	Description	Port
20h	Read Multiple Sectors, with retries	1F7h

Reads the number of sectors specified. If a data error is detected, the operation is retried automatically in an attempt to get valid data. The number of retries depends on the controller vendor.

Command	Description	Port
21h	Read Multiple Sectors, no retries	1F7h

Same as command 20h, but no retries are made if the data is bad.

Command	Description	Port
22h	Read Sector & ECC data, with retries	1F7h

Reads one sector including the ECC data bytes. The total number of bytes read is 512, plus the ECC of 4 or 7 bytes. A normal read is performed with command 20h, where the controller does not pass the ECC bytes to the user.

If a data error is detected, the operation is retried automatically in an attempt to get valid data. The number of retries depends on the controller vendor.

Command	Description	Port
23h	Read Sector & ECC data, no retries	1F7h

Same as command 21h, but the sector read includes 4 or 7 ECC bytes. The sector is 512 bytes plus the ECC bytes long.

Command	Description	Port
30h	Write Multiple Sectors, with retries	1F7h

Writes the number of sectors specified. If a data error is detected in locating the sector ID, the operation is retried automatically in an attempt to get valid ID data. The number of retries depends on the controller vendor.

Command	Description	Port
31h	Write Multiple Sectors, no retries	1F7h

Same as command 30h, except no retries are made if the sector ID data is bad.

Command	Description	Port
32h	Write Sector & ECC data, with retries	1F7h

Writes one sector including the ECC data bytes from the user. The controller does not generate the ECC bytes as occurs with command 30h. This means the sector supplied by the user is 512 bytes plus 4 or 7 ECC bytes.

If a data error is detected in locating the sector ID, the operation is retried automatically in an attempt to get valid ID data. The number of retries depends on the controller vendor.

Command	Description	Port
33h	Write Sector & ECC data, no retries	1F7h

Same as command 32h, except no retries are made if the sector ID data is bad.

Command	Description	Port
3Ch	Write Multiple Sectors & Verify (limited)	1F7h

This command writes the specified data, and then verifies the data after the write operation is complete. The write portion of the operation is similar to command 30h, Write multiple sectors. This command is not supported on most AT controllers.

Command	Description	Port
40h	Verify Multiple Sectors, with retries	1F7h

Reads and verifies the number of sectors specified. If a data error is detected, the operation is retried automatically in an attempt to get valid data. The number of retries depends on the controller vendor. No data is transferred by this command and DMA is not used during this command.

A verify is considered successful if the specified sectors are found, and the sector's ECC bytes are checked against the sector's data, and no errors are found. If an ECC error is found, the sector is read some number of times in an attempt to get valid data. Failure to get a valid ECC will fail the verify.

Command	Description	Port
41h	Verify Multiple Sectors, no retries	1F7h

Same as command 40h, but no retries are made if the data is bad.

Command	Description	Port
50h	Format Track	1F7h

Formats the specified track's sectors with sector ID information and initialized data. The Sector Count register, port 1F2h, is loaded with the number of sectors per track. The Sector Number register, port 1F3h, is not used by the format operation and is ignored.

A Sector Data Table must be provided with the format command, and includes two bytes of information for each sector in the track. The Sector Data Table is transferred into the controller by this command using the same process as used by write sector command. Table 11-6 in the description of the interrupt 13h, function 5 shows the layout of the Sector Data Table, and explains how interleave is set by the Sector Data Table.

Command	Description	Port
7xh	Seek	1F7h

Any command 70h up to 7Fh will position the head on the specified cylinder. The Sector Count register, port 1F2h, is not used by the Seek operation and is ignored.

An implied seek is automatically performed for all read, write, verify, and format commands, making it unnecessary to use this command immediately prior to those commands.

The drive does not need to be formatted for a Seek command to function correctly.

Command	Description	Port
90h	Drive Diagnostic	1F7h

This command activates the drive diagnostic for all drives attached to the controller. The diagnostic should be run with drive 0 selected, but the diagnostic is run on both drives if present. All other registers are ignored. The result of the diagnostic is returned in the Error register, port 1F1h. See Port 1F1h, input, for additional information.

Command	Description	Port
91h	Initialize Drive Parameters	1F7h

Loads the drive sector and head limits into the controller for the specified drive. Before the command is loaded, the Sector Count register, port 1F2h, is loaded with the number of sectors per track for the disk. The Drive and Head register, port 1F6, is loaded with the highest valid head number, which is the total number of heads, less one. This command ignores all other registers.

Command	Description	Port
92h	Download Microcode (limited)	1F7h

Change the controller's microcode. This command is very vendor specific. The head bits of the Head register are set to zero, and both Cylinder registers are also set to zero. The number of 512-byte increments to load is specified in 16 bits, where the high portion is stored in the Sector Number register, and the low portion is stored in the Sector Count register.

The feature register is set to "1" for temporary use of the download, whereas a value "7" indicates the download will be used both now and in the future. Both download types take effect immediately upon completion.

Command	Description	Port
94h	Standby Immediate (limited)	1F7h

The drive is set into standby mode. This is a 2-byte command and requires that the command E0h be sent immediately after 94h. If the drive motor is already off, no action occurs, otherwise the drive motor is turned off. This command ignores all other registers.

This command is not supported on most AT controllers, and is intended for laptops and other low-power designs.

Command	Description	Port
95h	Idle Immediate (limited)	1F7h

If the drive is in standby with the motor off, the motor is turned back on. This is a 2-byte command and requires the command E1h be sent immediately after 95h. This command ignores all other registers.

This command is not supported on most AT controllers, and is intended for laptops and other low-power designs.

Command	Description	Port
96h	Standby (limited)	1F7h

The drive is set into standby mode. This is a 2-byte command and requires the command E2h be sent immediately after 96h.

If the drive motor is already off, no action occurs. If the Sector Count register is non-zero, a countdown timer is enabled as soon as the drive becomes idle. At the end of the countdown the drive motor is turned off. This command ignores all other registers.

This command is not supported on most AT controllers, and is intended for laptops and other low-power designs.

Command	Description	Port
97h	Idle (limited)	1F7h

If the drive was in standby, with the motor off, the motor is turned back on. This is a 2-byte command and requires the command E3h be sent immediately after 97h.

This command is not supported on most AT controllers, and is intended for laptops and other low-power designs.

Command	Description	Port
98h	Check Power Mode (limited)	1F7h

Finds out the status of the specified drive, idle, or standby. This is a 2-byte command and requires the command E5h be sent immediately after 98h. This command ignores all registers, except the drive selection bit.

The status is returned in the Sector Count register. A value of zero indicates the drive is in standby mode, with the motor off, or is in transition to or from standby mode. A value of FFh indicates the drive is in idle mode with the motor running. This command is not supported on most AT controllers, and is intended for laptops.

Command	Description	Port
99h	Set Sleep Mode (limited)	1F7h

The controller and all drives are powered down. This is a 2-byte command and requires the command E6h be sent immediately after 99h. All other registers are ignored.

No further commands are accepted until a software or hardware reset occurs. All other registers are ignored by this command. This command is not supported on most AT controllers, and is intended for laptops.

Command	Description	Port
B0h	SMART Operations (limited)	1F7h

Control the various features of SMART (Self Monitoring, Analysis, Reporting Technology). The functions shown in Table 11-16 are available. Before activation, the hex function value is placed in the features register, the value 4Fh is stored in the Cylinder low register, and the value C2h is stored in the Cylinder high register.

Table 11-16. SMART Subfunctions

Function (hex)	Description
D0	Read Attribute Values *
D1	Read Attribute Thresholds *
D2	Disable Attribute Autosave (Sector count also set to 0) *
D3	Save Attribute Values *
D2	Enable Attribute Autosave (Sector count also set to F1h)
D8	Enable Operations
D9	Disable Operations
DA	Return Status

* *Functions which may not be supported with a SMART system (vendor optional)*

Command	Description	Port
C4h	Read Multiple Blocks (limited)	1F7h

This command is similar to the Read Multiple Sectors command, except interrupts are not generated at the end of every sector transfer. It is intended for those systems that use DMA for hard disk transfers. The Set Multiple Mode command C6h must have been issued prior to this command. See the Set Multiple Mode command C6h for additional information. This command is not supported on most AT controllers.

Command	Description	Port
C5h	Write Multiple Blocks (limited)	1F7h

This command is similar to the Write Multiple Sectors command, except interrupts are not generated at the end of every sector transfer. It is intended for those systems that use DMA for hard disk transfers. The Set Multiple Blocks Mode command C6h must have been issued prior to this command. See the Set Multiple Blocks Mode command C6h for additional information. This command is not supported on most AT controllers.

Command	Description	Port
C6h	Set Multiple Blocks Mode (limited)	1F7h

When supported, the controller provides a feature to send multiple groups of sectors at a time. The number of sectors per block is loaded into the Sector Count Register before this command is executed. Valid block sizes are 2, 4, 8, and 16. Larger blocks may be supported if the controller's internal buffer is greater than 8K. The drive bit is used in the Drive and Heads register. All other registers are ignored.

Following this command would be a Read or Write Multiple Blocks command C4h or C5h. This begins the transfer of the specified block of sectors, and the controller will only interrupt the system when each block completes. The total number of sectors transferred is specified by the Sector Count Register value when the Read or Write Multiple Block command executes.

If, for example, five sectors were transferred with a block size of 2, the first two sectors are transferred, followed by two more, and the last block would send the remainder, 1 sector. Only three interrupts would have been generated for this example, rather than the normal interrupt for each sector.

The Multiple Block feature is intended for higher performance when using DMA. This command is not supported on most AT controllers.

Command	Description	Port
C8h	Read DMA, with retries (limited)	1F7h

This command is similar to Read Multiple Sectors, with retries command 20h, except the DMA is set up by the hard disk BIOS prior to the read operation. Only one interrupt is generated at the completion of all the sectors sent. This command is not supported on most AT controllers.

Command	Description	Port
C9h	Read DMA, no retries (limited)	1F7h

Same as command C8h, but no retries are made if the data is bad. This command is not supported on most AT controllers.

Command	Description	Port
CAh	Write DMA, with retries (limited)	1F7h

This command is similar to Write Multiple Sectors, with retries command 30h, except the DMA is set up by the hard disk BIOS prior to the write operation. Only one interrupt is generated at the completion of all the sectors received. This command is not supported on most AT controllers.

Command	Description	Port
CBh	Write DMA, no retries (limited)	1F7h

Same as command CAh, except no retries are made if the sector ID data is bad. This command is not supported on most AT controllers.

Command	Description	Port
DCh	Removable Media Post-Boot (limited)	1F7h

This command is issued after the system boots to send vendor specific data to a removable media drive. This command is not supported on most AT controllers.

Command	Description	Port
DBh	Acknowledge Removable Media Change (limited)	1F7h

If a media change error occurred on a removable media drive, this command acknowledges that change, and clears the media change error bit 5 in the Error register port 1F1h. Only the drive bit is used in the Drive and Heads register. All other registers are ignored. This command is not supported on most AT controllers.

Command	Description	Port
DDh	Removable Media Pre-Boot (limited)	1F7h

This command is issued before the system reboots to send vendor-specific data to a removable media drive. This command is not supported on most AT controllers.

Command	Description	Port
DEh	Removable Media Door Lock (limited)	1F7h

Commands the selected drive to lock the door if the drive is currently ready and the door is unlocked. Only the drive bit is used in the Drive and Heads register. All other registers are ignored.

If the door is already locked, or the drive is not ready, the controller sets the drive not ready status in the Status register, port 1F7h. This command is not supported on most AT controllers.

Command	Description	Port
DFh	Removable Media Door Unlock (limited)	1F7h

Commands the selected drive to unlock the door if the drive is currently ready and the door is locked. Only the drive bit is used in the Drive and Heads register. All other registers are ignored.

If the door is already unlocked, or the drive is not ready, the controller sets the drive not ready status in the Status register, port 1F7h. This command is not supported on most AT controllers.

Command	Description	Port
E0h	Standby Immediate (limited)	1F7h

See identical command 94h.

Command	Description	Port
E1h	Idle Immediate (limited)	1F7h

See identical command 95h.

Command	Description	Port
E2h	Standby (limited)	1F7h

See identical command 96h.

Command	Description	Port
E3h	Idle (limited)	1F7h

See identical command 97h.

Command	Description	Port
E4h	Read Buffer (limited)	1F7h

Reads the contents of the controller's internal sector buffer. If the prior command was a Write buffer, the read buffer command will read the same 512 bytes previously written to the buffer. This command is not supported on most AT controllers.

Command	Description	Port
E5h	Check Power Mode (limited)	1F7h

See identical command 98h for details.

Command	Description	Port
E6h	Set Sleep Mode (limited)	1F7h

See identical command 99h for details.

Command	Description	Port
E8h	Write Buffer (limited)	1F7h

Writes to the controller's internal sector buffer. The write will expect 512 bytes to be transferred. This command is not supported on most AT controllers.

Command	Description	Port
E9h	Write Same (limited)	1F7h

This command writes the same data to multiple sectors. Only one sector is read into the controller, and that data is then used to write to all sectors specified. The Features register (port 1F1h) must have been loaded prior to this command with one of two values, 22h or DDh, or the command is aborted without any action. The Features register is loaded using command EFh.

With a Features register value of 22h, the write is similar to a normal write. The target disk address is used as the starting point, and the Sector Count specifies how many sectors to write with the same 512 bytes of information.

When the Features registers is set to value DDh, the controller will write the same 512-byte sector to every sector on the disk.

Only one interrupt is issued when the operation is complete. This command is not supported on most AT controllers.

Command	Description	Port
ECh	Get Device Information (limited)	1F7h

This command gets 256 words of device information that is stored on the device. The command will only work with drives like IDE that hold this data on the disk. This command is not supported on most old AT controllers.

The information returned through port 1F0h is described in Table 11-17. Items marked with an asterisk are not supported in the current ATA specifications and are considered obsolete.

Table 11-17. Drive Information

Offset (hex)	Size	Description	
0	word	Configuration bits	
		bit 15 = 0	ATA device
		1	ATAPI device
		14 = 1	Format speed tolerance gap required *
		13 = 1	Track offset option available *
		12 = 1	Data strobe offset available *
		11 = 1	Disk rotational speed tolerance is more than 0.5% *
		10 = x, 9 = x, 8 = x	Disk transfer rate *
			bit 10, bit 9, bit 8: megabits/second *
			0 0 1 = 5 or less
			0 1 0 = 10 or below and above 5
			1 0 0 = above 10
		7 = x, 6 = x	Drive type
			bit 7, bit 6
			0 1 = Fixed device
			1 0 = Removable media device
		5 = 1	Synchronized drive motor option enabled *
		4 = 1	Time to switch between heads is more than 15 us *
		3 = 0	MFM encoded *
		2 = x, 1 = x	Sectoring type *
			bit 2, bit 1
			0 1 = hard sectoring
			1 0 = soft sectoring
		0 = 0	unused
2	word	Total number of logical cylinders—If the dword at offset 78h exceeds 16,515,072, then this word will be set to 16,383.	
4	word	Unused	
6	word	Total number of logical heads—If the dword at offset 78h exceeds 16,515,072, then this word will be set to 16.	
8	word	Total bytes per track, unformatted *	
A	word	Total bytes per sector, unformatted *	
C	word	Total logical sectors per logical track—If the dword at offset 78h exceeds 16,515,072, then this word will be set to 63.	
E	3 words	Vendor specified, no standard	
14	10 words	Serial number, 20 ASCII characters, right justified; if first word is 0, serial number is not yet assigned by vendor	

Table 11-17. Continued

Offset (hex)	Size	Description
28	word	Buffer type * 0 = not specified 1 = single sector buffer, cannot transfer data through the system and disk at the same time 2 = multisector buffer, dual ported to allow to simultaneous access by both the drive and the system 3 = Same as 2 with read cache
2A	word	Buffer size on drive, in 512-byte pages; if set to zero, the buffer size is not specified *
2C	word	Number of ECC bytes passed on when using read/write with ECC commands; if set to zero, the number of bytes passed is not specified
2E	4 words	Drive's firmware revision, 8 ASCII characters; if first word is zero, the revision is not specified
36	20 words	Model number, 40 ASCII characters; if first word is zero, the model is not specified
5E	byte	Maximum number of sectors that can be transferred using the Read or Write Multiple blocks command
5F	byte	Vendor specified, no standard
60	word	32-bit I/O, 1=allowed, 0=16-bit only allowed *
62	word	Capabilities bit 15 = 0 unused 14 = 0 unused 13 = 0 Standby timer values are vendor specific 1 Standby timer values match ATA-3 or later standards 12 = 0 Future bit for advanced transfer mode 11 = 0 IORDY may be supported 1 IORDY is supported 10 = 1 IORDY can be disabled using the Set Features command 9 to 1 = x unused or obsolete 0 = 1 DMA supported *
64	word	Unspecified and/or unassigned
66	byte	Vendor specified, no standard
67	byte	Software controlled I/O data transfer cycle timing mode 0 = slow, 1 = medium, 2 = fast

Table 11-17. Continued

Offset (hex)	Size	Description
68	byte	Vendor specified, no standard
69	byte	DMA controlled data transfer cycle timing mode * 0 = slow, 1 = medium, 2 = fast
6A	word	Flags bits 15 to 2 = x unspecified and/or unassigned bit 0 = 0 Fields reported at offset 80h through 8Ch are valid 1 Fields reported at offset 80h through 8Ch may be valid bit 0 = 0 Fields reported at offset 6Ch through 75h are valid 1 Fields reported at offset 6Ch through 75h may be valid
6C	word	Number of current logical cylinders
6E	word	Number of current logical heads
70	word	Number of current logical sectors per logical track
72	dword	Current total number of sectors (must equal prior three words multiplied together)
76	byte	Number of sectors that can currently be transferred on a R/W multiple command during each interrupt. Must be zero if the R/W Multiple support (offset 5EH) is zero. The value is only valid if bit 0 in the Multiple Sectors byte at offset 77h is set.
77	byte	Multiple sectors bits 7 to 1 = x unused 0 = 1 Multiple sector setting is valid
78	dword	Total number of user addressable sectors when LBA mode active
7C	word	Unused
7E	byte	Multiword DMA transfer modes supported bit 7 = 1 Mode 7 supported 6 = 1 Mode 6 supported 5 = 1 Mode 5 supported 4 = 1 Mode 4 supported 3 = 1 Mode 3 supported 2 = 1 Mode 2 supported 1 = 1 Mode 1 supported 0 = 1 Mode 0 supported

Table 11-17. Continued

Offset (hex)	Size	Description		
7F	byte	Multiword DMA transfer mode active (only one bit can be set)		
		bit	7 = 1	Mode 7 active
			6 = 1	Mode 6 active
			5 = 1	Mode 5 active
			4 = 1	Mode 4 active
			3 = 1	Mode 3 active
			2 = 1	Mode 2 active
			1 = 1	Mode 1 active
			0 = 1	Mode 0 active
80	byte	Advanced PIO modes supported		
		bit	7 = 1	Mode A supported (future)
			6 = 1	Mode 9 supported (future)
			5 = 1	Mode 8 supported (future)
			4 = 1	Mode 7 supported (future)
			3 = 1	Mode 6 supported (future)
			2 = 1	Mode 5 supported (future)
			1 = 1	Mode 4 supported
			0 = 1	Mode 3 supported
81	byte	Reserved for future PIO mode support		
82	word	Minimum multiword DMA transfer cycle time per word in nanoseconds		
84	word	Manufacturer's recommended multiword DMA transfer cycle time per word in nanoseconds		
86	word	Minimum PIO transfer cycle time without flow control in nanoseconds		
88	word	Minimum PIO transfer cycle time with IORDY flow control in nanoseconds		
8A	22 bytes	Reserved for future command overlap and queuing		
A0	word	Major revision number of specification that the device conforms to (ATA-1 = 1, ATA-2 = 2, etc.). Value 0 or FFFFh indicates the device does not report the revision number.		
A2	word	Minor revision number of specification that the device conforms to. Value 0 or FFFFh indicates the device does not report the minor revision number.		

Table 11-17. Continued

Offset (hex)	Size	Description		
A4	word	Feature set support (only valid if words at this offset and offset A6 are not zero and not FFFFh)		
		bit	15 to 4 = 0	Reserved for future feature sets
			3 = 1	supports the power management feature set
			2 = 1	supports the removable media feature set
			1 = 1	supports the security feature set
			0 = 1	supports the SMART feature set (Self-Monitoring, Analysis, and Reporting Technology for the prediction and detection of device degradation and/or faults
A6	word	Feature set support (only valid if words at this offset and offset A4 are not zero and not FFFFh)		
		bit	15 = 0	
			14 = 1	
			13 to 0 = x	Reserved bits (unknown if ever used)
A8	90 bytes	Unused		
100	word	Security status		
		bits	15 to 9 = x	Unused or reserved
			8 = 0	Security level set to high
			1	Security level set to maximum
			7 = x	unused or reserved
			6 = x	unused or reserved
			5 = x	unused or reserved
			4 = 1	Security count expired
			3 = 1	Security frozen
			2 = 1	Security locked
			1 = 1	Security enabled
			0 = 0	Security supported

* *Obsolete items not supported in the latest ATA specifications*

Command	Description	Port
EDh	Media Eject (limited)	1F7h

After completing any pending operations, the drive door is unlocked (if applicable) and the media is ejected.

Command	Description	Port
EEh	Get Device Information DMA (limited)	1F7h

Get 256 words of parameter information from the device in DMA mode. See Command ECh for the information returned.

Command	Description	Port
EFh	Set Features (limited)	1F7h

This command controls various internal features of the controller. Other registers may contain values necessary for a feature, depending on the vendor. Not all features are supported by all vendors. Features that are enabled and disabled set internal flags in the controller. Once accepted, another Set Features command can be used without changing the prior feature setting. This command is not supported on most older AT controllers, but is supported on most EIDE controllers. Features codes are shown in Table 11-18.

Table 11-18. Feature Codes

Hex Value	Feature
1	Enable 8-bit data transfers instead of normal 16-bit transfers *
2	Enable write cache *
3	Set transfer mode based on value in Sector Count Register
4	Enable all automatic defect reassignment *
22	Write Same, user-specified area (see Write Same command, E9h) *
33	Disable Retries *
44	Specify length of ECC bytes returned on Read/Write with ECC
54	Set cache segments, value in the Sector Count Register *
55	Disable look-ahead feature
66	Disable reverting to power-on defaults
77	Disable ECC *
81	Disable 8-bit data transfers, use 16-bits (normal) *
82	Disable write cache *
84	Disable all automatic defect reassignment *
88	Enable ECC (normal) *
99	Enable Retries (normal) *
9A	Set device maximum average current (to control laptop power consumption) *
AA	Enable look-ahead feature
AB	Set maximum prefetech from Sector Count Register *
BB	Return 4 bytes on Read/Write with ECC commands
CC	Enable reverting to power-on defaults
DD	Write Same, entire disk (see Write Same command, E9h) *

** May not be supported on all EIDE controllers*

Command	Description	Port
F1h	Security Set Password (limited)	1F7h

★★★

Transfer the Password sector (512 bytes) to the disk if security is not in locked or frozen modes. The password sector contains the information shown in Table 11-19.

Table 11-19. Set Password Sector Data

Offset (hex)	Size	Description		
0	word	Control bits		
		bits	15 to 7 = x	unused or reserved
			8 = 0	Security level at high
			1	Security level at maximum
			7 to 1 = x	unused or reserved
			0 = 0	Set the user password
			1	Set the master password
2	32 bytes	Password bytes		
22h	478 bytes	Unused		

Command	Description	Port
F2h	Security Unlock (limited)	1F7h

★★★

Unlock a drive if currently locked. The password is passed in a 512-byte sector to the controller as shown in Table 11-20. If the password is accepted, the drive is unlocked. After five failed attempts, this command and the Security Erase Unit (F4h) commands are aborted until a hardware reset occurs.

Table 11-20. Password Sector Data

Offset (hex)	Size	Description		
0	word	Control bits		
		bits	15 to 1 = 0	Reserved for future
			0 = 0	Compare user password
			1	Compare master password
2	32 bytes	Password bytes		
22h	478 bytes	Unused (set to zero)		

Command	Description	Port
F3h	Security Erase Prepare (limited)	1F7h

This command is issued immediately before the Security Erase Unit (F4h) command is issued. It helps prevent accidental erasure of data. See Security Erase Unit for additional details.

Command	Description	Port
F4h	Security Erase Unit (limited)	1F7h

Erase all user data on the drive if the password matches. The password is passed in a 512-byte sector to the controller as shown in Table 11-19. The Security Erase Prepare command (F3h) must be issued immediately before this command, or the command is aborted.

Command	Description	Port
F5h	Security Freeze Lock (limited)	1F7h

When issued the device activates a frozen mode where other security commands are ignored until the device is powered down. Once power is restored, the freeze mode is automatically released.

Command	Description	Port
F6h	Security Disable Password (limited)	1F7h

Disable the ability to lock the drive. The password is passed in a 512-byte sector to the controller as shown in Table 11-19. If the password is accepted, the drive will no longer allow locking.

Port	Type	Description	Platform
320h	Input	Hard Disk Controller Status	PC/XT

This port is used by PC/XT-type controllers to get status from the controller. On a few commands, the register will return information specific to the command. In all other cases, the register returns a status byte. If the status indicates an error occurred, then the Sense Status command 3 should be issued to get additional information about the error.

When reading the input status byte, the controller's state will be changed indicating completion of the last command, and the busy flag is cleared.

Input (bits 0-7)

Byte 0—Status byte

bit	7 r = 0	unused
	6 r = 0	unused
	5 r = 0	Drive 0 status
	1	Drive 1 status

4 r = 0	unused
3 r = 0	unused
2 r = 0	unused
1 r = 0	No error has occurred
1 r = 1	Error occurred during the execution of a command (issue a Request Sense Status command to get the error information and location)
0 r = 0	unused

Port	Type	Description	Platform
320h	Output	Hard Disk Commands	PC/XT

This port is used by PC/XT-type controllers to specify the command to use along with necessary data.

Output (bits 0-7), Data Control Block (6 bytes, or 14 for initialization)

Byte 0—Command (described below in Table 11-20)

Byte 1—Drive and Head number

bit 7 = 0	always set to zero (unused)
6 = 0	always set to zero (unused)
5 = 0	Drive 0 select
1	Drive 1 select
4 = x	Head number (0 to 1Fh)
3 = x	
2 = x	
1 = x	
0 = x	

Byte 2—Cylinder and Sector number bits 6 and 7 = upper most 2 bits of cylinder number
0-5 = sector number (1 to 63)

Byte 3—Cylinder number (lower 8 bits)

Byte 4—Number of sectors to transfer (Read, Write, and Verify)
Interleave number 1 to 16 (format commands)

Byte 5—Control byte

bit 7 = 0	Attempt four retries on any disk access command
1	Disable retries
6 = 0	On read and verify commands, attempt one reread if an ECC error occurs before considering the read bad. Set this bit to zero on all other commands.
1	Do not attempt rereads if ECC error occurred.

5 = 0	unused			
4 = 0	unused			
3 = 0	unused			
2 = x	Set the step rate			
1 = x	bit 2	bit 1	bit 0	Step rate
0 = x	0	0	0	= 3 ms
	1	0	0	= 200 ms
	1	0	1	= 70 ms (normal)
	1	1	0	= 3 ms
	1	1	1	= 3 ms

The following bytes are only provided with the initialize command 0Ch.

Byte 6—Maximum number of cylinders in drive (low 8 bits)

Byte 7—Maximum number of cylinders in drive (high 8 bits)

Byte 8—Maximum number of heads

Byte 9—Cylinder where to start reduced write current (low 8 bits)

Byte A—Cylinder where to start reduced write current (high 8 bits)

Byte B—Maximum ECC burst data length (0Bh is normal)

Table 11-21. PC/XT Commands

Hex Value	Commands
0	Test if drive is ready
1	Recalibrate
3	Request sense status
4	Format drive
5	Verify multiple sectors
6	Format cylinder
7	Format cylinder with bad sectors
8	Read multiple sectors
A	Write multiple sectors
B	Seek
C	Initialize drive parameters
D	Get ECC burst error length
E	Read data from sector buffer
F	Write data to sector buffer
E0	Controller RAM diagnostic
E3	Drive diagnostic
E4	Controller internal diagnostics
E5	Read multiple sectors with ECC data
E6	Write multiple sectors with ECC data

Port 320h Command Detail

Command	Description	Port
0h	Test if Drive is Ready	320h

The controller updates hard disk controller status, which is read from port 321h. With this command, only bit 5, drive select of byte 1 needs to be defined. All other bits and bytes are don't cares.

Command	Description	Port
1h	Recalibrate	320h

Positions the head on cylinder 0. With this command, only bit 5, drive select in byte 1, and byte 5, the control byte must be defined. All other bits and bytes are don't cares.

Command	Description	Port
3h	Request Sense Status	320h

Commands the controller to get the four sense bytes. Along with the command byte, only bit 5, drive select in byte 1 needs to be defined. All other bits and bytes are don't cares.

When an error is detected, the sense data is obtained by the hard disk BIOS and the error byte converted into one of the standard error return codes. There is *not* a one-for-one correspondence in controller error codes and BIOS return status codes.

After this command block is issued, the four sense bytes can read from port 320h in sequence, and have the following contents:

Byte 0—Error byte

bit 7 = 0 No disk address was used by prior command

1 Prior command used a disk address (i.e., cylinders etc.)

6 = 0 unused

5 - 0 = Error code, hex (the number in parenthesis is the hex return status code returned by the disk BIOS)

- 0 No error detected (0)
- 1 Index signal missing—The index signal is normally asserted once every revolution just before the first sector appears. (20h)
- 2 Seek incomplete—No signal occurred from the drive that the commanded seek completed. (40h)
- 3 Write fault—During the last operation the drive signaled the controller with a write fault. (20h)
- 4 Drive not ready—After drive was selected, the drive failed to respond with a ready signal. (80h)

6	Recalibrate failure—After stepping the maximum number of cylinders outward, the drive failed to signal that it reached cylinder 0. (20h)
8	Drive is still seeking and is not ready. This status only occurs after a Test if Drive Ready command 0, and the drive is still seeking the specified cylinder. (40h)
10h	ID read error—The ECC failed on the sector ID. ECC can detect but not fix ID errors. (10h)
11h	Data error—The sector has an unrecoverable ECC error during a read operation. (10h)
12h	Missing address mark—No address mark was found that matched the request. (2)
14h	Sector not found—The cylinder and head were valid, but the controller could not find the specified sector. (4)
15h	Seek error—After a seek operation the cylinder and/or head address failed to match the specified seek address. (40h)
18h	Correctable data error—The desired data was read, and corrected by ECC. (11h)
19h	Bad track—During the last operation a bad track flag was detected. No retries were made. (0Bh)
20h	Invalid command. (1)
21h	Bad disk address—The cylinder, head, sector address is beyond the end of the disk (2)
30h	RAM error—The controller RAM diagnostic test E0h failed. (20h)
31h	Checksum error—The controller internal diagnostic test E4h failed, due to a checksum error of its internal program memory. (20h)
32h	Internal ECC error—The controller internal diagnostic test E4h failed its test of the ECC generator. (10h)

Byte 1—Current Drive and Head (if error, indicates position of error)

bit	7 = 0	unused
	6 = 0	unused
	5 = 0	Drive 0
	1	Drive 1

4 = x	Head number, 0 to 31
3 = x	
2 = x	
1 = x	
0 = x	

Byte 2—Cylinder and Sector (if error, indicates position of error)

bit 6 & 7 = cylinder bits 8 and 9

0 - 5 = sector number

Byte 3—Cylinder, low 8 bits of 10-bit number (if error, indicates position of error)

Command	Description	Port
4h	**Format Drive**	**320h**

Formats the drive. All six bytes of the Data Control Block must be used, except the sectors field in byte 2, which must be set to zero.

Command	Description	Port
5h	**Verify Multiple Sectors**	**320h**

Verifies ECC is valid for the specified sectors. All six bytes of the Data Control Block must be used.

Command	Description	Port
6h	**Format Cylinder**	**320h**

Formats the specified cylinder. All six bytes of the Data Control Block must be used, except the sectors field in byte 2, which must be set to zero.

Command	Description	Port
7h	**Format Cylinder with Bad Sectors**	**320h**

Formats the specified cylinder with each sector flagged with the bad sector mark. All six bytes of the Data Control Block must be used, except the sectors field in byte 2, which must be set to zero.

Command	Description	Port
8h	**Read Multiple Sectors**	**320h**

Reads the number of sectors specified. All six bytes of the Data Control Block must be used.

Command	Description	Port
Ah	**Write Multiple Sectors**	**320h**

Writes the number of sectors specified. All six bytes of the Data Control Block must be used.

Command	Description	Port
Bh	Seek	320h

Moves the drive head to the specified cylinder. All six bytes of the Data Control Block must be used, except the sectors field in byte 2, which must be set to zero. The sectors count value in byte 4 is a don't care.

Command	Description	Port
Ch	Initialize Drive Parameters	320h

Loads the drive parameters into the controller. This special case has a total of 14 bytes that must be sent. Bytes 1 through 5 of the data control block are don't cares, except for byte 1, bit 5, the drive select needs to be defined.

Command	Description	Port
Dh	Get ECC Burst Error Length	320h

Returns the controller's current setting of the ECC Burst Error Length. Bytes 1 through 5 of the data control block are don't cares. After the command is accepted, it reads port 320h to get the burst error length value. This value is the number of consecutive bits that were corrected.

Command	Description	Port
Eh	Read Data From Sector Buffer	320h

Reads the contents of the internal controller's sector buffer RAM. This is intended for diagnostic purposes only. Bytes 1 through 5 of the data control block are don't cares.

Command	Description	Port
Fh	Write Data From Sector Buffer	320h

Writes to internal controller's sector buffer RAM. This is intended for diagnostic purposes only. Bytes 1 through 5 of the data control block are don't cares.

Command	Description	Port
E0h	Controller RAM diagnostic	320h

Initiates the controller's internal diagnostic of its RAM. The Status register (read from port 320h) will provide the result of the test. Bytes 1 through 5 of the data control block are don't cares.

Command	Description	Port
E3h	Drive Diagnostic	320h

Initiates the specified drive's diagnostic. The Status register (read from port 320h) will provide the result of the test. Bytes 1 through 4 of the data control block are don't cares, except for byte 1, bit 5, the drive select needs to be defined. Byte 5, the control byte, must also be defined.

Command	Description	Port
E4h	Controller Internal Diagnostics	320h

Initiates the controller's internal diagnostic. The Status register (read from port 320h) will provide the result of the test. Bytes 1 through 5 of the data control block are don't cares.

Command	Description	Port
E5h	Read Multiple Sectors with ECC Data	320h

Reads the number of sectors specified. Each sector read also will include the sector's 4-byte ECC data. This means each sector will be 516 bytes long. All six bytes of the data control block must be used.

Command	Description	Port
E6h	Write Multiple Sectors with ECC Data	320h

Writes the number of sectors specified. Each sector written must include the sector's 4-byte ECC data, provided by the user. This means each sector read from memory will be 516 bytes long. All six bytes of the data control block must be used.

Port	Type	Description	Platform
321h	Input	Hard Disk Controller Hardware Status	PC/XT

Reads the status from the adapter card. When the lower nibble has the value 0Dh (busy latch, expecting input command, request ready) the controller is ready to receive the 6-byte control block. See port 320h for details on the control block.

While getting ready to send a control block, if the controller is not ready (as described above), then the status should be reread until the controller is ready or some predetermined timeout period elapses.

Input (bits 0-7)

bit	7 r = x	no connection, may have any value
	6 r = x	no connection, may have any value
	5 r = 1	Interrupt request 5 active

4 r = 1	DMA request 3 active
3 r = 0	Not busy
1	Busy latch set
2 r = 0	Controller expecting data (port 320h)
1	Controller expecting command (port 320h)
1 r = 0	Controller expecting input (port 320h)
1	Controller expecting output (port 320h)
0 r = 0	No request
1	request ready

Port	Type	Description	Platform
321h	Output	Hard Disk Controller Reset	PC/XT

Resets the hard disk controller. Any value may be sent as the value is ignored.

Port	Type	Description	Platform
322h	Input	Hard Disk Get Type Switches	PC/XT

Reads the switch settings on the adapter card. These switches specify the parameter table to use for drive 0 and drive 1. Each drive can choose from one of four fixed parameter tables. The BIOS uses this port to get the switch settings and determine which parameter table to use. See Table 11-7 for which table is selected based on the switch settings.

Input (bits 0-7)

bit 7 r = x	no connection, may have any value
6 r = x	no connection, may have any value
5 r = x	no connection, may have any value
4 r = x	no connection, may have any value
3 r = 0	switch 1 ON (drive 0)
2 r = 0	switch 2 ON (drive 0)
1 r = 0	switch 3 ON (drive 1)
0 r = 0	switch 4 ON (drive 1)

Port	Type	Description	Platform
322h	Output	Hard Disk Controller Make Busy	PC/XT

Any value output to this port sets a latch on the adapter card to indicate it is busy. After a command is loaded, and the command execution completes, the controller sends an interrupt request (IRQ 5 if enabled) to signal completion. The status must be read from the controller, which clears the busy latch.

Port	Type	Description	Platform
323h	Output	Hard Disk DMA and Interrupt Masks	PC/XT

This register controls if DMA and/or Interrupt requests are allowed.

Input (bits 0-7)

bit	7 r = x	unused
	6 r = x	unused
	5 r = x	unused
	4 r = x	unused
	3 r = x	unused
	2 r = x	unused
	1 r = 0	Disable Interrupt Request
	1	Allow Interrupt Request on IRQ 5
	0 r = 0	Disable DMA Request
	1	Allow DMA Request on channel 3

Port	Type	Description	Platform
276h	Input	Hard Disk Alternate Status, (4th controller)	AT/EISA

Alternate address for a fourth hard disk adapter. See port 3F6h, Input.

Port	Type	Description	Platform
276h	Output	Hard Disk Adapter Register, (4th controller)	AT/EISA

Alternate address for a fourth hard disk adapter. See port 3F6h, Output.

Port	Type	Description	Platform
277h	Input	Hard Disk Drive Address Register, (4th controller)	AT/EISA

Alternate address for a fourth hard disk adapter. See port 3F7h, Input.

Port	Type	Description	Platform
2F6h	Input	Hard Disk Alternate Status, (3rd controller)	AT/EISA

Alternate address for a third hard disk adapter. See port 3F6h, Input.

Port	Type	Description	Platform
2F6h	Output	Hard Disk Adapter Register, (3rd controller)	AT/EISA

Alternate address for a third hard disk adapter. See port 3F6h, Output.

Port	Type	Description	Platform
2F7h	Input	Hard Disk Drive Address Register, (3rd controller)	AT/EISA

Alternate address for a third hard disk adapter. See port 3F7h, Input.

Port	Type	Description	Platform
376h	Input	Hard Disk Alternate Status, (2nd controller)	AT/EISA

Alternate address for a second hard disk adapter. See port 3F6h, Input.

Port	Type	Description	Platform
376h	Output	Hard Disk Adapter Register, (2nd controller)	AT/EISA

Alternate address for a second hard disk adapter. See port 3F6h, Output.

Port	Type	Description	Platform
377h	Input	Hard Disk Drive Address Register, (2nd controller)	AT/EISA

Alternate address for a second hard disk adapter. See port 3F7h, Input.

Port	Type	Description	Platform
3F6h	Input	Hard Disk Alternate Status	AT/EISA

This port returns the same status information provided by the Hard Disk Status, port 1F7h. Unlike port 1F7h, reading port 3F6h does not clear a pending interrupt or imply an interrupt acknowledge.

If the Controller busy bit 7 is on, all other bits are undefined. In addition, when busy, reading any controller port 1F0h to 1F7h will return undefined results. When the busy bit transitions from busy to not busy, the remaining bits in this register, and the values in ports 1F0 to 1F7 will become valid 400 ns after the transition.

Input (bits 0-7)

bit	7 r = 0	Controller is not busy
	1	Controller busy, bits 0-6 undefined (see text)
	6 r = 0	Selected Drive not ready
	1	Selected Drive ready to respond to a command from the controller and if bit 4 is set, it is ready for a read, write or seek.
	5 r = 1	Write fault occurred from selected drive
	4 r = 1	Seek is complete on the selected drive and the heads are now at the requested position
	3 r = 1	Data Request is active—The controller indicates it is ready to send or receive words through its sector buffer. Refer to Data port 1F0h for details.
	2 r = 1	Corrected data—The data read from the disk had an ECC error that was corrected by the ECC algorithm. The condition does not stop a multisector data transfer.
	1 r = 1	Index pulse—This bit reflects the index pulse state and is set on once every revolution of the disk.
	0 r = 0	No error
	1	Error occurred in the previous command—The error register indicates the nature of the error. This bit is cleared when the next command is sent to the controller.

Port	Type	Description	Platform
3F6h	Output	Hard Disk Adapter Control Register	AT/EISA

This write-only register holds bits controlling reset, interrupt request, head information, and other options. The control byte from the disk parameter table is written to this port by the interrupt 13h handler before executing the command.

When interrupt requests are allowed (bit 1), the primary controller is connected to IRQ 14, which handles both a master and a slave drive. If a secondary controller is used (typically using port 376h for the Hard Disk Adapter Control Register), most adapters default to using IRQ 15 for the second controller. For third and fourth controllers, no standard is established, and each controller will normally require its own IRQ.

To reset the controller, set bit 2 on for 4.8 microseconds or longer, and then clear bit 2.

Output (bits 0-7)

bit	7 w = 0	unused
	6 w = 0	unused
	5 w = 0	unused
	4 w = 0	unused
	3 w = 0	Drive has 1 to 8 heads
	1	If the drive has more than 8 heads
	2 w = 0	Normal operation
	1	reset controller
	1 w = 0	Allow Interrupt Requests (typically IRQ 14 for primary controller)
	1	Disable Interrupt Request
	0 w = 0	unused

Port	Type	Description	Platform
3F7h	Input	Hard Disk Drive Address Register	AT/EISA

This port returns the drive select, drive head, and write status of the currently selected drive. These are read from the drive interface, and may not reflect exactly what is expected because of timing issues, controller caching, and other aspects. All six bits are returned in the inverted state. Not all controllers support this register.

This port is shared with the diskette controller. The diskette controller, if present, will return the diskette change state on bit 7. I've shown bit 7 as unused, tri-stated. This means if no diskette adapter is used, bit 7 can return any value.

Input (bits 0-7)

bit	7 r = x	Not connected—May return any value (see text)
	6 r = 0	Write in progress on drive
	5 r = x	Currently selected head (inverted)
	4 r = x	0000 = head 15
	3 r = x	0001 = head 14
	2 r = x	...
		1111 = head 0
	1 r = 0	Drive 1 is selected and active (slave drive)
	0 r = 0	Drive 0 is selected and active (master drive)

Port	Type	Description	Platform
3510h	Input	ESDI Hard Disk Status (16-bit)	PS/2

Reads status information from the controller after a command has completed execution. The controller flags the system with an interrupt request IRQ 14, interrupt 76h. Depending on the command issued, some number of words can be read back. See port 3510h, output, for specifics on each command and the data they return by reading this port.

Port	Type	Description	Platform
3510h	Output	ESDI Hard Disk Commands (16-bit)	PS/2

This 16-bit port is used to transfer the command block to the controller. The command process is started with a command request from the Attention register, port 3513h. The command block is then sent, one word at a time. A handshake is performed for each word transferred, so I/O delays are not necessary in sending command words.

Before each word of the command block is sent, the Basic Status register is read, and bit 2 examined. Bit 2 will be zero, indicating it is ready for the next command word. If bit 2 is not zero, the controller is not yet ready for the next word. The status should be reread continuously until the bit 2 is cleared, and the controller can accept the next command block word.

Output (bits 0-7), Command Control Block

The command block is two or four words, depending on the command. The most common command block is shown below. Any commands that differ from this structure are explained within the specific command.

Word 0—Command (described below)

Word 1—Number of Sectors to transfer

Word 2—Relative Sector Address, least significant word

Word 3—Relative Sector Address, most significant word

Hex Value	Command
0606	Park heads on drive 0
0607	Get command complete status on drive 0
0608	Get device status of drive 0
0609	Get configuration of drive 0
0615	Get manufacturing header for drive 0
0616	Low-level format drive 0
0617	Format prepare drive 0
0626	Park heads on drive 1
0627	Get command complete status on drive 1
0628	Get device status of drive 1
0629	Get configuration of drive 1
0635	Get manufacturing header for drive 1

Hex Value	Command
0636	Low-level format drive 1
0637	Format prepare drive 1
06E7	Get controller command complete status
06E9	Get configuration of controller
06EA	Get Programmable Option Select Information
06EB	Translate Relative Sector Address
4601	Read data from drive 0
4602	Write data to drive 0
4603	Verify data on drive 0
4604	Write with verify on drive 0
4605	Seek on drive 0
4621	Read data from drive 1
4622	Write data to drive 1
4623	Verify data on drive 1
4624	Write with verify on drive 1
4625	Seek on drive 1

Port 3510h Command Detail

★★★

Command	Description	Port
0606h	Park heads on drive 0	3510h

Drive 0 is sent a command to stop the motor. The drive will move the heads to its safe landing zone and the drive may shut off its motor. The drive will appear as Not Ready until power is removed. This means a power-down cycle must occur before the drive can be accessed again.

The Command Block for the Park Heads command uses only two words. The second word of the command block is set to zero.

★★★

Command	Description	Port
0607h	Get command complete status on drive 0	3510h

Commands the controller to return the Command Complete Status Block for drive 0. Only two words are used for this command, where the second word is set to zero.

Upon command completion, the Command Complete Status Block is read as a group of seven words from port 3510h. It is shown in Table 11-22.

Table 11-22. Command Complete Status Block

Offset	Size	Description
0	byte	07h (returns command value)
1	byte	Number of words in this status block (7)
2	byte	Command error code in hex (value in parentheses is the hex value return status code by the PS/2 BIOS; return status codes are explained in Table 11-5) 0 Successful, no errors (BB) 1 Invalid parameter (1) 2 unused or unknown function (BB) 3 Command not supported (1) 4 Command canceled (80) 5 unused or unknown function (BB) 6 Controller diagnostic failure, command rejected (20) 7 Format failed—requires format prepare command before format (D) 8 Format error—problem with primary map (D) 9 Format error—problem with secondary map (D) A Format error—diagnostic failure (D) B Format warning—secondary map too large (0) C Format warning—non-zero defect (0) D Format error—system checksum error (D) E Format warning—device incompatibility (0) F Format warning—push table overflow (0) 10 Format warning—more than 15 pushes in cylinder (0) 11 Internal hardware error (20) 12 Format warning—verify errors found (0) 13 Invalid device for command (1) FF Device error
3	byte	Command status codes in hex 1 Successful command completion 3 Successful command completion after ECC 5 Successful command completion after retries 6 Format partially complete 7 Successful command completion after ECC and retries 8 Command complete, with warning (see byte 2) 9 Abort complete A Reset complete B Data transfer ready, no status block C Command complete, with failure (see bytes 4 and 5) D DMA error—to fix, rerun entire command E Command block error (see byte 2) F Attention code bad

Table 11-22. Continued

Offset	Size	Description
4	byte	Device error code, group 1 (value in parentheses is the hex value return status code by the PS/2 BIOS; return status codes are explained in Table 11-5)
		0 No error (BB)
		1 Seek fault, but device detected (40)
		2 Interface fault due to parity, attention or command complete error (20)
		3 Unable to locate sector ID (4)
		4 Not formatted (2)
		5 Unrecoverable ECC error (10)
		6 Sector ID ECC error—ECC can detect but not correct sector ID errors (10)
		7 Relative Sector address out of range (1)
		8 Time out error (BB)
		9 Defective sector (A)
		A Disk changed on removable media (6)
		B Selection error (1)
		C Removable media write protected (3)
		D Write fault (CC)
		E Read fault (BB)
		F No index or sector pulse possibly due to defective drive or cable (2)
		10 Device not ready (10)
		11 Seek error, but adapter detected (40)
		12 Bad format (A)
		13 Volume overflow (BB)
		14 No data address mark found (2)
		15 Sector ID not found, No ID address mark (2)
		16 Device configuration data missing (BB)
		17 Missing first and last Relative Sector Address flags (4)
		18 No sector IDs found on track (4)
		81 Timeout—Waiting for stop
		82 Timeout—Waiting for data transfer to end
		84 Stopped while waiting for data transfer during format
		85 Timeout—Waiting for head switch
		86 Timeout—Waiting for DMA to complete

Table 11-22. Continued

Offset	Size	Description
5	byte	Device error codes, group 2 bit 7 = 0 Unused 6 = 0 Unused 5 = 0 Unused 4 = 1 Ready 3 = 1 Selected 2 = 1 Write fault 1 = 1 Track 0 flag 0 = 1 Seek or command complete
6	word	Number of sectors not processed due to error or operation canceled (returns zero for park heads and seek commands)
8	dword	Last Relative Sector Address Processed
C	word	Number of sectors requiring error recovery—Number of sectors that ECC corrected (returns zero for park heads and seek commands).

Command	Description	Port
0608h	Get device status of drive 0	3510h

Command the controller to return the Status Block for drive 0. Only two words are used for this command, where the second word is set to zero.

Upon command completion, the Status Block is read as a group of nine words from port 3510h. It is shown in Table 11-23.

Table 11-23. Device Status Block

Offset	Size	Description
0	byte	08h (returns command value)
1	byte	Number of words in this status block (9)
2	byte	Error bits bits 7-4 = 0 Unused bit 3 = 1 Timeout waiting for Command Complete line from the drive to become active bit 2 = 1 Parity error during data transfer bit 1 = 1 Timeout waiting for Transfer Acknowledge line from the drive to become inactive bit 0 = 1 Timeout waiting for Transfer Acknowledge line from the drive to become active

Table 11-23. Continued

3	byte	Unused
4	byte	Command error code (see Get Command Complete Status, command 607h for error codes)
5	byte	Command status byte (see Get Command Complete Status, command 607h for status codes)
6	word	ESDI standard status
8	word	ESDI drive vendor defined status #1
A	word	ESDI drive vendor defined status #2
C	word	ESDI drive vendor defined status #3
E	word	ESDI drive vendor defined status #4
10	word	ESDI drive vendor defined status #5

★★★

Command	Description	Port
0609h	Get configuration of drive 0	3510h

Command the controller to return the Configuration Status Block for drive 0. Only two words are used for this command, where the second word is set to zero.

Upon command completion, the Configuration Status Block is read as a group of six words from port 3510h. It is shown in Table 11-24.

Table 11-24. Configuration Status Block

Offset	Size	Description
0	byte	09h (returns command value)
1	byte	Number of words in this status block (6)
2	byte	Flags

bits 7-5 = 0 Unused

4 = 1 Invalid secondary defect map—The first sector of the secondary defect map was unreadable. Information such as the push table and the number of defects is not known.

3 = 1 Zero defects have been flagged

2 = 1 Skewed sectoring—The drive was formatted with sector skewing for drives that require long head switch times. For example, a skew of 2 would place the sectors as:

head	sector numbers									
0	1	2	3	4	5	6	7	8	9	10
1	9	10	1	2	3	4	5	6	7	8
2	7	8	9	10	1	2	3	4	5	6

Skewing is independent of interleave

Table 11-24. Continued

Offset	Size	Description		
			1 = 1	Drive has removable media
			0 = 0	Normal retries performed on read errors and position errors
			1	Disable all retries
3	byte	Number of spare sectors per cylinder		
4	dword	Total number of Relative Sector Addresses (usable sectors)		
8	word	Total number of cylinders		
A	byte	Number of tracks per cylinder		
B	byte	Number of sectors per track		

Command	Description	Port
0615h	Get manufacturing header for drive 0	3510h

Reads the manufacturing header and defect map 1 for drive 0. The manufacturing header is located at the beginning of defect map 1. Reading a single sector will obtain this header. The header data has the size of the defect map. Immediately following the header is the defect map 1. This command functions similar to a Read command, and the data is processed through DMA. Only two words are required for this command, where the second word indicates the number of sectors to read.

Command	Description	Port
0616h	Low level format drive 0	3510h

Performs a low-level format of the entire drive 0. Provides the option to include defect map information to skip defective sectors. See Format Prepare (command 0617h) for additional details.

The Command Block for the Low-level format command only requires two words. The second word of the command block specifies several options and the number of 4-byte defect entries. The second word has the following functions:

bit	15 = 0	Unused
	14 = 0	Unused
	13 = 0	Unused
	12 = 1	Send interrupt after every cylinder complete
	11 = 1	Perform surface analysis
	10 = 1	Save the results from the surface analysis
	9 = 1	Ignore secondary defect map during format
	8 = 1	Ignore primary defect map during format

7 = x	Number of 4-byte defect entries
6 = x	(see Table 11-8 under Interrupt 13h, function
5 = x	AH=1Ah in this chapter for the structure)
4 = x	
3 = x	
2 = x	
1 = x	
0 = x	

If the defect entries field is non-zero, then the format expects the defect map will be read through the DMA in exactly the same manner as a write command. Refer to Interrupt 13h, AH=1Ah (Low-Level Format ESDI Drive) for more in-depth explanation of the low-level format, and bit descriptions in the CL register, which are identical to those in the second command word.

Command	Description	Port
0617h	Format prepare drive 0	3510h

This command must be issued immediately prior to the Format Drive 0 command. Format prepare provides a safety interlock, so that a low-level format will not occur by accident. If Format prepare is not issued before the Format command, the format will not occur, and returns with a sequence error. The Command Control Block for Format prepare only uses two words, where the second word must be the value 55AAh.

In addition, the Format prepare passes the controller one or two sectors of data containing addresses of those sectors to be marked as defective by the format. This data is handled through DMA similar to a data write. The data uses a repeating structure of two-word Absolute Sector Addresses (ASA). After the last defect address, all remaining bytes contain FFs except for the last byte in each sector. The very last byte of each sector is a checksum of all prior bytes of the sector. When all 512 bytes of a sector are added up, and overflows are ignored, the result should be zero. Unused entries are padded with the dword FFFFFFFFh. Table 11-25 shows the contents of an example defect table using only one sector, although two are allowed.

Table 11-25. Defect Table Example of Absolute Sector Addresses

Offset	Size	Description
0	dword	First ASA
4	dword	Second ASA
1E4	dword	Last ASA
1E8	dword	Unused (set to 0FFFFFFFFh)
....all remaining unused dword entries are set to 0FFFFFFFFh		
1FC	word	0FFFFh
1FE	byte	0FFh
1FF	byte	Checksum of prior 511 bytes

Command	Description	Port
0626h	Park heads on drive 1	3510h

Drive 1 is sent a command to stop the motor and move the heads to its safe landing zone. See command 606h for details.

Command	Description	Port
0627h	Get command complete status on drive 1	3510h

Commands the controller to return the Command Complete Status Block for drive 1. See command 607h for details.

Command	Description	Port
0628h	Get device status of drive 1	3510h

Commands the controller to return the Status Block for drive 1. See command 608h for details.

Command	Description	Port
0629h	Get configuration of drive 1	3510h

Commands the controller to return the Configuration Status Block for drive 1. See command 609h for details.

Command	Description	Port
0635h	Get manufacturing header for drive 1	3510h

Reads the manufacturing header and defect map 1 for drive 1. See command 615h for details.

Command	Description	Port
0636h	Low level format drive 1	3510h

Performs a low-level format of the entire drive 1. See Format Prepare command 0637h and similar command 616h for additional details.

Command	Description	Port
0637h	Format prepare drive 1	3510h

This command must be issued immediately prior to the Format Drive 1 command. See similar command 617h for details.

Command	Description	Port
06E7h	Get controller command complete status	3510h

Commands the controller to return the configuration status block for the controller. Only two words are used for this command, where the second word is set to zero.

Upon command completion, the configuration status block is as a group of six words read from port 3510h. It is shown in Table 11-23 under Get configuration of drive 0 (0609h).

Command	Description	Port
06E9h	Get configuration of controller	3510h

Commands the controller to return the configuration status block for the controller. Only two words are used for this command, where the second word is set to zero.

Upon command completion, the configuration status block is read as a group of six words from port 3510h. It is shown in Table 11-26.

Table 11-26. Configuration Status Block—Controller

Offset	Size	Description
0	byte	E9h (returns command value)
1	byte	Number of words in this status block (6)
2	word	0 (unused)
4	dword	Controller microcode revision level
8	word	0 (unused)
A	word	0 (unused)

Command	Description	Port
06EAh	Get Programmable Option Select Information	3510h

Gets the contents of the Programmable Option Select (POS) registers. Only two words are used for this command. The second word is set to zero.

Upon command completion, the POS Information Status Block is read as a group of five words from port 3510h. It is shown in Table 11-27. If any POS register value is unused or unknown to the controller, the value is set to FFh.

Table 11-27. POS Information Status Block

Offset	Size	Description
0	byte	EAh (returns command value)
1	byte	Number of words in this status block (5)
2	word	0FFDDh (fixed value)
4	byte	POS Register 3
5	byte	POS Register 2
6	byte	POS Register 5 (unused and set to FFh)
7	byte	POS Register 4 (unused and set to FFh)
8	byte	POS Register 7 (unused and set to FFh)
9	byte	POS Register 6 (unused and set to FFh)

Command	Description	Port
06EBh	Translate Relative Sector Address	3510h

The ESDI drive maintains two types of addressing, Relative Sector Addresses (RSA) and Absolute Sector Address (ASA). The RSA is used to read, write, verify, and other normal actions. The Relative Sector Address hides defects and makes the entire disk appear as one long linear array. Should it be necessary to deallocate a defective block, the Absolute Sector Address is necessary. This function converts an RSA into ASA.

The second word of the Command Block is unused and should be set to zero. The third and fourth words contain the RSA to translate. When the translate command is complete, the resultant ASA can be obtained from the Command Complete Status Block. Use function 06E9h to get this status information. Word 4 has the least significant word, and word 5 has the most significant word.

Command	Description	Port
4601h	Read data from drive 0	3510h

Reads the specified number of sectors from drive 0. DMA is used for the data transfer.

Command	Description	Port
4602h	Write data to drive 0	3510h

Writes the specified number of sectors from drive 0. DMA is used for the data transfer.

Command	Description	Port
4603h	Verify data on drive 0	3510h

Verifies that the specified data can be read from drive 0 and the ECC codes are valid for each sector read. No retries are performed if an ECC error is detected. The disk data is not compared with the original data. DMA is not used for this command.

Command	Description	Port
4604h	Write with verify on drive 0	3510h

Writes the specified number of sectors from drive 0. A verify operation is automatically performed after all the sectors have been written. The verify operation reads the data from the disk and verifies the ECC is valid for each sector. The data is not compared with the original written data. If a verify error occurs, the write should be retried one or more times. DMA is used for the data transfer.

Command	Description	Port
4605h	Seek on drive 0	3510h

Positions the heads on drive 0 to the position indicated by the Relative Sector Address (RSA). A seek to an RSA of 0 is the same as a recalibrate.

Command	Description	Port
4621h	Read data from drive 1	3510h

Reads the specified number of sectors from drive 1. DMA is used for the data transfer.

Command	Description	Port
4622h	Write data to drive 1	3510h

Writes the specified number of sectors from drive 1. DMA is used for the data transfer.

Command	Description	Port
4623h	Verify data on drive 1	3510h

Verifies that the specified data can be read from drive 1 and the ECC codes are valid for each sector read. No retries are performed if an ECC error is detected. The disk data is not compared with the original data. DMA is not used for this command.

Command	Description	Port
4624h	Write with verify on drive 1	3510h

Writes the specified number of sectors from drive 1. A verify operation is automatically performed after all the sectors have been written. See similar command 4604h for details.

Command	Description	Port
4625h	Seek on drive 1	3510h

Positions the heads on drive 1 to the position indicated by the Relative Sector Address (RSA). A seek to an RSA of 0 is the same as a recalibrate.

Port	Type	Description	Platform
3512h	Input	ESDI Hard Disk Basic Status	PS/2

This port is used for handshaking and status of the controller. Before reading this port, interrupts must be disabled.

Input (bits 0-7)

bit 7	r = 0	DMA disabled (DMA control is set from port 3512h, output, bit 1)
	1	DMA enabled
6	r = 0	No interrupts pending
	1	Interrupt pending, do not send a command to the controller until the pending interrupt is cleared
5	r = 1	Command in progress—The controller is currently executing a command. This will be ON when the first command byte is sent, and cleared when the End-Of-Interrupt request code is sent to the Attention port 3513h
4	r = 0	Not busy—It is acceptable to send commands to the Attention port
	1	Attention port in use, and cannot be sent a command. This bit is set after a Command Request code is sent to the Attention port. It is cleared when a sector transfer is complete, or completion of the reset or abort command requests.
3	r = 0	No status available
	1	Status available from port 3510h—This flag is automatically cleared when port 3510h is read.
2	r = 0	Ready for Command at port 3510h
	1	Command interface port is busy, and cannot accept a command. It is automatically cleared when the controller has read the command and is ready to accept the next command.
1	r = 1	Transfer request—The controller is ready for a data transfer operation to occur.
0	r = 1	Interrupt request is active. This bit is cleared when the interrupt status port 3513h is read.

Port	Type	Description	Platform
3512h	Output	ESDI Hard Disk Basic Control	PS/2

This port is used to control interrupts and DMA, and to issue a reset to the controller.

Output (bits 0-7)

bit 7 w = 0		Normal operation
	1	Hardware reset of adapter, without clearing Programmable Option Select (POS) information. This bit is automatically set back to 0 by the action of the reset.
6 w = 0		unused
5 w = 0		unused
4 w = 0		unused
3 w = 0		unused
2 w = 0		unused
1 w = 0		Disable DMA request capability
	1	Enable DMA request capability—When enabled, a DMA request can be made by the controller. Depending on the adapter's configuration from POS, this bit can be automatically cleared at the completion of the disk controller's data transfer.
0 w = 1		Enable interrupt request support

Port	Type	Description	Platform
3513h	Input	ESDI Hard Disk Interrupt Status	PS/2

Gets the interrupt status and clears the current interrupt request. After a command has been executed, this port must be read to complete the current command cycle. The register holds basic error information if there was a problem with the command. After reading this port, get the status block by reading the Status Interface register port 3510h. Depending on the fault condition, the status block will pinpoint the area of the disk that contained the problem.

Input (bits 0-7)

bit 7 r = x, 6 r = x, 5 r = x: Device for which the command was completed

bit 7	bit 6	bit 5
0	0	0 = drive 0
0	0	1 = drive 1
1	1	1 = controller command

4 r = 0 Unused

3 r = x, 2 r = x, 1 r = x, 0 r = x: Cause of interrupt request

1 = successful completion
3 = successful completion with ECC
5 = successful completion with retries
6 = format partially completed, read status

7 = successful completion with ECC and retries
8 = command completed with warning
9 = abort command complete
A = reset complete
B = data transfer ready, no status block
C = command completed with failure
D = DMA error—Read Status Interface register. To correct condition, the entire command should be retried
E = command block error
F = attention error

Port	Type	Description	Platform
3513h	Output	ESDI Hard Disk Attention	PS/2

This port is used to initiate a command, complete the command process, and reset the adapter. The loaded function remains active until changed with a new request.

Before changing the Attention register, interrupts must be disabled, and the status read from the Basic Status register, port 3512h. The status must show the controller not busy (bit 4=0) and no interrupts pending (bit 6=0). When these conditions are meet, the attention register request can be made.

Command Request

A command request is used to ask the controller to accept a command block from the data port 3510h. Once the command block is loaded, another command request can be made for a non-busy device. This means the controller can be executing up to three commands at the same time, one for each drive 0 and 1, and one for the adapter.

When the request is complete, three actions occur. First, the adapter generates an interrupt request on IRQ 14 (if enabled) to inform the system that an operation is complete. Second, the Interrupt Status register at port 3513h will be updated to indicate the completed request status. Third, the hard disk status word at port 3510h will have the first word of the Command Complete status block, if available.

End-of-Interrupt Request

After a command has been executed and an interrupt generated indicating command completion, various registers hold information such as interrupt status and sense data from the controller. This data is kept until the End-of-Interrupt Request is issued. The controller will not allow another interrupt to occur until this request is issued to port 351h. If End-of-Interrupt Request is issued before all of the sense data words have been read, the controller assumes the remaining sense data words will not be requested by the system and are discarded.

Abort Command Request

When the controller fails to issue the command complete interrupt after a suitable timeout period, the Abort command should be issued to terminate the current command. After the Abort command has been accepted, the sense data read from port 3510h may help indicate what caused the problem. When the Abort command request is accepted and completed, an interrupt is generated.

Reset Request

Reset stops any current commands and resets the adapter similar to a power-on-reset. The reset runs the internal controller self-test and recalibrates all attached drives. Upon reset completion, interrupt IRQ 14 is issued. The result of the controller's self-test and reset is placed in the Interrupt status register at port 3513h.

Output (bits 0-7)

Bit				
bit 7 w = x	Device selection			
6 w = x	bit 7	bit 6	bit 5	
5 w = x	0	0	0 = drive 0	
	0	0	1 = drive 1	
	1	1	1 = adapter command	
4 w = 0	Unused			
3 w = 0	Unused			
2 w = x	Request code (see text)			
1 w = x	bit 2	bit 1	bit 0	
0 w = x	0	0	1 = Command request	
	0	1	0 = End-of-Interrupt	
	0	1	1 = Abort command	
	1	0	0 = Reset adapter	

Port	Type	Description	Platform
3518h	Input	ESDI Hard Disk Status (16-bit)	PS/2

Alternate address for a second hard disk adapter. See port 3510h, input.

Port	Type	Description	Platform
3518h	Output	ESDI Hard Disk Commands (16-bit)	PS/2

Alternate address for a second hard disk adapter. See port 3510h, output.

Port	Type	Description	Platform
351Ah	Input	ESDI Hard Disk Basic Status	PS/2

Alternate address for a second hard disk adapter. See port 3512h, input.

Port	Type	Description	Platform
351Ah	Output	ESDI Hard Disk Basic Control	PS/2

Alternate address for a second hard disk adapter. See port 3512h, output.

Port	Type	Description	Platform
351Bh	Input	ESDI Hard Disk Interrupt Status	PS/2

Alternate address for a second hard disk adapter. See port 3513h, input.

Port	Type	Description	Platform
351Bh	Output	ESDI Hard Disk Attention	PS/2

Alternate address for a second hard disk adapter. See port 3513h, output.

CHAPTER 12

Serial Ports

This chapter looks at the ordinary serial port, which on the surface has been documented fairly well. However, I've uncovered some interesting undocumented aspects of the serial port. This includes some high-performance FIFO modes, now supported in many newer modems and serial ports. I've also documented several common bugs that need special handling for older serial ports.

To help clarify the serial port, complete source code is provided for two utilities. The first describes all serial ports in the system and checks whether any have extended features. The second utility is used to find the maximum serial data transfer rate between two PCs, up to 115,200 baud!

I'll also show a slick debugging tool I wrote, SSPY, which displays the modem status lines for any serial port on screen. This TSR comes with complete source code, so it's easy to modify for special situations.

Introduction

All PCs are capable of operating up to four serial ports using standard serial I/O adapters. Serial ports are normally designed to the RS-232C specifications for electrical requirements and signal definitions. Other serial port specifications exist, such as RS-422, Bi-Sync, Synchronous Data Link Control (SDLC), IEEE-488 (GPIB), current loop, and others. For the most part, all of these alternative approaches have disappeared and are rarely used today. The BIOS only supports RS-232C serial ports, so additional drivers are required to support other standards. For some of these rarely used standards, the port summary includes registers reserved for these cards, but detailed functional information is not included.

The serial ports are used for modems, pointing devices like mice and trackballs, printers, networks, laptop data transfers, and many other applications. The maximum speed of the serial port depends on the baud rate generator in the serial port adapter, the BIOS software, and how fast the system can execute the serial BIOS code. In addition, if the system is processing other equal or higher priority code on a regular basis, the maximum reliable speed may be significantly reduced. Later we'll show a utility to determine the maximum reliable baud rate of the serial port.

Figure 12-1 shows the design of the serial port. The serial port operation is primarily handled by a UART (Universal Asynchronous Receiver/Transmitter) chip. The UART handles the conversion of serial data into bytes and bytes into serial data. The UART also provides control over a number of signal lines used to communicate with modems and other devices. The UART supports both the reception and transmission of data at the same time.

Original designs used a National Semiconductor 8250 chip. Later designs switched to a CMOS version, the 16450, which is functionally identical to the 8250. Some newer designs use a 16550 or other variant. These newer designs offer the same features as the 16450, but add additional buffering to reduce CPU overhead. I'll refer to all these chips and compatibles as a UART, except when explaining specific differences between different chips.

Figure 12-1. Serial Port

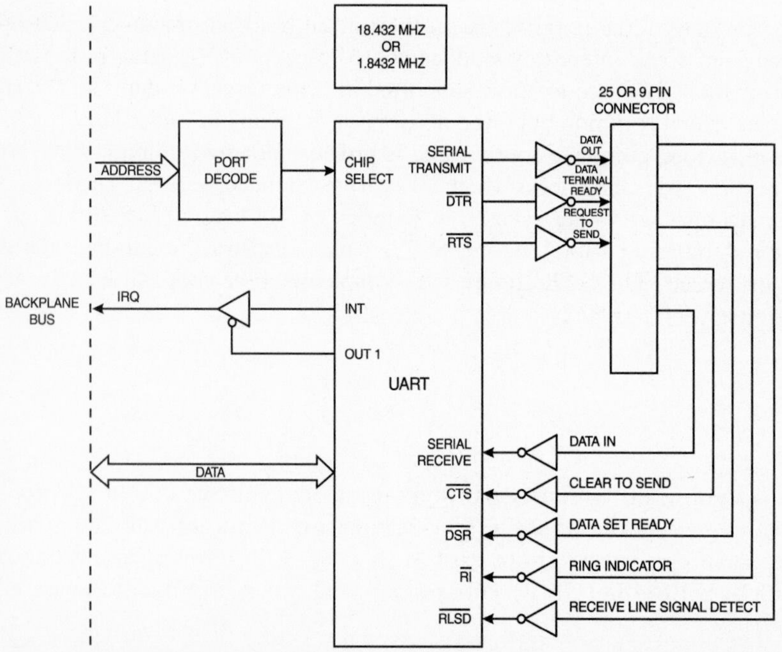

A portion of the system BIOS (interrupt 14h) provides services to communicate with the serial adapters.

Similar to parallel ports, POST checks if a serial port is attached, and records the I/O addresses of active ports in the BIOS data area. All systems support up to four serial ports. Additional ports are not supported by the BIOS.

Serial port numbering and access are a bit confusing. There are four possible serial ports, specified as port 1, 2, 3, or 4. To access the serial port hardware, four words in the BIOS data area hold the base I/O port address for the four possible serial ports. For example, to access serial port 2, you must first get the base I/O port value from the BIOS data area. This means a serial port has no fixed I/O port address.

Now to help confuse programmers further, all the BIOS routines use zero-based numbering to specify the port. To access port 1, a register is set up with 0.

BIOS Initialization

After a reset, the POST checks if any serial ports are installed. The POST examines I/O port group 3F8-3FFh first, and the I/O port group 2F8-2FFh second. To detect an active port, the Interrupt Identification Register is read from port 3FA or 2FAh. If bits 3 to 7 from this register are all zero, the POST considers the serial port active. Once it is determined the serial I/O group is active, the base I/O port address is stored in the lowest unused serial port BIOS RAM location. There are four words assigned in RAM starting at 40:0 to hold active serial port I/O addresses. Many vendors' POST will never check for serial ports 3 and 4, since IBM did not define a standard I/O port address for these ports.

In general, most systems only check for two ports, although newer systems often check four possible port addresses. MCA systems check eight different possible serial port addresses in an attempt to find up to four active serial ports. Table 12-1 shows the order in which BIOSes look for active ports. Only the base I/O port is shown in this table for each group. On the MCA system, once four ports are found, no other ports are checked.

Table 12-1. Order of Serial I/O Ports Checked By POST

Order Checked	Many Systems	Newer AT and EISA Systems	MCA Systems
1st	3F8h	3F8h	3F8h
2nd	2F8h	2F8h	2F8h
3rd	none	3E8h	3220h
4th	none	2E8h	3228h
5th	none	none	4220h
6th	none	none	4228h
7th	none	none	5220h
8th	none	none	5228h

At the completion of serial POST checks, the serial port addresses are saved. This typically results in one of the four cases shown in Table 12-2. Case 1 shows POST detecting two serial ports. Cases 2 and 3 show only one serial port being detected. Case 4 shows no serial ports detected.

Table 12-2. Possible POST Results of Serial Port Detection

RAM Address	Serial Port	Case 1 I/O Address	Case 2 I/O Address	Case 3 I/O Address	Case 4 I/O Address
40:0h	1	3F8h	3F8h	2F8h	0
40:2h	2	2F8h	0	0	0
40:4h	3	0	0	0	0
40:6h	4	0	0	0	0

These tests do not confirm whether a serial device is actually attached to the I/O port. The test only checks if the serial port hardware exists at the specified I/O address. The total number of active serial ports detected (0 to 4) is stored in the equipment byte at BIOS RAM location 40:10h, bits 9 through 11.

Serial BIOS

The serial BIOS provides simple abilities to transmit, receive, and control active serial ports. The BIOS supports up to four serial ports, which have their I/O port addresses previously stored in the BIOS data area. While sending or receiving data, the serial timeout values in the BIOS data area are used to prevent endless waits, should a device attached to the serial port fail to respond. A serial port might fail to respond if it is disconnected or a hardware failure occurred.

The BIOS functions do not use the interrupt feature of the serial port, but use timing loops in software. This requires constant polling of UART status through the BIOS routines. When the transmitter buffer is clear, another byte can be sent. Similarly, when the UART receive buffer is full, a byte can be read.

Most terminal emulation programs access UARTs directly and skip the serial BIOS routines entirely. This allows the software to maximize performance. In addition, baud rates higher than 9600 and interrupt control can be implemented when bypassing the BIOS.

All functions of the serial BIOS return the serial line status in AH. The line status is described in Table 12-3.

Table 12-3. BIOS Line Status in AH

bit	7 = 1	No response timeout error (bits 0 to 6 are indeterminate)
	6 = 1	The transmit holding register and the transmit shift register are both empty.
	5 = 1	Transmit buffer register is empty and ready to accept another byte for transmission.
	4 = 1	Break received. A break is signaled when an incoming signal remains low for longer than a full serial frame. This means the start bits, data bits, and parity bits are all low, and no stop bit (high) is received.
	3 = 1	Framing error occurred. While receiving data, the stop bit was detected as low, when the stop bit should always be a high signal. The UART will attempt to resynchronize on the next frame received. A framing error usually indicates a noisy or poor signal, or may indicate a mismatch in baud rates.
	2 = 1	Parity error occurred. The received data's parity bit does not match the parity specified.
	1 = 1	Overrun error occurred. A second byte was received before the byte previously received was read from the buffer. The new byte overwrites the prior byte, and the prior byte is lost. This usually indicates the system is too slow for the current baud rate, other interrupts in the system are slowing serial port response, or the port handler has software bugs.
	0 = 1	Data ready indicator. A received byte is now available to be read.

Except for the Send Byte and Receive Byte functions, all other functions return the modem status in AL as shown in Table 12-4. Bits 0 to 3 all indicate a state change since the last time the Modem Status Register was read. When this UART register is read by the BIOS, the bits are all cleared.

Table 12-4. BIOS Modem Status in AL

bit	7 = x	The state of the connector's Data Carrier Detect line
	6 = x	The state of the connector's Ring Indicator line
	5 = x	The state of the connector's Data Set Ready line
	4 = x	The state of the connector's Clear To Send line
	3 = 1	A change occurred on the Data Carrier Detect line
	2 = 1	Falling edge of a high to low signal on the ring detect line occurred
	1 = 1	A change occurred on the Data Set Ready line
	0 = 1	A change occurred on the Clear To Send line

Interrupt 14h provides the following services:

Function	Description	Platform
ah=0	Initialize Serial Port	All
ah=1	Send Byte	All
ah=2	Receive Byte	All

Function	**Description**	**Platform**
ah=3	Read Status	All
ah=4	Extended Initialize	MCA
ax=500h	Extended Control Read	MCA
ax=501h	Extended Control Write	MCA

Int	Func	Description	Platform
14h	0	Initialize Serial Port	All

Initializes the specified serial port with the speed, parity type, stop bits, and word length of the serial frame.

Called with: ah = 0

al = serial port register initialization value

bit 7 = x, 6 = x, 5 = x — Baud rate selection

bit 7	6	5	
0	0	0	= 110 baud
0	0	1	= 150 baud
0	1	0	= 300 baud
0	1	1	= 600 baud
1	0	0	= 1200 baud
1	0	1	= 2400 baud
1	1	0	= 4800 baud
1	1	1	= 9600 baud

4 = x, 3 = x — Parity selection

bit 4	3	
0	0	= no parity
0	1	= odd parity
1	0	= no parity
1	1	= even parity

2 = 0 Use one stop bit

1 Use two stop bits (or 1.5 bits if 5 bit data length is selected)

1 = x, 0 = x — data length

bit 1	0	
0	0	= 5 bits
0	1	= 6 bits
1	0	= 7 bits
1	1	= 8 bits

	dx	= serial port 0 to 3 (zero based, i.e., use 0 for port 1, etc.)
Returns:	ah	= line status (see Table 12-2)
	al	= modem status (see Table 12-3)

Int	Func	Description	Platform
14h	1	Send Byte	All

Sends a byte to the specified serial port. The modem control lines Data Terminal Ready and Request To Send from the attached serial device are checked to ensure both are high. The BIOS will wait up to 2 ms for these lines to become high before returning a timeout error. In addition, the UART's transmit buffer must become empty before a byte can be sent. The BIOS will wait up to 2 ms more for the transmit buffer to become clear before returning a timeout error.

The 2 ms delays are usually performed in crude software timing loops that vary considerably in different BIOSes. Be aware some serial devices incorrectly leave the DTR and RTS lines disconnected, making the BIOS transmit function unreliable. Should the lines "float" low, transmission is not possible. There is no easy fix for this, other than writing a custom routine with an option to ignore DTR and RTS. Better yet, complain to the vendor to fix the hardware problem!

Called with:	ah	= 1
	al	= byte to send
	dx	= serial port 0 to 3 (zero-based; i.e., use 0 for port 1, etc.)
Returns:	ah	= line status (see Table 12-2)
	al	= unchanged (byte that was sent)

Int	Func	Description	Platform
14h	2	Receive Byte	All

INT

Receives a byte from the specified serial port. Both the Data Terminal Ready status and Data Set Ready are checked. When both are high, a data byte is read from the UART. The BIOS will wait up to 2 ms for each signal to become high. If both status bits fail to become high within the timeout period, a timeout error is returned.

Called with:	ah	= 2
	dx	= serial port 0 to 3 (zero-based; i.e., use 0 for port 1, etc.)
Returns:	ah	= line status (see Table 12-2)
	al	= byte received

Int	Func	Description	Platform
14h	3	Read Status	All

Gets the current line and modem status of the specified serial port.

Called with: ah = 3
dx = serial port 0 to 3 (zero-based; i.e., use 0 for port 1, etc.)

Returns: ah = line status (see Table 12-2)
al = modem status (see Table 12-3)

Int	Func	Description	Platform
14h	4	Extended Initialize	MCA

This function adds more initialization options for the UART, unavailable in function 0. Most systems do not support extended serial initialization, although every MCA system will.

Called with:	ah = 4		
	al =	0	Break control off (normal)
		1	A break condition is transmitted by forcing the serial out line to "0." This will cause the break flag on the receiving UART's line status register to be set.
	bl =	0	one stop bit
		1	two stop bits (1.5 stop bits when 5 bit data length is selected)
	bh =	0	no parity bit
		1	odd parity (sum of data & parity bits must be an odd number)
		2	even parity (sum of data & parity bits must be an even number)
		3	sticky odd parity (the parity bit is sent as 0 and checked on incoming data as 0)
		4	sticky even parity (the parity bit is sent as 1 and checked on incoming data as 1)
	cl =	0	baud rate 110
		1	baud rate 150
		2	baud rate 300
		3	baud rate 600
		4	baud rate 1200
		5	baud rate 2400
		6	baud rate 4800
		7	baud rate 9600
		8	baud rate 19200
		9	baud rate 115200 (undocumented on PS/2 model 70 and possibly others)

	ch = 0	data length 5 bits
	1	data length 6 bits
	2	data length 7 bits
	3	data length 8 bits
	dx = serial port 0 to 3 (zero-based; i.e., use 0 for port 1, etc.)	
Returns:	ah = line status (see Table 12-2)	
	al = modem status (see Table 12-3)	

Int	Func	Description	Platform
14h	500h	Extended Control Read	MCA

INT III I

This function reads the extended modem control byte for a specified serial port. It is supported on all MCA systems and some AT+ systems.

Called with: ax = 500h
dx = serial port 0 to 3 (zero-based; i.e., use 0 for port 1, etc.)

Returns: ah = line status (see Table 12-2)
al = modem status (see Table 12-3)
bl = modem control register

bit		
	7 = x	Unused
	6 = x	Unused
	5 = x	Unused
	4 = 1	Loopback mode active (explained in later section)
	3 = 1	OUT2 (IRQ enabled)
	2 = x	OUT1 (unused and unconnected)
	1 = 1	Request To Send (RTS)
	0 = 1	Data Terminal Ready (DTR)

Int	Func	Description	Platform
14h	501h	Extended Control Write	MCA

INT III I

This function writes the extended modem control byte for a specified serial port. It is supported on all MCA systems and some AT+ systems.

Called with: ax = 501h
bl = modem control register

bit		
	7 = x	Unused
	6 = x	Unused
	5 = x	Unused
	4 = 1	Activate Loopback mode

3 = 1 OUT2 (enable IRQ)
2 = x OUT1 (unused and unconnected)
1 = 1 Request To Send (RTS)
0 = 1 Data Terminal Ready (DTR)

dx = serial port 0 to 3 (zero-based; i.e., use 0 for port 1, etc.)

Returns: ah = line status (see Table 12-2)
al = modem status (see Table 12-3)

The Serial Frame

The serial frame consists of a combination of the start, data, parity, and stop bits. One frame at a time is sent or received on the serial link. For transmission, the UART adds the start bit, optional parity bit, and stop bit to the data to be sent. On data reception, the UART checks the frame for various error conditions, and extracts the data from the frame.

The frame size depends on the various control options selected within the UART by software. The data portion can be from 5 to 8 bits long, a parity bit can be optionally included, and from 1 to 2 stop bits can be selected. This means the total frame can range from 7 bits up to 12 bits long. Figure 12-2 shows a typical serial frame. The values shown are those measured at the UART chip, which are inverted from the serial port connector. The idle state is 1 at the UART when no frames are being sent.

Figure 12-2. Typical Serial Frame

=0	bit 0	bit 1	bit 2	bit 3	bit 4	bit 5	bit 6	bit 7	odd	=1
Start	Data Byte								Parity	Stop

Control/Modem Signals

Six control lines and two data lines are used between the serial port and the attached device. It is not necessary to use all of these lines, but they provide a clear means of communicating with a modem or other attached device. When a control line is not used, the input is normally hardwired low at the connector. Tables 12-5 and 12-6 describe each line.

Table 12-5. Signals from a Device to the Computer

Signal	Abbreviation	Description
Clear To Send	CTS	The attached device is ready for the computer to send its data.
Data Carrier Detect	DCD	The attached device (modem) has established a link with another modem.
Data Set Ready	DSR	The attached device is powered on and ready for communications.
Ring Indicator	RI	The phone line connected to the attached device (modem) is ringing. This is typically used by communications software to automatically answer an incoming call.

Table 12-6. Signals from Computer to a Device

Signal	Abbreviation	Description
Data Terminal Ready	DTR	The computer signals the attached device that it is powered on and ready for communications.
Request To Send	RTS	The computer signals that it is ready to receive data.

For the RS-232C modem and control lines, a low signal, or "0" state on the connector is indicated with a level between -3 and -15 volts. A high signal or "1" state on the connector is indicated with a level between +3 and +15 volts.

To keep everyone a bit off balance, the data transmit and receive lines are inverted at the connector. This means when you transmit a byte with each bit set to logic "1", the voltage at the connector will be between -3 and -15 volts, just the opposite of modem and control lines! Almost everyone references transmit and receive logic levels at the UART instead of the connector, which is not inverted. Most serial ports on a system generate -12v and +12v for logic levels.

Sequence of Events—Serial Transmit

To transmit a byte over the serial link, the port is assumed to be initialized with the proper baud rate and serial frame options. I'll also assume that the byte will be transmitted on serial port 1.

1. First determine the serial I/O port base address, by reading a word from the BIOS data area at 40:0h for serial port 1. If the value is zero, there is no active serial port attached, and no data can be sent.

2. The two modem control lines Data Terminal Ready and Request To Send are set high. Data Terminal Ready informs the attached device that the computer is active and ready for communications. Request To Send tells the attached device that the computer wants to send data. These two lines are activated by writing the value 3 to the Modem Control port.
3. Next check the two status lines Clear To Send and Data Set Ready. These reside in the modem status register, bits 4 and 5. Data Set Ready indicates the attached device is powered up and ready. Clear to Send indicates the attached device is ready for data. These status lines should be checked for up to 2 ms or until they both become high. When both are high, the device attached to the serial port has signaled it is ready for a byte. A timeout error is signaled by software if either line remains low for more than about 2 ms.
4. Now that the attached device is ready to receive a byte, the UART must be checked to see if the transmit holding register is ready for a byte. The Line Status Register, bit 5, is set high when this holding register is empty and ready for a byte. Again, like step 3, if the transmit holding register fails to become available within 2 ms, the software should declare a timeout, and abort the transmission.
5. If no timeouts have occurred so far, the byte can be sent to the UART's transmit holding register.
6. The UART then transfers the byte from the transmit holding register into the transmit shift register, and sends the serial frame with the data byte over the serial link.

Sequence of Events—Serial Receive

To receive a byte from the serial link, the port is assumed to be initialized with the proper baud rate and serial frame options. I'll also assume that the byte comes from serial port 3.

1. First the serial I/O port base address is determined by reading a word from the BIOS data area at 40:4h for serial port 3. If the value is zero, there is no active serial port attached, and no data can be received.
2. The modem control line Data Terminal Ready is set high. This informs the attached device that the computer is active and ready for communications. This is done by writing the value 1 to the Modem Control port.
3. Next check Data Set Ready. This appears in the modem status register, bit 5. Data Set Ready indicates the attached device is powered up and ready. Data Set Ready should be checked until it becomes high, or up to 2 ms before a timeout is signaled.

4. The receive buffer is next checked to see if data has been received. The Line Status Register, bit 0, holds a data ready flag. It is set to one when the receive buffer has data. If the data ready flag fails to get set after 2 ms, then a timeout is signaled, and the operation aborted.
5. If no timeouts have occurred so far, the byte can be read from the UART's receive buffer.

Loopback Operations

The UART provides a special loopback mode to test the UART's internal transmit, receive and control circuitry. Loopback mode is activated from the BIOS function 5 (Extended Control) or activated directly by setting the modem control register (bit 4) high.

During loopback mode, a number of connections are forced to a specific state and/or disconnected from signals outside the UART chip. This allows a diagnostic test of the UART without affecting a device attached to the serial port connector. In loopback, the UART sets every output high, including Transmit out, -DTR, -RTS, -OUT1, and -OUT2. These are inverted by logic on the serial adapter card and the UART high outputs appear as a low signal on the respective connector pins. Transmit low represents the idle state for the serial link. When -OUT1 is set high, the interrupt request is also disconnected from the system.

The input lines CTS, DSR, DCD, and RI are disconnected from the connector during loopback. As part of the test, the UART connects these lines internally to the four modem control signals DTR, RTS, OUT1 and OUT2. In this manner a portion of the internal UART's control and status lines can be checked for stuck or crossed bits. This means that writes to the lower 4 bits of the Modem Control register (DTR, RTS, OUT1, OUT2) can be read from the upper four bits of the Modem Status register.

The receive input line is also disconnected from the connector during loopback mode. It is connected inside the UART directly to the internal transmit output. Serial bytes transmitted are immediately received. During loopback tests, receive and transmit interrupts are fully operational within the UART. The interrupt enable register still controls interrupt operation. As we noted earlier, the serial port hardware disconnects the interrupt request line from the system during loopback, so testing cannot cause actual system interrupt.

Baud Rates

The baud rate is the number of bits per second transferred over the serial link. To convert this to a number of bytes transferred per second, the baud rate is divided by the number of bits in the serial frame. One of the most common frames used include 8 bits of data, no parity bit, and one stop bit. Including the start bit, this adds up to 10 bits. This means 9600 baud can send 960 bytes per second. To put this in more meaningful terms, it will take over two seconds to fill a standard 2,000 character text screen at 9600 baud.

The UART has a built-in baud rate generator. The baud rate is set to match an attached device. Baud rates divisors are based on the crystal frequency. This crystal is chosen to ensure that a programmed divisor value will result in the same baud rate on any system. To determine a baud rate divisor for any baud rate, divide 115,200 by the desired baud rate.

For system-to-system transfers, the baud rates can be set to very high rates, usually limited only by the CPU speed of the slower of the two systems. For the maximum rate, 115,200 baud, the CPU must be able to read and store a byte every 87 microseconds.

Table 12-7 shows common baud rates, the divisor values for the UART, and the speed in bytes per second with a standard 10-bit serial frame.

Table 12-7. Baud Rates

Baud Rate	Divisor	Bytes Per Second	Typical Uses
50	2304 (900h)	5	antique teletypes
75	1536 (600h)	7.5	antique teletypes
110	1047 (417h)	11	very old teletypes
300	384 (180h)	30	old teletypes and obsolete terminals
1200	96 (60h)	120	old terminals, obsolete modems
2400	48 (30h)	240	obsolete terminals, modems, printers
4800	24 (18h)	480	obsolete terminals, modems, printers
9600	12 (0Ch)	960	terminals, modems, printers, faxes
14400	8	1440	high speed modems
19200	6	1920	high speed modems, data transfers
28800	4	2880	high speed modems, data transfers
38400	3	3840	high speed modems, data transfers
57600	2 *	5760	data transfers, ISDN modems
115200	1**	11520	data transfers, ISDN modems

** There is no divisor that will provide exactly 56000 baud. In this case, the divisor actually sets a baud rate of 57600, 2.86% faster than 56000. This is not a problem, as the system usually tolerates as much as 5% error in the baud rate.*

***Unavailable on original 8250 UART.*

Interrupt Control

The serial port can be configured to operate on an interrupt (rather than polled) basis. A serial port interrupt service handler gets control whenever errors occur, when a new byte has been received, when the UART is ready to transmit a new byte, or when the modem control line status changes. These four types of interrupt action can be selectively enabled and disabled by writing to the Interrupt Enable Register.

When any of the four types of interrupts occur, the adapter card triggers an interrupt request, typically IRQ 3 or 4. The software interrupt handler is called, typically at interrupts Bh or Ch for IRQs 3 or 4. The interrupt handler must be supplied by the application using that serial port with interrupt control. The BIOS does not provide any interrupt handling services for the serial ports.

Once an interrupt occurs, the handler must read the serial port's Interrupt Identification register to see the specific cause of the interrupt. Table 12-8 shows the possible results from reading this register. When multiple interrupts occur before reading the Interrupt Identification register, the highest priority function will be presented first.

Table 12-8. Interrupt Types and Actions

Interrupt Identification Register Bits 3	2	1	0	Priority Level	Type	Source	Action to Clear Interrupt
0	0	0	0	lowest	modem status	CTS, DSR, RI, or DCD goes high	read Modem status register
0	0	0	1	none	no interrupt active		
0	0	1	0	third lowest	transmit holding register empty	register becomes empty	read interrupt identification register or write into transmit holding register
0	1	0	0	second lowest	received data available	data received or FIFO trigger	read received data register or total level reached FIFO entries drops below trigger level
0	1	1	0	highest	receiver line status	Break interrupt or framing error or overrun error or parity error	read line status register
1*	1	0	0	second lowest	character timeout indications	At least one byte is in the receiver FIFO and none have been removed from or added to the FIFO during the last 4 character times	read the receiver buffer register

**Bit 3 is only defined on UARTs equipped with a FIFO, such as the 16550, and it is always zero on older parts.*

The system only reserves two IRQs for the four serial ports. IRQ 4 is normally associated with serial ports 1 and 3. IRQ 3 is normally associated with serial ports 2 and 4, but it is often used for other cards such as network adapters. Interrupt request lines 3 and 4 are the industry standard. Other IRQs could be used if the serial port adapter card provides such capability, although most do not.

Two or more serial ports can share the same interrupt on MCA systems. This is accomplished by chaining the interrupt handler to share the interrupt among multiple handlers. An application's serial port handler using serial port 1 must look at the Interrupt Identification Register for port 1. The Identification Register will indicate if an interrupt is active for serial port 1. If none is active, then some other serial port attached to the same interrupt will be responsible for handling the interrupt, and the port 1 handler performs no further actions.

As more ports share and use the same interrupt, the response time slows down for the oldest handler that hooks the interrupt. This may require reduced baud rates to avoid data loss when overruns occur. With very high baud rates, some applications will change the priority of the interrupt controller to make the serial port interrupt the highest priority. This means the serial port handler can service the serial port before any other interrupt, including the system timer. Chapter 17, Interrupt Control and NMI, explains more interrupt priorities.

FIFO Mode

The 16550 series of UARTs operate like the common 8250/16540 UART, but provides an optional "FIFO mode." Most older systems do not use the 16550 and cannot benefit from the FIFO mode of operation. In some cases, the 8250/16450 UART chip resides in a socket and can be replaced with the 16550.

A few systems use another alternative UART, the 82510. This Intel chip also provides 8250 compatibility and FIFO options. It is not as common as the 16550, but does show up in some systems. The 82510 is far more complex to program than other UARTs, providing lots of additional registers and modes. The balance of this section focuses on the more common 16550 FIFO UART. The BIOS interrupt service routines will not activate FIFO mode if available. The slow BIOS routines should be avoided if high performance is required.

With FIFO mode active, the UART will buffer up to sixteen bytes of receive data, and up to sixteen bytes of transmit data within the UART. This extra buffering allows the CPU additional time to process higher priority interrupts and other functions. Without the buffering, data received must be read before the next byte arrives. If the CPU remains busy for an extended period of time while handling a higher priority task, and two or more bytes are received during this time, an overrun occurs. The overrun error indicates bytes were lost since the CPU did not read the data from the UART while additional bytes arrived.

The serial port detector sample code later in this chapter shows how to detect if FIFO mode of operation is possible. Once it is determined FIFO mode is available, an alternate set of read and write routines could be substituted for the non-FIFO mode transmit and receive routines. These replacement routines can transfer multiple bytes of data at one time with the UART.

Like normal mode UART operation, the FIFO mode can be configured for interrupt or polled operation. In FIFO mode polled operation, the receive and transmit routines check the Line Status Register in the same way as the non-FIFO mode polled operation. The Line Status Register bit 0 is set when one or more bytes are in the receive FIFO. Bit 5 indicates when one or more bytes are in the transmit FIFO. Both FIFOs are used transparently by software. This allows activation of FIFO mode while still using the BIOS serial port handler.

For FIFO interrupt operation, a trigger level is set in the FIFO Control Register. The trigger level is the number of bytes needed in the receive FIFO before a received data available interrupt is generated. The UART can be programmed to interrupt the CPU when the receive FIFO has 1, 4, 8, or 14 bytes. To keep the interrupt rate low, a higher trigger level is used. A lower trigger level is used if the CPU does not respond quickly to the interrupt. Slow CPU response can occur if higher priority interrupts are allowed or if the system is slow due to CPU clock speed or CPU choice.

In FIFO interrupt mode, the UART will also issue a receive timeout interrupt if all three of the following conditions occur:

- The receive FIFO has one or more bytes.
- A byte has not been received over the link for the timeout period.
- The CPU has not read any bytes from the CPU in the timeout period.

The timeout period is the amount of time equivalent to receiving 4 frames in a row when no action occurs. This means the timeout is directly proportional to the baud rate. With a 10-bit frame at 9600 baud, the timeout period would be 4.2 ms. For other frames and baud rates the timeout period is calculated as:

$$\text{Timeout period (in ms)} = \frac{\text{Bits in frame}}{\text{Baud rate}} * 4 \text{ frames} * 1000 \text{ ms}$$

The timeout duration counter is reset when a new byte is received or when the CPU reads a byte from the receive FIFO. If a timeout interrupt does occur, it is reset when the CPU reads a byte from the receive FIFO.

In interrupt mode, the transmit FIFO will generate an interrupt when the FIFO becomes empty. The interrupt service routine can then transfer up to 16 bytes into the transmit FIFO.

BIOS Data Areas

Location	Description	Size
40:00h	Serial port 1	Word

This word value is used to store the first I/O port number for serial port 1. Normally serial port 1 is at I/O address 3F8h or 2F8h, but any serial I/O port can be stored in this word.

Location	Description	Size
40:02h	Serial port 2	Word

This word value is used to store the first I/O port number for serial port 2. Normally serial port 2 is at I/O address 2F8h, but any serial I/O port can be stored in this word.

Location	Description	Size
40:04h	Serial port 3	Word

This word value is used to store the first I/O port number for serial port 3. Any serial I/O port can be stored in this word.

Location	Description	Size
40:06h	Serial Port 4	Word

This word value is used to store the first I/O port number for serial port 4. Any serial I/O port can be stored in this word.

Location	Description	Size
40:7Ch	Serial 1 Timeout	Byte

This byte holds a fixed value used by the serial port interrupt 14h handler. When the serial port handler sends a character, the timeout value is used to wait for various status conditions change so a byte can be sent or received.

When transmitting a byte, the Data Terminal Ready (DTR) and Request To Send (RTS) lines are checked. If they both fail to become high within the timeout period, a timeout occurs and the BIOS returns a timeout error condition.

Similar actions occur while receiving a character. First the timeout value is used while waiting for Data Set Ready (DSR) line to become active. Then it uses the timeout value again to wait until the serial controller status indicates the receive buffer has a character. If either condition fails to occur within the timeout duration, the BIOS returns a timeout error condition.

The POST sets the initial value to one on most systems. Each count is equivalent to about 2 ms of delay. Since the timeout is based on instruction delays, the duration will vary depending on the system clock speed and BIOS implementation.

The timeout bytes are not supported on the original PC, but are supported in the XT and all later platforms.

Location	Description	Size
40:7Dh	Serial 2 Timeout	Byte

Refer to Serial 1 Timeout at RAM location 40:7Ch for details.

Location	Description	Size
40:7Eh	Serial 3 Timeout	Byte

Refer to Serial 1 Timeout at RAM location 40:7Ch for details.

Location	Description	Size
40:7Fh	Serial 4 Timeout	Byte

Refer to Serial 1 Timeout at RAM location 40:7Ch for details.

Debugging

Serial port routines are somewhat difficult to verify. Part of the difficulty stems from having to operate two independent systems. If either system's routines have coding errors, it is difficult to determine which system is causing the problem. It is also difficult to create all of the possible test error conditions to ensure the routines are properly coded.

Serial port analyzers can help quickly determine the source of a problem, but are quite expensive. Some of these analyzers are capable of generating error conditions for test purposes.

Recently serial analysis software has become available to run on a separate PC. This software can be used in place of a dedicated hardware analysis product. Although requiring a separate PC, the software is available for less that $300. One company that produces such a product is WCSC in Houston, Texas. Contact WCSC at 713-498-4832. An inexpensive (under $50) solution is a serial port tester. A serial port tester has LEDs that show the state of each of the 8 signal lines, high, low, or open. Using a debugger to single step the code while monitoring the signal states may help identify the source of a problem.

For debugging, we've included a third no-cost alternative, SSPY. SSPY continuously monitors the four modem input lines, DCD, RI, DSR, CTS, and also monitors the two output lines DTR and RTS. These are displayed on the screen. SSPY is a TSR that reads a specified serial port's UART status 18 times a second, without altering the state of the UART.

SSPY cannot detect defective hardware, cable shorts and opens, but helps isolate incorrect operation of a serial port routine. Run SSPY with the port to examine, 1 to 4. Once loaded, use the Scroll Lock key to activate. With Scroll Lock on, the status information is displayed on the top of the screen. Set Scroll Lock off to disable SSPY. SSPY's slight system overhead can cause problems on some systems at the highest data rates (38 Kbps and higher). Complete source code of SSPY is provided on the diskette if you desire to make any changes to SSPY.

In many cases, running at very slow baud rates can help clarify how two systems are communicating. Using the BIOS initialization function you can set a baud rate as low as 75 baud. This may still be too fast, especially if you are using a simple port tester. The subroutine in Code Sample 12-1 can be called to slow the baud rate to 2 bits per second, slow enough to see each bit in a frame of data.

UART Part Summary

Over the years there have been a number of improvements to the original 8250 UART. This list covers most of the 8250 variants in use on the PC platform. Keep in mind many different vendors supply these parts, usually with additional prefixes and suffixes, unique to each vendor.

Basic Number	**Description**
8250	Basic UART, with some performance limitations
16450	Improved performance version of 8250
16550	Added receive and transmit FIFOs to 16450
16552	Two 16550 UARTs in one part
16C454	Four 16450 UARTs in one part
16C554	Four 16550 UARTs in one part
16C1450	Improved 16450 with software-controlled power down and reset
16C1550	Improved 16550 with software-controlled power down and reset
82510	Added receive and transmit FIFOs to 16450 and power down modes (FIFO operation implemented differently than 16550)

Serial Port Connector

Although many programmers never deal with the hardware directly, it is often necessary to monitor signal lines and information directly at the connector. This can help resolve programming bugs and confirm valid operation. The serial port uses a 25-pin or 9-pin 'D' shell connector. The pinout for the 25-pin connector is shown in Table 12-9, and the 9-pin connector is shown in Table 12-10. The direction is relative to the system. This means an output sends a signal to the attached device. Functions are described in greater detail in the "Serial BIOS" section. Functions prefixed with a minus are active when low, and prefixed with plus when active denotes high.

Some serial adapter cards support current loop mode for old teletypes. The 9-pin connector does not have pins to support this mode of operation. Currently most serial port cards no longer support current loop mode.

Table 12-9. Serial Port 25-pin Connector

Pin	Direction	Function
2	output	Serial transmit line
3	input	Serial receive line
4	output	Request To Send (RTS)
5	input	Clear To Send (CTS)
6	input	Data Set Ready (DSR)
7	Ground	
8	input	Received Line Signal Detector
9	output	+Transmit Current Loop Data
11	output	-Transmit Current Loop Data
18	input	+Receive Current Loop Data
20	output	Data Terminal Ready (DTR)
22	input	Ring Indicator (RI)
25	input	-Receive Current Loop Data

Pins not shown are unused and not connected.

Table 12-10. Serial Port 9-pin Connector

Pin	Direction	Function
1	input	Received Line Signal Detector
2	input	Serial receive line
3	output	Serial transmit line
4	output	Data Terminal Ready (DTR)
5	Ground	
6	input	Data Set Ready (DSR)
7	output	Request To Send (RTS)
8	input	Clear To Send (CTS)
9	input	Ring Indicator (RI)

Warnings

Be sure there is sufficient delay between I/O accesses to the same UART, in case the system has a fast bus speed or has a UART with slow I/O handling. Before using a serial port, it is wise to check what kind of UART the system is using. There are a number of pitfalls in some chips that are easily avoided, once the chip is known. Code Sample 12-2 shows how to reliably determine which UART is present.

8250 Bugs The original 8250 UART has a number of bugs and restrictions, which can frustrate the unsuspecting programmer. All of these problems were corrected in newer UARTs, such as the 16450 and 16550. You can avoid these problems by using the system BIOS serial port functions or clearly understanding the limitations of the 8250.

These problems include:

- Invalid Transmit Holding Register Interrupts
- Enable Interrupt bit gets lost
- Limited baud rate
- Problems with 8-bit data length and parity enabled

First, when setting the Enable Transmit Holding Register Interrupt function in the Interrupt Enable Register, an interrupt is generated even if the transmit holding register is not empty! If this interrupt function is going to be used, the interrupt should be enabled only when the transmit holding register is empty. As an alternative, the interrupt handler could verify the transmit buffer is really empty, but this can reduce the maximum performance.

The UART may also miss the first time setting the Enable Transmit Holding Register Interrupt bit after the chip has first been powered up. To solve this bug, simply write to the Interrupt Enable Register twice in a row. It is acceptable to write to this register every time without any side effects. For example, the code might appear as:

```
mov     dx, 3F9h        ; Interrupt Enable Register
mov     al, 2           ; enable transmit empty int
out     dx, al          ; do-it!
jmp     short $+2       ; delay
out     dx, al          ; do-it again (bug fix)
```

Even though all UARTs can be programmed for baud rates up to 115,200, the 8250, 8250B and 8250C are limited by the manufacturer to a maximum of 56,000 baud. The 8250A does not have this limitation. In my tests, 56,000 baud is no problem as long as interrupts are not used and sufficient system real-time throughput is available.

In most cases, interrupts are necessary to work properly in today's environments. This drops the useful baud rate closer to 9600. This is caused by poor timing in the receiver portion of the UART, when clearing each interrupt. As compared with the 8250's successor, the 16450 UART receiver timing is 25 times faster! The transmitter timing in the 8250 is a bit better than the receiver and will likely work fine up to 38,400 baud with interrupt control.

Several respected engineers I've talked with have heard of problems with the original 8250 UART when using 8-bit data and parity. Using 7-bit data and parity or 8-bit data and no parity are always acceptable.

My own tests with an old 8250 chip were unable to reproduce any problem. Even with a maximum frame size of 8-bits, a parity bit, and two stop bits the transmit and receive functions worked fine. This included tests from 2400 to 56,000 baud, the maximum baud rate of the 8250 without using interrupts. Because I was unable to try every combination of functions and error conditions with all the different vendors' chips, it may be a real problem. On the other hand, because I was unable to find anyone who actually encountered the problem, the defect might be folklore without any real basis, or it might have been confused with some of the earlier problems I've described.

16550A Bad FIFO The 16550A UART works fine as 100% compatible replacement to the 16450, but due to a design flaw, the FIFO in this specific 16550 version does not operate correctly. All later variants including parts with suffixes AF, C, and CF corrected this problem. Fortunately, it is easy to detect chips that have the bad FIFO, as shown in code sample 12-2.

16550 FIFO Failed Transmit Byte When using the FIFO feature on all 16550 versions, there is one unusual situation that may prevent a byte from being transmitted! The problem occurs if a byte is being transmitted out of the UART shift register and the FIFO is now empty. If a single byte is loaded into the transmit FIFO, the UART should load the byte into the transmit shift register as soon as the prior byte is shifted out. In this special case, the new byte may not be transferred into the shift register, but simply remains in the FIFO.

When the next byte is loaded into the transmit FIFO, the UART resumes normal operation. The prior byte is correctly loaded into the shift register and sent.

There is no way to correct the failed transmit byte problem other than preventing the situation from occurring in the first place. One approach would check if the FIFO is empty when the last byte of a block is going to be sent. If it is, the software must wait one transmit frame to ensure the shift register is empty before loading the last byte into the FIFO.

Code Sample 12-1. Slow Baud Rate for Debugging

The following routine can be called to force the baud rate to a very slow rate. This is useful for debugging serial code. In this routine, we've set the baud rate to 2 baud (2 bits per second), which requires a divisor of E100h. The base I/O port address must be passed to the routine in the DX register.

```
;---------------------------------------------------------------
;    SLOW_BAUD
;        Set baud rate to 2, without changing any other settings
;
;        Called with:    dx = base I/O address of serial port
;
;        Returns:        New baud rate set
;
```

```
;       Regs used:      none

divisor equ     0E100h              ; divisor for 2 baud

slow_baud proc  far
        push    ax
        push    dx
        add     dx, 3               ; line control register
        in      al, dx
        or      al, 80h             ; set DLAB=1 to load baud
        IODELAY
        out     dx, al
        sub     dx, 3               ; divisor latch LSB
        mov     ax, divisor
        out     dx, al              ; set divisor LSB to 0
        inc     dx                  ; divisor latch MSB
        mov     al, ah
        out     dx, al              ; set divisor MSB to E1h
        add     dx, 2               ; line control register
        in      al, dx
        and     al, 7Fh             ; set DLAB=0, baud loaded
        IODELAY
        out     dx, al
        pop     dx
        pop     ax
        ret
slow_baud endp
```

Code Sample 12-2. Serial Port Detector

This routine checks all active ports, displays the port number, and determines the UART type. If this utility is run while a port is being used for another purpose, such as a mouse, the port operation might be briefly disrupted. SERTYPE will always return accurate information.

When SERTYPE is run, the serial port analysis results are displayed on screen. On one system SERTYPE appears as:

```
                 SERTYPE—Serial Port Analysis

 Serial Port      Active?           Basic UART Type
#1      03F8        Yes        8250A or 16450
#2      02F8        Yes        16550AF/C/CF with FIFO
#3      02E8        Yes        82510 with FIFO
#4                  No
```

What SERTYPE shows is the port number (1 to 4) and the related I/O port address. The UART is checked to see if it is actually present in the system. The Active state is set to YES when the UART properly responds to reads and writes to the baud rate register at the specified I/O port. When an active UART is detected, the routine then checks for the type of UART.

I've only included the most interesting part of SERTYPE in the book, the TESTPORT subroutine. TESTPORT determines if a given I/O port has an active UART and the type of UART. The entire SERTYPE source code is provided on the Undocumented PC diskette.

```
;-----------------------------------------------------------------
;    Testport
;       Check if the UART is responding and if so, test to
;       find out which chip it is equivalent to.
;
;       Called with:    dx = serial I/O port
;
;       Returns:        bl = chip type
;                            0 = no response, not a UART
;                            1 = 8250 (no scratch register)
;                            2 = 8250A or 16450
;                            3 = 16C1450
;                            4 = 16550 with defective FIFO
;                            5 = 16550AF/C/CF with FIFO
;                            6 = 16C1550 with FIFO
;                            7 = 16552 dual UART with FIFO
;                            8 = 82510 with FIFO

testport proc   near
```

```
        mov     bl, 0                   ; return value if no-response
        mov     di, dx                  ; save I/O port
        cli                             ; disable interrupts
        call    DLAB1                   ; Divisor Latch Access bit=1
        mov     ah, 5Ah                 ; test value 1
        call    IOtest                  ; write value, read it and compare
        jne     test_exit2              ; exit if not valid
        mov     ah, 0A5h                ; test value 2
        call    IOtest                  ; write value, read it and compare
        jne     test_exit2              ; exit if not valid
        sti                             ; enable interrupts

; now check if the scratch pad register is working (missing on 8250)

        inc     bl                      ; return 1 if 8250
        add     dx, 7                   ; point to scratch pad register
        mov     ah, 5Ah                 ; test value 1
        call    IOtest                  ; write value, read it and compare
        jne     test_exit2              ; exit if no scatch register
        mov     ah, 0A5h                ; test value 2
        call    IOtest                  ; write value, read it and compare
        je      scratch_ok
test_exit2:
        jmp     test_exit               ; exit if no scratch register

scratch_ok:
        mov     dx, di                  ; restore base I/O port

; check for 1655x and 82510 FIFO versions

        cli                             ; disable interrupts
        add     dx, 2                   ; interrupt ID register
        in      al, dx
        IODELAY
```

```
        and     al, 0C0h
        cmp     al, 0C0h            ; is 16550 FIFO already enabled ?
        je      is_1655x            ; jump if so

        mov     al, 1               ; try to enable FIFO on 1655x
        out     dx, al              ;  (if 82510 also set bank 0)
        IODELAY
        in      al, dx              ; read Interrupt Identification
        IODELAY
        mov     bh, al              ; save readback value
        mov     al, 0               ; Disable FIFO on 16550 or
        out     dx, al              ;   select bank 0 on 82510
        IODELAY
        and     bh, 0C0h
        cmp     bh, 0C0h            ; was FIFO enabled on 16550 ?
        je      is_1655x            ; jump if so
        cmp     bh, 40h             ; FIFO UART in some PS/2s ?
        je      is_16550C
        cmp     bh, 80h             ; 16550 with defective FIFO ?
        je      is_16550

; not 16550, so now check for possible 82510 by switching to bank
;  3 (which is only possible on a 82510)

        mov     al, 60h             ; select bank 3
        out     dx, al
        IODELAY
        in      al, dx              ; read back from port
        IODELAY
        mov     bh, al              ; save for later

        mov     al, 0               ; if 83510, return to
        out     dx, al              ;  bank 0
        IODELAY
```

```
        and     bh, 60h             ; now, did it goto bank 3?
        cmp     bh, 60h
        je      is_82510            ; jump if so (is 82510)

; no FIFO, so UART is 8250A or 16450 variant - Check if power down
;   bit functions on this UART, in the modem control register

no_FIFO:
        mov     dx, di
        add     dx, 4               ; select modem control register
        mov     al, 80h             ; see if power down mode allowable
        out     dx, al
        IODELAY
        in      al, dx              ; get modem register
        IODELAY
        mov     ah, al              ; save result
        mov     al, 0
        out     dx, al              ; turn power back on
        test    ah, 80h             ; did power down bit get set ?
        jnz     is_16C1450          ; jump if so

is_8250A:
        mov     bl, 2               ; set to 8250A/16450 UART
        jmp     test_exit

is_16C1450:
        mov     bl, 3               ; set to 16C1450 UART
        jmp     test_exit

is_16550:
        mov     bl, 4               ; set to 16550 with defective FIFO
        jmp     test_exit
```

```
; FIFO detected, and must be 16550 series

is_1655x:
        mov     dx, di
        call    DLAB1
        add     dx, 2
        mov     ah, 7
        call    IOtest              ; write value, read it
        mov     bh, al              ; save result for later
        mov     al, 0               ; reset register select
        out     dx, al
        cmp     bh, 7               ; did it work ?
        je      is_16552            ; if compare ok, is 16552

; Check if power down bit functions on this UART, in the modem
;   control register (only on 16C1550)

        mov     dx, di
        add     dx, 4               ; select modem control register
        mov     al, 80h             ; see if power down mode allowable
        out     dx, al
        IODELAY
        in      al, dx              ; get modem register
        IODELAY
        mov     ah, al              ; save result
        mov     al, 0
        out     dx, al              ; turn power back on
        test    ah, 80h             ; did power down bit get set ?
        jnz     is_16C1550          ; jump if so

is_16550C:
        mov     bl, 5               ; set to 16550AF/C/CF UART
        jmp     test_exit
```

```
is_16C1550:
        mov     bl, 6                   ; set to 16C1550
        jmp     test_exit

is_16552:                               ; set to 16552 UART
        mov     bl, 7
        jmp     test_exit

is_82510:
        mov     bl, 8                   ; set to 82510 UART

test_exit:
        mov     dx, di                  ; restore base port value
        call    DLAB0                   ; reset DLAB to 0
        sti                             ; enable interrupts in case off
        ret
testport endp

;-------------------------------------------------------------------
;    DLAB1
;       Set the Divisor Latch Access Bit to 1 without
;       changing other line control bits
;
;       Called with:    dx = serial I/O port
;
;       Regs Used:      al

DLAB1   proc    near
        push    dx
        add     dx, 3                   ; point to Line Control Reg
        in      al, dx                  ; get current state
        IODELAY
        or      al, 80h                 ; set DLAB to 1
        out     dx, al
```

```
        pop     dx
        ret
DLAB1   endp

;-------------------------------------------------------------------
;    DLAB0
;        Set the Divisor Latch Access Bit to 0 without
;        changing other line control bits
;
;        Called with:    dx = serial I/O port
;
;        Regs Used:      al

DLAB0   proc    near
        push    dx
        add     dx, 3                ; point to Line Control Reg
        in      al, dx               ; get current state
        IODELAY
        and     al, 7Fh              ; set DLAB to 0
        out     dx, al
        pop     dx
        ret
DLAB0   endp

;-------------------------------------------------------------------
;    IOtest
;        Write value al to port, then read back value and compare
;        to original value.
;
;        Called with:    ah = value to use for test
;                        dx = I/O port to test
;
;        Returns:        al = value read from port
;                        zero flag = 1 if register ok
```

```
IOtest  proc    near
        mov     al, ah              ; value to test
        out     dx, al              ; write value
        IODELAY
        in      al, dx              ; read back value
        IODELAY
        cmp     al, ah              ; compare if the same
        ret
IOtest  endp
```

Code Sample 12-3. Maximum Baud Rate Analyzer

The next two sample programs are used together to find the maximum sustained transfer rate between two computers. They work by sending 512 bytes at progressively higher baud rates between two systems until errors are detected.

The programs MAX_XMIT and MAX_RECV are provided on the diskette. Some of the code used to maximize performance may seem a bit strange. The source code is well-documented where odd approaches were used in coding the routines.

To boost performance, only RAM is used for data buffering. The transmit data comes from RAM, and the system receiving the data also places the data in RAM. A real communications package will likely send data to and from the disk, reducing the reliable transfer rate. The initial baud rate is 2400 since even the slowest system handles this rate.

To use these programs, one system runs MAX_XMIT, and the other runs MAX_RECV. The operation is interlinked to start when both programs are running by using the modem control signals. When the test is complete, both routines will exit. You can also use Ctrl-Break to exit.

The two systems should be connected with a null modem cable. This cable is generally available from any well-stocked computer store. Null modem cable connections are shown in Figure 12-3.

Figure 12-3. Null Modem Cable Connections

System 1	**Pin**		**Pin**	**System 2**
Transmit	2	→	3	Receive
Receive *	3	←	2	Transmit *
Request To Send	4	→ (also to pin 5)	8	Data Carrier Detect
Clear To Send	5	← (from pin 4)		
Data Set Ready	6	←	20	Data Terminal Ready
Data Carrier Detect	8	← (also to pin 5)	4	Request To Send
		→ (from pin 4)	5	Clear To Send
Data Terminal Ready	20	→	6	Data Set Ready

* *When system 1 runs the MAX_XMIT and system 2 runs MAX_RECV, this signal line is not used.*

```
;--------------------------------------------------------------
;                          MAX_XMIT
;--------------------------------------------------------------
;
;   This routine works with a companion routine MAX_RECV to find
;   the maximum sustained serial transfer rate between two
;   systems, connected by a null modem cable. Serial port 1 is
;   assumed unless command line indicates otherwise. From the
;   command specify port number x from 1 to 4:   MAX_XMIT  x
;
;   (c) Copyright 1994, 1996  Frank van Gilluwe
;   All Rights Reserved.

include undocpc.inc

cseg    segment para public
        assume  cs:cseg, ds:cseg, ss:tsrstk

max_xmit        proc    far

msg1    db      CR, LF
        db      'MAX_XMIT - Finds Maximum speed on serial link'
        db      CR, LF, '$'
```

```
msg2    db      CR, LF, '  Transmitter Loaded and ready.'
        db      '  Waiting for receiver MAX_RECV connection.'
        db      CR, LF
        db      '  (Press Ctrl-Break to exit)', CR, LF, '$'

msg3    db      'Testing at baud rate: $'
msgok   db      '  Test OK', CR, LF, '$'
msgfail db      '  Test failed', CR, LF, '$'
msgerr  db      '  Serial port not present', CR, LF, '$'

divisor db      30h, '2,400  $'  ; Table of divisors and baud

div2nd  db      18h, '4,800  $'  ;  rates to test
        db      0Ch, '9,600  $'
        db      8,   '14,400 $'
        db      6,   '19,200 $'
        db      3,   '38,400 $'
        db      2,   '57,600 $'
        db      1,   '115,200$'
divisor_end     label  byte

buffer  db      512 dup (31h)       ; buffer of bytes to send

start:
        mov     bx, 0               ; assume port 1
        cmp     byte ptr ds:[80h], 0  ; command line options ?
        je      max_skp1            ; jump if none
        mov     al, ds:[82h]        ; get command line value
        sub     al, 31h             ; convert to digit 0-3
        cmp     al, 3
        ja      max_skp1            ; skip if out of range
        mov     bl, al              ; save port number
max_skp1:
        push    cs
        pop     ds
```

```
        mov     ax, 40h               ; BIOS data area segment
        mov     es, ax
        mov     byte ptr es:[71h], 0  ; force break flag off
        OUTMSG  msg1                  ; output initial message

; get the serial base I/O port address and set up pointer

        shl     bx, 1                 ; setup to get I/O port
        mov     dx, es:[bx]           ; base I/O port address
        cmp     dx, 0
        jne     valid_port
        jmp     no_serial_port        ; exit if zero

valid_port:
        mov     bp, dx                ; save base port address
        mov     di, offset divisor ; pointer to divisor table

; inform the remote system that we are ready

        add     dx, 4                 ; modem control register
        mov     al, 3                 ;  set Request To Send &
        out     dx, al                ;  Data Terminal Ready

        OUTMSG  msg2                  ; output "waiting message"

; Now check if the remote system is ready. Data Set Ready and
;   Clear To Send lines must both be high.

next_block:
        mov     dx, bp

; Set up the modem with 8-bit, 1 stop bit, odd parity, and
;   set the current test baud rate divisor
```

```
        add     dx, 3               ; line control register
        mov     al, 10001011b       ;  8-bit, 1 stop, odd parity
        out     dx, al              ;  and DLAB=1 to load baud
        IODELAY
        mov     dx, bp              ; divisor latch LSB
        mov     al, [di]            ;  get divisor LSB
        out     dx, al              ;  set divisor LSB
        IODELAY
        inc     dx
        mov     al, 0               ;  divisor MSB is 0
        out     dx, al              ;  set divisor MSB
        IODELAY
        add     dx, 2               ; line control register
        mov     al, 00001011b       ;  turn DLAB off
        out     dx, al
        IODELAY

        add     dx, 3               ; modem status register

max_loop1:
        in      al, dx
        IODELAY
        not     al
        test    al, 0A0h            ; is remote system ready ?
        jz      ready_to_send       ; jump if so (DSR & DCD = 1)
        test    byte ptr es:[71h], 80h  ; did break occur ?
        jz      max_loop1           ; jump if not
        jmp     max_xmit_end        ; exit, ctrl-break

ready_to_send:
        OUTMSG  msg3                ; output Testing ...
        mov     dx, di
        inc     dx                  ; point to baud rate text
        mov     ah, 9
        int     21h                 ; output baud rate number
```

```
        mov     si, offset buffer  ; buffer of bytes to send
        mov     cx, 512            ; send 512 bytes
        call    send_block         ; transmit 512 bytes

; now wait until receiver indicates it has finished receiving the block

max_xmit_wait:
        test    byte ptr es:[71h], 80h  ; did break occur ?
        jnz     max_xmit_end       ; exit if so
        mov     dx, bp
        add     dx, 6              ; modem status register
        in      al, dx
        test    al, 80h            ; is remote system done, DCD=0
        jnz     max_xmit_wait      ; loop until done
        test    al, 20h            ; remote error ? DSR=0
        jz      max_xmit_fail      ; jump if so

; receiver happy, so output OK message and do next test

        OUTMSG  msgok
        add     di, offset div2nd - offset divisor
        cmp     di, offset divisor_end
        jb      next_blocka
        jmp     max_xmit_end
next_blocka:
        jmp     next_block

max_xmit_fail:
        OUTMSG  msgfail            ; baud rate failed

max_xmit_end:
        mov     dx, bp
        add     dx, 4              ; modem control register
        mov     al, 0              ;  set DTR off
```

```
        out     dx, al              ;  we're done!
        jmp     max_xmit_done

no_serial_port:
        OUTMSG  msgerr              ; output error message

max_xmit_done:
        mov     ah, 4Ch
        int     21h                 ; exit to DOS
max_xmit endp

;---------------------------------------------------------------------
;    SEND_BLOCK
;       Sends a block of data as fast as possible over the
;       serial link. Exit if Control-break detected or receive
;       Clear To Send no longer active.
;
;       Called with:    cx = number of bytes to transmit
;                       bp = base port I/O address
;                       ds:si = source of data
;
;       Returns:        bytes sent on serial link, unless
;                         control-break occurred
;
;       Regs used:      al, cx, dx, si

send_block proc near
        mov     dx, bp
        cld                         ; clear direction flag send_next:

send_next:
        add     dx, 5
wait_loop1:
        test    byte ptr es:[71h], 80h  ; did break occur ?
        jnz     send_exit           ; exit if so
```

```
        inc     dx                      ; modem status register
        in      al, dx
        IODELAY
        test    al, 80h                 ; remote problem ?, DCD=0
        jz      send_exit               ; jump if so
        dec     dx                      ; line status register
        in      al, dx
        IODELAY
        test    al, 20h                 ; xmit holding reg ready?
        jz      wait_loop1              ; jump if not

        mov     dx, bp                  ; transmit holding register
        lodsb                           ; get byte into al from [si]
        out     dx, al                  ; send byte
        IODELAY
        loop    send_next

send_exit:
        ret
send_block endp



;---------------------------------------------------------------------
;                           MAX_RECV
;---------------------------------------------------------------------
;
;   This routine works with a companion routine MAX_XMIT to find
;   the maximum sustained serial transfer rate between two
;   systems, connected by a null modem cable. Serial port 1 is
;   assumed unless command line indicates otherwise. From the
;   command specify port number x from 1 to 4:   MAX_RECV  x
;
;   (c) Copyright 1994, 1996  Frank van Gilluwe
;   All Rights Reserved.
```

```
include undocpc.inc
cseg    segment para public
        assume  cs:cseg, ds:cseg, ss:tsrstk

max_recv        proc    far

msg1    db      CR, LF
        db      'MAX_RECV - Finds Maximum speed on serial link'
        db      CR, LF, '$'

msg2    db      CR, LF, '  Ready to receive data.'
        db      '  Waiting for transmitter MAX_XMIT connection.'
        db      CR, LF
        db      '  (Press Ctrl-Break to exit)', CR, LF, '$'

msg3    db      'Testing at baud rate: $'
msgok   db      '  Test OK', CR, LF, '$'
msgfail db      '  Test failed - $'

msgovr  db      'Overrun error', CR, LF, '$'
msgpar  db      'Parity error', CR, LF, '$'
msgfra  db      'Framing error', CR, LF, '$'
msgdata db      'Data is invalid', CR, LF, '$'

msgerr  db      '  Serial port not present', CR, LF, '$'

divisor db      30h, '2,400  $'  ; Table of divisors and baud
div2nd  db      18h, '4,800  $'  ;  rates to test
        db      0Ch, '9,600  $'
        db      8,   '14,400 $'
        db      6,   '19,200 $'
        db      3,   '38,400 $'
        db      2,   '57,600 $'
        db      1,   '115,200$'
divisor_end     label  byte
```

```
buffer  db      512 dup (0h)        ; buffer of bytes to send

ctrlb   db      0                   ; 1=control break occurred

start:
        mov     bx, 0               ; assume port 1
        cmp     byte ptr ds:[80h], 0  ; command line options ?
        je      max_skp1            ; jump if none
        mov     al, ds:[82h]        ; get command line value
        sub     al, 31h             ; convert to digit 0-3
        cmp     al, 3
        ja      max_skp1            ; skip if out of range
        mov     bl, al              ; save port number
max_skp1:
        push    cs
        pop     ds
        mov     ax, 40h             ; BIOS data area segment
        mov     es, ax
        mov     byte ptr es:[71h], 0  ; force break off
        OUTMSG  msg1                ; output initial message

; get the serial base I/O port address and set up pointer

        shl     bx, 1               ; setup to get I/O port
        mov     dx, es:[bx]         ; base I/O port address
        cmp     dx, 0
        jne     valid_port
        jmp     no_serial_port      ; exit if zero

valid_port:
        mov     bp, dx              ; save base port address
        mov     si, offset divisor ; pointer to divisor table
```

```
; inform the remote system that we are ready
        add     dx, 4               ; modem control register
        mov     al, 1               ;  set Data Terminal Ready
        out     dx, al              ;  but not Ready To Send
        IODELAY

        OUTMSG  msg2                ; output "waiting message"

; Now check if the remote system is ready. Data Set Ready
;   will be high.

        mov     dx, bp
        add     dx, 6               ; modem status register

max_loop1:
        in      al, dx
        test    al, 20h             ; is remote system ready ?
        jnz     ready_to_recv       ; jump if so (DSR = 1)
        test    byte ptr es:[71h], 80h  ; did break occur ?
        jz      max_loop1           ; jump if not
        jmp     max_recv_end        ; exit, ctrl-break

; Set up the modem with 8-bit, 1 stop bit, odd parity, and
;   set the current test baud rate divisor

ready_to_recv:
        mov     dx, bp
        add     dx, 3               ; line control register
        mov     al, 10001011b       ;  8-bit, 1 stop, odd parity
        out     dx, al              ;  and DLAB=1 to load baud
        IODELAY
        mov     dx, bp              ; divisor latch LSB
        mov     al, [si]            ;  get divisor LSB
        out     dx, al              ;  set divisor LSB
        IODELAY
```

```
        inc     dx
        mov     al, 0                ;  divisor MSB is 0
        out     dx, al               ;  set divisor MSB
        IODELAY
        add     dx, 2                ; line control register
        mov     al, 00001011b        ;  turn DLAB off
        out     dx, al
        IODELAY

; flush anything in input buffer

        mov     dx, bp               ; load base address
        add     dx, 5                ; line status register
        in      al, dx
        test    al, 1                ; any received byte ?
        jz      skip_input           ; skip if not
        mov     dx, bp               ; receive register
        in      al, dx               ; flush receive buffer
skip_input:
        OUTMSG  msg3                 ; output Testing ...
        mov     dx, si
        inc     dx                   ; point to baud rate text
        mov     ah, 9
        int     21h                  ; output baud rate number

        mov     dx, bp
        add     dx, 5                ; line status register
        in      al, dx               ; a read clears error flags
        mov     di, offset buffer    ; buffer of bytes to receive
        mov     cx, 512              ; 512 bytes expected
        call    get_block            ; receive 512 bytes into ds:[di]

; check if any errors occurred and exit if so (al=line status)

        test    byte ptr es:[71h], 80h  ; did break occur ?
```

```
        jnz     max_recv_end        ; exit if so
        test    al, 0Eh             ; any errors on reception ?
        jnz     max_recv_fail       ; jump if so

        mov     cx, 512             ; check that the data is valid
        mov     di, offset buffer
        mov     al, 0

max_loop2:
        cmp     byte ptr [di], 31h ; correct value in buffer ?
        jne     max_recv_fail       ; jump if not
        mov     byte ptr [di], al   ; zero location for next test
        inc     di
        loop    max_loop2

; test successful, set RTS=0 output success and set next baud rate

        mov     dx, bp
        add     dx, 4               ; modem control register
        mov     al, 1               ;  set Data Terminal Ready
        out     dx, al              ;  but Request to Send now off

        OUTMSG  msgok
        add     si, offset div2nd - offset divisor
        cmp     si, offset divisor_end
        jae     delay_a_bit         ; jump if last divisor complete
        jmp     ready_to_recv

delay_a_bit:
        mov     cx, 0FFFFh          ; short delay to be sure
max_delay:                          ;  transmitter gets RTS=0
        loop    max_delay           ;  signal before we set
        jmp     max_recv_end        ;  DTR=0 as well
```

```
max_recv_fail:
        push    ax
        OUTMSG  msgfail                 ; output test failed message
        pop     ax
        mov     dx, offset msgovr       ; assume overrun error
        test    al, 2                   ; overrun error ?
        jnz     max_recv_fail2          ; jump if so
        mov     dx, offset msgfra       ; assume framing error
        test    al, 8                   ; framing error ?
        jnz     max_recv_fail2          ; jump if so
        mov     dx, offset msgpar       ; assume parity error
        test    al, 4                   ; parity error ?
        jnz     max_recv_fail2          ; jump if so
        mov     dx, offset msgdata      ; must be data error (al=0)
max_recv_fail2:
        mov     ah, 9
        int     21h                     ; output type of error

max_recv_end:
        mov     dx, bp
        add     dx, 4                   ; modem control register
        mov     al, 0                   ;  set DTR & RTS off to
        out     dx, al                  ;  tell transmitter to stop
        jmp     max_recv_done

no_serial_port:
        OUTMSG  msgerr                  ; output error message

max_recv_done:
        mov     ah, 4Ch
        int     21h                     ; exit to DOS
max_recv endp
```

```
;---------------------------------------------------------------
;    GET_BLOCK
;       Get a block of data as fast as possible over the
;       serial link. Exit if Control-break or errors are
;       detected. There are no timeouts.
;
;       Called with:    cx = number of bytes expected
;                       bp = base port I/O address
;                       es:di = destination of data
;
;       Returns:        bytes received on serial link, unless
;                         control-break occurred
;
;       Regs used:      ax, bx, cx, dx, di

get_block proc near
        push    si
        push    ds
        push    es

        mov     ax, ds
        mov     es, ax              ; es = buffer segment
        mov     ax, 40h
        mov     ds, ax              ; ds = BIOS data segment
        mov     si, 71h             ; offset of BIOS break flag
        mov     ah, 5               ; for adjusting DX
        mov     bh, 8Eh             ; test mask for errors & break
        mov     bl, 1               ; test mask if byte available

        mov     dx, bp
        add     dx, 4               ; modem control register
        mov     al, 3               ;  set Data Terminal Ready
        out     dx, al              ;  and Request to Send
```

```
        cld                             ; clear direction flag
        mov     dx, bp                  ; base I/O address

; The following loop is tightly optimized, with many fixed values
; pre-loaded into registers. In addition, the error conditions
; (bits 3-1 of the line status register) and the BIOS break bit 7
; at 40:71h are combined for a single exit test. This assumes no
; FIFO mode, where bit 7 of the line status register is always
; zero. The STOSB instruction loads AL into es:[di] and inc's DI.

get_next:
        add     dl, ah                  ; line status register
wait_loop1:
        in      al, dx                  ; get error & data ready bits
        or      al, [si]                ; insert break bit 7
        test    al, bh                  ; errors or break (bh=8E) ?
        jnz     get_exit                ; jump if so
        test    al, bl                  ; any received byte (bl=1) ?
        jz      wait_loop1              ; loop if not
        mov     dx, bp                  ; receive register
        in      al, dx                  ; get byte
        stosb                           ; store byte into es:[di]
        loop    get_next

        mov     al, 0                   ; no errors
get_exit:
        pop     es
        pop     ds
        pop     si
        ret
get_block endp
```

Port Summary

This is a list of I/O ports used for serial operations. Those marked with an asterisk in the platform column are rarely used today, and are shown for basic reference only. No additional detail is provided on these adapters.

RS-232 serial ports access a UART through 8 sequential I/O ports. The base I/O address refers to the first I/O port of the group. The most common base addresses are 3F8h and 2F8h, although others are also commonly used. This summary shows common base addresses. Each register with the group is explained in the section "UART Register Detail" following the summary.

Port	Type	Function	Platform
2E8-2EFh	I/O	RS-232 Serial port group	Adapter
2F8-2FFh	I/O	RS-232 Serial port group	Adapter
380h	I/O	SDLC Serial Port, 8255 Internal/External Sensing	*
380h	I/O	BiSync Serial Port, 8255 Internal/External Sensing	*
381h	I/O	SDLC Serial Port, 8255 External Modem Interface	*
381h	I/O	BiSync Serial Port, 8255 External Modem Interface	*
382h	I/O	SDLC Serial Port, 8255 Internal Control	*
382h	I/O	BiSync Serial Port, 8255 Internal Control	*
383h	I/O	SDLC Serial Port, 8255 Mode Initialization	*
383h	I/O	BiSync Serial Port, 8255 Mode Initialization	*
384h	I/O	SDLC Serial Port, 8253 Square Wave Generator Counter	*
384h	I/O	BiSync Serial Port, 8253 Unused Counter	*
385h	I/O	SDLC Serial Port, 8253 Inactivity Timeout 1	*
385h	I/O	BiSync Serial Port, 8253 Inactivity Timeout 1	*
386h	I/O	SDLC Serial Port, 8253 Inactivity Timeout 2	*
386h	I/O	BiSync Serial Port, 8253 Inactivity Timeout 2	*
387h	I/O	SDLC Serial Port, 8253 Timer Mode Set	*
387h	I/O	BiSync Serial Port, 8253 Timer Mode Set	*
388h	Input	SDLC Serial Port, 8273 Status	*
388h	Output	SDLC Serial Port, 8273 Command	*
388h	I/O	BiSync Serial Port, 8251 Data	*
389h	Input	SDLC Serial Port, 8273 Status	*
389h	Output	SDLC Serial Port, 8273 Parameter	*
389h	Input	BiSync Serial Port, 8251 Status	*
389h	Output	BiSync Serial Port, 8273 Command	*
38Ah	I/O	SDLC Serial Port, 8273 Transmit Interrupt Status	*
38Bh	I/O	SDLC Serial Port, 8273 Receive Interrupt Status	*
38Ch	I/O	SDLC Serial Port, 8273 Data	*
3A0h	I/O	BiSync Serial Port, 8255 Internal/External Sensing	*
3A1h	I/O	BiSync Serial Port, 8255 External Modem Interface	*

Port	Type	Function	Platform
3A2h	I/O	BiSync Serial Port, 8255 Internal Control	*
3A3h	I/O	BiSync Serial Port, 8255 Mode Initialization	*
3A4h	I/O	BiSync Serial Port, 8253 Unused Counter	*
3A5h	I/O	BiSync Serial Port, 8253 Inactivity Timeout 1	*
3A6h	I/O	BiSync Serial Port, 8253 Inactivity Timeout 2	*
3A7h	I/O	BiSync Serial Port, 8253 Timer Mode Set	*
3A8h	I/O	BiSync Serial Port, 8251 Data	*
3A9h	Input	BiSync Serial Port, 8251 Status	*
3A9h	Output	BiSync Serial Port, 8273 Command	*
3E8-3EFh	I/O	RS232 Serial port group	Adapter
3F8-3FFh	I/O	RS232 Serial port group	Adapter
3220-3227h	I/O	RS232 Serial port group	MCA only
3228-322Fh	I/O	RS232 Serial port group	MCA only
4220-4227h	I/O	RS232 Serial port group	MCA only
4228-422Fh	I/O	RS232 Serial port group	MCA only
5220-5227h	I/O	RS232 Serial port group	MCA only
5228-522Fh	I/O	RS232 Serial port group	MCA only

* *Obsolete adapter—for reference only*

UART Register Detail

This section details the UART registers used to access the RS-232 serial port. To access a specific register, the base I/O port is added to the UART register number. The base I/O port is saved in the BIOS data area for each of the four serial ports. For example, to access UART Modem Status register 6, the base I/O port is added to 6. For a base address of 2E8h, the Modem status is accessed at 2E8h+6, which is port 2EEh.

An overview of the UART registers is shown in Tables 12-11 and 12-12. Note that the Divisor Latch Access Bit (DLAB) found in register 3 controls access to different functions in registers 0 and 1, and in some cases, register 2.

Table 12-11. Overview of UART Registers, DLAB is 0

#	Register	Bit 7	Bit 6	Bit 5	Bit 4	Bit 3	Bit 2	Bit 1	Bit 0
0 R	Receiver Buffer	Data received (5 to 8 bits, bit 0 always least significant and is received first)							
0 W	Transmit Buffer	Data to send (5 to 8 bits, bit 0 always least significant and is sent first)							
1	Interrupt Enable	0	0	0 Timer (82510)	0 Transmit Machine (82510)	Modem Status	Receiver Line Status	Transmit Holding Register Empty	Received Data Available
2 R	Interrupt Identification	0 FIFO Enabled (1655x)	0 Bank Select (82510) 00 = bank 0 (default) 01 = bank 1 10 = bank 2 11 = bank 3 (registers for banks 1, 2, and 3 not shown)	0	0	Interrupt type 0000 = Modem status changed 0001 = No interrupt pending 0010 = Transmit holding register empty 0100 = Received data available 0110 = Receiver line status 1000 = Transmit machine (82510 only) 1010 = Timer Interrupt (82510 only) 1100 = Character time-out (1655x only)			
2 W	FIFO Control (1655x only)	Receiver trigger level 00 = 1 byte in FIFO 01 = 4 bytes in FIFO 10 = 8 bytes in FIFO 11 =14 bytes in FIFO		0	0	DMA mode select	Transmit FIFO reset	Receiver FIFO reset	FIFO enable
3	Line Control	DLAB (Controls registers 0 and 1)	Send Break	Parity bit mode 00 = odd 01 = even 10 = always 0 11 = always 1		Parity Enable	Number of Stop Bits	Character word length 00 = 5 bits 01 = 6 bits 10 = 7 bits 11 = 8 bits	
4	Modem Control	0 Reset & Power down (161450)	0	0 -Out 0 (82510)	Loop-back	-Out 2 Enable IRQ	-Out 1 Soft Reset (161450)	Request to Send	Data Terminal Ready
5	Line Status	0 Error in Receive FIFO (1655x)	Transmit Shift Register Empty	Transmit Holding Register Empty	Break Interrupt Occurred	Framing Error Occurred	Parity Error Occurred	Overrun Error Occurred	Received Data Ready
6	Modem Status	Data Carrier Detect	Ring Indicator	Data Set Ready	Clear To Send	Data Carrier Detect Changed	Ring Indicator Changed	Data Set Ready Changed	Clear To Send Changed
7	Scratch Pad Special Control	Data byte (unused by UART, unavailable in original 8250) Data byte (unused, address, or control character depending on options in 82510)							

Gray indicates advanced features and options only available on some UARTs.

Table 12-12. Overview of UART Registers, DLAB is 1

#	Register	Bit 7	Bit 6	Bit 5	Bit 4	Bit 3	Bit 2	Bit 1	Bit 0
0	Divisor Latch LSB	Least significant data byte of Divisor Word							
1	Divisor Latch MSB	Most significant data byte of Divisor Word							
2	Alternate Functions (16552)	0	0	0	0	0	Define OUT2 function 00 = Enable IRQ (default) 01 = Baud clock out 10 = Recv Ready out 11 = undefined		Write to both UARTs at the same time

Gray indicates advanced features and options only available on some UARTs.

Register	Type	Description	Platform
0	I/O	Transmit/Receive Buffers (DLAB=0)	Adapter

This is the first register of eight sequential I/O addresses controlling one serial port. An output to this register stores a byte into the UART's transmit holding buffer. An input gets a byte from the receive buffer of the UART. These are two separate registers within the UART.

To access this register, the Divisor Latch Access Bit (DLAB) must be zero. DLAB is bit 7 in the line control register 3.

Input (bits 0-7) Get Receive Buffer Data Byte

Output (bits 0-7) Store Transmit Buffer Data Byte

Register	Type	Description	Platform
0	I/O	Divisor Latch LSB (DLAB=1)	Adapter

This register holds the least significant byte of the baud rate divisor latch. To determine divisor for a given baud rate value, divide 115,200 by the desired baud rate. See the section on Baud Rates for more details and Table 12-7 for common baud rate divisors.

To access this register, the Divisor Latch Access Bit (DLAB) must be one. DLAB is bit 7 in the line control register 3.

I/O (bits 0-7) Baud Rate Divisor Latch (LSB)

Register	Type	Description	Platform
1	I/O	Interrupt Enable Register (DLAB=0)	Adapter

Interrupt operations of the serial port are controlled from this register. When specific operations occur in the UART, an interrupt can be triggered if enabled. Most serial port adapter cards can be jumpered to use IRQ 3 or IRQ 4. See register 2 and Table 12-8 for additional related details. After a hardware reset, all interrupts are disabled by setting all bits to zero.

To access this register, the Divisor Latch Access Bit (DLAB) must be zero. DLAB is bit 7 in the line control register 3.

See the warning section about bugs in early versions of the UART, relating to the setting of the Transmit holding register empty bit.

I/O (bits 0-7)

bit	7 r	= 0	Unused
	6 r	= 0	Unused
	5 r/w	= 0	Unused or 82510 Disable timer interrupt
		1	Enabled timer interrupt (82510 only)
	4 r/w	= 0	Unused or Disable transmit machine interrupt (82510 only)
		1	Enable transmit machine interrupt (82510 only)
	3 r/w	= 1	Enable "Modem status" interrupt
	2 r/w	= 1	Enable "Receiver line status" interrupt
	1 r/w	= 1	Enable "Transmit holding register empty" interrupt
	0 r/w	= 1	Enable "Received data available" interrupt. On the 16550 chip, this bit also enables timeout interrupt when in FIFO mode.

Register	Type	Description	Platform
1	I/O	Divisor Latch MSB (DLAB=1)	Adapter

This register holds the most significant byte of the baud rate divisor latch. To determine the divisor for a given baud rate value, divide 115,200 by the desired baud rate. See the section on Baud Rates for more details and Table 12-7 for common baud rate divisors.

To access this register, the Divisor Latch Access Bit (DLAB) must be one. DLAB is bit 7 in the line control register 3.

I/O (bits 0-7) Baud Rate Divisor Latch (MSB)

Register	Type	Description	Platform
2	Input	Interrupt Identification Register (DLAB = 0)	Adapter

The Interrupt Identification Register shows if an interrupt is currently pending, and what caused the interrupt. After a hardware reset, the interrupt identification register is set to 1, indicating no interrupt is pending.

Input (bits 0-7) Interrupt Identification Register (except 82510)

bit 7 r = x	Part Identification/FIF0 mode	
6 r = x	bit 7	bit 6
	0	0 = FIF0 off or not 16550
	0	1 = FIF0 on, 16550 compatible
	1	0 = FIF0 on, old 16550 (bad FIF0)
	1	1 = FIF0 on, newer 16550A or later
5 r = 0	Unused	
4 r = 0	Unused	

3 r = x	Interrupt Identification (Table 12-8 has more details)		
2 r = x	bit 3	bit 2	bit 1
1 r = x	0	0	0 = modem status
	0	0	1 = transmit holding register empty
	0	1	0 = received data available
	0	1	1 = receiver line status
	1	1	0 = character timeout (16550 only)
0 r = 0	Interrupt pending		
1	No interrupt pending		

* *Bit 3 is only defined on UARTs equipped with a FIFO, such as the 16550, and is always zero on older parts.*

Register	Type	Description	Platform
2	Output	FIFO Control Register (DLAB = 0)	Adapter

Writing sends a byte to the FIFO control register. It is only supported on the 16650 series of UARTs. When setting FIFO options, bit 0, the FIFO enable, must be set to one for any other bits to be changed during a write.

After a hardware reset, the FIFO control register is set to zero, indicating non-FIFO mode is active.

Output (bits 0-7) FIFO Control (only with 16650 series chips)

bit 7 w = x	Receiver FIFO interrupt trigger level	
6 w = x	bit 7	bit 6
	0	0 = 1 byte in FIFO triggers interrupt
	0	1 = 4 bytes in FIFO triggers interrupt
	1	0 = 8 bytes in FIFO triggers interrupt
	1	1 = 14 bytes in FIFO triggers interrupt
5 w = 0	Unused (writes ignored)	
4 w = 0	Unused (writes ignored)	

3 w = x	Sets the UART's receive and transmit ready lines to mode 0 or mode 1 operation. The two modes control how these lines reflect FIFO and holding register states. The lines from the UART are generally disconnected, so these functions are unimportant.
2 w = 1	Clear all contents of the transmit FIFO and reset its content counter to zero. The transmit shift register is not cleared, so an outgoing byte is unaffected. This bit is automatically reset to 0.
1 w = 1	Clear all contents of the receive FIFO and reset its content counter to zero. The receive shift register is not cleared, so an incoming byte is unaffected. This bit is automatically reset to 0.
0 w = 0	Disable FIFOs and clear FIFO contents
1	Enable both receive and transmit FIFOs

Register	Type	Description	Platform
2	I/O	Alternate Function Register (DLAB=1)	Adapter

The 16552 dual UART provides a new register, which does not appear on other parts. The alternate function register controls how the OUT2 pin will be used. This register also allows I/O writes to go into both UARTs at the same time. The alternate function register is only accessible when DLAB bit 7 is 1 (see register 3).

Bit 0 controls the dual UART write option. This is useful to speed the initialization process by cutting in half the number of registers needed to be programmed. The dual UART is normally accessed as two separate set of I/O ports, and appears functionally independent of each other, except for this feature. This bit is accessible from either register set. Setting or clearing this bit is only necessary once. When set, additional writes to either of the two sets of UART registers is duplicated in the other. Reads are unaffected. Keep in mind the DLAB bit should be written to ensure both UARTs are using the same DLAB state.

On other UARTs, this register does not exist. In these cases, the DLAB setting does not matter. Only the Interrupt Identification Register/FIFO control are accessible on non-16552 UARTs.

I/O (bits 0-7) Alternate Function Register (16552 only)

bit	7 r = 0	Unused
	6 r = 0	Unused
	5 r = 0	Unused
	4 r = 0	Unused
	3 r = 0	Unused

2 r/w = x	Output 2 type		
1 r/w = x	bit 2	bit 1	
	0	0 = Interrupt Enable (default)	
	0	1 = output baud rate clock * 16	
	1	0 = FIFO has receive data (can be used for DMA request)	
	1	1 = unused	
0 r/w = 0	Normal		
1	Any write to a single UART register is written to both UARTs at the same time (see text)		

Register	Type	Description	Platform
3	I/O	Line Control Register	Adapter

This register controls the construction of the serial frame. It is set to zero upon a hardware reset. Since a reset creates a rarely used 5 bit data with odd parity frame, the Line Control Register must be loaded with a value for the desired type of frame. The most common frame used today is 8 bit data, no parity, with 1 stop bit.

This register contains the Divisor Latch Address Bit (DLAB). The DLAB bit controls access to the baud rate generator divisor latches (DLAB must be set to 1), and access to the receive buffer, transmit holding register or interrupt enable register (DLAB must be set to 0).

I/O (bits 0-7)

bit 7 r/w = x	Divisor Latch Address Bit—DLAB (see text)
6 r/w = 0	Break control off (normal)
1	A break condition is transmitted by forcing the serial out low. The break flag is set in the receiving UART's line status register when the transmitter issues the break for a short duration. At a minimum, this duration should be two full character frames at the current baud rate.
5 r/w = 0	Disable Sticky parity bit operation
1	Sticky parity bit operation forces the parity bit equal to the inverse of bit 4 (if parity enabled). This means a fixed parity bit is included in the serial frame. The same bit value is always transmitted or checked for upon reception.
4 r/w = 0	Odd parity (if enabled)
1	Even parity (if enabled)
3 r/w = 0	No parity bit appears in the serial frame

1	Enable Parity—When transmitting, an addition parity bit is sent after the data bits. For receive, the parity bit is checked for validity.
2 r/w = 0	Use 1 stop bit in the serial frame
1	Use 2 stop bits in the serial frame (unless a 5 bit data length is set, then 1.5 stop bits are used)
1 r/w = x	Data length
0 r/w = x	bit 1 bit 0
	0 0 = 5 bits
	0 1 = 6 bits
	1 0 = 7 bits
	1 1 = 8 bits

Register	Type	Description	Platform
4	I/O	Modem Control Register	Adapter

This register provides a number of control functions. It is used to set the state of connector output lines RTS and DSR. One bit allows disabling the interrupt request line without disabling the internal UART interrupt state. A loopback bit is used to test the UART's internal transmit and receive operations. See the section on Loopback Operations for a full explanation of this feature. The register is zeroed after a hardware reset.

I/O (bits 0-7) Modem Control Register (except 16C1450/1550 series)

bit 7 r = 0	Unused
6 r = 0	Unused
5 r/w = x	Unused or on the 82510, used as the -OUT0 line
4 r/w = 1	Loopback between transmit and receive is enabled
3 r/w = 1	-OUT2 line, used to enable interrupt requests (IRQ)
2 r/w = x	-OUT1 line, unconnected and unused
1 r/w = x	Set the state of the Request To Send line on the connector (RTS)
0 r/w = x	Set the state of the Data Terminal Ready line on the connector (DTR)

The 16C1450 and 16C1550 series UARTs provide two additional functions with this register. A power down mode allows the system to save power. During power down, all registers are retained, but the oscillators are turned off. These parts allow a software controlled reset similar to a hardware reset. Bit 2 is used for reset, but with other UARTs, bit 2 controls the unused OUT1 line.

I/O (bits 0-7) Modem Control Register (16C1450/16C1550 series)

bit	7 r/w =	0	Power on, normal operation
		1	Power savings mode
	6 r =	0	Unused
	5 r =	0	Unused
	4 r/w =	1	Loopback between transmit and receive is enabled
	3 r/w =	1	Enable interrupt requests (IRQ)
	2 r/w =	0	Normal operation
		1	Reset UART (like a hardware reset)
	1 r/w =	x	Set the state of the Request To Send line on the connector (RTS)
	0 r/w =	x	Set the state of the Data Terminal Ready line on the connector (DTR)

Register	Type	Description	Platform
5	Input	Line Status	Adapter

This register holds status and error information relating to received and transmitted data. When the receiver line status interrupt is enabled, any set bits 1 to 4 cause the interrupt to occur. After a hardware reset, this register will have the value 60h, indicating no errors and the transmit buffer is empty.

A 16550 UART in FIFO mode changes the operation of the received error and break flags. When a byte is received and loaded into the FIFO, any related error conditions or break conditions are recorded with the saved byte. When the oldest byte in the FIFO is exposed (the byte the CPU will read), the related flag bits appear in this register, bits 1 to 4.

This register is intended for read operations only. The chip does allow a write to the register for chip testing at the factory. The chip manufacturers do not recommend writing to this port, and do not specify what will occur if a write is made. My own testing with a number of vendors' 16450 chips showed bits 0 to 4 writeable. No interrupts were generated by setting these bits high. The chip manufacturer also indicates some bits are not writeable in FIFO mode.

Input (bits 0-7)

bit	7 r =	0	Unused or a 16550 chip in non-FIFO mode
		1	In FIFO mode on a 16550, at least one error condition occurred, and is stored in the FIFO. This includes parity errors, framing errors, or a break indication.
	6 r =	0	The transmit holding register or transmit shift register has a byte

1	The transmit holding register and the transmit shift register are both empty. In FIFO mode the transmit FIFO must also be empty for this state to occur.
5 r = 0	The transmit holding register has a byte. This state is set whenever the CPU loads a byte for sending.
1	The transmit holding register is empty and is ready to accept a new byte for transmission. If the transmit holding interrupt is enabled, an interrupt request is made when this bit is 1. In FIFO mode, this bit is set to 1 only when the transmit FIFO is empty.
4 r = 0	Normal (no break detected)
1	Break received. A break is signaled when an incoming signal remains high for longer than a full serial frame. This means the start bits, data, and parity are all high, but no stop bit (low) is received. The break bit is cleared when this register is read.
3 r = 1	Framing error occurred. While receiving a data, the stop bit was detected as high, when the stop bit should always be a low signal. The UART will attempt to resynchronize on the next frame received. A framing error usually indicates a noisy or poor signal. The framing error bit is cleared when this register is read.
2 r = 1	Parity error occurred. The received data's parity bit does not match the parity specified by the line control register (port 3FBh). The parity error bit is cleared when this register is read.
1 r = 1	Overrun error occurred. A second byte was received before the CPU read the prior received byte from the buffer. The new byte overwrites the prior byte, and the prior byte is lost. In FIFO mode, an overrun only occurs if the received FIFO buffer is full. The overrun error is cleared when this register is read.
0 r = 0	No received data is available. In FIFO mode, the received FIFO is empty.
1	Data ready indicator. A received byte is now available to be read by the CPU.

Register	Type	Description	Platform
6	I/O	Modem Status	Adapter

This register holds modem status flags. These flags show the current control line's state, and if the line has changed state since this register was last read.

Whenever a changed state bit 0 to 3 is set, and if the modem status interrupt is enabled, an interrupt is generated. After the register is read or a hardware is reset, bits 0 to 3 are set to zero.

In loopback mode, bits 4 to 7 show the state of the modem control register This can be useful for testing for stuck or cross connected bits inside the UART. Table 12-13 shows how the bits connect in loopback mode.

Table 12-13. Bits in Loopback Mode

Modem Status Port 3FEh	Modem Control Port 3FCh
bit 7	bit 3, OUT2
bit 6	bit 2, OUT1
bit 5	bit 0, DTR
bit 4	bit 1, RTS

I/O (bits 0-7)

bit	7 r/w = x	The connector's Data Carrier Detect line. During loopback mode, the OUT2 state from within the UART appears.
	6 r/w = x	The connector's Ring Indicator line. During loopback mode, the OUT1 state from within the UART appears.
	5 r/w = x	The connector's Data Set Ready line. During loopback mode, the RTS state from within the UART appears.
	4 r/w = x	The connector's Clear To Send line. During loopback mode, the DTR state from within the UART appears.
	3 r/w = 1	A change occurred on the Data Carrier Detect line
	2 r/w = 1	Falling edge of a high to low signal on the ring detect line occurred
	1 r/w = 1	A change occurred on the Data Set Ready line
	0 r/w = 1	A change occurred on the Clear To Send line

Register	Type	Description	Platform
7	I/O	Scratch Pad Register	Adapter

This often-overlooked register accesses an 8-bit read/write register in the UART. It is not used by the UART for any purpose, and can be used to hold temporary data. If a non-zero value is read from this port, you can assume some other application is likely using this register. There is no mechanism to prevent two different applications from using this port.

One interesting aspect of this register is that its contents remain valid through a hardware reset! It is not cleared by the UART or the BIOS when a hardware reset occurs. When the system is first powered up, my tests show the register is always set to zero, but UART manufacturers do not explain if this is assured.

This register is not supported on the original 8250 UART. It is provided on replacement versions commonly in use today, such as the 8250A, 16450, and 16550 UARTs. The 82510 UART also provides this register, but provides two alternate functions when not using it as a 16450-compatible UART. Consult the Intel 82510 manual for details.

CHAPTER 13

System Functions

This chapter covers the general BIOS system functions (interrupt 15h), and various system I/O ports that fail to fit into any other category. A number of functions and ports have never been published before.

Included are various system control and status flags, math coprocessor functions, diagnostic codes, and POST operations. Code examples are included to help clarify the exact use of more complicated functions

BIOS Services

Interrupt 15h system services are quite varied and many functions are limited to specific platforms. Some very early 80286 AT BIOSes do not support some services supported by all later AT+ platforms. It is wise to write programs defensively and assume a function might not be supported if a program is intended to run on a wide range of systems. All functions return an error code if the function is not supported.

Interrupt 15h provides the following services:

Function	Description	Platforms
ah=0	Turn Cassette Motor On	PC
ah=1	Turn Cassette Motor Off	PC
ah=2	Read from Cassette	PC
ah=3	Write to Cassette	PC
ah=4	Build System Parameter Table	MCA
ah=5	Build Initialization Table	MCA
ah=Fh*	Format in Progress	ESDI Drives
ah=21h	Error Log Read/Write	MCA
ah=22h	Get Unknown Segment	PS/1
ah=23h	Miscellaneous Undocumented Functions	PS/1
ah=24h	A20 Control	PS/1
ah=40h	Laptop Profile Read/Write	Convertible
ah=41h	Laptop Wait for External Event	Convertible
ah=42h	Laptop Power Off Request	Convertible
ah=43h	Laptop Read System Status	Convertible
ah=44h	Laptop Modem Power Control	Convertible
ah=49h	Get BIOS Type	DBCS
ah=4Fh*	Keyboard Intercept	AT+
ah=50h	Font Subsystem Access	DOS/V only
ah=52h	Removable Media Eject*	EBIOS
ah=80h	Device Open	AT+
ah=81h	Device Close	AT+
ah=82h	Program Terminate	AT+
ah=83h	Event Wait	AT+
ah=84h	Joystick Support	AT+
ah=85h*	System Request Key Pressed	AT+
ah=86h	Wait	AT+
ah=87h	Access Extended Memory	AT+
ah=88h	Extended Memory Size	AT+
ah=89h	Switch to Protected Mode	AT+
ah=90h*	Device Busy	AT+
ah=91h*	Interrupt Complete	AT+
ah=C0h	Return System BIOS Configuration	AT+
ah=C1h	Return Extended BIOS Data Area	AT+
ah=C2h	Mouse BIOS Interface	PS/2
ah=C3h	Watchdog Timer Control	MCA, EISA
ah=C4h	Programmable Option Select	MCA
ah=C5h*	Begin System Interrupt	PS/2
ah=C8h	Cache Control	PS/2

Function	Description	Platforms
ah=C9h	Get CPU Stepping	Some 386+
ah=CAh	Read/Write CMOS memory	PS/1
ah=D8h	Access EISA System Information	EISA

---

* *These functions are call-backs made by the BIOS, and should not be issued by an application. The BIOS calls interrupt 15h with these function numbers. An application can hook interrupt 15h, to take some action when a call-back function is issued by the BIOS.*

Int	Func	Description	Platform
15h	0	Turn Cassette Motor On	PC

INT

Turns the cassette drive motor on. This is a very obsolete function only provided on the PC and PCjr.

Called with: ah = 0

Returns: if supported

ah = 0, carry = 0

if not supported

ah = 86h, carry = 1

Int	Func	Description	Platform
15h	1	Turn Cassette Motor Off	PC

INT

Turns the cassette drive motor off. This is a very obsolete function only provided on the PC and PCjr.

Called with: ah = 1

Returns: if supported

ah = 0, carry = 0

if not supported

ah = 86h, carry = 1

Int	Func	Description	Platform
15h	2	Read from Cassette	PC

INT

Reads a number of 256-byte blocks from the cassette drive. The number of bytes to read should be a multiple of 256. This is a very obsolete function only provided on the PC and PCjr.

Called with: ah = 2
cx = number of bytes to read
es:bx = buffer where to store data from cassette

Returns: es:bx = pointer to one byte beyond last byte read
dx = number of bytes actually read
if no error occurred
carry = 0
if error occurred
carry = 1
ah = error code
1 = CRC error
2 = Lost data transitions
4 = No data found (timeout error)
86h = function not implemented

Int	Func	Description	Platform
15h	3	Write to Cassette	PC

Writes a number of 256-byte blocks from the cassette drive. The number of bytes to write should be a multiple of 256. This is a very obsolete function only provided on the PC and PCjr.

Called with: ah = 3
cx = number of bytes to write
es:bx = buffer of data to write

Returns: cx = 0
es:bx = pointer to one byte beyond last byte written
if no error occurred
carry = 0
if error occurred
carry = 1
ah = error code
1 = CRC error
2 = Lost data transitions
4 = No data found (timeout error)
86h = function not implemented

Int	Func	Description	Platform
15h	4	Build System Parameter Table	PS/2

IBM's PS/2 has a second BIOS, built into the standard BIOS, commonly referred to as the ABIOS. It is only used by OS/2, although OS/2 works fine on systems without the ABIOS. This function creates a table of system parameters and pointers in a user-supplied buffer. A brief outline of the system parameter table is shown in Table 13-1. Refer to the IBM Personal System/2 and Personal Computer BIOS Interface Technical Reference for additional details about the Advanced BIOS (ABIOS).

Table 13-1. ABIOS System Parameter Table

Hex Offset	Size	Description
0	dword	Common start routine pointer
4	dword	Common interrupt routine pointer
8	dword	Common timeout routine pointer
C	word	Number of bytes required for Stack
E	16 bytes	Reserved by IBM
1E	word	Number of entries required in the initialization table (described in interrupt 15h, function 5)

Called with: ah = 4
ds:0 = pointer to RAM extension area (ds=0 if no RAM extension area)
es:di = pointer to user-supplied 32-byte buffer

Returns: if no error occurred
carry = 0
ah = 0
al = undefined
es:di = user buffer loaded with ABIOS system parameter table (see Table 13-1)
if error occurred
carry = 1
ax = undefined
if function not supported
carry = 1, ah = 80h or 86h

Int	Func	Description	Platform
15h	5	Build Initialization Table	PS/2

On a PS/2, this function loads initialization data and pointers into a user-supplied table. This is used for OS/2 only. See function 4 to get the number of entries that will be returned in the buffer. Each entry takes 24 bytes. See Table 13-2 for a single initialization table entry.

Table 13-2. ABIOS Initialization Table

Offset (Hex)	Size	Description
0	word	Device ID 0 = ABIOS internal calls 1 = Diskette drive 2 = Hard disk drive 3 = Video 4 = Keyboard 5 = Parallel port 6 = Serial port 7 = System timer 8 = Real-Time Clock 9 = System services A = Non-Maskable Interrupt B = Mouse E = CMOS RAM F = DMA 10h = Programmable Option Select (POS) 16h = Keyboard Password
2	word	Number of logical IDs
4	word	Device block length in bytes (0 indicates ABIOS patch or extension and no device driver block is needed)
6	dword	Pointer to routine to initialize device block and function transfer table
A	word	Request block length in bytes
C	word	Function transfer table length in bytes
E	word	Data pointers length in bytes
10	byte	Secondary Device ID
11	byte	Revision
12	6 bytes	Unused or undocumented

Called with: ah = 5

ds:0 = pointer to RAM extension area (ds=0 if no RAM extension area)

es:di = pointer to user-supplied buffer

Returns: if no error occurred
carry = 0
ah = 0
al = undefined
es:di = user buffer loaded with ABIOS initialization table (see Table 13-2)
if error occurred
carry = 1
ax = undefined
if function not supported
carry = 1, ah = 80h or 86h

Int	Func	Description	Platform
15h	F	Format in Progress	ESDI Drives

INT III I

The PS/2 ESDI hard disk BIOS will call interrupt 15h, AH=F, when each cylinder completes formatting. This allows a format program to display the status of the format by hooking interrupt 15h and watching for this function. The function also indicates if a surface analysis or format is in progress, and allows termination of the disk format.

A format program would first hook interrupt 15h, function F, and then issue the interrupt 13h low-level format ESDI drive command. When interrupt 15h, function F occurs, the format program can increment a count to keep track of which cylinder was just formatted. The format program might display a percent complete based on the number of total cylinders and the number of function F calls that the format program intercepts. After each interception the carry flag state is cleared to continue the format, or set to safely abort the format.

Other drive types, including most non-PS/2 ESDI drives, do not provide a function to format the entire drive at one time, and do not need this type of interface. Unlike most BIOS functions, this function is not intended to be called by an application program.

Called with: ah = Fh (called only by hard disk BIOS)
al = 1 if surface analysis
2 if low-level disk format

Returns: carry = 0 to continue the formatting or analysis
1 to end formatting or analysis
if function not supported
carry = 1, ah = 80h or 86h

Int	Func	Description	Platform
15h	21h	Error Log Read/Write	MCA

INT III I

The MCA system has the ability to log errors that occur during the Power-On-Self-Test (POST) into the extended CMOS data area. This function provides the ability to read and write to the error log. POST error codes are usually the same values that are output to the diagnostic port. See port 680h near the end of this chapter for typical POST codes. Be aware that different models and vendors may assign different error codes; there has been no consistent standard. To date, this function has only been supported on MCA systems.

INT	Subfunction	Description	Int	Function
	AL=0	Read Error Log	15h	AH=21h

Gets a pointer to the beginning of the error log list and finds the number of recorded errors. Each error word is comprised of a device code in the high byte and a POST device error code in the low byte.

Called with: ax = 2100h

Returns: if function supported

carry = 0

ah = 0

bx = number of error codes entries recorded in log

es:di = pointer to first error code word

if function not supported

carry = 1

ah = 80h or 86h

INT	Subfunction	Description	Int	Function
	AL=1	Write Error Log	15h	AH=21h

Writes an error code word into the error log.

Called with: ax = 2101h

bh = device code

bl = device error

Returns: if function supported, and successful

carry = 0

ah = 0

if function supported, but failed (log is full)

carry = 1

ah = 1

if function not supported

carry = 1

ah = 80h or 86h

Int	Func	Description	Platform
15h	22h	Get Unknown Segment	PS/1

INT

This undocumented function returns a segment value inside the BIOS. In one 486 PS/1, this value was F774, derived from segment F000 plus offset 7740h. F774:0 contains a near jump instruction into an area of zeros. This function may not be fully implemented or has some unknown purpose. It is never executed by the BIOS.

Called with: ah = 22h

Returns: if function supported

carry = 0

es = segment value (see text)

ax = 0

if function not supported

carry = 1

ah = 80h or 86h

Int	Func	Description	Platform
15h	23h	Miscellaneous Undocumented Functions	PS/1

INT

This group of functions appears in the IBM 486 PS/1 BIOS and may appear in other recent IBM BIOSes. There are four subfunctions.

AL=	Subfunctions
0	Get CMOS Registers 2D & 2E
1	Set CMOS Registers 2D & 2E
4	System Setup
5	Get Processor Speed

Subfunction	Description	Int	Function
AL=0	Get CMOS Registers 2D & 2E	15h	AH=23h

INT

Called with: ax = 2300h

Returns: if function supported

carry = 0

ax = 2300h

cl = CMOS register 2Dh (undocumented)

ch = CMOS register 2Eh (undocumented)

if function not supported

carry = 1

ah = 80h or 86h

Subfunction	Description	Int	Function
AL=1	Set CMOS Registers 2D & 2E	15h	AH=23h

Called with: ax = 2301h

cl = value to load CMOS register 2Dh (undocumented)

ch = value to load CMOS register 2Eh (undocumented)

Returns: if function supported

ax = 2301h

carry = 0

if function not supported

carry = 1

ah = 80h or 86h

Subfunction	Description	Int	Function
AL=4	System Setup	15h	AH=23h

Initiates system setup operations. This function displays information about the current system settings, and allows the user to change those settings. If the user elects to save the changes, CMOS memory is updated to reflect the new settings. This function will force the video mode to color text, using mode 3. Upon exit, video mode 3 is issued again to clear the screen.

Called with: ax = 2304h

dx = segment of 32 KB RAM buffer for operation

Returns: if function supported

carry = 0

ax = 3

bx, cx, dx, bp, ds, es are modified

if function not supported

carry = 1

ah = 80h or 86h

Subfunction	Description	Int	Function
AL=5	Get Processor Speed	15h	AH=23h

Returns the processor speed calculated by POST and normalized to standard speed values. Possible speeds include: 20, 25, 33, 40, 50, 66, and 80 MHz. If the speed was not measured or was too fast, the function returns the carry flag set.

Called with: ax = 2305h

Returns: if successful

carry = 0
ah = 23h
al = Processor speed in Megahertz

if unknown speed or speed above 80 MHz

carry = 1
ah = 23h
al = FFh

if function not supported

carry = 1
ah = 80h or 86h

Int	Func	Description	Platform
15h	24h	A20 Control	PS/1

These functions control the A20 gate. When enabled, all of extended memory is accessible. When disabled, the A20 address line is forced low to simulate an 8088 address map. This group of functions appears in the IBM 486 PS/1 BIOS and may appear on other recent BIOSes. A20 control has four subfunctions.

AL=	A20 Control Subfunctions
0	Disable A20
1	Enable A20
2	Get A20 Gate Status
3	Unknown Function

Subfunction	Description	Int	Function
AL=0	Disable A20	15h	AH=24h

Called with: ax = 2400h

Returns: if function supported

carry = 0
ah = 0

if function not supported
carry = 1
ah = 80h or 86h

Subfunction	Description	Int	Function
AL=1	Enable A20	15h	AH=24h

Called with: ax = 2401h

Returns: if function supported
carry = 0
ah = 0
if function not supported
carry = 1
ah = 80h or 86h

Subfunction	Description	Int	Function
AL=2	Get A20 Gate Status	15h	AH=24h

Called with: ax = 2402h

Returns: if function supported
carry = 0
ah = 0
al = 0 A20 disabled
1 A20 enabled
if function not supported
carry = 1
ah = 80h or 86h

Subfunction	Description	Int	Function
AL=3	Unknown Function	15h	AH=24h

On the IBM 486 PS/1, this function does nothing other than return the value 2 in BX. Other models might return other hard-coded values or perform other actions.

Called with: ax = 2403h

Returns: if function supported
carry = 0
ah = 0
bx = 2 (see text)

if function not supported
carry = 1
ah = 80h or 86h

Int	Func	Description	Platform
15h	40h	Laptop Profile Read/Write	Convertible

This function gets or sets the PC Convertible's system and modem profiles. Other laptop vendors may also use this function. It is not documented on any other platform. Most of the information for function 40h comes from the IBM technical reference, and is quite vague. Since the functions are only supported on the obsolete Convertible, I've somewhat glossed over these services. Function 40h has four subfunctions.

AL=	Laptop Subfunctions
0	Read System Profile
1	Write System Profile
2	Read Internal Modem Profile
3	Write Internal Modem Profile

Subfunction	Description	Int	Function
AL=0	Read System Profile	15h	AH=40h

Called with: ax = 4000h
Returns: if function supported
carry = 0
ah = 0
bx = profile information 1
cx = profile information 2
if function not supported or failed
carry = 1
ah = 80h or 86h

Subfunction	Description	Int	Function
AL=1	Write System Profile	15h	AH=40h

Called with: ax = 4001h
bx = profile information 1
cx = profile information 2

Returns: if function supported
  carry = 0
  ah = 0
 if function not supported or failed
  carry = 1
  ah = 80h or 86h

Subfunction	Description	Int	Function
AL=2	Read Internal Modem Profile	15h	AH=40h

Called with: ax = 4002h
Returns: if function supported
  carry = 0
  ah = 0
  bx = modem profile information
 if function not supported or failed
  carry = 1
  ah = 80h or 86h

Subfunction	Description	Int	Function
AL=3	Write Internal Modem Profile	15h	AH=40h

Called with: ax = 4003h
 bx = modem profile information
Returns: if function supported
  carry = 0
  ah = 0
 if function not supported or failed
  carry = 1
  ah = 80h or 86h

Int	Func	Description	Platform
15h	41h	Laptop Wait for External Event	Convertible

This function waits for an event to occur, and returns when the specified event occurs, or after an optional timeout period elapses. It is only supported on the PC Convertible, but other laptop vendors may also use this function. It is not documented on any other platform. Like function 40h, most of the function 41h information comes from the IBM technical reference, and is somewhat vague. Since the functions are only supported on the obsolete Convertible, I've skipped any detailed analysis of these subfunctions. Function 41h has ten subfunctions.

AL=	Laptop Wait Subfunctions
0	Return after any Event
1	Compare Memory, Return When Equal
2	Compare Memory, Return When Not Equal
3	Test Memory Bit, Return if Not Zero
4	Test Memory Bit, Return if Zero
10h	Return after any Event
11h	Compare Port, Return When Equal
12h	Compare Port, Return When Not Equal
13h	Test Port Bit, Return if Not Zero
14h	Test Port Bit, Return if Zero

Subfunction	Description	Int	Function
AL=0	Return after any Event	15h	AH=41h

INT

Called with: ax = 4100h
bl = timeout value in 55 ms steps (0 = no timeout)

Returns: if function supported, returns after event occurred
carry = 0
if function supported, but timed out
carry = 1
if function not supported
carry = 1
ah = 80h or 86h

Subfunction	Description	Int	Function
AL=1	Compare Memory, Return When Equal	15h	AH=41h

INT

Called with: ax = 4101h
bh = value to compare
bl = timeout value in 55 ms steps (0 = no timeout)
es:di = ptr to byte—wait until equals BH

Returns: if function supported, byte matches BH
carry = 0
if function supported, but timed out
carry = 1
if function not supported
carry = 1
ah = 80h or 86h

INT	Subfunction	Description	Int	Function
	AL=2	Compare Memory, Return When Not Equal	15h	AH=41h

Called with: ax = 4102h
bh = value to compare
bl = timeout value in 55 ms steps (0 = no timeout)
es:di = ptr to byte—wait until not equal to BH

Returns: if function supported, byte not equal to BH
carry = 0
if function supported, but timed out
carry = 1
if function not supported
carry = 1
ah = 80h or 86h

INT	Subfunction	Description	Int	Function
	AL=3	Test Memory Bit, Return if Not Zero	15h	AH=41h

Called with: ax = 4103h
bh = mask value
bl = timeout value in 55 ms steps (0 = no timeout)
es:di = ptr to byte—wait until value and BH not zero

Returns: if function supported, bit not zero
carry = 0
if function supported, but timed out
carry = 1
if function not supported
carry = 1
ah = 80h or 86h

Subfunction	Description	Int	Function
AL=4	Test Memory Bit, Return if Zero	15h	AH=41h

INT

Called with: ax = 4104h
bh = mask value
bl = timeout value in 55 ms steps (0 = no timeout)
es:di = ptr to byte—wait until value and BH is zero

Returns: if function supported, bit zero
carry = 0
if function supported, but timed out
carry = 1
if function not supported
carry = 1
ah = 80h or 86h

Subfunction	Description	Int	Function
AL=10h	Return after any Event	15h	AH=41h

INT

Same functionally as subfunction AL=0.

Subfunction	Description	Int	Function
AL=11h	Compare Port, Return When Equal	15h	AH=41h

INT

Called with: ax = 4111h
bh = value to compare
bl = timeout value in 55 ms steps (0 = no timeout)
dx = I/O port to read until equals BH

Returns: if function supported, byte matches BH
carry = 0
if function supported, but timed out
carry = 1
if function not supported
carry = 1
ah = 80h or 86h

Subfunction	Description	Int	Function
AL=12h	Compare Port, Return When Not Equal	15h	AH=41h

Called with: ax = 4112h
bh = value to compare
bl = timeout value in 55 ms steps (0 = no timeout)
dx = I/O port to read until it does not equal BH

Returns: if function supported, byte not equal to BH
carry = 0
if function supported, but timed out
carry = 1
if function not supported
carry = 1
ah = 80h or 86h

Subfunction	Description	Int	Function
AL=13h	Test Port Bit, Return if Not Zero	15h	AH=41h

Called with: ax = 4113h
bh = mask value
bl = timeout value in 55 ms steps (0 = no timeout)
dx = I/O port to read until value AND BH not zero

Returns: if function supported, bit not zero
carry = 0
if function supported, but timed out
carry = 1
if function not supported
carry = 1
ah = 80h or 86h

Subfunction	Description	Int	Function
AL=14h	Test Port Bit, Return if Zero	15h	AH=41h

Called with: ax = 4114h
bh = mask value
bl = timeout value in 55 ms steps (0 = no timeout)
dx = I/O port to read until value AND BH is zero

Returns: if function supported, bit zero
carry = 0
if function supported, but timed out
carry = 1
if function not supported
carry = 1
ah = 80h or 86h

Int	Func	Description	Platform
15h	42h	Laptop Power Off Request	Convertible

INT III I

Requests the laptop to power down. It is only supported on the PC Convertible, but other laptop vendors may also use this function. It is not documented on any other platform.

Called with: ah = 42h
al = 0 Use system profile for power down
1 Force power down, ignore profile
Returns: if function supported
ax = undefined
if function not supported
carry = 1
ah = 80h or 86h

Int	Func	Description	Platform
15h	43h	Laptop Read System Status	Convertible

INT III I

Read the system status. It is only supported on the PC Convertible, but other laptop vendors may also use this function. It is not documented on any other platform.

Called with: ah = 43h
Returns: if function supported
ah = undefined
al = status
bit 7 = 1 Low battery
6 = 1 Operating on external power
5 = 1 Standby power lost, clock wrong
4 = 1 Power activated by clock alarm
3 = 1 Internal modem is powered up
2 = 1 Serial & Parallel port powered up

1 = x unused
0 = 1 LCD not attached
if function not supported
carry = 1
ah = 80h or 86h

INT	Int	Func	Description	Platform
	15h	44h	Laptop Modem Power Control	Convertible

Controls the power to the internal modem. It is only supported on the PC Convertible, but other laptop vendors may also use this function. It is not documented on any other platform.

Called with: ah = 44h
al = modem power state
0 = off
1 = on and setup based on modem profile
Returns: if function supported
carry = 0
ah = 0
if function not supported or failed
carry = 1
ah = 80h or 86h

INT	Int	Func	Description	Platform
	15h	49h	Get BIOS Type	DBCS

This function is only available when the BIOS or operating system supports the Double Byte Character Set (DBCS). For example DOS/V makes DBCS support available on a standard AT or MCA system. This function works even if the DOS/V environment is set to English.

Called with: ax = 4900h
Returns: if function supported
carry = 0
ah = 0
bl = BIOS mode
0 = DOS/V
1 = Ordinary DBCS DOS BIOS (hardware DBCS support)
if function not supported
carry = 1
ah = 80h or 86h

Int	Func	Description	Platform
15h	4Fh	Keyboard Intercept	AT+

Beginning with the AT, IBM's engineers added the ability to hook the low-level keyboard stream. After the interrupt 9 keyboard BIOS routine reads a key scan code, the BIOS immediately makes a call to interrupt 15h, with AH=4Fh. The AL register has the scan code of the key that was read. The carry flag is set to indicate the key is valid. Multiple applications can hook interrupt 15h and look for function 4Fh. Should an important key combination occur, the application can take one of three actions:

1. Ignore the key, pass the key onto other hooked applications, and back to the BIOS keyboard handler to process. The carry flag is left on in this case.
2. Absorb the key, and appear as if the key never occurred. This is useful for TSR hot keys. The TSR internally records that the hot key occurred so the TSR can take an action at a later time. The TSR clears the carry flag to indicate there is no longer a key to process. Other applications that have hooked interrupt 15h and the BIOS keyboard handler will ignore the key. The keyboard BIOS will still be responsible for clearing the interrupt request.
3. Substitute a different key scan code for the one that occurred. In this scenario, the value in AL is changed, but the carry flag is left on. Any other applications hooking interrupt 15h after this application and the BIOS keyboard handler will see only the new key. Remember that the changed key must be a scan code value and not ASCII.

To see if the low-level keyboard handler supports this function, use interrupt 15h, function C0h to get the feature information byte 5. If bit 4 is set, then the keyboard BIOS supports the 4Fh keyboard intercept function. The system BIOS handling of this function will simply issue an IRET without any effect to registers or to the carry flag.

Called with: ah = 4Fh (called only by int 9)
al = keyboard scan code value
carry = 1 key is valid
0 key is invalid

Returns: al = same or altered scan code
carry = 1 to let keyboard BIOS process key
0 to make the key disappear
if function not supported (PC/XT)
carry = 1
ah = 80h or 86h

Int	Func	Description	Platform
15h	50h	Font Subsystem Access	DOS/V only

This function controls the DOS/V font system. It is only available when DOS/V is installed. This function has two subfunctions.

Subfunction	Description	Int	Function
AL=0	Get Read Font Function Address	15h	AH=50h

Called with: ax = 5000h

bh = font type

- 0 = Single Byte Character Set
- 1 = Double Byte Character Set

bl = 0

dh = font cell width

dl = font cell height

bp = code page

- 0 = Default code page
- 437 = US English
- 932 = Japanese
- 934 = Korea
- 936 = China
- 938 = Taiwan

Returns: if function supported, and successful

- carry = 0
- ah = 0
- es:bx = pointer to Read Font function

if function failed

- carry = 1
- ah = error code
  - 1 = BH font type not 0 or 1
  - 2 = BL not 0
  - 3 = DX font size invalid
  - 4 = BP code page invalid
  - 80h = function not supported (PC)
  - 86h = function not supported (XT)

Subfunction	Description	Int	Function
AL=1	Get Write Font Function Address	15h	AH=50h

Called with: ax = 5001h
bh = font type
0 = Single Byte Character Set
1 = Double Byte Character Set
bl = 0
dh = font cell width
dl = font cell height
bp = code page
0 = Default code page
437 = US English
932 = Japanese
934 = Korea
936 = China
938 = Taiwan

Returns: if function supported, and successful
carry = 0
ah = 0
es:bx = pointer to Write Font function
if function failed
carry = 1
ah = error code
1 = BH font type not 0 or 1
2 = BL not 0
3 = DX font size invalid
4 = BP code page invalid
80h = function not supported (PC)
86h = function not supported (XT)

Int	Func	Description	Platform
15h	52h	Removable Media Eject	EBIOS

This function is issued by the hard disk EBIOS when interrupt 13h, function 46h, eject removable media is issued. It should not be called by a program. Refer to the Chapter 11, Hard Disk System, for complete details.

Int	Func	Description	Platform
15h	80h	Device Open	AT+

The Device Open function is part of a protocol between an application and a multitasking operating system like OS/2. This function is issued by an application. The Device Open signals the OS that the caller is going to use a device.

When the operating system is installed, it hooks this function so that it gets Device Open requests from applications. When not hooked by a operating system, the system BIOS may return success or failure, depending on the specific BIOS. The BIOS performs no action, other than returning. IBM defined the following convention for use by a multitasking environment.

Called with: ah = 80h
bx = device ID
cx = process ID

Returns: if successful or not supported (AT+)
carry = 0
ah = 0
if function not supported (PC/XT)
carry = 1
ah = 80h or 86h

Int	Func	Description	Platform
15h	81h	Device Close	AT+

The Device Close function is part of a protocol between an application and a multitasking operating system like OS/2. This function is issued by an application. The Device Close signals the OS that the caller no longer needs the specified device.

When the operating system is installed, it hooks this function so that it gets Device Close requests from applications. When not hooked by an operating system, the system BIOS may return success or failure, depending on the specific BIOS. The BIOS performs no action, other than returning. IBM defined the following convention for use by a multitasking environment.

Called with: ah = 81h
bx = device ID
cx = process ID

Returns: if successful or not supported (AT+)
carry = 0
ah = 0
if function not supported (PC/XT)
carry = 1
ah = 80h or 86h

Int	Func	Description	Platform
15h	82h	Program Terminate	AT+

The Program Terminate function is part of a protocol between an application and a multitasking operating system like OS/2. This function is issued by an application. The Program Terminate signals the OS that the application is finished with all devices, and all devices can be closed. See functions 80h and 81h for additional details.

When the operating system is installed, it hooks this function so that it gets the Program Terminate request from an application. When not hooked by an operating system, the system BIOS may return success or failure, depending on the specific BIOS. The BIOS performs no action, other than returning. IBM defined the following convention for use by a multitasking environment.

Called with: ah = 82h
cx = process ID

Returns: if successful or not supported (AT+)
carry = 0
ah = 0
if function not supported (PC/XT)
carry = 1
ah = 80h or 86h

Int	Func	Description	Platform
15h	83h	Event Wait	AT+

This function is used to set a flag in user's memory when a time period elapses. The function returns to the user immediately after being issued. There are two subfunctions to begin or cancel the event wait.

Subfunction	Description	Int	Function
AL=0	Begin Event Wait	15h	AH=83h

This subfunction checks if the event wait function is available and, if so, sets up the CMOS RTC to issue interrupt 70h every 976 ms. The 32-bit countdown timer value is stored in the BIOS data area at 40:9Ch. The pointer to the user's flag byte is stored at 40:98h. The event wait in-use flag is bit 0 at address 40:A0h. These BIOS data items are shared with function 86h (Wait), such that only one function is allowable at one time. The in-use flag protects either function from overlapping a prior instance from another application.

After this subfunction is issued, interrupt 70h decrements the 32-bit counter every 976 microseconds. When the count reaches zero, the event elapsed bit 7 is set at the byte address of the supplied pointer. The caller is responsible to clear the event elapsed flag before issuing this function.

Some older PS/2 AT systems fail to support this function, and act as if the function is always in use.

Called with: ax = 8300h
cx:dx = 32-bit microsecond count (decremented by 976 every 976 ms)
es:bx = far pointer to byte in user memory

Returns: if successful
carry = 0
ah = 0
al = current contents of CMOS register B (see Chapter 15)
if function in use and unavailable
carry = 1
ax = 0
if function not supported (PC/XT)
carry = 1
ah = 80h or 86h

Subfunction	Description	Int	Function
AL=1	Cancel Event Wait	15h	AH=83h

Cancels the current event wait. In normal operation, when the event wait completes, it is automatically ready for the next user. This function is normally used to clear an event wait that has not yet elapsed. The subfunction turns off the periodic interrupt generated by the CMOS RTC and clears the BIOS data area's event in-progress bit 0, at 40:A0h. Only an event wait that was issued by the calling program should be canceled. Canceling an event wait from another application may cause that other program to hang.

The very first AT BIOS did not support this subfunction, and some PS/2 AT bus versions also fail to support this subfunction.

Called with: ax = 8301h

Returns: if successful
carry = 0
if function not supported
carry = 1
ah = 80h or 86h

Int	Func	Description	Platform
15h	84h	Joystick Support	AT+

INT

This function reads the switches and analog joystick position from up to four joysticks. With two joysticks, both an X and Y position for each joystick are supported. With four joysticks, only a single X position is available on each joystick. No checks are made by the BIOS to see if a joystick adapter or joystick is actually attached.

Subfunction	Description	Int	Function
AL=0	Read Joystick Switches	15h	AH=84h

INT

This subfunction simply inputs a byte from the joystick port 201h and strips off the lower four bits. What remains is the state of up to four switches, depending on the joysticks used.

Called with: ah = 84h
dx = 0

Returns: if successful
carry = 0
al = switch states
bit 7 = x joystick B, switch 2
6 = x joystick B, switch 1
5 = x joystick A, switch 2
4 = x joystick A, switch 1
3 = 0
2 = 0
1 = 0
0 = 0
if function not supported (PC/XT)
carry = 1
ah = 80h or 86h

Subfunction	Description	Int	Function
AL=1	Read Joystick Position	15h	AH=84h

INT

Checks the position of the four possible analog inputs from the joysticks. Each analog control has a variable resistor that connects to the joystick adapter. To measure the position, the resistor controls a timer that returns a different time delay depending on position. By measuring the time delay, the position is established. This involves disabling interrupts for a short period while each analog joystick position is timed.

Called with: ah = 84h
dx = 1

Returns: if successful
carry = 0
ax = Joystick A, X coordinate value
bx = Joystick A, Y coordinate value
cx = Joystick B, X coordinate value
dx = Joystick B, Y coordinate value
if function not supported (PC/XT)
carry = 1
ah = 80h or 86h

Int	Func	Description	Platform
15h	85h	System Request Key Pressed	AT+

When the Sys Req key is pressed, the low-level interrupt 9 keyboard handler issues this function. An application can hook this function to be notified whenever the Sys Req key state changes. It is not intended to be called directly by an application program. When called, the default system BIOS interrupt 15h handler performs no action.

Called with: ah = 85h (called only by int 9)
al = 0 Sys Req key now down
1 Sys Req key now released

Returns: if implemented
carry = 1
ah = 0
if function not supported (PC/XT)
carry = 1
ah = 80h or 86h

Int	Func	Description	Platform
15h	86h	Wait	AT+

Waits until the specified time period elapses. The caller does not regain control until the wait period elapses. See function 83h (Event Wait), for an alternative approach. A 32-bit counter holds the wait period value in microseconds.

When issued, the system BIOS checks if another wait is in-progress from this function or from function 83h. If so, the function returns without the wait occurring. When the wait is allowable, an operation identical to function 83h occurs, except the system BIOS has the event elapsed byte at address 40:A0h. The function waits in a tight loop until bit 7 is set, indicating the time period has elapsed, and then returns to the user.

The resolution of the wait function is 976 microseconds. This means the count is reduced by 976 every 976 microseconds until the count goes below zero. Some system BIOS services may call this function to time operations, like the diskette head settling. These internal BIOS routines are designed to switch to a software timing loop if the Wait function is already in use.

Called with: ah = 86h
cx:dx = 32-bit count in microseconds

Returns: if successful
carry = 0
ah = 0
al = undefined
if function in use and unavailable
carry = 1
ah = 0
if function not supported (PC/XT)
carry = 1
ah = 80h or 86h

Int	Func	Description	Platform
15h	87h	Access Extended Memory	AT+

INT
III I

This function can transfer up to 64K of data between the first 1 MB-address range and extended memory. On 386 and later systems, the function allows up to 128K, less one word, to be transferred. It can be very slow on 286 systems, as the system must go into protected mode, and the CPU goes through a slow reset process to get back to real mode. Be aware that interrupts are disabled while the block move occurs and may be disabled for an excessively long period.

Most programs today should use the old EMS standard or preferably the newer XMS memory standard to reliably coexist with other applications. Function 87h access to extended memory is not managed, and two applications that rely on accessing extended memory can easily corrupt each other's data stored in extended memory! This function can also cause a system to crash if a memory manager is in use and has already allocated extended memory. Most memory managers prevent this function from operating.

Since you're still reading, you must be a very brave soul to ignore my prior warnings, or else you're just interested in how this function works. This function is more complicated than other BIOS services. A set of descriptors are used to describe the source and destination of the memory in terms the CPU understands. This is shown in Table 13-3. You also need to know if the CPU is a 286 or 386 or later, since the descriptor changes between CPU families. I provide a real code example at the end of this function.

Table 13-3. Table Structure for Extended Memory Access

es:si Offset	Description
0	Unused descriptor (must be all zeros)
8	GDT descriptor (must be all zeros, filled in by BIOS)
10h	Source descriptor, where data comes from
18h	Destination descriptor, where data is placed
20h	Code descriptor (must be all zeros, filled in by BIOS)
28h	Stack descriptor (must be all zeros, filled in by BIOS)

Each descriptor holds the limit of access, the address to use, and a byte indicating how the section of memory can be accessed. The segment limit describes how much memory the descriptor can access. On a 286, the value FFFF sets the maximum limit, 64K. On a 386 or later, a limit of 1FFFFh makes a limit of 128K, the largest value supported by this BIOS function. Two descriptors are used to indicate the source memory location and the destination location. These are shown in Tables 13-4 and 13-5, depending on the system's CPU.

Table 13-4. 286 Descriptor for Extended Memory Access

Offset	Size	Description
0	word	Segment limit—the number of bytes minus one. Use the value FFFF to access 64K.
2	word	16-bit lower part of 24-bit physical address
4	byte	8-bit upper part of 24-bit physical address
5	byte	access rights byte, 93h = read/writeable
6	word	unused (must be zero)

Table 13-5. 386 and Later CPU Descriptor for Extended Memory Access

Offset	Size	Description
0	word	Segment limit, lower 16-bits of a 20-bit limit—the number of bytes minus one.
2	word	16-bit lower part of 32-bit physical address
4	byte	8-bit middle part of 32-bit physical address
5	byte	access rights byte, 93h = read/writeable
6	byte	low 4-bits are the upper most bits for the 20-bit segment limit. The upper 4-bits are flags that, for this function, should be set to zero.
7	byte	8-bit upper part of 32-bit physical address

Called with: ah = 87h
cx = number of words to transfer
es:si = pointer to 48-byte table of descriptors (see Table 13-3)

Returns: if successful
carry = 0
ah = 0
if function failed
carry = 1
ah = error code
1 = memory parity error occurred
2 = some other exception interrupt occurred
3 = turning on address line 20 failed (commonly referred to as the A20 gate)
if function not supported (pre-286 systems)
carry = 1
ah = 80h or 86h

As an example, a program might wish to save 32K from the display area into extended memory starting at the 4 MB address point. I've assumed the program has already used function 88h to check that the desired extended memory exists, and has checked that the CPU is a 386 or later.

```
        mov   ah, 87h            ; access extended memory
        mov   cx, 4000h          ; transfer 32K (16K words)
        push  cs
        pop   es
        mov   si, offset GDTdata ; es:si = pointer to our table
        int   15h                ; have BIOS perform move
        jc    failure
        .                        ; gets here if success
        .
failure:
        .                        ; gets here if problem

; User-supplied table of descriptors
GDTdata dw      4 dup (0)          ; unused descriptor
        dw      4 dup (0)          ; GDT descriptor
```

```
; start of source descriptor (for C8000h)
        dw      0FFFFh              ; seg limit, 20-bit value = 1FFFFh
        dw      08000h              ; source, 32-bit value = C8000h
        db      0Ch                 ; source, middle 8 bits
        db      93h                 ; access rights, read/write
        db      1                   ; flags and top of seg limit
        db      0                   ; source, top 8 bits

; start of destination descriptor (for 4000000h)
        dw      0FFFFh              ; seg limit, 20-bit value = 1FFFFh
        dw      0                   ; source, 32-bit value = 400000h
        db      40h                 ; source, middle 8 bits
        db      93h                 ; access rights, read/write
        db      1                   ; flags and top of seg limit
        db      0                   ; source, top 8 bits

; remainder of table
        dw      4 dup (0)           ; code descriptor
        dw      4 dup (0)           ; stack descriptor
```

INT

Int	Func	Description	Platform
15h	88h	Extended Memory Size	AT+

This function gets the total amount of extended memory in 1K blocks. When no application hooks this function, most BIOSes return the value stored in CMOS registers 30 and 31h. IBM's PS/2 and PS/1 use CMOS registers 35 and 36h to hold the amount of extended memory in the system.

Programs that use extended memory, such as memory managers, will reduce this value by the amount they use. Most memory managers consume all extended memory and (unless instructed otherwise with some sort of switch) will force this function to return a zero value.

Called with: ah = 88h

Returns: if successful

carry = 0

ax = number of 1K blocks of extended memory

if function not supported (pre-286 systems)

carry = 1

ah = 80h or 86h

Int	Func	Description	Platform
15h	89h	Switch to Protected Mode	AT+

This function switches the CPU into protected mode using information provided in a 64-byte table of descriptors. You should be familiar with protected mode, descriptors, and other CPU-specific aspects before using this function. The table of descriptors must be defined by the user prior to executing this function. The descriptor table is shown in Table 13-6. Remember that the format for the descriptor is different between the 286 and 386 or later CPUs. On 386 through Pentium Pro CPUs, the FS and GS segments are not valid until the user loads these descriptors after going into protected mode.

None of the system BIOS services are available while in protected mode. This means the user's code must handle all hardware interrupts. To accomplish this, the BIOS reloads the interrupt controllers with new user-supplied interrupt numbers. These new interrupt numbers are used as indexes into the user's Interrupt Descriptor Table (IDT). Both controllers are set to mask off all hardware interrupts. The user's code in protected mode has the responsibility to unmask hardware interrupts that are going to be supported. In addition, the user's protected mode interrupt descriptor table cannot overlap the real mode interrupt table.

The BIOS function activates address line 20, the A20 gate. The A20 line is locked to zero after POST completes, and is used to make the system appear like an 8088. Activating the A20 gate means the CPU can access all memory addresses in the system.

Once A20 is activated and the interrupt controllers are set, the BIOS sets up the BIOS CS descriptor for its own code. The BIOS loads the Global Descriptor Table register (GDTR) and Interrupt Descriptor Table Register (IDTR). The BIOS then activates protected mode. While in protected mode, the BIOS loads the user's data segments and finally returns to the caller in protected mode.

Table 13-6. Protected Mode GDT

es:si Offset	Description
0	Unused descriptor (must be all zeros)
8	Global Descriptor Table (GDT) descriptor (user supplied)
10h	Interrupt Descriptor Table (IDT) descriptor (user supplied)
18h	DS descriptor (user supplied)
20h	ES descriptor (user supplied)
28h	CS descriptor (user supplied)
30h	SS descriptor (user supplied)
38h	Temporary BIOS CS descriptor (BIOS defined, user values ignored)

Called with: ah = 89h
bh = first interrupt number for block of hardware interrupt requests IRQ 0 to 7
bl = first interrupt number for block of hardware interrupt requests IRQ 8 to 15
es:si = pointer to 64-byte table of descriptors (see Table 13-6)

Returns: if successful and in protected mode
carry = 0
ah = 0
al = undefined
bp = undefined
ds = 18h
es = 20h
ss = 28h
cs = 30h

if function unable to unlock A20 gate and remains in real mode
carry = 1
ah = FFh
al = undefined

if function not supported (pre-286 systems)
carry = 1
ah = 80h or 86h

Int	Func	Description	Platform
15h	90h	Device Busy	AT+

A number of BIOS routines begin an operation and will not return until the operation completes. This function provides a hook to let some other program or multitasking operating system gain control during the wait for the device operation to become complete. Only when a timeout period elapses or the device completes will this function return. If the device busy function is not hooked, the system BIOS simply returns and lets the calling routine wait for a timeout or device completion. This function is not intended to be called by a user application, but only by system BIOS code and some hardware device drivers.

For example, the diskette BIOS sets up a transfer of data from the diskette, and waits for the controller to interrupt the system when the data has been transferred. This may take up to 2 seconds, so interrupt 15h function 90h is issued. If no one hooked it, the system BIOS simply returns with the carry flag cleared, indicating the diskette BIOS must wait until a timeout period expires or the operation is complete.

Let's assume a multitasking operating system has hooked interrupt 15h, functions 90h and 91h. When an interrupt 15h, function 90h occurs, the operating system gets control and looks at the value passed in AL. For this example, the diskette interrupt has just been called. The diskette device type is 1, and the operating system can go off and run some other task for several seconds. In normal operation, the diskette service interrupt occurs before 2 seconds, and the diskette hardware interrupt handler issues interrupt 15h, with function 91h, and a device code of 1. The system sees this fact and records that the diskette function is now complete. The system returns from the interrupt 15h, function 91h so the interrupt handler can complete its operation. When convenient, the operating system returns to the caller of the interrupt 15h, function 90h, and sets the carry flag, indicating to the diskette BIOS that no further wait is required.

There are three classes for the device types defined in Table 13-7, as follows:

- Class 1: Non-reentrant devices, which only one user can access at a time. These devices use device type values 0 to 7Fh. All of these devices have a hardware interrupt handler that will issue interrupt 15h, function 91h, when the device completes.
- Class 2: Reentrant devices, which can be called multiple times. These devices use device type values 80h to BFh. All of these devices have a hardware interrupt handler that will issue interrupt 15h, function 91h, when the device completes. In addition, this class must provide a device control block in ES:BX to uniquely identify which instance of the device is being handled. This device control block format is specified by the operating system. The system BIOS does not contain any class 2 type devices.
- Class 3: Devices which do not have a hardware interrupt for the wait function and must simply wait a period of time. For example, when the diskette motor is turned on, the diskette BIOS will wait 2 seconds for the motor to get to speed before performing a write.

Table 13-7. Device Type Codes

Device Number	BIOS Interrupt	Device and Reason	Timeout?
0	13h	Hard disk BIOS, wait for data	yes
1	13h	Diskette BIOS, wait for data	yes
2	16h	Keyboard BIOS, wait for key	no
3		Mouse	yes
80h		Network	no
FCh	13h	Hard disk BIOS, reset	yes
FDh	13h	Diskette BIOS, motor start	yes
FEh	17h	Printer BIOS, busy printing	yes

Called with: ah = 90h (by BIOS or device driver)
al = device number (see Table 13-7)
es:bx = device control block, if al=80h to BFh

Returns: if wait has not been satisfied
carry = 0
if device completed or timeout period elapsed
carry = 1
if function not supported (pre-286 systems)
carry = 1
ah = 80h or 86h

Int	Func	Description	Platform
15h	91h	Interrupt Complete	AT+

A hardware device has issued an interrupt indicating it is complete. See function 90h for details of how this function is used. This function is not intended to be called by a user application, but by only system BIOS code and some hardware device drivers. Table 13-8 shows the device codes that are currently defined. Additional device codes should follow the class types described in function 90h.

Table 13-8. Device Type Codes

Device Number	BIOS Interrupt	Device
0	76h	Hard disk operation complete interrupt
1	Eh	Diskette operation complete interrupt
2	9	Keyboard BIOS, key has been pressed
3		Mouse interrupt
80h		Network interrupt

Called with: ah = 91h (by BIOS or device driver)
al = device number (see Table 13-8)
es:bx = device control block, if al=80h to BFh

Returns: if supported
ah = 0
carry = 0
if function not supported (pre-286 systems)
carry = 1
ah = 80h or 86h

Int	Func	Description	Platform
15h	C0h	Return System BIOS Configuration	some XTs, AT+

Gets a pointer to configuration information in the system BIOS ROM. This information often resides at F000:E6F5h, but starting with the PS/2, IBM no longer retains a fixed location for this table. The table is typically 10 bytes long. Table 13-9 shows the standard contents of the configuration table. Even though some fields have possible alternate values on older systems, only values possible on AT and later systems are shown, since this function is not available on older systems.

Table 13-9. BIOS ROM Configuration Information

Offset	Size	Description
0	word	Size of table following this word, in bytes
2	byte	Model byte F8 = PS/1, PS/2 and some clones F9 = PC Convertible FA = PS/2 Model 25 & 30 FC= AT, 286 XT, and most 286 to Pentium clones
3	byte	Submodel byte—varies considerably with different models and vendors
4	byte	BIOS revision number (0 for first release, but not supported by all vendors)
5	byte	Feature information 1 bit 7 = 0 DMA channel 3 not used by hard disk 1 Hard disk uses DMA channel 3 6 = 1 Two interrupt controllers present 5 = 1 Real-Time Clock is present 4 = 1 Keyboard BIOS calls interrupt 15h, function 4Fh on every key received 3 = 0 Wait for external event not supported 1 Wait for external event supported 2 = 0 No extended BIOS data area used 1 May use extended BIOS data area (usually 1 to 4K just below the top of main memory) 1 = 0 AT or ESDI bus 1 MicroChannel bus 0 = 0 unused

Table 13-9. Continued

Offset	Size	Description
6	byte	Feature information 2
		bit 7 = 0 unused
		6 = 0 interrupt 16h, function 9 not supported
		1 interrupt 16h, function 9 supported
		5 = 0 unused or unknown function
		4 = 0 unused or unknown function
		3 = 0 unknown function (set to 1 on a 486 PS/1)
		2 = 0 unused or unknown function
		1 = 0 unused or unknown function
		0 = 0 unused or unknown function
7	byte	Feature information 3
		bit 7 = 0 unused or unknown function
		6 = 0 unused or unknown function
		5 = 0 unused or unknown function
		4 = 0 unknown function (set to 1 on a 486 PS/1)
		3 = 0 unused or unknown function
		2 = 0 unused or unknown function
		1 = 0 unused or unknown function
		0 = 0 unused or unknown function
8	byte	Feature information 4 (unused, and set to zero)
9	byte	Feature information 5 (unused, and set to zero)

Called with: ah = C0h

Returns: if supported

carry = 0

ah = 0

es:bx = pointer to configuration table (see Table 13-9)

if function not supported or cannot be determined

carry = 1

ah = 80h or 86h

Int	Func	Description	Platform
15h	C1h	Return Extended BIOS Data Area	AT+

Get the segment where the extended BIOS data area resides. The extended BIOS data area has been used for mouse information, extra hard disk data, and other uses. BIOSes that require an extended BIOS data area take memory from the top of the main memory area in 1K increments. Most BIOSes that require an extended BIOS data area only use 1K, but I've see a few hogs that take 4K. Before executing this function, function C0h, feature byte at offset 5, bit 2 should be checked to verify if an extended BIOS data area is used.

Most of the better memory managers will eliminate or move the extended BIOS to high memory or to the bottom of main memory. The extended BIOS data area segment is stored in the BIOS data area at address 40:Eh. Refer to Chapter 6 on the contents of the Extended BIOS data area.

Called with: ah = C1h

Returns: if supported

carry = 0

es = segment of the extended BIOS data area

if function not supported or no extended data area

carry = 1

ah = 80h or 86h

Int	Func	Description	Platform
15h	C2h	Mouse BIOS Interface	PS/2

INT III

The PS/2 and later IBM offerings provide a built-in mouse port that is accessed through these eight services. Most clones that have a built-in mouse port also use these functions. Refer to Chapter 8, The Keyboard System, for details about the mouse interface that connects to the keyboard controller. These functions are intended for use by a mouse device driver, and are not intended for direct application use. Use the mouse device driver interface at interrupt 33h for application mouse handling.

Some technical documents use the more generic term of *pointing device*, which includes a mouse, trackball, and other such devices.

In my opinion, this interface approach is a rather weak design. When the mouse is enabled, continuous interrupts are sent even if no mouse actions occur. At the default sample rate, about 500 interrupts per second are generated. Most of the time the mouse is idle. This means the high interrupt rate needlessly adds system overhead, slowing down overall performance. This is especially true in protected or V86 modes.

When a mouse subfunction is called, the status in AH is returned as shown in Table 13-10.

Table 13-10. Mouse Status Return Codes

Value	Description
0	Successful operation, no errors
1	Invalid subfunction call (i.e., AL greater than 7)
2	Invalid input value (i.e., out of allowable range)
3	Interface error
4	Resend command received from mouse controller, the device driver should attempt command again.
5	Cannot enable mouse, since no far call has been installed
80h	Mouse service not implemented (PC)
86h	Mouse service not implemented

The Mouse BIOS interfaces provides eleven services:

AL=	**Mouse Subfunctions**
0, BH=0	Disable Mouse
0, BH=1	Enable Mouse
1	Reset Mouse
2	Set Sample Rate
3	Set Resolution
4	Get Device ID
5	Initialize Mouse
6, BH=0	Return Status
6, BH=1	Set Scaling Factor to 1:1
6, BH=2	Set Scaling Factor to 2:1
7	Set Mouse Handler Address

INT

Subfunction	Description	Int	Function
AL=0, BH=0	Disable Mouse	15h	AH=C2h

Sends a command to the keyboard/mouse controller to disable the mouse.

Called with: ax = C200h
bh = 0

Returns: if successful
carry = 0
ah = 0
if function not implemented
carry = 1
ah = 80h or 86h

INT

Subfunction	Description	Int	Function
AL=0, BH=1	Enable Mouse	15h	AH=C2h

Sends a command to the keyboard/mouse controller to enable the mouse. If a far call pointer has not been installed, using function C207h, the mouse will not be enabled. The error status will be set to 5 in this case.

Called with: ax = C200h
bh = 1

Returns: if successful
carry = 0
ah = 0
if function failed
carry = 1
ah = status (see Table 13-10)

Subfunction	Description	Int	Function
AL=1	Reset Mouse	15h	AH=C2h

INT

Resets the mouse and initializes values. This function also returns a device ID for the mouse in BX, but the IBM documentation indicates the BL portion is not important. The initialized mouse state after reset is disabled, sample rate set to 100 reports per second, 100 dpi resolution, and 1:1 scaling. This function is identical to function C205h, except the data package remains unchanged when using this function. See function C205h for more about the data package size.

Called with: ax = C201h
Returns: if successful
carry = 0
ah = 0
bh = 0 (device ID)
bl = x (invalid device ID low byte)
if function failed
carry = 1
ah = status (see Table 13-10)

Subfunction	Description	Int	Function
AL=2	Set Sample Rate	15h	AH=C2h

INT

Sets the rate at which the mouse should report position and button status information. The number of interrupts generated by the mouse port is approximately the sample rate times the packet size. With large sample rates and/or data packet sizes, the large number of interrupts being generated can affect overall system performance. This is especially true in protected or V86 modes.

Although the system BIOS limits this range, the mouse interface is capable of handling any sample rate from 1 to 255 reports per second. Unfortunately, direct programming of the keyboard/mouse controller is required. See Chapter 8, The Keyboard System, port 60h, command F3h for the low-level details.

Called with: ax = C202h
bh = sample rate value
0 = 10 reports per second
1 = 20 reports per second
2 = 40 reports per second
3 = 60 reports per second
4 = 80 reports per second
5 = 100 reports per second (default)
6 = 200 reports per second

Returns: if successful
carry = 0
ah = 0
if function failed
carry = 1
ah = status (see Table 13-10)

INT Subfunction	Description	Int	Function
AL=3	Set Resolution	15h	AH=C2h

Sets the resolution of the mouse. Lower numbers move the mouse faster across the screen for a given mouse motion. Higher numbers provide more precise control.

To program this value directly, see Chapter 8, The Keyboard System, port 60h, command E8h.

Called with: ax = C203h
bh = resolution
0 = 25 dpi, 1 count per millimeter
1 = 50 dpi, 2 counts per millimeter
2 = 100 dpi, 4 counts per millimeter (default)
3 = 200 dpi, 8 counts per millimeter

Returns: if successful
carry = 0
ah = 0
if function failed
carry = 1
ah = status (see Table 13-10)

Subfunction	Description	Int	Function
AL=4	Get Device ID	15h	AH=C2h

INT

This function returns a device ID for the mouse. The low-level commands actually get a two-byte ID number, but the lower byte is not returned using this function.

Called with: ax = C204h

Returns: if successful

carry = 0

ah = 0

bh = device ID (0 typical)

if function failed

carry = 1

ah = status (see Table 13-10)

Subfunction	Description	Int	Function
AL=5	Initialize Mouse	15h	AH=C2h

INT

Loads the mouse data package size and resets the mouse. The mouse can send from 1 to 8 bytes in each package of data depending on the design. This command sets the number of bytes per package. The value is typically sent once, and depends on the mouse and driver used.

The data package size is saved in the extended BIOS data area, at offset 27h on the PS/2 and PS/1 systems. Other vendors may use different areas to save this information.

Once the package is saved, this command issues a reset mouse command, C201h. The initialized mouse state after reset is disabled, sample rate set to 100 reports per second, 100 dpi resolution, and 1:1 scaling. See function C201h to reset the mouse without changing the data package size.

Called with: ax = C205h

bh = data package size in bytes (1 to 8)

Returns: if successful

carry = 0

ah = 0

if function failed

carry = 1

ah = status (see Table 13-10)

Subfunction	Description	Int	Function
AL=6, BH=0	Return Status	15h	AH=C2h

INT

Gets status of the mouse and current settings.

Called with: ax = C206h
bh = 0

Returns: if successful

carry = 0
ah = 0
bl = status byte
bit #7 = 0 unused
6 = 0 stream mode
1 remote mode
5 = 0 disabled
1 enabled
4 = 0 scaling set to 1:1
1 scaling set to 2:1
3 = 0 unused
2 = 1 left button pressed
1 = 1 unused
0 = 1 right button pressed
cl = resolution
0 = 25 dpi, 1 count per millimeter
1 = 50 dpi, 2 counts per millimeter
2 = 100 dpi, 4 counts per millimeter
3 = 200 dpi, 8 counts per millimeter
dl = sample rate value, in reports per second (i.e. 64h = 100 reports per second)

if function failed

carry = 1
ah = status (see Table 13-10)

INT Subfunction	Description	Int	Function
AL=6, BH=1	Set Scaling Factor to 1:1	15h	AH=C2h

To program 1:1 scaling directly, see Chapter 8, The Keyboard System, port 60h, command E6h.

Called with: ax = C206h
bh = 1

Returns: if successful
carry = 0
ah = 0
if function failed
carry = 1
ah = status (see Table 13-10)

Subfunction	Description	Int	Function
AL=6, BH=2	Set Scaling Factor to 2:1	15h	AH=C2h

INT

To program 2:1 scaling directly, see Chapter 8, The Keyboard System, port 60h, command E7h.

Called with: ax = C206h
bh = 2

Returns: if successful
carry = 0
ah = 0
if function failed
carry = 1
ah = status (see Table 13-10)

Subfunction	Description	Int	Function
AL=7	Set Mouse Handler Address	15h	AH=C2h

INT

A mouse device driver uses this function to load a pointer to code. The system BIOS will make a far call to the pointer value whenever a new mouse report is made. Data about the mouse status and position is stored on the stack.

A mouse report causes interrupt 74h to be issued. The system BIOS handler for interrupt 74h is responsible for issuing the far call, when enabled. Before the far call is made, the interrupt 74h handler pushes four words of data onto the stack, as shown in Table 13-11. The position within the stack is shown for each word at the entry to the far subroutine, before any additional information is stored on the stack. The far subroutine should save and restore any registers used.

Interrupts are enabled when the far call is made. The called subroutine should return with the stack in the same state it is called with, issuing an RETF upon exit. Interrupt 74h is responsible to remove the four excess words off the stack.

Table 13-11. Mouse Information in Stack at Far Call

Stack	Description			
Word 0	Status byte at [sp+Ah]			
		bits	15-8 = 0	unused
		bit	7 = 1	Y position data overflow
			6 = 1	X position data overflow
			5 = 1	Y position data negative
			4 = 1	X position data negative
			3 = 1	unused, but set to 1
			2 = 0	unused
			1 = 1	left button pressed
			0 = 1	right button pressed
Word 1	X position at [sp+8]			
		bits	15-8 = 0	unused
			7-0 = x	coordinate X position
Word 2	Y position at [sp+6]			
		bits	15-8 = 0	unused
			7-0 = x	coordinate Y position
Word 3	Z position at [sp+4] (future)			
		bits	15-0 = 0	unused

Called with: ax = C207h
es:bx = far pointer to subroutine

Returns: if successful
carry = 0
ah = 0
if function failed
carry = 1
ah = status (see Table 13-10)

INT

Int	Func	Description	Platform
15h	C3h	Watchdog Timer Control	MCA/EISA

This function controls the hardware watchdog timer. MCA and EISA systems provide an extra timer that can trigger NMI if not updated periodically. See Chapter 16, System Timers, for low-level details of timer 3.

The watchdog timer is used to trigger a non-maskable interrupt if a program goes into an endless loop while interrupts are disabled. It is up to the NMI handler to take whatever actions are deemed necessary. The BIOS POST defaults the watchdog timer to disabled. The system BIOS does not handle the NMI when a watchdog timeout occurs. It is left to the operating system or environment to take advantage of this feature by hooking interrupt 2, NMI. Two subfunctions disable and enable the watchdog timer.

Subfunction	Description	Int	Function
AL=0	Disable Watchdog Timer	15h	AH=C3h

INT

Called with: ax = C300h

Returns: if successful

carry = 0

ah = 0

if function not supported

carry = 1

ah = 80h or 86h

Subfunction	Description	Int	Function
AL=1	Enable Watchdog Timer	15h	AH=C3h

INT

Called with: ax = C301h

bx = initial count value (1-255 on MCA, 1-65535 on EISA)

Returns: if successful

carry = 0

ah = 0

if function not supported

carry = 1

ah = 80h or 86h

Int	Func	Description	Platform
15h	C4h	Programmable Option Select	MCA

INT

The Programmable Option Select (POS) system records information about each adapter in the system into extended CMOS memory. The POS system provides a mechanism to eliminate adapter switches and mediate potential I/O port conflicts.

The POS interface is comprised of three services:

AL=	POS Subfunctions
0	Get Base POS I/O port
1	Enable Slot for Setup
2	Enable Adapter

INT	Subfunction	Description	Int	Function
	AL=0	Get Base POS I/O port	15h	AH=C4h

In most cases the POS I/O port is fixed at 100h, but this function allows the POS base I/O port number to be changed in the future.

Called with: ax = C400h

Returns: if successful

- carry = 0
- al = 0
- dx = Base POS I/O port (typically 100h)

if failed

- carry = 1
- al = 0

if function not supported

- carry = 1
- ah = 80h or 86h

INT	Subfunction	Description	Int	Function
	AL=1	Enable Slot For Setup	15h	AH=C4h

Enables the specified slot for setup. To complete this action, issue subfunction 2. This uses the adapter enable and setup port 96h to signal setup for the specified adapter slot.

Called with: ax = C401h

bl = slot number 1 to 8

Returns: if successful

- carry = 0
- al = 1
- bl = slot number

if slot number out of range

- carry = 1
- al = 1
- bl = unchanged

if function not supported

- carry = 1
- ah = 80h or 86h

Subfunction	Description	Int	Function
AL=2	Enable Adapter	15h	AH=C4h

INT

This subfunction completes the setup operation initiated from subfunction 1. This is accomplished by sending a zero to port 96h to terminate the setup process. The system will not perform any function if subfunction 1 was not previously issued.

Called with: ax = C402h

Returns: if successful

carry = 0

al = 2

if failed

carry = 1

al = 2

if function not supported

carry = 1

ah = 80h or 86h

Int	Func	Description	Platform
15h	C5h	Begin System Interrupt	PS/2

INT

A number of interrupt routines within the system BIOS call this function to indicate that they are being issued. A TSR or operating system could potentially hook this function and prevent or alter various BIOS services.

Before calling this function, the BIOS first pushes the original AX value passed to the system service, and then issues interrupt 15h function C5h, with AL set to the interrupt code. The AX stack value is not always accessible, since it is possible for other TSRs to hook interrupt 15h. These TSRs will add additional information to the stack, and might even change to a new stack during execution.

If this function should be issued by an application, the system BIOS simply checks if AL is within the range 1 to 9, and returns with the carry cleared. For all other AL values, the system BIOS acts like an unsupported function.

Called with: ah = C5h (from system BIOS)

al = interrupt code from BIOS service

1 = interrupt 19h, bootstrap loader

2 = interrupt 14h, serial port services

3 = interrupt 16h, keyboard services

4 = interrupt 40h, diskette services

5 = interrupt 17h, printer services

6 = interrupt 10h, video services

7 = interrupt 12h, equipment information
8 = interrupt 11h, main memory size
9 = interrupt 1Ah, real-time-clock services

Returns: if BIOS supports this capability
carry = 0
if function not supported
carry = 1
ah = 80h or 86h

Int	Func	Description	Platform
15h	C8h	Cache Control	PS/1

This function controls the operation of the cache. These functions are undocumented and may change in different systems. Subfunctions 0 to 5 are not functional if the CPU is in protected mode, and will return an error.

Cache control has seven subfunctions:

AL=	Cache Control Subfunctions
0	Enable Cache
1	Disable Cache
2	Unknown Cache Subfunction
3	Unknown Cache Subfunction
4	Enable Cache with Prepare
5	Disable Cache with Prepare
6	Get Cache State

Subfunction	Description	Int	Function
AL=0	Enable Cache	15h	AH=C8h

Called with: ax = C800h

Returns: if successful
carry = 0
ax = 0
if cache previously failed POST tests
carry = 1
ax = C804h
if CPU is in protected mode
carry = 1
ax = C809h

if function not supported
carry = 1
ah = 80h or 86h

Subfunction	Description	Int	Function
AL=1	Disable Cache	15h	AH=C8h

INT

Called with: ax = C801h
Returns: if successful
carry = 0
ax = 1
if cache previously failed POST tests
carry = 1
ax = C803h
if CPU is in protected mode
carry = 1
ax = C809h
if function not supported
carry = 1
ah = 80h or 86h

Subfunction	Description	Int	Function
AL=2	Unknown Cache Subfunction	15h	AH=C8h

INT

Called with: ax = C802h
Returns: if successful
carry = 0
ax = 2
if failed
carry = 1
ax = C805h
if CPU is in protected mode
carry = 1
ax = C809h
if function not supported
carry = 1
ah = 80h or 86h

Subfunction	Description	Int	Function
AL=3	Unknown Cache Subfunction	15h	AH=C8h

Called with: ax = C803h

Returns: if successful

carry = 0

ax = 3

if failed

carry = 1

ah = C8h

al = 3, 4, or 5 depending on error

if CPU is in protected mode

carry = 1

ax = C809h

if function not supported

carry = 1

ah = 80h or 86h

Subfunction	Description	Int	Function
AL=4	Enable Cache with Prepare	15h	AH=C8h

Under some circumstances, performs some cache-related action. In all cases, cache is enabled.

Called with: ax = C804h

Returns: if successful

carry = 0

ax = 4

if CPU is in protected mode

carry = 1

ax = C809h

if function not supported

carry = 1

ah = 80h or 86h

Subfunction	Description	Int	Function
AL=5	Disable Cache with Prepare	15h	AH=C8h

Under some circumstances, performs some cache-related action. In all cases, cache is disabled.

Called with: ax = C805h

Returns: if successful

carry = 0

ax = 5

if failed

carry = 1

ax = C803h

if CPU is in protected mode

carry = 1

ax = C809h

if function not supported

carry = 1

ah = 80h or 86h

Subfunction	Description	Int	Function
AL=6	Get Cache State	15h	AH=C8h

INT

Called with: ax = C806h

Returns: if cache disabled

carry = 0

ax = 6

bh = unknown cache bit (0 or 1)

bl = 0

if cache enabled

carry = 1

ax = 6

bh = unknown cache bit (0 or 1)

bl = 1

if function not supported

carry = 1

ah = 80h or 86h

Int	Func	Description	Platform
15h	C9h	Get CPU Stepping	Some 386+

INT

This function, if supported, returns the CPU family and stepping number. The stepping number is the CPU revision. When a 386 or later CPU is reset, the CPU initializes the DX register with the stepping number in DL, and a family number in DH. If this value is not saved by the

BIOS very early in POST, it is lost. Newer 486s, and later CPUs such as Pentium and Pentium Pro, provide a new CPUID instruction to get this same information at any time.

IBM is one of the few vendors supporting this function in their latest BIOSes. The CPU-TYPE program, provided in this book, uses this function as one of its methods to help identify the stepping level of the CPU. If the returned value in CX is zero, the BIOS did not save the information from the CPU.

Called with: ah = C9h

Returns: if successful

carry = 0
ah = 0
ch = CPU family number (i.e. 4 = 486; 5=586/Pentium; etc.)
cl = CPU stepping number

if function failed

carry = 1
ah = 80h or 86h

Int	Func	Description	Platform
15h	CAh	Read/Write CMOS Memory	PS/1

Two subfunctions provide the ability to read and write CMOS memory registers E to 3Fh.

Subfunction	Description	Int	Function
AL=0	Read CMOS Memory Register	15h	AH=CAh

Called with: ax = CA00h
bl = CMOS register to read (E to 3F)

Returns: if successful

carry = 0
ah = 0
cl = CMOS register value

if failed

carry = 1
ah = error code

1 = CMOS lost power or checksum invalid
3 = register in bl too high
4 = register in bl too low
80h = function not supported (PC)
86h = function not supported (others)

Subfunction	Description	Int	Function
AL=1	Write CMOS Memory Register	15h	AH=CAh

INT

After writing the value to a CMOS register, this subfunction does not update the checksum in the CMOS memory. If POST had detected a checksum error in CMOS, this function is not usable.

A new checksum is not obtained before the write, so writes to different registers are allowed so long as a system reset does not occur. There is no function to create and save a new checksum.

Called with: ax = CA01h
bl = CMOS register (E to 3F)
cl = value to write

Returns: if successful
carry = 0
ah = 0
if failed
carry = 1
ah = error code
1 = CMOS lost power or checksum invalid
3 = register in bl too high
4 = register in bl too low
80h = function not supported (PC)
86h = function not supported (others)

Int	Func	Description	Platform
15h	D8h	Access EISA System Information	EISA

INT

On an EISA system, this function accesses extended CMOS memory that holds system and slot information. See the section on EISA system differences in Chapter 15, CMOS Memory and Real-Time Clock, for complete details of function D8h services.

Port Summary

Port	Type	Function	Platform
22h	Output	Chip Set Index Selection	AT+
23h	I/O	Chip Set Data	AT+
26h	Output	Power Management Index Selection	AT+
27h	I/O	Power Management Data	AT+
60h	Input	System switches	PC
60h	Output	POST diagnostic	XT
61h	I/O	Miscellaneous Functions & Speaker Control	AT+
61h	I/O	Miscellaneous Functions & Speaker Control	PC/XT
62h	Input	Miscellaneous System Port Functions	XT
62h	Input	Miscellaneous System Port Functions	PC
63h	Input	Miscellaneous System Port Functions	XT
64h	Output	System 8255 Mode Register	PC/XT
80h	Output	POST diagnostic	All
84h	Output	POST diagnostic	Compaq
84h	I/O	Synchronize Bus Cycle Register	EISA
90h	Output	POST diagnostic	All
91h	Input	Card Selected Feedback	MCA
92h	I/O	System Control	MCA/EISA
94h	I/O	System Control Enables	MCA
96h	I/O	Adapter Enable and Setup	MCA
E0h	I/O	Split Address Register	MCA
E1h	I/O	Memory Register	MCA
E3h	I/O	Error Trace Register	MCA
E4h	I/O	Error Trace Register	MCA
E5h	I/O	Error Trace Register	MCA
E7h	I/O	Error Trace Register	MCA
F0h	Output	Math Coprocessor—Clear Busy	AT+
F1h	Output	Math Coprocessor—Reset	AT+
F8h	I/O	Math Coprocessor—Opcode Transfer	AT+
FAh	I/O	Math Coprocessor—Opcode Transfer	AT+
FCh	I/O	Math Coprocessor—Opcode Transfer	AT+
100h	Input	Programmable Option Select 0	MCA
101h	Input	Programmable Option Select 1	MCA
102h	I/O	Programmable Option Select 2	MCA
103h	I/O	Programmable Option Select 3	MCA
104h	I/O	Programmable Option Select 4	MCA
105h	I/O	Programmable Option Select 5	MCA
106h	Input	Programmable Option Select 6	MCA
107h	Input	Programmable Option Select 7	MCA
178h	Output	Power Management Index Selection	AT+

Port	Type	Function	Platform
179h	I/O	Power Management Data	AT+
300h	Output	POST diagnostic	Award
461h	I/O	Extended NMI and Control	EISA
464h	Input	Last Busmaster Granted	EISA
465h	Input	Last Busmaster Granted	EISA
680h	Output	POST diagnostic	MCA
C80h	Input	System Board ID 1	EISA
C81h	Input	System Board ID 2	EISA
C82h	Input	System Board ID 3	EISA
C83h	Input	System Board ID 4	EISA

Port Detail

Port	Type	Description	Platform
22h	**Output**	**Chip Set Index Selection**	**AT+**

Many newer designs use an integrated chip set to perform a number of actions previously handled with a large number of ICs. These chip sets typically have additional functions and features requiring access. These registers are typically accessed by using two 8-bit I/O ports. The register index is written to this port, followed by access to that register through port 23h. Most of the registers are set up by the system BIOS POST operation.

The detailed functionality of the chip set's use of ports 22h and 23h is specific to each vendor. In general, only the system BIOS accesses the chip set, since the BIOS is configured for the specific chip set used. In most cases, the BIOS POST operation simply sets up the chip set values once, and does not access the chip set again.

Some vendors, like Intel, allow access to multiple chips through I/O ports 22h and 23h. A chip identification register controls which chip will respond to these ports. Once the chip ID is loaded into the ID register, only that chip will respond to ports 22h and 23h.

The Intel chip set uses the following chip selection IDs:

Chip ID	Registers Accessed
1	82359 EISA DRAM controller, general registers
2	82351 EISA local I/O support
A1	82359 EISA DRAM controller, EMS registers
FF	no chip is accessible (default)

The following example illustrates how a specific chip is selected and how the index and data registers are used. The EGA/VGA reserves 128K starting at segment A000, but a monochrome system only begins using video memory at segment B000. When using a monochrome adapter, it is nice to get an additional 64K of DOS memory, for a total of 704K. The following code will access the Intel 82359 DRAM controller and activate an additional 64K of RAM at address A000. The code will be different for other chip sets. This routine assumes the system currently has 640K of main memory, no extended BIOS data area is in use, and Upper Memory Blocks (UMB) are not used.

```
cli                               ; always disable interrupts
mov     al, 21h                   ; access the chip selection reg
out     22h, al                   ; set index = 21h
mov     al, 1                     ; select the DRAM controller chip
out     23h, al                   ; output to index 21h

mov     al, 42h                   ; access the video block reg
out     22h, al                   ; set index = 42h
mov     al, 0FFh                  ; set A000-AFFF to RAM
out     23h, al                   ; output to index 42h

mov     ax, 40h                   ; access BIOS data area
mov     es, ax
mov     word ptr es:[13h], 704 ; set the RAM to 704K

sti                               ; enable interrupts
```

The Intel chip sets allow the default ports 22h and 23h to be set to any other port 0 to FFh. The port numbers might be changed by POST should a hardware conflict exist, but this is rarely done in practice. This is controlled by the virtual index and data registers 22h and 23h.

The following summary of registers provides some ideas about what is controlled by a chip set. Other vendors provide different functions and controls, and use different register assignments. Cyrix also uses this port to access internal CPU registers. See Chapter 3 for more details.

Summary of Registers (Intel 82359 EISA DRAM Controller, General Registers)

Register	Function
0	DRAM memory array—row 1 type and population
1	DRAM memory array—row 2 type and population
2	DRAM memory array—row 3 type and population
3	DRAM memory array—row 4 type and population
4	DRAM speed detect and select
5	Line size—controls DRAM interleave
6	RAS lines mode

Register	Function
7	Block cache enable select—video, ROMs, and system BIOS
8	Mode register A—DRAM and cache control
9	Mode register B—cache, bust modes, and BIOS size
A	Mode register C—concurrency control, burst and cycle speed
10	Host timing
11	Host to system delay timing
12	System timing
13	DRAM Row precharge timing
14	DRAM Row timing
15	DRAM column timing
16	CAS pulse width
17	CAS to MDS delay
21	Chip selection register (set to 1 to access this chip)
22	Virtual index register
23	Virtual data register
28-2C	Parity error trap address
30	Read page hit cycle length
31	Read page miss cycle length
32	Read row miss cycle length
33	Write page hit cycle length
34	Write page miss cycle length
35	Write row miss cycle length
40	Lower memory block enable (0-7FFFF)
41	Lower memory block enable (80000-9FFFF)
42	Video memory block enable (A0000-AFFFF)
43	Video memory block enable (B0000-BFFFF)
44	ROM memory block enable (C0000-CFFFF)
45	ROM memory block enable (D0000-DFFFF)
46	BIOS memory block enable (E0000-EFFFF)
47	BIOS memory block enable (F0000-FFFFF)
4E	Remap memory (80000-FFFFF) to extended memory
50-53	Programmable attribute map 1 (caching, write protect, etc.)
54-57	Programmable attribute map 2 (caching, write protect, etc.)
58-5B	Programmable attribute map 3 (caching, write protect, etc.)
5C-5F	Programmable attribute map 4 (caching, write protect, etc.)
83-84	Split address register, address bits A20-32
85	Cache control
8B	System throttle
8C	Host throttle
8D	Host memory throttle watchdog
8E	Host system throttle

Register	Function
8F	Host system throttle watchdog
90	RAM enable
91	RAM disable
92-93	Elapsed time registers
94-95	Host memory request to ownership
96-97	System memory request to ownership
98-99	Host memory ownership
9A-9B	System bus ownership
9C-9D	Host request of system bus
9E-9F	Memory ownership transfer

Summary of Registers (Intel 82359 EISA DRAM Controller, EMS Registers)

Register	Function
0	EMS control (EMS=Expanded Memory Specification)
21	Chip selection register (set to "1" to access this chip)
22	Virtual index register
23	Virtual data register
80-8F	EMS page registers, pages 0-7

Summary of Registers (Intel 82351 EISA Local I/O Support)

Register	Function
21	Chip selection register (set to 2 to access this chip)
C0	Peripheral enable register A
C1	Peripheral enable register B
C2	Parallel configuration register
C3	Serial configuration register A
C4	Floppy disk controller configuration register
C5	Serial configuration register B
C6	COM3 chip select low port address
C7	COM3 chip select high port address
C8	COM4 chip select low port address
C9	COM4 chip select high port address
D0-D3	General chip select lines, mask registers 0-3
D4-D7	General chip select lines, low port address 0-3
D8-DB	General chip select lines, high port address 0-3
DC	Extended CMOS RAM page high port address
DD	Extended CMOS RAM page low port address
DF	Extended CMOS RAM access select high port address (low part of port address selects the RAM location)
E8-EB	EISA ID configuration registers (for ports C80-C83h)

Port	Type	Description	Platform
23h	I/O	Chip Set Data	AT+

This port is used with port 22h to access registers in the system's chip set. A register is previously specified with port 22h, and the data can then be written to or read using this port. See port 22h for details.

Port	Type	Description	Platform
26h	Output	Power Management Index Selection	AT+

Some laptops and other systems that use power management access a set of power management functions. First the register index is written to this port, followed by access to that register through port 27h. Other external power management designs often use other ports and register designations.

Summary of Registers (Intel 82347 Power Management Peripheral)

Register	Function
C0	Suspend and wakeup status, system state
C1	Power supply status, activity status, general purpose output and control
C2	Control bits
C3	Activity mask
C4	NMI mask
C5	I/O range for activity monitor
C6	On state—power output control bits
C7	Doze state—power output control bits
C8	Sleep state—power output control bits
C9	Suspend state—power output control bits
CA	Polarity control of power control bits
CB	Current output bits status
CC	Doze timer register (default—4 seconds)
CD	Sleep timer register (default—2 minutes)
CE	Suspend timer register (default—disabled)
CF	LCD display power timer register (default—2 minutes)
D0	EL display power timer register (default—2 minutes)

Port	Type	Description	Platform
27h	I/O	Power Management Data	AT+

For systems with power management, this port accesses the power management register specified in a prior write to port 26h. See port 26h for details.

Port	Type	Description	Platform
60h	Input	System switches	PC

The original PC retains a set of four registers for miscellaneous hardware functions on the PC. These four ports 60h to 63h are controlled through an 8255 peripheral interface chip or equivalent. Port 60h is dedicated for input switches on the motherboard. These switches are directly connected to port A on the 8255.

Most of this information is available using Interrupt 11h (get equipment information) and interrupt 12h (get main memory size).

Input (bits 0-7)

```
bit  7 r = x |  Number of diskette drives (when bit 0 = 1)
     6 r = x |      bit 7   bit 6
                    0       0 =  1 diskette drive
                    0       1 = 2 diskette drives
                    1       0 = 3 diskette drives
                    1       1 = 4 diskette drives
     5 r = x |  Video display type
     4 r = x |      bit 5   bit 4
                    0       0 = unused
                    0       1 = CGA, 40 columns by 25 rows
                    1       0 = CGA, 80 columns by 25 rows
                    1       1 = MDA, 80 columns by 25 rows
     3 r = x |  System motherboard memory size
     2 r = x |      bit 3   bit 2
                    0       0 = 16 KB
                    0       1 = 32 KB
                    1       0 = 48 KB
                    1       1 = 64 KB
     1 r = x    unused
     0 r = 0    boot from the BASIC ROM (no drives on system)
           1    boot from the diskette drive
```

Port	Type	Description	Platform
60h	Output	POST diagnostic	XT

During the Power-On-Self-Test (POST) values are output to this port as each test is made. Should a test fail (or hang the system), the last value will indicate the test that failed. The port number and values are very manufacturer-dependent, and may vary from model to model.

IBM XT BIOS Common POST Codes

The POST code is sent to port 60h. Only a limited number of POST codes were used with the XT. In addition, the system could send beep codes, and display additional error messages.

00h	Processor register tests
01h	BIOS ROM checksum (fails if bytes do not add to zero)
02h	Timer 1 tests
03h	DMA initialization and register test
04h	Memory test failure, lower 32K—alternates with the bit pattern used during the failure (one of: 00, 01, 55, AA, FF).
FFh	Processor register tests

Port	Type	Description	Platform
61h	I/O	Miscellaneous Functions & Speaker Control	AT+

This port controls the speaker and a group of unrelated internal system functions. On the AT this port connects to discrete hardware. Most current clones provide the hardware interface as an internal part of the chip set used. The primary programmer use is to generate sounds from the speaker.

When writing to this register be sure that bits 4 to 7 are always 0. Better yet, read the value and only alter the bits needed for the function desired.

Output (bits 0-3, 7), Input (bits 0-7)

bit	7 r	= 1	RAM parity error (only when enabled by bit 2)
	6 w	= 1	Clear IRQ 0 timer latch (MCA only)
	6 r	= 1	I/O parity error (only when enabled by bit 3)
	5 r	= x	Output of Timer 2 (8254 or equivalent)
	4 r	= x	Refresh request clock divided by 2
	3 r/w	= 0	Enable I/O parity check—Generate NMI if error
	2 r/w	= 0	Enable RAM parity check—Generate NMI if error
	1 r/w	= 1	Speaker data enabled
	0 r/w	= 1	Gate Timer 2 on

Code Example

Sends a tone to the speaker by toggling speaker enable bit on and off. This routine uses delays based on time to execute specific instructions and will change in pitch depending on the processor and CPU speed.

```
spkr_beep       proc    near
                mov     bx, 256           ; on/off cycle time duration
                mov     cx, bx            ; temporary register
                in      al, 61h           ; read port contents
                and     al, 0FEh          ; timer output to speaker off
                mov     dx, 80            ; loop count
spkr_cycle:
                or      al, 2
                out     61h, al           ; turn on speaker bit
spkr_on_delay:
                loop    spkr_on_delay     ; delay
                and     al, 0FDh
                out     61h, al           ; turn off the speaker bit
                mov     cx, bx            ; reset duration
spkr_off_delay:
                loop    spkr_off_delay    ; delay
                dec     dx
                jnz     spkr_cycle        ; loop 80 times
                ret
skpr_beep       endp
```

Port	Type	Description	Platform
61h	I/O	Miscellaneous Functions & Speaker Control	PC/XT

This port controls the speaker and a group of unrelated internal system functions. On the PC and XT this port is output port B of the 8255 peripheral interface chip. The primary programmer use is to generate sounds from the speaker.

When changing the value of this port, first read the current contents, and only change the bits needed before writing back the new value.

I/O (bits 0-7)

bit	7 r/w = 0	Disable system switches to port 60h, enable keyboard data, allow keyboard IRQ
	1	Enable system switches to port 60h, disable keyboard data path, clear keyboard IRQ
	6 r/w = 0	Hold keyboard clock low

5 r/w = 0	Enable I/O parity check—Generate NMI if error
4 r/w = 0	Enable RAM parity check—Generate NMI if error
3 r/w = 0	Cassette motor on (PC)
2 r/w = 0	Enable reading switches for RAM size (port 62h, bits 0-3)
1	Enable reading spare switch (port 62h, bit 0)
1 r/w = 1	Speaker data enabled
0 r/w = 1	Gate timer 2 output into speaker

Code Example

See port 61h AT+ code example

Port	Type	Description	Platform
62h	Input	Miscellaneous System Port Functions	XT

This port controls a group of unrelated functions on the XT and is no longer used on current systems. The input bits are from port C of the 8255 peripheral interface chip.

Input (bits 0-7)

bit	7 r = 1	RAM parity error (only when enabled by bit 4, port 61h)
	6 r = 1	I/O parity error (only when enabled by bit 5, port 61h)
	5 r = x	Output of timer 2 (8254 or equivalent)
	4 r = x	unused
	3 r = 1	System board RAM size type 1
	2 r = 1	System board RAM size type 0
	1 r = 1	Math Coprocessor installed, 8087
	0 r = 1	looping in POST (Power-On-Self-Test for diagnostic analysis)

Code Example

```
enable_RAM_parity:
                mov     al, 10h
                out     61h, al         ; enable RAM parity check
                .
                .
check_RAM_parity:
                in      al, 62h
                test    al, 80h         ; test for RAM parity error
```

```
        jnz parity_error            ; jump if error
        .                           ; fall through if ok
        .
```

Port	Type	Description	Platform
62h	Input	Miscellaneous System Port Functions	PC

This port controls a group of unrelated functions on the PC and is no longer used on current systems. The input bits are from port C of the 8255 peripheral interface.

Input (bits 0-7)

bit	7 r = 1	RAM parity error (only when enabled by bit 4, port 61h)
	6 r = 1	I/O parity error (only when enabled by bit 5, port 61h)
	5 r = x	Output of timer 2 (8254 or equivalent)
	4 r = x	Cassette data input
	3 r = x	Additional Memory x 32 MB
	2 r = x	bits 3-0 0000 = no extra memory
	1 r = x	1111 = 512K in addition to main
	0 r = x	

Port	Type	Description	Platform
63h	Input	Miscellaneous System Port Functions	XT

This port is used to read the system settings on the XT and is no longer used on current systems.

Input (bits 0-7)

bit	7 r = x	Number of diskette drives
	6 r = x	bit 7 bit 6
		0 0 = 1 diskette drive
		0 1 = 2 diskette drives
		1 0 = 3 diskette drives
		1 1 = 4 diskette drives
	5 r = x	Video display type at boot time
	4 r = x	bit 5 bit 4
		0 0 = unused
		0 1 = CGA, 40 columns by 25 rows

	1	0 = CGA, 80 columns by 25 rows		
	1	1 = MDA, 80 columns by 25 rows		
3 r = x	System motherboard memory size			
2 r = x	bit 3	bit 2 (64K chips)		(256K chips)
	0	0 =	16K	256K
	0	1 =	128K	512K
	1	0 =	192K	576K
	1	1 =	256K	640K
1 r = x	unused			
0 r = x	unused			

Port	Type	Description	Platform
64h	Output	System 8255 Mode Register	PC/XT

This port controls the operation of the 8255 peripheral interface chip or equivalent. Since the ports are dedicated and all operate in the basic input/output mode, this register is always loaded with 99h on the PC/XT.

Strobed mode and bidirectional modes are not supported and should never be programmed. During a hardware reset, all ports are set to input mode, so it is acceptable to read port 62h without having first set the mode register to 99h.

Output (bits 0-7)

bit	7 w = 1	Mode set active	
	6 w = x	Mode selection, port A, all, and port C, upper 4 bits	
	5 w = x	bit 6	bit 5
		0	0 = basic operation (normal)
		0	1 = strobed control (never used)
		1	x = bidirectional (never used)
	4 w = 0	Port A set for output	
	1	Port A set for input (normal)	
	3 w = 0	Port C, upper 4 bits, set for output (normal)	
	1	Port C, upper 4 bits, set for input	
	2 w = 0	Basic mode, port B and port C, lower 4 bits (normal)	
	1	strobed mode, port B and port C, lower 4 bits	
	1 w = 0	Port B set for output (normal)	
	1	Port B set for input	
	0 w = 0	Port C, lower 4 bits, set for output	
	1	Port C, lower 4 bits, set for input (normal)	

Code Example

```
init_8255:
                mov     al, 99h         ; command value
                out     64h, al         ; send to 8255
```

Port	Type	Description	Platform
80h	Output	POST diagnostic	All

During the Power-On-Self-Test (POST) values are output to this port as each test is made. Should a test fail (or hang the system), the last value will indicate the test that failed. The port number and values are very manufacturer-dependent, and may vary from model to model.

A number of diagnostic boards are available to display POST code. It is common for some sequential POST codes to be unused, depending on version and manufacturer.

AMI BIOS Common POST Codes

The POST code is sent to port 80h. When a failure occurs, the last code indicates the problem. Codes with an (F) indicate a failure is fatal. The information for these codes was derived in part from several motherboard user's manuals that document the AMI BIOS POST codes. It has been my experience that most AMI BIOSs with a 1990 date code or later follow these POST codes.

01h	Processor flag test failure (F)
02h	Processor register test failure (F)
03h	Main BIOS ROM checksum failure (F)
04h	Timer channel 2 failure
05h	Timer channel 2 not counting properly
06h	Timer channel 1 not counting properly (F)
07h	Timer channel 0, for DMA refresh, not counting properly (F)
08h	Parity status bit stuck (F)
09h	RAM refresh failure (F)
0Ah	Address low byte failure (F)
0Bh	Test of first 64K RAM failure, sequential data (F)
0Ch	Test of first 64K RAM failure, random data (F)
0Dh	RAM Parity error (F)
0Eh	Keyboard controller fails to respond (F)
0Fh	Keyboard controller self test failure (F)
10h	Keyboard controller mode cannot be set properly (F)
11h	Keyboard controller status not correct (F)
12h	CMOS memory read/write test failure (F)
13h	Video ROM detected, but checksum failed
14h	Video ROM does not return from initialization (F)
15h	Display memory read/write test failure

16h	Display cursor register read/write failure (CGA/MDA)
17h	Enter virtual mode (F)
18h	Enable 1 MB+ memory (A20 line) failure (F)
19h	All RAM test, address test failure
1Ah	All RAM test, sequential data pattern test failure
1Bh	All RAM test, random data test failure
1Ch	Parity error during RAM test
1Dh	Switching back to real mode
1Eh	Disable 1 MB+ memory (A20 line) failure
1Fh	DMA controller page register read/write test failure (F)
20h	DMA controller register latch test failure (F)
21h	DMA controller 1 test failure (F)
22h	DMA controller 2 test failure (F)
23h	Interrupt controller 1 mask register read/write test failure (F)
24h	Interrupt controller 2 mask register read/write test failure
25h	Spurious interrupts occurred on interrupt controller 1 (F)
26h	Keyboard failure
27h	Keyboard interface test failure
28h	Keyboard data line stuck
29h	Keyboard clock line stuck
2Ah	Keyboard key stuck down
2Bh	Parallel printer port setup
2Ch	RS-232 serial port setup
2Dh	Time and date setup
2Eh	Diskette controller and drive setup
2Fh	Hard disk controller and drive setup
30h	Detected ROM at C800h, but checksum failed
31h	ROM at C800 to E000 does not return from initialization (F)
32h	Detected ROM at E000h, but checksum failed
33h	ROM at E000 does not return from initialization (F)
34h	Boot via INT 19h (bootstrap loader)

AWARD BIOS Common POST Codes

The POST code is sent both to ports 80h and 300h, and the indicated test is performed.

01h	Processor flag tests
02h	Processor register tests
03h	Initialize chips, such as RTC, math, timers, DMA, interrupt controller, etc.
04h	Test memory refresh
05h	Keyboard initialization
06h	BIOS ROM checksum (fails if bytes do not add to zero, also separately checksums the sign-on message)
07h	Test CMOS interface and battery condition

08h	Setup and test first 256K of RAM, OEM chipset setup
09h	Early cache memory initialization
0Ah	Setup interrupt vectors
0Bh	Test CMOS RAM checksum
0Ch	Initialize keyboard and set num-lock status
0Dh	Initialize video interface based on CMOS type
0Eh	Test video memory and display sign-on message
0Fh	Test DMA controller 0
10h	Test DMA controller 1
11h	Test DMA page registers
12-13h	Unused
14h	Test the 8254 timer counter 2
15h	Test the 8259-1 interrupt mask bits
16h	Test the 8259-2 interrupt mask bits
17h	Test for stuck 8259 interrupt bits
18h	Test the 8259 interrupt controller
19h	Test for stuck NMI bits (from parity or I/O check)
1A-1Eh	Unused
1Fh	Set EISA mode if supported and check the EISA configuration memory interface and checksum. If EISA not supported, perform ISA tests and clear EISA mode flag.
20h	Initialize slot 0 (EISA only)
21h	Initialize slot 1 (EISA only)
22h	Initialize slot 2 (EISA only)
23h	Initialize slot 3 (EISA only)
24h	Initialize slot 4 (EISA only)
25h	Initialize slot 5 (EISA only)
26h	Initialize slot 6 (EISA only)
27h	Initialize slot 7 (EISA only)
28h	Initialize slot 8 (EISA only)
29h	Initialize slot 9 (EISA only)
2Ah	Initialize slot 10 (EISA only)
2Bh	Initialize slot 11 (EISA only)
2Ch	Initialize slot 12 (EISA only)
2Dh	Initialize slot 13 (EISA only)
2Eh	Initialize slot 14 (EISA only)
2Fh	Initialize slot 15 (EISA only)
30h	Determine size of base and extended memory
31h	Test base and extended memory (skipped if ESC pressed)
32h	Test EISA extended memory (skipped if in ISA mode, or ESC pressed)
33-3Bh	Unused
3Ch	Setup enabled
3Dh	Initialize and install mouse

3Eh	Initialize cache controller
3Fh	Setup shadow RAM according to setup
40h	Unused
41h	Initialize floppy controller and attached drives
42h	Initialize hard disk controller and attached drives
43h	Detect and initialize any serial and parallel ports
44h	Unused
45h	Detect and initialize math coprocessor
46h	unused
47h	Set system speed
48-4Dh	Unused
4Eh	If manufacturing jumper installed, reboot. Otherwise display on screen any non-fatal messages and enter setup
4Fh	Enter password (if so configured)
50h	Write CMOS values into RAM
51h	Enable parity check, enable NMI, enable cache
52h	Detect and initialize option ROMs from C800h to EF80h
53h	Copy time and date from CMOS to BIOS RAM
54-62h	Unused
63h	Set stack and boot via INT 19h (bootstrap loader)
64-CFh	Unused
B0h	Spurious interrupt occurred in protected mode
B1h	Unclaimed NMI
B2-BEh	Unused
BFh	Program chipset
C0h	Cache control (OEM specific)
C1h	Memory presence test (OEM specific)
C2h	Early memory initialization (OEM specific)
C3h	Extended memory initialization (OEM specific)
C4h	Special video display switch handling (OEM specific)
C5h	Early shadow (OEM specific for faster boot)
C6h	Cache programming (OEM specific)
C8h	Special speed switching (OEM specific)
C9h	Special shadow RAM handling (OEM specific)
CAh	Very early hardware initialization (OEM specific)
CB-E0h	Unused
E1h	Setup page 1
E2h	Setup page 2
E3h	Setup page 3
E4h	Setup page 4
E5h	Setup page 5
E6h	Setup page 6
E7h	Setup page 7

E8h	Setup page 8
E9h	Setup page 9
EAh	Setup page A
EBh	Setup page B
ECh	Setup page C
EDh	Setup page D
EEh	Setup page E
EFh	Setup page F
F0-FEh	Unused
FFh	Boot

IBM AT BIOS Common POST Codes

The POST code is sent to port 80h, and the indicated test is performed. I developed this list from the IBM AT BIOS, dated 6/10/85. Later IBM AT BIOS ROMs appear to use mostly the same codes. See Port 680h for codes used on IBM's MCA-based systems.

01h	Processor register tests, reset video
02h	BIOS ROM checksum (fails if bytes do not add to zero)
03h	CMOS read/write
04h	Timer 1 tests, check all count register bits on
05h	Timer 1 tests, check all count register bits off
06h	DMA 0 initialization and register test
07h	DMA 1 initialization and register test, start RAM refresh
08h	DMA page register test
09h	Memory refresh test
0Ah	Keyboard controller interface test, buffer cleared
0Bh	Keyboard controller, self test
0Ch	Keyboard controller, command test
0Dh	Keyboard controller, command test
0Eh	Memory test, first 64K
0Fh	Memory test, first 64K, cold boot
11h	Verify speed and refresh clock rates
12h	Protected mode register test, and initialize interrupt controller 1
13h	Initialize interrupt controller 2
14h	Set up all interrupt vectors to temporary handler
15h	Set up interrupt vectors 10h to 17h
16h	Verify CMOS battery status
17h	Verify CMOS checksum
18h	Disable parity
19h	Switch to protected mode
1Ah	Protected mode test
1Bh	Size RAM 0-640K and check for parity errors

1Ch	Check for main memory 512K or 640K
1Dh	Determine size of extended RAM
1Eh	Set extended memory size in CMOS locations 30h + 31h
1Fh	Test address lines for extended memory (A19 to A23)
20h	Switch back to real mode
21h	Read CMOS setup information and initialize video
22h	Video tests
23h	Check if video BIOS present
24h	Interrupt controller 0 and 1, read/write mask register
25h	Interrupt controller 0 and 1, read/write mask register
26h	Spurious interrupts detection
27h	Check for stuck NMI
28h	NMI is stuck or spurious NMI occurred
29h	Test timer 2
2Ah	Check timer 0 (RAM refresh speed) too slow
2Bh	Check timer 0 (RAM refresh speed) too fast
2Ch	Setup timer 0
2Dh	Check Keyboard controller status
2Eh	Unused
2Fh	Start of memory tests
30h	Start of memory tests, cold boot
31h	Enable protected mode
31h	Main memory test 0-640K (should have been 32h but coded wrong in BIOS)
32h	Unused
33h	Extended memory test
34h	Switch back to real mode
34h	Protected memory test passed (duplicate POST code)
35h	Start of keyboard test
35h	Protected memory test complete (duplicate POST code)
36h	Reset keyboard and check buffer full and stuck clock or data lines
37h	Keyboard not stuck
38h	Check for stuck key
39h	Check keyboard controller interface
3Ah	Setup BIOS interrupt vectors
3Bh	Check for optional ROMs at C800 to DF80, initialize other hardware
3Ch	Diskette drive tests
3Dh	Initialize diskette drive
3Eh	Initialize hard disk
3Fh	Initialize printer, time, date, and clear screen
40h	Unused
41h	Detect and checksum ROM at E000
42h	Initialize ROM at E000
43-DCh	Unused

DDh	Display RAM error address to this POST code port (DD is output, followed by the RAM address bytes, in a repeating sequence)
DE-EFh	Unused
F0h	Switch to protected mode
F1h	Test interrupt
F2h	Test General Protection Fault handler
F3h	Test protected mode instructions and control flags
F4h	Check memory bound operation
F5h	Test PUSHA and POPA instructions
F6h	Test access rights of description function correctly
F7h	Test ARPL instruction function
F8h	Test LAR instruction
F9h	Test LSL instruction
FAh	Protected mode memory address validity check

Phoenix ISA/EISA BIOS Common POST Codes

The POST code is sent to this diagnostic port. The indicated test is performed or test failure is indicated. This information was derived in part from Phoenix's BIOS technical reference.

01h	Test 16-bit CPU registers
02h	Read/write tests to CMOS register 0Eh
03h	Main BIOS ROM checksumed
04h	Test Timer 0
05h	DMA 0, channel 0 address and count register tests
06h	DMA page register tests
07h	Unused
08h	Memory DRAM refresh test
09h	Memory test, first 64K RAM
0Ah	Memory test failure, first 64K RAM
0B-0Ch	Unused
0Dh	Memory parity error, first 64K RAM
0Eh	Watchdog timer failure (EISA systems only)
0Fh	Forced software NMI port failure
10-1Fh	RAM test failure of 64K RAM, lower nibble indicates which bit 0-F failed in either the RAM chip or data line.
20h	DMA 1 initialization and register test (channels 1, 2, and 3)
21h	DMA 0 initialization and register test (channels 1, 2, and 3)
22h	Initialize and test interrupt controller 1, mask register
23h	Initialize and test interrupt controller 2, mask register
24h	Unused
25h	Setup BIOS interrupt vectors
26h	Unused
27h	Keyboard controller, self test

28h	Verify CMOS battery status and CMOS checksum
29h	Validate CMOS video configuration
2Ah	Unused
2Bh	Test video text memory area
2Ch	Video initialization in progress
2Dh	Test that the video retrace bit toggles
2Eh	Check if video BIOS present
2Fh	Unused
30h	Video BIOS detected and has been initialized
31h	Monochrome video operation set and operating
32h	Color 40 column mode video operation set and operating
33h	Color 80 column mode video operation set and operating
34h	Timer 0 with IRQ 0 tests
35h	Processor reset and recovery test
36h	A20 Gate line failure
37h	Unexpected interrupt occurred while in protected mode
38h	Memory test, above 64K
39h	Unused
3Ah	Test timer 2
3Bh	Test CMOS Real-Time Clock operating
3Ch	Test all installed serial ports
3Dh	Test all installed parallel ports
3Eh	Math Coprocessor integer load and store test

Port	Type	Description	Platform
84h	Output	POST diagnostic	Compaq

During the Power-On-Self-Test (POST) values are output to this port as each test is made. Should a test fail (or hang the system), the last value will indicate the test that failed. The port number and values may vary from model to model.

Port	Type	Description	Platform
84h	I/O	Synchronize Bus Cycle Register	EISA

This 8-bit register value has no function and can be written and read back. The act of reading the register will cause an extended I/O ready cycle to occur. This extended cycle will cause any buffers between EISA bus masters or DMA and main memory to be updated properly before the I/O cycle completes. The usefulness of this operation is unclear. This port may not be supported on all EISA implementations.

Port	Type	Description	Platform
90h	Output	POST diagnostic	Some PS/2

During the Power-On-Self-Test (POST) values are output to this port as each test is made. Should a test fail (or hang the system), the last value will indicate the test that failed. The port number and values are very manufacturer-dependent, and may vary from model to model. Port 90h is currently used on most PS/2 machines that have an ISA bus.

Port	Type	Description	Platform
91h	Input	Card Selected Feedback	MCA

When an adapter card's I/O is addressed, the card sends back a signal used to detect its presence. The card presence signal is recorded in this port. After this port is read, the presence bit is cleared. System I/O functions such as serial ports, parallel ports and the diskette controller also set this bit after being accessed.

Input (bit 0)

bit	0 r = 1	Selected card present

Port	Type	Description	Platform
92h	I/O	System Control	MCA/EISA

These bits control a number of unique system functions.

Input (bits 0-7) MCA

bit	7 r = x	Hard disk activity LED status
	6 r = x	bit 7 bit 6
		0 0 = off
		0 1 = on
		1 0 = on
		1 1 = on
	5 r = x	Unused (may be 0 or 1 depending on system)
	4 r = 1	Watchdog timeout occurred
	3 r = 0	Power-on-password accessible
	1	Power-on-password bytes inaccessible (see output for more details)
	2 r = x	Unused (may be 0 or 1 depending on system)
	1 r = 0	A20 address line disabled and forced to 0 (real mode)
	1	A20 address line enabled
	0 r = 0	Cold boot occurred
	1	Forced high speed reset (read by POST)

Output (bits 0-7) MCA

bit	7 w = x	Disk activity LED control
	6 w = x	bit 7 bit 6
		0 0 = off
		0 1 = on
		1 0 = on
		1 1 = on
	5 w = 0	Unused
	4 w = 0	Unused
	3 w = 1	Power-on-password bytes inaccessible. Password bytes are stored in CMOS registers 38h to 3Fh. Some systems also include bytes 36 and 37h. Once this bit is set to 1, the bit cannot be cleared except by a power-on-reset.
	2 w = 0	Unused
	1 w = 0	A20 address line disabled and forced to 0 (real mode)
	1	A20 address line enabled allowing access to memory above 1 MB.
	0 w = 0	Normal
	1	High speed reset—System is reset in 13.4 ms (used for switching from protected mode to real mode without going through the keyboard controller).

I/O (bits 0-7) EISA (undocumented, may differ by vendor)

bit	7 r/w = x	Hard disk activity LED status
	6 r/w = x	bit 7 bit 6
		0 0 = off
		0 1 = on
		1 0 = on
		1 1 = on
	5 r = 1	Unused or unknown
	4 r = 0	Unused
	3 r/w = 0	Power-on-password accessible
	3 w = 1	Power-on-password bytes inaccessible. Password bytes are stored in CMOS registers 38h to 3Fh. Some systems also include bytes 36 and 37h. Once this bit is set to 1, the bit cannot be cleared except by a power-on-reset.
	2 r = 1	Unused or unknown
	1 r/w = 0	A20 address line disabled and forced to 0 (real mode)
		A20 address line enabled
	0 w = 0	Normal

Port	Type	Description	Platform
94h	I/O	System Control Enables	MCA

This register controls setup and enabling certain motherboard functions.

Before going to motherboard setup mode (bits 7 or 5 set to 0), the adapter setup must be off. This can be verified by reading from port 96h that bit 3 is 0. If not, write 0 to port 94h to turn off adapter setup mode.

After motherboard setup is complete, this register should be written with the value FFh.

I/O (bits 0-7)

bit	7 r/w =	x	diskette drive controller, serial, parallel, and memory
		0	Setup mode (memory controlled through port 103h, others controlled through port 102h)
		1	Enable (default)
	6 r/w =	1	Unused
	5 r/w =	x	Video subsystem
		0	Setup mode (controlled through port 102h)
		1	Enable when port 102h bit 0 = 1 (default)
	4 r/w =	1	Unused
	3 r/w =	1	Unused
	2 r/w =	1	Unused
	1 r/w =	1	Unused
	0 r/w =	1	Unused

Port	Type	Description	Platform
96h	I/O	Adapter Enable and Setup	MCA

This register allows control and setup of each individual adapter card slot. It is also used to reset all adapter cards as a group.

Before going to setup mode on any adapter, system setup must be off. This can be verified by reading an FFh from port 94h. If any other value is returned, write an FFh to port 94h to exit system setup and video setup modes.

After adapter setup is complete, this register should be written with 00h.

I/O (bits 0-7)

bit	7 w =	0	normal
		1	activate the Channel Reset on all adapter slots
	6 r/w =	1	Unused
	5 r/w =	1	Unused
	4 r/w =	1	Unused
	3 r/w =	1	Send the card setup signal to slot specified in bits 0-2

2 r/w = x	Adapter card select			
1 r/w = x		bit 2	bit 1	bit 0
0 r/w = x		0	0	0 = slot 1
		0	0	1 = slot 2
		0	1	0 = slot 3
		0	1	1 = slot 4
		1	0	0 = slot 5 (not all systems)
		1	0	1 = slot 6 (not all systems)
		1	1	0 = slot 7 (not all systems)
		1	1	1 = slot 8 (not all systems)

Port	Type	Description	Platform
E0h	I/O	Split Address Register	MCA

This register specifies the starting address of the split memory block on PS/2 model 80 systems.

Split memory refers to the ability to split up first megabyte of memory for different uses. Most systems are set to have a full 640K of main memory, and use the remainder for shadowing the BIOS ROMs and extended memory. The types of splits are selected from the memory register at port E1h.

The split often leaves only a small 256K or 384K block to add to extended memory. Additional extended memory is provided in 1 MB sections on a 1 MB boundary. The memory block left from the split must be placed at the end of any other extended memory. This function assigns the placement of this extra block of memory.

Depending on the motherboard type, these functions differ. See port E1h to enable split memory.

I/O (bits 0-7)

bit	7 r/w = x	Unused		
	6 r/w = x	Unused		
	5 r/w = x	Memory (2 MB) for connector 2 (Type 2 motherboard)		
	4 r/w = x		bit 5	bit 4
			0	0 = 2 MB enabled
			0	1 = second 1 MB enabled of 2 MB
			1	0 = first 1 MB enabled of 2 MB
			1	1 = disabled or not installed
	3 r/w = x	Select which 1 MB extended memory area for split memory, 1 to 15. Zero is an invalid value when split memory is active.		
	2 r/w = x			
	1 r/w = x			
	0 r/w = x			

Port	Type	Description	Platform
E1h	I/O	Memory Register	MCA

This register allows control and status of motherboard memory on PS/2 model 80 systems. Depending on the motherboard type, these functions differ. When split memory is enabled, port E0h is used to specify where the memory above 1 MB should reside. Do not use split memory if the system has more than 16 MB total.

I/O (bits 0-7) Type 1 motherboard

bit 7 r/w = x | Memory (1 MB) for connector 2
6 r/w = x |

bit 7	bit 6
1	0 = installed
1	1 = not installed

5 r/w = x | Memory (1 MB) for connector 1
4 r/w = x |

bit 5	bit 4
1	0 = installed
1	1 = not installed

3 r/w = x | Split memory select and control of BIOS shadowing
2 r/w = x |
1 r/w = x

bit 3	bit 2	bit 1	ROM	Low Mem	Mem above 1 MB
0	0	1	= On	640 K	384 K
0	1	1	= On	512 K	512 K
1	0	0	= Shadowed	640 K	0 K
1	0	1	= On	640 K	0 K
1	1	0	= Shadowed	512 K	0 K
1	1	1	= On	512 K	0 K

0 r/w = 0 Enable memory parity checking
1 Clear memory parity error (and rewrite a 0 to re-enable)

I/O (bits 0-7) Type 2 motherboard

bit 7 r/w = x Unused
6 r/w = x Unused
5 r/w = x Memory Connector 1
4 r/w = x

bit 5	bit 4
0	0 = 2 MB enabled
0	1 = second 1 MB enabled of 2 MB
1	0 = first 1 MB enabled of 2 MB

3 r/w = x	Split memory select and control of BIOS shadowing						
2 r/w = x		bit 3	bit 2	bit 1	ROM	Low Mem	Mem above 1 MB
1 r/w = x		0	0	0	= Shadowed	640 KB	256 KB
		0	0	1	= On	640 KB	256 KB
		0	1	0	= Shadowed	512 KB	384 KB
		0	1	1	= On	512 KB	384 KB
		1	0	0	= Shadowed	640 KB	0 KB
		1	0	1	= On	640 KB	0 KB
		1	1	0	= Shadowed	512 KB	0 KB
		1	1	1	= On	512 KB	0 KB
0 r/w = 0	Enable memory parity checking						
1	Clear memory parity error (and rewrite a 0 to re-enable)						

Port	Type	Description	Platform
E3h	I/O	Error Trace Register	MCA

This is one of four error trace registers used on some MCA models. Specifically it is used on IBM's model 80, but not on models 50/60. The register holds the uppermost memory address bits on every rising edge of the ERS (errors) signal. A hardware reset forces this register to zero.

I/O (bits 0-7)

bit	7 r/w = x	Address bit 23
	6 r/w = x	Address bit 22
	5 r/w = x	Address bit 21
	4 r/w = x	Address bit 20
	3 r/w = x	Address bit 19
	2 r/w = x	Address bit 18
	1 r/w = x	Address bit 17
	0 r/w = x	Address bit 16

Port	Type	Description	Platform
E4h	I/O	Error Trace Register	MCA

This is one of four error trace registers used on some MCA models. See port E3h for details.

I/O (bits 0-7)

bit	7 r/w = x		Address bit 15
	6 r/w = x		Address bit 14
	5 r/w = x		Address bit 13
	4 r/w = x		Address bit 12
	3 r/w = x		Address bit 11
	2 r/w = x		Address bit 10
	1 r/w = x		Address bit 9
	0 r/w = x		Address bit 8

Port	Type	Description	Platform
E5h	I/O	Error Trace Register	MCA

This is one of four error trace registers used on some MCA models. See port E3h for details.

I/O (bits 0-7)

bit	7 r/w = x		Address bit 7
	6 r/w = x		Address bit 6
	5 r/w = x		Address bit 5
	4 r/w = x		Address bit 4
	3 r/w = x		Address bit 3
	2 r/w = x		Address bit 2
	1 r/w = 0		address captured was an I/O port
		1	address captured was memory
	0 r/w = 0		Grant
		1	Arbitration cycle for bus master control

Port	Type	Description	Platform
E7h	I/O	Error Trace Register	MCA

This is one of four error trace registers used on some MCA models. See port E3h for details. The register holds a single bit, the D/C signal line status when the edge of the ERS (errors) signal occurs. A hardware reset forces this register to zero.

I/O (bits 0-7)

bit	7 r/w = x		Unused
	6 r/w = x		Unused
	5 r/w = x		Unused
	4 r/w = x		Unused

3 r/w = x	Unused
2 r/w = x	Unused
1 r/w = x	Unused
0 r/w = 0	Bus cycle is Control for instruction fetch, halt, interrupt acknowledge
1	Bus cycle is Data for both memory and I/O access

Port	Type	Description	Platform
F0h	Output	Math Coprocessor—Clear Busy	AT+

A write to this port with the value zero will clear the math coprocessor's busy flag.

When the math coprocessor is either executing a given instruction or has encountered an error condition, a hardware busy line from the coprocessor to the main processor is asserted. In normal operation, the WAIT instruction is used to wait until the busy line is cleared by the completion of the current math coprocessor instruction. If an error occurred, then IRQ 13 (interrupt 75) is issued along with the busy signal. The busy line is left active until cleared by a write to this port with a data byte value of 0.

The BIOS normally processes the error condition of the math coprocessor. When interrupt 75 occurs, the BIOS will issue a write to port F0h to clear the busy flag, and issue an NMI (interrupt 2). This is done to retain software compatibility with older PC/XT computers.

Output (bits 0-7) Zero clears the busy flag

Port	Type	Description	Platform
F1h	Output	Math Coprocessor—Reset	AT+

Reset the math coprocessor. When a value of zero is written to port F1h, the math coprocessor is reset. If the math coprocessor was previously in protected mode, a reset will also switch the math coprocessor back to real mode.

The actions of this reset are identical to a power-on-reset or a system reset.

Output (bits 0-7) Zero resets the math coprocessor

Port	Type	Description	Platform
F8h	I/O	Math Coprocessor—Opcode Transfer	AT+

The processor communications with the math coprocessor through ports F8h, FAh, and FCh. Opcodes and operands are passed to the math coprocessor and results are passed back using these ports.

Port	Type	Description	Platform
FAh	I/O	Math Coprocessor—Opcode Transfer	AT+

See port F8h.

Port	Type	Description	Platform
FCh	I/O	Math Coprocessor—Opcode Transfer	AT+

See port F8h.

Port	Type	Description	Platform
100h	Input	Programmable Option Select 0	MCA

This port allows reading of the low byte of the adapter identification word. The specific adapter must have been previously placed into setup mode using port 96h.

Input (bits 0-7) Adapter ID low byte

Port	Type	Description	Platform
101h	Input	Programmable Option Select 1	MCA

This port allows reading of the high byte of the adapter identification word. The specific adapter must have been previously placed into setup mode using port 96h.

Input (bits 0-7) Adapter ID high byte

Port	Type	Description	Platform
102h	I/O	Programmable Option Select 2	MCA

This register is used for both the system board and adapter setup. For system setup, the system setup state must be activated using port 94h. To select a specific adapter, the adapter must have been previously placed into setup mode using port 96h.

I/O (bits 0-7) System Setup

bit	7 r/w = 0	Parallel port bidirectional mode
	1	Parallel port output only mode (default after POST)
	6 r/w = x	Parallel port assignment for IRQ 7
	5 r/w = x	bit 6 bit 5
		0 0 = Use as LPT 1, at address 3BCh-3BFh
		0 1 = Use as LPT 2, at address 378h-37Bh

	1	0 = Use as LPT 3, at address 378h-37Bh
	1	1 = invalid
4 r/w = 1		Enable parallel port (see bit 0)
3 r/w = 0		Serial port as COM2, at address 2F8h-2FFh with IRQ 3
1		Serial port as COM1, at address 3F8h-3FFh with IRQ 4
2 r/w = 1		Enable serial port (see bit 0)
1 r/w = 1		Enable diskette controller (see bit 0)
0 r/w = 0		System override disable (parallel, serial, and diskette are all disabled regardless of bits 1, 2 and 4)
1		Normal system enable

I/O (bits 0-7) Adapter Setup—Option select byte 1

bit	7 r/w = x	Defined by adapter card
	6 r/w = x	
	5 r/w = x	
	4 r/w = x	
	3 r/w = x	
	2 r/w = x	
	1 r/w = x	
	0 r/w = 0	Disable selected adapter card
	1	Enable selected adapter card

Port	Type	Description	Platform
103h	I/O	Programmable Option Select 3	MCA

This register is used for both the system board and adapter setup. For system setup, the system setup state must be activated using port 94h. To select a specific adapter, the adapter must have been previously placed into setup mode using port 96h.

I/O (bit 0) System Setup (PS/2 models 50/55/60)

bit	0 r/w = 0	Disable motherboard memory
	1	Enable motherboard memory

Input (bits 0-7) System Setup (PS/2 model 70, Types 1 and 2)

bit	7 r = x	Unused
	6 r = 0	If memory installed, connector 3, then 1 MB
	1	If memory installed, connector 3, then 2 MB
	5 r = 0	Memory is installed in connector 3
	4 r = x	Unused

3 r = 0	If memory installed, connector 2, then 1 MB
1	If memory installed, connector 2, then 2 MB
2 r = 0	Memory is installed in connector 2
1 r = 0	If memory installed, connector 1, then 1 MB
1	If memory installed, connector 1, then 2 MB
0 r = 0	Memory is installed in connector 1

Input (bits 0-7) System Setup (PS/2 model 80, Type 1); see ports E1 and E2h

bit	7 r = x	Unused
	6 r = x	Unused
	5 r = x	Unused
	4 r = x	Unused
	3 r = x	Memory (1 MB) for connector 2
	2 r = x	bit 3 bit 2
		0 0 = installed
		1 1 = not installed
	1 r = x	Memory (1 MB) for connector 1
	0 r = x	bit 1 bit 0
		0 0 = installed
		1 1 = not installed

Input (bits 0-7) System Setup (PS/2 model 80, Type 2); see ports E1 and E2h

bit	7 r = x	Unused
	6 r = x	Unused
	5 r = x	Unused
	4 r = x	Unused
	3 r = x	Memory (2 MB) for connector 2
	2 r = x	bit 3 bit 2
		1 0 = installed
		1 1 = not installed
	1 r = 1	Memory for connector 1 (must have 2 MB)
	0 r = 0	

I/O (bits 0-7) Adapter Setup—Option select byte 2 defined by specific adapter card

Port	Type	Description	Platform
104h	I/O	Programmable Option Select 4	MCA

This register is used for adapter setup on all models and for system setup on some models. For system setup, the system setup state must be activated using port 94h. The specific memory connector must also be selected using port 105h. To select a specific adapter, the adapter must have been previously placed into setup mode using port 96h.

I/O (bit 0) System Setup (PS/2 model 55)

bit		
7 r = x	Memory Card ID	
6 r = x		
5 r = x		
4 r = x		

bit 7	6	5	4	Size	Speed
0	0	0	1	= 2 MB	100 ns
0	0	1	0	= 1 MB	100 ns
0	1	0	1	= 2 MB	85 ns
0	1	1	0	= 1 MB	85 ns

bit	Description
3 r = x	Unused
2 r = x	Unused
1 r/w = 1	On 2 MB card, enable second 1 MB
0 r/w = 1	Enable first 1 MB

I/O (bits 0-7) Adapter Setup—Option select byte 3

bit	Description
7 r/w = x	Channel check active indicator
6 r/w = x	Channel check status-available indicator
5 r/w = x	Defined by adapter card
4 r/w = x	
3 r/w = x	
2 r/w = x	
1 r/w = x	
0 r/w = x	

Port	Type	Description	Platform
105h	I/O	Programmable Option Select 5	MCA

This register is used for adapter setup on all models and for system setup on some models. For system setup, the system setup state must be activated using port 94h. To select a specific adapter, the adapter must have been previously placed into setup mode using port 96h.

I/O (bit 0) System Setup (PS/2 model 55)

bit	7 r	= x	Unused
	6 r	= x	Unused
	5 r/w	= 0	Map 128 KB of memory at BIOS address and 256 KB above 1 MB
		1	Disable 384 KB of memory (leaves 640 KB main memory)
	4 r/w	= 1	BIOS shadow setup mode—address E0000-FFFFF read from ROM and if bit 5 = 0, writes go to RAM
		0	BIOS shadow enable—address E0000-FFFFF read from shadow RAM, and writes are disabled
	3 r	= x	Unused
	2 r/w	= x	Select memory connector 0-7 (see port 104h)
	1 r/w	= x	
	0 r/w	= x	

I/O (bits 0-7) Adapter Setup—Option select byte 4

Port	Type	Description	Platform
106h	Input	Programmable Option Select 6	MCA

This port specifies the low byte of the adapter subaddress extension word. The specific adapter must have been previously placed into setup mode using port 96h.

Input (bits 0-7) Adapter Subaddress extension low byte

Port	Type	Description	Platform
107h	Input	Programmable Option Select 7	MCA

This port specifies the high byte of the adapter subaddress extension word. The specific adapter must have been previously placed into setup mode using port 96h.

Input (bits 0-7) Adapter Subaddress extension high byte

Port	Type	Description	Platform
178h	Output	Power Management Index Selection	AT+

Some laptops and other systems that use power management access a set of power management functions. This is an alternate port depending on hardware implementation. It is identical to functions described for ports 26h and 27h.

Port	Type	Description	Platform
179h	I/O	Power Management Data	AT+

For systems with power management, this port accesses the power management register specified in a prior write to port 178h. See port 178h for details.

Port	Type	Description	Platform
300h	Output	POST diagnostic	Award

Diagnostic information during POST is sent to both ports 80h and 300h. Refer to port 80h for details.

Port	Type	Description	Platform
40Dh	Input	Stepping Level Register	EISA

Reads the stepping level (revision) of Intel's 82357 EISA Integrated System Peripheral chip. Unlikely to be implemented in other EISA designs.

Port	Type	Description	Platform
40Eh	I/O	Test Register 1	EISA

Undocumented test register for Intel's 82357 EISA Integrated System Peripheral chip. Unlikely to be implemented in other EISA designs.

Port	Type	Description	Platform
40Fh	I/O	Test Register 2	EISA

Undocumented test register for Intel's 82357 EISA Integrated System Peripheral chip. Unlikely to be implemented in other EISA designs.

Port	Type	Description	Platform
461h	I/O	Extended NMI and Control	EISA

This register controls various error conditions and status.

Output (bits 0-3), Input (bits 0-7)

bit	7 r	= 0	No Watchdog timeout or NMI not enabled
		1	Watchdog Timeout occurred—NMI pending
	6 r	= 0	No Bus timeout or NMI not enabled
		1	Bus Timeout occurred—NMI pending (see port 464h)
	5 r	= 0	No I/O port status or NMI not enabled
		1	I/O port status—NMI pending

4 r	= 1	Busmaster preemption timeout occurred
	x	Undefined if bit 6 = 0
3 r/w	= 0	Bus timeout disabled and cleared
	1	Bus timeout enabled—If NMI is enabled, and a timeout occurs, then an NMI interrupt is generated and status bit 6 is set.
	x	Undefined if bit 6 = 0
2 r/w	= 0	Watchdog timer disabled and cleared (default)
	1	Watchdog timer enabled—If NMI is enabled, and a timeout occurs, then a NMI interrupt is generated and status bit 7 is set.
1 r/w	= 0	NMI I/O port control disabled (default)
	1	NMI I/O port control enabled—If NMI is enabled, and an I/O port NMI is generated, status bit 5 is set.
0 r/w	= 0	Normal bus reset operation (default)
	1	Bus reset active

Port	Type	Description	Platform
464h	Input	Last Busmaster Granted	EISA

The last busmaster adapter, which had control of the bus, is recorded in this register with its bit set to 0. All other bits will be 1. The register is read-only.

When a bus timeout occurs, it is useful to identify which busmaster adapter caused the problem. This would be handled by the NMI routine after detecting a bus timeout.

Input (bits 0-7)

bit	7 r = 0	Busmaster 1 was last
	6 r = 0	Busmaster 2 was last
	5 r = 0	Busmaster 3 was last
	4 r = 0	Busmaster 4 was last
	3 r = 0	Busmaster 5 was last
	2 r = 0	Busmaster 6 was last
	1 r = 0	Busmaster 7 was last
	0 r = 0	Busmaster 8 was last

Port	Type	Description	Platform
465h	Input	Last Busmaster Granted	EISA

The last busmaster adapter, which had control of the bus, is recorded in this register with its bit set to 0. All other bits will be 1. The register is read-only.

It is useful should a bus timeout occur to identify which busmaster adapter caused the problem. This would be handled by the NMI routine after detecting a bus timeout.

Input (bits 0-7)

bit	7 r = 0	Busmaster 9 was last
	6 r = 0	Busmaster 10 was last
	5 r = 0	Busmaster 11 was last
	4 r = 0	Busmaster 12 was last
	3 r = 0	Busmaster 13 was last
	2 r = 0	Busmaster 14 was last
	1 r = 0	Busmaster 15 was last
	0 r = 1	Unused

Port	Type	Description	Platform
680h	Output	POST diagnostic	MCA

During the Power-On-Self-Test (POST) values are output to this port as each test is made. Should a test fail (or hang the system), the last value will indicate the test that failed. The port number and values are very manufacturer-dependent, and may vary from model to model. Port 680h is currently only used for machines that have an MCA bus.

The post codes that are sent to port 680h are also sent to the parallel printer 1, at I/O port 3BCh.

IBM MCA BIOS Common POST Codes

The POST code is sent to this port and the indicated test is performed. This list was developed from the IBM PS/2 BIOS, model 70, BIOS dated 2/7/89. Other IBM PS/2 MCA BIOS ROMs appear to use most of the same codes.

01h	Processor register tests
02h	BIOS ROM checksum (fails if bytes do not add to zero)
03h	System enable port test
04h	Programmable Option Select 2 test
05h	Adapter setup port test
06h	CMOS read/write
07h	Extended CMOS read/write
08h	DMA and page register tests
09h	DMA initialization
0Ah	Memory refresh test
0Bh	Keyboard controller interface test
0Ch	Keyboard controller, self test
0Dh	Keyboard controller, self test
0Eh	Keyboard controller, self test error

0Fh	System memory setup
10h	Test system memory (fault address sent to port 681h), clear video memory, initialize VGA controller
11h	Memory test failure
12h	Setup LDGT/LIDT/SGDT/SIDT for protected mode
13h	Initialize interrupt controller 1
14h	Initialize interrupt controller 2
15h	Interrupt vectors loaded with pointer to unused interrupt handler
16h	Set up interrupt vectors 10h to 1Fh
17h	Verify CMOS battery status
18h	Verify CMOS checksum
19h	CMOS battery defective or disconnected
1Ah	Cold boot—clear memory parity flags & IRQ 1 latch
1Bh	Enter protected mode
1Ch	Verify really in protected mode
1Dh	Determine low memory size
1Eh	Memory test with parity checking enabled
1Fh	BIOS shadowing setup
20h	Extended memory check
21h	DRAM address lines test
22h	Enable memory and I/O parity checking
23h	Warm boot loading of int vectors with unused handler
24h	CMOS battery status and checksum verification
25h	Cold boot Keyboard controller test
26-33h	Unused
34h	Descriptor tests ok
35h	Descriptor tests complete
36-3Fh	Unused
40h	Video initialization
41h	System board ID validity check
42h	Interrupt controller 0 and 1, read/write mask register 0
43h	Interrupt controller 0 and 1, read/write mask register FF
44h	Refresh clock test
45h	NMI test
46h	NMI test failed
47h	Timer 2 test—interface and count register
48h	Timer 2 test—output and not shorted to Timer 0 out
49h	Timer 0 test—interface and count register
4Ah	Timer 0 test—not shorted to Timer 2 out
4Bh	Timer 0 test—IRQ 0 operates
4Ch	Timer 3 test—Watchdog timer
4Dh	Timer 0 interrupt occurred verification
4Eh	Keyboard controller ready

4Fh	Soft reset test, cold boot
50h	Protected mode setup, cold boot
51h	Enter protected mode, cold boot
52h	Memory test in 64K sections, cold boot
53h	Memory test complete, cold boot
54h	System reset and resume real mode, cold boot
55h	Manufacturing test or normal test decision
56h	Keyboard power test and test if keyboard data line stuck
57h	Keyboard self-test
58h	Keyboard test successful
59h	Keyboard clock and data line tests
5Ah	Mouse test and initialization
5Bh	Mouse disabled, Keyboard enabled
5Ch	Set up interrupt vectors 8 to 0Fh
5Dh	Set up interrupt vectors 70 to 7Fh
5Eh	Set up interrupt vectors 2, 5, 18h, and zero vectors 60 to 6Fh
5Fh	Hard disk controller reset
60h	Hard disk 0 configuration setup
61h	Floppy drive reset
62h	Floppy drive test
63h	Floppy drive motor off
64h	Serial port tests and keyboard buffer initialization
65h	Timer 0 interrupt enabled (timer ticks), flag error if prior memory size error or invalid system configuration data
66h	Hard drives and floppy drives configured
67h	Set up interrupt vector 13h and initialize floppy drive(s)
68h	CPU Arbitration enabled
69h	Check for optional ROMs at C000 to DF80
6Ah	Serial and parallel ports testing
6Bh	Equipment byte determined and CMOS checksum verified
6Ch	Math coprocessor initialization
6Dh	Keyboard BIOS values initialized, IRQ 1 enabled (keyboard), printer ports initialized
6Eh	Proceed to bootstrap loader (load and run boot sector)
6Fh	Prepare for bootstrap load
70h	Area at 0:7C00 for bootstrap cleared
71h	Disk reset complete
72h	Sectors read into memory for bootstrap
73h	Bootstrap failed, go to ROM BASIC
74-BDh	Unused
BEh	Setup IDT and GDT and go into protected mode
BFh	Successfully entered protected mode
C0-E0h	Unused

F0h	Memory tests ok
F1h	Verify in protected mode
F2h	Interrupt 20h works (not DOS terminate)
F3h	Descriptor table setup
F4h	LDT and TS register test complete
F5h	Bound check tests
F6h	CPU register test ok
F7h	Verify access test complete
F8h	Privilege level test complete
F9h	Access rights test complete
FAh	Segment limit test complete

Port	Type	Description	Platform
681h	Output	POST Secondary Diagnostic	MCA

This port is used normally in conjunction with port 680h to provide additional information during some tests.

Port	Type	Description	Platform
C80h	Input	System Board ID 1	EISA

This byte with the byte from port C81h form a 3-character manufacturer ID. These bytes are compressed into 5-bit characters. Add 40h to each 5-bit character convert to ASCII letters A-Z.

To ensure valid information, write FFh to port C80h, followed by a read. If bit 7 is 1, no ID information is available.

Input (bits 0-6)

bit	7 r = 0	Fixed
	6 r = x	ID character 1
	5 r = x	
	4 r = x	
	3 r = x	
	2 r = x	
	1 r = x	Top 2 bits of ID character 2 (see port C81h)
	0 r = x	

Port	Type	Description	Platform
C81h	Input	System Board ID 2	EISA

This byte with the byte from port C80h form a 3-character manufacturer ID. These bytes are compressed into 5-bit characters. Add 40h to each 5-bit character convert to ASCII letters A-Z.

Input (bits 0-7)

bit	7 r = x	Bottom 3 bits of ID character 2 (see port C80h)
	6 r = x	
	5 r = x	
	4 r = x	ID character 3
	3 r = x	
	2 r = x	
	1 r = x	
	0 r = x	

Port	Type	Description	Platform
C82h	Input	System Board ID 3	EISA

This port is assigned by the individual EISA motherboard manufacturer for any special or unique capabilities.

Port	Type	Description	Platform
C83h	Input	System Board ID 4	EISA

This byte defines the EISA bus version. The first version is 1.

Input (bits 0-7)

bit	7 r = x	Manufacturer defined
	6 r = x	
	5 r = x	
	4 r = x	
	3 r = x	
	2 r = x	EISA bus version number
	1 r = x	
	0 r = x	

CHAPTER 14

Parallel Ports and Print Screen

Printer operations have changed very little since the first PC. The printer BIOS functions are reasonably straightforward, although I've explained the error information in more detail than previously available.

Several enhancements have been made over the years to parallel ports, including bidirectional data control and a fast port design that provides 10 times the performance over a normal parallel port. These capabilities are explained in detail.

I've created three small utilities to show different, less-known aspects of the parallel ports. This includes a filter TSR that converts the upper 128 IBM characters into printable characters on printers that do not support the complete IBM character set. Two other simple utilities will swap printers and detect the printers in the system and identify those ports that are bidirectional.

Introduction

The PC system design allows for up to four parallel ports. These parallel ports were intended for the attachment of printers. In addition, parallel ports are commonly used for copy protection keys, external tape backup devices, external CD-ROM drives, and other specialized data transfers.

Some parallel ports are designed for an optional extended mode. This allows full bidirectional data transfers. This is sometimes used for external disk and tape drives, network connections, and machine-to-machine data transfers. All MCA systems provide parallel ports with extended mode capability. Many newer systems also implement the "Fast Parallel Port" standard. This greatly boosts the maximum throughput on the parallel port.

Normally, the parallel port resides on a separate adapter card. The monochrome display adapter card has always been configured with a parallel port. On MCA systems at least one parallel port is built into the system motherboard. Most laptops also have a parallel port included as part of the system.

Figure 14-1 shows the design of the parallel port. The parallel port consists of a set of control and data latches to send signals to the parallel port connector. The same signals presented to the connector can be read to confirm proper operation. Additional status and control signals are read from the connector. When extended mode is available, and in a read mode, the latched data output is disabled so data can be read from the connector.

Figure 14-1. Parallel Port

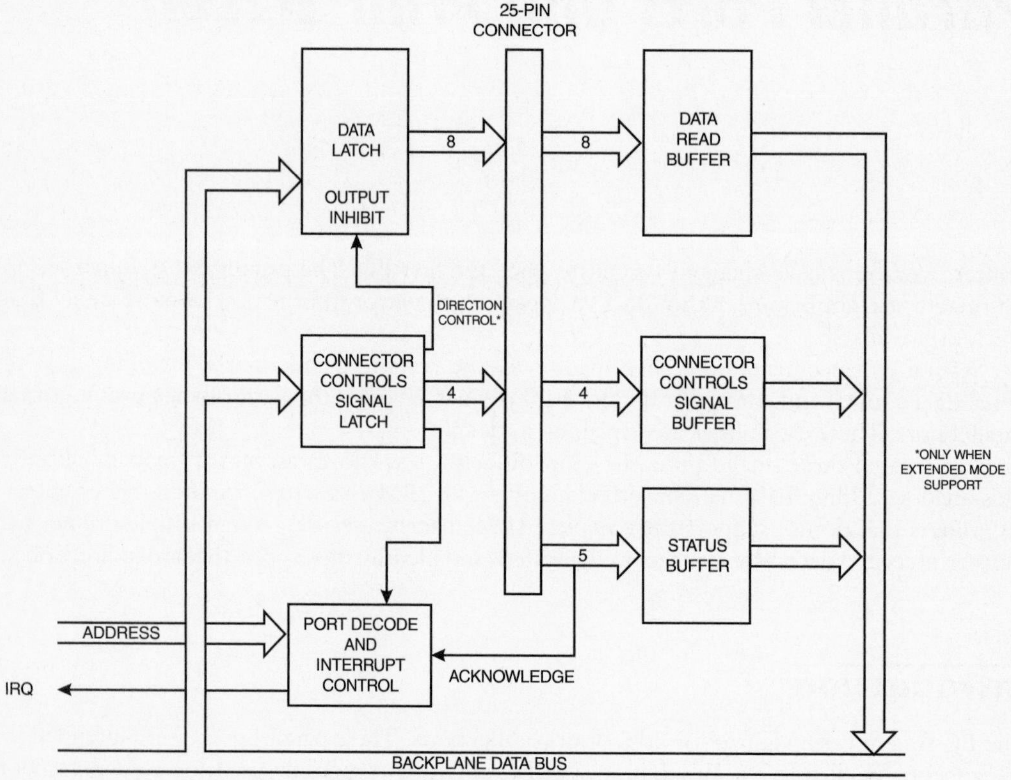

The system BIOS provides a special printer service, interrupt 17h, to initialize the printer, get printer status, and send data to the printer. For all other users of parallel ports, it is necessary to communicate directly with the I/O port addresses associated with the parallel port.

There are four possible parallel ports, numbered 1 to 4. These are accessed through consecutive sets of I/O port addresses. There is *no* direct mapping between I/O port addresses and the parallel port numbers. The I/O port associated with each parallel port number is determined by the system's Power-On-Self-Test (POST).

Many of the lowest-level routines are zero-based. To access parallel port 1, a register is loaded with 0.

BIOS Initialization

After a reset, the POST checks if any parallel ports are installed. The POST examines I/O port addresses 3BCh, 378h, and 278h in sequence. An active port is detected by writing a byte to the I/O port followed by a read from the same port. If the bytes match, the POST accepts the I/O port as having an active parallel port at the tested I/O address. The I/O address of the active port is then saved in the lowest unused parallel port BIOS RAM location. There are four words assigned in the BIOS RAM starting at 40:8. These bytes are used to hold the active parallel port I/O addresses.

What this all means is that parallel port 1 is associated with BIOS RAM address 40:8, port 2 with address 40:Ah, and port 3 with address 40:Ch. The contents of each word has the base I/O port address used to access the parallel port. A value of zero indicates no parallel port hardware was detected.

These tests do not confirm if a printer or any other device is actually attached to the I/O port. The test only checks if the parallel port hardware exists at the specified I/O address. The POST stores the total number of active parallel ports detected in the equipment byte at BIOS RAM location 40:10h, bits 14 and 15.

As an example, if a system has two parallel ports, using I/O addresses 378h and 278h, the parallel port RAM locations will have the following contents:

RAM Address	Parallel Port	I/O Port Address
40:8h	1	378h
40:Ah	2	278h
40:Ch	3	0
40:Eh	4	0

Can a System Have a Fourth Parallel Port ?

The original PC and XT systems allow a fourth parallel port. Starting with the AT, the word previously used to hold the fourth parallel port address in the BIOS RAM at 40:E was "reserved." The AT BIOS does not use this byte, so on AT machines it is easily used as a fourth parallel port.

The PS/2 was one of the first systems to actually use BIOS RAM word 40:E for the segment of the extended BIOS data area (EBDA). The EBDA is described in detail in Chapter 6. Many other BIOS manufacturers have followed suit, and it has become unsafe to use a fourth parallel port on AT+ systems, unless it is clearly known the BIOS manufacturer never uses this word for other purposes. Checking for a zero value at location 40:E may not be enough, because this may signal that there is no extended BIOS data area. Inserting an I/O port address in BIOS location 40:E could make the BIOS, or other software, believe this is the segment where the Extended BIOS data area begins. This could cause all sorts of weird effects and result in a hung system!

The POST does not check for a fourth parallel port. A system that has a fourth parallel port must check and load the I/O address of this port using a device driver, firmware, or other software means. Though not documented, the printer service handler, interrupt 17h, will normally support a printer attached to parallel port 4. The major known exception is on MCA systems, where the printer BIOS only supports three printers.

Printer BIOS

The printer BIOS is used to access a printer from any parallel port. The printer BIOS depends on the port addresses having been previously determined and saved in the BIOS RAM area at 40:8, as is done by POST. If an attempt is made to access a parallel port that does not exist (I/O port value of 0), the service returns without changing any register values.

All three printer BIOS services return the status of the printer in AH after the specified action was taken. The status is obtained by reading the printer status I/O port and inverting the state of the I/O error bit 3 and acknowledge bit 6. The resultant value is placed in AH. As an example, if the base I/O port was 278h, the status is read from port 279h. If the BIOS times out, the return status AH bit 0 is set to 1. This value is not read from the printer status I/O port, but is set by the BIOS. When bit 0 is set, it indicates a timeout condition occurred.

The returned status is defined as follows:

bit 7 = 0 Printer is busy This is an inversion of the line from parallel port connector pin 11 and is controlled by the printer. This bit is zero when the printer is busy and cannot accept data. The printer is busy when the printer is in a print operation, offline, or when an error occurred.

bit 6 = 1 Printer acknowledge This is an inversion of the line from the parallel port connector pin 10 and is controlled by the printer. A short 0.5 uS pulse from the printer indicates the printer is ready to receive data. If the interrupt is enabled for the parallel port, the act of acknowledgment will also generate a hardware interrupt.

bit 5 = 1 Out of paper This is directly read from the parallel port connector pin 12. This bit is set high when the printer runs out of paper. See the warnings section for potential problems.

bit 4 = 1 Printer selected This is directly read from the parallel port connector pin 13. This bit is set high by the printer when the printer is actively selected.

bit 3 = 1 I/O error This is an inversion of the line from the parallel port connector pin 15. When the printer is offline, paper is out, or a printer error is detected, this bit is set to 1.

bit 2 = x Unused
bit 1 = x Unused
bit 0 = 1 Timeout While printing a character, the printer remains busy longer than the timeout period. Unlike other status bits, this one is set by the BIOS service handler. When this bit is active, all other bits in the status byte are undefined. This means the timeout bit 0 must be checked before evaluating any other status bits. The timeout duration varies between systems, but the average duration is 40 uS. The timeout delay period is specified in the BIOS data area, starting at 40:78h.

Interrupt 17h provides the following three services:

Function	**Description**
ah=0	Print Character
ah=1	Initialize Printer
ah=2	Get Printer Status

Int	Func	Description	Platform
17h	0	Print Character	All

The print character function sends the byte in AL to the specified parallel port. If the printer is busy, the BIOS routine waits for the timeout period in case the printer becomes ready. If it becomes ready, the character is sent. If the timeout occurs, the BIOS sets the timeout status bit. The printer status is returned in AL. The status should be checked to ensure an error did not occur while attempting to print.

Called with:	ah = 0
	al = character to print
	dx = 0 to 3 for parallel port numbers 1 to 4 (port 4 not always supported)
Returns:	ah = printer status bits (explained in previous section)

Int	Func	Description	Platform
17h	1	Initialize Printer	All

This function initializes the printer at parallel port specified in DX. To perform the initialization, the printer BIOS sets the parallel port connector pin 16 low for a period greater than 50 uS.

Called with:	ah = 1
	dx = 0 to 3 for parallel port numbers 1 to 4 (port 4 not always supported)
Returns:	ah = printer status bits (explained in previous section)

INT

Int	Func	Description	Platform
17h	2	Get Printer Status	All

Gets the printer status in AH. Since this function simply reads the state of lines on the connector, a timeout cannot occur.

Called with:	ah = 2
	dx = 0 to 3 for parallel port numbers 1 to 4 (port 4 not always supported)
Returns:	ah = printer status bits (explained in previous section)

Print Screen

The system BIOS provides a print screen service, interrupt 5, to print the screen contents to the printer attached to parallel port 1. Print screen is normally called from the low-level keyboard BIOS, interrupt 9, when the Print Screen key is pressed. During the act of printing the screen, the print screen BIOS moves the cursor to the byte being read and sends that character to the printer. When the print screen is complete, the original cursor position is restored.

If an error condition occurs during the print screen operation, the print screen status byte at address 50:0 is set to FFh. The print screen BIOS then exits. Error conditions include a printer error, printer busy, or printer out of paper. While the print screen is in progress, the status byte at 50:0 is set to 1. If a print screen request is made while a prior print screen is in progress, the new request is ignored. This means you can easily lock out all print screen requests by simply loading the value 1 at address 50:0.

The original PC and XT print screen services will always assume the screen is 25 rows. AT+ systems use the video rows stored in the BIOS data area byte at 40:84. To allow the print screen to print more than 25 rows on PC or XT with an EGA/VGA/XGA adapter, an alternate print screen handler is available as part of the video BIOS. The alternate print screen is basically identical to the AT+ BIOS print screen. The video print screen version also checks the BIOS data area to get the number of video rows. To activate the alternate print screen the following code is used:

```
        mov     ah, 12h                 ; alternate select
        mov     bl, 20h                 ; install print screen
        int     10h                     ; video services
```

The alternate print screen has a quirk that fails to check if any TSR or other driver has already hooked interrupt 5. The install print screen function simply stuffs the interrupt vector with a pointer to the new print screen routine inside the video BIOS. This will cause problems if TSRs or drivers have previously hooked interrupt 5. The TSR will no longer get control before or after a print screen. AT+ systems eliminate the need for alternate print screen, avoiding this potential problem.

The print screen routine does not read data directly from the screen. Print screen uses the video BIOS interrupt 10h, function 8 to read the screen. On all systems, a check is made to see if the byte read from the screen is a zero. If so, it is converted to a space. Code Sample 14-1, later in this chapter, is a small TSR that further limits the printer to ASCII characters only, when a printer cannot handle the complete 256 character set.

Int	Description	Platform
5	Print Screen	All

INT

Prints the contents of the current video screen to the printer attached to parallel port 1. While processing the print screen, the status byte at 50:0 is set to 1. Print screen uses video services, interrupt 10h, to get the current rows and columns information and display contents. Actual printing is performed by the printer service routine, interrupt 17h.

Called with: nothing

Returns: Updates the print screen status byte at 50:0
- 0 = done
- 1 = already in progress or disabled
- FF = error occurred

BIOS Data Areas

Location	Description	Size
40:08h	Parallel Port 1	Word

BIOS

The base parallel I/O port number is stored in this word. Typical I/O address values are 3BCh, 378h, or 278h, but any parallel I/O port can be stored in this word. It is accessed as PRN or LPT1 from DOS.

Location	Description	Size
40:0Ah	Parallel Port 2	Word

BIOS

The base parallel I/O port number is stored in this word. Typical I/O address values are 378h or 278h, but any parallel I/O port can be stored in this word. It is accessed as LPT2 from DOS.

Location	Description	Size
40:0Ch	Parallel Port 3	Word

The base parallel I/O port number is stored in this word. Normally parallel port 3 is set to I/O address 278h, but any parallel I/O port can be stored in this word. It is accessed as LPT3 from DOS.

Location	Description	Size
40:0Eh	Parallel Port 4/Extended BIOS Pointer	Word

On AT+ systems, when an extended BIOS data area is used, this word holds the segment of the extended BIOS data area. The extended BIOS data area typically uses 1 KB of RAM at the top of main memory at 639 K. See Chapter 6, BIOS Data and Other Fixed Data Areas, for more about this area.

When the extended BIOS data is not supported (e.g., on an AT system), this word can be used to store a fourth parallel port I/O address. The I/O port address must be loaded by an application or driver. Unlike parallel ports 1, 2, and 3, POST does not set this word. It is accessed as LPT4 from DOS.

Location	Description	Size
40:78h	Parallel Printer 1 Timeout	Word

This byte holds a fixed value used by the printer BIOS, interrupt 17h. When the printer BIOS outputs a character to the printer, this value indicates the maximum delay while the printer is busy. If the printer is still busy after this delay period, the BIOS returns a failed error code.

The POST sets the initial value to 14h on most systems. Since the timeout is based on instruction delays, the duration will vary depending on the system clock speed. All AT+ systems and a few XT BIOSes use this byte. For a value of 14h, I've noted a timeout duration ranging from 20 to 50 uS on different systems.

Location	Description	Size
40:79h	Parallel Printer 2 Timeout	Word

See description under RAM address 40:78h.

Location	Description	Size
40:7Ah	Parallel Printer 3 Timeout	Word

See description under RAM address 40:78h.

Location	Description	Size
40:7Bh	**Parallel Printer 4 Timeout**	**Word**

See description under RAM address 40:78h. Some systems do not allow a fourth printer. In this case, the byte is unused or may be used for another unrelated purpose.

Location	Description	Size
50:00h	**Print Screen Status**	**Byte**

The print screen function is initiated by the low-level keyboard BIOS when the Print Screen key is pressed. The keyboard BIOS issues an interrupt 5, the print screen handler. This handler controls the status of the print screen operation through this status byte. It is accessed at address 40:100 as well as 50:0.

The byte holds the following values and functions.

0	= Print screen ready
1	= Print screen in progress or disable print screen
FFh	= Error occurred before printing began: Printer was busy or out of paper Error occurred while printing: The printer ran out of paper, or an error was signaled from printer, or a timeout occurred while waiting to become nonbusy

Parallel Port Timing

The process of sending bytes to a device attached to the parallel port, typically a printer, must follow a specific timing sequence. These timing requirements are shown in Figure 14-2, because the strobe and data line timing delays are performed in software.

If the busy line is low the first byte of data is output to the port (1). After a minimum time of 0.5 uS, the strobe line is set low for at least 0.5 uS (2). The act of making the strobe low will cause the connected device to set the busy line high. Once the device has processed the byte and is ready for the next byte, the device sets the acknowledge line low for a minimum of 0.5 uS (3). As the acknowledge line returns high, the device drops the busy line low (4). At this point another cycle can begin if additional bytes need to be sent to the device.

The timing requirements allow one byte to be transferred every 2 uS in the best case scenario. This assumes that the device responds with an acknowledgment immediately, without any delays between actions. The resultant theoretical maximum transfer rate is 500K bytes per second.

Figure 14-2. Software Timing

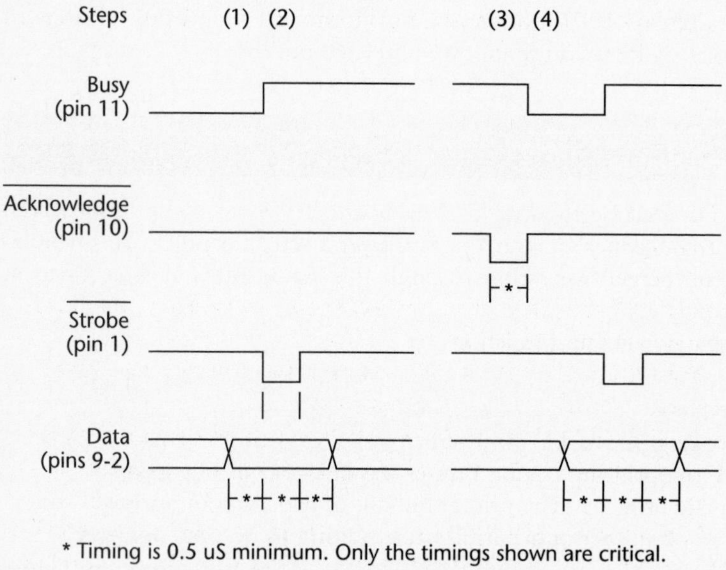

Typical transfer rates are much slower due to delays in device response and BIOS software timing. The BIOS uses timing partly dependent on instruction speed. To maintain the timing minimums, the BIOS software delays are designed to operate properly with the fastest possible processor. A BIOS designed for a range of CPU speeds from 20 MHz to 66 MHz must add significant delays at 20 MHz to make sure the 66 MHz system will work. CPU types will further affect the timing. A 80486DX is, of course, much faster than an 80386SX CPU, but the same BIOS code may be used in both systems. Most users can expect a best case transfer rate of about 150K bytes per second.

Parallel Port Connector

In the development of software to interface to the parallel port, it is helpful to understand which control lines are passed through the connector. The parallel port uses a 25-pin 'D' shell connector. The pinout for the connector is shown in Table 14-1. The direction is relative to the system. This means an output sends a signal to the attached device. Functions are described in greater detail in the section on the Printer BIOS. Functions prefixed with a minus are active when low, and prefixed with plus when active denotes high.

Table 14-1. Parallel Port Connector Functions

Pin	Direction	Function
1	output*	-Strobe—Pulsed low to signal the data is valid on the data lines.
2	output*	Data bit 0
3	output*	Data bit 1
4	output*	Data bit 2
5	output*	Data bit 3
6	output*	Data bit 4
7	output*	Data bit 5
8	output*	Data bit 6
9	output*	Data bit 7
10	input	-Acknowledgment—A 0.5 uS low pulse is sent from the printer to indicate it is no longer busy.
11	input	+Busy status—A high signal indicates the printer is in a print operation, offline or an error has occurred.
12	input	+Paper End—A high signal indicates the printer is out of paper.
13	input	+Select status—A high signal indicates the printer is currently selected.
14	output	-Auto feed—A low signal indicates the printer will automatically generate a carriage return after every linefeed. Not supported on some printers.
15	input	-Error—A low signal indicates the printer is offline, paper is out, or a printer error occurred.
16	output	-Initialize—A low signal for 50 uS or longer initializes the printer.
17	output	-Select—A low signal selects the printer. Not used on all printers.
18-25	Ground	

* *These pins are used as inputs in extended mode. Extended mode is not available on many systems.*

Fast Parallel Port

The standard parallel port design has limited performance, since some timing is performed in software. With a Fast parallel port design, the typical transfer rate is boosted from a slow 150K bytes/sec to a respectable 2M bytes/sec. The speed boost is accomplished by performing the data strobe operations automatically in hardware.

A standard parallel port is designed for attachment of a single device. The Fast port design provides the ability for bidirectional data transmission with up to 256 devices on a single parallel port connector.

The Fast port features are useful when connecting high speed devices to the parallel port such as external disk and tape drives, and transferring data between two systems. Laptops with limited expansion capabilities can benefit the most from a Fast port.

Five of the control pins at the 25-bit connector change in function when Fast port mode is enabled. These are shown in Table 14-2. When Fast port mode is off, the parallel port acts identical to the standard parallel port. This is the state after a hardware reset. When Fast port mode is activated, the following five connector pins change function.

Table 14-2. Fast Mode Connector Functions

Pin	Standard Function	Fast Function
1	-Strobe	-Write—Output line that signals the data on pins 2 to 9 has valid output data.
10	-Acknowledgement	-Interrupt Request—A low on this input line signals for a interrupt request if enabled.
11	+Busy	-Wait—Input line indicates the remote device is not ready.
14	-Auto Feed	-Data Strobe—This output indicates the data on pins 2 to 9 has valid data.
17	-Select	-Address Strobe—When low, the data on pins 2 to 9 is the address of the device (supporting up to 256 devices).

Intel supports the Fast parallel port, described as the Enhanced Parallel Port (EPP), on the 386SL and 486SL chip sets and other newer chipsets. Additional information is available on Compuserve in the IBMHW forum. Download a file called PARA14.ZIP.

Warnings

When reading the busy status from a parallel port, the status should be read twice in a row. This includes reading from ports 279h, 379h, and 3BDh. This improves the reliability on some parallel ports when the busy line may not be connected and is floating. Ignore the first read and use the value obtained from the second status read.

On some old Okidata printers, when the busy signal switches from high to low, the printer sends a 50 nS glitch on the paper out signal line. This may appear as a paper out from the BIOS or when directly reading the status from ports 279h, 379h, or 3BDh. Before declaring a paper out condition, check the status again for verification that the paper is truly out.

Code Sample 14-1. Print ASCII Only

This small TSR prevents non-ASCII characters from going to the printer. In addition, the TSR converts many of the IBM graphics characters into printable characters. This TSR is useful for printers than do not support the complete IBM character set.

```
;----------------------------------------------------------------------
;                          PRNASCII
;
;
;   TSR to convert non-ASCII characters to acceptable characters
;   for those printers that cannot print the entire IBM character
;   set.  Works with most programs and Print Screen.
;
;   (c) Copyright 1994, 1996  Frank van Gilluwe
;   All Rights Reserved.
include undocpc.inc

cseg    segment para public
        assume  cs:cseg, ds:cseg, ss:tsrstk



; This is the resident handler than converts characters to be
;   printed

int_17h_hook    proc    far
        pushf
        cmp     ah, 0                   ; printing a character ?
        jne     skip_change             ; jump if not

        cmp     al, 20h                 ; control character ?
        jb      control                 ; jump if so
        cmp     al, 7Fh                 ; in OK range
        jb      skip_change             ; jump if so
        je      set_space               ; if 7Fh, set to space
```

```
        sub     al, 80h             ; convert upper chars
        push    bx                  ;  into new chars
        mov     bx, offset new_chars
        xlat    cs:[bx]
        pop     bx
        jmp     finish_int17

control:
        cmp     al, 1Bh             ; escape ?
        je      skip_change         ; jump if so
        cmp     al, 08h             ; BS, HT, LF, VT, FF, CR ?
        jb      set_space           ; jump if not
        cmp     al, CR
        jbe     skip_change         ; if so, leave as-is
                                    ; all others switch to space
set_space:
        mov     al, ' '             ; switch to space

finish_int17:
skip_change:
        popf
        jmp     cs:old_int_17h      ; process old int_17h

int_17h_hook    endp

old_int_17h     dd      0           ; old pointer saved here

new_chars       db 'CueaaaaceeeiiiAA'   ;  80-8F
                db 'E AooouuyOU     '   ;  90-9F
                db 'aiounN  ?==  !<<>>'   ;   A0-AF
                db '###||||  ||      '   ;  B0-BF
                db '  _|__|||  _|_|_'   ;  C0-CF
                db '___    ||  ##**#'   ;  D0-DF
                db '                '   ;  E0-EF
```

```
                db '          ...  . '    ; f0-ff              F0-FF

;================================================================
; Start of non-resident installation portion

prnascii        proc    far

start:
        push    cs
        pop     ds

; get the current interrupt 17h vector and save

        mov     al, 17h
        mov     ah, 35h
        int     21h                     ; get current int 17h pointer
        mov     word ptr old_int_17h, bx
        mov     word ptr old_int_17h+2, es

; install our new interrupt 17h routine

        mov     dx, offset int_17h_hook
        mov     al, 17h
        mov     ah, 25h
        int     21h                     ; install our interrupt

        OUTMSG  msg1                    ; output installed message

; now determine the size to remain resident (paragraphs)
;   and become a TSR

        mov     dx, (offset start - offset int_17h_hook) SHR 4
        add     dx, 11h                 ; add PSP size + 1 paragraph
        mov     ax, 3100h               ; exit to DOS as tsr
```

```
        int     21h
prnascii        endp

msg1    db      CR, LF
        db      'PRNASCII TSR installed'
        db      ' - Print non-ASCII as ASCII.'
        db      CR, LF, '$'
cseg    ends

;=========================================================== stack ====

tsrstk  segment para stack
        db      150 dup (0)
tsrstk  ends
        end     start
```

Code Sample 14-2. Swap Printers

On systems with two printers, this program swaps printer 1 and printer 2. It is not a TSR, but simply changes the printer BIOS port address words and timeout bytes. Running the program twice restores operation to the original state. PRNSWAP works at the lowest hardware level, and other programs that intercept a parallel port, such as for network redirection, may not operate correctly with this utility.

```
;--------------------------------------------------------------------
;                            PRNSWAP
;
;
;    Swap the parallel ports for printers 1 and 2. (Not a TSR)
;
;    Assemble into a COM file.
;
;    (c) Copyright 1994, 1996  Frank van Gilluwe
;    All Rights Reserved.
```

```
include undocpc.inc

cseg    segment para public
        assume  cs:cseg, ds:cseg

        org     100h

prnswap proc    near

start:
        push    cs
        pop     ds

        mov     ax, 40h
        mov     es, ax              ; ES used for BIOS segment
        mov     dx, offset msg2     ; message if only 1 port

        mov     ax, es:[0Ah]        ; get parallel port 2 address
        cmp     ax, 0               ; is parallel port 2 active ?
        je      exit                ; jump if not

        xchg    ax, es:[8]          ; swap with port 1
        mov     es:[0Ah], ax        ; put old port 1 in port 2

        mov     al, es:[79h]        ; get printer timeout 2
        xchg    al, es:[8]          ; swap with timeout 1
        mov     es:[78h], al        ; put old timeout 1 in 2
        mov     dx, offset msg1     ; ports swapped message
exit:
        mov     ah, 9
        int     21h                 ; display message
        mov     ah, 4Ch
        int     21h                 ; exit
```

```
msg1    db      CR, LF, 'Printers 1 & 2 swapped.', CR, LF, '$'
msg2    db      CR, LF, 'Less than 2 active ports.', CR, LF, '$'

prnswap endp
cseg    ends
        end     start
```

Code Sample 14-3. Extended Mode Support Detect

This routine scans the four possible parallel ports to see if any ports are physically attached to the system. For attached active ports, the I/O address is shown, and the port is tested to see if the port supports extended bidirectional mode of operation. To test for extended mode, the extended read mode is set. Several data patterns are then written and read. In extended read mode, the output latches are not connected to the input latches. If extended mode is not supported, the reads will always match the writes. When PRNTYPE is run, the test results are displayed on screen. On one system the results appear as:

```
           PRNTYPE—Parallel Port Analysis
Parallel Port          Active?       Extended Mode?
#1    03BC               Yes               No
#2    0378               Yes               Yes
#3    0278               Yes               Yes
#4                       No                No
```

```
;-----------------------------------------------------------------
;                           PRNTYPE
;
;    Detect if active parallel ports and identify those ports
;    that support extended mode
;
;    Assemble into a COM file.
;
;    (c) Copyright 1994, 1996  Frank van Gilluwe
;    All Rights Reserved.
```

```
include undocpc.inc

cseg    segment para public
        assume  cs:cseg, ds:cseg

        org     100h

start:
        jmp     begin

msg1    db      CR, LF, CR, LF, TAB, TAB
        db      '    PRNTYPE - Parallel Port Analysis'
        db      CR, LF, CR, LF, TAB, TAB
        db      'Parallel Port    Active?    Extended Mode?'
        db      CR, LF, TAB, TAB
        db      '         '
        db      CR, LF, '$'

msg2    db      TAB, TAB, '#'
msgnum  db       '1        '
msghigh dw      '  '
msglow  dw      '  '
        db                   '      '
msgon   db                              'No           '
msgExt  db                                             'No '
        db      CR, LF, '$'

msg3    db      TAB, TAB
msg3num db      '#4  Likely Extended BIOS data area segment'
        db      CR, LF, '$'

prntype proc   near
```

```
begin:
        push    cs
        pop     ds
        OUTMSG  msg1                ; display initial message

        mov     ax, 40h
        mov     es, ax              ; ES used for BIOS segment

        mov     cl, '1'             ; printer number to check
        mov     si, 0               ; index for printer address

prnex_loop:
        mov     msgnum, cl          ; insert printer number
        mov     msghigh, '  '
        mov     msglow, '  '        ; blank port number
        MSGNO   msgon               ; assume not active
        MSGNO   msgExt              ; assume no extended support

        mov     dx, es:[si+8]       ; get parallel port address
        cmp     dx, 0               ; is parallel port active ?
        je      prnex_output        ; jump if not
        cmp     cl, '4'             ; last port ?
        jne     prnex_ok            ; jump if not
        cmp     dx, 1000h           ; port num too high ?
        ja      prnex_bios          ; if so, extended BIOS data
prnex_ok:
        MSGYES  msgon               ; parallel port active

        mov     bx, offset msghigh ; insert port number in line
        mov     al, dh
        call    hex                 ; convert to ASCII
        mov     bx, offset msglow
        mov     al, dl
        call    hex                 ; convert to ASCII
```

```
                                        ; now check extended support
        add     dx, 2                   ; set to control port
        in      al, dx
        IODELAY
        mov     ah, al                  ; save value to restore later
        or      al, 20h
        out     dx, al                  ; set extended read bit 5 on

        sub     dx, 2                   ; dx = read/write port #
        mov     al, 55h
        out     dx, al                  ; send value 55h
        IODELAY
        in      al, dx
        cmp     al, 55h                 ; read matches prior write ?
        jne     prnex_extended          ; jump if not

        mov     al, 0AAh
        out     dx, al                  ; send value AAh
        IODELAY
        in      al, dx
        cmp     al, 0AAh                ; read matches prior write ?
        je      prnex_restore           ; if so, no extended mode

prnex_extended:
        MSGYES  msgExt                  ; port supports extended mode

prnex_restore:
        add     dx, 2
        mov     al, ah
        out     dx, al                  ; restore to original state
        jmp     prnex_output

prnex_bios:
        OUTMSG  msg3                    ; Extended BIOS data area
```

```
        jmp     exit                    ; done!

prnex_output:
        OUTMSG  msg2                    ; display port line
        add     si, 2                   ; next index
        inc     cl
        cmp     cl, '4'                 ; are we done yet!
        ja      exit                    ; jump if so
        jmp     prnex_loop              ; go for next port

exit:
        mov     ah, 4Ch
        int     21h                     ; exit
prntype endp
```

Port Summary

This is a list of ports used for parallel ports.

Port	Type	Function	Platform
278h	I/O	Parallel Port Data	Adapter
279h	Input	Parallel Port Status	Adapter
27Ah	I/O	Parallel Port Control	Adapter
27Ch	I/O	Parallel Port Data (alternate)	Adapter
27Dh	Input	Parallel Port Status (alternate)	Adapter
27Eh	I/O	Parallel Port Control (alternate)	Adapter
378h	I/O	Parallel Port Data	Adapter
379h	Input	Parallel Port Status	Adapter
37Ah	I/O	Parallel Port Control	Adapter
37Ch	I/O	Parallel Port Data (alternate)	Adapter
37Dh	Input	Parallel Port Status (alternate)	Adapter
37Eh	I/O	Parallel Port Control (alternate)	Adapter
3BCh	I/O	Parallel Port Data	Adapter
3BDh	Input	Parallel Port Status	Adapter
3BEh	I/O	Parallel Port Control	Adapter

Port Detail

Port	Type	Description	Platform
278h	I/O	Parallel Port Data	Adapter

This I/O address port is part of three sequential I/O addresses for control of a parallel port. Depending on the number of other parallel ports, the POST will assign this I/O address as parallel port 1, 2, or 3.

This I/O address is used to transfer data to or from the device attached to the associated parallel port connector. Some newer systems provide extra hardware to support an extended mode of bidirectional operation. To send data through the parallel port, see the earlier section, Parallel Port Timing. See the Parallel Port Connector section for definitions of connector pin functions.

In a nonextended mode, a write to this port presents data to the parallel port connector. A read from this port obtains the data presented at the connector, normally the last byte written to this port. This allows confirmation that the latches are operating properly. With a series of data writes and reads, it is possible to test the output latches and the attached cable for possible shorts between data lines or between a line and ground.

When an extended mode is used, data output is latched, but only presented to the associated parallel port connector if the direction bit in the control port has been set to 0. If the direction bit is 0, a read from this port is identical to nonextended mode. The data is read from what was previously written to the port. If the direction bit is set to 1, a read from this port reads the byte from the device attached to the parallel connector.

I/O (bits 0-7) Data Byte

Port	Type	Description	Platform
279h	Input	Parallel Port Status	Adapter

This I/O address is read to get the status of the associated parallel port. An I/O read will input the current status from a number of lines on the parallel port connector. Refer to the section, Parallel Port Connector, for more about connector status bit functions. See the section on warnings for additional information.

Input (bits 0-7)

bit	7 r = 1	Device is Busy, inversion of the +Busy line, pin 11
	6 r = 1	Acknowledge completion, from -Acknowledge line, pin 10
	5 r = 1	Out of Paper, from +Paper End line, pin 12 (see section on Warnings about problems with Out of Paper)
	4 r = 1	Device Selected, from +Select line, pin 13
	3 r = 0	Error, inversion of the -Error line, pin 15

2 r = 0	Interrupt pending after acknowledge received (only on parallel ports that support extended mode)
1 r = x	Unused
0 r = x	Unused

Port	Type	Description	Platform
27Ah	I/O	Parallel Port Control	Adapter

The parallel port connector control pins are written using this port. The port also controls interrupt operation and extended mode direction control. The direction control bit 5 is unused in systems that do not support extended mode. See the section on the Parallel Port Connector for definitions of connector pin functions.

When the parallel port interrupt is enabled, the start of the acknowledge pulse triggers a hardware interrupt. A jumper usually exists to select which hardware interrupt request to use, IRQ 7, 5 or 2. Other selections may be available, depending on the card design. Newer chipsets, that include parallel ports, will often allow users to specify which IRQ is associated with each port, using the system BIOS setup utility.

On the combination MDA parallel port adapter and older systems that have a parallel port on the motherboard, the interrupt request is fixed at IRQ 7. The system BIOS does not use interrupts for any parallel port operations.

When reading this port, bits 0-3 are read directly from the connector pins, which should reflect the last value written to bits 0-3. This allows confirmation that the latches are operating properly. With a series of writes and reads, it is possible to test the output latches and the attached cable for possible shorts between control lines or between a line and ground.

Input (bits 0-7)

bit	7 r = x	Unused
	6 r = x	Unused
	5 r = x	Unused
	4 r = 1	Parallel port interrupt enabled
	3 r = 1	Select printer (inverted from pin 17)
	2 r = 0	Initialize printer (pin 16)
	1 r = 1	Automatic feed (inverted from pin 14)
	0 r = 1	Strobe (inverted from pin 1)

Output (bits 0-7)

bit	7 w = x	Unused
	6 w = x	Unused
	5 w = x	Extended mode direction control
	0	Data writes are presented to the connector

1	Data reads are read from the connector and the write latch is disconnected from the connector
4 w = 1	Enable parallel port interrupt
3 w = 1	Select printer (inverted to pin 17)
2 w = 0	Initialize printer (pin 16)
1 w = 1	Automatic feed (inverted to pin 14)
0 w = 1	Strobe (inverted to pin 1)

Port	Type	Description	Platform
27Ch	I/O	Parallel Port Data	Adapter

This port is a rarely used alternate to I/O address 278h.

Port	Type	Description	Platform
27Dh	Input	Parallel Port Status	Adapter

This port is a rarely used alternate to I/O address 279h.

Port	Type	Description	Platform
27Eh	I/O	Parallel Port Control	Adapter

This port is a rarely used alternate to I/O address 27Ah.

Port	Type	Description	Platform
378h	I/O	Parallel Port Data	Adapter

This I/O address port is part of three sequential I/O addresses for control of a parallel port. Depending on the number of other parallel ports, the POST will assign this I/O address as parallel port 1 or 2.

Refer to parallel port I/O address 278h for functional details.

Port	Type	Description	Platform
379h	Input	Parallel Port Status	Adapter

Refer to parallel port I/O address 279h for functional details.

Port	Type	Description	Platform
37Ah	I/O	Parallel Port Control	Adapter

Refer to parallel port I/O address 27Ah for functional details.

Port	Type	Description	Platform
37Ch	I/O	Parallel Port Data	Adapter

This port is a rarely used alternate to I/O address 378h.

Port	Type	Description	Platform
37Dh	Input	Parallel Port Status	Adapter

This port is a rarely used alternate to I/O address 379h.

Port	Type	Description	Platform
37Eh	I/O	Parallel Port Control	Adapter

This port is a rarely used alternate to I/O address 37Ah.

Port	Type	Description	Platform
3BCh	I/O	Parallel Port Data	Adapter

This I/O address port is part of three sequential I/O addresses for control of a parallel port. The POST will always assign this port group as parallel port 1, if present.

Refer to parallel port I/O address 278h for functional details.

Port	Type	Description	Platform
3BDh	Input	Parallel Port Status	Adapter

Refer to parallel port I/O address 279h for functional details.

Port	Type	Description	Platform
3BEh	I/O	Parallel Port Control	Adapter

Refer to parallel port I/O address 27Ah for functional details.

CHAPTER 15

CMOS Memory and Real-Time Clock

This chapter contains an extensive amount of undocumented information. I've included considerable information on the standard CMOS registers. Many of the CMOS registers have never been documented, yet contain useful information. In addition, you will find details on the little-known extended CMOS implementations on newer AT systems and MCA and EISA systems.

Sample routines are provided to reliably read and write CMOS memory. In addition, the CMOSVIEW utility program labels and displays the contents of the normal and extended CMOS memory registers.

The Real-Time Clock, which is part of the CMOS memory chip, is also covered in detail. This includes details on the many quirks and problems with the clock that can lead an unsuspecting programmer into creating unstable code.

Introduction

The system contains a small amount of CMOS memory that retains its data while the system power is off. This memory is used to record the type and number of diskette drives, hard disk size information, memory size and other important system data. This same CMOS chip also has a Real-Time Clock (RTC) that keeps the current time. The original AT uses a Motorola MC146818A Real Time Clock IC.

The RTC is powered by a battery in the computer when the power is off. The battery keeps the clock active and retains the CMOS memory contents. Should the battery fail while system power is off, the CMOS contents will be lost. Most BIOSes will identify that this has occurred during the BIOS Power On System Test (POST).

The clock registers can be accessed directly or through the Real-Time Clock BIOS. There are no documented BIOS services available to access the CMOS memory or the four status and control registers on the RTC. CMOS memory is accessed directly through I/O ports, described later in the chapter. IBM's PS/1 provides an undocumented BIOS access to CMOS memory. See Chapter 13, System Functions, interrupt 15, function CAh for details.

General Information About the Real-Time Clock (RTC)

Ten registers access the RTC time and date. All of the clock registers use BCD (Binary Coded Decimal) format. Four additional registers are used for status and control of the clock, alarm, and CMOS memory. These status and control registers are referred to as Registers A, B, C and D. All of the RTC registers are described in detail later in this chapter under port 70h's description.

The RTC has many quirks that require special programming to ensure reliable access. Using the RTC BIOS described in the next section avoids most of these headaches, and is highly recommended.

When loading any data or time register through I/O port 70h, the clock should be halted. This prevents the clock from updating a register in the middle of setting a new date or time. To stop the clock, set bit 7 of Register B to 1. When the update is complete, activate the clock by setting bit 7 of Register B to 0.

When saving a new date and time, avoid setting the RTC on the last day of the month within 2 seconds of the day rollover. At this critical point, if a new value is loaded, the value may be incorrectly altered due to internal hardware logic processing during the end of month change. If daylight savings time is going to be active, avoid setting the clock within 2 seconds of the daylight savings change or the internal counters may not be properly set up. The RTC uses the last Sunday in April as the point for switching to daylight savings time. Currently daylight savings time in the U.S.A. starts on the first Sunday in April. This makes the RTC's daylight savings option fairly useless.

Unfortunately, reading the clock values is a bit more tricky than changing them. Why make our lives as programmers easy? The RTC chip has an internal update cycle once every second which takes about 2 ms. During this internal update, reads from the time, date and alarm registers will get unpredictable data! If you just hope for the best, about 1 out of 500 tries will have bad data. Bad odds in my book, if you like stable repeatable operation.

OK, so you really would like to get a valid value when you read the clock. To do so, disable interrupts, go into a tight loop, reading Register A's Update in progress bit 7. When this transitions from high to low, you have all of 244 microseconds to read the clock register you want. To avoid these problems the Real-Time Clock BIOS functions can be used to read and write the clock values.

Real-Time Clock BIOS

The clock and alarm CMOS registers can be read or written using the BIOS interrupt 1Ah, time of day services. Access to the time services through interrupt 1Ah is recommended, instead of attempting to directly program the CMOS time registers.

Functions 0 and 1 are used to access the BIOS timer ticks count. The BIOS timer tick counter has nothing to do with the CMOS clock, as it is incremented by the system timer. Refer to Chapter 16, System Timers, for more about the system timer.

Interrupt 1Ah provides the following services:

Function	**Description**
ah=0	Get current clock count from BIOS RAM
ah=1	Set current clock count in BIOS RAM
ah=2	Read CMOS time
ah=3	Set CMOS time
ah=4	Read CMOS date
ah=5	Set CMOS date
ah=6	Set alarm time in CMOS
ah=7	Turn off alarm
ah=8	Set RTC activated power-on
ah=9	Read RTC alarm time and status
ah=A	Read days since 1980
ah=B	Set days since 1980

Int	Func	Description	Platform
1Ah	0	Get Current Clock Count	AT+

INT

This function reads the timer ticks count from the BIOS RAM double word at 40:6Ch. The function also returns the timer ticks' 24-hour rollover flag, stored in the BIOS RAM byte at 40:70h. The rollover flag is cleared after being read.

Only the operating system should use this call. Should an application use this call shortly after midnight, the 24-hour rollover flag is cleared by the act of reading the count. Later, when the operating system reads the information, the rollover flag is incorrectly set at zero. The end result is the operating system clock will appear to lose a day. A number of books recommend use of this subfunction, without realizing this serious problem.

We strongly suggest just reading the values directly from the BIOS RAM area. This is reliable and avoids interaction problems with the operating system. Remember to disable interrupts while reading the count and rollover flag. This prevents the timer ticks interrupt from updating the count and rollover flag in the middle of reading a portion of the information.

Called with:	ah = 0		
Returns:	ax = modified		
	cx = high word of timer ticks count		
	dx = low word of timer ticks count		
	al = 0	if count has not exceeded 24 hours since last read	
	1	if count exceeded 24 hours (this 24 hour overflow flag is cleared after being read)	

Int	Func	Description	Platform
1Ah	1	Set Current Clock Count	AT+

This function loads the specified double word count into the BIOS RAM timer ticks counter at 40:6Ch. The function also clears the timer ticks' 24-hour overflow flag at address 40:70h.

Called with:	ah = 1
	cx = high word of timer ticks count
	dx = low word of timer ticks count
Returns:	ax = modified

Int	Func	Description	Platform
1Ah	2	Read CMOS Time	AT+

The current time is read directly from the CMOS real-time clock. A successful read clears the carry flag.

The Real-Time Clock BIOS checks if an internal CMOS clock update is in progress. Depending on the technique used by the BIOS, if an update is in progress, the function may simply exit without getting the time. This is likely to occur about one out of every 500 tries. If the carry flag is set upon return, a second attempt will usually get successful results.

Called with:	ah = 2	
Returns:	if carry = 0	
		ax = modified
		ch = hours in BCD, 0 to 23 (assuming default 24 hour mode is set)
		cl = minutes in BCD, 0 to 59

dh = seconds in BCD, 0 to 59

dl = 0 if daylight savings time disabled

1 if daylight savings time enabled (see problems about daylight savings under the section General Information About the RTC)

if carry =1

ax = modified

clock update in progress or not running

Int	Func	Description	Platform
1Ah	3	Set CMOS Time	AT+

INT ▮▮▮ ▮

The specified time is written directly into the CMOS real-time clock. Unlike setting the timer ticks (function 1) this function permanently updates the time.

Called with: ah = 3

ch = hours in BCD, 0 to 23 (assuming the default 24 hour mode is set)

cl = minutes in BCD, 0 to 59

dh = seconds in BCD, 0 to 59

dl = 0 disable daylights savings time

1 enable daylight savings time (see problems about daylight savings under the section General Information About the RTC)

Returns: carry = 0

ax = modified

Int	Func	Description	Platform
1Ah	4	Read CMOS Date	AT+

INT ▮▮▮ ▮

The current date is read directly from the CMOS real-time clock. A successful read clears the carry flag.

The Real-Time Clock BIOS checks if an internal CMOS clock update is in progress. Depending on the technique used by the BIOS, if an update is in progress, the function may simply exit without getting the date. This is likely to occur about one out of every 500 tries. If the carry flag is set upon return, a second attempt will usually get successful results.

Called with: ah = 4

Returns: if carry = 0

ax = modified

ch = century in BCD, 19 or 20

cl = year in BCD, 0 to 99

dh = month in BCD, 1 to 12

dl = day in BCD, 1 to 31

if carry = 1
    ax = modified
    clock update in progress or not running

INT	Int	Func	Description	Platform
	1Ah	5	Set CMOS Date	AT+

The specified date is written directly into the CMOS real-time clock.

Called with: ah = 5
ch = century in BCD, 19 or 20
cl = year in BCD, 0 to 99
dh = month in BCD, 1 to 12
dl = day in BCD, 1 to 31

Returns: carry = 0
ax = modified

INT	Int	Func	Description	Platform
	1Ah	6	Set Alarm Time in CMOS	AT+

The CMOS RTC has a built-in alarm. Each day the current time equals the alarm time, interrupt 70h is called. To use the alarm feature, first set the alarm time using function 6. If setting the alarm was successful as indicated by the carry flag being cleared, interrupt 4Ah is then vectored into a user-supplied alarm handler. If setting of the alarm failed with the carry flag set, the error condition indicates the alarm cannot be used. An alarm in use by another program should never be reset, because this function only allows one user at a time.

When use of the alarm is complete, interrupt 1Ah, function 7 is used to disable the alarm. It's a good practice to return the interrupt 4Ah vector to its original value.

Each of the alarm registers has a special don't-care mode. By loading any value from C0h to FFh into a register, the register is ignored when determining an alarm time. For example, to make the alarm occur 15 minutes after the hour, every hour, the hours register CH is loaded with FFh, the minutes register CL is loaded with 15h and the seconds register DH is loaded with 0.

Called with: ah = 6
ch = hours in BCD, 0 to 23, or FFh
cl = minutes in BCD, 0 to 59, or FFh
dh = seconds in BCD, 0 to 59, or FFh

Returns: if carry = 0
    ax = 0

if carry = 1

ax = modified

Alarm already enabled. This indicates another application is already using the alarm, the clock update is in progress, or the clock is not running.

Int	Func	Description	Platform
1Ah	7	Turn off Alarm	AT+

INT

The alarm function is disabled. See interrupt 1Ah, function 6, to set an alarm.

Called with: nothing

Returns: carry = 0

ax = modified

Int	Func	Description	Platform
1Ah	8	Set RTC Activated Power-On	PC Convertible

INT

Sets the time for the laptop power activation after a shutdown has occurred.

Called with: ah = 8

ch = hours in BCD, 0 to 23

cl = minutes in BCD, 0 to 59

dh = seconds in BCD, 0 to 59

Returns: carry = 0 if successful

Int	Func	Description	Platform
1Ah	9	Read RTC Alarm Time and Status	Limited

INT

Reads the RTC alarm time. The function is only supported on the PC Convertible and PS/2 model 30. The PC convertible also indicates whether an active alarm will power up the system or not.

Called with: ah = 9

Returns: ch = hours in BCD, 0 to 23

cl = minutes in BCD, 0 to 59

dh = seconds in BCD, 0 to 59

dl = 0 if alarm not enabled

1 if alarm enabled

2 if alarm enabled and will power-on system

Int	Func	Description	Platform
1Ah	Ah	Read Days Since 1980	XT/MCA

Gets the number of days since January 1, 1980. Only IBM XTs with BIOSes dated 1/10/86 or later support this function. The AT does not support this function, but all PS/2 and MCA bus machines support this function.

Called with: ah = 0Ah

Returns: cx = count of days since 1980

Int	Func	Description	Platform
1Ah	Bh	Set Days Since 1980	XT/MCA

Sets the number of days since January, 1, 1980. Only XTs with BIOSes dated 6/10/85 or later support this function. The AT does not support this function, but all PS/2 and MCA bus machines support this function.

Called with: ah = 0Bh

cx = count of days since 1980

Returns: nothing

EISA System Differences

The EISA system contains an additional 8K of CMOS memory to store special BIOS information and slot configuration data. The exact approach to accessing CMOS memory is left to the BIOS manufacturer (so much for standards). The approach used by most manufacturers is to have 32 banks of 256 registers. This is described in the ports section, port 8xxh and C00h.

The information stored in extended CMOS is normally handled by a special configuration program that reads and writes to CMOS memory. The configuration program uses three EISA BIOS interrupt services to read and write this information to the additional CMOS memory.

Int	Func	Description	Platform
15h	D800h	Read Slot Configuration Information	EISA

This function reads configuration information about a specific board slot. The function also indicates the number of subfunctions for getting addition configuration information from function AX=D801h.

Called with: ax = D800h

cl = board slot number (1=slot 1)

Returns: carry = 1 unable to get information
carry = 0 successful
ah = 0 success in getting information
al = 0 when board ID readable and not duplicated
bx = revision level of configuration utility
cx = checksum of configuration file
dh = number of functions on this board (see Read Function below)
dl = function information byte
di,si = board ID, 4 bytes

Int	Func	Description	Platform
15h	D801h	Read Function Configuration Information	EISA

INT III I

Each board has significant additional information that can be read using this function, with the subfunction specified in CH.

Called with: ax = D801h
cl = board slot number (1=slot 1)
ch = subfunction number
0 = I/O port requirements
1 = ROM, IRQ and DMA information
2 = RAM and ROM information
3 = IRQ and I/O port information
ds:si = ptr to where data should be written (buffer should hold at least 320 bytes)

Returns: carry = 1 unable to get information
carry = 0 successful
ah = 0 success in getting information
ds:si buffer now has the information requested

The contents of the buffer returned are summarized here. Each subfunction returns the same type of initial information. All of the subfunction information was derived from the EISA specification, v3.12. This document has a few inconsistencies, which may indicate errors. Be cautious in using this information. For further details, consult the latest EISA specifications.

Beginning buffer contents, all subfunctions:

Offset	**Bytes**	**Description**
0h	2	Board ID, first and second bytes
2h	1	Product number, first and second hex digits
3h	1	Product number, third digit and revision

Offset	Bytes	Description
4h	1	ID and slot information
5h	1	ID information, miscellaneous
6h	1	Configuration Utility revision level, major
7h	1	Configuration Utility revision level, minor
8h	1	first selection
9h	1	second selection
Ah	1	third selection (not used on some subfunctions)
Bh	1	fourth selection (not used on some subfunctions)
Ch	1	fifth selection (not used on some subfunctions)
Dh	21	unused
21h	1	Function information
23h	80	ASCII type and subtype string (see chart below)

ASCII Type Information

Device Type	Description
COM,ASY	Serial port, ISA compatible with 8250
COM,ASY,FIFO	Serial port, ISA compatible with 16550 (FIFO)
COM,SYN	SDLC port, ISA compatible
KEY,xxx,KBD=yy	Keyboard, xxx=number of keys (083/084/101/103) yy=two letter country codes: AE=Arabic, English AF=Arabic, French AU=Australia BE=Belgium BF=Belgium, Flemish CE=Canadian, English CF=Canadian, French CH=China DN=Denmark DU=Dutch EE=European English FN=Finland FR=France GR=Germany HA=Hungary IT=Italy IS=Israel A=Kanji LA=Latin America ME=Middle East NE=Netherlands NO=Norway PO=Portugal SP=Spain SW=Sweden ST=Switzerland SF=Swiss, French SG=Swiss, German TA=Taiwan UK=United Kingdom US=United States
CPU,80386SX	386 microprocessor, SX version
CPU,80386	386 microprocessor
CPU,80486SX	486 microprocessor, SX version
CPU,80486	486 microprocessor
CPU,PENTIUM	Pentium microprocessor
JOY	Joystick

Device Type	Description
MEM	System memory
MSD,DSKCTL	Hard disk controller, ISA compatible
MSD,FPYCTL	Floppy disk controller, ISA compatible
MSD,TAPCTL	Tape controller, primary
NET,ETH	Network, Ethernet
NET,TKR	Network, Token Ring
NET,ARC	Network, Arcnet
NPX,387	Math coprocessor, 387
NPX,387SX	Math coprocessor, 386, SX version
NPX,W1167	Math coprocessor, Weitek 1167
NPX,W3167	Math coprocessor, Weitek 3167
OSE	Operating system or environment
PAR	Parallel port, ISA compatible
PAR,BID	Parallel port, bidirectional
PTR,8042	Mouse controller
SYS	System board
VID,MDA	Video, Monochrome
VID,MDA,MGA	Video, Monochrome, Hercules graphics
VID,CGA	Video, CGA, no write sync needed during retrace
VID,CGA,RTR	Video, CGA, write sync needed during retrace
VID,EGA	Video, EGA
VID,VGA	Video, VGA

Subfunction 0, Secondary Portion of Buffer

Offset	Bytes	Description
73h	91	unused
104h	1	IOPORT 1 initialization byte
105h	2	IOPORT 1 address, 16-bit
107h	1	IOPORT 1 value, 8-bit
108h	1	IOPORT 2 initialization byte
109h	2	IOPORT 2 address, 16-bit
10Bh	2	IOPORT 2 value, 16-bit
10Dh	2	IOPORT 2 mask, 16-bit
10Fh	1	IOPORT 3 initialization byte
110h	2	IOPORT 3 address, 16-bit
112h	1	IOPORT 3 value, 8-bit
113h	1	IOPORT 3 mask, 8-bit
114h	1	IOPORT 4 initialization byte
115h	2	IOPORT 4 address, 16-bit
117h	1	IOPORT 4 value, 8-bit
118h	1	IOPORT 4 mask, 8-bit

Offset	Bytes	Description
109h	1	IOPORT 5 initialization byte
11Ah	2	IOPORT 5 address, 16-bit
11Ch	1	IOPORT 5 mask, 8-bit
10Dh	1	IOPORT 6 initialization byte
11Eh	2	IOPORT 6 address, 16-bit
120h	1	IOPORT 6 value, 8-bit
121h	1	IOPORT 6 mask, 8-bit
122h	1	IOPORT 7 initialization byte
123h	2	IOPORT 7 address, 16-bit
125h	1	IOPORT 7 value, 8-bit
126h	1	IOPORT 7 mask, 8-bit

Subfunction 1, Secondary Portion of Buffer

Offset	Bytes	Description
73h	1	Memory configuration (ROM = 18h)
74h	1	ROM memory size
75h	3	ROM start address (in paragraphs)
78h	2	ROM size/1024
7Ah	56	unused
B2h	1	IRQ number (value ORed with 20h)
B3h	1	reserved
B4h	12	unused
C0h	1	DMA channel number
C1h	1	DMA mode type

Subfunction 2, Secondary Portion of Buffer

Offset	Bytes	Description
73h	1	Memory configuration (RAM = 19h)
74h	1	RAM memory size
75h	3	RAM start address (in paragraphs)
78h	2	RAM size/1024

Subfunction 3, Secondary Portion of Buffer

Offset	Bytes	Description
B2h	1	IRQ number (value ORed with 20h)
B3h	1	reserved
B4h	20	unused
C8h	1	Port IO range entry
C9h	2	Port address, 16-bit

Int	Func	Description	Platform
15h	D803h	Write Function Configuration Information	EISA

Configuration information is written to the extended CMOS memory area on the EISA motherboard. A buffer passed to this function must contain the data to be written into CMOS. The slot is specified as a value in the buffer. The length of the buffer will vary depending on a number of variable length fields in the buffer.

Called with: ax = D803h
cx = 41h
ds:si = ptr to where data is read from

Returns: if successful (i.e. the information was stored)
carry = 0
ah = 0
if failed
carry = 1

A number of specified bytes indicate the length of subsequent sections, so the offsets are not shown.

Bytes	Subfunction	Description
2		Board ID, first and second bytes
1		Product number, first and second hex digits
1		Product number, third digit and revision
1		ID and slot information
1		reserved
1		Configuration Utility revision level, major
1		Configuration Utility revision level, minor
2		Length of function 0 entry (starting with the next byte, until function 1 entry)
1	0	Length of next selection fields, bytes
1	0	first selection
1	0	second selection
?	0	additional selections
1	0	Function 0 information byte (21h)
1	0	Length of following ASCII type string
?	0	ASCII type and subtype string (see prior chart)
1	0	IOPORT 1 initialization byte
2	0	IOPORT 1 address, 16-bit
1	0	IOPORT 1 value, 8-bit
1	0	IOPORT 2 initialization byte

Bytes	Subfunction	Description
2	0	IOPORT 2 address, 16-bit
2	0	IOPORT 2 value, 16-bit
2	0	IOPORT 2 mask, 16-bit
1	0	IOPORT 3 initialization byte
2	0	IOPORT 3 address, 16-bit
1	0	IOPORT 3 value, 8-bit
1	0	IOPORT 3 mask, 8-bit
1	0	IOPORT 4 initialization byte
2	0	IOPORT 4 address, 16-bit
1	0	IOPORT 4 value, 8-bit
1	0	IOPORT 4 mask, 8-bit
1	0	IOPORT 5 initialization byte
2	0	IOPORT 5 address, 16-bit
1	0	IOPORT 5 mask, 8-bit
1	0	IOPORT 6 initialization byte
2	0	IOPORT 6 address, 16-bit
1	0	IOPORT 6 value, 8-bit
1	0	IOPORT 6 mask, 8-bit
1	0	IOPORT 7 initialization byte
2	0	IOPORT 7 address, 16-bit
1	0	IOPORT 7 value, 8-bit
1	0	IOPORT 7 mask, 8-bit
2		Length of function 1 entry (starting with the next byte, until function 2 entry)
1	1	Length of next selection fields, bytes
1	1	first selection
1	1	second selection
?	1	additional selections
1	1	Function 1 information byte (0Fh)
1	1	Length of following ASCII type string
?	1	ASCII type and subtype string (see prior chart)
1	1	ROM Memory Configuration byte (18h)
0	1	ROM memory size
3	1	ROM start address (in paragraphs)
2	1	ROM size/1024
1	1	IRQ number (value ORed with 20h)
1	1	reserved
1	1	DMA channel number
1	1	DMA mode type

Bytes	Subfunction	Description
2		Length of function 2 entry (starting with the next byte, until function 3 entry)
1	2	Length of next selection fields, bytes
1	2	first selection
1	2	second selection
?	2	additional selections
1	2	Function 2 information byte (03h)
1	2	Length of following ASCII type string
?	2	ASCII type and subtype string (see prior chart)
1	2	Memory configuration RAM (19h)
1	2	RAM memory size
3	2	RAM start address (in paragraphs)
2	2	RAM size/1024
2		Length of function 3 entry (starting with the next byte, until end)
1	3	Length of next selection fields, bytes
1	3	first selection
1	3	second selection
?	3	additional selections
1	3	Function 3 information byte (15h)
1	3	Length of following ASCII type string
?	3	ASCII type and subtype string (see prior chart)
1	3	IRQ number (value ORed with 20h)
1	3	reserved
1	3	Port IO range entry
2	3	Port address, 16-bit
2		Last function length (fixed at 0)
2		Configuration file Checksum, 16-bit

System Data Areas

Many of the CMOS registers are read during POST. Some of the information is copied from CMOS registers into the BIOS data area at segment 40h. Refer to Chapter 6, BIOS Data and Other Fixed Data Areas, for a complete listing of these BIOS data areas.

Extended CMOS Registers

Many systems today include more CMOS registers than the original 64 registers provided in AT compatibles. There are three common methods used today, divided between newer AT compatibles, MCA, and EISA systems. The CMOSVIEW program displays all of the standard 64 CMOS registers and any other extended CMOS registers detected. Key portions of CMOSVIEW are shown in code examples later in this chapter.

AT Extended CMOS Memory Many AT compatibles today provide an additional 64 registers. These are accessed through the identical method used for the first 64 registers. Port 70h is loaded with an address between 40h to 7Fh to access these extra registers. In examinations of a number of system that support 128 registers, these are typically used to store information about third and fourth drives, as well as items specific to the motherboard's chipset.

MCA Extended CMOS Memory Most MCA systems include an additional 2K of CMOS memory. This is used for storage of slot configuration information. Some of this information is duplicated in the regular CMOS memory, such as Programmable option select information for card slots 0 to 3. See ports 74h, 75h, and 76h described later in this chapter to access this memory and for further details.

EISA Extended CMOS Memory The EISA standard defines an additional 8K of CMOS for system and slot configuration information. See ports 8xxh and C00h described later in this chapter to access this memory.

Warnings

Interrupts All interrupts must be disabled while accessing CMOS registers. When accessing a CMOS register, an output to port 70h selects which register to use. This is followed by reading or writing the register through port 71h. Should an interrupt occur between these two I/O port accesses AND the interrupt handler accesses CMOS, the wrong register will be read or written by your code.

In addition to disabling interrupts, the Non-Maskable-Interrupt (NMI) should be disabled. The NMI is primarily used to trap RAM parity errors and math coprocessor errors. These are very unlikely to occur while accessing CMOS. Unfortunately, the NMI disable is a write only flag, so the prior state is never known. Those hardware guys never seem to learn we hate write-only information! The common approach everyone uses is to assume NMI has been enabled. This means NMI is always enabled after CMOS is accessed.

In reviewing the steps taken to access a CMOS register, you must first disable interrupts using a CLI instruction. The CMOS register is selected with NMI disabled. It so happens NMI is controlled by bit 7 of port 70h, the same port used to specify the CMOS register! When the CMOS access is complete, port 70h is rewritten with bit 7 cleared to re-enable NMI. General interrupts are then enabled using an STI instruction. All of this is taken care of in our READ_CMOS and WRITE_CMOS routines in the next section.

CMOS Checksum Most BIOS vendors use a checksum on CMOS registers above 10h. This is done to detect CMOS memory problems and possible invalid writes into a CMOS register. The BIOS manufacturers believe that only the CMOS system setup program they provide should alter CMOS registers. To this end, the checksum spans different registers and is stored in vendor-designated CMOS registers. One of the BIOS power-on tests ensures the CMOS register checksum is valid. If the checksum is invalid the BIOS usually stops the system from proceeding until the CMOS memory is reloaded with correct values.

Many BIOS vendors, such as AMI and Phoenix, add up the CMOS registers from 10h to 2Dh. The word total of these values is saved in registers 2Eh and 2Fh. Register 2Eh holds the high checksum byte, and register 2Fh holds the low checksum byte. IBM's PS/1 486 BIOS uses two sets of checksums for registers 10h-31h and 40-5Fh. The word checksum for 10h to 31h has the high byte stored in CMOS register 32h, and the low byte is stored in register 33h. For the word checksum of registers 40h to 5Fh, the high checksum byte is stored in register 60h, and the low checksum byte is stored in 61h. Unless you are absolutely sure where and how the checksum is constructed, individual CMOS memory writes should be avoided unless you restore them to the original values before the next system boot.

Clock Registers There are several unusual restrictions in both setting and reading the clock registers. See the section at the beginning of this chapter on General Information About the Real-Time Clock. Also note that reading status registers C and D may cause several bits to be changed. Refer to Status Register C and D under port 70h for details.

Code Sample 15-1. Read CMOS

```
;-------------------------------------------------------------
;   READ_CMOS
;         read the contents of a specific CMOS register
;
;         Call with:      al = CMOS address to read
;
;         Returns:        ah = Contents of register
;                              NMI enabled, if disabled

read_CMOS         proc    near
          or      al, 80h                ; disable NMI
```

```
        cli                             ; disable interrupts
        out     70h, al                 ; al= register to read
        IODELAY
        in      al, 71h                 ; returns contents of reg
        mov     ah, al
        mov     al, 0
        IODELAY
        out     70h, al                 ; enable NMI
        sti                             ; enable interrupts
        ret
read_CMOS       endp
```

Code Sample 15-2. Write CMOS

```
;-----------------------------------------------------------------
;    WRITE_CMOS
;       write to a CMOS register
;
;       Call with:      al = CMOS register to read
;                       ah = Value to write
;
;       Returns:        NMI enabled, if disabled

write_CMOS      proc    near
        cli                             ; disable interrupts
        or      al, 80h                 ; disable NMI
        out     70h, al                 ; al= register to read
        mov     al, ah
        IODELAY
        out     71h, al                 ; write register
        mov     al, 0
```

```
        IODELAY
        out     70h, al             ; enable NMI
        sti                         ; enable interrupts
        ret
write_CMOS      endp
```

Code Sample 15-3. Display AT CMOS

This routine displays the standard CMOS registers from Eh to 3Fh. If extended CMOS registers 40h to 7Fh are detected, these are also displayed. The complete program is provided on the diskette in the CMOSVIEW.ASM file. The diskette includes data definitions and additional required subroutines.

```
;-------------------------------------------------------------------
;
;    DISPLAY_CMOS
;       display the CMOS RAM memory contents; that may be
;       redirected to a file.
;
;       Called with:    nothing
;
;       Returns:        CMOS register values sent to std output
;
;       Regs used:      all
;
;       Subs used:      hex, read_CMOS, write_CMOS

display_CMOS    proc    near
        push    cs
        pop     ds
        push    cs
        pop     es

        OUTMSG  disp_CMOS_head      ; output header string
```

```
; first check if CMOS limit is 3Fh or 7Fh. If the register sets
;   Eh to 3Fh are identical to 4Eh to 7Fh, only 64 registers are
;   supported, otherwise 128 registers likely supported

        mov     cl, 0Eh             ; start at CMOS location 0E
        mov     ch, 7Fh             ; assume limit for 128 regs
        mov     al, cl

disp_CMOS_size:
        call    read_CMOS           ; get location value in ah
        mov     bh, ah              ; temp save in bh
        add     cl, 40h             ; switch to possible upper set
        call    read_CMOS           ; get location value in ah
        sub     cl, 40h
        cmp     ah, bh              ; are registers the same ?
        jne     disp_CMOS_128       ; if not, 128 regs supported
        inc     cl
        cmp     cl, 3Fh             ; are we done ?
        je      disp_CMOS_size      ; loop if not

        mov     ch, 3Fh             ; set limit for 64 regs
        jmp     disp_CMOS_regs

; the registers fail to compare so it looks like 128 registers,
;   but to be sure, write a value and confirm it is written.

disp_CMOS_128:
        mov     al, 7Fh             ; select very last location
        call    read_CMOS           ; get location value in ah
        mov     bh, al              ; save it for later
        not     ah                  ; invert current value
        mov     bl, ah              ; save for compare
        call    write_CMOS
        call    read_CMOS
```

```
        cmp     bl, ah              ; was value written ?
        je      disp_CMOS_skp1      ; jump if so, 128 registers
        mov     cl, 3Fh             ; limit is 64 registers
disp_CMOS_skp1:
        mov     ah, bh
        call    write_CMOS          ; restore original value

; now output the registers, starting at E

disp_CMOS_regs:
        mov     cl, 0Eh             ; start at CMOS location E

disp_CMOS_loop:
        mov     al, cl
        mov     bx, offset disp_CMOS_loc
        call    hex                 ; convert loc to ASCII hex
        mov     al, cl
        call    read_CMOS           ; get location value in ah
        mov     al, ah
        mov     bx, offset disp_CMOS_value
        call    hex                 ; convert value to ascii hex

        cmp     cl, 40h             ; insert line feed after 3F
        jne     disp_CMOS_skp2
        OUTMSG  crlf
disp_CMOS_skp2:
        cmp     cl, 40h             ; 40h+ are vendor specific
        ja      disp_CMOS_skp3      ;   so reuse text
        mov     si, offset msgE
        mov     di, offset disp_CMOS_type
        mov     dx, offset msgF - offset msgE
        mov     al, cl
        sub     al, 0Eh
        mul     dl                  ; ax = dl*al
```

```
        add     si, ax
        push    cx
        mov     cx, dx
        cld
        rep     movsb                   ; transfer type string
        pop     cx
disp_CMOS_skp3:
        OUTMSG  disp_CMOS_text          ; output info line
        inc     cl
        cmp     cl, ch                  ; all done ?
        jbe     disp_CMOS_loop

        ret
display_CMOS    endp
```

Code Sample 15-4. Display Extended MCA CMOS

This routine displays the 2048 CMOS registers from MCA systems. The complete program is provided on the diskette in the CMOSVIEW.ASM file. The diskette includes data definitions and additional required subroutines.

```
;-----------------------------------------------------------------------
;    DISP_MCA_CMOS
;       display the extended CMOS RAM memory contents on a MCA
;       system.
;
;       Called with:    nothing
;
;       Returns:        CMOS register values sent to std output
;
;       Regs used:      all
;
;       Subs used:      hex
```

```
disp_MCA_CMOS    proc    near
        push    cs
        pop     ds
        push    cs
        pop     es

; output the registers, starting at 0

        mov     cx, 0                   ; extended CMOS location 0

d_MCA_loop1:
        mov     bx, offset disp_eCMOS
        mov     al, ch
        call    hex                     ; convert reg to ASCII hex
        add     bx, 2
        mov     al, cl
        call    hex                     ; convert reg to ASCII hex
        add     bx, 4

d_MCA_loop2:
        mov     al, cl
        cli                             ; disable interrupts
        out     74h, al                 ; set low portion of register
        mov     al, ch
        out     75h, al                 ; set high portion of register
        IODELAY
        in      al, 76h                 ; get port value
        sti                             ; enable interrupts
        call    hex
        add     bx, 3
        inc     cx
        test    cl, 7                   ; 8th value in line ?
        jnz     d_MCA_skp1              ; jump if not
        inc     bx
```

```
d_MCA_skp1:
        test    cl, 0Fh             ; 16 values output ?
        jnz     d_MCA_loop2
        OUTMSG  disp_eCMOS_all      ; output line of 16 registers
        cmp     cx, 800h            ; all registers output ?
        jb      d_MCA_loop1         ; loop if not

d_MCA_done:
        ret
disp_MCA_CMOS    endp
```

Code Sample 15-5. Display Extended EISA CMOS

This routine displays 8K of extended CMOS memory from EISA systems. The complete program is provided on the diskette in the CMOSVIEW.ASM file. The diskette includes data definitions and additional required subroutines.

```
;-------------------------------------------------------------------
;    DISP_EISA_CMOS
;       display the extended CMOS RAM memory contents on a EISA
;       system.
;
;       Called with:    nothing
;
;       Returns:        CMOS register values sent to std output
;
;       Regs used:      all
;
;       Subs used:      hex

disp_EISA_CMOS    proc    near
        push    cs
        pop     ds
```

```
        push    cs
        pop     es

; output the registers, starting at 800, bank 0

        mov     cl, 0                   ; extended CMOS bank 0
d_EISA_next_bank:                       ;   (1 of 32 banks)
        mov     dx, 800h                ; ports 800 to 8FF
d_EISA_loop1:
        mov     bx, offset disp_eCMOS
        mov     al, cl                  ; get bank number
        call    hex                     ; convert to ASCII
        add     bx, 2
        mov     byte ptr [bx], '-'      ; separator
        inc     bx
        mov     byte ptr [bx], '8'      ; always 800-8FFh
        inc     bx
        mov     al, dl
        call    hex                     ; convert reg to ASCII hex
        add     bx, 4

d_EISA_loop2:
        cli                             ; disable interrupts
        push    dx
        mov     dx, 0C00h
        mov     al, cl                  ; bank select
        out     dx, al
        pop     dx
        IODELAY
        in      al, dx                  ; get register
        sti                             ; enable interrupts
        call    hex
        add     bx, 3
        inc     dx
```

```
        test    dl, 7               ; 8th value in line ?
        jnz     d_EISA_skp1         ; jump if not
        inc     bx
d_EISA_skp1:
        test    dl, 0Fh             ; 16 values output ?
        jnz     d_EISA_loop2
        push    dx
        OUTMSG  disp_eCMOS_all      ; output line of 16 registers
        pop     dx
        cmp     dx, 900h            ; 256 registers output ?
        jb      d_EISA_loop1
        OUTMSG  crlf                ; insert a blank line
        inc     cl
        cmp     cl, 32              ; all 32 banks output ?
        jb      d_EISA_next_bank
        ret
disp_EISA_CMOS    endp
```

Port Summary

Port	Type	Function	Platform
70h	Output	CMOS Memory Address and NMI Enable	AT+
71h	I/O	CMOS Memory Data	AT+
74h	Output	Extended CMOS Address LSB	MCA
75h	Output	Extended CMOS Address MSB	MCA
76h	I/O	Extended CMOS Data Register	MCA
8xxh	I/O	Extended CMOS Registers	EISA
C00h	Output	Extended CMOS Bank Select	EISA

Port Detail

Port	Type	Description	Platform
70h	Output	CMOS Memory Address	AT+

To access this memory, the RAM address is first written to port 70h. Then port 71h is used to read or write the RAM location previously specified.

Output (bits 0-7) CMOS address and NMI

bit	7 w =	0	Allow Non-Maskable Interrupt, NMI interrupt 2
		1	NMI disabled (used in normal access to CMOS RAM)
	6 w =	x	Unused (upper CMOS address bit for extended CMOS on some systems)
	5 w =	x	CMOS RAM address for the next read or write
	4 w =	x	
	3 w =	x	
	2 w =	x	
	1 w =	x	
	0 w =	x	

The following lists summarizes CMOS locations. The original AT contained 64 bytes of RAM and clock information. Some current systems contain additional memory for other options.

Register Summary—Time and Date

Address	Register Description
00h	Seconds
01h	Seconds alarm
02h	Minutes
03h	Minutes alarm
04h	Hours
05h	Hours alarm
06h	Day of week
07h	Day of the month
08h	Month
09h	Year
0Ah	Status Register A
0Bh	Status Register B
0Ch	Status Register C
0Dh	Status Register D

Register Summary—CMOS Memory

In the few technical references that show CMOS registers, many are identified with the dreaded *Reserved* word. Reserved entries are often just unused entries, although they are also used to hold specific features and options provided by some BIOSes. I've referred to nonconsistent "reserved" registers as "Vendor specific," and provided some of the popular uses by major BIOS manufacturers.

Be aware that most BIOSes today are tuned to a specific motherboard and CPU. This means that a BIOS with a specific release date can be configured in different ways that provide conflicting use of CMOS registers! The BIOS release date in ASCII is usually found at address

F000:FFF5. Never assume every BIOS from a single vendor with the same date code uses CMOS registers in the same manner.

To find out the CMOS register values on your specific system, you can use the CMOSVIEW utility included on the diskette. The output can be piped to a file. Then reboot the system and go into the BIOS setup program. Change one flag or value, and return to DOS. Run CMOSVIEW again, and compare the results between the prior saved settings and the current settings to see exactly where the information is stored.

With a quickly hacked-together batch file and a difference program, I've found it takes about three to four hours to trace down most flags and values in a BIOS. Be aware that some values, such as chipset settings and RAM refresh settings may make the system unstable. You may also need to boot through a diskette drive for some tests. For example, changing the hard drive settings could affect (i.e., destroy) information on the hard drive!

Address	**Register Description**
0Eh	Diagnostic status byte
0Fh	Shutdown status byte
10h	Diskette drive types (drive A & B)
11h	Vendor Specific
12h	Hard disk type
13h	Vendor Specific
14h	Equipment byte
15h	Base memory, low
16h	Base memory, high
17h	Extended memory, low
18h	Extended memory, high
19h	Hard disk 0 extended type
1Ah	Hard disk 1 extended type
1Bh	Vendor Specific
1Ch	Vendor Specific
1Dh	Vendor Specific
1Eh	Vendor Specific
1Fh	Vendor Specific
20h	Vendor Specific
21h	Vendor Specific
22h	Vendor Specific
23h	Vendor Specific
24h	Vendor Specific
25h	Vendor Specific
26h	Vendor Specific
27h	Vendor Specific
28h	Vendor Specific
29h	Vendor Specific
2Ah	Vendor Specific
2Bh	Vendor Specific

Address	Register Description
2Ch	Vendor Specific
2Dh	Vendor Specific
2Eh	CMOS checksum, high (except MCA)
2Fh	CMOS checksum, low (except MCA)
30h	Extended memory, low
31h	Extended memory, high
32h	Date century byte (ISA); CRC high (MCA)
33h	Power on information flags (ISA); CRC low (MCA)
34h	Vendor Specific
35h	Vendor Specific
36h	Vendor Specific
37h	Date century byte (MCA)
38h	Vendor Specific
39h	Vendor Specific
3Ah	Vendor Specific
3Bh	Vendor Specific
3Ch	Vendor Specific
3Dh	Vendor Specific
3Eh	Vendor Specific
3Fh	Vendor Specific
40h to 7Fh	Vendor Specific (Extended CMOS)

Register Detail

Register	Description	Type
00h	Seconds	CMOS

This location contains the RTC's current seconds value in BCD format. The valid range is 0 to 59. See General Information about restrictions on reading and writing to this location.

Register	Description	Type
01h	Seconds alarm	CMOS

This location contains the RTC's alarm seconds value in BCD format. The valid range is 0 to 59. The alarm can be programmed a number of different ways. See Registers A to D for more details. If the top two bits are set to 1 (values C0h to FFh), this seconds register is ignored as part of the alarm. See General Information for the Real-Time Clock for restrictions on reading and writing to this location.

Register	Description	Type
02h	Minutes	CMOS

This location contains the RTC's current minutes value in BCD format. The valid range is 0 to 59. See General Information for restrictions on reading and writing to this location.

Register	Description	Type
03h	Minutes alarm	CMOS

This location contains the RTC's alarm minutes value in BCD format. The valid range is 0 to 59. The alarm can be programmed a number of different ways. See Registers A to D for more details. If the top two bits are set to 1 (values C0h to FFh), this minutes register is ignored as part of the alarm. See General Information for restrictions on reading and writing to this location.

Register	Description	Type
04h	Hours	CMOS

This location contains the RTC's current hours value in BCD format. The valid range is 1 to 12 in 12-hour mode. Bit 7 of the byte is 0 if AM, and 1 if PM. The range in 24-hour mode is 0 to 23. Register B, bit 1 controls if 12 or 24-hour mode is used. See General Information for restrictions on reading and writing to this location.

Register	Description	Type
05h	Hours alarm	CMOS

This location contains the RTC's alarm hours value in BCD format. The valid range is 1 to 12 in 12-hour mode. Bit 7 of the byte is 0 if AM, and 1 if PM. The range in 24-hour mode is 0 to 23. Register B, bit 1 controls if 12 or 24-hour mode is used. The alarm can be programmed a number of different ways. See Registers A to D for more details. If the top two bits are set to 1 (values C0h to FFh), this hours register is ignored as part of the alarm. See General Information for restrictions on reading and writing to this location.

Register	Description	Type
06h	Day of the week	CMOS

This location indicates the day of week. Even though the day of week can be determined from the date, this register can be incorrectly set to the wrong day of the week. Generally, the operating system ignores this byte and performs its own determination of the day of week from the date. See General Information for restrictions on reading and writing to this location.

Value	Day of Week
1	Sunday
2	Monday
3	Tuesday
4	Wednesday
5	Thursday
6	Friday
7	Saturday

Register	Description	Type
07h	Day of the month	CMOS

This location contains the RTC's current day of the month in BCD format. The valid range is 1 to 31. See General Information for restrictions on reading and writing to this location.

Register	Description	Type
08h	Month	CMOS

This location contains the RTC's current month in BCD format. The valid range is 1 to 12. See General Information for restrictions on reading and writing to this location.

Register	Description	Type
09h	Year	CMOS

This location contains the RTC's current year in BCD format. The valid range is 0 to 99. See General Information for restrictions on reading and writing to this location.

Register	Description	Type
0Ah	Status Register A	CMOS

This register controls the operation of the RTC. None of these bits are affected by a hardware reset. Note that bit 7 is read only, and is not changed by a write to this register.

bit	7 r = 1	Update in progress. With the PC, this will remain high for about 2 us every second. The clock should only be updated within 244 us after this bit transitions from high to low.
	6 r/w = 0	Divider control—Sets the internal divider for the specific crystal selected. On the PC, a 32.768 kHz crystal is used, so bits 6, 5 and 4 should be 010. Other values will yield a considerably slower clock.
	5 r/w = 1	

4 r/w = 0	bit 6 bit 5 bit 4 0 0 0 = divide clock by 128 over normal 0 1 1 = divide clock by 32 over normal 0 1 0 = normal Other combinations are for test modes.	
3 r/w = x	Rate selection divider control—Used to set how fast the periodic interrupt occurs. This is normally set to 6 (0110b) to generate an interrupt every 976 us.	
2 r/w = x		
1 r/w = x		
0 r/w = x	Lower Nibble	

0	= no periodic rate interrupt generated	
1	= 3.90625	ms
2	= 7.8125	ms
3	= .122070	ms
4	= .244141	ms
5	= .488281	ms
6	= .976562	ms (default)
7	= 1.953125	ms
8	= 3.90625	ms
9	= 7.8125	ms
A	= 15.625	ms
B	= 31.25	ms
C	= 62.5	ms
D	= 125.0	ms
E	= 250.0	ms
F	= 500.0	ms

Register	Description	Type
0Bh	Status Register B	CMOS

This register controls the operation of the RTC. Bits 7, 2, 1, and 0 are not affected by a hardware reset. Bits 6, 5, 4, and 3 are all set to 0 after a hardware reset.

bit 7 r/w = 0	Clock update occurs every second
1	Halt clock (used to update clock to a new time or date). This also forces bit 3 to 0, turning off the interrupt after update feature, if enabled.

6 r/w = 0	Prevent the periodic interrupt from occurring. A hardware reset sets this bit to zero. (default)
1	Enable the periodic interrupt . The interrupt is toggled at the rate specified in Register A, rate divider control, normally every 976.562 uS.
5 r/w = 0	Disable alarm interrupt (default)
1	Enable alarm interrupt. When the three alarm registers match the current time, the interrupt is issued. When a seconds alarm register is in the don't care state, the interrupt is issued once every second when the remaining registers match.
4 r/w = 0	Disable update complete interrupt (default)
1	Enable issuing a interrupt every time the clock update has been completed (once a second). This flag is cleared if bit 7 is set to 1.
3 r/w = 0	Square wave disable (default)
1	Square wave enable. Since the chip's square wave output pin is normally not connected on the motherboard, the square wave function is unavailable.
2 r/w = 0	Time and calendar are stored as BCD values (default)
1	Time and calendar are stored as binary (never used)
1 r/w = 0	Hours are stored in 12-hour mode
1	Hours are stored in 24-hour mode (default)
0 r/w = 0	Daylight savings time disabled (default)
1	Daylight savings time enabled. As noted earlier, the internal time changes are made on dates no longer used in the U.S. When active, on the last Sunday in April, at 1:59:59 a.m., the time will switch to 3:00:00 a.m. On the last Sunday in October, at 1:59:59 a.m., the time will switch to 1:00:00 a.m.

Register	Description	Type
0Ch	Status Register C	CMOS

This register has the current flag status for interrupt operation. Register C is read-only. All bits are cleared after a read occurs, or after a hardware reset occurs.

bit	7 r = 0	Interrupt request not active. The periodic (bit 6), alarm (bit 5), and updated ended (bit 4) flags are all 0.
	1	Interrupt request active, any bit 6, 5, or 4 is set to 1, and IRQ 8 is activated.

6 r = 1	This Periodic Interrupt Flag is set once every periodic cycle as set by Register A rate selection bits. Register B, bit 6 must also be set to 1 for this to occur. When set, bit 7 is also set to 1, and IRQ 8 becomes active.
5 r = 1	This Alarm Flag indicates the alarm time matches the current time. Register B bit 5 must also be set to 1 for this to occur. When set, bit 7 is also set to 1, and IRQ 8 becomes active.
4 r = 0	This Update-Ended flag is set after each clock update cycle, when Register B, bit 4 is also set to a 1. When set, bit 7 is also set to 1, and IRQ 8 becomes active.
3 r = 0	Unused
2 r = 0	Unused
1 r = 0	Unused
0 r = 0	Unused

Register	Description	Type
0Dh	Status Register D	CMOS

Valid RAM and Time RTC register. Register D is read only and is not affected when a hardware reset occurs. After a read occurs, bit 7 is set to 1.

bit	7 r = 0	The contents of RAM and the time are not valid since power was lost to the RTC chip. This occurs if the system power was off and the battery was disconnected, dead, or the battery voltage is insufficient to operate the RTC.
	1	RTC power has been stable since the last read of this register.
	6 r = 0	Unused
	5 r = 0	Unused
	4 r = 0	Unused
	3 r = 0	Unused
	2 r = 0	Unused
	1 r = 0	Unused
	0 r = 0	Unused

CMOS Memory

The following CMOS RAM locations contain nonvolatile information for the main system BIOS.

Register	Description	Type
0Eh	Diagnostic Status	CMOS

This byte contains failure information during the system's POST (Power On System Test).

bit	7 r/w = 1	The RTC lost power and its contents are no longer valid.
	6 r/w = 1	CMOS RAM checksum is bad.
	5 r/w = 1	Incorrect configuration information detected.
	4 r/w = 1	Memory size does not match configuration record.
	3 r/w = 1	Hard disk drive 0 (C:) adapter or drive failed initialization preventing the normal boot up.
	2 r/w = 1	Time or Date found to be invalid.
	1 r/w = 1	Adapters do not match the configuration (MCA/EISA only)
	0 r/w = 1	Timeout reading an adapter ID (MCA/EISA only)

Register	Description	Type
0Fh	Shutdown Status	CMOS

This byte contains a code indicating where the system should return after a system shutdown occurred. It is used by the BIOS to go through a reset and possibly take alternate action other than a normal reset. This is also useful for returning to real mode from protected mode by issuing a reset.

Codes 0, 4, 5, 9, and Ah are generally consistent with different BIOS manufacturers. Other codes may vary in function between different BIOS manufacturers and microprocessors.

After a reset, some functions will jump or call the address previously stored in the double word at 40:67h. POST will have both interrupts disabled and NMI disabled when the jump or call is made. To enable NMI, issue an OUT to port 70h, with value 0. Then issue an STI to enable interrupts. For code 5, the user must also restore the interrupt mask registers. Some functions issue an End-Of-Interrupt (EOI) to the interrupt controller, while others do not. See the specific function for EOI handling. Before passing control through the jump or call, POST will have set the stack SS:SP to 0:400h. This means the top of the interrupt vector table is used as a temporary stack. The user should be sure to change the stack pointer to a more appropriate location as soon as practical.

code	0 = Proceed with normal POST (soft reset)
	1 = Initialize chip set for real mode operation
	2 = Shutdown after memory test
	3 = Shutdown with memory error
	4 = Jump to disk bootstrap routine

5 = Jump to DWORD pointer at 40:67h (EOI was issued and keyboard has been flushed)

6 = Jump to DWORD pointer at 40:67h (no EOI issued)

7 = Return to BIOS extended memory block move (interrupt 15h, function 87h was in progress)

8 = Return to POST memory test

9 = Return to BIOS extended memory block move (interrupt 15h, function 87h was in progress)

A = Jump to DWORD pointer at 40:67h (no EOI issued)

B = Return as if IRET was issued through 40:67h

C = Return as if RETF was issued through 40:67h

Register	Description	Type
10h	Diskette Drive Type	CMOS

Defines the type of diskette drives installed. Only the values valid for a specific BIOS are permitted. You cannot insert a 5 in CMOS for 2.88 MB drives on a BIOS that does not support 2.88 MB drives.

bit	7 r/w = x	Diskette type, drive 0	
	6 r/w = x	Upper Nibble	
	5 r/w = x	0	No drive
	4 r/w = x	1	360 KB 5.25" drive
		2	1.2 MB 5.25" drive
		3	720 KB 3.5" drive
		4	1.44 MB 3.5" drive
		5	2.88 MB 3.5" drive
	3 r/w = x	Diskette type, drive 1	
	2 r/w = x	Lower Nibble	
	1 r/w = x	0	No drive
	0 r/w = x	1	360 KB 5.25" drive
		2	1.2 MB 5.25" drive
		3	720 KB 3.5" drive
		4	1.44 MB 3.5" drive
		5	2.88 MB 3.5" drive

Register	Description	Type
11h	Vendor Specific	CMOS

This is a vendor-specific CMOS location, and may be unused on some systems. A number of BIOS examples follow, but some BIOS vendors use different flags for specific motherboards, even when they have the same date code!

AMI BIOS, dated 11-11-92

bit	7 r/w = 1	Mouse enabled (if BIOS supports mouse)
	6 r/w = 1	Test memory above 1 MB
	5 r/w = 1	Generate tick sound during memory test
	4 r/w = 1	Memory parity check enabled
	3 r/w = 1	At boot up, display which key to use for Setup
	2 r/w = x	Specify location of user-defined hard disk data only when the system BIOS is not shadowed in RAM. When shadowing is on, the user disk data is stored in the shadowed RAM area, and this bit is ignored.
	0	Store user-defined disk type information at 0:300h
	1	Store at top of main memory (640K becomes 639K)
	1 r/w = 1	If any error during boot, ask to press F1 to continue
	0 r/w = 0	Num lock off at boot up time
	1	Num lock on at boot up time

Phoenix BIOS, dated 1-11-96

bit	7 r/w = x	PCI slot 1—latency timer
	6 r/w = x	for timer values 0 to F8h, multiple value by 8
	5 r/w = x	
	4 r/w = x	
	3 r/w = x	
	2 r/w = 1	PCI slot 1—master enabled
	1 r/w = 0	Unused or unknown function
	0 r/w = 1	PCI slot 1—default latency timer active

Register	Description	Type
12h	Hard Disk Type	CMOS

Defines a type number for hard disks 0 and 1. The type specifies an entry in a ROM table of disk type information.

bit 7 r/w = x	Hard disk type, drive 0		
6 r/w = x	Upper Nibble		
5 r/w = x		0	No drive
4 r/w = x		1 to 0Eh	Types 1 to 14
		0Fh	Types 16 to 255 as specified in drive 0 extended type CMOS register 19h
3 r/w = x	Hard disk type, drive 1		
2 r/w = x	Lower Nibble		
1 r/w = x		0	No drive
0 r/w = x		1 to 0Eh	Types 1 to 14
		0Fh	Types 16 to 255 as specified in drive 1 extended type CMOS register 1Ah

Most BIOS manufactures DO NOT have the same contents in their drive tables. There are usually changes in the table data between BIOS versions from the same manufacturer. The organization of these tables does appear consistent.

Each type entry is comprised of the following 14 bytes of information (see also Table 11-3 for further details):

Offset	Size	Description
0	word	number of cylinders
2	byte	number of heads
3	word	low write current, cylinder begin (XT only, unused all others)
5	word	precompensation cylinder
7	byte	error correction burst length (XT only, unused all others)
8	byte	disk information bits bit 7 = 1 for no retries bit 6 = 1 for no retries bit 5 = 1 when bad map is at last cylinder + 1 bit 4 = 0 unused bit 3 = 1 if number of heads is greater than 8 bit 2 = 0 must be zero (no reset) bit 1 = 0 must be zero (disable IRQ) bit 0 = 0 unused
9	byte	normal timeout (XT only, unused all others)
A	byte	format timeout (XT only, unused all others)
B	byte	check timeout (XT only, unused all others)
C	byte	number of sectors per track
D	byte	unused

Note that the precompensation and landing zone cylinders value is obsolete. Current drives do not care about or use these values. If this information is not known, set each to the same value as the total number of cylinders.

Most newer BIOSes reserve up to four type numbers as a custom entry. This allows setting a custom drive type. This works especially well for IDE drives, where the exact cylinders, heads, and sectors per track have little meaning. Values that multiply together to define the total capacity of the drive is what matters, and a custom setting allows maximizing the useful capacity of the drive. Also refer to the vendor-specific locations starting at 1Bh.

Register	Description	Type
13h	Vendor Specific	CMOS

This is a vendor specific CMOS location, and may be unused on some systems. A number of BIOS examples follow, but some BIOS vendors use different flags for specific motherboards, even if they have the same date code!

AMI BIOS, dated 11-11-92

bit 7 r/w = 1 — Force the initial keyboard repeat rate and delay

6 r/w = x, 5 r/w = x — Set the delay before keyboard repeat occurs

bit 6	bit 5
0	0 = 250 ms
0	1 = 500 ms
1	0 = 750 ms
1	1 = 1000 ms

4 r/w = x, 3 r/w = x, 2 r/w = x — Set the repeat rate

bit 4	bit 3	bit 2
0	0	0 = 6 char/sec
0	0	1 = 8 char/sec
0	1	0 = 10 char/sec
0	1	1 = 12 char/sec
1	0	0 = 15 char/sec
1	0	1 = 20 char/sec
1	1	0 = 25 char/sec
1	1	1 = 30 char/sec

1 r/w = 0 — Lower two bits of repeat rate.

0 r/w = 0 — Controls finer resolution, but bits are not set by the BIOS configuration program. See Port 60h, Command F3h for all repeat values (Chapter 8, The Keyboard System).

PS/2 MCA BIOSes

This is a reserved byte for internal POST operations.

bit	7 r/w = 1	POST sets VGA pel information
	6 r/w = 0	RTC lost battery power
	5 r/w = 1	Go to ROM BASIC from POST
	4 r/w = 0	POST sets typematic rate: 10.9 cps with a delay of 500 ms
	1	POST sets typematic rate: 30 cps with a delay of 250 ms
	3 r/w = x	Unused or unknown function
	2 r/w = x	Unused or unknown function
	1 r/w = 1	Password for network installed
	0 r/w = 1	Password after Power-on installed

Compaq BIOS

Some COMPAQ systems use this location to indicate that a second hard disk controller is present. In this case one controller is used for Drive 0, and a second controller for drive 1. To detect a Compaq system, look for the string 03COMPAQ at F000:FFE8.

byte =	zero if no 2nd controller
	non-zero if 2nd controller used

Phoenix BIOS, dated 1-11-96

bit	7 r/w = x	PCI slot 2—latency timer
	6 r/w = x	for timer values 0 to F8h, multiple value by 8
	5 r/w = x	
	4 r/w = x	
	3 r/w = x	
	2 r/w = 1	PCI slot 2—master enabled
	1 r/w = 0	Unused or unknown function
	0 r/w = 1	PCI slot 2—default latency timer active

Register	Description	Type
14h	Equipment Byte	CMOS

This contains information about the attached diskette drives, primary display type at bootup, and other information. The POST uses this entry to create the equipment word at 40:10h. Interrupt 11h can be used to read the equipment information from 40:10h.

bit	7 r/w = x	Diskette drives installed	
	6 r/w = x	bit 7	bit 6
		0	0 = 1 diskette drive installed

	0	1 = 2 diskette drives installed
	1	x = Unused
5 r/w = x	Primary video display	
4 r/w = x	bit 5	bit 4
	0	0 = video card with BIOS ROM (EGA/VGA+)
	0	1 = 40 columns by 25 rows, color, CGA
	1	0 = 80 columns by 25 rows, color, CGA
	1	1 = 80 columns by 25 rows, monochrome
3 r/w = 0	Unused (most systems) or ignore POST keyboard tests (AMI BIOS)	
1	Test keyboard (AMI BIOS)	
2 r/w = 0	Unused	
1 r/w = 1	Standard math coprocessor installed	
0 r/w = 0	No diskette drive for boot	
1	diskette drive installed for boot	

Register	Description	Type
15h	Base Memory—Low	CMOS

Used with register 16h to create a word indicating the size of base memory in 1,024-byte multiples. A typical value is 0280h indicating 640 KB of base memory. The POST stores this word into the BIOS memory area at 40:13h. The value at 40:13h can be read using Interrupt 12h, Get Memory Size.

Register	Description	Type
16h	Base Memory—High	CMOS

Used with register 15h to create a word indicating the size of base memory in 1 KB multiples. See CMOS register 15h for more information.

Register	Description	Type
17h	Extended Memory—Low	CMOS

Used with register 18h to create a word indicating the size of extended memory in 1,024-byte multiples. For example, 3C00h indicates 15 MB of extended memory. Many older BIOSes only support 15 MB as a maximum. Most newer BIOSes can accept up to 63 MB of extended memory, the limit of this word. Beyond 63 MB there is no standard.

Register	Description	Type
18h	Extended Memory—High	CMOS

Used with register 17h to create a word indicating the size of extended memory in 1 KB multiples. See CMOS register 17h for more information.

Register	Description	Type
19h	Hard Disk 0 Extended Type	CMOS

Non-MCA Systems

Drive type byte, types 16 to 255 when high nibble of hard disk type, register 12h is Fh. See CMOS register 12h.

MCA Systems

This register holds the adapter card ID for card slot 0. This byte is duplicated in extended MCA CMOS register 0. Refer to port 76h, register 0 for details.

Register	Description	Type
1Ah	Hard Disk 1 Extended Type	CMOS

Drive type byte, types 16 to 255 when low nibble of hard disk type, register 12h is Fh. See CMOS register 12h.

On MCA systems, this register holds the adapter card ID for card slot 0. This byte is duplicated in extended MCA CMOS register 1. Refer to port 76h, register 1 for details.

Register	Description	Type
1Bh	Vendor Specific	CMOS

This is a vendor-specific CMOS location, and may be unused on some systems.

AMI BIOS, dated 11-11-92

This byte holds the low portion of the cylinders word for hard disk 0. It is only used when type 47 is specified (user defined) for hard disk 0.

Phoenix BIOS, dated 9-28-95

This byte holds the low portion of the cylinders word for hard disk 3.

Phoenix BIOS, dated 1-11-96

This byte holds the low portion of the cylinders word for hard disk 0. It is only used when type 47 is specified (user defined) for hard disk 0.

MCA Systems

This register holds the adapter card ID for card slot 1. This byte is duplicated in extended MCA CMOS register 23h. Refer to port 76h, registers 23h for details.

Register	Description	Type
1Ch	Vendor Specific	CMOS

This is a vendor-specific CMOS location, and may be unused on some systems.

AMI BIOS, dated 11-11-92

This byte holds the high portion of the cylinder word for hard disk 0. It is only used when type 47 is specified (user defined) for hard disk 0.

Phoenix BIOS, dated 9-28-95

This byte holds the high portion of the cylinders word for hard disk 3.

Phoenix BIOS, dated 1-11-96

This byte holds the high portion of the cylinders word for hard disk 0. It is only used when type 47 is specified (user defined) for hard disk 0.

MCA Systems

This register holds the adapter card ID for card slot 1. This byte is duplicated in extended MCA CMOS register 24h. Refer to port 76h, register 24h for details.

Register	Description	Type
1Dh	Vendor Specific	CMOS

This is a vendor-specific CMOS location, and may be unused on some systems.

AMI BIOS, dated 11-11-92

Number of heads for hard disk 0. It is only used when type 47 is specified (user defined) for hard disk 0.

Phoenix BIOS, dated 9-28-95

This byte holds the low portion of the cylinder number for the write precompensation word on hard disk 3.

Phoenix BIOS, dated 1-11-96

This byte holds the low portion of the cylinders word for hard disk 1. It is only used when type 47 is specified (user defined) for hard disk 1.

MCA Systems

This register holds the adapter card ID for card slot 2. This byte is duplicated in extended MCA CMOS register 46h. Refer to port 76h, register 46h for details.

Register	Description	Type
1Eh	Vendor Specific	CMOS

This is a vendor-specific CMOS location, and may be unused on some systems.

AMI BIOS, dated 11-11-92

This byte holds the low portion of the cylinder number for the write precompensation word on hard disk 0. It is only used when type 47 is specified (user defined) for hard disk 0.

Phoenix BIOS, dated 9-28-95

This byte holds the high portion of the cylinder number for the write precompensation word on hard disk 3.

Phoenix BIOS, dated 1-11-96

This byte holds the high portion of the cylinders word for hard disk 1. It is only used when type 47 is specified (user defined) for hard disk 1.

MCA Systems

This register holds the adapter card ID for card slot 2. This byte is duplicated in extended MCA CMOS register 47h. Refer to port 76h, register 47h for details.

Register	Description	Type
1Fh	Vendor Specific	CMOS

This is a vendor-specific CMOS location, and may be unused on some systems.

AMI BIOS, dated 11-11-92

This byte holds the high portion of the cylinder number for the write precompensation word for hard disk 0. It is only used when type 47 is specified (user defined) for hard disk 0.

Phoenix BIOS, dated 9-28-95

This byte holds the low portion of the cylinder number for the write precompensation word on hard disk 0. It is only used when type 47 is specified (user defined) for hard disk 0. Along with register 20h, a value of 0FFFh indicates no write precompensation.

Phoenix BIOS, dated 1-11-96

This byte holds the low portion of the cylinder number for the write precompensation word for hard disk 1. It is only used when type 47 is specified (user defined) for hard disk 1.

MCA Systems

This register holds the adapter card ID for card slot 3. This byte is duplicated in extended MCA CMOS register 69h. Refer to port 76h, register 69h for details.

Register	Description	Type
20h	Vendor Specific	CMOS

This is a vendor-specific CMOS location, and may be unused on some systems.

AMI BIOS, dated 11-11-92

This byte holds the disk information flags for hard disk 0. It is only used when type 47 is specified (user defined) for hard disk 0.

bit	7 r/w = 1	No retries
	6 r/w = 1	No retries
	5 r/w = 1	Bad map is at last cylinder plus 1
	4 r/w = 0	Unused
	3 r/w = 1	If number of heads is greater than 8
	2 r/w = 0	Unused
	1 r/w = 0	Unused
	0 r/w = 0	Unused

Phoenix BIOS, dated 9-28-95

This byte holds the high portion of the cylinder number for the write precompensation word on hard disk 0. It is only used when type 47 is specified (user defined) for hard disk 0. Along with register 1Fh, a value of 0FFFh indicates no write precompensation.

Phoenix BIOS, dated 1-11-96

This byte holds the high portion of the cylinder number for the write precompensation word for hard disk 1. It is only used when type 47 is specified (user defined) for hard disk 1.

MCA Systems

This register holds the adapter card ID for card slot 3. This byte is duplicated in extended MCA CMOS register 6Ah. Refer to port 76h, register 64h for details.

Register	Description	Type
21h	Vendor Specific	CMOS

This is a vendor-specific CMOS location, and may be unused on some systems.

AMI BIOS, dated 11-11-92

This byte holds the low portion of the cylinder number for the landing zone word for hard disk 0. It is only used when type 47 is specified (user defined) for hard disk 0.

MCA Systems

This holds the Programmable Option Select configuration byte 2 to be sent to adapter card slot 0 byte POST. It is duplicated in extended MCA CMOS register 3.

Register	Description	Type
22h	**Vendor Specific**	**CMOS**

This is a vendor-specific CMOS location, and may be unused on some systems.

AMI BIOS, dated 11-11-92

This byte holds the high portion of the cylinder number for the landing zone word for hard disk 0. It is only used when type 47 is specified (user defined) for hard disk 0.

Phoenix BIOS, dated 9-28-95

bit	7 r/w = x	Sectors per track, low portion hard disk 1
	6 r/w = x	(high four bits are in register 23h)
	5 r/w = x	Sectors per track, hard disk 0
	4 r/w = x	
	3 r/w = x	
	2 r/w = x	
	1 r/w = x	
	0 r/w = x	

MCA Systems

This holds the Programmable Option Select configuration byte 3 to be sent to adapter card slot 0 byte POST. It is duplicated in extended MCA CMOS register 4.

Register	Description	Type
23h	**Vendor Specific**	**CMOS**

This is a vendor-specific CMOS location, and may be unused on some systems.

AMI BIOS, dated 11-11-92

This byte holds the number of sectors per track for hard disk 0. It is only used when type 47 is specified (user defined) for hard disk 0.

Phoenix BIOS, dated 9-28-95

bit	7 r/w = x	Sectors per track, low portion, hard disk 2 (high two bits are in register 24h)
	6 r/w = x	
	5 r/w = x	
	4 r/w = x	
	3 r/w = x	Sectors per track, high portion, hard disk 1 (high two bits are in register 22h)
	2 r/w = x	
	1 r/w = x	
	0 r/w = x	

MCA Systems

This holds the Programmable Option Select configuration byte 4 to be sent to adapter card slot 0 byte POST. It is duplicated in extended MCA CMOS register 5.

Register	Description	Type
24h	Vendor Specific	CMOS

This is a vendor-specific CMOS location, and may be unused on some systems.

AMI BIOS, dated 11-11-92

This byte holds the low portion of the cylinder word for hard disk 1. It is only used when type 47 is specified (user defined) for hard disk 1.

Phoenix BIOS, dated 9-28-95

bit	7 r/w = x	Sectors per track hard disk 3
	6 r/w = x	
	5 r/w = x	
	4 r/w = x	
	3 r/w = x	
	2 r/w = x	
	1 r/w = x	Sectors per track, high portion, hard disk 2 (low four bits are in register 23h)
	0 r/w = x	

MCA Systems

This holds the Programmable Option Select configuration byte 5 to be sent to adapter card slot 0 byte POST. It is duplicated in extended MCA CMOS register 6.

Register	Description	Type
25h	Vendor Specific	CMOS

This is a vendor-specific CMOS location, and may be unused on some systems.

AMI BIOS, dated 11-11-92

This byte holds the high portion of the cylinder word for hard disk 1. It is only used when type 47 is specified (user defined) for hard disk 1.

Phoenix BIOS, dated 9-28-95

bit	7 r/w = x	Number of heads for hard disk 1, when type 47 specified (value 0 = 1 head; value F = 16 heads)
	6 r/w = x	
	5 r/w = x	
	4 r/w = x	
	3 r/w = x	Number of heads for hard disk 0, when type 47 specified (value 0 = 1 head; value F = 16 heads)
	2 r/w = x	
	1 r/w = x	
	0 r/w = x	

MCA Systems

This holds the Programmable Option Select configuration byte 2 to be sent to adapter card slot 1 byte POST. It is duplicated in extended MCA CMOS register 26h.

Register	Description	Type
26h	Vendor Specific	CMOS

This is a vendor-specific CMOS location, and may be unused on some systems.

AMI BIOS, dated 11-11-92

This byte holds the number of heads for hard disk 1. It is only used when type 47 is specified (user defined) for hard disk 1.

MCA Systems

This holds the Programmable Option Select configuration byte 3 to be sent to adapter card slot 1 byte POST. It is duplicated in extended MCA CMOS register 27h.

Register	Description	Type
27h	Vendor Specific	CMOS

This is a vendor-specific CMOS location, and may be unused on some systems.

AMI BIOS, dated 11-11-92

This byte holds the low portion of the cylinder number for the write precompensation word for hard disk 1. It is only used when type 47 is specified (user defined) for hard disk 1.

Phoenix BIOS, dated 9-28-95

bit	7 r/w = x	Number of heads for hard disk 3, when type 47 specified (value 0 = 1 head; value F = 16 heads)
	6 r/w = x	
	5 r/w = x	
	4 r/w = x	
	3 r/w = x	Number of heads for hard disk 2, when type 47 specified (value 0 = 1 head; value F = 16 heads)
	2 r/w = x	
	1 r/w = x	
	0 r/w = x	

MCA Systems

This holds the Programmable Option Select configuration byte 4 to be sent to adapter card slot 1 byte POST. It is duplicated in extended MCA CMOS register 28h.

Register	Description	Type
28h	Vendor Specific	CMOS

This is a vendor-specific CMOS location, and may be unused on some systems.

AMI BIOS, dated 11-11-92

This byte holds the high portion of the cylinder number for the write precompensation word for hard disk 1. It is only used when type 47 is specified (user defined) for hard disk 1.

Phoenix BIOS, dated 9-28-95

bit	7 r/w = 0	Unused or unknown function
	6 r/w = x	Multisector transfers, hard disk 1 0 = disabled 1 = 2 sectors 2 = 4 sectors 3 = 8 sectors 4 = 16 sectors
	5 r/w = x	
	4 r/w = x	
	3 r/w = 0	Unused or unknown function
	2 r/w = x	Multisector transfers, hard disk 0 0 = disabled 1 = 2 sectors 2 = 4 sectors 3 = 8 sectors 4 = 16 sectors
	1 r/w = x	
	0 r/w = x	

MCA Systems

This holds the Programmable Option Select configuration byte 5 to be sent to adapter card slot 1 byte POST. It is duplicated in extended MCA CMOS register 29h.

Register	Description	Type
29h	Vendor Specific	CMOS

This is a vendor-specific CMOS location, and may be unused on some systems.

AMI BIOS, dated 11-11-92

This byte holds the disk information flags for hard disk 1. It is only used when type 47 is specified (user defined) for hard disk 1.

bit	7 r/w = 1	No retries
	6 r/w = 1	No retries
	5 r/w = 1	Bad map is at last cylinder plus 1
	4 r/w = 0	Unused
	3 r/w = 1	If number of heads is greater than 8
	2 r/w = 0	Unused
	1 r/w = 0	Unused
	0 r/w = 0	Unused

Phoenix BIOS, dated 9-28-95

bit	7 r/w = 0	Unused or unknown function
	6 r/w = x	Multisector transfers, hard disk 3
	5 r/w = x	0 = disabled
	4 r/w = x	1 = 2 sectors
		2 = 4 sectors
		3 = 8 sectors
		4 = 16 sectors
	3 r/w = 0	Unused or unknown function
	2 r/w = x	Multisector transfers, hard disk 2
	1 r/w = x	0 = disabled
	0 r/w = x	1 = 2 sectors
		2 = 4 sectors
		3 = 8 sectors
		4 = 16 sectors

MCA Systems

This holds the Programmable Option Select configuration byte 2 to be sent to adapter card slot 2 byte POST. It is duplicated in extended MCA CMOS register 49h.

Register	Description	Type
2Ah	Vendor Specific	CMOS

This is a vendor-specific CMOS location, and may be unused on some systems.

AMI BIOS, dated 11-11-92

This byte holds the low portion of the cylinder number for the landing zone word for hard disk 1. It is only used when type 47 is specified (user defined) for hard disk 1.

MCA Systems

This holds the Programmable Option Select configuration byte 3 to be sent to adapter card slot 2 byte POST. It is duplicated in extended MCA CMOS register 4Ah.

Register	Description	Type
2Bh	Vendor Specific	CMOS

This is a vendor-specific CMOS location, and may be unused on some systems.

AMI BIOS, dated 11-11-92

This byte holds the high portion of the cylinder number for the landing zone word for hard disk 1. It is only used when type 47 is specified (user defined) for hard disk 1.

Phoenix BIOS, dated 1-11-96

This byte holds the low portion of the cylinder number for the write precompensation word for hard disk 0. It is only used when type 47 is specified (user defined) for hard disk 0.

MCA Systems

This holds the Programmable Option Select configuration byte 4 to be sent to adapter card slot 2 byte POST. It is duplicated in extended MCA CMOS register 4Bh.

Register	Description	Type
2Ch	Vendor Specific	CMOS

This is a vendor-specific CMOS location, and may be unused on some systems.

AMI BIOS, dated 11-11-92

This byte holds the number of sectors per track hard disk 1. It is only used when type 47 is specified (user defined) for hard disk 1.

Phoenix BIOS, dated 1-11-96

This byte holds the high portion of the cylinder number for the write precompensation word for hard disk 0. It is only used when type 47 is specified (user defined) for hard disk 0.

MCA Systems

This holds the Programmable Option Select configuration byte 5 to be sent to adapter card slot 2 byte POST. It is duplicated in extended MCA CMOS register 4Ch.

Register	Description	Type
2Dh	Vendor Specific	CMOS

This is a vendor-specific CMOS location, and may be unused on some systems.

AMI BIOS, dated 11-11-92

This byte holds various system flags as follows:

bit	7 r/w = 1		Weitek math coprocessor present
	6 r/w = 0		Normal diskette seek at bootup
		1	Skip diskette seek at bootup for faster boot
	5 r/w = 0		System boot sequence, first drive C:, then drive A:
		1	System boot sequence, first drive A:, then drive C:
	4 r/w = 0		Slow system clock at bootup
		1	Fast system clock at bootup (normal)
	3 r/w = 1		External cache memory enabled
	2 r/w = 1		Internal cache memory enabled (486 or later CPUs)
	1 r/w = 0		Normal A20 gate through keyboard controller
		1	Fast A20 gate switch allowed bypassing slow keyboard A20 control (only when motherboard supports fast A20 control)
	0 r/w = 0		Disable system turbo switch
		1	Allow system turbo switch to function

MCA Systems

This holds the Programmable Option Select configuration byte 2 to be sent to adapter card slot 3 byte POST. It is duplicated in extended MCA CMOS register 6Ch.

Register	Description	Type
2Eh	Checksum—High	CMOS

Non-MCA Systems

This register is used with register 2Fh to create a word indicating the sum of CMOS registers 10h through 2Dh.

MCA Systems

This holds the Programmable Option Select configuration byte 3 to be sent to adapter card slot 3 byte POST. It is duplicated in extended MCA CMOS register 6Dh.

Register	Description	Type
2Fh	Checksum—Low	CMOS

Non-MCA Systems

This register is used with address 2Eh to create a word indicating the sum of CMOS registers 10h through 2Dh.

MCA Systems

This holds the Programmable Option Select configuration byte 4 to be sent to adapter card slot 3 byte POST. It is duplicated in extended MCA CMOS register 6Eh.

Register	Description	Type
30h	Extended Memory Detected—Low	CMOS

Non-MCA Systems

Used with register 31h to create a word indicates the size of extended memory in 1,024-byte multiples. It is calculated every time the POST is run. For example, 3C00h indicates 15 MB of extended memory. Many older BIOSes can only handle 15 MB as a maximum. Most newer BIOSes can accept up to 63 MB of extended memory. Interrupt 15h, function 88h can be used to get this word from CMOS.

MCA Systems

This holds the Programmable Option Select configuration byte 5 to be sent to adapter card slot 3 byte POST. It is duplicated in extended MCA CMOS register 6Fh.

Register	Description	Type
31h	Extended Memory Detected—High	CMOS

Non-MCA Systems

Used with register 30h to create a word indicates the size of extended memory in 1,024-byte multiples. See CMOS address 30h for more information.

MCA Systems

This holds the Programmable Option Select byte 2 for the motherboard.

Register	Description	Type
32h	Century/Checksum	CMOS

Non-MCA Systems

This byte contains the BCD value for the date century. For example, the year 1995 will have the value 19h.

MCA and PS/1 Systems

This byte contains the high byte of the CRC word. This CRC covers the bytes 10h to 31h of the CMOS RAM.

Register	Description	Type
33h	Vendor Specific	CMOS

This is a vendor-specific CMOS location, and may be unused on some systems.

IBM AT (Original)

The original IBM AT defines these bytes as follows (very obsolete today).

bit	7 r/w = 0	512K base memory system
	1	640K base memory system
	6 r/w = 1	Display a user message in SETUP program
	5 r/w = 0	Unused
	4 r/w = 0	Unused
	3 r/w = 0	Unused
	2 r/w = 0	Unused
	1 r/w = 0	Unused
	0 r/w = 0	Unused

AMI BIOS, dated 12-12-91

bit	7 r/w = 1	640K system (as opposed to a 512K system)
	6 r/w = 0	Unused or unknown function
	5 r/w = x	Slow RAM refresh option
	4 r/w = x	bit 5 bit 4
		0 0 = 15 S
		0 1 = 30 S
		1 0 = 60 S
		1 1 = 120 S
	3 r/w = 1	System cachable enabled

	2 r/w = 1	Video cachable enabled
	1 r/w = 0	Unused or unknown function
	0 r/w = 0	Unused or unknown function

AMI BIOS, dated 6-6-92

bit	7 r/w = 1	640K system (as opposed to a 512K system)
	6 r/w = 0	Unused or unknown function
	5 r/w = 0	DRAM write CAS pulse = 1T (20/25 MHz)
	1	DRAM write CAS pulse = 2T (33-50 MHz)
	4 r/w = 0	Unused or unknown function
	3 r/w = 1	Automatic configuration enabled—from setup menu, allows the option of loading all of the BIOS defaults into CMOS, or loading maintenance values into CMOS. Maintenance values are the most stable values that can be set, but often create the poorest system performance.
	2 r/w = 0	Unused or unknown function
	1 r/w = 0	Unused or unknown function
	0 r/w = 0	Unused or unknown function

AMI BIOS, dated 11-11-92

This register is set at value 0FBh, and does not change with setup options.

MCA Systems

This byte contains the low byte of the CRC word. This CRC covers the bytes 10h to 31h of the CMOS RAM.

Register	Description	Type
34h	Vendor Specific	CMOS

This is a vendor-specific CMOS location, and may be unused on some systems.

AMI BIOS, dated 6-6-92

bit	7 r/w = 1	Boot sector virus protection enabled (this bit is also used for password control on some systems)
	6 r/w = 1	Password required at bootup (when supported)
	5 r/w = 1	Shadow adapter ROM at C800 for 32K bytes
	4 r/w = 1	Slow CPU, under 25 MHz (unused in some versions)
	3 r/w = 1	Shadow adapter ROM at D000 for 32K bytes
	2 r/w = 0	Unused or unknown function
	1 r/w = 1	Shadow adapter ROM at D800 for 32K bytes
	0 r/w = 1	BIOS cachable option enabled (unused in some versions)

AMI BIOS, dated 11-11-92

This register is set at value 0, and does not change with setup options.

MCA and PS/1 Systems

bit	7 r/w = x	Number of serial ports detected by POST (0 to 8)
	6 r/w = x	
	5 r/w = x	
	4 r/w = x	
	3 r/w = x	Status of BIOS interrupt 15h, function 87h, access extended memory, before system is reset to get back to real mode
	2 r/w = x	
	1 r/w = x	
	0 r/w = x	

Register	Description	Type
35h	Vendor Specific	CMOS

This is a vendor-specific CMOS location, and may be unused on some systems.

AMI BIOS, dated 12-12-91

bit	7 r/w = 1	Shadow adapter ROM at E000 for 32K bytes
	6 r/w = 0	Unused or unknown function
	5 r/w = 1	Shadow adapter ROM at E800 for 32K bytes
	4 r/w = 0	Unused or unknown function
	3 r/w = 1	Automatic configuration function enabled
	2 r/w = 1	Shadow video ROM area at C000h for 32K bytes
	1 r/w = 0	Unused or unknown function
	0 r/w = 0	Unused or unknown function

AMI BIOS, dated 6-6-92

bit	7 r/w = 1	Shadow adapter ROM at E000 for 32K bytes
	6 r/w = 0	DRAM write cycle, 0 wait state (20/25 MHz)
	1	DRAM write cycle, 1 wait state (33-50 MHz)
	5 r/w = 1	Shadow adapter ROM at E800 for 32K bytes
	4 r/w = 0	Unused or unknown function
	3 r/w = 1	Video cachable option enabled
	2 r/w = 1	Shadow video ROM area at C000h for 32K bytes
	1 r/w = 0	Unused or unknown function
	0 r/w = 0	Unused or unknown function

AMI BIOS, dated 11-11-92

This register is set at value 0Fh, and does not change with setup options.

Register	Description	Type
36h	Vendor Specific	CMOS

This is a vendor-specific CMOS location, and may be unused on some systems.

AMI BIOS, dated 12-12-91

bit	7 r/w = 0	Unused or unknown function
	6 r/w = 0	Unused or unknown function
	5 r/w = x	ISA bus speed
	4 r/w = x	bit 5 bit 4 bit 3
	3 r/w = x	0 0 0 = 7.15 MHz
		0 0 1 = CLK/2 (2 MHz)
		0 1 0 = CLK/3 (3 MHz)
		0 1 1 = CLK/4 (4 MHz)
		1 0 0 = CLK/5 (5 MHz)
		1 0 1 = CLK/6 (6 MHz)
		1 1 0 = CLK/8 (8 MHz)
		1 1 1 = CLK/10 (10 MHz)
	2 r/w = x	16-bit ISA command wait states
	1 r/w = x	bit 2 bit 1
		0 0 = 1 wait state
		0 1 = 2 wait states
		1 0 = 3 wait states
		1 1 = 4 wait states
	0 r/w = 0	Unused or unknown function

AMI BIOS, dated 6-6-92

bit	7 r/w = x	DRAM speed option
	6 r/w = x	bit 7 bit 6
		0 0 = Slowest (50 MHz)
		0 1 = Slower (40 MHz)
		1 0 = Faster (33 MHz)
		1 1 = Fastest (25 MHz)
	5 r/w = 0	Unused or unknown function
	4 r/w = 0	Cache read cycle, 1T (20-25 MHz or 33 MHz with 64/256 KB cache)

1	Cache read cycle, 2T (40-50 MHz or 33 MHz with 128 KB cache)			
3 r/w = 0	Cache write cycle, 3T (33-50 MHz)			
1	Cache write cycle, 2T (20-25 MHz)			
2 r/w = x	ISA bus speed			
1 r/w = x		bit 2	bit 1	bit 0
0 r/w = x		0	0	0 = 7.15 MHz
		0	1	0 = CLK/4
		0	1	1 = CLK/6
		1	0	0 = CLK/5

AMI BIOS, dated 11-11-92

This register is set at value 0, and does not change with setup options.

EISA Systems

On some EISA systems, locations 36h through 3Fh are used for password control and are made inaccessible by the BIOS once the POST completes. See port 92h in Chapter 13, System Functions.

MCA Systems

This byte contains the high byte of the amount of extended memory detected by POST. The combined low and high bytes are multiplied by 1,024 to get the total bytes of extended memory.

Register	Description	Type
37h	Date Century	CMOS

This is a vendor-specific CMOS location, and may be unused on some systems.

EISA Systems

On some EISA systems, this register is used for the password. See register 36h.

MCA Systems

This byte contains the BCD value for the date century. For example, the year 1997 will have the value 1Bh.

Register	Description	Type
38h	Vendor Specific	CMOS

This is a vendor-specific CMOS location, and may be unused on some systems.

EISA Systems

On some EISA systems, this register is used for the password. See register 36h.

MCA Systems

Each POST code is stored here during power-up operations. Refer to the POST codes for PS/2 MCA systems under the system chapter, port 680h.

Register	Description	Type
39h	Vendor Specific	CMOS

This is a vendor-specific CMOS location, and may be unused on some systems.

EISA Systems

On some EISA systems, this register is used for the password. See register 36h.

MCA Systems

On some MCA systems, the password is stored in this register.

Register	Description	Type
3Ah	Vendor Specific	CMOS

This is a vendor-specific CMOS location, and may be unused on some systems.

EISA Systems

On some EISA systems, this register is used for the password. See register 36h.

MCA Systems

On some MCA systems, the password is stored in this register.

Register	Description	Type
3Bh	Vendor Specific	CMOS

This is a vendor-specific CMOS location, and may be unused on some systems.

EISA Systems

On some EISA systems, this register is used for the password. See register 36h.

MCA Systems

On some MCA systems, the password is stored in this register.

Register	Description	Type
3Ch	Vendor Specific	CMOS

This is a vendor-specific CMOS location, and may be unused on some systems.

Award BIOS, dated 9-14-87

bit	7 r/w = 0	Unused or unknown function			
	6 r/w = 0	Unused or unknown function			
	5 r/w = x	System speed selection			
	4 r/w = x		bit 5	bit 4	bit 3
	3 r/w = x		0	0	0 = no change
			0	0	1 = low speed
			1	1	1 = high speed
	2 r/w = x	Action when error detected during POST			
	1 r/w = x		bit 2	bit 1	bit 0
	0 r/w = x		0	0	1 = halt on all errors
			0	1	0 = do not halt on any error
			0	1	1 = halt for all except keyboard error
			1	0	1 = halt for all except disk error
			1	1	1 = halt for all except a disk or keyboard error

EISA Systems

On some EISA systems, this register is used for the password. See register 36h.

MCA Systems

On some MCA systems, the password is stored in this register.

Register	Description	Type
3Dh	Vendor Specific	CMOS

This is a vendor-specific CMOS location, and may be unused on some systems.

EISA Systems

On some EISA systems, this register is used for the password. See register 36h.

MCA Systems

On some MCA systems, the password is stored in this register.

Register	Description	Type
3Eh	Vendor Specific	CMOS

This is a vendor-specific CMOS location, and may be unused on some systems.

Award BIOS, dated 9-14-87

This location is used for a single byte checksum of key reserved bytes.

AMI BIOS (most)

This register holds the upper byte of a word checksum of registers 34h to 3Dh. Registers 34h to 3Dh are added together to get this word checksum value. On AMI BIOSes that use extended registers 40h to 7Fh, some portion of the extended registers are checksumed, and the upper byte of the word checksum is stored here.

EISA Systems

On some EISA systems, this register is used for the password. See register 36h.

MCA Systems

On some MCA systems, the password is stored in this register.

Register	Description	Type
3Fh	Vendor Specific	CMOS

This is a vendor-specific CMOS location, and may be unused on some systems.

AMI BIOS (most)

This register holds the lower byte of a word checksum of registers 34h to 3Dh. Registers 34h to 3Dh are added together to get this word checksum value. On AMI BIOSes that use extended registers 40h to 7Fh, some portion of the extended registers are checksumed, and the upper byte of the word checksum may be stored here.

EISA Systems

On some EISA systems, this register is used for the password. See register 36h.

MCA Systems

This byte contains the checksum of CMOS bytes 38h to 3Eh. Should these seven CMOS byte values add up to zero, the checksum is ignored.

Registers	Description	Type
40h	Vendor Specific	Extended CMOS

When this register exists, it is a vendor-specific CMOS location, and may be unused.

Phoenix BIOS, dated 9-28-95

This byte holds the low portion of the cylinders word for hard disk 0. It is only used when type 47 is specified (user defined) for hard disk 0.

Phoenix BIOS, dated 1-11-96

bit	7 r/w = x	Transfer mode, hard disk 1	
	6 r/w = x	bit 7	bit 6
		0	0 = standard

	0	1 = PIO 1	
	1	0 = PIO 2	
	1	1 = PIO 3	
5 r/w = 0	Unused or unknown function		
4 r/w = x	Transfer mode, hard disk 0		
3 r/w = x	bit 4	bit 3	
	0	0 = standard	
	0	1 = PIO 1	
	1	0 = PIO 2	
	1	1 = PIO 3	
2 r/w = 0	Unused or unknown function		
1 r/w = 0	Unused or unknown function		
0 r/w = 0	Unused or unknown function		

Registers	Description	Type
41h	Vendor Specific	Extended CMOS

When this register exists, it is a vendor-specific CMOS location, and may be unused.

Phoenix BIOS, dated 9-28-95

This byte holds the high portion of the cylinders word for hard disk 0. It is only used when type 47 is specified (user defined) for hard disk 0.

Phoenix BIOS, dated 1-11-96

bit 7 r/w = 0	Unused or unknown function		
6 r/w = 0	Unused or unknown function		
5 r/w = 0	Unused or unknown function		
4 r/w = 1	Unused or unknown function		
3 r/w = 0	Unused or unknown function		
2 r/w = 0	Unused or unknown function		
1 r/w = x	Keyboard repeat rate (also see register 42h)		
0 r/w = x	bit 1	bit 0	bit 7 (register 42h)
	0	0	0 = 30 cps
	0	0	1 = 26.7 cps
	0	1	0 = 21.8 cps
	0	1	1 = 18.5 cps
	1	0	0 = 13.3 cps
	1	0	1 = 10 cps
	1	1	0 = 6 cps
	1	1	1 = 2 cps

Registers	Description	Type
42h	Vendor Specific	Extended CMOS

When this register exists, it is a vendor-specific CMOS location, and may be unused.

Phoenix BIOS, dated 9-28-95

This byte holds the low portion of the cylinders word for hard disk 1. It is only used when type 47 is specified (user defined) for hard disk 1.

Phoenix BIOS, dated 1-11-96

bit	7 r/w = x	Keyboard repeat rate (see register 41h)
	6 r/w = 0	Unused or unknown function
	5 r/w = 0	Unused or unknown function
	4 r/w = 0	Unused or unknown function
	3 r/w = 0	Unused or unknown function
	2 r/w = 0	Unused or unknown function
	1 r/w = 0	Unused or unknown function
	0 r/w = 0	Unused or unknown function

Registers	Description	Type
43h	Vendor Specific	Extended CMOS

When this register exists, it is a vendor-specific CMOS location, and may be unused.

Phoenix BIOS, dated 9-28-95

This byte holds the high portion of the cylinders word for hard disk 1. It is only used when type 47 is specified (user defined) for hard disk 1.

Registers	Description	Type
44h	Vendor Specific	Extended CMOS

When this register exists, it is a vendor-specific CMOS location, and may be unused.

Phoenix BIOS, dated 9-28-95

This byte holds the low portion of the cylinder number for the write precompensation word on hard disk 1. It is only used when type 47 is specified (user defined) for hard disk 1. Along with register 45h, a value of 0FFFh indicates no write precompensation.

Registers	Description	Type
45h	Vendor Specific	Extended CMOS

When this register exists, it is a vendor-specific CMOS location, and may be unused.

Phoenix BIOS, dated 9-28-95

This byte holds the high portion of the cylinder number for the write precompensation word on hard disk 1. It is only used when type 47 is specified (user defined) for hard disk 1. Along with register 45h, a value of 0FFFh indicates no write precompensation.

Registers	Description	Type
46h	Vendor Specific	Extended CMOS

When this register exists, it is a vendor-specific CMOS location, and may be unused.

Phoenix BIOS, dated 9-28-95

This byte holds the low portion of the cylinders word for hard disk 2.

Registers	Description	Type
47h	Vendor Specific	Extended CMOS

When this register exists, it is a vendor-specific CMOS location, and may be unused.

Phoenix BIOS, dated 9-28-95

This byte holds the high portion of the cylinders word for hard disk 2.

Phoenix BIOS, dated 1-11-96

bit	7 r/w = 0	Unused or unknown function
	6 r/w = 0	UART 2, infrared mode
	1	UART 2, standard mode
	5 r/w = 0	Unused or unknown function
	4 r/w = 1	Unused or unknown function
	3 r/w = 0	Unused or unknown function
	2 r/w = 0	Unused or unknown function
	1 r/w = 0	Unused or unknown function
	0 r/w = 0	Unused or unknown function

Registers	Description	Type
48h	Vendor Specific	Extended CMOS

When this register exists, it is a vendor-specific CMOS location, and may be unused.

Phoenix BIOS, dated 1-11-96

bit	7 r/w = x	Keyboard repeat delay	
	6 r/w = x	bit 7	bit 6
		0	0 = 250 ms delay

	0	1 = 500 ms delay
	1	0 = 750 ms delay
	1	1 = 1 second delay
5 r/w = x	Boot up sequence	
4 r/w = x	bit 5	bit 4
	0	0 = boot A: if present, otherwise boot C:
	0	1 = boot from C: only
	1	0 = boot C: if valid, otherwise boot A:
3 r/w = x	LPT port mode	
2 r/w = x	bit 3	bit 2
	0	0 = output only
	0	1 = bi-directional
	1	1 = ECP
1 r/w = x	Motherboard IDE controller	
0 r/w = x	bit 1	bit 0
	0	0 = disabled
	0	1 = set as the primary controller
	1	0 = set as the secondary controller

Registers	Description	Type
51h	Vendor Specific	Extended CMOS

When this register exists, it is a vendor-specific CMOS location, and may be unused.

Phoenix BIOS, dated 1-11-96

bit	7 r/w = 0	Other large disk mode
	1	DOS large disk mode
	6 r/w = 0	Unused or unknown function
	5 r/w = 0	Unused or unknown function
	4 r/w = 0	Unused or unknown function
	3 r/w = 0	Unused or unknown function
	2 r/w = 0	Unused or unknown function
	1 r/w = 0	Unused or unknown function
	0 r/w = 0	Unused or unknown function

Registers	Description	Type
52h	Vendor Specific	Extended CMOS

When this register exists, it is a vendor-specific CMOS location, and may be unused.

Phoenix BIOS, dated 1-11-96

bit	7 r/w = 1	BIOS summary display enabled
	6 r/w = 1	Floppy seek at boot check enabled
	5 r/w = 1	Stop if POST errors enabled
	4 r/w = 1	Display prompt at boot for entering setup
	3 r/w = 0	Unused or unknown function
	2 r/w = 0	Unused or unknown function
	1 r/w = 1	Plug & Play feature enabled
	0 r/w = 1	Diskette controller enabled

Registers	Description	Type
53h	Vendor Specific	Extended CMOS

When this register exists, it is a vendor-specific CMOS location, and may be unused.

Phoenix BIOS, dated 1-11-96

bit	7 r/w = 0	Unused or unknown function
	6 r/w = 0	Unused or unknown function
	5 r/w = 1	LBA mode enabled for hard disk 1
	4 r/w = 1	LBA mode enabled for hard disk 0
	3 r/w = 0	Unused or unknown function
	2 r/w = 0	Unused or unknown function
	1 r/w = 1	32-bit access enabled for hard disk 1
	0 r/w = 1	32-bit access enabled for hard disk 0

Registers	Description	Type
54h	Vendor Specific	Extended CMOS

When this register exists, it is a vendor-specific CMOS location, and may be unused.

Phoenix BIOS, dated 1-11-96

bit	7 r/w = 1	Write protect MBR on hard disk 0
	6 r/w = 0	Unused or unknown function
	5 r/w = 0	Hard disk 1 parameters set by user
	1	Hard disk 1 parameters set automatically
	4 r/w = 0	Num lock set off
	1	Num lock set on
	3 r/w = 0	Unused or unknown function
	2 r/w = 0	Unused or unknown function

1 r/w = 0	Unused or unknown function
0 r/w = 0	Hard disk 0 parameters set by user
1	Hard disk 0 parameters set automatically

Registers	Description	Type
58h	Vendor Specific	Extended CMOS

When this register exists, it is a vendor-specific CMOS location, and may be unused.

Phoenix BIOS, dated 9-28-95

bit	7 r/w = x	Transfer mode, hard disk 0
	6 r/w = x	bit 7 bit 6
		0 0 = standard
		0 1 = PIO 1
		1 0 = PIO 2
		1 1 = PIO 3
	5 r/w = 0	Unused or unknown function
	4 r/w = 0	Unused or unknown function
	3 r/w = 0	Unused or unknown function
	2 r/w = 0	Unused or unknown function
	1 r/w = 0	Unused or unknown function
	0 r/w = 0	Unused or unknown function

Registers	Description	Type
59h	Vendor Specific	Extended CMOS

When this register exists, it is a vendor-specific CMOS location, and may be unused.

Phoenix BIOS, dated 9-28-95

bit	7 r/w = x	Transfer mode, hard disk 3 (see register 62h for states)
	6 r/w = 0	Unused or unknown function
	5 r/w = x	Transfer mode, hard disk 2
	4 r/w = x	bit 5 bit 4
		0 0 = standard
		0 1 = PIO 1
		1 0 = PIO 2
		1 1 = PIO 3
	3 r/w = 0	Unused or unknown function
	2 r/w = 0	Unused or unknown function
	1 r/w = 0	Unused or unknown function
	0 r/w = 0	Unused or unknown function

Registers	Description	Type
5Ah	Vendor Specific	Extended CMOS

When this register exists, it is a vendor-specific CMOS location, and may be unused.

Phoenix BIOS, dated 9-28-95

bit	7 r/w = 0	Unused or unknown function
	6 r/w = 0	Unused or unknown function
	5 r/w = 0	Unused or unknown function
	4 r/w = 0	Unused or unknown function
	3 r/w = 0	Unused or unknown function
	2 r/w = 0	Unused or unknown function
	1 r/w = 0	Unused or unknown function
	0 r/w = 1	32-bit access enabled for hard disk 3

Registers	Description	Type
5Dh	Vendor Specific	Extended CMOS

When this register exists, it is a vendor-specific CMOS location, and may be unused.

Phoenix BIOS, dated 9-28-95

bit	7 r/w = x	Num lock state	
	6 r/w = x	bit 7	bit 6
		0	0 = automatic
		0	1 = on
		1	0 = off
	5 r/w = 0	Unused or unknown function	
	4 r/w = 0	Bootup sequence—boot A: if present, otherwise boot C:	
	1	Bootup sequence—boot C: if valid, otherwise boot A:	
	3 r/w = 0	Unused or unknown function	
	2 r/w = 0	Unused or unknown function	
	1 r/w = 0	Unused or unknown function	
	0 r/w = 0	Unused or unknown function	

Registers	Description	Type
5Eh	Vendor Specific	Extended CMOS

When this register exists, it is a vendor-specific CMOS location, and may be unused.

Phoenix BIOS, dated 9-28-95

bit	7 r/w = 1	Shadow memory at D800h for 16 KB
	6 r/w = 1	Shadow memory at D400h for 16 KB
	5 r/w = 1	Shadow memory at D000h for 16 KB
	4 r/w = 1	Shadow memory at CC00h for 16 KB
	3 r/w = 1	Shadow memory at C800h for 16 KB
	2 r/w = 0	Unused or unknown function
	1 r/w = 0	Unused or unknown function
	0 r/w = 0	Unused or unknown function

Registers	Description	Type
5Fh	Vendor Specific	Extended CMOS

When this register exists, it is a vendor-specific CMOS location, and may be unused.

Phoenix BIOS, dated 9-28-95

bit	7 r/w = 0	Unused or unknown function
	6 r/w = 0	Unused or unknown function
	5 r/w = 0	Unused or unknown function
	4 r/w = 0	Unused or unknown function
	3 r/w = 0	Unused or unknown function
	2 r/w = 0	Unused or unknown function
	1 r/w = 0	Unused or unknown function
	0 r/w = 1	Shadow memory at DC00h for 16 KB

Registers	Description	Type
60h	Vendor Specific	Extended CMOS

When this register exists, it is a vendor-specific CMOS location, and may be unused.

Phoenix BIOS, dated 9-28-95

bit	7 r/w = 0	Unused or unknown function
	6 r/w = 0	Unused or unknown function
	5 r/w = 0	Unused or unknown function
	4 r/w = 1	Shadow memory at C000h for 32 KB
	3 r/w = 0	Unused or unknown function
	2 r/w = 1	Memory cache enabled
	1 r/w = 0	Unused or unknown function
	0 r/w = 0	Unused or unknown function

Registers	Description	Type
61h	Vendor Specific	Extended CMOS

When this register exists, it is a vendor-specific CMOS location, and may be unused.

Phoenix BIOS, dated 9-28-95

bit	7 r/w = 1	32-bit access enabled for hard disk 2
	6 r/w = 1	32-bit access enabled for hard disk 1
	5 r/w = 1	32-bit access enabled for hard disk 0
	4 r/w = 0	Unused or unknown function
	3 r/w = 0	Unused or unknown function
	2 r/w = 0	Unused or unknown function
	1 r/w = 0	Unused or unknown function
	0 r/w = 0	Unused or unknown function

Registers	Description	Type
62h	Vendor Specific	Extended CMOS

When this register exists, it is a vendor-specific CMOS location, and may be unused.

Phoenix BIOS, dated 9-28-95

bit	7 r/w = 0	Hard disk 2 parameters set by user
	1	Hard disk 2 parameters set automatically
	6 r/w = 0	Unused or unknown function
	5 r/w = 0	Unused or unknown function
	4 r/w = 1	LBA mode enabled for hard disk 3
	3 r/w = 1	LBA mode enabled for hard disk 2
	2 r/w = 1	LBA mode enabled for hard disk 1
	1 r/w = 1	LBA mode enabled for hard disk 0
	0 r/w = x	Transfer mode, hard disk 3

bit 0	bit 7 (register 59h)
0	0 = standard
0	1 = PIO 1
1	0 = PIO 2
1	1 = PIO 3

Register	Description	Type
63h	Vendor Specific	CMOS

When this register exists, it is a vendor-specific CMOS location, and may be unused.

AMI BIOS, dated 11-11-92

bit	7 r/w = 0	Unused or unknown function
	6 r/w = 0	Unused or unknown function
	5 r/w = 1	Fast system timing enabled
	4 r/w = 1	Burst ready to VL ready return enabled
	3 r/w = 0	Unused or unknown function
	2 r/w = 1	Main memory cutoff at 15 MB enabled
	1 r/w = 0	Cache set to write-back
	1	Cache set to write through
	0 r/w = 1	High performance ISA bus enabled (fast).

Phoenix BIOS, dated 1-11-96

bit	7 r/w = 0	Unused or unknown function
	6 r/w = 1	PCI slot 1—default latency timer active
	5 r/w = 0	Unused or unknown function
	4 r/w = 0	Unused or unknown function
	3 r/w = 0	Unused or unknown function
	2 r/w = 0	Unused or unknown function
	1 r/w = 0	Unused or unknown function
	0 r/w = 0	Unused or unknown function

Registers	Description	Type
64h	Vendor Specific	Extended CMOS

When this register exists, it is a vendor-specific CMOS location, and may be unused.

AMI BIOS, dated 11-11-92

bit	7 r/w = 0	Unused or unknown function
	6 r/w = 0	Unused or unknown function
	5 r/w = 0	Unused or unknown function
	4 r/w = x	ISA bus speed vs. CPU speed
	3 r/w = x	
	2 r/w = x	

bit 4	bit 3	bit 2
0	0	0 = automatic
0	1	0 = 1/6
0	1	1 = 1/5
1	0	0 = 1/4
1	0	1 = 1/3
1	1	0 = 1/2

	1 r/w = 0	Unused or unknown function
	0 r/w = 0	Unused or unknown function

Phoenix BIOS, dated 1-11-96

bit	7 r/w = 0	Unused or unknown function
	6 r/w = 0	Unused or unknown function
	5 r/w = x	PCI slot 1—latency timer
	4 r/w = x	to get timer values 0 to F8h, multiply this value by 8
	3 r/w = x	
	2 r/w = x	
	1 r/w = x	
	0 r/w = 1	PCI slot 1—master enabled

Registers	Description	Type
67h	Vendor Specific	Extended CMOS

When this register exists, it is a vendor-specific CMOS location, and may be unused.

Phoenix BIOS, dated 1-11-96

bit	7 r/w = x	Sectors per track, low portion, hard disk 0
	6 r/w = x	(high two bits are in register 68h)
	5 r/w = x	
	4 r/w = x	
	3 r/w = 0	Unused or unknown function
	2 r/w = 0	Unused or unknown function
	1 r/w = 0	Unused or unknown function
	0 r/w = 0	Unused or unknown function

Registers	Description	Type
68h	Vendor Specific	Extended CMOS

When this register exists, it is a vendor-specific CMOS location, and may be unused.

Phoenix BIOS, dated 1-11-96

bit	7 r/w = x	Sectors per track hard disk 1
	6 r/w = x	
	5 r/w = x	
	4 r/w = x	
	3 r/w = x	
	2 r/w = x	
	1 r/w = x	Sectors per track, high portion, hard disk 0
	0 r/w = x	(low four bits are in register 67h)

Registers	Description	Type
6Ah	Vendor Specific	Extended CMOS

When this register exists, it is a vendor-specific CMOS location, and may be unused.

Phoenix BIOS, dated 1-11-96

bit	7 r/w = x	Number of heads for hard disk 0, when type 47 specified (value 0 = 1 head; value F = 16 heads)
	6 r/w = x	
	5 r/w = x	
	4 r/w = x	
	3 r/w = 0	Unused or unknown function
	2 r/w = 0	Unused or unknown function
	1 r/w = 0	Unused or unknown function
	0 r/w = 0	Unused or unknown function

Registers	Description	Type
6Bh	Vendor Specific	Extended CMOS

When this register exists, it is a vendor-specific CMOS location, and may be unused.

Phoenix BIOS, dated 1-11-96

bit	7 r/w = 0	Unused or unknown function
	6 r/w = 0	Unused or unknown function
	5 r/w = 0	Unused or unknown function
	4 r/w = 0	Unused or unknown function
	3 r/w = x	Number of heads for hard disk 0, when type 47 specified (value 0 = 1 head; value F = 16 heads)
	2 r/w = x	
	1 r/w = x	
	0 r/w = x	

Registers	Description	Type
6Ch	Vendor Specific	Extended CMOS

When this register exists, it is a vendor-specific CMOS location, and may be unused.

Phoenix BIOS, dated 1-11-96

bit	7 r/w = 0	Unused or unknown function
	6 r/w = x	Multisector transfers, hard disk 0
	5 r/w = x	0 = disabled
	4 r/w = x	1 = 2 sectors

2 = 4 sectors
3 = 8 sectors
4 = 16 sectors
3 r/w = 0 Unused or unknown function
2 r/w = 0 Unused or unknown function
1 r/w = 0 Unused or unknown function
0 r/w = 0 Unused or unknown function

Registers	Description	Type
6Dh	Vendor Specific	Extended CMOS

When this register exists, it is a vendor-specific CMOS location, and may be unused.

Phoenix BIOS, dated 1-11-96

bit 7 r/w = 0 Unused or unknown function
6 r/w = 0 Unused or unknown function
5 r/w = 0 Unused or unknown function
4 r/w = 0 Unused or unknown function
3 r/w = 0 Unused or unknown function
2 r/w = x Multisector transfers, hard disk 1
1 r/w = x 0 = disabled
0 r/w = x 1 = 2 sectors
2 = 4 sectors
3 = 8 sectors
4 = 16 sectors

Registers	Description	Type
70h	Vendor Specific	Extended CMOS

When this register exists, it is a vendor-specific CMOS location, and may be unused.

AMI BIOS, dated 11-11-92

bit 7 r/w = x Memory region shadowing, segment C000h, for 32 KB
6 r/w = x bit 7 bit 6
0 0 = disable shadowing
0 1 = read-only shadowing

	1	0 = cacheable
	1	1 = memory shadowing
5 r/w = x	Memory region shadowing, segment C800h, for 32 KB	
4 r/w = x	bit 5	bit 4
	0	0 = disable shadowing
	0	1 = read-only shadowing
	1	0 = cacheable
	1	1 = memory shadowing
3 r/w = x	Memory region shadowing, segment D000h, for 32 KB	
2 r/w = x	bit 3	bit 2
	0	0 = disable shadowing
	0	1 = read-only shadowing
	1	0 = cacheable
	1	1 = memory shadowing
1 r/w = x	Memory region shadowing, segment D800h, for 32 KB	
0 r/w = x	bit 1	bit 0
	0	0 = disable shadowing
	0	1 = read-only shadowing
	1	0 = cacheable
	1	1 = memory shadowing

Registers	Description	Type
71h	Vendor Specific	Extended CMOS

When this register exists, it is a vendor-specific CMOS location, and may be unused.

AMI BIOS, dated 11-11-92

bit 7 r/w = x	Memory region shadowing, segment E000h, for 64 KB	
6 r/w = x	bit 7	bit 6
	0	0 = disable shadowing
	0	1 = read-only shadowing
	1	0 = cacheable
	1	1 = memory shadowing
5 r/w = x	Memory region shadowing, segment F000h, for 64 KB	
4 r/w = x	bit 5	bit 4
	0	0 = disable shadowing
	0	1 = read-only shadowing
	1	0 = cacheable
	1	1 = memory shadowing

3 r/w = 0	Unused or unknown function			
2 r/w = x	CPU frequency setting			
1 r/w = x		bit 2	bit 1	bit 0
0 r/w = x		0	0	0 = 25 MHz
		0	0	1 = 33 MHz
		0	1	0 = 40 MHz
		0	1	1 = 50 MHz
		1	0	1 = 66 MHz
		1	1	1 = Automatic detection

Registers	Description	Type
72h	Vendor Specific	Extended CMOS

When this register exists, it is a vendor-specific CMOS location, and may be unused.

Phoenix BIOS, dated 1-11-96

bit	7 r/w = x	COM 2 operation			
	6 r/w = x		bit 7	bit 6	bit 5
	5 r/w = x		0	0	0 = disabled
			0	1	0 = use port 2F8h and IRQ 3
			1	0	0 = use port 2E8h and IRQ 3
			1	0	1 = automatic
	4 r/w = x	COM 1 operation			
	3 r/w = x		bit 4	bit 3	bit 2
	2 r/w = x		0	0	0 = disabled
			0	0	1 = use port 3F8h and IRQ 4
			0	1	1 = use port 3E8h and IRQ 4
			1	0	1 = automatic
	1 r/w = 0	Unused or unknown function			
	0 r/w = 0	Unused or unknown function			

Registers	Description	Type
73h	Vendor Specific	Extended CMOS

When this register exists, it is a vendor-specific CMOS location, and may be unused.

Phoenix BIOS, dated 1-11-96

bit	7 r/w = 0	Unused or unknown function
	6 r/w = 0	Unused or unknown function

5 r/w = 0	Unused or unknown function			
4 r/w = 1	Unused or unknown function			
3 r/w = 0	Unused or unknown function			
2 r/w = x	LPT port mode			
1 r/w = x		bit 2	bit 1	bit 0
0 r/w = x		0	0	0 = disabled
		0	0	1 = port 378h, IRQ 7
		0	1	0 = port 278h, IRQ 7
		0	1	1 = port 3BCh, IRQ 7
		1	1	1 = automatic

Registers	Description	Type
75h	Vendor Specific	Extended CMOS

When this register exists, it is a vendor-specific CMOS location, and may be unused.

Phoenix BIOS, dated 1-11-96

This register, along with registers 76h and 77h, holds a modified checksum of most (all?) registers from 40h through 74h.

Registers	Description	Type
76h	Vendor Specific	Extended CMOS

When this register exists, it is a vendor-specific CMOS location, and may be unused.

Phoenix BIOS, dated 1-11-96

This register, along with registers 75h and 77h, holds a modified checksum of most (all?) registers from 40h through 74h.

Registers	Description	Type
77h	Vendor Specific	Extended CMOS

When this register exists, it is a vendor-specific CMOS location, and may be unused.

Phoenix BIOS, dated 1-11-96

This register, along with registers 75h and 76h, holds a modified checksum of most (all?) registers from 40h through 74h.

Registers	Description	Type
7Ah	Vendor Specific	Extended CMOS

When this register exists, it is a vendor-specific CMOS location, and may be unused.

Phoenix BIOS, dated 9-28-95

bit	7 r/w = 0	Unused or unknown function
	6 r/w = 0	Unused or unknown function
	5 r/w = 0	Unused or unknown function
	4 r/w = 1	Unused or unknown function
	3 r/w = 0	Unused or unknown function
	2 r/w = 0	Unused or unknown function
	1 r/w = 0	Hard disk 1 parameters set by user
	1	Hard disk 1 parameters set automatically
	0 r/w = 0	Hard disk 0 parameters set by user
	1	Hard disk 0 parameters set automatically

Registers	Description	Type
7Ch	Vendor Specific	Extended CMOS

When this register exists, it is a vendor-specific CMOS location, and may be unused.

Phoenix BIOS, dated 9-28-95

This register, along with register 7Dh, holds a modified checksum of most (all?) registers from 40h through 7Bh.

Registers	Description	Type
7Dh	Vendor Specific	Extended CMOS

When this register exists, it is a vendor-specific CMOS location, and may be unused.

Phoenix BIOS, dated 9-28-95

This register, along with register 7Ch, holds a modified checksum of most (all?) registers from 40h through 7Bh.

Port	Type	Description	Platform
71h	I/O	CMOS Memory Data	AT+

Port 70h selects which CMOS memory address to use. Port 71h is then used to read or write the data from the previously selected address. See Port 70h, READ_CMOS and WRITE_CMOS examples earlier in the chapter for more details.

Port	Type	Description	Platform
74h	Output	Extended CMOS Address LSB	MCA

Most MCA systems contain an additional 2K CMOS RAM memory area. To access this memory, the least significant address byte is output to port 74h. See port 76h for details.

Output (bits 0-7) Extended CMOS address LSB

Port	Type	Description	Platform
75h	Output	Extended CMOS Address MSB	MCA

Most MCA systems contain an additional 2K CMOS RAM memory area. To access this memory, the most significant address byte is output to port 75h. See port 76h for details.

Output (bits 0-7) Extended CMOS address MSB

bit	7 w = 0	Unused
	6 w = 0	Unused
	5 w = 0	Unused
	4 w = 0	Unused
	3 w = 0	Unused
	2 w = x	Upper 3 bits of CMOS extended memory address
	1 w = x	
	0 w = x	

Port	Type	Description	Platform
76h	I/O	Extended CMOS Data Register	MCA

This register is used to write and read data bytes from the 2K extended CMOS memory. To select an address, an 11-bit address must be set by writing to ports 74h and 75h.

The extended CMOS memory is used for additional configuration and system information beyond the standard CMOS memory on most MCA systems. The primary function of this extra CMOS memory is to store information from the adapter description files. To my knowledge, of all the MCA systems, only the IBM model 50 computer fails to support extended MCA CMOS memory.

Register Summary Extended MCA CMOS Memory Registers not included in the list are generally unused, but may be used in future systems. Registers with an asterisk denote registers not explained in detail, since the function is identical to an earlier described register in the list below. For example, disk 1 registers are identical to disk 0 registers, other than the disk number.

Register	Description
00h	Card slot 0, LSB adapter ID
01h	Card slot 0, MSB adapter ID
02h	Card slot 0, POS bytes used
03h	Card slot 0, POS byte 2
04h	Card slot 0, POS byte 3
05h	Card slot 0, POS byte 4

Register	Description
06h	Card slot 0, POS byte 5
23h*	Card slot 1, LSB adapter ID
24h*	Card slot 1, MSB adapter ID
25h*	Card slot 1, POS bytes used
26h*	Card slot 1, POS byte 2
27h*	Card slot 1, POS byte 3
28h*	Card slot 1, POS byte 4
29h*	Card slot 1, POS byte 5
46h*	Card slot 2, LSB adapter ID
47h*	Card slot 2, MSB adapter ID
48h*	Card slot 2, POS bytes used
49h*	Card slot 2, POS byte 2
4Ah*	Card slot 2, POS byte 3
4Bh*	Card slot 2, POS byte 4
4Ch*	Card slot 2, POS byte 5
69h*	Card slot 3, LSB adapter ID
6Ah*	Card slot 3, MSB adapter ID
6Bh*	Card slot 3, POS bytes used
6Ch*	Card slot 3, POS byte 2
6Dh*	Card slot 3, POS byte 3
6Eh*	Card slot 3, POS byte 4
6Fh*	Card slot 3, POS byte 5
8Ch*	Card slot 4, LSB adapter ID
8Dh*	Card slot 4, MSB adapter ID
8Eh*	Card slot 4, POS bytes used
8Fh*	Card slot 4, POS byte 2
90h*	Card slot 4, POS byte 3
91h*	Card slot 4, POS byte 4
92h*	Card slot 4, POS byte 5
AFh*	Card slot 5, LSB adapter ID
B0h*	Card slot 5, MSB adapter ID
B1h*	Card slot 5, POS bytes used
B2h*	Card slot 5, POS byte 2
B3h*	Card slot 5, POS byte 3
B4h*	Card slot 5, POS byte 4
B5h*	Card slot 5, POS byte 5
D2h*	Card slot 6, LSB adapter ID
D3h*	Card slot 6, MSB adapter ID
D4h*	Card slot 6, POS bytes used
D5h*	Card slot 6, POS byte 2
D6h*	Card slot 6, POS byte 3
D7h*	Card slot 6, POS byte 4

Register	Description
D8h*	Card slot 6, POS byte 5
F5h*	Card slot 7, LSB adapter ID
F6h*	Card slot 7, MSB adapter ID
F7h*	Card slot 7, POS bytes used
F8h*	Card slot 7, POS byte 2
F9h*	Card slot 7, POS byte 3
FAh*	Card slot 7, POS byte 4
FBh*	Card slot 7, POS byte 5
161h	Extended CMOS CRC high byte
162h	Extended CMOS CRC low byte
163h	Size of extended memory, LSB
164h	Size of extended memory, ISB
165h	Size of extended memory, MSB
166h	Disk 0, maximum cylinders, LSB
167h	Disk 0, maximum cylinders, MSB
168h	Disk 0, maximum heads
16Bh	Disk 0, write precomp cylinder, LSB
16Ch	Disk 0, write precomp cylinder, MSB
16Eh	Disk 0, control byte
172h	Disk 0, landing zone cylinder, LSB
173h	Disk 0, landing zone cylinder, MSB
174h	Disk 0, sectors per track
176h*	Disk 1, maximum cylinders, LSB
177h*	Disk 1, maximum cylinders, MSB
178h*	Disk 1, maximum heads
17Bh*	Disk 1, write precomp cylinder, LSB
17Ch*	Disk 1, write precomp cylinder, MSB
17Eh*	Disk 1, control byte
182h*	Disk 1, landing zone cylinder, LSB
183h*	Disk 1, landing zone cylinder, MSB
184h*	Disk 1, sectors per track
186h	POST CMOS presence test
18Eh	Total MCA slots
389h	Error log number (0 to 5)
38Ah	Error log group 0
39Eh*	Error log group 1
3B2h*	Error log group 2
3C6h*	Error log group 3
3DAh*	Error log group 4
3EEh*	Error log group 5

* *Not explained (see prior text)*

Register Detail

Register	Description	Type
00h	Card slot 0, LSB adapter ID	Extended MCA CMOS

This register holds the adapter card ID for card slot 0. The least significant byte of the ID word is stored here, with the most significant byte stored in extended register 1. The value is stored by the reference diskette provided with the adapter.

Register	Description	Type
01h	Card slot 0, MSB adapter ID	Extended MCA CMOS

See extended MCA register 0.

Register	Description	Type
02h	Card slot 0, POS bytes used	Extended MCA CMOS

This register specifies the number of Programmable Option Select (POS) bytes to be loaded by POST from extended CMOS into the adapter in card slot 0. The POS bytes are specified in the extended MCA CMOS registers following this register.

POS bytes are originally installed into CMOS by a setup program provided with the adapter. They serve the same purpose as switches on AT style cards, and may include port selections, IRQ usage, DMA channels, and other information specific to the system and adapter card.

Register	Description	Type
03h	Card slot 0, POS byte 2	Extended MCA CMOS

Programmable Option Select byte 2 for card slot 0.

Register	Description	Type
04h	Card slot 0, POS byte 3	Extended MCA CMOS

Programmable Option Select byte 3 for card slot 0.

Register	Description	Type
05h	Card slot 0, POS byte 4	Extended MCA CMOS

Programmable Option Select byte 4 for card slot 0.

Register	Description	Type
06h	Card slot 0, POS byte 5	Extended MCA CMOS

Programmable Option Select byte 5 for card slot 0.

Register	Description	Type
161h	Extended CMOS CRC high byte	Extended MCA CMOS

A word is stored in this and the next register as part of the CRC mechanism. The value is selected so the CRC of extended CMOS registers 0 to 162h becomes zero. It is calculated and written by the reference diskette.

Register	Description	Type
162h	Extended CMOS CRC low byte	Extended MCA CMOS

See register 161h.

Register	Description	Type
163h	Size of extended memory, LSB	Extended MCA CMOS

When a system has more than 63 MB of extended memory, this and the next two registers form a 24-bit value of the number of 1,024-byte groups of actual extended memory.

The original AT design only provided a word for extended memory in regular CMOS memory registers 17h and 18h. By definition, it is limited to specifying a maximum of 64 MB of extended memory. With a 24-bit value, the system provides the capability of up to 16 GB of extended memory, a limit unlikely to be reached in the next year or two. To put the size of memory in perspective, at $3 per megabyte, 16 GB of memory would cost about $50,000.

Register	Description	Type
164h	Size of extended memory, ISB	Extended MCA CMOS

Inner byte of the 24-bit extended memory size. See register 163h.

Register	Description	Type
165h	Size of extended memory, MSB	Extended MCA CMOS

Most significant byte of the 24-bit extended memory size. See register 163h.

Register	Description	Type
166h	Disk 0, maximum cylinders, LSB	Extended MCA CMOS

This register holds the low portion of the total number of cylinders for hard disk 0.

Register	Description	Type
167h	Disk 0, maximum cylinders, MSB	Extended MCA CMOS

This register holds the high portion of the total number of cylinders for hard disk 0.

Register	Description	Type
168h	Disk 0, maximum heads	Extended MCA CMOS

This register holds the total number of heads for hard disk 0.

Register	Description	Type
16Bh	Disk 0, write precomp cylinder, LSB	Extended MCA CMOS

This register holds the low portion of the cylinder number for write precompensation for hard disk 0.

Register	Description	Type
16Ch	Disk 0, write precomp cylinder, MSB	Extended MCA CMOS

This register holds the high portion of the cylinder number for write precompensation for hard disk 0.

Register	Description	Type
16Eh	Disk 0, control byte	Extended MCA CMOS

This register holds the disk information flags for hard disk 0.

bit	7 r/w = 1	No retries
	6 r/w = 1	No retries
	5 r/w = 1	Bad map is at last cylinder plus 1
	4 r/w = 0	Unused
	3 r/w = 1	If number of heads is greater than 8
	2 r/w = 0	Unused
	1 r/w = 0	Unused
	0 r/w = 0	Unused

Register	Description	Type
172h	Disk 0, landing zone cylinder, LSB	Extended MCA CMOS

This register holds the low portion of the cylinder number for the landing zone for hard disk 0.

Register	Description	Type
173h	Disk 0, landing zone cylinder, MSB	Extended MCA CMOS

This register holds the high portion of the cylinder number for the landing zone for hard disk 0.

Register	Description	Type
174h	Disk 0, sectors per track	Extended MCA CMOS

This register holds the number of sectors per track for hard disk 0.

Register	Description	Type
186h	POST CMOS presence test	Extended MCA CMOS

The post writes and reads a value at this location to confirm extended MCA CMOS is present.

Register	Description	Type
18Eh	Total MCA slots	Extended MCA CMOS

The total number of MCA adapter slots on this system.

Register	Description	Type
389h	Error log number (0 to 5)	Extended MCA CMOS

Errors detected by POST are stored in one of six log groups. This register specifies which log group was used last.

Register	Description	Type
38Ah	Error log group 0	Extended MCA CMOS

This register is the start of 20 registers used to store error information from the system BIOS.

Port	Type	Description	Platform
8xxh	I/O	Extended CMOS Registers	EISA

The ports 800h to 8FFh are used to access the current bank of 256 extended CMOS memory locations in many EISA systems. Refer to port C00h for additional details. A partial list of extended CMOS memory locations is shown for bank 0.

Bank 0 Port	Description
800h	Extended configuration bits
801h	Extended configuration bits
802h	Extended configuration bits
803h	Extended configuration bits

Bank 0 Port	**Description**
821h	Checksum of first 32 locations
87Ah	Checksum high byte, all extended CMOS except the checksum. (excludes bank 0, bytes at ports 800 to 87Fh)
87Bh	Checksum high byte, all extended CMOS except the checksum. (excludes bank 0, bytes at ports 800 to 87Fh)

Port	Type	Description	Platform
C00h	I/O	Extended CMOS Bank Select	EISA

EISA systems have an additional 8 KB of CMOS RAM for extended configuration data and slot configuration data. The exact method of access to the extended CMOS memory is not specified by the EISA specification. The individual manufacturer has been left to decide both the method and ports to use (so much for complete standards)!

Most manufacturers use port C00h for extended memory bank selection. The 8K CMOS RAM is divided into 32 banks, each containing 256 registers. Bank 0 is used for additional configuration information not in the main CMOS memory. The other banks (1 to 1Fh) are used for slot configuration information. The bank selection remains unchanged until a system reset occurs or another bank selection is made. The current bank selection can be read, but if there is doubt as to the current bank selected its faster to just reselect the desired bank.

When accessing Extended CMOS memory, the bank is selected followed by an input or output to the desired register through ports 800h to 8FFh. Interrupts must be disabled during this process. Otherwise an interrupt could occur after the bank select, but before access to the specific memory location is made. If the interrupt service routine changed the bank selection, when the current process resumes, the wrong bank of CMOS memory will be accessed. The extended CMOS memory can also be accessed by the EISA BIOS. Interrupt 15h services are used for this purpose. They are described in detail earlier in this chapter in the section on EISA system differences.

CHAPTER 16

System Timers

The system timers are used for a variety of purposes, from system timing to serving as watchdog timers. I'll show how they are used and the different modes of operation available. Unlike most other technical references, I'll show what is actually possible, since a number of limitations have been imposed by the motherboard design. This chapter will also explore the subtle and not so subtle differences between the AT, MCA, and EISA systems.

A utility is provided to demonstrate how to set up and use the timers. It provides a very accurate means to time an event, such as a subroutine, precisely on all CPUs. If you are using a Pentium or Pentium Pro, you should look at the undocumented Read Time Stamp Counter instruction, in Chapter 3, for an alternate super precise timer.

Introduction

Every PC system includes at least one 8254 Programmable Interval Timer or equivalent. This timer contains three independent 16-bit timers. Timer 0 is used as the primary system timer, and timer 1 is used for DRAM refresh on ISA systems and is not supported on MCA systems. Timer 2 is for general application use, including speaker tones. MCA and EISA systems also provide a fourth counter, timer 3, that is used as a Watchdog timer. EISA systems also have a fifth counter, timer 5 (not 4), used for optional CPU speed control. The first three timers are connected in hardware in different ways as shown in Figure 16-1.

Figure 16-1. Timing System

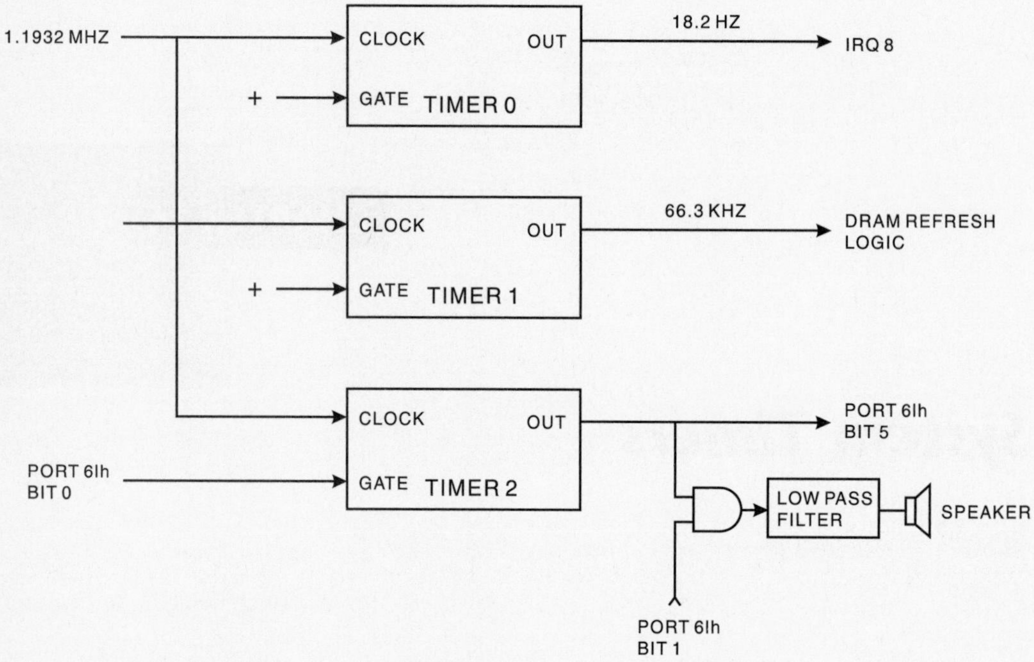

Figure 16-2 shows the internal logic of one timer channel. Each timer contains a mode and status register, along with a 16-bit counter. The counter is loaded from a separate input latch. In some modes of operation, the counter is automatically reloaded from this input latch at the end of a count. The contents of the counter can be latched into the counter output latch for reading by the CPU. Different modes of operation control the actions of the various registers, the latches, and the counter.

Modes of Operation

The 8254 timer controller has six modes of operation for each channel. Due to the way the chip is connected in hardware, some modes are not practical for a specific channel. For all the diagrams below, only the lower 8-bit counts are shown. Binary counting mode is assumed, although BCD counting is also available as a programmable option. BCD counting is rarely used, and is not shown.

Figure 16-2. Internal Timer Logic

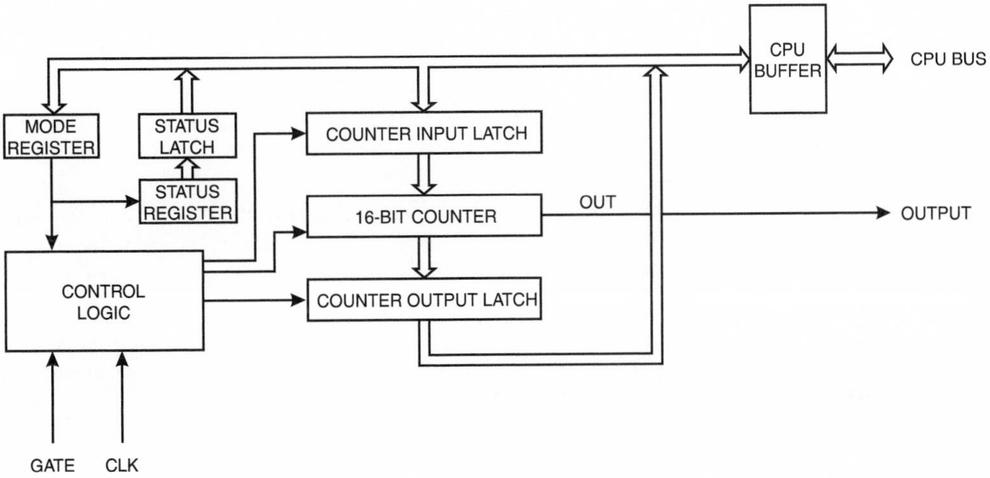

Mode 0: Single Timeout

This mode is used to trigger an event, such as an interrupt, after a preset interval. This interval can be up to 54.9 ms long, when using a starting count of 0. All timers, 0, 1, 2, 3, and 5 can use single timeout mode.

A countdown value is loaded into the timer. For the timing diagram in Figure 16-3, the loaded count value is 4. The output line is low. While the gate line is high, the timer counter decrements at 1.1932 MHz. When the timer reaches a zero count, the output line goes high. While counting, if the gate line goes low, the count stops until the gate line again returns to high.

Figure 16-3. Timing Diagram, Mode 0

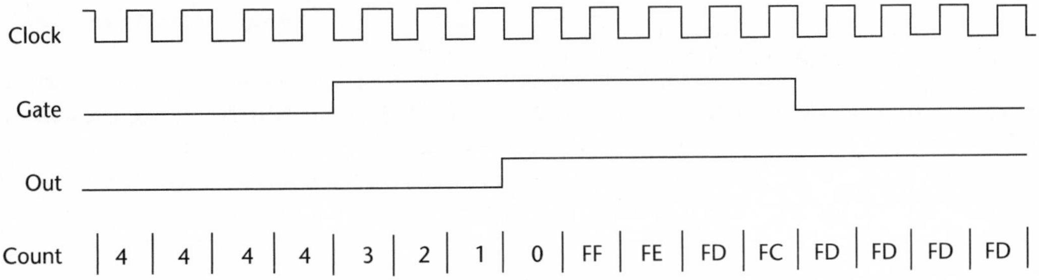

Mode 1: Retriggerable One-Shot

This mode uses the gate line to trigger an output of fixed duration. Once the output duration is complete, the timer is ready to generate another one-shot when next triggered on the gate line. The maximum duration of the output pulse is 54.9 ms long, using a starting count of 0. The counter is always decremented before checking if the counter value is zero, to stop the count. When the check finds a zero value, the count stops.

Normally only timer 2 can be used for this mode, because timer 2 is the only timer with a settable gate line. An output to port 61h, bit 0, controls the gate line on timer 2. EISA systems timers 3 and 5 typically use this mode as well.

A count value is loaded into the timer. For the timing diagram in Figure 16-4, the loaded count value is 3. The output line is initially high. The gate line is used to trigger the one-shot. When the gate line goes high, the next clock cycle starts the counter decrementing and the output line is set low. The gate line would normally be set low shortly thereafter to prepare for another one-shot once the countdown completes. When the count reaches zero, the output line returns high. The timer is automatically restored to the loaded value, and becomes ready for the next trigger to begin the process again.

Figure 16-4. Timing Diagram, Mode 1

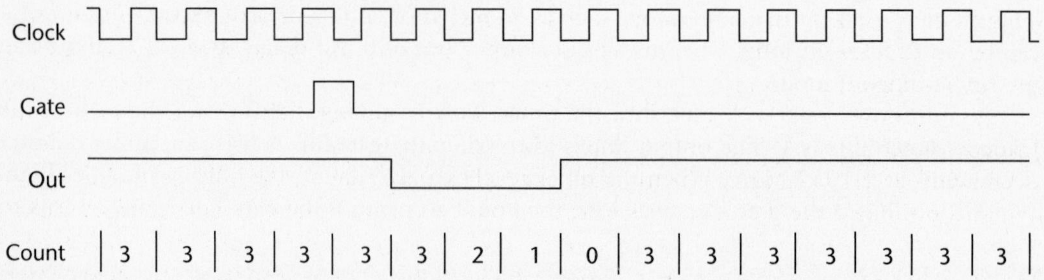

Mode 2: Rate Generator

The Rate Generator mode is used to create a short periodic output pulse. With a maximum count of 0, an output occurs every 54.9 ms. Timers 0, 1, and 2 can use rate generator mode. On EISA machines timers 3 and 5 can also use this mode.

The count value is loaded into the timer. For the timing diagram in Figure 16-5, the loaded count value is 3. The output line is initially set high. When the countdown reaches 1, the output line goes low for one count. The output line then returns high. The count value is automatically reloaded, and the countdown automatically resumes. Should the gate line go low (timer 2 only), the count is temporarily halted, until the gate line returns high. If the output is low when the gate goes low, the output is immediately set high (not shown). Do not load a count value of 1, as unpredictable results can occur.

Figure 16-5. Timing Diagram, Mode 2

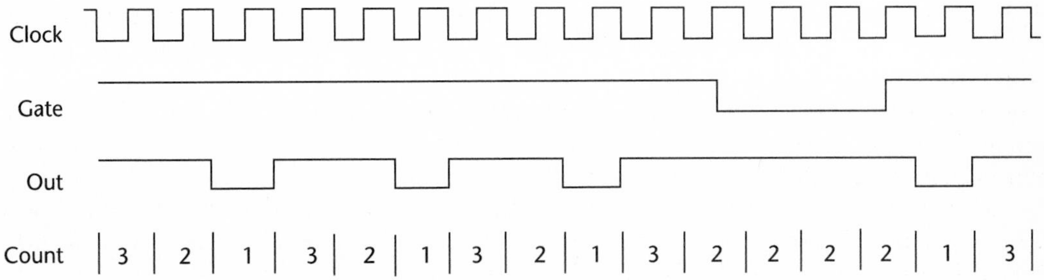

Mode 3: Square Wave Mode

The square wave mode is used to create a periodic square wave output. This mode is normally used with timer 0 to generate the system timer interrupt. With the maximum count of 0, IRQ 0 is triggered every 54.9 ms. This means that interrupt 8 is triggered at a rate of 18.2 times per second. Timers 0, 1 and 2 can use square wave mode. On EISA systems, timers 3 and 5 can also use this mode.

Operation differs slightly depending on whether the loaded count value is an even or odd value. First, we'll examine the even count value case. The even count value is loaded. For the example in Figure 16-6 this is 6. The value is then transferred into the counter. The output line is initially set high. The counter is decremented twice each clock. When the count expires, the output line is toggled from its prior state. The counter is automatically reloaded, and the process continues.

In the second case, an odd count is loaded. The output line is initially set high. On the next clock, the odd value, less one, is transferred into the counter. Like the even case, the count is decremented twice each clock. The output goes low one clock pulse after the count expires. The count is automatically reloaded with the odd value, less one. The count is decremented twice each clock. When the count expires (without a clock pulse delay) the output returns high. The process then repeats. For odd counts, the timer's output line will be high for (N+1)/2 counts. The output line will return low for (N-1)/2 counts. N is the loaded count value.

Should the gate line go low (timer 2 only), the count is temporarily halted, until the gate line returns high. If the output line is high while the gate goes low, the output line is forced to the low state (not shown). Do not load a count value of 1, as unpredictable actions will occur.

Figure 16-6. Timing Diagram, Mode 3

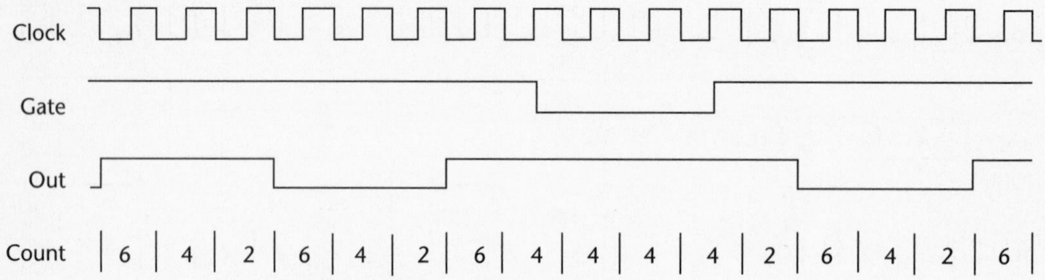

Mode 4: Software Triggered Strobe

This mode is used to pulse the output after a time delay initiated by software. This time delay can be up to 54.9 ms. Timers 0, 1, and 2 can use software triggered strobe mode. On EISA systems, timers 3 and 5 can also use this mode.

A delay value is loaded. For the example in Figure 16-7, the loaded count value is 6. The output is initially set high. The loaded value is transferred to the counter, and the counter immediately begins counting downward. When the count switches from 1 to 0, the output goes low for one cycle. No further action occurs until a new count is loaded by software. Should the gate line go low (timer 2 only), the count is temporarily halted, until the gate line returns high.

Figure 16-7. Timing Diagram, Mode 4

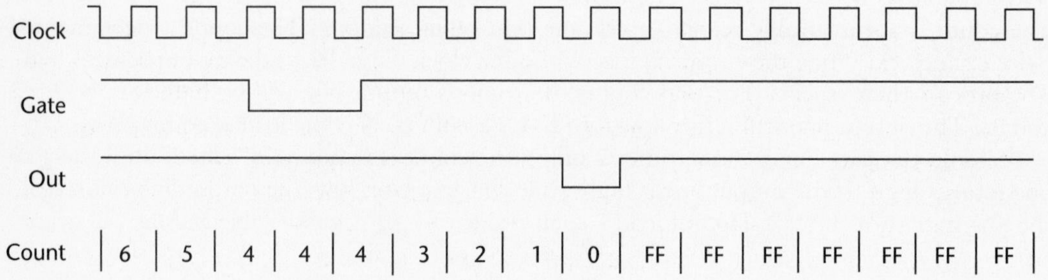

Mode 5: Hardware Retriggerable Strobe

This mode is used to pulse the output after a time delay initiated by the gate line trigger. This time delay can be up to 54.9 ms. Only timer 2 can be used for this mode, because only timer 2 has a settable gate line. An output to port 61h, bit 0, controls the gate line.

A delay value is loaded. For the example in Figure 16-8, the loaded count value is 5. The output is initially set high. The rising edge of the gate line triggers the loaded value to be transferred into the counter. Then the counter immediately begins counting downward. When the count switches from 1 to 0, the output goes low for one cycle. No further action occurs until there is another rising edge of the gate trigger.

Figure 16-8. Timing Diagram, Mode 5

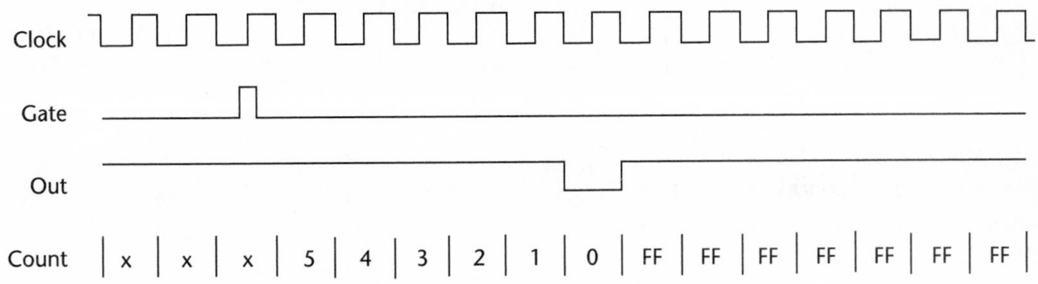

Common Operations—All Modes

The gate line operation for each mode is summarized in Table 16-1. Timers 0 and 1 have their gate lines permanently tied high. Timer 2's gate line is controlled by writing to port 61h at bit 0. Timer 3's gate line is connected to the output of timer 0 (MCA only). On EISA systems, timer 3's gate line is permanently tied high, while timer 5's gate line is connected to the refresh request output of timer 1.

Table 16-1. Gate Operation

		Action		
Mode	**Trigger**	**Low**	**Rising**	**High**
0	level sensitive	stops count		enables counting
1	rising edge		1) begin counting 2) output goes low on next clock	
2	level sensitive and rising edge	1) stops count 2) output goes immediately high	begin counting	enables counting
3	level sensitive and rising edge	1) stops count 2) output goes immediately high	begin counting	enables counting
4	level sensitive	stops count		enables counting
5	rising edge		begin counting	

The count value loaded has different limits depending on the mode of operation. Table 16-2 shows these limits. The largest initial count is 0 as shown below. On modes 2 and 3 the count is reloaded after the count expires. In all other modes, the counters continue to decrement, even after a specific action has occurred. These nonperiodic modes cause the count to wrap after a count of 0 to FFFF if binary, and 9999 if BCD operation is enabled.

Table 16-2. Initial Count Limits

			Maximum Number of Counts		
Mode	**Minimum**	**Maximum***	**16-Bit Binary**	**4-Digit BCD**	**Action after Count Expires**
0	1	0	65536	10000	wraps
1	1	0	65536	10000	wraps
2	2	0	65536	10000	reloads
3	2	0	65536	10000	reloads
4	1	0	65536	10000	wraps
5	1	0	65536	10000	wraps

** The maximum number of counts occurs at zero, because the counter is decremented before checking if the new counter value is zero.*

Timer 0—System Timing

Timer 0 is fed from a fixed frequency 1.1932 MHz clock, regardless of the CPU system speed. Timer 0 is set to mode 3 operation by POST to output a square wave signal cycling at 18.207 times a second. This square wave signal is connected to the interrupt controller through IRQ 0. Once each cycle the timer causes interrupt 8 to be triggered. This is used to maintain the system time and to perform specific timing services such as how long the diskette motor remains on. In addition, interrupt 8 calls interrupt 1Ch, the user timer tick interrupt.

Programs that wish to perform their own low resolution timing can hook interrupt 1Ch to be triggered every 54.926 ms (18.207 times per second). For higher resolution timing, timer 2 is normally used.

See warning section about how some systems use mode 2 for timer 0, instead of the IBM standard of mode 3.

Timer 1—DRAM Refresh

Like timers 0 and 2, timer 1 is fed from a fixed frequency 1.1932 MHz clock, regardless of the CPU system speed. On an AT system, timer 1 is normally set to mode 2 operation by POST to output a pulse signal once every 15.09 uS. A rate value of 12h is loaded to accomplish this. Other systems may used other modes or timing values depending on the refresh design.

The output of timer 1 is then fed into the DRAM refresh circuits on the motherboard. Programming this timer for a different periodic rate or mode can cause the DRAM refresh operations to cease to operate, such that all DRAM memory contents will be lost. For this reason, I strongly suggest avoiding the use of timer 1.

Timer 2—General Use and Speaker

Timer 2 is available for general program use. Its input is fed from a fixed frequency 1.1932 MHz clock, regardless of the CPU system speed. Timer 2's gate line is controlled by port 61h, bit 0. Timer 2's output can be read by reading a byte from port 61h and examining bit 5.

In addition, the output can be gated into the speaker to generate tones and other simple effects. When port 61h, bit 1 is set to 1, timer 2's output is gated to the speaker. When using mode 3, periodic square wave, the frequency is set by loading a 16-bit count value = 1,193,200 Hz/output frequency (Hz).

For example, to generate a 2 KHz tone, the 16-bit value loaded into the timer is 1,193,200 divided by 2,000, or 597.

Timer 3—Watchdog Timer (MCA Only)

The watchdog timer is used to detect a system problem, such as software in an endless loop, with interrupts disabled. The watchdog works by checking that the system timer 0 is being serviced regularly. Should the watchdog detect that IRQ 0 is not being serviced fast enough (i.e., lost timer ticks), the timer overflow initiates a Non-Maskable Interrupt (NMI).

This timer only operates in mode 0, and only has an 8-bit counter. It is connected as shown in Figure 16-9.

Figure 16-9. Watchdog Timer Connections

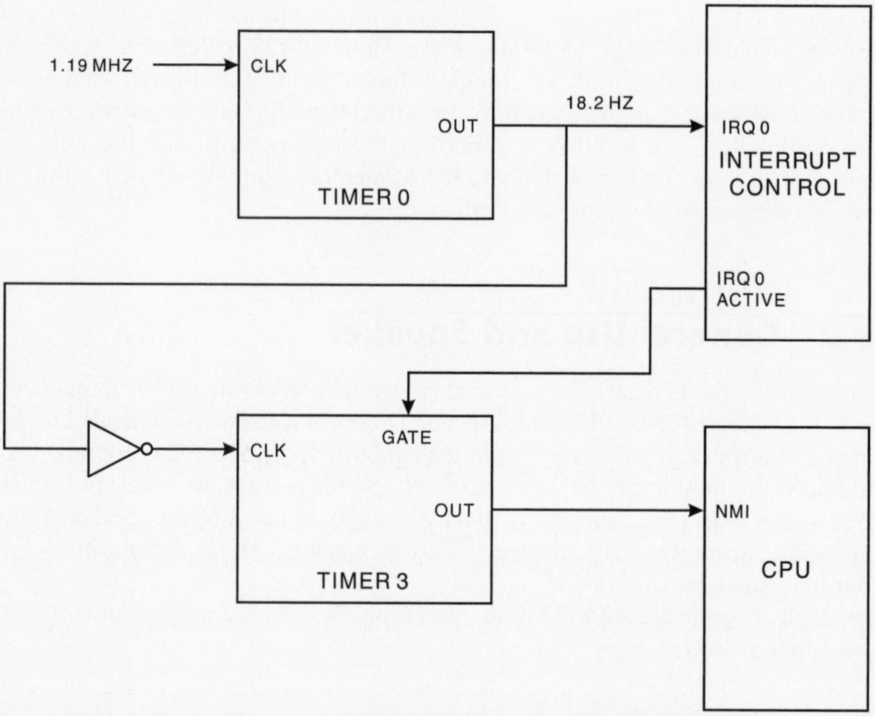

In normal operation, each trigger of IRQ 0 will initiate the interrupt 8 timer service routine. At the completion of the timer service routine, the IRQ 0 line is cleared. This same line is fed to timer 3's gate. Since no clock occurred from timer 0 while timer 3's gate was active, timer 3 remains in the same state.

Should the system become hung, IRQ 0 is not serviced, and the IRQ 0 active line remains high. The next clock from timer 0 output is allowed to clock timer 3 down. Once the preset count is exhausted, timer 3's output goes high, causing an NMI. The BIOS NMI service handler can then take appropriate action such as resetting the system.

The output of timer 3 can be examined by reading from port 92h and examining bit 4.

Timer 3—Watchdog Timer (EISA Only)

The watchdog timer is used to detect a system problem, such as software in an endless loop, with interrupts disabled. Its gate is hard-wired on, with an input clock of 298.3 KHz. Its output is fed through the NMI gate controlled by port 70h, to the CPU's NMI. When active, this timer must be periodically updated to prevent a watchdog timeout from occurring.

The watchdog timer feature is enabled by first setting this timer into mode 1 operation. An initial count is loaded and the Extended NMI control register at port 461h, bit 2 is set on. A new count should be periodically loaded to prevent a timeout. The watchdog timer decrements one count every 3.352 uS.

When a timeout does occur, if the Extended NMI control allows NMI, a NMI is sent to the CPU. If the NMI occurred due to a watchdog timeout, bit 7 of port 461h will be 1. Details of port 461h are shown in Chapter 13 (System Functions).

Though this timer is intended for use only as a Watchdog timer, it is a full 16-bit timer. The timer supports all modes and operations of a standard 8254 timer.

Timer 4—Not Implemented (EISA Only)

There is no timer 4 on EISA systems, even though they have timers 3 and 5.

Timer 5—CPU Speed Control (EISA Only)

This counter is reserved by the BIOS for CPU speed control. Timer 5 can be used by the motherboard designer for alternate purposes. It is not available for general use.

Timer 5 is a full function 16-bit timer/counter that can operate in all modes. The counter is gated from the output of the refresh timer 1. Its input clock is the BCLK line supplied to the backplane, typically 8 MHz.

Timer 5 is set for mode 1, retriggerable one-shot operation, when used for CPU speed control. Every time the system issues a refresh request, the one-shot trips and stops the CPU for the duration of the one shot. In this manner the CPU is slowed down in a ratio to the initial count value.

Typical Timer Setup and Operation

1. First the gate to timer 2 is turned off. An input from port 61h gets the current settings for all the bits of port 61h. Bit 0, the timer 2 gate value is set to 0, and the new byte is written back to port 61h (this prevents other nonrelated bits in port 61h from being changed).

2. Next, timer 2's command mode is set by outputting a command byte to port 43h. The command 0B6h indicates the counter is set for mode 3: periodic square wave, binary count mode, and read/writes to port 42h are made first with the least significant byte, followed by the most significant byte (command bytes are described in the port summary section for port 43h).

3. The starting count value is written to timer 2. For this example, the 16-bit counter value will be 1000h. The least significant byte is written first by outputting 00h to port 42h. Second, the most significant byte 10h is output to port 42h.
4. The Gate to timer 2 is enabled. An input from port 61h gets the current settings. Bit 0, the timer 2 gate value is set to 1, and the new byte is written back to port 61h.
5. The timer proceeds to generate a square wave output, at 291 Hz.
6. The output of timer 2 can be polled by reading port 61h and examining bit 5.

   As an alternative, the output of timer 2 can be gated into the motherboard speaker. The current contents of port 61h are read, and bit 1 is set to 1. The byte is then written back to port 61h, enabling the speaker.

Typical Uses

Dedicated timers 0, 1, 3, and 5 are used by the system and are not available for general program use. Timer 2 is available for programs. Some of its uses include:

- Generation of speaker tones—The timer is set for mode 3, periodic square wave output, and the speaker is gated on.
- Pollable timing—The counter is loaded with the time, and a mode such as 4 or 5 is set. The timer is started, and the output state change can be polled in software.
- Precise event timing—Mode 0, single timeout is selected. The timer is loaded with its maximum value, 0. At the start of an event, timer 2's gate is switched to high. At the end of the event, the gate line is set back low. The difference in counts between the start and end multiplied by .838 uS will yield the event duration. The maximum event duration is 54.9 ms before the counter stops.
- High interrupt rate control—In this special case, timer 0 is used. For example, if you would like to have complex sound effects, such as speech, the system timer can be made to generate interrupts at a much higher rate. At a rate of about 10 KHz, it is possible to generate reasonable speech and complex music out of the built-in speaker. This is how most games accomplish special sound effects without any special sound cards. See Code Sample 16-3 for an example of how this is accomplished.

Access

The BIOS directly controls operation of timers 0, 1, and 3 for internal systems use. There are no BIOS interrupt service routines or functions to provide direct user control of any timer. See Chapter 15, CMOS Memory and Real-Time Clock, for BIOS timing services using the real-time clock.

Warnings

The timer count value can be inaccurate if read while the counter changes value. Use the latched method to ensure accurate values. Commands 0xh, 4xh, or 8xh control the output latches for timers 0, 1, and 2, respectively (see port 43h).

A bug was introduced in many, if not all, AMI BIOSes starting in 1994 with the use of timer 0. Instead of using the IBM-defined standard mode 3, mode 2 is programmed by the AMI BIOS. While this still produces a timer tick at the same interval, every 54.926 ms, the internal counter counts down at half the rate of the rate in mode 3! Applications that access timer 0 and fail to consider this problem will have the timing run at half speed on these systems.

Unfortunately, you cannot read the mode that was set by the BIOS, so a "timing check" must be performed to detect the mode in use. For high resolution timing and sound effects, programs that read the timer 0 current count must compensate on systems that use mode 2. Code Sample 16-2 shows how this timing check is made.

Code Sample 16-1. Precise Event Timing

This small program sets up the timer for measurement of a software event. TIMEVENT can be used to profile execution of a section of code. Should the event take longer that 54 ms, the overflow is detected. TIMEVENT first reads the last event value and displays the event duration. TIMEVENT then resets the timer for the next event. The accuracy will be +/– 838 ns, which is one clock cycle of the timer.

To start event timing, the following code activates the counter:

```
in      al, 61h             ; read the current contents
or      al, 1               ; set gate bit on
out     61h, al             ; activate counter
```

To stop the event timing, the following code disables the counter:

```
in      al, 61h             ; read the current contents
and     al, 0FEh            ; set gate bit off
out     61h, al             ; disable the counter
```

The program TESTCASE has the start/stop event timing code to measure the time required for DOS to output one character to the display. The TIMEVENT program below initializes the timer and measures the duration of an event. TESTCASE and the subroutines called within TIMEVENT are not shown here, but are included with sources on the supplied diskette.

To try out TIMEVENT on your machine, run TIMEVENT, then TESTCASE, and then TIMEVENT again. These actions will appear similar to those shown in Figure 16-10.

Figure 16-10. Results of TIMEVENT

```
C:\ >  timevent
Last event duration exceeded 54,142 uS   Counter reset for next event.

C:\ >  testcase
TESTCASE - Use TIMEVENT before and after to measure the duration that
DOS takes to output the character "X" to the screen.

X

C:\ >  timevent
Last event duration = 40.134 uS          Counter reset for next event.
```

```
;----------------------------------------------------------------------
;                           TIMEVENT
;----------------------------------------------------------------------
;
;    Program displays any previous event duration, and resets
;    the timer to time the next event duration.
;
;    Build as a COM program.
;
;    (c) Copyright 1994, 1996  Frank van Gilluwe
;    All Rights Reserved.
include undocpc.inc

cseg    segment para public
        assume  cs:cseg, ds:cseg

        org     100h                    ; .COM type program
```

```
timevent proc   far

; first, check if timer has overflowed

start:
        in      al, 61h
        test    al, 20h               ; check Timer 2 output status
        jz      timeskp1              ; jump if not overflowed
        mov     dx, offset ovrflow    ; output overflow message
        jmp     timeskp2

; read Timer 2 counter contents

timeskp1:
        mov     al, 80h               ; latch output command
        out     43h, al               ; send command
        IODELAY
        in      al, 42h               ; get lsb of counter
        IODELAY
        mov     dl, al
        in      al, 42h               ; get msb of counter
        mov     dh, al                ; dx = counter value
        mov     ax, 0FFFFh            ; starting value
        sub     ax, dx                ; ax = duration count

; multiply the duration count ax by 838 to get microseconds

        mov     bx, 838
        mul     bx                    ; dx:ax = ax * bx
        call    make_decimal          ; convert dx:ax to decimal
        mov     dx, offset event      ; duration message
timeskp2:
        mov     ah, 9
        int     21h                   ; display message
```

```
; now re-set Timer 2 mode and count for the next duration

        mov     al, 0B0h            ; Timer 2 command, mode 0
        out     43h, al             ; send command
        IODELAY
        mov     al, 0FFh            ; counter value FFFF
        out     42h, al             ; send lsb to counter
        IODELAY
        out     42h, al             ; send msb to counter

        mov     ah, 4Ch
        int     21h                 ; DOS terminate
timevent endp

event           db      CR, LF
                db      'Last event duration = '
out_value       db      '           uS   '
                db      '   Counter reset for next event'
                db      CR, LF, '$'

ovrflow         db      CR, LF
                db      'Last event duration exceeded 54,142 uS'
                db      '   Counter reset for next event'
                db      CR, LF, '$'
```

Code Sample 16-2. Timer 0 Mode

Timer 0 on most systems is set by the BIOS to mode 3. Some systems will erroneously set mode 2, which will affect any timing based off of reading the current timer 0 count. The mode does not affect the system timer duration, which issues an interrupt 8 every 54 ms. See warnings for more about the mode problem. This routine finds out if timer 0 is set to mode 3 or mode 2. To run the test, type TIMERTST at a DOS prompt. Figure 16-11 shows the result of running TIMERTST on one system.

Figure 16-11. Results of TIMERTST

```
C:\ >  timertst
TIMER 0 MODE TEST                                    V1.00 (c) 1996 FVG
-----------------------------------------------------------------
Current Mode: 2
```

```
;--------------------------------------------------------------------
;                           TIMERTST
;--------------------------------------------------------------------
;    Find out if timer 0 is in normal mode 3, or if it is
;    running at half speed mode 2.  The mode does not affect
;    how often the timer issues timer ticks for interrupt 8.
;
;    (c) Copyright 1996  Frank van Gilluwe
;    All Rights Reserved.

include undocpc.inc

cseg    segment para public
        assume  cs:cseg, ds:cseg

        org     100h                ; Assemble into a COM file.

timertst proc   far

start:
        call    calibrate           ; determine timer mode 2 or 3
        jnc     output_msg          ; jump if normal timer mode 3
        dec     mode_value          ; detected timer mode 2
output_msg:
        mov     dx, offset timer_mode
        mov     ah, 9
        int     21h                 ; display message
```

```
        mov     ah, 4Ch
        int     21h                     ; DOS terminate
timertst endp



timer_mode      db      CR, LF, CR, LF
                db      'TIMER 0 MODE TEST          '
                db      '           v1.00 (c) 1996 FVG'
                db      CR, LF
                db      '---------------------------'
                db      '---------------------------'
                db      CR, LF
                db      'Current mode: '
mode_value      db      '3 '
                db      CR, LF, '$'

;-------------------------------------------------------------------
;   CALIBRATE
;   Check if timer 0 is in normal mode 3, or if in mode 2
;   which counts at half the speed of mode 3 operation.
;   Both modes issue the system interrupt at the same rate.
;
;       Called with:    nothing
;
;       Returns:        carry = 0  normal, mode 3
;                               1  mode 2 operation
;
;       Regs used:      ax, bx, cx, dx
;
;       Subs called:    none

calibrate proc  near
        push    es
        mov     cx, 20h                 ; cx:dx = max limit in case cache
        xor     dx, dx                  ;  masks timer ticks (200000h)
```

```
        mov     ax, 40h             ; use BIOS data in segment 40h
        mov     es, ax
        mov     ax, es:[6Ch]        ; get low portion of timer ticks

        ; go into tight loop looking for timer tick (54 ms) occurs

cal_nochange:
        cmp     ax, es:[6Ch]
        jne     cal_change          ; wait for change
        sub     dx, 1
        sbb     cx, 0
        jcxz    cal_done            ; skip process, cache interfers
        jmp     cal_nochange

        ; timer tick just occurred, so save current value

cal_change:
        mov     bx, es:[6Ch]        ; save new value
        mov     cx, -1              ; min value register

cal_loop:
        mov     al, 0
        out     43h, al             ; latch timer information
        IODELAY
        in      al, 40h             ; get low byte, timer 0
        mov     ah, al
        IODELAY
        in      al, 40h             ; get high byte, timer 0
        xchg    ah, al
        cmp     cx, -1              ; first time timer was read?
        jne     cal_notfirst        ; jump if not
        cmp     ax, 2
        jbe     cal_loop            ; wait until timer resets
```

```
cal_notfirst:
        cmp     ax, cx              ; see if new value less than last
        ja      cal_rolled          ; jump if timer rolled
        mov     cx, ax              ; save new minimum
        jmp     cal_loop

        ; The timer just rolled once - if mode 3, no int 8 will
        ;   have occurred yet (it takes two rolls of the timer)
        ;   If the timer was in mode 2, int 8 will occur on the
        ;   first timer roll.

cal_rolled:
        IODELAY                     ; give a little time for int 8 to
        IODELAY                     ;   be processed if timer mode 3
        mov     ax, es:[6Ch]        ; get low portion of timer ticks
        cmp     ax, bx              ; has timer ticks changed ?
        je      cal_done            ; jump if not, must be mode 3
        stc                         ; timer in mode 2!
        jmp     cal_done2
cal_done:
        clc
cal_done2:
        pop     es
        ret
calibrate endp

cseg    ends

        end     start
```

Code Sample 16-3. Fast Interrupt Handler

Some applications require a considerably faster interrupt rate than the standard system clock of 18.2 times per second. The CMOS clock can only be used to generate a periodic interrupt every 976 us, and a few other fixed periods (see CMOS register 0Ah). In addition, the PC and

XT do not include a CMOS clock, and add-in cards may not follow the AT standard. One solution speeds up the system clock interrupt.

To get control at a much higher rate, several actions are necessary. First, let's assume a rate 50 times the normal is desired, or a trigger every 1,099 uS. A program must hook the interrupt 8 service routine. Unlike a normal hook, the speed-up TSR must only pass control to the original service routine once every fifty times. This assures the original system timing is preserved. Next, timer 0 at I/O port 40h is loaded with a count of 1311. This is determined by dividing 65,536 by 50. The hooked interrupt 8 will be called every 1,099 uS, and some short action, such as sending a bit to the speaker, can be performed.

Be aware that problems often develop as the interrupt rate is pushed higher and higher. Depending on the CPU, CPU speed, the time required by the system, and your interrupt 8h handlers, the system can easily run out of time to process anything else and can even miss timer ticks. Games and other programs that speed up timer 0 will normally perform a check of the system to see how far they can push the clock rate. If the system cannot support the highest desired rate, a lower rate is selected. For products that speed up timer 0 for sound effects, the sound quality is lowered when the system can't handle the highest speed desired.

One key warning is required. Only one program can safely speed up the system clock. There is no defined means to share a sped-up system clock timer. To detect if another program has sped up the clock, it is necessary to hook both interrupt 8 and 1Ch. The code must check that, for each interrupt 8 encountered, one interrupt 1Ch also occurs. If interrupt 8h is issued more frequently than 1Ch, another program has beaten you to this trick!

The original interrupt 8h must be restored when the program terminates. You should also prevent abnormal exits, such as Control-Break, from exiting without interrupt restoration.

My example below writes two different color characters on top of each other on the screen. By alternating very quickly, the two characters overlap, appearing as a white overstrike character on top of a green text character. Although this demo is not very practical, the code demonstrates the ability to crank the interrupt rate significantly beyond the normal speed.

To use this program for other purposes, simply replace the DEMO_TWO_CHAR subroutine with your own routine. The NEWRATE specifies the multiplication factor of the standard system timer 0 rate. A NEWRATE value of 10 means your interrupt 8 routine will be called 182 times per second. The complete source code is found in the file TMRFAST.ASM. Even though TMRFAST is constructed as a TSR, it is not necessary to use the speed-up technique as a TSR. For a non-TSR application, before exiting to DOS, the original interrupt 8 vector must be replaced.

```
;---------------------------------------------------------------
;                          TIMER FAST
;---------------------------------------------------------------
;
;     This program demonstrates how to get interrupt control
;     at frequency higher than the normal 18 times a second, by
```

```
;    speeding up system timer 0. In this example, interrupts
;    occur at 50 times normal, or 910 times per second.
;
;    (c) Copyright 1994, 1996  Frank van Gilluwe
;    All Rights Reserved.

include undocpc.inc

NEWRATE equ     50                  ; number of times to increase
                                    ;  the interrupt rate

cseg    segment para public
        assume  cs:cseg, ds:cseg, ss:tsrstk

countdown       dw      NEWRATE     ; countdown timer
old_int_8       dd      0           ; old pointer saved here

;-------------------------------------------------------------
; This is the resident handler for handling interrupt 8

int_8_hook    proc    far
        pushf

; code which occurs at fast rate inserted here in place
;   of demo_two_char

        call    demo_two_char       ; demo program

; Upon completion of the fast rate code call the old
;   interrupt 8 routine ONLY at the original 18.2 times
;   per second rate.

        dec     cs:[countdown]
        jnz     int_8_exit
```

```
        mov     cs:[countdown], NEWRATE    ; reload counter
        popf
        jmp     cs:[old_int_8]      ; process old interrupt 8

int_8_exit:
        cli                         ; disable interrupts
        push    ax
        mov     al, 20h             ; end-of-interrupt command
        out     20h, al             ; issue command to controller
        pop     ax
        popf
        iret
int_8_hook    endp

;-------------------------------------------------------------------
; This demo program quickly alternates between the "/" character
;    and letters of the alphabet to give the visual appearance
;    of strike-through. Any two characters could be
;    "overlapped" using this routine. Also notice three colors
;    appear in a single text cell (black, white and green).

democount       dw      0
demochar        db      'A'         ; character to display
SLASH_ATTRB     equ     0Fh         ; attribute, bright white
CHAR_ATTRB      equ     0Ah         ; attribute, green

demo_two_char   proc    near
        push    ax
        push    di
        push    es

        mov     ax, 40h
        mov     es, ax              ; point to BIOS memory area
        mov     ax, 0B800h          ; assume color text video area
```

```
        cmp     byte ptr es:[49h], 7  ; mono video mode ?
        jne     demo1                 ; jump if not
        mov     ax, 0B000h            ; use monochrome segment
demo1:
        mov     es, ax                ; load screen segment
        mov     di, 79 * 2            ; point to end of first line
        mov     al, '/'               ; strike-through character
        mov     ah, SLASH_ATTRB       ; attribute
        test    cs:[democount], 1     ; toggle between chars
        jz      demo2                 ;  depending on count
        mov     al, cs:[demochar]
        mov     ah, CHAR_ATTRB        ; character attribute
demo2:
        cld
        stosw                         ; store AX to screen at es:[di]
        inc     cs:[democount]
        mov     ax, cs:[democount]
        cmp     ax, 182*(NEWRATE/10) ; 1 second elapsed ?
        jb      demo3                 ; jump if not
        mov     cs:[democount], 0     ; reset democount
        inc     cs:[demochar]         ; use a different char
demo3:
        pop     es
        pop     di
        pop     ax
        ret
demo_two_char   endp

;==============================================================
; Start of non-resident installation portion

tmrfast proc    far

start:
```

```
        push    cs
        pop     ds

; get the current interrupt 8 vector and save

        mov     al, 8
        mov     ah, 35h
        int     21h                 ; get current int 8 pointer
        mov     word ptr old_int_8, bx
        mov     word ptr old_int_8+2, es

; install our new interrupt 8 routine
        mov     dx, offset int_8_hook
        mov     al, 8
        mov     ah, 25h
        int     21h                 ; install our interrupt

        OUTMSG  installmsg          ; display installed message

; now reset timer 0 to the faster rate

        cli                         ; disable interrupts
        mov     al, 36h             ; command for 16-bit,
        out     43h, al             ;  mode 3, binary operation
        IODELAY
        mov     ax, 65535/NEWRATE  ; counter value
        out     40h, al             ; load timer 0 count LSB
        IODELAY
        mov     al, ah              ; get most significant byte
        out     40h, al             ; load timer 0 count MSB
        sti                         ; enable interrupts

; now determine the size to remain resident (paragraphs)
;   and become a TSR
```

```
        mov     dx, (offset start - offset countdown) SHR 4
        add     dx, 11h              ; add PSP size + 1 paragraph
        mov     ax, 3100h            ; exit to DOS as tsr
        int     21h
tmrfast endp
installmsg db   CR, LF
        db      'TIMER FAST Installed - Demonstrates fast '
        db      'interrupt 8 handler.', CR, LF
        db      '   Makes the top right corner of screen '
        db      'overlap two colors and characters.', CR, LF, '$'
cseg    ends
```

Port Summary

This is a list of ports used to control the timers.

Port	Type	Function	Platform
40h	I/O	Timer 0—System Ticks	All
41h	I/O	Timer 1—DRAM Refresh	All except MCA
42h	I/O	Timer 2—General Use	All
43h	Output	Timers 0-2 Mode Control	All
44h	I/O	Timer 3—Watchdog	MCA
47h	Output	Timer 3—Mode Control	MCA
48h	I/O	Timer 3—Watchdog	EISA
4Ah	I/O	Timer 5—CPU Speed Control	EISA
4Bh	I/O	Timers 3 & 5—Mode Control	EISA

Port Detail

Port	Type	Description	Platform
40h	I/O	Timer 0—System Ticks	All

Timer 0 is used for system clocking. It is normally programmed for mode 3, periodic square wave operation. The Count is loaded with 0, to generate a pulse 18.2 times per second. Refer to the subsection on system timing for more details on timer 0, and how some systems use the less-compatible mode 2.

Input (bits 0-7)—Read Count Register 0

The command byte written to port 43h controls how information is read from this port.

1xh = reads the least significant byte only

2xh = reads the most significant byte only

3xh = the first read gets the least significant byte, and the second read gets the most significant byte.

Output (bits 0-7)—Write Count Register 0

The command byte written to port 43h controls how information is written to this port.

1xh = writes the least significant byte and the most significant byte is set to zero

2xh = writes the most significant byte and the least significant byte is set to zero

3xh = the first write sets the least significant byte, and the second write sets the most significant byte.

To help clarify this, the following code fragment shows how timer 0 is changed to 1820.7 times per second. The timer must be loaded with a count of 655 to accomplish this (1193200/ 1820.7 = 655). Mode 3 will be used, since this provides a continuous square wave output to trigger the interrupt. See Code Sample 16-3 for a complete program using this mechanism.

```
        mov     al, 36h             ; command for 16-bit,
        out     43h, al             ;  mode 3, binary operation
        IODELAY
        mov     ax, 655             ; counter value
        out     40h, al             ; load timer 0 count LSB
        IODELAY
        mov     al, ah              ; get most significant byte
        out     40h, al             ; load timer 0 count MSB
```

Port	Type	Description	Platform
41h	I/O	Timer 1—DRAM Refresh	PC/XT/AT/EISA

Timer 1 is used for DRAM refresh. It is normally programmed for mode 2, rate generator operation. The count is loaded with 12h, to generate a pulse every 15 uS. Refer to the subsection on timer 1, DRAM Refresh, for more details.

Input (bits 0-7)—Read Count Register 1

The command byte written to port 43h controls how information is read from this port.

5xh = reads the least significant byte only

6xh = reads the most significant byte only

7xh = the first read gets the least significant byte, and the second read gets the most significant byte.

Output (bits 0-7)—Write Count Register 1

The command byte written to port 43h controls how information is written to this port.

5xh = writes the least significant byte and the most significant byte is set to zero

6xh = writes the most significant byte and the least significant byte is set to zero 7xh = the first write sets the least significant byte, and the second write sets the most significant byte.

Port	Type	Description	Platform
42h	I/O	Timer 2—General Use	All

Timer 2 is used for speaker operations and general use. Refer to the subsection on timer 2, General Use and Speaker, for more details.

Input (bits 0-7)—Read Count Register 2

The command byte written to port 43h controls how information is read from this port.

9xh = reads the least significant byte only

Axh = reads the most significant byte only

Bxh = the first read gets the least significant byte, and the second read gets the most significant byte.

Output (bits 0-7)—Write Count Register 2

The command byte written to port 43h controls how information is written to this port.

9xh = writes the least significant byte and the most significant byte is set to zero

Axh = writes the most significant byte and the least significant byte is set to zero Bxh = the first write sets the least significant byte, and the second write sets the most significant byte.

Port	Type	Description	Platform
43h	Output	Timers 0-2 Mode Control	All

The three timers, 0, 1, and 2, are controlled by modes set using this port. See the subsection on Modes of Operation.

Output (bits 0-7)

bit 7 w = x	Command			
6 w = x				
5 w = x				
4 w = x				
3 w = x	Mode selection			
2 w = x		bit 3	bit 2	bit 1
1 w = x		0	0	0 = Mode 0
		0	0	1 = Mode 1
		0	1	0 = Mode 2
		0	1	1 = Mode 3
		1	0	0 = Mode 4
		1	0	1 = Mode 5
		1	1	0 = Mode 2
		1	1	1 = Mode 3
0 w = 0	Binary Counter mode (16-bit)			
1	BCD Counter mode (4 Binary Coded Decimal digits)			

Command Summary

The *x* in the following commands specifies the timer mode and binary/BCD bit. This lower nibble of data is explained in the command detail.

Number	Port 43h Commands
0xh	Counter Latch Timer 0
1xh	Timer 0 LSB Mode
2xh	Timer 0 MSB Mode
3xh	Timer 0 16-bit Mode
4xh	Counter Latch Timer 1
5xh	Timer 1 LSB Mode
6xh	Timer 1 MSB Mode
7xh	Timer 1 16-bit Mode
8xh	Counter Latch Timer 2
9xh	Timer 2 LSB Mode
Axh	Timer 2 MSB Mode
Bxh	Timer 2 16-bit Mode
Dxh	General Counter Latch
Exh	Latch Status of Timers

Command Detail

Command	Description	Port
0xh	Counter Latch Timer 0	43h

The timer 0 counter value is transferred into the output latch register. The latched value is held until read by port 40h or a new counter value is loaded into timer 0. Subsequent counter latch commands are ignored until the value is read. The lower 4 bits of this command byte are ignored.

Using this command differs from a general read of the counter. When not latched, the value read from port 40h is the immediate contents of timer 0.

Command	Description	Port
1xh	Timer 0 LSB Mode	43h

Timer 0 is set to read and write the least significant byte only. When writing timer 0 count, the most significant byte is automatically set to zero. The remaining bits control the mode of operation for timer 0.

bit 7 w = 0	Command			
6 w = 0				
5 w = 0				
4 w = 1				
3 w = x	Mode selection			
2 w = x		bit 3	bit 2	bit 1
1 w = x		0	0	0 = Mode 0
		0	0	1 = Mode 1 (not applicable)
		0	1	0 = Mode 2
		0	1	1 = Mode 3
		1	0	0 = Mode 4
		1	0	1 = Mode 5 (not applicable)
0 w = 0	Binary Counter mode (16-bit)			
1	BCD Counter mode (4 Binary Coded Decimal digits)			

Command	Description	Port
2xh	Timer 0 MSB Mode	43h

Timer 0 is set to read and write the most significant byte only. When writing timer 0 count, the least significant byte is automatically set to zero. The remaining bits control the mode of operation for timer 0.

bit 7 w = 0	Command			
6 w = 0				
5 w = 1				
4 w = 0				
3 w = x	Mode selection			
2 w = x		bit 3	bit 2	bit 1
1 w = x		0	0	0 = Mode 0
		0	0	1 = Mode 1 (not applicable)
		0	1	0 = Mode 2
		0	1	1 = Mode 3
		1	0	0 = Mode 4
		1	0	1 = Mode 5 (not applicable)
0 w = 0	Binary Counter mode (16-bit)			
1	BCD Counter mode (4 Binary Coded Decimal digits)			

Command	Description	Port
3xh	Timer 0 16-bit Mode	43h

★★★

Timer 0 is set to read and write the entire 16-bit counter. For both reads and writes, the least significant byte is sent first, followed by the most significant byte. The remaining bits control the mode of operation for timer 0.

bit 7 w = 0	Command			
6 w = 0				
5 w = 1				
4 w = 1				
3 w = x	Mode selection			
2 w = x		bit 3	bit 2	bit 1
1 w = x		0	0	0 = Mode 0
		0	0	1 = Mode 1 (not applicable)
		0	1	0 = Mode 2
		0	1	1 = Mode 3 (typical)
		1	0	0 = Mode 4
		1	0	1 = Mode 5 (not applicable)
0 w = 0	Binary Counter mode (16-bit)			
1	BCD Counter mode (4 Binary Coded Decimal digits)			

Command	Description	Port
4xh	Counter Latch Timer 1	43h

The timer 1 counter value is transferred into the output latch register. The latched value is held until read by port 41h or a new counter value is loaded into timer 1. Subsequent counter latch commands are ignored until the value is read. The lower 4 bits of this command byte are ignored.

Using this command differs from a general read of the counter. When not latched, the value read from port 41h is the immediate contents of timer 1.

Command	Description	Port
5xh	Timer 1 LSB Mode	43h

Timer 1 is set to read and write the least significant byte only. When writing timer 1 count, the most significant byte is automatically set to zero. The remaining bits control the mode of operation for timer 1.

bit 7	w = 0	Command			
6	w = 1				
5	w = 0				
4	w = 1				
3	w = x	Mode selection			
2	w = x		bit 3	bit 2	bit 1
1	w = x		0	0	0 = Mode 0
			0	0	1 = Mode 1 (not applicable)
			0	1	0 = Mode 2
			0	1	1 = Mode 3
			1	0	0 = Mode 4
			1	0	1 = Mode 5 (not applicable)
0	w = 0	Binary Counter mode (16-bit)			
	1	BCD Counter mode (4 Binary Coded Decimal digits)			

Command	Description	Port
6xh	Timer 1 MSB Mode	43h

Timer 1 is set to read and write the most significant byte only. When writing timer 1 count, the least significant byte is automatically set to zero. The remaining bits control the mode of operation for timer 1.

bit	7 w = 0	Command		
	6 w = 1			
	5 w = 1			
	4 w = 0			
	3 w = x	Mode selection		
	2 w = x	bit 3	bit 2	bit 1
	1 w = x	0	0	0 = Mode 0
		0	0	1 = Mode 1 (not applicable)
		0	1	0 = Mode 2
		0	1	1 = Mode 3
		1	0	0 = Mode 4
		1	0	1 = Mode 5 (not applicable)
	0 w = 0	Binary Counter mode (16-bit)		
	1	BCD Counter mode (4 Binary Coded Decimal digits)		

Command	Description	Port
7xh	Timer 1 16-bit Mode	43h

Timer 1 is set to read and write the entire 16-bit counter. For both reads and writes, the least significant byte is sent first, followed by the most significant byte. The remaining bits control the mode of operation for timer 1.

bit	7 w = 0	Command		
	6 w = 1			
	5 w = 1			
	4 w = 1			
	3 w = x	Mode selection		
	2 w = x	bit 3	bit 2	bit 1
	1 w = x	0	0	0 = Mode 0
		0	0	1 = Mode 1 (not applicable)
		0	1	0 = Mode 2 (typical)
		0	1	1 = Mode 3
		1	0	0 = Mode 4
		1	0	1 = Mode 5 (not applicable)
	0 w = 0	Binary Counter mode (16-bit)		
	1	BCD Counter mode (4 Binary Coded Decimal digits)		

Command	Description	Port
8xh	Counter Latch Timer 2	43h

The timer 2 counter value is transferred into the output latch register. The latched value is held until read by port 42h or a new counter value is loaded into timer 2. Subsequent counter latch commands are ignored until the value is read. The lower 4 bits of this command byte are ignored.

Using this command differs from a general read of the counter. When not latched, the value read from port 42h is the immediate contents of timer 2.

Command	Description	Port
9xh	Timer 2 LSB Mode	43h

Timer 2 is set to read and write the least significant byte only. When writing timer 2 count, the most significant byte is automatically set to zero. The remaining bits control the mode of operation for timer 2.

bit	7 w = 1	Command			
	6 w = 0				
	5 w = 0				
	4 w = 1				
	3 w = x	Mode selection			
	2 w = x		bit 3	bit 2	bit 1
	1 w = x		0	0	0 = Mode 0
			0	0	1 = Mode 1
			0	1	0 = Mode 2
			0	1	1 = Mode 3
			1	0	0 = Mode 4
			1	0	1 = Mode 5
	0 w = 0	Binary Counter mode (16-bit)			
	1	BCD Counter mode (4 Binary Coded Decimal digits)			

Command	Description	Port
Axh	Timer 2 MSB Mode	43h

Timer 2 is set to read and write the most significant byte only. When writing timer 2 count, the least significant byte is automatically set to zero. The remaining bits control the mode of operation for timer 2.

bit	7 w = 1	Command
	6 w = 0	
	5 w = 1	
	4 w = 0	

3 w = x	Mode selection		
2 w = x	bit 3	bit 2	bit 1
1 w = x	0	0	0 = Mode 0
	0	0	1 = Mode 1
	0	1	0 = Mode 2
	0	1	1 = Mode 3
	1	0	0 = Mode 4
	1	0	1 = Mode 5
0 w = 0	Binary Counter mode (16-bit)		
1	BCD Counter mode (4 Binary Coded Decimal digits)		

Command	Description	Port
Bxh	**Timer 2 16-bit Mode**	**43h**

Timer 2 is set to read and write the entire 16-bit counter. For both reads and writes, the least significant byte is sent first, followed by the most significant byte. The remaining bits control the mode of operation for timer 2.

bit 7 w = 1	Command		
6 w = 0			
5 w = 1			
4 w = 1			
3 w = x	Mode selection		
2 w = x	bit 3	bit 2	bit 1
1 w = x	0	0	0 = Mode 0
	0	0	1 = Mode 1
	0	1	0 = Mode 2
	0	1	1 = Mode 3
	1	0	0 = Mode 4
	1	0	1 = Mode 5
0 w = 0	Binary Counter mode (16-bit)		
1	BCD Counter mode (4 Binary Coded Decimal digits)		

Command	Description	Port
Dxh	**General Counter Latch**	**43h**

This command is used to transfer counter contents into the output latch. The counters for timer 0, 1, and 2 can be latched independently or in combination. Similar to commands 0xh, 4xh and 8xh, the latched value is held until read by the respective timer port 40h to 42h or a new counter value is loaded into the timer. Subsequent counter latch commands are ignored for any timers that have already been latched but have not yet been read.

bit	7 w = 1	Command
	6 w = 1	
	5 w = 0	
	4 w = 1	
	3 w = 1	Select Counter 2
	2 w = 1	Select Counter 1
	1 w = 1	Select Counter 0
	0 w = 0	Unused

Command	Description	Port
Exh	Latch Status of Timers	43h

This command latches the status of the selected timer(s) into the output latch. Once a timer's status has been latched, the status is read from the respective timer port 40h to 42h. Subsequent status latch commands are ignored for any timers that have already been latched but have not yet been read.

bit	7 w = 1	Command
	6 w = 1	
	5 w = 1	
	4 w = 0	
	3 w = 1	Select Counter 2
	2 w = 1	Select Counter 1
	1 w = 1	Select Counter 0
	0 w = 0	Unused

When the status is latched by this command, the status is read from the respective port 40h to 42h. This status byte contains the current mode information in bits 0-5, and other information shown below.

bit	7 r = x	State of timer's output pin	
	6 r = 0	Null Count, a new count has been loaded into counter	
	1	Count has not been loaded into counter	
	5 r = x	Read/Write mode	
	4 r = x	bit 5	bit 4
		0	1 = read/write most significant byte only
		1	0 = read/write least significant byte only
		1	1 = read/write least significant byte first, then most significant byte

3 w = x	Mode selection			
2 w = x		bit 3	bit 2	bit 1
1 w = x		0	0	0 = Mode 0
		0	0	1 = Mode 1
		0	1	0 = Mode 2
		0	1	1 = Mode 3
		1	0	0 = Mode 4
		1	0	1 = Mode 5
		1	1	0 = Mode 2
		1	1	1 = Mode 3
0 w = 0	Binary Counter mode (16-bit)			
1	BCD Counter mode (4 Binary Coded Decimal digits)			

Port	Type	Description	Platform
44h	I/O	Timer 3—Watchdog	MCA

Timer 3 is used for the watchdog timer. Timer 3 has restricted operation and modes. Refer to the subsection on timer 3, watchdog (MCA), for more details.

Input (bits 0-7)—Read Count Register 3 (8-bit counter only)

Output (bits 0-7)—Write Count Register 3 (8-bit counter only)

Port	Type	Description	Platform
47h	Output	Timer 3—Mode Control	MCA

The mode of timer 3 is set using this port.

Output (bits 0-7)

bit	7 w = x	Command
	6 w = x	
	5 w = x	
	4 w = x	
	3 w = 0	Unused
	2 w = 0	Unused
	1 w = 0	Unused
	0 w = 0	Unused

Command Summary

Number	Port 47h Commands
00h	Counter Latch Timer 3
10h	Timer 3 Mode

Command Detail

Command	Description	Port
00h	Counter Latch Timer 3	47h

Timer 3's counter value is transferred into its output latch. The latched value is held until read by port 44h or a new counter value is loaded into timer 3. Subsequent counter latch commands are ignored until the value is read. The lower 4 bits of the command byte are ignored and are normally set to zero.

Using this command differs from a general read of the counter. When not latched, the value read from port 44h is the immediate contents of timer 3.

Command	Description	Port
10h	Timer 3 Mode	47h

Timer 3 is set to read and write the counter byte. The remaining command bits are unused. Timer 3 is fixed in hardware as an 8-bit counter, binary counting, mode 0 operation.

bit	7	w = 0	Command
	6	w = 0	
	5	w = 0	
	4	w = 1	
	3	w = 0	Unused
	2	w = 0	Unused
	1	w = 0	Unused
	0	w = 0	Unused

Port	Type	Description	Platform
48h	I/O	Timer 3—Watchdog	EISA

Timer 3 is used for the watchdog timer. Timer 3 has restricted operation and useful modes. Timer 3's input clock is 298.3 KHz, and the gate line is always on. Refer to the subsection on the timer 3, watchdog (EISA), for more details.

Input (bits 0-7)—Read Count Register 3

The command byte written to port 4Bh controls how information is read from this port.

1xh = reads the least significant byte only

2xh = reads the most significant byte only

3xh = the first read gets the least significant byte, and the second read gets the most significant byte.

Output (bits 0-7)—Write Count Register 3

The command byte written to port 4Bh controls how information is written to this port.

1xh = writes the least significant byte and the most significant byte is set to zero

2xh = writes the most significant byte and the least significant byte is set to zero

3xh = the first write sets the least significant byte, and the second write sets the most significant byte.

Port	Type	Description	Platform
4Ah	I/O	Timer 5—CPU Speed Control	EISA

Timer 2 is used for optional CPU speed control or other functions determined by the motherboard designer. Refer to the subsection on timer 5.

Input (bits 0-7)—Read Count Register 5

The command byte written to port 4Bh controls how information is read from this port.

9xh = reads the least significant byte only

Axh = reads the most significant byte only

Bxh = the first read gets the least significant byte, and the second read gets the most significant byte.

Output (bits 0-7)—Write Count Register 5

The command byte written to port 4Bh controls how information is written to this port.

9xh = writes the least significant byte and the most significant byte is set to zero

Axh = writes the most significant byte and the least significant byte is set to zero

Bxh = the first write sets the least significant byte, and the second write sets the most significant byte.

Port	Type	Description	Platform
4Bh	Output	Timers 3 & 5 Mode Control	EISA

The two timers, 3 and 5, are controlled by the mode set using this port. See the subsection on Modes of Operation.

Output (bits 0-7)

bit 7 w = x	Command				
6 w = x					
5 w = x					
4 w = x					
3 w = x	Mode selection				
2 w = x		bit 3	bit 2	bit 1	
1 w = x		0	0	0 = Mode 0	
		0	0	1 = Mode 1	
		0	1	0 = Mode 2	
		0	1	1 = Mode 3	
		1	0	0 = Mode 4	
		1	0	1 = Mode 5	
		1	1	0 = Mode 2	
		1	1	1 = Mode 3	
0 w = 0	Binary Counter mode (16-bit)				
1	BCD Counter mode (4 Binary Coded Decimal digits)				

Command Summary

Number	Port 4Bh Commands
0xh	Counter Latch Timer 3
1xh	Timer 3 LSB Mode
2xh	Timer 3 MSB Mode
3xh	Timer 3 16-bit Mode
8xh	Counter Latch Timer 5
9xh	Timer 5 LSB Mode
Axh	Timer 5 MSB Mode
Bxh	Timer 5 16-bit Mode
Dxh	General Counter Latch
Exh	Latch Status of Timers

Although the 4Bh commands are very similar to the 43h commands, there are subtle differences as to which modes are not allowed or are typical.

Command Detail

Command	Description	Port
0xh	Counter Latch Timer 3	4Bh

The timer 3 counter value is transferred into the output latch register. The latched value is held until read by port 48h or until a new counter value is loaded into timer 3. Subsequent counter latch commands are ignored until the value is read. The lower 4 bits of the command byte are ignored.

Using this command differs from a general read of the counter. When not latched, the value read from port 48h is the immediate contents of timer 3.

Command	Description	Port
1xh	Timer 3 LSB Mode	4Bh

Timer 3 is set to read and write the least significant byte only. When writing timer 3 count, the most significant byte is automatically set to zero. The remaining bits control the mode of operation for timer 3.

bit				
7 w = 0	Command			
6 w = 0				
5 w = 0				
4 w = 1				
3 w = x	Mode selection			
2 w = x		bit 3	bit 2	bit 1
1 w = x		0	0	0 = Mode 0
		0	0	1 = Mode 1
		0	1	0 = Mode 2
		0	1	1 = Mode 3
		1	0	0 = Mode 4
		1	0	1 = Mode 5 (not applicable)
0 w = 0	Binary Counter mode (16-bit)			
1	BCD Counter mode (4 Binary Coded Decimal digits)			

Command	Description	Port
2xh	Timer 3 MSB Mode	4Bh

Timer 3 is set to read and write the most significant byte only. When writing timer 3 count, the least significant byte is automatically set to zero. The remaining bits control the mode of operation for timer 3.

bit	7 w = 0	Command			
	6 w = 0				
	5 w = 1				
	4 w = 0				
	3 w = x	Mode selection			
	2 w = x		bit 3	bit 2	bit 1
	1 w = x		0	0	0 = Mode 0
			0	0	1 = Mode 1
			0	1	0 = Mode 2
			0	1	1 = Mode 3
			1	0	0 = Mode 4
			1	0	1 = Mode 5 (not applicable)
	0 w = 0	Binary Counter mode (16-bit)			
	1	BCD Counter mode (4 Binary Coded Decimal digits)			

Command	Description	Port
3xh	Timer 3 16-bit Mode	4Bh

Timer 3 is set to read and write the entire 16-bit counter. For both reads and writes, the least significant byte is sent first, followed by the most significant byte. The remaining bits control the mode of operation for timer 3.

bit	7 w = 0	Command			
	6 w = 0				
	5 w = 1				
	4 w = 1				
	3 w = x	Mode selection			
	2 w = x		bit 3	bit 2	bit 1
	1 w = x		0	0	0 = Mode 0
			0	0	1 = Mode 1 (typical)
			0	1	0 = Mode 2
			0	1	1 = Mode 3
			1	0	0 = Mode 4
			1	0	1 = Mode 5 (not applicable)
	0 w = 0	Binary Counter mode (16-bit)			
	1	BCD Counter mode (4 Binary Coded Decimal digits)			

Command	Description	Port
8xh	Counter Latch Timer 5	4Bh

The timer 5 counter value is transferred into the output latch register. The latched value is held until read by port 4Ah or a new counter value is loaded into timer 5. Subsequent counter latch commands are ignored until the value is read. The lower 4 bits of this command byte are ignored.

Using this command differs from a general read of the counter. When not latched, the value read from port 4Ah is the immediate contents of timer 5.

Command	Description	Port
9xh	Timer 5 LSB Mode	4Bh

Timer 5 is set to read and write the least significant byte only. When writing timer 5 count, the most significant byte is automatically set to zero. The remaining bits control the mode of operation for timer 5.

bit				
7 w = 1	Command			
6 w = 0				
5 w = 0				
4 w = 1				
3 w = x	Mode selection			
2 w = x		bit 3	bit 2	bit 1
1 w = x		0	0	0 = Mode 0
		0	0	1 = Mode 1
		0	1	0 = Mode 2
		0	1	1 = Mode 3
		1	0	0 = Mode 4
		1	0	1 = Mode 5
0 w = 0	Binary Counter mode (16-bit)			
1	BCD Counter mode (4 Binary Coded Decimal digits)			

Command	Description	Port
Axh	Timer 5 MSB Mode	4Bh

Timer 5 is set to read and write the most significant byte only. When writing timer 5 count, the least significant byte is automatically set to zero. The remaining bits control the mode of operation for timer 5.

bit 7 w = 1	Command			
6 w = 0				
5 w = 1				
4 w = 0				
3 w = x	Mode selection			
2 w = x		bit 3	bit 2	bit 1
1 w = x		0	0	0 = Mode 0
		0	0	1 = Mode 1
		0	1	0 = Mode 2
		0	1	1 = Mode 3
		1	0	0 = Mode 4
		1	0	1 = Mode 5
0 w = 0	Binary Counter mode (16-bit)			
1	BCD Counter mode (4 Binary Coded Decimal digits)			

Command	Description	Port
Bxh	Timer 5 16-bit Mode	4Bh

Timer 5 is set to read and write the entire 16-bit counter. For both reads and writes, the least significant byte is sent first, followed by the most significant byte. The remaining bits control the mode of operation for timer 5.

bit 7 w = 1	Command			
6 w = 0				
5 w = 1				
4 w = 1				
3 w = x	Mode selection			
2 w = x		bit 3	bit 2	bit 1
1 w = x		0	0	0 = Mode 0
		0	0	1 = Mode 1 (typical)
		0	1	0 = Mode 2
		0	1	1 = Mode 3
		1	0	0 = Mode 4
		1	0	1 = Mode 5
0 w = 0	Binary Counter mode (16-bit)			
1	BCD Counter mode (4 Binary Coded Decimal digits)			

Command	Description	Port
Dxh	General Counter Latch	4Bh

This command is used to transfer counter contents into the output latch. The counters for timer 3 and 5 can be latched independently or in combination. Similar to commands 0xh and 8xh, the latched value is held until read by the respective timer port 48h or 4Ah or a new counter value is loaded into the timer. Subsequent counter latch commands are ignored for any timers that have already been latched but have not yet been read.

bit	7	w = 1	Command
	6	w = 1	
	5	w = 0	
	4	w = 1	
	3	w = 1	Select Counter 5
	2	w = 0	Unused
	1	w = 1	Select Counter 3
	0	w = 0	Unused

Command	Description	Port
Exh	Latch Status of Timers	4Bh

This command latches the status of the selected timer(s) into the output latch. Once a timer's status has been latched, the status is read from the respective timer port 48h or 4Ah. Subsequent status latch commands are ignored for any timers that have already been latched but have not yet been read.

bit	7	w = 1	Command
	6	w = 1	
	5	w = 1	
	4	w = 0	
	3	w = 1	Select Counter 5
	2	w = 0	Unused
	1	w = 1	Select Counter 3
	0	w = 0	Unused

When the status is latched by this command, the status is read from the respective port 48h or 4Ah. This status byte contains the current mode information in bits 0-5 and other information shown below.

bit	7	r = x	State of timer's output pin
	6	r = 0	Null Count, a new count has been loaded into counter

1	Count has not been loaded into counter			
5 r = x	Read/Write mode			
4 r = x	bit 5	bit 4		
	0	1 = read/write most significant byte only		
	1	0 = read/write least significant byte only		
	1	1 = read/write least significant byte first, then most significant byte		
3 w = x	Mode selection			
2 w = x	bit 3	bit 2	bit 1	
1 w = x	0	0	0 = Mode 0	
	0	0	1 = Mode 1	
	0	1	0 = Mode 2	
	0	1	1 = Mode 3	
	1	0	0 = Mode 4	
	1	0	1 = Mode 5	
	1	1	0 = Mode 2	
	1	1	1 = Mode 3	
0 w = 0	Binary Counter mode (16-bit)			
1	BCD Counter mode (4 Binary Coded Decimal digits)			

CHAPTER 17

Interrupt Control and NMI

Interrupt control manages the hardware interrupt processes of the computer. I'll show the basic operation of the interrupt controllers, the Non-Maskable Interrupt (NMI), and the basics for programming the interrupt controller for special high-performance needs. The interrupt control differences between the PC, AT, MCA, and EISA architectures are also explained.

One problem some programmers encounter is the need to redirect hardware interrupts to alternate vectors. This is done to boost system performance or to avoid conflicts in special situations. I'll explain how to accomplish this and show several real-world examples.

Introduction

The computer system is designed so hardware devices such as the keyboard or a serial port can request servicing on a timely basis. This is accomplished using interrupt control. This avoids having the CPU waste time checking or polling for hardware that may need servicing on a non-predictable basis. Essentially, a hardware device interrupts the current process in the CPU, and a service handler routine is run. Once the hardware device has been serviced, the CPU resumes its prior task.

Interrupt control handles eight hardware interrupts on PC/XT systems and fifteen on AT+ class machines. Many of the hardware interrupt lines are dedicated to specific functions, such as timers, the keyboard, and disk drive operations. Some of these hardware lines are available on the motherboard backplane, so adapter cards can also use the hardware interrupt system. The PCI bus provides programmable connection of interrupt ports to each PCI card slot. This allows a "Plug-n-Play" BIOS to configure PCI cards automatically.

Interrupt control is handled through one or two 8259 interrupt controller chips. These interrupt controller chips perform the task of managing multiple interrupt requests (IRQs) and the presentation of interrupts to the CPU.

To control interrupt operation, the 8259 has a number of internal registers. These registers control which hardware interrupts are allowed, priority levels, types of hardware interrupts, and which specific interrupt software routine the CPU should process (1 out of 256).

A Typical Interrupt Occurrence

Figure 17-1 shows the sequence of events when an interrupt is initiated. Assume the adapter card has jumpered its interrupt to IRQ 5, the interrupt controller was initialized, and is not active with any other requests. In addition, the interrupt controller's mask register allows interrupt 5. (The mask register is used to allow or to lock out interrupts.)

The complete processing of a single interrupt occurs in the following sequence:

1. The adapter card requests service, by driving the hardware IRQ 5 backplane line from low to high.
2. The IRQ 5 line is connected to the interrupt controller. The edge-triggered request is recorded in the controller's Interrupt Request Register. In this case, the Interrupt Request Register bit 5 is set to one.
3. The interrupt controller first checks the Interrupt Mask Register to see if IRQ 5 is allowed. Assuming the mask bit is clear for IRQ 5 to allow the request, the controller proceeds to the next check.
4. The controller checks if any higher priority interrupts are active or in progress. If so, no further action occurs until all higher priority interrupts are serviced.
5. If no higher priority interrupts are active, the controller flags the CPU over the dedicated INT hardware line leading to the CPU.
6. The CPU returns an acknowledgment to the interrupt controller if the CPU has hardware interrupts enabled.
7. The CPU interrupt acknowledgment causes the controller to send the interrupt byte value Dh back to the CPU. In this case, IRQ 5 links to interrupt D. In addition, the controller's In-Service Register (ISR) IRQ 5 bit is activated (on). Lastly, the controller's Interrupt Request Register (IRR) IRQ 5 bit is cleared, indicating the interrupt is actively being serviced.
8. The CPU interrupts the current process, saves the current instruction address and flags on the stack, and then calls the interrupt service handler at vector Dh. The far

address of the interrupt D is stored at the bottom of memory at segment 0, offset 4 * Dh (i.e., at 0000:0034).

9. The called interrupt service handler performs all necessary actions. One of the key actions the handler must take is to remove the interrupt request made by the adapter. This is typically done when the necessary interrupt service handler action is completed, such as reading or writing a byte to the adapter. The IRQ 5 line from the adapter now goes low.

10. At the end of the service handler routine, the handler sends the value 20h to port 20h to signal the End Of Interrupt (EOI) to the interrupt controller.

11. The EOI command from the CPU clears the IRQ 5 In-Service bit. This clears the way for the interrupt controller to accept another interrupt from IRQ5 or any lower priority interrupt.

12. The service handler routine issues an IRET instruction, so the processor restores the flags and returns to the previously interrupted process.

Figure 17-1. Sequence of an Interrupt

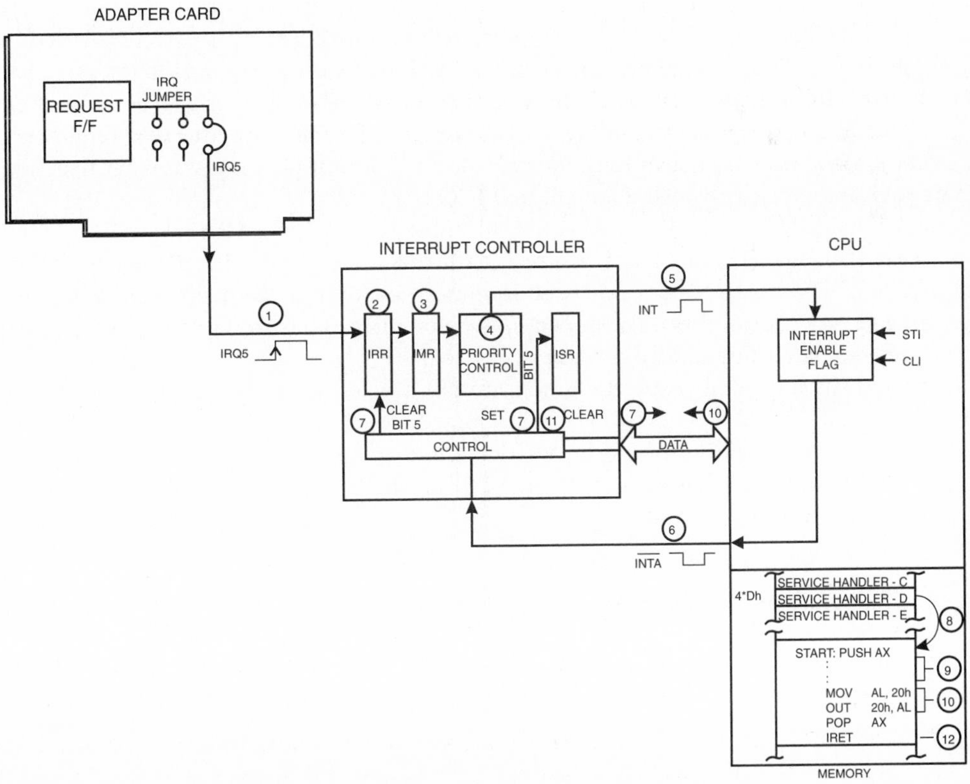

Edge/Level Control

A hardware interrupt is generated whenever an IRQ line becomes active. Each interrupt controller has the ability to trigger this event in two different ways. This selection is made using the initialization command word 1 at port 20h or A0h. This selection is normally based on the hardware system design and should not be changed.

Edge Triggered The first approach to detecting an interrupt request uses the rising edge of an IRQ line. This is called edge triggering. The IRQ line can remain high without triggering another interrupt. This is the approach used on all PC/XT/AT type machines, and it is the default on EISA machines.

Only one device can use a single edge-triggered interrupt on the PC, XT, and AT. Should two devices attempt to use the same IRQ, with each sending a different signal, the high and low signals conflict. This puts the IRQ line in an indeterminate state that may fail to trigger the interrupt.

Level Triggered The second approach to interrupt request detection is based on the state of the request line. When the IRQ is set high, an interrupt request is signaled. Should the IRQ remain high after the interrupt is serviced and cleared, another interrupt will be issued. The advantage of this approach is that it allows multiple hardware devices to share the same IRQ line. MCA systems are designed this way. EISA systems can optionally select level triggering on an individual interrupt basis. Interrupts from PCI bus slots are also level triggered.

To share a hardware interrupt, the system is designed so multiple adapters can drive the same interrupt request line without conflict. This is accomplished by using an active pull-down design. The design safely allows multiple adapters to trigger the same interrupt request at the same time. In addition, each adapter must provide an interrupt pending status bit that is readable by software, typically by using a dedicated I/O port.

The interrupt service handler for the adapter must check whether the interrupt was caused by its related adapter. The interrupt pending status bit is read from the adapter to make this determination. If the adapter did not issue the interrupt, the service handler must ignore the interrupt and pass control down the hooked interrupt chain. This allows other service handlers for the same interrupt to handle the request.

Interrupt sharing will increase the time to respond, referred to as interrupt latency. This is usually acceptable for devices that do not need immediate servicing, such as serial devices at low baud rates. Interrupt sharing should be avoided when an adapter needs to keep the interrupt latency to a minimum.

NMI—Non-Maskable Interrupt

The CPU has a separate hardware Non-Maskable Interrupt (NMI) line, independent of the interrupt controller. When NMI goes active, the processor vectors to the interrupt 2 handler.

This is used primarily by the BIOS to trap memory parity errors and I/O channel parity errors. The NMI can be masked off using a flag bit in port 70h.

The type of error that will trigger an NMI, such as a memory parity error, can be independently enabled or disabled. Refer to ports 61h and 461h in Chapter 13, System Functions.

Since NMI is normally shared, when an NMI occurs, all possible sources should be checked. Once the cause is identified and handled, the NMI can be cleared. When the handler's IRET is executed, new NMIs are allowed. If any remaining NMIs are pending, another NMI interrupt will immediately occur. Due to the hardware design, it is possible to get a phantom NMI after a valid NMI. If no source of the NMI is found, then the NMI handler should just exit normally.

When NMI is enabled, the system flags should be checked to determine the interrupting cause. Table 17-1 shows the most common functions on AT+ systems.

Table 17-1. NMI Status Bits

Port	Bit	Function
61h	7	1 = RAM parity error occurred
61h	6	1 = I/O Channel parity error occurred
461h	7	1 = Watchdog timeout occurred (EISA only)
461h	6	1 = Bus timeout occurred (EISA only)
461h	5	1 = I/O port status (EISA only)

Floating Point Coprocessor and NMI

The math coprocessor generates an interrupt in the event of an error. On all systems, a program that uses the math coprocessor must hook interrupt 2 (NMI) to catch possible math coprocessor error conditions. Since NMI is shared with other functions such as parity errors, the hooked routine must check to see what caused the interrupt. If the math coprocessor did not issue the interrupt, the prior interrupt 2 handler must be called.

On the PC and XT, the error interrupt line was connected to the CPU's NMI input (through a software controlled gate). On the AT, and all later systems, the math coprocessor error line is connected to IRQ 13 (interrupt 75h). To maintain compatibility with software designed for the PC and XT, the BIOS installs a service handler for interrupt 75h. When a math error occurs, the BIOS handler interrupt 75h removes the interrupt request, and issues an End-Of-Interrupt to the interrupt controller. At this point, the BIOS routine issues an interrupt 2 to simulate the NMI action of the PC and XT systems. The BIOS code fragment to handle interrupt 75h will appear similar to:

```
int_75h_entry:
        push    ax
        mov     al, 0
```

```
out     0F0h, al            ; clear math IRQ
mov     al, 20h
out     0A0h, al            ; issue EOI to controller 2
out     20h, al             ; issue EOI to controller 1
pop     ax
int     2                   ; issue NMI for compatibility
iret                        ; all done!
```

If you look at an 80286 or a later CPU manual, it describes the math coprocessor interrupt at decimal 16 (10h). This conflicts with what we just described and overlaps with the video services interrupt 10h! The 80286, and all later CPUs, have a separate math error interrupt in the processor. If this special error input were used, the CPU would issue interrupt 10h. No AT+ system uses this method because of the conflict it causes.

MCA System Differences

Unlike AT system's IRQ edge triggering, all MCA IRQ lines are level triggered. This means the hardware must remove its request before the interrupt service routine completes, otherwise the interrupt occurs again. Level triggered IRQ has two advantages over edge triggered. It is less susceptible to spurious noise, and it provides the option for multiple devices to share a single IRQ.

The nonmaskable interrupt can be triggered by one additional source in MCA systems. The watchdog timer's output (timer 3) is connected to the NMI. If the watchdog timeout occurs, NMI is triggered. Refer to System Timer 3 in Chapter 16, System Timers, for more details.

EISA System Differences

EISA systems offer the ability to control each individual IRQ line's trigger mechanism. Ports 4D0h and 4D1h allows the IRQ line to be edge triggered or level triggered. Internal trigger selection for IRQ 0, 1, 2, 8, and 13 is fixed by the motherboard designer, and should never be changed.

The NMI can be triggered by three additional sources in an EISA system. This includes the bus timeout, the watchdog timer, and I/O port status. Refer to port 461h in Chapter 13, System Functions, for additional details. The NMI is also triggered, if enabled, by a software write of any value to port 462h.

PCI System Differences

Level triggering is used for all interrupts from each PCI card slot. Because most PCI systems still have separate AT bus slots, the AT bus interrupts must remain edge triggered. Each PCI slot provides access to four interrupts. These four interrupts can be routed to any available IRQ through a programmable interrupt router. This router is typically part of the PCI chipset, and varies in capabilities and operation depending on the chipset vendor and implementation. The Plug and Play BIOS is responsible for resolving conflicts and assignment of IRQs to PCI cards. With level triggering, multiple PCI cards can share an interrupt if necessary.

When a specific IRQ is assigned to a PCI card, the router disconnects the IRQ from the AT backplane. This helps avoid a conflict between a PCI and AT type card when both are attempting to use the same IRQ.

Typical Uses

The hardware interrupts requests (IRQs) are divided into two classes. The first group of IRQs includes dedicated functions, such as processing the timer ticks for the clock, and keyboard servicing, among others. A second class of IRQs are provided for optional adapter cards. Most cards provide a means to select from one of the available IRQ lines in order to avoid conflicts with other adapter cards. In most cases, the IRQ selection is made manually using a specific switch or jumper on the adapter card. MCA, EISA, PCI, and a few other systems can select the IRQ through installation software.

The system BIOS initializes and programs the interrupt controller. In most cases the only non-BIOS access to the interrupt controller is sending the command to clear the current interrupt and checking the interrupt in progress bits. In rare cases, software may also program the interrupt controller.

Tables 17-2 and 17-3 summarize the users of interrupt requests and each associated interrupt. Interrupt request lines attached to the system are directly connected to hardware on the motherboard. Other interrupt request lines are available to adapter cards through the backplane. Only the most common adapter usage is shown, but many other adapter cards use IRQ lines.

Table 17-2. Original PC Interrupt Request Users

Int Request	Line Attached to	Interrupt Controller	Int Vector	Source of IRQ
IRQ 0	System	1	8	System timer 0 output
IRQ 1	System	1	9	Keyboard
IRQ 2	Backplane	1	A	Parallel port 2
IRQ 3	Backplane	1	B	Serial port 2
IRQ 4	Backplane	1	C	Serial port 1

Table 17-2 Continued

Int Request	Line Attached to	Interrupt Controller	Int Vector	Source of IRQ
IRQ 5	Backplane	1	D	Hard disk
IRQ 6	Backplane	1	E	Diskette controller
IRQ 7	Backplane	1	F	Parallel port 1

IRQ 2 to 7 are available in any adapter slot.

Table 17-3. AT+ Interrupt Request Users

Int Request	Line Attached to	Interrupt Controller	Int Vector	Source of IRQ
IRQ 0	System	1	8	System timer 0 output
IRQ 1	System	1	9	Keyboard controller
IRQ 2	System	1	none	Cascade for controller 2
IRQ 3	Backplane	1	B	Serial ports 2 & 4, Network card
IRQ 4	Backplane	1	C	Serial ports 1 & 3
IRQ 5	Backplane	1	D	Parallel port 2, Network card
IRQ 6	Backplane	1	E	Diskette controller
IRQ 7	Backplane	1	F	Parallel port 1
IRQ 8	System	2	70	CMOS Real-Time Clock
IRQ 9	Backplane	2	A/71	EGA/VGA vertical retrace option
IRQ 10	Backplane-16	2	72	
IRQ 11	Backplane-16	2	73	
IRQ 12	Backplane-16	2	74	Motherboard mouse port
IRQ 13	System	2	75	Math coprocessor error, DMA
IRQ 14	Backplane-16	2	76	Hard disk controller (primary)
IRQ 15	Backplane-16	2	77	Hard disk controller (secondary)

IRQ 3 to 7, and 9 are available in any slot. IRQ 10, 11, 12, 14, and 15 are only available to a 16-bit card in a 16-bit adapter slot on AT+ systems. PCI card slots provide configurable access to IRQs.

Since IRQ 2 is used to cascade interrupt controller 2 to controller 1, it is not available for use. Because of a clever design, IRQ 2 is made to appear available. IRQ 9 is now connected to the same backplane line as was originally marked IRQ 2 in the PC/XT. To maintain full compatibility with the original PC, if an adapter uses the hardware line for IRQ 2/9 (one line), interrupt 71h is issued. The BIOS interrupt 71h handler calls the interrupt Ah handler, where IRQ 2 would have gone on the original PC. In this manner, use of IRQ 2 by an adapter card appears to function the same on both PC/XT and AT class machines. No software changes are necessary.

Interrupt Data Areas

Interrupt vectors are stored at the bottom 1K of memory, holding 256 interrupt pointers. In addition, the BIOS on most systems uses a byte to record occurrences of unused software and hardware interrupts. Table 17-4 briefly summarizes these locations. A complete listing of interrupt vectors is shown in Chapter 7, Interrupt Vector Table.

Table 17-4. BIOS Data Areas

Address	Size	Name	Function
0:0	dword	Int vector 0	Divide error
0:4	dword	Int vector 1	Debug
0:8	dword	Int vector 2	Non-Maskable Interrupt
	.		
	.		
0:3FCh	dword	Int vector FF	Unused vector
40:6Bh	byte	Unused_int	The interrupt number is stored here if a hardware interrupt occurs that has no related interrupt service routine. If a software interrupt occurs without an interrupt service routine, the value FFh is stored in this byte.

Warnings

Noise Glitches Although a noise glitch should never occur, a poor bus design or badly designed adapter card could cause an occasional glitch to occur on an IRQ line. The noise glitch will trigger an invalid interrupt. If the glitch occurs on IRQ 0 to IRQ 7, interrupt F will be called. If the glitch occurs on IRQ 8 to IRQ 15, interrupt 77h will be called. The service handler for interrupts Fh and 77h should read the In-Service register to confirm that a real interrupt occurred. An invalid interrupt has In-Service bit 7 cleared, and a valid interrupt has bit 7 set. See command 3 of port 20h to read the In-Service register for interrupt F. For interrupt 77h, use command 3 of port A0h to read the In-Service register in the second interrupt controller.

Interrupt Priorities It is usually best to avoid changing the interrupt priorities. It is difficult to know whether some other hardware device relies on the default priority levels. Be aware that no priority management is provided, should different programs need to change priorities. The last program to change the priorities cannot provide notification to other programs that may have already changed the priorities.

Programs that use the serial ports at high baud rates often change the interrupt priority, because bytes will be lost if the serial port is not serviced frequently enough. In this case the keyboard and system timer are usually placed at a lower priority than the serial port.

COM2, IRQ 3 It has been reported that IRQ 3 (interrupt Bh) for COM 2 can cause problems to software when a DOS extender such as PharLap or Rational Systems is in use. This is most likely because INT 0Bh is also the protected-mode Segment Not Present exception. For users of IRQ 3, it is recommended that the In-Service bit be checked before assuming a real interrupt occurred. The following code fragment will assure correct operation in these circumstances, for a normal nonshared IRQ 3:

```
int_Bh_entry:
        push    ax
        cli                             ; disable interrupts
        mov     al, 0Bh                 ; command to read ISR
        out     20h, al
        IODELAY
        in      al, 20h                 ; get In-Service Register
        sti                             ; enable interrupts
        test    al, 8                   ; is IRQ 3 in-service ?
        jz      int_Bh_exit             ; jump if not

         user code goes here

int_Bh_exit:
        pop     ax
        iret
```

CPU Overlaps and IRQ 5 There is an overlap of interrupt usage for interrupts 5 through 10h. Intel specifically indicated all interrupts 0 to 1Fh were reserved for future CPU internal use. However, IBM ignored this in the PC design and proceeded to use many of these interrupts for other purposes. For example, the PC defined interrupt 5 as the print screen function, an overlap with the 80286's bound-range-exceeded interrupt. The 80386 and higher processors define many more interrupts that overlap with the PC's BIOS interrupts. IRQ 0 through 7 are preset to use interrupt vectors 8 to Fh, the same vectors reserved for a number of processor fault conditions.

Surprisingly, these interrupt overlaps do not cause many problems. Most of the processor fault interrupts are restricted to protected or V86 modes. This means that only developers who write protected mode software need to be concerned with overlaps. The one exception is interrupt D. This is used by the 80386 and later processors for the General Protection (GP) fault.

General protection faults can occur in both real and protected modes. Since the sort of things that trip the GP fault are serious errors, it is generally ignored in real mode. The type of errors include things like accessing a data word at offset FFFFh or an instruction length of over 15 bytes. GP faults also occur when any protected mode instruction is used in V86 mode.

If very high interrupt rates or extremely quick response is required, avoid the use of IRQ 5 (interrupt D) when the system is in virtual (V86) mode. This may be difficult to do, because so few IRQs are available for use. On machines with the 386 or later CPU operating in V86 mode, interrupt D is used for the GP fault. This interrupt is generated by the processor to handle various processor faults, and passed to the protected mode manager to deal with. The system operates in V86 mode with any 386 memory manager.

Due to the design of the processor in V86 mode, the protected mode manager is given control before the user's interrupt service routine. For interrupt D, the protected mode manager must determine whether a fault occurred, and pass control to the original interrupt service routine if no fault is found. Unfortunately, determining what caused the GP fault requires a considerable amount of code to find out whether a fault occurred and to take any necessary action. This causes a significant response delay on slower systems when passing control back to the original interrupt service routine.

Most floating point libraries emulate the floating point processor when the FPU is not present. For any floating point instruction, an interrupt is issued to get to the appropriate emulation routine. This can add extensive delays in V86 mode, with the additional overhead required to process each interrupt.

All other interrupts are subject to a some delay due to V86 mode. Again, the processor gives control first to the protected mode manager, which must then pass control back to the original interrupt service handler. Since little, if any, action is necessary by the protected mode manager for any interrupt other than D, this effect is often minimal. The Pentium processor appears to provide a new mechanism to avoid going into protected mode for every interrupt. Though it does not help the problem with interrupt D, it can help ensure maximum interrupt response for many other interrupts.

Code Sample 17-1. IRQ Redirection

IRQ_REDIRECT boosts the performance of the hardware device attached to IRQ 5, by separating IRQ 5 from the processor's general protection fault interrupt D. After IRQ_REDIRECT is run, when the hardware device issues a IRQ, the interrupt controller uses interrupts 50h through 57h instead of interrupts 8 to F. This keeps the protected mode manager from having to perform extra processing each time IRQ 5 occurs, since IRQ5 no longer uses interrupt D. The code fragment for these routines resides in IRQREDIR.ASM on the supplied diskette.

```
;--------------------------------------------------------------
;    IRQ_REDIRECT
;        Redirect IRQ 0 through 7 to an alternate set of
;        interrupt vectors. This may boost performance when the
;        system is in V86 mode if IRQ 5 is used for high
;        interrupt rates. See the Warnings section for more
;        about the conflict between IRQ 5 and interrupt 0Dh.
;
;        Some software such as OS/2, Desqview, DoubleDOS, and the
;        IBM 3270 emulator perform a similar task, usually to get
;        these functions before any application can. This is
;        useful when multitasking software must appear to share
;        hardware with software applications that never intended
;        this!  Do not use this with any of those programs.
;
;        Notes: 1) No check is made to see if interrupt 50h to
;                  57h is in use before the vectors are changed.
;               2) Any program or TSR that hooks interrupts 8 to
;                  0Fh after IRQ_redirect is run, will never get
;                  access to that interrupt! See the notes immediately
;                  after this listing for an alternative approach.
;
;        Regs used:      ax, cx, di, si, ds, es

IRQ_redirect    proc    near
        cli                             ; disable interrupts

                                        ; Program int controller 1
                                        ; -----------------------
        in      al, 21h                 ; get current interrupt mask
        mov     ah, al                  ; save for later
        IODELAY
        mov     al, 11h                 ; Init command 1, cascade &
        out     20h, al                 ;   require 4th init byte
```

```
        IODELAY
        mov     al, 50h                 ; Init command 2
        out     21h, al                 ;   switch IRQ's to int 50h
        IODELAY
        mov     al, 4                   ; Init command 3
        out     21h, al                 ;   slave controller on IRQ 2
        IODELAY
        mov     al, 1                   ; Init command 4, normal EOI
        out     21h, al                 ;   nonbuffered, 80x86
        IODELAY
        mov     al, ah                  ; Operation command 1
        out     21h, al                 ;   restore interrupt mask

                                        ; Now copy interrupt vectors
                                        ; -------------------------
        xor     ax, ax
        mov     es, ax                  ; set segment registers to
        mov     ds, ax                  ;   point to interrupt table
        mov     cx, 8 * 2               ; number of words to transfer
        mov     si, 8 * 4               ; start at interrupt 8
        mov     di, 50h * 4             ; xfer to interrupt 50-57h
        cld
        rep     movsw                   ; transfer interrupt vectors
        sti                             ; enable interrupts
        ret
IRQ_redirect    endp
```

As an alternative, each interrupt 50h to 57h could call one of eight interrupt routines. These, in turn, call the vector installed at 8 through F. This approach can be used for multitasking or when it is necessary to get interrupt control before or after anyone else who might hook the vector of interest. Instead of copying the vectors as was done above, interrupts 50 through 57h point to eight routines similar to the interrupt 51h routine below.

```
;-------------------------------------------------------------
;     INTERRUPT_51h
;         Alternate code - see text in book
```

```
;
;       Registers used: all

Interrupt_51h   proc    far

; <<<< possible code here, for operations prior to anyone else >>>>

        push    ax
        push    es
        mov     ax, 0
        mov     es, ax                  ; segment of int table
        mov     ax, es:[9 * 4]          ; current int 9 offset
        mov     cs:[old_int_9_off], ax  ; save
        mov     ax, es:[9 * 4 + 2]      ; current int 9 segment
        mov     cs:[old_int_9_seg], ax  ; save
        pop     es
        pop     ax
        pushf
        call    dword ptr cs:[old_int_9_off] ; call current int9

; <<<< possible code here, for operations after anyone else >>>>

        ret     2                   ; get rid of extra flags
Interrupt_51h   endp

old_int_9_off   dw      0           ; temporary int 9 offset
old_int_9_seg   dw      0           ; temporary int 9 segment
```

Normally, interrupts are hooked by a TSR or driver to get control when a specific interrupt occurs. Hooking interrupts is a well-defined means to get control. These code examples are not recommended as approaches to getting control, except in the most unusual case.

Port Summary

This is a list of ports used to control the 8259 interrupt controller(s).

Port	Type	Function	Platform
20h	Input	8259-1 Read Interrupt Request/Service Registers	All
20h	Output	8259-1 Interrupt Command	All
21h	Input	8259-1 Interrupt Mask Register	All
21h	Output	8259-1 Interrupt Commands	All
70h	Output	NMI Enable	AT+
A0h	Input	8259-2 Read Interrupt Request/Service Registers	AT+
A0h	Output	8259-2 Interrupt Command	AT+
A0h	Output	Non-Maskable Interrupt Control	PC/XT
A1h	Input	8259-2 Interrupt Mask Register	AT+
A1h	Output	8259-2 Interrupt Commands	AT+
462h	Output	Trigger NMI	EISA
4D0h	I/O	8259-1 IRQ Trigger Type	EISA
4D1h	I/O	8259-2 IRQ Trigger Type	EISA

Port Detail

Port	Type	Description	Platform
20h	Input	8259-1 Read Interrupt Request/ Service Registers	All

This function reads the contents of the Interrupt Request Register (IRR) or the Interrupt Service Register (ISR). You specify which register to read by sending a command to port 20h. A command value of 0Ah selects IRR, and value 0Bh selects ISR. Once a command is sent, multiple reads can be made to get the contents of the same register. It is not necessary to resend the register selection command.

Refer to Port 20h, Output commands 0Ah and 0Bh for more details about these registers.

Port	Type	Description	Platform
20h	Output	8259-1 Interrupt Command	All

This controls initialization and operation of the interrupt controller for interrupt request lines 0 to 7. The most common use is the issuance of the End-of-Interrupt, command 20h. This is accomplished by:

```
        mov     AL, 20h
        out     20h, AL                 ; issue EOI
```

Initialization

Normally only the BIOS, during a reset, will initialize the interrupt controller. The initialization process requires sending an 8-bit command to port 20h, followed by two to three 8-bit commands to port 21h in sequence. Only allowable options are shown, as other selections are not compatible with PC platforms. See port 21h for the other initialization bytes.

Output (bits 0-7), Initialization command 1

bit	7 w = 0	Unused
	6 w = 0	Unused
	5 w = 0	Unused
	4 w = 1	Signifies—Initiate Initialization
	3 w = 0	Edge triggered mode (PC, XT, AT)
	1	Level triggered mode (MCA)
	x	Unused (EISA—controlled from port 4D0h)
	2 w = 0	Unused
	1 w = 0	Cascade mode (when two controllers are used, AT+)
	1	Single mode (when only one controller, PC/XT)
	0 w = 1	Require 4th initialization byte

Normal Operation

Once the interrupt controller has been initialized, this port accepts a number of commands. The commands are detailed after the bits are defined for each command.

Output (bits 0-7), Operation command 2

bit	7 w = x	Subcommand (* indicates rarely used commands)		
	6 w = x	bit 7	bit 6	bit 5
	5 w = x	0	0	0 = rotate in auto-EOI mode (clear)*
		0	0	1 = nonspecific EOI
		0	1	0 = no operation*
		0	1	1 = specific EOI*
		1	0	0 = rotate in auto-EOI mode (set)*
		1	0	1 = rotate on nonspecific EOI*
		1	1	0 = set priority command
		1	1	1 = rotate on specific EOI*
	4 w = 0	Signifies—Command 2		
	3 w = 0			

2 w = x	Priority level (commands: set priority, rotate on specific EOI)
1 w = x	bit 2 bit 1 bit 0 lowest highest
0 w = x	0 0 0 = IRQ 0 IRQ 1
	0 0 1 = IRQ 1 IRQ 2
	0 1 0 = IRQ 2 IRQ 3
	0 1 1 = IRQ 3 IRQ 4
	1 0 0 = IRQ 4 IRQ 5
	1 0 1 = IRQ 5 IRQ 6
	1 1 0 = IRQ 6 IRQ 7
	1 1 1 = IRQ 7 IRQ 0 (default)
	In-Service bit to reset (command: specific EOI)
	bit 2 bit 1 bit 0
	0 0 0 = Reset In-Service bit 0
	0 0 1 = Reset In-Service bit 1
	0 1 0 = Reset In-Service bit 2
	0 1 1 = Reset In-Service bit 3
	1 0 0 = Reset In-Service bit 4
	1 0 1 = Reset In-Service bit 5
	1 1 0 = Reset In-Service bit 6
	1 1 1 = Reset In-Service bit 7

Output (bits 0-7), Operation command 3

bit 7 w = 0	fixed
6 w = x	Special mask mode
5 w = x	bit 7 bit 6
	0 x = no action
	1 0 = clear special mask mode
	1 1 = set special mask mode
4 w = 0	Signifies—Command 3
3 w = 1	
2 w = 0	no poll command
1 w = x	Read specified register
0 w = x	bit 1 bit 0
	0 x = no action
	1 0 = read interrupt request register
	1 1 = read in-service register

Command Summary

Number	Port 20h Commands
00h	Rotate in Automatic EOI Mode (clear)
0Ah	Read Interrupt Request Register
0Bh	Read Interrupt In-Service Register
20h	End Of Interrupt Command
40h	No Operation
48h	Clear Special Mask Mode
60h	Specific EOI—IRQ 0
61h	Specific EOI—IRQ 1
62h	Specific EOI—IRQ 2
63h	Specific EOI—IRQ 3
64h	Specific EOI—IRQ 4
65h	Specific EOI—IRQ 5
66h	Specific EOI—IRQ 6
67h	Specific EOI—IRQ 7
68h	Set Special Mask Mode
80h	Rotate in auto-EOI mode (set)
A0h	Rotate on nonspecific EOI
C0h	IRQ 0 Lowest Priority
C1h	IRQ 1 Lowest Priority
C2h	IRQ 2 Lowest Priority
C3h	IRQ 3 Lowest Priority
C4h	IRQ 4 Lowest Priority
C5h	IRQ 5 Lowest Priority
C6h	IRQ 6 Lowest Priority
C7h	IRQ 7 Lowest Priority
E0h	EOI and IRQ 0 Lowest Priority
E1h	EOI and IRQ 1 Lowest Priority
E2h	EOI and IRQ 2 Lowest Priority
E3h	EOI and IRQ 3 Lowest Priority
E4h	EOI and IRQ 4 Lowest Priority
E5h	EOI and IRQ 5 Lowest Priority
E6h	EOI and IRQ 6 Lowest Priority
E7h	EOI and IRQ 7 Lowest Priority

Command Detail

Command	Description	Port
00h	Rotate in Automatic EOI Mode (clear)	20h

★★★

This command is technically available in the 8259, but Automatic EOI mode is not a real option on any PC system, making this command unusable. If the interrupt controller is in automatic EOI mode, it issues an End-Of-Interrupt command as soon as the interrupt acknowledge is returned from the CPU. A bug in early 8259 chips, with a copyright prior to 1985, prevented automatic EOI from working in the second interrupt controller when two controllers are used. Hopefully, all these old chips are history by now.

Command	Description	Port
0Ah	Read Interrupt Request Register	20h

★★★

After this command is issued, the next read from port 20h will get the contents of the Interrupt Request Register. When an interrupt request is made, the associated bit is set on. Interrupts should be disabled before issuing this command, and can be re-enabled after the register is read from port 20h.

The Interrupt Request register is useful to see if any hardware interrupts are pending while interrupts are disabled. The register can also be used inside an interrupt service handler to identify if lower-priority interrupts are pending.

Input (bits 0-7)

bit	7	w = 1 IRQ 7 requests service
	6	w = 1 IRQ 6 requests service
	5	w = 1 IRQ 5 requests service
	4	w = 1 IRQ 4 requests service
	3	w = 1 IRQ 3 requests service
	2	w = 1 IRQ 2 requests service
	1	w = 1 IRQ 1 requests service
	0	w = 1 IRQ 0 requests service

Command	Description	Port
0Bh	Read Interrupt In-Service Register	20h

★★★

After this command is issued, the next read from port 20h will get the contents of the Interrupt In-Service Register. This register contains the interrupts that are currently being serviced.

In most cases, only one interrupt is being serviced, but should a higher-priority interrupt occur during the processing of a lower-priority interrupt, multiple interrupts will be indicated in this register. The Interrupt In-Service register is also used on 80286 or later systems to determine whether an interrupt was caused by hardware or by a CPU exception. If the interrupt occurs without having the related in-service bit set, it indicates the CPU caused the interrupt and not the hardware.

An End-Of-Interrupt (EOI) command clears the current highest priority in-service bit.

Input (bits 0-7)

bit	7	w = 1	IRQ 7 in-service
	6	w = 1	IRQ 6 in-service
	5	w = 1	IRQ 5 in-service
	4	w = 1	IRQ 4 in-service
	3	w = 1	IRQ 3 in-service
	2	w = 1	IRQ 2 in-service
	1	w = 1	IRQ 1 in-service
	0	w = 1	IRQ 0 in-service

★★★

Command	Description	Port
20h	End-Of-Interrupt Command (EOI)	20h

At the end of a hardware interrupt service routine, the routine issues an End-Of-Interrupt (EOI) command for IRQ 0 to 7. This instructs the interrupt controller to accept additional interrupts, and accept lower priority interrupts that were locked out during the processing of the current interrupt.

When using IRQ 8 to 15, it is necessary to first issue a EOI command to the second interrupt controller (port A0h), followed by another EOI to the master interrupt controller (port 20h).

★★★

Command	Description	Port
40h	No Operation	20h

This subcommand performs no operation. It is a rarely, if ever, used command.

★★★

Command	Description	Port
48h	Clear Special Mask Mode	20h

Restores controller to normal operations. See Set Special Mask Mode for details of this operation.

★★★

Command	Description	Port
60-67h	Specific EOI	20h

Resets one specific In-Service bit for an IRQ, allowing a new interrupt to be serviced. Commands 60h through 67h relate to IRQ 0 through 7, respectively. For the PC family, command 20h, general EOI is normally used instead of these commands to clear the appropriate In-Service bit.

Command	Description	Port
68h	Set Special Mask Mode	20h

Activates Special Mask Mode operation. In some cases, an interrupt service routine may wish to allow lower priority interrupts to occur during a portion of the current service routine. Normal operation prevents any other lower interrupt requests from processing until the current higher priority interrupt routine is complete. With the special mask mode set, the mask register can be updated (port 21h) to disable the current request, and allow any others requests, including those of a lower priority level.

Before the completion of the service routine that initiated the special mask mode, the routine must clear special mask mode and restore the mask register to the prior state.

Command	Description	Port
80h	Rotate in Auto-EOI Mode (set)	20h

This command is technically available in the 8259, but Automatic EOI mode is not a real option on any PC system, making this command unusable.

Command	Description	Port
A0h	Rotate on nonspecific EOI	20h

This command performs two actions. When issued at the end of an interrupt service routine, the interrupt controller switches the completed interrupt to the lowest priority and then accepts additional interrupts.

This is a rarely used command in the PC environment. To use this method requires that all interrupt service routines issue this command upon completion. It is not practical to use this option unless you are creating a custom system BIOS. Instead, all BIOS routines use the non-specific EOI command, 20h.

Command	Description	Port
C0-C7h	IRQ Lowest Priority	20h

Sets one IRQ to the lowest priority. Commands C0h through C7h relate to making IRQ 0 through 7 the lowest priority. The action is summarized in Table 17-5.

Table 17-5. Commanded Priority

Command	Priority Lowest Highest
C0h	0 7 6 5 4 3 2 1
C1h	1 0 7 6 5 4 3 2
C2h	2 1 0 7 6 5 4 3
C3h	3 2 1 0 7 6 5 4

Table 17-5 Continued

Command	Priority Lowest Highest
C4h	4 3 2 1 0 7 6 5
C5h	5 4 3 2 1 0 7 6
C6h	6 5 4 3 2 1 0 7
C7h	7 6 5 4 3 2 1 0

Command	Description	Port
E0-E7h	EOI and Set Lowest Priority	20h

This command performs two actions. It is issued at the end of an interrupt service routine to perform the same actions as a specific EOI and allow the next interrupt. See commands 60h to 67h for more about specific EOI. The second action is to set an IRQ to the lowest priority. Commands E0h through E7h relate to making IRQ 0 through 7 the lowest priority. The action is summarized in Table 17-6.

These commands are not normally used in the PC family environment. They are intended for systems in which all interrupts have a equal priority. If all eight interrupts were always active, each would be assured of being serviced once every eight times.

Table 17-6. EOI and Commanded Priority

Command	Priority Lowest Highest	Specific EOI
E0h	0 7 6 5 4 3 2 1	IRQ 0
E1h	1 0 7 6 5 4 3 2	IRQ 1
E2h	2 1 0 7 6 5 4 3	IRQ 2
E3h	3 2 1 0 7 6 5 4	IRQ 3
E4h	4 3 2 1 0 7 6 5	IRQ 4
E5h	5 4 3 2 1 0 7 6	IRQ 5
E6h	6 5 4 3 2 1 0 7	IRQ 6
E7h	7 6 5 4 3 2 1 0	IRQ 7

Port	Type	Description	Platform
21h	Input	8259-1 Interrupt Mask Register	All

The interrupt mask register indicates which interrupt requests are allowed (value 0) and which are disabled (value 1).

Input (bits 0-7) Interrupt Mask Register

bit	7	w = 0 IRQ 7 Enabled
	6	w = 0 IRQ 6 Enabled
	5	w = 0 IRQ 5 Enabled
	4	w = 0 IRQ 4 Enabled
	3	w = 0 IRQ 3 Enabled
	2	w = 0 IRQ 2 Enabled
	1	w = 0 IRQ 1 Enabled
	0	w = 0 IRQ 0 Enabled

Port	Type	Description	Platform
21h	Output	8259-1 Interrupt Commands	All

This controls initialization and operation of the interrupt controller for interrupt request lines 0 to 7.

Initialization

After the initialization command is sent from port 20h, two to three additional bytes complete the process. Initialization command byte 3 is skipped when using single mode as specified in the initialization command 1, bit 1=1 (PC/XT).

Output (bits 0-7), Initialization command 2

bit	7	w = 0	Specify group of 8 interrupts for this controller
	6	w = 0	bits 7 6 5 4 3
	5	w = 0	0 0 0 0 0 = use vectors 0-7
	4	w = 0	0 0 0 0 1 = use vectors 8-F (normal)
	3	w = 1	. . . . .
			1 1 1 1 1 = use vectors F8-FF
	2	w = 0	Unused
	1	w = 0	Unused
	0	w = 0	Unused

Output (bits 0-7), Initialization command 3

bit	7	w = 0	no slave attached to IRQ 7
	6	w = 0	no slave attached to IRQ 6
	5	w = 0	no slave attached to IRQ 5
	4	w = 0	no slave attached to IRQ 4
	3	w = 0	no slave attached to IRQ 3

2 w = 0	no slave attached to IRQ 2 (PC/XT default)
1	slave controller attached to IRQ 2 (AT+ default)
1 w = 0	no slave attached to IRQ 1
0 w = 0	no slave attached to IRQ 0

Output (bits 0-7), Initialization command 4

bit	7 w = 0	Unused
	6 w = 0	Unused
	5 w = 0	Unused
	4 w = 0	Not special fully nested mode
	3 w = x	Buffered mode
	2 w = x	bit 3 bit 2
		0 x = nonbuffered (AT+)
		1 0 = buffered (PC/XT)
	1 w = 0	Normal End Of Interrupt (EOI)
	1	Automatic End Of Interrupt (not supported on any system)
	0 w = 1	80x86 mode

Normal Operation

Once the interrupt controller has been initialized, individual interrupt request lines can be disabled or enabled. Setting a bit to 1 disables the request. At the end of the BIOS POST operations, all interrupts are enabled.

Output (bits 0-7), Operation command 1

bit	7 w = 0	Enable IRQ 7
	6 w = 0	Enable IRQ 6
	5 w = 0	Enable IRQ 5
	4 w = 0	Enable IRQ 4
	3 w = 0	Enable IRQ 3
	2 w = 0	Enable IRQ 2
	1 w = 0	Enable IRQ 1
	0 w = 0	Enable IRQ 0

Port	Type	Description	Platform
70h	Output	NMI Enable	AT+

NMI is enabled automatically at the end of POST. A write to this port will set the state of NMI. Because CMOS memory can only be accessed with additional reads or writes to port 71h, the value for the lower 7 bits is unimportant.

Output (bits 0-7) CMOS address and NMI

bit	7	w = 0	Allow Non-Maskable Interrupt, NMI interrupt 2
		1	NMI disabled (used in normal access to CMOS RAM)
	6	w = x	Unused
	5	w = x	CMOS RAM address (see port 70h in CMOS chapter)
	4	w = x	
	3	w = x	
	2	w = x	
	1	w = x	
	0	w = x	

Port	Type	Description	Platform
A0h	Input	8259-2 Read Interrupt Request/ Service Registers	AT+

This command reads the contents of the Interrupt Request Register (IRR) or the Interrupt Service Register (ISR). Specify which register to read by sending a command to port A0h. A command value of 0Ah selects IRR, and value 0Bh selects ISR. Once a command is sent, multiple reads can be made to get the contents of the same register. It is not necessary to resend the register selection command.

Refer to Port A0h, Output commands 0Ah and 0Bh for more details about these registers.

Port	Type	Description	Platform
A0h	Output	8259-2 Interrupt Command	AT+

This controls initialization and operation of the interrupt controller for interrupt request lines 8 to 15.

Initialization

Normally only the BIOS, during a reset, will initialize the interrupt controller. The initialization process requires sending an 8-bit command to port A0h, followed by two to three 8-bit commands to port A1h, in sequence. Only allowable options are shown, as other selections are not compatible with PC platforms. See port A1h for the other initialization bytes.

Output (bits 0-7), Initialization command 1

bit	7	w = 0	Unused
	6	w = 0	Unused
	5	w = 0	Unused
	4	w = 1	Signifies—Initiate Initialization
	3	w = 0	Edge triggered mode (AT)
		1	Level triggered mode (MCA)
		x	Unused (EISA—controlled from port 4D1h)
	2	w = 0	Unused
	1	w = 0	Cascade mode (when two controllers are used, AT+)
	0	w = 1	Require 4th initialization byte

Normal Operation

Once the interrupt controller has been initialized, this port accepts a number of commands. The commands are detailed after the bits are defined for each command.

Output (bits 0-7), Operation command 2

bit	7	w = x	Subcommand (* indicates rarely used commands)				
	6	w = x	bit 7	bit 6	bit 5		
	5	w = x	0	0	0 = rotate in auto-EOI mode (clear)*		
			0	0	1 = nonspecific EOI		
			0	1	0 = no operation*		
			0	1	1 = specific EOI*		
			1	0	0 = rotate in auto-EOI mode (set)*		
			1	0	1 = rotate on nonspecific EOI*		
			1	1	0 = set priority command		
			1	1	1 = rotate on specific EOI*		
	4	w = 0	Signifies—Command 2				
	3	w = 0					
	2	w = x	Priority level (commands: set priority, rotate on specific EOI)				
	1	w = x	bit 2	bit 1	bit 0	lowest	highest
	0	w = x	0	0	0 =	IRQ 8	IRQ 9
			0	0	1 =	IRQ 9	IRQ 10
			0	1	0 =	IRQ 10	IRQ 11
			0	1	1 =	IRQ 11	IRQ 12
			1	0	0 =	IRQ 12	IRQ 13

1	0	1 =	IRQ 13	IRQ 14
1	1	0 =	IRQ 14	IRQ 15
1	1	1 =	IRQ 15	IRQ 8 (default)

In-Service bit to reset (command: specific EOI)

bit 2	bit 1	bit 0
0	0	0 = Reset In-Service bit 0
0	0	1 = Reset In-Service bit 1
0	1	0 = Reset In-Service bit 2
0	1	1 = Reset In-Service bit 3
1	0	0 = Reset In-Service bit 4
1	0	1 = Reset In-Service bit 5
1	1	0 = Reset In-Service bit 6
1	1	1 = Reset In-Service bit 7

Output (bits 0-7), Operation command 3

bit 7 w = 0 — fixed

6 w = x, 5 w = x — Special mask mode

bit 7	bit 6
0	x = no action
1	0 = clear special mask mode
1	1 = set special mask mode

4 w = 0, 3 w = 1 — Signifies—Command 3

2 w = 0 — no poll command

1 w = x, 0 w = x — Read specified register

bit 1	bit 0
0	x = no action
1	0 = read interrupt request register
1	1 = read in-service register

Command Summary

Number	Port A0h Commands
00h	Rotate in Automatic EOI Mode (clear)
0Ah	Read Interrupt Request Register
0Bh	Read Interrupt In-Service Register
20h	End-Of-Interrupt Command
40h	No Operation
48h	Clear Special Mask Mode
60h	Specific EOI—IRQ 8

Number	Port A0h Commands
61h	Specific EOI—IRQ 9
62h	Specific EOI—IRQ 10
63h	Specific EOI—IRQ 11
64h	Specific EOI—IRQ 12
65h	Specific EOI—IRQ 13
66h	Specific EOI—IRQ 14
67h	Specific EOI—IRQ 15
68h	Set Special Mask Mode
80h	Rotate in auto-EOI mode (set)
A0h	Rotate on nonspecific EOI
C0h	IRQ 8 Lowest Priority
C1h	IRQ 9 Lowest Priority
C2h	IRQ 10 Lowest Priority
C3h	IRQ 11 Lowest Priority
C4h	IRQ 12 Lowest Priority
C5h	IRQ 13 Lowest Priority
C6h	IRQ 14 Lowest Priority
C7h	IRQ 15 Lowest Priority
E0h	EOI and IRQ 8 Lowest Priority
E1h	EOI and IRQ 9 Lowest Priority
E2h	EOI and IRQ 10 Lowest Priority
E3h	EOI and IRQ 11 Lowest Priority
E4h	EOI and IRQ 12 Lowest Priority
E5h	EOI and IRQ 13 Lowest Priority
E6h	EOI and IRQ 14 Lowest Priority
E7h	EOI and IRQ 15 Lowest Priority

Command Detail

★★★

Command	Description	Port
00h	Rotate in Automatic EOI Mode (clear)	A0h

This command is technically available in the 8259, but Automatic EOI mode is not a real option on any PC system, making this command unusable. See command 00h under port 20h for details.

★★★

Command	Description	Port
0Ah	Read Interrupt Request Register	A0h

After this command is issued, the next read from port A0h will get the contents of the Interrupt Request Register. When an interrupt request is made, the associated bit is set on. Interrupts should be disabled before issuing this command, and can be re-enabled after the register is read from port 20h.

Input (bits 0-7)

bit 7 w = 1 IRQ 15 requests service
6 w = 1 IRQ 14 requests service
5 w = 1 IRQ 13 requests service
4 w = 1 IRQ 12 requests service
3 w = 1 IRQ 11 requests service
2 w = 1 IRQ 10 requests service
1 w = 1 IRQ 9 requests service
0 w = 1 IRQ 8 requests service

Command	Description	Port
0Bh	Read Interrupt In-Service Register	A0h

After this command is issued, the next read from port A0h will get the contents of the Interrupt In-Service Register. This register contains the interrupts that are currently being serviced. Interrupts should be disabled before this command, and can be re-enabled after the register is read from port 20h.

In most cases, only one interrupt is being serviced, but should a higher priority interrupt occur during the processing of a lower priority interrupt, multiple interrupts will be indicated in this register.

An End-Of-Interrupt (EOI) command clears the current highest priority in-service bit.

Input (bits 0-7)

bit 7 w = 1 IRQ 15 in-service
6 w = 1 IRQ 14 in-service
5 w = 1 IRQ 13 in-service
4 w = 1 IRQ 12 in-service
3 w = 1 IRQ 11 in-service
2 w = 1 IRQ 10 in-service
1 w = 1 IRQ 9 in-service
0 w = 1 IRQ 8 in-service

Command	Description	Port
20h	End-Of-Interrupt Command (EOI)	A0h

At the end of a hardware interrupt service routine, the routine issues an End-Of-Interrupt (EOI) command for IRQ 8 to 15. This informs the interrupt controller to accept additional interrupts, and accept lower priority interrupts that were locked out during the processing of the current interrupt.

When using IRQ 8 to 15, it is necessary to first issue an EOI command to the second interrupt controller (port A0h), followed by another EOI to the master interrupt controller (port 20h).

★★★

Command	Description	Port
40h	No Operation	A0h

This command performs no operation. It is a rarely, if ever, used command.

★★★

Command	Description	Port
48h	Clear Special Mask Mode	A0h

Restores controller to normal operations. See Set Special Mask Mode for details of this operation.

★★★

Command	Description	Port
60-67h	Specific EOI	A0h

Resets one specific In-Service bit for an IRQ. Commands 60h through 67h on port A0h relate to IRQ 8 through 15, respectively. For the PC family, command 20h, general EOI is normally used instead of these commands to clear the appropriate In-Service bit.

★★★

Command	Description	Port
68h	Set Special Mask Mode	A0h

Activates Special Mask Mode operation. In some cases, you might want an interrupt service routine to allow lower priority interrupts to occur during a portion of the current service routine. Normal operation prevents any other lower interrupt requests to be processed until the current higher-priority interrupt routine is complete. With the special mask mode set, the mask register can be updated (port A1h) to disable the current request and allow any other requests, including those of a lower-priority level.

Before the completion of the service routine that initiated the special mask mode, the routine must clear special mask mode and restore the mask register to the prior state.

★★★

Command	Description	Port
80h	Rotate in Auto-EOI Mode (set)	A0h

This command is technically available in the 8259, but Automatic EOI mode is not a real option on any PC system, making this command unusable.

Command	Description	Port
A0h	Rotate on nonspecific EOI	A0h

This command performs two actions. When issued at the end of an interrupt service routine, the interrupt controller switches the completed interrupt to the lowest priority and then accepts additional interrupts.

This is a rarely used command in the PC environment. To use this method requires that all interrupt service routines issue this command upon completion. Instead all the BIOS routines use the nonspecific EOI command, 20h. It is not practical to use this option unless you are creating a custom system BIOS.

Command	Description	Port
C0-C7h	IRQ Lowest Priority	A0h

Sets one IRQ to the lowest priority. Commands C0h through C7h relate to making IRQ 8 through 15 the lowest priority on interrupt controller 2. In a system with two controllers, IRQ 8 to 15 form a group that appears to the system having the priority level of IRQ 2. The default priority is shown in Table 17-7. This default is the way systems are configured most of the time.

Table 17-7. Interrupt Default Priorities

Controller 1 Request	Controller 2 Request	Default Priority
IRQ 0		1 (highest)
IRQ 1		2
IRQ 2		chain to 2nd controller
	IRQ 8	3
	IRQ 9	4
	IRQ 10	5
	IRQ 11	6
	IRQ 12	7
	IRQ 13	8
	IRQ 14	9
	IRQ 15	10
IRQ 3		11
IRQ 4		12
IRQ 5		13
IRQ 6		14
IRQ 7		15 (lowest)

Command	Description	Port
E0-E7h	EOI and Set Lowest Priority	A0h

This command sets a specific EOI for IRQ 8 to 15, and also sets the lowest priority for interrupt controller 2. See commands E0-E7h under port 20h for details. These commands are not normally used in the PC family environment.

Port	Type	Description	Platform
A1h	Input	8259-2 Interrupt Mask Register	AT+

The interrupt mask register indicates which interrupt requests are allowed (value 0) and which are disabled (value 1).

Input (bits 0-7) Interrupt Mask Register

```
bit  7 w = 0 IRQ 15 Enabled
     6 w = 0 IRQ 14 Enabled
     5 w = 0 IRQ 13 Enabled
     4 w = 0 IRQ 12 Enabled
     3 w = 0 IRQ 11 Enabled
     2 w = 0 IRQ 10 Enabled
     1 w = 0 IRQ 9 Enabled
     0 w = 0 IRQ 8 Enabled
```

Port	Type	Description	Platform
A1h	Output	8259-2 Interrupt Commands	AT+

This controls initialization and operation of the interrupt controller for interrupt request lines 8 to 15.

Initialization

After the initialization command is sent from port A0h, three additional bytes complete the 8259 initialization.

Output (bits 0-7), Initialization command 2

```
bit  7 w = 0 |  Specify group of 8 interrupts for this controller
     6 w = 1 |     bits  7  6  5  4  3
     5 w = 1 |           0  0  0  0  0 = use vectors 0-7
     4 w = 1 |              .....
     3 w = 0 |           0  1  1  1  0 = use vectors 70-77h (normal)
                            .....
                         1  1  1  1  1 = use vectors F8-FFh
```

2 w = 0	Unused	
1 w = 0	Unused	
0 w = 0	Unused	

Output (bits 0-7), Initialization command 3

bit	7 w = 0	Unused			
	6 w = 0	Unused			
	5 w = 0	Unused			
	4 w = 0	Unused			
	3 w = 0	Unused			
	2 w = 0	Slave controller ID			
	1 w = 1		bit 2	bit 1	bit 0
	0 w = 0		0	1	0 = slave on IRQ 2

Output (bits 0-7), Initialization command 4

bit	7 w = 0	Unused		
	6 w = 0	Unused		
	5 w = 0	Unused		
	4 w = 0	Not special fully nested mode		
	3 w = 0	Buffered mode		
	2 w = 0		bit 3	bit 2
			0	x = nonbuffered
	1 w = 0	Normal End Of Interrupt (EOI)		
	1	Automatic End Of Interrupt (not supported on any system)		
	0 w = 1	80x86 mode		

Normal Operation

Once the interrupt controller has been initialized, individual interrupt request lines can be disabled or enabled. Setting a bit to 1 disables the request.

Output (bits 0-7), Operation command 1

bit	7 w = 0	Enable IRQ 15
	6 w = 0	Enable IRQ 14
	5 w = 0	Enable IRQ 13
	4 w = 0	Enable IRQ 12
	3 w = 0	Enable IRQ 11
	2 w = 0	Enable IRQ 10
	1 w = 0	Enable IRQ 9
	0 w = 0	Enable IRQ 8

Port	Type	Description	Platform
462h	Output	Trigger NMI	EISA

Any write to this port when NMI is enabled causes an NMI to occur. The actual value written is ignored.

Port	Type	Description	Platform
4D0h	I/O	8259-1 IRQ Trigger Type	EISA

This register controls the triggering type for each IRQ line. Clear the bit to program edge sensitive (AT bus compatible, default mode). Set the bit to program level sensitive mode (PCI bus slot usage of an interrupt).

Before writing this register, read the contents first. Do not change the state of IRQ 0, 1, 2 bits, as these are set by the motherboard manufacturer's BIOS to reflect the specific board design.

I/O (bits 0-7) IRQ Trigger Type

bit 7 r/w = 0 IRQ 7 edge sensitive triggering
6 r/w = 0 IRQ 6 edge sensitive triggering
5 r/w = 0 IRQ 5 edge sensitive triggering
4 r/w = 0 IRQ 4 edge sensitive triggering
3 r/w = 0 IRQ 3 edge sensitive triggering
2 r/w = x IRQ 2 triggering (do not change)
1 r/w = x IRQ 1 triggering (do not change)
0 r/w = x IRQ 0 triggering (do not change)

Port	Type	Description	Platform
4D1h	I/O	8259-2 IRQ Trigger Type	EISA

This register controls the triggering type for each IRQ line. Clear the bit to program edge sensitive (ISA bus compatible, default mode). Set the bit to program level sensitive mode (PCI bus slot usage of an interrupt).

Before writing this register, read the contents first. Do not change the state of IRQ 8 or IRQ 13, as these are set by the motherboard manufacturer's BIOS to reflect the specific board design.

I/O (bits 0-7) IRQ Trigger Type

bit 7 r/w = 0 IRQ 15 edge sensitive triggering
6 r/w = 0 IRQ 14 edge sensitive triggering
5 r/w = x IRQ 13 triggering (do not change)
4 r/w = 0 IRQ 12 edge sensitive triggering
3 r/w = 0 IRQ 11 edge sensitive triggering
2 r/w = 0 IRQ 10 edge sensitive triggering
1 r/w = 0 IRQ 9 edge sensitive triggering
0 r/w = x IRQ 8 triggering (do not change)

CHAPTER 18

DMA Services and DRAM Refresh

In talking with other software engineers, I was surprised to find a number of common misconceptions about how Direct Access Memory (DMA) operates. This chapter will thoroughly explain how the DMA system works. Few programmers will ever find it necessary to directly program the DMA system, but understanding it is important to many subsystems of the PC.

Over the years there have been a number of changes, which I detail for the PC, AT, EISA, and MCA systems. In addition, the Virtual Device Specification is briefly covered. The Virtual Device Specification solves some messy issues with protected mode software and DMA. A short example program is detailed to provide a real-world look at how to control the DMA system. This is followed by an extensive reference to the more than 75 I/O ports used to program the DMA system across different PC platforms.

Introduction

Direct Memory Access provides a method for high speed transfer of data between memory and the I/O bus. A DMA controller performs these transfers on the physical memory without processor involvement.

A special IC, the 8237 DMA controller, performs the data transfers automatically, once set up. Older pre-AT class machines used only one DMA chip. This provides four separate DMA channels capable of making 8-bit memory transfers (DMA-1). Starting with the AT class machines, and all current PCs, a second DMA controller was added (DMA-2). This second controller provides four additional DMA channels, each capable of 16-bit memory transfers. One of the 16-bit channels is reserved to chain from the first DMA controller, DMA-1. This leaves a total of seven channels available for use.

Each DMA controller has a number of registers to control the DMA operations, to specify the number of bytes/words to transfer, and to designate the memory addresses for the transfer. These registers are all accessed through I/O ports. The operation of channels 0 to 3 differs from channels 4 to 7 as shown in Table 18-1.

Table 18-1. DMA Usage and Limits

Channel Number	Function	Systems	DMA Chip	Data Size	Maximum Block
0	DRAM refresh	PC	1	8	64 K
	Unassigned, all others	XT+			
1	Unassigned	all	1	8	64 K
2	Diskette	all	1	8	64 K
3	Hard disk	all	1	8	64 K
	Unassigned, all others	AT+			
4	Cascade from DMA-1	AT+	2	16	128 K
5	Hard disk	PS/2	2	16	128 K
	Unassigned, all others	AT/EISA			
6	Unassigned	AT+	2	16	128 K
7	Unassigned	AT+	2	16	128 K

The 8237 DMA Controller can only address 64 K different memory addresses with its internal 16-bit address registers. To access the entire 16 MB address space (1 MB on 8088-class machines) a separate page register is used for each DMA channel. Each page register adds 8 more address bits for each channel. The page register associated with each DMA channel is loaded to the specific bank of memory to use. This means that DMA transfers on channels 0 to 3 must occur within a 64 K block on a 64 K boundary. The 16-bit channels 5 to 7 must occur within a 128 K address block on a 128 K boundary. Tables 18-2 and 18-3 show the ports and address lines controlled by the page register during a DMA transfer.

Table 18-2. Original PC Page Registers

		Page Register to Address Bits							
Page Register	**Port**	**0**	**1**	**2**	**3**	**4**	**5**	**6**	**7**
DMA Channel 0	80h	a16	a17	a18	a19	x	x	x	x
DMA Channel 1	81h	a16	a17	a18	a19	x	x	x	x
DMA Channel 2	82h	a16	a17	a18	a19	x	x	x	x
DMA Channel 3	83h	a16	a17	a18	a19	x	x	x	x

Table 18-3. AT/EISA/MCA Page Registers

		Page Register to Address Bits							
Page Register	**Port**	**0**	**1**	**2**	**3**	**4**	**5**	**6**	**7**
DMA Channel 0	87h	a16	a17	a18	a19	a20	a21	a22	a23
DMA Channel 1	83h	a16	a17	a18	a19	a20	a21	a22	a23
DMA Channel 2	81h	a16	a17	a18	a19	a20	a21	a22	a23
DMA Channel 3	82h	a16	a17	a18	a19	a20	a21	a22	a23
RAM Refresh*	8Fh	a16**	a17	a18	a19	a20	a21	a22	a23
DMA Channel 5	8Bh	a16**	a17	a18	a19	a20	a21	a22	a23
DMA Channel 6	89h	a16**	a17	a18	a19	a20	a21	a22	a23
DMA Channel 7	8Ah	a16**	a17	a18	a19	a20	a21	a22	a23

* *DMA Channel 4 is reserved for cascading DMA-1 to DMA-2, and the page register is reserved for RAM refresh.*

** *Non-zero values written to bit 0 of the page register are always output as a zero for channels 4 to 7. This ensures that the DMA transfer is on a 128 K address boundary.*

All DMA memory transfers must occur within the first 16 MB of address space. No provisions have been made to support DMA addresses beyond 16 MB. In addition, channels 4 to 7 must align addresses on a word boundary. These channels also are only available for 16-bit data transfers. They cannot be used with 8-bit I/O adapters.

The DMA system can perform three types of transfers: reads, writes, and verifies. These are shown in Table 18-4. A DMA read transfers data from memory to I/O. A DMA write performs the opposite operation of transferring data from I/O into memory. The verify operation is like a DMA read, but no I/O write occurs. The adapter is able to read the data and perform a verify operation within the adapter. Even though many diskette and hard disk adapters use DMA, they rarely use the DMA verify function.

Table 18-4. Memory and I/O Transfer Types

Transfer Type	Source	Destination
Read	Memory	I/O
Write	I/O	Memory
Verify	Memory	none

Confusion Resolved

One of the more confusing concepts about DMA is that data transfers between memory and I/O occur on the *same* bus. These are commonly referred to as the memory bus, and separately referred to as an I/O bus or channel. There is only one physical data and address bus in the system.

Separate control lines indicate whether the address is for a memory access or for an I/O access. Four lines control whether the address/data bus is for an active memory read or write, or for an I/O read or write. I/O reads and writes normally occur using the CPU's IN or OUT instructions to a specific port address.

Unlike the CPU, the DMA controller has the ability to activate both the memory and the I/O access lines at the same time! To transfer a byte from memory to the adapter card, the Memory Read line and the I/O write lines are active at the same time. The adapter card will get a DMA acknowledge on its specific DMA channel when the transfer is being made. No port address is associated with the I/O transfer. In this manner, a transfer occurs between memory and the adapter card.

A Typical I/O-to-Memory Transfer

Figure 18-1 shows the sequence of events when a DMA is initiated, and performs a data transfer from an adapter card's I/O directly into memory. This is considered a DMA write. DMA channel 3 is used in this example, and no other DMA transfers are in progress.

The complete processing of this transfer occurs in the following sequence:

1. A device driver initialization routine programs the DMA chip, setting up the following information:

   Base address in memory where first write should begin: The lower 16-bits are programmed into the DMA controller, channel 3. The upper address bits are programmed into the page register 3. Count of bytes to transfer on the request, less 1, is placed into the DMA controller, channel 3. The transfer mode is selected as "demand mode" (single and block modes are other options).

   The direction of count is set to increment (decrement is the other option).

   The transfer type is "write" (read and verify are other options).

   The DMA Mask is updated to allow DMA Request 3 (DREQ 3).

Figure 18-1. DMA Transfer Sequence

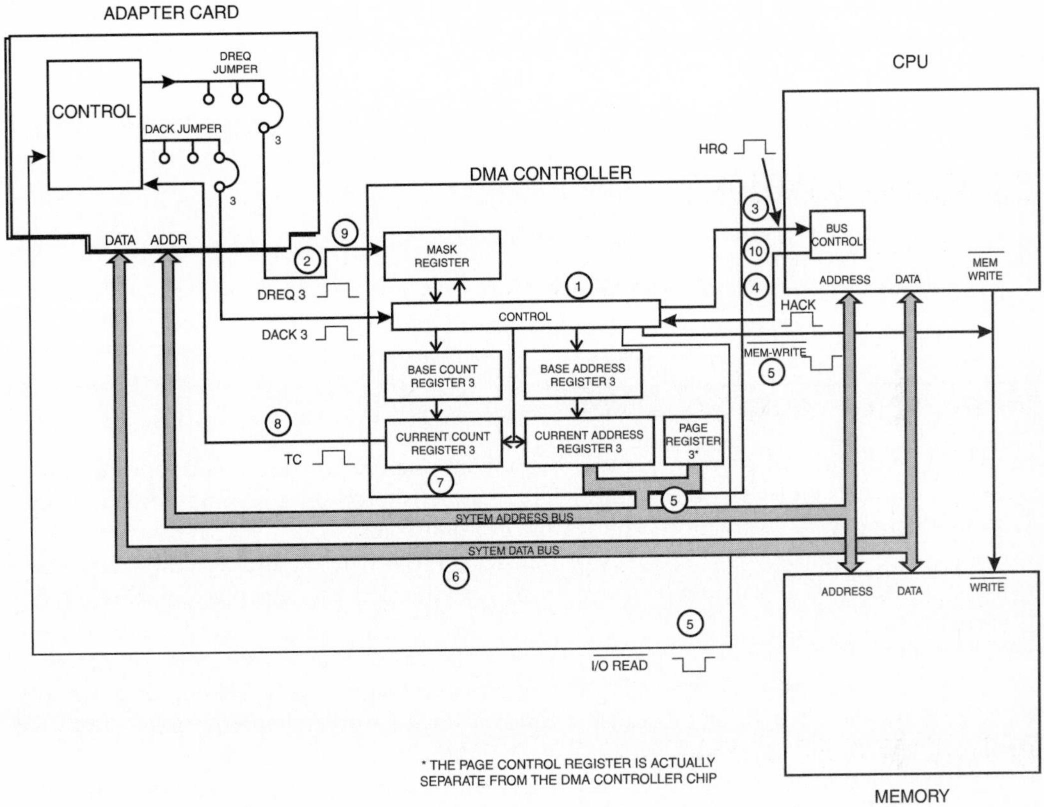

2. The adapter card requests DMA service by asserting a high on the DMA request line 3 (DREQ 3).
3. The DMA controller verifies that DREQ 3 is allowed, and then asks the CPU to go into a hold mode by asserting the Hold Request line (HRQ).
4. The CPU responds by asserting the Hold Acknowledge (HLDA) and goes into a bus hold state.
5. An address generated by the DMA system is passed onto the bus. The memory write and I/O read control lines are also activated. The DMA acknowledge (DACK 3) signal is activated, so the adapter card is aware that the transfer is now in progress.

6. The data is transferred directly from the adapter to memory without passing through the DMA controller. The CPU interleaves normal cycles and bus holds cycles as the transfer proceeds, under control of the DMA controller.
7. The transfer completes when the DMA controller's count completes or, if the transfers are going too fast for the adapter, the adapter can temporarily stop the transfer by dropping the DREQ 3 line.
8. At completion, the DMA controller asserts the Terminal Count (TC) line to signal the adapter card that the transfer is complete. The hold request (HRQ) and DMA acknowledge (DACK 3) lines are deactivated.
9. The adapter turns off the request, DREQ 3.
10. The CPU resumes normal bus control.

Memory-to-Memory DMA

The DMA controller can transfer memory bytes from one memory address to another, using two DMA channels under software control. This feature is rarely used because it is slower than an 80386's string move instruction. This feature can only transfer one byte per transfer cycle, as opposed to the 80386's MOVSD ability to transfer up to 4 bytes at a time. When a memory-to-memory transfer is in progress, no memory-to-I/O transfers can take place, further limiting its usefulness.

Using memory-to-memory transfers can be a source of strange problems. In almost all cases, applications that use memory-to-I/O transfers never expect to be held up by a memory-to-memory transfer. The delay can cause a timeout error or other unpredictable actions and data loss.

Memory-to-memory transfers can only be performed with channels 0 and 1. On the original PC, DMA channel 0 was used for DRAM refresh. This makes memory-to-memory transfers much trickier, because the refresh must be disabled while performing the DMA transfer. With long transfers and refresh disabled, the DRAM may lose its contents causing a system crash. In general it's best to avoid memory-to-memory DMA.

To enable memory-to-memory transfers, the Command Register bit 0 is set. The Channel 0 Base Address Register is loaded with the source memory address, and Channel 1's Base Address contains the destination address. Channel 1's Base Word Count Register holds the number of bytes to transfer less 1. The transfer is initiated by setting the DREQ 0 bit high using the Request Register.

Modes of Operation

The DMA controller offers four transfer modes: single, block, demand, and cascade. In addition, an Autoinitialization option can be used in the first three modes. The transfer begins when the channel's DREQ becomes active. These selections are made for each channel using the mode registers at ports Bh and D6h.

Autoinitialization

Autoinitialization provides a means to restart a transfer by loading the base address and count register into the current address and current count registers. If autoinitialize is enabled for the channel and a Terminal Count (TC) occurs, the registers are transferred. A TC occurs when the word count rolls over from 0 to FFFF.

Single Transfer Mode

As the name implies, this sets up the DMA for a single byte or word transfer for each DREQ. The current address is adjusted for the next memory address. The current count register is decremented once. If this causes a TC, by rolling from 0 to FFFF, an autoinitialize will occur if autoinitialization has been set on.

Should the DREQ line be held active, the DMA controller releases the bus at the conclusion of the single transfer. The CPU is allowed one bus cycle. The DMA then reasserts control and performs the next single transfer.

Block Transfer Mode

When the DREQ becomes active the transfer begins. Transfers continue until TC is reached, by rolling from 0 to FFFF. In this manner, up to 64 K bytes can be transferred at a time on channels 0 to 3, or 64 K words on channels 5 to 7. If autoinitialization is programmed, at the end of the transfer when TC occurs, the channel will autoinitialize. If the DREQ is still active or when DREQ next goes active, the next block transfer will begin.

Demand Transfer Mode

When the DREQ becomes active the transfer begins. Transfers continue until TC is reached or the DREQ becomes inactive. This allows the I/O device to regulate the transfers. If a slow I/O device runs out of data, the adapter deactivates its DREQ line. When the adapter is ready to send more data, the DREQ is reasserted, and the transfer continues. If autoinitialization is programmed, at the end of the transfer when TC occurs, the channel will autoinitialize. If the DREQ is still active or when DREQ next goes active, the next block of transfers will begin.

Cascade Mode

This is used on systems with two DMA controllers such as the AT and EISA systems. Channel 4 is connected in hardware to properly cascade the two DMA controllers. When the DMA controllers are initialized, the BIOS sets channel 4 into cascade mode. Channel 4's cascade mode settings should never be changed, otherwise DMA channels 5, 6, and 7 will become unusable.

MCA System Differences

MicroChannel systems replaced the dual 8237 DMA controllers with custom logic to simulate the same functional operations. All of the standard DMA ports and registers operate alike on MCA systems. In addition, MCA DMA allows special extended functions accessed through ports 18h and 1Ah.

There are few major differences between the 8237 DMA controllers and MCA systems. MCA systems provide the ability to program the transfer size (byte or word) for each channel. The size is still dependent on the connected hardware, but this provides additional flexibility.

The MCA system also allows transfers to a specific I/O address. In this case, the DMA transfer is routed through a temporary register for the channel. Because two bus accesses are required for each transfer, making a DMA transfer to a specific I/O address will be slower than standard DMA. The advantage is that many more hardware devices can share a single DMA port. Currently very few devices, if any, use this alternative method.

MCA systems have an arbitration system to control bus access to multiple DMA users. Competing devices are assigned different priorities to resolve these conflicts. In addition, the motherboard has the two highest levels of bus arbitration preassigned for refresh and NMI. Table 18-5 shows the default arbitration levels, with FEh the highest priority and 0Fh the lowest. DMA channels 0 and 4 can be assigned any priority level from 0 to Eh. The priorities are set using port 18h, function 80h for channel 0, and function 84h for channel 4.

Table 18-5. MCA DMA Arbitration Levels

Level	Function
FEh	RAM Refresh
FFh	NMI
0	DMA Channel 0 (default level, but changeable)
1	DMA Channel 1
2	DMA Channel 2
3	DMA Channel 3
4	DMA Channel 4 (default level, but changeable)
5	DMA Channel 5
6	DMA Channel 6
7	DMA Channel 7
8-Eh	Unused
Fh	Reserved for CPU use

EISA System Differences

EISA systems fully support two 8237 equivalent DMA controllers and all related operations. No software changes are necessary for DMA transfers written for other AT-type machines to run on an EISA machine. EISA does add a host of nice enhancements, including 32-bit wide

DMA transfers into any 32-bit address. This is a major extension over the standard 16-bit wide, 24-bit address limits of AT-type systems. In addition, EISA systems offer a unique DMA burst mode that provides up to 33 times the transfer speed over standard DMA.

The enhancements are great, except for several critical considerations. Code that relies on the unique EISA enhancements will, of course, only work on an EISA machine. For an EISA adapter card, this may be acceptable, but on any other AT-type card, EISA extensions add significant complications. The second, and more critical problem is with the processor's virtual mode. In this case, the physical memory address used by the DMA is usually different from the virtual address used by the device driver. There is no clear specification to handle these cases on an EISA machine. The section on Virtual DMA Services goes into much greater detail about this problem. Unfortunately, it is not clear if VDS specifications will always handle these new EISA features.

Cycle Timing Modes

One of the extended features the EISA system offers is faster transfer rates. EISA provides a number of new DMA timing modes, referred to as Type A, B, and C. These new timing modes are not generally compatible with AT adapters, but EISA adapters can take advantage of these new modes. One major advantage of these new modes is the EISA DMA can translate smaller I/O data sizes into the full 32-bit width of the memory system. Table 18-6 shows the typical transfer rates that can be achieved on a EISA system.

Table 18-6. EISA DMA Transfer Rates

Mode	I/O Data Width	Transfer Rate
AT Compatible	8-bit	1.0 MB/sec
	16-bit	2.0 MB/sec
Type A	8-bit	1.3 MB/sec
	16-bit	2.6 MB/sec
	32-bit	5.3 MB/sec
Type B	8-bit	2.0 MB/sec
	16-bit	4.0 MB/sec
	32-bit	8.0 MB/sec
Type C, Burst DMA	8-bit	8.2 MB/sec
	16-bit	16.5 MB/sec
	32-bit	33.0 MB/sec

There are some limits on the combinations of timing mode, DMA transfer mode, the data size, and the transfer type. AT compatible timing mode only allows 8-bit data with normal addresses or 16-bit data with shifted addresses, which is not shown on the table. A shifted address is the ability to access a larger address range. For example, a word address does not need the lowest bit if all data is word aligned. By "shifting" the address up by one bit, twice as much memory can be accessed. The timing modes combinations that are allowable are shown in Table 18-7.

Table 18-7. Allowable Advanced EISA Combinations

Transfer Types	DMA Mode	Timing Mode	Address Option	Data Size (bits)
Read/Write/Verify	Single	A	normal	8
Read/Write/Verify	Single	A	shifted	16
Read/Write	Single	A	normal	16
Read/Write	Single	A	normal	32
Read/Write/Verify	Single	B	normal	8
Read/Write/Verify	Single	B	shifted	16
Read/Write	Single	B	normal	16
Read/Write	Single	B	normal	32
Read/Write/Verify	Demand	A	normal	8
Read/Write/Verify	Demand	A	shifted	16
Read/Write	Demand	A	normal	16
Read/Write	Demand	A	normal	32
Read/Write/Verify	Demand	B	normal	8
Read/Write/Verify	Demand	B	shifted	16
Read/Write	Demand	B	normal	16
Read/Write	Demand	B	normal	32
Read/Write	Demand	C	normal	8
Write	Demand	C	shifted	16
Read	Demand	C	normal	16
Read/Write	Demand	C	normal	32
Read/Write/Verify	Block	A	normal	8
Read/Write/Verify	Block	A	shifted	16
Read/Write	Block	A	normal	16
Read/Write	Block	A	normal	32
Read/Write/Verify	Block	B	normal	8
Read/Write/Verify	Block	B	shifted	16
Read/Write	Block	B	normal	16
Read/Write	Block	B	normal	32
Read/Write	Block	C	normal	8
Write	Block	C	shifted	16
Read	Block	C	normal	16
Read/Write	Block	C	normal	32

EISA FIFO Transfers

EISA systems offer a mechanism to create a First-In-First-Out (FIFO) buffer, or a ring buffer. The DMA system transfers information into the buffer while the software is reading out the oldest information from the buffer. The start of the buffer is defined by the Base address register, and the size is defined by the Base count register. When a single DMA block transfer completes, as defined by the current count reaching its limit, the DMA autoinitializes and continues to load additional data at the beginning of the buffer.

Meanwhile, software reads data from the buffer. The software settable stop register indicates the next data location to read. Software should read the DMA's Current address register to prevent reading an empty buffer. After software reads from the buffer, it updates the value in the stop register to the next sequential unread address. The DMA controller uses this address to prevent overwriting data that has not been read by the CPU.

Should the CPU not read data fast enough, allowing the buffer to fill to capacity, the DMA would expect to do a transfer to the same address as the stop register. The DMA controller detects this problem and stops the transfer. The channel is automatically disabled. A DMA overrun is very likely, and the software should check for this condition by looking at the Mask status register.

Figure 18-2 shows a typical FIFO configuration before the transfer begins and after DMA has been started. The software has begun to read some of the DMA transferred data.

Figure 18-1. Typical FIFO Buffer Configuration

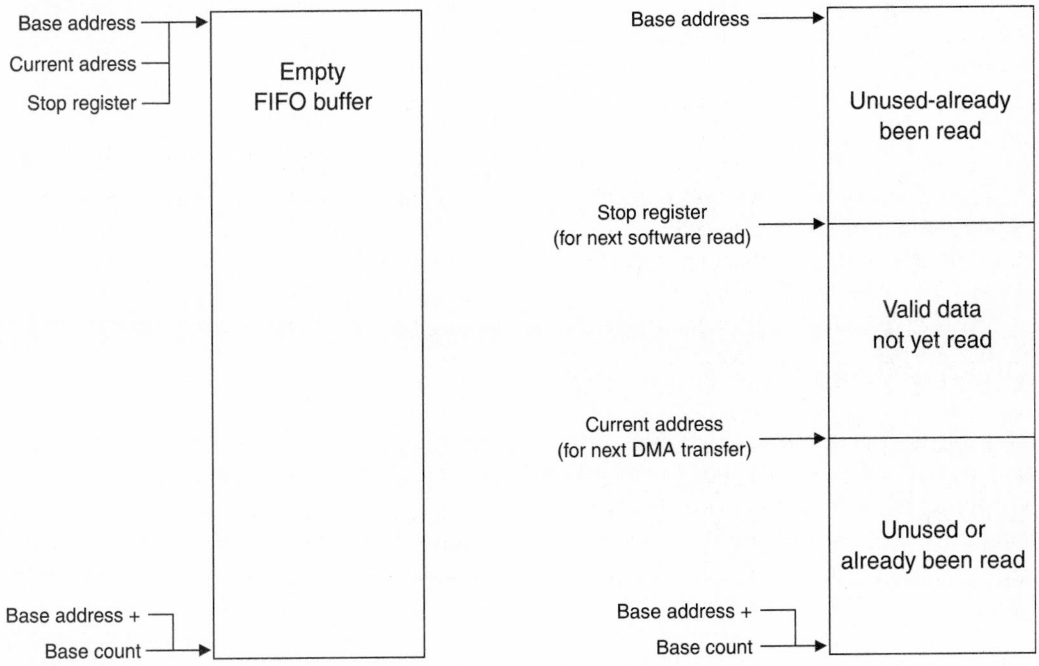

EISA Chained Transfers

With chained transfers, an EISA system can transfer data to many different areas in memory in a single continuous transfer. This works by having the DMA controller interrupt the software for new information while the current transfer is in progress. The software loads the new set of information and when the current transfer is complete, this new information is automatically loaded and the transfer continues.

The specific actions necessary to make this happen are:

1. For the first block to transfer, the base address and count are loaded.
2. The channel's chaining mode bits are set to enable chaining (ports 40Ah or 4D4h, bits 3 & 2 = 01). This copies the base and count registers into the current base and current count registers.
3. The next base address and count are loaded for the second block transfer.
4. The process is launched by setting the channel's chaining mode bits to signify the update is complete (ports 40Ah or 4D4h, bits 3 & 2 = 11). This causes the first transfer to begin.
5. When the first transfer is complete, the previously loaded base and count are automatically loaded into the current address and current count registers. This new transfer then proceeds.

   These actions also cause a DMA interrupt to be initiated on IRQ 13, interrupt 75h. The interrupt handler must check the chaining interrupt status register (port 40Ah) to confirm the interrupt was caused by chaining, and from which channel. With this knowledge, the handler can then load the next set of base address and count values.
6. The channel's chaining mode bits are again set to signify the update is complete (ports 40Ah or 4D4h, bits 3 & 2 = 11). This causes the interrupt to be cleared, and the process continues at step number 5.

Virtual DMA Services (VDS)

Now life gets a lot more complicated. DMA memory transfers occur between *physical* memory and an I/O channel. Memory management software, 386 DOS extenders, and Windows enhanced mode all create a virtual memory map, usually quite different than physical memory. Since most systems with a 386 or better CPU normally operate in virtual mode (V86), this can pose a major problem. The DMA system has no knowledge of virtual addresses, and software device drivers have no knowledge of the physical system!

Two procedures have evolved to solve this dilemma. The first is automatically handled by the virtual memory manager, and the second provides a special interface called Virtual DMA Services (VDS).

Memory managers, such as Max8 (386Max), EMM386, Memory Commander, QEMM, and a few others cleverly solve the problem by trapping all I/O operations to the DMA system. When a device driver writes to a DMA chip, the memory manager intercepts the information, and, if necessary, translates the virtual address into a physical address. The memory manager then writes the new information into the DMA controller's registers.

If the physical address is outside the range of the DMA controller, the virtual memory manager will use a temporary buffer within the range of the DMA controller. Every virtual memory manager allocates a 16K buffer for this purpose, so it is very important that the driver only transfers a maximum of 16K bytes in any single transfer. If more than 16K is attempted, and the buffer is required, a General Protection Fault will occur, halting the system. The user will have to reset the system, which usually creates a very annoyed user! Most of these memory managers offer a way to expand the buffer to handle the maximum transfer size of 128K, but this wastes extended memory and requires the user to explicitly change the default settings of the memory manager.

A major problem occurs with the DMA translation method just discussed if an adapter card provides its own DMA controller, commonly referred to as a busmaster DMA controller. The virtual memory manager only has knowledge of the two DMA controllers on the motherboard. Fortunately, the problem was detected early on when IBM added SCSI support to the PS/2 line. IBM developed the Virtual Device Standard (VDS) as the solution.

VDS is a set of INT 4Bh functions provided by the VDS implementor (the memory manager) to communicate the physical and virtual relationships to the busmaster DMA's driver. Any busmaster DMA driver that fails to use VDS when physical memory does not match the virtual memory will likely cause serious system stability problems and hang the system. The reverse is also true; if the virtual memory manager does not provide VDS services, a busmaster DMA transfer is likely to crash the system. All of the major memory managers—like Max8 (386Max), Memory Commander, QEMM, and the versions of EMM386 provided with DOS 5.0 and later—provide VDS support. So does the Windows enhanced mode virtual DMA Device (VDMAD) VxD.

VDS services are provided through software interrupt 4Bh, function ah=81h. If VDS is active, location 40:7Bh, bit 5 will be 1. In this case, the busmaster DMA driver should use VDS services to perform the proper DMA transfer.

Refer to the full VDS specification for the use and operations required. The VDS specification is free and available from both Microsoft and IBM. Refer to the bibliography for part numbers to order. A brief summary of functions is shown in Table 18-8.

Table 18-8. Summary of VDS Services (Interrupt 4Bh)

AX=	Description
8102h	Get VDS Version
8103h	Lock DMA Region
8104h	Unlock DMA Region
8105h	Scatter/Gather Lock Region
8106h	Scatter/Gather Unlock Region
8107h	Request DMA Buffer
8108h	Release DMA Buffer
8109h	Copy into DMA Buffer
810Ah	Copy out of DMA Buffer
810Bh	Disable DMA Translation
810Ch	Enable DMA Translation

Typical Uses

In pre-AT class machines, one DMA channel was used to refresh the dynamic memory. The diskette adapter in all machines also uses a DMA channel to transfer data to and from the diskette controller. Some of the other optional DMA users include the old SDLC (Synchronous Data Link Controller), a number of network adapter cards, digital sound cards, scanners, and the hard disk adapter on the PC/XT and many PS/2 systems.

DMA BIOS Data Areas

DMA operations generally do not use any BIOS data. The one exception is when Virtual DMA services are used. A byte normally reserved for printer number 4's timeout is reused for VDS information. This is generally acceptable, because most AT+ systems provide only capabilities for three printer ports. VDS will never be available on a system equipped with any CPU less than an 80386.

When a memory manager is installed, it must hook interrupt 4Bh. This interrupt may already be used for another service handler, so the vector must be checked to see if it is used. If so, the interrupt must be chained. If not, the memory manager can point the interrupt vector 4Bh directly to the VDS service handler. On a MCA system, the VDS_flags bit 3 is used to flag the VDS implementor on how to hook interrupt 4Bh. If bit 3 is 0, then the interrupt has not been intercepted. The contents of vector 4Bh are checked (address 0:12Ch). If the contents are 0:0, or the segment is E000, or F000, hooking the interrupt is not permitted. If the VDS_flags bit 3 is 1, then interrupt 4Bh should be chained.

Location	Description	Size
40:7Bh	Virtual DMA Flags	Byte

These flags are used for the VDS service provider.

bit	7 = x	Unused
	6 = x	Unused
	5 = 0	VDS is unavailable
	1	VDS is active
	4 = x	Unused
	3 = 0	Int 4Bh is not intercepted
	1	Chaining required
	2 = x	Unused
	1 = x	Unused
	0 = x	Unused

Warnings

Avoid reading and writing the Address and Count registers when a DMA request could occur. To accomplish this the controller can be disabled (see Command register at ports 8h/D0h, bit 2) or you can mask the channel (see ports Ah/D4h). Interrupts should also be disabled when programming the DMA controller to avoid an interrupt handler from changing operations midstream.

The number of transfers is always *one more* than loaded into the count register. To transfer 200 bytes or words, a count of 199 is used. A count of 0 performs one transfer.

Although the DMA system can transfer up to 128 K bytes per transfer, it is wise to limit the transfers to 16K bytes per transfer. See the section on Virtual DMA Services for additional details.

Refrain from using large block transfers. Large counts with demand mode can also cause problems, if the I/O device is fast. When large block/demand mode transfers occur other critical devices cannot get bus control like RAM Refresh. EISA systems can perform large block transfers in extended modes Types A, B, or C without this concern.

Busmaster DMA cards, which contain their own DMA controller, should check if VDS is active. If VDS is active, VDS services should be used to ensure reliable operation.

On an AT-type system DMA channels 2 and 4 are reserved by the system, but the remaining channels are not assigned. Unfortunately, there is no mechanism to tell which DMA channels are being used by other adapters in the system. Like I/O ports, any hardware/software package should offer the ability to select alternate DMA channels. It is also extremely helpful if the BIOS, device driver, or TSR shows which DMA channel it is using during the display of the sign-on or copyright message. This will not automatically solve conflicts, but an informed user will be more likely to avoid overlaps when selecting additional DMA channels.

For example, Novell's IPX network TSRs show which DMA channel the software is set to use (if any). The IPX software can redisplay the important current selections at the DOS prompt by using the I command line option. On the other end of the spectrum are short-lived manufacturers (we hope) who enjoy forcing the customer to find the manual, kill the system, remove the card and locate the appropriate jumpers, just to see which DMA channel was used! It is equally bad to require the user to insert a diagnostic diskette and run a special program to get this information. You will not endear yourself to your customers if you hide this critical information. For new equipment, strongly consider Plug and Play support to automatically assign the DMA channels.

Do not totally depend on any diagnostic package to find unused DMA channels. If they do detect a DMA channel in use, the information is accurate. But there is no sure way to detect dormant DMA users. Channels may appear unused, but might become active at a later time.

Code Sample 18-1. DMA Transfer Setup

This sample subroutine shows how an adapter card would set up the DMA controller for a 16-bit I/O-to-memory data transfer.

```
;-----------------------------------------------------------------
;    DMA_READ
;        Set up DMA for a 16-bit adapter to memory transfer, using
;        DMA channel 5 that is activated by the hardware DMA
;        request 5 (DRQ 5) line.
;
;         Notes: 1) operation for AT+ systems only (not for PC/XT)
;                2) ds:si must be word aligned, with si bit 0 = 0
;                3) ds:si + dx must not cross a 128 KB boundary
;
;        Called with:    ds:si = memory buffer to read into
;                        dx    = count, number of WORDS (not bytes)

DMA_read        proc    near
        cli
        mov     al, 00000101b       ; set channel 5 mask bit
        out     0D4h, al            ;  to disable DMA
        IODELAY
        out     0D8h, al            ; clear byte flip/flop
                                    ;  (al value unimportant)
        IODELAY
        mov     al, 01001001h       ; mode byte: single mode,
                                    ;  increment, no autoinit,
                                    ;  read, channel 5
        out     0D6h, al
        IODELAY
                                    ; Convert es:si to 32-bit
                                    ;  linear and output to DMA-2
        mov     ax, ds
        mov     cl, 4
```

```
        rol     ax, cl
        push    ax
        and     al, 0Fh              ; al = address bits a16 to a23
        out     08Bh, al             ; load channel 5 page register
        IODELAY
        pop     ax
        and     ax, 0FFF0h           ; segment * 16
        add     ax, si               ; ax = address bits a0 to a15
        out     0C4h, al             ; output low address byte
        IODELAY
        mov     al, ah
        out     0C4h, al             ; output high address byte
        IODELAY
                                     ; Send Count of Words to DMA-2

        mov     ax, dx               ; get count
        dec     dx                   ; adjust, since DMA count
                                     ;   is 1 more
        out     0C6h, al             ; output low count byte
        IODELAY
        mov     al, ah
        out     0C6h, al             ; output high count byte
        IODELAY
        mov     al, 00000001b        ; clear channel 5 mask bit
        out     0D4h, al             ;  to enable DMA
        IODELAY
                                     ; Now it's up to hardware!
        sti
        ret
DMA_read        endp
```

Port Summary

This is a list of standard DMA port assignments. Some differences occur between ports used for AT+ class machines and the original PC. These have multiple entries for different platforms.

Port	Type	Function	Platform
00h	I/O	DMA-1 Base and Current Address, channel 0	All
01h	I/O	DMA-1 Base and Current Count, channel 0	All
02h	I/O	DMA-1 Base and Current Address, channel 1	All
03h	I/O	DMA-1 Base and Current Count, channel 1	All
04h	I/O	DMA-1 Base and Current Address, channel 2	All
05h	I/O	DMA-1 Base and Current Count, channel 2	All
06h	I/O	DMA-1 Base and Current Address, channel 3	All
07h	I/O	DMA-1 Base and Current Count, channel 3	All
08h	Input	DMA-1 Status Register	All
08h	Output	DMA-1 Command Register	PC/XT/AT/EISA
09h	Output	DMA-1 Request Register	PC/XT/AT/EISA
0Ah	Output	DMA-1 Mask Register Bit	All
0Bh	Output	DMA-1 Mode Register	All
0Ch	Output	DMA-1 Clear Byte Flip/Flop	All
0Dh	Input	DMA-1 Temporary Register	All
0Dh	Output	DMA-1 Master Disable	All
0Eh	Output	DMA-1 Clear Mask Register	All
0Fh	Output	DMA-1 Write All Mask Bits	All
18h	I/O	DMA Extended Function Register	MCA
1Ah	I/O	DMA Extended Function Execute	MCA
80h	I/O	DMA page register channel 0	PC
81h	I/O	DMA page register channel 2	AT+
81h	I/O	DMA page register channel 1	PC
82h	I/O	DMA page register channel 3	AT+
82h	I/O	DMA page register channel 2	PC
83h	I/O	DMA page register channel 1	AT+
83h	I/O	DMA page register channel 3	PC
87h	I/O	DMA page register channel 0	AT+
89h	I/O	DMA page register channel 6	AT+
8Ah	I/O	DMA page register channel 7	AT+
8Bh	I/O	DMA page register channel 5	AT+
8Fh	I/O	DMA page register channel 4 (refresh)	AT+
90h	Input	DMA Arbitration Status	MCA
90h	Output	DMA Arbitration Register	MCA
C0h	I/O	DMA-2 Base and Current Address, channel 4	AT+
C2h	I/O	DMA-2 Base and Current Count, channel 4	AT+
C4h	I/O	DMA-2 Base and Current Address, channel 5	AT+
C6h	I/O	DMA-2 Base and Current Count, channel 5	AT+

Port	Type	Function	Platform
C8h	I/O	DMA-2 Base and Current Address, channel 6	AT+
CAh	I/O	DMA-2 Base and Current Count, channel 6	AT+
CCh	I/O	DMA-2 Base and Current Address, channel 7	AT+
CEh	I/O	DMA-2 Base and Current Count, channel 7	AT+
D0h	Input	DMA-2 Status Register	AT+
D0h	Output	DMA-2 Command Register	AT/EISA
D2h	Output	DMA-2 Request Register	AT/EISA
D4h	Output	DMA-2 Mask Register Bit	AT+
D6h	Output	DMA-2 Mode Register	AT+
D8h	Output	DMA-2 Clear Byte Flip/Flop	AT+
DAh	Input	DMA-2 Temporary Register	AT+
DAh	Output	DMA-2 Master Disable	AT+
DCh	Output	DMA-2 Clear Mask Register	AT+
DEh	Output	DMA-2 Write All Mask Bits	AT+
401h	I/O	DMA-1 Base and Current Count, channel 0, high	EISA
403h	I/O	DMA-1 Base and Current Count, channel 1, high	EISA
405h	I/O	DMA-1 Base and Current Count, channel 2, high	EISA
407h	I/O	DMA-1 Base and Current Count, channel 3, high	EISA
40Ah	Input	DMA Chaining Interrupt Status	EISA
40Ah	Output	DMA-1 Chaining Mode Register	EISA
40Bh	Output	DMA-1 Extended Mode Register	EISA
40Ch	Input	DMA Chaining Terminal Count Action Status	EISA
481h	I/O	DMA page register channel 2, high	EISA
482h	I/O	DMA page register channel 3, high	EISA
483h	I/O	DMA page register channel 1, high	EISA
487h	I/O	DMA page register channel 0, high	EISA
489h	I/O	DMA page register channel 6, high	EISA
48Ah	I/O	DMA page register channel 7, high	EISA
48Bh	I/O	DMA page register channel 5, high	EISA
4C6h	I/O	DMA-2 Base and Current Count, channel 5, high	EISA
4CAh	I/O	DMA-2 Base and Current Count, channel 6, high	EISA
4CEh	I/O	DMA-2 Base and Current Count, channel 7, high	EISA
4D4h	Input	DMA Chaining Status	EISA
4D4h	Output	DMA-2 Chaining Mode Register	EISA
4D6h	Output	DMA-2 Extended Mode Register	EISA
4E0-4E2h	I/O	DMA-Stop Register, channel 0	EISA
4E4-4E6h	I/O	DMA-Stop Register, channel 1	EISA
4E8-4EAh	I/O	DMA-Stop Register, channel 2	EISA
4EC-4EEh	I/O	DMA-Stop Register, channel 3	EISA
4F4-4F6h	I/O	DMA-Stop Register, channel 5	EISA
4F8-4FAh	I/O	DMA-Stop Register, channel 6	EISA
4FC-4FEh	I/O	DMA-Stop Register, channel 7	EISA

Port Detail

Port	Type	Description	Platform
00h	I/O	DMA-1 Base and Current Address, Channel 0	All

Channel 0 DMA is an unassigned channel on AT/EISA/MCA bus machines, used for high-speed transfers between memory and the I/O bus.

Channel 0 DMA is used by the system for RAM refresh on obsolete PC/XT systems. A system timer is programmed to periodically request a dummy DMA transfer. This generates memory read cycles. The memory reads serve to keep the dynamic memory contents valid, as the RAM requires periodic read/writes or the contents are lost.

Input (bits 0-7)—Read Current Address Register

Read the 16-bit Current Address Register for DMA channel 0. The first 8-bit read will return the low portion of the word, and the second read will return the upper portion of the word.

The Current Address Register holds the current memory address used in a DMA transfer. It is automatically incremented or decremented after each DMA memory transfer.

Output (bits 0-7)—Write both Base and Current Address Registers

Two sequential 8-bit I/O writes load a 16-bit value into both the Base Address Register and the Current Address Register. The first 8-bit write loads the low portion of the word, and the second 8-bit write loads the high portion of the word. The Base Address Register is Write-Only.

The Base Address Register is used to hold the original value of the Current Address Register, and is not incremented or decremented during the DMA transfer.

Port	Type	Description	Platform
01h	I/O	DMA-1 Base and Current Count, Channel 0	All

This port controls the Base and Current Count registers for DMA channel 0. See Port 0h for the usage of DMA channel 0.

Input (bits 0-7)—Read Current Count Register

Read the 16-bit Current Count Register for DMA channel 0. The first 8-bit read will return the low portion of the word, and the second read will return the upper portion of the word.

The Current Count Register holds the remaining number of transfers to occur plus 1. A value of 100h indicates 101h transfers remain. This register is decremented after each transfer. When the register rolls from 0 to FFFFh, the transfer is complete.

Output (bits 0-7)—Write both Base and Current Count Registers

Two sequential 8-bit I/O writes load a 16-bit value into both the Base Count Register and the Current Count Register. The first 8-bit write loads the low portion of the word, and the second 8-bit write loads the high portion of the word. The Base Count Register is Write-Only.

The Base Count Register is used to hold the original value of the Current Count Register.

Port	Type	Description	Platform
02h	I/O	DMA-1 Base and Current Address, Channel 1	All

Channel 1 DMA is used by the SDLC (Synchronous Data Link Control) for high-speed transfers between memory and the I/O bus. If SDLC is not used, channel 1 is available for other adapter cards.

Input (bits 0-7)—Read Current Address Register (see port 0)

Output (bits 0-7)—Write both Base and Current Address Registers (see port 0)

Port	Type	Description	Platform
03h	I/O	DMA-1 Base and Current Count, Channel 1	All

This port controls the Base and Current Count registers for DMA channel 1. See Port 2h for the usage of DMA channel 1.

Input (bits 0-7)—Read Current Count Register (see port 1)

Output (bits 0-7)—Write both Base and Current Count Registers (see port 1)

Port	Type	Description	Platform
04h	I/O	DMA-1 Base and Current Address, Channel 2	All

Channel 2 DMA is a used by diskette services for high-speed transfers between memory and the I/O bus.

Input (bits 0-7)—Read Current Address Register (see port 0)

Output (bits 0-7)—Write both Base and Current Address Registers (see port 0)

Port	Type	Description	Platform
05h	I/O	DMA-1 Base and Current Count, Channel 2	All

This port controls the Base and Current Count registers for DMA channel 2. See Port 4h for the usage of DMA channel 2.

Input (bits 0-7)—Read Current Count Register (see port 1)

Output (bits 0-7)—Write both Base and Current Count Registers (see port 1)

Port	Type	Description	Platform
06h	I/O	DMA-1 Base and Current Address, Channel 3	All

On the AT+ systems, DMA channel 3 is an unassigned channel, used for high-speed transfers between memory and the I/O bus.

The PC/XT's hard disk adapter card uses channel 3 for transferring data between the disk controller and memory.

Input (bits 0-7)—Read Current Address Register (see port 0)

Output (bits 0-7)—Write both Base and Current Address Registers (see port 0)

Port	Type	Description	Platform
07h	I/O	DMA-1 Base and Current Count, Channel 3	All

This port controls the Base and Current Count registers for DMA channel 3. See Port 6h for the usage of DMA channel 3.

Input (bits 0-7)—Read Current Count Register (see port 1)

Output (bits 0-7)—Write both Base and Current Count Registers (see port 1)

Port	Type	Description	Platform
08h	Input	DMA-1 Status Register	All

The DMA Status Register hold flags (bits 0-3) indicate when each channel has reached the Terminal Count (transfer completed). When this register is read, these lower four bits are cleared.

The status register also contains flags for pending DMA requests on each of the four channels. DMA requests occur by asserting the desired DMA channel request line.

Input (bits 0-7)

bit	7 r = 1	DMA Channel 3 request
	6 r = 1	DMA Channel 2 request
	5 r = 1	DMA Channel 1 request
	4 r = 1	DMA Channel 0 request
	3 r = 1	DMA Channel 3 has reached terminal count
	2 r = 1	DMA Channel 2 has reached terminal count
	1 r = 1	DMA Channel 1 has reached terminal count
	0 r = 1	DMA Channel 0 has reached terminal count

Port	Type	Description	Platform
08h	Output	DMA-1 Command Register	PC/XT/AT/EISA

This 8-bit register controls the operation of the DMA. The register is cleared by a hardware reset or a Master Disable instruction (port 0Dh). The command value used by PCs is 0. Normally all bits are left at 0, except bit 2 is typically set to 1 to disable the controller while writing to DMA registers. This register is write-only, and is not supported on MCA systems.

Output (bits 0-7)

bit	7 w = 0	DACK sense active low (default)
	1	DACK sense active high
	6 w = 0	DREQ sense active high (default)
	1	DREQ sense active low
	5 w = 0	Late write selection
	1	Extended write selection
	x	if bit-3 = 0 (default)
	4 w = 0	Fixed priority (default)
	1	Rotating priority
	3 w = 0	Normal timing
	1	Compressed timing
	x	if bit-1 = 0 (default)
	2 w = 0	Controller enable (default)
	1	Controller disable
	1 w = 0	Channel 0 address hold disable
	1	Channel 0 address hold enable
	x	if bit-0 = 0 (default)
	0 w = 0	Memory-to-memory transfers disabled (default)
	1	Memory-to-memory transfers enabled

Port	Type	Description	Platform
09h	Output	DMA-1 Request Register	PC/XT/AT/EISA

In addition to initiating a request for DMA service by asserting a hardware request line, software can also initiate a DMA request. The Request Register is used to both set and clear any channel's request bit. The DMA controller does need to be in Block mode to use this function, as set in the Mode Register (port Bh). This register is write-only and is not supported on MCA systems.

Output (bits 0-7)

bit	7 w = x	Unused
	6 w = x	Unused
	5 w = x	Unused
	4 w = x	Unused
	3 w = x	Unused
	2 w = 0	Clear request bit
	1	Set request bit
	1 w = x	Select channel number
	0 w = x	bit 1 bit 0
		0 0 = channel 0
		0 1 = channel 1
		1 0 = channel 2
		1 1 = channel 3

Port	Type	Description	Platform
0Ah	Output	DMA-1 Mask Register Bit	All

The mask register is used to disable or enable individual incoming requests. Setting a mask bit on disables the selected channel. A hardware reset disables all channels by setting all mask bits. This register is write-only.

Output (bits 0-7)

bit	7 w = x	Unused
	6 w = x	Unused
	5 w = x	Unused
	4 w = x	Unused
	3 w = x	Unused
	2 w = 0	Clear mask bit
	1	Set mask bit

1 w = x	Select channel number		
0 w = x		bit 1	bit 0
		0	0 = channel 0
		0	1 = channel 1
		1	0 = channel 2
		1	1 = channel 3

Port	Type	Description	Platform
0Bh	Output	DMA-1 Mode Register	All

The Mode Register indicates the mode of operation for each of the four DMA channels 0 to 3. Each channel has a separate 6-bit mode register, each is loaded through the Mode Register port. This register is write-only.

Output (bits 0-7)

bit	7 w = x	Mode type selection		
	6 w = x		bit 7	bit 6
			0	0 = demand mode select
			0	1 = single mode select
			1	0 = block mode select
			1	1 = cascade mode select (not valid)
	5 w = 0	Address increment select		
	1	Address decrement select (invalid in EISA 32-bit and EISA normal address 16-bit transfer modes)		
	4 w = 0	Autoinitialization disable		
	1	Autoinitialization enable		
	3 w = x	Transfer type		
	2 w = x		bit 3	bit 2
			0	0 = verify
			0	1 = write
			1	0 = read
			1	1 = not valid
			x	x = if in cascade mode (bits 6 & 7)
	1 w = x	Select channel number		
	0 w = x		bit 1	bit 0
			0	0 = channel 0
			0	1 = channel 1
			1	0 = channel 2
			1	1 = channel 3

Port	Type	Description	Platform
0Ch	Output	DMA-1 Clear Byte Flip-Flop	All

An output of any value to this port causes the internal First/Last flip-flop to be cleared in DMA controller 1. This is done before any 8-bit reads or writes to 16-bit registers that require two successive 8-bit port accesses to complete the word transfer. After the flip-flop is cleared, a 16-bit DMA register is accessed by reading or writing the low byte followed by the high byte. The flip-flop can only be cleared, and is not readable.

Port	Type	Description	Platform
0Dh	Input	DMA-1 Temporary Register	All

The Temporary Register holds data during memory-to-memory data transfers. After the transfer is completed, the Temporary Register holds the last data transfer. The Temporary Register can be read when the DMA controller is not performing a DMA transfer. The register is cleared by a reset, and is read-only.

Port	Type	Description	Platform
0Dh	Output	DMA-1 Master Disable	All

Writing any value to this port resets DMA controller 1. This command has the same action as a hardware reset. The mask register is set (channels 0 to 3 disabled). The Command, Status, Request, Temporary, and the Byte flip-flop are all cleared. This register is write-only.

Port	Type	Description	Platform
0Eh	Output	DMA-1 Clear Mask Register	All

Writing any value to this port clears the mask register. Clearing the Mask Register will enable all four channels to accept DMA requests. This register is write-only.

Port	Type	Description	Platform
0Fh	Output	DMA-1 Write All Mask Bits	All

The mask register is used to disable or enable individual incoming requests. Setting a mask bit on disables the selected channel. A hardware reset disables all channels by setting all mask bits. This register is write-only.

Output (bits 0-7)

bit	7 w = x	Unused
	6 w = x	Unused

5 w = x	Unused
4 w = x	Unused
3 w = 0	Channel 3 clear mask bit (enabled)
1	Channel 3 set mask bit
2 w = 0	Channel 2 clear mask bit (enabled)
1	Channel 2 set mask bit
1 w = 0	Channel 1 clear mask bit (enabled)
1	Channel 1 set mask bit
0 w = 0	Channel 0 clear mask bit (enabled)
1	Channel 0 set mask bit

Port	Type	Description	Platform
18h	Output Register	DMA Extended Function	MCA

MCA machines replace the pair of 8237 DMA controllers with custom logic to simulate the base functions of the 8237 and add a number of extensions. This register allows alternate access to the DMA registers and extensions.

An output to this port initiates an extended command for a specific DMA channel. Depending on the command, the command byte may be followed by one to three reads or writes to port 1Ah to complete the operation.

Output (bits 0-7)

bit 7 w = x	Extended command 0 to F			
6 w = x				
5 w = x				
4 w = x				
3 w = 0	Unused			
2 w = x	Select channel number			
1 w = x		bit 2	bit 1	bit 0
0 w = x		0	0	0 = channel 0
		0	0	1 = channel 1
		0	1	0 = channel 2
		0	1	1 = channel 3
		1	0	0 = channel 4
		1	0	1 = channel 5
		1	1	0 = channel 6
		1	1	1 = channel 7

Extended Command Summary

The *x* in the command numbers below represents the channel number for the command, from 0 to 7.

Number	Port 18h Commands
0xh	I/O Address Register
2xh	Base and Current Address Write
3xh	Base Address Read
4xh	Base and Current Count Write
5xh	Base Count Read
6xh	Status Register Read
7xh	Extended Mode Register
80h	Arbitration Level—Channel 0
84h	Arbitration Level—Channel 4
9xh	Mask Register Disable Channel
Axh	Mask Register Enable Channel
Dxh	Master Disable

Extended Command Detail

★★★

Command	Description	Port
0xh	I/O Address Register	18h

The I/O address register allows setting an I/O port address for a DMA transfer. There is a 16-bit I/O address register for each of the 8 DMA channels. When set to 0000, the DMA operation for the channel is identical to the standard 8237 DMA found on AT/EISA machines. Non-zero values indicate the DMA action will occur to the specific port.

When a specific port address is used, each byte/word of the transfer must be stored in the DMA channel's temporary register. Use of this mode of operation will be slower than standard DMA because two bus accesses are required for each transfer. The big advantage is avoiding conflicts with other DMA users.

The following steps are taken to read or write a specific I/O address register, associated with a DMA channel *x*. All reads and writes must be in single bytes.

Step	Read Address Register
1	Output to port 18h, value 0xh
2	Input from port 1Ah, a0-a7
3	Input from port 1Ah, a8-a15

Step	Write Address Register
1	Output to port 18h, value 0xh
2	Output to port 1Ah, a0-a7
3	Output to port 1Ah, a8-a15

Command	Description	Port
2xh	Base and Current Address Write	18h

This command loads a 24-bit value into both the Base and Current address registers. It is similar in function to the standard 16-bit Base and Current address write specified with ports 0, 2, 4, 6, C0h, C4h, C8h or CCh, followed by a write to the page registers starting at port 81h.

The following steps occur to write a specific Base and Current address register, associated with DMA channel *x*. All writes must be in single bytes. The address bits differ between 8- and 16-bit transfers, as shown.

Step	For 8-bit DMA transfer
1	Output to port 18h, value 2xh (*x* = channel 0-7)
2	Output to port 1Ah, a0-a7
3	Output to port 1Ah, a8-a15
4	Output to port 1Ah, a16-a23

Step	For 16-bit DMA transfer
1	Output to port 18h, value 2xh (*x* = channel 5-7)
2	Output to port 1Ah, a1-a8
3	Output to port 1Ah, a9-a16
4	Output to port 1Ah, a17-a23

Command	Description	Port
3xh	Base Address Read	18h

This command reads the Base address register. There is no equivalent command on the 8237 DMA controller.

The following steps are taken to read a specific 24-bit Base address register, associated with DMA channel *x*. All reads and writes must be in single bytes. The address bits differ between 8- and 16-bit transfers, as shown.

Step	For 8-bit DMA transfers
1	Output to port 18h, value 3xh (*x* = channel 0-7)
2	Input from port 1Ah, a0-a7
3	Input from port 1Ah, a8-a15
4	Input from port 1Ah, a16-a23

Step	For 16-bit DMA transfers
1	Output to port 18h, value 3xh (*x* = channel 5-7)
2	Input from port 1Ah, a1-a8
3	Input from port 1Ah, a9-a16
4	Input from port 1Ah, a17-a23

Command	Description	Port
4xh	Base and Current Count Write	18h

This loads a 16-bit value into both the Base and Current count registers. It is similar in function to the standard 16-bit Base and Current count write specified with ports 1, 3, 5, 7, C2, C6, CA or CEh.

The following steps are taken to write a specific Base and Current count register, associated with DMA channel *x*. All writes must be in single bytes.

Step	Write Base and Current Count
1	Output to port 18h, value 4xh (*x* = channel 0-7)
2	Output to port 1Ah, count bits 0-7
3	Output to port 1Ah, count bits 8-15

Command	Description	Port
5xh	Base Count Read	18h

This command reads the Base count register. There is no equivalent command on the 8237 DMA controller.

The following steps are taken to read a specific 16-bit Base count register, associated with DMA channel *x*. All reads or writes must be in single bytes.

Step	Read Base Count
1	Output to port 18h, value 5xh (*x* = channel 0-7)
2	Input from port 1Ah, count bits 0-7
3	Input from port 1Ah, count bits 8-15

Command	Description	Port
6xh	Status Register Read	18h

The DMA Status Register hold flags (bits 0-3) of channels which have reached the Terminal Count (transfer completed). When this register is read, these four lower bits are cleared.

The status register also contains flags for pending DMA requests on each of the four channels. DMA requests occur by asserting the desired DMA channel request line.

The following steps are taken to read one of the two status registers. When a DMA channel, 0 to 3 is specified, all the information for channels 0 through 3 are returned, the same as using a status read with port 8. When a DMA channel, 4 to 7 is specified, all the information for channels 4-7 are returned, the same as using a status read with port D0h. All reads must be in single bytes.

Step	Status for Channels 0-3
1	Output to port 18h, value 50h-53h
2	Input from port 1Ah, status

bit	7 r = 1	DMA Channel 3 request
	6 r = 1	DMA Channel 2 request
	5 r = 1	DMA Channel 1 request
	4 r = 1	DMA Channel 0 request
	3 r = 1	DMA Channel 3 has reached terminal count
	2 r = 1	DMA Channel 2 has reached terminal count
	1 r = 1	DMA Channel 1 has reached terminal count
	0 r = 1	DMA Channel 0 has reached terminal count

Step	Status for Channels 4-7
1	Output to port 18h, value 54h-57h
2	Input from port 1Ah, status

bit	7 r = 1	DMA Channel 7 request
	6 r = 1	DMA Channel 6 request
	5 r = 1	DMA Channel 5 request
	4 r = 1	DMA Channel 4 request
	3 r = 1	DMA Channel 7 has reached terminal count
	2 r = 1	DMA Channel 6 has reached terminal count
	1 r = 1	DMA Channel 5 has reached terminal count
	0 r = 1	DMA Channel 4 has reached terminal count

Command	Description	Port
7xh	Extended Mode Register	18h

★★★

MCA systems provide an extended mode register for each channel. The extended mode register has some similarities to the mode register on the 8237 DMA controller. When the standard mode register is programmed, the MCA system reformats the information and places it into the related extended mode register.

The following steps are taken to read or write a specific extended mode register, associated with DMA channel *x*. All read and writes must be in single bytes.

Step	Read Mode Register
1	Output to port 18h, value 7xh (*x* = channel 0-7)
2	Input from port 1Ah, mode byte

Step	Write Mode Register
1	Output to port 18h, value 7xh (*x* = channel 0-7)
2	Output to port 1Ah, mode byte

Extended Mode byte:

bit	7 r/w = 0		Unused
	6 r/w = 0		8-bit transfer
		1	16-bit transfer
	5 r/w = 0		Unused
	4 r/w = 0		Unused
	3 r/w = 0		Read memory transfer
		1	Write memory transfer
	2 r/w = 0		Read verification operation
		1	Data transfer operation
	1 r/w = 0		Unused
	0 r/w = 0		No I/O address (address = 0)
		1	Use specified I/O address

Command	Description	Port
80h	Arbitration Level—Channel 0	18h

This sets channel 0's arbitration level for virtual DMA operations. There is no equivalent function on the 8237. There are no arbitration level registers for channels 1, 2, 3, 5, 6, or 7.

Step	Read Arbitration Level
1	Output to port 18h, value 80h
2	Input from port 1Ah, level

Step	Write Arbitration Level
1	Output to port 18h, value 80h
2	Output to port 1Ah, level

Arbitration level byte:

bit	7 r/w = 0	Unused
	6 r/w = 0	Unused
	5 r/w = 0	Unused
	4 r/w = 0	Unused
	3 r/w = x	Arbitration level 0-14
	2 r/w = x	
	1 r/w = x	
	0 r/w = x	

Command	Description	Port
84h	Arbitration Level—Channel 4	18h

This sets channel 4's arbitration level for virtual DMA operations. There is no equivalent function on the 8237. There are no arbitration level registers for channels 1, 2, 3, 5, 6, or 7.

Step	Read Arbitration Level
1	Output to port 18h, value 84h
2	Input from port 1Ah, level

Step	Write Arbitration Level
1	Output to port 18h, value 84h
2	Output to port 1Ah, level

Arbitration level byte:

bit	7 r/w = 0	Unused
	6 r/w = 0	Unused
	5 r/w = 0	Unused
	4 r/w = 0	Unused
	3 r/w = x	Arbitration level 0-14
	2 r/w = x	
	1 r/w = x	
	0 r/w = x	

Command	Description	Port
9xh	Mask Register Disable Channel	18h

The mask register is used to enable or disable individual incoming requests. This command sets a specific mask bit to disable the selected channel. Ports Ah and D4h provide similar functions on the 8237 DMA controller.

Command	Description	Port
Axh	Mask Register Enable Channel	18h

The mask register is used to enable or disable individual incoming requests. This command resets a specific mask bit to enable the selected channel. Ports Ah and D4h provide similar functions on the 8237 DMA controller.

Command	Description	Port
Dxh	Master Disable	18h

This command has the same effect as a hardware reset. The mask register is set and all channels in the group are disabled. The Command, Status, Request, Temporary, and the Byte flip-flop are all cleared. Ports Dh and DAh provide similar functions on the 8237 DMA controller.

To disable channels 0-3 as a group, use any command D0h to D3h. To disable channels 4-7 as a group, use any command D4h to D7h.

Port	Type	Description	Platform
1Ah	I/O	DMA Extended Function Execute	MCA

This port is used to read and write bytes based on a previously set command from port 18h. Refer to port 18h for details.

Port	Type	Description	Platform
80h	I/O	DMA page register channel 0	PC/XT

This register holds the address bits A16-A19 to use for DMA transfers to memory for channel 0. The lower 16 bits of address are generated by the DMA controller.

Port	Type	Description	Platform
81h	I/O	DMA page register channel 2	AT+

This register holds the address bits A16-A23 to use for DMA transfers to memory for channel 2. The lower 16 bits of address are generated by the DMA controller. This allows DMA transfers in the first 16 MB of memory.

Port	Type	Description	Platform
81h	I/O	DMA page register channel 1	PC/XT

This register holds the address bits A16-A19 to use for DMA transfers to memory for channel 1. The lower 16 bits of address are generated by the DMA controller.

Port	Type	Description	Platform
82h	I/O	DMA page register channel 3	AT+

This register holds the address bits A16-A23 to use for DMA transfers to memory for channel 3. The lower 16 bits of address are generated by the DMA controller. This allows DMA memory transfers in the first 16 MB of memory.

Port	Type	Description	Platform
82h	I/O	DMA page register channel 2	PC/XT

This register holds the address bits A16-A19 to use for DMA transfers to memory for channel 2. The lower 16 bits of address are generated by the DMA controller.

Port	Type	Description	Platform
83h	I/O	DMA page register channel 1	AT+

This register holds the address bits A16-A23 to use for DMA transfers to memory for channel 1. The lower 16 bits of address are generated by the DMA controller. This allows DMA memory transfers in the first 16 MB of memory.

Port	Type	Description	Platform
83h	I/O	DMA page register channel 3	PC/XT

This register holds the address bits A16-A19 to use for DMA transfers to memory for channel 3. The lower 16 bits of address are generated by the DMA controller.

Port	Type	Description	Platform
87h	I/O	DMA page register channel 0	AT+

This register holds the address bits A16-A23 to use for DMA transfers to memory for channel 0. The lower 16 bits of address are generated by the DMA controller. This allows DMA memory transfers in the first 16 MB of memory.

Port	Type	Description	Platform
89h	I/O	DMA page register channel 6	AT+

This register holds the address bits A17-A23 to use for DMA transfers to memory for channel 6. The lower 16 bits of address are generated by the DMA controller. This allows DMA memory transfers in the first 16 MB of memory.

Port	Type	Description	Platform
8Ah	I/O	DMA page register channel 7	AT+

This register holds the address bits A17-A23 to use for DMA transfers to memory for channel 7. The lower 16 bits of address are generated by the DMA controller. This allows DMA memory transfers in the first 16 MB of memory.

Port	Type	Description	Platform
8Bh	I/O	DMA page register channel 5	AT+

This register holds the address bits A17-A23 to use for DMA transfers to memory for channel 5. The lower 16 bits of address are generated by the DMA controller. This allows DMA memory transfers in the first 16 MB of memory.

Port	Type	Description	Platform
8Fh	I/O	DMA page register channel 4 (refresh)	AT+

Since channel 4 is used for a cascade from DMA controller 1 to DMA controller 2, this register is used instead for dynamic RAM refresh as part of the refresh controller on some systems.

Port	Type	Description	Platform
90h	Input	DMA Arbitration Status	MCA

This register is used to read the arbitration status.

Input (bits 0-7)

bit	7 r = 1	CPU cycles are enabled during arbitration
	6 r = 1	NMI occurred, so arbitration has been masked
	5 r = 1	A bus timeout occurred. Bit 6 is cleared.
	4 r = 0	Unused
	3 r = x	Returns the arbitration level of the last
	2 r = x	grant state. (0 to 15)
	1 r = x	
	0 r = x	

Port	Type	Description	Platform
90h	Output	DMA Arbitration Register	MCA

This register is used to change arbitration information.

Output (bits 0-7)

bit	7 w = 0	Disable CPU cycles during arbitration (default)
	1	Enable CPU cycles during arbitration
	6 w = 0	Normal operation (default)
	1	Enter arbitration state, the CPU controls the channel (used for diagnostics only)
	5 w = 0	Normal arbitration cycle (300 uS minimum, default)
	1	Extended arbitration cycle (600 uS minimum)

4 w = 0	Unused
3 w = 0	Unused
2 w = 0	Unused
1 w = 0	Unused
0 w = 0	Unused

Port	Type	Description	Platform
C0h	I/O	DMA-2 Base and Current Address, Channel 4	AT+

Channel 4 DMA is used for a cascade function from DMA controller 1. Channel 4 is unavailable for other uses.

Port	Type	Description	Platform
C2h	I/O	DMA-2 Base and Current Count, Channel 4	AT+

Channel 4 DMA is used for a cascade function from DMA controller 1. Channel 4 is unavailable for other uses.

Port	Type	Description	Platform
C4h	I/O	DMA-2 Base and Current Address, Channel 5	AT+

On AT and EISA systems DMA channel 5 is an unassigned channel, used for high-speed transfers between memory and the I/O bus.

On the PS/2, channel 5 is used for hard disk DMA operations.

Input (bits 0-7)—Read Current Address Register (see port 0)

Output (bits 0-7)—Write both Base and Current Address Registers (see port 0)

Port	Type	Description	Platform
C6h	I/O	DMA-2 Base and Current Count, Channel 5	AT+

On AT and EISA systems DMA channel 5 is an unassigned channel, used for high-speed transfers between memory and the I/O bus.

On the PS/2, channel 5 is used for hard disk DMA operations.

Input (bits 0-7)—Read Current Count Register (see port 1)

Output (bits 0-7)—Write both Base and Current Count Registers (see port 1)

Port	Type	Description	Platform
C8h	I/O	DMA-2 Base and Current Address, Channel 6	AT+

Channel 6 DMA is an unassigned channel, used for high-speed transfers between memory and the I/O bus.

Input (bits 0-7)—Read Current Address Register (see port 0)
Output (bits 0-7)—Write both Base and Current Address Registers (see port 0)

Port	Type	Description	Platform
CAh	I/O	DMA-2 Base and Current Count, Channel 6	AT+

Channel 6 DMA is an unassigned channel, used for high-speed transfers between memory and the I/O bus.

Input (bits 0-7)—Read Current Count Register (see port 1)
Output (bits 0-7)—Write both Base and Current Count Registers (see port 1)

Port	Type	Description	Platform
CCh	I/O	DMA-2 Base and Current Address, Channel 7	AT+

Channel 7 DMA is an unassigned channel, used for high-speed transfers between memory and the I/O bus.

Input (bits 0-7)—Read Current Address Register (see port 0)
Output (bits 0-7)—Write both Base and Current Address Registers (see port 0)

Port	Type	Description	Platform
CEh	I/O	DMA-2 Base and Current Count, Channel 7	AT+

Channel 7 DMA is an unassigned channel, used for high-speed transfers between memory and the I/O bus.

Input (bits 0-7)—Read Current Count Register (see port 1)
Output (bits 0-7)—Write both Base and Current Count Registers (see port 1)

Port	Type	Description	Platform
D0h	Input	DMA-2 Status Register	AT+

The DMA Status Register hold flags (bits 0-3) indicating when each channel has reached the Terminal Count (transfer completed). When this register is read, these lower four bits are cleared.

The status register also contains flags for pending DMA requests on each of the four channels. DMA requests occur by asserting the desired DMA channel request line.

Input (bits 0-7)

bit	7 r = 1	DMA Channel 7 request
	6 r = 1	DMA Channel 6 request
	5 r = 1	DMA Channel 5 request
	4 r = 0	DMA Channel 4 used for cascade
	3 r = 1	DMA Channel 7 has reached terminal count
	2 r = 1	DMA Channel 6 has reached terminal count
	1 r = 1	DMA Channel 5 has reached terminal count
	0 r = 0	DMA Channel 4 used for cascade

Port	Type	Description	Platform
D0h	Output	DMA-2 Command Register	AT/EISA

This 8-bit register controls the operation of the DMA. The register is cleared by a hardware reset or a Master Disable instruction (port 0DAh). The command value used by PCs is 0. Normally all bits are left at 0, except bit 2 is typically set to 1 to disable the controller while writing to DMA registers. This register is write-only, and is not supported on MCA systems.

Output (bits 0-7)

bit	7 w = 0	DACK sense active low (default)
	1	DACK sense active high
	6 w = 0	DREQ sense active high (default)
	1	DREQ sense active low
	5 w = 0	Late write selection
	1	Extended write selection
	x	if bit-3 = 0 (default)
	4 w = 0	Fixed priority (default)
	1	Rotating priority
	3 w = 0	Normal timing
	1	Compressed timing
	x	if bit-1 = 0 (default)

2 w = 0	Controller enable (default)
1	Controller disable
1 w = 0	Channel 4 address hold disable
1	Channel 4 address hold enable
x	if bit-0 = 0 (default)
0 w = 0	Memory-to-memory transfers disabled (default)
1	Memory-to-memory transfers enabled

Port	Type	Description	Platform
D2h	Output	DMA-2 Request Register	AT/EISA

In addition to initiating a request for DMA service by asserting a hardware request line, software can also initiate a DMA request. The Request Register is used to both set and clear any channel's request bit. The DMA controller does need to be in Block mode to use this function, as set in the Mode Register (port D6h). This register is write-only and is not supported on MCA systems.

Output (bits 0-7)

bit 7 w = x	Unused		
6 w = x	Unused		
5 w = x	Unused		
4 w = x	Unused		
3 w = x	Unused		
2 w = 0	Clear request bit		
1	Set request bit		
1 w = x	Select channel number		
0 w = x		bit 1	bit 0
		0	0 = channel 4
		0	1 = channel 5
		1	0 = channel 6
		1	1 = channel 7

Port	Type	Description	Platform
D4h	Output	DMA-2 Mask Register Bit	AT+

The mask register is used to disable or enable individual incoming requests. Setting a mask bit on disables the selected channel. A hardware reset disables all channels by setting all mask bits. This register is write-only.

Output (bits 0-7)

bit	7 w = x	Unused
	6 w = x	Unused
	5 w = x	Unused
	4 w = x	Unused
	3 w = x	Unused
	2 w = 0	Clear mask bit (enable channel)
	1	Set mask bit (disable channel)
	1 w = x	Select channel number
	0 w = x	bit 1 bit 0
		0 0 = channel 4
		0 1 = channel 5
		1 0 = channel 6
		1 1 = channel 7

Port	Type	Description	Platform
D6h	Output	DMA-2 Mode Register	AT+

The Mode Register is used to indicate the mode of operation for each of the four DMA channels 4 to 7. Each channel has a separate 6-bit mode register, each loaded through the Mode Register port. This register is write-only.

Output (bits 0-7)

bit	7 w = x	Mode type selection
	6 w = x	bit 7 bit 6
		0 0 = demand mode select
		0 1 = single mode select
		1 0 = block mode select
		1 1 = cascade mode select (channel 4 only)
	5 w = 0	Address increment select
	1	Address decrement select (invalid in EISA 32-bit and EISA normal address 16-bit transfer modes)
	4 w = 0	Autoinitialization disable
	1	Autoinitialization enable
	3 w = x	Transfer type
	2 w = x	bit 3 bit 2
		0 0 = verify
		0 1 = write

	1	0 = read
	1	1 = not-valid
	x	x = if in cascade mode (bits 6 & 7)
1 w = x	Select channel number	
0 w = x	bit 1	bit 0
	0	0 = channel 4
	0	1 = channel 5
	1	0 = channel 6
	1	1 = channel 7

Port	Type	Description	Platform
D8h	Output	DMA-2 Clear Byte Flip/Flop	AT+

An output of any value to this port causes the internal First/Last flip-flop to be cleared in DMA controller 2. This is done before any 8-bit reads or writes to 16-bit registers that require two successive 8-bit port accesses to complete the word transfer. After the flip-flop is cleared, a 16-bit DMA register is accessed by reading or writing the low byte followed by the high byte. The flip-flop can only be cleared, and is not readable.

Port	Type	Description	Platform
DAh	Input	DMA-2 Temporary Register	AT+

The Temporary Register holds data during memory-to-memory data transfers. After the transfer is completed, the Temporary Register holds the last data transfer. The Temporary Register can be read when the DMA controller is not performing a DMA transfer. The register is cleared by a reset, and is read-only.

Port	Type	Description	Platform
DAh	Output	DMA-2 Master Disable	AT+

Writing any value to this port resets DMA controller 2. This command has the same action as a hardware reset. The mask register is set (channels 4 to 7 disabled). The Command, Status, Request, Temporary, and the Byte flip-flop are all cleared. This register is write-only.

Port	Type	Description	Platform
DCh	Output	DMA-2 Clear Mask Register	AT+

Writing any value to this port clears the mask register. Clearing the Mask Register will enable channels 5, 6, and 7 to accept DMA requests. This register is write-only.

Port	Type	Description	Platform
DEh	Output	DMA-2 Write All Mask Bits	AT+

The mask register is used to disable or enable individual incoming requests. Setting a mask bit on disables the selected channel. A hardware reset disables all channels by setting all mask bits. This register is write-only.

Output (bits 0-7)

bit	7 w = x	Unused
	6 w = x	Unused
	5 w = x	Unused
	4 w = x	Unused
	3 w = 0	Channel 7 clear mask bit (enabled)
	1	Channel 7 set mask bit
	2 w = 0	Channel 6 clear mask bit (enabled)
	1	Channel 6 set mask bit
	1 w = 0	Channel 5 clear mask bit (enabled)
	1	Channel 5 set mask bit
	0 w = 0	Channel 4 clear mask bit (enabled)
	1	Channel 4 set mask bit (recommended)

Port	Type	Description	Platform
401h	I/O	DMA-1 Base and Current Count, Channel 0, high	EISA

The EISA system adds an additional 8 bits to the 16-bit count registers at port 1 to provide a 24-bit count. Depending on the size of the transfer, up to 64 MB can be transferred at a time (32-bit transfer * max count of 16 M).

Input (bits 0-7)—Read Current Count Register

Read the high 8-bits of the 24-bit Current Count Register for DMA channel 0.

Output (bits 0-7)—Write both Base and Current Count Registers

The high 8-bits of both 24-bit count registers is written. If chaining mode is active only the base count is written. The Base Count Register is write-only.

Port	Type	Description	Platform
403h	I/O	DMA-1 Base and Current Count, Channel 1, high	EISA

This port controls the 24-bit Base and Current Count registers for DMA channel 1. Port 401h has further details.

Input (bits 0-7)—Read Current Count Register

Output (bits 0-7)—Write both Base and Current Count Registers

Port	Type	Description	Platform
405h	I/O	DMA-1 Base and Current Count, Channel 2, high	EISA

This port controls the 24-bit Base and Current Count registers for DMA channel 2. Port 401h has further details.

Input (bits 0-7)—Read Current Count Register

Output (bits 0-7)—Write both Base and Current Count Registers

Port	Type	Description	Platform
407h	I/O	DMA-1 Base and Current Count, Channel 3, high	EISA

This port controls the 24-bit Base and Current Count registers for DMA channel 3. Port 401h has further details.

Input (bits 0-7)—Read Current Count Register

Output (bits 0-7)—Write both Base and Current Count Registers

Port	Type	Description	Platform
40Ah	Input	DMA Chaining Interrupt Status	EISA

When chaining mode is used and a Terminal Count occurs (transfer count completes), IRQ 13 is activated. In addition, a bit is set in this interrupt status register for the specific channel. It is cleared automatically when the chaining mode for that channel is set to programming complete "11" or chaining is disabled or terminated "00". This register is read-only.

Input (bit 0-7)

bit	7 r = 1	DMA Channel 7 chained interrupt occurred
	6 r = 1	DMA Channel 6 chained interrupt occurred
	5 r = 1	DMA Channel 5 chained interrupt occurred

4 r = 0	Unused
3 r = 1	DMA Channel 3 chained interrupt occurred
2 r = 1	DMA Channel 2 chained interrupt occurred
1 r = 1	DMA Channel 1 chained interrupt occurred
0 r = 1	DMA Channel 0 chained interrupt occurred

Port	Type	Description	Platform
40Ah	Output	DMA-1 Chaining Mode Register	EISA

This register controls chained DMA transfers. Refer to the section on EISA Chained Transfers for further details. This register is write-only.

Output (bits 0-7)

bit	7 w = 0	Unused
	6 w = 0	Unused
	5 w = 0	Unused
	4 w = 0	Signal last transfer complete on IRQ 13 (default)
	1	Signal last transfer complete on Terminal Count line
	3 w = x	Chaining mode
	2 w = x	bit 3 bit 2
		0 0 = Disable or terminate chaining
		0 1 = Enable chaining for programming
		1 0 = Invalid mode
		1 1 = Programming complete, begin
	1 w = x	Channel select
	0 w = x	bit 1 bit 0
		0 0 = channel 0
		0 1 = channel 1
		1 0 = channel 2
		1 1 = channel 3

Port	Type	Description	Platform
40Bh	Output	DMA-1 Extended Mode Register	EISA

This register controls advanced features for channels 0-3 on the EISA DMA controller. A binary value of "000000xx" is used for AT compatibility, and is the default for each channel after a hardware reset. Some combinations are not valid. Refer to Table 18-7 for these limitations. The DMA Master clear does not affect this information. This register is write-only.

On AT systems, only 8-bit transfers are allowed for channels 0 to 3. EISA provides a number of options to allow 16-bit transfers with the address shifted by 1-bit so that 64 K words can be addressed. This is similar to the standard AT support for channels 5, 6, and 7.

Output (bits 0-7)

bit	7 w = 0	Stop register disabled
	1	Stop register enabled (see EISA FIFO Transfers)
	6 w = 0	Terminal Count (TC) line outputs when TC reached
	1	Terminal Count line is an input to terminate a transfer
	5 w = x	Cycle timing mode
	4 w = x	bit 5 bit 4
		0 0 = AT bus compatible
		0 1 = type A
		1 0 = type B
		1 1 = type C, burst DMA
	3 w = x	Address translation and I/O transfer size
	2 w = x	bit 3 bit 2
		0 0 = normal addresses, 8-bit (AT)
		0 1 = shifted addresses, 16-bit (AT)
		1 0 = normal addresses, 32-bit
		1 1 = normal addresses, 16-bit
	1 w = x	Channel select
	0 w = x	bit 1 bit 0
		0 0 = channel 0
		0 1 = channel 1
		1 0 = channel 2
		1 1 = channel 3

Port	Type	Description	Platform
40Ch	Input	DMA Chaining Terminal Count Action Status	EISA

The Chaining mode register, bit 4, specifies the action when a Terminal Count (TC) occurs. The status for all channels of this selection is read from this port. A "1" indicates the channel will flag the TC line when TC occurs. A "0" indicates the channel will flag IRQ 13 when TC occurs. This register is read-only.

Input (bit 0-7)

bit	7 r = 0	DMA Channel 7 chaining TC flags IRQ 13
	6 r = 0	DMA Channel 6 chaining TC flags IRQ 13
	5 r = 0	DMA Channel 5 chaining TC flags IRQ 13
	4 r = 0	Unused
	3 r = 0	DMA Channel 3 chaining TC flags IRQ 13
	2 r = 0	DMA Channel 2 chaining TC flags IRQ 13
	1 r = 0	DMA Channel 1 chaining TC flags IRQ 13
	0 r = 0	DMA Channel 0 chaining TC flags IRQ 13

Port	Type	Description	Platform
481h	I/O	DMA page register channel 2, high	EISA

This register holds the address bits A24-A31 for DMA transfers for channel 2. Always write this register after the base and low page registers are written. A write to this channel's base address register or a write to the low page register at port 81h automatically clears this register. This ensures compatibility with DMA on AT systems.

Port	Type	Description	Platform
482h	I/O	DMA page register channel 3, high	EISA

This register holds the upper 8 bits of the 32-bit address register for channel 3. See port 481h for details.

Port	Type	Description	Platform
483h	I/O	DMA page register channel 1, high	EISA

This register holds the upper 8 bits of the 32-bit address register for channel 1. See port 481h for details.

Port	Type	Description	Platform
487h	I/O	DMA page register channel 0, high	EISA

This register holds the upper 8 bits of the 32-bit address register for channel 0. See port 481h for details.

Port	Type	Description	Platform
489h	I/O	DMA page register channel 6, high	EISA

This register holds the upper 8 bits of the 32-bit address register for channel 6. See port 481h for details.

Port	Type	Description	Platform
48Ah	I/O	DMA page register channel 7, high	EISA

This register holds the upper 8 bits of the 32-bit address register for channel 7. See port 481h for details.

Port	Type	Description	Platform
48Bh	I/O	DMA page register channel 5, high	EISA

This register holds the upper 8 bits of the 32-bit address register for channel 5. See port 481h for details.

Port	Type	Description	Platform
4C6h	I/O	DMA-2 Base and Current Count, Channel 5, high	EISA

This port controls the 24-bit Base and Current Count register for DMA channel 5. Port 401h has further details.

Input (bits 0-7)—Read Current Count Register

Output (bits 0-7)—Write both Base and Current Count Registers

Port	Type	Description	Platform
4CAh	I/O	DMA-2 Base and Current Count, Channel 6, high	EISA

This port controls the 24-bit Base and Current Count register for DMA channel 6. Port 401h has further details.

Input (bits 0-7)—Read Current Count Register

Output (bits 0-7)—Write both Base and Current Count Registers

Port	Type	Description	Platform
4CEh	I/O	DMA-2 Base and Current Count, Channel 7, high	EISA

This port controls the 24-bit Base and Current Count register for DMA channel 7. Port 401h has further details.

Input (bits 0-7)—Read Current Count Register

Output (bits 0-7)—Write both Base and Current Count Registers

Port	Type	Description	Platform
4D4h	Input	DMA Chaining Status	EISA

Chaining Status is a set of flags indicating whether chaining mode is active on each channel or not. This register is read-only.

Input (bits 0-7) Chaining Status

bit	7 r = 1	DMA Channel 7 chaining active
	6 r = 1	DMA Channel 6 chaining active
	5 r = 1	DMA Channel 5 chaining active
	4 r = 0	Unused
	3 r = 1	DMA Channel 3 chaining active
	2 r = 1	DMA Channel 2 chaining active
	1 r = 1	DMA Channel 1 chaining active
	0 r = 1	DMA Channel 0 chaining active

Port	Type	Description	Platform
4D4h	Output	DMA-2 Chaining Mode Register	EISA

This register controls chained DMA transfers. Refer to the section on EISA Chained Transfers for further details. This register is write-only.

Output (bits 0-7)

bit	7 w = 0	Unused
	6 w = 0	Unused
	5 w = 0	Unused
	4 w = 0	Signal last transfer complete on IRQ 13 (default)
	1	Signal last transfer complete on Terminal Count line
	3 w = x	Chaining mode
	2 w = x	bit 3 bit 2
		0 0 = Disable or terminate chaining
		0 1 = Enable chaining for programming
		1 0 = Invalid mode
		1 1 = Programming complete, begin
	1 w = x	Channel select
	0 w = x	bit 1 bit 0
		0 0 = channel 4
		0 1 = channel 5
		1 0 = channel 6
		1 1 = channel 7

Port	Type	Description	Platform
4D6h	Output	DMA-2 Extended Mode Register	EISA

This register controls advanced features for channels 4-7 on the EISA DMA controller. A binary value of "000001xx" is used for AT compatibility, and is the default for each channel after a hardware reset. Some combinations are not valid. Refer to Table 18-7 for these limitations. The DMA Master clear does not affect this information. This register is write-only.

On AT systems, 16-bit transfers occur with the address shifted by 1-bit so that 64 K words can be addressed. EISA offers this same compatibility mode, but also offers a normal non-shifted 16-bit mode. This could be used for non-word-aligned transfers.

Output (bits 0-7)

bit	7 w = 0	Stop register disabled	
	1	Stop register enabled (see EISA FIFO Transfers)	
	6 w = 0	Terminal Count (TC) line outputs when TC reached	
	1	Terminal Count line is an input to terminate a transfer	
	5 w = x	Cycle timing mode	
	4 w = x	bit 5	bit 4
		0	0 = AT bus compatible
		0	1 = type A
		1	0 = type B
		1	1 = type C, burst DMA
	3 w = x	Address translation and I/O transfer size	
	2 w = x	bit 3	bit 2
		0	0 = normal addresses, 8-bit (ISA)
		0	1 = shifted addresses, 16-bit (ISA)
		1	0 = normal addresses, 32-bit
		1	1 = normal addresses, 16-bit
	1 w = x	Channel select	
	0 w = x	bit 1	bit 0
		0	0 = channel 4
		0	1 = channel 5
		1	0 = channel 6
		1	1 = channel 7

Port	Type	Description	Platform
4E0-4E2h	I/O	DMA-Stop Register, Channel 0	EISA

The DMA Stop Register is used to build a FIFO buffer in the lower 16 MB of memory. Should the DMA transfer reach the address stored in the stop register (buffer full), the transfer is stopped and the channel is disabled. The stop register is built from three 8-bit ports, and must align on a double word boundary.

Port 4E0h—DMA channel 0 stop address a0 to a7 (a0 and a1 are ignored)
Port 4E1h—DMA channel 0 stop address a8 to a15
Port 4E2h—DMA channel 0 stop address a16 to a23

Port	Type	Description	Platform
4E4-4E6h	I/O	DMA-Stop Register, Channel 1	EISA

This is the stop register for channel 1. See port 4E0-4E2h for details.

Port 4E4h—DMA channel 1 stop address a0 to a7 (a0 and a1 are ignored)
Port 4E5h—DMA channel 1 stop address a8 to a15
Port 4E6h—DMA channel 1 stop address a16 to a23

Port	Type	Description	Platform
4E8-4EAh	I/O	DMA-Stop Register, Channel 2	EISA

This is the stop register for channel 2. See port 4E0-4E2h for details.

Port 4E8h—DMA channel 2 stop address a0 to a7 (a0 and a1 are ignored)
Port 4E9h—DMA channel 2 stop address a8 to a15
Port 4EAh—DMA channel 2 stop address a16 to a23

Port	Type	Description	Platform
4EC-4EEh	I/O	DMA-Stop Register, Channel 3	EISA

This is the stop register for channel 3. See port 4E0-4E2h for details.

Port 4ECh—DMA channel 3 stop address a0 to a7 (a0 and a1 are ignored)
Port 4EDh—DMA channel 3 stop address a8 to a15
Port 4EEh—DMA channel 3 stop address a16 to a23

Port	Type	Description	Platform
4F4-4F6h	I/O	DMA-Stop Register, Channel 5	EISA

This is the stop register for channel 5. See port 4E0-4E2h for details.

Port 4F4h—DMA channel 5 stop address a0 to a7 (a0 and a1 are ignored)
Port 4F5h—DMA channel 5 stop address a8 to a15
Port 4F6h—DMA channel 5 stop address a16 to a23

Port	Type	Description	Platform
4F8-4FAh	I/O	DMA-Stop Register, Channel 6	EISA

This is the stop register for channel 6. See port 4E0-4E2h for details.

Port 4F8h—DMA channel 6 stop address a0 to a7 (a0 and a1 are ignored)
Port 4F9h—DMA channel 6 stop address a8 to a15
Port 4FAh—DMA channel 6 stop address a16 to a23

Port	Type	Description	Platform
4FC-4FEh	I/O	DMA-Stop Register, Channel 7	EISA

This is the stop register for channel 7. See port 4E0-4E2h for details.

Port 4FCh—DMA channel 7 stop address a0 to a7 (a0 and a1 are ignored)
Port 4FDh—DMA channel 7 stop address a8 to a15
Port 4FEh—DMA channel 7 stop address a16 to a23

APPENDIX A

Programs on Disk

This appendix summarizes the files on the accompanying diskette.

Executable Program Summary

Program Name	Description	Chapter Described
a20test	Tests the keyboard controller's ability to change A20 *	8
beep*x*	Demonstration programs for assembly and C	3
biosview	Displays key BIOS values and full descriptions *	6
cmosview	Displays main and extended CMOS registers *	15
cpurdmsr	Finds and describes model-specific registers *	4
cpurdtsc	Tests undocumented Pentium time stamp counter	4
cputest	Looks for undocumented opcodes *	4
cputype	Identifies information about CPU *	4
cpuundoc	Tests all known undocumented instructions *	4
ctrl2cap	TSR to swap Ctrl and Caps Lock	8
disktest	Tests for BIOS problem, sector reads *	10, 11
iodelay	Short delay for I/O on any CPU	3

Program Name	Description	Chapter Described
iospy	TSR to monitor I/O port states	2
irqredir	Changes IRQ redirection	17
keybios	Checks for extended keyboard support	8
keyscan	Shows Kscan or scan code for any key pressed *	8
max_recv	Used to find maximum serial transfer rate	12
max_xmit	Used to find maximum serial transfer rate	12
prnascii	TSR to allow printing of non-ASCII	14
prnswap	Swaps the parallel ports *	14
prntype	Information about parallel ports	14
sertype	Information about serial ports *	12
sspy	TSR to display serial port status	12
systype	Shows system type, BIOS, disk and video info *	4, 9, 10, 11
testcase	Test case for the event timer program TIMEVENT	16
timevent	High precision event duration timer	16
tmrfast	Makes system timer 50 times faster	16
unpc	Views I/O ports, runs other tests	2

* *New, modified and/or enhanced from* The Undocumented PC, *first edition*

Interesting Subroutines

Subroutine Name	Description	Parent Program
biosinfo	Identifies the BIOS manufacturer and date. In some cases this routine also identifies the chipset, LBA support, and motherboard manufacturing location	systype.asm
cache_d_size	Measures the size of the internal CPU cache	cputype.asm
check_A20	Finds out whether A20 is currently enabled or not	a20test.asm
cpu386	Short version of cpuvalue, to identify the CPU 8088 to 80386+. Does not test for CPUs above 80386.	systype.asm
cpu_cache	Determines if the CPU cache is enabled	cputype.asm
cpuq	CPU prefetch queue size is measured	cputype.asm
cpumode	Returns if CPU in real, protected, or V86 mode	cputype.asm
cpuspeed	Determines the CPU speed in MHz	cputype.asm
cpustep	Identifies the CPU revision	cputype.asm
cpuvalue	Gets the current CPU type, 8088 to P7 and other variants, the instruction set supported by the CPU, and whether CPU supports the CPUID instruction	cputype.asm
cpuvendor	Identifies the CPU manufacturer	cputype.asm
disktype	Gets the type of diskette drive, 320K to 2.88M	systype.asm

Subroutine Name	Description	Parent Program
dma_read	Shows how to perform a DMA transfer	dma_read.sub
fpuloc	Determines if floating point is inside CPU	cputype.asm
fputype	Identifies the floating-point processor	cputype.asm
hdconvert	Unscrambles BIOS head position	systype.asm
hdsktype	Gets the type of hard disk and size	systype.asm
iodelay	Subroutine for a short 1 uS delay	iodelay.asm
key9	Checks if int 16h, function 9 is available	keybios.asm
keyboard_cmd	Sends a command to the keyboard keyview.asm	controller
keyboard_read	Reads a byte from the keyboard	keyview.asm
keyboard_write	Writes a byte to the keyboard	keyview.asm
keytype	Checks for extended keyboard support	keybios.asm
PCI_detect	Checks if the motherboard has a PCI bus	systype.asm
read_CMOS	Reads the contents of a specific CMOS register	cmosview.asm
serslow	Slows the UART to 2 bits per second	serslow.sub
setLEDs	Controls LEDs on the keyboard for debugging a port	keyview.asm
sysvalue	Gets the type of system: PC, XT, AT, EISA, MCA, or PCI	systype.asm
testport	Identifies UART chip type	sertype.asm
video_type	Gets the type of video, MDA to XGA, and more	systype.asm
write_CMOS	Writes the contents to a specific CMOS register	cmosview.asm

Detailed Explanations of Executable Programs

A20TEST

This program shows the current A20 state, and as long as the CPU is not in V86 mode, it attempts to change the state through the keyboard controller. Upon completion, the A20 state is returned to its prior value.

BEEPx

Three programs demonstrate the operation of interrupts and I/O ports in both assembly and C. The programs are BEEPA.ASM, BEEPB.C and BEEPM.C. The last two programs are for Borland C and Microsoft C. Beep*x* uses the timer to generate a 2 second 5 KHz beep.

BIOSVIEW

Displays the current BIOS values in low memory, with detailed descriptions. The best way to view this output is to redirect the output to a file. For example, “BIOSVIEW > BIOSDATA.TXT”.

CMOSVIEW

Displays the contents of CMOS with documented function names. See Chapter 15 for vendor-specific functions, which vary depending on the BIOS manufacturer. CMOSVIEW also checks for three alternate extended CMOS data areas and displays any extended data found.

CPURDMSR

Some 386+ CPUs support new instructions, Read and Write Model Specific Registers (RDMSR and WRMSR). These access special functions for the CPU. The instruction is called with ECX set to the register to look at. This test program looks through every possible combination to see which registers, if any, are used by the CPU. Any found registers are presented with the current 64-bit register value and description (when known).

Use "CPURDMSR +" to display every test made. This runs about 30 times slower than the default, which only displays once every 65,536 tests—unless a register is found. Use "CPURDMSR -" to test and display the 32 hidden registers starting at 80000000h.

CPURDTSC

The Pentium processor uses a new instruction, RDTSC, to read the Time Stamp Counter. This routine continuously displays the values from the Time Stamp Counter until Ctrl-Break is pressed.

CPUTEST

Locates potential hidden instructions on 80286 and later CPUs. This program works by seeing if any unused opcodes do not trip the bad opcode interrupt. Known Intel-documented instructions and known undocumented instructions are ignored. This program also ignores MMX instructions, when the CPU indicates MMX instructions are supported. Use CPUUNDOC to show and test validity of known undocumented instructions.

CPUTYPE

Displays information about the CPU. Demonstrates the results of a number of individual detection subroutines. Information includes the CPU class (as stated by the manufacturer), the true instruction set supported (relative to Intel), the CPU vendor, internal CPU speed, prefetch queue size, CPU step and revision, L1 cache state and L1 measured cache size. In addition, the routine identifies if the CPUID, Cyrix ID registers, or MMX instructions are supported. Additional information is provided if CPUID or Cyrix ID registers are available.

Use the command line option "-" to prevent a test that requires the use of protected-mode instructions that might not be handled correctly in V86 mode. Use the option "+" to show the raw timing values for the internal CPU speed and L1 cache sizing tests.

CPUUNDOC

Tests all known undocumented instructions for the current CPU. Most tests verify how each undocumented instruction functions, as described in Chapter 3, The CPU and Undocumented Instructions.

CTRL2CAP

TSR to swap the functions of the Ctrl and Caps Lock keys. Demonstrates the use of interrupt 15h, 4Ah to hook into scan codes.

DISKTEST

Reads sectors from the specified disk to test how the BIOS responds. The test looks for problems when more than one track is read at a time, using the BIOS service interrupt 13h. Many systems show different limitations. Works with both diskette and hard disk drives, although diskette drives take a few minutes to test. Specify the disk number on the command line, 0 and 1 for diskette drives, and 80, 81, etc. for hard disk drives.

IODELAY

Shows the use of the IODELAY subroutine. This example is not really useful, but just shows how IODELAY would be used when accessing I/O ports on the same device in quick succession.

I/O SPY

This TSR displays the current state of specific ports. The specified port is read 18 times/second. Up to eight ports can be monitored at one time. Many command line options. See full description in Chapter 2.

IRQREDIR

Redirects IRQ 0 through 7 to an alternate set of interrupt vectors. This may boost performance when the system is in V86 mode if IRQ 5 is used for high interrupt rates. See the warnings section in Chapter 17 for more about the conflict between IRQ 5 and interrupt 0Dh.

KEYBIOS

Checks the BIOS to see if interrupt 16h extended BIOS services are available. Specific services are checked including functions 5, 9, 10h, 11h, and 12h.

KEYSCAN

Displays the current keyboard controller command byte, then turns off normal keyboard controller translation, and displays the untranslated code when a key is pressed. Escape key exits program. This is for all computers equipped with a keyboard controller, but not for PC/XT. Program also shows how to turn on and off the keyboard LEDs.

Use the command line option "-k" to leave translation active and show the scan code of a pressed key.

MAX_RECV

This routine works with a companion routine, MAX_XMIT, to find the maximum sustained transfer rate between two systems, connected by a null modem cable. Serial port 1 is assumed unless port 1 to 4 is specified on the command line.

MAX_XMIT
This routine works with a companion routine, MAX_RECV, to find the maximum sustained transfer rate between two systems, connected by a null modem cable. Serial port 1 is assumed unless port 1 to 4 is specified on the command line.

PRNASCII
TSR to convert non-ASCII characters to acceptable characters for those printers that cannot print the entire IBM character set. Works with most programs and Print Screen.

PRNSWAP
Swaps the parallel ports for printers 1 and 2. PRNSWAP is not a TSR.

PRNTYPE
Detects any active parallel ports and identifies those ports which support extended mode.

SERIAL TYPE
Reports active serial port I/O addresses and identifies the UART type.

SERIAL SPY
TSR to display the current modem input and output states of a specific port. To use, specify which port, from 1 to 4, to monitor on the command line.

SYSTYPE
Determines the system bus type, BIOS vendor and date, diskette types, hard disk types, video display type and, in some cases, the video display vendor.

TESTCASE
Program used to show how TIMEVENT can monitor the duration of a section of code. To use, first run TIMEVENT. Then run TESTCASE. Then run TIMEVENT again to see the time it took to run a section of code in TESTCASE.

TIMEVENT
Program displays any previous event duration, and resets the timer to time the next event duration. See TESTCASE.

TMRFAST
Demonstration program to show how to boost the system interrupt rate beyond the normal 18.2 times per second. Useful when higher interrupt rates are needed without affecting the rest of the system. Demonstration puts a white overstrike character on a changing green character, with a black background. This is performed in text mode by quickly swapping characters at 910 times per second, which is 50 times the normal system clock rate.

UNPC
Views I/O ports, runs utilities, and displays information. This is also the fastest way to run programs and look at the source code of many utilities included in the book.

APPENDIX B

Glossary

General Abbreviations

ABIOS A portion of the system BIOS on IBM's PS/2 systems. It is only used by OS/2.

AT Advanced Technology is a designation used by IBM for their first 286-based PC, which offered the first 16-bit adapter bus. Many new machines are commonly referred to as AT compatible, even when they use a 386 or later CPU. ISA (Industry Standard Architecture) is an outgrowth of the basic AT design, and the two abbreviations are used interchangeably.

AT+ 286 or later PC, including the AT, ISA, EISA, and MCA bus designs

ATA (AT Attachment) ATA defines the commands and physical aspects of internal block devices. The most common block device is the IDE hard drive.

BIOS Basic Input/Output System, which provides the lowest level software control of the computer's hardware.

CMOS In the context of a PC, a nonvolatile memory device used to store a small amount of system configuration information (it really stands for Complimentary Metallic Oxide Semiconductor).

CRC Cyclic Redundancy Check—Data used to verify that no data corruptions have occurred in a block of data. Commonly used on diskette drives.

CTS Clear To Send—An input line from the serial port connector

DAC Digital to Analog Converter, used in VGA for the generation of colors.

DBCS Double Byte Character Set

DMA Direct Memory Access

dpi dots per inch, used as a measure of resolution for the mouse, displays, and other devices.

DPMI DOS Protected Mode Interface. A standard for providing services to programs running in protected mode under DOS.

DSR Data Set Ready—An input line from the serial port connector

DTR Data Terminal Ready—An output line to the serial port connector

EBDA Extended BIOS Data Area—Reserved area at the top of main memory for use by the system BIOS.

ECC Error Checking and Correction for hard disk drives—A method where burst errors are detected and corrected. Common methods can detect and correct a damaged sequence of up to 11 bits.

EISA Extended Industry Standard Architecture—An independent standard to define the hardware and bus design of a 32-bit AT design with extensions beyond the standard AT/ISA.

ESDI Enhanced Small Device Interface—A mostly obsolete hard disk drive interface

FEP Front End Processor (for the input of Japanese DBCS characters)

FIFO First-In-First-Out queue

FPU Floating-point Processor

GDT Global Descriptor Table

HLDA Hold Acknowledge from CPU

HMA High Memory Area, consisting of 64 KB less 16 bytes and starting at the 1 MB address boundary.

ICE In-Circuit-Emulator, the ultimate in debuggers

IDT Interrupt Descriptor Table

Int Interrupt

IOPL I/O Privilege Level (0 to 3, where 0 is highest privilege level)

IRQ Interrupt Request (a hardware line)

ISA Industry Standard Architecture—An independent standard to define the hardware and 16-bit bus design of the AT for IBM AT clones.

kbps thousand bits per second

LBA Logical block addressing—used to reference a block device, such as a hard drive, as a linear mapping of sectors.

LIDT Local Interrupt Descriptor Table

LSB Least Significant Byte/Bit (depending on context)

mbps million bits per second

MCA Micro Channel Architecture—A bus standard used in the discontinued PS/2 systems. Incompatible with AT style adapter cards, but otherwise software compatible with AT systems.

MSB Most Significant Byte/Bit (depending on context)

NMI Non-Maskable Interrupt

PC Personal Computer—IBM's computer that helped make this book possible.

PCI Peripheral Component Interconnect—An alternate card bus standard to ISA. It is typically found on most Pentium class systems today.

pel a pixel or dot on the video display

PIO Programmed Input/Output—A form of data transfers that are made through I/O ports rather than through memory.

POS Programmable Option Select, a new feature of PS/2 MCA systems

POST Power-On-Self-Test performed by the BIOS immediately after power up or reset.

RGB Red-Green-Blue, usually in reference to the older EGA form of accessing the display with three color components: Red, Green, and Blue. Sometimes used in the form IRGB, where "I" stands for Intensity.

RI Ring Indicator—An important line from the serial port connector

RSIS Relocated Screen Interface Specification

RTC Real-Time Clock (CMOS clock)

RTS Request To Send—An output line to the serial port connector.

SCSI Small Computer System Interface—Primarily used to connect to disk drives, tape backup systems, and CD ROM drives

TSR Terminate and Stay Resident (memory-resident) program

UART Universal Asynchronous Receiver Transmitter—Hardware for serial port operation

V86 Virtual-86 mode. An operating mode on 386 and later CPUs that provides a simulation of the 8088 environment under a supervisor program

VCPI Virtual Control Program Interface—A common method for protected mode DOS programs and memory managers to coexist.

VDS Virtual DMA Specification. VDS is used to manage DMA operations and memory when 386 or later systems have memory paging active.

VESA Video Electronics Standards Association. A group of video card manufactures offering a common high resolution standard.

VxD Virtual Device Driver—A 32-bit Windows device driver.

XT IBM's followup to the original PC, which supports a hard disk. Most XTs are 8088 based, although a few were made with the 80286. All adapter cards are 8-bit in design.

YUV A color standard used on standard NTSC televisions. Y controls brightness, and U and V control color.

Common Chip Numbers and Functions

This list covers many common LSI parts used in various subsystems that are accessed through the I/O port bus. It does not include CPUs, RAM, or EPROM. New chip sets replace many of these parts with far fewer chips, while providing the same functionality. Only the original chip vendor or most common manufacturer is listed. In most cases, other vendors supply identical parts and use a slight variant of the part number shown.

765 Diskette controller (NEC)

6845 Video controller for CGA and MDA (Motorola)

8031 Microcontroller, used in keyboards and motherboard keyboard controller (Intel, ROM version)

8042 Microcontroller, used on motherboard keyboard controller (Intel)

8048 Microcontroller, for older keyboards (Intel)

8051 Microcontroller, used in keyboards and motherboard keyboard controller (Intel, EPROM version)

8237 DMA controller (various)

8250 UART for serial port (National Semiconductor)

8254 Programmable Interval Timer with 3 Timers/Counters (Intel)

8255 An interface chip that provides three 8-bit ports to hardware. Used only on the PC/XT. On later systems, some I/O ports are still described as 8255, even though chip sets and other approaches replace the actual 8255 with a functional equivalent (Intel)

8259 Programmable Interrupt Controller (Intel)

8272 Diskette controller (Intel)

16450 UART for serial port (National Semiconductor)

16550 UART for serial port, with optional FIFO mode (National Semiconductor)

16552 Dual UART for serial port, each with optional FIFO mode (Western Digital)

72065B Diskette controller (NEC)

72077 Diskette controller with 2.88 MB support (Intel)

82510 UART for serial port, with optional FIFO mode (Intel)

146818 CMOS Real-Time Clock and CMOS memory (Motorola)

161450 UART for serial port, similar to 16450, but includes software power down control (Startech Semiconductor)

161550 UART for serial port, similar to 16550, but includes software power down control (Startech Semiconductor)

APPENDIX C

Bibliography

The following books and standards are some of the better sources for additional information. The approximate cost without shipping, when known, and a phone number for ordering are included. Contact the listed company for latest pricing. My personal comments are not necessarily a complete description of the reference.

At the end of this appendix is a list of products that are discussed in the book, vendor contacts, and useful internet web sites.

BIOS and System

Extended Industry Standard Architecture Specification, Washington D.C.: BCPR Services. ($125) Contact BPCR Services at 713-251-4770.

This is mostly a hardware specification for the EISA bus. It does contain information about EISA I/O ports and some EISA-unique interrupts are covered here. 550 pages.

MCDA Starter Kit, Redding, CA: Micro Channel Developers Association. ($580) Contact MCDA at 800-438-6232 or 916-222-2262.

This kit includes all MCA documents produced by the Micro Channel Developers Association, an independent organization that promotes the Micro Channel architecture. Individual documents are also available. Documents are oriented much more toward hardware vendors than toward programmers. Contact MCDA for more information. Substantial discounts to MCDA members. I have not checked if this organization still exists because IBM abandoned the MCA architecture in 1995.

Anderson, Don, *PCMCIA System Architecture, Second Edition*, Reading, MA: Addison-Wesley Publishing Co., 1995. ISBN 0-201-40991-7. ($30) Addison-Wesley's order desk number is 880-358-4566.

PC Card standards and design details. 440 pages.

Shanley, Tom, and Anderson, Don, *PCI System Architecture, Third Edition*, Reading, MA: Addison-Wesley Publishing Co., 1995. ISBN 0-201-40993-3. ($35) Addison-Wesley's order desk number is 880-358-4566.

PCI system in detail, mostly from a hardware perspective. 560 pages.

Shanley, Tom, *Plug and Play System Architecture*, Reading, MA: Addison-Wesley Publishing Co., 1995. ISBN 0-201-41013-3. ($30) Addison-Wesley's order desk number is 880-358-4566.

Details the Plug and Play system. 327 pages.

Schmidt, Friedhelm, *The SCSI Bus and IDE Interface*, Reading, MA: Addison-Wesley Publishing Co., 1995. ISBN 0-201-42284-0. ($35) Addison-Wesley's order desk number is 880-358-4566.

While the IDE information provided is mostly at a hardware and timing level, the chapters on SCSI go into considerable detail. 304 pages.

Phoenix Technologies Ltd. and IBM, *Bootable CD-ROM Format Specification Version 1.0.* 1995. Available from the Phoenix Web site in Acrobat format.

Details about a BIOS supporting a bootable CD-ROM and other non-hard disk boot devices. 20 pages.

Phoenix Technologies Ltd., *Enhanced Disk Drive Specification Version 1.1.* 1995. Available from the Phoenix Web site in Acrobat format.

Details about BIOS extensions for supporting drives greater than 504 MB. 16 pages.

Phoenix Technologies Ltd., *System BIOS for IBM PCs, Compatibles, and EISA Computers, Second Edition.* Reading, MA: Addison-Wesley Publishing Co., 1991. ISBN 0-201-57760-7. ($27) Addison-Wesley's order desk number is 800-358-4566.

Covers basic BIOS services functions and brief summaries on BIOS data areas and interrupts. Minimal information on I/O ports. 360 pages.

Technical Reference—Options and Adapters, IBM Corporation. 1984. Order number 6322509 for two-volume set. ($150) IBM's order desk is at 800- 426-7282.

Details adapter cards, primarily for the PC/XT systems. Includes schematics and adapter BIOS listings, which must be used for complete understanding because the related documentation is usually missing important details.

Technical Reference—Personal Computer AT, IBM Corporation. 1985. Order number 6280070 and supplement 6280099. ($186) IBM's order desk number is 800-426-7282.

The most detailed programmer's reference IBM has ever produced. This is the last manual with both schematics and BIOS listings. Considerable information appears removed from schematics, and the listings can be difficult to follow, but half a pie is better than none! All IBM system references have since been sanitized to remove most if not all lower-level information, and they specify 'reserved' much too freely.

Personal System/2 and Personal Computer BIOS Interface Technical Reference, IBM Corporation. Second Edition 1988. Order number S68X2341 and supplement 15F2161. ($178) IBM's order desk number is 800-426-7282.

A good source of information on BIOS interfaces to IBM's line of personal computers. No listings or schematics are provided. Generally the information included is accurate, but it lacks detail on how to write software to use functions. The only IBM-published source of information on the PS/2 BIOS. It is a bit out of date, and no new edition has been released as of November 1993.

Personal System/2 Hardware Interface Technical Reference, IBM Corporation. 1988. Order number 68X2330 with 1991 update number 04G3281. ($160) IBM's order desk number is 800-426-7282.

Details the MicroChannel architecture and subsystems on the PS/2 MCA systems. Includes detailed VGA/XGA information, IBM's SCSI, and a few other adapters. Although the information is useful, it is sadly missing fine details. No listings or schematics are included.

Brown, Ralf, and Jim Kyle, David Maxey, Raymond J. Michels, Andrew Schulman, *Undocumented DOS, Second Edition.* Reading, MA: Addison-Wesley Publishing Co., 1994. ($45) Addison-Wesley's order desk number is 800-358-4566.

This is the only book to go into extreme detail about DOS and underlying undocumented structures and functions. Excellent reading. 800 pages.

AX Technical Reference Guide, Second Edition, AX Conference Office, 1991. ($25) Order from Pacific Software Publishing at 206-232-3989.

This book covers the AX system, a standard based on the AT design for the Japanese marketplace. Many major Japanese vendors used to (and still do?) support this standard. DOS/V now provides much of the AX functionality on a standard AT system, diminishing the need for AX. This reference covers all AX specific features and software functions. 494 pages.

Interrupts and Services

Brown, Ralf, and Jim Kyle. *PC Interrupts, Second Edition.* Reading, MA: Addison-Wesley Publishing Co., 1994. ISBN 0-201-62485-0. ($40) Addison-Wesley's order desk number is 800-358-4566.

This book does an excellent job of summarizing interrupts for the PC, peripherals, adapters, and many application programs. A must on your bookshelf. 1216 pages.

Virtual DMA Services, version 1.00 (no date), Redmond, WA: Microsoft Corporation. Part number 098-10869.

Documents the functions for virtualized DMA services. 25 pages. Recent users have reported that this document is now out of print.

Peripherals

ATA (AT Attachment) Standard with Extensions, New York, NY: American National Standards Institute. 1994. Specification X3T9.2948D. ($25) To order from Global, call 800-624-3974 or 714-261-1455.

A proposed common standard for IDE hard disk controllers attached to the AT bus. Details low-level I/O, commands, disk drive interface, timing, electrical interfaces, and connectors. 102 pages.

ESDI Fixed Disk Drive Adapter/A Technical Reference, IBM Corporation. 1987. Order number 68X2234. ($14) IBM's order desk number is 800-426-7282.

Details much of the low-level I/O interface of IBM's PS/2 ESDI controller. Leaves numerous areas used by the PS/2 BIOS undefined or reserved, and does not explain any interrupt 13h BIOS functions.

Peripheral Components, Mt. Prospect, IL: Intel Corporation. 1993. Intel order number 296467-004. ($25) To order, call McGraw-Hill at 800-822-8158.

Hardware coverage of various key chips, including 8237 DMA controller, 8254 Timer/counter, 8259 interrupt controller, and chip sets for the PC. One source for many of the lowest-

level details. Be aware that many functions and operations detailed are not applicable due to hardware implementation in the PC architecture. 1600 pages.

SCSI-2 Common Access Method Transport and SCSI Interface Module, New York, NY: American National Standards Institute. 1992. Specification X3.232- 199x draft. ($25) To order from Global, call 800-624-3974 or 714-261-1455.

A proposed common standard for SCSI-2 disk controllers not specific to the PC. Unless you are into SCSI, this document is a tough read. 70 pages.

Processor Related

Cyrix Cx486DLC Microprocessor Data Sheet, Richardson, TX: Cyrix Corporation. 1992. Order number 94076-01. To order, call Cyrix at 214- 994-8387.

Covers hardware and software aspects of the Cyrix 486. 150 pages.

Cyrix 5x86 Microprocessor Data Book, Richardson, TX: Cyrix Corporation. 1995. Order number 94214-00. To order, call Cyrix at 214- 994-8387.

Covers hardware and software aspects of the Cyrix 5x86. 66 pages.

Cyrix 6x86 Microprocessor Data Book, Richardson, TX: Cyrix Corporation. 1995. Order number 94175-00. To order, call Cyrix at 214- 994-8387.

Covers hardware and software aspects of the Cyrix 6x86. 226 pages.

Intel486 SL Microprocessor SuperSet System Design Guide, Mt. Prospect, IL: Intel Corporation. 1992. Intel order number 241326-001. ($25) To order call McGraw-Hill at 800-822-8158.

This book is mostly oriented toward hardware designers (OK, so are all Intel manuals). Some useful information is provided for programmers as well. 230 pages.

Pentium Processor User's Manual, Mt. Prospect, IL: Intel Corporation. 1993. Intel order number 241430-001. ($86 for a three-volume set) To order call McGraw-Hill at 800-822-8158.

The best Intel CPU book to date. The descriptions are clearer than many of their past processor books. Unfortunately, like most Intel documentation, no index is provided, so plan on a lot of hunting. 1640 pages.

This is the first major manual from Intel I've seen that hides considerable programming information. An almost unobtainable Appendix H includes extensive additional documentation for those lucky programmers who are able to get it, and are willing to sign long nondisclosures. Be prepared for frustration without it. A few tidbits were moved from Appendix H in the 1995 edition of these manuals, but sadly, much is still missing.

Pentium Pro Family Developer's Manual—Specifications, Mt. Prospect, IL: Intel Corporation. 1996. Intel order number 242690 ($28). To order call McGraw-Hill at 800-822-8158.

Primarily hardware details, not very useful to most programmers.

Pentium Pro Family Developer's Manual—Programmer's Reference Manual, Mt. Prospect, IL: Intel Corporation. 1996. Intel order number 242691 ($27). To order call McGraw-Hill at 800-822-8158.

Basic instruction set reference.

Pentium Pro Family Developer's Manual—Developer's Manual, Mt. Prospect, IL: Intel Corporation. 1996. Intel order number 242692. To order call McGraw-Hill at 800-822-8158.

Excellent programmer's guide to the Pentium Pro CPU. First Intel book I've seen that has an index (Thank you, Intel)! Includes many details left out of the original Pentium manual, but these new features and options are only covered briefly. 480 pages.

Hummer, Robert L. *The Processor and Coprocessor.* Emeryville, CA: Ziff-Davis Press, 1992. ISBN 1-56276-016-5. ($50)

The best I've seen on the 80x88 processor family and all instructions. Covers the 8088 through the 80486 in depth, and all math coprocessors. 761 pages.

Microprocessor Report. *Understanding x86 Microprocessors.* Microprocessor Report. Emeryville, CA: Ziff-Davis Press, 1993. ISBN 1-56276-158-7. ($50)

This book is a collection of 99 articles published between 1987 and 1993 in the Microprocessor Report newsletter. Interesting reading, with some articles on undocumented programming information. 286 pages.

Video

Hercules Monochrome Technical Reference, Hercules Computer Technology, Customer Service Dept., 2550 Ninth St., Berkeley CA 415-540-6000

Covers the Monochrome Hercules Adapter.

Ferraro, Richard F., *Programmer's Guide to the EGA and VGA Cards, Third Edition.* Reading, MA: Addison-Wesley Publishing Co., 1994. ISBN 0-201-62490-7. ($45) Addison-Wesley's order desk number is 800-358-4566.

Good in-depth information on how to program the EGA, VGA, and SVGA down to the chip level. Excellent source for small and not-so-small nuances between all the major chip vendors. 1602 pages.

VESA Super VGA Standard, #VS891001 Video Electronics Standards Association, 1330 South Bascom Ave., San Jose, CA 408-971-7525.

A must for anyone programming the SVGA, although written from a hardware perspective. 25 pages.

Video Cursor Interface, #VS911021 Video Electronics Standards Association, 1330 South Bascom Ave., San Jose, CA 08-971-7525.

Covers a general-purpose interface to make mouse device drivers work in all SVGA resolutions. 26 pages.

VESA XGA Extensions Standard, Video Electronics Standards Association, 1330 South Bascom Ave., San Jose, CA 408-971-7525.

Defines registers for the VESA XGA standard. 34 pages.

Products

"COMM-DRV," WCSC, 2470 S. Dairy Ashford, Suite 188, Houston, TX 77099. 713-498-4832.

One of a number of useful utilities used to help develop and debug serial port software with a second PC. Call the vendor for a complete list of products.

"LIMSIM," Larson Computing, 1556 Halford Ave., #142, Santa Clara, CA 95051. 408-737-0627.

This memory manager is the only one to provide real-mode paging as described in Chapter 3. An interesting product, but no longer produced.

"Memory Commander," Mix Software, 1132 Commerce Dr., Richardson, TX 75081. 214-783-6001.

This memory manager replaces the basic memory manager supplied with DOS. It provides the unique ability to add from 100K to 300K of additional DOS main memory to current applications. This means a single application can have, in the best case, up to 900K of contiguous DOS memory.

"PocketPOST," Data Depot, 1525 Sandy Lane, Clearwater, FL 34615. 813-446-3402.

Provides an adapter card to monitor BIOS Power-On-Self-Test codes. Comes with detailed manual on POST codes for standard as well as a number of less familiar BIOS manufacturers.

"Sourcer," V Communications, Inc., 4320 Stevens Creek Blvd., Suite 120, San Jose, CA 95129. 408-296-4224.

This is the commenting disassembler I developed for V Communications. Sourcer takes binary files, such as EXEs, COMs, and device drivers, and generates commented assembly language code. It supports code written for the 8088 through the Pentium Pro, and related math coprocessors. Several options are available for BIOS analysis, Windows files (EXEs, DLLs, VxDs, and Win32 executables), and OS/2 files.

"ViewComm," Greenleaf Software, 16479 Dallas Parkway, Suite 570, Dallas TX 75248. 214-248-2561.

This is a serial port Datascope software that monitors and captures the operations of the serial port. Greenleaf also offers a variety of serial port software and libraries.

Electronic Access, Companies

Advanced Micro Devices—www.amd.com

Cyrix Corporation—www.cyrix.com

Intel Corporation—www.intel.com; Compuserve forums, INTEL and INTELC (for developers)

International Business Machines Corporation—www.ibm.com

Phoenix Technologies Ltd.—www.ptltd.com

Texas Instruments—www.ti.com

V Communications, Inc.—www.v-com.com

Western Digital—www.wdc.com

Electronic Access, Other

Plug and Play—Compuserve forum, PLUGPLAY

Various undocumented CPU information—www.x86.org and http://cnit2.uniyar.ac.ru/user/BobbyZ/download/4p_v331.zip

Index

Addison-Wesley warrants the enclosed disk to be free of defects in materials and faulty workmanship under normal use for a period of ninety days after purchase. If a defect is discovered in the disk during this warranty period, a replacement disk can be obtained at no charge by sending the defective disk, postage prepaid, with proof of purchase to:

Addison Wesley Longman, Inc.
Editorial Department
Developers Press
One Jacob Way
Reading, MA 01867

After the 90-day period, a replacement will be sent upon receipt of the defective disk and a check or money order for $10.00, payable to Addison Wesley Longman, Inc.

Addison-Wesley makes no warranty or representation, either express or implied, with respect to this software, its quality, performance, merchantability, or fitness for a particular purpose. In no event will Addison-Wesley, its distributors, or dealers or the author be liable for direct, indirect, special, incidental, or consequential damages arising out of the use or inability to use the software. The exclusion of implied warranties is not permitted in some states. Therefore, the above exclusion may not apply to you. This warranty provides you with specific legal rights. There may be other rights that you may have that vary from state to state.